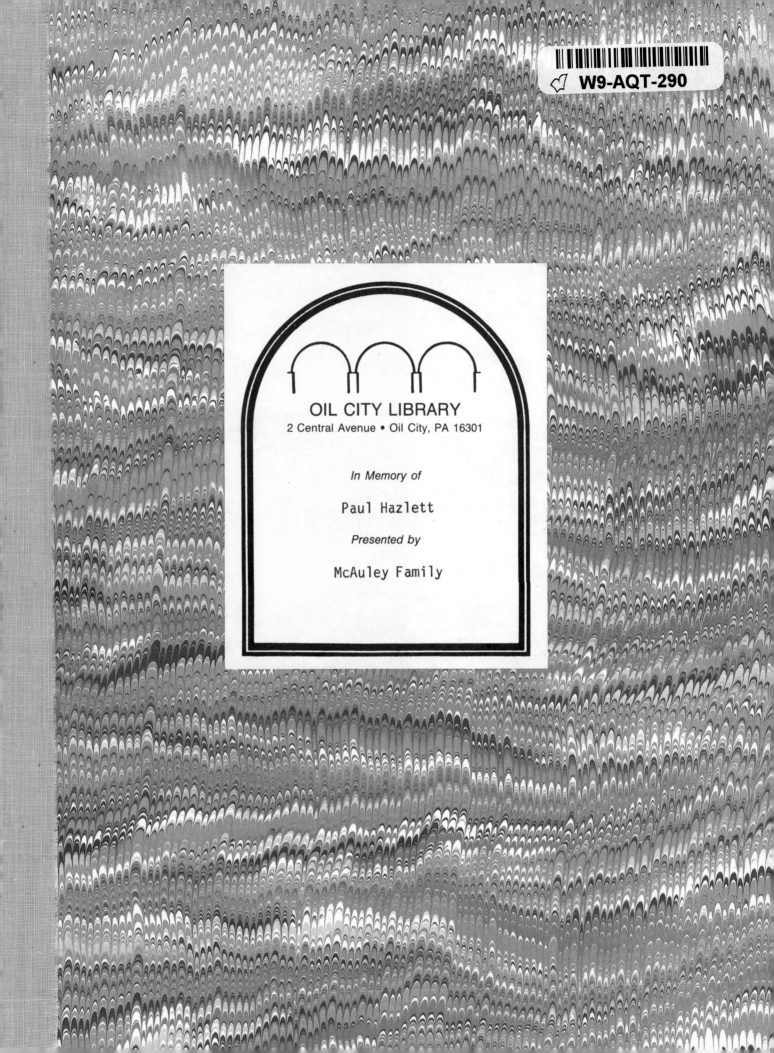

America's Hundred Thousand

America's Hundred Thousand

The US Production Fighter Aircraft of World War II
Francis H. Dean

DATA CONTRIBUTIONS BY

GOVERNMENT ORGANIZATIONS

-UNITED STATES AIR FORCE MUSEUM
-NATIONAL AIR AND SPACE MUSEUM
-NATIONAL AERONAUTICS AND SPACE ADMINISTRATION
-NAVAL AVIATION MUSEUM
-WASHINGTON NAVY YARD
-UNITED STATES MARINE CORPS MUSEUM
-NATIONAL ARCHIVES
-USAF HISTORICAL RESEARCH CENTER, MAXWELL AFB, ALA.

PRIVATE ORGANIZATIONS

-SAN DIEGO AEROSPACE MUSEUM

CORPORATIONS

-GRUMMAN CORPORATION
-LOCKHEED CORPORATION

-NORTHROP CORPORATION
-LING-TEMCO-VOUGHT CORPORATION

PRIVATE INDIVIDUALS

-GLEN HOLCOMBE, BOEING CO., RET.
-RONALD MCCANN, BOEING CO. RET.
-JOHN SCHNEIDER, BOEING CO., RET.
-JIM MAAS, AAHS
-HENRY BORST, H.V. BORST &ASSOCIATES
-BIRCH MATTHEWS, TRW, RET., AAHS
-JOSEPH WEATHERS, AAHS
-RAY WAGNER, AAHS
-HAROLD ANDREWS, NAVAIR RET. AAHS
-CLARENCE E. "BUD" ANDERSON, COL.USAAF RET.
-DONALD S. LOPEZ, NASM
-MILTON SHEPARD, BOEING CO. RET.,AAHS
-BILL SKELLY, BOEING CO., RET.
-HANK MACK, EX 1ST LT. USAAF
-WILLIAM B. CHURCHMAN III, ex-USMC
-ROBERT DEAN
-CHRIS WHEAL, ex-USN
-SAM ORR, PHOTOGRAPHER

COVER ARTWORK BY

Steve Ferguson, Colorado Springs, CO

DEDICATION

This book is dedicated to my sister-in-law, Helen Gardner Farrell, a very special friend.

Book Design by Ian Robertson.

Copyright © 1997 by Francis H. Dean.
Library of Congress Catalog Number: 96-67103

Printed in the United States.
ISBN: 0-7643-0072-5

We are interested in hearing from authors with book ideas on related topics.

Published by Schiffer Publishing Ltd.
77 Lower Valley Road
Atglen, PA 19310
Phone: (610) 593-1777
FAX: (610) 593-2002
Please write for a free catalog.
This book may be purchased from the publisher.
Please include $2.95 postage.
Try your bookstore first.

Contents

ACKNOWLEDGEMENTS

Several people whose patient assistance, or tolerance, allowed me to finally put this book together must be acknowledged. Tolerance is mentioned because the effort extended over several years, and I suspect some, including my very patient wife, felt there never would be a conclusion.

The project started in 1989, three years after my retirement from the aero industry. Besides the "work" part in industry I've been most interested all my life in aviation history, and was elated in 1962 upon finding an organization of fellow enthusiasts, the American Aviation Historical Society which I promptly joined and have enjoyed ever since.

In no particular order I would like to thank the following people for encouragement, assistance, and good advice, some of which I may not have followed.

Glen Holcombe of Boeing assisted early on in providing for the loan of several key NACA reports. Ron McCann, late of Boeing and a self-styled "P-40 nut", assisted on P-40 matters and references. John Schneider, long my boss at Boeing and once a Curtiss employee, drew from his volumnious files on aircraft to provide World War II era material. I had little Brewster data until AAHS friends put me in touch with Jim Maas. The large amount of material Jim kindly provided allowed inclusion of the interesting Brewster fighter. "Hank" Borst, my boss for years at Curtiss Wright, opened his extensive library of technical data, including NACA and other reports (like P-47 flying qualities), and provided moral support and computer help as well as his experience as an author. Birch Matthews, ex-Bell aircraft and TRW engineer and AAHS member, himself an aviation writer, was very generous with supply of pertinent fighter materials, especially but not limited to the Bell aircraft, and gave freely of good advice and encouragement. My long time AAHS friend Joe Weathers loaned an invaluable fighter report and manuals along with great photographic support. Author and historian Ray Wagner helped greatly with Republic weight and performance information. Hal Andrews, ex-NavAir and very long time AAHS friend who has helped so many people, enthusiastically supported me with historical material of all kinds and the usual good advice. A Boeing friend and World War II fighter pilot Pete Howell put me in touch with Col.(Ret.) Clarence "Bud" Anderson, World War II ace in the ETO and recent author of a fine book. Bud set me straight in several areas with particular reference to the P-39

and P-51. Another WWII fighter pilot, Don S. Lopez of the NASM and an author himself kindly consented to answer a detailed questionaire on P-40 flying qualities. He flew that aircraft in China. What a great help! Christopher Wheal, an ex-USN pilot who has been flying a Wildcat at air shows, provided a copy of an excellent NAA report on P-51 flying qualities. Milt Shepard, late of Boeing and now deceased came through with valuable government fighter procurement reports. My good friend and reference for all powerplant questions Boeing retiree Bill Skelley provided excellent wartime data on the Allison V-1710 engine and its installations. A local gentleman, wartime P-38 pilot Hank Mack kindly reviewed a P-38 handling qualities section and provided valuable critical comments to enhance it, particularly noting where improvements were made on late versions of that aircraft. Sam Orr, a good friend from Boeing and now in Oklahoma gave me constant support in the photographic area and I cannot thank him enough. A friendly piece of help came from Bill Churchman in the form of pilot manuals. Bill is a former USMC Corsair (and sometimes Hellcat) pilot.

I should also not forget the corporations and government organizations and museums that provided helpful data. Grumman did the most; Lockheed, Northrop, and LTV also provided information. The USAF Museum helped early on, also NASM, NASA, Naval Aviation Museum, USMC Museum, Washington Navy Yard, National Archives, and the USAF Historical Research Center. Mr. Larry Wilson of NASM went out of his way to find pertinent material and I thank him kindly. The San Diego Aerospace Museum helped through Ray Wagner.

A special thank you is due the very helpful folks at my local Rachael Kohl Library who never failed to acquire reference material I requested no matter how far away it was!

I sincerely hope I have left no one out and that none of my friends are too disappointed in my effort.

In particular I should like to acknowlege the support of my family. My wife Evie almost never showed the exasperation she must have felt on so many occasions. My son Bob was constantly helpful in getting me to master the mechanics of typing, computers, printers, and the like. Because of him I am reasonably computer literate.

1

INTRODUCTION

There were over 100,000 of them, 100,000 US fighter airplanes! For six years they filled the skies of a warring world. Built by Americans, they were flown by the pilots of many countries.

There were eleven distinct fighter types put out by nine US companies. Of these seven were for the Army and four for the Navy. Individual numbers produced varied from just over 500 to over 15,000. But the total was over 100,000 fighter planes, and such production will never happen again. Today no one could pay for that number even if they were desired.

Six of the producing companies were located in the eastern US with three on the west coast, but licensing and subcontracting soon spread manufacture of fighter planes or their components all over the country. Five piston engine models by four manufacturers, along with three propeller designs, powered these fighters. Innumerable firms joined in making parts. Around-the-clock production of these deadly machines, much of the work done by women, was only a small but vital part of the American home front effort in World War II.

A few of these fighters remain today, flying at air shows, competing in air races, and reposing in museums, but the number is dwindling as attrition takes place, though some have been rebuilt almost from scratch. Time is near up for the men who flew them in combat. There has been continuing interest, however, by younger men in these sleek machines designed over fifty years ago, evidenced by crowds at "warbird" air shows and air races. Today remaining fighter aircraft are piloted by well-heeled hobbyists, and tales of past glory in combat continue.

In the forty-five years since the wide-ranging conflicts of World War II there have been many efforts to record various fighter characteristics, performance, and combat records. Here, for United States production fighters of the period, we set down an exceptionally detailed record of development and operational history, examine major factors affecting performance, lay out extensive definition of their characteristics, and make comparisons.

Problems arose in the effort. Major among them was acquisition of full and accurate aircraft data. Many inaccurate or unqualified numbers have crept into fifty years of literature. Today records are buried in obscure archives or destroyed, even though museums and interested individuals do their best to preserve them. Without exception, manufacturers of World War II fighters have more cru-

cial matters than history to consider. And four companies have gone out of business. Government and military organizations do their best to help the historian, but some material is not available. It would have been ideal to consider the characteristics of major foreign types against which the US planes were pitted in World War II, and make direct comparisons. This required an additional effort greater than the writer wished to address.

So here's to America's Hundred Thousand; the Lightnings and Airacobras, the Warhawks, Thunderbolts, and Mustangs, the Black Widows and Kingcobras! And to the Buffalos, the Wildcats, Corsairs, and Hellcats. And to the men and women who designed, built, serviced, and flew them. It was a magnificent effort in a time well past—something of which Americans can still be proud!

PROJECT ARRANGEMENT

The project is divided into five sections: Fighter Introductions, History, Factors, Figures, and Comparisons.

It was felt necessary to INTRODUCE, up front, the eleven aircraft types about which information has been gathered to provide a refresher for knowlegeable aviation buffs, and a quick first look for others. Some may be familiar with one or two, and know little about others; some may have a passing acquaintance with all, and wish to know more. In any case introduction of each fighter helps set a stage for material presented later.

The HISTORY section contains a summary and pictures of "production" inter-war fighters. Since production was so minor in those times, any type that was produced in an amount of twenty-five or more articles is included. The section provides a backdrop for the World War II major production types and a view of the progress of technology in the pre-war era. Monthly production of the World War II types is then shown as contrast. The HISTORY section also includes an extensive illustrated review of fighter types that were in development during the wartime period but did not make production status. The number and design variety of these piston engined models is surprising. There was a tremendous effort involved in the new project area as well as in fighter production, and in retrospect one is given some reason to wonder whether all this work was necessary.

The fighter FACTORS section is the semi-technical part, but hopefully not too much so for an interested person of average intelligence without technical background. An understanding of the forces acting on fighters in flight is helpful in seeing why some performed better than others. An effort has been made to keep explanations as straightforward and uncomplicated as possible. The section is not intended to be a textbook, but rather an overview of major factors in World War II fighter design. In particular the sections on engine supercharging and aircraft weight and balance are considered important to understanding the fighters.

Fighter FIGURES is the largest section, where, for each of the eleven production types, aircraft performance and design data along with handling characteristics are contained. In addition sketches, photos, and schematic diagrams of aircraft structures and systems are provided. These descriptions define state of the art of fighter design a half century ago. In each fighter section except one is contained an extensive chronology for the type from inception to the end of the war.

The handling qualities section contains references to a fighter conference or meet. This occurred at Patuxent River in Maryland where the Navy flight test center was and is located. It was the site of one of several conferences, this one in October 1944. Most all fighters were there, and a large number of contractor and service pilots made evaluations and reported. Some results noted are based on those pilot reports. A limited amount of data is taken from an earlier conference at Eglin Field in Florida, January 1944, the USAAF test center of that time. For the most part performance data were taken from USAAF or USN official documents. In a few instances manufacturers information was used. Performance information is often controversial. Performance presented is typical for an aircraft in good condition, and is qualified as to aircraft weight and power setting. All performance is at standard atmosphere conditions.

The final section makes COMPARISONS between the eleven US production types, mainly in the areas of fighter performance, but also included are comparisons of major program milestones for each type. Finally a general evaluation of the types is given based on the comments of the large number of World War II pilots attending the October, 1944 Fighter Conference conducted at Naval Air Station, Patuxent River, Maryland.

THE HUNDRED THOUSAND

The 100,000 figure is derived from the production figures for eleven US World War II fighter types as follows:

Aircraft	Production	Ranking
P-38 Lightning	10037	6
P-39 Airacobra	9529	7
P-40 T'Hawk-Warhawk	13143	3
P-47 Thunderbolt	15683	1
P-51 Mustang	15486	2
P-61 Black Widow	706	10
P-63 Kingcobra	3303	9
F2A-/229/339 Buffalo	509	11
F4F-/FM- Wildcat	7905	8
F4U-/FG-/F3A- Corsair	11514	5
F6F- Hellcat	12275	4
Total Production	100,090	

LOCKHEED P-38 LIGHTNING, AN INTRODUCTION
With a fifty-two foot wingspan, the P-38 was the biggest of the single seat fighters, and the most recognizeable. Its two inline engines and twin tail boom arrangement could hardly be missed. Depending on the war-time tactical situation, this could be a plus or a minus. P-38s patrolled over the invasion beaches of Europe on D-day in 1944 so friendly gunners could recognize them. On the other hand, early recognition at a distance by German fighter pilots over Europe was often seen as a tactical deficit for the aircraft.

go fast! When first flown it was the sleekest thing around, and its mission was interception of high altitude bombers. From the start P-38s were equipped with turbosuperchargers maintaining engine power at high altitudes for good climb and high speed, and these were kept aboard through the life of the aircraft. This very factor however, high altitude performance, got the P-38 in serious trouble with compressibility before other fast US high altitude fighters encountered the problem.

Lockheed P38H Lightning, Ser. 42-67079, Mfr. Photo. Showing a clean-lined elegance, the big Lightning displays its high aspect ratio wing, concentrated nose armament, turbosuperchargers atop booms, and Prestone cooler ducts alongside. Mirrored surface inboard on starboard engine nacelle allowed the pilot to check gear status. The high aspect ratio wing conferred lower induced drag characteristics, helping in turning and climbing flight as well as increasing range capability.

The P-38 was a study in contrasts, and any discussion will bring out more diversity of views on the airplane than most other US fighters. Their performance in North Africa, and particularly in Europe was certainly less than a full success, whereas in the Pacific they were seen as almost ideal fighter planes. The opposition encountered formed a significant part of this difference. The same characteristics that gave the P-38 long range, good load-carrying abilities, and excellent mission flexibility also limited its use as an agile air-to-air fighter.

The P-38 was the earliest, in first flight date, of the 400 mph US Army fighters, and thus a true hallmark in United States fighter design. It got high up while still retaining enough engine power to

Its 1930s profile wing sections ran into compressibility quickly because of the low critical Mach number of the wing combined with a relatively low speed of sound at high altitude and the winter cold of European skies. This problem, particularly on early P-38 variants, affected operational capability. At high altitudes the pilots didn't dare to dive, fearing the onset of compressibility as the sleek heavy machine plunged downward. The German pilots knew of the P-38 problem, and when required dove away without fear of being followed. Since much of the Pacific Theatre had warmer temperatures, and operations tended to be at lower altitudes, the speed of sound was greater (it varies only with temperature), and P-38s did not encounter the problem as often. Late in the war P-38s incorporated a fix of sorts, compressibility dive flaps under the wings, which when extended provided better characteristics in high speed dives and recoveries.

The P-38 had a layout that bothered some pilots. The first worry was its twin powerplants. On many occasions it was great to have two engines, but not on takeoff where the perils of a possible engine failure leaving a sudden big difference of thrust between propellers, plus high rolling torque just after leaving the ground, scared the daylights out of young inexperienced pilots. It was almost a sure way to auger in, and it sometimes happened. Another factor worrisome to pilots was the long horizontal tail running between the booms. It sometimes seemed like a big knife ready to slice up a pilot trying to bail out.

Some pilots felt twin liquid-cooled engines made the aircraft twice as susceptible to a critical hit from enemy fire as a single engine machine, and that the twin engine safety feature quickly disappeared if the hit engine caught on fire. They were quick to point out that on earlier models there was no fire extinguishing system aboard. There were probably more pilots, however, who valued the perceived twin engine safety over water and forbidding terrain.

Another concern for pilots of all but the latest models of the P-38 was the electrical generator on one engine only. The failure of that engine meant single engine flight on just the battery. A low battery could be extra trouble, including problems with control of the Curtiss Electric propellers.

The P-38's guns were concentrated in the nose, an arrangement allowed by the twin engine configuration, and they could blast a big hole. Pilots liked this feature—a tight pattern at all ranges. But bringing these guns to bear on an enemy aircraft could present a problem because the P-38 was a big aircraft to horse around. Its major agility problem involved starting to roll into a turn. Because of the wide spanwise distribution of weight, powerplants and booms way out on the wings, the aircraft did not start rolling quickly after an aileron control input. It had lots of roll inertia and it hesitated. This initial hesitation could mean real trouble in aerial combat where smaller lighter single engine enemy fighters could flick quickly into the rolling motion required to start turning in a hurry. It was a deadly game of split seconds, and in this initial moment the P-38 lost. Late models were equipped with power-assisted ailerons to give the pilot more muscle. On these, roll performance at high speed improved considerably, but the P-38 never became a world-beater in roll.

Once in a turn the P-38 was excellent, and a skilled pilot could pull the big fighter around in tight circles without stalling. Even if he did stall, it was no catastrophe. The aircraft just mushed outward. Two factors contributed to this fine turning performance. The twin propellers gave zero net torque reaction (one propeller's torque cancelled torque of the other opposite-turning propeller). So when the P-38 slowed down in a tight wind-up turn on the point of a stall, there was less tendency to flick roll out of the turn in stall departure as single engine fighters often did. The other factor was the high lift coefficient of the wing with use of a maneuver setting on the big tracked Lockheed/Fowler flaps. The pilot could quickly drop some flap, thereby increasing both wing section curvature and wing area. In addition, slipstream of the two propellers over most

of the wing helped maintain airflow at low speeds. So wing lift soared, the stall speed went down, and that big brute of a fighter cranked around in a tight turn.

The virtues of the P-38, particularly long range and endurance compared to other Allied fighters of the early war period, generated constant demands for the airplane in all theatres. The P-38 would perform missions no other fighter could tackle. Allocations of the limited numbers available were made only after considerable sweat. Load-carrying was greater than contemporaries of late 1942 and early 1943. It could carry ammunition and bombs over extra distance, hit the enemy in his rear areas, and fight its way back. The photo versions provided badly-needed fast high altitude long range reconnaisance capability. The P-38 was the long range fighter of the early part of the war.

Losses of P-38s were high in North African fighting, and for a time all the production capacity was required for resupply. Factors in this high attrition were primitive basing conditions, first combat for inexperienced US pilots, susceptibility of two liquid-cooled engine installations to ground fire (countering this was good single engine flight capability), mission constaints hampering flexibility of flight operations—they were tied too closely to the bombers, not enough airplanes, and, certainly not least, opposition by seasoned enemy pilots flying very good fighter aircraft.

Later European operations in the bomber escort role were successful in the early stages, but troubles soon began with the onset of winter. Powerplants failed with excessive frequency at the higher altitudes, the cockpits were cold and transparencies froze over in winter high altitude flying, pilots were fatigued from long missions, and work load was often high. P-38 cockpits were judged poorest in arrangement of the US fighters. Pilots couldn't dive the aircraft from high altitude without compressibility worries and attendant loss of control. Added to these factors were the problems of easy recognition and slow initial roll into turns noted earlier. The powerplant problems were probably the most frustrating. Finally in 1944 the British-based P-38s in the Eighth Air Force were withdrawn from their strategic escort role in favor of P-51s, and given to the Ninth Air Force where they performed well through the remainder of the war in varied tactical mission assignments.

In the Pacific the P-38 was the Army Air Force fighter king through most of the war. Its long range twin engine capability was just fine for distant over-water operations in island-hopping campaigns. After a few early debacles where US pilots tried to mix it up in tight aerobatic combat with the nimble Japanese fighters and lost, the American fighter tactics changed to take advantage of the fast high-flying P-38's best performance features. They introduced combat on their own terms, slashing through enemy formations from above, doing great damage with concentrated firepower, and kept going without losing speed to later zoom back up again for altitude advantage.

P-38 operations continued through the war with considerable success, and the aircraft was hailed as one of the great US fighter planes of the war. The type disappeared almost immediately from US service ranks after the war, however, in favor of the P-47 and P-51 fighters and its own follow-on, the P-80 jet-powered Shooting Star. Better reliability and maintainability of single engine aircraft were among the factors in selection of what would be retained in the post-war US fighter forces.

The P-38 is a seldom-seen aircraft today, but a few still remain to commemorate an unusual and interesting fighter airplane design.

BELL P-39 AIRACOBRA, AN INTRODUCTION

Smallest of the Army fighters and, with the P-38, one of the new breed of planes using a tricycle landing gear, the P-39 was a rather handsome mid-engine ship with a cannon barrel poking out its pointed nose. If looks would do it, the P-39 should have been a super fighter!

The experimental airplane, the XP-39, had a turbosupercharged Allison engine providing the potential of near 400 mile per hour speed at high altitude. But an early Army decision removed the turbosupercharger from the design, leaving only the normal single stage unit integral in the engine. The Airacobra was thus relegated

to a low to middle altitude role with performance falling off rapidly above 17000 feet. But it was the fastest of the early US single engine fighters down low, and packed a good sized punch with its nose cannon, making it a premier ground attack fighter.

There was a great deal of over-optimistic propaganda put out early on the P-39, along with many publicity photos emphasizing its sleek lines. All of this seemed to make out the aircraft as a world-beater, which it was not. The pendulum quickly swung the other way when, based on early combat results, it was labeled a great disappointment.

As with the P-38, the Airacobra was a worrisome aircraft to many young service pilots when first introduced, and there were a batch of accidents; they felt the aircraft was tricky to fly. One problem with the P-39 involved its particularly cramped cockpit for a large man. Rumor said large pilots acquired a permanent hunched over appearance after a lot of P-39 flying. But a more troublesome

Bell P-39C Airacobra, Mfr. Photo via Birch Matthews. One of the first limited production batch, this early Airacobra shows off its special features: tricycle landing gear (novel for the time), exhaust stacks of the mid-located engine, a cannon barrel protruding through the propeller spinner nose, and auto-type cockpit doors. The C version was unique in having all guns in the fuselage nose; later models had wing machine guns, too.

factor was lack of adequate stall warning coupled with very sensitive controls. When stalled it could quickly snap over and start to spin, particularly if expenditure of nose gun ammunition had pushed the center of gravity rearward. There were also stories of strange gyrations that could take place, including tumbling, an uncontrolled motion where the aircraft was said to pitch end for end. Some service pilots maintained they had tumbled the plane, or had seen one tumble. In some cases recovery was eventually made, and in others pilots managed to depart the aircraft. Company test pilots denied such maneuvers could take place. But the stories have persisted through the years. The rationale was the aircraft weight distribution longitudinally was unusual with the engine behind the pilot, and firing off nose ammunition moved the center of gravity well aft. In any case worried pilots sang "It would tumble and spin and soon auger in."

The Army requested the National Advisory Committee for Aeronautics, the predecessor of todays NASA, to test the P-39 and report on flying qualities. NACA reported the stall characteristics were quite normal, but there was no warning of a stall. It was possible, however, to get the airplane out of the spin resulting from a stall departure using normal recovery techniques, though considerable altitude was lost in recovery. The report also noted extreme control sensitivity with very small fore-aft stick motions covering the full lift coefficient range of the wing from high speed to stall.

Early P-39 versions, including the export P-400 type refused by the British, were available just after the Pearl Harbor attack and thus deployed quickly to the Southwest Pacific, there to fight alongside P-40 and Wildcat fighters against the Japanese. Certain facts were learned quickly about the P-39 by the American Pacific forces. It normally could not climb quickly enough to intercept high-flying (about 25000 feet) Japanese bombers, and so usually missed them altogether. Time to climb to 25000 feet was about 15 minutes. It could not maneuver as well as Japanese fighters during close-in aerial combat (nor could other US fighters); it was short-legged on range, though somewhat faster than the Japanese aircraft at low altitudes—if given time to accelerate. To make matters worse, the P-400 Airacobra version, due to lack of any supply of high pressure cylinders, had no oxygen for pilots. It was thus limited to little more than 10000 foot altitude capability.

All this was very upsetting to local air commanders, and to pilots, but there was no help for it. In retrospect the performance shortfall, principally due to engine power limitations without auxiliary stage supercharging, should not have been surprising. Shortly the P-39 was transferred to a tactical ground support role where it raised hob with enemy forces, using its excellent low level speed and heavy nose armament to great advantage. It could also lug a centerline-mounted 500 pound bomb. Fighting performance of the P-39 was exemplary once assigned its proper role. But the airplane has been labeled a failure since it performed poorly in missions it clearly was not designed to handle.

Original Army plans envisioned sending US P-39 aircraft by air to England along with the P-38s in 1942 for Operation Bolero, using big ferry fuel tanks beneath the fuselage. But these plans changed, and Airacobras were used in the Southwest Pacific, Alaska, the Canal Zone, Mediterranean areas, at many remote islands in the Pacific defence chain, and in the continental US as defense and training fighters. It had been decided, properly, that low level short range Airacobras were unsuitable for missions over Europe.

A large part , almost exactly half, of P-39 production went to the USSR. They were properly used in Russian operations and well liked, their principal role being ground attack. The planes were considered structurally rugged, but like other aircraft with liquid-cooled engines, their cooling systems were vulnerable to gunfire. German fighter pilots on the Russian front claimed they ran up big scores against Airacobras.

Another role for the P-39 was advanced fighter training in the US. It was considered a very nice-flying aircraft at low and moderate altitudes by experienced pilots. Only a light touch on the controls was required as the airplane was very responsive. It was different from most fighters in that there were no hydraulically-operated items except wheel brakes. Landing gear and flap operation was electric. When the nose guns of early models were fired acrid fumes leaked into the cockpit. The propeller gearbox drive shaft ran forward at engine speed between the pilot's legs. Though some were nervous about this, records show the arrangement almost never caused trouble.

The mechanical gun-charging system on the P-39 was operated manually via cables from low in the cockpit, and was awkwardly located and hard to operate. In addition the 37mm cannon was for a long time unreliable, and often there was a stoppage after expenditure of a few rounds. The alternate 20 mm cannon installation was more popular with many pilots, being reliable, faster-firing, and longer ranged.

The final models of the P-39 employed a single lever synchronizing the propeller and throttle controls with the object of lessening pilot workload, an arrangement also employed on the follow-on P-63 fighter.

The P-39 was a boldly designed innovative airplane for its time, but lack of adequate engine supercharging and fuel capacity severely limited operational capability. Its reputation as a tricky airplane to fly would not alone have been limiting, since there were others in somewhat the same category, and experienced pilots handled them well. In spite of its limitations, thousands were built by Bell Aircraft on a very efficient production line until supplanted in 1944 by a similar looking but quite different P-63 airplane.

A few Airacobras survived the war to be used as civil racers for a time, and some were provided to foreign air forces, notably that of Italy, but none were in the postwar USAAF.

CURTISS P-40, AN INTRODUCTION

The P-40 was different from the P-38 and P-39 fighters in being more evolutionary than revolutionary in concept and design. Whereas the P-38 was Lockheed's first single seat fighter and the P-39 Bell's first, the P-40 had fighter ancestors back to just after World War I. Its direct antecedent was the Army's P-36, standard equipment in the late 1930s, using a Pratt and Whitney aircooled radial engine, and reportedly a fine handling aircraft with unspectacular speed performance. High speed was around 300 mph at 10000 feet altitude.

Spurred by reports of high performance in European fighters using inline liquid cooled V-12 engines (neglected by the Army since the days of the old Curtiss Conqueror), and now interested in the new Allison V-12 and what its slim contour might do for a P-36, the Army ordered one modified with the Allison as the XP-40. As with the P-39, the Allison was equipped only with a single stage single speed integral supercharger. After considerable development on the new installation, the P-40 emerged with significant speed improvement and retained most of the P-36's good handling characteristics. It became the new standard Army fighter with first production deliveries in the spring of 1940. Subsequent versions had more armament and some armor, making them heavier and slightly slower, but when the Japanese struck the US at Pearl Harbor in December 1941 the P-40 was the Army's fighter. There had been to that time 2810 P-40s built compared to 796 P-39s and only 167 P-38s. We went to war with what we had!

Export versions of the P-40, the Tomahawks, had been in combat with the British in North Africa since the spring of 1941, and were regarded there as pretty fair low to medium altitude fighters and ground attack machines, particularly against the Italians, but no match for the latest German equipment at higher altitudes. In China with Chennault's Flying Tigers the P-40s wove a legend, particularly because of the Chennault flyers intelligent use of their capabilities. When the Japanese invaded the Southwest Pacific the P-40 was thrown into a series of losing battles against larger numbers of enemy aircraft. With armor and bullet-proof tanks it was hundreds of pounds heavier than the opposing fighters, and could not climb or maneuver with them. And, like the P-39, it often could not climb in time to intercept high flying enemy bombers. On the plus side the P-40 was faster in level flight and diving than Japanese airplanes of the early wartime period. In addition it was rugged and armored, so normally held its own in fights of near equal

Curtiss H81 A-2 Tomahawk, Mfr. Photo via John Schneider. A Tomahawk destined for Britain sits on the tarmac at Buffalo near the end of 1940, about a year before Pearl Harbor. Curtiss was the only American company turning out substantial numbers of fighters at this time. British H81 versions started their fighting in North Africa. Armament was two heavy caliber fuselage machine guns and four rifle caliber wing guns as shown here.

numbers. Like other US fighters with liquid cooled engines, however, a hit in the P-40 cooling system would disable the airplane quickly. Comments in reports of May 1942 from the Pacific on the P-40 included; "Performance above 18000 feet sluggish, rate of climb too low at all altitudes, wing loading too high to maneuver with enemy fighters, 40 to 50 mph faster than the Japanese at medium altitudes; hit and run tactics must be employed against the maneuverable Japanese fighters". Reports also stated three to four enemy aircraft were being downed for every P-40 lost in combat.

P-40s were exported to Russia where they were used extensively, however it was reported P-39s were preferred by the Russians, perhaps because the P-40 lacked a cannon. Flying qualities of the P-40 were reasonably docile; it was usually labeled as pleasant to fly. It was lighter than late model P-51s. It had to be retrimmed for just about any change in airspeed or engine power, and in a dive there was a large directional trim change, so pilots had to get used to standing on one rudder pedal. Elevator forces tended to get heavy in a dive pullout. On takeoff, like other high-powered single engine fighters, the P-40 pilot really had to use trim and rudder pedal to hold against propeller torque reaction, a lesson learned early. Although P-40 stall characteristics were gentle given well coordinated pilot control, the airplane could snap roll if handled poorly, and then would spin in a manner the manual described as "extremely violent". Normal procedures could effect a recovery within two turns however. The P-40 was known to pilots as a ground-looper, and crosswind landings were especially difficult to handle. Where young pilot-trainees worried about a takeoff engine failure in a P-38, and stalling out and tumbling in a P-39, they were concerned about ground-looping on landing in a P-40. The P-40 was considered more difficult to land than other US Army fighters.

The P-40 went through constant design changes into late 1944 when production was finally stopped. Major changes in appearance up front accompanied Allison's revision of engine-propeller reduction gearing from internal to external spur drive characterized by a raised spinner and a deeper airscoop underneath. If the carburetor air scoop was atop the cowl, the plane was powered by an Allison engine with downdraft carburetor. If there was no upper cowl scoop, the airplane had a Packard Merlin with single stage two speed supercharger and updraft carburetor fed by air coming in the underneath scoop. The Merlin-powered F and L versions had slightly better altitude performance because of the two supercharger speeds.

The destabilizing effect of the big scoop up front required increasing tail volume (the product of tail arm and tail area) to gain back stability lost, and after considerable experimentation, including NACA tests, fuselage length was increased twenty inches, and other tail modifications made. The designer of the P-36 and early P-40s, Don Berlin (who had left Curtiss), always maintained if the front scoop had been properly designed the length increase would have been unnecessary. The additional length again substantially changed the appearance of the fighter, but overall performance changed little through the later versions of the aircraft.

P-40 fighters were employed just about everywhere in the world but the European Theatre. They fought in North Africa and throughout the Mediterranean, in the campaigns for Sicily and Sardinia, over the Anzio beachead, and did yeoman fighter-bomber service up the Italian peninsula until replaced by P-47s. At times they were the only US fighters in the China-Burma-India Theatre, were used effectively in the Southwest Pacific by US, Australian, and New Zealand forces, also in Russia, and were employed in large numbers as fighter-trainers in the US throughout the war. The P-40 was the first fighter a great number of US pilot-trainees flew, and it was regarded kindly by most.

There was a great deal of post-war criticism about the P-40 being kept in production until late 1944, long after it was considered a first-line fighter by the USAAF. However these fighters were used effectively in many areas of the world where nothing else would have been available, in addition to their use in the training role. Curtiss-Wright was frustrated in continual efforts to provide a production line sucessor to the P-40 via the XP-46 and P-60 series. It never did get a new fighter design into production as its nearby neighbor, Bell Aircraft, managed to do with the P-63 follow-on to the P-39.

The P-40 served honorably around the world as a rugged short-legged middle-altitude fighter in the 350 mph high speed category. It could double quite nicely in the light fighter-bomber class.

One famous Japanese fighter pilot gave the P-40 high praise when he indicated how unhappy he was anytime he had to face a well-piloted P-40 airplane. German pilots in the North African campaigns were more disdainful of the P-40, and several German aces with high scores claimed P-40 types made up large portions of their victory totals.

By wars end P-40s were generally out of service except as trainers, and none were retained by the USAAF, though Curtiss made late efforts to sell some as two-place trainers. There are a few in museums, and several in flight status as hobbyist airplanes, but none of the early Tomahawk type seem to have survived.

REPUBLIC P-47 THUNDERBOLT, AN INTRODUCTION

The P-47 Thunderbolt, known as the Jug (for Juggernaut, presumeably) was big and heavy for a single engine fighter. When you stood next to it the airplane looked more like a big brute than other fighters. It was comparable in load-carrying capability to the P-38, and also being turbosupercharged had excellent performance at high altitudes. It was marginally faster, but poorer in climb and had less range. The P-47 sported heavy firepower, being able to deliver thirteen pounds of lead per second from eight .50 caliber wing machine guns, and in spite of excellent high altitude performance was used most extensively in ground attack.

The Jug was an evolutionary design, in many respects a blow-up of predecessor Seversky/Republic fighter aircraft starting with the P-35 and later the P-43 Lancer. There was a family look—the radial engine, capacious fuselage, and eliptical wing planform, even the tail shaping. Its eight guns were certainly a firepower advance compared to two or four guns of its predecessors. Turbosupercharging of a radial engine had been employed in its limited-production antecedent, the Lancer, where even the location of the turbo unit was similar—way to the rear under the fuselage.

Except for the P-61 and Navy Hellcat, the P-47 was the last US fighter into combat, nine months behind the Allison-powered P-51. First flight was in spring 1941, first production in early spring 1942, and first combat in spring 1943. It was the most-produced US fighter of World War II, barely beating out the P-51. The main plant in Farmingdale, Long Island and a new "from scratch" facility at Evansville, Indiana produced practically all the aircraft, with Curtiss at Buffalo contributing a few in a poor effort.

Hopes were high for the P-47 when introduced into the European Theatre. After initial problems were sorted out, the aircraft started to prove itself as a tough customer and a match for enemy fighters. But it did have drawbacks, one a great ability to go downhill, but poor capability in climb. Even more important, it lacked range, and in 1943 fighter range was the critical item. Alone in England at the time as an escort fighter for Eighth Air Force heavy bombers (the P-38s had earlier departed for North Africa), the P-47 could not go the escort distance required, and losses of unescorted bombers were high. Emergency measures succeeded in adding droppable tanks of various types to the Jugs, extending their escort radius. Later internal fuel tankage was also increased, but the range problem was never fully solved as escort distances required steadily increased. It remained for the new Merlin-powered P-51 to solve the problem later, and the P-47, except for one group, was replaced in Eighth Air Force and turned over to Ninth Air Force for tactical duties. It served admirably as the best ground-attack fighter the Army had.

P-47s also fought in the Mediterranean area, including the Italian campaign, as well as in the invasion of southern France. Entered into the western Pacific in July 1943 with the Fifth Air Force, the Jug was again criticized for lack of range. P-47s were in China starting in spring 1944, and the British operated some in the Far East. About 200 got to Russia.

Later in the war, under threat of Thunderbolt order cancellations because of limited range, Republic brought out a new version for the Pacific, the P-47N, with a bigger wing and much more internal fuel. This model entered Pacific combat late in the war. The

Republic P-47N Thunderbolt, Ser. 44-88908, F. Dean coll. Its big four-blade Curtiss Electric propeller nearly touching the ground, this Jug is doing a bit of flat-hatting. One identification characteristic of the N version, clearly shown here, was the squared-off wingtips. Barely visible is the larger dorsal fin on this late long range model meant for operating over Pacific distances. This final Thunderbolt version was Republic's answer to criticism of the P-47's lack of legs.

aircraft had staying power and served well after the war with USAAF and USAF units. Some were provided to other countries like Brazil and Iran.

The P-47 used the popular and reliable Pratt and Whitney R-2800 Double Wasp engine, the only Army single seat production fighter to do so, and this contributed greatly to its success.

The Jug got into trouble with compressibility soon after production started because, like the P-38, it could fly high and dive fast, and did not have the new laminar flow wing design. One was tested, but never made it to production. Along the way underwing dive flaps were added, and pilots rated them very effective. P-47D variants were the most produced, and regarded with affection by most Jug pilots. It was relatively quiet in the big cockpit, though lack of leg room was noteably apparent. It was forgiving to fly and the engine was a favorite. Other attributes included rugged structure and good armor, dear to the heart of every fighter pilot. Pilots also liked the electrically operated bubble canopy installed on late D models. They loved the good visibility, but complained about excess cockpit heat when flying low in warmer climates.

The conversion from earlier "razor-back" versions to newer bubble canopy aircraft reduced the turtledeck stabilizing area aft on initial airplanes. The airplane could get into a snap roll if flown in an uncoordinated manner allowing over ten degrees yaw at high speeds. A dorsal fin was soon added to restore adequate lateral-directional stability characteristics.

Some World War II pilot comments on the P-47 are interesting:

-"Best all-around fighter above 25000 feet."
-"Best armor installation."
-"Has a large turning circle; poor maneuverability; not for a dog-fight; stalls in a steep turn at three g."
-"Good dive and zoom performance."
-"Performance not so good at low altitude; mediocre rate of climb."

It is interesting to note that the P-47, designed as a high altitude fighter with a second stage supercharger, was used most effectively as a tactical ground support fighter-bomber aircraft throughout the latter part of the war. In a tribute to its flexibility the P-47 was retained in service long after cessation of hostilities, serving in Reserve and Air National Guard units with distinction. The big Jug was not the most spectacular airplane, but got many jobs done well.

Strangely there are very few of these planes preserved today compared to P-51 Mustangs, even though slightly more P-47s were built. One reason, perhaps; the P-47 was never used for postwar racing like the Mustang.

NORTH AMERICAN P-51 MUSTANG, AN INTRODUCTION
The P-51 Mustang has had, in postwar years, the best name recognition of US World War II fighters. Extensive use as an air racer

North American P-51D Mustang Ser. 44-74629, USAF photo via Dave Menard. A post-war "Spam-Can" with buzz markings on the fuselage and USAF on the wing. Though we are unable to see here, many post-war P-51s had a fixed tail wheel. The planform of the laminar flow airfoil wing is well shown including a forward rake of the leading edge inboard and the protrusions giving away the six gun armament. Merlin engined Mustangs provided the solution to US bomber escort problems.

and collector's airplane has for decades provided it wide visual recognition. Even a car was named for it, the mid-1960s Ford Mustang still marketed today.

The Mustang's debut in the fall of 1940 was inauspicious as a British-ordered US design, and the first from-scratch fighter ever from North American, a company then noted for producing trainer airplanes.

Powered by the same Allison engine with single stage single speed supercharging as the P-39 and P-40 airplanes, it seemed this slick-looking machine might fall into the mold of just another medium altitude fighter, and US Army interest was not high; two aircraft were ordered for testing. As British Allison powered Mustangs entered war service real virtues began to show; they performed very well in army cooperation and low level reconnaisance missions. They were fast, handled well, and were liked by UK pilots. The British Mustang was the first US designed fighter sufficiently favored by England to operate in the "big" European war—a harbinger of things to come.

The US Army showed appreciation of the type by ordering a batch as dive bombers, this apparently due to a temporary lack of fighter funds. A-36 attack/dive bomber aircraft served in the Mediterranean areas shortly after the fall of North Africa to the Allied forces. Other early P-51 types were shipped to the backwater China-Burma-India Theatre, some as dive bombers and some as fighters.

Luckily it came to be recognized in 1943 by a few observers that if the sleek Mustang airframe with its new laminar flow wing design (and the lowest flat plate drag area of any US fighter) were combined with a high altitude engine like the Rolls Royce Merlin in the Spitfire Mark 9, it should make a very good all-around fighter airplane. And again, the Mustang with its low drag had potential for long range capability at a time when there was no really successful strategic escort fighter for US bombers over Europe. P-38s and P-47s both had problems as escorts. The British installed Merlins in Mustang test aircraft. After some development work the Merlin engine, with a two-stage supercharger and critical altitude near 30000 feet, combined beautifully with the Mustang airframe. A superior fighter was born and put into production in the US powered by a Packard Motor Car Company produced Merlin.

The first Merlin Mustangs were very fine performers, bettering their enemy opposition in all performance factors but climb and roll rate, but suffered from poor cockpit visibility and, with only four guns, marginal hitting power. Worse, the gun installation was subject to jams during combat maneuvers. Extra internal fuel had been added in a fuselage tank well aft of the center of gravity and, while excellent range for bomber escort was obtained, care had to be used in flying the normally stable aircraft when the aft tank was full. Under this condition, and until about half the fuel in this tank was burned off, the airplane was unstable and difficult to fly. Aft tank fuel was always burned first—hopefully accomplished before encountering enemy aircraft.

The pilot vision and gun problems were solved admirably in the "Spam-can", the P-51D model, by providing a full bubble canopy, going to six guns, and correcting jamming problems by completely modifying the gun installation. Thus was born what is usually called the best all-around US Army fighter airplane of the war for air to air combat and escort.

With a combination of full internal fuel and largest external drop tanks, the P-51D, and its similar counterpart the P-51K, could go anywhere the bombers needed to go, stay with them near the target and fight off enemy aircraft, and then return with the "heavies".

Unfortunately the Army got off to a slow start in recognizing the full potential of the Mustang, and Merlin Mustangs did not enter service in large numbers in Europe until the spring of 1944. Even at a far-along stage of the war the Army was sending the first Merlin Mustangs to the Ninth (tactical) Air Force in England instead of the Eighth (strategic) Air Force which so sorely needed an effective long range escort fighter, and had to borrow planes from the Ninth.

Eventually, with minor exceptions, the P-51D/K Mustang was to equip the whole Eighth Air Force Fighter Command, and slowly percolated into other areas of the war. It was later used as an escort for B-29s in very long range missions over Japan during the war's final stages.

Mustangs were retained in the Air Force for a long time after World War II, and fought with distinction in the Korean conflict. Even today the Mustang is known as a premium piston engined fighter, a combination of the then-best of British and US technology in a deadly and handsome fighter airplane. As racer airplanes, with many modifications, P-51s have taken honors from wars end up to the present time, and many near stock versions can be seen at air shows today.

Norhtrop P-61 Black Widow, Ser. 42-39728, Mfr. photo via F. Dean coll. As the only US warplane designed from the start as a night fighter, its black paint job seems appropriate for the job. With the size and weight of a World War II medium bomber, the performance of the Widow was not up to that of other late model US fighters, but its benign flying qualities were praised by its pilots. With a crew of three, two big Double Wasp engines, radar in the nose, and very heavy armament, the P-61 was quite an airplane for it time. Production was minimal compared to most other US wartime fighters.

P-61 BLACK WIDOW, AN INTRODUCTION

The P-61 Black Widow night fighter could easily be mistaken for a medium bomber as its size was in that class. It was arranged like a P-38 with twin engines and twin tail booms, but similarity ended there. The P-61 had twin row R-2800 radial engines and a relatively large fuselage carrying three people, radar, four fixed cannon, and a flexible four-gun turret. It was a lot of airplane and complex for its day, even including an autopilot and a remote gun firing control system.

The P-61 did not evolve from predecessor types, and was built by a relatively fledgling company. Its reason for being was night fighting, a problem that bothered the British and others from the war's early stages. Requirements were set by observations of the problem of trying in England to down night raider aircraft. The airplane had to carry airborne interception radar to acquire targets at night after being directed into an area by a ground radar controller, to have enough performance to stay with an acquired target, and required overwhelming firepower to down an intruder. It also had to defend itself, have good all-weather capability, provide sufficient loiter time, and not require excessive pilot workload. A big order for the time, and the Northrop company, selected to develop and produce the P-61 because they were not then occupied with a major program, came up with quite an airplane. It took time, however, and the plane did not get into combat until the last year of the war. In spite of its relative complexity, the P-61 did not take much extra development time compared to other fighters.

Innovations were many in the Widow, among them use of spoilers for lateral control with only small "tickler" ailerons to give the pilot feel. Since spoilers could be located ahead of instead of outboard of the flaps like conventional ailerons, a very long span flap system gave excellent low speed flying qualities.

The P-61 could do all sorts of acrobatics with ease, and was noted for gentle stall behavior. Pilots praised flying qualities, but were not excited about performance. It was excellent as a turning aircraft, and capable of giving some single engine fighters a terrific battle. The firepower of the Black Widow was tremendous, though for awhile the turret had to be omitted because in certain positions it excited turbulent airflow that vibrated the tail. This problem was later solved, and the four .50 calibers went back on the airplane. The fixed belly cannon were fired by the pilot, and the remotely-controlled top turret, arranged to fire through a full 360 degrees, was normally the gunner's weapon, though it could be handed off for control by either the pilot or the radio operator in the aft end. The gunner sat aft of and above the pilot in a tandem arrangement, and the radio operator could either face aft or forward in the rear portion of the central crew nacelle.

P-61 aircraft started percolating into European and Pacific Theatres squadron by squadron in the middle of 1944 to replace cobbled-up light bombers like the P-70 that pioneered Army night fighting efforts. The new airplane's successes were sporadic, and their victories were numbered in the isolated ones and twos, so their impact in the combat zones was minimal. Many times, because of their heavy firepower, they were used in daylight ground interdiction missions rather than as night fighters. In the Pacific particularly, range was a problem, and the P-61, with two big thirsty engines, was no exception. Sometimes the turret system was removed, and jury-rigged extra internal fuel tanks were located in the turret area. Later versions had provisions for external drop tanks to gain range.

Responding to criticism that the P-61 was too low and slow to be an effective night fighter, Northrop installed turbosupercharged R-2800 engines in a late version. The modifications gave the Widow quite a boot at altitude, but only a few of this version were produced before the war ended.

Perhaps the most-remembered incident in P-61 Pacific wartime history occurred during the campaign to retake the Philippines. General MacArthur, not satisfied with the performance of P-61s

stationed there, asked for replacement by Navy F6F-5N night fighters for a time. The exchange was made, and the Widows in question were sent temporarily to duty in a back-water area while the Hellcats took over. A reverse switch was made later.

Since production of the Widow was not large by wartime standards (about 650 aircraft), and arrival in combat areas was late, the aircraft had only a minor impact on war fortunes. It was, however, a significant milestone in the history of US military aircraft, being the first true night fighter to come into Army service, and the first to integrate the complex radar, flight control, and weapons fire control subsystems into an aircraft designed from scratch for night fighting. Given the combination of requirements and the state of the art of all the necessary components, the P-61 was notable indeed. And Northrop put these elements into one of the nicest-flying aircraft ever produced in the wartime era.

Bell P-63A Kingcobra, Ser. 42-68941, Mfr. photo. An updated and completely redesigned version of the Airacobra, the P-63 had the same basic design theme of a mid-located buried engine with a forward extension shaft to the propeller, this arrangement to allow installation of a cannon firing through the nose. Important changes to correct some P-39 deficiencies were additional engine supercharging and a new laminar flow airfoil wing design. But internal fuel capacity was still modest, thereby severely limiting combat radius capability.

BELL P-63 KINGCOBRA, AN INTRODUCTION

The P-63 Kingcobra was unique in one respect; it was the result of a second chance given a company to produce a wartime US Army fighter, the first being the P-39. Only Grumman had a similar second shot, with its Hellcat succeding the Wildcat for the Navy. The P-63 got into production only in 1944 when the P-39 was phased

out, and then was used only sparingly by the USAAF and never in combat groups. Of roughly 3300 wartime Kingcobras produced, fully 2400 of them reached Russia, almost all ferried over the Alaska-Siberia route. Records of use by the USSR are obscure.

A larger leaner Airacobra with the same general arrangement— the Allison engine again mounted aft of the pilot—the Kingcobra incorporated many improvements over its older brother. Although arrangement was similar, all parts were new and different. The wing had a new laminar flow airfoil section to delay onset of compressibility, and the engine was equipped with a new auxiliary-stage supercharger to hold power at altitude and thereby obtain increased airplane speed up high, thus correcting the primary deficiency of the earlier Airacobra. In addition, pilot workload was reduced by inclusion of automatic manifold pressure control and a single lever combining throttle and RPM control.

A good deal of effort by Bell and the NACA went into getting good flying qualities for the P-63, and they pretty much succeeded. The type was universally regarded as a nice-flying airplane with the best rate of roll of any Army production fighter.

By the time Bell got the P-63 into production there was some very tough US fighter competition in being, namely the Merlin-powered Mustang, also with a laminar flow wing and an auxiliary-stage supercharger. And this competition flew faster and higher. And to cap it off the P-51 had much better combat radius capability.

P-63 aircraft were tested at Eglin Field, Florida where it was suggested unless improvements could be made in several areas to make it fully competitive with the latest P-51 models, P-63 production should be cancelled. It was not cancelled, but most went to Russia to satisfy what was at times an almost insatiable demand for fighter aircraft. In the spring of 1944, when faced with Russian requests for more fighters, General Hap Arnold, head of the USAAF, suggested they be given as many used P-39 and P-63 aircraft as were in the US.

A major deficiency of the P-63 was lack of range, and this at a time when more and more range was demanded of fighters. Little more internal fuel capacity was provided than in the earlier short-legged P-39. Drop tanks would be added under the fuselage, and later under the wings, but adding more internal fuel for the return leg of a mission was difficult if not impossible.

Like the Airacobra the P-63 carried a lot of punch in the nose with a 37mm cannon firing through the hollow propeller shaft, this being the central theme of Bell fighter philosophy from the start. Unique among the second generation fighters, the P-63 retained two synchronized .50 caliber nose guns, the last US World War II production fighter to do so. In addition, a podded .50 caliber gun could be carried under each wing. The Army test people at Eglin Field did not like this arrangement, and wanted internally-mounted wing machine guns like contemporary fighters.

It is interesting that among many Russian complaints about US fighters was one that P-63s were structurally weak. Aft fuselages of P-63s going to Russia were strengthened in Alaska in late 1944. It was true the US supplied a less-favored fighter to the USSR, the P-63 instead of the P-51. When commanders in the Pacific were crying for more long range P-38s, the Washington Air Force offered a batch of P-63s. There is no record of a response, but P-63 aircraft were never operated by Army Air Force combat units in Pacific areas, nor by the US in any combat zone. Late in the war some Kingcobras were delivered to the Free French Air Force.

A few P-63 airplanes remained in military service after the war, but not for long. An interesting use of specially designed Kingcobras with thicker metal skinning and special pilot protection was that of "pinball" target aircraft for bomber gunner training using frangible bullets. In gunnery practice the bombers would actually fire to hit attacking P-63s, and light up the fighter if hits were scored. Some aircraft were used in postwar development projects, and a very few in air racing, but the type disappeared quickly from use.

Brewster 339D Buffalo, photo via P.M. Bowers. An export version of the US Navy F2A-2/3, the aircraft shown is at the Newark, NJ, airport where Brewster did assembly work in a large hangar. The bulbous fuselage resulted from use up front of a large diameter nine cylinder Wright Cyclone engine. Much maligned, the Brewster fighter certainly had its faults, but also had the misfortune of nearly always being badly outnumbered by the enemy in the early Asia-Pacific fighting.

BREWSTER F2A- BUFFALO, AN INTRODUCTION

The Brewster F2A- airplane, along with its competitor, the Grumman F4F-, was a pioneer in US naval aviation as one of two new monoplane fighters competing for production. Tested by the Navy in early 1938, and shortly after by the National Advisory Committee for Aeronautics (NACA, now NASA), the Brewster fighter was slightly modified and approved for production, thus beating out the F4F- initially.

A stubby rotund fighter with a fixed wing (the Navy was not ready to fold fighter wings) and sprightly performance, the F2A- was one of only two World War II US fighters powered with the single row nine cylinder Wright Cyclone engine (the other was certain versions of the Wildcat), and thus started out with a large diameter up front. Another distinguishing feature of the Brewster, one to cause almost continuous trouble on aircraft carriers as time progressed, was the arrangement of the wide-tread landing gear which seldom gave ground looping problems like its Wildcat contemporary. The wheels retracted into lower forward pockets in the fuselage like the Grumman, but there similarity ended. Long sloped struts supported wheels of the Brewster in a manner sure to put members in bending from vertical landing loads. The restraint against drag loads was close coupled, throwing high forces into the wing fittings. Carrier landings were rather violent affairs, and landing gear failures were frequent.

In original form, the F2A-1, the Brewster fighter managed to exceed, after modifications, a 300 mph high speed—the very desireable goal of those days. It was considered to handle very well, and be a delightfully maneuverable airplane. One pilot flew it two hours on a first flight simply because he enjoyed it so much. Most early versions (forty-four of fifty-four ordered) were fitted with commercial-equivalent engines, and sent in 1940 to Finland to aid that small country's fight against invading Russians. Reports indicated these Model 239 aircraft acquitted themselves well in northern fighting, though winter weather gave some trouble.

The first version the US Navy obtained in any quantity was the F2A-2 with uprated engine, though numbers of Brewster aircraft were never large. Prior to weighty combat modifications these aircraft were considered excellent flying machines, at least at low and moderate altitudes where Cyclone power held up.

The British started receiving export versions, having already taken over an order destined for Belgium after that country was over-run by German forces. British evaluation of their 339E version noted it made a very nice training airplane, but not a front line fighter for European use. Thus the Brewster airplanes were sent as desperately needed reinforcements to the Far East. These aircraft, along with Brewster fighters exported to the Netherlands East Indies, were among forces catching the full brunt of initial Japanese offensives to the south. Completely overwhelmed by fast-striking superior forces, including the excellent Japanese Zero fighter, the 339s and other Allied warplanes did not last long. In the Dutch East Indies, Singapore, and Burma the Brewsters, together with other hastily-gathered forces, fought and lost. As at Midway later on, where the Marines operated later F2A-3 versions against Japanese attackers, Brewster fighters were up against greater numbers and the result was inevitable. They were used at a time in the war when the Allies were rocked back on their heels and losing badly.

After the US Navy decided to take F2A-2 and F2A-3 aircraft off carriers and replace them with Wildcats, they were given to the Marines as land-based fighters. Shortly after the Midway battle in mid-1942, the Brewsters were taken from front line service and used as fighter trainers in the continental US, many based at Florida naval stations. By this time most were beat up and regarded as maintenance headaches. Gradually all were replaced with Wildcats. Manufacture of the type was stopped, and Brewster retooled to start making Corsairs under licence.

The Brewster fighters had basic design problems dogging them from the start. A single piece wing design gave rise to British criticism that any damage meant a whole new wing, and the fuel tanks designed integrally with the wing beams made it difficult if not impossible to make them self-sealing against gunfire. The US Navy on later models went as far as to add new tanks in places where they could be protected, while leaving the original unprotected ones in place and limiting their use. The single stage engine supercharger, while two-speed, still made certain that power available, and thus performance, fell off quickly with altitude—this as opposed to the two-stage supercharger used with the Wildcat engine. The many failures of landing gear on carriers made the aircraft less than popular at sea. And, like other US fighters, Wildcat included, weight added to bring the aircraft up to modern wartime standards reduced combat capabilities significantly. Performance and flying qualities deteriorated, and the type was reduced from the nice-flying maneuverable fighter of 1939 to an overloaded, marginally stable, and disliked has-been of 1942.

Brewster had the dubious distinction, after producing some Corsairs and a dive bomber, of being the only military aircraft company to go out of business during the war.

No example of a Brewster fighter can be seen in the US today, perhaps a reflection of the low esteem in which it was generally held. One does remain in a museum in Finland, however, in a tribute to the good service it provided that country.

Eastern FM-1 Wildcat, Henry McGrew photo via Joe Weathers. Cuising high over the California coastline in 1944, this GM-Eastern-built Wildcat shows the pilot with cockpit canopy open and definitely "behind the eight ball". Attached to Marine Squadron VMF-112, the FM-1 was a General Motors equivalent to the F4F-4 with four guns installed instead of six. A well-remembered characteristic of the Wildcat was its manually-retracted narrow tread landing gear.

GRUMMAN F4F- WILDCAT, AN INTRODUCTION

The F4F- had the distinction of being the oldest, in first flight date, of US wartime production fighters, and narrowly missed being a biplane. Although other monoplanes had been tested by the Navy, the F4F- was one of the first serious attempts, along with the contemporary Brewster, to develop a monoplane carrier deck fighter airplane. It was lucky the Navy started when they did, because development to a first production aircraft took almost two and one half years. The Wildcat was just in time for US entry into World War II. There were not many available; about four hundred had been produced by Grumman. Nowhere near that number were with fleet operating squadrons at the time of the Pearl Harbor attack.

A squat and chubby aircraft in the Grumman mold of the times, the Wildcat, in its initial F4F-3 form, was a sprightly machine with a fixed mid-wing, limiting severely the number stowable aboard fleet carriers. It used a two-stage two-speed supercharged Twin Wasp engine that gave respectable performance at altitude, and a hand-cranked narrow-tread retractable main landing gear never to be forgotten by any who flew the aircraft. A Navy commander cracked, late in the war, there were only two kinds of Navy fighter pilots— those who had ground looped the aircraft, and those who were going to. Armament consisted of four .50 caliber wing guns, each with a substantial supply of ammunition. A F4F-3A version was put out with less engine supercharging to cover for temporary production problems with the two-stage engine. These were either in-

termingled with Navy -3s or tossed off to the Marine Corps, which operated Wildcats from shore bases instead of carriers. Since the British had no modern carrier fighters, they also needed Wildcats (initially named Martlets by them), and many were exported. In contrast to Brewster fighters, the Wildcats operated well from carrier decks. Decent visibility, good low speed handling qualities, and a strong energy-absorbing landing gear gave pilots a good chance to avoid operational accidents at sea. Navy pilots were pleased with their mounts, and in initial encounters with Japanese aircraft the -3s gave a good account of themselves, even against the new and surprising enemy Zero fighter.

Several design modifications combined to change the attitude of Navy fighter pilots, all adding weight to the Wildcat. Protection for pilots and fuel tanks had to be added in the form of armor plate and self-sealing to withstand fire from enemy planes. Pilots had no quarrel here, though loss of performance from extra weight was not welcome. Next was the need for more fighters per carrier, necessitating wing folding. A power fold system was tested, but deemed not operationally necessary, so lighter weight manual folding by plane handlers was adopted. Another substantial weight penalty was then thrust upon the F4F-. The British felt four guns were not sufficient, and wanted six in their export versions. Grumman gave them a six gun installation, and to standardize production the US Navy Bureau of Aeronautics agreed to use the six gun arrangement, with much less ammunition per gun, in US Navy F4F-4 airplanes. Weight went up again. This upset US carrier pilots, and unhappiness was rampant over decreased performance of the F4F-4 Wildcat, including less range (the self-sealing tanks had less capacity) and less rounds per gun. Gradually pilots learned to accept shortcomings of the new production Wildcat, love it for its virtues, and let development of good fighting tactics, aerial marksmanship, rugged structure, and gunfire protection make up for known performance deficiencies. The Wildcat had to last until new fighters could be sent to handle the enemy. This meant hanging in there with the Marines until Corsairs arrived in early 1943, and at sea with the Navy until Hellcats got there in late 1943. During these months the Wildcat acquitted itself well, downing many more enemy aircraft (a 6.9:1 ratio in the air was claimed) than were lost to enemy action.

When Grumman tapered off Wildcat production, Eastern Aircraft Division of General Motors picked up the slack, and after producing a version like the F4F-4 (the FM-1 with only four guns!), put out over 4000 of an updated model for small escort carriers used by both US and Royal Navys. The FM-2 differed in having the nine-cylinder Wright R-1820 engine with a single stage two speed supercharger and was revised somewhat in other ways, but pilots still had to cope with the hand-cranked landing gear. One pilot commented, after flying a Corsair in a mock dogfight with an FM-2, there was no way he could stay on its tail. Escort carriers with FM-2s aboard tried to stay out of the way of enemy fighters, however.

The Wildcats, like their Army counterparts the P-39 and P-40, held the line as best they could until later US fighters could get into the fray. When the chips were really down, as at Guadalcanal in the Solomon Islands, Marine and Navy Wildcat fighters performed well under extremely adverse circumstances.

Eastern produced so many FM-2 Wildcats that a healthy supply remained after the war as surplus. Many were bought for a song by civilian enthusiasts, and a few remain on flight status today as hobbyist planes.

Civil Vought F4U-1D Corsair, photo via Mfr. A refurbished civilian Corsair shown post-war in a photo supplied by Ling Temco Vought. A slim forward fuselage was gained by locating the fuel tank and cockpit in tandem, the tank properly being over the wing. The semi-bubble cockpit enclosure yielded better forward visibility than on previous "birdcage" versions, but the pilot still sat further aft than in other US fighters. The hallmark gulled wing shows well in this photo.

VOUGHT F4U- CORSAIR, AN INTRODUCTION

In October 1940 the experimental model of the Corsair, the XF4U-1, excited both the Navy and its manufacturer, Chance Vought, by flying over Connecticut at a level flight speed of slightly over 400 mph. Whether this airplane or the Lockheed YP-38 was the first US fighter to exceed the magic 400 mph number is a question, but certainly the Corsair prototype was the first Navy fighter to do so.

The key to achieving such speed was the then-new eighteen-cylinder Pratt and Whitney Double Wasp air-cooled radial engine of near 2000 horsepower. This engine was equipped with a two-stage supercharger so the Corsair could fly high enough into thin air to go fast.

The Vought fighter was large, and distinctive in appearance because of an inverted gull wing, designed to reduce length of main landing gear required for ground clearance of a large propeller. In the prototype all fuel was carried in the wing, but for production it was decided to increase wing armament, and the space required necessitated displacement of a large part of the fuel to a fuselage location. Vought designers had the choice of locating this displaced fuel some distance from the center of gravity and suffering considerable CG travel with fuel burnoff, or locating the fuel at the longitudinal center of gravity and allowing the new tank to displace the cockpit well aft. Back the cockpit went, and this, combined with a low "birdcage" canopy design, gave rise to a continuing major complaint against the Corsair—poor pilot visibility. Later, raising the pilot, redesigning the canopy, and lengthening the tail wheel strut somewhat alleviated the problem, but the aircraft never had really good visibility.

Intended as the Navy's premier carrier fighter, the F4U- for a long time was a disappointment in this respect, but as a Marine land-based combat plane in the Pacific it would prove its worth. The F4U- did not inhabit carrier decks in any quantity until very late in the war when improved Corsairs gradually displaced the Grumman Hellcat.

Early problems with the Corsair included the poor visibility (one pilot said the only decent view was straight up, and Charles Lindbergh once compared Corsair forward visibility to that of his Spirit of Saint Louis), cowl flap actuators that leaked fluid over the windshield, a stiff bouncy landing gear, and a highly unsymmetrical stall pattern that could suddenly flip a pilot on his back in an underspeed landing or a sharp turn. The cowl flap problem was fixed fairly quickly by actuation redesign, and the stall problem solved later by using a spoiler strip on the right wing leading edge, but the springy landing gear lasted quite a while, with land-based Marine Corsairs bouncing all over Pacific island airstrips. Marine landings were often spectacular and sometimes deadly. It was not uncommon for new pilots to lose control in landing and smash into the jungle or parked airplanes. As time passed softer oleo shock struts were developed, and the problem went away.

In the air the Corsair was an effective fighter. It had the speed, altitude capability, and range to work well against the Japanese as a land-based aircraft. Though it could not dogfight close-in with them any more effectively than other US fighter planes, it had the ability to initiate and to break off combat, and deliver heavy firepower. Shortly after Southwest Pacific introduction by Marines in February 1943, the Corsair started making a good reputation in air combat. It had a very good roll rate and low maneuvering stick forces. Like other high speed high altitude fighters the F4U- could get into compressibility by diving near vertically from altitudes over 25000 feet. It accelerated quite rapidly and soon the critical Mach number

was reached. More than one pilot returned with tail parts missing; a common effect was the shredding of elevator fabric trying to pull out of a steep dive. Squadrons started prohibiting pilots from making high altitude vertical dives after incurring casualties. Many pilots considered late Corsair versions the best of all the US aerial combat machines. Except at altitudes above 25000 feet there was little to choose between the Corsair and the Army Merlin-powered P-51 in speed, and head-to-head performance tests showed the Navy aircraft could outclimb the P-51. The US Navy evaluated the P-51B against the Corsair at Patuxent River, Maryland, and decided the Corsair was superior for their purposes with the Mustang noted as not suitable. Below very high altitudes P-47 pilots became reluctant to tangle with Corsairs in mock combat during training. In April, 1944 the US Navy conducted further tests of the Corsair landing aboard an escort carrier planes with "de-bounced" landing gear oleo struts. These tests were sufficiently successful to clear the F4U- for carrier use. At the end of 1944 the Navy finally decided to dramatically increase the number of fighters on carriers because of heavy losses from Japanese kamakaze attacks, and to allow Marine squadrons with their Corsairs to operate from the carriers. The F4U- finally made it to sea! Two Marine squadrons went aboard the carrier Essex right after Christmas of 1944, but operational accidents were frequent.

The "bent-wing" Corsair was quickly adapted to ground attack missions as the war progressed and participated heavily, both from land and carrier bases, in the later major campaigns. Charles Lindbergh, working at the time for Vought, visited the Pacific in late 1944, and demonstrated capability of the Corsair in carrying and dropping both a 2000 pound and a 3000 pound bomb load, and in one instance with a special rack carried 4000 pounds, a 2000 pound bomb on center and two 1000 pounders. The last World War II version of the Corsair was the F4U-4, a considerably improved machine, but combat action of this aircraft was limited to the last four months of the war. The Corsair had the distinction of being the longest-produced piston engine fighter of the war and immediate post-was period, and was clearly the US Navy's preferred fighter for many years. The Navy used the Grumman Hellcat to continually goad Vought people into improving the Corsair design, particularly noting the excellent cockpit arrangement, good visibility forward, and superior carrier compatibility features of the Grumman fighter. The consensus seemed to be that the Corsair was a better all-around fighter for the expert pilot in the air, but the Hellcat was the preferred machine for the run-of-the-mill naval fighter pilot to minimize operational and training losses of fighters while still being able to clobber the enemy.

GRUMMAN F6F- HELLCAT, AN INTRODUCTION

If ever there was a fighter aircraft to successfully fill a wartime need it was the Hellcat. Next to last of US World War II fighters in first flight date (the P-63 was last), the F6F-, through prodigious efforts of all concerned, went from first flight to first Pacific combat in little more than a year. In addition the aircraft was not only a combat success but was successful in all operational aspects. Its benign flying characteristics were just what the Navy needed to introduce a new fighter to carrier flight decks while training a huge contingent of new naval fighter pilots. A replacement for the Wildcat, the design started as an improvement of that aircraft with a more powerful engine to cope with greater weight being imposed on the F4F-, but shortly was "improved" to a completely new design. The plane was sorely needed; the Wildcat was hard-pressed to cope with Japanese opposition, and the Corsair, though capable as a land-based fighter, was deemed unacceptable for operation aboard US aircraft carriers until very late in the war. The new Grumman had to be capable of handling the Japanese Zero models and other enemy fighters and of minimizing our own operational casualties. In these matters it was to prove successful indeed.

Like the Corsair the Hellcat was a big fighter. Its wingspan was slightly greater than the F4U- and and the wing had twenty square feet more area. Empty and gross weights were nearly the same, but the two aircraft were entirely different in looks. The Hellcat was definately a descendant of its stubby Grumman predecessors. The cockpit was placed at the highest point of a somewhat humpbacked fuselage to assure best possible visibility and fuel was located under the cockpit, yielding a deep fuselage with a less than handsome but functional appearance.

Although the Hellcat had the same engine and two stage supercharging system as the Corsair, slightly higher drag area made for lower speed performance, but the larger Hellcat wing with the

Grumman F6F-5 Hellcat, USN photo via Joe Weathers. A stubby looking Hellcat flying lead in formation with a Helldiver, an Avenger, and a Bearcat near Pensacola. Grmman chose to put the pilot over the fuselage fuel tank and wing as opposed to the Corsair arrangement, thus accounting for the deeper F6F- fuselage and better pilot forward vision. The good-tempered Hellcat was a fine aircraft both for training large numbers of new inexperienced Navy fighter pilots and for fighting the Japanese on better than equal terms.

same gross weight, and thus lower wing loading, provided a tighter turning capability and lower landing speeds. But the Hellcat, particularly the later F6F-5 version, was a fighter to take on the Japanese Zeke 52 and win, even at twice the weight of the enemy craft. It was much faster at all altitudes, had a better rate of climb at medium and higher altitudes, dove faster, and zoomed better. At lower speeds the Japanese aircraft was more maneuverable, but the Hellcat gained superiority in this respect at the higher speeds. So it was again a case of the Hellcat pilot using appropriate tactics to exploit areas of fighting advantage and to minimize those of performance disadvantage. The record of the airplane in combat indicated F6F- pilots were very successful in using its fighting capabilities since a victory-to-loss ratio of 19:1 was claimed! It should be kept in mind, however, that the Hellcat did not enter combat until twenty months after Pearl Harbor, thus escaping the particularly tough times of 1942 and early 1943 when US forces in the Pacific were heavily outnumbered.

Grumman passed off Wildcat production to Eastern Aircraft Division of General Motors and concentrated on production of the F6F- airplane. By the end of 1943 they had exceeded total Corsair production for that year by over 200 aircraft. In 1944 they produced over 700 more Hellcats than Vought and Goodyear produced Corsairs. The new Grumman plant put out 500 aircraft in January of 1944 alone, and increased the figure to 555 Hellcats in December, the highest monthly rate achieved for a Navy fighter to that time, about nine planes every twelve hours, day and night. During its wartime career relatively few changes were made to the F6F-. Water-alcohol injection systems were added to the powerplants of most -3 versions retrospectively and factory-installed in all -5s. Other changes from F6F-3 to F6F-5 models included a new pinched-in more streamlined engine cowling, a new very smooth paint finish for better drag characteristics, an improved windshield, new spring tab equipped ailerons for a better roll rate at high speeds, strengthened tail structure, and a larger sheet of armor plate behind the cockpit. Without detailed study the general observer would notice no difference between the versions. Pilots had interesting comments about the F6F- aircraft. One found it much less exciting to fly than the Wildcat. Another, in comparing Corsair and Hellcat noted the former was a "high strung predator" while the F6F- was "a nice safe pussycat". Pussycat or not, Grumman's second World War II fighter was the carrier deck airplane needed to win the Navy's air war in the Pacific, and achieved the noteable objective of killing many more enemy pilots than those of the US. Hellcats stayed in the Navy after the war and flew with reserve squadrons for a number of years, their final use being special purpose drone aircraft. Very few are preserved, and it is rare to see one in flying condition.

2

FIGHTER HISTORY

FIGHTER FORBEARS

It is of interest to review the eleven US World War II production fighter types against background represented by American-produced fighters (called pursuits) in the twenty year period leading up to World War II, the so-called inter-war years. Twenty-eight "production" types were manufactured by the US aviation industry for the US Army, US Navy, and export to foreign military services. See Table 1. Compared to World War II production inter-war output of fighters was puny, so "production" arbitrarily means twenty-five aircraft or more. Money was tight, military appropriations were very small, and in the second half of the period America was bogged down in "The Great Depression". Strangely perhaps, greater technical progress in fighter design occurred during that half.

Except for planes covered by America's Hundred Thousand, from 1920 to 1940 only 4149 "production" fighters were turned out, an average of about 207 per year. The Army obtained 1694 of these, the Navy 1262, and 1193 were exported. The largest number procured by the Army were 366 of the Boeing P-12 variety, and for the Navy it was 188 of the Boeing F4B-, the seagoing version of the P-12. Of the twenty-eight fighter types, two Army and three Navy were two-seaters, the rest single seat. In all, 989 of the Army's 1694 fighters were low wing monoplanes; all the Navy fighters were biplanes. The companies that manufactured these fighters were led by Curtiss, with 1827 airplanes. Next in line was Boeing with 1201; the Seattle company never built another production fighter

TABLE 1
US PRODUCTION FIGHTERS OF THE INTER-WAR YEARS, 1920 TO 1940

TYPE	YEAR	WING	ENG. COOLING	US SERVICE	US TOTAL	EXPORT TOTAL	NOTES
CURTISS-ORENCO D	1920	BIPL.	LIQUID	ARMY	50	—	ORENCO DESIGN.
VOUGHT VE-7	1920	BIPL.	LIQUID	NAVY	128	—	ORIGINALLY TWO SEAT
BOEING MB-3A	1921	BIPL.	LIQUID	ARMY	200	—	THOMAS MORSE DESIGN
EBERHARDT SE-5A	1922	BIPL.	LIQUID	ARMY	50	—	WWI SOPWITH FIGHTER
CURTISS TS-1	1922	BIPL.	AIR	NAVY	43	—	SOME BY N.A.F.
BOEING PW-9	1923	BIPL.	LIQUID	ARMY	113	—	
CURTISS PW-8	1923	BIPL.	LIQUID	ARMY	28	—	SKIN COOLING
BOEING FB-	1925	BIPL.	LIQUID	NAVY	42	—	FB-6 AIR COOLED
CURTISS P-1	1925	BIPL.	LIQUID	ARMY	93	17	HAWK
CURTISS F6C-	1925	BIPL.	LIQUID	NAVY	75	—	-4 AIR COOLED
BOEING F2B-	1926	BIPL.	AIR	NAVY	33	2	
BOEING F3B-	1928	BIPL.	AIR	NAVY	74	—	
BOEING F4B-	1928	BIPL.	AIR	NAVY	188	—	NAVY VERSION OF P-12
BOEING P-12	1929	BIPL.	AIR	ARMY	366	32	ARMY F4B-
CURTISS F8C-	1929	BIPL.	AIR	NAVY	96	—	-1&-3 NOT INCLUDED.
BERL. JOYCE P-16	1931	BIPL.	LIQUID	ARMY	25	—	TWO PLACE
CURTISS P-6E	1932	BIPL.	LIQUID	ARMY	46	—	UPDATED HAWK
GRUMMAN FF-	1932	BIPL.	AIR	NAVY	28	—	RETRACT. GEAR
CURTISS BFC/BF2C-	1932	BIPL.	AIR	NAVY	67	264	BF2C- GEAR RETRACT.
BOEING P-26	1932	MONO.	AIR	ARMY	139	12	WIRE-BRACED WING
GRUMMAN F2F-1	1933	BIPL.	AIR	NAVY	56	—	
CONSOLIDATED PB-2A	1933	MONO.	LIQUID	ARMY	54	—	CANTILEVER WING
GRUMMAN F3F-	1935	BIPL.	AIR	NAVY	166	—	IMPROVED F2F-1
SEVERSKY P-35	1936	MONO.	AIR	ARMY	136	61	SOME EXPORTS RECLAIMED
CURTISS P-36	1937	MONO.	AIR	ARMY	243	778	INCL. FIXED GEAR EXPORTS
CURTISS WR. CW-21	1938	MONO.	AIR	(EXP)	—	27	TO N.E.I. 3 TO CHINA
VULTEE P-66	1939	MONO.	AIR	ARMY	145	—	RECLAIMED FR. EXPORT
REPUBLIC P-43	1940	MONO.	AIR	ARMY	272	—	P-47 PARENT

Fig.1 Curtiss-Orenco D, US Army photo via M.Copp. Using a 300 horsepower Wright Hispano engine and a design revised from the original Ordnance Engineering Company airplanes, fifty of these D model fighters were produced by Curtiss in 1920-1921. A 2840 pound biplane with a flat nose radiator, the D had a high speed of 139 mph. Small bombs are loaded under the fuselage of the airplane pictured.

after its P-26 of the early 1930s, being known thereafter as a builder of bombers and transports. Next was Seversky/Republic with 469 fighters, and then 250 from Grumman and 145 from Vultee. The remainder, from Vought, Consolidated, Eberhardt, and Berliner-Joyce, totaled 257 pursuit aircraft.

Figures 1 and 2 show the Curtiss-built Ordnance Engineering Company (Orenco) Model D fighter of 1920. The aircraft was designed by Orenco, but Curtiss was the low bidder on a production lot, and, in the custom of those times, got the contract. The Model D was a conventional double-bay biplane of wooden construction similar to aircraft of World War I.

About the same time the Navy was getting production quantities of the Vought VE-7 airplane shown in Figure 3, another two-bay biplane design of wood construction. It was really a two-seater convertible for use as a single-seater of sorts, and, as necessary in the pre-aircraft carrier days of the Navy, could be employed as a seaplane equipped with floats.

Fighters for the Army were normally designed back then by the Engineering Division of the Army Signal Corps and let out for production bids. Boeing got started in fighters by winning a production contract for the MB-3A fighter after the Thomas-Morse Company had built prototypes. It was the first "mass-produced"

Fig.2 Curtiss-Orenco D, US Army photo via M.Copp. Tip balanced ailerons on upper wings of this double-bay biplane and a fire extinguisher handy to the pilot on the fuselage right side are two features of the Model D. The aircraft had a first flight in late 1920. Wing span weas thirty-three feet.

Fig.3 Vought VE-7, Mfr.photo via Bill Vance. Manufactured by Lewis and Vought Company of Long Island City, New York with help from the Naval Aircraft Factory in Philadelphia, the VE-7 was first produced as the two seat training aircraft shown, but later "fighter" modification converted it to a single seat VE-7S. With the Wright Hisso E engine of 180 horsepower and a speed of 120 mph, the aircraft served in the two earliest Navy fighter squadrons. In 1922 a VE-7 made the first carrier takeoff from a stationary USS Langley, the Navy's first carrier.

Fig.3A Vought VE-7, Mfr. photo via Bill Vance. The VE-7 served the Navy for several years and participated in many early experiments with items such as flotation equipment, carrier arresting gear, and operations from a carrier in general. When used as a VE-7F fighter the front cockpit was covered and a fixed forward firing .30 caliber machine gun was added.

post-war fighter for the Army, shown in Figure 4 as a stubby double-bay biplane of conventional layout built of wood from the forests of the Pacific Northwest at Boeing's Seattle factory.

In a seeming reversion to World War I, the Eberhardt Company turned out fifty fighters of British Sopwith SE-5 design in 1922 for the Army. The SE-5, Figure 5, was a good fighter by late World War I standards, but hardly a progressive design for 1922. It was a trim-looking wooden single-bay biplane.

The Navy's Curtiss TS-1, Figure 6, was a convertible land- or sea-based twin float airplane powered by an air cooled radial engine, an early trend-setter for Navy powerplants. Basically a design of the Navy, production, such as it was, got split between Curtiss and the Naval Aircraft Factory at Philadelphia. TS-1s were for a time based aboard battleships.

The next two aircraft, the Boeing PW-9 and Curtiss PW-8, Figures 7 through 12 , were competitors for Army fighter contracts.

Fig.4 Boeing MB-3A Special, US Army photo via R. Besecker. As was customary back then production contracts were open for award to the lowest bidder no matter who designed the aircraft. In this manner Boeing won a fiercely contested production contract for 200 Thomas Morse MB-3A fighters after the latter had produced fifty MB-3s in 1920. The MB-3A was powered by a Wright Hispano engine of 300 horsepower giving it a high speed of 141 mph. It was considered an excellent fighter.

Fig.5 Eberhardt SE-5A/SE-5E, US Army photo via Sam Orr. The British SE-5A of late World War I was used in post-war Army pursuit squadrons back in the US for a time with the Eberhardt Company assembling fifty from spare parts. These planes, labeled SE-5Es, were powered by a 180 horsepower Wright Hispano engine, weighed 2100 pounds, and could make a speed of 120 mph. Design-wise they did nothing to advance the state of the art.

Fig.6 Curtiss TS-1, photo via F. Dean coll. Designed at the Naval Aircraft Factory, most TS-1 airplanes came from the Curtiss shops, and were noteable in being powered by the 200 horsepower Lawrence J-1 radial engine, the predecessor of many radial engines to come. Distinguished by a lower wing spaced off the fuselage by struts and incorporating the fuel tank, the TS-1 served the Navy as a fighter through most of the 1920s, and some were converted for racing.

Fig.6A Curtiss TS-1 Seaplane, National Archives photo via Joe Weathers. Adapted to twin floats also designed at the NAF, a TS-1 fighter taxis in after a flight. The unusual lower wing-fuselage design is readily apparent as is the fuel tank in the center section of that wing. With only one aircraft carrier in the US Navy at the time the flexibility of having fighters convertable to float operation seemed adviseable. At one time TS-1s served on battleships as well.

Fig.7 Boeing XPW-9, photo via P.M.Bowers. The PW stood for Pursuit, Water-cooled engine, and this photo shows one of three 1923 Boeing prototypes for what was to be a very successful US Army fighter. A trim single bay tapered wing biplane powered by a 440 horsepower Curtiss D-12 engine, the XPW-9 was a then-modern fighter much to the Army's liking with a maximum speed of 161 mph.

Fig.7A Boeing PW-9, photo via Bill Vance. Boeing produced a total, including prototypes, of 113 PW-9 aircraft in five variants from 1923 through 1927. This was big business in fighters for that company and again firmly established them in the fighter field after a great start producing the earlier MB-3A. This flight photo shows clean aircraft lines for the period. A Fokker influence seems apparent.

Fig.8 Boeing PW-9C, photo via P.M.Bowers. A fine photo showing the rakish lines of a PW-9C, the most-produced PW-9 variant with thirty-nine aircraft delivered in 1927. Changes over earlier versions included a stronger fuselage, but improvements usually meant greater weight, in this case over 200 pounds more than the prototypes and a performance penalty resulted.

Fig.9 Curtiss XPW-8, Mfr.photo via F.Dean coll. The first of three Curtiss prototypes of the competitor to the Boeing PW-9. Also powered by the Curtiss D-12 watercooled engine, the XPW-8 took some features from the Curtiss racers of the period. It differed from the PW-9 in having a thin airfoil double bay constant chord wing arrangement using skin cooling like the racers.

Fig.9A Curtiss XPW-8A, Mfr. photo via J. Schneider. A second PW-8 prototype was quite different from the first, though skin cooling across the center portion of the upper wing was retained. That feature cleaned up the powerplant contours in the forward fuselage. The big difference was a good looking single bay wing arrangement. A split axle landing gear is well illustrated here. Two cowl gun blast tube muzzles are obvious.

The Boeing featured a simplified interplane strut system and tapered wings; the Curtiss machine stuck with a double-bay constant chord wing of less advanced form. Clean fuselage lines of the PW-8 resulted from "skin-cooling"; the radiators for the engine coolant were spread over the upper wing surface. This very vulnerable cooling system, also used in Curtiss racers of the period, was to quickly disappear. The Boeing PW-9 clearly won the production competition with four times Curtiss PW-8 output.

Shortly after these machines came out, the Boeing FB-1/-6 series of fighters appeared for the Navy. They were single-bay tapered wing types like the PW-9s, covertible to twin-float seaplanes. The FB-5, Figure 13, was the "production" version of the series, others being for powerplant experiments, including radial engine testing.

The same year, 1925, Curtiss got the single-bay tapered wing message, put the water-cooling radiator under the engine like the Boeings, and a series of P-1 Hawk fighters, like the P-1B shown in Figures 14 and 15 , was produced for the Army. All were powered by vee-type liquid-cooled Curtiss D-12 engines. (The Curtiss P-3 series, with very few built, explored radial engines). At the same time Curtiss started producing the Hawk, Figure 16, in the F6C-series, -1 through -4, for the Navy. As shown in Figure 17 the naval Hawk could convert to twin floats. Except for minor equipment the Army and Navy Hawks were almost identical. The Navy -4, Figure 18, changed to the new Pratt and Whitney Wasp radial air-cooled engine. Production Navy piston-engined fighters from then on would be powered by that type of engine, based on the Navy's consider-

Fig.10 Curtiss PW-8, photo via M. Copp. The production PW-8 of 1924, if one can call twenty-five airplanes production, retained the double bay wing with skin cooling atop the upper panel and incorporated a drive strut between upper and lower ailerons. It was soon realized skin cooling was impractical on service aircraft for several reasons, including presentation of too much gunfire-vulnerable area.

Fig.10A Curtiss PW-8, photo via Joe Christy. Side view of this PW-8 shows it as a family predecessor to the Curtiss biplane Hawk series. Blade twist of the Curtiss-Reed metal propeller shows up and tells us the propeller rotation was right handed looking from the cockpit. Note on this airplane exhaust gasses were routed aft of the pilot via a long pipe. The standard PW-8 provided 161 mph on its 460 horsepower.

Fig.11 Curtiss PW-8 with turbosupercharger, US Army photo via M.Copp. A PW-8 pursuit with a turbosupercharger, one of several Army aircraft so tested in the inter-war period. All supercharger components were located up front alongside the engine. Though testing showed real performance benefits at altitude, weight penalties were severe and reliability was poor because high temperature materials development was not sufficient. Dr. Sanford Moss of General Electric company was persistant, however, and there were to be more test installations.

Fig.12 Curtiss PW-8 with turbosupercharger, US Army photo via M. Copp. In contrast to the production PW-8 with smooth nose contours, the test installation pretty well mucked up the forward fuselage. The basic compressor and turbine unit is shown mounted on the right side of the cowling. Exhaust entered the turbine using the pipes shown. Intake air went through the compressor and intercooler (ahead of the turbo) and into the engine carburetor. It appears the skin cooling was not used and a water radiator was patched on underneath.

ation of less powerplant weight, easier maintenance, and less gunfire vulnerability than liquid-cooled engines.

Boeing broke into the radial engine powered Navy fighter business with the F2B-1 shown in Figure 19, quickly followed by a larger number of an improved F3B-1 model, Figures 20 through 22 , again with the Wasp engine. On the heels of these two Boeing Navy fighters came the famous Boeing F4B- and P-12 series with Wasp engines; the former for the Navy and the latter for the Army. A stubby clean-cut design with reversion to constant-chord wings, Figures 23 through 29, these airplanes were favorites of service pilots. Provided in various models over several years, both Army and Navy versions carried successive improvements in structural

and powerplant areas, all-metal fuselages and ring cowlings being among these. Production totaled 554 airplanes, by far the greatest number of biplane fighters produced in the inter-war years, keeping Boeing happily in military business. Many a famous World War II Army Air Force or Naval Air officer started his career in Boeing P-12 or F4B- fighters.

About the same time the P-12 series started, Curtiss was developing a two-seat fighter for the Navy, the F8C- Helldiver shown in Figure 30 . Perhaps influenced by the success of the two-seat Bristol Fighter of World War I, the Navy wanted to give the two-place fighter another try. It became apparent after some in-service use the Helldiver could not match the speed and agility of single-

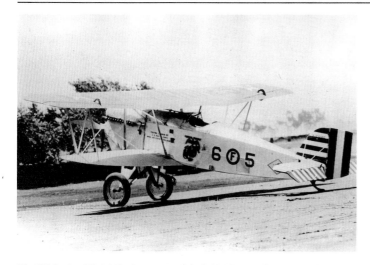

Fig.13A Boeing FB-1, Mfr.photo via Herb Fyfield. The initial airplanes of a famous series, ten Boeing FB-1 fighters were produced for the Navy. These airplanes were similar to the Army PW-9, and since they were not provided with carrier gear the FB-1s were turned over to the Marine Corps. The airplane in the photo has the markings of that service, though the tail stripes are novel.

Fig.13B Boeing FB-3, Mfr.photo via Herb Fyfield. The FB-3 is shown on twin floats, a then-required adaptation for Navy fighter types. It used the big 525 horsepower Packard 2A-1500 engine with an underslung water radiator. So there would be no mistakes weight and loading data for the airplane was stenciled on the fabric just outside the cockpit. Note the airframe similarities to the Army PW-9 airplanes.

Fig.13C Boeing FB-3, Mfr.photo via Herb Fyfield. The FB-3 airplanes, all two of them, lead up to the FB-5, the real "production" version. Another view of the FB-3 shows clean powerplant lines and the absence of a propeller spinner. The strut bracing for the floats is straightforward and the front struts are provided with steps. The intermediate FB-2 airplanes, two of which were delivered, had been designed to meet the requirements of carrier operations and used the D-12 engine.

Fig.13D Boeing FB-4, Mfr.photo via Herb Fyfield. Not to be caught short with the wrong engine, one of the FB- series, the -4, was tested by Boeing with both Wright P-1 and Pratt and Whitney Wasp radials. This 1926 Boeing photo shows the test aircraft with the Wright engine. The handwriting of the radial engine was getting clearer on the wall for the Navy.

Fig.13E Boeing FB-5, Mfr.photo via Herb Fyfield. The FB-5, shown here as a twin float seaplane, was the production version of the FB- series with twenty-seven airplanes ordered by the Navy for fighter squadrons. Equipped with the water cooled Packard engine tested on FB-3s, the FB-5 in landplane form was equipped for carrier operations. The Navy got its new airplanes in late 1926 and early 1927. Two .30 caliber guns were mounted in the fuselage. High speed as a landplane was 169 mph.

Fig.13F Boeing FB-6, USN photo via Joe Weathers. The Navy was starting to find what it really wanted in an engine to power its fighters. The FB-6 airplane was the FB-4 with the new Pratt and Whitney R-1340 Wasp under test. The lesser weight of the air cooled radial engine compared to a heavy water cooled Packard powerplant was an important advantage.

Fig.14 Curtiss P-1 Hawk, photo via F. Dean coll. The P-1 Hawk of 1925 reflected a change from the production PW-8 airplanes but was actually developed from the third PW-8 prototype which had a new tapered wing and an underslung tunnel radiator like the Boeing PW-9 series instead of the straight two-bay wing with skin cooling. Note the split axle landing gear and the external belly fuel tank. Ten P-1 fighters were produced.

Fig.14A Curtiss P-1A Hawk, US Army photo via F.Dean coll. Minor improvements were incorporated in the batch of twenty-five P-1A fighters like the one pictured. P-1As were ordered and delivered in 1926. The Curtiss V-1150 D-12 vee-type water cooled engine developed a maximum of 435 horsepower and provided a P-1A high speed of 161 mph. The Hawks had vertical rudder stripes with the Curtiss name imprinted, and this one has a missing spinner nose section.

Fig.14B Curtiss P-1B Hawk, Mfr.photo via J. Schneider. Curtiss got another Hawk order in 1927 for twenty-five more aircraft of the P-1B variety. With a new D-12 engine version and larger diameter wheels the B was little different from earlier Hawks, about 80 pounds heavier, and a few miles an hour slower than the earlier P-1. The manufacturers photo shows a factory-new fighter.

Fig.14C Curtiss P-1B Hawk, photo via P.M.Bowers. A ground crewman helps a taxiing P-1B onto the hardstand area. Note the mud collected on the wheels, the attach fitting under the fuselage for the absent external fuel tank, and the new standard for rudder stripes that continued until World War II.

Fig.14D Curtiss P-1B Hawk, US Army photo via F. Dean coll. Flight view of a P-1B Hawk shows the new tapered wing arrangement which stayed about the same on all the Curtiss biplane fighters. The large print legend on the fuselage was standard for Army aircraft and identified the military serial number, manufacturer and Army model. In this case F.A.D. stood for the Army Fairfield Air Depot in Ohio. With wheel covers removed the "sporty" wire wheels are revealed!

Fig.15 Curtiss P-1C Hawk, Mfr.photo via J. Schneider. Minor powerplant revisions and the addition of wheel brakes were among the improvements in the P-1C Hawk. Thirty-three aircraft of this variety were produced in 1929, the last Army order for D-12 powered Hawks. The facing up "C" on the fuselage was a zipper in the fabric for storage compartment access. A hand crank for engine starting is located alongside the engine accessory compartment.

Fig.15A Curtiss P-1C Hawk, Mfr.photo via F. Dean coll. The P-1C Hawk looked no different from its predecessors; there were no great technological advances through the 1920s; Curtiss was content to make minor changes and produce a few Hawks every year. The P-1C was the last production version; the P-1D, E, and F versions were the same airplanes with powerplant revisions used as advanced trainers.

Fig.15B Curtiss P-1C Hawk, photo via Chuck Mandrake. A well used P-1C Hawk sitting in a field of Boeing fighters. Boeing always had a big margin in numbers of single seat fighters produced in the 1920s. They put out almost four times as many as Curtiss, but none of the numbers were very high in those times.

Fig.16 Curtiss F6C-2 Hawk, F.Dean coll. Along with the Army the US Navy ordered the Curtiss Hawk to the extent of five F6C-1 and four F6C-2 fighters, the latter fitted out for carrier use. The -2 shown here had a series of hooks along the landing gear cross axle to guide the plane along wires running the length of the carrier deck. There was no tail hook. It can be seen there was little difference in appearance from the Army aircraft.

Fig.17 Curtiss F6C-1 Hawk, Mfr.photo via J.Schneider. In 1925 the Navy still felt it wise to assure their fighter aircraft could operate from the water as well as from land or an aircraft carrier. In this Curtiss photo the Hawk is equipped with twin floats as part of the overall evaluation of the type. The F6C-3 was the developed version of the D-12 powered Navy Hawk, and thirty-five of these were produced and used by both the Navy and Marine Corps.

Fig.18 Curtiss F6C-4 Hawk, photo via F.Dean coll. A fundemental change occurred in the F6C-4 model where the new air cooled Pratt and Whitney Wasp radial engine was installed on the Navy Hawk and thirty-one fighters were ordered. With the advantages of lower powerplant weight and less gunfire vulnerability as well as the promise of greater reliability, the Wasp powered F6C-4 was one of the trend-setters for the Navy's future.

Fig.19 F2B-1 prototype, Mfr.photo via Herb Fyfield. The Navy wanted a new fighter powered with the Wasp radial engine after evaluation of the FB-6 tests with that engine. The experimental prototype was the initial F2B-1 shown. Strenuous efforts to streamline the new radial engine resulted in a large propeller spinner which started off a bullet-shaped fuselage. A clean tapered single bay wing cellule was employed.

Fig.19A Boeing F2B-1 prototype, Mfr.photo via Herb Fyfield. Another view of the F2B-1 prototype showing how difficult it was to streamline the new radial engine. The engine cylinders hung out in the breeze and were truly air cooled. There were individual cylinder exhaust stacks. The fuselage structure consisted of bolted aluminum members, a new form of construction. First flight of the F2B-1 prototype occurred in November of 1926 with flight testing successful enough to warrant going into production.

Fig.19B Boeing F2B-1, Mfr.photo via Herb Fyfield. The production aircraft started deliveries early in 1928, and several changes were made from the prototype including removal of the big propeller spinner, some fuselage recontouring, and addition of balance area atop the rudder. The production F2B-1 obtained a high speed of 158 mph out of its 425 horsepower Wasp engine and weighted 2800 pounds fully loaded. An agile fighter, it was the mount of "The Three SeaHawks", an early Navy acrobatic flight demonstration team.

Fig.20 XF3B-1, Mfr.photo via Herb Fyfield. Not resting on their laurels, Boeing brought out another private venture fighter for Navy tests in early 1927. It resembled the F2B-1 with tapered wings and a Wasp engine. Flotation gear was mounted on the fuselage sides. The airplane was one of the last types convertible to seaplane operations, using a single main and wingtip floats. The cross-axle landing gear was adaptable to the multiple hook arrangement required for carrier operations. The X aircraft was delivered as the first production F3B-1.

Fig.21 Boeing F3B-1, Mfr.photo via Herb Fyfield. The Navy ordered a production batch of seventy-three fighters in mid-1927 and the F3B-1 started service in the fall of that year with deliveries coming through 1928 and into early 1929. In this photo some of the changes for production are evident, including new constant chord wing panels with upper wing sweepback and a new vertical tail with balanced rudder. Hooks on the landing gear crossbar for carrier landing work are evident in this photo.

Fig.21A Boeing F3B-1, photo via F.Dean coll. The F3B-1 aircraft were in service for several years and after fleet service some were also used as transports, command aircraft, and hacks. The aircraft shown was attached to the Anacostia Naval Air Station near Washington D.C., and is gussied up with a ring engine cowl and wheel pants that were definitely not standard.

Fig.22 Boeing F3B-1, photo via F.Dean coll. An F3B-1 of the Aircraft Battle Force, probably a command plane, equipped with a ring cowl. In mid-1928 there were only four F3B-1s with Squadron VF-2B on carrier Langley along with nine Vought FU-types, but in the spring of 1929 all three carriers, Lexington, Saratoga, and Langley had fighter complements of F3B-1s, a total of sixty-three aircraft.

Fig.22A Boeing F3B-1, USN photo via F.Dean coll. Fine flight view of an F3B-1 of VF-2 from carrier Langley and the nineteenth aircraft, probably used as a command plane of the Aircraft Battle Force. A landing gear crossbar to carry landing arrestor hooks is no longer needed as the more modern tail arresting hook is now employed to match the new cross-wires on the carriers.

Fig.23A Boeing F4B-1, photo via F.Dean coll. This early F4B-1, photographed prior to squadron service, has gotten rid of the propeller spinner, and is minus a tail hook, but retains the engine cylinder fairings of the prototype. Instead of a bomb an external fuel tank is attached on centerline. The bolted square aluminum tubes used for the fuselage structure were a Boeing innovation. Wings were framed in wood; they and the fuselage were fabric covered.

Fig.23 Boeing XF4B-1/Model 83, Mfr.photo via Milt Sheppard. The start of a long series of Boeing fighters for both Army and Navy, one of two prototypes for the series. After initial testing the aircraft was delivered as a production F4B-1. Noteable prototype features included a tail skid and tail hook, a 500 pound dummy bomb under the fuselage, a propeller spinner, and cylinder fairings in an attempt to slick up that radial engine installation.

Fig.23B. Boeing F4B-1, USN photo via Milt Sheppard. An F4B-1 on a carrier takeoff with external fuel tank aboard, this 1-B-7 aircraft from the VB-1B Red Ripper Squadron of the Battle Fleet. There are no more propeller spinners or engine cylinder aft fairings aboard. Tail hook and tail skid show up as do corrugated aluminum skinned vertical tail surfaces. The slot allowing actuation of the variable incidence horizontal tail surfaces used to trim the aircraft is also evident.

Fig.24. Boeing F4B-2, photo via F.Dean coll. The next Boeing fighter was the F4B-2, forty-six of which were delivered starting in January, 1932. With the same 500 horsepower Wasp engine of the -1 the -2, though 75 pounds heavier, was about ten mph faster, the speed increase effected at least partly by addition of a ring cowl on the engine. Other changes included a new cross-axle landing gear, a tail wheel, and Frise ailerons.

Fig.24A Boeing F4B-2, Mfr.photo via Herb Fyfield. An F4B-2 fighter at the Boeing plant prior to delivery. In the background are two roughly equivalent P-12 fighters for the Army also ready for delivery. The Navy F4B-1 spawned the Army P-12 series. In mid-1931 eighteen F4B-2s of Squadron VF-6B comprised the fighter force of carrier Saratoga; a mixed force of -1 and -2 aircraft were with VF-5B on the Lexington. The F4B-2s left first line service and were used in training by 1935.

Fig.25 Boeing F4B-4, F.Dean coll. via Milt Sheppard. After twenty-one F4B-3 versions incorporating all metal fuselages were ordered by the Navy with deliveries starting at the end of 1931 the defining version of the series appeared in July of the next year. The F4B-4 was distinguished by the same metal semi-monocoque fuselage, new tail surfaces, a more powerful Wasp engine, and a very large pilot headrest and radio antenna.

Fig.25A. Boeing F4B-4, photo via R. Besecker. This close-up picture of an F4B-4 emphasizes the stubby character of the little fighter with the big headrest. The external fuel tank is under the fuselage and wing bomb racks have been added. The F4B-4 was the Navy's first line fighter aboard carriers from 1932 to 1936 when the single seat Grumman biplane fighters took over.

Fig.26. Boeing F4B-4, F.Dean coll. Running up the engine on the parking line, a Navy F4B-4 pilot is ready to go. The armament was two fuselage cowl machine guns with blast tubes leading between engine cylinders within the ring cowl, one of which can be seen in the photo. Either two .30 caliber or one .50 caliber and one .30 caliber could be installed. Two 116 pound bombs could also be carried, one under each wing.

Fig.26A. Boeing F4B-4, photo via R.Besecker. In 1935 four special F4B-4 aircraft with highly polished fuselages were based at Naval Air Station Anacostia near Washington, D.C. in Navy Squadron VX-4. They were used as high level "staff transports" which meant getting in some flying time for high ranking Navy brass. Behind this Anacostia-based Boeing biplane is a sample of the then-future, Boeing's newer monoplane Army fighter, the P-26A.

Fig.27. Boeing P-12, Mfr. photo via Milt Sheppard. Perceiving the success of Navy F4B-1 prototypes, the Army tested one and ordered ten P-12 land-based versions with deliveries started early in 1929. With a span of only thirty feet and a length of about twenty, the little 2540 pound fighter with an early Wasp engine was quite an impressive performer. The engine cylinder fairings on the plane pictured were later dispensed with.

Left: Fig.27A Boeing P-12 replica, photo via P.M.Bowers. A very carefully done and attractive P-12 replica, restored from a Boeing 100, in a taxi photo taken in recent years; there is little if anything to tell it is not a 1929 photo however. Serial No. AC29-354 duplicates the second aircraft of the small batch ordered, the 354th aircraft purchased by the Army in 1929.

Right: Fig.27B. Boeing P-12 replica, photo via P.M.Bowers. Another view of the Boeing 100 redone as an Army P-12 of 1929. The large-size lettering on the aft fuselage was standard marking for Army aircraft of the period. Just aft a hole for the variable incidence stabilizer drive can be seen. All F4B- and P-12 fighter ailerons were on the upper wing only but were actuated through lower wing control runs to interplane drive struts for the ailerons located just aft of the wing N struts.

Fig.27C Boeing XP-12A, Mfr.photo via Herb Fyfield. The tenth P-12 airplane of the original order shown here was fancied up with special features in an attempt to reduce drag. Changes included an uprated Wasp engine enclosed in a special long chord cowling, a fuselage rounded out with addition of fairing strips, modified ailerons, and a shortened landing gear. A crash ended testing, and no production followed.

Fig.27E Boeing P-12B, Mfr.photo via Herb Fyfield. Another view of the P-12B at the Boeing plant. The aircraft was a fine acrobatic type with sensitive controls. It was said it could be put through a loop directly after takeoff. With a 525 horsepower Pratt and Whitney Wasp a speed of about 167 mph could be achieved; P-12B gross weight was 2640 pounds, a real lightweight.

Fig.27D Boeing P-12B, Mfr.photo via Herb Fyfield. An order for a large (by 1920s standards) number of P-12B aircraft was obtained by Boeing in 1929 with deliveries of ninety aircraft completed in 1930. The order was based on the Army's satisfactory experience with the P-12 airplanes. Tail and landing gear revisions were made, and cylinder fairings were eliminated. This P-12B was photographed just outside the Boeing flight test hangar.

Fig.27F Boeing P-12B, photo via F. Dean coll. One of a lineup of P-12B aircraft in Army squadron service, this P-12B has been retrofitted with the engine ring cowl of later versions. It seems the fuel tank carried underneath the fuselage was an ever-present appendage. The landing gear was a split axle type; the propeller is all metal, either fixed pitch or ground adjustable two position.

Fig. 28 Boeing P-12C, Mfr.photo via Milt Sheppard. A factory photo of the P-12C now equipped with a standard engine ring cowl, the 1931 version of the Boeing fighter. The Army liked the type so well it ordered another ninety-six airplanes. The P-12C was very much like the P-12B, though updates were made during the service life of the airplanes.

Fig.28A Boeing P-12C, Mfr.photo via F.Dean coll. Here a P-12C has been updated with the vertical tail of a D airplane. These aircraft served in the Army squadrons for several years piloted by men who were to be USAAF leaders in World War II. Most regarded the P-12 type with considerable affection.

Fig.28D Boeing P-12E, photo via F.Dean coll. A particularly famous variant and one getting the largest Army order of one hundred and ten aircraft in 1931 was the P-12E. A noteable technical improvement was the new all metal semi-monocoque fuselage structure. A large headrest incorporated storage space directly behind the pilot. The arrow insignia on the fuselage identified aircraft assigned to Wright Field in Dayton, Ohio, the Air Corps test center.

Right: Fig.28B Boeing P-12C, photo via P.M.Bowers. Another runup photo of a P-12; noteable is a change to cross-axle landing gear and there is still a tail skid. The pace of fighter development was slower in the depression era when appropriation of funds was particularly tight.

Right: Fig.28C Boeing P-12D, photo via F.Dean coll. The next version of the popular Boeing fighter was the P-12D of which thirty-five were ordered in 1931. They were little different from the P-12C except for a higher compression Wasp engine and a taller more rounded vertical tail. This photo emphasizes the small size of the fighter and the closeness of the cockpit around the pilot who flew with his shoulders out in the breeze, particularly if he was a fairly large man.

Fig.28E Boeing P-12E, Mfr. photo via Herb Fyfield. A P-12E at the Boeing plant; the standard fighter for the Army Air Corps of the mid-1930s with a maximum speed of 189 mph, an overall length of twenty feet, three inches, and a gross weight of 2680 pounds. The engine was still the 525 horsepower Wasp. Late models got tail wheels and parking brakes.

Fig.28F Boeing P-12E, Curtiss photo via F.Dean coll. Closeup view of a P-12E with someone facing aft in the cockpit , reason unknown. Details of propeller, engine cowling, and cross-axle landing gear are well shown. A bomb rack is seen inboard under the lower wing. Detailed attention to streamlining is shown by fairings at strut junctions with wing and fuselage. A small venturi tube to obtain suction for instruments is forward of the squadron insignia.

Fig.28G Boeing P-12E, photo via P.M.Bowers. A well-used P-12E with squadron badge almost obliterated parked on the flight line personifies the flavor of the times with the pilot's parachute dropped on a lower wing. Chutes were heavy and bulky, and pilots often left them on the airplane or nearby ground. The object on the horizontal tail is unidentified.

Fig.28H Boeing P-12E, photo via P.M. Bowers. A tail skid is still used on the P-12E in this fine view, but it is unusual to see no external fuel tank on the aircraft. What appears as a bomb rack is installed beneath the fuselage. Tail surfaces are all metal, and the horizontal stabilizer is no longer a variable incidence type.

Fig.29 Boeing P-12F, Mfr.photo via Herb Fyfield. A factory fresh P-12F fighter at Boeing, its metal fuselage gleaming, sits in the sunlight in Seattle (a somewhat un-usual experience!). With the depression deepening only twenty-five F models were delivered to the Army in 1932, these powered with a mechanically supercharged Wasp engine uprated to 600 horsepower.

Fig.29A Boeing P-12F, photo via P.M.Bowers. With landing lights and wing bomb racks added, one of the last "production" P-12 models, a P-12F, runs up ready for takeoff. This version was as up-to-date as the aircraft got, and hundreds of young air-minded boys and men around the country found it a thing of beauty. Many models of Boeing P-12s were made.

Fig.29B Boeing XP-12G, photo via F.Dean coll. A P-12B airframe converted to incorporate for test a turbosupercharger and three blade propeller to absorb the increased horsepower thereby available at altitude. This installation was one of a continuing series of experiments conducted through the inter-war period on turbo-superchargers which culminated in their use with production aircraft during World War II. This XP-12G was later reconverted to a P-12B when testing ended.

Fig.29C Boeing P-12K, photo via F.Dean coll. Seven P-12E airplanes were con-verted by the Army to use fuel injected engines and labeled P-12Ks. Outwardly they resembled a standard P-12E. A civilian photographer got close enough to snap a picture of the P-12K running up; this was accomplished much more easily in the 1930s than today. The Wright Field arrow denotes aircraft home base.

Fig.29D Boeing P-12K, photo via R. Besecker. No, this is not a Flying Tiger aircraft; the tiger emblem on the fuselage is the badge of the 24th Fighter Squadron. This P-12K in squadron service was converted from a P-12E that still had a tail skid instead of a tail wheel. The pilot is ready to move out; his helmet is on and goggles are down.

Fig.29E Boeing Model 218, Mfr.photo via Herb Fyfield. Sitting outside the Boeing flight test hangar is a 1930 export fighter developed along with the P-12 series. The Boeing 218 shows a ring cowl, an all metal fuselage used in development testing of this feature, and a tail hook for carrier operations as well as a tail wheel. Testing by the Army and Navy led to service aircraft orders. The Model 218 was sold to China in 1932.

Fig.30A Curtiss XF8C-4, Mfr.photo via J.Schneider. This dynamic run-up photo by the Curtiss photographer depicts the prototype of the first production Helldiver. It was strengthened as a result of the XF8C-2 crash and had its first flight in the summer of 1929. The XF8C-4 carried a single flexible machine gun for the rear seat man and two .30 caliber fixed forward-firing machine guns in the upper wing, not shown in this photo.

Fig.30 Curtiss XF8C-2, Mfr.photo via F. Dean coll. The prototype of the Curtiss Helldiver series, this aircraft resulted from a Navy desire to test the merits of a two seat fighter and dive bomber combination. Curtiss designed a scaled-down version of their Falcon observation type resulting in the aircraft shown. The unusual long chord engine cowling was tested but not used in production. The XF8C-2 crashed as a result of a high speed dive.

Fig.30B Curtiss F8C-4 Helldiver, photo via F.Dean coll. A production Helldiver, one of twenty-five put out by Curtiss and originally equipped for carrier operations. Eighteen were aboard the carrier Saratoga in mid-1931, but they were replaced by single seat Boeing fighters in 1932. Upper wing sweep is emphasized in this photo and one of the fixed wing guns is in place. The carrier hook has been removed. A 500 pound bomb could be carried.

Fig.30C, Curtiss F8C-5 Helldiver, photo via F.Dean coll. Sixty-three -5 Helldivers were ordered by the Navy, but by the time they started off the production line the -4 Helldiver had been judged inadequate in performance for a fighter. The F8C-5 was shortly relegated to land-based duty as an observation plane. The aircraft shown is a special version equipped with a forward cockpit enclosure.

Fig.30D, Curtiss XF8C-8 Helldiver, photo via F.Dean coll. This airplane was one of four 575 horsepower Wright Cyclone powered Helldivers used as special command aircraft. This one has the two wing guns with special covers, the rear gun stowed, and wheels covered with large size pants. The Navy hung many designations on the Cyclone powered Helldivers, including XF8C-7, XF8C-8, XF10C-1, XS3C-1, and O2C-2; it didn't know whether the type was a fighter, a scout, an observation plane, or what, but Navy brass no doubt had a fine time flying the four planes.

Fig.31, Berliner-Joyce XP-16, photo via P.M.Bowers. The prototype aircraft of a two seat fighter design ordered by the Army and delivered in 1930, powered by a liquid cooled twelve cylinder Curtiss V-1570 Conqueror engine of 600 horsepower. The gap between wings was increased to lessen interference drag by gulling both upper and lower surfaces off the fuselage as shown in the photo and avoiding the necessity for cabane struts from fuselage to upper wing. A three blade propeller and a split axle landing gear were also featured.

Fig.31A Berliner-Joyce P-16, photo via F.Dean coll. This view of the production aircraft, twenty-five of which were delivered in 1932, shows the two cockpits of the P-16. Though the aircraft had a top speed of 170 mph or more, it weighed over 1300 pounds more than a Boeing P-12E and over 550 pounds more than a Curtiss P-6E. Agility suffered, and the rear gunner was judged not useful in combat maneuvers. The P-16 still had a tail skid instead of a tail wheel.

Fig.31B Berliner-Joyce P-16, photo via P.M.Bowers. The side elevation of a P-16 does not disclose a windshield for the rear seat man. It must have been quite breezy at 150 to 170 mph! It may be that after a time the aircraft was flown as a single seater. A large sized and unhandsome external fuel tank was used with the P-16; it is doubtful it was droppable in flight.

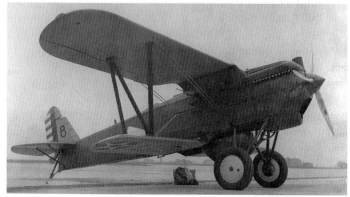

Fig.31C Berliner-Joyce P-16, photo via P.M.Bowers. This P-16 photo shows clearly the absence of cabane struts from fuselage to upper wing usually employed on biplanes to gain sufficient gap aerodynamically between wings and to allow the pilot some forward vision. Both wings were gulled to provide the necessary gap. Gulling the upper wing allowed the pilot to see straight forward but blocked angular vision.

Fig.32 Curtiss P-6E Hawk, Mfr.photo via J.Schneider. After a long series of experimental fighters, most of these from a batch of eighteen P-6 aircraft delivered in 1929, Curtiss came up with an Army production order of forty-six P-22 fighters, shortly redesignated as P-6Es. The P-6 series were all Curtiss V-1570 Conqueror-powered Hawks, differentiating them from the earlier P-1 series Hawks with Curtiss D-12 engines. The P-6Es were delivered to the Army in 1932. Pictured is the final P-6E, Serial 32-377. The legend on the side of this airplane says it is a P6-E. That is wrong; it is a P-6E; small point of course.

place fighters. The Navy changed the Curtiss models into observation and dive bombing airplanes, but did not altogether abandon their two-seat thinking.

Shortly the Army had to try the two-seat formula, and in 1931 the Berliner-Joyce Company obtained an order for twenty-five two-place P-16 fighters as shown in Figure 31. The P-16, a clean-looking single-bay biplane with inline engine and wings tied directly to the fuselage, was not a big success.

After considerable experimentation with prototypes, Curtiss finally won an order for a developed version of their basic Hawk, the handsome P-6E shown in Figures 32 to 35. It was equipped with a V-12 liquid-cooled Curtiss Conqueror engine, the small radiator allowed by Prestone coolant, and wheel pants on the single-leg fixed gear.

A more significant development at about the same time, though perhaps not as pretty, was the FF-1 for the Navy, the first of the long Grumman fighter line. A two-place single-bay biplane, the FF-1, shown in Figure 36 , had a ring-cowled radial engine, an enclosure over the cockpits, and the first retractable landing gear on a US production fighter, making it the speediest in the services. Again the Navy found two seats not to their liking for a fighter, and the design became a fast scout airplane.

Curtiss stuck to their basic Hawk design, and produced for the Navy a slick new version with the required radial engine and the wheels spatted. This was the 1933 Goshawk shown in Figures 37 through 40 and labeled first by the Navy as an F11C-2, then changed

to BFC-2 to include a light bombing mission. Curtiss made money in the depression by a significant number of export orders obtained for this type, mainly from South America. They went on to improve the Goshawk by following Grumman's lead and incorporating retractable landing gear in the biplane along with more metal construction. This was the BF2C-1, the BF standing for bomber-

Fig.32A Curtiss P-6E Hawk, photo via F.Dean coll. Along with the Boeing P-12s and the few two-place P-16s, the P-6Es were the final fighter biplanes used by the Army. Though there were many more P-12s the P-6Es got their share of the spotlight in the weariness of the Great Depression. Often considered the handsomest of the inter-war biplanes, the P-6E tended to be a darling of young air enthusiasts and modelers of the 1930s. With a smoothly contoured nose, a small radiator allowed by using Prestone instead of water, and single leg streamlined landing gear with panted wheels, the P-6E looked good even with the older Hawk series wings and tail.

Fig.33 Curtiss P-6E Hawk, photo via R. Besecker. Running up on a snowy field with the pilot glancing over his shoulder, this P-6E Hawk is ready to go! The groove in the fuselage just below the exhaust stacks (two stacks per cylinder) provides clearance for the path of bullets out of side-mounted machine guns and blast tubes. The radiator is neatly cowled beneath the engine and the external belly fuel tank is in place. P-6E fighters weighed over 750 pounds more than the Boeing P-12E, were a few miles per hour faster, but were also a bit larger and somewhat less maneuverable.

Fig.33A Curtiss P-6E hawk, US Army photo via M. Copp. This flight photo of a P-6E Hawk adorned with the great horned owl badge of the 17th Pursuit Squadron and the clawed wheel pants symbolizes the popularity of the type with the US public. It was featured in newsreels and at flight demonstrations for air shows. A P-6E in good shape could almost but not quite touch 200 mph in level flight at a modest altitude.

Fig.34 Curtiss P-6E hawk, photo via R. Besecker. Parked on the line a P-6E Hawk shows it had a three blade fixed pitch propeller, an upper air intake for the carburetor of the V-12 engine, and open-sided wheel pants (on some airplanes). The wings were essentially the same as those of the P-1 series. The P-6E was about 500 pounds heavier than P-1s. With fighters grossing out not much more than a ton and a half this was a large difference.

Fig.35 Curtiss P-6E Hawk, photo via R. Besecker. The P-6E never did get a metal semi-monocoque fuselage like the Boeing P-12E. Several of the aircraft were employed for experiments- turbosupercharging, other engine modifications, enclosed cockpits, and extra wing machine guns. Some aircraft were flown with ski landing gear. The projections below the fuselage aft of the external fuel tank were chutes for dropping flares.

Fig.36A Grumman FF-2, photo via F. Dean coll. An FF-2 running up shows the large diameter single row nine cylinder Cyclone engine and the deep belly with pockets to house the new retractable landing gear wheels. The FF-2 was a dual control trainer version of the FF-1 and received a great deal of use right into early World War II. The FF-1 Grummans paved the way for scout versions, labeled SF-1s, of which thirty-three were built. These aircraft could make over 200 mph top speed.

Fig.36 Grumman FF-1, Mfr.photo via F.Dean coll. A new era for US Navy fighters started with the advent of the first Grumman product under a spring 1931 contract for an XFF-1. Grumman was new in the business of producing whole planes, but the XFF-1 had a combination of two seats under an enclosed canopy, a ring-cowled Cyclone engine, all metal fuselage, and a fully retractable landing gear all of which proved irresistable. Prototype first flight was on December 29, 1931 and the first of twenty-seven FF-1 production models appeared in the spring of 1933, serving successfully on aircraft carrier Lexington in 1934.

Fig.37 Curtiss XF11C-1, photo via F.Dean coll. The Army Curtiss Hawks were watched carefully by the Navy who decided to purchase two radial engined versions for test. One was the aircraft shown, an XF11C-1 powered by a twin row Wright R-1510 engine of 600 horsepower. It consisted of much the same old Hawk type wings and tail but with the fuselage adapted to the new radial engine and a cantilever leg landing gear with big open-sided pants. The aircraft first flew in March, 1932 and had a high speed just over 200 mph. It was later redesignated as a BFC-1 bomber-fighter, but was never produced in quantity.

Fig.38 Curtiss XF11C-2 Goshawk, photo via F.Dean coll. The -2 prototype of the Hawk is seen with an external fuel tank between landing gear legs and the big Wright Cyclone up front. This aircraft had been a Curtiss company demonstrator since early 1932 and was purchased by the Navy for testing. It passed muster and twenty-eight production F11C-2 fighters were ordered with deliveries starting late in 1932.

Fig.37A Curtiss XF11C-1 and F11C-2, Mfr.photo via J.Schneider. The two Navy Hawks, XF11C-1 and F11C-2 flying together at the end of 1932 show the main variation in configuration was the different engine cowling with the twin row R-1510 on the -1 versus the single row Wright Cyclone on the -2. The Cyclone had 100 more horsepower. The -1 was about 240 pounds heavier, but performance was almost identical.

Fig.38A Curtiss F11C-2 Goshawk, USN photo via F.Dean coll. The rakish lines of this Curtiss product made it everyone's favorite for awhile. Perhaps it was those great big wheel pants. There still was no real technological advance in structural materials or concepts; the fuselage was steel tubing with light forming stringers aft and aluminum cover panels up front, and the wings were fabric covered wooden structures. In June of 1933 there were fourteen F11C-2s with the Fleet Battle Force on carrier Saratoga.

Fig.39 Curtiss Cuba Hawk II, Len Povey photo via Joe Christy. Curtiss exported quite a few Curtiss Hawk II aircraft in the early and middle 1930s including some to Turkey, Cuba, China, and two to Germany. This Cuban Hawk flew for the Batista government when American Len Povey took over the Cuban Air Force. Ernst Udet of Germany ordered two Hawks after seeing one perform dive bombing demonstrations at the National Air Races.

Fig.39A Curtiss Turkey Hawk II, Mfr. photo via F.Dean coll. An export Hawk II was photographed in July, 1932 ready to go overseas adorned with the Turkish insignia. Curtiss sold nineteen of these striking biplane fighters to the Turks. Such sales helped the company financially during the dark days of the depression. The flattened external fuel tank is smoothly integrated with the fuselage contour. These Hawks had a big propeller and a long landing gear, making for a large nose-up three point angle.

Fig.39B Curtiss Turkey Hawk II, photo via R.Besecker. A dynamic view of the silver colored Hawk II for Turkey in 1932 running up its big Cyclone engine with individual exhaust stacks barking away. This was every boy's idea of a fighter aircraft in 1932. Besides those to Turkey, fifty Hawk IIs went to China between March, 1933 and September, 1933. Three were exported to Bolivia, four to Chile, and so on.

Fig.39C Curtiss Hawk II seaplane, Mfr.photo via J.Schneider. A Hawk II seaplane demonstrator undergoing flight tests shows how the fighter could be adapted to twin floats. There were quite a few struts, of course! Note also the ventral fin adding stabilizing area aft to offset the forward volume of the floats, and the water rudders on the floats. Columbia bought twenty-six seaplane versions delivered from October of 1932 to mid-1934. Without engines they cost from $13,000. to $16,000. In those days a dollar bought something!

fighter, shown in Figures 41 and 42. Export versions of this aircraft were also sold overseas. The BF2C-1 disappeared rather quickly from the Navy as vibration response of its new metal-framed wing matched Cyclone engine exitations, giving the airplane a bad vibration problem.

At the same time, 1932, the Army and Boeing combined to make a technology advance of sorts; the Boeing P-26 single-place low wing monoplane was put into production. The P-26, shown in Figures 43 through 46, featured a thin wire-braced wing and fully-panted fixed landing gear, along with all-metal construction and ring-cowled Wasp radial engine. This popular "Peashooter" became

the standard Army fighter. A few were still around when the US entered World War II. It was the last US Army open-cockpit fighter.

A year after introduction of the P-26, the Navy and Grumman came out with the F2F-1 carrier fighter, a compact little radial engined biplane in the FF-1 mold except single seat. Close cowling of the two-row radial, retractable landing gear, and a fully enclosed cockpit distinguished the F2F-1, shown in Figure 47.

The same year the Army ordered from Consolidated a plane to set the style for future US fighters except in one respect—it was a two-seater. The PB-2 (PB standing for pursuit, biplace) had it all, or almost. Shown in Figures 48 through 52, the PB-2/-2A was a

Fig.40 Curtiss BFC-2 Goshawk, photo via F.Dean coll. The Navy decided their F11C-2 aircraft should be revamped and redesignated BFC-2 to denote addition of a light bombing mission to that of a fighter. BFC- meant bomber-fighter by Curtiss. Ten additional aircraft were delivered directly as BFC-2s. The main changes involved raising the turtledeck aft of the pilot, adding a partial pilot enclosure, and slightly revising the landing gear. Note this BFC-2 airplane of the High Hat Squadron has its variable incidence stabilizer set at full negative angle.

Fig.40A Curtiss BFC-2 Goshawk, photo via P.M.Bowers. A favorite target for aviation photographers of the period, this BFC-2 was the initial airplane of the final batch of ten ordered, and was delivered in early 1933. With the standard Hawk span of thirty-one feet, six inches and a gross weight of just over 4100 pounds, the BFC-2 could make 205 mph. Twenty BFC-2 airplanes were with VB-2B on the carrier Saratoga in the middle of 1935, and most were aboard a year later. They were still around in 1937.

Fig.41 Curtiss XF11C-3, Mfr.photo via F.Dean coll. With Grumman fighters starting a retractable landing gear trend, Curtiss was instructed to hold back the final F11C-2 and equip it with such a gear. The result was the XF11C-3 prototype depicted here. The arrangement was quite like the Grumman with the forward fuselage deepened to accept the bulk of the retracted wheel. Delivered to the Navy in mid-1933, the XF11C-3 weight increased about 375 pounds and speed went up about ten mph versus the F11C-2.

Fig.41B Curtiss BF2C-1, Photo via F.Dean coll. A BF2C-1 without the external fuel tank illustrates the forward fuselage contouring to achieve the gear retraction and still carry a central store such as a tank. Later a semicircular ring was added in that area to smooth airflow. Racks for light bombing are underwing. Curtiss made an advance by framing the BF2C-1 wings in aluminum alloy rather than wood, only to find the natural frequency of the structure was sympathetic to Cyclone engine vibrations when cruising. The BF2C-1s therefore did not last long.

Fig.41A Curtiss BF2C-1, photo via P.M.Bowers. A good side view of the BF2C-1 production version of the XF11C-3 with delivery of twenty-seven aircraft starting in the fall of 1934. Note the way the external fifty gallon fuel tank nestled between the deepened fuselage sections on each side. The BF2C-1s were aboard the new carrier Ranger in June, 1935 as squadron VB-5B, but were out of the Fleet Battle Force by the next year. Vibration and landing gear problems were cited as reasons for their withdrawal.

Fig.42 Curtiss Siamese Hawk III, Mfr.photo via J.Schneider. Curtiss did not do well with their US Navy BF2C-1s, but they hit a jackpot in export sales with the Hawk III equivalent (with wooden-framed wings). The aircraft shown was for Siam, now Thailand, which ordered twenty-four samples delivered between August, 1935 and February, 1936. One was exported to Turkey in 1935, ten went to Argentina in 1936, and by far the largest number, 102 aircraft, went to China from early 1936 to the middle of 1938 to assist that country in fighting the Japanese.

Fig.43 Boeing Y1P-26, Mfr.photo via F.Dean coll. As a private venture for the Boeing Company, three XP-936/YIP-26 aircraft were constructed using government furnished engines and equipment. First prototype flight came in March, 1932. As the photo shows, this Boeing fighter was a low wing open cockpit all metal design with fixed landing gear. Wire bracing tied wings, landing gear, and fuselage together. The prize was to be a production contract for a fighter to replace P-6 and P-12 biplanes in the Army.

Fig.44 Boeing P-26A, photo via P.M.Bowers. After extensive performance, structural, and operational tests of the prototypes, which were purchased by the Army in mid-1932, a contract for a very large number for the period of a production fighter, 111 aircraft, was gained by Boeing in January of 1934. The production model, the P-26A with a new version of the Pratt and Whitney R-1340 Wasp engine, revised landing gear fairing, a much higher pilot's headrest to provide turnover structure, and certain structural and equipment changes including flotation bags, won the prize of being the new standard Army fighter.

Fig.44A Boeing P-26A, photo via P.M.Bowers. On the P-26A wire bracing ran from low tubular structure behind the landing gear shock struts up and outboard to the wing spars, and from the spar fittings up and in to fuselage upper longeron tie points as well as between gear legs. The P-26A was about forty mph faster than the biplanes it was intended to replace with approximately the same installed horsepower. As in at least two later notable World War II fighters Boeing chose a semielliptical wing planform to achieve optimum aerodynamic span loading.

Fig.44B Boeing P-26A, photo via F.Dean coll. The P-26A was somewhat of a technology advance with its all metal structure and low wing monoplane configuration, but still had the open cockpit, fixed landing gear, and thin wire braced wing, all items from the past. The two bladed fixed pitch P-26A propeller was ground adjustable. Armament consisted of the usual two fixed synchronized fuselage machine guns, one of which could be .50 caliber. A bomb rack could be fitted between the landing gear legs. Wing flaps were added as a retrofit on all P-26As after some airplanes had been produced.

Fig.44C Boeing P-26A, photo via F.Dean coll. In a 1960s visit to an Air Force general's office the author found a beautiful flight photo of a P-26A "Peashooter" on the wall. Asked about the picture, the general related his flying the little Boeing in Hawaii was a truly fond memory and a career highlight. Apparently there were many ex-Air Corps officers who shared the same feelings. The P-26 type was the last open cockpit Army production fighter; it was also Boeing's last production fighter.

Fig.45 Boeing P-26B, photo via F.Dean coll. The photo shows a P-26B of the 17th Pursuit Squadron in the First Pursuit Group with some of the colorful markings then prevalent. The entrance door to the pilot's cockpit is open and the aft end of the centerline stores rack shows just behind the landing gear fairing. Many Air Corps squadrons used the P-26 in front line service until the type was replaced by P-35 and P-36 fighters in 1940. The P-26B had a fuel-injected engine; twenty-five were produced.

Fig.45A Boeing P-26C, photo via F.Dean coll. An excellent run-up picture of a P-26C with the pilot in full winter flight gear ready to battle the open cockpit elements aloft. This aircraft also has the great snow owl badge of the 17th Pursuit Squadron. The locale is believed to be Boeing field. P-26 aircraft could also be equipped with skis. Though P-26s were out of US service when Pearl Harbor took place, some were operating for a time in the Philippines against the Japanese until overwhelmed.

Right: Fig.46, civil Boeing P-26A, photo via P.M.Bowers. This restored P-26A was once operated in Guatamala and later returned to the US for display in Air Corps 17th Attack Group markings by the Air Museum in California. Except for the pilot's modern headgear and perhaps a bit of wrong background it could almost be the 1930s! A dozen Boeing Model 281 versions were exported in the mid-1930s; eleven of these went to China and fought the Japanese.

Left: Fig.47 Grumman F2F-1, photo via F.Dean coll. After two seat FF-1 production was complete Grumman had a single seat fighter of the same general configuration well in work, and after successful tests of a prototype XF2F-1 a production order for fifty-four F2F-1 aircraft was obtained from the Navy in May of 1934. Powered with a 650 horsepower closely cowled Pratt and Whitney Twin Wasp Junior engine and capable of a high speed of about 230 mph at just under two tons gross weight, the F2F-1 went into service in early 1935. In June of that year thirty-nine F2F-1s were serving aboard the carriers Lexington and Ranger. Five years later twenty-one of them were still aboard the Lexington. The stubby little fighter from Grumman served the Navy well.

Fig.48 Consolidated P-30, photo via F.Dean coll. Developed from the configuration of the earlier YP-24 and YIP-25 two seat fighter projects, the Consolidated P-30 represented a step forward in fighter plane design, and in 1933 the Army ordered four aircraft for tests of this two seat low cantilever wing monoplane with retractable landing gear and cockpit enclosures. The powerplant was a liquid cooled Curtiss Conqueror of 675 horsepower driving a two blade controllable pitch propeller. These airplanes were later redesignated as PB-2s, for pursuit, bi-place, second model.

Fig.49A Consolidated PB-2A, photo via F.Dean coll. An in-service PB-2A in a view showing the turbosupercharger installation mounted alongside the engine compartment. The PB-2A was notable in being the first turbosupercharged production fighter in US service. It was also the first production fighter having a cantilever wing. With a forty-five foot wing span and a gross weight of over three tons it was the largest and heaviest production fighter to date, and with the turbo unit no doubt the most complex, and one suspects the source of many turbo problems.

Left: Fig.49 Consolidated PB-2A, photo via P.M.Bowers. Originally called a P-30A as a modification of the P-30, fifty-two of these production fighters were delivered in 1935 from Consolidated's new San Diego plant in spite of the fact many felt the rear seat man imposed too great a weight penalty and couldn't do his job in high speed maneuvers. A big difference from the P-30 involved the powerplant; the PB-2A had a 700 horsepower turbosupercharged Curtiss Conqueror engine driving a three blade propeller for good high altitude performance.

Fig.49B. Consolidated PB-2A, Another photo of a PB-2A with its turbosupercharged Conqueror engine. The turbo was a very neat package. Note that engine exhaust is piped back to the turbine (exhaust from the other side crosses over) and induction air is taken in from the side screened inlet to the compressor, and thence to the carburetor. The exhaust waste gates can also be seen. The propeller here is a fixed pitch ground adjustable type, to be later replaced by a variable pitch constant speed model.

Fig.50 Consolidated PB-2A, photo via P.M. Bowers. A two seat PB-2A sits in the sun with a cover thrown over the rear cockpit and the front canopy slid back, perhaps to try and keep internal heat down. Armament was the usual two fixed forward firing synchronized nose guns along with the post-mounted rear seat flexible gun. With the exception of control surface covering structure and skin was all metal. The legend on top of the engine cowling says PRESTONE, referring to the engine coolant.

Fig.51 Consolidated PB-2As, Curtiss Propeller Div. photo via F.Dean coll. The lineup of PB-2A fighters looked like quite a display of air power, but Curtiss Wright used the photo to advertise the fact their Curtiss Electric constant speeding variable pitch propellers were aboard. Without question these new propellers provided a significant performance increase. The deep underslung scoops provided oil cooler air on one side and air for the Prestone radiator on the other. Blast tubes for the two nose guns protruded forward to just behind the propeller.

low wing cantilever monoplane of all-metal construction with enclosed cockpits and retractable main landing gear. It was powered by a turbosupercharged liquid-cooled Curtiss Conqueror V-12 engine swinging a three-blade constant speed controllable pitch Curtiss propeller, the latter a significant new advance. Here the Army had something—a modern high altitude fighter in a "production" quantity of fifty-four aircraft, these the first planes built at Consolidated's newly-constructed plant in San Diego, California. The trouble was the Army later found they really didn't want the rear seat and gunner; he was of no use during high speed maneuvering or at high altitude, and was quite a weight penalty. Consolidated later covered over the rear seat on one airplane, Figure 52, and entered it in the next fighter competition, to no avail.

In 1933 Grumman and the Navy, sticking to the biplane formula one last time, got the follow-on development to the F2F-1, the F3F- series, into production. This type became the standard carrier fighter in the years just prior to World war II. The F3F-1, -2, and -3 were all marginal improvements over their predecessor. The earlier version, F3F-1, employed a Pratt and Whitney two-row radial engine, and is shown in Figure 53. The F3F-2, Figure 54, used a more powerful Wright Cyclone engine. This was the peak of, and

Fig.52 Consolidated PB-2A Single Seat, photo via F.Dean coll. Consolidated entered a single seat version of its PB-2A in a 1936 fighter competition to replace the Boeing P-26 airplanes. Essentially all that was done was to cover the rear cockpit and substitute sheet metal skinning for some Plexiglas on the enclosure. It was still a big heavy aircraft competing against new prototypes from the other manufacturers and had little chance against the competition except, perhaps, for price and high altitude speed.

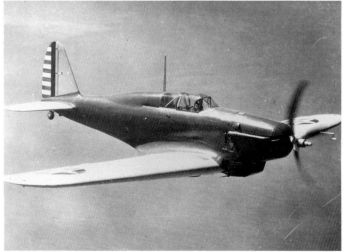

Fig.52A Consolidated PB-2A Single Seat, photo via Jon Davis. A flight view of the single place PB-2A shows Consolidated didn't expend much effort in grooming a fighter competition contender. The aircraft was one of the losers and the Seversky P-35 was the winner. Note the interesting pilot's canopy on the PB-2A. It is the result of a designer's successful effort to keep transparency areas as either flat or single curvature panels. The tubular structure aft of the pilot is a turnover post.

Fig.53 Grumman F3F-1, via F.Dean coll. The next effort in the Grumman fighter line was the F3F-1, an aircraft using the same 700 horsepower Pratt and Whitney Twin Wasp Junior as the F2F-1 but new larger wings and fuselage. Though the change did not help carrier deck spotting problems it did help correct some F2F-1 flying quality problems. After the loss of two XF3F-1 prototypes the third completed tests successfully and in August, 1935 the US Navy ordered fifty-four production aircraft. Performance was similar to the F2F-1 with a high speed of about 230 mph.

Right: Fig.54 Grumman F3F-2, photo via F.Dean coll. The major difference apparent in the -2 version of this Grumman fighter was a new powerplant to wring more performance out of the basic design, particularly at altitude. An 850 horsepower Wright Cyclone together with a three blade propeller increased speed to over 250 mph and helped altitude capability as well. Tested in early 1937, the F3F-2 aircraft appeared late that year after a Navy order for eighty-one airplanes. In mid-1938 the F3F-2 was in service aboard the USS Enterprise with Squadron VF-6 and was still there a year later. The aircraft shown is one of that squadron. Twenty-seven of a final F3F-3 version were ordered later with minor modifications.

Fig.54A Grumman F3F-2, USN photo via J.Weathers, The stubby F3F-2 is shown with a light bomb under each wing and machine gun blast tube muzzles poking through the upper cowling of the engine. The starboard gun was a .50 caliber weapon and the port gun a .30 caliber. A telescopic sight protrudes through the pilot's windshield. The retractable landing gear was hand cranked up by the pilot; a horn sounded if he reduced throttle to land and had forgotten to lower the gear.

Fig.54B Civil Grumman Gulfhawk G-32, photo via P.M.Bowers. This aircraft is a civilian version of the Navy F3F-2 series using a similar Wright Cyclone engine. It was used as a demonstrator Gulf Oil aircraft by expert pilot Al Williams. As a last gasp of the biplane era it is beautifully preserved by the National Air and Space Museum in Washington, D.C.

Fig.55 Seversky P-35, photo via P.M. Bowers. As the winner of a pursuit competition for a P-26 replacement after a drawn-out selection process Major Alexander de Seversky's P-35 was ordered into production on June 30,1936. The order went to a company who previously never had a fighter contract. The P-35 was powered by a 950 horsepower Pratt and Whitney Twin Wasp engine, spanned thirty-six feet, grossed out at 5600 pounds, and achieved a high speed of 281 mph. This beautiful runup photo shows the P-35 to advantage.

the end of biplane fighters in the US, and these Grummans were used by the Navy as fighter trainers early in World War II.

After a protracted fighter competition in 1935 and 1936 for an Army replacement of the Boeing P-26 airplane, where several low wing monoplanes were in the running, the Army selected the product of a relative newcomer to the fighter business, the Seversky P-35, shown in Figures 55 through 60. The P-35 combined all the new features of then-modern fighter planes, all-metal structure, single seat, cantilever low wing monoplane layout, retractable landing gear, and a fully-enclosed cockpit. It still had the old faithful

arrangement of only two guns in the fuselage nose as on all predecessors, but there was design provision for wing-mounted guns in addition. The P-35 was powered by a two-row Pratt and Whitney air-cooled radial engine in a smooth NACA-developed long chord cowling. A four-gun export version, of which some went to Sweden, was taken over by the Army just before World War II, and labeled a P-35A. These met their demise, along with a few P-26 airplanes, early in the Philippines fighting going up against the Japanese.

Fig.56 Seversky P-35, photo via P.M. Bowers. Though the P-35 did not achieve the desireable 300 mph high speed it was a significant advance over previous Army fighters, being 50 mph faster than the Boeing P-26 using an additional 350 horsepower. Further it had all the elements of the modern World War II type fighter plane for the first time with the exceptions of sufficient armament, armor, and supercharging. There was the all metal cantilever low wing construction, the retractable landing gear (though not retracted flush), nicely cowled engine, enclosed cockpit, and constant speed propeller. This photo of a P-35 was taken three months before Pearl Harbor.

Fig.56A Seversky P-35, photo via P.M. Bowers. This three quarter rear view of a P-35 emphasizes the clean lines of the Seversky aircraft, civil versions of which were used for racing and establishing various record flights. Metal workmanship was excellent. It was a sensitive aircraft to fly with marginal but positive stability characteristics, and was known as a ground-looper. Armament was the standard two cowl machine guns. The aft fuselage contained a large access door, the outlines of which can be seen in the photo, and a second man could be flown as a passenger within the spacious fuselage.

Fig.57 Seversky P-35, photo via R.Besecker. This P-35 picture is noteable in that the landing gear aft fairings normally under the wings are missing. The P-35 main gear retracted straight aft with wheels entering the wing only slightly. The mostly exposed wheels were faired both forward and, normally, aft as can be seen in flight photos. There have been claims both that the gear bumps were big drag producers and that they actually reduced drag due to an area rule effect. The former is true; the so-called Whitcombe effect takes place near transonic speeds which of course the P-35 could not achieve.

Fig.57A Seversky P-35, photo via Andre La Clair. A 1939 flight photo of the Commander's aircraft of the 17th Pursuit Squadron, First Pursuit Group, based at Selfridge Field, Michigan shows the P-35 to advantage, including the degree to which the landing gear retracted. Rows of these P-35s were seen in late pre-war years publicity photos, sometimes giving young Americans the impression we had lots of air power and that it was superior to all others. It wasn't.

Fig.57B Seversky P-35, photo via Andre La Clair. Another First Pursuit Group P-35 in 1939 from the 94th Pursuit Squadron at Selfridge Field, a main fighter base of the Army Air Corps. P-35 aircraft were distinguished by semi-elliptical wing planforms, this shape used on just about all Seversky aircraft as one way to get optimum spanwise aerodynamic loading. The P-35 was essentially the grandfather of the World War II P-47 which also had that wing planform.

Fig.57C Seversky P-35, Dave Menard photo via R. Besecker. This P-35 has been restored to pristine condition by the Air Force Museum in Ohio and exhibited there as a good example of a late 1930s production fighter. Markings are those of the First Pursuit Group where the P-35 achieved some temporary fame. These aircraft never saw war service; some survived into early wartime as trainers and service hacks. At least one USAAF commander kept a P-35 as a personal run-around. Charles Lindbergh flew the P-35 for a time, but liked it much less than the Curtiss P-36.

Fig.58 Seversky S-2 Racer, photo via P. M. Bowers. The S-2 was a racing version of the P-35; the main change was a revised cut-down canopy. In 1937 Major de Seversky asked civilian pilot Frank Fuller to race the S-2. Fuller flew it to sixth place in the 1937 Thompson Trophy Race, but he won first prize in the 1937 and 1939 Bendix Trophy Races and came in second in the 1938 Bendix. The S-2 airplane was the "Drake Bullet" in the MGM movie Test Pilot.

Fig.59 Seversky DS Doolittle Special, photo via P.M. Bowers. Another civil version of the P-35 was the DS, ordered from Seversky in 1936 by the Shell Oil Company for executive use of pilot employee Jimmy Doolittle and for testing of the new 100 octane aviation fuel under development by the company. The DS was equipped with the single row nine cylinder R-1820 Wright Cyclone engine, making for a larger diameter nose than the P-35 fighter and S-2 racer which both used the twin row fourteen cylinder Pratt and Whitney R-1830. The DS was later sold to Ecuador.

Fig.60 Seversky/Republic EP-1, photo via W. Dunton. The version of the P-35 exported to Sweden is pictured, the photo taken in the 1980s in Sweden. The aircraft was saved by them as a museum exhibit. In late 1939 and early 1940 Sweden ordered a total of 120 EP-1s differing from the P-35 in powerplant details, increased fuselage length, and armament. Sweden got only sixty of the fighters, which they called J-9s; the US government took over the remainder as P-35A fighters.

Fig.60A Republic P-35As, photo via Andre La Clair. These P-35A aircraft are at Nichols Field near Manila in the Philippine Islands in 1941. Taken over from the Swedish EP-1 order, forty-five aircraft were sent to the Philippines in 1940 to bolster Pacific defenses. Note the wing guns. A few P-35As were also sent to Ecuador where they served for several years. The aircraft sent to Manila were soon wiped out in early 1942 by the Japanese invaders.

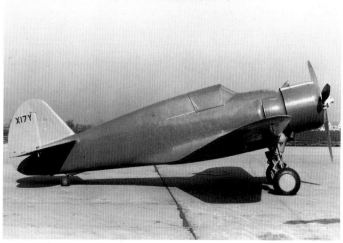

Fig.61 Curtiss Model 75, Mfr.photo via J. Schneider. The original version of the Curtiss entrant in the 1935/1936 fighter competition designed under the guiding hand of Don Berlin who was hired by Curtiss at least partly because of his Northrop experience with advanced metal structural design techniques needed for the new fighter project. The engine installed was the new 900 horsepower twin row Wright R-1670 designed as competition for the Pratt and Whitney R-1535 Twin Wasp Junior two row engine. It turned out to be a poor powerplant choice, no doubt pushed upon the designers by Curtiss Wright management. The plane first flew in April, 1935.

Fig.61A Curtiss Model 75B, Mfr.photo via J.Schneider. The same basic airframe at the same Curtiss plant location ready for the fighter competition of 1936. The 1935 competition was postponed because no entrant was really ready with a definitive prototype in 1935, except perhaps Curtiss. The difference in nose contours is the primary outward change, though canopy modification is also evident. After trying the Pratt and Whitney R-1535 engine with an unsatisfactory result Don Berlin settled on an 850 horsepower Wright R-1820 Cyclone, this accounting for the greater engine cowl diameter. The prototype lost the competition to the Seversky P-35.

Fig.61B Curtiss Y1P-36, photo via R.Besecker. In spite of the production win in 1936 by Seversky, the Army liked the Curtiss product well enough to ask for three service test aircraft fitted with the Pratt and Whitney R-1830 Twin Wasp engine, as it turned out a quite agreeable combination. In a 1937 fighter competition the Y1P-36 came out on top.

Fig.61C Curtiss Y1P-36, USAF photo via C. Mandrake. Like its Seversky P-35 competitor, the Y1P-36 represented the new look as regards then-modern fighters-a clean cantilever low wing all metal single seat monoplane with enclosed cockpit and retractable landing gear. The Curtiss airplane twisted the landing gear wheel ninety degrees to lay flat and flush in the wing without the large protuberances of the Seversky aircraft. Performance of the two was quite comparable with the P-36 having a speed edge. Service tests of Y1P-36s started in February of 1937.

Fig.61D Curtiss P-36A, photo via P.M.Bowers. As a result of Y1P-36 service tests the Army, favorably impressed, ordered a production batch of 210 P-36A versions in the summer of 1937 and production aircraft appeared in the spring of 1938. External changes appeared minor; cowl flaps were added and cowl machine gun and exhaust stack fairings were revised. The Curtiss propeller was made standard equipment. But structural beef-up, equipment additions, and other revisions added 575 pounds to gross weight. High speed was around 300 mph.

Fig.61E Curtiss P-36A, photo via P.M.Bowers. A beautifully refurbished P-36A painted up in camouflage originally used for the 1939 National Air Races and on display at the USAF Museum in Ohio. Handling qualities were excellent; roll acceleration and roll rate were exceptional and overall maneuverability was considered very good. Col. Charles Lindbergh flew a P-36A extensively and preferred it to the P-35.

Fig.61F Curtiss P-36A, photo via P.M. Bowers. Another view of the Air Force Museum refurbished P-36A showing the badge of the 27th Fighter Squadron and the two stripes of the squadron leader's airplane. The concave cutouts covered with Plexiglas just aft of the cockpit gave the pilot some degree of rear quarter vision and were carried through into the P-40 series. The P-36A, like the P-35, was still a two gun airplane, with one .50 caliber and one .30 caliber fuselage weapon. Four P-36As managed to get airborne during the Pearl Harbor attack, but that was the extent of their USAAF combat service.

Fig.61G Curtiss P-36B, US Army photo via F. Dean coll. This aircraft was a P-36A equipped for testing a new version of the Twin Wasp engine that provided slightly more power and had a new blower drive. The P-36B was accepted by the Army in November, 1938. It became an ordinary squadron airplane and for a time was painted in camouflage colors.

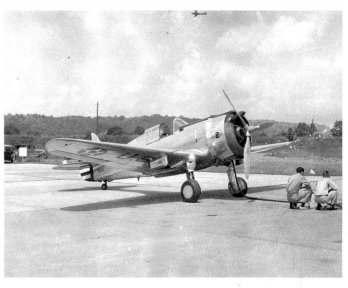

Fig.62. Curtiss P-36C, photo via R. Besecker. The P-36C version could easily be distinguished by noting the addition of two .30 caliber wing machine guns with ammunition containers in small underwing pods. It was powered with a new uprated R-1830 engine delivering a maximum of 1200 horsepower. Including the test aircraft thirty-one of the original 210 planes ordered were provided as P-36Cs.

Fig.62A Curtiss P-36C, photo via P.M.Bowers. The famous number sixty-nine of the 27th Pursuit Squadron in camouglage. This P-36C is the real squadron commander's airplane the Air Force Museum's P-36A is marked to resemble. The paint was washable so the aircraft could be cleaned off afterwards we are told. One wonders how hard some Air Corps crew chiefs might have worked on that project! The turtle painted on the wing gun ammunition pod apparently meant the airplane had crossed the equator at some time.

Fig.62B Curtiss P-36Cs, US Army photo via C.Mandrake. A flight photo of the 27th Pursuit Squadron taken in 1939 showing the various camouflage patterns displayed at the 1939 National Air Races. To the extent it can be discerned all aircraft appear to be P-36Cs with wing guns. Pictures like this were good pre-war propaganda for the public, but the fact was America had considerably less than 300 modern fighter planes in the Army in 1939, counting P-35s and P-36s; the first production P-40 was not test flown until April, 1940.

Curtiss disappointment in losing a fighter competition to Seversky was soon soothed by award of a then-large contract for their P-36 pursuit airplane, shown in Figures 61 through 63. The P-36 was similar in configuration to the P-35, and used the same basic engine; together they filled out the thin Army fighter ranks of the last pre-war years. Some pilots preferred one type and some the other; Col. Charles Lindbergh preferred the P-36, a particularly nice-

flying aircraft. A few P-36s got involved in fighting during the Japanese attack on Pearl Harbor; earlier many more Hawk 75A export versions had fought for France in the losing battle against Germany in the European war. Some fought with other countries. A lighter fixed-gear version was exported, mostly to China. The P-35 airplane might be considered the grandfather of the World War II P-47 Thunderbolt, with the P-43 Lancer the father in between, and the P-

Fig.62C Curtiss P-36C, photo via F. Dean coll. A P-36C fighter in an early camouflage scheme with the Army star on the fuselage. In the second half of 1940 and through 1941 P-40s were rapidly replacing P-36s in the squadrons and the latter were considered second line fighters. This P-36C was used for tests of various camouflage schemes and was painted in olive drab above and gray below. It appears the USAAF stenciled model data near the cockpit has been obliterated.

Fig.62D Curtiss P-36Cs, USAAF photo via Joe Christy. Taken three and a half months after Pearl Harbor, this early wartime picture of three P-36Cs (one tenth of the entire P-36C fleet!) shows what appears to be an overall olive drab paint job with the national insignia on the fuselage. The central red circle of pre-war days seems already to have been painted out, though there is a faint indication remaining. In the scary early days of war with rumors everywhere anything that seemed remotely modern was put into the air for America's defense.

Fig.63 Civil Curtiss 75A, Mfr.photo via F.Dean coll. This "P-36 type" was a Curtiss demonstrator aircraft, company owned and used for many different tests, mostly of powerplants and related items. Based at Caldwell Wright Airport in northern New Jersey adjacent to the new Curtiss Propeller Division plant, the 75A, NX22028, was at one time equipped with a geared two stage supercharger as the 75R for entry in a fighter competition. As shown it was powered with a Wright Cyclone engine swinging a Curtiss Electric propeller.

Fig.63A Curtiss H75A-4, Mfr.photo via H. Andrews. Many H75A "Hawk" aircraft were exported from late 1938 through 1941 with France obtaining the most, well over 600 airplanes in four variants, some powered with Pratt and Whitney Twin Wasps and others with Wright Cyclones. The photo shows a Cyclone powered airplane for France. These aircraft fought the Germans over France and later the Americans in North Africa.

Fig.63B Curtiss H75A-9, photo via Joe Christy. The export Hawks got to some strange places in World War II. The aircraft shown is one of ten Cyclone powered H87A-9 fighters destined for Iran, but taken over by the British in early 1941 and ending up in India. Other H75As went to places like Norway, Finland, the UK, Peru, Germany, Netherlands East Indies, and so on. The total exports of Hawk 75 fixed gear and 75A retractable gear fighters amounted to 778 airplanes and made Curtiss Wright quite a bit of money.

Fig.63C Curtiss H75H Hawk, Mfr.photo via Joe Christy. The Curtiss Airplane Division put out a simplified export version of the Army P-36 in 1937 with a fixed panted main landing gear. Two demonstrator aircraft were built; one got to China and was used by Gen. C.L.Chennault. The other was the aircraft in the photo, the Argentine demonstrator as it looked in May, 1937. It was delivered about a month later. Argentina built twenty more under license about three years later.

Fig.63D Curtiss H75O Hawk, Mfr.photo via Joe Christy. One of the export aircraft built by Curtiss for Argentina and delivered near the end of 1938. A total of ninety-three fixed gear versions were exported or built under license; fifty of these were operated by Argentina (H75H and H75O), thirty-one by China against the Japanese (H75H and H75M), and twelve by Siam/Thailand (H75N). High speed was about 280 mph; armament varied.

Fig.64 Civil Seversky AP-4, Mfr.photo via P.M.Bowers. A company demonstrator entered into the 1939 fighter competition, the AP-4 was essentially a prototype for the Republic P-43 Lancer production aircraft. It had inwardly retracting flush landing gear and was powered by a turbosupercharged Pratt and Whitney Twin Wasp engine. The turbo unit was located in the belly of the aircraft behind the wing trailing edge.

Fig.64A Republic YP-43, Mfr.photo via F.Dean coll. One of thirteen service test YP-43 fighters redesigned from the AP-4 demonstrator but having the same basic turbosupercharged powerplant. Changes included revised fuselage and canopy lines, engine air induction system revisions, two wing .30 caliber machine guns added to the two fuselage guns, and a new more powerful version of the R-1830 engine. The first service test aircraft was delivered in September, 1940 with all completed by the next spring.

Fig.64C Republic P-43A Lancer, photo via F.Dean coll. After fifty-four P-43 production aircraft were delivered more P-43 types were ordered to fill the Republic production line gaps until the P-47 Thunderbolt program could get under way. In the fall of 1941 eighty P-43A versions, one of which is shown in the photo, started appearing and later 125 P-43A-1 variants were produced for export to China, most of which reached the Far East. Production at Farmingdale, Long Island was completed in March of 1942. Combat reports from China provided mixed reviews; one problem involved leaky fuel tanks.

36 spawned the P-40. The Lancer, Figure 64, was an interim fighter improved over the P-35 by the addition of a turbosupercharger, flush retracting landing gear, and other modifications. It filled the Republic (was Seversky) production line until the Thunderbolt got started, with output totaling 272 aircraft. P-43s served US home defense squadrons early in the war, and some were sent to China to help fight the Japanese.

Two other low-production US fighters were manufactured in the period just before US entry into World War II, the Curtiss-Wright (St. Louis) CW-21, and the Vultee Model 48, later the P-66. Both were in the latest configuration of all-metal low wing single seat monoplanes with retractable landing gear and, in these cases, air-

cooled radial engines. The CW-21 was designed as a bomber interceptor for export, and had a high rate of climb. Shown in two versions, Figures 65 through 67, the CW-21 was slated for production in China, but this never came about. Most of the limited number of aircraft produced went to the Netherlands East Indies where they were destroyed by the invading Japanese. The rather slick looking P-66, Figures 68 through 70, were intended for Sweden, but production aircraft were taken over by the US which eventually sent most to China. The prototype Vultee fighter was interesting as an experiment in attempting to fair over a radial engine to make it look like the pointed nose of an inline engine installation, while attempting to cool it. The attempt was not successful, and the air-

Fig.64B Republic P-43 Lancer, photo via P.M.Bowers. A fine view of one of the fifty-four P-43 airplanes ordered in 1940 and delivered in 1941. Notable are the protrusions representing the two .50 caliber cowl guns; the two .30 caliber wing guns are not mounted. The propeller is a Curtiss type; the bump under the belly aft is the turbosupercharger unit. These aircraft were not considered combat-ready, but were revised for a photo reconnaissance role as P-43Bs with fuselage cameras. High speed was about 350 mph at 20000 feet altitude. With turbosupercharging the service ceiling was over 35000 feet.

Fig.65 Curtiss Wright CW-21 Demon, Mfr.photo via F. Dean coll. The St. Louis Division of Curtiss Wright developed a single seat interceptor fighter for the export market during 1938 which flew first in January of 1939. Based on earlier two place trainer designs, the CW-21 employed a much more powerful engine, the Wright R-1820 Cyclone of 1000 horsepower. With a gross weight of only about 4250 pounds the climb rate of the interceptor was exceptional, about 4500 feet per minute at sea level. High speed was approximately 300 mph. The landing gear retracted into large underwing bulges.

Fig.65A Curtiss Wright CW-21 Demon, Mfr. photo via Art Krieger. China desperately needed fighter aircraft to combat the Japanese invaders and ordered three CW-21s plus parts with the intention of assembling them in China, and Curtiss Wright delivered these in 1939. The CW-21 was equipped with two synchronized fuselage cowl guns, one of .50 caliber and the other .30 caliber, and the eighty gallon fuel tank was unprotected against gunfire. There were no external store stations.

Fig.66 Curtiss CW-21 Demon, Mfr.photo via F. Dean coll. A flight photo of the prototype CW-21 interceptor shows the bulbous Cyclone radial engine up front, the much reduced fuselage cross section near the empennage, and a fixed tail wheel. The pilot sat aft of the wing trailing edge, further aft than most pilot locations. This factor limited pilot visibility, but the location allowed the fuselage fuel tank to be over the wing.

Fig.67 Curtiss Wright, CW-21B Demon, Mfr.photo via J.Schneider. A revised version of the Demon interceptor was put out in late 1939, and in 1940 Curtiss Wright obtained an order for twenty-four CW-21B models from the Netherlands East Indies. The major change readily apparent was in the landing gear which now retracted inward and flush with the wing lower surface. The tail wheel was also modified. Two wing guns could be provided in addition to the cowl machine guns. By the time of Pearl Harbor seventeen of the two dozen CW-21Bs were in the Netherlands East Indies. Like other fighters there they were shortly overwhelmed by the Japanese invaders of Java in early 1942. Three other CW-21B interceptors got to China.

Fig.68 Vultee 48X Vanguard, Bill Larkins photo via M. Sheppard. The prototype Vultee fighter is shown running up in September, 1939. The aircraft shared some common parts with Vultee trainers, but the most interesting aspect was the powerplant installation. The reduction gear nose case of the Pratt and Whitney Twin Wasp was extended and the engine cowling faired down to the propeller spinner to make the airplane appear as if powered by a V-12 liquid cooled engine. A variable area lower scoop collected cylinder cooling air. The experiment did not work; the engine did not cool properly, and the configuration was abandoned.

Fig.69 Vultee 48 Vanguard, Mfr.photo via F.Dean coll. A Vultee publicity photo of the production Model 48 with a conventional radial engine cowling. It is certainly doubtful the fighter would be armed during high RPM runup of the Twin Wasp engine! The aircraft in the photo is in Chinese markings, and after aborted assignments to Sweden and England almost all of the 144 Model 48s went to China under Lend Lease as P-66s. Two .50 caliber fuselage guns were supplemented by four .30 caliber wing guns in this fighter.

plane was put into production with a standard radial engine cowling.

This short survey of US "production" fighters between the two great wars leads directly to the aircraft covered herein as AMERICA'S HUNDRED THOUSAND, the eleven production types of World War II. It is seen even minor production in the war period exceeded individual type production of 1920 to 1940. The small peacetime aircraft industry which produced 2956 fighters for the US services and 1193 exports expanded quickly into a giant producer of 100000 fighters!

Fig.69A Vultee P-66 Vanguard, photo via F.Dean coll. Of the total number of Vultee fighters produced in late 1941 and early 1942 a few remained in the US to be employed as fighter trainers during the worrysome early war months when everything available was utilized. The P-66 in this photo shows the results of typical hard use of training aircraft. Note main landing gear fairings have been discarded, and tape over wing gun ports has been pierced in gunnery training.

Fig.70 Vultee P-66 Vanguards, USAF photo via Bob Martin. The legend on this official photo says "Newly assembled Vultee P-66s are lined up on the parking apron at Karachi Air Base, India for final touches", and is dated 25 October, 1942.

FIGHTER PRODUCTION

Production of fighters during World War II, like that of other aircraft types, and military hardware in general, was little short of breathtaking. From a very modest start at the beginning of the European war in 1939, American production accelerated slowly at first, and then with great rapidity to a massive outpouring of fighters in 1944 and 1945. In December of 1944 the P-51 Mustang alone was being produced at a rate of one every sixty-two minutes, almost a plane hourly. In mid-1941 there were no Mustangs; by that December of 1944 nearly 9500 had been built. At the time of Pearl Harbor, December 1941, not one production Thunderbolt fighter existed; by the very same December of 1944 over 12000 P-47s had been turned out. For the eight US fighter types produced in very large numbers, and employed by US airmen in combat (the P-61, P-63, and F2A- are here excluded), there had been a total of only 4743 fighter airplanes put out by the month of US war entry; at the end of 1944, three years later, factories had turned out, for the eight types, a total of 75,718 fighters, a sixteen-fold increase.

Production numbers for the "big eight" of US machines are given in Table 2. The P-61 and F2A- are omitted because they were not manufactured in very large numbers (a few hundred each), and

FIGHTER ACCEPTANCES

YEAR	MONTH	P-38	P-39	P-40	P-47	P-51	F4F-	F4U-	F6F-
1940	Jan.								
	Feb.								
	Mar.								
	Apr.								
	May			11					
	Jun.			25					
	Jul.			56			2		
	Aug.			104			33		
	Sep.	1	1	114			29		
	Oct.		2	135			21	1	
	Nov.			168			2		
	Dec.		10	165			19		
Year	Total	1	13	778			106	1	
Cum.	Total	1	13	778			106	1	
1941	Jan.	1	3	155			31		
	Feb.		6	153			25		
	Mar.	2	11	133			25		
	Apr.	4	1	186			47		
	May	4	15	146			37		
	Jun.	4	37	125			29		
	Jul.	23	50	81			32		
	Aug.	26	158	179		2	31		
	Sep.	12	128	254		6	18		
	Oct.	3	198	270		25	6		
	Nov.	74	128	281		37	15		
	Dec.	54	191	285	1	68	28		
Year	Total	207	926	2248	1	138	324		
Cum.	Total	208	939	3026	1	138	430	1	
1942	Jan.	116	179	317		84	63		
	Feb.	127	113	295		84	81		
	Mar.	100	141	348	5	52	90		
	Apr.	100	52	396	1	86	98		
	May	100	86	385	10	84	107		
	Jun.	105	227	282	26	84	132		
	Jul.	170	255	135	38	76	100	2	
	Aug.	80	309	143	61	24	135	9	
	Sep.	132	-	416	67	60	127	13	1
	Oct.	145	3	360	66	-	164	32	1
	Nov.	144	268	376	116	-	196	54	1
	Dec.	160	299	404	142	-	177	68	7
Year	Total	1479	1932	3854	532	634	1470	178	10
Cum.	Total	1687	2871	6883	533	772	1900	179	10
1943	Jan.	175	330	315	170	-	38	39	12
	Feb.	168	385	314	151	-	54	75	35
	Mar.	193	472	324	232	70	80	77	81
	Apr.	122	511	325	244	121	103	115	131

YEAR	MONTH	P-38	P-39	P-40	P-47	P-51	F4F-	F4U-	F6F-
	May	84	312	380	307	121	120	139	150
	Jun.	180	439	400	307	20	121	169	180
	Jul.	264	503	337	382	91	98	196	210
	Aug.	102	501	463	434	175	170	200	250
	Sep.	155	280	400	496	201	159	271	295
	Oct.	351	420	378	496	284	156	285	345
	Nov.	387	403	422	549	295	193	336	400
	Dec.	316	391	200	660	332	245	385	458
Year	Total	2497	4947	4258	4428	1710	1537	2293	2547
Cum.	Total	4184	7818	11141	4946	2482	3437	2466	2557
1944	Jan.	317	351	275	651	370	235	436	500
	Feb.	313	350	241	633	380	282	510	510
	Mar.	352	300	283	648	482	303	578	512
	Apr.	342	252	203	623	407	300	569	515
	May	352	201	200	601	580	300	596	500
	Jun.	355	150	73	600	581	300	431	499
	Jul.	367	112	97	600	569	300	487	477
	Aug.	400	13	155	600	700	300	388	496
	Sep.	397	-	202	594	665	300	390	501
	Oct.	364	-	193	494	763	210	401	550
	Nov.	325	-	80	377	765	150	342	525
	Dec.	300	-	-	644	720	150	312	555
Year	Total	4186	1729	2002	7065	6982	3130	5380	6140
Cum.	Total	8368	9547	13143	12026	9464	6567	7906	8697
1945	Jan.	301			480				
	Feb.	253			544				
	Mar.	289			539				
	Apr.	252			591				
	May	225			528				
	Jun.	175			415				
	Jul.	118			305				
	Aug.	53			157				
	Sep.	-			67				
	Oct.	-			25				
	Nov.	-			1				
	Dec.	-			5				
Year	Total	1669	0	0	3657	6103	1337	3578	3578
Cum.	Total	10037	9547	13143	15683	15567	7904	11484	12275

Notes
P-38 grand total includes three aircraft not accounted for in monthly totals.
F4F- figures include FM-1 and FM-2 aircraft by Eastern Aircraft.
F4U- figures include FG- and F3A- aircraft by Goodyear and Brewster.

the P-63 is left out because it was not used by USAAF combat groups. These numbers are shown in Graphs 1 and 2, where cumulative production numbers are indicated.

It is clearly seen the Curtiss P-40 was the US Army and export fighter of major significance before we entered the war in December, 1941, with the Bell P-39 trailing well behind. A very modest number of Grumman Wildcats had been produced, and anything else was really insignificant. Over 3000 P-40s had come off the line with less than 1000 Airacobras, and about 400 Wildcats.

The P-40 was a real phenomenon. It had such a lead in production that cumulative numbers accepted were not exceeded by any other type until it was out of production near the end of 1944. The P-39 was always about a year behind in cumulative production, and acceptances were stopped about the same time as the P-40. Certainly from a numbers viewpoint the importance to the US and its allies of the P-40 in the early and middle parts of the war can

hardly be overestimated. Peak monthly production of P-40s hit about 400 aircraft, or about thirteen a day, all made in Buffalo, New York. The P-39 was next, and cumulative numbers produced were not exceeded by a type other than the P-40 until the middle of 1944 when P-47 Thunderbolt production totals finally beat out the Airacobra. Bell was near Curtiss in Buffalo, certainly a city of supreme importance to the war effort for at least the first half of the conflict. Buffalo was producing almost all the Army fighters!

Lockheed P-38 production was slow in getting started, partly no doubt because of its relative twin engine twin boom complexity. It took until July 1942 to get 1000 Lightnings produced, this at a time when almost 2000 P-39s and over 5000 P-40s had come off the lines. And a little over a year later, in August, 1943, P-47 Thunderbolt production caught up with the P-38 and swiftly passed it. Since the P-38, P-39, P-40, and early P-51 were all powered by Allison V-1710 engines (except for two P-40 versions), the produc-

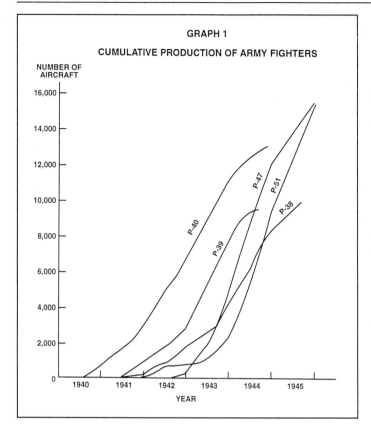

GRAPH 1

CUMULATIVE PRODUCTION OF ARMY FIGHTERS

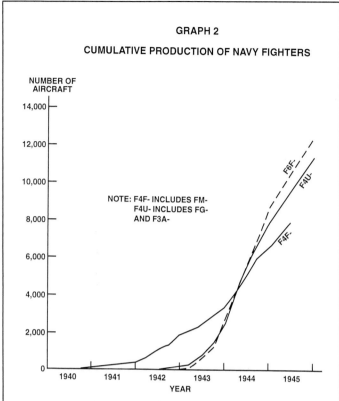

GRAPH 2

CUMULATIVE PRODUCTION OF NAVY FIGHTERS

NOTE: F4F- INCLUDES FM-
F4U- INCLUDES FG-
AND F3A-

tion strain on Allison Division of General Motors was great. They were equal to the task, however, and by the end of 1943 had put out a total of 43,500 V-1710 engines versus the 26,600 Allisons required up to that time. This was a ratio of about 1.6 to 1, which provided for engine spares.

Yearly production of early P-47s and Allison-powered P-51s was about the same (500-plus and 600-plus respectively) at the end of 1942, but Thunderbolt numbers spurted way ahead of the P-51 in 1943, mainly because of the North American changeover from Allison to Packard-Merlin engined Mustangs. At 1943 years end almost 5000 Thunderbolts had been accepted against half that number of P-51 aircraft. But in the next year, 1944, North American made up the slack with a prodigious second half effort, pouring out Merlin Mustangs at an average rate of almost 700 a month, and at the end of the year P-47 and P-51 cumulative production was just about the same at near 7000 aircraft each. With the switch to the P-47N Pacific version, Republic production dropped somewhat in 1945 off their 1944 600-a-month average pace, while P-51s rolled out the doors at about the previous rate. In the end production totals for the two fighters were closely similar at well over 15000 apiece, each more than any other US type. The P-40 rang in third with a little over 13000 accepted.

On the Navy fighter side the Grumman/Eastern Wildcat was the lone aircraft turned out in the war's early stages, passing 2000 total units in early 1943 and a 3000 mark by the end of that year. Navy Vought Corsair production got off to a slow start, even with later assistance from Goodyear and Brewster. After the first year of American participation in the war, less than 200 Corsairs had been built, and these were not carrier-based, so the 1900 Wildcats

produced to that time, less considerable attrition in service, had to suffice. During 1943 help started to come in the form of production quantities, about 2500 each, of land-based Corsairs and carrier-compatible F6F- Hellcats. In 1944 production of the two newer types proceeded apace with cumulative turnout almost exactly equal at mid-year, after which Hellcat output from the single Grumman plant began to slowly outstrip that of the combined Vought and Goodyear plants. At the end of America's biggest production year, 1944, cumulative Corsair production was 7900 fighters, and for the Hellcat 8700. End-of-war rounded totals were about 11500 for the Corsair and 12300 for the Hellcat. They thus placed fourth and fifth behind three Army fighters (P-47, P-51, and P-40) for total wartime production honors. The remaining US fighters, P-38, P-39, and Wildcat, each totaled in the 8000 to 10000 aircraft range.

The output of all US fighters, including minor types, during the war rose spectacularly through the period, ending of course at AMERICA'S HUNDRED THOUSAND. Approximate figures, rounded to the nearest thousand, are impressive: 1940-2000 fighters, 1941-4000, 1942-10000, 1943-24000, 1944-39000, 1945-21000.

What happened to them? There is no detailed breakdown known, but categories of disposal can be noted. Certainly there were a great number of combat losses, but non-combat attrition was higher. Training accidents accounted for large numbers. At war's end some were kept in service, but huge numbers were scrapped, others given to foreign governments, some were kept in western storage. A few were purchased by civilian hobbyists at very low prices. A very few were saved for museums and rest there today.

FIGHTER FAILURES

THE EXPERIMENTAL LOW WING MONOPLANES

Along with production types of the inter-war years and of World War II, there were a large number of US fighter projects built as experimental and service test aircraft that for a variety of reasons never reached production. We will look at piston-engined low wing monoplanes in this category, listed in Table 3.

The first American low wing fighter monoplane, built for the Army, was the Detroit-Lockheed YP-24. The thick cantilever wooden wing was that of the popular Lockheed civil monoplanes of the time like the Sirius, and the retractable landing gear was also similar. The aircraft, shown in Figure 71, was a tandem two-seater with enclosed cockpits and a V-12 Conqueror engine up front. Af-

TABLE 3
US EXPERIMENTAL PISTON-ENGINE LOW WING MONOPLANE FIGHTERS, 1930-1945

TYPE	KEY DATE	NOTES
LOCKHEED	YP-24 DELIVERED SEPT.'31	FIRST ARMY CANTILEVER LW MONOPLANE
CONSOLIDATED	Y1P-25 DELIVERED DEC. '32	DEVEL. OF YP-24. TO P-30/PB-2A
CURTISS	XP-31 TESTED DEC. '32	LOST OUT TO BOEING P-26 FOR PROD.
BOEING	XF7B-1 FIRST FLT.SEPT.'33	TESTED, NOT ACCEPTED BY NAVY.
BOEING	XP-29 FIRST FLT.JAN. '34	COMPLETELY MODERNIZED P-26.
NORTHROP	XFT-1/-2 FIRST FLT.JAN. '34	FOR NAVY TEST; DEVELOPMENT PROBLEMS
VOUGHT	V-141 FIRST FLT.MAR. '36	FROM A NORTHROP DESIGN.
CURTISS	XP-37 FIRST FLT.APR. '37	PRODUCTION REJECTED IN FAVOR P-40.
VOUGHT	V-143 FIRST FLT.JUNE '37	DEVELOPED V-141 FOR EXPORT.
SEVERSKY	NF-1 TESTED SEPT. '37	NAVAL VERSION OF ARMY PROD. P-35.
CURTISS	75R TESTED FEB. '39	P-36/75A WITH NEW POWERPLANT.
SEVERSKY	XP-41 ACCEPTED MAR. '39	LAST ARMY P-35 MODIFIED. NO PROD.
CURTISS	XP-42 DELIVERED MAR. '39	ARMY P-36 WITH REVISED NOSE FAIRING
GRUMMAN	XF5F-1 FIRST FLT.APR. '40	REJECTED IN FAVOR OF LATER XF7F-1.
BELL	XFL-1 FIRST FLT.MAY '40	NAVAL VERSION OF ARMY P-39
CURTISS	XP-46 FIRST FLT.FEB. '41	PRODUCTION REJECTED FOR P-40E.
GRUMMAN	XP-50 FIRST FLT.FEB. '41	TWO ENGINE LIKE XF5F-1; CRASHED.
CURTISS	XP-60 FIRST FLT.SEPT.'41	MANY DIFFERENT DEVELOPMENT VERSIONS
LOCKHEED	XP-49 FIRST FLT.NOV. '42	RE-ENGINED P-38; NO PRODUCTION.
CONVAIR	XP-54 FIRST FLT.JAN. '43	TWIN BOOM PUSHER; REJECTED.
NORTHROP	XP-56 FIRST FLT.MAR. '43	PUSHER SEMI-FLYING WING TYPE.
CURTISS	XP-55 FIRST FLT.JUL. '43	PUSHER; DEVELOPMENT PROBLEMS.
CURTISS	XP-62 FIRST FLT.JUL. '43	ENGINE TYPE NEEDED FOR B-29s.
FISHER/GM	XP-75 FIRST FLT.NOV. '43	NOT NEEDED WITH MERLIN P-51
MCDONNELL	XP-67 FIRST FLT.JAN. '44	TWIN ENGINED. DEVELOPMENT PROBLEMS
REPUBLIC	XP-72 FIRST FLT.FEB. '44	P-47 VERSION WITH WASP MAJOR ENGINE
BELL	XP-77 FIRST FLT.APR. '44	LIGHTWEIGHT FIGHTER, WOODEN.
CURTISS	XF14C-2 ACCEPTED JULY '44	PERFORMANCE NOT UP TO LATE CORSAIRS
BOEING	XF8B-1 FIRST FLT.NOV. '44	TOO LATE FOR WW II ACTION.
LOCKHEED	XP-58 ACCEPTED DEC. '44	BIG TWO-PLACE P-38 TYPE. NO REQ'T.
CURTISS	XF15C-1 FIRST FLT.FEB. '45	PISTON ENGINE PLUS JET TYPE.

Fig.71 Detroit-Lockheed XP-900/YP-24, US Army photo via F. Dean coll. The first low wing monoplane fighter built for Army tests was known in the company as the XP-900 and as the YP-24 by the Army. With metal covered fuselage and tail surfaces the YP-24 had a thick wooden cantilever wing based on the civil Lockheed Altair design. Mockup inspection took place in March, 1931, and the 600 horsepower Curtiss Conqueror-powered two place fighter was delivered to the Army in late September, 1931. It had a gross weight of 4360 pounds and a high speed of 214 mph. After three weeks of tests at Wright Field, Dayton, Ohio the test pilot bailed out after failing to be able to lower the landing gear. The Detroit-Lockheed company folded after the crash of the airplane.

Fig.72 Consolidated Y1P-25, photo via F.Dean coll. After the demise of Detroit-Lockheed the Army requested Consolidated to pick up the YP-24 design and improve it, and provided them a contract for two aircraft, one the Y1P-25 fighter and the other the XA-11 attack plane. Consolidated did a redesign including a remodeled fuselage, a new all metal wing, and, for the fighter, a turbosupercharged Conqueror engine. The photo shows the collector which routed the exhaust across to the turbo unit on the far side of the aircraft.

Fig.73 Consolidated Y1P-25, Mfr.photo via F.Dean coll. Another view of the Y1P-25 shows the turbosupercharger mounted on the left side of the engine compartment. The wing was still thick, but it was all metal. Air inlets for coolant radiator and oil cooler are low under the engine. The 5100 pound fighter had a high speed of 247 mph at altitude. The Y1P-25 was destroyed in an early 1933 accident, but paved the way for an Army order of four similar P-30 fighters, later redesignated as PB-2s.

ter a few flights an Army test pilot bailed out under orders because the landing gear would not extend, and the single prototype was lost. Soon after Detroit-Lockheed went bankrupt.

The promise of the YP-24 did not die, however, since some of the design team moved to Consolidated Aircraft, then in Buffalo, New York. They started work on a successor aircraft with a metal fuselage, and a turbosupercharger on the Conqueror engine. The airplane, a real stride forward, is shown in Figures 72 and 73 as the Y1P-25 pursuit, still in two-seater mold. This model did not go into production either, however a later derivative P-30/PB-2A shown in the inter-war fighters section made the grade after further development. The two-seat arrangement was, however, never to be used after the PB-2A model.

About the time of the Y1P-25 development, the Army conducted a competition for a single seat monoplane successor to the P-12 biplane then in extensive service. Competing against a new Boeing entry, the XP-26, was the Curtiss XP-31 Swift fighter, first powered by a radial engine, later the Curtiss Conqueror V-12. Shown in Figures 74 through 76, the Swift had a thin low wing of metal construction, a faired fixed landing gear, and enclosed cockpit. It was both overweight and disappointing in performance; the Boeing P-26 won the competition and production contracts to be the new standard Army fighter.

Boeing was not so successful with their next fighter effort. The XF7B-1 Navy fighter prototype was to provide that service with its first monoplane fighter and replace the F4B- biplanes then in ser-

Fig.74 Curtiss XP-934/XP-31 Swift, Mfr.photo via J.Schneider. A company-funded fighter project to compete against the Boeing P-26 design, the Curtiss XP-934 at the Army's request was fitted first with a 700 horsepower Wright Cyclone radial engine as shown here. The all metal fighter had a thin wing strut-braced to a less than handsome panted landing gear. The wing design included both flaps and leading edge slats. In mid-1932 the Swift was ready for testing, but performance fell short and plans for an engine change were put into effect.

Fig.75 Curtiss XP-934/XP-31 Swift, Mfr.photo via J.Schneider. The Swift is shown after a quick change to the liquid cooled Curtiss Conqueror engine of 600 horsepower in an effort to improve streamlining and thus performance. This picture was taken before the plane was officially sold to the Army early in 1933; the legend stenciled on the fuselage says US Army XP-934 but the serial number space is blank. The aircraft was a mixture of old and new; tail surfaces were all metal but strut-braced and the tail wheel was fixed but panted along with the main landing gear.

Fig.76 Curtiss XP-934/XP-31 Swift, Mfr.photo via J.Schneider. A fine flight photo of the Swift, which with a high speed of about 210 mph was over 20 mph slower than Boeing's P-26A, and thus not so Swift. The cleanly cowled Conqueror had a carburetor air scoop on top, an oil cooler faired neatly in a duct, and a coolant radiator in a deep narrow scoop between landing gear legs. Here the pilot demonstrates how the cockpit hatch slides aft to open.

Fig.76A Curtiss XP-934/XP-31 Swift, Mfr.photo via J.Schneider. In this flight photo of the Swift low speed features of the new all metal thin wing are demonstrated. The plain flaps are lowered and the full span automatic slats on the leading edge are extended. The slats were great unless they worked unsymmetrically left versus right wing. The Curtiss A-8/A-12 attack aircraft had similar wing characteristics. Other unusual Swift features were the packaged .30 caliber guns alongside the fuselage just below the cockpit.

vice. A closed cockpit all-metal low wing monoplane with retractable landing gear, along with the mandated radial engine, the XF7B-1, Figures 77 and 78, appeared to be showing the Navy the wave of the future. That service was not ready for the change, however, and was quick to point out deficiencies for sea-going use, including unsatisfactory flight characteristics, high landing speed, extra shipboard space required, and lack of visibility from the enclosed cockpit. The design was modified to employ an open cockpit, but Navy interest was lacking.

Boeing put out a very similar fighter airplane for the Army as a significant improvement over the P-26. The XP-29 fighter, Figures 79 through 83, cleaned up the P-26 arrangement nicely by enclosing the cockpit, making the wing fully cantilever, and retracting the landing gear as on the Navy XF7B-1. The P-29 incorporated all features of later World War II fighters (with exception of armament) with performance significantly exceeding then-current production aircraft. After Army testing in various versions, including a

Fig.78 Boeing XF7B-1, Mfr.photo via F.Dean coll. Engine cowling, open cockpit, and landing gear changes are seen in this photo of the XF7B-1 after 1934 modifications at Boeing. It was early 1935 before the fighter was dive tested, and after a high speed dive damage to the aircraft was sufficient to make repairability questionable. Shortly the decision wasa made, based on the Navy's overall evaluation, to do no further work on the project. The Navy did not seem to have their heart in a monoplane project, and biplane fighters ruled the day for some time afterwards.

Fig.77 Boeing XF7B-1, Mfr.photo via F. Dean coll. Boeing attempted to interest the Navy in a low wing monoplane as they had the Army with the P-26, and succeeded in obtaining an order for an XF7B-1 prototype in March of 1933. The XF7B-1 was an all metal fighter with an enclosed cockpit and semi-retractable landing gear. It was powered with a cowled Wasp engine of 550 horsepower driving a two blade Hamilton variable pitch propeller. It first flew in September of 1933 and was ready for Navy tests in November. The Navy complained about high landing speed and poor visibility. Wing flaps were added and the fighter was modified to open cockpit configuration.

Fig.79 Boeing XP-940/XP-29, Mfr. photo via F.Dean coll. Generally similar to the Navy XF7B-1, though far from identical, the XP-29 was offered to the Army in 1934 as an advanced all metal low wing monoplane fighter with enclosed cockpit and retractable landing gear. With the ubiquitous Pratt and Whitney Wasp engine of 475 horsepower, a gross weight of 3160 pounds, and a high speed of 220 mph, the XP-29 looked like it could be successful, but the Army wanted changes. The airplane was shortly revised to a YP-29A with a Wasp engine of higher power and an open cockpit. This aircraft, Serial 34-24, became a plain P-29A, but no production resulted. Note the fixed pitch propeller.

Fig.80 Boeing YP-29, photo via F. Dean coll. A nice runup shot of another of the three Boeing prototypes, Serial 34-23, with the arrow denoting Wright Field as a base. The airplane had major differences from the XP-29, including a shorter chord engine cowl, but the most striking change was the cockpit enclosure. It seemed the designer did not know where to stop, and except for space occupied by an elaborate turnover structure the YP-29 almost looked like a two seat aircraft.

modified closed cockpit and open cockpit, the aircraft was rejected for production.

A new fighter from Northrop was tested by the Navy at the same time the Army was testing the P-29. This was the stubby little XFT-1, made compact for carrier stowage. A concession to conservatism was heavily panted fixed landing gear in the style of other Northrop airplanes of that time. The XFT-1 is seen in Figure 84. Other than landing gear, the little Northrop also had all the features of a World War II fighter. Again the Navy was not ready to step up to monoplanes, and was wary of certain aircraft characteristics. An XFT-2 modification, Figure 85, was made by Northrop, but the airplane crashed and development ended. Another fighter was built

by Northrop, Model 3A, with retractable gear and other refinements; it was shortly lost on a test flight over the Pacific Ocean. Vought purchased the design from Northrop and a slightly modified version, the Vought V-141 shown in Figure 86, was manufactured as a prototype for the current Army fighter competition where it lost to the Seversky P-35. A new version with fuselage and tail modification, the V-143, was produced by Vought to capture orders in the export market, but none were forthcoming.

Curtiss first flew their advanced XP-37 prototype, Figures 87 through 91, in spring 1937. The airplane was intended as a fast high-altitude fighter exploiting the virtues of a turbosupercharger on the then-new Allison V-12 engine. Racer-looking, it was fast for

Fig.81 Boeing YP-29, photo via P.M.Bowers. Looking quite like a modern fighter the YP-29 is shown during engine runup. With a 575 horsepower Wasp, a weight of about 3300 pounds, and a maximum speed of 244 mph, the YP-29 was no more than ten mph faster than the in-service P-26A. The cantilever wing, retractable landing gear, and large cockpit canopy made the gross weight over 300 pounds greater than that of the P-26A.

Fig.82 Boeing P-29 photo via F. Dean coll. The same aircraft, Ser.34-23, as a P-29. Bearing the Wright Field arrow and starting to look a bit worn, the P-29 was not slated for production. Wing flaps were added, as they had been on P-26As, because of complaints about high landing speed. The P-29 experimental fighter had a semi-elliptical wing planform as one means of obtaining acceptable spanwise aerodynamic loading.

Fig.83 Boeing YP-29B, Boeing tried hard with the P-29 series of three aircraft. The third aircraft, Ser.34-25, is shown with an open cockpit and a pilot's headrest built up for an overturn structure like the P-26 series. The Boeing Company did everything possible, including installing a new wing on the YP-29B, but the aircraft ended up as a ground trainer with no production resulting from all Boeing's efforts.

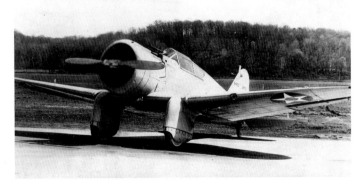

Fig.84 Northrop XFT-1, photo via F.Dean coll. The Navy gave out a contract in May, 1933 to Northrop for development of a small all metal low wing single place monoplane fighter, the XFT-1. Navy fighters had to be compact so as to take up a minimum of valuable carrier stowage space., and Northrop came up with a design thirty-two feet in span and only twenty-one feet long. Unfortunately powered with the Wright R-1510 engine, a design failure, the fighter was quickly seen to have major stability problems and a to spin easily due in part to the large side area of the fixed landing gear pants, a Northrop hallmark of that time.

Fig.85 Northrop XFT-2, photo via F.Dean coll. Re-engined with a Pratt and Whitney R-1535 of 650 horsepower and with other revisions the XFT-2 was again tested by the US Navy in the spring of 1936. There was no great change in configuration, however, and in spite of efforts to make fixes flying quality problems persisted. The airplane crashed in July of 1936 on a flight intended to return it to Northrop; this ended efforts to develop the aircraft further.

Fig.86 Vought V-141, Mfr.photo via Bill Vance. Looking like the Northrop XFT-1 Navy airplane but with retractable landing gear because it was basically a Northrop design (Vought purchased the Northrop 3-A design rights after that aircraft disappeared over the Pacific Ocean on a test flight) the V-141 was one of the losers in the 1935/1936 Army fighter competition. Powered with the fourteen cylinder 750 horsepower Pratt and Whitney R-1535 Twin Wasp Junior engine and with a wing span of thirty-three feet, six inches and a length of twenty-two feet, two inches, the V-141 looked every inch a modern fighter, but was never put into production. A later version, the V-143 with a longer fuselage, was offered on the export market, but again no production resulted.

Fig.87 Curtiss XP-37, Mfr.photo via Joe Christy. In April, 1937 Curtiss delivered an XP-37 fighter to the Army; this aircraft was the original Model 75 prototype airframe with a much-modified fuselage accomodating a turbosupercharged Allison V-12 liquid cooled engine of 1150 horsepower. Including all necessary powerplant items in a neatly streamlined fuselage required pushing the cockpit back far aft, as can be seen in the photo. The plane was damaged, returned to Curtiss and repaired, and went back to Wright Field in June of 1937.

Right: Fig.88 Curtiss XP-37, photo via F.Dean coll. Curtiss designer Don Berlin wanted an advanced type to replace the P-36, and knowing the Army was interested in Allison engine powered fighters, proposed a high altitude version with a turbosupercharger, the XP-37. Although the XP-37 proved to provide a high speed of 340 mph at altitude with a gross weight of 6640 pounds there were problems of powerplant unreliability and of poor pilot visibility with the far aft cockpit location.

Left: Fig.89 Curtiss XP-37, US Army photo via P.M.Bowers. As evidenced in the photo the XP-37 cut a rather handsome figure. The powerplant installation was quite complex within the nicely streamlined nose. The supercharger was cleanly buried beneath the engine with exhaust from both sides of the engine ducted forward and down to the turbine with waste gate gases exiting aft. The unit can be seen in the belly of the forward fuselage just above the right landing gear leg in the picture.

Fig.90 Curtiss YP-37, USAF photo via R. Besecker. The Army was sufficiently impressed with XP-37 performance potential to order in 1938 a service test batch of thirteen YP-37 versions with certain improvements including new versions of the Allison engine and of the turbosupercharger, revised cooling, and a two foot longer rear fuselage behind the pilot. Delivered in 1939, these YP-37s were about 500 pounds heavier and slightly slower. The basic problem was not really fixed, however; there were still turbosupercharger failures with regulators not performing properly and turbine buckets flying off.

Fig.91 Curtiss YP-37, Mfr.photo via J.Schneider. The long nose ahead of the cockpit evidenced in this company photo was required to pack in items such as a Prestone cooling radiator and supercharger air-to-air intercooler between compresser and carburetor behind the engine as well as an engine oil cooler, oil tank, and fuselage fuel tank. Side and lower scoops fed cooling air through these components as required with this air exiting via circumferential louvres near the rear of the powerplant bay. By late 1941 or early 1942 the XP-37 and all but one YP-37 had been disposed of by the Army.

its time, and thirteen YP-37 service test airplanes were ordered. The aft-located cockpit, pushed back by the powerplant installation, made for poor forward visibility, and the turbo installation gave trouble; the Army decided not to order production, and standardized on the P-40 instead.

Looking to supply the first Navy low wing monoplane fighter after success in winning an Army production order for the P-35, Seversky supplied their NF-1 for test. Shown in Figure 92, the NF-

1 was a navalized P-35 with a Wright Cyclone engine in place of the Twin Wasp on the Army version. The airplane performed poorly in competitive tests, and the Navy had no real interest; it was buying biplane fighters for carrier squadrons from Severskys nearby neighbor, Grumman.

In early 1939 Curtiss submitted a modified 75A demonstrator aircraft, basically like the Army production P-36, to the Army as an entry in their pursuit competition. The major modification, an aux-

Fig.92 Seversky XNF-1, photo via Andre La Clair. Though Seversky obtained an Army production contract for P-35 fighters, they had no such luck with the Navy. After first appearing in July, 1937 a company owned prototype was delivered to Anacostia, Maryland in September for the start of Navy tests. The fighter was powered by a 950 horsepower Wright Cyclone engine, had two cowl guns, and had yet another variation of Seversky's ever-changing semi-retractable landing gear. It was dubbed XNF-1 by the company, presumeably meaning experimental Navy fighter the first.

Fig.92A Seversky XNF-1, USN photo via J. Weathers. Equipped with a tail hook, the Seversky fighter is shown during Navy tests sporting no more than a civil registration and the company name. Both windshield and landing gear fairings as well as wing dihedral were revised during the testing. A Navy-type telescopic sight has also been installed. The XNF-1 was similar in dimentions to the Army P-35 and normal gross weight was about 5200 pounds.

Fig.92B Seversky XNF-1, USN photo via J. Weathers. The XNF-1 displayed poor performance for a new monoplane fighter, diappointing both the builder and the Navy. Highest speed reached in tests was 267 mph at medium altitude. This speed was hardly greater than that obtained from the latest Grumman biplane going into Navy service. Later Brewster and Grumman monoplane fighters would exceed the Seversky's performance.

iliary second stage mechanical supercharger with intercooler "patched on" under the aircraft for enhanced altitude power of the Twin Wasp engine changed the label to 75R, Figures 93 and 94. The competition was won by the aircraft that developed into the Republic P-43. The Curtiss 75R returned to the Caldwell, New Jersey airport owned by Curtiss-Wright to be used through the war as a powerplant test bed.

A failed Seversky attempt to win Army production contracts past the P-35 was the XP-41 prototype of 1939, Figure 95. This was the last airframe on the P-35 contract with major modifications made in landing gear and powerplant. A sideways-retracting gear folded into the wing root to replace the large gear-fairing bumps under the P-35 wing. A new version of the Pratt and Whitney Twin Wasp radial engine with a two stage mechanical supercharger was

Fig.93 Curtiss H75R, photo via Joe Christy. A company owned H75A airplane, civil registration NX22028, was used for years as a powerplant test plane at Caldwell Wright Airport in northern New Jersey. In January, 1939 the aircraft was provided to the Army at Wright Field in their markings for tests with a new Pratt and Whitney R-1830 Twin Wasp engine version equipped with a two stage mechanical supercharger somewhat like that later used on the Grumman Wildcat to provide increased performance at altitude.

Fig.94 Curtiss H75R, photo via Joe Christy. The company 75A/75R was equipped with a modified P-36A engine cowling and sported two large protrusions on the fuselage belly. It is believed the large forward scoop served a modified engine oil cooling and induction air system, the large bump under the engine accessory compartment housed the auxiliary blower (the first stage blower was integral with the engine) of the two stage mechanically driven supercharger, and the underwing heat exchanger pod housed the supercharger intercooler. After Army testing the plane returned to Curtiss Wright. The author saw it briefly in New Jersey in early 1948.

Fig.95 Seversky XP-41, photo via F. Dean coll. The last P-35 production aircraft was held back for modification into an XP-41 with changes in powerplant and landing gear. Delivered to the Army in March of 1939, the XP-41 had an inward retracting main landing gear folding flush, a Curtiss Electric propeller, and a Pratt and Whitney Twin Wasp having a mechanical supercharger which was either a two stage unit as used in the Grumman F4F-3, or a single stage two speed type as used on the F4F-3A. With a gross weight of 7200 pounds the XP-41 achieved a high speed of 323 mph, reportedly at 15000 feet, which makes use of a single stage two speed mechanical supercharger more likely.

Fig.95A Seversky AP-9, photo via P.M.Bowers. A company demonstrator sent to the 1938-1939 Army fighter competition in early 1939. A revised landing gear and wing cleaned up the P-35 configuration. The powerplant included an 825 horsepower Pratt and Whitney Twin Wasp with a single stage mechanical type supercharger integral with the engine and a Hamilton Standard propeller. Neither the XP-41 nor the AP-9 generated any new Army business; the Army selected the Curtiss P-40 as the competition winner.

installed to provide significant increases in altitude performance over the production P-35. At that time, however, the Army was preoccupied with altitude performance potential of the turbosupercharged Allison V-12 engines in their new XP-38 and XP-39 fighter prototypes and passed the XP-41 by. Seversky got the message, installed a turbosupercharged Twin Wasp in their AP-4 fighter prototype and its direct successor, the Republic P-43 Lancer, and left two-stage mechanical supercharger installations to the Navy.

At the same time the search was on for other new and efficient fighter powerplant alternatives, including the possibility of streamlining a radial engine to look like a V-12 installation with a pointed nose. A Curtiss P-36 fighter was modified with a special extended-shaft engine, faired cowling, air scoop below, and a large spinner, and labeled the XP-42, Figures 96 through 98. Several variations were tried by Curtiss and the NACA at Langley Field, Virginia, but until an annular inlet system was used (Figure 98), cooling the engine evenly was always a problem, and time passed the XP-42 by. The approach was also tried on the Vultee 48 (later P-66) prototype with the same unfavorable result, and the 48 reverted to a conventional radial engine cowling arrangement.

A radically different approach to naval fighter design was attempted in 1940 by Grumman, resulting in the XF5F-1 Skyrocket

Fig.96 Curtiss XP-42, Mfr.photo via F.Dean coll. A P-36A was converted by Curtiss to see if an air cooled radial engine installation could be revised to low drag nose contours competitive with those of liquid cooled installations. The initial attempt with an extended nose case on the Twin Wasp engine and a lot of fairing up front is shown in the photo. The low scoop for engine cooling air was right behind the propeller, and air was dumped through conventional adjustable cowl flaps and fixed exit slots. Twin carburetor air intakes were located atop the cowl. From powerplant aft the aircraft was strictly a P-36A.

Fig.96A Curtiss XP-42, Mfr. photo via J.Schneider. An underneath view of the XP-42 in its original configuration shows the shape of the duct for cooling air. The XP-42 was delivered to the Army in March of 1939. Gross weight was about 6300 pounds and the best speed obtainable was about 315 mph using the R-1830 Twin Wasp engine of 1050 horsepower, very slightly better than that of a P-36C type.

Fig.97. Curtiss XP-42, photo via F.Dean coll. This fine picture was taken at the 1939 National Air Races where some of the latest Army Air Corps and Navy aircraft types showed up, and it was a time when it was not difficult for private citizen photographers to take pictures. Note the XP-42 nose has been completely redone with much more pleasing contours including a new propeller spinner, new carburetor air intake, and a new cooling air scoop below.

Fig.97A Curtiss XP-42, photo via F. Dean coll. Another photo of the modified XP-42 showing it was based at Wright Field in Ohio, but also giving a view of the right side exit slot for cooling air that had passed over the engine and through the engine accessory compartment. Cowl flaps are open; the exit slot is located about eighteen inches aft of these flaps. Proper engine cooling was not achieved, however, and symmetrical inlets had to be considered.

prototype shown in Figures 99 and 100. Twin radial engines, a truncated forward fuselage, a folding wing, and twin tails distinguished this all-metal monoplane. Grumman and the Navy flight tested and modified the single prototype over an extended period. This twin-engined fighter experience led not to Skyrocket production, but to a later twin-engined Grumman XF7F-1 airplane, a different and more powerful design.

Flying for the first time in early 1940 like the Skyrocket was Bell Aircraft's single entry in the naval fighter arena, the XFL-1 Airabonita shown in Figures 101 and 102. The XFL-1 was a navalized version of the Army P-39 airplane and, had it been produced in quantity, would have broken the Navy's aircooled engine habit. A major difference from the P-39 was incorporation of tail-down landing gear in place of the nose wheel arrangement of the Army airplane. With the advent of the XF4U-1 radial engined Vought

prototype with impressive speed and altitude performance, the Bell airplane with its liquid-cooled engine and less performance lost its appeal. After failing carrier qualification tests it remained just another experimental fighter.

The Army and Curtiss planned the XP-46 fighter as a smaller, lighter, and faster more heavily armed replacement for the P-40. Development of this racy-looking airplane, Figures 103 and 104, using two prototypes, was slow, with requirements changing based on war experience of the British, and Curtiss preoccupied with P-40 production demands. A decision had to be made between quickly switching production lines to a P-46, or a revised P-40D and E model. The easier change to P-40D/E was decided upon, and the P-46 lost out. It is interesting to note the aft radiator location on the XP-46 similar to that on the early XP-40 and the P-51 Mustang.

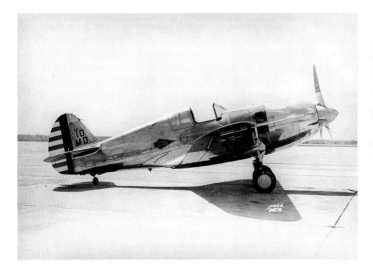

Fig.98. Curtiss XP-42, NACA photo via M. Copp. The NACA was asked to examine prospects of properly cooling the XP-42 powerplant and several cowl/spinner configurations were tested. One of these, a long nose version, is shown in the photo using large propeller blade cuffs to assist cooling, another new spinner, and a narrow air inlet annulus around the spinner giving high inlet air velocity. It certainly slicked up the airplane as far as looks were concerned.

Fig.98A Curtiss XP-42, NACA photo via M.Copp. Another view of the XP-42 under NACA test with the narrow annulus high inlet velocity design. The final cowl was a much shorter version with a wider annulus providing a lower velocity inlet. In mid-1941 a high speed of about 340 mph was achieved. By this time the faster P-40 series was in full production and the XP-42 remained just a series of experiments.

Fig.99 Grumman XF5F-1 Skyrocket, Mfr.photo via F.Dean coll. A twin engined fighter ordered by the Navy at the same time, June, 1938, as the Vought XF4U-1 Corsair. It was radical thinking indeed, since only that same month the first production order was given for Brewster F2A-1 monoplanes and this was well before any Grumman F4F-3 Wildcat production orders. So the Navy wanted to test a twin engined folding wing fighter monoplane when all they were flying was single engined biplanes! Grumman came up with the XF5F-1 in the highly unusual configuration shown powered by two 1200 horsepower Wright Cyclone engines. It grossed a bit over 10000 pounds and had a spread wing span of forty-two feet.

Fig.99A Grumman XF5F-1 Skyrocket, Mfr.photo via F.Dean coll. Flight view of the Skyrocket reveals its unusual configuration with a short nose not even extending to the wing leading edge. The XF5F-1 flew first in April, 1940 but powerplant cooling difficulties were encountered, presaging a long list of test problems and resulting aircraft modifications. In the spring of 1942 many changes had been made, including a lengthened nose, addition of propeller spinners, and armament revisions. With wartime pressure on for Wildcat production the XF5F-1 program went slowly. The thought of twin engine training for all their carrier pilots must have scared many Navy men to death!

Fig.100 Grumman XF5F-1 Skyrocket, Mfr.photo via F. Dean coll. A well publicized dramatic photo of the Skyrocket in 1940 made a large segment of the American public just know that our Navy had the latest and greatest fighter aircraft! The original configuration before nose lengthening is shown. In 1942 testing of the XF5F-1 was ordered to aid design of Grumman's latest XF7F-1 Tigercat twin engined fighter. Accidents plagued the Skyrocket, and after about 200 flights the project was abandoned. High speed was reported as 360 to 380 mph at medium altitude.

Fig.101 Bell XFL-1, Mfr.photo via F.Dean coll. In November of 1938 the Navy took the step, unprecedented for many years, of ordering development of a fighter with a liquid cooled engine, though not without misgivings. Further they awarded the contract to a company with no previous association with the Navy or its specialized requirements. The fighter was the Bell XFL-1 naval variant of the Army P-39 Airacobra. The XFL-1, sometimes called the Airabonita, differed from the P-39 in several ways; the most apparent was a change from tricycle to "conventional" tail down landing gear insisted on by the Navy. The photo shows the single prototype XFL-1 aircraft.

Fig.101A Bell XFL-1, Mfr.photo via J. Weathers. A flight photo taken about two months into the flight test program started in May, 1940 shows the XFL-1 in its earliest configuration. Oil and Prestone coolers are under the wing, not flush and inside the airplane like the P-39 arrangement. Changing from tricycle gear to conventional caused major problems in aircraft balance and wing structural design. Wing area and span were greater than those of the P-39. Inadvertant inflation of flotation air bags almost caused a crash on the first flight before they were torn away.

Less than a year after the Grumman XF5F-1 first flight, the company flew, in early 1941, their only prototype fighter for the Army. This was the XP-50, shown in Figures 105 and 106 as a twin engine aircraft somewhat like the earlier Navy Skyrocket, but incorporating a nose wheel landing gear, a more extended fuselage nose, and turbosuperchargers on the two radial engines. The aircraft looked like a hot item, but during a flight test a turbo exploded and the aircraft was lost. No further XP-50 aircraft were made by Grumman; the project was dropped, and Grumman went on to a later twin-engined fighter for the Navy, the XF7F-1.

The epitome of lost opportunity was reached by Curtiss in their XP-60 series of fighters which represented the company's attempts through the war to provide a viable successor to the P-40. The approach was to use laminar flow wing sections and a more powerful engine with better altitude performance. Starting in late 1941 with the first flight of an XP-60 airplane, and ending with a few test flights of a YP-60E version, the P-60 prototype airplanes, looking quite different from one another—see Figures 107 through 114—variously used Allison or Rolls Royce liquid cooled V-12s, and Pratt and Whitney radial engines. The P-60 story was one of unavailable engines, delayed propeller deliveries, cancelled production orders, accidents, changing directions from the Army, and of airplane performance no better than current production fighters. Curtiss never got into production of any P-60, and P-40 output continued unabated until late summer of 1944 without a Curtiss fighter replacement.

In late 1942 a variant of the Lockheed P-38 production fighter had its first flight using experimental twelve-cylinder inverted vee

Fig.102 Bell XFL-1, Mfr.photo via F.Dean coll. Another flight photo shows a very small carburetor air intake aft of the canopy, later changed to the P-39 design. A major problem was inadequate directional stability. Shortly before this photo was taken the plane was almost lost due to stability problems. In May, 1941 the XFL-1 failed its carrier qualification tests and was declared unsatisfactory for use as a carrier aircraft. It sat at Norfolk NAS and Patuxent NAS until 1944 when it was striken from service.

Fig.103 Curtiss XP-46 Mockup, Mfr.photo via F.Dean coll. A wooden mockup for the XP-46, the planned Curtiss replacement for the P-40 using the Allison V-1710 engine version ultimately used in the P-40E. Full scale mockups of new aircraft with one wing only were common at the time. Considerably smaller and lighter than the P-40, though not as much so as originally planned, the XP-46 was to carry heavy armament; the mockup shows no less than six guns on a side, five in one wing!

Fig.104 Curtiss XP-46, Mfr.photo via J.Schneider. The XP-46 at the Curtiss plant in 1941. Two prototypes, one an XP-46A without armament, were ordered in September, 1939. First flight of the XP-46A took place in February, 1941, well after Curtiss was committed to mass production of P-40 models. The XP-46 prototypes were character-ized by inward retracting landing gear and an aft-mounted cooling radiator like the P-51. There was an upper nose scoop for carburetor air and a larger scoop under the nose for oil cooler air. At a normal gross weight of 7320 pounds high speed was 355 mph at 12000 feet, and it offered virtually no improvement over the then-current P-40 version in performance.

Fig.105 Grumman XP-50, Mfr.photo via F.Dean coll. One of the aircraft in a fighter competition won by the Lockheed XP-49, the Grumman XP-50 had twin turbosu-percharged engines, twin tails, and a tricycle landing gear like the P-38, but from there on resemblance ended. This runup photo shows the XP-50 looked a little like Grumman's Navy XF5F-1. Ordered in November, 1939, it first flew in February of 1941.

Fig.106 Grumman XP-50, Mfr.photo via F.Dean coll. Flight photo of the XP-50 reveals a trim looking aircraft with the pilot sitting high on the fuselage in a spa-cious cockpit typical of Grumman designs. Armament consisted of two 20mm. can-non and two .50 caliber machine guns in the nose. With normal gross weight just over 10500 pounds, wingspan was forty-two feet, and a high speed of 424 mph at 25000 feet was claimed, this performance due to turbosupercharged engines hold-ing their power up to that altitude. In mid-1941 a turbosupercharger explosion in the right side engine during a test flight caused damage sufficient to make the pilot bail out, and the aircraft was lost.

Fig.107 Curtiss XP-60, Mfr.photo via F.Dean coll. The XP-60 was to be a successor to the P-40 with new features, including an advanced powerplant combined with a new wing using laminar flow airfoil sections. The XP-60, shown in November of 1941 two months after its first flight and still adorned with the old rudder stripes, was powered with a 1300 horsepower Rolls Royce Merlin with a single stage two speed supercharger. High speed was claimed as 380 mph at 20000 feet.

Fig.108 Curtiss XP-60, Mfr.photo via J.Schneider. Another later view of the XP-60 at the Curtiss plant shows much of a P-40 fuselage including cockpit, along with a cowling for the new Merlin engine and combined scoop for Prestone cooling radiator and carburetor air, a new inward-retracting landing gear, a longer laminar flow wing of over forty-one foot span, and a new higher aspect ratio vertical tail for improved effectiveness. Gross weight was 9350 pounds.

Fig.109 Curtiss XP-60A, photo via F. Dean coll. The XP-60A was a much different aircraft from the XP-60 and looked it. Powered by a turbosupercharged Allison V-1710 engine of 1425 horsepower with a four blade propeller and a totally new fuselage, the P-60A appeared less than handsome, but because of the turbo installation a top speed of 420 mph at 29000 feet was claimed. Just before Pearl Harbor the Army provided Curtiss with a contract for 1950 P-60A fighters, but shortly, in January of 1942 there was concern about conflicts with P-40 production and the contract was reduced to only three aircraft. In addition Curtiss was asked to produce Republic P-47 Thunderbolts.

Left: Fig.110 Curtiss XP-60C, Mfr.photo via F.Dean coll. One of three XP-60A aircraft allowed by the new Army development contract turned into an XP-60C, this being an XP-60A airframe powered by a Pratt and Whitney R-2800 engine driving a six bladed dual rotation propeller to cancel out propeller torque reaction. First flight took place in January, 1943. High speed of the XP-60C was over 400 mph at 20000 feet, but the Army already had a high altitude R-2800 powered fighter in production with similar or better performance in the Republic P-47, which Curtiss now produced.

Fig.111 Curtiss XP-60C, Mfr.photo via J.Schneider. Another view of the XP-60C shows a cleanly cowled installation of the Double Wasp engine, the dual rotation propeller, the inwardly-retracting main landing gear, and four .50 caliber wing machine gun armament (half that of the P-47). The choice of a dual rotation propeller was probably unfortunate; they were apt to be heavy, complex, and unreliable. Army testing of the XP-60C did not go well. Poor powerplant performance and deteriorating wing finish were two of the problems encountered. No production was forthcoming.

Fig.112 Curtiss XP-60D, photo via F. Dean coll. The XP-60D airplane was the XP-60 using a new variant of the Packard V-1650 Merlin engine which hardly changed its appearance. Both three and four bladed propellers were tried. Converted in 1943, the XP-60D fighter had a short history as it crashed in May of that year.

Fig.113 Curtiss XP-60D, Mfr.photo via F. Dean coll. This photo of the XP-60D was taken about three months before its demise. A P-40 heritage is evident and from the three quarter rear angle it resembles a P-40F with revised landing gear and empennage. Normal gross weight was just under 10000 pounds, wing span was forty-five feet five inches, and a high speed of 390 mph was claimed.

liquid-cooled engines made by Continental instead of the regular Allisons. Original plans were to use new experimental Pratt and Whitney engines with twenty-four cylinders each, but this development was stopped.

Flight tests with Continental engines indicated no performance improvement over production P-38s, and the single prototype XP-49, shown in Figures 115 and 116, was used as a test bed for the Continental, which never did get into production.

In January 1943 Vultee started flight testing a large and unusual looking fighter with a single pusher propeller, twin booms and tails like a P-38, and a tricycle landing gear. The airplane was the XP-54, bigger than a P-38 (Figure 117), with an inverted gull wing like a Navy Corsair. Use of an experimental turbosupercharged liquid-cooled Lycoming engine pretty much assured the fighter

would not go into production. Only two prototypes were built, and flight test performance was below expectations. Then engine development was cancelled, resulting in stoppage of work on the aircraft in 1944.

Another unusual fighter, shown in Figure 118, was Northrop's XP-56.Though not a flying wing because of a bulbous center fuselage, the plane was an unusual almost-tailless pusher type with dual-rotation propeller driven by a Double Wasp engine, a tricycle landing gear, and all-magnesium airframe.

With a combination of these and other advanced or unusual features many development problems arose on the two aircraft built. A very limited amount of flight testing took place. The first aircraft was destroyed in a taxi accident, and after work lagged on the second, the XP-56 project was abandoned.

Fig.114 Curtiss XP-60E, Mfr.photo via F. Dean coll. Another XP-60A airframe became first an XP-60B and was later changed to XP-60E with a first flight in May, 1943. With a Pratt and Whitney R-2800 Double Wasp engine this airplane looked much like the XP-60C except Curtiss got smarter and used a four blade single rotation propeller. With a gross weight of 10500 to 11500 pounds the E model had a maximum speed of 410 mph at 20000 feet. Army evaluation of the aircraft in early 1944 resulted in many negative comments. Later Curtiss expressed the desire to abandon further P-60 series development as having no future, but a final version, the YP-60E, was completed per Army requirement and flown in the summer of 1944. This fighter had a bubble canopy and was later sold privately after the war for use as a racer, but the aircraft crashed in 1947.

Fig.115. Lockheed XP-49, Mfr.photo via F.Dean coll. First envisioned as a P-38 variant with two twenty-four cylinder Pratt and Whitney X-1800 engines, the initial version of the XP-49 won first place in a 1938 twin engine fighter design competition along with the Grumman XP-50. Shortly there was a change to Continental twelve cylinder inverted vee-type engines which were predicted to power the aircraft to 458 mph at 20000 feet. It was also supposed to have a pressurized cabin and include armament of two 20mm. cannon and four .50 caliber machine guns. The armament was never installed. A contract was given Lockheed in January, 1940 and the Continental powered XP-49 flew first in November, 1942. During tests high speed turned out to be about 400 mph at 15000 feet, a disappointing result.

Fig.116 Lockheed XP-49, Mfr.photo via F. Dean coll. After a series of minor test mishaps including a hydraulic failure leading to an emergency landing, the XP-49 resumed testing in February, 1943. It became apparent the new aircraft would not provide any performance margin over the Allison powered P-38 aircraft sufficient to justify production with a new and unproved engine. The XP-49 was then relegated to service as a two seat test bed for the Continental engine, and was down for long periods. Shortly after an in-flight engine failure in 1944 and a determination there was no production future for the Continental engine the aircraft development was stopped.

Fig.117 Convair XP-54 Swoose Goose, Mfr.photo via Jon Davis. In a 1940 competition for new fighters of unusual configuration the Vultee XP-54 design won over the Curtiss XP-55 and the Northrop XP-56. Two prototypes were ordered, one in January, 1942 and another in March, 1942. The photo shows the single engine twin boom pusher propeller configuration of the XP-54. Larger than a twin engined P-38, the Convair fighter was powered by a turbosupercharged Lycoming 2300 horsepower engine with dual propellers and a pressurized cockpit, a combination not making for a simple aircraft. The nose contained very heavy armament and an electrically powered elevator raised the pilot seat into the pressurized cockpit. Leading edge ducting fed the oil cooler, coolant radiator, and intercooler. First flights of the two aircraft were in January, 1943 and May, 1944 with the second aircraft flying only once. Testing showed performance of the 18300 pound aircraft was disappointing with a high speed of 380 to 400 mph, and the prototypes were used for engine and armament tests only.

A third fighter of unusual configuration was the Curtiss XP-55 Ascender, a tail-less pusher with tricycle landing gear like the XP-56. A major difference was addition of moveable elevator surfaces at the fuselage nose as shown in Figure 119. Curtiss took a conservative approach and first constructed a piloted low-powered flying model called the 24-B which was extensively tested to determine flying qualities of the unusual arrangement. With this data in hand three XP-55 prototypes were constructed. Flights of the first plane started in mid-1943. Shortly thereafter, in spite of all the earlier data collected, the aircraft crashed after pitching into an inverted position during stall tests. Testing continued with another aircraft modified, but poor stall characteristics and Allison engine cooling problems dogged the aircraft. Since performance was no better than types in production, there was no advantage in continuing development, and the XP-55 program was stopped.

Fig.118 Northrop XP-56, Mfr.photo via Jon Davis. Another very unorthdox fighter configuration was exemplified in Northrop's tail-less XP-56, two of which were ordered, the first in September, 1940 and the other much later in February, 1942. The only conventional aspect was use of a Pratt and Whitney Double Wasp engine of 2000 horsepower. The photo shows the second prototype with increased vertical surface area. The first XP-56 flew initially in September, 1943 at Muroc dry lake in California. After a few very short flights it was destroyed in a high speed taxi accident. The second aircraft underwent limited tests in early 1944, but many problems were evident and shortly the project was discontinued.

Fig.118A Northrop XP-56, Mfr.photo via F.Dean coll. The second prototype aircraft shown at Muroc test center in 1944. Wing root ducts fed cooling air to the buried R-2800 engine. A construction novelty was use of magnesium alloy for airframe structure; another feature was use of wingtip air bellows to achieve aircraft directional control. NACA Ames was asked to study the XP-56, but wartime pressures delayed further work. Wing span was forty-two and a half feet and maximum gross weight was six tons. The limited testing never provided good performance data.

Fig.119 Curtiss XP-55 Ascender, Mfr.photo via H.Andrews. Placing second to the XP-54 in the 1939-1940 unorthodox fighter aircraft design competition was the Curtiss XP-55 Ascender. The photo shows well the general arrangement of the rather light 7700 pound gross weight class swept wing pusher design. The distinctive forward elevator surface was a variable incidence type with small moveable trailing edge surfaces. The engine was an Allison V-1710 of 1275 horsepower driving a jettisonable single rotation propeller. Rudders were located on vertical surfaces near the wingtips.

Fig.119A Curtiss XP-55 Ascender, Mfr.photo via H.Andrews. The first of three prototypes was initially flown in July of 1943 after a large number of test flights had been made at Muroc in early 1942 by a manned flying scale model of the configuration known as the CW-24B. Operation of the forward surface was tricky, and the initial XP-55 flipped on its back during stall tests, would not recover, and crashed.

Fig.119C Curtiss XP-55 Ascender, Mfr.photo via H.Andrews. Close view of an XP-55 nose shows details of forward fuselage, nose landing gear, and the forward elevator which has been increased in area and somewhat revised in planform from earlier versions. Elevators are interconnected left and right and driven to vary incidence by an actuating mechanism in the fuselage. Each contains a smaller trimming surface on the inboard trail edge. Such forward surfaces are highly destabilizing unless left to float free. Note the B-26, the old B-18, and B-17s in the background.

Fig.119B Curtiss XP-55 Ascender, Mfr.photo via H.Andrews. A well known photo of the second XP-55 fighter which first flew in January, 1944 shows the high degree of wing sweep required to provide a tail arm for rudder control of the aircraft. Outboard surface vertical areas were augmented by dorsal and ventral surfaces on the aft fuselage. Planned armament was four .50 caliber machine guns in the nose. Many flying qualities problems arose, most concerned with unwanted stall characteristics, including no warning and a difficult recovery. The XP-55 also grew considerably over intended design weight.

A relatively conventional fighter design of which several prototypes were made was the Fisher/General Motors P-75 Eagle shown in Figures 120 through 125. The Eagle was a large aircraft with a buried engine aft of the pilot driving a dual rotation propeller via an extension shaft like the Bell P-39 and P-63. It used an engine which was two Allison V-12s mated into a "W" of twenty-four cylinders. The mission of the P-75 was long range bomber escort. The concept was to use major parts from existing aircraft wherever possible, and plans were laid for large scale production. First flying in late 1943, Eagle prototypes developed many problems requiring redesign, and about a year later P-75 production plans were shelved, since production Merlin-powered Mustangs were working out well in escort missions.

In 1941 Curtiss contracted with the Army to build a fast heavily armed high altitude fighter using a new turbosupercharged two-row Wright Cyclone engine and a pressurized cabin. The result was the XP-62, a big machine with long tapered wings for high altitude work, as shown in Figure 126. Later a production contract for P-62 fighters was cancelled so Curtiss could build Thunderbolts, and the airplane development lagged; first flight took place in mid-1943 without the pressure cabin. With demand for the engine used in the P-62 for the high priority B-29 bomber program, it became clear the project was going nowhere, and in 1944 it was terminated.

The first aircraft put out by the new McDonnell Aircraft Corporation was a large twin-engined fighter of exotic appearance designated the XP-67 and shown in Figures 127 through 129. Again the engine choice helped doom the project, since inverted V-12 Continental models were strictly experimental items. The complication of turbosuperchargers on these engines did not help the situation, and engine fires dogged development testing. The first of two XP-67 aircraft did not fly until January 1944. Tests during 1944 showed disappointing performance, and late in the year the first

Fig.119D Curtiss XP-55 Ascender, Mfr.photo via H. Andrews. An excellent view of the XP-55 powerplant installation, main landing gear, and wing flaps. Hinged panels are open to show good access to many components. The lower hinged panel includes ducting to coolant radiators for the Allison engine with upper ducting feeding oil cooler and carburetor. The engine mount is a system of built up beams that also supported the radiators. Note also the cooling air fan blades just forward of the Curtiss propeller spinner and the segments providing variable exit area. The XP-55, like the other unorthodox fighters, did not live up to expectations. Engine cooling was a problem. One XP-55 remains in the collection of the National Air and Space Museum.

Fig.120 General Motors/Fisher XP-75 Eagle, photo via Jon Davis. Don Berlin of P-40 fame had left Curtiss and gone to General Motors where he made a proposal to the Army that a new fighter using the GM/Allison V-3420 (side-by-side V-1710s) and parts from various in-production aircraft be tested. This fighter, the XP-75 Eagle, would use P-40 wings, an A-24 empennage, and F4U-1 landing gear. Two prototypes were ordered and the first flew in late 1943. The XP-75 is shown in the flight photo with a mid-fuselage engine and extension propeller shaft like the P-39 driving a dual rotation propeller. Note the P-40 outer wing panels and Dauntless tail, also the rather strange cockpit canopy. Many problems were encountered during flight test.

Fig.121 General Motors/Fisher XP-75 Eagle, photo via F. Dean coll. Ground view of an XP-75 (there turned out to be eight prototypes in all) shows modified rudder and cockpit canopy. Split flaps are down. Mid-fuselage protrusions are exhaust stacks of the W-type engine, two V-types side by side. Some exhausts are just above the wing. Bumps just behind the dual rotation propeller are two of the four .50 caliber nose machine guns. In addition there were six wing .50s. Wing span was forty-nine feet and the big fighter grossed about seven tons. It was being groomed as an escort fighter.

Fig.122 General Motors/Fisher XP-75A, photo via F. Dean coll. Side view of another Eagle prototype shows new modifications. The A-24 tail is gone, though the P-40 wing and part of the Corsair landing gear still seem to be aboard. The bubble canopy is new. The large belly scoop housed Prestone radiator and oil cooler. Prototype high speed was 400 to 430 mph depending on configuration.

Fig.123 General Motors/Fisher P-75A Eagle, photo via F. Dean coll. The final configuration of the Eagle is shown with all the "fixes" in place. Most of the original Don Berlin concept had been removed in the renovations, however. The tail has again been revised with increased area and a dorsal fin. First flight of this production version did not come until the fall of 1944 at a time when the Merlin powered P-51s were doing just fine as escort fighters.

Fig.124 General Motors/Fisher P-75A Eagle, photo via Jon Davis. A large unwieldy fighter with a twenty-four cylinder liquid cooled engine and dual rotation propeller was probably the last thing the USAAF needed in late 1944. After completion of six "production" P-75A aircraft, one of which had crashed, the Army found the good sense to stop the program. This photo shows well the features of the final configuration which managed to just about touch 400 mph at medium altitude. The span and aspect ratio of the horizontal tail seems quite extraordinary in the picture.

Fig.125 General Motors/Fisher P-75A Eagle, USAF Museum photo via D. Menard. One of the six P-75A fighters has been preserved and rests with the Air Force Museum at Wright-Patterson AFB where this photo was taken. Ports for five of the ten .50 caliber machine guns can be seen, two in the fuselage nose just aft of the rear section of the Aeroproducts dual rotation propeller, and three in the wing. General Motors manufactured the airframe, the engine, and the propeller. One suspects it probably could not have gotten out of its own way against a bunch of slashing ME-109 and FW-190 fighters.

Fig.126 Curtiss XP-62 Mfr.photo via F. Dean coll. Development of the Curtiss XP-62 fighter was originally discussed between the Army and Curtiss in 1941. The mission was that of a heavily armed high altitude interceptor fighter, and the design therefore included a sharply tapered high aspect ratio wing with a fifty-three foot span, a high powered turbosupercharged two row Wright R-3350 Double Cyclone engine with a dual rotation propeller, a pressurized cabin, and eight .50 caliber wing machine guns. Only one prototype was built; a second was cancelled in July, 1942 when plans for production were put aside. Curtiss was directed to produce P-47s. Some flight tests were conducted starting in mid-1943, but by 1944 the project was cancelled.

Fig.127 McDonnell XP-67 Mfr.photo via F.Dean coll. The first design of the then-new McDonnell Aircraft Corporation, the XP-67 was a very large twin engined single seat fighter. As shown in this front view of the aircraft during taxi, the XP-67 had tricycle landing gear and large engine nacelles blended into the wings, and wings blended into the fuselage with large fairings.

prototype was destroyed by fire. The Army decided to stop all work on the XP-67.

Republic had been studying advanced versions of their P-47 Thunderbolt production fighter, and in 1943 received an order for two XP-72 prototypes, intended as the next step in fighters. The big change was a new powerplant installation, and except for that the airplane looked much like a P-47, using essentially the same wing as a P-47D. The new engine was a four-row twenty-eight cylinder radial from Pratt and Whitney known as the Wasp Major. Powerplant features included either a four blade single rotation or a six blade dual rotation propeller, a cooling fan behind the spinner, and an aft-located auxiliary-stage supercharger with blower driven by the engine via an extension shaft running aft. Testing of two prototypes,

one shown in Figure 130, took place in 1944. Although the XP-72 was a very fast high altitude piston engine fighter, its performance was outclassed by the new jet-powered Lockheed P-80 fighter then under development, and the Army cancelled the XP-72 program.

Bell Aircraft took on design of a small light-fighter in 1942 with the idea of saving critical materials in wartime. Powered by a Ranger inverted-vee air-cooled engine, made in large part of wood, and provided with tricycle landing gear, the XP-77, shown in Figure 131, was the victim of changing requirements and various delays. The first prototype did not fly until spring of 1944. After one of the two aircraft crashed late that year, and long after worries about aluminum shortages had subsided, the contract for the light-fighter was cancelled.

Fig.128 McDonnell XP-67, Mfr.photo via F.Dean coll. Two prototypes of the XP-67 were ordered in October, 1941, and the choice of an experimental engine type along with many complex features just about doomed the long range fighter from the start. It was a large heavy aircraft with a span of fifty-five feet and a normal gross weight of eleven tons. Contributing to this weight were two turbosupercharged Continental twelve cylinder inverted vee type liquid cooled engines rated at 1350 horsepower and using exhaust jet thrust augmentation, a pressurized cabin, and an unbelievably heavy six 37 mm. cannon armament. After many development problems the first XP-67 flew in January, 1944. This flight view shows the large size of the engine nacelles.

Fig.129 McDonnell XP-67, Mfr.photo via F.Dean coll. The smooth airfoiled contouring of the XP-67 shows up in this flight photo. Very limited flight testing interposed with several development problems needing fixes proceeded through 1944 until September when the first aircraft was destroyed in a fire. Since the air war was being won by production-type aircraft, the performance of the XP-67 was disappointing, and the second aircraft had not flown it was determined the program should be ended.

Fig.129A McDonnell XP-67, Mfr. photo via F. Dean. This flight photo showing a plan view of the XP-67 provides a good description of the aircraft and indicates exceptionally liberal use of large airfoiled fairings blending lines of major bodies. The large fighter came up over forty mph short of expected high speed capability; flight tests yielded just over 400 mph at 25000 feet.

Fig.130 Republic XP-72 Mfr. photo via Jon Davis. A P-47 Thunderbolt with the then-new 3000 to 3500 horsepower Pratt and Whitney R-4360 four row air cooled twenty-eight cylinder Wasp Major radial engine, the XP-72 was a fighter that might have gone places had not the jet age caught up with it. The first of two prototypes was flown only four and one half months before the jet powered Lockheed XP-80, and the second flew two weeks after the XP-80. The engine of the Republic fighter was equipped with a large supercharger secondary blower directly shaft-driven by the engine. The prototypes were tested with both a single rotation four blade and a dual rotation six blade propeller, the latter to cancel out the tremendous torque reaction. The XP-72 claimed 490 mph at 25000 feet; the jet XP-80 502 mph at 21000 feet. There was no XP-72 production.

The Navy contracted with Curtiss just after the US entered World War II to produce a fighter capable of operating at very high altitude. This became the XF14C-1 design with an experimental liquid-cooled Lycoming engine. Later, because the engine devel-opment was lagging, a change was made to the big eighteen cylinder two-row Wright Double Cyclone radial air cooled engine with a turbosupercharger. This version was the XF14C-2 with a dual rotation propeller and inwardly retracting landing gear. A pressure

Fig.131 Bell XP-77, Mfr. photo via Jon Davis. In late 1941 and early 1942 there was fear of a possible shortage of aluminum due to the submarine menace. Studies were being made of fighters constructed of wood, and in August, 1942 Bell got authorization to produce six XP-77 light fighters powered by Ranger V-770 twelve cylinder inverted vee air cooled engines of 520 horsepower and made principally of laminated wood bonded with resins. The little single seat fighter had a tricycle landing gear and a wing span of only twenty-seven and a half feet, and weighted under two tons gross. High speed was 330 mph and armament consisted of two .50 caliber guns. In mid-1943 procurement was reduced to two aircraft; the first XP-77 flew in the spring of 1944. Later that year one prototype crashed. No aluminum shortage occurred, and by the end of 1944 the project was cancelled.

Fig.132 Curtiss XF14C-2, Mfr. photo via J. Schneider. Curtiss obtained a Navy development contract for a high altitude carrier fighter in June, 1941. It was for the XF14C-1, designed to use the new 2200 horsepower liquid cooled Lycoming XH-2470 engine under development. Over two years later it was decided the -1 airplane would be unsatisfactory and the design was reworked to use a turbosupercharged Wright Double Cyclone engine driving a dual rotation propeller and redesignated XF14C-2. The first of two prototypes flew in mid-1944, but by the this time not only was there no need for the plane, but the R-3350 Double Cyclone engines were all needed for the B-29 bomber program.

Fig.133 Lockheed XP-58 Chain Lightning, photo via F.Dean coll. Designed as a long range escort fighter and also as a destroyer of enemy bombers, the XP-58 was a product of thinking that said a fighter should have a lot of everything, apparently including complexity. Looking like a big P-38, the aircraft was to have several different engine types considered during its gestation, but finally ended up with two Allison V-3420 twenty-four cylinder 3000 horsepower engines. The photo shows one of two XP-58 prototypes taxiing out for a test flight. Maximum loaded weight was almost twenty tons, more than the weight of most medium bombers.

Fig.134 Lockheed XP-58 Chain Lightning, Mfr.photo via F. Dean coll. Shown in the yard of a camouflaged Lockheed plant, the XP-58 displays some of its features, including the upper of two gun turrets, turbosuperchargers in a P-38-like location, and a similar location of Prestone coolers on twin booms. The two place cabin was to be pressurized. First flight of an XP-58 did not take place until June, 1944. The test program was conducted without armament or a pressurized cabin. Both 37mm. and 75mm. cannon were considered as armament possibilities.

cabin was planned for operation at 40000 feet, but was not incorporated initially. The big XF14C-2, shown in Figure 132, did not fly until the middle of 1944, a time when the Wright engines were destined for B-29 bombers. And since a need for the Navy to fly at extreme altitudes did not appear as the war moved on, the Curtiss XF14C-2 was shortly discontinued.

Another first flight took place about the same time as the XF14C-2; this was the Lockheed XP-58, called Chain Lightning. Intended as a high altitude bomber destroyer using heavy armament, the XP-58, shown in Figures 133 through 135, had the size and weight of a medium bomber. The arrangement of the two seat aircraft was like the P-38, but the two turbosupercharged engines were each the equivalent of two P-38 Allisons, being vee types mated

in a side-by-side "W" arrangement. In late 1944 a lot of development was still needed on the XP-58 and its systems. There turned out to be no need for this type of bomber destroyer late in the war. Production fighters were doing well in this role, and work on the single big XP-58 was discontinued.

In spring 1943 the Boeing Company started work on the last fighter to carry their name. This was the XF8B-1 for the Navy shown in Figures 136 and 137. A big airplane with gross weight over ten tons, the XF8B-1 was intended as a long range multi-purpose new-carrier fighter to attack Japan. It used the big four-row Wasp Major engine driving counter-rotating propellers, and carried heavy armament along with a sizeable bomb load if required. The first of three aircraft flew near the end of 1944, but no production order

Fig.135 Lockheed XP-58 Chain Lightning, photo via F. Dean coll. The XP-58 was an imposing aircraft as shown here with a wing span eighteen feet greater than the already good-sized P-38 and a wing area of 600 square feet, dimensions well worthy of a medium bomber! High speed was claimed to be 420 mph or more at 25000 feet, but it is not clear that such performance was demonstrated during flight tests. There was no need for a fighter like the XP-58 in 1944 and by the end of that year the development was abandoned.

Fig.136 Boeing XF8B-1, Mfr.photo via F. Dean coll. A wind tunnel model of Boeing's last fighter for the US Navy is mounted and ready for testing in 1943. Note the model is powered and has a dual rotation propeller. The XF8B-1 was designed as a long range carrier based single seat fighter to operate from the then-latest big carriers against the Japanese homeland.

Fig.137 Boeing XF8B-1, Mfr.photo via F. Dean coll. A dynamic photo showing the big Boeing fighter running up for vibration tests of the thirteen foot six inch diameter dual rotation Aeroproducts propeller. The object on the front of the propeller hub is a "pineapple" housing electrical slip rings tranferring blade-mounted strain gage data to a fixed (non-rotating) point. The shock cord keeps the pineapple housing and brushes from rotating. The engine is the big twenty-eight cylinder four row Pratt and Whitney "corncob" R-4360 of 3000 horsepower. Landing gear mechanism twisted the retracting wheels to lay flat in the wing.

Fig.137A Boeing XF8B-1, Mfr.photo via P.M. Bowers. Three prototypes were to be delivered to the Navy according to a contract of May,1943. The first flew in November, 1944; the other two were not completed until after the war. The dual rotation propeller was installed so six blades could absorb the very high engine power and to negate torque reaction. Note in the photo there are two men under the bubble canopy; one prototype was fitted with an observer's jump seat, but as seen it was a tight fit. With war's end no XF8B-1 production ensued.

was forthcoming. In-service production aircraft were doing the job. The XF8B-1 was comparable to the later Douglas AD-series Skyraider attack airplanes.

The last of the wartime monoplane fighter projects never to achieve production status first flew early in 1945, and was another Curtiss effort for the Navy. Curtiss probably had the record for number of failed wartime prototype projects, and the XF15C-1, shown in Figure 138, was the final one before the jet era. Like the Ryan FR-1 Fireball (which started into limited production shortly before the war ended), the Curtiss fighter was a "composite-powered" aircraft with a Double Wasp piston engine up front and a British jet engine in the tail. Of three prototypes built, the first crashed in May, 1945. With new higher performance all-jet fighters in the mill after the war, the Navy lost interest in the composite-powered formula, and development of the last Curtiss naval fighter was dropped.

In retrospect it is amazing that in just a fourteen year period, 1931 to 1945, there was such a formidable array of thirty-one dif-

Fig.138 Curtiss XF15C-1, Mfr.photo via J.Schneider. Late in the war the US Navy became interested in the possibilities of composite-powered aircraft, a combination of a piston and a jet, the former for long range cruise and the combination for bursts of speed. Conceptually the Curtiss XF15C-1 was similar to the Ryan FR-1 Fireball. Three Curtiss prototypes powered by a Double Wasp and a British jet engine in the lower tail end were ordered in April, 1944. Flight testing without the jet started in early 1945; with that engine mounted tests resumed in May. The first prototype crashed that month and extensive modifications, including a new tail, were made in the other aircraft. Further testing difficulties ensued, and the Navy lost interest in the Curtiss fighter. One aircraft is preserved in the New England Air Museum.

ferent unsuccessful fighter monoplane prototypes put forth, these in addition to AMERICA'S HUNDRED THOUSAND, the eleven production fighters. And this was only fighters! In this period the US aviation industry, spurred first by threat of war, then by actual war, was nothing if not prolific. Because of continually increasing complexity and cost of aircraft in later times up to the present day, never again will there be so many experimental fighter projects with so much diversity of character. In light of hindsight it is easy to say many wartime projects should never have been started, but at the time it was impossible to predict the flow of wartime events around the world and how trends of fighter design would be influenced.

3

FIGHTER FACTORS

THE AIR IN WHICH THEY FLEW

The characteristics of the air through which fighters flew were important to their performance. These characteristics were not constant day-to-day and varied from sea level to high altitude. Two major factors are worth remembering. Both air density and temperature decreased as the plane went higher. The density (number of air particles in a cubic foot) decreased as the plane ascended; about 26% less at 10000 feet and fully 63% less at 30000 feet. Anyone who has climbed a mountain knows how breathing becomes more difficult up high because of reduced air density. Similarly it gets colder with increases in altitude; the drop is about three degrees F. for every 1000 feet up. Again, a person feels this quickly in a mountain climb. See Graph 3.

But the numbers do not remain constant day-to-day and season-to-season. They also vary around the world and with weather. So nothing was constant in the atmosphere where the fighters flew. A pilot could not be sure of temperature and density of the air in which he would be flying. But he did know the higher he flew the colder and thinner the air would become.

To make matters workable for comparative analysis of aircraft by engineers and technicians an artificial "standard" atmosphere was devised years before World War II. This standard allowed aeronautical people to talk about things like fighter performance on a common relative basis. All figures quoted herein are based on this standard atmosphere. When a fighter was flight tested, all measured performance was later corrected to standard atmosphere conditions. Years later, after World War II, we had not only a standard atmosphere, but also standard hot and standard cold atmospheres, all with different temperature and density values at the same altitude. But we will use the old standard atmosphere as first devised.

The decrease in air density with altitude let fighter aircraft fly faster as they went higher—if engine power and propeller performance held up. This was because up high airplane drag at any speed went down; there were less air particles, and thus less air resistance. The maximum speeds of the eleven fighters we are considering were invariably gained at the highest altitude maximum engine power with good propeller performance could be held. The 400 mph fighters of World War II developed this performance at altitude, not sea level.

A pilot could not read his real (or true) airspeed, TAS, when he was flying up high. He had to read what the air speed measuring system on the aircraft told him. This was "indicated" airspeed (IAS), a smaller number than true airspeed if he was anywhere above sea level, and the higher the greater the difference. If he flew at sea level his indicated air speed, IAS, was the same as his true air speed, TAS, the latter being his real speed going through the air. Of course this assumed his air speed indicator on the instrument panel displayed the proper indicated speed; there was usually an installation correction on the instrument reading.

We will not consider the effect of wind to correct true air speed to ground speed (how fast the plane is traversing over the ground). To make things easy we will always assume the fighters are flying in zero wind conditions.

An important effect of the decrease in temperature with altitude is the change it makes in the speed of sound in air. This speed turns out to be important because the air pressure disturbances the plane makes going through the air all travel at the speed of sound. This speed depends only on air temperature. If temperature is low as at high altitude the speed of sound is also lower. In the standard atmosphere at sea level it is 761 mph; at 30000 feet 678 mph. The

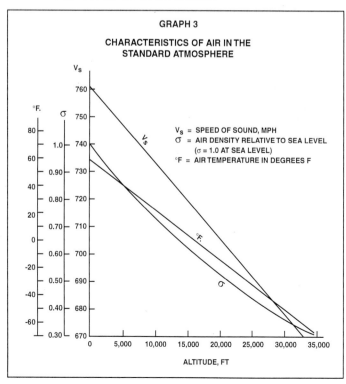

GRAPH 3

CHARACTERISTICS OF AIR IN THE
STANDARD ATMOSPHERE

V_S = SPEED OF SOUND, MPH
σ = AIR DENSITY RELATIVE TO SEA LEVEL
(σ = 1.0 AT SEA LEVEL)
°F = AIR TEMPERATURE IN DEGREES F

ALTITUDE, FT

closer World War II fighter aircraft got to the speed of sound the more trouble arose. Trouble started when the plane was traveling at true airspeeds between 65 and 75% of the speed of sound, sometimes at lesser speeds. (See the section on COMPRESSIBILITY). A fighter going at 400 mph TAS was in more trouble the higher he flew. The cold air over Europe at 30000 feet in dead of winter was colder than air at the same altitude in summer in the SW Pacific. The speed of sound was lower in the first case, and planes at high altitude tended to get into trouble quicker in the European winter air. We are talking here about the real world and not about standard atmosphere conditions.

It can thus be seen the air in which planes operated had a great effect on their performance and flying qualities, even without considering weather variations. It also had a significant effect on fighter pilots, many of whom almost froze at high altitude without sufficient cockpit heating, and also got pretty warm flying low in a closed cockpit in summer conditions with no air conditioning.

THRUST

Thrust is the force that counters drag and makes fighters go; the more thrust the faster the speed. Thrust is generated by combined effort of a piston engine and its propeller. The more horsepower developed by the engine at its output shaft, and the higher the efficiency of the propeller, the more thrust force produced. Engine power developed depends on output shaft torque (twist) times shaft revolutions per minute. This power can vary depending on where the pilot puts the throttle lever, the supercharger control lever, and the propeller RPM control. It also depends on how high the plane is flying and other factors. Maximum engine powers at sea level for US World War II fighter aircraft were in the range 1000 to 2000 horsepower. Typical propeller efficiencies were around 80%, sometimes lower and sometimes a little higher, depending on many factors. This meant about 80% of the available engine power was converted into useful thrusting power by the propeller.

An example of thrust force developed by a Curtiss P-40 fighter flying at 280 mph using 900 horsepower with an 80% propeller efficiency is: (neglecting any thrust from exhaust stacks)

THRUST (LB.)= 375 x PROP. EFFICIENCY x ENGINE HP / TAS
= 375 x .80 x 900 / 280
= 964

(The 375 is there to make the answer come out OK when speed is in mph)

In this case if the P-40 was flying at a steady speed, the air drag on the plane would be the same as the thrust, or 964 LB. (Again neglecting exhaust stack jet thrust.) So thrust came from a combination of engine power and the efficiency of conversion of this power by the propeller. A look at the engines and propellers used in US World War II fighter aircraft is in order.

ENGINES

Table 4 shows characteristics of engines used in US fighter aircraft, including takeoff powers. There were four fighter engine manufacturers during the war: Allison, Packard, Pratt and Whitney, and Wright. Allison was a division of General Motors, and a relatively recent entry into the big-time of engine production, though they had been making a small number of development engines during the 1930s. Their product was the V-1710, a liquid-cooled 12-cylinder vee-type engine of 1710 cubic inches displacement. Packard was a motor car company which for the war produced the Rolls Royce Merlin V-1650 engine under license from the British. Negotiations between Rolls and Ford Motor Company to produce the Merlin in the US had earlier fallen through. The Merlin was also a liquid-cooled 12-cylinder vee-type engine. Pratt and Whitney was part of the United Aircraft Corp. (now United Technologies) and a split-off from Wright years before. A veteran producer by World War II, Pratt made two engine models for fighters, both of them twin-row radials. These were the 14-cylinder R-1830 Twin Wasp (also used on the B-24 bomber), and the considerably larger R-2800 18-cylinder Double Wasp engine. Wright, the engine-manufacturing arm of the Curtiss-Wright Corp., was an old-line outfit. Their only fighter engine was the R-1820 Cyclone, a nine-cylinder single-row radial also used in the B-17 bomber.

The US Army used both liquid-cooled V-type engines and air-cooled radials. In earlier years the Army had gone to liquid-cooled powerplants for fighters, then went back to radials, and not too long before the war, no doubt influenced by trends in Britain and Germany, switched again to the liquid-cooled Vee-type in a push for more nose streamlining and speed. The US Navy, many years before the war, made a firm decision to use radial air-cooled engines in their fighters (as well as all other types of Navy planes), and never deviated on any production aircraft.

As with their airplanes, fighter pilots had favorite engines; there was often great loyalty to an engine type that may have saved their skin a time or two. During a 1944 fighter conference at Patuxent River, Md. a large group of service and company test pilots was asked to name the powerplant inspiring the most confidence. Eighty-one percent voted (between Double-Wasp, Merlin, and Allison V-1710; Wright was not mentioned). The R-2800 was by far the favored engine; 79% voted for it, with 17 % opting for the Merlin, and 1% for the V-1710. There is no question pilots worried about vulnerability of cooling systems in liquid-cooled engines, especially in the face of heavy fire directed at them during ground-attack missions.

The output power of an engine was defined by pressure in the intake manifold leading to the cylinders, and speed of rotation of the output shaft. Engine performance charts were made up on the basis of manifold pressure (usually expressed in inches of mercury) and engine revolutions per minute. Both items were easily measureable on the airplane, and indicated to the pilot on his instrument panel by a manifold pressure gage and a tachometer. Graph 4 gives a simplified picture of typical engine performance showing how power was determined by absolute manifold pressure and RPM. Engine ratings were established for wartime military piston engines

TABLE 4
FIGHTER ENGINES

AIRCRAFT	ENG.MFR.	MODEL	NR.CYL.	MAX. HP	SUPERCHARGING	NOTES
P-40F,L	PACKARD	V-1650	12	1300	MECH 1 STAGE 2 SPEED	MERLIN
P-51B,D,K	PACKARD	V-1650	12	1490	MECH 2 STAGE 2 SPEED	MERLIN
P-39,-40 P-51,-51A	ALLISON	V-1710	12	1150	MECH 1 STAGE 1 SPEED	NO NAME
P-63	ALLISON	V-1710	12	1325	MECH/HYDR. VAR.SPEED	"
P-38	ALLISON	V-1710	12	1475	MECH 1 STAGE & TURBO	"
F2A- FM-2	WRIGHT	R-1820	9	1350	MECH 1 STAGE 2 SPEED	CYCLONE
F4F-3A	P & W	R-1830	14	1050	MECH 1 STAGE 2 SPEED	TW.WASP
F4F-3,-4	P & W	R-1830	14	1200	MECH 2 STAGE 2 SPEED	TW.WASP
P-61,F4U- F6F-	P & W	R-2800	18	2100	MECH 2 STAGE 2 SPEED	DBLE.WASP
P-47, P-61C	P & W	R-2800	18	2100	MECH 1 STAGE & TURBO	DBLE.WASP

as shown in Table 5 in order of decreasing manifold pressure and RPM, and thus of decreasing power. The "War Emergency" or "Combat" power setting was an emergency rating available for a limited time to get out of trouble in combat. The throttle lever was pushed full forward through a detent (such as lockwire) for extra power corresponding to manifold pressure and engine speed values near structural limits. The broken detent left a record, and the engine was subjected to subsequent special examination. On some of the later fighter aircraft Combat Power was achieved by injecting a mixture of water and alcohol into the cylinders to suppress engine detonation at very high power. This was also called ADI for anti-detonation injection.

Take-off power rating was just that—the engine power used to take the fighter off the ground under ordinary circumstances. Military Power setting was the maximum throttle position allowed for other than the special combat emergency noted above, or take-off. Application of this power was allowed for a longer period of time as seen in Table 5. Normal Power was the highest continuous power setting allowed; it could be used for high speed cruising. There was no time limit. The more economical cruise powers most often used were expressed as certain percentages of Normal Power.

Most sets of piston engine exhaust stacks would provide (if a turbosupercharger was not employed) something like 100 to 150 pounds of additional thrust if they were properly shaped and dumped exhaust mostly rearward. If a turbosupercharger was used these gases were routed to drive the turbine instead of going directly overboard.

Typical fuel consumption for high powered fighter engines during World War II was about .42 to .82 pounds per horsepower per hour, the first figure being for most economical cruise power and the second for Military or Takeoff Power. Since a gallon of gasoline weighs six pounds, these figures translated into .077 to .137 gallons per horsepower per hour. Consumption depended heavily on the condition of the engine and how it was operated. A combination of low RPM and fairly high manifold pressure gave low fuel consumption and did not seem to hurt the engines. The Japanese knew this and used these settings frequently for long range

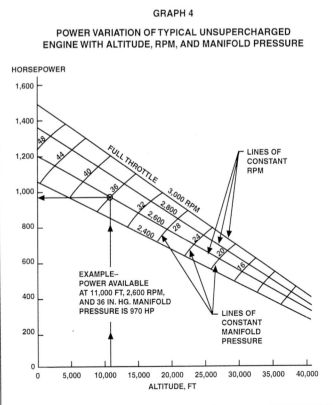

GRAPH 4

POWER VARIATION OF TYPICAL UNSUPERCHARGED ENGINE WITH ALTITUDE, RPM, AND MANIFOLD PRESSURE

TABLE 5
TYPICAL ENGINE RATING CHART

RATING/PWR.SET.	MAX.TIME(MIN.)	HP	RPM	ALTITUDE (FT.)	MANIFOLD PRESS."HG.
WAR EMERGENCY OR COMBAT	5	1800	3000	SEA LEVEL	76
TAKEOFF	5	1325	3000	SEA LEVEL	54
MILITARY	15	1100	3000	27000	52
100% NORMAL RATED OR MAX.CONTINUOUS	UNLIMITED	1000	2600	23000	43

NOTES: The numbers shown as an example are for the Allison V-1710-117 engine used in a Bell P-63 aircraft.
The WAR EMERGENCY, or COMBAT power setting was often, though not always, attained using water-alcohol injection in the engine.

cruising, and Charles Lindbergh taught the same cruise methods to US pilots in the Pacific.

Powerplants could be handfuls to take care of in flight—lots of items to monitor and control—particularly in earlier model aircraft where nothing was automatic. The pilot was in the loop for everything, and it is almost a wonder he had time to fight! It has been said for the twin-engined P-38 if the pilot was small he had to be a multi-armed ape to keep ahead of everything. For the powerplant alone the typical single engine fighter pilot had to handle throttle lever, mixture control, and supercharger lever on the throttle quadrant at his left, the increase/decrease RPM control for the propeller governor, carburetor air control, cooling airflow control flap or flaps, fuel selector valve, and droppable fuel tanks release handle. He had to monitor, at a minimum, gages showing oil pressure, cylinder head temperature, fuel quantity, manifold pressure, and RPM.

Most fighter engines were geared, that is, crankshaft speed had to be reduced through gearing to an output shaft speed depending on the specific installation, this done to keep propeller tip speeds at acceptable values. Propellers rotated at a speed from about 44% to 67% of engine crankshaft speed.

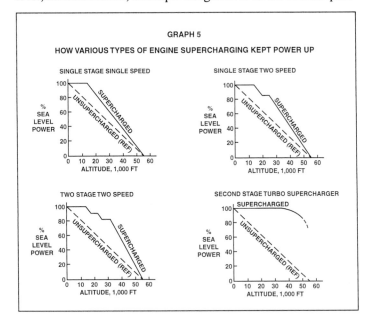

GRAPH 5
HOW VARIOUS TYPES OF ENGINE SUPERCHARGING KEPT POWER UP

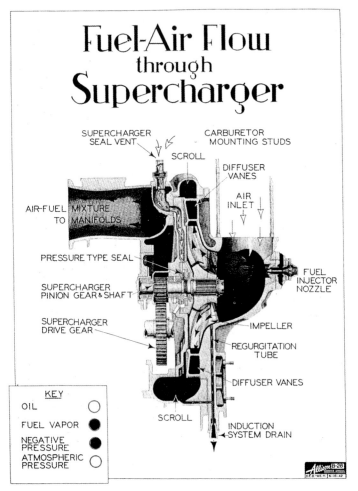

Fig. 139

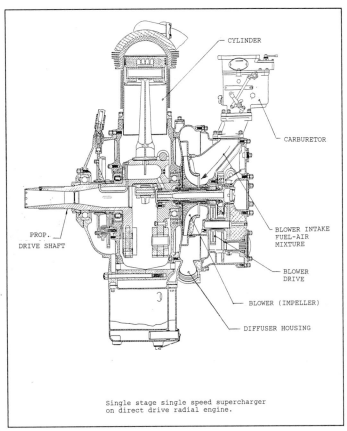

CYLINDER

CARBURETOR

PROP.
DRIVE SHAFT

BLOWER INTAKE
FUEL-AIR
MIXTURE

BLOWER
DRIVE

BLOWER (IMPELLER)

DIFFUSER HOUSING

Single stage single speed supercharger
on direct drive radial engine.

Fig. 140

SUPERCHARGERS

Supercharging the piston engines of World War II fighter aircraft was an all-important factor in providing required performance at high altitude. An unsupercharged engine would lose about half its sea level power at 20000 feet altitude and almost three quarters sea level power at 30000 feet—an unacceptable situation. On the other hand, if full sea level power could be maintained high up, reduction of drag in the thinner air at altitude allowed the fighter to go faster and faster. Even if sea level power could not be fully maintained as the airplane climbed to high altitude, a means of lessening the abrupt power fall-off of the unsupercharged engine (to zero at 55000 feet) was a great asset. Graph 5 shows how supercharging kept altitude power available up.

All five basic engine models used in the eleven US production fighters were supercharged to one degree or another (see Table 4). Supercharging compressed the fuel-air mixture entering the engine intake manifold and cylinders so power could be maintained, or at least its drop-off with altitude minimized. Since the amount of air in each cubic foot of space decreased dramatically as the airplane climbed to altitude, the engine gasped for air unless a compressor forced (or "boosted") more into the manifold and cylinders. The compressors used were commonly called "blowers". They were of the centrifugal type where air or a fuel-air mixture was introduced at the center and thrown radially outward on a high speed spinning rotor disc containing a series of vanes into a surrounding diffuser. See Figures 139 and 140. In the process the mix was compressed

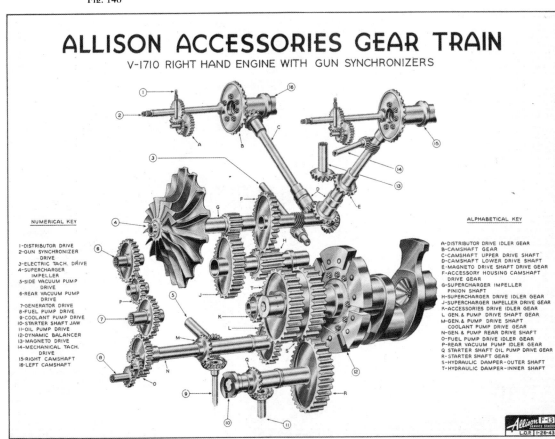

ALLISON ACCESSORIES GEAR TRAIN
V-1710 RIGHT HAND ENGINE WITH GUN SYNCHRONIZERS

NUMERICAL KEY

1-DISTRIBUTOR DRIVE
2-GUN SYNCHRONIZER DRIVE
3-ELECTRIC TACH. DRIVE
4-SUPERCHARGER IMPELLER
5-SIDE VACUUM PUMP DRIVE
6-REAR VACUUM PUMP DRIVE
7-GENERATOR DRIVE
8-FUEL PUMP DRIVE
9-COOLANT PUMP DRIVE
10-STARTER SHAFT JAW
11-OIL PUMP DRIVE
12-DYNAMIC BALANCER
13-MAGNETO DRIVE
14-MECHANICAL TACH. DRIVE
15-RIGHT CAMSHAFT
16-LEFT CAMSHAFT

ALPHABETICAL KEY

A-DISTRIBUTOR DRIVE IDLER GEAR
B-CAMSHAFT GEAR
C-CAMSHAFT UPPER DRIVE SHAFT
D-CAMSHAFT LOWER DRIVE SHAFT
E-MAGNETO DRIVE SHAFT DRIVE GEAR
F-ACCESSORY HOUSING CAMSHAFT DRIVE GEAR
G-SUPERCHARGER IMPELLER PINION SHAFT
H-SUPERCHARGER DRIVE IDLER GEAR
J-SUPERCHARGER IMPELLER DRIVE GEAR
K-ACCESSORIES DRIVE IDLER GEAR
L GEN. & PUMP DRIVE SHAFT GEAR
M-GEN.& PUMP DRIVE SHAFT
COOLANT PUMP DRIVE GEAR
N-GEN. & PUMP REAR DRIVE SHAFT
O-FUEL PUMP DRIVE IDLER GEAR
P-REAR VACUUM PUMP IDLER GEAR
Q STARTER SHAFT OIL PUMP DRIVE GEAR
R-STARTER SHAFT GEAR
S-HYDRAULIC DAMPER-OUTER SHAFT
T-HYDRAULIC DAMPER-INNER SHAFT

Allison F-3 SERVICE SCHOOL
L.O.P. 1-26-43

Fig. 141

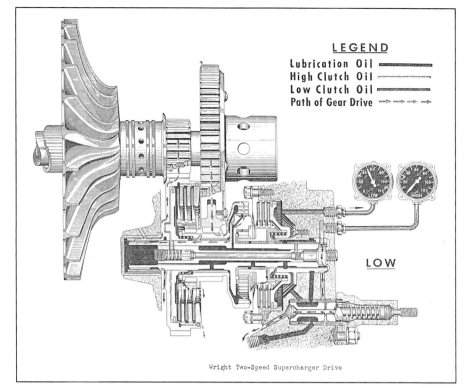

LEGEND
Lubrication Oil
High Clutch Oil
Low Clutch Oil
Path of Gear Drive

LOW

Wright Two-Speed Supercharger Drive

Fig. 142

The next form of supercharging, a little heavier and more complex, was the single-stage two-speed type (Figure 142). The only difference from above was the blower could be run at two different gear ratios to the crankshaft instead of one. This was accomplished by a clutch and gear drive arrangement similar to that of a straight-stick automobile, and the pilot had a control in the cockpit to mechanically change gears in flight. As altitude increased he shifted from "low" to "high", and the blower ran at an even higher speed relative to the engine, thereby compressing more air and keeping the power up. This helped up to a point (critical altitude) where the single-stage blower ran out of capability even at its higher speed. Single-stage two-speed supercharging was employed in the Rolls Royce/Packard V-1650-1 Merlin used in the P-40F and P-40L, the Wright R-1820 Cyclone versions used in the Brewster F2A-2 and F2A-3 and some export Buffalo aircraft, and in the F4F-3A Wildcat version with the Pratt and Whitney R-1830 Twin Wasp engine. The later FM-2 Wildcat made by Eastern Division of General Motors also employed a single-stage two-speed supercharger in its R-1820 Cyclone. It helped, but marginally. Power could be maintained up to about an 18000 foot critical (start of full throttle) altitude.

In the middle 1930s the US Navy and Pratt and Whitney had been looking for better fighter engine performance at altitude, and developed a two-stage two-speed supercharger. In England Rolls Royce was also working on two-stage systems to further boost engine power at altitude (the Merlin 61). Later, Allison in the US developed a two-stage system. This type was also known as "auxiliary-stage" supercharging with the second of the two stages being the auxiliary blower. This supercharging was responsible for the successful altitude performance—holding near sea level power up to 25000 feet or more—of several of our later wartime fighter aircraft such as the F6F- Hellcat, F4U- Corsair, P-61 Black Widow, the P-51B/C/D Mustangs, and the P-63 Kingcobra, and it was pioneered in the USN for production in the Grumman F4F-3 and F4F-4 Wildcat versions. In England this supercharging in the Merlin 61/Spitfire IX gave the aircraft a critical altitude of just about 30000 feet.

There were three different versions of two-stage mechanical supercharging, or in one case hydromechanical. The first type (Figure 143) used in the Merlin P-51s employed two blower discs in tandem on the same shaft behind the engine. These were always connected to the engine crankshaft by one of two sets of speed-up gearing which was designed to shift automatically between the lower and higher speed (gear ratio) depending on altitude. So this setup was like the single-stage, two-speed units just described except for use of two blowers in tandem instead of one. As outlined previously the intake air went into the carburetor where it was mixed with fuel, and then entered the blower system where in this case it

because air velocity turned into air pressure. Most often the blowers were driven by the engine crankshaft through speed-up gearing. See Figure 141. A blower speed of over 25000 RPM was not uncommon. Though this mechanical drive took power from the engine, the compression added more power than the blower drive took out, thus providing a net gain.

Fighter engines were designed to operate at part throttle at sea level because of structural limits. With supercharging the engine power output could be held constant by opening throttle as airplane altitude increased, up to the point where full throttle was applied. This was the so-called "critical" or "full-throttle" altitude, after which the power fell off with increasing altitude even under full throttle conditions.

The simplest and lightest form of supercharging used a single-stage (single-rotor) single-speed blower located behind the engine cylinders. (Figure 140). The blower rotated any time the engine ran, since it was geared to the crankshaft, Figure 141 . If the engine speeded up so did the blower and vice-versa. So it was really single gear ratio, not single speed. The fuel-air mixture entered the blower from the carburetor (Figures 139 and 140) and, compressed, entered the engine intake manifold and then the cylinders. This so-called single-stage single-speed system was used on Allison V-1710 engine versions in the Bell P-39, Curtiss P-40 (except F and L models), the early North American Mustangs (P-51 and P-51A), and also on the earliest experimental versions of the Brewster F2A- and Grumman F4F- using Wright R-1820 Cyclone and Pratt and Whitney R-1830 Twin Wasp engines respectively. In these cases the supercharger held sea level power up to 12000-15000 feet critical altitude after which it fell off rapidly. Performance of these aircraft fell off above that altitude accordingly.

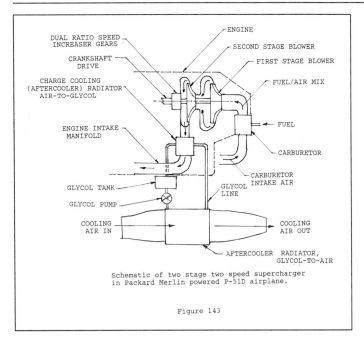

DUAL RATIO SPEED INCREASER GEARS
CRANKSHAFT DRIVE
CHARGE COOLING (AFTERCOOLER) RADIATOR AIR-TO-GLYCOL
ENGINE
SECOND STAGE BLOWER
FIRST STAGE BLOWER
FUEL/AIR MIX
ENGINE INTAKE MANIFOLD
FUEL
CARBURETOR
GLYCOL TANK
GLYCOL PUMP
CARBURETOR INTAKE AIR
GLYCOL LINE
COOLING AIR IN
COOLING AIR OUT
AFTERCOOLER RADIATOR, GLYCOL-TO-AIR

Schematic of two stage two speed supercharger in Packard Merlin powered P-51D airplane.

Figure 143

was more highly compressed by the tandem blowers. The greatest compression of the fuel-air mixture occurred of course when the system switched to high speed at the higher altitudes. The two blowers worked on the mixture so hard in this two-stage system that its temperature rose considerably along with its pressure. A method was needed to cool the charge mixture to the proper temperature before it entered the engine cylinders. The arrangement employed was called an aftercooler system—the "after" because it was placed in line after the blowers did their work. After compression the mixture passed through a charge-cooling radiator, then on to the intake manifold. The aftercooling was completely separate from the basic engine liquid-cooling system. It included an engine-driven pump, a header tank, lines, the charge-cooling radiator, the aftercooler radiator, and glycol coolant. The charge-cooling radiator was an air-to-glycol heat exchanger. The coolant was then routed through a glycol-to-air aftercooler radiator (heat exchanger). Air ducted from the outside was rammed through the aftercooler radiator, and this overall cooling system reduced the temperature of the compressed mixture to a point where it could safely enter the engine intake manifold and cylinders without causing detonation. In the Merlin Mustang aircraft the aftercooler radiator was located, along with other cooling items, in the large scoop below the fuselage just aft of the wing. This supercharger system was heavier and more complex than single stage types, but it did a good job in keeping power up

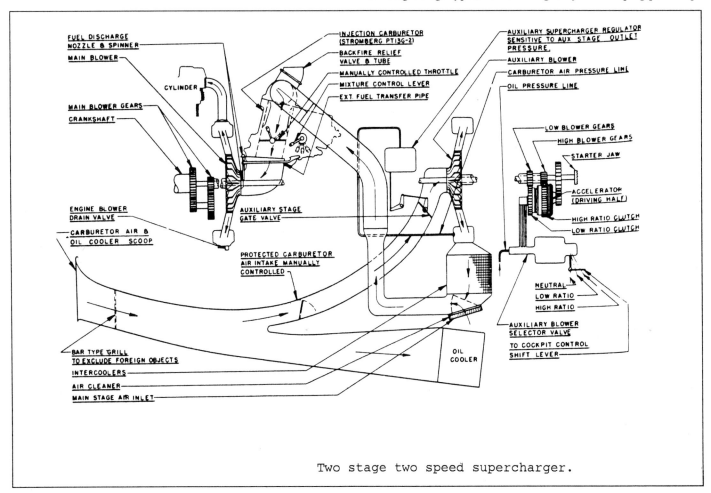

FUEL DISCHARGE NOZZLE & SPINNER
MAIN BLOWER
CYLINDER
MAIN BLOWER GEARS
CRANKSHAFT
INJECTION CARBURETOR (STROMBERG PT13G-2)
BACKFIRE RELIEF VALVE & TUBE
MANUALLY CONTROLLED THROTTLE
MIXTURE CONTROL LEVER
EXT FUEL TRANSFER PIPE
AUXILIARY SUPERCHARGER REGULATOR SENSITIVE TO AUX STAGE OUTLET PRESSURE
AUXILIARY BLOWER
CARBURETOR AIR PRESSURE LINE
OIL PRESSURE LINE
LOW BLOWER GEARS
HIGH BLOWER GEARS
STARTER JAW
ACCELERATOR (DRIVING HALF)
HIGH RATIO CLUTCH
LOW RATIO CLUTCH
ENGINE BLOWER DRAIN VALVE
CARBURETOR AIR & OIL COOLER SCOOP
AUXILIARY STAGE GATE VALVE
PROTECTED CARBURETOR AIR INTAKE MANUALLY CONTROLLED
NEUTRAL
LOW RATIO
HIGH RATIO
AUXILIARY BLOWER SELECTOR VALVE
TO COCKPIT CONTROL SHIFT LEVER
BAR TYPE GRILL TO EXCLUDE FOREIGN OBJECTS
INTERCOOLERS
AIR CLEANER
MAIN STAGE AIR INLET
OIL COOLER

Two stage two speed supercharger.

Fig. 144

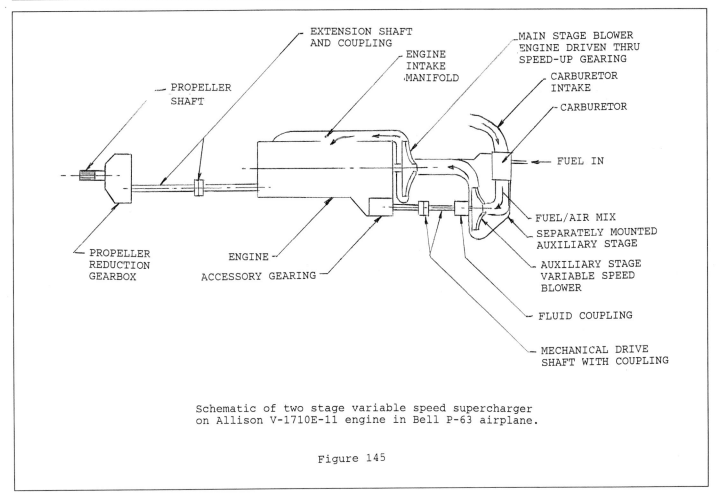

Schematic of two stage variable speed supercharger
on Allison V-1710E-11 engine in Bell P-63 airplane.

Figure 145

with increasing altitude to about 25000-29000 feet and made these Mustang versions very fast fighter airplanes at altitude.

A second type of two-stage supercharging was developed by the USN and Pratt and Whitney for the R-1830 and R-2800 engines used in the major Navy fighters of World War II—the Wildcat, Hellcat, and Corsair. In this system, again with additional weight and complexity involved to keep power up at altitude, there were two blowers (Figure 144 .) The "main" blower was always speed-up geared to the engine crankshaft, and thus ran whenever the engine turned over. The "auxiliary" (second-stage) blower and its two sets of different speed-up gearing could be clutched to and declutched from the crankshaft via a control in the cockpit. The first-stage blower was located between the carburetor and the engine cylinders, and thus compressed the fuel and air mixture. The second (auxiliary) stage blower was placed between an outside air intake and an air-to-air intercooler which was a heat exchanger. The intercooler's function was to cool, by close passage of outside air, the charge air compressed by the auxiliary-stage blower before it entered the carburetor. In this scheme the main blower compressed a fuel-air mixture whereas the auxiliary blower compressed air only. The system had three modes of operation as follows:

Neutral Blower was used at takeoff and low altitude. Operation was similar to a single-stage supercharger; the second-stage was declutched, inoperative, and thus in "neutral". Intake air was routed directly to the carburetor, through the main blower, and on to the cylinders.

Low Blower was employed at medium altitude starting around 5000 and lasting to about 18000 feet. Intake air came directly from an outside scoop into the auxiliary blower which had been connected to the crankshaft through gearing. A cockpit-controlled shift lever operated a hydraulic "low-ratio" clutch. The compressed and heated air was cooled by passage through the intercooler and then routed through the carburetor, into the operating main blower and to the engine cylinders. Charge air was thus compressed by two blowers, one ahead of the carburetor and one after it.

High Blower came into play at high altitude. Operation was similar to Low Blower mode except the cockpit shift lever was moved to a high-ratio position to clutch in another set of gearing and speed up the auxiliary blower for additional air compression.

The third type of two-stage variable-speed supercharging was utilized in the Bell P-63 Kingcobra fighter to ensure the good high altitude performance its predecessor, the P-39 Airacobra, had lacked. This system was similar in some respects to that above for the Navy fighters, and in some to the two-stage unit in the Merlin Mustangs. There were differences, however. The P-63 used a version of the Allison V-1710 as had the P-39. To add an "auxiliary" stage of supercharging to supplement the existing single-stage blower in the V-1710, Allison used a mechanical drive shaft and hydraulic cou-

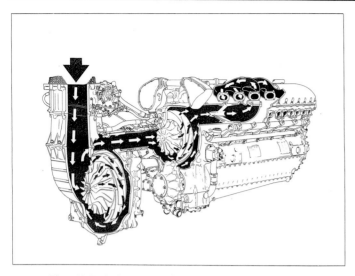

Fig. 146: Fuel-Air Flow Diagram-V-1710-93 and -117 Engines

pling from the engine aft to a separately-housed new blower. (Figures 145 through 147). The engine charge air flow passed through the carburetor before going through the two stages of supercharging. There was no intercooler system. Control of the P-63 system was automatic with the auxiliary blower cutting in at 7000 feet altitude, and operating at a smoothly variable ever higher speed as the plane increased its altitude. The hydraulic coupling allowed variable speed operation. High power could be maintained up to an altitude of about 25000 feet.

Perhaps the best-known supercharging system, and certainly the one providing US World War II fighters with the most power available at the highest altitude was the turbosupercharger. This system was employed on the P-38 Lightning, P-47 Thunderbolt, and on a few late-model P-61C Black Widow fighters. The P-38 had turbosuperchargers on its two Allison V-1710 powerplants, and the others had turbos on Pratt and Whitney R-2800 engines. The B-17 and B-24 bombers and later the B-29 airplanes also had turbosuperchargers, so a tremendous number of these units were produced during the war. Although the Navy did some experimenting with turbosuperchargers, the Army had been intrigued with the concept since just after World War I. General Electric Companys Dr. Sanford Moss spent years in the 1920s and 1930s developing test installations on Army airplanes, often hampered by lack of funds and of advanced materials technology . But by World War II the turbosupercharger was ready, and was used extensively. Turbosupercharging could maintain sea level engine power to 30000 feet or above, thereby providing altitude performance superior to other types of supercharging used on US production fighters. It did, however, preclude use of engine exhaust gases to give jet thrust directly through exhaust stacks. As in other two-stage systems, two blowers or compressors were used. The standard first stage blower integral to the engine was retained. The auxiliary-stage blower was driven not mechanically from the engine, but by engine exhaust gases ducted to a turbine wheel on the same shaft as the auxiliary blower. (Figures 148 and 149). The gases drove the turbine wheel which drove the compressor (auxiliary blower). Exhaust gases then exited through

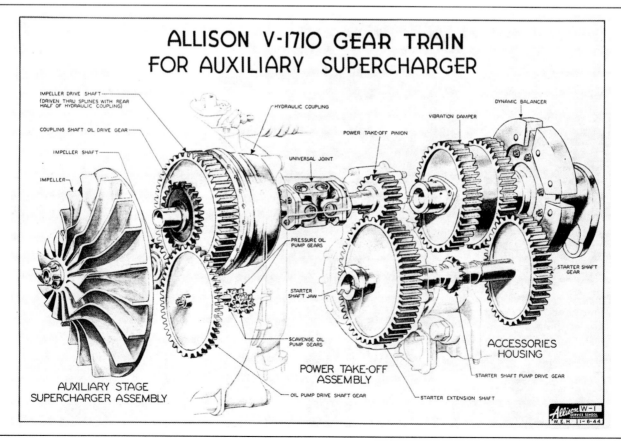

ALLISON V-1710 GEAR TRAIN
FOR AUXILIARY SUPERCHARGER

IMPELLER DRIVE SHAFT
(DRIVEN THRU SPLINES WITH REAR HALF OF HYDRAULIC COUPLING)

HYDRAULIC COUPLING

DYNAMIC BALANCER

COUPLING SHAFT OIL DRIVE GEAR

VIBRATION DAMPER

IMPELLER SHAFT

POWER TAKE-OFF PINION

IMPELLER

UNIVERSAL JOINT

PRESSURE OIL PUMP GEARS

STARTER SHAFT JAW

STARTER SHAFT GEAR

SCAVENGE OIL PUMP GEARS

ACCESSORIES HOUSING

AUXILIARY STAGE SUPERCHARGER ASSEMBLY

POWER TAKE-OFF ASSEMBLY

OIL PUMP DRIVE SHAFT GEAR

STARTER SHAFT PUMP DRIVE GEAR

STARTER EXTENSION SHAFT

Allison W-1 SERVICE SCHOOL
W.E.H. 11-6-44

Fig. 147

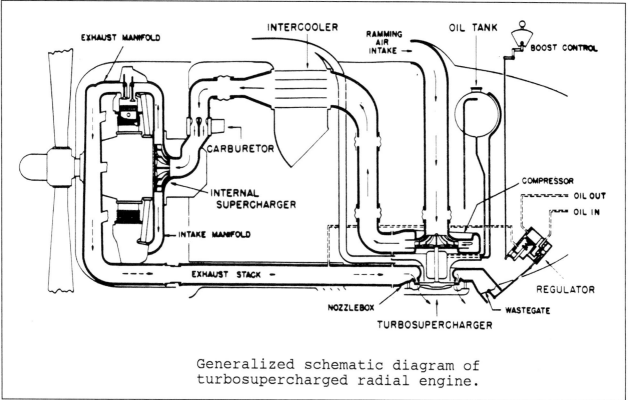

EXHAUST MANIFOLD
INTERCOOLER
RAMMING
AIR
INTAKE →
OIL TANK
BOOST CONTROL
CARBURETOR
INTERNAL
SUPERCHARGER
INTAKE MANIFOLD
COMPRESSOR
OIL OUT
OIL IN
REGULATOR
EXHAUST STACK
WASTEGATE
NOZZLEBOX
TURBOSUPERCHARGER

Generalized schematic diagram of
turbosupercharged radial engine.

Fig. 148 (Above)

Fig. 149 (Below)

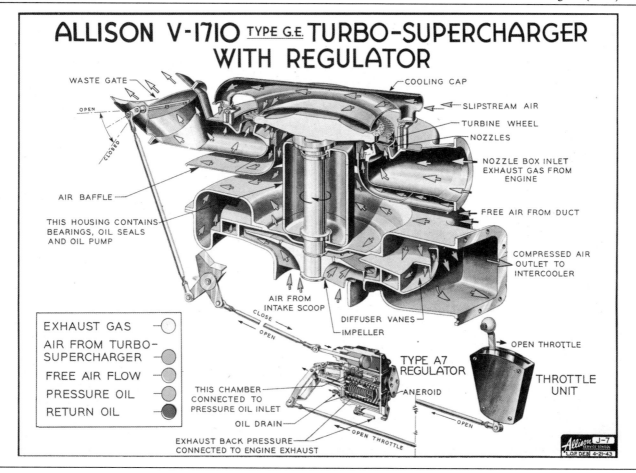

ALLISON V-1710 TYPE G.E. TURBO-SUPERCHARGER WITH REGULATOR

WASTE GATE
OPEN
CLOSED
COOLING CAP
SLIPSTREAM AIR
TURBINE WHEEL
NOZZLES
NOZZLE BOX INLET
EXHAUST GAS FROM
ENGINE
AIR BAFFLE
FREE AIR FROM DUCT
THIS HOUSING CONTAINS
BEARINGS, OIL SEALS
AND OIL PUMP
COMPRESSED AIR
OUTLET TO
INTERCOOLER
AIR FROM
INTAKE SCOOP
CLOSE
OPEN
DIFFUSER VANES
IMPELLER
OPEN THROTTLE

EXHAUST GAS
AIR FROM TURBO-
SUPERCHARGER
FREE AIR FLOW
PRESSURE OIL
RETURN OIL

TYPE A7
REGULATOR
ANEROID
THROTTLE
UNIT
THIS CHAMBER
CONNECTED TO
PRESSURE OIL INLET
OIL DRAIN
OPEN
OPEN THROTTLE
EXHAUST BACK PRESSURE
CONNECTED TO ENGINE EXHAUST

Allison J-7
SERVICE SCHOOL
L.O.P. D.E.B. 4-21-43

a waste gate. The turbine and compressor could be speed-controlled using a valve to vary the inlet flow or the exit orifice of the waste gate. Compressed air from the blower was collected in a surrounding shroud and piped to an air-to-air intercooler similar to those earlier described. This unit cooled the compressed air sufficiently for it to enter the carburetor, and from there proceed to the integral main blower, intake manifold, and engine cylinders.

The turbosupercharger units, consisting of compressor/blower and turbine wheel with housing, were produced by the General Electric Company who came out with improved versions through the war. Since they were gas-driven they could be installed remote from the engine, and were so located on P-38 and P-47 fighters. On the P-38 units were mounted well aft of the engines at the top of the tail booms. On the P-47 the unit was contained in the lower fuselage just forward of the tail wheel. A lot of air ducting was involved in both installations, and a turbo installation added considerable weight and complexity to any powerplant system, but above 25000 feet a turbosupercharger really made a fighter look good by holding engine power up.

The supercharging system in a World War II piston-engined fighter made a difference. If a single-stage unit was employed the plane was lighter and simpler, but effectively limited in performance anywhere over medium altitude. If some kind of two-stage unit was installed the aircraft could get up high where the air was thin and really move out!

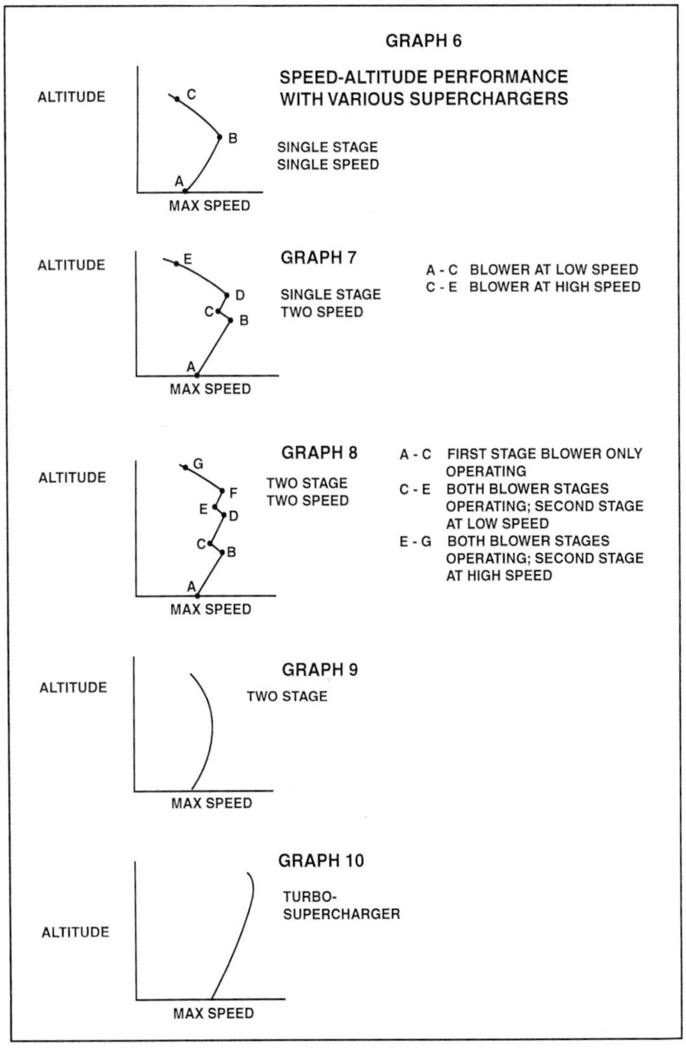

To illustrate the performance differences effected by the different types of supercharging Graphs 6 through 10 give typical forms of speed variation with altitude.

The simplest system, the single-stage single-speed supercharger used in the P-39, most P-40s, and Allison P-51s gave typical performance as shown in Graph 6. Maximum speed capability increased from A to B because because engine power available was constant, propeller performance varied little, and air density (and thus airplane drag) decreased with gain in altitude between the two points. Highest airplane speed occurred at point B. Maximum speed attainable decreased from B to C because engine power available fell off very quickly, and more than countered further decrease in air density with altitude for drag reduction.

In a fighter with an engine having a single-stage two-speed supercharger speed capability versus altitude typically looked as shown in Graph 7.

Examples were Merlin P-40s F and L, Brewster F2A-, and some early Grumman Wildcat airplanes. From A to B maximum speed increased for the reasons mentioned earlier. At B power and thus speed started to fall off until at C the supercharger was shifted into higher blower speed. This action temporarily, from C to D, boosted power available and thus speed. At point D even the higher blower speed couldn't further increase engine performance, and speed fell off rapidly to point E at the higher altitudes.

With a fighter using a two-stage two-speed mechanical supercharger, such as the P-61. most F4F-s, and F4U- and F6F- airplanes, the typical speed-altitude curve is shown in Graph 8. In this case there are three modes of operation as described in the legend of that figure. From A to C the operation was just like the single-stage single-speed supercharger case, and speed variation with altitude was the same. As power began to fade from B to C, at C the second-stage blower was clutched in and power increased up to D, where again it started to fade until at E the speed of that second blower was increased. At F the limit of power was reached using both blowers, and power and speed capability fell off rapidly to G.

One fighter type used a somewhat different two-stage mechanical supercharger. The P-63 aircraft incorporated an infinitely variable speed second-stage blower as earlier noted. This feature smoothed out the variation in power available as altitude increased so the maximum speeds available also varied smoothly as shown in Graph 9.

A fighter with a turbosupercharger, like P-38, P-47, and late P-61, provided constant powerplant output up to high altitude. If propeller performance held up well the maximum speed capability of the plane just kept increasing as air density and airplane drag decreased with altitude. The result was a smooth speed versus altitude curve as shown in Graph 10. The quick fall-off of speed shown at high altitude in this figure happened because rotational speed of the second-stage blower could not be further increased. It was at a structural limit.

GRAPH 6

SPEED-ALTITUDE PERFORMANCE WITH VARIOUS SUPERCHARGERS

SINGLE STAGE SINGLE SPEED

GRAPH 7

SINGLE STAGE TWO SPEED

A - C   BLOWER AT LOW SPEED
C - E   BLOWER AT HIGH SPEED

GRAPH 8

TWO STAGE TWO SPEED

A - C   FIRST STAGE BLOWER ONLY OPERATING
C - E   BOTH BLOWER STAGES OPERATING; SECOND STAGE AT LOW SPEED
E - G   BOTH BLOWER STAGES OPERATING; SECOND STAGE AT HIGH SPEED

GRAPH 9

TWO STAGE

GRAPH 10

TURBO-SUPERCHARGER

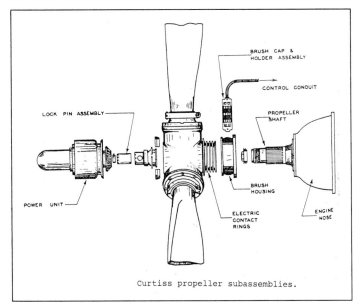

Fig. 150

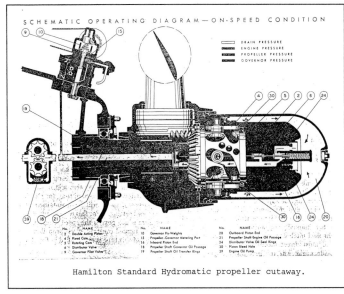

Fig. 152

PROPELLERS

US World War II fighter aircraft propellers were produced by three manufacturers: Hamilton Standard Division of United Aircraft Corporation, an old-line producer, Curtiss Propeller Division of Curtiss-Wright Corporation, also in the business awhile, and a relative newcomer, Aeroproducts Division of General Motors Corporation. Together these outfits made the propellers for all the fighters.

Hamilton and Aeroproducts types were hydraulic; Curtiss produced an electrically operated propeller. Props were either three or four-bladed, made in diameters of about ten to thirteen feet, and turned at RPM values producing tip rotational speeds (at zero forward speed) of 800 to 950 feet per second. Forward speed added to this tip speed, so the fighter didn't have to fly forward very fast for

propeller tip speeds to approach the speed of sound, which at sea level in standard atmosphere is 1116 feet per second. Blade tips were solid or near solid metal, and tip sections were very thin, so although propeller efficiency reduced from tip losses during high airplane speeds, compressibility effects were minimal. But a great deal of noise could be generated by blade tips along with a loss in efficiency when operating at or near sonic speeds. Propeller blades were made either of solid aluminum alloy or hollow steel; propeller hubs were steel. Blades varied considerably in width; many of the early fighters used rather narrow "toothpick" blades, but later in the war blade widths increased in newer designs. These were often called "paddle" blades. Blade widths were defined in terms of "activity factor" (AF). A narrow blade might have a low value of

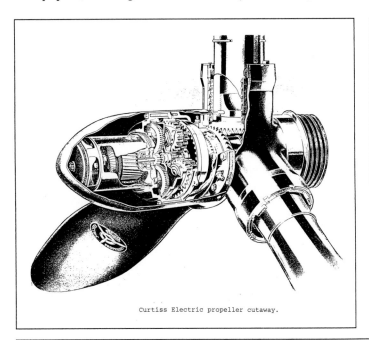

Curtiss Electric propeller cutaway.

(Left) Fig. 151

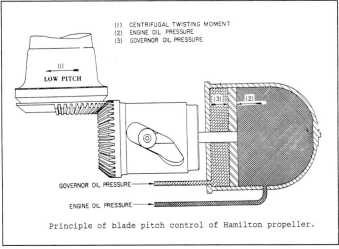

Principle of blade pitch control of Hamilton propeller.

Fig. 153

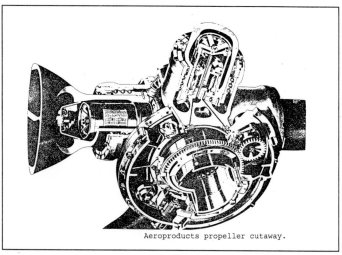

Aeroproducts propeller cutaway.

Fig. 154

80 to 100 AF; a paddle blade might be 130 to 150 AF or so. Activity factor described the ability of the blade to absorb power at zero forward speed. So as engine powers increased and propellers were limited in diameter by aircraft dimensional limits, the number of blades and their width tended to increase. This was called an increase in "solidity" of the propeller (more of the prop disc was solid). This increase caused flight stability problems in later fighter versions, because propellers on the nose were always a very destabilizing component of the aircraft, larger higher solidity ones more so than smaller.

All propellers were the constant speed controllable pitch variety, and on US single engine fighters all rotated right hand looking from the cockpit. Constant speed types had been developed in the 1930s, and were a huge advance over earlier fixed pitch or two-position models since they provided high propeller efficiency at various flight speeds and altitudes.

The Curtiss Electric propeller (Figures 150 and 151) changed blade angle (pitch) using an electric motor with friction brake on

the front of the hub, along with several stages of planetary reduction gearing to reduce motor speed . Reduction gearing output drove a slow-turning bevel gear within the hub. This gear meshed with a bevel gear on the inner end of each blade. Pitch change rate was two to three degrees per second. Electrical power from the aircraft DC system was fed through brushes mounted on the engine nose which rode on slip rings around the back end of the hub, and run out to the rotating electric motor and brake.

The Hamilton Hydromatic propeller (Figures 152 and 153) used engine oil pressure and governor-boosted oil pressure to act on a piston within a closed dome forward of the prop hub. The oil passed through hydraulic "transfer rings" to get to the rotating hub. The piston force was transmitted to a cam and follower system transferring axial into rotary motion and to a bevel drive gear which meshed with bevel gears on the blade butts like the Curtiss type. These blade bevel gears drove blade angle change as required. As with the Curtiss, blades were socketed within bearings inside the hub barrels.

The Aeroproducts design (Figures 154 and 155) consisted of a self-contained "regulator" unit mounted on the engine nose behind the hub, a hydraulic pump driven by propeller rotation, a governor controlling oil flow, and blade pitch change mechanisms socketed inside each blade root end. These involved hydraulic pistons and splined drives attached to blade gears. The design was self-contained, using a separate propeller oil system rather than engine oil as on the Hamilton propeller.

Propeller blades of all manufacturers had a natural tendency to go to flat (low) pitch. If this happened it meant an overspeed , or runaway propeller—one of the much-feared results of propeller failure. An overspeeding propeller would cause high drag, and the aircraft would quickly lose altitude, usually with disasterous results. In addition high overspeeding increased blade centrifugal force loads on the hub and could result in blade loss. The reason propellers had this flat pitch tendency was something called centrifugal twisting moment (part of centrifugal force) on a whirling blade. This CTM tended to make the blade twist in its socket towards low pitch, or flat blade angle, so the pitch change mechanisms of propellers had to hold against this tendency and a resulting run-away propeller. In the Curtiss prop the blades were held, in the absence of a signal to change pitch, by the irreversibility of the high ratio (about 7500 to one) planetary reduction gearing driven by the electric motor and by the friction brake on the motor. In the hydraulic propellers pressure locked and held the blades in fixed pitch when there was no signal for angle change.

On a single engined fighter there was no need for propeller feathering (blade pitch changed all the way up to an edge-on position). On the twin-engined P-38 and P-61 airplanes a feathering feature was required to stop propeller windmilling and reduce drag if one engine was shut down. No propeller reversing was used on the US production fighters.

Propeller governors maintained speed of the propeller and engine system at values set by the pilots cockpit control. The governor compared pilots desired RPM set by this control with actual prop RPM at that instant. If they were the same the governor did nothing. If they were different than desired the governor sent a sig

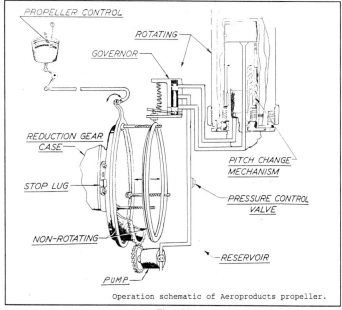

PROPELLER CONTROL

ROTATING

GOVERNOR

REDUCTION GEAR CASE

STOP LUG

NON-ROTATING

PUMP

PITCH CHANGE MECHANISM

PRESSURE CONTROL VALVE

RESERVOIR

Operation schematic of Aeroproducts propeller.

Fig. 155

nal to the propeller to make it change blade angle (higher angle if prop speed was too high and lower if speed was too low) and thus wash out the difference in desired and actual speeds to zero. If the propeller speed was momentarily too high, increasing blade angle would quickly slow down the engine-propeller system by increasing propeller torque (twisting requirement) load on the engine. The electric propeller governor sent an electrical signal to the motor on the front of the hub; the hydraulic propeller governors sent a pressure signal to their pitch change mechanisms via hydraulic lines.

There were large numbers of complaints about propellers by pilots during the war, probably all justified. Electric props froze up at extreme altitudes; hydraulic props sometimes leaked oil all over windshields—they tended to be one of the problem areas on the fighters, and from the maintenance and reliability standpoint at least, the services were not unhappy with the post-war changes to jet aircraft.

Propeller blades of World War II fighters were designed aerodynamically as a compromise between take-off and high speed performance. As might be expected, the blade design characteristics to optimize takeoff thrust capability were different than those for getting best high speed performance. And the airplane climb condition also had to be considered. Increasing blade width (chord) resulting in higher activity factor could also improve takeoff and climb performance, but a penalty in high speed efficiency might result. Higher activity factor propellers on later P-47 aircraft made a very significant improvement in the rather poor climbing performance of early P-47 versions.

For the P-51D Mustang the propeller takeoff performance, as an example, was 3.3 pounds of thrust per horsepower, or a total of about 4900 pounds of thrust, at the very start of a take-off run (zero speed), reducing to 2.8 pounds thrust per horsepower , or 4200 pounds of thrust, at 80 mph in the take-off run. The propeller effi-

ciency at high speed would be something like 70 to 80 percent. Complex analysis of a blade design, called "strip analysis", could be used to predict flight efficiency at various conditions with good accuracy, given good blade sections airfoil data. This result had to be corrected by an installation factor which would account for the effect on efficiency of the body behind the propeller.

Of the eleven production fighters those five using inline V-12 engines (Allisons and Merlins) had propeller "spinners", pointed-nose aluminum fairings, covering propeller hubs and rotating with them. Spinners brought nose lines of these aircraft neatly to a near-point at the fuselage forward extremity. Spinner support bulkheads bolted to the propeller hub, and holes in the spinner skin were provided so blades could clear and rotate for pitch change.

The other six production aircraft with radial engines did not have a full spinner with exception of some early Brewster F2A-aircraft. Propeller hubs were generally bare, and the only concession to streamlining was the bullet-fairing over the power units of some Curtiss propellers, and the dome ahead on the Hamilton models. Aeroproducts propellers had nothing ahead of the hub front face. If there was no spinner on a fighter it was easy to recognize from a distance or in a photo which of the prop types was installed on the fighter plane. Another way was to check the decals on the blades if they were visible.

Another part of some propeller installations deserves mention—blade cuffs. These were aerodynamic fairings placed over the inboard sections of propeller blades adjacent to the hub or spinner surface in the area where the blade had to have a circular cross-section to fit into a barrel of the hub. Cuffs were used to streamline these inboard sections and provide air pumping action to help cool radial engines. An example was the Grumman Wildcat. Some cuffs were molded on, others clamped on a blade cuff support flange.

DRAG

Aerodynamic drag on aircraft is the force opposing thrust in straight steady flight as the result of air resisting passage of the plane. The creation of sleek streamlined yet practical forms designed to pass through the air with a minimum of resistance (drag) had been a subject of study for many years, and the advent of World War II intensified this work.

Drag of an airplane is broken into two parts, zero-lift drag and drag due to lift. The two parts are called, respectively, profile drag and induced drag.

First consider profile drag. It is broken into two more parts, pressure drag and skin friction drag. Parts of an airplane all have some of each. Consider some extreme examples to illustrate the two types. Hold up a thin flat plate like a sign against some wind, or stick the flat of your hand out the window of a fast-moving car and against the wind. With the thin flat plate or your palm, all the drag you feel, or practically all, is pressure drag. If the plate is very thin there is no friction drag. Now turn that thin flat plate edge-on to the wind, or stick your hand from the car with fingers pointed straight into the wind. Here all drag, or practically all, is friction drag. There is, of course, much less drag in the second case, but we

are talking about the origin of the force, not the amount. So a body which is very short (in the direction of the airflow), but wide and high, that is, blunt, has mostly pressure drag in an airstream, whereas a very long slender body has mostly friction drag. Shapes of parts of fighter airplanes, like fuselages, wings, and tails are more slender than short blunt shapes so they tend to produce more friction drag than pressure drag going through the air, though there is some of each. See Figure 156.

Pressure drag is characterized by burbling or eddy-making instead of smooth flow behind the body. Frictional drag has to do with the "boundary layer" of air right next to the body surface. This adjacent air layer is slowed down by the body. Stickiness (viscosity) of the air makes particles at or near the body surface slow down or even stop right at the surface. This slow-down causes the friction drag. If this slow boundary layer right next to the surface is relatively smooth-flowing it is called "laminar" (flow in nice smooth adjacent layers). But often the layer thickens and becomes turbulent, increasing the friction drag. A factor called Reynolds Number has a lot to do with whether the boundary layer is laminar or turbulent and thus the amount of drag involved. This factor takes into

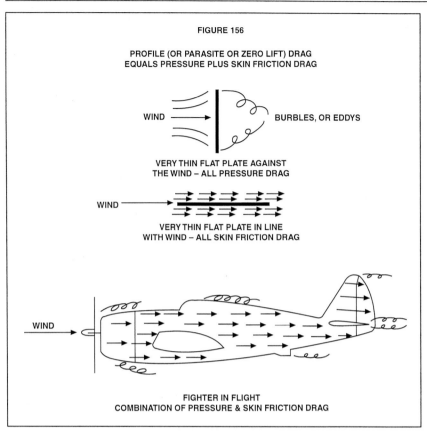

FIGURE 156

PROFILE (OR PARASITE OR ZERO LIFT) DRAG
EQUALS PRESSURE PLUS SKIN FRICTION DRAG

WIND → ← BURBLES, OR EDDYS

VERY THIN FLAT PLATE AGAINST
THE WIND – ALL PRESSURE DRAG

WIND →

VERY THIN FLAT PLATE IN LINE
WITH WIND – ALL SKIN FRICTION DRAG

WIND →

FIGHTER IN FLIGHT
COMBINATION OF PRESSURE & SKIN FRICTION DRAG

account both the viscosity and the density of the air along with the size and speed of the body in the airstream. RN increases with density, size and speed. A typical RN for a World War II fighter is about five to eight million, and drag goes down as the RN gets higher. Graph 11 shows this variation.

The total profile (zero-lift) drag of an aircraft is the sum of the drag of its parts (wing, tail, fuselage, canopy, antennas, etc.) plus the interference drag between the various parts, plus drag of any little lumps and bumps not already counted, plus drag from air leakage through any cracks and holes. So drag is not easy to estimate, and is best obtained by testing—wind tunnel model or full-scale.

The profile drag discussed above (pressure plus friction) is sometimes called "parasite drag". It is useless and thus "parasitic" from a pure aerodynamic standpoint, though the parts involved may have a very practical function. A flying wing design attempts to minimize parasite drag.

At the higher flight speeds a correction has to be made on profile or parasite drag because of compressibility of the air. (See the later section on compressibility). Up to speeds about 50% of the speed of sound in air (Mach 0.50) the correction is mini-

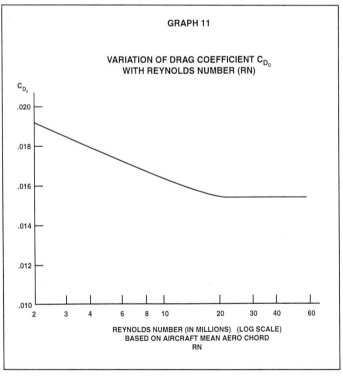

GRAPH 11

VARIATION OF DRAG COEFFICIENT C_{D_0}
WITH REYNOLDS NUMBER (RN)

C_{D_0}

REYNOLDS NUMBER (IN MILLIONS)   (LOG SCALE)
BASED ON AIRCRAFT MEAN AERO CHORD
RN

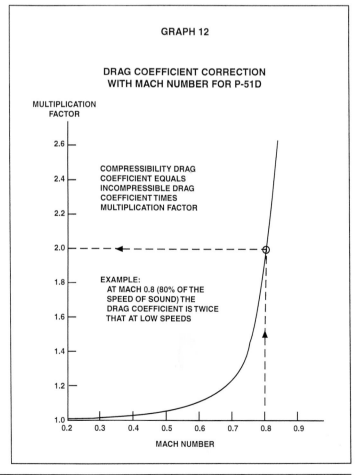

GRAPH 12

DRAG COEFFICIENT CORRECTION
WITH MACH NUMBER FOR P-51D

MULTIPLICATION
FACTOR

COMPRESSIBILITY DRAG
COEFFICIENT EQUALS
INCOMPRESSIBLE DRAG
COEFFICIENT TIMES
MULTIPLICATION FACTOR

EXAMPLE:
AT MACH 0.8 (80% OF THE
SPEED OF SOUND) THE
DRAG COEFFICIENT IS TWICE
THAT AT LOW SPEEDS

MACH NUMBER

TABLE 6
FIGHTER DRAG DATA (CLEAN IN-SERVICE AIRCRAFT)

FIGHTER	Cdo*	S WING AREA,SQ.FT.	f=C$_{Do}$S SQ.FT.	HP	HP/f	REFERENCE
P-51D	.0176	233.19	4.10	1500	366	1
P-39	.0217	213.2	4.63	1150	248	2
P-63	.0203	248.0	5.03	1500	298	3
P-40	.0242	236.0	5.71	1150	201	4
F2A-	.0300	208.9	6.27	1200	191	5
P-47	.0213	300.0	6.39	2000	313	6
F4F-	.0253	260.0	6.58	1200	182	3
F4U-	.0267	314.0	8.38	2000	239	3
P-38	.0270	327.5	8.84	2300	260	7
F6F-	.0272	334.0	9.08	2000	220	3
P-61	.0244	664.0	15.94	4000	251	7

REFERENCES: 1. North American Report NA-46-130, 2/6/46.
2. NACA Report ACR5D04
3. NACA Report L5A30,2/45.
4. NACA Report ACR,10/40.
5. NACA Report ACR 3I30, 3/43.
6. Air Corps Technical Report 4677,9/11/41.
7. Boeing in house drag data.

*Cdo is the zero lift drag coefficient at moderate speeds.

mal. Above that speed the correction gets large for World War II fighter designs. At 75% of the speed of sound (Mach 0.75) the correction required is very large, the drag value being about 1.4 times the low speed (incompressible) drag value. Graph 12 shows this correction for a P-51D Mustang fighter. The increment varied for the different fighters depending on relative cleanliness. If the plane was very clean and the airfoil one of the then-new laminar flow sections, the profile drag rise due to compressibility (and therefore the correction factor at a given Mach number) would be less. If the fighter had a sharply changing contour somewhere, or if the wing airfoil sections were of an older type, the local Mach number at the critical point, and the resulting drag correction factor, could be very high. The correction always increased drag.

Profile drag (in pounds) is obtained by multiplying the equivalent flat plate area of the fighter (fe, in square feet) by the dynamic pressure (q, in pounds per square foot). The first factor, fe, equals the profile (zero lift) drag coefficient times the airplane wing area, Sw. Values of fe and Sw for the various US fighters are shown in Table 6. The fe values range from just over four square feet for the P-51 fighter to almost sixteen square feet for the big twin engined P-61. The second factor, q, or dynamic pressure, is the force on each square foot of fighter flat plate area from the air moving relative to the speeding plane. It is reasonable that the dynamic pressure q increases with thicker or denser air so it tends to be greater at sea level and decreases at progressively higher altitudes. Even more important, q increases with airplane speed, in fact so quickly that it increases with the speed squared (speed times speed; if the speed

doubles, q is four times as great). So the value of q , and thus the profile drag of a given fighter design varies with altitude and speed of the plane. An aircraft flying high and slow therefore suffers the least profile drag and one flying low and fast incurs the most.

Now consider induced drag. It is the result of, and a penalty from, the wing producing lift to support the plane in the air. It must be added to profile drag to obtain the total drag of the fighter plane as it speeds along. Induced drag varies primarily with three factors. It increases greatly with the amount of lift generated by the wing, and decreases with longer wing spans and with greater dynamic pressures, q. So where increased fighter wing lift , compared to normal level flight, is required, as in climbing, turning, or pulling out of a dive (demonstrated in a later section), the induced drag is considerably greater than normal. This part of total drag is minimized by designing the plane with a long wing span (the P-38 had particularly good induced drag characteristics), and by flying at a high dynamic pressure, q, that is low down and fast. Figure 157 illustrates cases of low and high induced drag.

It is seen that increased dynamic pressure has a large and an opposite effect on the profile and induced portions of total drag by increasing the former and reducing the latter. Similarly a lower q will reduce profile and increase induced drag. In low speed flight therefore induced drag tends to predominate whereas at high speed most all drag is of the profile variety. There is a speed in between where the two types of drag are just equal, and this is where the best/highest ratio of lift to drag of the plane is obtained, a flight condition where peak aerodynamic efficiency occurs. This speed

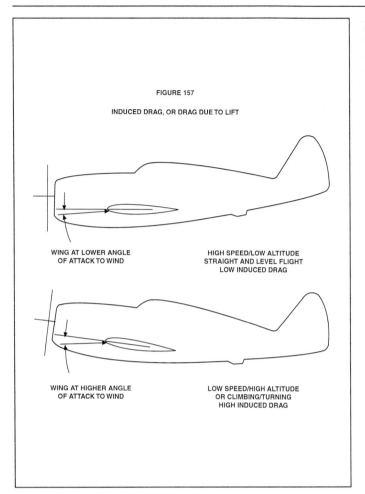

FIGURE 157

INDUCED DRAG, OR DRAG DUE TO LIFT

WING AT LOWER ANGLE
OF ATTACK TO WIND

HIGH SPEED/LOW ALTITUDE
STRAIGHT AND LEVEL FLIGHT
LOW INDUCED DRAG

WING AT HIGHER ANGLE
OF ATTACK TO WIND

LOW SPEED/HIGH ALTITUDE
OR CLIMBING/TURNING
HIGH INDUCED DRAG

for maximum lift/drag ratio is close to that for best fighter range; typically this speed is quite modest, a low cruise speed. Best lift/drag ratio of US fighters in World War II was approximately twelve to fourteen to one, which among other things meant these fighters could glide over a distance of twelve to fourteen miles for every mile of altitude lost after engine failure.

This discussion has presented some factors involved in estimating airplane drag, and has shown drag comparisons of the World War II fighters. It was necessary to estimate drag so that sufficient thrust capability to counter drag and achieve the desired speed could be installed in the airplane. Drag estimates could be made by initial analysis based on experience as a first shot, but subsequent testing work was then and is now required to make good estimates. Then confirmation or correction was made based on actual flight tests. One good way to obtain drag values in flight test was to use an engine incorporating a thrustmeter in its nose section based on the principle of a hydraulically balanced piston. Propeller thrust could be read directly in terms of hydraulic pressure, and in steady level flight drag is equal to propeller thrust plus any additional thrust from jet exhaust stacks.

LIFT (IN STEADY LEVEL FLIGHT)

Lift in steady level flight is the force opposing aircraft weight; it holds the plane up. Lift is generated by airflow over the wing surfaces, this airflow being generated by the speed of the plane. As shown in Figure 158 the direction of lift is at a right angle, or 90 degrees, to the direction of the incoming airstream, and thus can directly oppose and counteract the weight of the aircraft. The amount of wing lift generated depends on three factors. The lift coefficient, shown in Graph 13 for a typical fighter of the time, depends on the angle of the wing to the airstream and whether wing flaps are retracted or down. The second factor is the same dynamic pressure, q, noted in the previous section. Recall that the value of dynamic pressure depends on air density (airplane altitude) and speed, in fact the squared value of speed (speed times itself). If speed doubles the dynamic pressure is four times as great. The third factor is the wing area of the fighter; the greater the area the more wing lift, in direct proportion. Graph 13 shows that the lift coefficient increases directly as the wing angle to the airstream (angle of attack) increases, at least up to a point where the angle gets so large that airflow breaks down and burbles behind the wing. Typically this angle is about fifteen degrees. The wing then stalls and loses lift starting at a lift coefficient of about 1.2, corresponding to 15 degrees nose up.

The figure also shows how the relationship of lift coefficient and angle of attack changes if wing flaps are lowered full down. Things vary some depending on just what type of flaps are used on the particular fighter, but the picture shown is representative. For any given angle flaps down gives a significantly larger lift coefficient, and similarly for any given coefficient the angle of attack required is less. At fifteen degrees lift coefficient with flaps dropped could increase from approximately 1.2 to 1.8, a gain of 50 percent.

So lift equals lift coefficient times dynamic pressure q times wing area. A fighter flying at a two degree angle of attack (a 0.25 lift coefficient) at 300 mph at sea level and having 300 square feet of wing area (a P-47, say) would be at a q of about 205 pounds per square foot and have a wing lift of 15375 pounds (0.25x205x300). If that fighter was to be able to land at sea level with flaps full down at that weight and a speed of 110 mph (in this case the dynamic pressure q is 31 pounds per square foot) the wing would have to develop a lift coefficient of 1.65 (15375/31x300). Graph 13 shows that the wing could develop this lift coefficient at an angle of attack just under thirteen degrees, leaving a margin from this point to the stall of about two degrees.

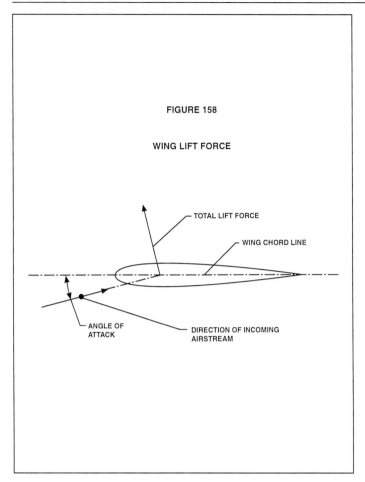

FIGURE 158

WING LIFT FORCE

TOTAL LIFT FORCE

WING CHORD LINE

ANGLE OF ATTACK

DIRECTION OF INCOMING AIRSTREAM

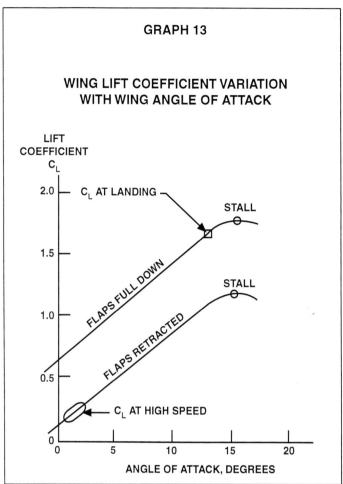

GRAPH 13

WING LIFT COEFFICIENT VARIATION WITH WING ANGLE OF ATTACK

LIFT COEFFICIENT C_L

2.0 — C_L AT LANDING

STALL

FLAPS FULL DOWN

1.5

STALL

FLAPS RETRACTED

1.0

0.5

C_L AT HIGH SPEED

0

0   5   10   15   20

ANGLE OF ATTACK, DEGREES

LIFT (IN MANEUVERING FLIGHT)

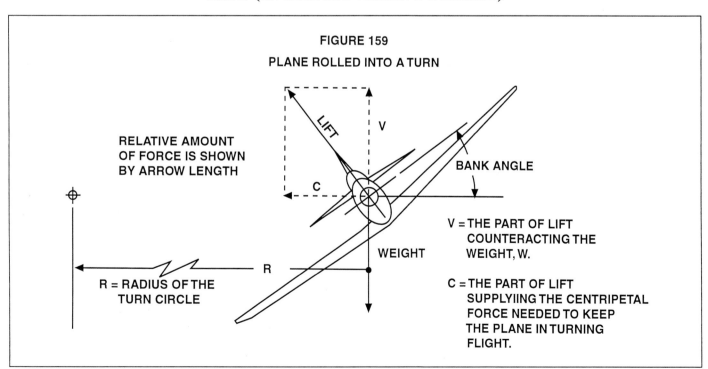

FIGURE 159

PLANE ROLLED INTO A TURN

LIFT

V

C

BANK ANGLE

RELATIVE AMOUNT OF FORCE IS SHOWN BY ARROW LENGTH

WEIGHT

V = THE PART OF LIFT COUNTERACTING THE WEIGHT, W.

R

R = RADIUS OF THE TURN CIRCLE

C = THE PART OF LIFT SUPPLYIING THE CENTRIPETAL FORCE NEEDED TO KEEP THE PLANE IN TURNING FLIGHT.

A fighter plane spends part of its time maneuvering as opposed to one g straight and level flight. During maneuvers additional lift must be generated by the wing. Maneuvering means making the aircraft depart from straight into curving flight such as turning, or pulling out from a dive. Rolling is another matter because a curved flight path is not involved, and it will be discussed in another section. However an airplane must start a roll to get into a turn.

The case of turning flight will be considered. Figure 159 shows a sketch of an aircraft rolled into a turn. It is turning in a circle with the radius R. The lift force of the wing has to supply two components as shown. First, the vertical part of lift has to oppose and just equal the weight of the plane, or it will fall. From the diagram it is seen lift must be greater than weight of the aircraft. The lift arrow, L, is longer than the weight arrow, W, to make things all balance properly. The other part of the lift force is pointed inwards towards the center of the turning circle. This force, C, constitutes the "centripetal" (not centrifugal) force needed to keep the fighter in turning flight. Since lift force is always perpendicular (at right angles or 90 degrees) to the wing, one can see why the plane must be rolled over to put this lift force L at an angle to get into the turn. The centripetal force, C, keeps pulling the plane around. If it wasn't there the fighter would go straight again. This would be accomplished by rolling out of the turn and leveling the wings, making the lift go straight up again, and the centripetal force go to zero. Lets understand the difference between centripetal force and centrifugal force. Contrary to what one might think, there is no centrifugal force on the fighter plane. Consider a boy whirling a stone around tied to the end of a string. The string force on the stone keeping it going around in a circle is the centripetal force. There must be an opposing force in this case. The string force trying to pull the boys hand outward is the opposing centrifugal force. In the turning fighter case the horizontal part of the lift force keeping it in the turn is the centripetal force, as stated. There is no boy, no string, and no centrifugal force on the plane. The plane is always accelerating inward towards the center of the circle, and an acceleration always goes with a net force, in this case, centripetal force. It can be seen from the diagram the tighter the turn desired, the greater the bank angle required of the fighter. This means that while the same lift part is still needed to counter the weight, the horizontal centripetal force must increase to tighten the turn, and thus the wing lift force (L=C qS) must also increase. Looking again at the parts making up wing lift, it can be seen the wing area normally can't increase (there is an exception to this as we will see later), the q (speed and altitude) won't change much right off, so the lift coefficient must increase. Without flaps down the lift coefficient can't go too high, or the wing will stall out (the so-called high speed stall), the demands for lift exceeding what it can supply, and then perhaps the plane will go into a spin.

There was a way to obtain more lift to make sharp turns, and for one the Lockheed P-38 used it. The previous discussion about lift coefficient presumed no use of wing flaps. If flaps were partially deflected a higher lift coefficient could be obtained at the same wing angle of attack (see Graph 13), and thats what the P-38 would do. A fast-acting system lowered the flaps to an eight degree maneuver setting. Further, the Fowler type of flap employed slid back on tracks to increase wing area some, and that also increased lift force, as seen from the lift force expression noted earlier. These factors were important in accounting for the good turning performance of the big P-38 fighter. Other types could and did lower their flaps in some turns.

The centripetal force required in turning depends on four factors: airplane weight, airplane speed squared (speed times speed), the number of gs pulled in the turn, and the radius of the turn. This force is directly proportional to weight and the square of the speed (that is it increases with increases in these factors), and is inversely proportional to the gs pulled and the turn radius (that is the force increases with decreases in the latter two factors). In other words centripetal force equals airplane weight times airplane true speed (TAS) squared all divided by the number of gs times the turn radius. It seems quite reasonable that the heavier the fighter and the greater its speed the more centripetal force would be required to hold it in a turn, though it may seem less logical that the force required increases if less gs are pulled and the radius of turn is not as tight.

In maneuvering flight the "g-loading" on plane and pilot in a turn must be considered, since the g effect on the pilot is a factor limiting tightness of the turn, and particularly since a g-suit was not always part of the World War II fighter pilot's equipment. It was often a case of tense your muscles and try to keep blood from leaving your head with consequent graying or blacking out if unsuccessful.

The fighters were structurally good for limit loads of seven to eight g positive (meaning ultimate breaking load capability of 1.5 times that, or ten and one half to twelve g), and therefore were not normally the deciding factor. Late model P-51s typically had somewhat less structural capacity because of overloaded airframes.

On the other hand a "standard" pilot's limits were about 70 seconds at four g, 20 seconds at five g, and eight seconds at seven g before blackout. Some pilots had more tolerance than others. There were probably very few turns over five to six g.

We should get a feel for g's. Everyone has experienced forces due to g's, so-called inertia forces, riding in autos and other vehicles, and in rides at a carnival. A roller coaster provides an opportunity to experience g forces. The g stands for the acceleration of a body due to gravity, a specific case of acceleration used as a measuring unit and pegged at 32.2 feet per second per second. Straight and level flight takes place at one g vertical acceleration where airplane weight is just equalled by lift as we have seen. It has become convenient for pilots and engineers to measure any acceleration, like that in turning flight, in terms of these standard acceleration units. In a turn the forces on airplane and pilot are directly proportional to the number of gs. In certain kinds of pushover maneuvers the forces due to vertical g can momentarily go to zero such that the pilot would be "weightless". A dive pullout would also be a common maneuver for a fighter aircraft. While in a steep zero-lift dive it will be in one g normal flight. The flight path of the plane is essentially in a straight line—downward. But it must get into a curved flight path to recover from the dive, or sooner or later it will hit the ground. We will look at the case where the plane is just at the bottom of the pullout, and is flying level (though now well above

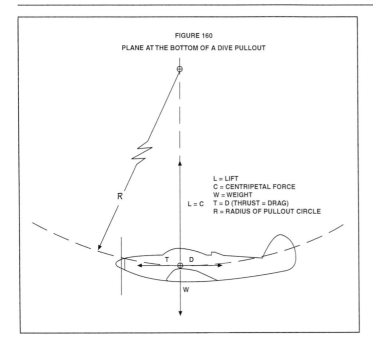

FIGURE 160
PLANE AT THE BOTTOM OF A DIVE PULLOUT

L = LIFT
C = CENTRIPETAL FORCE
W = WEIGHT
L = C   T = D (THRUST = DRAG)
R = RADIUS OF PULLOUT CIRCLE

one g). To keep things simple assume that the plane's thrust now just equals its drag. Figure 160 shows the diagram of the forces acting in the aircraft at this point. The vertical forces are the weight W pulling down as usual, and the wing lift, L, which is the centripetal force keeping the plane in the curved flight path required to pull out of its dive. Because the pilot is pulling more than one g the wing lift (centripetal force) L is greater than the aircraft weight W as shown on the diagram. If it was a three g pullout at this point L would be three times W.

The required centripetal force is the lift of the wing; the two are equal in this case. If this fact is expressed properly in terms of algebra it will result that the required radius (and thus the altitude at which the pullout must be started) can be calculated. The distance turns out to be twice the fighter wing loading (weight over wing area) divided by the wing lift coefficient, the air density, and the number of gs pulled. Assume a P-47 Thunderbolt with a weight of 15000 pounds and a wing area of 300 square feet, a resulting wing loading of 15000/300 or 50 pounds per square foot, and that the highest available wing lift coefficient without getting to a high speed stall is 1.0 and the pilot can stand a five g pullout. Also assume the pilot is daring and will pull out just at sea level. Then he better start at an altitude of:

$$2 \times 50/1.0 \times .002378 \times 5 = 8410 \text{ feet.}$$
(The .002378 is sea level air density)

This figure is optimistic since a lower air density factor corresponding to an average altitude of about 4200 feet should have been used, but it does show the pilot had better have started to pull out of his dive well above an altitude of 8000 feet!

These simple examples of maneuvers requiring curved flight, turning and dive pullout, give a feel for the way the wing has to generate lift much greater than required for straight and level flight. These maneuvers in various curved flight paths with g loading on plane and pilot can govern wing sizing for the aircraft in initial design. This is why the wing loading, W/S, is so important. Since the US fighters of World War II were designed either before the war or in its early stages the choice of wing size was usually based on gross weight of early versions, unless the designers were blessed with great foresight. If weight increased, and it always did, the wing loading increased and reduced the maneuverability of the plane. US fighters tended to have higher wing loadings than early Japanese fighters, and higher than British fighters too. This is why these planes could often out-turn US machines.

LINEAR ACCELERATION

In the sections on thrust and drag expressions for these forces were developed. It was stated that under conditions of steady level flight thrust and drag forces were equal. The words "steady flight" meant the airplane was in "dynamic equilibrium" horizontally. It was in unaccelerated flight; speed was neither increasing or decreasing, but the plane was just moving along steadily. So for that case thrust equaled drag, or T = D.

The capability to accelerate quickly was an asset for a fighter, so factors influencing accelerative capability will be examined.

Acceleration was mentioned in the section on lift in conjunction with curved flight like turns or dive pull-outs. In those cases acceleration was radial, that is, towards the center of the turn or the pull-out circle, and was associated with centripetal force. Radial acceleration was a somewhat difficult concept to grasp, but the concept of linear acceleration is more easily visualized. It is like a race car accelerating up to speed in a straight line in a drag race.

Consider a fighter cruising at 250 mph at sea level using moderate engine power. Suddenly, due to an emergency, perhaps the appearance of an enemy plane, the fighter pilot wants to accelerate quickly in a straight line and evade by slamming throttle forward to full power and resetting the propeller control to maximum RPM. We'll check initial acceleration in a typical example.

Acceleration is produced by the excess of propeller thrust from the higher power over the drag force on the fighter. The net accelerating force is thrust minus drag. See Figure 161. The acceleration thus provided is the net force divided by the "mass" (weight/g) of

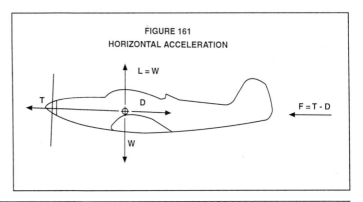

FIGURE 161
HORIZONTAL ACCELERATION

L = W

T   D

F = T - D

W

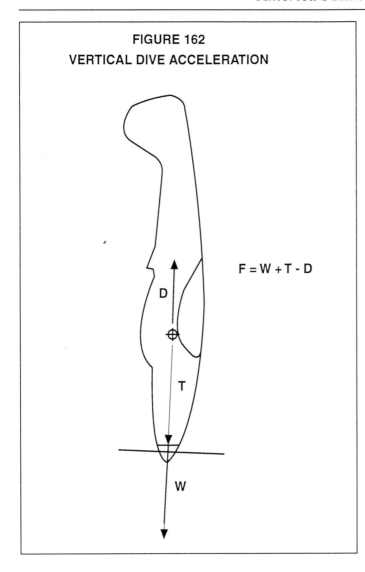

FIGURE 162
VERTICAL DIVE ACCELERATION

$$F = W + T - D$$

in 1000 feet in about 2.7 seconds. We could go on and calculate speed values after the next one thousand feet and so on right up to the maximum level flight speed of the aircraft, but the idea has been shown. The acceleration would be proportional to the net force in each case.

It is of interest to tip the plane over into a vertical zero-lift dive and see what happens by calculating it's acceleration in the same manner. Making the dive vertical instead of shallow keeps the forces acting on the plane simple. They are shown in Figure 162. Here the net force equals thrust plus weight minus drag. Substituting in the proper P-38L values as before we can calculate the acceleration as 3840 pounds thrust plus 16880 pounds weight minus 1398 pounds of drag (a net force of 19332 pounds) divided by a mass of 524.2 slugs, or 36.9 feet per second per second downward, a much greater value than the horizontal case of course. Calculation thus shows a significant speed increase in the first one thousand feet of the dive with the aircraft going from 250 to 311 mph, a gain of 61 mph. At an average speed of 280.5 mph (411.5 feet per second) for the thousand feet the elapsed time is 2.43 seconds (1000/411.5). Again we could go on and by successive steps of substituting increasing speeds back in the analysis, one thousand feet by one thousand feet, obtain acceleration and new speed values for a long dive. It would not be long, however, before the P-38 got itself into compressibility trouble (especially if dive flaps were not extended) as dive speed rapidly increased. Compressibility is described in the next section.

For an intermediate angle of dive, say 45 degrees, we show the diagram of forces acting in Figure 163. The procedure is the same. The net force acting along the direction of flight, 45 degrees below the horizontal, is calculated and that force is equal to the mass, W/g, times the acceleration. The net force F acting along the straight line flight path is: Thrust plus 0.707 x weight minus drag. (The .707 comes from the 45 degree angle). In this case only part of the weight (70.7% of it) is helping make a net force along the flight path. The other part of the weight is balancing out, or countering, the lift force L. The resulting acceleration and speed increase in one thousand feet will be somewhere in between the results of the two cases above.

the plane. So acceleration equals thrust minus drag divided by weight/32.2. Using expressions developed earlier for thrust and drag forces it is possible to calculate initial acceleration. Assume a 16880 pound gross weight P-38L Lightning fighter at sea level going suddenly from a 250 mph moderate cruise condition to full COMBAT power setting of the engines. The calculated initial acceleration would equal 3840 pounds of thrust minus 1676 pounds of drag (a net force of 2164 pounds) divided by a mass of 524.2 (16880/32.2) slugs, or 4.13 feet per second per second, corresponding to 0.128g (4.13/32.2) in the fore-aft direction. A slug is a unit of mass and is tied in with the word "sluggish". The more slugs the more sluggish the plane. The pilot would feel the acceleration by being pressed back in his seat a bit, the way we have all felt some acceleration in the seat of an airliner on its takeoff run. The acceleration above is the initial value. As time elapses the speed will increase from the 250 mph due to acceleration, and this action will in turn change the acceleration from moment to moment. If we estimate the new speed after a distance of one thousand feet is covered (assuming a constant acceleration over that distance for a simple approximation) we would find the speed to be 258 mph. The P-38 gained eight mph

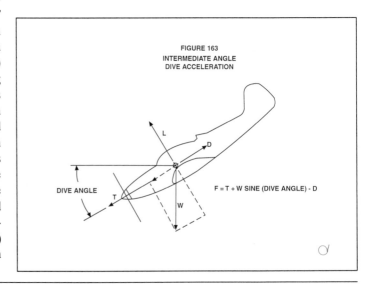

FIGURE 163
INTERMEDIATE ANGLE
DIVE ACCELERATION

DIVE ANGLE

$$F = T + W \text{ SINE (DIVE ANGLE)} - D$$

Another case can be made for zoom climb flight where the plane is going upward after pulling out of a dive and losing speed, that is, decelerating. In this case it can be seen, by mentally revising the force diagram, that a portion of the weight is assisting the drag instead of the thrust, and the plane will slow down.

Most common maneuvers can be made up of combinations of the simple cases shown in this section and the one on lift in accelerated flight. These would include maneuvers like an Immelman turn, a split S, and so on.

COMPRESSIBILITY

With the low maximum speeds of fighter aircraft before World War II, usually well under 350 mph and often under 300 at moderate altitudes, airplane performance analysts could assume air was an incompressible fluid. Calculations based on this assumption were quite accurate. As fighters grew more powerful and their lines became sleeker, the situation started to change. The advent of more efficient engine supercharging got fighters up higher, particularly those intended as intercepters of ever higher flying bombers.

The wing airfoil shapes used before the war were designed for moderate speeds with emphasis on good lift-to-drag ratios and safe low speed characteristics. Analysis of very high speed flight in the 1930s was almost all for ballistics work on artillery shells.

Dives from high altitude of new design aircraft in the late 1930s and early 1940s first brought out troubles with air compressibility. P-38 problems came first in the US, but were shortly followed by those appearing on other high speed high altitude types. In a typical case of a high speed dive from way up, the aircraft would start to vibrate badly; control was lost with the stick or column flailing wildly in the cockpit (or frozen rigidly in place). The plane would often nose down more steeply in the dive; this was called "tuck-under". The pilot could do nothing to recover, and some men were lost. If the aircraft hung together it might come out of compressibility (a general term used at the time for problems caused by high speed flight) at lower altitudes in warmer denser air. The pilot might have a chance to regain control if he was lucky and didn't run out of air space. It was a scary business.

These problems started to occur at Mach numbers over about 0.6 and were fully developed around a speed of Mach 0.7 to 0.8. Mach number is simply the percentage of the speed of sound in air at which the plane is flying. If the speed of sound was 734 mph (it is at 10000 feet altitude in standard atmosphere) and the plane was flying at 350 mph true airspeed at that altitude, it would be flying at 350/734 or Mach 0.48. The reason the speed of sound comes into play is simple—pressure disturbances in air travel at that speed, and the flow field around an airplane in flight is a bunch of pressure disturbances. In slow speed flight the pressure changes in the airflow, due to the presence of a wing leading edge, say, propagate forward at the speed of sound to warn the air particles further upstream that the wing is coming, and they better get ready to split up and flow smoothly around it, and similarly for other parts of the airplane. And at moderate speeds they have time to do so. In high speed flight, say at a high percentage of the speed of sound (high subsonic Mach number), the wing is coming at those upstream par-

ticles almost as fast as the Mach 1.0 message that it is coming gets to them. So the air particles arrive at that wing leading edge before they quite know what to do, and tend to pile up and "compress" near the leading edge. It is sort of like Lucy Arnez in that famous assembly line scene trying to put the cakes in the boxes with the line speeding up. After piling up the air has to break loose and continue on past the wing. This situation brings on a very abrupt pressure change at the wing leading edge which is the essence of a local "shock wave". These abrupt discontinuities of flow can start anywhere on the aircraft, but are usually initiated where there is a rather sudden change of airplane contour. Along with the wing leading edge, the top of the windshield at the front of the cockpit canopy was another popular spot for a local shock to form. At these kinds of points on the aircraft the local Mach number could get very near 1.0 even though the airplane as a whole was still at only Mach 0.75. The local particles of air had to speed up well past the "free stream" speed to get around any local discontinuity, and then keep on going downstream.

These local pressure discontinuities at high subsonic (below Mach 1.0) airplane speed destroyed wing lift, increased airplane drag, and severely disturbed the trim, or balance, of the aircraft. The unsteady nature of the airflow caused vibration. On World War II fighters things got to be a mess in a hurry, as earlier indicated. The older aircraft designs with the earlier airfoil contours tended to get into trouble first (at lower Mach numbers); the later designs with the so-called laminar flow wing airfoil sections (P-51 and P-63 fighters) were able to delay the onset of severe compressibility up to a higher speed—which was their principal advantage—but they too encountered the problem.

The two Army high altitude fighters with the older-style wing airfoil shapes, P-38 and P-47, "solved" the problem of encountering compressibility, or Mach effects, in high speed high altitude dives by a straightforward expedient later in the war—adding enough drag on the airplane selectively by incorporating extendable dive flaps under their wings. The pilot was thereby able to slow the plane down sufficiently to keep it out of the worst of the trouble until a lower, warmer, safer altitude with a faster speed of sound was reached. The flaps were designed so nose-down pitching (tuck-under) of the plane could be countered as well. This was a fairly satisfactory fix for wartime expediency, but it was not the longer range solution to problems of high speed flight. These solutions would have to wait until after the war and newer airplanes.

WEIGHT

GENERAL

It is difficult to over-emphasize the impact of weight on aircraft performance. In a fighter plane, where performance is an over-riding consideration, weight assumes special significance. Three aspects of fighter weight will be considered: The composition, or breakdown of weight, and how bookkeeping was accomplished; empty weight growth of the fighters through the war years; and the effect of a weight increase on aircraft performance. An attempt was made to obtain weight details for US World War II fighters. Where available, these have been obtained from manufacturers data , a difficult task over forty-five years later. But efforts have met with some success, and results are presented in a later section.

FIGHTER WEIGHT BREAKDOWN

It is important to understand weight accounting. The total loaded weight of the airplane was called "gross weight", or in the case of the British, "all-up weight". Gross weight will be used here. It can vary widely for an airplane depending on mission requirements. Gross weight is composed of two parts—"empty weight" and "useful load". Useful load is the part performing a useful function in getting the plane somewhere and fighting. Empty weight goes along for the ride as a necessary evil to make the plane work properly. So:

GROSS WEIGHT = EMPTY WEIGHT + USEFUL LOAD

Generally the higher percentage of useful load to gross weight, or put another way, the lower the empty weight to carry a specific useful load, the more efficient the fighter—given similar structural design factors.

We will look at the empty weight part of an airplane first. It was composed of three kinds of parts: airframe (structure), powerplant, and fixed equipment. Table 7 shows the major components of empty weight. The aircraft structural groups are self-explanatory. The tail group included the vertical and horizontal surfaces and fixed and moveable portions. In a conventionally-arranged fighter the landing (or alighting) gear group included main and tail gear with shock struts, rolling elements, retraction means, and braking systems. In nose-wheel planes like the P-38 and P-39, the "auxiliary gear" was the nose wheel assembly instead of the tail wheel. In a conventional arrangement the body, or fuselage, group included structure up through the firewall in the nose, and the engine section items forward of that area like the engine mount and cowling parts. In planes like the P-39 and P-63 the engine section weight was relatively light because of the mid-location of the engine.

The series of group items under the heading of powerplant included the installation of the engine plus subsystems required to make the engine work. The installed engine required a charge air intake along with an exhaust system and engine isolator mounts. The engine accessories included items like oil and fuel pumps mounted on accessory drive pads provided at the engine rear face. Under engine controls weight of the throttle and mixture linkages from the cockpit were considered as well as supercharger controls. The propeller weight had to include the unit itself, propeller gover-

nor and controls. and a spinner if required. Starting system weight included items required to fire up the engine. In later airplanes a water injection (anti-detonant) system was added, and the weight of its components (except the fluid mixture itself) had to be considered. In an air-cooled engine weight of the cooling system was either zero or very low. Engine cylinder baffling was normally considered part of engine weight, and the cowl flap actuating system weight could be put in other groups. But liquid-cooled engines were another matter, and cooling system weight there was substantial, including the coolers themselves, lines, pumps, and for this case the coolant fluid. Fluid weight was carried here because it was not expendable, as opposed to water injection fluid. The supercharger was often carried as part of engine weight if it was fully integral, but could also be listed separately. The lubrication system is self-explanatory, and the fuel system, less fuel, was accounted for as a powerplant item, including all tanks and lines for internal fuel (and self-sealing where applicable), valves, controls, and so on.

It can be seen there could be a problem of allocation, that is, sometimes components could logically be placed in one group or another. And there were items which, if the weights engineer was not thorough, could "fall through the crack". So great care had to

TABLE 7.

EMPTY WEIGHT GROUP BREAKDOWN

AIRFRAME (STRUCTURE)	WING GROUP TAIL GROUP BODY (FUSELAGE) GROUP LANDING (ALIGHTING) GEAR GROUP ENGINE SECTION
POWERPLANT	ENGINE INSTALLATION ENGINE ACCESSORIES POWERPLANT CONTROLS PROPELLER (S) STARTING SYSTEM ATER INJECTION (ADI) SYSTEM COOLING SYSTEM LUBRICATION SYSTEM FUEL SYSTEM
FIXED EQUIPMENT	INSTRUMENTS SURFACE CONTROLS ELECTRICAL SYSTEM HYDRAULIC SYSTEM COMMUNICATIONS/RADIO (Army only) ARMAMENT PROVISIONS (INCL. GUNFIRE PROT.) FURNISHINGS ANTI-ICING EQUIP'T TOWING/HOISTING GEAR ARRESTING GEAR FLOTATION PROVISIONS SERVICE PICKUP
Adds to:	EMPTY WEIGHT

be taken in accounting for all components in the aircraft, and in specifying what group included which items. We will stay with group totals, and not get into further detail.

The third major portion of empty weight was fixed equipment. Running down groups included in the list of Table 7 will show most as self-explanatory. The instrument group included the panel and any sub-panels. Surface controls weight encompassed cockpit stick and rudder pedals, bell cranks, control rods, cables, pulleys, fittings, and so on, but not the control surfaces themselves. On late-model P-38 airplanes surface controls would include aileron boost system components. Electric and hydraulic systems were the so-called utility systems. In the case of the P-39 airplane there were no

hydraulics except wheel brakes (included in the landing gear group) so hydraulics system weight was zero. If there was a pneumatic system (as the FM-2 flap actuation) it would be added in fixed equipment, but that was unusual, and not part of the normal breakdown format. The communications listing is interesting in that the Army and Navy differed in book-keeping this item. The Army listed radio weights in empty weight, and the Navy listed them under useful load. This is one of the few instances where military service weight formats were different. A second item with variation in listing is armament provisions weight. In some cases (as with P-39) armor and bullet-proof glass weights were listed as empty weight fixed equipment, while in others (like P-63) these weights were in

TABLE 8
USEFUL LOAD BREAKDOWN

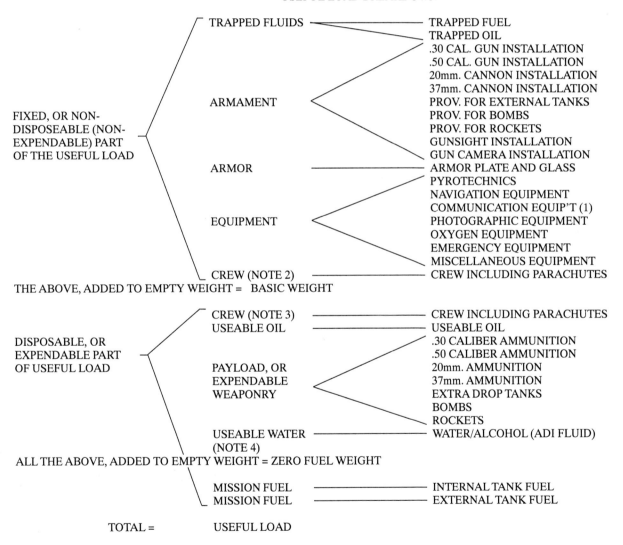

NOTE 1: For US Navy only; carried in empty weight by USAAF.
NOTE 2: US Navy only.
NOTE 3: USAAF only.
NOTE 4: For engine water injection system if used.

USEFUL LOAD ABOVE PLUS EMPTY WEIGHT = GROSS WEIGHT

TABLE 9
BASELINE GROSS WEIGHTS

AIRCRAFT	BASELINE GROSS WT.LB.	BASELINE USEFUL LOAD LB.	UL/GW
P-38J	17699	4919	.278
P-39D-2	7793	2135	.274
P-39Q-1	7570	1886	.249
P-40	7173	1806	.252
P-40B	7624	2009	.264
P-40C	8013	2246	.280
P-40E	8289	2221	.268
P-40F	8678	2102	.242
P-40K	8522	2155	.253
P-40L	8120	1635	.201
P-40M	8541	2155	.252
P-40N	8354	2148	.257
P-47D (UP TO -25)	13582	3625	.267
P-47D (-25 & UP)	14411	4212	.292
P-51A	8633	2200	.255
P-51D	10176 (NO RACKS)	2916	287
A-36	9030	2380	.264
P-61A	29249	8284	.283
P-61B	31103	9103	.293
P-61C	33144	9144	.273
P-63A-10	8989	2295	.255
239	5276	1532	.290
F2A-2	6637	2061	.310
F3A-3	6906	2174	.315
F4F-3	7543	2117	.281
F4F-3A	7320	2136	.292
F4F-4	7973	2194	.275
FM-2	7487	2039	.272
F4U-1 (EARLY)	12676	3913	.309
F4U-1D	12289	3318	.270
F4U-4	12281	3114	.254
F6F-3	12213	3262	.267
F6F-5	12483	3404	.273

Note: No external loads on airplane; full to capacity ammunition load, and full to capacity internal fuel only.

useful load. So comparisons had to be made carefully. Furnishings included accomodations for the pilot, like a seat, certain emergency items, and air conditioning—which in World War II fighters meant ventilation and heating equipment only. Anti-icing usually meant an alcohol-slinging system for the propeller and windshield. Towing, tiedown, and hoisting items were part of the airplane handling gear, as for instance tow or tiedown rings on the landing gear or other hard points. Arresting and catapulting gear weight was included for Navy fighters used on carriers, and flotation gear weight for aircraft-integral inflatable bags or special sealing to keep a ditched aircraft afloat. After early use on Grumman Wildcats, flotation bags were removed because of inadvertant inflations, and never again included. The last item, service pick-up, accounted for weight accumulated during service use—things like dirt and mud. Often no allocation was made for this weight.

This summary gives an idea how empty weight of a US fighter was broken down, and is much the same for aircraft of today. Empty weight had an uncomfortable habit of growing as new versions of the fighter were produced. This will be discussed later.

Useful load was the other part of gross weight. Table 8 gives a breakdown of useful load items. This part was split into disposeable

or expendable items, and those that were not. In the one category, for instance, would be machine guns, which were not expendable and came back with the aircraft on completion of the mission. In the other category was ammunition for the guns, which would normally be expended during the mission. At least that was the assumption. One can see other differences by reviewing the list in Table 8. Generally speaking, if one added all non-expendable items of useful load to empty weight, he got to the "Basic Weight" of the fighter. But there was an exception. The Navy categorized the pilot in the non-disposeable part of useful load, and thus part of Basic Weight; the Army put the pilot in the disposeable portion, and thus not part of Basic Weight. This difference is indicated in Table 8. Basic Weight was a term used in both services. Review of the expendable category of useful load items will show (with the exception of Army Air Force pilot!) they are truly disposeable items—oil consumed by the engine, ammunition fired off, bombs or external fuel tanks dropped, rockets fired, water injection fluid consumed, and fuel burned during the mission. There are two other types of weights noted in Table 8: "Tactical Weight Empty" was defined in the Army as Basic Weight plus crew (pilot only, most often) and useable oil; and "Zero Fuel Weight" was simply Gross Weight minus all useable fuel.

Perusal of Table 8 shows there can be many gross weights for an aircraft depending on whether it carries a partial or full load of ammunition, whether bombs or rockets are carried, and whether it carries a partial or full load of fuel. Size and weight of fuel drop tanks varied widely. So gross weight of World War II fighters could vary a great deal. For instance weight of the Lockheed P-38L Lightning could range from 15500 pounds (structural design gross weight with partial internal fuel and ammunition) to 21600 pounds (ferry gross weight with full large extra fuel tanks). So just about any gross weight in between could be considered "right". And many different gross weights have been cited in the literature for the fighters.

As a first approximation, the allowable limit load factor of a fighter varies directly as gross weight. If gross weight is on the lower side limit load factor is high, usually around seven and a half to eight. If gross weight is a maximum load factor goes down to five or so. The load factor (full name is the "positive flight symmetrical maneuver limit load factor") is the number of vertical g's the airplane can stand, say in a dive pull-out, without exceeding limit strength values of critical structural parts. If the plane is loaded to high gross weight, it can't stand as many g's as if lightly loaded. Fighters with heavy external loads were limited to gentle maneuvers producing low g levels., often because of structural limits on load attachment parts.

To make comparisons in performance between different fighter aircraft, gross weights had to be on a rational common basis, or comparisons would not be fair, since weight made considerable difference in performance. For purposes of any comparisons herein we will use "baseline" gross weight values computed as follows:

    1.No external loads, such as bombs, tanks or rockets.
    2.Useful load to include full to capacity ammunition
     and internal fuel load.

"Baseline" gross weight is terninology used strictly for our purposes; it was never used in World War II military terminology. Rationale for the ground rules noted: No fighter pilot would take off without having, as a minimum, a full load of ammunition for his weapons and a full load of fuel in his internal tanks—to do otherwise would not be safe in wartime. Of course in many cases the pilot would want in addition underwing stores of weapons or drop tanks. But for our purposes that complicates matters such as drag, and fighters would not, at least in World War II, enter air-to-air combat with external stores underwing. See Table 9 for baseline gross weights of some of the fighters.

FIGHTER EMPTY WEIGHT GROWTH

One of the biggest problems for World War II fighters was empty weight growth. This affliction was common on just about all types, but on some more than others. Results of reviewing empty weights of successive fighter variants are shown in Table 10. Increases in weight came about because of several factors, major among them addition of self-sealing fuel tanks and protective armor, additional or heavier guns, fittings for underwing stores, addition of systems such as water injection, design modifications, and structural beef-up to take care of weight additions. It seemed to pyramid up. The planes designed well before start of US hostilities had the biggest weight growth facors because features later found needed in air combat were not envisioned during initial design. As combat experience was gained, particularly that of the British, it became clear certain additional offensive and defensive features were required, all costing weight. Another reason earlier designed fighters had greater weight increases was they were in production longer. There were efforts made during the war to reduce weight, but in the end to little avail. Most consisted of stripping out guns or other equipment, and often this weight would be added back in the field. Another factor—it was extremely difficult to introduce weight-saving changes in a high-speed wartime production line. If changes could not be incorporated with relative ease later in a modification center, they were often not made. Efforts were made to hold down weight growth in the hope that increases in engine power output would help counter weight trends.

Inspection of Table 10 shows most empty weight growth factors varied from 10 to 40% with earlier designs being worse. Two of the most criticized fighter aircraft, the Brewster F2A- Buffalo and the Bell P-39 Airacobra show up as the greatest offenders, and weight growth was doubtless a considerable factor influencing their combat performance. With the possible exception of the Vought F4U- Corsair, all the worst offenders, with over 20% weight growth factor, are what could be called "first-generation" fighters. The three types usually noted as premier designs are in the middle of the pack with more moderate growth factors in the 11 to 14% range. The later designs are the best, with the Grumman F6F- Hellcat the most notable example of holding the line on empty weight growth.

Increases in empty weight posed a problem of what to do about gross weight, which ultimately affected performance. If empty weight increased one could either hold gross weight (and performance) constant by reducing useful load the same amount, or hold the same useful load and let the gross weight increase the same amount as empty weight. With real war missions to perform demanding the greatest combination of fuel for range and firepower to fight—all part of useful load—it was clear this weight had to be held fixed, and gross weight had to increase along with empty weight. This is what happened almost invariably. The total loaded aircraft got heavier and heavier as the war progressed, and performance and handling qualities tended to degrade. In some cases performance was held with greater engine power, but there was no such help for handling qualities unless major aircraft changes were to be made.

TABLE 10
FIGHTER EMPTY WEIGHT GROWTH

MODEL	EMPTY WEIGHT (LB.)
XP-38	11507
YP-38	11196
P-38	11672
XP-38A	11507
P-38D/E	11780
P-38F	12264
P-38G	12200
P-38H	12380
P-38J	12780
P-38L	12800

EW GROWTH=12800/11507x100=11.2%

XP-39	3995
XP-39B	4530
YP-39	5042
P-39C	5070
P-39D/F	5462
P-39D-2	5658
P-39K	5658
P-39L	5733
P-39M	5610
P-39N	5657
P-39Q	5645

EW GROWTH=5733/3995x100=43.5%

XP-40	5417
P-40	5376
P-40B	5590-5615
P-40C	5767-5812
P-40D	5970
P-40E	6069-6350
P-40F	6576-6590
P-40K	6367-6400
P-40L	6480-6485
P-40M	6386-6464
P-40N	6200-6206

EW GROWTH=6590/5417x100=21.7%

XF4F-2	4035
XF4F-3	4863
F4F-3	5238-5426
F4F-3A	5216-5184
F4F-4	5779
FM-1	5895
FM-2	5328-5448
FM-2	5473-5542

EW GROWTH=5542/4863x100=14.0%

XF4U-1	7505
F4U-1	8763-8873
F4U-1D	8971-8982
F4U-4	9167-9205
F4U-4B	9132

EW GROWTH=9205/7505x100=22.%

MODEL	EMPTY WEIGHT (LB.)
XP-47B	9190
P-47B	9346
P-47C	9900
P-47D RAZOR.	9957-10000
P-47D BUB.	10000-10199
P-47M	10423

EW GROWTH=10423/9190x100=13.4%

XP-51	6278
P-51	6550
P-51A	6433
XP-51B	7038
P-51B/C	6985-6988
P-51D/K	7125-7205

EW GROWTH=7205/6278x100=14.8%

XP-61	21695
YP-61/P-61	21910
P-61A	20965
P-61B	21215-22000
P-61C	24000

EW GROWTH=24000/21695x100=10.6%

XP-63A	6185-6188
P-63A	6325-6694
P-63C	6800
P-63D	7076
P-63E	7300

EW GROWTH=7300/6185x100=18.0%

XF2A-1	3711-3722
F2A-1	3783-3785
239	3744
339B	4020
F2A-2	4150
F2A-2 COMBAT	4576
339E	4268
339D	4282
F2A-3	4732-4765
F2A-3	4848-4879

EW GROWTH=4879/3711x100=31.5%

F6F-3	8951
F6F-5	9079-9238

EW GROWTH=9238/8951x100=3.2%

GROWTH RANKING, WORST TO BEST

MODEL	% E. W. GROWTH
P-39	43.5
F2A-	31.5
F4U-	22.7
P-40	21.7
P-63	18.0
P-51	14.8
F4F-	14.0
P-47	13.4
P-38	11.2
P-61	10.6
F6F-	3.2

EFFECT OF GROSS WEIGHT INCREASE ON PERFORMANCE

Increases in gross weight of fighter aircraft reduce performance in several ways. Table 11 summarizes the effect of a 1000 pound gross weight increase (in the range of 8000 to 12000 pounds gross weight) for a P-51D Mustang fighter. The effect on speed is there, but is not dramatic. The big effects come in climb and takeoff and landing performance. Though not shown in the table, a weight increase would impact severely on maneuver performance as reference to the section on lift in maneuvering flight will show.

TABLE 11
EFFECT OF 1000 POUND G.W. INCREASE ON P-51D AIRPLANE (CLEAN)

PERFORMANCE ITEM	RESULT OF 1000LB. INCREASE
1. Maximum Speed(WE Power,24,500')	Reduction of about 3 MPH.
2. Climb Rate (WE Power)	Reduction of 370 to 590 FT./MIN.
3. Climb Time to 25000'	Increase of 1.4 to 1.6 MIN.
4. Take-off Ground Distance	Increase of 225 to 300 FT.
5. Take-off Over 50' Obstacle	Increase of 280 to 460 FT.
6. Stalling Speed (50 DEG. Flap)	Increase of 5.2 MPH.
7. Landing Over 50' Obstacle	Increase of 200 FT.
8. Fuel Consumption in Cruise	Loss of .072 MI./ LB.Fuel
9. Fuel Consumption at 5000'	Increase of 22 LB. Fuel / HR.

BALANCE AND THE CENTER OF GRAVITY

We'll discuss only longitudinal, or fore and aft, center of gravity and not vertical or lateral location since the latter are of secondary importance. The longitudinal center of gravity (CG) is the fore-aft point on the aircraft where the whole plane will balance on a knife edge—like the center point of a balanced see-saw. Weights of all the planes parts aft of the CG times their distances to it will exactly equal weights of all the parts forward of the CG times their respective distances from it. On a World War II fighter plane the CG had to be located approximately one quarter of the way back of the average wing chord, the chord being the fore-aft dimension of the wing. Actually the wing chord used was the "mean aerodynamic chord", a bit different from the average chord of the wing, but for our purposes this has little importance. The chord of the wing was abbreviated MAC. All parts had to be arranged fore and aft so they would balance around a point close to 1/4 MAC, or more exactly weights of all plane parts not expendable had to be so balanced. See Figure 164. This was essentially everything in Basic Weight of the aircraft. (Refer to the WEIGHT section).

It was important to locate the longitudinal CG of all basic weight items near the point noted (1/4 MAC) to assure reasonable stability and control qualities in the aircraft. This was done by carefully laying out the aircraft in a side view drawing, positioning all parts in their fore-aft location, calculating all weights and distances from the desired CG location, and moving them so balance was attained.

Consideration could then go to expendable items—those burned, dropped, or shot off during flight (like internal fuel, ammunition, and external fuel and drop tanks). The purest and most desireable procedure was to locate these items at or very close to the 1/4 MAC longitudinally. The airplane CG then would not move forward or aft if fuel was burned off from internal or external tanks, or if ammunition was shot off from the guns. In this ideal arrangement longitudinal stability and control characteristics would stay constant because the CG would not move. One primary design rule was to avoid balancing non-expendable items (like guns) with an expendable item (like fuel). The pilot was treated as non-expendable since though he left the plane after landing, he did not normally leave it in the air! He could be located anywhere along the length of the aircraft the designer thought was desireable from other considerations, like vision. This meant the internal fuel tank or tanks should be located on , or as close as possible to, the CG, and that ammunition be also located in line with the CG. If the plane was equipped with wing guns it was easy because ammunition for these, located adjacent to them in the wings, fell naturally close in line with the desired CG. But if the guns were located in the nose, and the ammunition for these was close by, a problem could arise with unwanted CG movement aft when ammunition was expended. Drop tanks under wings or fuselage (or bombs or rockets) were normally not a problem as they located naturally in line with the CG. When they were dropped there was little if any shift in CG location. Fuel location internally, particularly when there was a lot required, could be a real design problem and cause considerable heartburn to de-

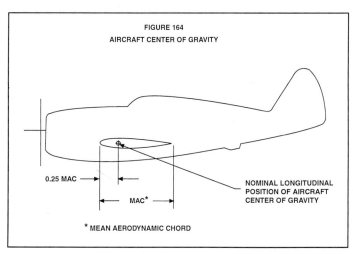

FIGURE 164
AIRCRAFT CENTER OF GRAVITY

0.25 MAC

MAC*

NOMINAL LONGITUDINAL
POSITION OF AIRCRAFT
CENTER OF GRAVITY

* MEAN AERODYNAMIC CHORD

signers. The greater the amount of internal fuel located any fore or aft distance from the CG, the more CG would travel one way or the other as fuel burned off, and flying characteristics could vary widely and deteriorate quickly. The plane could go unstable longitudinally or directionally, and be very hard to control with normal stick and rudder pedal forces, and either way make the pilot work extra hard or bring on dangerous conditions. The allowable CG travel longitudinally, as defined by pilot-tolerable handling qualities, had to be greater than and outside of the actual CG travel. Said another way, the allowable CG envelope had to be outside the possible limits of the actual CG envelope.

We'll check how US production fighters stacked up in terms of actual CG travel, but first another consideration regarding internal fuel. Some fighters ended up needing more fuel than originally designed into them, notably P-38, P-47, and P-51 aircraft used for bomber escort. To keep bomber losses to a minimum, they needed fighter escort all the way. Though additional fuel in drop tanks helped to a point, escort distance required steadily increased. Soon escort fighter radius was limited by internal tankage needed for the return trip after using drop tank fuel for the outbound leg. So internal fuel capacity became critical. Adding more was difficult, particularly in the hurry of wartime. This aspect will be discussed airplane by airplane below.

The Lockheed P-38 airplane initially carried all internal fuel tanks in wing sections inboard of the booms centered near the 1/4 MAC location, so fuel burn-off caused almost no change in CG location, a fine situation. Cannon and machine gun ammunition was located well forward in the nose, however. This ammounted to 715 pounds several feet ahead of the CG that could be fired off, and the airplane CG slid back when this happened with stability getting worse. With a new requirement for more internal fuel, Lockheed engineers searched for space. The solution was elegant—they removed intercoolers for the engine supercharging system from the forward wing sections outboard of the booms and put additional fuel tanks in their place, close in line with the 1/4 MAC. So like the old wing fuel, burn-off of the new wing fuel would not move the CG perceptibly. Intercoolers were redesigned and newly located in the forward sections of the engine nacelles with the oil coolers, changing the look of the intake area. The P-38 continued to live with the ammunition location problem, which was handleable.

The Bell P-39, a much smaller and lighter aircraft of modest range, had all internal fuel in the inboard sections of the wings each side in a location well lined up with the CG. Thus there was almost no change in center of gravity location with fuel burn-off. The ammunition for the main part of its armament, two .50 caliber machine guns and a 37mm cannon was located well forward of the CG, however. This ammunition weight totaled 189 pounds, and when it was all fired off the CG moved back a fair amount. It has been reported this aft CG movement caused significantly adverse flying characteristics, some of these, such as possibilities for snap rolls, spins, and possible tumbling, causing arguments even today. Ammunition for the .30 caliber wing guns or the later .50 calibers caused no problem as it was lined up just about on the CG.

The Curtiss P-40 was built in two basic models, the early Tomahawk type, and the later Kittihawk/Warhawk version. On the early

configuration there were two nose guns, but ammunition storage was just forward of the cockpit and only a short distance ahead of the CG, so shooting off the 228 pounds of nose .50 caliber ammunition moved the CG back very little. Wing gun ammunition in all models (and later versions had all wing guns and no nose installation) was closely alligned with the aircraft CG, and expenditure produced no perceptable CG change. So the P-40 ammunition situation was good as regards CG shift; there was very little. All P-40 models had three fuel tanks, two in the wing roots right around the CG, and one in the fuselage just aft of the cockpit near the wing trailing edge. The center of the wing tanks was close to the longitudinal CG, and thus burnoff caused little shift, but using the fuselage tank would cause a substantial CG shift forward as the fuel was burned.

In the Republic P-47 the 1020 pounds of ammunition for the eight machine guns was placed just about on the 1/4 MAC line of the aircraft, and thus caused desireably little shift of CG when expended. The early P-47 versions had about two thirds of their fuel in a main fuselage tank forward of and slightly under the cockpit, and nicely in line with the aircraft CG. The remaining third of internal fuel was in another fuselage tank under the cockpit, but aft of the CG near the wing trailing edge. When fuel was used from this tank the CG moved forward somewhat. When Republic added more fuel internally to increase ability to escort bombers they were able to add 65 gallons to the main tank in a way that was ideal; the addition was almost over the nominal CG, and the situation was improved so about 3/4 of internal fuel was perfectly positioned. The remaining quarter in the auxiliary tank was still aft, causing a CG shift when fuel was used from that tank.

The North American P-51 airplane was built in several models with varying degrees of CG shifting possible from expenditure of ammunition or fuel. The four variations of importance were (1) P-51 with four 20mm cannon, (2) P-51A with nose and wing guns and ammunition, (3) P-51B/C with wing guns only and wing fuel tanks only, and (4) P-51B/C/D/K with wing guns only and both wing fuel tanks and a fuselage auxiliary fuel tank. The four cannon in the P-51 wings had ammunition containers just aft of the front spar not far back of the quarter chord line. Fuel was located inboard in the wings in the same allignment longitudinally as the ammunition. Expenditure of either caused a slight but not troublesome forward shift in CG. The armament of the P-51A was different though the fuel location was the same. The .30 and .50 caliber wing gun ammunition in the A model was located just aft of the main spar again so shift in CG was small and in the forward direction with expenditure of the ammo. There were also two .50 caliber guns in the lower nose with ammunition for these stored three or four feet forward of the 1/4 MAC line. Firing these guns would drive the CG aft significantly, but if wing guns were fired at the same time that would compensate somewhat. In the early P-51B/C models all guns were in the wings, so ammunition for them was just aft of the quarter chord line in a decent position, and fuel was in the same longitudinal location with respect to the CG. Getting rid of disposeables in this case meant the CG slid forward only a little. The problems really set in with the addition, on most Merlin Mustang aircraft, of an 85 gallon tank in the fuselage aft of the pilot. This modification significantly increased escort range of the airplane, but since the tank was well aft of the quarter chord the aft CG location with this tank full resulted in stability and control problems in the early part of the mission. As the the CG moved forward with fuel burn-off from that tank, the aircraft handled better. North American had been unable, in the layout of the P-51, to do what Lockheed and Republic accomplished in the P-38 and P-47 by adding extra internal fuel weight almost on the aircraft CG and thus minimizing CG travel.

The Northrop P-61 Black Widow, a large twin-engined night fighter airplane, had a commendable distribution of both ammunition and fuel disposeables. Internal fuel was located between wing spars in the inboard wing sections just aft of the quarter chord so there was only slight forward travel of CG with fuel burn-off. Location of ammunition for the four belly 20mm cannon and four .50 caliber upper turret was longitudinally the same as fuel, though in the fuselage. Thus with ammunition shot off and/or fuel consumed the aircraft CG would move only slightly forward, not a bad situation.

The Bell P-63 was built in the same configuration as the earlier P-39, though a larger and heavier machine. Ammunition and fuel locations were basically the same. So there was little CG travel with fuel consumed, but again the ammunition supply for the 37mm cannon and nose machine guns was well forward, and the CG travelled aft when the fuselage nose weapons were fired, disposing of a total of 705 pounds. Ammunition for the wing podded guns was close in line with the CG and thus posed no problem.

The Brewster F2A- Buffalo had two fuselage guns and two in the wings. The wing was located well forward on the fuselage so ammunition for fuselage guns was closely alligned with the wing quarter chord, and ammunition for the wing guns was only slightly aft of the 1/4 MAC point. Thus the ammunition situation was excellent, and expenditure of rounds would not materially alter the CG. The F2A- fuel was located inboard in the wing between spars so it was close to the 1/4 MAC nominal location of the CG. Burn-off of that fuel would hardly affect CG location, a good situation.

But in later models fuel was added in a fuselage tank and two wing leading edge tanks. All were ahead of the 1/4 MAC point so when fuel was burned from these the CG would move aft. Since additional tankage was small movement was not large however.

The Grumman F4F- Wildcat had all guns, four or six depending on the version, in the wings and ammunition located at about 50% chord; there was a slight CG shift forward when guns were fired. The main fuselage tank was located under the cockpit floor a little aft of 1/4 MAC. So the airplane CG would move slightly forward with fuel burn-off. These CG shifts were not a real big problem however.

The Vought F4U- Corsair started with fuel in the wings, two guns in the nose, and one gun in each wing in the experimental model. Additional firepower was desired for the production aircraft, and six wing guns were installed with fuselage weapons omitted. The change displaced most fuel from the wings (only two small tanks were left in outboard panels). Space had to be made for a main tank in the fuselage. It was located just in line with the 1/4 MAC, displacing the pilot aft since fuel was a disposeable item while the pilot was not. This change resulted in the farthest aft cockpit with respect to the wing of any US World War II fighter plane , and pilot visibility problems throughout the life of the aircraft. It does serve to show, however, how vital it was to locate heavy disposeable items (in this case fuel) very near the desired aircraft CG. So fuel was in the right place and wing ammunition lined up just aft of it longitudinally , so CG travel due to using fuel and shooting guns was minimal, with movement only slightly forward.

The Grumman F6F- Hellcat had six wing guns and ammunition for these was located slightly aft of the 1/4 MAC. So the CG shift from shooting was minimal. There were three fuel tanks in the Hellcat fuselage. Two were almost perfectly in line with the 1/4 MAC, so emptying them caused an almost imperceptable change in CG location. The third tank, containing a bit less than a third of total tankage, was a couple of feet aft of the aircraft 1/4 MAC, and thus burn-off of this fuel caused some forward CG shift.

STABILITY AND CONTROL

INTRODUCTION
Flying qualities of World War II fighters had to do with performance, but mostly with stability and control. Stability and control requirements for US service aircraft were getting standardized when war hit. Tremendous research was accomplished in this area during wartime.

Fighters needed a degree of stability to provide steadiness as gun platforms and weapons launchers. They also needed the degree of control to make agile air combat machines. Flying qualities of some fighters were fairly good, and some not so good. In another section data is presented describing their flight and ground handling characteristics.

TRIM
A fighter was said to be in trim when cockpit stick and rudder pedal forces were zeroed out in any steady flight condition such as cruise or climb. Cockpit control forces in temporary maneuvering might not be trimmed out unless forces became extremely high, but in some cases pilots were constantly re-trimming. The pilot rotated trim wheels in the cockpit for pitch, roll, and yaw; these connected to trim tabs on elevator, aileron, and rudder respectively. Tabs were small moveable surfaces set into main control surfaces. Angular deflection of a tab by the trim wheel changed the equilibrium trail angle of the main surface, thereby changing the control moment (the effect of the control) on the whole airplane, and relieving the pilot of constantly holding against a control force.

As with all conventional airplanes of the war period, net lift force on the wing acted behind the fore-aft center of gravity, resulting in a nose-down pitching moment (a moment is a force times a distance). This effect had to be counteracted by a download (or negative lift) on the horizontal tail. When the aircraft was in normal cruise trim, the wing lift, the weight, the tail download force, and the moments of these forces about the pitch axis all had to be in balance, or the plane would upset. The wing had to generate extra lift to not only counter the aircraft weight but also the download on the horizontal tail.

AIRPLANE AXES

In discussing stability and control there are standard conventions of description. One has to do with the axis system of the aircraft, and with motions about the axes. There are three axes: longitudinal, lateral, and directional. Think of the longitudinal axis as a long rod running fore and aft through the fuselage from nose to tail about which the aircraft can roll. Also consider the lateral (pitch) axis as a long rod running sideways through the wing from tip to tip about which the aircraft can nose up and down, and the directional (yaw) axis as a vertical rod running up and down through the fuselage intersecting the lateral axis at the wing. See Figure 165. Rotational motions of the airplane are considered about or around these axes: rolling motion about the longitudinal, pitching motion about the lateral, and yawing motion about the directional axis. The three types of stability are spoken of as longitudinal, lateral, and directional; these are stabilities about lateral, longitudinal, and directional axes respectively. Similarly longitudinal control inputs by elevators, lateral control inputs by ailerons, and directional control inputs by rudder are also about lateral, longitudinal, and directional axes respectively. With this as background we can discuss stability and control of fighter aircraft.

STATIC STABILITY

If a statically stable airplane is moved about any of the axes, either in pitch, roll, or yaw, and then the input or upset is stopped, the plane will recover and move back to its original position. On the other hand, an unstable aircraft will keep turning in the direction towards which it was disturbed. A neutrally stable airplane, if disturbed, will move to a new position and then stop moving, but will not return to its original position. See Figure 166. The disturbance causing the aircraft to depart from its original position could arise from various sources, such as gusts or turbulence in the air, or a momentary slow pilot input.

Instability about any axis could be a real problem for the pilot. He could be continually trying to correct airplane rotations by using his controls, and could easily over-control the plane. If the plane was directionally unstable for instance, a slight air disturbance on one side would, say, cause it to yaw to the left, and keep yawing to the left with no natural tendency to return. If the pilot corrected using opposite rudder and then stopped the correction, the plane would come back in response, go through its original zero yaw position, and then start yawing nose-right. The pilot would have a tough time controlling his plane in yaw, and trying to get into position to fire his guns and hit a target would be difficult. The size of the vertical tail, the side area of the aft fuselage, and their distances

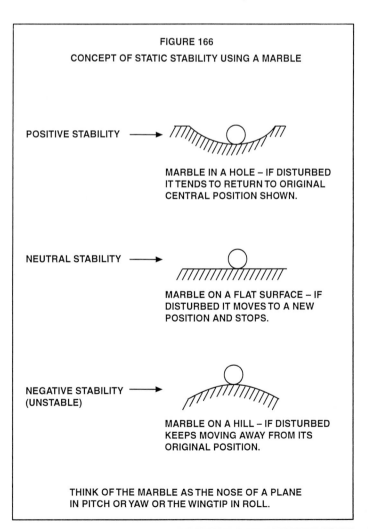

FIGURE 166
CONCEPT OF STATIC STABILITY USING A MARBLE

POSITIVE STABILITY ⟶

MARBLE IN A HOLE – IF DISTURBED IT TENDS TO RETURN TO ORIGINAL CENTRAL POSITION SHOWN.

NEUTRAL STABILITY ⟶

MARBLE ON A FLAT SURFACE – IF DISTURBED IT MOVES TO A NEW POSITION AND STOPS.

NEGATIVE STABILITY (UNSTABLE) ⟶

MARBLE ON A HILL – IF DISTURBED KEEPS MOVING AWAY FROM ITS ORIGINAL POSITION.

THINK OF THE MARBLE AS THE NOSE OF A PLANE IN PITCH OR YAW OR THE WINGTIP IN ROLL.

FIGURE 165
AIRPLANE AXES

Z
ROLL MOTION
YAW MOTION
X
Y   LATERAL AXIS
PITCH MOTION
Y
X   LONGITUDINAL AXIS
Z
DIRECTIONAL AXIS

- ROLLING ROTATES THE AIRCRAFT AROUND THE LONGITUDINAL AXIS X – X
- PITCHING ROTATES THE AIRCRAFT AROUND THE LATERAL AXIS Y – Y
- YAWING ROTATES THE AIRCRAFT AROUND THE DIRECTIONAL AXIS Z – Z

aft of the plane's center of gravity were stabilizing factors in yaw, and the side area of the fuselage ahead of the center of gravity was a destabilizing factor. In addition, during any yawed flight the propeller generated an in-plane (of the disc) force, called side force, which was highly destabilizing, that is, it contributed strongly to instability. Static stability was a matter of degree; it could be very strong (lots of tail-feathers on the arrow), in fact too strong, and take away from easy controllability and agility of the fighter. It also could be very weak, bordering on neutral stability, making the aircraft very controllable and agile.

One noteable case of loss of directional (weathercock) stability came up with the continuing development of the P-51 Mustang fighter. In the later models the change from a three-blade to a four-blade higher activity factor propeller along with modification from a high aft turtledeck to a bubble canopy degraded static yaw stability of earlier versions. This was the result of decreased fuselage projected side area aft of the center of gravity together with greatly increased propeller side force of the Merlin-powered versions. A dorsal fin was added to the vertical tail which improved the situation by adding stabilizing area aft. Moving the center of gravity aft by adding weight in the rear also gave a problem because the distance from CG back to the stabilizing areas was decreased; for instance the distance to the center of the vertical tail area was reduced. Problems arose when an 85 gallon capacity rear fuselage (aft of CG) fuel tank was added to the Merlin P-51s to increase range. When the tank was full the aircraft was difficult to fly because of statically unstable longitudinal and directional characteristics. As fuel in that tank burned off the center of gravity moved forward and things got better. Fuel in the rear tank was limited to a maximum of 35 gallons at the time of entering combat, and hopefully fuel was managed to make this happen.

Static longitudinal (pitching) stability, having to do with nose up and down movements about the lateral axis, was a situation similar to yaw stability. Here the relative size of flat surfaces like wing, horizontal tail, the projected horizontal surfaces of the fuselage, and their distances forward and aft of the CG along with the propeller were items of concern. The wing normally had a natural stabilizing (nose down) pitching moment about the CG, and this effect was assisted by area of the horizontal tail located aft. But here again the propeller side force had a strong destabilizing effect. A positive degree of static longitudinal stability was desireable so the pilot could easily keep the nose from wandering off a target, and fly the plane without tiring effort, such as having to cope with control reversals.

Lateral (roll) static stability about the longitudinal axis was controlled by the amount of dihedral (up-slope angle from root to tip) designed into the wing. When the fighter was disturbed in roll it would try and slip to the lower wing side. This action tended to increase lift on the low-side wing and right the plane. If the wing and center of gravity was low on the fuselage, the case on the majority of fighters, the side component of wind due to the slip also tended to right the plane.

Terms often used when defining characteristics of aircraft were "stick-free" and "stick-fixed" stability. The first case referred to when the cockpit control stick was released by the pilot and allowed to move freely. The second applied when the stick was held firmly in place by the pilot. Aircraft flight stability characteristics could be considerably different in the two cases, with stick-free cases normally yielding poorer stability.

Lateral and directional stability were highly inter-related in practice, with a lot of cross-coupling. The subject is more complex than need be further related here, so we will conclude with the basic static stability definition: If the plane was statically stable it would tend to return naturally to its original position after having been disturbed regardless of axis involved. If not statically stable the aircraft would wander after a disturbance, and be difficult to fly.

DYNAMIC STABILITY

A second type of stability was called dynamic stability. The word dynamic was used because alternating or oscillatory (back and forth) motions were involved. A plane susceptible to such motions about any axis because of an initial disturbance, and one which continued back and forth motions long after the disturbance had abated, was dynamically unstable. It would be an uncomfortable aircraft to fly in, and perhaps impossible to fight well with. Proper dynamic stability characteristics were important to a fighter.

A typical testing procedure to evaluate a dynamic characteristic, say stick-free dynamic longitudinal stability about the pitch axis, was for the pilot to apply a sudden large control force on the stick and elevators, quickly take it out (neutralize the stick) and then release it. If the plane was stable in this mode the elevator would then not oscillate about its hinges, nor would the aircraft nose hunt past the horizon more than, say, one cycle up and down. In other words, no continual snaking motion was allowed after the upset, and the motion had to damp out (decrease in magnitude) quickly. If there was quick damping of the motion in one or one and a half cycles, the dynamic stability in that mode was pretty good. If there was continual wandering with no damping, or such a small amount of damping that many oscillatory motions were necessary before the plane settled down again, there was a dynamic stability problem.

After a sudden large lateral stick input, takeout, and release, the aileron system should not oscillate, and the plane should not roll back and forth in an oscillating fashion, but rather the initial roll motion should damp out quickly. Similarly the dynamic stability in yaw would be tested with a sudden kick of a rudder pedal, and the resulting motion should die out quickly.

Some of the dynamic motions could be combined, with oscillation occuring about two of the airplane axes at once. Two common motions in this category were: Spiral divergence where the plane would roll and yaw away from its course with no automatic recovery, and Dutch roll, which was a very uncomfortable combination of motions. Further discussion of dynamic stability, a rather complex subject, will be left to the specialized texts, but some reports of fighter flying qualities make reference to dynamic stability, and one should recognize, at least in a general way, what is involved.

AIRCRAFT CONTROL

Fighter aircraft had to be highly maneuverable as well as reasonably stable, or they could never get into position to hit a target with weapons, nor would they be able to successfully evade an enemy. Controls of the aircraft had to be sufficiently powerful that all basic maneuvers could be performed in a responsive manner, including those required at low speed, such as take-off and landing, and those necessary during high speed aerial combat.

All US World War II production fighters had similar flight control systems. The control stick (or column in the cases of P-38 and P-61) was mechanically linked to the elevators and ailerons (and spoilers on the P-61) for pitch and roll control respectively, and cockpit rudder pedals mechanically actuated the rudder. Connecting components included bellcranks, control rods, cables, and pulleys with no hydraulic power boosting elements, except for ailerons of late-model P-38s. Control surfaces were normally balanced about their hinge lines. In many cases surfaces contained balance tabs. These were small surfaces set into main surfaces and hinged to them. They should not be confused with trim tabs since functions were different. Unlike trim tabs balance tabs were not connected to a cockpit control. They were set up with mechanical linkage to the main surface only, so they could move angularly in a direction opposite to the surface when it moved, and thereby reduce pilot effort in moving it. Sometimes a refinement called a spring tab was used. See Figure 167. These were also hinged to the main surface and inset. Linkage and a spring were arranged so spring

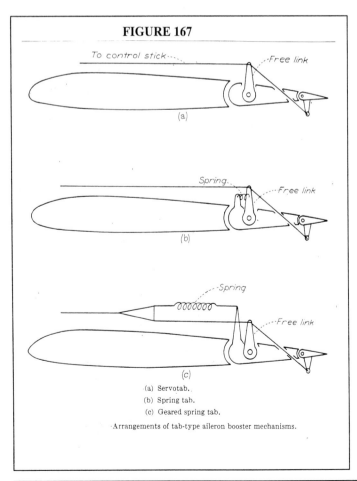

FIGURE 167

To control stick

Free link

(a)

Spring

Free link

(b)

Spring

Free link

(c)

(a) Servotab.
(b) Spring tab.
(c) Geared spring tab.
Arrangements of tab-type aileron booster mechanisms.

force aided in using tab balance to lessen pilot control force required at high speed.

Control force feel through the speed range and over the spectrum of aircraft maneuvers had to be such that stick or pedal forces were neither too light or too heavy. On the one hand the pilot could inadvertantly overstress the plane (or himself) in a very abrupt maneuver if stick forces were too light. On the other, if control forces were greater than an average pilot could handle, say at high speed, the maneuverability of the fighter would suffer. All this was difficult to arrange in the unboosted systems of the time, and control forces required of pilots varied widely.

In some airplanes, notably the P-51, pilots were sometimes overstressing the airplane during particularly violent maneuvers with structural failures resulting. Designers modified flight controls for both elevators and rudder to alleviate the situation. They added a 20 pound metal bobweight in the elevator control system to make it harder for the pilot to move them. When he moved the stick he had to swing the bobweight, which action opposed his applied force. Many pilots did not like exerting the extra stick force, but less airplane structure got broken. In the rudder system designers changed the tab to an anti-balance type. This arrangement worked just opposite to the balance tab described above. Linkage between the tab and main rudder surface was set up so the tab moved in the same direction as the rudder, thus increasing required pedal force. This change helped keep vertical tails on.

Depending on a variety of factors, control stick forces a pilot had to exert during, say, a turning maneuver, varied considerably between fighter types. Stick loads were usually expressed in terms of stick force per g of acceleration. As a turn would tighten into smaller and smaller radius of curvature (a so-called wind-up turn) and g forces increased, stick forces tended to increase proportionately. As well as the difference between types in stick force per g, there was considerable difference in pilot preference. Some liked heavier forces; some liked lighter. But pilots did not have to continually put up with heavy control forces in combat maneuvers if they often used elevator and other trim wheels in the cockpit. One combat veteran employed the elevator trim wheel of his Merlin-powered Mustang constantly in maneuvers during air battles over Europe. Another pilot, flying a Mustang many years after the war and new to it, commented on high stick forces. Theoretically it could have been the same airplane, with one pilot constantly re-trimming and the other not. Some discussions about maneuvering stick forces could depend on the amount of trimming by the pilots. There were other factors—longitudinal location of the aircraft center of gravity (forward locations gave higher stick forces and extreme aft locations could even reverse the sense of elevator stick force), and presence or absence of a bobweight were two of these.

Another important aspect of control system design, again say for elevators, was control sensitivity. This varied considerably. How far forward or aft did the control stick have to be moved for full angular throw of the elevators? It was a function of the mechanical "gear ratio" in the system—crank arm lengths, cable arrangements, etc. The P-39 Airacobra was noted for very sensitive controls; it took only about an inch of stick movement to go from high speed to stall. On the P-51 the stick could be moved the same amount and

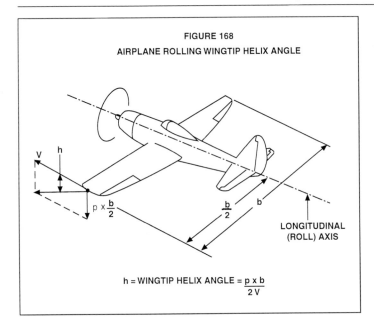

FIGURE 168
AIRPLANE ROLLING WINGTIP HELIX ANGLE

LONGITUDINAL
(ROLL) AXIS

$$h = \text{WINGTIP HELIX ANGLE} = \frac{p \times b}{2V}$$

nothing much would happen. Some pilots liked great control sensitivity; others did not.

Control in roll was particularly important for fighters. A large amount of research and testing was devoted to improving rolling performance during World War II. If a fighter could not roll quickly into a turn it could be in trouble in combat. Any major directional change had to be preceded by rolling action , so it was one key to agility. Roll controllability will be discussed in some detail.

There are two aspects to rolling motion of a fighter, both important, but the first probably more so. First the plane has to accelerate from zero up to a steady rolling velocity, and second continue to roll at that steady rate. It goes from steady level flight with no roll up to a steady value of roll rate limited by damping from drag of the wing flat area. It rolls around with either full aileron deflection, or deflection limited by lateral stick force the pilot can exert. The first (acceleration) part of the roll should take place very quickly if the plane is to have good performance. This phase might end in a quarter of a full roll or less. The two important factors determining this initial rotational acceleration are the magnitude of rolling forces about the airplane longitudinal (X) axis generated by displacement of the ailerons and the moment of inertia of the fighter about this axis. Roll acceleration is increased by a high rolling moment (torque) from aileron rolling forces M, and decreased by high lateral inertia I of the airplane. That is, the acceleration is proportional to M/I. The value of M depends on the distance across the wing between ailerons, their areas, details of their design, and how much they can be deflected with the available 'ilot force. Important details of design include shaping of leading and trailing edges. The included bevel angle of the trailing edge is important as is the exact shape of the gap between wing and aileron, and whether there is a seal across the gap. The moment of inertia, I, depends on the lateral (spanwise) weight distribution of the aircraft. It is proportional to the weight outboard times the square of the distance of this weight from the longitudinal (X) axis or centerline of the fighter. If most weight is close in to the aircraft centerline, as with a single engined fighter

with no external stores underwing, the I is relatively small and the plane will accelerate more quickly in roll. External stores outboard, as on many fighters, or gun pods way outboard, as on the Bell P-63, greatly increased lateral moment of inertia. And twin engined fighters like the P-38 and P-61 had high roll moments of inertia. So it is seen that the P-38, with a high percentage of total weight outboard in twin booms (all propulsion items) would tend to have poorer initial roll acceleration. And there was a definite initial hesitation of the P-38 entering a roll, a detriment to air combat effectiveness. In final models Lockheed added power boost to the aileron control system, thereby significantly increasing the value of the M term to increase initial roll acceleration at high speed. But the I could not be changed without completely revising the whole twin boom configuration of that aircraft.

The second part of rolling a fighter is the constant roll velocity phase noted earlier. The plane has stopped accelerating around its roll axis, and is rolling at a steady rate, neither faster nor slower. Forces from action of deflected ailerons are just balanced by damping drag forces of the wing flat area as it rolls around.

A criteria used during the war to measure roll capability was the helix, or total, angle made by the airplane wingtip as it swept around. It was worked out as follows—see Figure 168. Assume the fighter is rolling to the left, that is, left wingtip going down, and its speed of rotation is p, as indicated in the figure. The wingspan of the airplane is b. Translating the rolling velocity p into a linear speed at the left wingtip—the speed at which the wingtip is going down— is p times its distance from the center of the rotation. The distance is half the wingspan, or b/2, and the linear speed is then p times b/2. The forward speed of the wingtip, V, is the speed of the total plane, since the tip is part of it. So the overall speed of the wingtip is the addition of forward speed and rolling speed, shown as R in the figure. Speeds are shown as arrows in the figure and add as

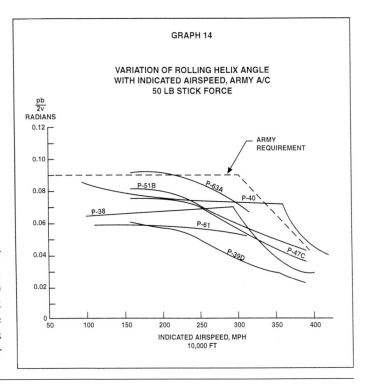

GRAPH 14

**VARIATION OF ROLLING HELIX ANGLE
WITH INDICATED AIRSPEED, ARMY A/C
50 LB STICK FORCE**

$\frac{pb}{2v}$
RADIANS

ARMY REQUIREMENT

P-51B
P-63A
P-40
P-38
P-61
P-39D
P-47C

INDICATED AIRSPEED, MPH
10,000 FT

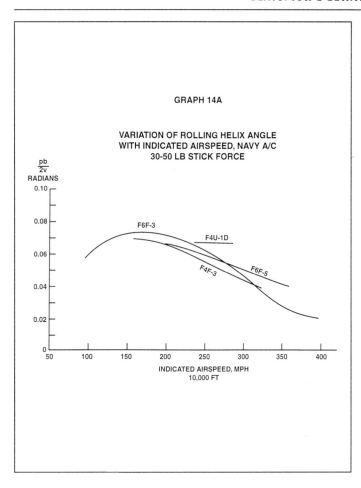

GRAPH 14A

VARIATION OF ROLLING HELIX ANGLE
WITH INDICATED AIRSPEED, NAVY A/C
30-50 LB STICK FORCE

vectors to R. The angle of this total speed R is proportional to the factor pb/2V, as is the wingtip helix angle.

So the measure selected for steady roll performance was pb/2V, which in essence indicates how fast the plane is rolling compared to how fast it is flying forward.

The military had a requirement for the pb/2V of fighters at that time. Desired values were .09 up to 300 mph IAS and .05 at 400 mph, the latter because fast rolls were tougher to do at very high speeds. Taking a case of the Army value of .09 at the highest speed required, 300 mph, we will see how fast a typical fighter would have to roll to meet the specification. Using a typical fictitious span of 40 feet we will roll the plane at sea level where true and indicated speeds are the same. The speed is 440 feet per second. So pb/2V is .09, or p=.09x2x440/40=1.98 radians per second, where a radian is 57.3 degrees. So the roll velocity v is 1.98 times 57.3, or 113 degrees per second. So the time for a full roll of 360 degrees is 360/113, or 3.18 seconds. That was a good roll time for a US World War II fighter, and thats what the Army wanted. Charts of pb/2V values for some of the fighters are shown in Graphs 14 and 14A, where it is seen desired roll performance was not often obtained in the wartime production types. Peak values varied from about .06 for the P-39D aircraft to around .09 for the P-63A.

This short discussion of fighter stability and control gives a general idea of what was involved in this very important area, and points out a few of the factors to be considered.

ARMAMENT

In World War II a fighter's primary reason for being was air combat with enemy aircraft employing guns to down the opposition. A secondary role that evolved was attack of ground targets using guns, bombs, and rockets. Weapons used in the primary role were machine guns and cannon mounted variously in the fuselage area or in or under the wings. In only one case, the Northrop P-61 night fighter, was a moveable gun turret employed in addition to fixed guns. We will take a short look at gun-type weapons used on the fighters. They ranged from .30 caliber through .50 caliber machine guns and 20 millimeter up to 37 millimeter cannon. Some weapon characteristics are listed in Table 12.

The .30 caliber machine gun fell by the wayside as the war progressed. So did the synchronized fuselage gun. Early models of the Bell P-39 the Curtiss P-40 and the P-51 used .30 caliber wing guns, but limitations in range and hitting power of this weapon were very evident. With half again the range and two and one half times the hitting power (based on delivered projectile weight per second), the advantages of .50 caliber over .30 caliber could not be ignored. Changes to all .50 caliber gun armament were made in later models of the planes mentioned, and other US models used the .50 caliber machine gun from the start. The extra weight and size of this weaponry and the additional space required for a given number of rounds of ammunition just had to be accomodated. The

.50 caliber gun was more difficult to install in fighter wings—for instance .50 caliber guns in P-51B and C models were inclined (rolled) over at an angle to better fit wing contours which complicated the ammunition belt feed and made it subject to jams. The problem was later corrected on the D model Mustangs.

But the .50 caliber gun was the favored weapon, though 20mm cannon started to gain popularity for installations later in the war. Of the eleven US fighters, fully eight (all except P-38, P-39, and P-61) either both started and ended, or ended using all .50 caliber weapons. All except five (P-40, P-47, P-63, F2A-, and F4F-) used the 20mm cannon at one time or another. The 37mm cannon was used in most (including the final) variants of the P-39. When the P-63 came along to replace the P-39 the 37mm nose cannon stayed on in spite of a relatively low rate of fire and shorter range than the 20mm weapon. As to the two types of cannon, 20mm and 37mm, on P-39 versions there were supporters on both sides of the fence. Initial jamming problems of the 37mm weapon made many pilots scramble for the 20mm alternate. It took awhile to fix the 37mm problems. The P-39 in early models was the only fighter with three different size weapons aboard, making it more difficult for armorers and logistics in the field. The cannon arrangement on the P-39 and its younger brother the P-63 was interesting. It was integrated into the basic concept of these airplanes. An airplane was built

TABLE 12
WEAPON CHARACTERISTICS

ITEM	.30 CAL.GUN	.50 CAL.GUN	20mm CANNON	37mm CANNON
APPROX WT.(LB)	24.1	70.	129.	238.
APPROX. OA LENGTH "	40.2	54.	78.	101.
RATE OF FIRE RDS./ MINUTE	1200	800-900	600	90
MUZZLE VELOCITY FT./SECOND	2,660	2,550-2,840	2920	1250-2700
AMMO. TYPE	AP OR TRACER	AP OR TRACER	EXPLOSIVE OR TRACER	EXPLOSIVE OR TRACER
WT. OF BELTED AMMO. LB./RD.	.065	.30-.311	.54-.616-.766	1.72-2.00
WT. OF AMMO. WITHOUT BELT LB./RD.	.056	.261	.66	1.40
WT. OF PRO-JECTILE LB./RD. / GRAINS/RD.	.0314/220	.106/709-743	.29	1.10
PROJECTILE WT. OF FIRE PER GUN PER SECOND	.628	1.59	2.90	1.65
MAX. EFFECTIVE PRACTICAL RANGE YARDS.	200	300	1200	300
MAX. EFFECTIVE THEORETICAL RANGE, YARDS	600	900	2400	600

around a gun, rather than making an airplane and hanging guns on it. The cannon barrel, 20mm or 37mm, ran through the center of the propeller reduction gearbox and of the propeller. In the Curtiss propeller installation the propeller hub, pitch change mechanism, electric motor, and the reduction gearbox of the engine were all specially built with a hole in the center to accept the cannon barrel. This arrangement meant no synchronizing system was required for the cannon. On the P-38 no synchronizing system was needed for either 20mm cannon or four .50 caliber machine guns since they were grouped in the nose inboard of the propeller arcs. The concentrated fire of this arrangement, allowed because the P-38 was twin-engined, was a distinct plus in hitting power. There was no bullet dispersion at any feasible range.

With wing guns installed on a fighter firepower was dispersed. Decisions had to be made on gun allignment to set the pattern of fire and convergence range. Space and weight limitations on storage of ammunition meant weapon firing time was limited, and limits were shorter than one might imagine. Table 13 displays firing times for fighter weapons based on full loads of ammunition and assuming synchronization did not restrict rates of fire. About fifteen to thirty seconds was the typical total firing time for .50 cali-

ber guns with about fifteen to twenty for 20mm cannon (the Airacobra allowed only six seconds!) Fighter pilots had to be careful and not waste ammunition with over-long bursts!

Table 14 shows weights of projectile fire, with all guns firing, thrown by various aircraft. Relative figures for the "premier" aircraft of the eleven fighter types, P-38, P-47, and P-51 for the Army, and F4U- and F6F- for the Navy, are of particular interest. The leader in throw weight per time was the P-47 Thunderbolt with 12.72 pounds per second of lead. The others are closely similar at 9.26 to 9.54 pounds per second.

Guns had to be charged before they were fired electrically. In some aircraft charging the guns was done on the ground before the flight, and they could not be recharged in the air. This was sometimes the case with wing guns. In other fighters a gun recharging system was provided. Some were mechanical cable systems running from handles in the cockpit out to each wing gun. These could be difficult to use either because of awkward positions of the handles, or the large amount of pilot force required, or both. An improvement was a hydraulic gun charging system with actuators at each gun to supply the muscle. Pilot controls would be mounted near the instrument panel.

TABLE 13
FIRING TIME AVAILABLE
(Rates of fire are: 37mm cannon 1.5 RDS/SEC; 20mm cannon 10 RDS/SEC; .50cal. machine gun 15 RDS/SEC; and .30cal. machine gun 20 RDS/SEC.)

AIRCRAFT	37mm CANNON		20mm CAMMON		.50 cal MG.		.30cal.MG.	
	RDS.PER GUN	FIRE TIME sec.	RDS.PER GUN	FIRE TIME sec.	RDS.PER GUN	FIRE TIME sec.	RDS.PER GUN	FIRE TIME sec.
P-38D-L	-	-	150	15	500	33.3	-	-
P-39D-N	30	20	-	-	200	13.3	1000	50
P-400	-	-	60	6	200	13.3	1000	50
P-39D-1,-2	-	-	60	6	200	13.3	1000	50
P-39Q	30	20	-	-	200	fus.13.3		
					300	wg. 20	-	-
P-40	-	-	-	-	200	13.3	500	25
P-40B,C,G	-	-	-	-	380	25.3	490	24.5
P-40D	-	-	-	-	615	41	-	-
P-40E-N	-	-	-	-	281	18.7	-	-
P-47B-N	-	-	-	-	267	17.8	-	-
P-51	-	-	125	12.5	-	-	-	-
P-51A	-	-	-	-	315	21	-	-
P-51B,C	-	-	-	-	315	21	-	-
P-51D,K	-	-	-	-	313	20.9	-	-
P-61A,B,C	-	-	200	20	560	37.3	-	-
P-63A,C	58	38.6	-	-	225	15	-	-
F2A-2	-	-	-	-	250	fus.16.7	-	-
					200	wg. 13.3	-	-
F2A-3	-	-	-	-	250	fus.16.7	-	-
					400	wg. 26.7	-	-
F4F-3	-	-	-	-	430	28.7	-	-
F4F-4	-	-	-	-	240	16	-	-
FM-2	-	-	-	-	430	28.7	-	-
F4U-1,-4	-	-	-	-	400	26.7	-	-
F6F-3,-5	-	-	-	-	400	26.7	-	-
F6F-5, mix.	-	-	225	22.5	400	26.7	-	-

Stoppages which prevented guns from firing sometimes occurred. At times these could be cleared by recharging if the pilot had a system available. It was often hard to know which gun had stopped firing, depending on how the guns were grouped. Usually the pilot could tell which side in case of wing guns.

Weapon stoppages could be caused by many factors—the cold air of high altitude preceded by dampness, problems with gun feed or ejection mechanisms, high g forces on linked ammunition, and so on. Noteable examples of problems were those of the Bell P-39 cannon in the early days, feed problems on early Wildcats, and the firing stoppages on the P-51B/C Mustangs during combat maneuvering.

Most all fighters ended up with gun heater systems using either electrical heating pads or hot air ducting. Some gun heaters were direct wired without pilot control. These went a long way towards solving the cold at altitude problem.

GUN SIGHTING AND GUNSIGHTS

Fighter guns were alligned in their mounts to achieve a desired firing pattern, and the airplane gunsight had to be lined up with them. The firing pattern depended on location of the weapons on the airplane, and on the pilots or air commanders philosophy on how to maximize hits on enemy aircraft. If weapons were close together in the nose of the aircraft, as on the P-38, no big decision

had to be made; guns were mounted parallel, so a tightly concentrated pattern resulted at all practical firing ranges. With the more usual location of guns out along the wing, decisions had to be made whether to keep them parallel and shoot a "box" pattern, or angle them slightly inwards to concentrate fire at a certain range. Various allignments were employed. The sight had to be set to allign with the guns at a certain flight condition since the pitch angle of the fighter varied with speed and altitude. Some average condition, such as, say, the pitch attitude for two thirds of maximum speed at a medium altitude, might be selected.

Gunsights improved over the wartime period, but very slowly, and it was late in the war before US fighter pilots got real help in the form of a radically new sighting system. A few pilots were natural born aerial marksmen, and did well even with relatively crude sights, but most pilots were only fair to poor gunners. Being an excellent flyer did not necessarily mean a pilot could consistently shoot down his opposition, though excellent flying ability did increase odds that a firing solution could be made simpler, such as a dead-astern close-in zero deflection shot.

For most of the war, that is, up until the last year, gunsights were in one form or another of the "ring and bead " type, the earlier being strictly mechanical, and the other electro-optical (the latter used very extensively). Each provided the image of a circular ring, or reticle, enclosing a central dot or "pipper". The idea was to line

TABLE 14
FIGHTER PROJECTILE THROW WEIGHTS

AIRCRAFT	NO. OF WEAPONS	.30CAL	.50CAL	20MM	37MM	TOTAL LB./SEC
			POUNDS PER SECOND			
P-38	4 .50 CAL & 1 20 MM	-	6.36	2.90	-	9.26
P-39D	4 .30 CAL, 2 .50 CAL & 1 37 MM	2.51	3.18	-	1.65	7.34
P-39D-1	4 .30 CAL, 2 .50 CAL & 1 20 MM	2.51	3.18	2.90	-	8.59
P-39Q	4 .50 CAL & 1 37MM	-	6.36	-	1.65	8.01
P-40E-N	6 .50 CAL	-	9.54	-	-	9.54
P-47	8 .50 CAL	-	12.72	-	-	12.72
P-51	4 20 MM	-	-	11.60	-	11.60
P-51B/C	4 .50 CAL	-	6.36	-	-	6.36
P-51D/K	6 .50 CAL	-	9.54	-	-	9.54
P-61A/B/C	4 .50 CAL & 4 20MM	-	6.36	11.60	-	17.96
P-63A/C	4 .50 CAL & 1 37MM	-	6.36	-	1.65	8.01
F2A-2/3	4 .50 CAL	-	6.36	-	-	6.36
F4F-3	4 .50 CAL	-	6.36	-	-	6.36
F4F-4	6 .50 CAL	-	9.54	-	-	9.54
F4U-1/1D	6 .50 CAL	-	9.54	-	-	9.54
F4U-1C	4 20MM	-	-	11.60	-	11.60
F6F-3/5	6 .50 CAL	-	9.54	-	-	9.54
F6F-5 (mix)	4 .50 CAL & 2 20MM	-	6.36	5.80	-	12.16

up the pipper on the target in the center of the ring and fire just as in using a rifle. In the mechanical ring and bead type carried over from World War I and the inter-war years, two separate supports were spaced out longitudinally and mounted on the cowling forward of the cockpit windshield. The pilot looked through his windshield and made the proper eye allignment. Provision was made for mounting these mechanical sighting elements on fighters well along in the war as backup systems; these installations including P-40s, Airacobras, and Mustangs.

In the electro-optical reflector sight the concept was the same, but the ring and bead were inside the cockpit and both in the same plane—they were not separated longitudinally. Atop the cockpit coaming behind the windshield, and behind the windshield armor glass if this was separate, and sloped back like them, a thin flat transparent glass reflector plate was mounted. A light projector was placed below and behind this plate, and angled in a manner to project an image upon it. The pattern on the projector glass was a circle with a central dot, and this was projected by a light bulb onto the sloped reflector plate so the pilot, in a central position, saw a circle of light on the plate with a pipper dot in the middle. Some installations had a dark glass that could be slipped against the reflector plate to provide "sunglasses" on a very bright day. The projector bulb usually had a dual filiment and switch, and a spare bulb was stored near the sight, since lights out meant no sight. The intensity of light projection on the reflector plate could be adjusted using a rheostat control on the bulb, a dimmer switch. The electric sight was still pretty crude and really told the pilot nothing more than the outside ring and bead type. He still had to guess target range and deflection angle, or lead, the latter being the same lead the duck hunter had to estimate. Deflection shooting was definitely an art with little help from the sight.

In the middle of 1944 US fighter pilots started to get a new sight of British design, the K-14 gyro lead-computing unit; these were first installed on Eighth Air Force Mustangs after some initial mounting difficulties were overcome. The new piece of equipment did wonders for the accuracy of American shooters, and dramatically increased aerial victories over the enemy.

The K-14 projected a central dot or pipper within a circle of small diamonds. The pilot maneuvered the aircraft to put the pipper on the target. The sight had a target size selector preset by the pilot to enemy aircraft type or target wingspan. Rotation of a throttle twist grip adjusted the diameter of the circle of diamonds to bracket the enemy. The sight computed target range and required lead angle, the pipper moving to the proper lead. The pilot adjusted flight path to again center the pipper and have it on target, and pressed the firing switch on the stick. The sight had the advantage of allowing high-angle deflection shooting with good accuracy, even by previously mediocre pilot marksmen. The new sight was used to the end of the war and for several years after.

4

FIGHTER FIGURES

THE P-38

Table 15 shows P-38 Lightnings made up ten percent of America's Hundred Thousand, the most-produced US twin-engined fighter. About two thirds of these were the late P-38J and P-38L models with intercoolers relocated from wing leading edges to engine nacelles, giving that "deep chin" look along with providing increased internal fuel capacity. Almost all P-38s were kept in American hands, including the 500 very useful F-5 reconnaissance versions.

les, the largest of these external tanks giving late P-38s a maximum total fuel capacity over 1000 gallons, or three tons of gasoline.

The striking aspect of a P-38, as shown in the three view drawings, was its configuration. Early bomber interception requirements including high speed and good climb dictated use of two engines based upon a large total power demand, and turbosuperchargers were considered necessary to maintain power available for speedy high altitude performance. Once two long liquid cooled and turbo-

TABLE 15
LOCKHEED P-38 LIGHTNING MODELS

CO. MODEL	MIL.DESIG.	EXPORT DES.	NO. A/C	FIRST DEL.	NOTES
022-64-01	XP-38	—	1	AUG.1939	NO ARMAMENT. CRASHED
122-62-02	YP-38	—	13	SEP.1940	SERVICE TEST, MANY CHGS.
222-62-02	P-38	—	30	JUN.1941	ARMOR ADDED, TRAINERS
622-62-10	XP-38A	—	(1 CONV.)	DEC.1942	19TH P-38, PRESS. CABIN
222-62-08	P-38D	—	36	JUL.1941	LEAKPROOF TANKS, TRAINER
222-62-09	P-38E	—	210	OCT.1941	COMBAT-READY , F-4 ADDL.
322-61-04	—	P-322	143	DEC.1941	UK, NO TURBOSUPERCHARGER
322-60-09/-15	P-38F	—	527	FEB.1942	UPRATED ENG.; WING RACKS
322-68-19	P-38G	—	1082	JUN.1942	ENGINE CHANGE
322-60-19	—	322-60-19	1	APR.1942	BRITISH, 524 CANC.
	P-38H	—	601	MAR.1943	POWERPLANT CHGS.
422	P-38J	—	2970	SEP.1943	DEEP CHIN, BRAKES, BOOST
	XP-38K	—	1	1943	NEW ENGINES, LARGER PROP
422	P-38L	—	3923	JUN.1944	ROCKETS, 113 BY VULTEE
	P-38M	—	(75 CONV.)	FEB.1945	2-PL CONV. NITE-FTR. L.
			TOTAL—9538		

NOTES- THREE P-322 A/C GOT TO THE UK.; 23 P-322 KEPT THEIR SAME-ROTATION ENGINES REMAINDER CONVERTED WITH NEW ENGINES FOR USAAF.
-500 F-4 AND F-5 RECON. VERSIONS ALSO PRODUCED, MAKING A TOTAL OF 10,038 A/C PRODUCED.

P-38 PRODUCTION BY YEAR

YEAR	FIGHTER AIRCRAFT	PHOTO AIRCRAFT	TOTAL
1940	1	0	1
1941	205	2	207
1942	1264	214	1478
1943	2213	284	2497
1944	4186	-	4186
1945	1669	-	1669
TOTALS	9538	500	10038

NOTE- SOME REFERENCES, INCLUDING LOCKHEED, SAY 10.037 AIRCRAFT WERE PRODUCED.

Table 16 shows the P-38 was a very big single seat fighter, over ten feet greater in span than a P-47 with almost ten percent more wing area than the Thunderbolt.

Fuel capacity figures in Table 17 present some interesting aspects. Earliest P-38s with unprotected tanks had 400 or more gallons of internal capacity; this reduced drastically to 300 gallons when self-sealing tanks were substituted in the same inboard wing spaces. The original capacity was finally regained when additional tanks were located in outer wing panel leading edges in place of intercoolers; these were moved into the engine nacelles. Another significant factor was addition of two under-wing drop tank shack-

supercharged engines were selected and a tricycle landing gear arrangement chosen, packaging all components, propulsion and main gear, made for very long nacelles in a conventional arrangement. So going a few more feet aft with twin booms, not particularly novel in aviation of the past, resulted quite naturally. The long narrow chord horizontal tail connecting the booms made the elevator particularly effective, and, for a fighter, the unusually high aspect ratio wing conferred aerodynamic benefits in both climbing and turning flight. Whether two booms or a conventional twin nacelle and single tail layout made little difference in lateral, or spanwise, inertia characteristics. Either way rolling performance was hurt. The initial roll

TABLE 16
P-38J PHYSICAL DATA

WING SPAN	52'0"	MAIN WHEEL TIRE SIZE	36"
OVERALL LENGTH	37'9 15/16"	AUX. WHEEL TIRE SIZE	27"
HEIGHT	9'10 3/8"	MAIN SHOCK STRUT TRAVEL	10"
LANDING GEAR TREAD	16' 6"	AUX. SHOCK STRUT TRAVEL	12"
WHEELBASE	10' 0.83"	TOTAL HORIZ. TAIL AREA	78.54 SQ.FT.
PROPELLER DIAMETER	11' 6"	HORIZ.TAIL ASPECT RATIO	6.02
TAIL SPAN	21' 9"	STABILIZER INCIDENCE	0 DEG.
GROSS WING AREA	327.5	SQ.FT. STABILIZER AREA	53.99 SQ.FT.
WING ROOT CHORD	117"	ELEVATOR AREA	24.55 SQ.FT.
WING TIP CHORD	36"	ELEVATOR TAB SPAN	47.69"
WING ASPECT RATIO	8.24	ELEVATOR TAB CHORD	5.25"
WING TAPER RATIO	3.25:1	ELEVATOR TAB AREA	1.74 SQ.FT.
WING MEAN AERO. CHORD	84.25"	ELEVATOR MOVEMENT	23DEG.UP 8.5DN
WING ROOT AIRFOIL	NACA 23016	HORIZ. TAIL CHORD	45"
ROOT THICKNESS RATIO	16%	HORIZ. STABILIZER CHORD	25"
WING TIP AIRFOIL	NACA 4412	ELEVATOR CHORD	20"
TIP THICKNESS RATIO	12%	ELEV.TAB MOVEMENT	25DEG.UP 25DN.
WING ROOT INCIDENCE	2 DEG.	TOTAL VERTICAL TAIL AREA	48.78 SQ.FT.
WING TIP INCIDENCE	2 DEG.	VERTICAL FIN OFFSET	0 DEG.
WING DIHEDRAL	5 DEG.40MIN.	TOTAL RUDDER AREAS	21.36FT
WING LEADING EDGE SWEEP	5DEG.11.5MIN.	MIN.RUDDER ASPECT RATIO	2.06
WING TRAILING EDGE SWEEP	9DEG.35MIN.	MIN. RUDDER TAB HEIGHT	30.75"
TOTAL AILERON AREA	25.44 SQ.FT.	RUDDER MOVEMENT 28DEG.L	28DEG R.
AILERON SPAN, EACH	107"	RUDDER TAB MOVE.25DEG.L	25DEG R.
AILERON MOVEMENT	20 DEG.DN,25 UP	RUDDER OVERALL HEIGHT	84.98"
AILERON TAB AREA	0.5 SQ.FT.	WING MAIN SPAR LOC.	35% CHORD
FLAP SPAN, INBOARD	69.25"	PROP-FUSELAGE CLEARANCE	9.62"
FLAP SPAN, OUTBOARD	61.25"	MIN. PROP GND.CLEARANCE	9.0"
FLAP CHORD, RETRACTED	23.5"	C/L FUS. TO C/L NACELLE	8 FT.
MAX. FUSELAGE WIDTH	38"	FIN AREA TOTAL	27.42 SQ.FT.
MAX. FUSELAGE DEPTH	72"		

TABLE 17
P-38 FUEL CAPACITIES

MODEL	MAX INTERNAL FUEL(US GAL.)	MAX EXTERNAL FUEL(US GAL.)
XP-38	400	—
YP-38	410	—
P-38	410	—
XP-38A	400	—
P-38D	300	—
P-38E	300	—
P-38F	300	300
P-38G	300	600
P-38H	300	600
P-38J	410	600
P-38L	410	600

time constant suffered with respect to those of smaller single engine fighters with little weight outboard of the fuselage. An advantage was a twin engined layout allowed concentrated unsynchronized fire power in the central nose. This was a distinct plus for the P-38.

The cutaway drawing of a P-38 shows the central fuselage pod carried a large and easily accessible weapons bay up front for a cannon and four machine guns plus ammunition storage containers. The pilot's cockpit was located just aft of this bay. A nose landing gear bay filled out a large section of available space beneath both weapons bay and cockpit with the retracted wheel nestling just under the pilot's seat. Radio gear and hydraulic subsystems equipment, along with a stowed pilot access ladder filled out the aft space available.

Each outboard boom of the P-38 was packed with required items. The forward bay ahead of the firewall and just aft of propeller and spinner started off with a coolant tank wrapped around the engine reduction gearing, then came the long Allison V-12 engine and accessories. Behind the engine was a large oil tank, and alongside the engine mounting structure. Below the engine was the oil cooler and associated ducting, and on late models the intercooler for the induction system with its associated air ducting was situated in this area. Back of the engine firewall came upper space for the wing structural carrythrough and above and just aft of that the turbosupercharger installation with input and output ducting to and from the engine. A large space below was reserved for a main land-

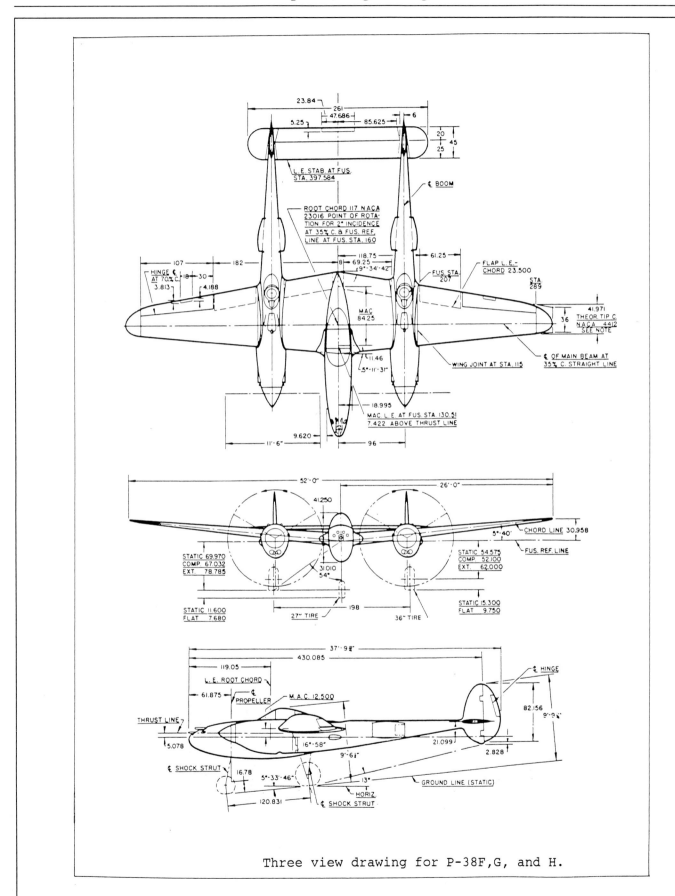

Three view drawing for P-38F,G, and H.

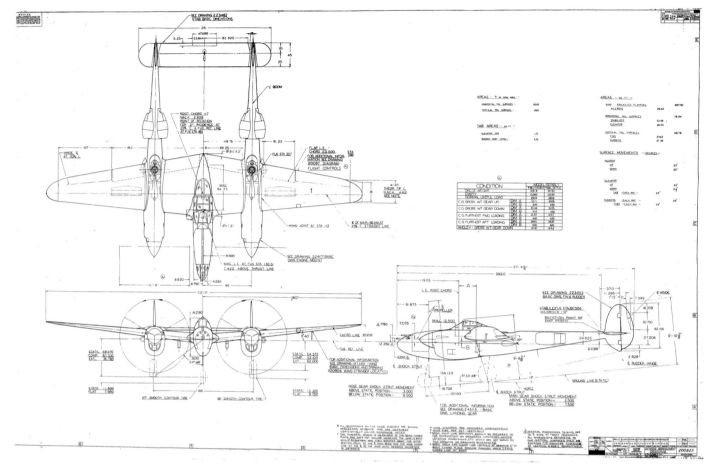

Three view drawing for P-38J and L.

ing gear bay where the retracted wheel folded into a space just aft of the wing trailing edge. The next bay aft contained the glycol coolers for the engines and their air ducts and associated actuators. Finally at the extreme rear of each boom was space for equipment like the battery, special equipment stowage, and oxygen bottles. In addition flight control runs to the tail were routed through each boom aft and engine controls routed forward. Nacelles were tightly packed, and particularly in the powerplant areas space was tight and hard to work in.

Table 18 indicates the progression of Allison V-12 models used in P-38s along with power ratings. It shows where a COMBAT rating was introduced, very high short-time power, sometimes called WAR EMERGENCY. Horsepowers and altitudes at which they could be maintained steadily increased, though cooling problems limited attainable powers at least temporarily; relocation of the intercoolers helped here. Curtiss Electric propellers stayed aboard all P-38 versions. Since these depended for blade angle change on aircraft electrical power things improved substantially when on late models two generators were installed instead of one. Engines and propellers were handed left and right which did not improve logistics.

The curves of Graphs 15 and 16 show P-38 high speed and steady climb performance from near sea level to high altitude. Speed

capability increased steadily from 330-340 mph at low altitude to 400 mph or more at 25000 to 30000 feet because the turbosuperchargers kept engine power up. Above 25000 feet cooling or supercharger impeller or turbine speeds became limiting, and airplane high speed capability started to fall off. Near 30000 feet speeds over Mach 0.60 could be reached in steady level flight, and any diving or maneuvering could start the P-38 into the area of possible compressibility troubles.

Graph 16 indicates climb rates of late models at MILITARY power started well over 3000 feet per minute down low, gradually falling off up to 25000 feet; from there on up climb rate reduced quickly. At COMBAT power low altitude climb rates exceeded 3500 feet per minute. For World War II the P-38 was a pretty fast climbing airplane. Late model climb times are shown in the curves as three and a half, seven, and 11.5 minutes to 10000, 20000, and 30000 feet respectively.

Curves of Graph 17 indicate range performance for P-38s with different amounts of takeoff fuel. Under the stated conditions, somewhat impractical since there is no fuel reserves allowance, range varied from 800 miles on just internal fuel for early versions and increased in later models to 2200 miles with maximum internal and external fuel. Combat radii are specified in the table as 275 miles on internal fuel or 650 miles with a total of 740 gallons internally

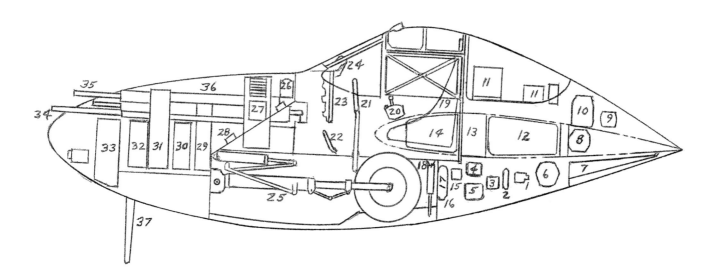

1. Flap Control hydraulic valve.
2. Fuel strainer
3. Fuel selector hydraulic valve
4. Flap control hydraulic valve
5. Landing gear control hydraulic valve
6. Hydraulic system accumulator
7. Access ladder stowage
8. Flap motor and gearbox
9. Gear emergency extension hydraulic reservoir
10. Main hydraulic reservoir
11. Radio
12. Wing main fuel tank (outside of pod)
13. Main spar (carries through fuselage)
14. Wing reserve fuel tank (outside of pod)
15. Electric auxiliary fuel pump
16. Subsystems component bay
17. Hydraulic filter
18.
19. Pilot's seat
20. Throttle quadrant
21. Pilot's control column
22. Pilot's rudder pedals
23. Instrument panel
24. Gunsight
25. Retracted nose landing gear
26. Cannon hydraulic charging reservoir
27. Cannon ammunition container
28. Machine gun solonoid
29.
30. Machine gun ejection chute
31. Machine gun ammunition box
32. Machine gun ejection chute
33. Cannon ballast space
34. Cannon barrel
35. Left upper gun barrel
36. Armament bay
37. Radio antenna

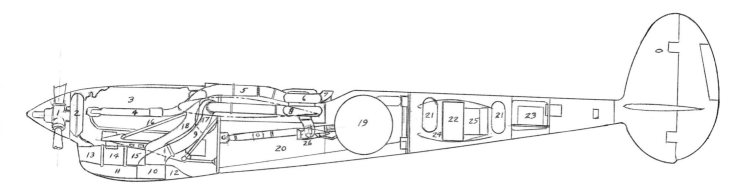

1. Curtiss Electric propeller
2. Coolant header tank
3. Allison V-1710 engine
4. Engine exhaust manifold
5. Exhaust duct to turbine
6. Turbosupercharger turbine section
7. Turbine exhaust waste gate
8. Turbosupercharger compressor
9. Turbine to intercooler duct
10. Intercooler
11. Intercooler cool air duct
12. Intercooler cooling air exhaust
13. Left side oil cooler intake duct
14. Left side oil cooler
15. Left side oil cooler exhaust
16. Engine mount
17. Oil tank (behind duct)
18. Intercooler to carburetor duct
19. Retracted main gear wheel
20. Main landing gear bay
21. Oxygen bottle
22. Coolant radiator (both sides)
23. Battery (left boom)
24. Cooling air intake
25. Cooling air exhaust
26. Air intake to turbosupercharger compressor.

Inboard profile drawings of the P-38L

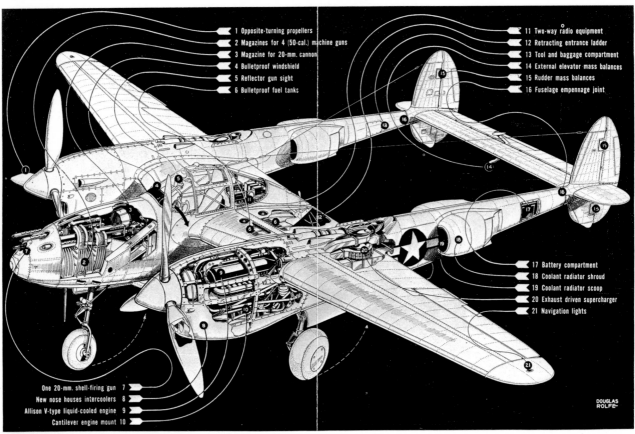

1 Opposite-turning propellers
2 Magazines for 4 (50-cal.) machine guns
3 Magazine for 20-mm. cannon
4 Bulletproof windshield
5 Reflector gun sight
6 Bulletproof fuel tanks

11 Two-way radio equipment
12 Retracting entrance ladder
13 Tool and baggage compartment
14 External elevator mass balances
15 Rudder mass balances
16 Fuselage empennage joint

One 20-mm. shell-firing gun 7
New nose houses intercoolers 8
Allison V-type liquid-cooled engine 9
Cantilever engine mount 10

17 Battery compartment
18 Coolant radiator shroud
19 Coolant radiator scoop
20 Exhaust driven supercharger
21 Navigation lights

DOUGLAS ROLFE

LOCKHEED P-38 LIGHTNING
ARMY AIR FORCES TWIN ENGINE FIGHTER
World War II

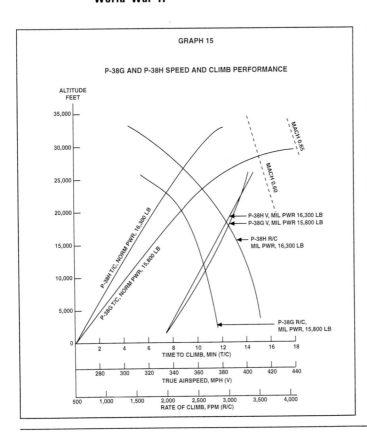

GRAPH 15

P-38G AND P-38H SPEED AND CLIMB PERFORMANCE

ALTITUDE FEET

MACH 0.65
MACH 0.60

P-38H V, MIL PWR 16,300 LB
P-38G V, MIL PWR 15,800 LB

P-38H R/C MIL PWR, 16,300 LB

P-38H T/C, NORM PWR, 16,300 LB
P-38G T/C, NORM PWR, 15,800 LB

P-38G R/C, MIL PWR, 15,800 LB

TIME TO CLIMB, MIN (T/C)
TRUE AIRSPEED, MPH (V)
RATE OF CLIMB, FPM (R/C)

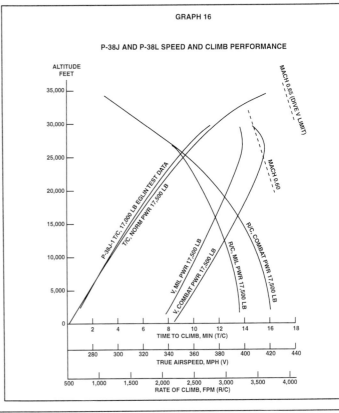

GRAPH 16

P-38J AND P-38L SPEED AND CLIMB PERFORMANCE

ALTITUDE FEET

MACH 0.65 (DIVE V LIMIT)
MACH 0.60

P-38J-1 T/C, 17,000 LB EGLIN TEST DATA
T/C, NORM PWR 17,500 LB

V, MIL PWR 17,500 LB
V, COMBAT PWR 17,500 LB
R/C, MIL PWR 17,500 LB
R/C, COMBAT PWR 17,500 LB

TIME TO CLIMB, MIN (T/C)
TRUE AIRSPEED, MPH (V)
RATE OF CLIMB, FPM (R/C)

TABLE 18
P-38 PROPULSION DATA

MODEL	ENGINE	RATING	HP	ERPM	ALTITUDE'	MAP"HG.	AUX.SUPER.
XP-38	AL.V-1710-11/15	TO.	1150	3000	SEA LEVEL		GE B-1 TURBO.
		MILITARY	1150	3000	25000		
		NORMAL	1000	2600	25000		
YP-38,P-38	V-1710-27/29	TO.	1150	3000	SEA LEVEL		GE B-2 TURBO
P-38D,P-38E	(F-2)	MILITARY	1150	3000	25000		
		NORMAL	1000	2600	25000		
P-322	V-1710-C15	TO.	1150	3000	SEA LEVEL		—
		MILITARY					
		NORMAL	930	2600	15000	35.3	
P-38F	V-1710-49/53	TO.	1325	3000	SEA LEVEL	47.0	GE B-13 TURBO
	(F-5)	MILITARY	1325	3000	25000	47.0	
		NORMAL	1000	2600	25000	37.8	
P-38G	V-1710-51/55	TO.	1325	3000	SEA LEVEL	47.0	GE B-13 TURBO
	(F-10)	MILITARY	1325	3000	25000	47.0	
		NORMAL	1100	2600	25000	41.0	
P-38H	V-1710-89/91	TO	1425	3000	SEA LEVEL	54.0	GE B-33 TURBO
	(F-17)	COMBAT	1600	3000	26500	60.0	
		MILITARY	1240	3000	25000	54.0	
		NORMAL	1100	2600	34000	44.0	
P-38J,	V-1710-89/91	TO	1425	3000	SEA LEVEL	54.0	GE B-33 TURBO
(SOME P-38L-5)		COMBAT	1600	3000	26500	60.0	
		MILITARY	1425	3000	26500	54.0	
		NORMAL	1100	2600	32500	44.0	
XP-38K	V-1710-75/77	TO	1425	3000	SEA LEVEL	54.0	
P-38L	V-1710-111/113	TO	1425	3000	SEA LEVEL	54.0	GE B-33 TURBO
P-38M	(F-30)	COMBAT	1600	3000	28700	60.0	
		MILITARY	1425	3000	29000	54.0	
		NORMAL	1100	2600	33800	44.0	

NOTE: PROPELLERS—CURTISS THREE BLADE ELECTRIC, MODEL C532D. DIAMETER 11'6" EXCEPT XP-38K 12'6" SOLID ALUMINUM BLADES ON PROD. MODELS, DESIGN 88996 LEFT HAND, AND 89303 RIGHT HAND.

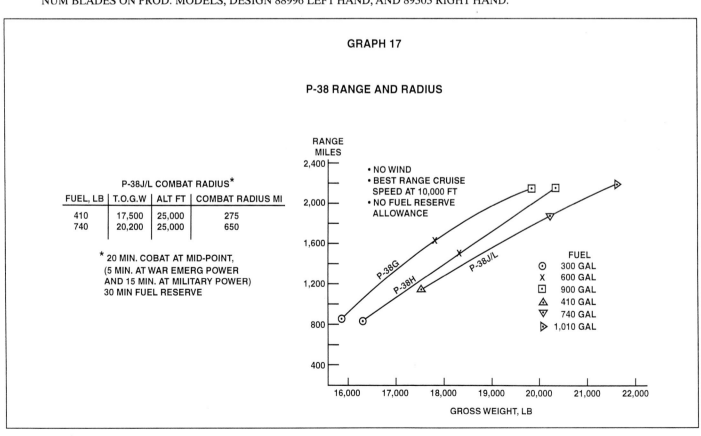

GRAPH 17

P-38 RANGE AND RADIUS

P-38J/L COMBAT RADIUS*

FUEL, LB	T.O.G.W	ALT FT	COMBAT RADIUS MI
410	17,500	25,000	275
740	20,200	25,000	650

* 20 MIN. COBAT AT MID-POINT,
(5 MIN. AT WAR EMERG POWER
AND 15 MIN. AT MILITARY POWER)
30 MIN FUEL RESERVE

RANGE MILES

• NO WIND
• BEST RANGE CRUISE SPEED AT 10,000 FT
• NO FUEL RESERVE ALLOWANCE

FUEL
⊙ 300 GAL
X 600 GAL
⊡ 900 GAL
△ 410 GAL
▽ 740 GAL
▷ 1,010 GAL

GROSS WEIGHT, LB

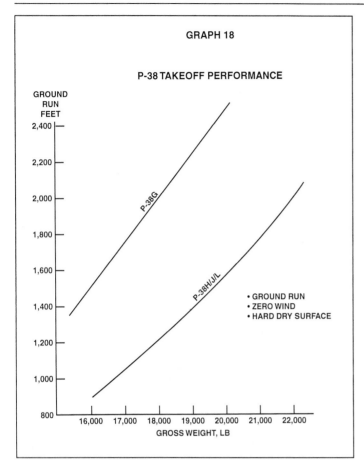

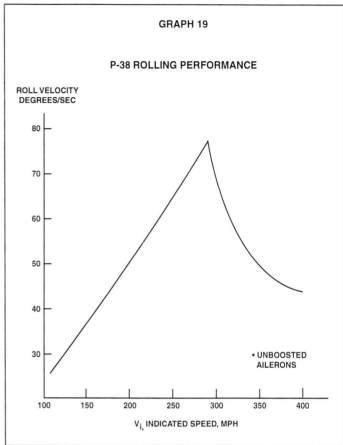

and externally. For these radii a fuel reserve allowance is made as well as midpoint time allotted for combat at high power settings.

Graph 18 shows P-38 takeoff performance against aircraft gross weight in terms of ground run required with zero wind on improved fields. These curves show takeoff got considerably shorter in late versions. In all practical cases of aircraft gross weight, however, ground runs were over 1000 feet.

A curve of steady state rolling performance, degrees of roll per second against indicated airspeed, is shown in Graph 19 for a P-38 without the aileron boost feature added later on P-38J-25 and subsequent Lightning versions. The inverted vee shape of the curve reflects two factors. On the left, or "up" side, ailerons are constantly at maximum deflection (to almost 300 mph IAS), and up to the peak rate of about 77 degrees per second (a 4.7 second roll) the pilot can exert sufficient control wheel force to hold this full deflection. The actual value of control wheel force used in this curve is unknown, but roll rates at higher speeds represented by the "down" side of the curve are all at constant maximum pilot wheel force, and decrease rapidly. So, at the lower speeds maximum aileron deflection limits roll rate, and at high speeds the pilot's available muscle limits it. Installing an aileron power boost system, as Lockheed did

in late models, substantially raised roll rate values on the "down" side of the curve by hydraulically boosting the pilot's muscle a considerable amount. Unfortunately data on the boosted system performance is not available.

Table 19 details empty and basic weights of a P-38J along with group weights of an early service test YP-38 for comparison. The J model empty weight increased almost 600 pounds over the YP-38. Most all group weights increased, particularly the fuel system weight, reflecting installation of more fuel capacity as well as use of gunfire-protected tanks. The reason for the change in surface control weights is unknown.

Using the P-38J (and L) basic weight of 14100 pounds, Table 20 shows five typical loading conditions bringing the aircraft to various gross weights. They range from just over 16000 pounds to more than 21000 pounds. The light gross weight is achieved by limiting both .50 caliber ammunition and internal fuel and oil to less than full capacity, probably not a really practical case in wartime. The first alternate loading case similarly limits internal fuel. Second and third alternate loadings shown are quite practical, the latter with two 165 gallon drop tanks underwing. Loading for a ferry mission results in the highest takeoff gross weight.

TABLE 19
P-38 WEIGHTS

EMPTY AND BASIC WEIGHTS (LB.)				
GROUP	YP-38	P-38J		
Wing	1821.6	1859.6		
Tail	418.3	417.2		
Fuselage	1376.3	1453.6		
Landing Gear	836.6	885.9		
Engine Section	445.3	471.0		
Engines	2536.7	2730.0		
Engine Accessories	661.2	321.3		
Engine Controls	81.0	80.8		
Propellers	692.5	827.3		
Starting	81.0	82.3		
Cooling	863.6	1065.1		
Supercharging	(with access.)	613.5		
Lubricating	161.9	194.1		
Fuel System	121.4	505.8		
Surface Controls	431.8	234.4		
Instruments	54.0	73.2		
Hydraulics	27.0	209.0		
Electrical	296.9	321.1		
Communication	81.0	161.9		
Armament Provisions	121.4	175.5		
Furnishings	54.0	95.8		
Other	35.0	1.5		
EMPTY WEIGHT (P-38J)	11,196.0	12,780.0		

EMPTY WEIGHT (P-38J)	12,780.0
Trapped Oil	60.0
Trapped Fuel	20.0
Cal..50 Gun Install.	(4) 425.0
20 mm. Cannon Install.	(1) 196.0
Gun Sight	3.0
Gun Camera	12.0
Prov. for Drop Tanks	56.0
Armor/BP Glass	245.0
Pyrotechnics	
Navig. Equipment	
Photo Equipment	
Oxygen Equipment	303.0
Emerg. Equipment	
Misc. Equipment	
BASIC WEIGHT (P-38J)	14,100.0

WTS. OF OTHER VERSIONS

VERSION	EMPTY	BASIC
XP-38	11,507	
P-38	11,672	
XP-38A	11,507	
P-38D	11,780	12,700
P-38E	11,780	12,700
P-38F	12,264	13,000
P-38G	12,200	13,500
P-38H	12,380	13,700
P-38L	12,800	14,100

TABLE 20
TYPICAL P-38J ALTERNATE LOADS
(POUNDS)

MISSION	NORMAL	1ST. ALTERNATE	2ND ALTERNATE	3RD.ALTERNATE	FERRY
Pilot	200	200	200	200	200
Useable Oil	128	195	195	195	195
Gun Ammo.	249	622	622	622	—
20mm. Ammo.	92	92	92	92	—
Bomb Instl.	—	—	—	—	—
Rocket Instl.	—	—	—	—	—
Drop Tanks	—	—	—	175	310
Fuel,Int.L.E.	—	—	690	690	690
Fuel,Int.Front	720	720	720	720	720
Fuel,Int.Rear	660	1080	1080	1080	1080
Fuel,Ext. Drop	—	—	—	1980	3744
TOT.DISP.LOAD	2049	2909	3599	5754	6939
GROSS WEIGHT	16149	17009	17699	19854	21039
USEFUL LOAD	3369	4229	4919	7074	8259

Note: The above use the P-38J BASIC WEIGHT of 14,100 lb.
       Gas weighs 6.0 pounds per gallon
       Oil weighs 7.5 pounds per gallon

800 Rounds of .50 cal. ammo weighs 249 lb.; 2000 rounds weighs 622lb.
150 Rounds of 20mm. ammo weighs 92lb.

P-38 MAJOR MODEL-TO-MODEL CHANGES

YP-38 Two radiators in each boom in place of one. New cowl lines. New brakes. Engine reduction gearing change. Raised thrust line. Propeller rotation reversed. Redesigned canopy. Revised structural design. Turbosupercharger installation revised. Armament changed. Thirty thousand drawing changes from XP-38 to YP-38.

P-38 Pilot armor and bullet-proof windshield added. Armament changed again.

P-38D New wing-fuselage fillets at leading edge. Redesign of elevator mass-balance. Horizontal tail incidence changed downward from 1 deg.15' to 0 deg. Self-sealing fuel tanks added. New low-pressure oxygen system. New propellers. Heavier armor. Retractable landing light in place of droppable flares. Elevator control system changes.

P-38E Nearly 2000 changes; many in cockpit. Armament change; 37mm. cannon to 20mm. Nose section completely redesigned with greater ammunition capacity. Heated weapons. Revised hydraulic and electrical systems. SCR-274N radio added. Oxygen system change.

P-38F Powerplant model change. External store stations added.

P-38F-5 New A-12 oxygen system added.

P-38F-13 Instruments modified.

P-38F-15 Maneuver flap setting introduced.

P-38G-3 New B-13 turbosuperchargers, allowing cruising at higher power.

P-38G-5 New radio. New A-9 oxygen system. Revised turbosupercharger. Instrument changes.

P-38G-10 External bomb capacity upped to 3200 pounds total. Last 200 G models modified to carry two 300 gallon drop tanks.

P-38H New B-33 turbosuperchargers. New automatic engine controls. Automatic oil cooler exit flap operation. New engine version. Electrical system changes. M-2C cannon replaced M-1 model.

P-38J New propellers. New higher capacity coolant radiators.

P-38J-10 New flat windshield. Improved cockpit heating. Control wheel revised. Improved electrical system with generator on each engine instead of on only one.

P-38J-15 New wing leading edge fuel tanks. Intercoolers moved from wings to engine nacelles. Revised cowl lines.

P-38J-25 Underwing dive recovery flaps incorporated. Power-boosted ailerons added.

XP-38K Revised powerplant with new larger propellers..

P-38L Automatic powerplant controls. Uprated engines. Flush landing light in left wing. Tail warning radar added. New turbo regulator.

P-38L-5 Underwing rocket-launcher system added. Five rockets per side.

P-38M Night fighter equipment added to P-38L-5 version. Two-place, revised canopy, radar.

LOCKHEED P-38 CHRONOLOGY

Mar '36 Design work on project M12-36 leads up to Lockheed Model 22.

Jan '37 Army interceptor specification is sent to manufacturers.

Feb '37 Army announces a design competition for a new interceptor.

'37 Lockheed's Hall hibbard starts design studies for the plane.

Apr 13, '37 Kelly Johnson completes an Aerodynamic and Performance Study of the Lockheed Model 22 Pursuit Aircraft.

Jun 23, '37 Lockheed wins a $163000 XP-38 prototype aircraft contract.

Sep 23, '37 Allison V-1710-C7 and C9 engines are selected for the XP-38.

Jul 31, '38 The completed XP-38 is secretly trucked to March Field, Cal.

Jan 27, '39 Army Lt.Ben Kelsey takes the XP-38 on a first flight.

Feb 11, '39 After 11 hours 50 minutes XP-38 time Kelsey takes it on a two stop transcontinental speed dash of seven hours and two minutes air time and crashes short of Mitchell Field, N.Y.

Apr 27, '39 A new contract for thirteen YP-38s is valued at $2,180,725.

Jun 26, '39 A Model Specification is issued for the P-38 version.

Jul '39 The first YP-38 design drawings are released to the shop.

Aug 10, '39 Sixty-six production 222 planes are ordered. The first 20 of these are P-38 models.

Oct 20, '39 A Lockheed YP-38 Model Specification 1611 is approved.

Jan 1, '40 Lockheed now employs 7464 people with numbers increasing.

Feb '40 Fabrication on YP-38s is started.

Mar '40 The British order 143 Model 322 planes with no turbosuperchargers.

Jun 5, '40 US approval is given for UK purchase of an additional 524 Lightning MK.2 airplanes with engine turbosuperchargers.

Aug 5, '40 Army decides all P-38 machine guns are to be .50 caliber and that defensive armor is to be fitted on the planes.

Aug 30, '40 Army orders 607 more P-38s now to use a 20 mm. cannon.

Sep 16, '40 Test pilot Marshall Headle pilots the first YP-38 flight.

Jan 1, '41 Lockheed now employs 16959 people and is still growing.

Jan '41 The second YP-38 goes to Wright Field, Dayton, Ohio.

Mar '41 The first YP-38 is accepted and held at Lockheed for test.

Apr 8, '41 The British informally test the YP-38 at Wright Field.

Jun '41 All YP-38s are delivered; most go to Selfridge Field, Mi.

Jun 28, '41 Tail buffet is occurring. After dive tests wing-fuselage fillets provide an acceptable solution to the problem.

Jul '41 Delivery of the P-38 version commences from Lockheed.

Aug '41 Five British 322-61s roll off the Lockheed assembly line.

Aug '41 Delivery begins of P-38D versions.

Aug 15, '41 Only 39 Lightnings have been delivered to this time.

Aug 30, '41 All P-38D airplanes have now been delivered.

Sep '41 P-38s and P-38Ds go to Louisiana Army summer maneuvers.

Sep 8, '41 The second British 322 is now flying. The first had been used for the tail buffeting tests.

Oct 31, '41 Of 1000 P-38s on order 80 have been delivered.

Oct 31, '41 Production changes allowed October delivery of three P-38s.

Nov '41 Lockheed employment now totals 40307 people.

Nov 4, '41 Lockheed test pilot Ralph Virden is killed in a dive crash of the first YP-38. A compressibility problem is suspected.

Nov '41 The P-38E appears. Acceptances of P-38s rise to 74 planes.

Dec '41 Employment at Lockheed and Vega has risen to 53221.

Dec '41 The first British Model 322-61 is delivered in England.

Dec 7, '41 USAAF inventory of P-38s at the time of Pearl Harbor is 69 in active service including some D models; the only unit fully equipped is the First Pursuit Group, Selfridge Field.

Dec 8, '41 Initial elements of the First Pursuit Group from Selfridge arrive at San Diego to defend the west coast from Japanese attack. Group movement is complete by December 22, 1941.

Dec '41 The first F-4 photo version of the P-38E model is produced.

Dec 31, '41 The total of P-38s produced is 207 including exports.

Jan '42 The second British 322-61 airplane arrives in Britain.

Feb '42 Production of the P-38F with a maneuver flap is started.

Mar '42 Studies are made of a twin float P-38E seaplane for the Pacific. A raised-tail airplane is tested.

Mar '42 Deliveries commence from Lockheed of the P-38F model.

Apr 7, '42 F-4 Photo Lightnings of Flight A, 8th Photo Squadron with 75 gallon drop tanks arrive in Australia under Maj. K. Prolifka and by April 16 start reconnaissance missions over eastern New Guinea and New Britain. These are the first Lightnings in the Pacific. Later F-4s operate very successfully with the 435th Bombardment Squadron.

Apr 15, '42 A decision is made to fly P-38s of the First Pursuit Group (and P-39s of the 31st Group) along with B-17s across the Atlantic Ocean to England. A hundred new P-38Fs are being prepared for the trip at Lockheed.

Apr '42 The third British 322-61 Lightning arrives in the UK.

May '42 The XP-38A with pressurized cabin is converted from a P-38.

May 29, '42 The first P-38E combat deployment to Alaska takes place. The planes are winterized and equipped with drop tanks. Twenty-five aircraft of the 54th Sdn. 343rd Fighter Group, 11th AF go north to Elmendorf Field at Anchorage.

Jun 11, '42 The First Fighter (was Pursuit) Group after returning east is again turned to the west coast because of the Japanese Midway threat. They are stopped at Charlotte, N.C. June 3rd then ordered to Bangor, Maine.

Jun '42 Twenty F-5A photo planes are put in line ahead of P-38G-1s.

Jun 9, '42 The ground echelon of the First Fighter Group arrives in UK.

Jun 15, '42 The First Ftr.Gp. has a full P-38 complement at Bangor, Me.

Jun 18, '42 Eighth AF Fighter Command orders 80 P-38Fs to go along with 49 B-17s and 52 C-47s across the Atlantic as part of Bolero.

Jun 23, '42 Initial P-38Fs of First FG fly from Presque Isle, Me. to Goose Bay, Labrador on a first leg of a trans-Atlantic flight to the United Kingdom.

Jul '42 Fourth and last 322-61 airplane arrives in England.

Jul '42 The 14th Fighter Group with new P-38F and P-38G Lightnings assembles at March Field, Cal. for a mass flight to the UK. It includes the 48th, 49th, and 50th Squadrons.

Jul 31, '42 The 27th Sdn. of First FG stays in Iceland to act as a defense unit; it is relieved Aug.26 by the 50th Fighter Sdn. of the 14th Fighter Group as the latter flies to England.

Jul 15, '42 Six P-38s come down on the east coast ice cap of Greenland and are lost; the pilots walk out to safety. Of 186 P-38s sent over the Atlantic in 1942 only these and one other are lost. The planes carry two 165 gallon drop tanks.

Jul 22, '42 Twenty-eight P-38s of the 14th FG with an escort of six B-17 aircraft start the trip from Maine via Goose Bay and Iceland to Stornaway, Scotland. All the planes make it.

Aug '42 Twenty F-5A-3 photo Lightnings are started in production.

Aug '42 The British contract for 524 Lightning IIs is cancelled.

Aug '42 Gen. Kenney pleads for P-38s for the 5th AF to Gen. Arnold.

Aug 9, '42 A first Alaskan combat victory for P-38s occurs when two Lightnings shoot down two Japanese flying boats.

Aug 22, '42 The 67th Fighter Squadron, made up of P-38s and Bell P-400s, arrives at Henderson Field on Guadalcanal in the Solomons.

Aug 28, '42 The First FG in England is now ready for combat operations.

Aug 29, '42 Two P-38s of the 94th Sdn.,First FG attempt to intercept German aircraft over England, but do not make contact.

Aug 31, '42 A total of 164 P-38s along with 119 B-17s and 103 C-47s have now crossed the Atlantic by air, and the First and 14th FGs are established in the United Kingdom.

Sep 2, '42 The First FG flies an initial mission from England, a 32 aircraft sweep over France with no contacts. A total of 340 sorties are flown in the next few days with two non-combat Lightning crashes.

Sep 14, '42 The four fighter groups of the 8th Air Force are transferred to the 12th Air Force and slated for shipment to North Africa for Operation Torch. They operate in the UK until Oct.10. Eventually only the Fourth Fighter Group stays in England.

Sep 16, '42 The P-38 groups in England become fully operational.

Oct '42 The 14th FG is moved to Lands End in the UK for deployment to North Africa. It then departs for Gibraltar.

Oct '42 Difficulties occur getting P-38s ready in the Pacific. About 60 planes are in-theatre but not in combat. Problems include fuel tank leaks, superchargers, coolers, inverters, and armament.

Oct '42 Gen. Hap Arnold replies to P-38 requests from the South Pacific that if these were granted the planned invasion of North Africa would have to be abandoned.

Oct 15, '42 P-38s finally fly a B-17 escort mission after a few fighter sweeps over France.

Oct 22, '42 All early P-38s through the D are now in restricted use.

Oct 25, '42 Fifteen P-38s are now serving with the 339th Squadron in the South Pacific. They are being inserted by squadron only.

Oct 31, '42 The P-38Fs in England are withdrawn from combat status so as to be part of Operation Torch in North Africa.

Oct 31, '42 P-38s of the 339th FS arrive at Guadalcanal's Henderson Field in the Solomon Is., SW Pacific.

Nov '42 P-38s of the 78th FG are also ferried from England to North Africa along with most pilots as replacements, but the 78th as a unit stays in England.

Nov '42 P-38s in Tunisia are being used for weather reconnaissance.

Nov 13, '42 Major Dale Brannon brings in eight P-38s of the new 339th Fighter Squadron to Henderson Field on Guadalcanal. They stay until Nov.22 and return in December.

Nov 14, '42 The two P-38F FGs, First and 14th, transfer from the UK to North Africa. One 14th squadron is still in Iceland.

Nov 16, '42 The 14th FG is operational in North Africa after having flown down the previous day. The First FG took off on the 13th and settled near Oran. Ground personnel came ashore on the 8th with the landings.

Nov 18, '42 The 48th Sdn.,14th FG goes on a first North African mission.

Nov 21, '42 The 49th Sdn.,14th FG escorts A-20s to Bizerte and downs five enemy aircraft but loses five P-38s.

Dec '42 Raised tail P-38 tests for a seaplane version are stopped.

Dec '42 P-38s escort B-17s over Tunis and Bizerte in North Africa. P-38 attrition is high and the type is in very short supply.

Dec '42 P-38s in North Africa are used on anti-shipping missions.

Dec '42 The 82nd FG arrives in North Africa. On the flight from the UK the 80 P-38s shoot down two German JU-88s over the Bay of Biscay. Most 82nd planes are used as replacements for lost First and 14th FG aircraft, and the 82nd gets replacements directly from the United States.

Dec 21, '42 With a mix of P-38s and P-39s the 70th FS flies into Guadalcanal's Henderson Field. P-38s are scarce because of the demands of the North African campaign which has priority.

Dec 27, '42 P-38s of the 39th FS, 35th FG fly their first combat mission in the SW Pacific. In the Papua, New Guinea campaign nine Japanese fighters and two dive bombers are claimed for the loss of one Lightning.

Dec 31, '42 Gen. Harmon visits Guadalcanal and praises the P-38 as giving excellent service in several roles with minimum maintenance. Harmon now has about 41 P-38s but could use 100.

Dec 31, '42 Lockheed has produced 1264 P-38s in the last year; 179 of 186 have gotten to England by air over the Atlantic. In December alone 475 P-38s have been shipped to the UK by sea.

Jan '43 The P-38 shortage is acute. Only 90 are available to the three No. African FGs as the Casablanca Conference is held. Gen. Arnold orders all P-38s down from England, even updated P-38Es, also planes of the reserve 78th FG just arrived in England along with aircraft from the US.

Jan '43 In the SW Pacific the 9th Sdn. of the 49th FG is supplied with P-38s to replace P-40 aircraft used up until now.

Jan '43 The 13th Air Force is formed in the South Pacific, and the 339th Sdn. is equipped with the few P-38s available.

Jan 1, '43 Gen. Whitehead of the 5th Air Force says "We have whipped the Jap" after a second victory by P-38s in New Guinea.

Jan 9, '43 P-38s and P-40s over Lae, New Guinea have a good day. P-38s score at least 13 victories. Lt. Richard Bong of the 49th GP claims the downing of three enemy aircraft.

Jan 17, '43 The 17th Photo Reconnaissance Squadron arrives at Henderson Field, Guadalcanal with F-5 Lightning photo aircraft.

Jan 23, '43 The 48th Sdn.,14th FG in North Africa has lost 13 pilots and about 20 aircraft since Nov.18 with five lost this date, and morale hits rock bottom. The 14th GP is pulled from combat; flying personnel are re-assigned though ground people are held. A third squadron, the 37th, is added, and the group is refitted using men and aircraft from the 78th FG to replace the heavy losses.

Feb '43 Gen. Kenney of the 5th Air Force in the SW Pacific is told that because of the critical North African situation he can expect no more P-38s until summer. He is given permission to activate the 475th FG for which P-38s would probably be available in June. Kenney is operating under a replacement schedule of 15 P-38s a month initiated in January, and has received only eight replacement Lightnings so far.

Feb '43 The 13th Photo Sdn. in the 8th Air Force now has enough F-4 and F-5 Lightnings to start high altitude reconnaissance missions. The best altitude for the F-5 is found to be 25000 feet. Higher altitudes are apt to mean engine trouble.

Mar '43 The 80th Sdn.,8th FG in the Pacific changes over from P-39s to P-38 Lightning aircraft.

Mar '43 In Washington on a visit Gen.Kenney asks Gen.Hap Arnold for a full group of P-38s. Arnold says he can give him planes but no personnel. Kenny says send the aircraft, he would find the people. Later Kenney scrapes all over Australia for personnel to make up the new group.

Mar 4, '43 Fifth AF P-38 units participating in the Battle of the Bismark Sea are the ninth and 39th Squadrons of the 49th FG.

Mar 28, '43 The 13th Photo Sdn., 8th AF undertakes a first operational mission from the UK over the coast of France.

Apr '43 Deliveries start of the P-38H Lightning model.

Apr '43 The refitted and rested 14th FG is back in North African fighting. Group aircraft often carry bombs during missions.

Apr 5, '43 Twenty-eight P-38s of the First FG escorting B-25s find enemy fighters escorting transports north of Cape Bon in No. Africa and destroy 17 aircraft for a loss of four P-38s. Eleven of the total are enemy transports.

Apr 9, '43 First FG P-38s shoot down 28 enemy planes in No. Africa little more than two weeks before German resistance ends.

Apr 11, '43 The 80th FS, 8th FG, newly operational with P-38s, scores its first victories, downing four Japanese aircraft.

Apr 18, '43 Eighteen P-38s, eight each from the 12th and 339th FSs and two from the 70th FS, fly a circuitous low level over-water 435 mile route to the Bougainville coast north of Kahili and shoot down a bomber carrying Japanese Admiral Yamamoto and kill him. One Lightning is lost.

Apr 26, '43 P-38s with bombs destroy many German Siebel ferries in the eastern Mediterranean area.

May '43 New aircraft are on the way to Gen. Kenney in the SW Pacific for his first all P-38 outfit, the 475th FG.

May 11. '43 The 11th Air Force in Alaska has one P-38 at Unmak, one at Adak, and 24 at Amchitka, along with some F-5A photo planes.

May 13, '43 Eleven P-38s along with other Army and Marine aircraft break up an enemy attack over Guadalcanal, shooting down 16 E/A.

Jun '43 The 13th Photo Sdn. in the UK has suffered high losses: Two F-5s in April, one in May, and four in June. The squadron has only eleven aircraft left.

Jun 9, '43 A directive is issued ordering a P-38 outfit to China to serve with the new (activated in March) 14th AF. Personnel are to come mostly from the three Mediterranean groups with others directly from the United States.

Jun 15, '43 The Far East Air Force is formed to plan for the air part of the invasion of the Philippines with P-38s in the planning.

Jun 21, '43 P-38s of the 80th Sdn.,8th FG shoot down 13 enemy airplanes in Pacific combat.

Jul '43 P-38s and supporting transports start a trip from the eastern Mediterranean via India to the 14th Air Force in China.

Jul '43 All three P-38 fighter groups in the Mediterranean Theatre fly ground attack missions over Sicily prior to invasion.

Jul '43 The 13th Air Force in the Central Pacific now has on hand less than 20 P-38 fighters.

Jul '43 P-38s are extremely active during the Sicily invasion in both bomber escort and ground attack roles. Gen Spaatz says "the P-38 is in a class by itself".

Jul 7, '43 The Italians claim destruction of 17 P-38s in the last five days of combat action.

Jul 21, '43 In the Pacific P-38s of the 35th FG move to their new base at Tsili-Tsili (Maralinen), and 39th and 8th Sdn. P-38s escort B-25s on a raid over Bogadjim shooting down 22 E/A.

Jul 23, '43 P-38s of the 39th and 8th Sdns., 49th FG get 12 more Pacific victories over Japanese aircraft.

Jul 28, '43 Dick Bong of the 9th Sdn.,49th FG. now has a total of 16 enemy aircraft shot down.

Aug '43 Ten P-38J versions are completed in the Lockheed experimental shops.

Aug '43 Two groups of P-38s, the 20th and 55th FGs, fly to England. Aircraft of the 20th are new P-38H-5 models.

Aug '43 A 5th Air force decision is made to keep P-38s in the 475th FG and the 80th Sdn.,8th FG, and to have the 9th and 39th Sdns. convert to the P-47 when it becomes available.

Aug '43 The Mediterranean theatre is told it will get no more P-38s until October because they are urgently needed in the UK for bomber escort.

Aug 15, '43 The 475th FG becomes operational in the Fifth AF with 115 P-38s available for three squadrons assembled at the Eagle Farm line in Brisbane, Australia. The group goes on a first mission the next day.

Aug 17, '43 Ninety-nine P-38s from six squadrons raid Wewak, New Guinea from bases at Dobadura and Port Moresby escorting medium bombers. Next day 74 P-38 aircraft cover bombers on another Wewak raid. They down 15 of the enemy and lose two P-38s.

Aug 25, '43 P-38s of the First and 82nd FGs attack Foggia, Italy fields.

Aug 30, '43 Forty-eight P-38s of the First FG escort bombers to Aversa, Italy and destroy eight enemy planes, but 13 Lightnings are lost on the mission.

Aug 31, '43 The 475th FG P-38s of 5th Air Force claim a total score of 53 enemy aircraft brought down.

Sep '43 A total of 212 P-38s are now in the SW Pacific. The number is to reduce from attrition in the following months and P-38 needs elsewhere allow little replacement.

Sep '43 In the Pacific P-38s start escorting bombers attacking the big enemy base at Rabaul.

Sep '43 The P-38 is regarded as the most valuable fighter covering the Italian invasion beaches because it has a combat radius, including 10 minutes of combat, of 350 miles. It can reach the beaches and remain over them an hour, including the 10 minutes of aerial fighting.

Sep '43 All of the 55th FG and its P-38s are now in the UK.

Sep 5, '43 P-38 losses in the Mediterranean Theatre are high, 60 planes in August, and 24 in the week ending this date. There are less than 250 of the type in the theatre; replacements are not making up for losses.

Sep 11, '43 In the 10th AF in India P-38s of the 459th FS are activated as a fourth squadron of the 80th FG. The P-38s have come from the Mediterranean to Bengal, India replacing P-40s.

Sep 21, '43 The 82nd FG P-38s escort bombers to Cancello, Italy and claim a total of 28 enemy aircraft destroyed.

Oct '43 There are few P-38 replacements in the Pacific. From October to December only 45 Lightnings reach Gen. Kenney's 5th Air Force in Australia.

Oct '43 Constant 5th AF raids on the big Japanese base at Rabaul are covered by P-38s as follows: 47 Lightnings on Oct.3, 54 on Oct.24, 50 on Oct.25, 75 on Oct.29, 80 on Nov.1, and 67 on Nov.5.

Oct '43 P-38s of the 449th FS in the 14th AF are reassigned to the newly-arrived 51st FG. They fly to Hong Kong as escorts and also act as interceptors against enemy air raids.

Oct 9, '43 Seven P-38s of the 14th FG provide top cover for British Fleet units in the eastern Mediterranean, and during an encounter with enemy aircraft down 12 of them.

Oct 15, '43 The 55th FG goes operational in England with first use of P-38H models; the 343rd Sdn. has P-38H-1s. With two 75 gallon drop tanks the aircraft of the 55th can escort bombers 450 to 520 miles compared with the P-47's 340 miles. However there are seven P-47 groups already operational.

Oct 21, '43 In the last five days the 55th FG has flown P-38 fighter sweeps and limited bomber escort missions. Many mechanical difficulties are encountered.

Oct 30, '43 Gen. Hap Arnold decides to stop P-38 (or P-51) allocations to theatres other than Europe for the remainder of 1943. In the Mediterranean, where there are only three groups of P-38s, the P-47 will be introduced.

Nov '43 Gen. Harmon of the 5th AF, SW Pacific sees a solution to his fighter problems in replacing P-39 Airacobras with more P-38 Lightnings, but now comes up against the demand for ETO escort fighters, and must make do with what he has.

Nov '43 In the Pacific the 9th and 39th Fighter Sdns.convert from P-38s to P-47 fighters with considerable pilot unhappiness.

Nov 1, '43 During the US invasion of Bougainville in the Solomons eight P-38s and eight Kittihawks from Munda and Vella Lavella prevent enemy aircraft from attacking.

Nov 3, '43 The 15th Air Force is activated to attack Italy; among units transferred are the three P-38 groups in the Mediterranean.

Nov 3, '43 P-38s of the 55th FG escort bombers to Wilhelmshaven, Germany and see initial combat, shooting down three planes without loss to themselves.

Nov 5, '43 After a US carrier plane attack on Japanese Rabaul 67 P-38s escort 27 B-24s to bomb the base again.

Nov 5, '43-Three P-38 squadrons of the 55th FG totaling 48 aircraft take off to escort bombers to Munster. Some planes turn back with engine trouble and only one squadron contacts the bombers, but they manage to shoot down five of the enemy with no loss of Lightnings.

Nov 9, '43 The 55th FG loses two P-38s during operations over Europe.

Nov 13, '43 Forty-eight P-38s escort bombers over Germany to Bremen in poor weather at 26000 feet altitude. It is a bad day all around with seven Lightnings lost to the enemy and two to unknown causes. Sixteen planes return damaged.

Nov 20, '43 The 459th Sdn.,80th FG, the only P-38 squadron of the 10th Air force in India, flies its first combat mission.

Nov 26, '43 P-38s of the 449th Sdn.,14th Air Force in China escort B-25 bombers on a first raid over Formosa. Ten enemy aircraft are destroyed on the ground and 12 more in air battles.

Nov 29, '43 The 55th FG and some of the 20th FG, 8th AF use their P-38s to escort bombers to Bremen. At 31000 feet over Holland they are attacked by German aircraft. They shoot down three, but lose seven P-38s, bringing 55th FG losses to 18 planes with four others written off on return. Many losses are due to powerplant problems. Engines appear unreliable when conducting operations above 20000 to 25000 feet.

Dec '43 P-38 groups transferred to the new 15th AF move to new bases in southern Italy.

Dec '43 A P-38 assembly and modification line is established by the 8th AF Service Command at Burtonwood in the UK to speed aircraft to the groups.

Dec '43 F-4 and F-5 photo Lightnings of the 13th PR Sdn.,8th AF in England have been averaging about 50 sorties a month.

Dec '43 A third squadron of F-5 Lightnings is added to the 7th Photo Reconnaissance Gp., 8th AF in the United Kingdom.

Dec 9, '43 The 459th FS, 10th AF in India scores its first victories.

Dec 15, '43 P-38 units in the Mediterranean Theatre 12th AF consist of the 90th PR Wing with four squadrons of F-5s, two in the 3rd PR Gp. and two in the 5th PR Gp. For the new 15th AF there is the 14th and 82nd FGs. At the end of the year 2/33 Sdn. of the Free French AF is added using F-5 photo Lightnings.

Dec 17, '43 Only 31 Air Solomons (AIRSOLS) P-38s are available with just 12 operational. There are few replacements for attrition.

Dec 26, '43 P-38s of the 475th FG and 80th FS provide air support for the invasion of New Britain in the Solomon Islands.

Dec 26, '43 The 459th FS P-38s in India participate in a large raid near Maymyo in Burma.

Dec 28, '43 The 20th FG, 8th Air Force flies its first mission as a group with P-38Js. Since early November it had attached a training squadron to the 55th FG on missions over Europe.

Dec 31, '43 The P-38s of the 475th FG, 5th AF claim 46 victories for the month of December. The 80th FS claims 18 for the same time.

Dec 31, '43 The 13th Air Force in the Pacific, including the 18th and 347th FGs with P-38s, now have a total of about 50 Lightning fighters, thus showing how short these groups are of assigned aircraft. The 13th AF is preparing to move to New Guinea.

Jan '44 P-38s of the 459th FS, 10th AF see little action in the period January through March, but move to a new base at Chittagong near the Bay of Bengal and Burma.

Jan 29, '44 On a bomber escort mission to Frankfort, Germany P-38s have a successful day; fighters of the 20th FG shoot down 10 enemy aircraft for a loss of four of their own of which two are due to a collision.

Jan 30, '44 A quarter of the P-38s escorting bombers over Europe return early due mainly to powerplant failures from bitter cold.

Jan 31, '44 It is decided to have four P-38 groups in the 8th AF and three in the 9th AF. The 9th has no P-38s at this time.

Feb '44 P-38s in the 339th FS, 14th AF are now based at Suichwan, China. They counter Japanese raids and fly ground attack missions.

Feb '44 The supply of P-38s in the SW Pacific area is now down to a total of 150 aircraft.

Feb 4, '44 Nearly half of the 20th and 55th FGs Lightnings on escort need to abort with powerplant problems due to severe cold weather. P-38s now limit operation to 30000 feet because of potential powerplant troubles, leaving enemy aircraft the chance to dive at them from 35000 feet.

Feb 8, '44 A P-38 pilot of the 20th FG shoots down four enemy aircraft in one day over Europe, a single mission record for 8th AF.

Feb 11, '44 Enemy aircraft diving from above shoot down eight P-38s of the 20th FG as they escort bombers to Frankfort, Germany.

Feb 23, '44 P-38s fly their first dive bombing attack on the Japanese base at Rabaul.

Mar '44 F-5 photo Lightnings are being used for mapping the French coast prior to the Normandy invasion.

Mar '44 In the SW Pacific B-24s are now raiding the huge Japanese base at Truk. P-38s and other fighters now raid Rabaul.

Mar '44 The Townsville, Australia Air Depot completes long range modifications (internal fuel tanks added in outer wing panel leading edges) on 56 P-38s. These planes are sent to New Guinea. Additional P-38J versions with these modifications are slated to arrive in Brisbane March 11, and can be sent there shortly after. An additional 37 P-38s up there can be modified. The longer range aircraft are assigned to the 80th and 475th FGs and by the end of the month groups at Nadzab, New Guinea have 106 longer range P-38s for escort missions.

Mar 3, '44 P-38s of the 55th FG fly over Berlin, Germany though many pilots have to drop out before getting there due to engine problems. They are the only aircraft to reach Berlin; the bombers turn back at Hamburg. The fighter pilots are almost frozen stiff from cold cockpits.

Mar 3, '44 The 364th FG goes operational with P-38s, but is plagued with engine failures. The group commander is killed in a crash when both his engines fail. Sixteen aircraft fail to return from missions in the month of March. The group stays down at lower warmer altitudes.

Mar 11, '44 Between this date and May 26 459th FS P-38s in India fly a total of 58 combat days and destroy 128 enemy aircraft including 60 air victories.

Mar 13, '44 The 459th FS in India is detached from the 80th FG. It is to be operated under administrative control of 10th AF, but under tactical control of the British 3rd Tactical Air Force.

Apr '44 Lockheed converts two P-38J-20 aircraft as test night fighters with radar located aft of the nose gear.

Apr 2, '44 Twelve P-38s of the 14th FG, 15th AF escort bombers to Steyr in Austria. During a big air battle they shoot down 12 of the enemy without loss to themselves.

Apr 7, '44 P-38s of the 14th FG down six enemy planes while escorting bombers over Italy.

Apr 8, '44 Forty-eight P-38s of the 20th FG go on a strafing mission to airfields west of Berlin, Germany and destroy many planes.

Apr 10, '44 In the first operational use of a droop-snoot P-38 by 8th AF the 55th FG bombs an airfield in France. The plane carries a bombsight and bombardier, and the other P-38s carry a 1000 pound bomb and one drop tank. Later the 20th FG also gets a P-38 conversion to the droop-snoot configuration.

Apr 12, '44 Gen. Eisenhower goes for a flight in a droop-snoot P-38.

Apr 20, '44 Two Lightning groups, the 20th and 55th, conduct droop-snoot led bombing attacks over Europe.

Apr 25, '44 The 474th FG is the first P-38 unit to join the 9th Tactical Air Force being primed for the invasion of Europe in June.

Apr 27, '44 Twelve P-38 droop-snoot bombing missions have been laid on in the preceeding week with mixed success.

Apr 28, '44 Chateaudun, France is bombed by P-38s lead by a droop-snoot aircraft; 49 1000 pound bombs are dropped from 18000 feet.

May '44 Two P-38 outfits go operational with the 9th Tactical AF this month, the 370th FG on May 1, and the 367 FG on May 9, thus joining the big build-up preparing for invasion D-day.

May '44 In the Pacific the 9th FS reconverts from P-47s to P-38s.

May '44 The 35th and 36th Squadrons of the 8th FG (a two-squadron group) are now using P-38s, bringing the total Lightning strength of the 5th AF in the Pacific to seven squadrons.

May '44 Thirteen P-38 fighter groups are now in service overseas with the US Army Air Forces.

May 21, '44 P-38s of the 55th FG, 8th AF destroy 23 locomotives, damage 15, leave 16 trains afire, and shoot up four river steamers and 14 barges in a pre-invasion strike.

May 26, '44 The 8th Air Force in England now has a full complement of fighter groups with the 479th FG going operational. The force is now 15 groups, four P-38, four P-47, and seven P-51. Total effective strength is 885 fighters.

May 29, '44 P-38s of the 55th FG in the UK go on a mission to Denmark and back for a 1040 mile round trip.

May 31, '44 Eighth Air Force F-5 Lightning photo planes carry out very low altitude missions over the planned invasion beaches to assess German defenses.

Jun '44 The 15th Air force in Italy which has been suffering for lack of long range fighters finally gets replacements of late-model P-38s for older versions. These replacements have the extra internal fuel tanks in their outer wing panels.

Jun '44 The 8th AF conversion of fighter groups from P-38 to P-51 is started. From now until December 1944 seven P-38 and P-47 groups make the change. Many P-38s and P-47s are sent to the 9th AF which frequently complains they are in poor shape.

Jun '44 Thirty-nine P-38s of the 82nd FG are selected to bomb oil refineries at Ploesti, Roumania with 39 P-38s of the First FG flying cover. The raid is not too successful. Some damage is done, and 29 enemy aircraft are downed, most all by the First FG. Losses are high however; eight planes from the 82nd and 14 from the First.

Jun '44 New dive flaps designed to minimize P-38 compressibility troubles begin to reach combat units, and pilots are generally pleased. The P-38J-25 versions are flap-equipped at the factory; anything earlier is a retrofit.

Jun '44 Deliveries of the P-38L start. This model has dive flaps and incorporates the new boosted ailerons to improve roll rate.

Jun 6, '44 Eighteen P-38s of the 459th FS in India go on a mission to Heho in Burma and have a last big air battle with enemy fighters before the monsoons. Capt. W.F.Duke, leading ace of the 10th AF with 10 victories, is lost. After this the Burma air war simmers down. P-38s then do ground support missions.

Jun 6, '44 P-38 units now in the 8th AF in England are: Seventh Photo Reconn. GP with F-5s at Mount Farm, 20th FG at King's Cliffe, 364th FG at Honington, 479th Bomb Group at Wattisham (with some P-38s), and the 496th Ftr. Training Gp. at Goxhall with P-38s and P-51s.

Jun 6, '44 P-38s are assigned as fighter cover over the English Channel as the big invasion of Europe is started and are the first aircraft to be painted in invasion stripes. The P-38 was selected for easy recognition by Allied gunners. Patrols last until June 11 and are very dull.

Jun 11, '44 P-38s of the 55th FG go on a droop-snoot fighter-bomber mission and encounter enemy fighters. They shoot down three FW-190s for the loss of two Lightnings.

Jun 15, '44 The 15th AF in Italy has three P-38 groups, the First, 14th, and 82nd of the 306th Fighter Wing. In addition it has the 154th Weather Reconnaissance Squadron with P-38s and the 15th Combat Mapping Squadron with F-5 Photo Lightnings.

Jun 26, '44 Two thousand P-38L aircraft are ordered from the Convair plant in Nashville, Tenn.

Jul '44 The 339th FS P-38s evacuate Suichwan, China, and retreat to Chengkung in western China because of enemy advances. A flight of eight P-38s is detached to Yunnanyi to assist ground forces in Burma.

Jul '44 P-38 groups in the 8th AF start conversion to P-51s. The P-38 ratio of victories to losses from all causes is roughly one to one.

Jul 3, '44 C.A.Lindbergh works with pilots of the 8th and 475th FGs in the Pacific to show them how to extend P-38 range. He shows how round trips of 1280 miles can be attained. After a six hour 50 minute flight on July 1, CAL lands with 210 gallons still in his tanks. He uses a low 1600 RPM with auto-lean mixture and careful throttle action, and shows how nine hours endurance is possible.

Jul 7, '44 A particularly successful 8th AF mission takes place when P-38s fly B-24 escort to Halle and Bernberg, Germany. The Lightnings claim 18 enemy aircraft downed without a loss.

Jul 20, '44 Eighth AF 55th and 364th FGs have converted from P-38 to P-51 and have flown their first mission with the Mustang.

Jul 21, '44 The 20th FG, 8th AF flies a last mission with P-38s.

Jul 22, '44 P-38s of the 14th and 82nd FGs, 15th AF go on a shuttle bombing mission to Russia. They strafe a German airfield on the way out and destroy many enemy planes. On the return they down 12 of the enemy in air combat.

Jul 29, '44 A 479th FG aircraft has the first P-38 encounter with a German ME-163 rocket-powered interceptor near Meresberg and gets away successfully.

Jul 29, '44 Thirteen P-38s of the 339th FS, 14th AF in China escort B-24s raiding Hainan Island. Twenty-five Japanese aircraft attack and the 339th downs seven, making a total score of 74 enemy aircraft destroyed by them.

Aug '44 P-38s of the 82nd FG in the 15th AF are now encountering little enemy opposition, and from this time until war's end score few air victories.

Aug '44 Production cost of a P-38 is now $97,147. compared to a P-40 which costs $44,892.

Aug 5, '44 Photos from F-5 Lightnings over Pelelieu in the Pacific indicate the enemy still has 36 aircraft on the island.

Aug 18, '44 Fifteenth AF P-38s start flying ground support missions over Yugoslavia and Hungary to aid Allied advances.

Aug 23, '44 F-5 photo Lightnings are making reconnaissance flights over southern Mindanao as a prelude to a Philippines invasion.

Aug 31, '44 Including planes in transit to the Pacific, the Far East Air Force now has 497 P-38s, the greatest number of any fighter type.

Sep '44 Fifty-eight P-38s escort B-24s in a raid over Davao in the Philippines and destroy three enemy aircraft in a combined effort of the 5th and 13th Air Forces.

Sep '44 A P-38J is modified by Lockheed to be a two seater equipped with wing radar.

Sep '44 Gen. Whitehead of the Far East Air Force requests P-38s to make the 49th FG an all P-38 outfit. Two squadrons have been flying weary P-40s. P-38s are obtained and the P-40s are transferred to the 82nd and 110th Reconn. Sdns. (which had been using P-39s) until these units can get their new F-6A reconnaissance Mustangs.

Sep '44 All groups in the Pacific with a P-38 squadron now get equipped with a full complement of P-38 Lightnings.

Sep 13, '44 The 479th FG of 8th Air Force has obtained some P-51s. At this date it is flying two P-38 squadrons and one of P-51s.

Sep 15, '44 Thirteenth AF P-38s from Sansapor in the Pacific have flown 172 missions and dropped 119 1000 pound bombs and 53 500 pound bombs on two airfields at Namlea the past two weeks.

Oct '44 P-38 range has been stretched with added internal and external fuel tanks prior to the Hollandia operation, and cruise control techniques give more radius capability for Pacific operations.

Oct 4, '44 Just before the invasion of Leyte in the Philippines Morotai is occupied, and Wama opened for fighters. Among others P-38s of the 8th FG are assigned to relieve Navy CVEs for air defense.

Oct 9, '44 The last P-38s in the 479th FG fly a final mission for the 8th AF over Europe, but the 9th AF continues to use P-38s as tactical support aircraft and F-5 photo planes continue to serve the 8th AF.

Oct 10, '44 One hundred and six B-24s with 31 P-38s and some P-47s raid Balikpapan in Borneo on a very long range mission of 830 miles to the target. The Lightnings use one 310 gallon and one 165 gallon drop tank under their wings. The P-38s are from the 9th, 80th, and 432nd Squadrons based at Sansipor.

Oct 16, '44 Fifth AF P-38s of the 35th, 36th, and 38th Squadrons staging from Morotai conduct long range fighter sweeps over Mindanao in the Philippines, strafing ground and coastal traffic in support of the Leyte invasion.

Oct 26, '44 Fifth AF P-38s of the 7th and 9th FSs stage up to Morotai ready to go to Leyte in the Philippines.

Oct 27, '44 Thirty-four P-38s of the 49th FG land at Tacloban on Leyte, P.I.; one crashes on landing. They refuel and take off again to shoot down four enemy aircraft. The 85th Fighter Wing under which the 49th FG operates has the assignment of defending Leyte against enemy intrusion.

Oct 28, '44 Twelve P-38s of the 49th FG blow up a big enemy ammunition dump on Ormoc in the Philippines.

Oct 29, '44 P-38s of the 49th FG score their 500th victory over Tacloban on Leyte.

Oct 30, '44 Only 20 P-38s remain in service at Tacloban Airfield on Leyte due to damage from Japanese strafing and accidents.

Oct 30, '44 The 36th Squadron of the 8th FG based on Morotai with P-38s flies a strafing strike against Sandakan Airfield on the northern tip of Borneo and a nearby harbor and sink a ship.

Nov 1, '44 In the Pacific 42 P-38s of the 8th FG fly from Morotai and strafe enemy airfields on Leyte, shooting down seven planes in the air and destroying about 75 on the ground.

Nov 1, '44 The two P-38 groups in the 13th AF do not get in on early action around Leyte in the Philippines, but conduct strikes at central P.I. bases and in the Celebese. This date they hit Cebu and down some enemy aircraft.

Nov 2, '44 In air battles around the Philippine invasion area P-38s of the 49th FG shoot down 26 enemy planes.

Nov 7, '44 P-38s of the 82nd FG, 15th AF in a mission over Yugoslavia tangle in error with Russian fighters and shoot down two, losing two of the Lightnings.

Nov 14, '44 The other two squadrons (431st and 433rd) of the 475th FG have arrived in Leyte over the last five days. The enemy is fighting hard for control of the air, and US fighter strips are very muddy.

Nov 21, '44 Steel matting is finally laid at Dulag airstrip providing a base for 475th FG P-38s and relieving the congestion at Tacloban on Leyte, Philippine Islands.

Nov 31, '44 The 475th FG in the Pacific claims their P-38s have destroyed 70 enemy aircraft. This claim will rise to over 90 in the next month.

Dec '44 In the previous six months 265 new P-38 combat pilots have come into the Far East Air Force. In the next six months (January to June, 1945) an additional 489 P-38 pilots will be received by FEAF.

Dec '44 F-5 Lightnings of the 8th Photo Squadron fly from Tacloban to Luzon, P.I. and photograph areas suitable for invasion.

Dec 7, '44 The landing at Ormoc is supported by the very daring fighter cover of P-38s from the 49th and 475th FGs; the P-38s claim a total of 53 enemy planes shot down out of 75 attackers.

Dec 12, '44 Gen. MacArthur presents P-38 pilot Maj. Richard Bong with the Congressional Medal of Honor at Tacloban Airstrip on Leyte. Bong has 38 victories; in the next week he scores twice again for a total of 40 and is sent back to the US. During this period Maj. Thomas McGuire, leading the 431st Squadron of P-38s, has 31 victories.

Dec 23, '44 The 8th FG is now based on Hill and Elmore Fields on Mindanao, P.I. just a week after its invasion by US forces. Their new P-38J and P-38L Lightnings escort C-47 aircraft. The 36th Squadron takes care of air defense.

Dec 25, '44 Forty-four P-38s are part of a force of 105 fighters and bombers attacking an enemy fleet offshore which threatens the Mindoro, P.I. beachhead. Losses are heavy and include seven P-38s.

Dec 26, '44 Aircraft based on Leyte increase the tempo of attacks on the island of Luzon, P.I. P-38s of the 431st Squadron are led by Maj.McGuire who shoots down four enemy aircraft for a total of 38 victories. Twelve days later on January 7, 1945 McGuire is lost in a low altitude combat.

Dec 30, '44 The 80th FS gets its final combat victory.

Dec 31, '44 Lockheed has produced 4186 P-38 aircraft in 1944.

Dec 31, '44 The Far East Air Force now has 470 P-38s including those in transit from the States. Forty-seven late model P-38J and P-38L aircraft are released to them by the 7th Air Force.

Dec 31, '44 In this year Lockheed has employed more than 60000 people in 100 locations on five continents.

Jan 1, '45 The 8th FG in the Philippines is short 17 P-38s and enemy raids the next two nights destroy 15 more. Replacements are obtained from Leyte for these heavy 310th Wing losses.

Jan 17, '45 P-38s of the 18th FG along with other aircraft arrive at Lingayen Airstrip on Luzon just a week after the start of the invasion of that island. Enemy resistance is light.

Jan 21, '45 The 8th and 49th FGs send about 80 P-38s on a sweep of southern Formosa. An earlier carrier aircraft raid has been made and the P-38s find no opposition. Later this day 49 P-38s from these two groups escort bombers to Formosa and no opposition is encountered.

Feb '45 The 367th and 370th FGs of the 9th Tactical Air Force in Europe convert from P-47s (the 367th) and from P-38s (the 370th) to P-51s. Only the 474th FG flies P-38s until the end of World War II.

Feb 5, '45 A P-38L-5 is converted into a night fighter and makes its first flight as a P-38M prototype.

Apr '45 Azon guided bombs are used on ten P-38s modified in a fast 51 day conversion effort to a bombardier nose, M-9 bomb sight, a bomb directional control unit, and a transmitter.

May 18, '45 At the battle for Ipo on Luzon in the Philippines, 5th AF P-38s using napalm, along with P-47s, fly at 50 to 100 foot altitudes and devastate enemy areas with fires.

Jul '45 The character of the air war is changing. The once-common P-38s (and P-39s) have virtually disappeared.

Jul '45 In the last eight months the number of P-38s in the China/Burma/India Theatre has been: Dec.1944-92, Jan.1945-109, Feb.-140, Mar.-205, Apr.-190, May-225, Jun.-280, Jul.-231. At the end of July the 10th AF has 103 P-38s and the 14th AF in China has 19.

Aug '45 Squadrons of the 343rd FG, 11th AF in the Aleutian Islands are now supplied with P-38L-5 models, including the 11th FS on Shemya. Earlier models are returned to the States.

Aug '45 P-38 production is halted. Convair has completed 113 P-38Ls to June. Besides the US a small number of P-38s have flown for China, the Free french, and the UK.

Aug '45 The P-38 is the first USAAF type to land in Japan.

Aug 14, '45 Five P-38s of the 35th FS escort two rescue planes and meet six enemy planes near Japan, downing four. These are the last victories for fighters of the 5th Air Force.

'45 Fifty P-38Ls go to Italy and a few go to Honduras.

'49 Over 150 P-38L-5s are scrapped by 5th AF in Korea.

'49 The few F-38J and F-38L aircraft in the Air Force inventory are declared surplus.

P-38 HANDLING QUALITIES AND CHARACTERISTICS

HANDLING QUALITIES
GROUND HANDLING

Taxi characteristics were good. Differential engine power could be used to save the brakes when turning. The airplane could be turned sharply and full brake power used without upset because of the tricycle landing gear. Since the attitude of the P-38 was fairly level during taxi visibility on the ground was good. The pilot could see well enough forward to taxi straight ahead, and he could see both wingtips. Seventy-five percent of one large pilot group rated the P-38 good in ground handling. The roll-up side windows of the cockpit could be left down for hot weather taxi, but had to be rolled closed before takeoff or tail buffeting would result.

TAKEOFF AND CLIMB

Because of the two opposite rotating propellers there was no net torque reaction on the airplane, so the P-38 was steady as a rock on takeoff. The procedure was to either keep flaps retracted or set them in half down position, hold with the brakes, run up to 45 to 54 inches of manifold pressure and 3000 RPM, release the brakes, and go to 60 inches manifold pressure as the roll started. Turbosuper-

chargers were seldom used on takeoff of early models since they could cut in and out and upset thrust symmetry. This problem was later solved. The control column was eased back at 70 mph, and

Fig.38-1 Lockheed XP-38 Lightning, Ser.37-457, Mfr. Photo via Hal Andrews. One of the few views of the prototype aircraft. This airplane was fated to crash at the end of a transcontinental west-to-east speed dash in February of 1939 with very few hours of previous testing. Then Army Lt. Ben Kelsey survived the crash near Mitchel Field, Long Island.

Fig.38-3 Lockheed YP-38 Lightning, Mfr. Photo via Hal Andrews. This run-up picture of a YP-38 shows the Lightning configuration well, including turbosupercharger locations atop the booms near the wing trailing edge and Prestone radiator duct exit flaps wide open for ground cooling. Gleaming natural Alclad finish and old-style tail stripes distinguished the service test airplanes.

Fig.38-1A Lockheed XP-38 Lightning, photo via Joe Christy. Another view of the prototype Lightning before its epic transcontinental flight. The slim lines of engine nacelle and boom are evident as is the small size of the coolant radiator housing relative to later versions. Propeller blades swept downward past the fuselage on the XP-38; later airplanes reversed propeller direction of rotation.

lift-off would occur at 90 to 100 mph IAS. The single engine control speed was 120 to 125 mph IAS, that is, the speed at which rudder and aileron power were sufficient to continue under control if an engine failed. At speeds under 120 mph IAS an engine failure would yaw the airplane and put it into a half roll and an inverted crash. One solution was to keep the plane on the ground until it was over 120 mph IAS, then pull into the air and retract the gear. Above 120 mph IAS the pilot had a chance to survive an engine failure if his reactions were quick. Procedures for engine failure on takeoff were: With a failure before lift-off the throttles were chopped and the airplane braked, with the gear retracted if the plane was going off the runway. With a failure after leaving the ground but before reaching the safe single engine speed of 120 to 125 mph IAS, throttles were chopped and the aircraft landed straight ahead. With a failure after leaving the ground and reaching 120 mph IAS or above, power was reduced quickly enough on the good engine to

regain control, after deducing which engine had failed, then power was gradually reapplied holding rudder and trimming with rudder tabs while feathering the propeller on the dead engine. Rolling forces also had to be trimmed out. It was unwise to turn into a dead engine while coming around to land.

Upon normal takeoff the airplane was cleaned up quickly and climbout at best speed established. The P-38 had good acceleration qualities. On early models an initial climb rate of up to 2800 feet per minute could be attained using MILITARY power, and well over 3000 feet per minute for the latest versions.

TRIMMING
The P-38 could be trimmed out to be pleasant to fly, and trimmability was rated good to fair by the majority of pilots in one survey. No adjustment of rudder or elevator trim was required with power or speed changes.

Fig.38-2 Lockheed YP-38 Lightning, Mfr.Photo via F.Dean coll. Front view of one of the service test YP-38s with many changes from the experimental prototype, in fact a major redesign. The first YP-38 airplane did not fly until nineteen months after the prototype crash. Note the blade cuffs near the propeller spinners. The pilot has his hands on the control wheel and column which was used in place of a stick on P-38s.

Fig.38-4 Lockheed YP-38 Lightning, Mfr.photo via F.Dean coll. Flight photo of a service test airplane shows no armament yet installed. Major revisions from the prototype are apparent, including new cowl and canopy lines and changes in the turbosupercharger installation. Larger coolers are now on both sides of the boom. All YP aircraft had been delivered by June of 1941.

Fig.38-5 Lockheed RP-38 lightning, P.M.Bowers photo via Hal Andrews. One of thirty plain P-38 aircraft used as trainers and put in a restricted (R) category, this airplane lasting into the spring of 1943 in dull olive drab paint. Some armor and a bullet-resistant windshield was installed in this version.

Fig.38-6 Lockheed XP-38A Lightning, Ser.40-762, Mfr.Photo via Hal Andrews. A P-38 modified to provide cockpit pressurization, the conversion taking place in 1942. As with other cabin pressurization efforts, the project was not carried through into production. A camouflage pattern is readily discernable in this photo.

DIVE AND RECOVERY

Due to its weight and streamlined design the P-38 accelerated rapidly in a dive. At a Mach number of 0.65, that is 65 percent of the speed of sound in air, airplane drag started to increase sharply with the onset of compressibility. This Mach number corresponded to 440 mph true airspeed (290 mph IAS) at 30000 feet, or 460 mph TAS (360 mph IAS) at 20000 feet. In one g diving flight (no pullup attempted) shocks started forming at Mach 0.67 and aircraft buffeting commenced at Mach 0.675. At flight above one g, as in a dive pullout or a turn, buffeting developed at a lower Mach number. At 30000 feet a pullout maneuver over three g got the P-38 in trouble. At lower altitudes the safe limits of speed and g level without compressibility buffet occurrence expanded, since there were higher temperatures where for a given speed Mach number decreased. The speed of sound was greater lower down. In any case compressibility buffet could be stopped by reducing speed or g level. If a high speed dive was continued past placarded limits compressibility effects really took over. At Mach 0.74 a nose down pitching tendency, or "tuck-under", started to steepen the dive. A typical experience for a P-38 pilot going after an enemy plane in a near-vertical dive,

perhaps trying to follow an enemy "split-S" maneuver from high altitude, was to have his aircraft start to vibrate and buck severely with the control column flailing back and forth and the wheel taken right out of his hands. Sometimes bucking was so severe the pilot might think he had lost tail surfaces. Then if the aircraft hung together control could finally be re-established in the warmer denser air of lower altitude, but the enemy would likely have disappeared. The elevator trim tab could be used to recover at lower altitudes but use resulted in a five g pullout. So dive speeds were restricted to the equivalent of Mach 0.65, and the restriction was placarded in the cockpit.

In late model P-38s, some P-38J and all P-38L models, a dive recovery flap system was added under the wings on each side just outboard of the booms. These flaps when extended lessened the lift loss in compressibility and delayed onset of the tuck-under tendency. They also added drag which together with higher allowable dive speed permitted dives at steeper angles. Flaps were extended just before or just after starting a dive. If the P-38 was already in buffet and the flaps were extended buffeting would momentarily increase, then diminish and the tuck-under tendency would reduce.

Fig.38-7 Lockheed P-38D lightning, P.M.Bowers photo via Hal Andrews. One of three dozen aircraft delivered in the summer of 1941, and which participated in the Army summer war games down south. Leakproof fuel tanks were now installed and reduced fuel tank capacity by one quarter. D models were never used operationally and served as trainers.

Fig.38-8 Lockheed P-38 lightning, Ser.40-744, USAAF via F.Dean coll. The first P-38 airplane was used as a test bed with installation of a second cockpit in the port boom, apparently to test pilot reactions to an asymmetric location for some other intended application.

Fig.38-8A Lockheed 322 Lightning, USAAF photo via Joe Weathers. One of the 143 airplanes intended for export to the British and taken over by the USAAF for stateside training. These aircraft were originally bereft of turbosuperchargers and had same-rotation propellers, but the Army installed opposite rotation engines in most, including this one, after taking them over.

But even with flaps deployed it was not wise to exceed placarded speeds by more than 20 mph. With flaps extended before diving angles of dive up to 45 degrees could be safely attained, whereas without flaps maximum dive angle was 15 degrees. If the 45 degree dive angle was exceeded and speeds attained of more than 20 mph above placard a dangerous buffet of the airplane and tuck-under would occur even with dive flaps extended. In general reduction of power improved aircraft characteristics in a dive.

A large number of US service, British, and company test pilots evaluated a P-38L airplane equipped with dive flaps in 1944. They rated divingacceleration, dive stick forces, and dive recovery good. Four pilots reported dive flaps made recovery "effortless". In spite of this a pilot survey ranked the P-38 last of all fighters tested in a category "best stability and control in a dive".

MANEUVERING

The P-38 was a delightful aircraft to fly in aerobatics because it was stable and no maneuver was restricted except dives past placarded limits. Loops, Immelmans, and rolls were permitted, but extreme care had to be taken in maneuvers requiring a downward recovery because loss of altitude was great. Pilots were warned not to attempt aerobatics below 10000 feet altitude unless they were very familiar with how fast the P-38 could lose altitude. The airplane was great for precision maneuvers like loops, aileron rolls, and Cuban eights. It was particularly good in vertical maneuvers with fine ability to change vertical direction and had excellent zoom climb characteristics. As an example, however, of how 1944 service and test pilots rated P-38L in maneuverability: Of 28 flight evaluators only two rated it good, ten said fair, while the others

Fig.38-9 Lockheed P-38E, F.Dean coll. Many changes went into the E version which brought the Lightning up to a partial combat standard and can be thought of as the first real production version. The armament installation was standardized as one 20 mm cannon and four .50 caliber machine guns grouped closely in the nose, and ammunition capacity was increased. There were no external store stations, however.

Fig.38-9A Lockheed P-38E Lightning, USAAF photo via Joe Christy. In the spring of 1942 the defenses of Alaska were strengthened by deployment of Lightning fighters to Anchorage. Four of twenty-five P-38E fighters of the 343rd Fighter Group are shown here. Usually regarded as the initial combat-ready version, slightly over 200 P-38E models were built.

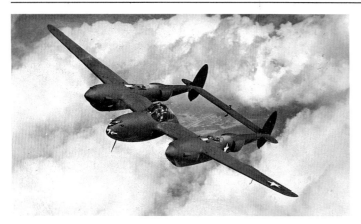

Fig.38-10 Lockheed P-38F Lightning, Mfr.Photo via F. Dean coll. The first fully combat ready Lightning with uprated engines and, importantly, two wing store stations, one between the fuselage and each boom. In this photo there are drop tanks aboard, but they are hidden from view by the fuselage and the port boom. Late versions of the F also incorporated a wing flap maneuver setting.

Fig.38-11 Lockheed P-38F Lightning, Mfr. Photo via Joe Christy. This view of the same P-38F airplane shows off the new drop tank installation, giving the Lightning some long legs for trans-Atlantic flight operations to start implementing the UK buildup of forces known as Operation Bolero. Deliveries of the F version got under way in early spring of 1942 with over 500 ultimately produced. Flights to England started in June of that year.

gave it a poor rating. The P-38 was a large heavy fighter not suited for quick "snap" or "slam-bang" maneuvers, and had a particularly slow initial response in roll due to a high lateral inertia characteristic. The problem was a slow start into a roll and thus an inability to switch quickly from one attitude to another, as in reversing from a turn in one direction to one in the other. As one pilot said "It was disconcerting to have a fighter barreling in on you, crank the wheel over hard, and just have the P-38 sit there. Then, after it slowly rolled the first five or ten degrees of bank it would turn quickly, but the hesitation was sweat-producing". Many combat losses, particularly in North Africa, were attributed to this creaky initial rate of roll. Another pilot noted "The first ten degrees of bank came very slow". Power boosted ailerons, introduced the same time as dive

recovery flaps, gave the P-38 pilot a lot more "muscle" to improve roll characteristics at high speeds, but did nothing to improve them at low and moderate speeds where maximum roll performance was dependent only on full aileron deflection instead of pilot effort. The P-38, particularly in early versions, could not roll into a dive fast enough to catch enemy aircraft diving down and away to evade, as in a split-S maneuver.

Once rolled into a turn, however, the P-38 could then turn very tightly for such a large fighter, particularly at low altitudes, and was touted when driven by some of its best pilots as able to stay with most any good single engine fighter in turning flight. Reputedly some pilots even utilized differential engine power in turning. Also, starting early in P-38 airplane design evolution with the F-15

Fig.38-11A Lockheed P-38F Lightnings, Mfr.photo via Joe Christy. A rather dramatic photo of a P-38F with others trailing below and behind taken from the ventral position in a Lockheed Hudson. The nose armament of four machine guns grouped around a centrally located 20 mm. cannon is well shown as are cooling air inlets and turbosuperchargers atop the nacelles.

Fig.38-12 Lockheed P-38F Lightning, Ser.41-7586, Mfr.Photo via Hal Andrews. This attractive flight view of the F version with drop tanks is interesting in that the main landing gear doors under the starboard boom are drooping down, a not unknown problem with some fighters, including P-51s. The P-38F aircraft got their first chance to fight in the North African campaign under some difficult conditions late in 1942.

Fig.38-13 Lockheed P-38G Lightning, Ser.42-12687, F. Dean coll. via Joe Christy Lightning production really got going with the G version. Powerplant changes were incorporated. Deliveries started in mid-1942 and continued into the next year with over 1000 produced. Drop tank pylons were revised on late versions for greater load capacity so the external fuel load could be increased from 300 to 600 gallons, or twice the internal capacity.

Fig.38-14 Lockheed P-38H Lightning, Ser.42-67079, Mfr. photo via F. Dean coll. More powerplant changes with uprated engines, including a new COMBAT power rating and updated turbosuperchargers characterized the P-38H. Here the limits were being pushed on the capability of the intercoolers in wing leading edges, and the H was the final model of that design. Leaks in the intercooling systems plagued operations in the Pacific for a time.

variant, the aircraft was fitted with an eight degree MANEUVER flap setting for its big Lockheed-Fowler flap system which could be used up to a speed of 250 mph IAS. Deployment of this flap provided substantial improvement in turning capability without stalling. The P-38 possessed very gentle characteristics in turns. It had been known in combat, when in clean configuration and well piloted, to stay inside of and behind a turning enemy aircraft at 1000 feet altitude and 100 mph. It would shudder on the edge of a stall, but never snapped into a spin because, contrary to single engine fighters, it had no propeller net torque reaction. If the P-38 stalled in a very tight turn it would just mush outward, and forward stick pressure would unstall it with little loss of altitude. A pilot could rack the airplane around using an "in and out of stall turn" to safely effect a very tight turning circle.

Elevator control for maneuvering was very effective, and the cockpit control column had considerable travel. The P-38 was considered fairly heavy on the controls, especially on the ailerons before power boost was installed. After this installation most pilots rated aileron control force characteristics and effectiveness very good, and the aircraft scored high in a category "best ailerons at 350 mph IAS", but rather poorly in another, " best ailerons at low speed". Rudder force and effectiveness characteristics were good. With an interesting commentary on the first use of power-boosted control on a US fighter, one test pilot new to the P-38L noted "Pleasant aircraft to fly except for queer ailerons".

Fig.38-15 Lockheed P-38H Lightning, Ser. 42-67079, Mfr. photo via Hal Andrews Displaying the familiar twin boom configuration, this P-38 Lightning cruises over the hills of California posing for a company photo shoot. When one sees how long the combination of inline engine, supercharger, coolers, and main landing gear bay would have made "conventional" nacelles it is an easy stretch to get to a proper tail location via twin booms.

Fig.38-15A Lockheed P-38H Lightning, USAAF photo via Joe Christy. Coming out in April of 1943, the P-38H was characterized primarily by changes in powerplant including addition of a COMBAT rating for the engines amounting to short time use of 1600 horsepower each at 60 inches of manifold pressure. This version deployed to England in August with the 20th Fighter Group.

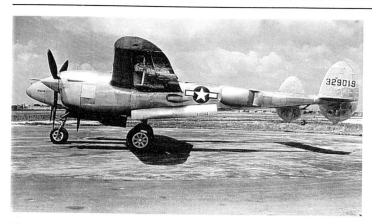

Fig.38-16 Lockheed P-38J Lightning, Ser.43-29019, photo via Hal Andrews. Major changes were involved when the J version appeared in 1943. A rather elegant solution to the problems of intercooler limitations and combat radius limits was effected in this model when new design coolers were located in the nacelle chins leaving space inside the wing leading edges for over 100 gallons of additional fuel. The deeper chin of the P-38J can be seen in the photo.

Fig.38-17 Lockheed P-38J Lightning,Ser.42-104309, Mfr.photo via Hal Andre With all the improvements the Lightning had gained weight with the J version a most 1600 pounds greater in empty weight than the service test YP-38 airplan Two other major changes appreciated by pilots were much improved cockpit he ing and use of an electrical generator on each engine, though some pilots felt the cockpit arrangement had gotten "lousier and lousier". The deeper forward cowli is apparent in this photo.

APPROACH AND LANDING

Landing a P-38 was normally simple and easy, and landing with an engine out was still considered not especially difficult. Many pilots gave the P-38 a good rating on approach and landing characteristics, though not all were happy with aileron performance at 100 mph IAS. The wide tread main landing gear and nose wheel configuration were very helpful in landing, and brakes were very effective. Tricycle gear reduced the potential of ground looping in cross-wind landings. The landing approach was made with gear down and flaps set to the MANEUVER position at 120 mph IAS. When on the final leg flaps were lowered full down, and the aircraft came over the fence at 110 mph IAS, flared to about 80 mph and touched down, main wheels first and slightly tail low to keep the nose wheel off. If the flaps happened to be left up in error or due

to battle damage extreme tail down landings were possible. Und such conditions the lower tail fins could hit the ground. Landin engine-out was similar to a two engine landing , but once commit ted there was no going around under 500 feet with flaps down. A NORMAL RATED power setting, 44 inches of manifold pressur and 2600 RPM on the good engine, the P-38 could barely ho altitude with gear down and flaps up. With both gear down, an flaps down at all, the aircraft would sink. Since in the single engin case thrust was assymmetrical it was important to avoid using ex cessive power on the good engine at low airspeed or aircraft con trol problems would result. For single engine final approach the P 38 was trimmed directionally and held manually against propell torque, otherwise the plane could roll on its back with throttl chopped.

Fig.38-18 Lockheed P-38J Lightning,Ser.42-68008, F. Dean coll. The P-38 really matured with the J version where most every Lightning problem had been tackled by the designers. In the final Js two new features were added, power-boosted ailerons to give a needed substantial roll rate increase at the higher speeds, and underwing dive recovery flaps to provide a means of improving diving characteristics.

Fig.38-19 Lockheed P-38J Lightning, Ser.43-28256, photo via P.M. Bowers. An un usual airplane-to airplane shot provides some indication of pilot vision limitation in the lower rear quarters due to the twin boom arrangement. A weaving fligh pattern was sometimes used to periodically uncover blind spots. The small air i take just below the wing trailing edge served the engine air induction system. Th photo shows the port supercharger installation in the near airplane.

Fig.38-18A Lockheed P-38J Lightning, USAAF photo via Joe Christy. Servicing a P-38J of the 8th Air Force, a ground crewman fills the port drop tank. In this version the new wing leading edge fuel tanks were installed and the intercoolers moved to the engine nacelles, providing a new look to the aircraft. Note also a new flat windshield is installed.

STALLS AND SPINS

P-38 stall characteristics were rated by pilots as very good. Near stall speed the wing center section stalled first, and warning was given by noticeable shaking of the aircraft. The ailerons remained effective. In clean configuration the one g stall, whether in power on or off condition, resulted in the P-38 mushing straight forward. With a dirty aircraft one g stall there was a slight tendency for one wing to drop, but no tendency to spin. The nose then dropped slightly and as speed increased the wing would come up. In a high speed stall the result was the same, and as noted earlier, the plane could be urged around, shuddering all the way, in a tight "in and out of stall" turn.

Stalling with only one engine operating was a different and nerve wracking experience. The dead engine wing would drop vi-

Fig.38-20 Lockheed P-38J Lightnings, USAAF photo via Joe Christy. Peel-off shot of P-38J airplanes provides an idea of how relatively easy Lightning identification was compared to single engine fighters. There were few aspects where this twin boom twin tail airplane could not be readily identified from a considerable distance and this could provide an advantage to the enemy. These aircraft are still carrying drop tanks. The J really had legs; it could cruise eight hours or more.

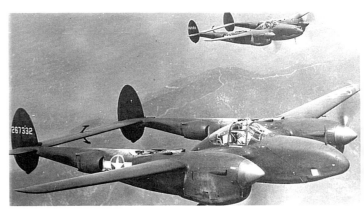

Fig.38-21 Lockheed F-5E Lightning, Ser.42-67332, Mfr photo via F. Dean coll. The F-5E was a photo reconnaissance version of the P-38J with cameras installed in the fuselage nose section. F-4 and F-5 aircraft made tremendously important contributions to war efforts. Through most of the war Lightnings had no equal for long range reconnaissance at high speeds and altitudes. Without armament, they evaded by use of these capabilities, but losses were sometimes high.

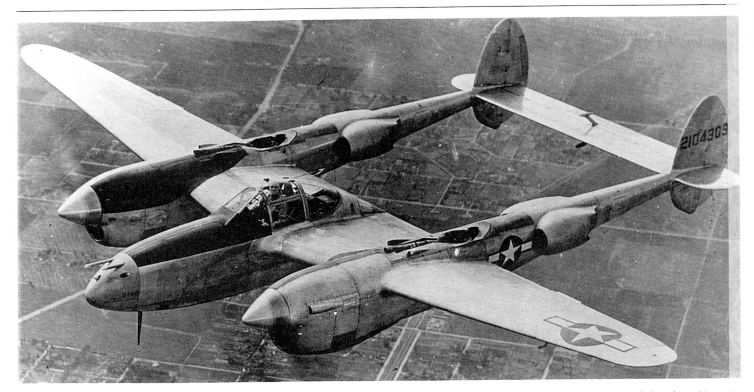

Fig.38-22 Lockheed P-38J lightning,Ser.42-104309, Mfr. photo. Another Lockheed photo of the then-new P-38J showing off its new features including deep chin cowls, larger Prestone cooler installations, and flat panel windshield. The twin booms were pretty well packed with powerplant items, retracted main landing gear, cooling radiators and duct controls, oxygen bottles, battery, control runs, and tool and baggage stowage spaces.

ciously past the vertical, and the only way to recover was to back off power on the good engine and wait until speed built up so control could be regained. At least 2000 feet of altitude would be lost in such a stall.

Deliberate spinning of the P-38 was prohibited because the spin tended to flatten out after two or three turns. When that occurred the control column was forced back, and engine power had to be used to get it forward. Before the spin flattened out recovery could be made without using engine power by applying full opposite rudder and easing the control column forward.

CHARACTERISTICS

COCKPIT

The P-38 cockpit was comfortable as far as roominess was concerned, though some pilots thought the cabin roof was too low. But in cold weather at altitude it was, as one pilot put it, "the world's coldest airplane". Both cockpit heating and transparency defrosting were totally inadequate. There were instances where half-frozen pilots had to be lifted from their cockpits after long high altitude escort missions. Frosting over of transparencies made a pilot a sitting duck for enemy attacks. Another pilot said "Cockpit comfort was miserable".

Since the P-38 was a twin engine fighter there were of necessity more controls and displays than on single engine machines. Someone counted 21 dials and 69 controls of various sorts. A large number of pilots considered the cockpit layout poor. One pilot with considerable P-38 experience said "The cockpit had gotten lousier and lousier (with successive models), and you could see fewer gages". At a 1944 gathering of fighter pilots 55 percent rated the P-38 cockpit worst in arrangement of the many fighter types present, and noted it had the least convenient landing gear and flap controls of all.

VISIBILITY

As noted earlier P-38 ground taxi visibility was very good because of the attitude provided by a tricycle landing gear. In-flight visibility was excellent in the forward and downward directions, but very poor to the side, and particularly to the lower rear quarters. Certainly pilots did not consider the P-38 good in all-around visibility. Rear quarter views were so poor that resort was often made to weaving flight to periodically uncover blind spots where enemy fighters might hide.

POWERPLANT OPERATION

This aspect of P-38 operation was generally considered good at low to moderate altitudes, but at high altitude there was almost constant trouble. One distinguished 8th Air Force pilot said "At low and medium altitudes they were fine, but at high altitude they were hopeless". A major reason the P-38 was removed from 8th Air Force bomber escort missions over Europe and transferred to tactical missions in the 9th Air Force was the engine problem. The situation was not nearly as bad in other theatres of operation. Another aspect of the powerplant problem was that maintenance on P-38 powerplants was "something to behold". It was an extremely close-cowled engine with "much piping and no space" and "truly a crew chief's nightmare", and there were two of them per airplane.

VULNERABILITY/ARMOR

In 1944 a P-38 combat pilot said of the plane "African experience was that the aircraft was used at low level on many occasions, and we found it quite vulnerable to ground fire, even small arms fire". One view of P-38 vulnerability went like this: "Having two engines doubled the chance of being hit in an engine or its subsystem, like cooling. However instead of being able to come home on the other engine the damaged engine caught fire, forcing you to bail out. They never put fire extinguishers on that aircraft". In some circles it was a standing joke that "The P-38 was designed with two engines so you could come back on one".

Like other fighters powered with liquid-cooled engines, a hit in a P-38 cooling system disabled the powerplant very quickly, and those systems were strung out over two thirds of each P-38 boom. Lockheed went to some lengths to prove the P-38 configuration less vulnerable than more conventional layouts. One study showed most fighters got a preponderance of hits in the aft fuselage, and since the P-38 did not have any aft fuselage—.

In 1944 the P-38 was placed last of US fighter types by a large group of pilots in the categories "best fighter-bomber", and "best strafer". This may have been partially because of vulnerability aspects mentioned above.

GUN PLATFORM AND WEAPOPN PERFORMANCE

The airplane was generally regarded as a pretty fair gun platform. One experienced pilot said it was better than the P-40 or Merlin powered P-51. Most pilots rated "fair". But there was no question about pilots liking the machine gun and cannon installation in the nose. There were comments as "A P-38 plus was accurate concentrated firepower", and "It had a honey of a gun installation where you could see where the bullets went". It had the same pattern at all firing ranges. In an installation where there might seem to be no adverse factors one was found (this for some earlier models) "If one gun stopped firing the pilot couldn't find which it was, so he had to go through the slow and difficult procedure of charging them all again using a single gun charge lever on the upper right section of the instrument panel".

Enemy fighters became wary of meeting the concentrated firepower of the P-38 in head-on attacks, and wary also of pulling up ahead of a P-38 since the fire from this aircraft could be so deadly.

GENERAL COMMENTS

Two engines gave pilots a feeling of safety when flying over long stretches of water or rough terrain.

Fig.38-23 Lockheed P-38J lightning, Ser.42-68008, Mfr. photo. Late airplanes were again in natural metal finish like the one in this company picture of the J Lightning. As shown extensive use was made of black anti-glare paint ahead of the cockpit and on the inboard upper quadrants of the engine nacelles. The ideal location for concentration of firepower in the nose is evident; enemy pilots quickly realized it was unwise to pull up anywhere in front of a Lightning.

Fig.38-24, Lockheed P-38L Lightning, Ser.44-26361, photo via R.Besecker. A good photo of the final P-38 version. A much-needed new turbosupercharger regulator was provided along with engine uprating, automatic engine controls, and tail warning radar. Powerplant problems with Lightnings at high altitude in Europe had been legion, to the point where they were relegated from strategic to tactical air forces. It was hard to differentiate between J and L aircraft. One easy way was to note the flush landing light in the port wing leading edge of the P-38L.

Some pilots considered the P-38 a complete failure in Europe mainly because of powerplant troubles.

Bailout was a psychological hazard because of the horizontal tail and the elevator external balance.

Fighter pilots in 1944 commenting on the P-38: Low maneuverability. Speed OK for Japanese. Good fighter-bomber and fair for sweeps but poor for escort.

The lack of a second electrical generator on early P-38 models resulted in many accidents, particularly when generator failure caused propeller malfunctions.

In Europe very high altitude operation was causing powerplant failures every few hours.

Pilots who got in a jam were very grateful for the fine P-38 stalling characteristics.

The attitude in some circles was they would rather have a plane that went like hell and had a few things wrong with it than one that didn't and still had a few things wrong.

The Germans could escape a P-38, with its slow initial roll capability and diving limitations by using a split S maneuver.

The P-38 just did not adapt to high altitude operations over Europe.

Lightning pilots often got so cold over Europe they lost the will to fight.

At low altitudes it was hard to beat a P-38; it could perform fairly tight maneuvers.

P-38 pilots were unable to perform a split S until the airplane was provided with dive flaps.

One tough problem with P-38s was engine failure.

It was a fine airplane, long ranged, a steady gun platform, and no propeller torque problem.

The introduction of the P-38 into the Pacific really changed the air combat situation.

Single engine landings were not uncommon with the P-38.

Cockpit arrangements in early and late P-38s were considered poor.

The Japanese felt the P-38 confronted them with a frighteningly effective weapon.

All problems concerning heating and defrosting were entirely cleaned up on the P-38L-5. It was a shirtsleeves aircraft in the Aleutians.

Powerplant fire sensing and extinguishing equipment was installed in late model P-38s, including the P-38L-5.

Bailout instructions, based on Lockheed testing, were to crawl out on the left wing and slide off. The airstream carried you under the horizontal stabilizer except under compressibility conditions.

Those of us who trained from the beginning in P-38s were heirs to combat experience brought back by earlier pilots and knew its limitations. The fully developed J and L aircraft had a reputation of combat success, witness Bong and Mcguire. It was a joy to fly and we had full confidence in it.

Galland's opinion of the P-38 was like that for the ME-110. Twin engined fighters were no match for the single engined variety.

Losing an engine on takeoff was the predominent concern, and some new pilots were lost due to such failures.

Some pilots found a combination of maneuver flap setting and differential throttle use allowed the P-38 to out-turn German fighters.

In China it was found the P-38s used up too much of the limited fuel supplies, and the P-51 was preferred.

Pilots felt the P-38 could not match the Zero in low altitude maneuvers, but at high altitude the Lightnings could always dive away to evade.

The latest P-38's new cannon gave a problem. Ejected shell casings during firing struck airplane surfaces.

There were pilots who felt the P-38 was the most versatile fighter of all, but that turbosupercharged twin engines made it too complicated.

The sound of a P-38 was a pleasant smooth purr compared to other fighters.

Fig.38-24A Lockheed P-38L lightning, USAAF photo via Joe christy. Things were really tough in Europe during the winter of 1944-1945, one of the worst on record, and maintenance on a P-38 outdoors was not pleasant work. Heaters and flexible ducting were utilized to direct hot air where needed. Armament bay doors of this P-38L, the final basic version, are up to expose weapons and ammunition containers. The work stand was nothing fancy!

On takeoff the speed built up quickly and there was no requirement to hold the rudder against torque.

The cockpit was comfortable compared to the P-39 and P-47. Visibility was good except where the engine nacelles blocked the view. The P-38 performed well in both power on and power off stalls. In both low and high speed stalls it gave plenty of warning, and was still under control.

For a large two engine machine the P-38 was very aerobatic and could make a believer out of a pilot.

Visibility on landing was very good; it came over the fence at about 90 mph.

The fact that the P-38 could not turn as tightly as a Zero did not matter, though models with aileron boost and maneuver flap setting could probably come close. The hit and run approach worked well and was recommended for use.

European P-38 pilots were hampered by dive compressibility and cold cockpit problems before the latest models came along. In the Pacific operations were normally conducted at lower altitudes and the problems did not surface. Very high speed dives into compressibility were not necessary to out-dive the Japanese.

After the new wing leading edge tanks were introduced and careful cruise control techniques used the P-38 could reach a 1000 mile radius. Mission durations of eight to nine hours were possible, but pilot comfort limits tended to take over.

The P-38 was a Pacific favorite. One happy pilot felt it was the best fighter of all even after flying the P-51.

It was foolhardy to try and out-maneuver Japanese single engine fighters with a P-38. The rule was to avoid pulling up at angles above thirty degrees.

Gen. George Kenney knew Gen. Hap Arnold didn't think highly of the P-38 as a fighter, but Kenney liked it more and more all the time, particularly after early bugs were eliminated. Kenney continually pleaded for more P-38s, and later argued vehemently against the threat of stopping P-38 production.

Kelly Johnson's explanation for the P-38 twin boom configuration was that after stringing together a long turbosupercharged engine, radiators, and landing gear bay he had almost reached a logical tail location anyway.

Lockheed decided that since they could not solve the compressibility problem directly they would provide flaps to slow the plane in dives and skirt the problem.

Some military pilots were reluctant to fly the P-38 because of its reputation in compressibility.

Germans felt the P-38 could out-turn an ME-109, but its slow initial roll reaction normally prevented it from catching the smaller fighter. They also though it was suicide to go head-on against the very heavy firepower of a P-38.

P-38 STRUCTURAL DESCRIPTION
(Metal is aluminum alloy unless otherwise noted)

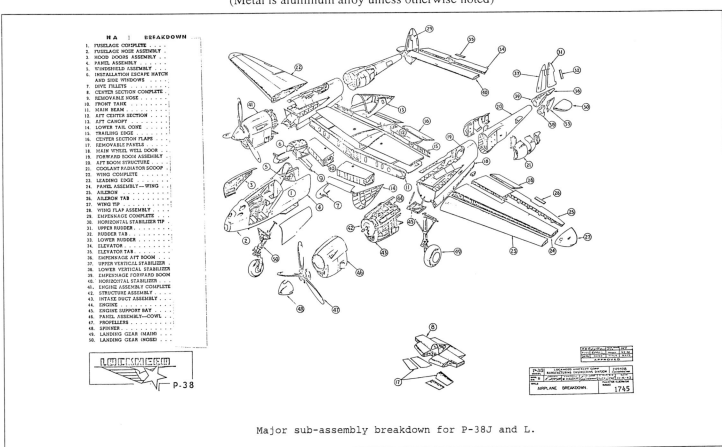

Major sub-assembly breakdown for P-38J and L.

WING GROUP

The wing consisted of a center section, two outer panels, and removeable wingtips. The wing center section was jig-mated, riv-

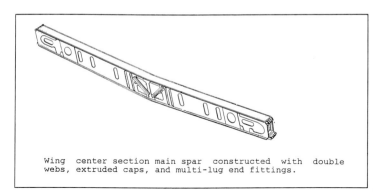

Wing center section main spar constructed with double webs, extruded caps, and multi-lug end fittings.

eted, and bolted to the fuselage and to the forward sections of the two tail booms.

The primary structural elements of the wing were the main beam, or spar, located at 35% of wing chord, and a front and rear shear beam. The main wing beam in the center section was a built-up double-web box type with upper and lower extruded cap strips of a channel shape and tapering ftom 7/8 to 7/16 inches thick. These cap strips were joined by five intermediate bulkheads. The center thirty inches of the front beam web was a built-up truss section. The main beam had upper and lower fittings at the cap strips at each end to attach to the outer wing panels at the boom locations. These were multiple-lug pin-jointed types. The main beam depth varied from nineteen inches at its center to thirteen and one half inches at the outboard ends.

A forward shear beam in the wing center section extended only from the crew nacelle out to the booms on each side, and did not extend outboard. It was of single web and extruded cap construc-

Fig.38-24B Lockheed P-38L Lightning, Warren Thompson photo via Joe Weathers Nose closeup of G.I.Miss U. shows the generous proportions of both the decorative young lady and the wing-to-fuselage fillet found necessary early in the P-38 program to eliminate buffet downstream. The P-38L had an empty weight 1300 pounds heavier than the prototype, and for a ferry flight took off at a gross weight of over 21000 pounds.

Fig.38-24C Lockheed P-38L Lightning, photo via P.M. Bowers. The P-38L restored for display by the USAF Museum shows a pristine paint job with two Japanese flags on the nose. The dark line under the wing inboard of the national insignia is the outer edge of the starboard dive flap used on late J and all L models. When extended the two-section flap formed a shallow V.

tion. The rear shear beam was also a single web and extruded cap structure, and supported the center section wing flaps. The ends of this beam were joined to mating outer panel beams at the booms by steel fittings bolted at top and bottom beam caps.

Longitudinal ribs were used in the center section except between the main beam and the rear shear beam and spanwise between wing stations 17 and 68 (inches from the centerline respectively) on each side. This was the location of the main fuel tanks. There were also no ribs between the main beam and forward shear beam between wing stations 18.5 and 79.5 on each side where the reserve fuel tanks were located. A corrugated inner skin replaced rib strength over the main fuel tanks, and hat-section formers were employed over the reserve tank area to provide required support. The skin of the wing center section was a double-layer type composed of a corrugated inner skin and a smooth butt-jointed flush-riveted outer covering. Corrugations were .064 and the outer skin .040 inches thick. In later models hard-point provisions at the spar lower cap locations in the wing center section were made to support attaching shackles to carry underwing stores, one location either side.

The spars of each outer wing panel, the main wing beam and the rear shear beam, joined the corresponding beams of the wing center section at the forward boom locations. The main beam in the outer panel continued straight outboard, and was of single-web modified Wagner type construction with extruded top and bottom cap strips of double reinforced L-shaped sections which reduced uniformly in section going outboard. The outer half of the caps were of sheet angle rather than extrusions. At the inboard end of the outer wing panel main beam all vertical shear was carried through a diagonal hat-section member to the top beam fitting; the bottom beam attach fitting secured the lower side of the wing. The pin-jointed main beam fitting was an aluminum forging in the center section and a steel fitting in the outer section. The attach pins were also of steel.

Fig.38-25 Lockheed P-38L, Martin and Kelman photo via Hal Andrews. Almost 4000 of the Lightning fighters were of the L variety which appeared in mid-1944 with only about a year left in the war. Gen. Kenney of 5th Air Force in the Pacific fought hard against the inclinations of some to stop P-38 production. This picture of a P-38L shows an early version of under-wing rocket mounts, later modified to zero-length lauchers, five beneath each wing.

Fig.38-26 Civil Lockheed P-38L, Ser.44-53095, Ron McCann photo. This photo of a civilian P-38L at an airshow in the 1980s illustrates how difficult it could be to get a good ground shot that fully shows the P-38 confiqfuration. One boom masks much of the remainder of the aircraft. A P-38 is a rare sight indeed at one of today's air shows.

The rear shear beam in the outer panel ran parallel to the wing trailing edge to a point near the inner end of the aileron where it was spliced to a lighter outboard section. The load at the splice was carried through the surface structure and the ribs. The rear beam used cap strips of bent up sheet angles with a web strengthened by vertical angle stiffeners. The rear shear beam sections of center and outer wing panels were joined by steel fittings bolted together at the top and bottom caps. For additional joint strength nine upper and nine lower forged aluminum bathtub fittings were provided along the upper and lower skin lines and carried well back from the joint line. The inner and outer bathtubs were bolted together with internal wrenching tension bolts.

Like the center section, the skin of the outer panels was a double layer with corrugated inner skins and butt-jointed flush-riveted outer skins varying in thickness from .040 to .020 inches. The outer panel torque box was formed by the main and aft beams and the upper and lower stressed skin and stringer combination between beams.

Wing panel trailing edge sections were made up of ribs and skin on the upper surface with intercostal stiffeners between the ribs. In the later P-38 models the wing leading edge contained shells, and was composed of chordwise corrugations and smooth skin with few ribs. In the outer wing panels the outer skin was attached to fourteen ribs at twelve inch spacing which were formed from sheet stock. In the latest P-38s space was provided in the leading edge sections of the outer panels for an additional fuel tank replacing the intercoolers located there on earlier models.

Wingtips were all metal with smooth outer skins spot-welded to beaded inner skins joined at their periphery and stiffened by two channel-section internal spanwise formers. The tips were joined to the wing outer panels by multiple screws around the upper and lower skin line contours. A wingtip light was part of the assembly.

Wing flaps were the Lockheed-Fowler type which rolled aft and down from the trailing edge on tracks beneath the wing, extending the wing area. The flaps were divided into four panels which were interconnected and operated together. They were installed on each side between wing stations 8.0 and 77.25 in the wing center section, and between 118.75 and 180.0 on each side in the wing outer panels. Flaps were made up of a main spar with sheet metal web and caps, sheet metal ribs, and stringers covered with flush-riveted metal skin. At each end the flap sections were attached to carriages which rolled in tracks built into the wing structure. The carriages were linked by preformed tinned carbon steel cables to

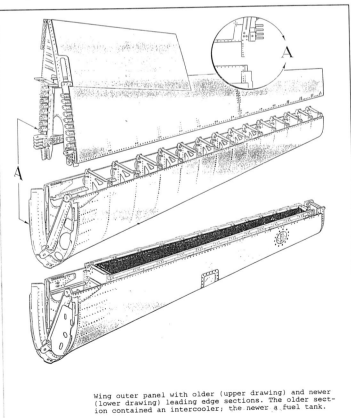

Wing outer panel with older (upper drawing) and newer (lower drawing) leading edge sections. The older section contained an intercooler; the newer a fuel tank.

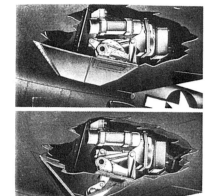

Dive recovery flap with electric actuator and drive linkage, shown retracted and extended.

Fig.38-27 Civil lockheed P-38L, R. Besecker photo, Reno, Nevada. A nicely restored L version is shown at the 1971 Reno Air Races. Tail stripes from the pre-war era are painted on. Expensive to operate, the P-38s were not much favored as postwar racers as compared to other fighter types. Protruding behind the port engine nacelle in the down position is the retractable pilot access ladder at the back end of the central pod.

push-pull tubes, traveling in roller brackets on the aft face of the rear shear beam. The push-pull tubes were actuated by long irreversible screw actuators driven by a hydraulic motor housed under the upper rear crew nacelle section. The wing flaps had three automatic positions, UP, DOWN, and MANEUVERING. The flaps could also be placed in any intermediate position by using the cockpit control. When fully extended the flap leading edge corresponded approximately to the basic wing trailing edge. The flap control system consisted of a four-way selector valve , a piston-type hydraulic drive motor, and a travel limit valve. The motor was mounted on the flap drive gearbox which was bolted to the wing center section aft shear beam.

The ailerons extended on each side from just outboard of the flaps in the outer wing panels to the wingtip assemblies. They were all-metal statically and dynamically balanced assemblies built up of ribs, stringers, and flush riveted metal skin with internal single spars of sheet metal angles and stamped ribs. Ailerons were piano-hinged to the wings and four internal balance weight assemblies extended from their forward edges. A moveable trim tab, metal-covered, was provided slightly inboard of mid-span on both ailerons. Late models equipped with an aileron power-boost system did not have trim tabs however.

Dive recovery flaps were used on late P-38J and all P-38L models. The flaps extended to an angle of 40 degrees and were

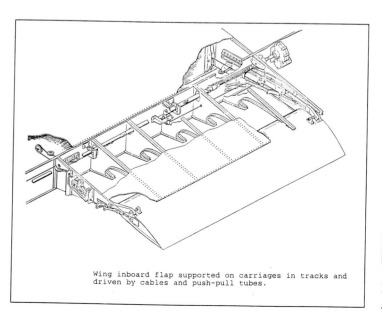

Wing inboard flap supported on carriages in tracks and driven by cables and push-pull tubes.

Fig.38-28 Civil Lockheed P-38L, R. Besecker photo, Reno, Nevada. Another 1971 view of Scrapiron IV with suitable nose adornment. The pilot's entrance hatch is shown open. Below that side windows could be cranked down as on an automobile. This airplane appears in like-new condition, reflecting the careful attention given these "warbirds" by their civilian hobbiest owners.

Fig.38-29. Lockheed P-38L, Photo via P.M.Bowers. After World War II a few P-38s were provided to Honduras in Central America. This airplane is believed to be one of those "rescued" from Honduran service and brought home. It is doubtful that turbosuperchargers remained with the aircraft at this stage. They would be a needless complication.

composed of two hinged panels called a flap panel and a brace panel mounted on the lower surface of each outer wing just outboard of the booms. Fabricated of three layers of sheet metal and flush riveted, the flap and brace panels together had a chord of fifteen and a half inches, eight and a half for the flap and the remainder for the brace panel. When the flap system was retracted it lay flat and flush against the wing lower surface. When deployed the two flap sections moved to form a vee cross-section projecting into the airstream. Dive flap span was 58 inches on each side of the aircraft. Spanwise they extended about as far as the regular inboard landing flap behind them, but were located so the forward piano hinge line was along the wing main beam at 35% chord. Flaps were actuated by an electrically-driven screw-jack mechanism and linkage. The actuating system, including the 24 volt DC motor, was located within the wing behind the main beam.

TAIL GROUP

The tail, or empennage, group consisted of the forward empennage booms (actually the rear ends of the tail booms), the horizontal stabilizer and elevator, the upper and lower vertical fins on each side, and the upper and lower rudder assemblies on each side.

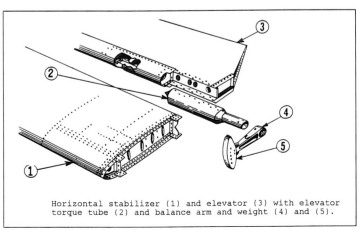

Horizontal stabilizer (1) and elevator (3) with elevator torque tube (2) and balance arm and weight (4) and (5).

The horizontal stabilizer was a built-up all metal structure with two spars having single stamped webs and sheet metal angle caps. The flush riveted stringer-stiffened skin varied in thickness from .032 to .020 inches. Stamped ribs were employed. The rounded horizontal stabilizer tips outboard of the booms were interchangeable right and left.

The elevator was a single-panel all-metal structure attached to the horizontal stabilizer by ball bearing hinges. The elevator was moved by torque tubes at each end and driven by cables. The elevator tab was located on the airplane centerline in the trailing edge. It was attached to the elevator by a steel hinge pin, and connected to the cable actuating system by a push-pull tube. The inboard ends of the elevator torque tube were carried in bearings on the stabilizer rear spar. The torque tube balance arm, attached to the outboard end of the tube by two taper pins, contained a bearing that slipped over a pin to the empennage boom. The arms extended forward, and the control cables and balance weights were fastened to them.

Upper and lower vertical fins (vertical stabilizers) were all-metal built-up structures with multiple spars having stamped webs and sheet metal angle caps and ribs. Skins were flush riveted metal stiffened by bulb angle sections and ribs were stampings. Similar construction was employed for the upper and lower rudder assemblies. The vertical fins, constructed in upper and lower sections, were interchangeable left and right. Located in the upper fin sections were the rudder tab actuating units, navigation lights showing on the outboard sides only, and control pulleys. Each lower fin section carried an elevator control pulley and a steel shoe or cap to protect the lower tip in the event of a tail-down landing. The rudder hinge brackets and the rudder torque tubes were attached to the fin rear spars.

The rudders were constructed in two sections, upper and lower, and were interchangeable left and right. The rudders were attached to the vertical stabilizers by ball bearing hinges, and to the torque tubes by screws. A counterbalance area extended forward of the hinge line of both upper and lower rudder sections. Upper and lower

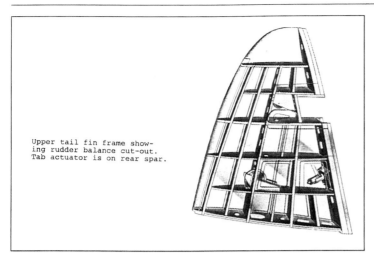

Upper tail fin frame showing rudder balance cut-out.
Tab actuator is on rear spar.

sections were tied together by screws. Tabs on each upper rudder section were attached to the rudder by a hinge and steel hinge pin. Tabs were connected to their actuating units by a push-pull tube. Rudder torque tubes, bearings, brackets, and arms were assembled as units and attached to the fins by bolts. The control arm projected outboard from each tube and was connected by a push-pull tube to walking beams in the boom. The empennage booms each consisted of forward and aft parts which were joined at boom station 430. The empennage booms formed tail cones to the aft boom sections. The tail cones faired to a trailing edge flush with the horizontal stabilizer tip and with the elevator when it was in neutral position. The horizontal stabilizer tip was attached to both parts of the empennage boom.

FUSELAGE GROUP

The basic fuselage was an all-metal semi-monocoque gondola-type structure, framed primarily by hydro-press stamped bulkheads with transverse partitions between different compartments for additional strength. Longitudinal stringers of bent-up sheet metal were employed, and covering skin sheets were butt-jointed and flush riveted. Skin thicknesses varied from .025 to .051 inches. The large armament compartment doors in the forward section were built up of a smooth outer skin and a formed inner skin strengthener. Both were stamped from .040 inch thick material and riveted and spot welded. These hinged doors were secured by Dzus fasteners. The nose wheel well down under the forward section was similar in construction except the outer skin was .032 and the inner skin was .040 inches thick. A firewall was located between the armament compartment and the pilot and this was reinforced with armor plate.

The lower section of the fuselage contained the nose gear, a compartment for receiving ejected cannon shell cases and links, major units of the hydraulic system, fuel system components, and engine control and flight surface control parts. The upper section contained, forward to aft, the armament, cockpit, and radio compartments.

The aft section of the fuselage enclosed the flap motor drive and the mounting ladder. The ladder was pivoted and spring-loaded so that it retracted into the aft cone of the gondola. A hand hold was

provided in the aft end of that body for assistance in climbing the ladder.

The windshield was composed of three separate glass panels. The front panel was constructed of five layers of glass set in vinyl plastic, and was bullet-proof. The arrangement for earlier models was different where there was a curved plexiglass enclosure and a separate flat glass shield mounted inside the cabin ahead of the pilot. Side windshield panels were similar, but with two layers of glass. They were mounted in synthetic sponge rubber within a metal frame and held in place with metal strips. The side windows of the cockpit enclosure fit in slots between the front shear beam and main wing beam locations. The windows were raised and lowered by a hand crank and locked in position by a ratchet and pawl. The cockpit hatch used for ingress and egress was a moulded plastic panel fitted to a metal frame and was hinged at the rear. A telescopic stop was incorporated in the hatch hinge system. A pin and cable assembly on the forward framing, controlled from either inside or outside the hatch, locked the hatch in the down position. A red-painted emergency handle was provided in the cockpit to release the hatch and let it raise about two inches to a point where in-flight air pressure would tear the hatch away and provide emergency egress. Access to the cockpit from outside was obtained by use of two small handles located on the forward side of the framing channel. When these were turned latch pins retracted to release the hatch.

The fixed aft canopy covering the radio compartment was made up of two plastic panels of moulded sheet set in metal frames and secured by Airloc fasteners for quick removal. A synthetic rubber liner cemented to the metal frame provided the seal between framework and panels. An armored headrest was mounted between the pilot and radio compartments. The pilot's seat was of moulded plastic, and both seat and back were protected by 3/8 inch thick face-hardened steel armor plate. A seat belt and a shoulder harness were provided and a pilot relief tube was located at the left edge of the seat.

Fig.38-30 Lockheed P-38L, photo via P.M.Bowers. A fine view of another ex-Honduran aircraft with the rudder insignia of that country still apparent. Turbosuperchargers have definitely been removed from this airplane, in fact the whole engine induction system has been revised as exemplified by absence of an air intake under the wing trailing edge and re-skinning of the boom in that area.

Fig.38-31 Civil Lockheed P-38L, Ser.44-53095, Ron Mccann photo. An expensive hobby sitting at a 1980s air show, and a rarity! This Fork-Tailed Devil displays details of landing gear and boom. The reinforced bumper shown at the bottom of the tail fin catered to a case of excessive tail-down landing which could occur if the plane was landed with wing flaps shot up and inoperable, or if the pilot just forgot to lower flaps.

The nose gear compartment and door were located forward on the gondola underside. The door was operated by a hydraulic cylinder connected directly to its aft end. A hydraulic latching device held the door in the closed position after the gear was retracted.

FORWARD BOOMS

The forward boom assemblies extended from the engine firewalls aft to station 265 just forward of the coolant radiators, and were jig-mated to the wing center section. These sections contained the main landing gear and supercharger installations. Stressed skin construction was used throughout, including the inside skins of the wheel wells. The portion of the upper surface of the booms exposed to supercharger heat was made from .018 inch thick stainless steel. Internal construction consisted of stamped metal bulkheads and bulb-angle stringers with the bulkheads spaced about fifteen inches on centers. The covering skins were .032 inches thick.

The main landing gear retracted aft into the forward boom wheel wells. The two landing gear doors in each boom were hinged to the lower boom channels, and operated automatically with gear movement. A hydraulic cylinder located in the aft end of the wheel well operated the front and rear door carriage through a linkage of cables and rods.

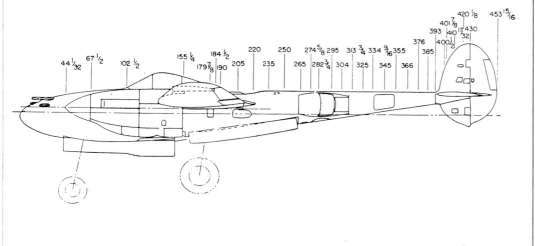

Station locations on an early P-38 boom. Intercoolers are in the wing leading edges here.

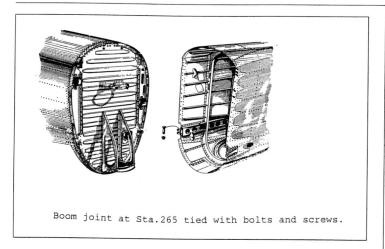

Boom joint at Sta.265 tied with bolts and screws.

Nose landing gear.

AFT BOOMS

The aft boom assemblies were also of semi-monocoque stressed skin construction, and extended from the forward boom at station 265 to station 393 where the empennage boom started. The attachment to forward and empennage booms was made in both cases by screws and stop nuts through the skins and webs, and by bolts through two forged fittings that mated with fittings on the adjacent boom sections. Coolant radiator frames were supported by brackets attached to formers at stations 282 and 295. A baggage compartment was located in the right hand aft boom between stations 325 and 366. There was an access door on the left hand side of the boom. The top liner panel was tied to the structure with Dzus fasteners and could be removed for access to flight controls components above that area. Each end of the baggage compartment was closed off by a bulkhead, the forward portion carrying the aircraft data case. A similar compartment for stowage of the battery was located in the left hand boom accessable through a door on the outboard side. A manhole located at station 282 in the underside of each aft boom provided access to the interior. The aft booms also provided space for large oxygen supply bottles.

ENGINE SECTION

The engine sections were located ahead of the forward boom assemblies. The engines were supported on forged aluminum alloy mounts of triangular shape that were bolted to fittings at the forward corners of the support bay. The bay was also made of forged aluminum alloy, and was joined by two large machine bolts to heavy fittings on the forward boom wheel well channel members. Both the support bay and the longitudinal trusses were supported by tubular diagonal hangers bolted at their upper ends to fittings on the cross-members of the forward boom. Engines were mounted by eight 7/16 inch bolts along with vibration isolators.

The engine cowling sections were made up of metal sheets formed and tied to pressed metal support strips by flush quick-disconnect fasteners. The lower cowl sections incorporated the air scoops for oil coolers, and in the later models, the air-to-air intercoolers of the supercharging system.

LANDING GEAR

The fully retractable landing gear was of the tricycle type, consisting of a nose gear located under the fuselage gondola and two main gears at the forward boom assembly underside locations. When retracted the landing gear units were all enclosed in their respective wheel wells by flush automatically operated doors.

The nose landing gear retracted aft with the strut trunnion mounted in fittings in the gear well. Below the oleo shock strut a single side fork supported an axle for the self-castoring nose wheel. The nose gear assembly included a torque scissors and a shimmy damper, but had no brakes or steering system. The gear hydraulic actuating cylinder included a built-in downlock. A hydraulic up-

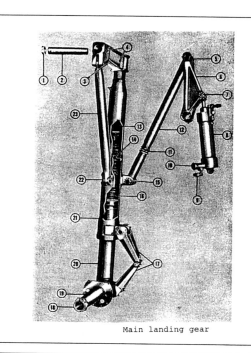

Main landing gear

Fig.38-32 Lockheed P-38M, Ser.44-27234, Mfr.photo via F. Dean coll. Starting in early 1945 a batch of 75 planned P-38L aircraft were converted to a night fighter configuration by the addition of a second crew member acting as radar operator and sitting in a cramped looking area aft of the pilot and under a bubble canopy. The radar scanner was located in a pod just under the aircraft nose.

lock system was also included.

The main landing gear retracted aft into wells in the forward boom assemblies. At the upper end of a main gear assembly a fulcrum forging was pinned to gear attach fittings in the boom structure. The main vertical strut was an oleo shock unit with the piston extending down to support an axle for a single wheel overhung on the outboard side. Torque scissors connected the oleo piston and housing. A tubular side load strut extended from a lug on the outboard side of the oleo up to the fulcrum forging, and a drag link ran from an oleo aft lug to an upper drag link pin. A hydraulic retracting actuator modified the drag link system geometry to retract the gear. A landing gear lever in the cockpit controlled the extension and retraction of all three wheels. A lever lock was in place whenever the left main shock strut was compressed. The lock could be released by rotating a control knob. A position indicator and a warning light were located in the cockpit. Normal power came from an engine-driven hydraulic pump; auxiliary power from a hand pump pressure through the same system, and emergency power from the hand pump via an emergency system with separate reservoir and

P-38 SYSTEMS DESCRIPTION

hydraulic lines.

PROPULSION SUBSYSTEMS

ENGINE

The two engines were 1200 to 1500 horsepower class Allison V-1710 liquid cooled twelve cylinder vee-type inline models of 5.5 inch bore and 6.0 inch stroke. They were equipped with auxiliary stage turbosupercharging and operated at a maximum RPM of 3000. The right side engine rotated counterclockwise and the left engine

rotated clockwise looking from the rear. Each engine had a self-contained single stage supercharger with an 8.1 to 1 gear ratio driving a nine and one half inch diameter impeller located in the engine accessory housing. The propeller reduction gear ratio was 2.1 to 1 and the integral gearboxes were such that propellers rotated in the opposite direction to the crankshaft. Magnetos were pressurized Bendix Scintilla type and turned at 1.5 times crankshaft speed. AC or Champion spark plugs were specified.

Allison V-1750-F5R engine showing splined propeller shaft.

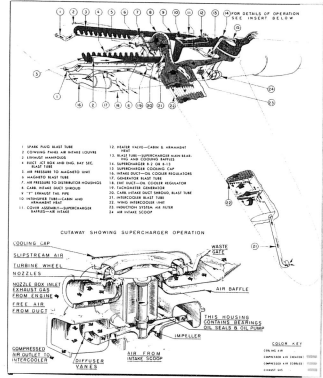

Fig.38-33 Lockheed P-38M Lightning, Ser.44-27234, Mfr. photo via F. Dean coll. Another view of the black-painted night fighter, this showing the radar antenna arrays under the wings. This version of the P-38 was one final attempt to prolong the life of the type, but Lightnings disappeared rather quickly from the scene postwar. Simpler more easily maintainable P-47s and P-51s were the immediate postwar fighters favored with the Lockheed jet P-80 to be operational soon.

CUTAWAY SHOWING SUPERCHARGER OPERATION

Induction and exhaust systems for early P-38s with wing leading edge intercoolers.

ENGINE INDUCTION SYSTEM

Charge air for the engines entered the induction system through an airscoop located on the outboard side of the boom below the wing trailing edge. If an air filter was in use, the air passed through and on via ducting to the compressor of the turbosupercharger. After compression the air was routed through pressure-tight ducting to an intercooler unit. On the early P-38s the intercoolers were lo-

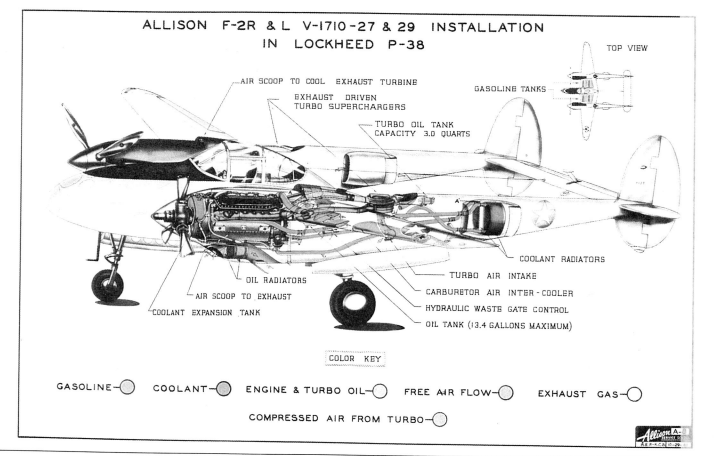

Fig.38-34 Lockheed P-38L Lightning, Ron McCann photo. Several years ago this P-38L was restored to be mounted at the main entrance of McGuire AFB in central New Jersey in honor of World War II ace Major Tommy McGuire. The project caused considerable dissent from those who did not wish to see a rare bird mounted outside in the elements. A rather sturdy but unhandsome support structure is evident. How the P-38 fares today is not known.

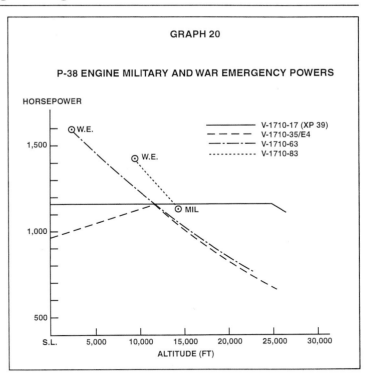

cated in the wing leading edges outboard of the nacelles; in later models they were moved to the engine nacelles under the engines where they were bolted via four shock mounts to the engine mounts. The intercoolers on the later models were of the core type and were equipped with electrically-operated airflow exit control flaps. These controlled carburetor air temperature. Compressed hot air from the turbosupercharger compressor passed through the tubes of the intercooler and was cooled sufficiently to make it suitable for engine operation. From the intercooler the air was delivered by pressure-

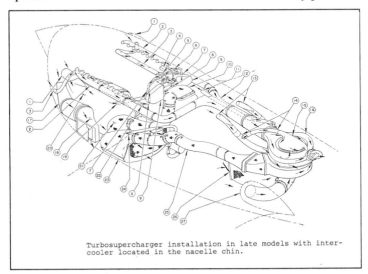

Turbosupercharger installation in late models with inter-cooler located in the nacelle chin.

(1) scoop-exhaust manifold and shroud
(2) exhaust manifold
(3) spark-plug blast tube
(4) electrical relay box
(5) magneto
(6) magneto blast tube
(7) air pressure to distributor housing
(8) air pressure to magneto unit
(9) distributor housing
(10) carburetor intake duct
(11) intensifier tube-cabin & armament heat
(12) exhaust Y tail pipe
(13) cover assembly-supercharger baffles
(14) blast-tube supercharger main bearing and cooling baffles
(15) cooling cap supercharger
(16) B-33 supercharger
(17) intake scoop-oil-cooler regulator
(18) exit duct-oil-cooler regulator
(19) duct to electrical oil-cooler relay
(20) intake scoop-intercooler
(21) exit duct-intercooler
(22) blast tube to tachometer generator
(23) intercooler unit
(24) generator blast tube
(25) intake duct-intercooler
(26) air filter
(27) supercharger air-intake scoop

tight ducting to the engine carburetor and from there the fuel-air mixture went to the integral supercharger described above and then on to the engine intake manifold.

ENGINE EXHAUST SYSTEM
Exhaust manifolds from the engine cylinder banks converged in a Y to a single shrouded duct which carried the exhaust gases from that point to the turbosupercharger nozzle box at the top of the nacelle. In the turbo unit the gases drove the turbine wheel, which in turn drove the compressor on the same shaft, and then passed out the waste gate and dumped overboard.

ENGINE MOUNTED ACCESSORIES
The engine-mounted or engine-driven accessories included: fuel pump, lubrication oil pump, coolant pump, hydraulic pump, electrical generator (on one engine for early airplanes, on two engines for late models) propeller speed governor, magnetos, tachometer generator, and Bendix-Stromberg carburetor. Two generators were used only on late J and all L model P-38s. A hydraulic pump was mounted on each engine.

ENGINE CONTROLS
The engine throttle control in the cockpit was mechanically connected to the supercharger pressure regulator by pulley and cable and linkage runs through the inboard wing sections to the boom, so separate lever control of the supercharger was eliminated. Late model aircraft using a COMBAT power rating had turbosupercharger regulators incorporating two overspeed controls; the basic one regulated to 24000 turbo RPM and the COMBAT one to 26400 RPM. The late airplanes also had automatic manifold pressure regulators. With these two regulators each manifold pressure had a correspond

ALLISON V-1710 MODEL F LOCATION OF ACCESSORIES

1-MECHANICAL TACH. DRIVE (NOT SHOWN)
2-MIXTURE CONTROL CONNECTION
3-FUEL VAPOR VENT
4-FUEL PRESSURE CONNECTION
5-FUEL INLET
6-THROTTLE CONNECTION
7-MIXTURE TEMPERATURE CONNECTION
8-REAR VACUUM PUMP FLANGE
9-OIL PRESSURE CONNECTION
10-GENERATOR FLANGE
11-STARTER FLANGE
12-FUEL PUMP FLANGE
13-OIL INLET
14-VACUUM PUMP OIL DRAIN
15-COOLANT INLET
16-OIL DRAIN
17-COOLANT PUMP SEAL DRAIN
18-SIDE VACUUM PUMP FLANGE
19-OIL VENT CONNECTION
20-ELECTRIC TACH. DRIVE FLANGE
21-DISTRIBUTOR DRAIN
22-SPARK PLUG COOLING MANIFOLD INLET
23-COOLANT OUTLET
24-PROP. GOVERNOR DRIVE (IN VEE)

ing cockpit throttle position. This relationship was fixed up to the critical altitude, which was defined as the altitude where the overspeed governor took control to hold turbo RPM at either 24000 or 26400 RPM. The manifold pressure automatically dropped about one and one half inches for every 1000 feet above critical altitude.

Engine controls mechanically linked to the engine were those for mixture and for the propeller governor. The runs were of the pulley and cable type out to the booms where they reverted to rods and bellcranks. Carburetor air temperature control via the intercooler flaps was electrical. Other engine controls were those for oil dilution, oil cooler flaps for temperature control (automatic with manual backup), the carburetor air filter control, and engine coolant temperature control (automatic with manual backup). The air filter control was a knob in the cockpit that actuated air intake duct valves in the boom via pulleys, cable, and control rods out through the wing.

PROPELLER

The propellers were Curtiss C532D Electric three blade 11'6" diameter constant speed selective pitch and full feathering models. The left side propeller rotated counterclockwise viewed from the aft side and the right side propeller rotated clockwise from the rear.

These opposite turning propellers meant that blades on each side were handed differently. The blades were solid aluminum alloy; hubs were alloy steel mounted on an SAE #50 splined shaft. Left hand blades were of the 88996 design and right hand blades an 89303 design. The propellers operated from the aircraft electrical system. Hubs and inboard blade sections were covered by streamlined rotating metal spinner assemblies tied to the hub by bulkheads. Propeller blade angle settings at the 42 inch blade radius station were 22.7 degrees low pitch, 57.7 degrees high pitch, and 87.5 degrees feather position.

PROPELLER CONTROLS

A propeller speed governor was mounted on each engine nose. Control of the engine/propeller set speed was made from two propeller levers mounted in the cockpit on the throttle quadrant and mechanically linked to the governors via a pulley and cable system in the wing and a rod and bellcrank system in the boom. Output of the governors was transmitted electrically to the propellers whenever the cockpit propeller switches were set to automatic constant speed. The switches could also be set to manually increase or decrease blade pitch or be set in fixed pitch. Other cockpit switches

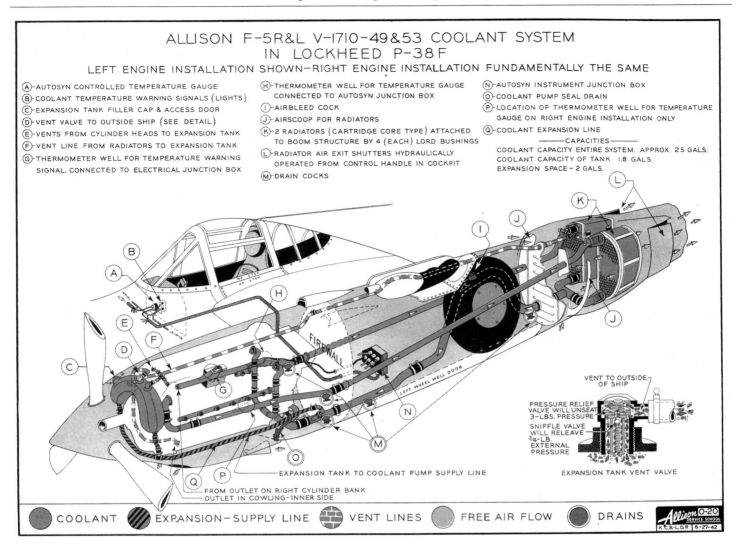

ALLISON F-5R&L V-1710-49&53 COOLANT SYSTEM
IN LOCKHEED P-38F
LEFT ENGINE INSTALLATION SHOWN—RIGHT ENGINE INSTALLATION FUNDAMENTALLY THE SAME

(A)-AUTOSYN CONTROLLED TEMPERATURE GAUGE
(B)-COOLANT TEMPERATURE WARNING SIGNALS (LIGHTS)
(C)-EXPANSION TANK FILLER CAP & ACCESS DOOR
(D)-VENT VALVE TO OUTSIDE SHIP (SEE DETAIL)
(E)-VENTS FROM CYLINDER HEADS TO EXPANSION TANK
(F)-VENT LINE FROM RADIATORS TO EXPANSION TANK
(G)-THERMOMETER WELL FOR TEMPERATURE WARNING
    SIGNAL. CONNECTED TO ELECTRICAL JUNCTION BOX

(H)-THERMOMETER WELL FOR TEMPERATURE GAUGE
    CONNECTED TO AUTOSYN JUNCTION BOX
(I)-AIRBLEED COCK
(J)-AIRSCOOP FOR RADIATORS
(K)-2 RADIATORS (CARTRIDGE CORE TYPE) ATTACHED
    TO BOOM STRUCTURE BY 4 (EACH) LORD BUSHINGS
(L)-RADIATOR AIR EXIT SHUTTERS HYDRAULICALLY
    OPERATED FROM CONTROL HANDLE IN COCKPIT
(M)-DRAIN COCKS

(N)-AUTOSYN INSTRUMENT JUNCTION BOX
(O)-COOLANT PUMP SEAL DRAIN
(P)-LOCATION OF THERMOMETER WELL FOR TEMPERATURE
    GAUGE ON RIGHT ENGINE INSTALLATION ONLY
(Q)-COOLANT EXPANSION LINE
            —CAPACITIES—
COOLANT CAPACITY ENTIRE SYSTEM. APPROX. 25 GALS.
COOLANT CAPACITY OF TANK 1.8 GALS.
EXPANSION SPACE - 2 GALS.

VENT TO OUTSIDE
OF SHIP
PRESSURE RELIEF
VALVE WILL UNSEAT
3-LBS. PRESSURE
SNIFFLE VALVE
WILL RELEAVE
¾-LB.
EXTERNAL
PRESSURE
EXPANSION TANK VENT VALVE

EXPANSION TANK TO COOLANT PUMP SUPPLY LINE
FROM OUTLET ON RIGHT CYLINDER BANK
OUTLET IN COWLING-INNER SIDE

COOLANT   EXPANSION–SUPPLY LINE   VENT LINES   FREE AIR FLOW   DRAINS   *Allison* O-20 SERVICE SCHOOL   K.C.B-L.O.R. 6-27-42

were used to signal a propeller to go to the feather blade angle. To prevent any pilot from feathering the wrong propeller in case of an engine failure late model airplanes were equipped with indicator lights to glow over the proper feathering switch when either a hard left or hard right rudder was applied to overcome the yaw caused by engine failure.

ENGINE STARTING SYSTEM

The engine starters were of the electric inertia type with booster coils. Standard procedure was to start the left hand engine first by holding a cockpit starter switch to LH until the inertia starter reached maximum RPM, then push the ENGAGE switch to clutch in the starter, and prime the engine. Then the right hand engine was started similarly. If there wasn't sufficient battery power for starting an inertia starter handcrank or an external energy source could be used. The handcrank was stowed in the left main landing gear wheel well. Manual crank extensions were accessible through doors in the engine cowl panels.

ENGINE WATER INJECTION SYSTEM

No water injection system was used.

ENGINE COOLING SYSTEM

Certain parts of the engine were cooled by an auxiliary system of nacelle scoops and ducts provided to conduct cooling air to various sections of the engine. Air was directed to the spark plugs, magnetos, distributors, and to the cap baffles of the turbosuperchargers. The cooling air was dumped overboard after use.

The main cooling system for the engine used Ethelyn Glycol as the liquid cooling medium. It consisted primarily of a coolant supply reservoir, a half-donut shaped tank just behind the propeller spinner in the upper part of the nacelle, lines to and from the engine inlets and outlets, valves, drain cocks, vents and breather lines, and coolant radiators. On late model aircraft the reservoir was pressurized. The coolant was forced through the system by an engine-driven

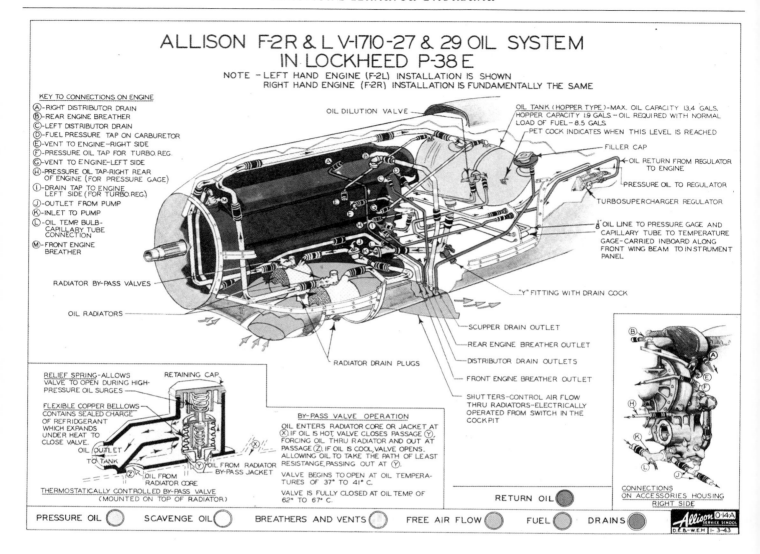

ALLISON F-2R & L V-1710-27 & 29 OIL SYSTEM IN LOCKHEED P-38E

NOTE – LEFT HAND ENGINE (F-2L) INSTALLATION IS SHOWN
RIGHT HAND ENGINE (F-2R) INSTALLATION IS FUNDAMENTALLY THE SAME

KEY TO CONNECTIONS ON ENGINE
(A)-RIGHT DISTRIBUTOR DRAIN
(B)-REAR ENGINE BREATHER
(C)-LEFT DISTRIBUTOR DRAIN
(D)-FUEL PRESSURE TAP ON CARBURETOR
(E)-VENT TO ENGINE-RIGHT SIDE
(F)-PRESSURE OIL TAP FOR TURBO. REG.
(G)-VENT TO ENGINE-LEFT SIDE
(H)-PRESSURE OIL TAP-RIGHT REAR OF ENGINE (FOR PRESSURE GAGE)
(I)-DRAIN TAP TO ENGINE LEFT SIDE (FOR TURBO.REG.)
(J)-OUTLET FROM PUMP
(K)-INLET TO PUMP
(L)-OIL TEMP BULB-CAPILLARY TUBE CONNECTION
(M)-FRONT ENGINE BREATHER

OIL DILUTION VALVE

OIL TANK (HOPPER TYPE)-MAX. OIL CAPACITY 13.4 GALS. HOPPER CAPACITY 1.9 GALS – OIL REQUIRED WITH NORMAL LOAD OF FUEL – 8.5 GALS
-PET COCK INDICATES WHEN THIS LEVEL IS REACHED
-FILLER CAP
-OIL RETURN FROM REGULATOR TO ENGINE
-PRESSURE OIL TO REGULATOR
TURBOSUPERCHARGER REGULATOR
-OIL LINE TO PRESSURE GAGE AND CAPILLARY TUBE TO TEMPERATURE GAGE-CARRIED INBOARD ALONG FRONT WING BEAM TO INSTRUMENT PANEL

RADIATOR BY-PASS VALVES
OIL RADIATORS

"Y" FITTING WITH DRAIN COCK

RADIATOR DRAIN PLUGS

-SCUPPER DRAIN OUTLET
-REAR ENGINE BREATHER OUTLET
-DISTRIBUTOR DRAIN OUTLETS
-FRONT ENGINE BREATHER OUTLET
-SHUTTERS-CONTROL AIR FLOW THRU RADIATORS-ELECTRICALLY OPERATED FROM SWITCH IN THE COCKPIT

RELIEF SPRING-ALLOWS VALVE TO OPEN DURING HIGH-PRESSURE OIL SURGES
RETAINING CAP
FLEXIBLE COPPER BELLOWS-CONTAINS SEALED CHARGE OF REFRIDGERANT WHICH EXPANDS UNDER HEAT TO CLOSE VALVE.
OIL OUTLET TO TANK
OIL FROM RADIATOR BY-PASS JACKET
OIL FROM RADIATOR CORE
THERMOSTATICALLY CONTROLLED BY-PASS VALVE (MOUNTED ON TOP OF RADIATOR)

BY-PASS VALVE OPERATION
OIL ENTERS RADIATOR CORE OR JACKET AT (X). IF OIL IS HOT, VALVE CLOSES PASSAGE (Y), FORCING OIL THRU RADIATOR AND OUT AT PASSAGE (Z). IF OIL IS COOL, VALVE OPENS, ALLOWING OIL TO TAKE THE PATH OF LEAST RESISTANCE, PASSING OUT AT (Y).
VALVE BEGINS TO OPEN AT OIL TEMPERA-TURES OF 37° TO 41° C.
VALVE IS FULLY CLOSED AT OIL TEMP OF 62° TO 67° C.

RETURN OIL

CONNECTIONS ON ACCESSORIES HOUSING RIGHT SIDE

Allison SERVICE SCHOOL D.E.B-W.E.H 1-3-43

| PRESSURE OIL | SCAVENGE OIL | BREATHERS AND VENTS | FREE AIR FLOW | FUEL | DRAINS |

pump. Coolant radiators of the core type were located in the forward sections of the aft booms, one on either side of each boom. Two lines ran into each cooler and two came out, were interconnected, and ran forward to the engine. Radiators were located in short air ducts with fixed inlets and variable area exits. The flaps to vary exit area were moved by a hydraulic actuator driving linkage to them. An actuator was in the center of each boom. If the cockpit coolant flap switch was set to ON, the flaps could be moved to full open or full closed position. They went to a middle position if hydraulic pressure failed.

ENGINE LUBRICATION SYSTEM

A circulating oil system cooled by air lubricated each engine separately, the oil being pushed through the system by an engine-driven oil pump. The major system components for each engine were a 13 gallon oil tank, two oil cooling radiators, a bimetal line thermostat or automatic temperature regulator, check valve, strainer, oil lines, vents and breathers. Each engine incorporated an oil scavenge pump.

The aluminum alloy oil tank was located high and aft of the engine; the two oil coolers were located behind a forward cowl scoop under and just aft of the propeller spinners. Cooling air entered the forward scoop, passed through the two oil coolers, and exited overboard through oil cooler air exit flaps. Normal system operation was automatic with exit flaps moved by an electric motor-driven actuator. If the normal system failed cockpit switches could revert the system from automatic to manual control over the flaps.

An oil dilution system was controlled by cockpit switches.

ENGINE FIRE SENSING AND EXTINGUISHING SYSTEMS

No such systems were included on early models. Late versions like P-38L incorporated both sensing and extinguishing systems.

FUEL SYSTEM

The major components of the fuel system were tanks, lines, valves, and pumps. The two main fuel tanks, self-sealing and each of 90 gallon capacity, were located in the wing center section inboard of

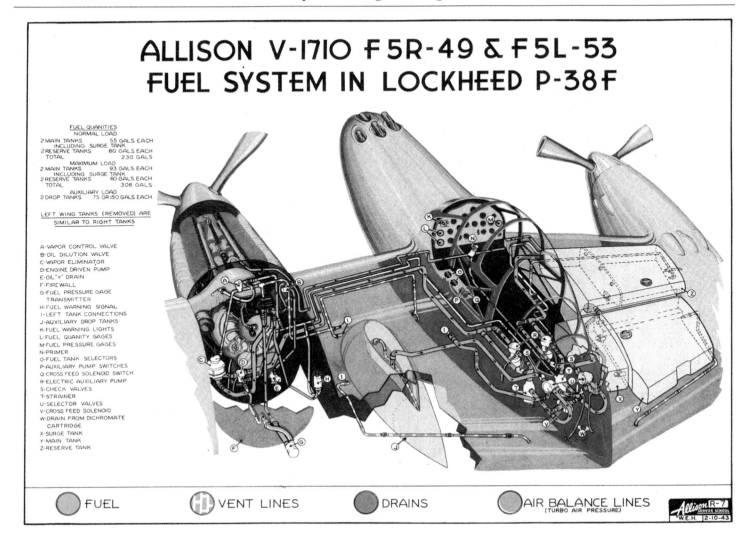

ALLISON V-1710 F5R-49 & F5L-53 FUEL SYSTEM IN LOCKHEED P-38F

FUEL QUANITIES
NORMAL LOAD
2 MAIN TANKS   55 GALS. EACH
   INCLUDING SURGE TANK
2 RESERVE TANKS   60 GALS. EACH
TOTAL   230 GALS.
MAXIMUM LOAD
2 MAIN TANKS   93 GALS. EACH
   INCLUDING SURGE TANK
2 RESERVE TANKS   60 GALS. EACH
TOTAL   306 GALS.
AUXILIARY LOAD
2 DROP TANKS   75 OR 150 GALS EACH

LEFT WING TANKS (REMOVED) ARE
SIMILAR TO RIGHT TANKS

A - VAPOR CONTROL VALVE
B - OIL DILUTION VALVE
C - VAPOR ELIMINATOR
D - ENGINE DRIVEN PUMP
E - OIL "Y" DRAIN
F - FIREWALL
G - FUEL PRESSURE GAGE
      TRANSMITTER
H - FUEL WARNING SIGNAL
I - LEFT TANK CONNECTIONS
J - AUXILIARY DROP TANKS
K - FUEL WARNING LIGHTS
L - FUEL QUANITY GAGES
M - FUEL PRESSURE GAGES
N - PRIMER
O - FUEL TANK SELECTORS
P - AUXILIARY PUMP SWITCHES
Q - CROSS FEED SOLENOID SWITCH
R - ELECTRIC AUXILIARY PUMP
S - CHECK VALVES
T - STRAINER
U - SELECTOR VALVES
V - CROSS FEED SOLENOID
W - DRAIN FROM DICHROMATE
      CARTRIDGE
X - SURGE TANK
Y - MAIN TANK
Z - RESERVE TANK

FUEL   VENT LINES   DRAINS   AIR BALANCE LINES (TURBO AIR PRESSURE)

Allison R-7 SERVICE SCHOOL W.E.H. 2-10-43

---

the booms between the main wing beam and the aft shear beam. The two reserve tanks, each self-sealing and of 60 gallon capacity, were located in the wing center section between the wing main beam and the forward shear beam. On late models (some J and all L versions) an additional tank was located in each outboard wing panel leading edge section where the intercoolers had been placed on earlier models. These outer wing tanks were self-sealing and each carried 55 gallons. Each of the six tanks on the late models contained an electrically-driven fuel booster pump. Total internal capacity on the earlier models was 300 gallons; on the later J and L airplanes it was 410 gallons. A drop tank could be carried under each wing center section, except on the earliest versions, each external tank of a capacity up to 300 gallon size, making the maximum late-version airplane fuel load 1010 gallons. Smaller drop tanks could be and most often were carried, including 150 and 75 gallon sizes. The single drop tank electrical boost pump was located in the aft fuselage. A fuel pump and strainer were located on each engine. A separate fuel system was provided for each engine, but the fuel could

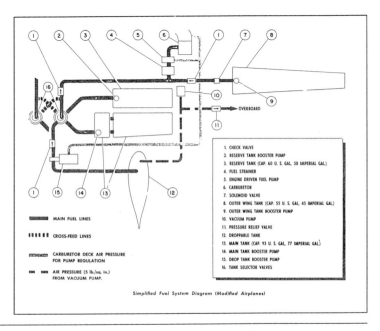

1. CHECK VALVE
2. RESERVE TANK BOOSTER PUMP
3. RESERVE TANK (CAP. 60 U.S. GAL. 50 IMPERIAL GAL.)
4. FUEL STRAINER
5. ENGINE DRIVEN FUEL PUMP
6. CARBURETOR
7. SOLENOID VALVE
8. OUTER WING TANK (CAP. 55 U.S. GAL. 45 IMPERIAL GAL.)
9. OUTER WING TANK BOOSTER PUMP
10. VACUUM PUMP
11. PRESSURE RELIEF VALVE
12. DROPPABLE TANK
13. MAIN TANK (CAP. 93 U.S. GAL. 77 IMPERIAL GAL.)
14. MAIN TANK BOOSTER PUMP
15. DROP TANK BOOSTER PUMP
16. TANK SELECTOR VALVES

OVERBOARD

▬▬▬ MAIN FUEL LINES

▪▪▪▪ CROSS-FEED LINES

▬▬▬ CARBURETOR DECK AIR PRESSURE
      FOR PUMP REGULATION

▬ ▬ AIR PRESSURE (5 lb./sq. in.)
      FROM VACUUM PUMP.

Simplified Fuel System Diagram (Modified Airplanes)

LOCKHEED P-38 E INSTRUMENT PANEL & CONTROLS

1-FUEL PRESSURE WARNING
2-RESERVE FUEL TANK GAGES
3-MAIN FUEL TANK GAGES
4-OIL SHUTTER POSITION INDICATOR
5-PROPELLER GOVERNOR CONTROLS
6-COOLANT SHUTTER CONTROLS
7-PROPELLER CIRCUIT BREAKERS
8-PROPELLER FEATHER SWITCHES
9-PROPELLER CONTROL SWITCHES
10-MANUAL MIXTURE CONTROLS
11-THROTTLES
12-FUEL TANK SELECTOR
13-ENGINE PRIMER
14-PARKING BRAKE
15-GENERATOR SWITCH
16-OIL SHUTTER SWITCH
17-IGNITION SWITCHES
18-OIL DILUTION SWITCHES
19-STARTER SWITCHES
20-COOLANT TEMPERATURE WARNING
21-COOLANT TEMPERATURE GAGE
22-TACHOMETER
23-MANIFOLD PRESSURE GAGE
24-OIL PRESSURE GAGE
25-FUEL PRESSURE GAGE
26-OIL TEMPERATURE GAGE
27-CARBURATOR AIR TEMPERATURE GAGE
28-VOLTMETER
29-AMMETER

1. Standby magnetic compass.
2. Suction gage.
3. Clock.
4. Gyro Horizon.
5. Manifold pressure gages (left and right).
6. Tachometers (left and right).
7. Engine gage right engine (oil temperature and pressure and fuel pressure).
8. Coolant temperature gage.
9. Carburetor air temperature gage.
10. BC-608 contactor.
11. Generator switches.
12. Ammeters.
13. Compass correction cards.
14. Engine gage left engine (oil temperature and pressure and fuel pressure).
15. Rate of climb indicator.
16. Bank and turn indicator.
17. Airspeed indicator.
18. Directional gyro.
19. Remote indicating compass.
20. Front (reserve) fuel tanks quantity gage.
21. Rear (main) fuel tanks quantity gage.
22. Hydraulic pressure gage.
23. Altimeter.
24. Landing gear warning light.
25. Landing gear warning light test button.
26. Spare bulb.

Typical Instrument Panel (P-38J-25 Panel Shown)

also be cross-fed to the opposite engine with an engine out or when operating on drop tank fuel. Tank selector valves and boost pump switches were at the left side of the cockpit. Low level warning lights were also provided. A drop tank release switch and button were provided on the left side of the cockpit.

FIXED EQUIPMENT SUBSYSTEMS

INSTRUMENTS

The instruments varied some between models. Those listed are for the J model. Flight instruments included: Standby magnetic compass, clock, gyro horizon, rate of climb indicator, bank and turn indicator, airspeed indicator, directional gyro, remote indicating compass, and altimeter. Engine instruments were: Dual manifold pressure gages, dual tachometers, engine gages (showing oil temperature, oil pressure, and fuel pressure), coolant temperature gages, and fuel quantity gages. Other instruments included: Suction gage, ammeters, and hydraulic pressure gage.

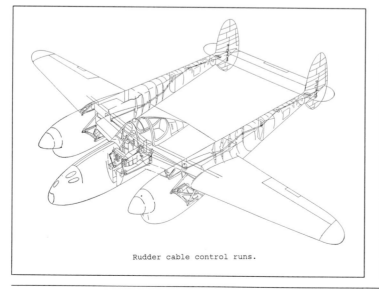

Rudder cable control runs.

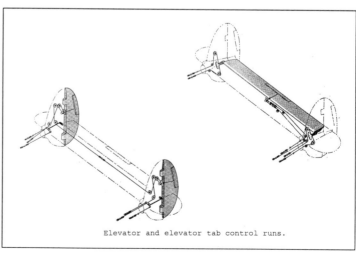

Elevator and elevator tab control runs.

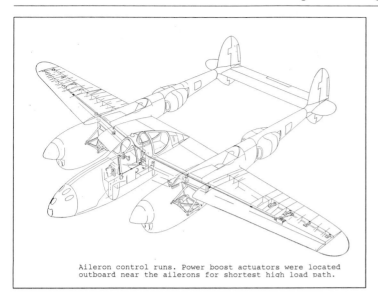

Aileron control runs. Power boost actuators were located outboard near the ailerons for shortest high load path.

SURFACE CONTROLS

Surface controls included the control wheel and column and rudder pedals in the cockpit, and control runs to the various surfaces, ailerons, elevator, and rudders. Tab controls were also included.

Rudder pedals were clamped between hangars that swung on

anti-friction bearings supported on fuselage frame webs and a casting on the airplane centerline. Pedals were adjustable to five positions to match leg length. They were interconnected by cranks and a walking beam. Adjustable stops limited their travel. Rudder cables were extra-flexible pre-formed tinned 3/16 inch diameter and were bolted in pairs to a forked mast extending forward on the outboard side of each pedal assembly. Cables ran through the wing and boom. In the empennage at boom station 402 the cables were attached to walking beams pivoted in the horizontal stabilizer. A push-pull tube connected to each walking beam was attached to the control arms on the torque tubes of the rudders, and thus could actuate them. The rudder trim tabs were cockpit-adjustable using a hand crank. The crank was geared to operating drums which were connected by cables running aft to drums in the fins and then to a revolving drum on an acme-threaded push-pull rod which moved the tab.

The elevators were controlled by fore-aft movement of a cockpit control column. The column was a hollow inverted L-shaped member made of alumunum alloy tubing. It was mounted on the right side of the fuselage on two ball bearing mounts located below the cockpit floor and between the outer skin and the nose wheel well web. The lower extremity of the column was the attachment point for the elevator control cables. Threaded adjustable stops limiting the fore and aft movement of the column were located below the floor and were reached through the wheel well. Elevator control cables ran around pulleys through the fuselage, out the inboard

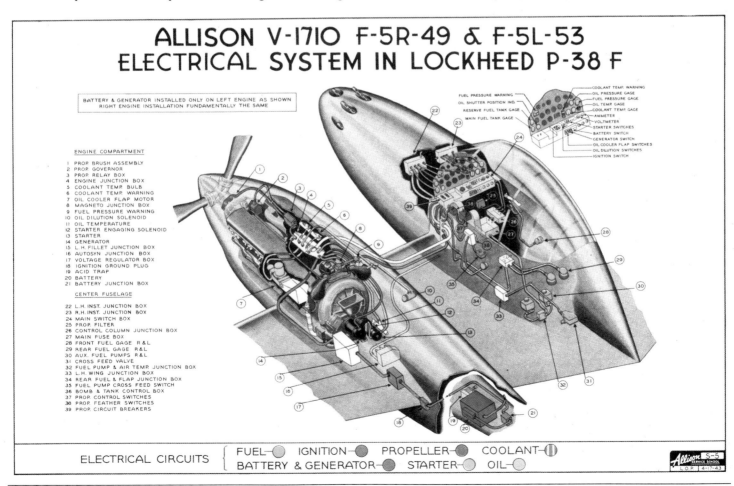

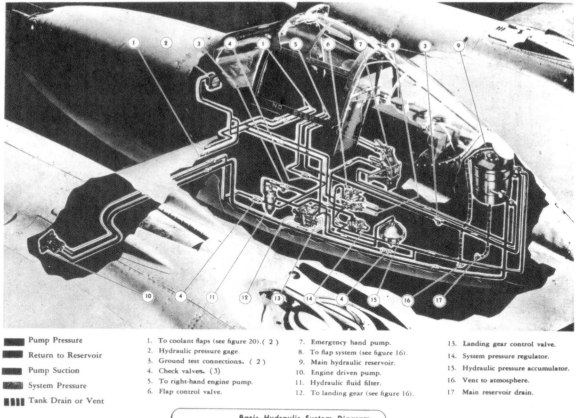

Pump Pressure

Return to Reservoir

Pump Suction

System Pressure

Tank Drain or Vent

1. To coolant flaps (see figure 20). (2)
2. Hydraulic pressure gage.
3. Ground test connections. (2)
4. Check valves. (3)
5. To right-hand engine pump.
6. Flap control valve.
7. Emergency hand pump.
8. To flap system (see figure 16).
9. Main hydraulic reservoir.
10. Engine driven pump.
11. Hydraulic fluid filter.
12. To landing gear (see figure 16).
13. Landing gear control valve.
14. System pressure regulator.
15. Hydraulic pressure accumulator.
16. Vent to atmosphere.
17. Main reservoir drain.

Basic Hydraulic System Diagram

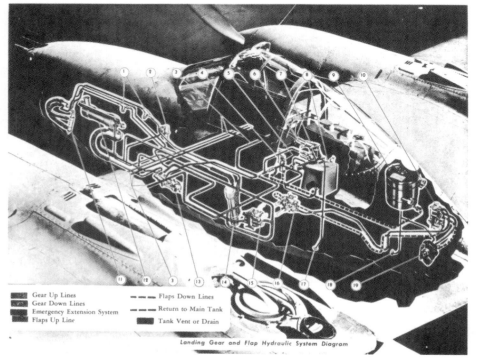

Gear Up Lines

Gear Down Lines

Emergency Extension System

Flaps Up Line

‒ ‒ ‒ **Flaps Down Lines**

‒ · ‒ **Return to Main Tank**

Tank Vent or Drain

Landing Gear and Flap Hydraulic System Diagram

wing sections near the main beam, then aft over pulleys in the booms along the inboard side of the wells for the main wheels, then up into the top section of the booms and over pulleys in the vertical stabilizer sections and down to the horizontal stabilizer. Here the cables were connected to the elevator balance arms at upper and lower ends in a manner where cable movement caused elevator movement. An elevator trim tab control wheel was in the cockpit. Cables from the control ran over pulleys under the floor, out the left wing down the boom aft into the horizontal stabilizer, and to the tab-actuating drum and screw arrangement.

Early models of the airplane used the same kind of mechanical cable and pulley drive from the cockpit wheel control to the ailerons as employed for rudders and elevator. Late models were changed to incorporate a power-assisted, or boosted, control system for the ailerons as described below:

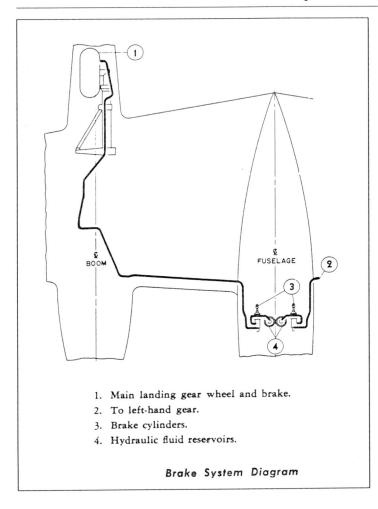

1. Main landing gear wheel and brake.
2. To left-hand gear.
3. Brake cylinders.
4. Hydraulic fluid reservoirs.

Brake System Diagram

tuation for the tabs similar to that for the tail surfaces.

Model A-4 autopilots were installed on the F-5 photo versions of the Lightning.

ELECTRICAL SYSTEM The electrical system was a single wire airframe ground return type operating on 24 volts DC. On P-38H and earlier aircraft and on early P-38J models the system was powered by one generator on the left engine and by a battery in the left boom. On photo versions the battery was located in the fuselage nose. 'Late models of P-38J and all P-38L aircraft had a 100 ampere generator on each engine and a battery in the boom. Cockpit switches could cut out battery or generators from the system. The ignition master switch was independent of the electrical system. Fuses were used in early models and were located in the nose wheel well. Later versions used circuit breakers in the cockpit, and these were of the push-to-reset type.

The electrical system was used to power landing, recognition, position, and cockpit lights and an inverter to provide 115 volt AC power for the remote compass. Power was also provided for communication, navigation, and identification gear, and for armament systems control, starters, dive flaps, auxiliary fuel pumps, turbo regulators, oil cooler and intercooler exit flap actuators, pitot tube heating, instruments, and propellers.

HYDRAULIC SYSTEM

The hydraulic system, with ten gallons capacity, operated between pressures of 1100 to 1400 pounds per square inch with a typical operating pressure of 1350 psi. Surge to 1600 psi. was permitted. The system normally operated the landing gear, landing gear doors, wing flaps, coolant radiator exit flap actuators, and on control boosted aileron airplanes, the aileron boost using pressure from the two engine-driven variable-volume hydraulic pumps and hydraulic fluid from the top half of the main hydraulic fluid reservoir located high in the aft part of the fuselage pod. The hydraulic system was capable of extending the wing flaps to the MANEUVER position of eight degrees in three seconds and retracting them in four seconds. Other major components of the system, accumulator, valves, filters, aluminum alloy lines, nose gear actuators, and flap drive were located in the lower and the aft fuselage. If the normal hydraulic system had a failure the auxiliary system could be used. It operated the same items and used the same lines except a hand-powered hydraulic pump supplied the pressure, and the fluid came from the bottom of the main hydraulic fluid reservoir. Sufficient pressure could not be built up, however, unless the aileron boost was off, and the flow to the coolant flap actuators was limited. If both normal and auxiliary hydraulic modes failed an emergency system could be used to extend the landing gear. The system had a separate reservoir and separate lines. Pressure was supplied by the hand pump in the cockpit.

PNEUMATIC SYSTEM

There was no pneumatic system in the airplane except the vacuum pump for the instruments.

Aileron action was initiated by movement of the partial wheel at the top of the L-shaped control column. A 144 degree turn of the wheel gave full aileron throw. Pulleys and cables within the column carried the control run to turnbuckles fastened to both ends of a cable running aft to pulleys under the main wing beam, up through holes in the lower beam cap, and around a reduction drum inside the beam. From this point out to each aileron the right and left hand systems were independent, and either side could be disabled without affecting the other. From the reduction drum aileron cables were routed via pulleys and fairleads outboard and aft to the quadrant of the aileron booster unit. The boost system used the main hydraulic system pressure to supplement pilot force on the wheel; the boost did about 85 percent of the job. Operation was such that the pilot maintained feel, but could produce much more force at the ailerons. A booster unit in the wing consisted of a quadrant and bellcrank assembly, a control valve, an actuating cylinder assembly, and a bypass control to shunt hydraulic fluid through the actuator to maintain unboosted control if hydraulic pressure was lost. Booster units were connected to the ailerons by push-pull tubes.

Drives from the cockpit control to both aileron trim tabs were mechanical cable and pulley systems using a drum and screw ac-

COMMUNICATION, NAVIGATION, AND IDENTIFICATION EQUIPMENT

Typical communication equipment consisted of either an SCR-522 or SCR-274N command radio set. In addition an SCR-695A radio and a Detrola 438 beacon receiver were normally provided. Sometimes when operating with British units a B-606 contacter was installed. An MN-26Y radio compass could also be installed for ferry flights. Radio equipment was located high in the after section of the fuselage pod.

ARMAMENT PROVISIONS

The aircraft was equipped with four .50 caliber machine guns and one 20 mm. cannon in the gondola nose. Five hundred rounds of ammunition were available for each machine gun and one hundred and fifty rounds were carried for the cannon. The weapons were concentrated in a 20 inch by 8 inch rectangular pattern area in the fuselage pod nose, and they fired straight ahead, neither converging or diverging in pattern.

The gun compartment was located in the upper forward part of the gondola with weapon barrels protruding out of the upper nose. Machine gun ammunition was contained in four drawer-type trays, and cannon ammunition was also served from such a container. Expended links and cartridge cases were discharged through chutes leading to openings in the skin below the armament compartment. Expended cannon shell cases and links were discharged into a compartment between the bulkheads on the lower right side of the fuselage.

Sighting was done by means of a Lynn electric gunsight installed on the aircraft just aft of the bulletproof windshield.

Streamlined bomb supports with Type D-820 Interstate bomb shackles inside were attached to the underside of the wing center section on each side midway between the fuselage and the boom. They could carry bombs (on later models) from 100 to 2000 pounds each. An M-6 gun camera was mounted in the left drop tank/ bomb support fairing. It could be operated from the cockpit either independently or in conjunction with the guns. P-38H airplanes were equipped with a machine gun charger that could be operated in flight, but later versions had to have their guns and cannon charged before taking off. In the H model the charger was operated by pulling out the charging selector in the cockpit and turning it to the gun to be charged, pulling the charging handle back and pushing it forward, then repeating the procedure for other guns. Cannon and gun firing buttons were on the control wheel. In early versions the guns were heated. To drop bombs the arming switch was set and the bomb selector switch set for the bomb to be dropped and the release button on the control wheel pushed. Bombs were not to be dropped at speeds over 400 mph IAS, and dives were to be kept to less than thirty degrees from the horizontal with dive flaps up.

The P-38L was equipped to carry ten 2.75 inch HVAR rockets, five under each wing on zero-length launchers.

PASSIVE DEFENSE SYSTEM

Passive defense items included the self-sealing fuel tanks, armor plate, and bullet-resistant glass. The armor plate consisted of small

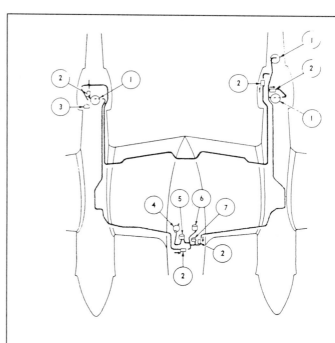

1. Oxygen bottles.
2. Check valves.
3. Refill connection.
4. Demand type oxygen regulator.
5. Oxygen flowmeter.
6. Oxygen pressure gage.
7. Pressure warning light.

Oxygen System Diagram

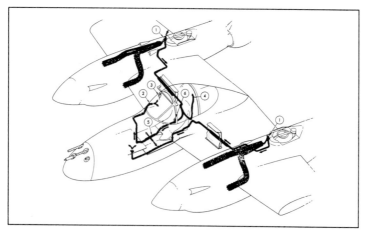

Heat System Diagram

1. Heat by-pass (shut-off) valves (2)
2. Windshield defroster tube
3. Cockpit heat control
4. Flexible hatch defroster tube

5. Foot heat shut-off valve
6. Gun (or camera) heat control
   (Cockpit heat control on late airplanes)

pieces of face-hardened steel attached separately to facilitate removal and replacement. The pilot was protected from frontal attack by armor plate mounted on the aft bulkhead of the armament compartment and by a bullet-resistant glass windshield. Two pieces of armor plate lined the back and bottom of the pilot's seat, and a single piece of plate mounted behind and above the seat provided additional protection from the rear. Armor plate on the inboard sides of the turbosuperchargers, or circular deflectors on the units protected the pilot from any broken turbo blades.

FURNISHINGS
Furnishings consisted of the pilot's seat and pilot restraint harness system, flare pistol, glare shield, rear view mirror, and other small items. The seat was adjustable in height. A relief tube was provided.

HEATING/VENTILATING/COOLING
Cockpit heat was supplied by an intensifier tube in the right engine exhaust (both engines in late models) and controlled by the pilot. Heat outlets were arranged to supply warm air to the windshield and the removeable hatch via a flexible tube. A foot outlet could be closed off by using a heat control on the floor. On late airplanes a heated flying suit plug and rheostat were supplied. Ventilating air entered from a port on the left wing-fuselage fillet. The flow control was in the cockpit. There was no cooling system.

CO2 SYSTEM
There was no such system.

ICE PROTECTION SYSTEM
There was no ice protection system other than those mentioned under heating above.

AIRCRAFT HANDLING SYSTEM
Hoist hard points were provided. Towing and tiedown fittings were provided on the landing gear.

FLOTATION GEAR
No flotation gear was provided.

ARRESTING GEAR
No arresting gear was provided.

PHOTOGRAPHIC EQUIPMENT
The fighter versions of the Lightning carried no photo equipment other than a gun camera. Special F-4 or F-5 photo versions were produced or converted where photo equipment replaced guns in the fuselage nose in three compartments. A typical arrangement, for the F-5B model, had one six inch K-17 chart camera in the forward compartment. The center compartment accomodated two six inch K-17 chart cameras or one twelve inch or twenty-four inch reconnaissance camera. The aft compartment was provided with two twenty-four inch K-17 or one twenty-four inch K-18 reconnaissance camera. Cockpit controls were provided for all the camera equipment.

OXYGEN SYSTEM
The capacity of the oxygen system was sufficient to supply the pilot for about six hours at 25000 feet to 30000 feet altitude. Three bottles, two in the left boom and one in the right boom, provided the supply at a pressure of 400 to 450 pounds per square inch. A refill connection was provided in the right boom. Lines ran from the supply bottles across the inner wing to the fuselage where the other system components were located, flowmeter, pressure gage, pressure warning light, and a regulator unit. The pilot used a demand-type oxygen mask.

REFERENCES, P-38

1. *Lockheed Newsbureau Press Release*, undated.
2. *Fighter Conference*, NAS Patuxent River, Md., proceedings of, Oct.'44
3. *The Lockheed P-38 Lightning*, Hall L. Hibbard, Aviation Mag. reprint.
4. *Forktailed Devil;The P-38* Martin Caidin Ballantine Books Inc. NY 1971
5. *Tactical Planning Characteristics and Performance Chart, P-38*, USAAF 29 June, 1945
6. *Allison Engine Pilot's Notes, P-38*, Issued March 31, 1942
7. *Allison Service School Handbook ALD-SSH-5*, 5th ed. Dec.1, 1943
8. *Aircraft Designer's Data book*, Leslie Neville, McGraw Hill, NY, 1951
10. *Industrial Aviation Magazine*, Aug.1944, Design Analysis of the P-38 Lightning, Joseph Johnson.
11. *Aero Digest Magazine*, May 1, and May 15, 1945, Portfolio of Design Features, Lockheed P-38L Lightning
12. *Erection and Maintenance Instructions for P-38 Series through P-38G-15, F-4, F-5A Series Airplanes*, Dec.25,1943
13. *Journal of the American Aviation Historical Society*: Summer,1963 Spring,1969, and Spring,1972
14. *The Dragon's Teeth; The Creation of US Airpower for World War II*, Benjamin Kelsey (Brig. Gen. USAAF, Ret.)
15. *Basic Weight Check List and Loading Data for P-38 through L Series* 25 Feb. 1945, TO No. 01-75F-5
16. *Air International Magazine*, May 1981, Lightning-Lockheed's Innovattive Fighter
17. *Air Force Magazine*, April 1943, Battle Reports from P-38 Pilots in the SW Pacific.
18. *Pilot's Flight Operating Instructions for Army Models P-38H, P-38J P-38L-1,L-5 and F-5B Airplanes*
19. *Aerospace Historian Magazine*, Dec.1986, The P-38, the P-39, and The F4U-, Paul S. Bechtel.
20. *Airpower Magazine*, Nov.1972, Forktailed Devil, Bob Davidson.
21. *Airpower Magazine*, Nov.1973, Man-Made Lightning, Warren M. Bodie.
22. *Airpower Magazine*, Mar.1976, Sept.1976, Nov.1976, and Wings Magazine, Aug.1976, Dec.1976, Skybolt, The Story of Lockheed's P-38 Lightning, Warren M. Bodie.
23. *Zero*, by Masatake Okumiya and Jiro Horikoshi with Martin Caidin, Ballantine Books, 1956.
24. *Days of the Ching Pao*, by Malcomb Rosholt, Rosholt House II, Graphic Communications Publishing Div. Appleton, Wisc. 1978.
25. *Crosswinds, An Airman's Memoir*, by Najeeb E. Halaby, Doubleday and Co. Inc. NY, 1978.
26. *Pacific Sweep*, by William N. Hess, Doubleday and Co.Inc. Garden City, NY, 1974.
27. *Letter from Mr. Hank Mack*, former Lt. USAAF, and P-38 pilot.
28. *General Kenney Reports, A Personal History of the Pacific War* by George C. Kenney, Duell, Sloan, and Pearce, NY, 1949.
29. *Kelley, More Than My Share of It All*, by Clarence L. Johnson with Maggie Smith, Smithsonian Institution Press, Wash.DC,1985
30. *Pilot*, by Tony LeVier, Bantam Books

THE P-39

TABLE 21
P-39 AIRACOBRA MODELS

CO. MODEL	MIL. DESIG.	EXP.DESIG.	NO.OF A/C	FIRST DEL.	NOTES
4	XP-39	—	1	APR.1939	WITH TURBO. TO XP-39B
4	XP-39B	—	(1 conv'd)	NOV.1939	MOD.XP-39, NO TURBO
12	YP-39	—	13	SEP.1940	LIKE ABOVE, SERV.TEST
12	XP-39A	—	(canceled)	—	HI-ALT. DEL.AS YP-39
12	P-39C	—	20	JAN.1941	WAS P-45. SIM. TO YP-3
15	P-39D	—	863	APR.1941	SELF-SEAL TKS. DROP TK.
14A	P-39D-1	—	(incl.above)	1941	LEND-LEASE,20MM CANNON.
14A-1	P-39D-2	—	(incl.above)	JUN.1942	" " ,ENG.GEAR CHG.
14	—	P-400	675	JUL.1941	UK,BUT MANY TO US,USSR
23	XP-39E	—	3	FEB.1942	RESEARCH FOR P-63
15B	P-39F	—	229	DEC.1941	D MODEL WITH AEROPROP
15B	P-39J	—	25	1942	D WITH ENGINE CHG.
26	P-39K	—	210	JUL.1942	D MODEL WITH AEROPROP
26	P-39L	—	250	JUL.1942	D-2 WITH CURTISS PROP.
26	P-39M	—	240	NOV.1942	NEW ENGINE VERSION
26	P-39N	—	500	NOV.1942	POWERPLANT CHANGES
26	P-39N-1	—	900		
26	P-39N-5	—	695		
	P-39Q-1	—		MAY.1943	WING ARMAMENT CHANGE
	P-39Q-5				
	P-39Q-10				
	P-39Q-15		4905		(ALL Q VERSIONS)
	P-39Q-20				
	P-39Q-25				
	P-39Q-30				

NOTES—Three P-39C to UK for test July 1941. Approximate distribution of P-400 80 plus (94?) to RAF, 212 to USSR, 54 lost at sea, 315 to USAAF.

Table 21 summarizes P-39 variants and numbers produced. Total Airacobra production was 9.6 percent of America's Hundred Thousand with the late-model N and Q versions making up 7000 of over 9500 built. The P-400 was the early export model soon rejected by England and then used by Russia and US Pacific forces. Table 22 gives total production by year. In the end Russia got about half the Airacobras, 4789 aircraft after losses in delivery. As the table shows, most went via an Alaska-Siberia (ALSIB) route, though a substantial number passed through Iran on another way to Russia. A few took the very dangerous northern ship route to the USSR.

Physical dimensions of the P-39 given in Table 23 show the fighter was relatively small, with a wingspan of only 34 feet.

TABLE 22
APPROXIMATE AIRACOBRA ACCEPTANCES BY YEARS

YEAR	NUMBER OF AIRCRAFT
1940	13
1941	926
1942	1932
1943	4947
1944	1729

AIRACOBRA EXPORTS TO RUSSIA (WITHOUT P-400)

ROUTE	DELIVERED AT FACTORY	LOSSES EN ROUTE	TO RUSSIA
ALASKA-SIBERIA(ALSIB)	2689	34	2655
SHIP(NORTH RUSSIA)	120	12	108
SHIP(VIA IRAN)	2115	91	2026
TOTALS	4824	137	4789

TABLE 24
P-39 FUEL CAPACITIES
(US GALLONS)

MODEL	MAXIMUM INTERNAL FUEL		EXTERNAL FUEL
XP-39	200		—
XP-39B	200		—
YP-39	170		—
P-39C	170		—
P-39D	120		95
P-39D-2	120		175
XP-39E	150		—
P-39F	120		175
P-39K	120		175
P-39L	120		175
P-39M	120		175
P-39N	87	(see note)	175
P-39Q-1	87	"	175
P-39Q-5	110		175
P-39Q-10/-15	120		175
P-39Q-20/-30	120		175

NOTE: Kits were made available to bring capacity back up to 120 gallons.

TABLE 23
P-39 PHYSICAL DATA

		TOTAL FLAP SPAN	179.2"
WING SPAN	34'0"	FLAP AVERAGE CHORD	19.5"
OVERALL LENGTH	30'2"	FLAP MAXIMUM DEFLECTION	43DEG.
HEIGHT, LEVEL T.L.	11'2"	MAX. FUSELAGE WIDTH	34.75"
TREAD, LANDING GEAR	11'4"	MAX. FUSELAGE DEPTH	70.66"
WHEELBASE	9'11.75"	MAIN WHEEL TIRE SIZE	26"
PROPELLER DIAMETER	10'4.5"	NOSE WHEEL TIRE SIZE	19"
TAIL SPAN	13'0"	MAIN SHOCK STRUT TRAVEL	8"
GROSS WING AREA	213.22 SQ.FT.	NOSE SHOCK STRUT TRAVEL	10"
NET WING AREA	197.7 SQ.FT.	TOTAL HORIZ. TAIL AREA	40.04 SQ.FT.
WING ROOT CHORD,C/L	100.0"	HORIZ. TAIL ASPECT RATIO	4.225
WING CHORD, STA.22	98.66"	STABILIZER INCIDENCE	+2.25DEG.
WING TIP CHORD	50.0"	STABILIZER AREA	23.90 SQ.FT.
WING ASPECT RATIO	5.42	ELEV.AREA(INC.TAB & BAL.)	16.22 SQ.FT.
WING TAPER RATIO	2.0:1.0	ELEVATOR BALANCE AREA	4.30 SQ.FT.
WING MEAN AERO. CHORD	80.64"	ELEVATOR TAB AREA (BOTH)	0.86 SQ.FT.
WING ROOT AIRFOIL	NACA 0015	ELEVATOR MOVEMENT	35DEG.UP,15 DN.
ROOT THICKNESS RATIO	15%	HORIZ. TAIL MAX. CHORD	52.25"
WING TIP AIRFOIL	NACA 23009	STABILIZER MAX. CHORD	43.875"
TIP THICKNESS RATIO	9%	ELEVATOR MAX. CHORD	15.66"
WING ROOT INCIDENCE	2 DEG.	ELEV.TAB MOVEMENT	20DEG.UP,20 DN
WING TIP INCIDENCE	2 DEG.	TOTAL VERTICAL TAIL AREA	18.97 SQ.FT.
WING DIHEDRAL(.30cTOP)	4 DEG.	VERTICAL FIN OFFSET	1.5DEG. LEFT
WING L.E. SWEEP	4 DEG.35'9"	VERTICAL FIN AREA	7.94 SQ.FT.
TOTAL AILERON AREA	15.46 SQ.FT.	RUDDER AREA(INC.TAB&BAL.)	11.07 SQ.FT.
AILERON SPAN, EACH	79.55"	RUDDER BALANCE AREA	1.52 SQ.FT.,
AILERON AVERAGE CHORD	1.17 FT..	RUDDER TAB AREA	0.37 SQ.FT.
AILERON TOT.BAL. AREA	3.64 SQ.FT.	RUDDER MOVEMENT	30DEG.L.30DEG.R.
AILERON AREA (AFT H/L)	11.94SQ.FT.(2)	FIN MAXIMUM CHORD	43.875"
AILERON MOVEMENT	20DEG. UP,10DN.	RUDDER MAXIMUM CHORD	26.44"
AILERON TAB AREA	0.904 SQ.FT.	RUDDER TAB MOVEMENT	20DEG.L,20R.
AILERON TAB MOVEMENT	10DEG.UP,10DN.	RUDDER OVERALL HEIGHT	44.52"
FLAP AREA, TOTAL	26.2 SQ.FT.	PROPELLER-GROUND CLEAR.	9.0 IN.

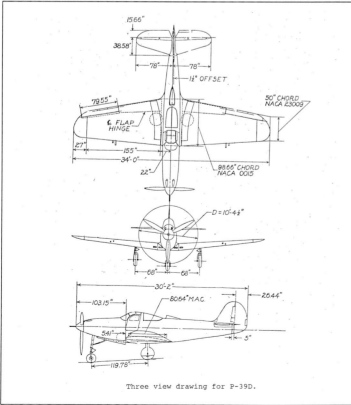

Three view drawing for P-39D.

Fuel capacities of Airacobra models are given in Table 24. The reduction in internal capacity from experimental aircraft to first real production model, the P-39D, is dramatic indeed, 200 gallons down to 120, much of the reduction from use of self-sealing tanks. This cut-back of capacity guaranteed short range on internal fuel alone, and effectively fixed return distance of a radius mission, assuming a dropped external tank at mission mid-point. The external tank on production models was a centerline-mounted type of up to 175 gallons, or greater capacity than internal tankage in this case. Limited fuel capacity and resulting short range was one basic fault of the Airacobra.

The three view drawing shows the P-39 as a smoothly streamlined aircraft with a minimum of external projections. Only the cockpit enclosure and the carburetor intake protruded beyond basic contours. Cooling air entered flush wing inlets and exited under the aircraft. Tricycle landing gear was novel when the P-39 first emerged; the scheme worked well in the aircraft layout.

The Airacobra inboard profile illustrates salient design aspects. Central themes included a cannon forward on centerline and an engine aft of the pilot with output shaft driving forward between his legs to a propeller reduction gearbox in the nose. The cannon barrel ran through the center of the reduction gearbox and the propeller hub. Forward upper cowl synchronized machine guns were also installed. The nose gear retracted aft with wheel nestled near the pilot's feet after full retraction. The wing center section and

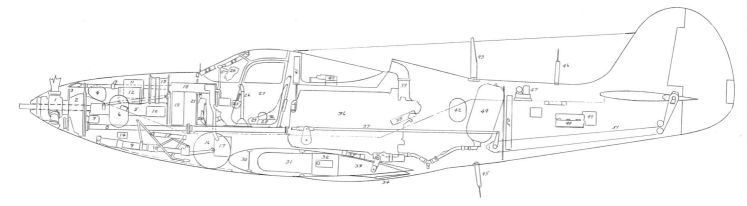

1. Curtiss Electric propeller.
2. Propeller reduction gearbox.
3. Gearbox armor plates.
4. Gearbox oil tank.
5. 37mm. cannon.
6. Oxygen tank.
7. Propeller governor.
8. Propeller gearbox drive shaft.
9. Nose gear shock strut (retracted).
10. Glycol tank.
11. Battery.
12. Data case.
13. 37mm. cannon magazine.
14. Battery switch solonoid.
15. Nose gear retracting cylinder.
16. Nose gear wheel (retracted).
17. Electrical junction box.
18. Machine gun, .50 caliber.
19. Machine gun ammunition box.
20. Rudder pedals.
21. Forward armor plate.
22. Armor plate.
23. Armor glass.
24. Gunsight.
25. Throttle quadrant.

26. Elecator control system cables.
27. Cabin door.
28. Trim wheel console.
29. Pilot's seat.
30. Wing forward spar.
31. Coolant radiator air intake.
32. Coolant radiator.
33. Coolant radiator air exit duct.
34. Cooling air exit shutter.
35. Engine tool kit.
36. Allison V-1710 engine.
37. Elevator system push rod.
38. Airplane tool kit.
39. Carburetor air intake duct.
40. Radio.
41. Wing flap drive.
42. Glycol tank.
43. Radio mast.
44. Engine oil tank.
45. SCR-515 Transmitter antenna.
46. SCR-515 Receiver antenna.
47. Dynamotor.
48. Radio.
49. First aid kit.
50. Mooring kit.

coolers passed through the fuselage beneath the cockpit. There was no fuselage space for fuel; it was located in outer wing panel tanks.

As data on P-39 model engines in Table 25 indicates, after a turbosupercharger was removed from the prototype the Allison V-12 engine was left with just an integral single stage single speed supercharger impeller. Then the best that could be done in successive engine models was to provide marginal increments in power available at medium altitudes. Improvements can be gaged by noting engine MILITARY power rating changed from 1150 horsepower at 12000 feet to 1125 horsepower at 15500 feet from D to Q model Airacobras. As with most fighters a COMBAT, or WAR EMERGENCY rating was added on the later P-39 versions. Graph 20 plots MILITARY power and COMBAT power versus altitude for certain P-39 engine models. A sharp drop-off of the engine power above 12000 feet is seen, this being the reason for poor Airacobra performance above medium altitudes.

The curves of Graph 21 show the speed and climb performance of Airacobras. High speed of the P-39D increased rapidly from just over 300 mph at sea level to more than 360 mph at approximately 12000 feet where engine power started to decline. Above that altitude maximum speed dropped, so that around 28000 feet it was back to that at sea level. Here although air resistance was much less the power was way down. For late model N and Q airplanes in-

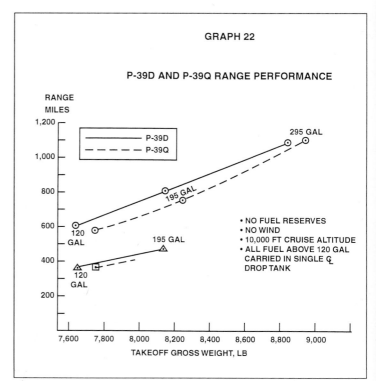

TABLE 25
P-39 ENGINE DATA

A/C MODEL	ENGINE	RATING	MIN.	HP	RPM	ALTITUDE'	MAP,"HG.	SUPERCHARGER
XP-39	V-1710-17	T.O.	5	1150	3000	SEA LEVEL		2ND STAGE TURBO
		MILITARY	15	1150	3000	25000		
		NORMAL	—	1000	2600	25000		
XP-39B YP-39	V-1710-37	T.O.	5	1090	3000	SEA LEVEL		1-STAGE,1-SPEED
		MILITARY	15	1090	3000	13300		
		NORMAL	—	960	2600	12000		
P-39C,D, D-1,F, P-400	V-1710-35 V-1710E4 (GR=1.8:1)	T.O.	5	1150	3000	SEA LEVEL		1-STAGE,1-SPEED
		MILITARY	15	1150	3000	12000		
		NORMAL	—	1000	2600	10800		
P-39D-2,K P-39L	V-1710-63 (GR=2.0:1)	T.O.	5	1325	3000	SEA LEVEL	51.0	1-STAGE,1-SPEED
		WAR EMERG	5	1590	3000	2500	61.0	
		MILITARY	15	1150	3000	12000	42.0	
		NORMAL	—	1000	2600	11000		
P-39M-1,-2	V-1710-83	T.O.	5	1200	3000	SEA LEVEL		1-STAGE,1-SPEED
		WAR EMERG	5	1420	3000	9500		
		MILITARY	15	1125	3000	14600		
		NORMAL	—	1000	2600	13800		
P-39N,Q	V-1710-85	T.O.	5	1200	3000	SEA LEVEL	50.5	1-STAGE,1-SPEED
		WAR EMERG	5	1420	3000	9700	57.0	
		MILITARY	15	1125	3000	15500	44.5	
		NORMAL	—	1000	2600	14000	39.2	

NOTE: NORMAL power could be used for an unlimited amount of time.

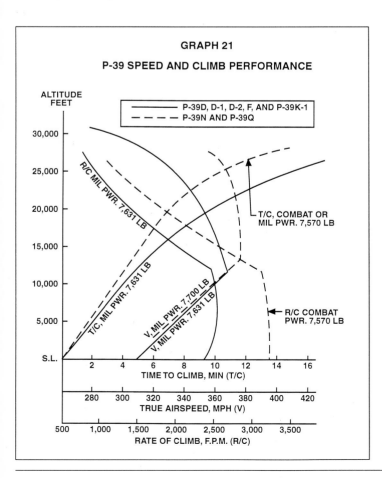

GRAPH 21

P-39 SPEED AND CLIMB PERFORMANCE

creased engine performance above 12000 feet provided some extra speed capability, so the Airacobra could make about 375 mph up to 20000 feet before speed fell off at higher altitudes. The USAAF speed estimates shown for the P-39Q may be optimistic. The early P-39D could climb at 2400-2500 feet per minute up to 12000 feet, after which climb rate, like speed, fell off sharply with increasing altitude, dipping to under 1000 feet per minute at 25000 feet. Rate of climb figures for a late Q model at COMBAT power show substantial performance increases with values well over 3000 feet per minute to 12000 feet, thereafter reducing sharply. Climb times for the early P-39D were four minutes to 10000 feet, and just under 10 minutes to 20000 feet. Higher powers of late models improved these figures by almost a minute to 10000 feet and over two and one half minutes to 20000 feet. At low to medium altitudes it is seen the Airacobra provided good performance for an early design. Had engine power held up to greater altitudes, speed capability would have been excellent. As an example the XP-39 prototype with a turbosupercharger clocked about 390 mph at 20000 feet altitude.

The chart of Graph 22 shows range characteristics of P-39 aircraft on a very optimistic basis, that is, ranges shown should be reduced by at least 10 percent. The data shows that a maximum of about 600 miles could be attained on internal fuel alone (120 gallons) flying at engine power settings for best range , probably about 60 percent of NORMAL, or MAXIMUM CONTINUOUS, power. With the largest centerline drop tank of 175 gallons added to the 120 gallons of internal fuel range at low power and slow speed could be extended to about 1050 miles. This was really ferry range,

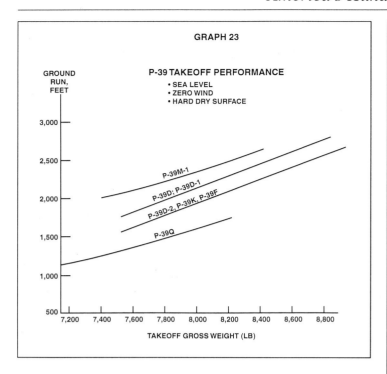

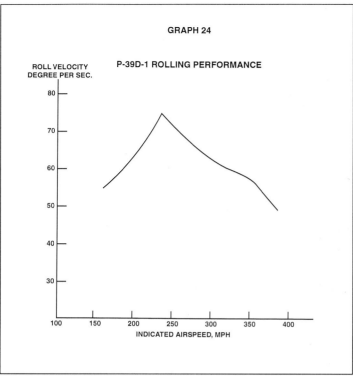

and with 10 percent fuel reserves the range would reduce to around 950 miles maximum. The P-39 was a short range airplane.

Graph 23 shows curves of Airacobra takeoff ground run performance under no wind and improved runway conditions. Data for different models varies considerably, but at the most practical gross weights ground runs from just over 1300 feet to around 2100 feet are indicated, with the P-39Q data from the pilot's manual showing the lowest numbers. Takeoff runs required were considerably in excess of those for Navy fighters.

Steady state roll performance of a P-39D is indicated by the curve of Graph 24 with a typical inverted vee shape. A peak roll rate of 75 degrees per second (a 4.8 second roll) is shown at 235 mph IAS, not a particularly good performance. At the left side of

the curve high point, that is at the lower speeds, rates are determined by maximum aileron deflection. At the high point and at all speeds greater than 235 mph the pilot is exerting a 50 pound lateral stick force. A more muscular pilot could attain faster rolls at the higher speeds.

Available empty and basic weight information for Airacobra models is given in Table 26, including group weight breakdowns for early versions P-39D and export P-400. Note there is no weight allocation for "engine section" because of the mid-fuselage engine location. There is also no weight allocation for "supercharging" because the single stage unit was integral with the engine and accounted for in engine weight. There is no "hydraulic system" weight listed since the P-39 used no hydraulics. (The braking system was

TABLE 27
TYPICAL P-39 ALTERNATE LOADS (LB.)

AIRCRAFT	P-39D-2		P-39Q-1		
MISSION	NORMAL	OVERLOAD	NORMAL	BOMBER	FERRY
PILOT	160	160	200	200	200
USEABLE OIL	70.5	118.5	62	62	103
AMMO,.30CAL.	260 (4000rd.)	260	—	—	—
AMMO,.50CAL.	129 (400rd.)	129	—	(1000rd)	(1000rd)
AMMO,20mm.	32.4 (60rd)	32.4	370	370	370
AMMO,37mm.	—	—	— (30rd.)	— (30rd)	—
BOMB INSTLN.	—	—	—	516	—
DROP TANK	—	45	—	—	45
ROCKET INSTLN.	—	—	—	—	—
INTERNAL FUEL	624 (104 GAL)	720(120GAL)	522 (87GAL)	522	522
EXTERNAL FUEL	—	546 (91GAL)	—	—	450(75G.)
TOT.DISPOSE.LOAD	1275.9	2010.9	1154	1670	1690
GROSS WEIGHT	7697.4	8432.4	7570	8086	8106
EMPTY WEIGHT	5658.0	5658.0	5684	5684	5684
USEFUL LOAD	2039.4	2774.4	1886	2402	2422

TABLE 26
P-39 EMPTY AND BASIC WEIGHTS(LB.)

MODEL	P-39D	P-39D-2	P-400	P-39Q-1
GROUP				
WING	934.6	934.2	930.0	
TAIL	116.0	116.0	114.0	
FUSELAGE	618.3	627.6	622.9	
LANDING GEAR	516.6	514.8	514.8	
ENGINE SECTION	——	——	——	
ENGINE	1408.5	1435.0	1397.0	
ENG. ACCESSORIES	115.6	119.2	119.2	
ENGINE CONTROLS	30.3	30.3	30.3	
PROPELLER	398.0	399.3	399.3	
STARTING SYSTEM	43.6	47.2	47.2	
COOLING SYSTEM	322.0	323.3	326.3	
SUPERCHARGING	——	——	——	
LUBRICATING SYS.	56.2	63.6	60.6	
FUEL SYSTEM	289.2	291.7	267.3	
INSTRUMENTS	60.3	57.5	45.6	
SURFACE CONTROLS	108.0	115.0	110.0	
HYDRAULIC SYSTEM	——	——	——	
ELECTRICAL SYSTEM	225.0	274.6	278.0	
COMMUNICATION	62.0	80.2	35.0	
ARMAMENT PROV.	177.2	146.6	204.9	
FURNISHINGS	41.6	50.7	47.6	
OTHER	——	31.0	——	
EMPTY WEIGHT	5523.0	5658.0	5550.0	5684
4 .30 CAL MG	92.8	94.9	94.9	——
2 .50 CAL MG	161.0	138.7	138.7	(4) 297
1 20mm CANNON	——	131.2	127.2	——
1 37mm CANNON	238.4	——	——	238
GUNSIGHT	4.4	4.9	2.3	4
ARMOR/BP GLASS	262.2	246.4	265.6	193
PYROTECHNICS	——	10.0	10.0	
OXYGEN EQUIPMENT	8.2	8.2	30.0	——
MISC.EQUIP.(RADIO)	——	129.2	109.9	——
BASIC WEIGHT	6290.0	6421.5	6328.6	6416

included in landing gear weight). Once the Airacobra got to full production empty weight changed little, varying from 5500 to 5700 pounds, and similarly with basic weight, this running from 6300 to 6400 pounds. Note how much more the 37mm cannon weighed than the 20mm type.

Alternate loads are shown for typical cases of both early and late Airacobras in Table 27. An allocation of only 160 pounds for a pilot (with chute) on the P-39D-2 is highly optimistic, and was later corrected to a standard 200 pounds, the latter also including the 20 pound chute. Though the armament complements on the two aircraft variants are different, weight of ammunition is quite similar, 421 pounds for the D-2 and 370 for the Q-1. Strangely, even though internal fuel capacity of the P-39 aircraft was usually a low 120 gallons, the P-39Q-1 capacity was reduced even more to 87 gallons, presumeably in an effort to save weight, and this capacity is shown in the table. A kit was available to restore the capacity to 120 gallons. One alternate loading of the Q-1 illustrates the ability of the Airacobra to carry a 500 pound bomb on its centerline rack. With 87 gallons of gas it could not carry the bomb very far.

P-39 MAJOR MODEL-TO-MODEL CHANGES

XP-39B/YP-39 (FROM XP-39)—New engine version, turbosupercharger deleted, new radiator location, carburetor air intake moved aft of canopy, wingspan reduced 22 inches, length increased 13 inches, cockpit enclosure lowered, main wheel closure doors added, turnover beam added, vertical tail contour modified, armament installed.

P-39C—Armor glass added behind windshield.

P-39D—Self-sealing fuel tanks and armor added, provision made for centerline store. .30 cal. armament changed from nose to four in wings.

P-39D-1—Dorsal fillet added to vertical tail.

P-39D-2—Uprated engine and revised propeller reduction gearing.

XP-39E—Major modifications including engine, supercharging, laminar flow wing, revised airframe contours, and other test items for P-63.

P-39F—Aeroproducts propeller in place of Curtiss type, revised exhaust. The -2 version had field modifications for rear fuselage camera installations.

P-39J—Like D model except new engine version with automatic manifold pressure regulation.

P-39K—Like F model with new engine version.

P-39L—Like K except Curtiss propeller in place of Aeroproducts model.

P-39M—Like L except new engine version and reduction gear changes.ʹ

P-39N-0—Like M except engine change and Aeroproducts propeller. Fuel reduced in some aircraft.

P-39N-5—Some armor removed; kits to restore full internal fuel.

P-39Q-1—Podded .50 caliber wing guns, less fuel (kits to restore), full armor complement.

P-39Q-5—Less armor, kits to restore full fuel.

P-39Q-10—Fuel back to full 120 gallons internal capacity, automatic speed/boost control, throttle and RPM control coordination (kits to restore separate control quadrant).

P-39Q-15—Minor equipment changes.

P-39Q-20—Podded .50 caliber guns omitted.

P-39Q-21 to -25—Four blade propeller, no wing guns.

P-39Q-30—No wing guns, cut-down diameter three blade propeller.

P-39 CHRONOLOGY

Oct10,'35-Larry Bell founds Bell Aircraft in Buffalo NY after Consolidated moves from Buffalo to San Diego, Cal. Some workers stay with Bell.

Jun '36-Headed by Chief Engineer Robert Woods and Harlan Poyer, design work is started at Bell. The company employs about 60 people.

Mar13,'37-Bell receives an invitation to bid on a new Army pursuit airplane.

Mar18,'37-Bell submits a new pursuit proposal, the Model 4, to the Army.

Oct 7, '37-A contract is signed by Bell and the Army for a new pursuit design. The contract calls for a single prototype aircraft and support data.

Dec 2, '38-A decision is made to incorporate a 37mm. cannon in the design in place of the 23mm. gun originally contemplated.

Apr 6, '39-Bell test pilot James Taylor flies the new XP-39 prototype in its initial test flight. No armament is included.

Apr15, '39-The US War Dept. announces that the Bell XP-39 has been under test at Wright Field in Dayton, Ohio, and describes the aircraft.

Apr27, '39-The prototype XP-39 is returned to Bell in Buffalo for modifications

Apr27, '39-The Army orders 13 YP-39 aircraft for service tests; one of these is to be a YP-39A with a different version of the Allison engine.

Aug10, '39-A first production order comes for the Airacobra: 80 P-45 models, later to be changed to 20 P-39C and 60 P-39D versions.

Nov25, '39-The XP-39B aircraft makes it's first flight; this is the original XP-39 with many changes.

Jan , '40-Bell Aircraft is growing and now employs 1200 people.

Jan , '40-The Army decides to eliminate the turbosupercharger, as used on the XP-39, from the Airacobra design.

Feb 1, '40-Capt. G.E.Price of the Army puts the XP-39B through flight tests including high speed dives.

Apr13, '40-France orders 170 export Bell Model 14 Airacobras equipped with the 20MM. Hispano cannon.

Jun , '40-The French Airacobra contract is taken over by the British RAF, and the order is increased to 675 aircraft. For a short time the plane is called the Caribou, but is switched back to Airacobra.

Sep13, '40-The first YP-39 version is flown. It has full armament aboard.

Sep14, '40-The US Army orders an additional 623 Airacobras with wing guns and leakproof tanks to be added to the design.

Dec , '40-The final YP-39 is delivered. The YP-39A is never developed and the plane is delivered as a YP-39.

Dec31, '40-Twenty-four Airacobras have been produced by Bell thus far. Deliveries in 1940 are worth $5 million.

Jan , '41-Bell Aircraft has plenty of business with orders for about 1600 A/C worth $60 million and now has over 5000 employees. The Airacobra requires over 9000 parts.
Jan , '41-The first P-39C Airacobra is delivered to the USAAC.

Mar , '41-All 20 P-39C's are delivered and go to the 31st Pursuit Group at Selfridge Field, Michigan. Later 3 of these A/C go to England.

Apr , '41-The first P-39D versions are delivered to the US Army; these A/C have self-sealing fuel tanks.

Jun11, '41-Bell obtains orders for Model 14A UK Lend-Lease aircraft: 494 P-39D-1 and -2 Airacobra models.

Jul 6, '41-The first of the 3 P-39C's in the UK are tested by the British; they are disappointed in the 359mph top speed attained.

Jul30, '41-The first Airacobra I's get to England. High speed is 355 MPH. It is faster than a Spitfire VB at low altitude, slower over 15000FT., and poorer in climb.

Aug25, '41-Bell obtains a contract for 1800 P-39G/Model26 A/C, later delivered as P-39K,L, and M versions.

Sep , '41-A single RAF squadron (#601) changes over to Airacobras from Hurricanes; eleven aircraft are received by this month.

Oct 9, '41-The first RAF Airacobra operations take place. Nine barge-strafing sorties are undertaken from 10/9 to 10/11.

Dec , '41-Deliveries are now being made of the P-39F version of the Airacobra.

Dec , '41-Airacobras are taken out of RAF service. They are labelled unsatisfactory. Deliveries stop at about 80 aircraft and 179 British A/C are taken over by the USAAF; 212 go to Russia, and 54 planes are lost at sea during delivery.

Dec 7, '41-The total number of Airacobras built for the US Army as of the day of the Pearl Harbor attack is 600. Five pursuit groups are equipped with P-39Ds; the 8th at Mitchell Field, L.I., the 31st and 52nd at Selfridge Field, Michigan, the 36th in Puerto Rico, and the 53rd at McDill Field, Florida.

Dec23, '41-The first batch of 100 P-400's (ex-UK A/C) and 90 P-39D's sent to the Southwest Pacific arrive in Australia.

Dec31, '41-Bell has produced a total of 926 Airacobras in 1941. The company made 429 P-39Ds and 229 P-39Fs. Bell now has nearly 10,000 employees and a new plant is located at Niagara Falls.

Jan29, '42-The 70th Pursuit Sdn. with 25 crated P-39s debarks at Suva in the Fiji Is. The squadron is sent to act as a defense force.

Feb , '42-Russia is complaining that Airacobras sent them have arrived without any spare parts.

Feb , '42-The 35th Fighter Gp. with Bell P-400s reaches Australia.

Feb 9, '42-The first P-39 of the 70th Pursuit Group in the Fiji Is. is now assembled and ready to fly.

Feb26, '42-The first XP-39E model has a first flight.

Feb26, '42-The 67th Pursuit Sdn. arrives in Melbourne Australia with 25 P-400s

Mar , '42-Three P-39D squadrons go to Panama where they will stay for the duration of the war.

Mar10, '42-The last of the three fighter groups assigned to Australia, the 8th, with P-39 and P-400 aircraft, disembarks at Brisbane. It is not yet considered ready for combat.

Mar15, '42-The 67th Pursuit Sdn.(now Fighter Sdn.) arrives in New Caledonia from Australia.

Mar18, '42-Of the 90 P-39s and more than 100 P-400s, all have now arrived in Australia, and on this date 33 P-39s and 52 P-400s are in commission.

Mar20, '42-The first XP-39E crashes and a replacement aircraft is ordered.

Mar24, '42-Gen. HC Davidson of the 7th AF Interceptor Command in Hawaii expresses dissatisfaction with the P-39D (and the P-40) as interceptors-neither could operate at high altitudes. The first P-39Ds to arrive in Hawaii are those of the 47th Sdn.,15th Fighter Group.

Apr , '42-P-39s of the 8th Ftr. Gp. fly up from Townsville Australia to Port Moresby, New Guinea. The P-39s are mostly well-used aircraft; many of the pilots have not trained as fighter pilots, and there are many operational losses. Eleven A/C are lost from Australia to New Guinea

Apr 2, '42-The first flight of the second XP-39E airplane takes place. This aircraft has an Allison engine with a 2-stage supercharger.

Apr15, '42-It is planned that the 31st and 52nd Fighter Gps., to be equipped with P-39F aircraft, will fly across the Atlantic to the UK with large 150 gal. slipper tanks under their bellies along with P-38s as part part of the Operation Bolero buildup of forces in the UK.

Apr30, '42-By this time the Army has accepted a total, including versions for export, of 1411 Airacobras. Besides those sent overseas the P-39 constitutes the main body of the fighter command A/C in the US.

Apr30, '42-Twenty-six P-39s of the 8th Ftr. Gp. are now at Port Moresby, New Guinea, and 13 of the Airacobras carry out a strafing mission over Lae and Salamaua. In combat with enemy Zeros at low altitude they claim the downing of 3 enemy A/C, but lose 4 from loss of coolant.

May , '42-The Australian Air Force obtains 22 P-39D, P-39F, and P-400 aircraft from the US 5th Air Force in the local area.

May , '42-Airacobras available in the S.W.Pacific area are: The 8th Ftr.Gp. with 100 A/C, half at Port Moresby, New Guinea, and half at Townsville Australia; and the 35th Ftr.Gp. with 100 A/C at Sydney Australia.

May , '42-The 70th Ftr.Sdn. on Fiji Is. has all its P-39 A/C operational. Also the 67th Ftr.Sdn. on New Caledonia with Airacobras is now settled in.

May , '42-The 52nd Ftr.Gp. has moved its P-39s to Grenier Field, N.H. in preparation for the transatlantic Bolero flights. The 31st Ftr. Gp. with P-39Ds has been conducting fuel consumption tests in New Orleans, La.. This group is to pick up new P-39F A/C at Bell.

May 1, '42-The 39th and 40th Squadrons of the 8th Ftr Gp. are at Port Moresby.

May31, '42-The 7th Air Force in Hawaii has, for fighter strength, in addition to 101 P-40's, 17 operational P-39's out of 22 in the area.

May31, '42-In the SW Pacific 20-25 P-39s have now been lost in combat, 8 lost in forced landings, and 3 more have been destroyed on the ground.

May31, '42-The first flights of the 35th Ftr.Gp., equipped with P-400's, have arrived in relief of 8th Ftr. Gp. pilots and planes.

Jun , '42-The 8th Ftr. Gp. returns to Townsville from Port Moresby to recover from fatigue and disease.

Jun 1, '42-P-39F and P-39J A/C of the 57th Ftr.Sdn.,54th Ftr.Gp. are enroute to Alaska from the west coast to counter a Japanese threat to the Aleutians. There are 30 P-39s, 15 at Anchorage and 15 at Kodiak. The Airacobras start escorting bombers on raids to Kiska Island.

Jun 2, '42-The P-400's of the 35th Ftr.Gp. go into combat for the first time.

Jun 4, '42-The 31st Ftr.Gp. is ordered to proceed to England by air.

Jun11,'42-The 31st Ftr.Gp. is ordered to stop preparations for flying their P-39's across the Atlantic. The big 150 gal external ferry fuel tanks will not be ready. The group is to prepare to go to the UK by ship and leave their Airacobras in the US. They will fly Spitfires.

Jun30,'42-Ninety-three P-400 Airacobras have gotten to Russia by this time.

Jun30,'42-Bell Aircraft has 227 Airacobra acceptances by the Army in this month- a record number up to this date.

Jun30,'42-During this month at least 20 P-39s and P-400s have been destroyed in the Southwest Pacific.

Jul ,'42-The first P-39K and P-39L versions are delivered by Bell this month

Jul ,'42-Enemy bombers come over Port Moresby and Darwin Australia at 22000 feet or higher. P-39s and P-400s can seldom get to the bombers, reaching them only four times in nine raids, even with 30 minute warning. The P-39s always seem to be looking up at the bombers.

Jul 2,'42-Two squadrons of the 35th Ftr.Gp.,equipped with P-400s, move up to Port Moresby in New Guinea.

Jul15,'42-Personnel of the 52nd Ftr.Gp. are on their way to England without their P-39 A/C. They are slated to fly Spitfires.

Jul18,'42-In the SW Pacific, the US has, for fighter strength, besides P-40s, 83 P-400s of the 35th Ftr.Gp., two of whose squadrons are based at Port Moresby in New Guinea.

Jul21,'42-The Japanese land at Buna in New Guinea. The only A/C available, the 39th and 40th Squadrons of the 35th Ftr.Gp. with P-400s and P-39s heavily strafe invasion barges and enemy troups.

Jul31,'42-Eight Airacobras have been lost to enemy action in July.

Aug ,'42-Along with P-40s, P-39s cover the US invasion of Vella Lavella in the lower Solomons.

Aug ,'42-Thirty-eight P-39s are now based at New Caledonia in the Pacific.

Aug ,'42-In the UK the former P-39-equipped 31st and 52nd Ftr.Gps. are using British Spitfires and flying from RAF airfields.

Aug ,'42-Gen.Kenney of the 5th AF in SW Pacific assures Gen.Hap Arnold of the usefulness of the P-40 and to a lesser extent of the P-39, but he really wants P-38s.

Aug 8,'42-P-400s make good strafer A/C; 32 Airacobras from the 35th Ftr.Gp. fly from Port Moresby thru a gap in the Owen Stanley mountains to the Kokoda area and strafe enemy supply dumps. Sixteen of the A/C are equipped with bomb racks and dive bomb the enemy.

Aug17,'42-Airacobra pilots are frustrated when for the 78th time enemy bombers hit Seven Mile Airdrome at Port Moresby, Australia, and though the fighters have adequate warning they are unable to intercept.

Aug21,'42-Only one Army squadron with 16 P-39s is stationed on Fiji Is.; New Caledonia has only 27 P-400s , 2 P-39s, and 2 P-43s , and half of the P-400s are going to Guadalcanal.

Aug22,'42-The first five P-400s arrive at Henderson Field on Guadalcanal in the Solomons, having been escorted from New Caledonia via Espiritu Santo by a B-17. The unit is part of the 67th Ftr.Sdn., 347th Ftr.Gp headed by Capt. Dale Brannon.

Aug25,'42-The fighter situation is critical in the South Pacific with few reinforcements in sight—nothing more than 30 P-39s diverted to New Caledonia from allocations intended for Australia. These are scheduled to arrive in Noumea in late September.

Aug27,'42-Nine more P-400s of the 67th Ftr.Sdn. arrive at Henderson Field on Guadalcanal, completing the squadron. They have no altitude capability above about 12000 ft. because the pilots have no oxygen. The US Marine Corps has operational control at Henderson.

Aug31,'42-After four days of operations from Henderson Field the Guadalcanal P-400s of the 67th Ftr.Sdn. are down to only 3 operational aircraft Four A/C have been lost and six damaged.

Sep 2,'42-On Guadalcanal Gen. Vandergrift assigns P-400s of the 67th Sdn. to ground support duties where they excell. They can take off from muddy fields, fly fast at low altitudes, and bomb and strafe ground troops, barges, transports, and destroyers.

Sep13,'42-Towards the end of an enemy attack on Bloody Ridge, Guadalcanal, three P-400s pounce in with a strafing attack that all but annihilates the last of the enemy concentration.

Sep14,'42-Fourteen Airacobras with 14 P-38s escort a deck-level bombing raid of 12 B-24s on a successful bombing raid of the Japanese on Kiska Is. in the Aleutians. The fighters shoot down 5 Rufe float planes, but 2 P-38s collide and are lost.

Sep19,'42-Bell flies the third XP-39E model for the first time.

Oct ,'42-P-39D aircraft of the 33rd Sdn. stationed in Iceland shoot down two German reconnaissance bombers.

Oct ,'42-Two USAAF Ftr.Gps.,the 81st and 350th, are equipped in England with P-400 and P-39D-1 Airacobras that had been waiting to go to Russia.

Oct ,'42-The 7th Air Force under Gen.R. Douglas is providing local defense for central Pacific bases with a force of 319 fighters including a squadron of P-39s. (Others are P-40s and a squadron of P-70s.)

Oct13, '42-Japanese Betty bombers raid Henderson Field, Guadalcanal throughout the day. P-400 pilots are frustrated in their 12000 ft. limits and cannot reach the high-flying bombers. The P-39s go higher, but cannot get at them either. The next night enemy cruisers shell the airfields. Four P-39s are lost by this enemy action.

Oct16, '42-P-400s and P-39s from Henderson Field make seven separate attacks on enemy positions on Guadalcanal. They strafe and bomb the Japanese with little let-up and with good effectiveness.

Oct23, '42-The enemy raids Henderson Field with 16 bombers and 24 fighters, and are met by 24 Marine Wildcats and 4 Airacobras. Twenty-two enemy A/C are shot down with no US losses. The 67th Ftr.Sdn gets occasional replacements of P-400s and manages to keep 6 to 8 aircraft bombing and strafing the enemy.

Oct26, '42-The Cactus Air Force, as the Guadalcanal air contingent is called, is again in desperate straits. There are 3 P-400s and 3 P-39s operational as well as only 13 Wildcats.

Oct27, '42-Today the operational contingent of P-39s and P-400s has doubled at Henderson Field with six each now available for combat. There are 46 P-39s at New Caledonia with 12 en route to Guadalcanal.

Oct ,'42-Bell Aircraft conducts a series of spin tests of the P-39 based on an Army request to demonstrate spin recovery. Several A/C have been lost in spins. Bell concludes that no basic design deficiencies exist that would prohibit spin recovery.

Nov ,'42-The first P-39M versions of the Airacobra are now being delivered.

Nov 7, '42-P-39s covering a bomber attack on an enemy warship in the Solomons area shoot down five enemy float fighters going after the TBF's.

Nov20,'42-Airacobra strength on Guadalcanal has risen to 16 P-39s , one P-400.

Nov24,'42-Airacobras on Guadalcanal continually strike at enemy troops all along the local coast and fly up to 11 missions a day per aircraft.

Dec ,'42-The 54th Ftr.Gp. returns from Alaska to the US and will act as a replacement training unit.

Dec ,'42-Airacobras on Guadalcanal assume a large part of the ground support burden, helping both Marine and Army troops. Early in the US offensive P-39s and Marine SBDs strike regularly at Japanese positions around Kokumbona, getting high praise from the Marines. On D-day the P-39s, carrying 500 lb. bombs, team up with SBDs and assist a successful infantry attack on the hills of Mt. Austen.

Dec21,'42-Part of the 70th Ftr.Sdn. arrives on Guadalcanal with their P-39s.

Dec24,'42-Nine P-39s , 4 P-38s , and 4 F4Fs escort 9 SBDs to the Japanese base at Munda, catch the enemy by surprise, and knock off 24 Zeros, 10 on the ground. That afternoon 4 F4Fs and 4 P-39s escort SBDs on a barge-attack mission.

Dec31,'42-Bell deliveries total over $20 million in 1942. Almost half of all Bell shop workers are women. Powered assembly lines are now employed. In 1942 1972 Airacobras have been built for a total of 2898 A/C.

Jan ,'43-The two P-39/P-400 groups, the 81st and 350th, fly from England to North Africa and lose 15 A/C (interred in Portugal) along the way, including the C.O. of the 81st.

Jan ,'43-The cost of a P-39 is variously estimated at $50,666 to $60,000.

Jan 3, '43-The P-39s of the 12th Fighter Squadron reach Henderson Field on Guadalcanal in the Solomon Islands.

Jan26,'43-The fighter strength of the 12th Air Force in North Africa has now built to 23 P-39s and 52 P-40s. The Airacobras pose a problem of use; finally it is given the specialty of "rhubarbs"-strafing and reconnaisance missions at very low altitudes. The A/C is considered quite resistant to flak.

Mar ,'43-Production has just started by Bell on the P-39Q version of the A/C.

Mar 4,'43-P-39s of the 40th Ftr.Sdn. 35th Group have been among the active AAF fighter participants in the Battle of the Bismark Sea.

Apr ,'43-The French in No. Africa are supplied with 90 P-39N Airacobras. Later, in 1944 they will also get 75 P-39Qs.

Apr ,'43-The Soviet 16th Guards Fighter Air Regiment receives P-39's delivered thru Iran. The Commander of the Soviet Air Force in the Stalingrad area says there is absolutely no criticism of the Airacobra but they have too few of them.

Apr30,'43-Bell produces 511 P-39N aircraft in this month.

May ,'43-P-39Q airplanes are being delivered from the Bell factory.

May ,'43-In North Africa the 2nd Air Defense Wing with it's P-39s of the 350th Ftr.Gp. is given responsibility for the very active Algiers region west to Spanish Morocco. The P-39s are used for convoy escort, patrol, and scrambles, but they are not able to intercept high-altitude enemy reconnaisance aircraft.

May ,'43-The Russians request delivery of 500 P-39s per month.

May13,'43-On Guadalcanal in the SW Pacific the Japanese conduct a 24 A/C fighter sweep over Henderson Field. Among the intercepting aircraft are 12 P-39s together with Corsairs, Wildcats, Lightnings, and P-40's. In furious air battles the enemy loses 16 planes.

Jun ,'43-P-39Ns of the 18th Ftr.Gp. are now at Henderson Field, Guadalcanal

Jul 4,'43-The Bell tech rep with 5th Air Force reports to Gen. Kenney that his P-39s and P-400s all had averaged about 300 hours of combat flying, and that they are getting tired.

Jul19,'43-Russia requests that the US send P-39s in lieu of P-40s.

Jul31,'43-Gen. Wurtsmith has 565 A/C in 5th Air Force which includes 70 P-39 and 30 P-400 airplanes, but more than half of these are in depot, and few of the remainder can really be counted on for combat. Gen. Kenney writes to Gen. Arnold "With the possible exception of Gen. Chennault, I don't believe any one else is flying stuff as old and worn out as these youngsters out here are."

Aug14,'43-Japanese aircraft attack the Maralinan airsrip on eastern New Guinea near Salamawa. Radar warning to 36 P-39 fighters saves the field from serious damage when the attackers are dispersed.

Oct 5,'43-The airbase at Nadzeb, New Guinea is the new home of the 2nd Air Task Force with 8 runways and many dispersal areas. On this date the Hdqtrs. Sdn. of 35th Ftr.Gp. P-39s comes in from Tsili Tsili. Before the month ends two sqadrons of P-39s are providing base fighter defense.

Oct 4,'43-The anti-barge campaign is going well in the central Solomons area. Four P-39s and 4 Corsairs destroy 16 barges on a single mission along western Choiseul. The P-39 pilots find their nose cannon is very effective against light water surface craft.
Oct30,'43-Twelve P-39s strafe enemy shipping in Tonoki harbor, Bougainville.

Nov ,'43-Gen. Harmon has the problem in the Solomons of inadequate fighter aircraft. He regards the P-39 and P-40 as useful for certain purposes, but unequal to the heavy demands currently made

on them. The P-39 is practically useless above 17000 ft., and Harmon believes its poor performance reflects adversely on the AAF fighter force as a whole. He wants later A/C, but none are available.

Nov ,'43-After the initial landings on Bougainville fighters are directed to strafe targets of opportunity as they return to base. Just as on Guadalcanal the P-39s prove highly useful for this work.

Nov 1,'43-In the 12th Air Force in the Mediterranean the 12th Fighter Command includes the 350th Ftr.Gp. with P-39s in its 63rd Ftr. Wing. The 12th also has the 154th Recon.Sdn. with P-39s operating in the 12th Air Training Command.

Dec15,'43-The newly-created 15th Air Force in Italy includes three squadrons of P-39s attached to the 5th Bomb Group. The 332nd Ftr.Gp. with 75 P-39Q aircraft, scheduled for arrival this month, is late and will not arrive for several weeks.

Dec17,'43-Airsols(Air Solomons) fighter strength in the Pacific includes, among other types, 69 P-39s of which 51 aircraft are operational.

Dec18,'43-P-39 Airacobras of the 46th and 47th Ftr.Sdns. escort Army A-24 dive bombers from Makin Is. in the Marshalls to attack the bypassed islands of Mille and Jaluit held by the enemy. From this date until Feb.12,1944 the P-39s fly a total of 635 sorties plus 114 aborts.

Dec31,'43-In 1943 Bell Aircraft has produced more fighters than any other US company. They have put out 4945 P-39s and and 28 P-63 Kingcobras.

Jan11,'44-The P-39 units in the Mediterranean Allied Air Forces are: 3 Sdns. attached to the 5th Bomb Wing; the 350th Ftr.Gp., 2 Sdns. in the French Air Force of the Coastal Air Force; and some P-39s attached to the 287th Wing, RAF.

Jan29,'44-In support of the US landings on Kwajalein Is. the 46th and 72nd Ftr.Sdns. with P-39 Airacobras assist in conducting continuous daylight combat patrols over Japanese-held Mille Is. The patrols continue until February 1,1944.

Feb ,'44-The peak inventory of P-39s in the USAAF inventory is reached-2150 Airacobras are in service. A large number are being used as fighter trainers in the continental United States.

Feb ,'44-The 332nd Ftr.Gp. with P-39Q-20 Airacobras joins the 15th AF, Italy

Mar ,'44-The 71st Tactical Reconnaissance Sdn. of the 82nd Tactical Reconn. Group is operating P-39Q-5 aircraft in the Pacific.

Mar 8,'44-P-39's drop 500 pound bombs on enemy troops and artillery attacking the US perimeter on Bougainville in the Solomons.

Mar 8, '44-With the completion of an airstrip on Nissan even the short-range P-39s are able to strike at the big enemy base at Rabaul. There is no fighter opposition but plenty of AA. The Airacobras go on their first mission this date. The fighters are taking over here because the B-24's are devoting their attention to the enemy base at Truk.

Mar15, '44-P-39s, along with P-40s are still being used in support of US ground troops on Bougainville in the SW Pacific.

Apr, '44-The Italian Air Force 4th Stormo at Naples receives 149 Airacobras from the US 15th AF(now re-equipping with P-47s). These include the 75 P-39Qs brought into the theatre in February by the 332nd Ftr.Gp. along with P-39Ns for the remainder.

Apr, '44-In the Pacific the P-39s of the 82nd and 110th Reconn.Sdns. are approaching 400 flying hours and are about worn out. They have been extremely valuable in close-support work. Gen. Whitehead wants P-51s as replacements, but because of ETO demands on Mustangs this is not possible. The 82nd and 110th will have to make do with P-40N cast-offs when available from the 7th and 8th Ftr.Sdns. until they can get F-6D reconnaissance Mustangs late in the year.

Jun, '44-The last of the P-39Q Airacobra versions go to the 12th Air Force in the Mediterranean which has been using them for ground support work.

Jun, '44-The Bell P-39 is going out of production after a total of 9558 units have been delivered. Of this total 4924 (aside from P-400s) have been allocated to Russia under Lend-Lease. Approximately 4758 A/C actually reached Russia. Unit costs have varied between $51000 and $72000. The Bell factory will switch to production of P-63 aircraft.

Jun20, '44-The 9th,10th, and 12th Gruppos of the Italian AF start training in their newly-acquired P-39s and practice through September. There are many accidents-primarily due to engine problems.

Jun28, '44-The 82nd Recon.Sdn. along with their P-39s , considered invaluable for close-support work, move up to Owi in New Guinea along with some P-61s of the 421st Night Fighter Squadron.

Aug, '44-All USAAF Groups are now converted from P-39s to more advanced fighter A/C. The last P-39 missions are flown in New Guinea by the 347th Ftr.Gp.

Aug, '44-The last P-39Q-30 is officially delivered to the USAAF.

Sep 8, '44-The first operational mission for P-39s in the Italian Air Force takes place—Italian Macchi fighters provide top cover. Losses due to engine troubles are still high. Ten aircraft are lost in November.

Oct, '44-P-39s in Soviet service are now being replaced by Russian-designed fighters.

Dec, '44-P-39Q aircraft are being used by the Free French Air Force (GC11/6) in southern France.

Dec, '44-Most P-39 aircraft in the continental US are being used as proficiency trainers.

Apr, '45-The Italian Air Force 4th Stormo P-39s are active in ground-strafing enemy positions and installations. On VE-Day the 4th has a strength of 83 P-39s of which 60 are serviceable. In 1946 all the P-39s are replaced by P-38's. The P-39s serve at the Italian fighter school until 1951, and then are scrapped.

P-39 HANDLING QUALITIES AND CHARACTERISTICS

HANDLING QUALITIES
GROUND HANDLING

On hard surfaces P-39 taxi characteristics were very good. Many pilots thought they were the best of US fighters, with comments like "The P-39 was the best in ground handling"; "The plane taxied beautifully"; and "The plane moved like a race car on the ground". Also "I think I liked the P-39 the best insofar as ground handling is concerned". The tricycle landing gear arrangement provided good taxi visibility for the pilot so S-turns were not required to see ahead. But at soft spongy forward airstrips in the Pacific there were complaints about the P-39 and its brother the P-400. The main wheel tires were considered too small and narrow, more so than the P-40, causing the plane to bog down easily, and the nose gear was labeled too delicate for forward areas. Many nose gears broke at the base of the oleo strut while taxiing over rough ground. On the other hand cases were cited where a tricycle gear P-39 could take off in poor conditions where tail-down fighters could not. As with all powerful single engine US fighters, the P-39 tended to swing left with a sudden throttle application due to propeller torque reaction. While taxiing the trim tabs were set for takeoff, rudder tab for right rudder and elevator tab for slightly nose up.

TAKEOFF AND CLIMB

For P-39 takeoff flaps were left up or lowered no more than one quarter. After runup and magneto checks brakes were released, and the aircraft gained speed rapidly on hard surfaces. On a takeoff run

Fig.39-1 Bell XP-39 Airacobra, Ser.38-326, Mfr.photo via F. Dean coll. The experimental prototype after some modifications. Notable features include the cuffed propeller blades, later abandoned, the long forward cover on the nose landing gear, and the single air intake of early design at each wing inboard leading edge. Not visible, but included in the design was a turbosupercharger to allow the fighter to perform well at altitude.

Fig.39-2 Bell XP-39B Airacobra, Ser.38-326, Mfr. photo via F.Dean coll. The prototype Airacobra with revised nose landing gear covers, plenty of cooling louvres for the engine compartment, narrow chord vertical fin and rudder, and early carburetor air intake fairing. When the P-39 first appeared the tricycle landing gear configuration was novel, though far from unheard of. Curtiss pushers used it many years earlier.

the nose wheel was raised slightly early to save tire wear. There was the usual tendency to pull to the left which disappeared as speed increased. Torque swings were corrected by a combination of right rudder and right brake. The P-39 was eased into the air at 100 mph IAS and cleaned up after gaining some altitude. Best initial climb speed of about 162 mph IAS was quickly established with throttle adjusted to climb power. Speed for best climb reduced slightly as altitude was gained.

TRIMMING
P-39 trimmability was good. Elevator tab action allowed stick force to be trimmed to zero throughout the speed range. Aileron trim changes with speed or power were negligible to 400 mph IAS. Above that speed there was an erratic trim force change, possibly caused by aileron fabric bulging. There were directional trim changes in climbing and diving, but they were not extreme.

Fig.39-3 Bell XP-39B Airacobra, Ser.38-326, Mfr.photo via F. Dean coll. The sleek lines of the modified prototype are evident in this photo and in early 1940 it was not surprising the airplane was labeled as a "super-fighter" and a potential "world-beater" by the US aviation press. The single wing leading edge air intakes were modified, but propeller blade cuffs stayed on. The big change of course was the absence of the turbosupercharger from the powerplant, making for a lower and slower airplane.

DIVE AND RECOVERY
The aircraft could be dived to a recommended limit speed of 475 mph IAS. During the dive throttle was set to at least 20 inches of mercury manifold pressure to assure the engine would run smoothly when throttle was increased after pulling out. Prior to diving the P-39 was trimmed nose heavy to reduce severity of the pullout, making it more difficult to pull excessive g levels by increasing stick force required. During a dive left rudder had to be held since the aircraft tended to yaw to the right. Although the P-39 was a clean airplane, and thus accelerated quickly in a dive, it would not normally encounter compressibility at the low to medium altitudes where it usually operated. However it could reach the noted high limit dive speed of 475 mph IAS with a corresponding Mach number close to 0.80, the terminal Mach number of the airplane. In a series of high speed test dives a P-39N was taken from 28000 to 34000 feet down to 10000 to 12000 feet at engine conditions varying from part to full throttle. The dives took less than a minute, and peak Mach numbers ranged from 0.76 to 0.80 at about 15000 feet. This meant the Airacobra was reaching a true airspeed of about 560 mph. The g levels encountered at pullout varied from 4.4 to 7.0, the latter figure nearing the allowable flight limit load factor of 8.0. Compressibility was encountered during these dives. The drag divergent Mach number of the P-39N, where drag coefficient started to increase rapidly, was 0.62. At the highest dive Mach number reached, about 0.80, the airplane drag coefficient was almost triple its low speed value. The test aircraft was not specially cleaned up; a bomb rack and sway braces were mounted under the fuselage and test booms were installed on the wings. If there were severe flight control problems from compressibility they were not mentioned in the pilot's report, though other tests showed at 410 mph IAS speeds on the P-39D there was aileron structural deformation and aileron fabric bulging.

MANEUVERING
The P-39 would easily perform most all fighter maneuvers, including loops, slow rolls, and Immelmann turns. Snap rolls were not

Fig.39-4 Bell YP-39 Airacobra, Mfr.photo via B. Matthews. One of the thirteen service test Airacobras in October 1940, its gleaming metal skin reflecting careful Bell craftsmanship. Armament does not appear to be installed. Propeller blade cuffs are discarded, the carburetor intake recontoured, and the chords of vertical tail surfaces substantially increased. In addition skin louvres in the powerplant area have disappeared.

recommended, and outside loops and deliberate spinning of the airplane were prohibited. But a wartime pilot said "Loops, spins, rolls, both slow and snap (the latter strictly forbidden, but we did them anyway), you name them; I've done them all". The P-39 was considered slightly less maneuverable than the P-40.

An outstanding characteristic of the P-39 was extreme control sensitivity; a P-39D fore-aft stick movement of only one inch would change the wing lift coefficient from a high speed value of 0.20 to a near stall 1.40 with a normal airplane center of gravity location. One pilot put it this way "You moved the stick on a P-39 one eighth of an inch and you could throw it into a spin before you knew what was happening". In addition stick forces were light. At a normal center of gravity location fore-aft stick force per g in a turn was less than two pounds, where the normally allowed minimum was three pounds per g. Aileron stick forces were also light; a force under 30

pounds yielded maximum structurally permissible aileron deflection at high speeds. "The slightest lateral pressure on the stick would sent the ball skidding unless coordinated properly with rudder". Rudder forces were also well within maximum allowed limits with plenty of rudder control available. The combination of light control forces and very sensitive stick-to-elevator "gearing' was undoubtedly a large part of why the P-39 was considered, in the words of one experienced Air Force veteran, "A tricky airplane to fly". A P-39 pilot noted practically all he had to do was "think" the plane through maneuvers. Another indicated Airacobras handled "terrifically" under 15000 feet. Still another pilot, experienced in several fighter types, said "Of all the airplanes I ever flew, I think I liked the P-39 the best insofar as flying and general performance are concerned". Really good pilots seemed to like the plane and have little trouble with it; others had difficulty and didn't like it. Although the

Fig.39-5 Bell YP-39 Airacobra, Mfr.photo via B. Matthews. The manufacturer's legend on this photo indicates the airplane is a "YP-39 and P-39C", indicating there was precious little difference between the two. Here the new dual air intakes at the wing root are shown, the ducts therefrom leading to oil and Prestone coolers, and the car-type cockpit door is apparent. The YP-39s appeared in the September to December, 1940 time period.

Fig 39-6. Bell YP-39 Airacobra, Mfr.photo via F. Dean coll. A service test airplane in flight, showing off clean lines. The low drag coefficient of the Airacobra was bested only by the later P-51 Mustang of the US world War II fighters. All was not well with the P-39, however; empty weight was over a thousand pounds greater than the prototype, even with the turbosupercharger taken out in the YP-39, and the fuel tank capacity had dropped by thirty gallons.

Fig.39-7 Bell YP-39 Airacobra, Mfr.photo via B. Matthews. Another flight photo of the P-39 in natural metal finish and old style Army Air Corps stars and tail stripes. These were the kind of photos making air-minded young Americans of 1940 believe US fighters had to be superior to anything that flew. The mid-fuselage location of the engine made for clean nose lines and a unique cannon installation, but prevented a fuel tank from being located in the fuselage, as was done on other single engine US fighters.

aircraft was sensitive and "tricky" to fly with a normal center of gravity location, it was stable in longitudinal and lateral/directional modes, both stick-fixed and stick-free. There were rudder reversals at low speed and large sideslip angles, and marginal dihedral effect in some conditions, however these were considered manageable. At aft center of gravity conditions, as when all nose ammunition had been fired, flight stability characteristics deteriorated. Controls became even more sensitive, and as one pilot put it "The plane was very sensitive to flat spins when the nose ammo had been expended", and another "After you'd spend some ammunition the center of gravity would slide back and the plane would do strange things". There has always been dispute as to just what kind of maneuvers these strange things were, snap rolls, pure tumbles, flat spins, or

some combination, but it was not wise to try acrobatics with a tail-heavy aircraft.

The P-39D was deficient in roll rate compared to USAAF requirements. Its time constant to start rolling was extremely fast, but maximum roll rate was about 75 degrees per second at 235 mph IAS, reducing to about 50 degrees per second at 385 mph IAS, slower than some other fighters, including the P-40. One pilot said, however "It would do rolls as good as the P-63"; the latter was a very good performer in roll.

APPROACH AND LANDING
Maximum gear down speed was 200 mph IAS. With gear and flaps down and idle power on approach, the glide path was very steep

Fig.39-7A Bell YP-39 Airacobra, Mfr.photo via Herb Fyfield. Clean lines of the service test Airacobra in its natural metal finish are evident in this photo showing the planform of the smallest US Army production fighter. In spite of the turbosupercharger removal from X to Y airplanes empty weight rose over 1000 pounds. It rose again almost 500 pounds from the Y airplanes to the production P-39D.

Fig.39-8 Bell P-39C Airacobra. photo via F. Dean coll. The first Airacobra to get into limited service use was the P-39C, of which twenty were delivered early in 1941. These were the first to get the full Army paint job. Here we see the first photo indicating armament installed. A 37mm cannon barrel pokes from the spinner nose, and the bumps above the nose indicate presence of four machine guns synchronized to fire through the propeller. Armor glass was added behind the windshield on the C airplanes.

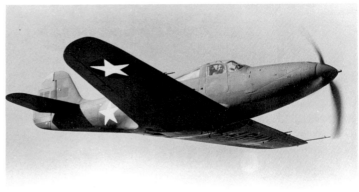

Fig.39-9 Bell P-39C Airacobra, Mfr.photo via F. Dean coll. Bell employees move an early model Airacobra with service unit markings on the vertical tail. A clear view of the armament installation shows the P-39C as the only version with all guns in the fuselage. There were two .50 caliber and two .30 caliber machine guns in the nose. In later versions the rifle caliber guns were moved to the wings with four installed.

Fig.39-10 Bell P-39D Airacobra, Mfr. photo via F. Dean coll. The Airacobra got into large scale production with the D version, shown here in flight, starting in the spring of 1941. This was the initial combat-ready model with armor and self-sealing fuel tanks, and provision for a centerline store. Internal fuel capacity was again reduced. In addition the .30 caliber guns were removed from the nose and two were installed mid-span in each wing. The censor has obliterated the airplane serial number on the tail, a common wartime procedure on photo negatives.

and glide attitude very nose high. A speed of 130 mph IAS had to be maintained to keep enough elevator control to level out. If a power-on approach was made with the aircraft in landing attitude, a speed of 110 mph IAS was required. In a normal landing the nose of the P-39 was well up, and the main wheels touched first at 95 to 100 mph IAS. The aircraft, without pilot action, would then pitch down onto the nose wheel with no tendency to bounce or ground loop. The tricycle gear was of great value in making safe landings. Braking during the runout was accomplished by intermittent action to prevent overheating or lockup. It sounded easy, but a veteran pilot said "Too many inexperienced pilots met their fate during operational training, mostly in the landing pattern. The final turn often induced a tendency to feed in too much bottom rudder, resulting in a sudden snap roll".

STALLS AND SPINS

At normal weight unaccelerated stall speeds were about 105 mph IAS flaps up and 90 mph IAS flaps down. Another reason P-39 aircraft were considered tricky, as a flight test report indicated "Stalls always developed with no warning of approach, no buffeting of the aircraft or controls. At the stall break the ailerons floated such that the stick moved in the direction of the roll-off, but the action was too late to constitute a warning". So not only could the pilot, by a very small aft stick movement get to a stall, but he had no advance warning of it happening. One g and accelerated stalls were similar; there was no warning of a high speed stall either. One pilot said "The P-39 would do the most wicked stall of any airplane I ever saw. That is why there were so many stall-spin accidents". Another noted "Its controls were extremely delicate. The slightest hint of

Fig.39-10A Bell P-39D Airacobra, photo via Jon Davis. A well-used P-39D, probably a D-1 or D-2 Lend-Lease version with the 20 mm. nose cannon. The Allison engine had a MILITARY rating of 1150 horsepower at 12000 feet; at 25000 feet that figure went down to 650. At the same time climb rate went down from almost 2500 feet per minute to under 1000.

Fig.39-11 Bell P-400 Airacobra, Mfr.photo via F. Dean coll. One of the British-ordered P-400 Airacobras, this airplane has been modified from standard configuration with a large fairing around the engine exhaust stacks and a completely different vertical tail. In the fall of 1941 an RAF squadron put P-400s into operation from England, was dissatisfied with the type, and took Airacobras out of service.

Fig.39-12 Bell P-400 Airacobra, Mfr. photo via F.Dean coll. A P-400 for Britain cavorts through the clouds. These aircraft were fitted for a 20mm cannon instead of the 37mm gun in the US models. It is not clear just what the British expected out of the P-400, given its single stage single speed mechanical supercharged engine. It was faster than the then-current Spitfires down low, but lost out in performance at the higher altitudes.

Fig.39-14 Bell Model 14, Mfr. photo via F. Dean coll. Apparently a company demonstrator aircraft this unmarked Airacobra had no fittings for centerline store carriage apparent, nor is a cannon installed. The sideways vee-shaped links on all the landing gears are torque scissors to keep shock strut pistons, forks, and wheel assemblies from turning with respect to the shock strut body.

abruptness on the pilot's part would instigate a high speed stall; result, a snap roll". The P-39 at one g stall mushed considerably, and had a simultaneous mild roll and downward pitch; it would then return to level flight, and a pitching motion would start as the stall progressed. In high speed stalls this pitching would be accompanied by yawing and rolling motions. Stall recovery could be made by promptly using down elevator; ailerons were ineffective, and using the rudder only increased oscillatory motions, as would use of up elevator. If the pilot did not get out of stall, a spin which quickly flattened out would result, particularly if the center of gravity was aft. A wartime pilot in training related "We bounced some P-39s. One of them stalled in a tight turn and went into a flat spin. We

received orders not to attack P-39s as they were susceptable to flat spins after they had expended their ammunition". The center of gravity had moved aft. Another said "One other characteristic was its tendency to flat spin. This was unrecoverable, as demonstrated many times". Other pilots commented "Stall it on a steep turn coming in for a landing, and thats it. You won't get out", but also "The airplane was honest in stalling whether high speed or straight-away stall". Other comments denoted pilot's concerns "It had a pronounced stalling tendency in steep turns; a pilot entering a tight turn never knew whether he would make it around or get into a high speed stall. Notoriously tricky in the hands of a careless operator", and "It was very important to keep the nose down in recov-

Fig.39-13 Bell P-400 Airacobra, Mfr. photo via B.Matthews. In standard configuration a P-400 for Britain poses for a Bell photographer. Of this production model where 675 aircraft were built starting in mid-1941, some were lost during sea shipment, over 200 got to Russia where they were more appreciated, and near the same number were appropriated by the USAAF because they were urgently needed in the South Pacific with US war entry after Pearl harbor.

Fig.39-15 Bell XP-39E, Mfr. photo via F. Dean coll. The third of three much modified experimental aircraft built by Bell to remedy some of the deficiencies of the
basic Airacobra. They acted as predecessor aircraft for the later P-63 Kingcobra.
The initial airplane first flew in February 1942 and crashed soon after, the third
airplane being a replacement. New wings and two stage engine superchargers were
among items tested.

Fig.39-16 Bell P-39F, Ser.41-7246, Photo via F. Dean coll. Appearing about the
time of Pearl Harbor the P-39F, shown here with drop tank aboard, revised horn-
type exhaust stacks, and flash hiders on the .50 caliber nose guns, used an
Aeroproducts Unimatic hydraulically operated propeller instead of a Curtiss Electric type. The length of the nose gear strut is emphasized here-they were known to
snap on occasion operating from rough South Pacific airfields.

ering from a stall or spin. If the nose was brought up too quickly in
recovering from a normal stall or spin, the P-39 could go into a flat
spin".

In a spin the P-39 was a problem, particularly for young inexperienced service pilots. This fact was recognized by the USAAF
when they urgently requested Bell in October, 1942 to demonstrate
spin recovery techniques. Several recoveries were demonstrated by
Bell pilots. It was concluded in-service recovery problems were
due either to faulty pilot technique, insufficient altitude for recovery, or improper loading so the center of gravity was too far aft, and
that the aircraft had no basic design deficiency to prohibit recovery.
But as the pilot's manual noted "If recovery technique is not closely
followed the aircraft might not recover from the spin". Proper recovery method was to cut power, put the propeller in low RPM,
pull the stick full back, wait for the spin to be slowest, and apply
opposite rudder (it was very important to apply the rudder at just
the right time), wait for the rudder effect to be noticeable, and then
apply full forward stick and set the ailerons against the spin. If this

was all done properly the aircraft would recover in half a turn; if
not, well, as the old drinking song said of the P-39 "It would tumble
and spin, and soon auger in".

CHARACTERISTICS
COCKPIT
The cockpit of the Airacobra was designed for pilots not over five
feet eight inches in height. This is why there were jokes about P-39
pilots, particularly the larger ones, being identified by a permanently hunched-over appearance. A pilot noted "It was a very small
cockpit". A very large man would have to leave out his parachute
before entering a P-39 cockpit. In early Airacobra versions the
weight allocation for a pilot was only 160 pounds. This was raised
in later versions to the standard 200 pounds including parachute. It
is doubtful P-39 pilots were specially selected for small size. But
certainly the Airacobra had a small cockpit compared with other
US fighters, and was not altogether comfortable for large pilots.
Most agreed the unusual car door entrance and exit was satisfac-

Fig.39-17 Bell P-39F Airacobra, photo via B. Matthews. An excellent view of an
Airacobra in flight. Sway braces for an external store are seen below the fuselage.
By the time this F model was operating the central red circle in the US star insignia
had disappeared to avoid any resemblance to a Japanese "meatball". The aircraft
is also minus a USAAF serial number on the tail.

Fig.39-18 Bell P-39F Airacobra, Ser.42-7248, P.M.Bowers photo via H.Andrews/B.
Matthews. Some D and F aircraft were modified for photo reconnaissance missions
with cameras in the lower aft fuselage, including the one pictured. Since the Airacobra
now had an internal fuel capacity of only 120 gallons it was quite usual to carry an
external fuel tank as seen here. Tank sizes from 75 to 175 gallons could be carried
with the smaller sizes mostly fitted. The car-type right side door is open on this
aircraft.

Fig.39-19 Bell P-39K Airacobra, Ser.42-4395, photo via F. Dean coll. The K version of the airplane was essentially a D with an Aeroproducts propeller in place of the Curtiss type, of which there was at that time a shortage. The 210 Ks started showing up in mid-1942. Another change was a new Allison engine version with increased takeoff power and the addition of a WAR EMERGENCY power rating for five minute periods. Outward appearance was unchanged.

Fig.39-20 Bell P-39K Airacobra, P.M. Bowers photo via B. Matthews. This striking view of an Airacobra was taken stateside in mid-1944. Considerable numbers of the Bell machine were used for fighter pilot training in the US, and this aircraft was probably one. Pilots had widely varying opinions, ranging from those who would have liked to fly it into combat to those who absolutely hated it. Almost all agreed it was tricky to fly.

tory. Another uncomfortable factor for pilots was that on early models acrid smoke and fumes reached the cockpit when nose weapons were fired. Later versions had improved fume tightness. A complaint was that gun charging handles were too low. They were hard to operate; too much force was required. The pilot had to duck down to use them, diverting his attention and making him temporarily vulnerable. From the psychological viewpoint some pilots worried about the drive shaft running at engine speed between their legs from engine forward to propeller reduction gearbox. They felt it made an annoying noise as well.

VISIBILITY
Pilot visibility was good. As noted earlier forward visibility for taxi was facilitated by the tricycle landing gear. Many pilots were complimentary about in-flight visibility. "Absolutely fabulous; you could see everything", "Visibility was excellent. You could look past your tail", "Very good", and again "When you were flying you could see everything", and "Visibility was outstanding". The P-39 canopy

was a first step towards later full blown bubble canopies, but visibility was interrupted by framing required at the upper door sections and heavy overturn framing just aft of the pilot. This could be annoying during formation flying if continuous pilot head movement was required to spot a nearby aircraft. An interesting contribution to good rearward visibility was use of thick armor glass aft of the pilot instead of steel armor plate. One pilot commented that visibility from a P-39 was better than from a P-38 or an F4U-. This in itself did not appear to be very high praise.

VULNERABILITY/ARMOR
As with all liquid cooled engine fighters, The P-39 cooling system was vulnerable to a hit which could quickly knock out the powerplant. The combat report on the Airacobra's first encounter with Japanese fighters in the Pacific said "All P-39s before going down had apparently been hit in the cooling system, as Glycol spray could be seen streaming from behind. All P-39s shot down were hit

Fig.39-21 Bell P-39K Airacobra, Ser.42-4321, P.M. Bowers photo via B. Matthews. Another K model Airacobra photographed in the summer of 1944 looking a little tired, no doubt after some hard usage as a fighter-trainer. The drop tank stayed aboard to give the pilot some reasonable flight endurance. Note the horizontal bar is now on the well-worn national insignia. The war was one year from ending, and P-39 production had stopped in June 1944 in favor of the P-63 fighter.

Fig.39-22 Bell P-39L Airacobra, Ser.42-4460, photo via B. Matthews. A service-worn P-39L sits on a hardstand area. Pretty much another version of the D and K models, 250 Ls were produced at about the same time as the K, these with the Curtiss Electric propeller, making the P-39 an almost all-electric airplane. Flaps were electrically powered on all variants as was the landing gear retraction system. And there were a few pilots that got these functions mixed up.

Fig.39-23 Bell P-39 Airacobra Ser.42-4520, photo via B. Matthews. "Evelyn" was probably used as a trainer in the mid-to-late war period stateside. Many US pilots who flew Merlin P-51s in combat did their fighter training in Airacobras, among them Gen.Chuck Yeager, who apparently was one of the few who fell and stayed in love with the P-39.

Fig.39-23A Bell P-39M Airacobra, Curtiss photo via H.Andrews. The P-39M started in production near the end of 1942; this photo was taken during the 1942-1943 winter in snowy Buffalo, New York. In the cockpit is Herb Fisher, not a Bell but a Curtiss test pilot, sampling the wares of close neighbor Bell Aircraft and getting a change from testing production P-40 aircraft.

in the engine and cooling system". A very severe verdict on Airacobra vulnerability was given by one experienced German pilot who had fought against Russian P-39s when he said "You could hit them anyplace and they would tumble in". A report from the Pacific in early 1942 noted the perceived vulnerability of the aft-mounted engine as extremely undesireable. The thesis was because there were so many attacks from the rear the aft engine was vulnerable since it was behind pilot armor instead of ahead of it like more conventional front-mounted engines. The report noted armoring the engine at the rear would cost too much weight. But at least on some later P-39s protective armor was placed aft to protect the large oil tank and incidently the engine. A pilot reported that in North Africa P-39s doing low level strafing missions were considered quite resistant to ground fire. However another said "In North Africa the German 109s shot them down almost at will".

GUN PLATFORM AND WEAPON PERFORMANCE

One pilot did say if anyone ever hit his target with the 37 mm. nose cannon he never saw it, but this may have been as much from erratic weapon firing performance as from aircraft gun platform qualities. Pilots had some definite opinions on the 37 mm. cannon. "We had some problems with jamming but you could clear a jam instantly" (by charging). "The muzzle velocity was less than 1000 feet per second" (low), "The cannon turned out to be a complete loss; I never got over three shots before it jammed". "I couldn't make the cannon work. I never got over one shot". "We could get one round out of the cannon, and then it would jam." Also "I never had the jamming problem". Early Pacific combat reports noted the 37 mm. cannon was "An extremely desireable weapon, but bugs are still being eliminated". In all cases a 37 mm. hit brought down an enemy aircraft (not surprisingly), and it was effective in ground

Fig.39-24 Bell P-39N Airacobra Ser.42-9382, photo via B. Matthews. A major production version with over 2000 articles manufactured in the early parts of 1943, the P-39N had powerplant changes, an Aeroproducts propeller, and another reduction in fuel capacity to only 87 gallons internally, apparently to reduce weight. There were second thoughts because kits were made available to restore tankage to 120 gallons. The Aeroproducts logo can be seen on the propeller blades. Aeroproducts was part of General Motors.

Fig.39-25 Bell P-39N Airacobra, Ser.42-18799, photo via P.M. Bowers. An Airacobra sits at a South Pacific airfield. P-39 airplanes from the 18th Fighter Group were based at Henderson Field on Guadalcanal, though it is not clear that site is pictured. The 5th Air Force had 70 P-39s at the end of July, 1943. More than half of these were in depot for maintenance and most all were very well worn.

Fig.39-26 Bell P-39 Airacobra, photo via P.M. Bowers/B. Matthews. Another well-worn Airacobra in flight, this with an empty centerline store station. The P-39 was small and light compared to the other US fighters, and thus tended to carry lighter useful loads for lesser distances. However with their potent nose armament they were fine ground support aircraft. Some P-39Ns went to the Italians in 1944; the French had received some in early 1943.

Fig.39-27 Bell P-39Q Airacobra, Ser.44-3572, photo via F. Dean coll. The final version of the Airacobra, built in greater quantity than all other versions combined, appeared in the spring of 1943. It looked much like the other P-39s except for substitution of a pod-mounted .50 caliber gun under each wing for the previous two .30 calibers in the wing. There were variations in amounts of fuel and armor, and equipment changes between the P-39 sub-variant airplanes. A few had four bladed propellers, and there were slight propeller diameter changes.

attack. The rate of fire was slow, however, and considerable stoppage trouble was experienced, "due, it is believed, to the newness of the gun". The malfunctions were later traced to the ejector mechanism, and a redesign was effected in 1943. The cannon was considered difficult to recharge in flight because of high pilot force required. Some Airacobras, noteably the P-400 and other export versions, used the 20 mm. cannon which many pilots preferred because of better reliability, longer range, and a flatter shell trajectory. Recommendations back from the Pacific included a desire for gun heaters, hydraulic charging systems, and a request that the two .30 caliber guns in each wing be exchanged for a .50 caliber because the smaller gun did not have enough hitting power. One pilot noted "The .30 calibers didn't seem to do that much". This was done using a pod installation on later P-39Q Airacobras. The change made life a little easier for armorers. They then had only to deal with two sizes of ammunition instead of the previous three on any

one aircraft. A jam of one podded P-39Q .50 caliber wing gun during firing caused the aircraft nose to drift off in a yaw from unsymmetrical recoil force. There were reports the P-39 nose weapons bay was a difficult place in which to work.

GENERAL COMMENTS

The P-39 had a reputation as a tricky airplane to fly and being not at all docile, and many pilots didn't like it. Some absolutely hated it. The word was to fly it as if you were petting a rattlesnake.

Other pilots had a good feeling about the P-39, saying they were one of the finest planes built and a pleasure and not difficult to fly. There were pilots who said it was a sweet airplane, most enjoyable to fly, the very best, a nice airplane, a fun plane, and had nothing but praise for it.

But it was said you had to know how to handle it. Those most admiring of the P-39 would admit they seemed to be in the minority.

Fig.39-26A Bell P-39N Airacobras, Curtiss photo via H. Andrews. Showing that Curtiss and Bell shared the same modification center is this photo of P-39Ns in the foreground and Curtiss C-46A Commando transports behind. It also is a fine illustration of how access to powerplant and other bays of the Airacobra was gained. Cockpit doors are also missing.

Fig.39-28 Bell P-39Q Airacobra, Ser.42-19483, Mfr.photo via F. Dean coll. A Q model Airacobra outside the plant with a wrapping around the nose gear shock strut and torque scissors for reasons unknown. An Aeroproducts decal is on one propeller blade; the Curtiss blade decals were perfectly round. The Italian Air Force received 75 P-39Q Airacobras in April of 1944. Some served through the end of the war and a few lasted as trainers until 1951.

It has been stated the P-39 was the single exception to the rule that all US World War II fighters had good safe characteristics.

The P-39 was cited as a disappointment with slow climb, low ceiling, and relatively poor maneuverability, and thus proved a poor mount for its pilots.

Stalin to Churchill, October 5,1942: "We have not enough fighters for the protection of our forces from the air. Even the bravest troops are helpless if they lack the air protection. We more particularly require Spitfires and Air-Cobras."

The word was: Stay under 15000 feet and above 300 mph with the P-39 and the Zero couldn't get to you.

When used in a proper manner the P-39 was impressive.

Stalin to Roosevelt, October 7,1942: "But at the same time we are extremely in need of an increase in deliveries of pursuit planes of modern type such as Airacobra."

The Russians liked the P-39 even though German aircraft on the eastern front were reported to have picked them off with ease.

Invaluable for ground support, the P-39 with its heavy armament was a good strafer.

Very good performance at 5000 to 10000 feet and mincemeat above 15000 feet seemed to be the P-39 story.

One P-39 deficit was its short mission radius.

Some pilots noted the P-39 had a vibration problem; others never experienced it.

In spite of reports from service pilots Bell Aircraft maintained the P-39 would not tumble, no matter how hard their test pilots tried to do so. They attempted to counter tumbling rumors, insisting there was no documented evidence of a P-39 tumble. But rumors have persisted that P-39s would tumble.

Army pilots told stories of stalling and tumbling, doing snap rolls or other gyrations that seemed like tumbles. Some thought they had tumbled but were not sure. The gyrations seemed like a tumble. One pilot reported he saw a P-39 tumble and crash.

A pilot noted he had seen a P-39 "do something of the sort", going out of control. Questioned further he indicated it was an unusual maneuver where the pilot said later he had tumbled. But he could

not say for sure it was "an end over end maneuver", though he could understand why the pilot might feel he had tumbled and how "the legend could build".

> Don't give me a P-39
> With an engine that's mounted behind
> It will tumble and roll
> And dig a big hole
> Don't give me a P-39.
>
> Don't give me a P-39
> It will tumble and spin
> And soon auger in
> Don't give me a P-39.

The pilot who test flew British P-400 aircraft extensively never experienced tumbling or any other strange maneuver.

Luckily, perhaps, exit from a P-39 in flight was considered very easy.

A story was circulated in North Africa about the P-39 pilot who had sold his plane to an Arab but borrowed it back to fly missions.

One combat pilot's experience with the P-39 was bad. He noted it lacked range to get to the fight, had a low ceiling and climb rate, and was nothing special in diving. Poor climb rate was a very common complaint.

Adm.J.S.McCain: "P-400s no good at altitude and disheartening to the brave men who fly them."

Marine Gen.Vandergrift: "P-400 entirely unsuitable for Operations Cactus (Guadalcanal). Will not be employed further except in extreme emergency." A few days later Vandergrift stated his revised opinion that P-400s were useful for ground attack work.

Some detractors called the P-39 a flying electrical system looking for a place to go haywire. Some also said it was unstable.

German pilots reported on the Russian front they knocked P-39s down almost at will, and in North Africa they reported they were always looking down at P-39s, which gave them no trouble.

P-39 STRUCTURAL DESCRIPTION

(All metals are aluminum alloy unless otherwise noted)

WING GROUP

The wing group was made up of a center section, two outer wing panels, wing tips, ailerons and flaps.

The wing center section extended twenty-two inches outboard on each side from the aircraft centerline, and became an integral part of the fuselage during manufacture. The center section consisted of a forward part and a trailing edge part. The forward part was made up of a forward beam, or spar, a rear beam (both running spanwise), two inner bulkhead-type ribs, and two outer bulkhead-type ribs at the mating stations to the outer panels. The forward beam consisted of extruded top and bottom metal caps and four web panels. The inboard web sections were solid; the outer sections were three layers laminated with formed flanges, and were cut by large oval holes to accomodate oil cooler ducting. Four steel wing bolt fittings tied the forward beam into the fuselage structure.

The rear spar consisted of a two-layer formed steel web riveted back-to-back with aluminum cap strips. Steel was employed in the webs because of large cutouts required-two (one per side) square inboard holes for radiator air ducting and two circular holes for oil cooler ducting. Eight forged steel fittings for wing-fuselage attach bolts were riveted to the steel webs lying up against the cap strips and side flanges. The left and right inboard bulkhead-type ribs had metal webs with extruded forming members. Outboard center section ribs were constructed of reinforced webs where wing bolts ran through from outer wing panel beams to fittings in the center section beams. Outer rib framing members were extruded metal. Top and bottom center section skins were of formed metal sheet reinforced with angle-section stringers and reinforced sections where holes were cut out for wing bolt access doors. The trailing edge portion of the wing center section consisted of a single auxiliary

Fig.39-29 Bell P-39Q Airacobra, Ser.42-21244, P.M.Bowers photo via B. Matthews. This P-39Q shows the contour of the wing .50 caliber machine gun pod. The left side cockpit door is slightly ajar, and one engine compartment cowl panel has been removed. The glycol tank was located in this area, and just behind that the large engine oil tank. Cowl panels were secured by quick attach/detach quarter-turn fasteners.

Fig.39-30 P-39Q Airacobra, Ser.44-3919, photo via Birch Matthews. Except for the wing gun pods the final Airacobra model looked much like the earlier versions. The last P-39 missions in the Pacific were flown in New Guinea in the summer of 1944, and the last P-39 was delivered to the USAAF in August of that year. A couple of months later the Russsians phased out their hard-working Airacobras and replaced them with Soviet fighters.

beam acting as a fuselage carry-through member for the outer panels auxiliary beams. This trailing edge beam was built up of a formed sheet web with tee and angle section caps. Each side was cut through in the web area to accomodate radiator air ducts. Extruded channel sections tied the trailing edge beam to the outboard ribs at the splice joint, and forged fittings were riveted to the beam for additional wing splice bolts. The two engine oil coolers, one on each side, were strapped into the compartments formed by the rib/bulkheads just ahead of this auxiliary beam.

The outer wing panels were joined to the center section at wing station 22 with four large and six small bolts at each of the three beam/spar locations. The outer panels had three spars to match the chordwise locations of those in the center section, the front beam, rear beam, and auxiliary beam. The front and rear beams consisted of solid stringer-reinforced metal webs and flanged extruded and milled cap strips. Flange thicknesses varied from a maximum of 0.87 inches inboard to .0154 inches at the wingtips. The aft auxiliary beam in the outer panels was made up of a solid web with formed cap strips. The top cap was in dual sections from the in-

board splice rib to just beyond the fifth rib going outboard. In the trailing edge assembly an intercostal beam was installed which formed a compartment with the auxiliary beam for the flap-actuating push-pull rod assembly. Short beams ran between the three inboard ribs at the trailing edge to support the wing catwalk

The metal strips forming the wing trailing edges inboard of the ailerons were drawn pieces clamping around and riveted to the skin. The thirteen principal wing ribs were pressed and beaded metal and ranged from .072 inches thick at the inboard splice to .064 inches thick at the tip splice. The ribs or partial ribs were numbered one through ten with additional ribs at 7.5, 8.5, and 9.5. Compartments formed by front and rear beams and ribs 2 to 7.5 accomodated the aircraft self-sealing fuel cells. A bulkhead between ribs 4 and 5 formed a compartment for the main landing gear retracting spindle assembly. Twin .30 caliber machine guns were installed between ribs 7.5 and 8 with a false-rib bulkhead between them. An intercostal beam of formed, blanked, and beaded metal sheet webbing between capstrips ran between ribs 8 and 10 midway between front and rear beams, forming a compartment along with the front beam to accomodate wing ammunition boxes for the thirty caliber guns. Landing gear wells in the wing between ribs 1 and 2 were shaped of formed and drawn capstrips with formed sheet webs. Two angle-shaped stringers extended from rib number 1 over the top of the wheel to the outer periphery to reinforce the wing catwalk. The skins on the wing's lower surface were in three major sections—forward and aft of the rear beam, and the leading edge. Each section consisted of two panels, inboard and outboard. Lower wing skin thickness ranged from .051 to .025 inches. The upper skin panels were similar. Access panels and doors required for fuel tanks and guns had local skin reinforcements. Spanwise stringers were Z-sections, rolled or drawn. All skins were flush riveted.

The wing tips were made up of two ribs and three spanwise tapering beams. The splicing ribs to the outer wing panels were built up of .064 inch sheet webbing and rolled capstrips. The internal rib was made up of three sections of formed beaded sheet stock

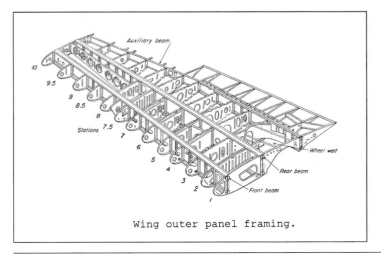

Wing outer panel framing.

with beaded lightning holes. The tip edge of the assembly was a formed strip enclosing the skin. Tip skins were flush riveted and .032 inches thick.

The fabric covered ailerons were single spar metal structures of the Frise type with built-up ribs tied together with gusset plates. Ribs were capped with metal channel assemblies used in conjunction with thin metal retainer strips to tie down the fabric covering and give a flush surface. Leading edge ribs were formed and blanked sheet riveted to the .040 inch thick beam. Trailing edges were formed strips enclosing the fabric. Controllable tabs of laminated phenolic plastic were located on the trail edge of each aileron inboard. They acted as a servo control through a linkage to rotate the tab to an angle opposite to aileron movement, and reduced energy required by the pilot to move the aileron. An additional servo tab of laminated plastic, not pilot-controlled, was located just inboard of the trim tabs. These tabs were actuated by a linkage attached to the aileron hinge bracket maintaining the tab at a fixed neutral setting regardless of aileron position.

Split trailing edge wing flaps formed the rear surface of the outer wing panels. The flaps extended from rib 1 to the inboard ends of the ailerons. The flaps were connected to the lower flange of the auxiliary beam by a full flap-length piano hinge. Flaps were operated by a push-pull tube and an electrically-driven connecting link mechanism. Tthe single flap beam was a formed channel section of .040 inch gage. Ribs were solid sheet sections in two parts, riveted forward and aft of the beam, and stringers were formed channel sections. Flap skin was a solid panel of .025 inch metal. A doubler sheet with lightning holes was riveted to the ribs foreward of the flap beam. Flaps were stressed so a full extension of 43 degrees could be effected up to 150 mph IAS.

TAIL GROUP

The tail group consisted of a horizontal stabilizer, two elevators, the vertical stabilizer or fin, the rudder, and an empennage fillet assembly.

Fig.39-30A *Bell P-39Q Airacobra, R. Besecker photo. Painted and serialed as a P-39J, this restored Airacobra at the USAAF Museum was, according to an informant, a P-39Q though no podded wing gun is apparent. Neither, however, are the .30 caliber wing guns used on all models prior to the Q. The P-39 is a rare bird indeed today.*

The horizontal stabilizer was built as a single unit with sections cut away in the center to permit access of the vertical stabilizer to the fuselage. The stabilizer was a two spar unit of conventional stressed skin design. The forward spar or beam was built in three flanged sections of heavy gage sheet. The center section was short, perpendicular to the aircraft centerline, and to which were attached two outer beam sections with pronounced sweepback approximately parallel to the leading edge. A series of false ribs of formed and blanked sections formed the leading edge. The rear spar of .072 inch gage sheet was in two half sections spliced with a riveted plate. Each half section had a solid sheet tip riveted on. About halfway from the center on each side, forged steel hinge fittings for the elevator attachment were fastened to the rear spar. The front and rear spars were tied together with a series of blanked and formed ribs. Zee-shaped stringers supported a flush-riveted skin. The leading edge metal skin was a single formed section on each side, extending from the top flange of the front beam around the forming ribs to the bottom flange. From the front beam to the rear edge the skin was in four sheet sections, two on each side, top and bottom. Stabilizer tips were single formed sections riveted to the single rib of the stabilizer proper. Four threaded studs, two on each spar beam, provided for stabilizer attachment to the fuselage with lock nuts.

The elevators were similar in construction to the ailerons and were fabric covered. Right and left elevators were joined at the control quadrant by tubular steel members spliced by forged flanged steel collars. The left elevator had a trim tab fastened to an auxiliary spar just forward and inboard of the trailing edge section. Two hinge settings were installed on the main beam and attached to the horizontal stabilizer. A mass-balance, constructed of a tubular-shaped weight used for static and dynamic balancing, was located in the most forward section of the leading edge.

The fin, or vertical stabilizer, was similar in construction to the horizontal stabilizer except that the spars were one-piece. A hole

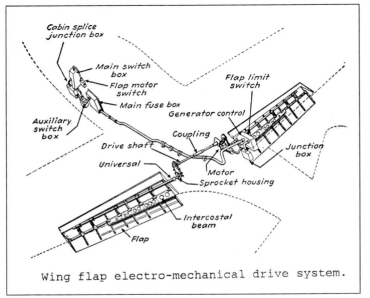

Wing flap electro-mechanical drive system.

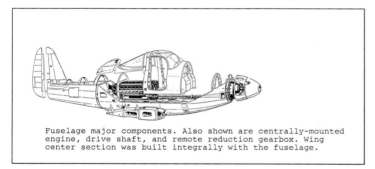

Fuselage major components. Also shown are centrally-mounted engine, drive shaft, and remote reduction gearbox. Wing center section was built integrally with the fuselage.

Fig.39-31 Bell TP-39Q Airacobra, P.M. Bowers photo via R. Besecker. Throughout the war attempts were made, either by the manufacturers or in field conversions, to make two place aircraft out of single seat fighters. Reasons varied, but one was obviously for training purposes. An illustration of how to make an ugly duckling of an attractive airplane is given here. An additional canopy is built forward and the gun bay cleaned out. Note the extra dorsal fin area to counter destabilizing effects of the forward enclosure.

was cut in the skin for a navigation light. Cast fittings were installed on the projecting ends of the main and rear spars for bolt and nut attachment to the aft fuselage. Two hinge fittings were riveted to the aft flange of the rear beam for rudder attachment. Extruded ribs were used in the fabric-covered rudder, however, the top and bottom portions were covered by formed and beaded metal sheet. Two hinge fittings were installed on the rudder main spar for fastening to the vertical stabilizer, and rudder control quadrants were installed on the main beam. The auxiliary spar supported a plastic trim tab, and a round mass-balance weight was mounted in the most forward section of the leading edge.

An empennage fillet assembly was comprised of nine pieces of formed sheet and formers which were attached by flush screws and channel nuts.

FUSELAGE GROUP
The fuselage was made up of forward and aft major sections spliced together aft of the cabin. The forward section was the largest part, containing the center wing section, extension shaft and propeller reduction gearbox mounts, nose wheel attachment fittings, and sup-

ports and brackets for many system components as well as for the pilot's cabin, nose armament components, and cooling system parts.

The forward section was comprised primarily of two built-up longitudinal beams which were of cradle shape in side profile. Each beam was made up of angle sections tied with virtually solid heavily reinforced webbing. A series of formed bulkheads imparted the cross-sectional shape. Two of these bulkheads were main structural members located where the wing center section beams were tied in; these were steel castings and became an integral part of the wing center section upon assembly. A heavy gage stamped deck plate was riveted to the tops of the bulkheads and extended the full length of the beams. A forged angle member was mounted to the rear of the beam to form the engine bed. The skin of the forward fuselage

Fig.39-32 Bell civil P-39Q Airacobra, R. Besecker photo. Handsomely restored and sporting the early national insignia on the fuselage, this Confederate Air Force Airacobra appeared at the Reno Air Races in the 1970s. Landing gear and flaps on the P-39 were operated by electro-mechanical systems; other than for wheel brakes there was no hydraulic system on the aircraft.

section consisted of formed sheet from .032 to .051 inches thick riveted to the bulkheads. The two longitudinal beams were maintained rigidly parallel by tubular spreader bars, a forward bulkhead, and the aft splicing bulkhead. In addition the wing center section, coolant radiator supports, and the pilot cabin (joined later) also acted as tying members. Superimposed on the forward fuselage, but designed as an integral part of it, the pilot cabin was attached just forward of the engine compartment. Fumetight bulkheads were provided between the engine compartment and the cabin, and between the cabin and armament compartment forward.

The aft fuselage section supported the tail, or empennage, and contained the radio installation. It was of semi-monocoque construction and had eight principal forming bulkheads. The forward splicing bulkhead had a beaded sheet web and a number of drilled stiffeners for bolts joining the aft and forward fuselage sections. The two most forward bulkheads were tied by two longitudinal bulkheads to form a compartment for the engine oil tank. The skins of the aft section were .032 inches thick formed sheet throughout, and were all flush riveted.

The cabin section was in two parts-the forward cabin for the pilot, a permanent built-up structure superimposed upon and forming an integral part of the forward fuselage ahead of the engine, and the removeable aft cabin enclosure directly over the engine and joining the forward section at the turnover beam. The forward cabin section was comprised of drawn metal frames for the glass and Plexiglass enclosures, as well as the formed side skins forward of the doors. Directly ahead of the pilot was a windshield of one quarter inch laminated shatterproof glass; the two side windshield panels were of one quarter inch convex Plexiglass, and directly overhead a 5/32 inch Plexiglass panel was formed to the cabin contour. All panels were set in rubber channel retainer strips. The doors located on both sides of the cabin were the metal automobile type. Both had a 21/64 inch roll-down laminated glass panel operable on the ground or in the air at any speed up to design high speed in level flight. Emergency door release handles, painted red, were just for-

Fig.39-34 Bell civil P-39Q racer Cobra II, photo via P.M. Bowers. A real hot-rod of an airplane, Cobra II piloted by Tex Johnson showed what a highly modified P-39 race plane could do at sea level, winning the 1946 Thompson Trophy Race at a speed of 373.9 mph. The Allison V-1710E-30 engine delivered about 2000 horsepower. Note the extra cooler under the fuselage.

Fig.39-33 Bell civil P-39Q Airacobra, R. Besecker photo. The CAF Airacobra at Reno in 1976 showing mid-engine exhaust streaks back to the side insignia. Split-type flaps are lowered. Central location of engine with shaft drive forward to the remote gearbox facilitated cannon installation but precluded use of a fuselage fuel tank installation as used in P-40, P-47, and the later P-51s.

ward of each door frame in the cockpit. When the handle was pulled out and turned 90 degrees the hinge pin was parallel with the door release slot, and the door was free to be pushed outward away from the aircraft. Both doors were held tightly closed by latches at the top to prevent opening at high speeds; the fastenings were broken when emergency handles were operated. The main instrument panel was a metal one-piece unit flexibly mounted on three Lord mounts just below the center windshield. An auxiliary instrument panel was set to the right of the main panel and attached directly to the fuselage. A left hand panel mounted electrical switches.

The cabin was designed to accomodate a pilot five foot eight inches in height with a parachute. The turnover structure was made up of two main beams of heavy gage tied together by a number of formed and blanked bulkhead sections and skin flush riveted to the beams and bulkheads. Additional strength was provided by crossed streamline wire bracing running from the top of each side of the assembly to the bottom of the other.

The aft cabin was a shallow streamlined structure conforming to the fuselage contours. It was enclosed by two convex panels of 5/32 inch thick Plexiglass, and consisted of channel formers and a beaded metal deck plate for housing a portion of the radio installation. This removeable aft cabin joined the forward section at the turnover beam.

LANDING GEAR GROUP

The aircraft was equipped with a fully retractable tricycle landing gear consisting of a nose gear assembly and two main gear assemblies along with retracting mechanisms.

The nose gear was a self-castoring non-steerable type retracting up and aft into a forward fuselage bay. The 19 inch diameter nose wheel was magnesium alloy and could swivel 60 degrees each side of center. the gear included a Cleveland Pneumatic air-oil shock strut hinged to the forward fuselage inside the nose wheel well, and was retracted by a linkage assembly. A centering cam was installed

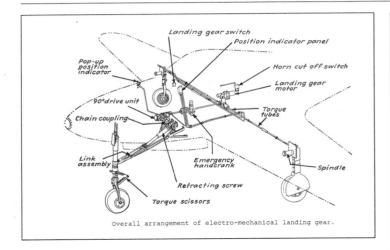

Overall arrangement of electro-mechanical landing gear.

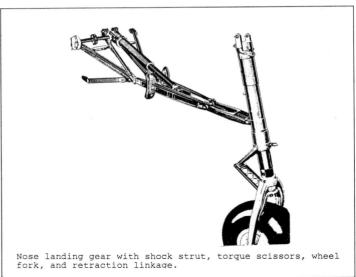

Nose landing gear with shock strut, torque scissors, wheel fork, and retraction linkage.

in the oleo strut keeping the wheel in a central position and preventing it from hitting the airplane during retraction. An adjustable Houde Engineering shimmy damper was installed in the lower end of the strut piston tube. The nose wheel fork was a steel forging bolted to the lower end of the strut assembly. The nose wheel was carried on a steel tube axle which slid through the fork ends and was held in place by a large nut lockwired to the fork. A high pressure dual-seal safety tube was used inside the tire. An anti-torque scissors assembly was used between the body of the shock strut and the wheel fork. The nose wheel retracting linkage consisted of a retracting screw actuator installed in the forward fuselage and driven by the landing gear electric motor through torque tubes and a 90 degree gear drive. The actuating screw was attached to the main leg of the nose wheel linkage assembly. A coupling shaft linked

the retracting screw and gear drive. The retracting linkage consisted of a short link attached to the oleo strut, to which was attached a larger, or main link, hinged in turn to two A-frame fittings in the fuselage. The nose gear fairing was in two sections. One was bolted to the top of the nose wheel strut and lay flush with the underside of the fuselage after gear retraction. The other section consisted of right and left hand doors hinged to the forward section of the fuselage at four hinge points. These doors were actuated by a spring-loaded arm contacting the wheel in the opening and closing cycles.

The main landing gear assemblies retracted up and inboard into the outer wing panels. The main gear struts were Cleveland

Fig.39-35 Bell civil P-39Q racer, photo via P.M. Bowers. The Airacobra NX92848, ex-Cobra II, continued its racing career in 1947 and 1948, coming in third in the 1947 Thompson barely behind two Goodyear Corsair racers with 4000 horsepower R-4360 Wasp Major engines. The Bell racer averaged almost 390 mph. In 1948 it had to quit on the next to last lap, but had done one earlier lap at 413 mph.

Pneumatic units attached to a fitting of the spindle assembly in the wing panel by four bolts. The forged steel single-side landing gear fork was attached to the piston tube of each strut which operated with the wheel. Conventional torque scissors were used. Main wheels were magnesium alloy equipped with disc-type hydraulic brakes. The casings were 26 inches by six inches six-ply rayon with high pressure puncture-proof tubes. Three types of interchangeable tires could be used: treaded for ice or snow-packed fields, flat contour for desert or sandy fields, and smooth contour for normal operations. Each main wheel brake assembly had eleven plates, six stationary steel discs, and five moveable brass discs. The stationary discs were held in place by six slots on the inner side which slid over six tongues on the axle hub. The moveable discs had six tongues on the outer edge which slid into six corresponding slots in the brake drum. The main wheels retracted into the wing by means of a worm sector gear which was installed with a spindle assembly on the aft face of the rear main beam by twelve nuts and bolts. Each strut was attached to a fitting of the spindle assembly by four nuts and bolts. A worm gear installed on the spindle assembly was actuated by the landing gear electric motor by means of torque tubes. The worm gear rotated the sector gear, which in turn retracted or extended the wheels. The landing gear was operated by a reversible 24-volt motor providing 3/4 horsepower at 3800 RPM. A clutch and reduction gear with a 40 to one ratio were incorporated in the assembly. The clutch was designed to slip at an output torque of 700 inch-pounds at the output shaft. The motor was mounted on the forward fuselage deck at the right side of the engine. An operating control switch was mounted just forward of the left hand cabin door in the cockpit. An emergency hand crank was equipped with a ratchet, and could be reversed by a switch on the crank. A clutch handle was located near the hand crank on the cabin floor to change from electric to manual operation and back. The main wheel fairing was made up of three sections. Two were attached to the main wheel strut at two places. The lower section of the fairing lapped over the upper section, but the two were not connected in any way, the overlap permitting motion of the oleo strut without damage or buckling. The lower section was attached to the main wheel axle and to the upper portion of the fork by a link assembly. The upper section of the fairing was attached to the strut in two places by clamps. The third section of the fairing, known as the "flipper door", was hinged to the lower surface of the wing center section, near the wing splice ribs. It opened toward the aircraft centerline, and was actuated by the main wheel during extension and retraction. The wheel extended and allowed the spring-loaded arm of the door to straighten, forcing the door open. Upon retraction the tire came in contact with the spring-loaded arm, and caused it to fold upward, drawing up the door.

ENGINE SECTION

Because the engine was mounted in the center of the fuselage there was no conventional engine section. The engine was mounted on Fabreeka pads and tied down by eight bolts in four pairs to the fuselage bed. Removeable cowl panels secured by quarter-turn quick-disconnect fasteners allowed ready access to the engine compartment aft of the cockpit area.

P-39 SYSTEMS DESCRIPTION

PROPULSION SUBSYSTEMS

ENGINE

The engine was an 1100 to 1300 horsepower class Allison V-1710 liquid-cooled twelve-cylinder vee-type inline model of 5.5 inches bore and 6.0 inches stroke. It was equipped with an integral single stage single speed supercharger, and operated at a maximum crankshaft RPM of 3000. It had an 8.8:1 gear ratio to the blower which was nine and one half inches in diameter. The propeller reduction gear ratio was either 1.8:1 or 2:1 depending on the version, and the reduction gear assembly was mounted separately ten feet ahead of the basic engine as a separately lubricated unit. The two-section connecting shaft contained a flanged coupling and a central bearing support. The SAE #50 splined gearbox output shaft rotated clockwise looking from the rear.

ENGINE INDUCTION/INTAKE SYSTEM

A ram intake air scoop on top of the fuselage aft of the cockpit enclosure directed air via a duct to the engine carburetor. The forward face of the duct had a door controlled from the cockpit which could close off the cold outside air and admit alternate warm air from the engine compartment.

ENGINE EXHAUST SYSTEM

The exhaust system was made up of six (sometimes twelve) stacks on each side protruding from the skin line, formed and directed aft to provide jet thrust force in flight. Each unit was of seam-welded stainless steel with mounting flanges welded on to attach to the engine exhaust ports.

ENGINE-MOUNTED ACCESSORIERS

The engine-mounted or -driven accessories included fuel pump, starter, magnetos, lubrication pump, vacuum pump, electrical generator, tachometer generator, and carburetor. The propeller speed governor and a lube pump were mounted on the separate reduction gearbox.

ENGINE CONTROLS

Engine controls for throttle and mixture were located together on a quadrant at the left side of the cockpit, and mechanical drives ran aft from there to control levers on the engine carburetor. A friction-adjusting nut on the quadrant prevented creeping due to vibration. On very late P-39 models the throttle and propeller control were linked together to provide a coordinated control as later used on the P-63 fighter. Kits were supplied to return to the conventional arrangement.

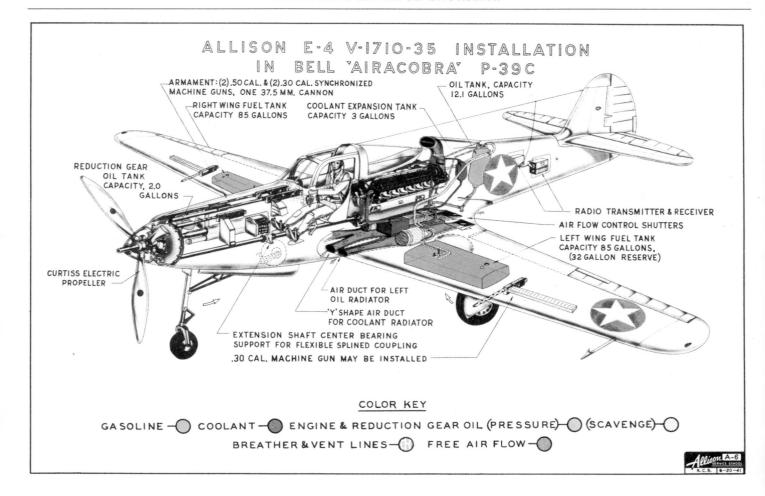

ALLISON E-4 V-1710-35 INSTALLATION
IN BELL 'AIRACOBRA' P-39C

ARMAMENT: (2).50 CAL. & (2).30 CAL. SYNCHRONIZED
MACHINE GUNS, ONE 37.5 MM. CANNON

RIGHT WING FUEL TANK
CAPACITY 85 GALLONS

COOLANT EXPANSION TANK
CAPACITY 3 GALLONS

OIL TANK, CAPACITY
12.1 GALLONS

REDUCTION GEAR
OIL TANK
CAPACITY, 2.0
GALLONS

RADIO TRANSMITTER & RECEIVER

AIR FLOW CONTROL SHUTTERS

LEFT WING FUEL TANK
CAPACITY 85 GALLONS,
(32 GALLON RESERVE)

CURTISS ELECTRIC
PROPELLER

AIR DUCT FOR LEFT
OIL RADIATOR

'Y' SHAPE AIR DUCT
FOR COOLANT RADIATOR

EXTENSION SHAFT CENTER BEARING
SUPPORT FOR FLEXIBLE SPLINED COUPLING

.30 CAL. MACHINE GUN MAY BE INSTALLED

COLOR KEY

GASOLINE —◯— COOLANT —◯— ENGINE & REDUCTION GEAR OIL (PRESSURE) —◯— (SCAVENGE) —◯—

BREATHER & VENT LINES —◯— FREE AIR FLOW —◯—

Allison A-6
SERVICE SCHOOL
K.C.B. | 6-20-41

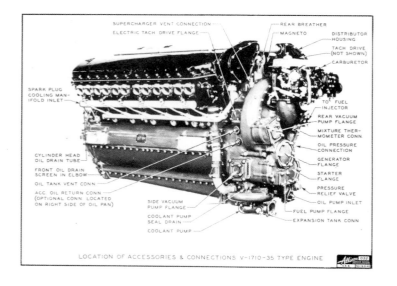

SUPERCHARGER VENT CONNECTION

ELECTRIC TACH DRIVE FLANGE

REAR BREATHER

MAGNETO

DISTRIBUTOR
HOUSING

TACH DRIVE
(NOT SHOWN)

CARBURETOR

SPARK PLUG
COOLING MAN-
IFOLD INLET

TO FUEL
INJECTOR

REAR VACUUM
PUMP FLANGE

MIXTURE THER-
MOMETER CONN.

OIL PRESSURE
CONNECTION

CYLINDER HEAD
OIL DRAIN TUBE

GENERATOR
FLANGE

FRONT OIL DRAIN
SCREEN IN ELBOW

STARTER
FLANGE

OIL TANK VENT CONN.

PRESSURE
RELIEF VALVE

ACC. OIL RETURN CONN.
(OPTIONAL CONN. LOCATED
ON RIGHT SIDE OF OIL PAN)

OIL PUMP INLET

SIDE VACUUM
PUMP FLANGE

FUEL PUMP FLANGE

COOLANT PUMP
SEAL DRAIN

EXPANSION TANK CONN.

COOLANT PUMP

LOCATION OF ACCESSORIES & CONNECTIONS V-1710-35 TYPE ENGINE

Allison 932
SERVICE SCHOOL

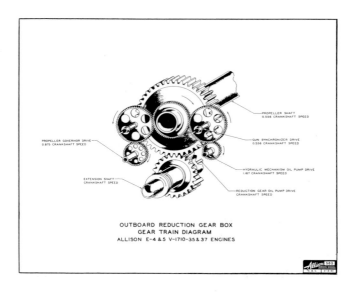

PROPELLER SHAFT
0.556 CRANKSHAFT SPEED

PROPELLER GOVERNOR DRIVE
0.875 CRANKSHAFT SPEED

GUN SYNCHRONIZER DRIVE
0.556 CRANKSHAFT SPEED

HYDRAULIC MECHANISM OIL PUMP DRIVE
1.167 CRANKSHAFT SPEED

EXTENSION SHAFT
CRANKSHAFT SPEED

REDUCTION GEAR OIL PUMP DRIVE
CRANKSHAFT SPEED

OUTBOARD REDUCTION GEAR BOX
GEAR TRAIN DIAGRAM
ALLISON E-4 & 5 V-1710-35 & 37 ENGINES

Allison 588
SERVICE SCHOOL

PROPELLER

The aircraft was equipped with either a Curtiss C532S propeller using three model 614 hollow steel blades in a diameter of 10 feet 4 and 1/2 inches or an Aeroproducts propeller with three A-20-156-17 hollow steel blades. Both propellers were governor-controlled constant-speed types, with the Curtiss being electrically operated from the aircraft system, and the Aeroproducts type a self-contained hydraulic unit. The Aeroproducts propeller diameter varied between aircraft models from 10 feet 5 inches to 11 feet 7 inches. A few late models were equipped with four blade Aeroproducts propellers. Both propeller types had an automatic constant speeding mode and a manual selective pitch mode of operation. Both propellers were of special hollow-hub design to allow the barrel of the centrally-mounted cannon to protrude through the nose of the aircraft. In the Curtiss design both the electric motor and its reduction gearing on the hub front had to be designed as annular ring units with a hole in the center for the cannon barrel. Both propellers mounted an aerodynamic spinner supported by the hub.

PROPELLER CONTROLS

A mechanical control linkage ran from the propeller lever in the cockpit to the propeller governor mounted on the reduction gearbox to set the desired system speed.

ENGINE STARTING SYSTEM

An electrically-operated inertia-type starter was employed. The starter was mounted near the bottom right hand side of the engine accessory housing. It was energized by pressing downward on the starter pedal on the right side of the floor with the heel of the right foot until the starter was energized sufficiently (by sounding as though it had reached maximum RPM) to turn over the engine. Then the pedal was depressed forward with the toe to engage the starter to engine gearing via a clutch, and was held until the engine was firing regularly. The pedal was then released. A hand crank could also be used in starting, and this was located in a compartment inside the trailing edge of the right wing. A handcrank extension shaft with a sleeve was permanently installed, and had a sleeve bearing support inside the fuselage. It was accessible through a hinged door on the fuselage right side near the wing trailing edge. On some models a mechanism was installed for lifting the starter brushes to prevent generation of a charge while the starter was being cranked manually. A lever located in a side access door next to the starter door was operated when the hand crank was being used. When the starter was engaged and the engine started the lever was operated to return the brushes to normal position. An electric receptacle located in the left wing trail edge fillet could be used in conjunction with an outside battery for cold weather starting. The receptacle was connected to the electrical inertia starter mechanism.

ENGINE WATER INJECTION SYSTEM

No water injection system was installed.

ENGINE COOLING SYSTEM

A high temperature (185-257 deg.F.) liquid Prestone cooling system was provided for the engine. The radiator was of the cartridge

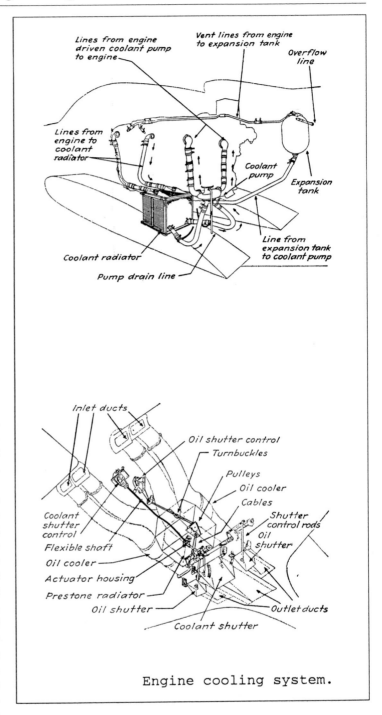

Engine cooling system.

core type, constructed in two sections and assembled as a single unit in a mounting cradle set on four flexible vibration isolators below the engine between the fuselage longitudinal main beams and aft of the wing rear beam carry-through structure. The Prestone coolant was carried in lines from the outlet at the top forward end of each engine cylinder head to the radiator. Coolant entered the radiator through a compound inlet on each side of the top and flowed down and rearward, returning to the coolant circulating pump inlet collector. The Prestone expansion tank mounted high and aft of the

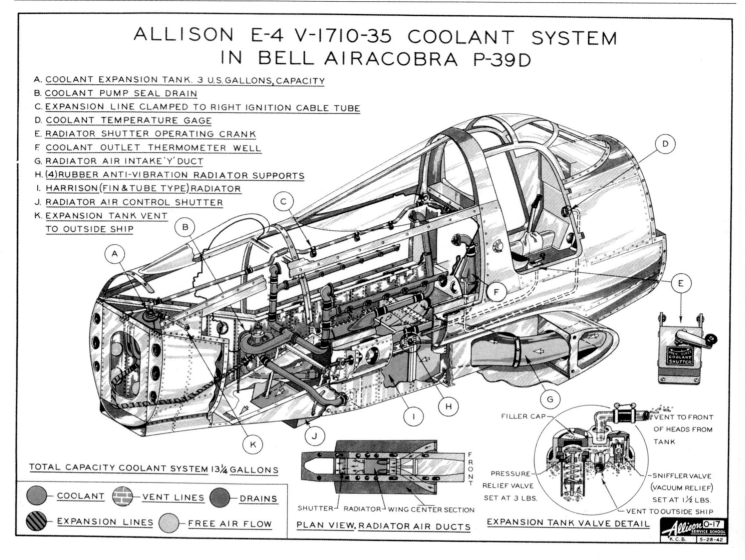

ALLISON E-4 V-1710-35 COOLANT SYSTEM IN BELL AIRACOBRA P-39D

A. COOLANT EXPANSION TANK. 3 U.S.GALLONS, CAPACITY
B. COOLANT PUMP SEAL DRAIN
C. EXPANSION LINE CLAMPED TO RIGHT IGNITION CABLE TUBE
D. COOLANT TEMPERATURE GAGE
E. RADIATOR SHUTTER OPERATING CRANK
F. COOLANT OUTLET THERMOMETER WELL
G. RADIATOR AIR INTAKE 'Y' DUCT
H. (4)RUBBER ANTI-VIBRATION RADIATOR SUPPORTS
I. HARRISON(FIN & TUBE TYPE) RADIATOR
J. RADIATOR AIR CONTROL SHUTTER
K. EXPANSION TANK VENT TO OUTSIDE SHIP

TOTAL CAPACITY COOLANT SYSTEM 13¾ GALLONS

COOLANT   VENT LINES   DRAINS
EXPANSION LINES   FREE AIR FLOW

PLAN VIEW, RADIATOR AIR DUCTS
SHUTTER   RADIATOR   WING CENTER SECTION

EXPANSION TANK VALVE DETAIL
FILLER CAP
VENT TO FRONT OF HEADS FROM TANK
PRESSURE RELIEF VALVE SET AT 3 LBS.
SNIFFLER VALVE (VACUUM RELIEF) SET AT 1½ LBS.
VENT TO OUTSIDE SHIP
Allison SERVICE SCHOOL O-17
K.C.B. 5-28-42

engine was arranged so when filled to filler neck level with the aircraft level it would contain the proper amount of coolant and expansion space. The system was vented automatically to prevent air locks, allow expansion, relieve pressure above three pounds per square inch, and prevent a re-entrance of air. Automatic relief and sniffle valves were included in the cooling system filler unit on top of the tank. The coolant pump was a centrifugal type mounted on the bottom of the accessory housing on the rear left side of the engine. Two separate air ducts, one on each side of the fuselage at the leading edge of the wing center section, ran aft in the wing and converged in front of and connected to the radiator with an air-tight seal, providing a cooling air supply. A radiator air exit flap, or shutter, control was located on the cockpit floor. It consisted of a gearbox with a small handcrank. The gearbox output drove a flexible shaft extending aft to a screw jack actuating a trunnion on the shutter operating arm to control the exit flap opening. The shutter was located at the air exit point of the radiator, and could completely restrict air flow through the radiator by closing, or provide full air flow when opened. All coolant lines were of aluminum alloy tub-

ing. A coolant temperature thermometer was in the system and registered on a cockpit indicator.

ENGINE LUBRICATION SYSTEM

Engine oil was circulated by a main pressure pump with built-in check valve, and a scavenge pump located at the lower right side of the engine accessory housing. Oil was supplied to the "in" side of the pump from the tank and lubricated the engine, then left the engine from the main scavenge pump "out" side, and was delivered equally to two oil coolers. From the oil coolers two lines tied into a single line returning oil to the top of the tank. The main oil tank was located in the aft fuselage behind the engine accessory bay on centerline with a capacity of 13.8 gallons. Oil level was measured by a flexible bayonet-type rod located in the top casting of the tank, which was constructed of seam-welded magnesium alloy sheet. The tank was constructed to make it impossible to fill the expansion space if the aircraft was level. The two oil coolers were cylindrical units secured by straps and mounted in the aft part of the wing center section. They incorporated an independent automatic, ther-

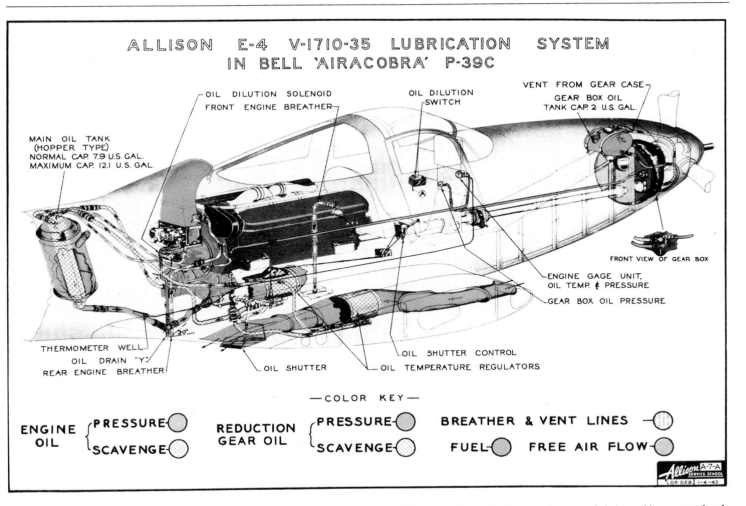

ALLISON E-4 V-1710-35 LUBRICATION SYSTEM IN BELL 'AIRACOBRA' P-39C

mostatically-controlled by-pass valve that circulated oil along the cooler coils until it was cooled. Cooling air entrance ducts were located one in each outer wing panel leading edge and connected to the front of each cooler. Each exit duct left the outer wing panel between front and rear wing spars and joined the duct section connected to the coolers. Air exhausted overboard through the two flap-type shutters aft of the coolers on the underside of the wing center section. The shutters were operated together by a lever control in the right forward face of the turnover beam near the cabin floor, and could fully open or completely restrict air flow through the coolers.

A solonoid-operated oil dilution valve was maintained in the system for cold-weather starting. Oil dilution was implemented by controlled addition of engine oil to the oil-inlet line using a toggle switch in the cockpit.

An oil thermometer was incorporated and registered on an oil temperature gage in the cockpit. An oil system drain was provided at a low point, and a bypass surge valve included to provide a by-pass to the tank if oil pressure exceeded 60 psi. Two engine breather pipes were connected to the engine at the top, one forward and one aft; they drained down and exited under the aircraft. Oil lines were all of aluminum alloy tubing. A Pesco oil separator was incorporated mounted on the left hand deck of the fuselage.

The propeller reduction gearbox was lubricated by a completely separate oil circulating system with its own tank, sump, and integral pump. The reduction gearbox oil tank was located just aft of the gearbox and was constructed of magnesium alloy sheet with welded seams. Oil lines for this independent system were aluminum alloy tubing with brass liners at each connection. A line ran from the gearbox to the cockpit to record oil pressure.

ENGINE FIRE SENSING AND EXTINGUISHING SYSTEMS
There were no sensing or extinguishing systems on the aircraft.

FUEL SYSTEM
The fuel tank system was composed internally of two 60 gallon capacity units, each consisting of six leakproof bags, built integrally into each outer wing panel, providing a total internal capacity of 120 US gallons . A few models of N and Q airplanes had a reduced capacity of 87 to 110 gallons, but were later kitted up to the more standard 120 gallon capacity. A droppable auxiliary tank of 75 to 175 US gallon capacity could be carried by the bomb rack on the airplane centerline. The left wing tank 60 gallons included a 20 gallon reserve capacity. The left wing tank system was equipped with two finger-type fuel strainers, one providing for normal fuel consumption and the other for reserve fuel consumption. The right

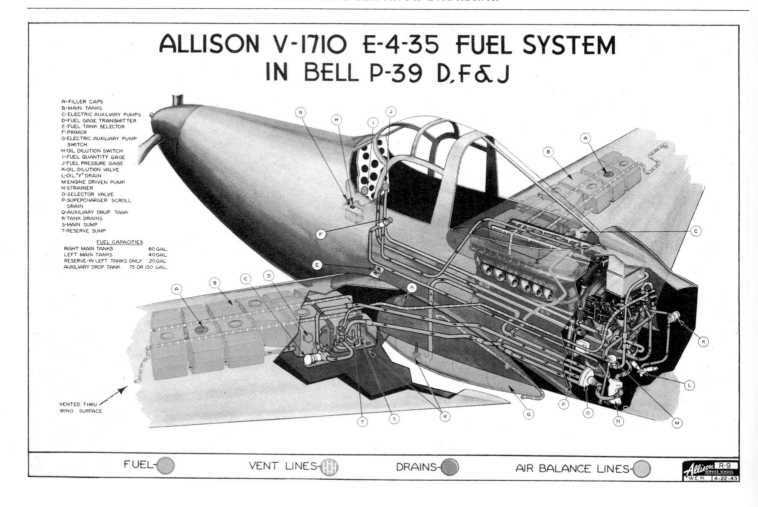

ALLISON V-1710 E-4-35 FUEL SYSTEM IN BELL P-39 D, F & J

A-FILLER CAPS
B-MAIN TANKS
C-ELECTRIC AUXILIARY PUMPS
D-FUEL GAGE TRANSMITTER
E-FUEL TANK SELECTOR
F-PRIMER
G-ELECTRIC AUXILIARY PUMP
    SWITCH
H-OIL DILUTION SWITCH
I-FUEL QUANTITY GAGE
J-FUEL PRESSURE GAGE
K-OIL DILUTION VALVE
L-OIL "Y" DRAIN
M-ENGINE DRIVEN PUMP
N-STRAINER
O-SELECTOR VALVE
P-SUPERCHARGER SCROLL
    DRAIN
Q-AUXILIARY DROP TANK
R-TANK DRAINS
S-MAIN SUMP
T-RESERVE SUMP

FUEL CAPACITIES
RIGHT MAIN TANKS   60 GAL.
LEFT MAIN TANKS   40 GAL.
RESERVE-IN LEFT TANKS ONLY 20 GAL.
AUXILIARY DROP TANK   75 OR 150 GAL.

VENTED THRU WING SURFACE

FUEL-   VENT LINES-   DRAINS-   AIR BALANCE LINES-

Allison R-9 SERVICE SCHOOL W.E.H. 4-22-43

wing tank system included only one fuel strainer providing for consumption of the entire tank capacity on that side. Each tank was provided with a liquidometer unit with a resistance strip and moveable contact arm at the end of which was installed a pivoting cork float actuating the contact arm in accordance with fuel level in the tank. Contact arm position was transmitted electrically to a cockpit indicator. Electrical connectors were installed in shielded conduits between each tank unit and the cockpit indicator.

Fuel was supplied to the carburetor by a pressure pump located on the rear of the engine accessory housing either by two fuel booster pumps in the wing outer panels (in some models), or by a single booster pump in the wing center section (on other models). The booster pumps were electrically driven and were used for starting the engine, warm weather takeoff, and high altitude flying to prevent vapor lock. A fuel strainer, an air vapor eliminator, and an air vapor valve were included, the last two installed to provide a steady fuel flow when the fuel selector valve was actuated to switch fuel intake from an empty tank to a full one. A vent line from the carburetor to the left wing tank was routed through the air vapor control valve which prevented vapor in that tank from backing up into the carburetor. A fuel pressure warning switch and a cockpit warning light was also provided to warn of low fuel pressure conditions. A fuel primer pump was installed at the lower right hand side of the radio control panel. It was hand-operated, drew fuel from the booster pump, and injected it into the engine intake manifold system.

FIXED EQUIPMENT SUBSYSTEMS

INSTRUMENTS
Flight instruments consisted of: Altimeter, turn indicator, climb indicator, air speed meter, clock, bank and turn indicator, flight indicator, and remote reading compass. Engine instruments carried were: Gearbox pressure gage, suction gage, coolant temperature gage, carburetor air temperature gage, manifold pressure gage, engine gage unit, and tachometer. Other instruments were: Ammeter, liquidometer, and oxygen pressure and flow indicator. An engine-mounted vacuum pump supplied the vacuum for instruments where required.

SURFACE CONTROLS
The surface controls system started in the cockpit with stick-type control for elevators and ailerons, and rudder pedals for rudder con-

trol. The stick was attached to a control column with a yoke at the cockpit floor through which the engine drive shaft ran from engine to propeller gearbox. Control column travel was restrained by four stop bolts, two regulating fore-aft movement and two lateral movement. Rudder pedals were adjustable in five positions over a range of six and one half inches. The main control cables were made of extra-flexible corrosion-resistant steel, and control cable oulleys were mounted on ball bearings.

Control of the elevators was effected via a push-pull tube assembly attached to the bottom of the control column yoke and running aft through the fuselage to a quadrant in the aft fuselage section. From this quadrant a duplicate cable system extended along the aft fuselage, around a set of pulleys at the tail, and upward to an elevator control quadrant at the elevator splice bar on centerline.

The trim tab on the left elevator was controlled from the cockpit via a wheel and sprocket-driven chain which was connected by turnbuckles to control cables supported by pulleys and running aft through the fuselage. The cables were connected to a straight-drive unit from where a flexible drive shaft ran to the trim tab screw actuator mounted on the spar of the left elevator.

BELL P-39 F
INSTRUMENT PANEL & CONTROLS

1 THROTTLE
2-MANUAL MIXTURE CONTROL
3-PROPELLER GOVERNOR CONTROL
4-CARBURATOR HEAT CONTROL
5-ELECTRIC FUEL PUMP SWITCH
6-FUEL TANK SELECTOR
7-ENGINE PRIMER
8-OIL DILUTION SWITCH
9-PROPELLER CONTROL SWITCH
10-PROPELLER CIRCUIT BREAKER
11-GENERATOR SWITCH
12-MANIFOLD PRESSURE GAGE
13-FUEL TANK GAGE
14-IGNITION SWITCH
15-COOLANT TEMPERATURE GAGE
16-PARKING BRAKE
17-TACHOMETER
18-OIL TEMPERATURE GAGE
19-FUEL PRESSURE GAGE
20-OIL PRESSURE GAGE
21-FUEL PRESSURE WARNING
22-FUEL PRESSURE TEST SWITCH
23-OIL PRESSURE GAGE-REDUCTION GEAR
24-STARTER SWITCH
25-COOLANT SHUTTER CONTROL
26-OIL SHUTTER CONTROL

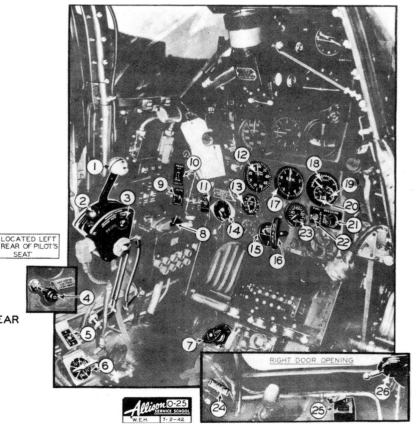

LOCATED LEFT REAR OF PILOT'S SEAT

RIGHT DOOR OPENING

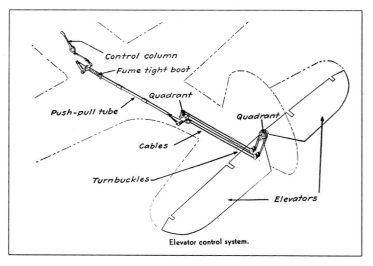

Elevator control system.

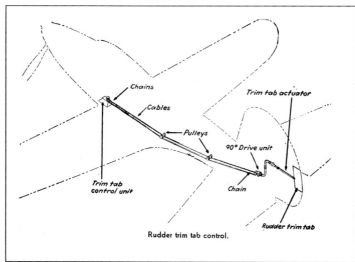

Rudder trim tab control.

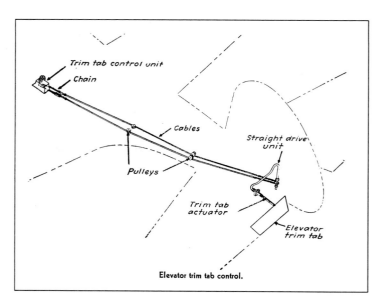

Elevator trim tab control.

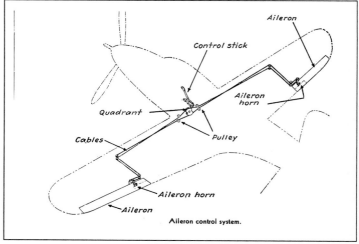

Aileron control system.

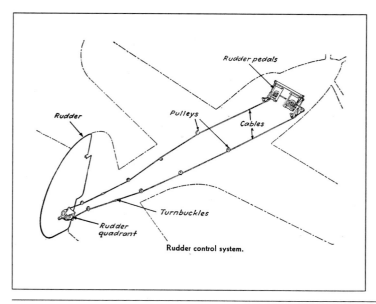

Rudder control system.

Lateral movement of the stick and control column actuated an aileron link rod connected to a quadrant in the fuselage. Control cables ran outboard from this quadrant along the leading edge of each outer wing panel. At wing station 7.5 the cables made a turn 90 degrees aft over pulleys and ran to a quadrant located on the forward side of the wing auxiliary spar. The quadrant actuated a linkage connected to a fitting on the aileron leading edge.

A control from the cockpit actuated trim tabs on both ailerons. A sprocket-drive chain was tied to control cables at the wing leading edge. The cables ran outboard to wing station 7.5 where they made a 90 degree turn aft and ran to the wing auxiliary spar, where they attached to a chain on a sprocket-drive unit mounted on the forward side of the spar. A flexible drive shaft connected the sprocket-drive to an actuator mounted on the aileron spar, which in turn moved the tab.

The rudder pedals drove two links connected to two quadrants in the center section of the fuselage. Control cables connected to the quadrants extended aft through the fuselage guided and supported by pulleys to the control quadrant on the rudder main spar. A continuous system was thus formed to drive the rudder.

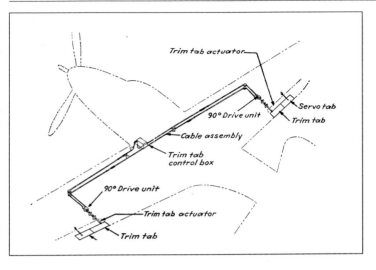

lage. The chain actuated a 90 degree drive unit which connected to the trim tab actuator on the rudder spar aft face via a flexible drive shaft.

ELECTRICAL SYSTEM

The electrical system was a DC single-wire ground return type with conductors shielded and protected by rigid or flexible conduits. The electrical switch controls were mounted to the left of the main instrument panel in the cockpit. The 24 volt battery was mounted in the forward fuselage between the .50 caliber guns under the gun compartment cowl and aft of the reduction gearbox. The battery was drained to a glass bottle and vented to the outside. Standard electrical plugs were used where disconnections were required to remove assemblies. A ground wire was attached to the nose landing gear fork on some models; on others a special static-conducting tire was used for grounding. The main fuse panel, including spares, was on the left side of the nose landing gear well.

Items powered electrically included landing gear retraction and extension, wing flaps, aircraft lights, fuel boost pumps, engine starter, radio gear, and the Curtiss Electric propeller.

To control the rudder trim tab from the cockpit, a sprocket-driven chain ran from the cockpit to a point just aft of the fuselage turn-over beam where it was connected to control cables running aft through the fuselage and connected to a chain in the aft fuse-

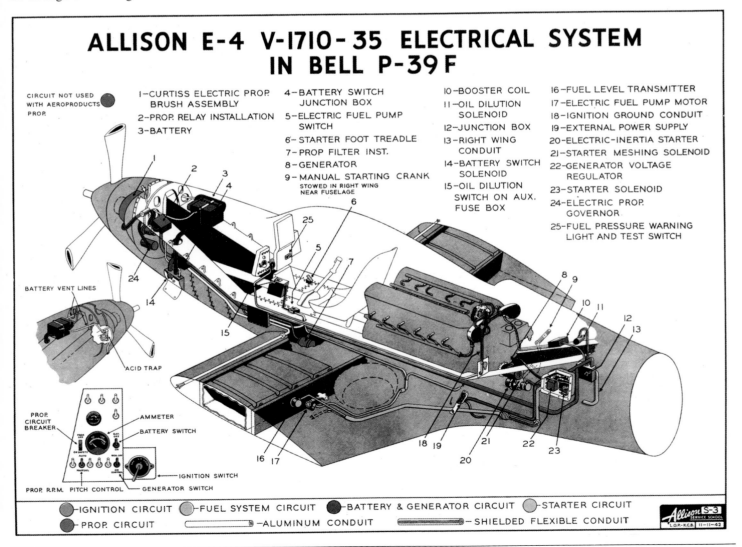

ALLISON E-4 V-1710-35 ELECTRICAL SYSTEM IN BELL P-39F

CIRCUIT NOT USED WITH AEROPRODUCTS PROP.

1 – CURTISS ELECTRIC PROP. BRUSH ASSEMBLY
2 – PROP. RELAY INSTALLATION
3 – BATTERY
4 – BATTERY SWITCH JUNCTION BOX
5 – ELECTRIC FUEL PUMP SWITCH
6 – STARTER FOOT TREADLE
7 – PROP FILTER INST.
8 – GENERATOR
9 – MANUAL STARTING CRANK STOWED IN RIGHT WING NEAR FUSELAGE
10 – BOOSTER COIL
11 – OIL DILUTION SOLENOID
12 – JUNCTION BOX
13 – RIGHT WING CONDUIT
14 – BATTERY SWITCH SOLENOID
15 – OIL DILUTION SWITCH ON AUX. FUSE BOX
16 – FUEL LEVEL TRANSMITTER
17 – ELECTRIC FUEL PUMP MOTOR
18 – IGNITION GROUND CONDUIT
19 – EXTERNAL POWER SUPPLY
20 – ELECTRIC-INERTIA STARTER
21 – STARTER MESHING SOLENOID
22 – GENERATOR VOLTAGE REGULATOR
23 – STARTER SOLENOID
24 – ELECTRIC PROP. GOVERNOR
25 – FUEL PRESSURE WARNING LIGHT AND TEST SWITCH

BATTERY VENT LINES
ACID TRAP
PROP. CIRCUIT BREAKER
AMMETER
BATTERY SWITCH
PROP. R.P.M. PITCH CONTROL
GENERATOR SWITCH
IGNITION SWITCH

⬤ – IGNITION CIRCUIT   ⬤ – FUEL SYSTEM CIRCUIT   ⬤ – BATTERY & GENERATOR CIRCUIT   ⬤ – STARTER CIRCUIT
⬤ – PROP. CIRCUIT   ▭ – ALUMINUM CONDUIT   ▭ – SHIELDED FLEXIBLE CONDUIT

Allison S-3 SERVICE SCHOOL L.O.P.-K.C.B. 11-11-42

An electrical generator was mounted on the engine accessory drive housing. The generator control panel was installed in the left side of the fuselage. The generator relay was operated by a switch on the electrical control panel in the cockpit. A battery-operated booster coil unit was mounted in a shielded box on the inclined deck aft of the engine. The circuit was connected so the coil was energized when the pedal starter switch was depressed forward, bringing the solonoid-operated meshing mechanism on the starter into operation.

A retractable landing light was installed flush with the lower surface of the left wing outer panel. Extension and retraction were controlled by an electric motor.

HYDRAULIC SYSTEM
Except for the main wheel brake system, there were no hydraulics in the aircraft.

PNEUMATIC SYSTEM
A vacuum pump mounted on the rear of the engine supplied the vacuum necessary for some instrument operation. It included a suction line from the instrument panel and an exhaust line to the Pesco oil separator. A relief valve was mounted on the vacuum pump.

COMMUNICATION, NAVIGATION, AND IDENTIFICATION SYSTEMS
The electronics gear varied with model, but typically the following would be carried: SCR-535A radio recognition set with detonator and crash inertia switch, SCR-522A command radio set, and SCR-274N radio.

ARMAMENT PROVISIONS
Provision was made for installation of a 37mm cannon, or alternatively a 20mm cannon on export models, located on the aircraft centerline with barrel projecting through the reduction gearbox and propeller hub. Provision was also made for two .50 caliber M-2 machine guns in the forward fuselage just ahead of the pilot and synchronized to fire through the propeller arc. Provision for wing armament of two .30 caliber machine guns on each side was made on all early models up through N. On the Q models the wing installation was normally replaced with a single external under-wing pod-mounted .50 caliber machine gun on each side, though on some versions all wing armament was deleted.

The cannon and wing guns were manually charged using pull handles in the cockpit. The 37mm cannon was loaded on the ground by pulling the charging handle once and the loading handle once which put a live round in the chamber. If there was a jam in the air, both handles were pulled again. The cockpit handles were directly and mechanically connected to the gun. The charging system for the .30 caliber wing guns consisted of mechanical linkage and cables running out the wing leading edge section and then aft to the gun breeches. The .50 caliber fuselage guns protruded aft into the cockpit and the gun charging levers were directly accessible to the pilot. The guns were charged by pulling the operating handles completely rearward. The .50 caliber nose guns in later models were equipped with flame-suppressor blast tubes. An impulse-type synchronizer was used on these guns, the tubes fabricated from chrome-moly steel and clamped to the gun barrels at twelve inch intervals. Exhaust louvres were used in the gun compartment cowl to evacuate fumes. The .50 caliber wing podded guns in the late models were manually charged from the outside before takeoff. A small door in the pod fairing provided access to the charging handles on the guns.

Guns were fired electrically using solonoid units actuated by two firing switches on the pilot's control stick, one for the cannon as a button on top, and a trigger type on the stick forward section for the machine guns; it would fire all machine guns selected by toggle switches. In the event a gun jammed the others would continue to operate.

The magazine for the 37mm cannon was an oval section endless belt type installed around the front machine gun barrels and contained 30 rounds. An ejection compartment for the links and cases was located between web and outer skin of a longitudinal beam. Each .50 caliber nose gun had a separate ammunition case with 200 rounds capacity. Ejection chutes carried off links and cases. Both chutes deposited their contents into a triangular space between longitudinal beams and outer skin.

For aircraft with .30 caliber guns in the wings, each set of .30s had an ammunition box located outboard of the guns between front and rear spars. The box capacity was 1000 rounds, 700 rounds of which were considered alternate load. Ejection chutes were installed for the wing guns, the links dropping inboard from the respective guns and the cases dropping straight down. Four small doors on each lower wing surface ejected the contents overboard.

The .50 caliber guns under the wings of late models were provided with 300 rounds of amminition per gun.

Provisions were made for carrying a 500 or 600 pound bomb under the fuselage as an alternate to a fuel drop tank. A type B-7 bomb shackle was installed on the lower surface of the wing center section, and included a spring-loaded hook device which released the bomb automatically when the bomb release handle in the cockpit at the left side of the instrument panel was pulled up and aft. An armed/safe lever in the cockpit was used to arm the bomb.

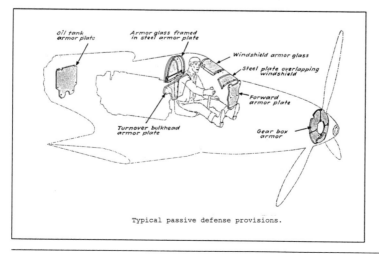

Typical passive defense provisions.

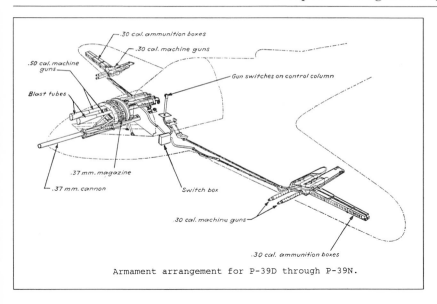

.30 cal. ammunition boxes
.30 cal. machine guns
.50 cal. machine guns
Blast tubes
Gun switches on control column
.37 mm. magazine
.37 mm. cannon
Switch box
.30 cal. machine guns
.30 cal. ammunition boxes

Armament arrangement for P-39D through P-39N.

HEATING/COOLING/VENTILATION

Cockpit heating was provided by two three inch diameter metal tubes which took hot air from directly behind the Prestone radiator and directed it to two ducts on the cabin floor behind the pilot's seat. The hot air ducts extended between the engine and the fuselage longitudinal beams. Cool air was supplied to the cabin by two ducts taking air from the cooling duct just forward of the Prestone radiator. The same ducts that transmitted the hot air also transmitted the cool air. The selection of hot, cold, or mixed air was controlled by two butterfly flaps, one on each duct "Y" at the union of hot and cold air ducts. The flaps were operated by handles at the right of the pilot seat via direct mechanical linkage. Air was exhausted from the cockpit through ducts over the rudder pedal well leading to the cannon and .50 caliber guns. Air supply to the cockpit was constant flow and only the temperature was regulated. The two flexible heater tubes leading into the gun compartment extended upward and joined together at another duct attached to the pan and feed chute assembly of the .50 caliber guns. That duct had two flanged outlets which heated the guns. The forward end of the duct extended downward to the left, tapering out fan-shaped to heat the cannon installation. The air was then drawn forward and expelled overboard via four external louvres.

ICE PROTECTION SYSTEM

Ice protection equipment included a glycol spray spray system for the windshield and a propeller deicing system. Both were supplied from a single glycol tank in the gun compartment of the fuselage. The windshield system included a hand pump on the instrument panel, a nozzle on the windshield above the armor plate, and a deicing rheostat on the instrument panel. Use of the pump sprayed several streams of fluid up on the glass. Propeller deicing equipment (on the Aeroproducts propeller installation) included an electrically-driven pump and filter, a nozzle assembly, a slinger ring on the propeller assembly, and a cockpit switch. Use of the motor-pump unit sent fluid from the glycol tank forward to the slinger ring which splashed it on the blades. There was no other airframe ice protection system.

HOISTING/TOWING/LEVELING

Hard point and other provisions were made to accomplish all of these.

FLOTATION GEAR

No flotation gear was carried.

ARRESTING GEAR

No arresting gear was provided..

PASSIVE DEFENSE SYSTEM

The armoring provisions of the aircraft consisted of seven parts—reduction gearbox armor, cockpit forward bulkhead armor plate, lower windshield armor plate, windshield armor glass, armor plate behind the pilot, turnover bulkhead armor plate, and oil tank armor plate. The armor at the reduction gearbox consisted of five pieces of 5/8 inch homogeneous steel forming a circle just ahead of the gearbox. The forward fume-tight bulkhead armor plate was fastened to the bulkhead forward side, and was a single piece of 5/8 inch thick face-hardened steel plate. A 7mm thick non-magnetic homogeneous piece of armor plate was installed on the fuselage outer surface just forward of, and overlapping, the lower part of the windshield. The forward armor glass was 1 and 1/2 inches thick and was located forward of and above the gun sight support casting and at the top of the transverse windshield frame. The aft armor glass, 2 and 1/2 inches thick, was located in the curve of the fuselage turnover beam just aft of the pilot. It carried a frame of steel armor plate and was held in place by screws and nuts to the turnover beam. The glass allowed pilot vision to the rear areas. Below this and aft of the pilot a body protecting turnover armor plate was located, consisting of two pieces of 1/4 inch thick face-hardened steel plate bolted to the aft face of the turnover bulkhead. A 1/4 inch thick face-hardened steel plate was bolted to the bulkhead just aft of the oil tank to protect it from rear gunfire.

FURNISHINGS

The pilot's seat was a metal bucket type, and was not adjustable. The safety harness, a B-11 Sutton type, was fastened to the seat with a roller mechanism. It was released or locked by a control under the seat. A relief tube was located beneath the right side of the pilot seat, and a first aid kit was mounted on the left hand cabin door. A signal light was placed on the right hand door, and a flashlight was clamped at the left side of the cabin.

USEFUL LOAD SUBSYSTEMS
GUNS, BOMBS, AND ROCKETS
As noted previously, early aircraft carried one 37mm or 20mm cannon, two .50 caliber machine guns, and four .30 caliber machine guns. Late models had a cannon and four .50 caliber machine guns. All production models could carry a 500 or a 600 pound bomb. No rockets were carried on any model.

GUN SIGHT/GUN CAMERA
An electrically operated gun sight controlled by a switch panel rheostat was located above the main instrument panel in line with the pilot's eyes. No gun camera was installed.

PYROTECHNICS
Some models of the Airacobra, including the P-39D-2 and the P-400, carried a signal pistol with several rounds in the cockpit.

PHOTOGRAPHIC EQUIPMENT
No photo equipment was carried on standard factory models. Some aircraft were modified in the field to carry cameras in the fuselage.

OXYGEN SYSTEM
A low pressure oxygen system was installed using anywhere from one to four D-2 type bottles with an A-12 demand regulator. Oxygen bottles were located in the armament compartment in the fuselage forward section. Additional bottles could be located in the leading edge section of the wing.

A different higher pressure system was installed in the P-400 export version.

REFERENCES, P-39

1. The P-39 in Action, Ernie McDowell
2. Operation Pinball, Ivan Hickman, Motorbooks International
3. Airplane Engine Performance Data, Allison Engineering Co. Spec.130-D April 19, 1940.
4. Airplane Engine Performance Data, Allison Engineering Co. Report 14-943-503, Oct.23, 1942.
5. Airplane Engine Performance Data, Allison Engineering Co. Spec.130-E Oct. 1, 1941
6. Tactical Planning Characteristics and Performance Chart, P-39, Aug.21, 1944
7. Tactical Planning Characteristics and Performance Chart, P-39, June 29, 1945.
8. NACA Report ACR, Oct. 1940.
9. Army Aircraft Characteristics, Report No. TSEST-A2, Revised Dec.1947 AMC Flight Data Branch, Wright Air Development Center.
10. Nanette, Edwards Park, W.W. Norton & Co. NY,NY.
11. Airacobra in Retrospect, Birch J. Matthews, TRW Systems Group.
12. Aircraft Designers Data Book, Neville, McGraw-Hill, NY, 1951.
13. USAAF Technical Order 01-11OFB-2, P-39
14. Report on First Action Against Japanese by P-39 Type Airplane, May 4, 1942, Hdqtrs, 3rd Fighter Command, Townsville, Queensland, Austr.
15. Report on Combat Qualities of P-39 and P-40 airplanes, May 11, 1942 Hdqtrs, Pursuit Section, N.E.Area, Townsville, Queensland, Australia.
16. Bell Aircraft Corp. Report 14-945-001-2, June 1,1942, P-39D-2 Detail Specification
17. Bell Aircraft Corp. Report 14-942-001, July 28, 1941, Actual Weight and Balance, Model 14, Aircraft AH-621.
18. NACA Wartime Report MR, Sept.1945, Measurements of the Flying Qualities of a Bell P-39D-1 Airplane.
19. NACA Advance Confidential Report (ACR)5D04
20. Pilot's Flight Operating Instructions for Army Model P-39Q-1 Airplane.
21. Historical Aviation Album, Vol.II, Paul R. Matt Temple City, Cal.1965
22. To Fly and Fight, Col.Clarence Anderson with Joseph Hamelin, St. Martins Press, NY 1990.
23. The P-38, The P-39, and The F4U-, Paul S. Bechtel, Aerospace Historian, Winter, Dec. 1986.
24. Air Classics Magazine, Mar.1966, *How the Air Corps Shot Down Bell's Airacobra*, Tice.
25. *Roosevelt and Hopkins*, by Robert E.Sherwood, Harper and Brothers, NY.1948
26. *Yeager*, Gen. Chuck Yeager and Leo Janos, Bantom Books Inc.1985
27. *Airacobra Advantage, The Flying Cannon*, by Rick Mitchell, Pictorial Histories Publishing Co. Missoula, Montana
28. *The Cactus Air Force*, Thomas G. Miller Jr. Harper and Rowe New York, 1969.
29. *Pacific Sweep*, by William N. Hess, Doubleday & Co. Garden City New York, 1974

THE P-40

The many versions of the P-40, variously Tomahawks, Kittihawks, and Warhawks, along with quantities of each manufactured, are set down in Table 28 . The P-40 types altogether constituted over 13 percent of America's Hundred Thousand. Aside from the XP-40 (a modified P-36 airplane), the rest of the P-40s separate into company models H81 and H87. The H81 aircraft covered P-40, P-40B, P-40C, P-40G, and export Tomahawks. The domestic USAAF H81 versions had no popular name. Later H87 types started with the P-40D and covered all subsequent machines. The designs were quite different and could be characterized as wholly different aircraft. H81 aircraft were distinguished by three projections on the upper cowl just behind the propeller, two being .50 caliber gun blast tube fairings and the other a central carburetor air intake with circular inlet. The lower nose scoop of H81 aircraft was shallower and wider than H87s which had a deep chin scoop. If an H87 was Allison-powered a flattened carburetor scoop perched atop the upper cowl just behind the propeller; if the upper cowl line was smooth not interrupted by a scoop the H87 was Merlin-powered. H87 types were broken into short and long fuselage versions, the short fuselage airplanes having incurred some flying quality difficulties; the 20 inch longer fuselage and revised tail arrangement was designed to alleviate these. The other outwardly apparent change in H87 type P-40s came early in the P-40N series. To improve aft visibility the rear fuselage deck was cut down and extra transparent area was

TABLE 28
P-40 MODEL DESIGNATION, QUANTITIES, AND DELIVERY DATES

COMPANY DESIGNATION	US MILITARY DESIGNATION	EXPORT DESIGNATION	NO. OF AIRCRAFT	FIRST DELIVERY	NOTES
H75P	XP-40	—	(1)	OCT.'38	10TH P-36 CONVERTED
H81	P-40	—	200	JUN.'40	FIRST PROD. AIRCRAFT
H81	P-40A	—	(1)	MAR.'42	P-40 40-326 TO RECONN.
H81A-1	—	TOMAHAWK I		SEP.'40	FRENCH,NO WG.GUNS,TO UK.
H81A-1	—	TOMAHAWK IA	140	SEP.'40	UK,WING GUNS,ARMY CO-OP.
H81A-1	—	TOMAHAWK IB		SEP.'40	UK, FOUR WING GUNS.
H81B	P-40B	—	131	JAN.'41	2 WG.GUNS,ARMOR,SS TANKS
H81A-2	—	TOMAHAWK IIA	110	OCT.'40	EXPORT VERSION OF P-40B.
H81B	P-40C	—	193	MAR.'41	US,4 WG.GUNS, DROP TANK.
H81A-3	—	TOMAHAWK IIB	930	MAY,'41	EXPORT VERSION OF P-40C.
H81A-G	P-40G	—	44	AUG,'41	P-40,H81A-2 4 GUN WINGS.
H87A-2	P-40D	—	22	JUL,'41	NEW CONFIG.4WG GUNS ONLY
H87A-2		KITTIHAWK I	20	AUG,'41	EXPORT VERSION OF P-40D.
H87A-3	—	KITTIHAWK I	540	'41	UK DIRECT BUY, 6 WG GUN.
H87B-2	P-40E	—	820	AUG,'41	USAAF 6 GUN VERSION.
H87A-4	P-40E-1	KITTIHAWK IA	1500	DEC,'41	LEND-LEASE P-40E
H87B-2	P-40ES	—	(2)		2 SEAT E,DIR. FR.FACTORY
H87B-3	XP-40F	WARHAWK	(1)	NOV,'41	CONV. D, MERLIN ENGINE.
H87B-3	YP-40F	WARHAWK	(1)		3RD.P-40F, COOL.SYS.CHG.
H87B-3	P-40F	WARHAWK	1311	JAN,'42	FIRST 699 SHORT FUSELAGE
H87B-3	—	KITTIHAWK II	250		EXPORT P-40F.
	P-40K-1,-5	WARHAWK	800	MAY,'42	SHORT FUS.600K-1,200K-5.
	P-40K-10,-15	WARHAWK	500	OCT,'42	LONG FUS.335K-10,165K-15
	XP-40K	WARHAWK	(1)		PROD.K-10, COOLING MODS.
87B-3	P-40L-1,-20	WARHAWK	600	JAN,'43	STRIPPED,MERLIN,SHT/LG F
	—	KITTIHAWK III	21		RAF VERSION OF P-40K.
87B-3	—	KITTIHAWK II	100		RAF VERSION OF P-40L.
	P-40M-1,-10	WARHAWK	5	NOV,'42	USAAF, ALLISON ENGINE.
	—	KITTIHAWK III	595		LEND-LEASE M TO UK, 6GUN
87V	P-40N-1	WARH.& KITTI. IV	400	MAR,'43	FASTEST,LIGHT, LESS FUEL
87W	P-40N-5	WARHAWK	1100	MAY,'43	AFT WINDOW CHANGE.
	P-40N-10	WARHAWK	100	AUG,'43	WINTERIZED
	P-40N-15	WARHAWK	377	SEP,'43	SOME -16 RECONN. MODELS.
	P-40N-20	WARHAWK	1523	SEP,'43	AUTOMATIC ENG. CONTROLS.
	P-40N-25	WARHAWK	499	JAN,'44	3 to 2-PLACE -26
	P-40N-30	WARHAWK	500	APR,'44	22 A/C to 2-PLACE -31
	P-40N-35	WARHAWK	500	JUL,'44	
	P-40N-40	WARHAWK	216	OCT,'44	CUT BACK FROM 1000 ORDER
	TP-40N	WARHAWK	(-)		CONVERTED 2-PL. N'S
87W	XP-40N	WARHAWK	(1)	P-40N	WITH BUBBLE CANOPY
87X	XP-40Q	WARHAWK	(3)		REVISED DESIGN, BUBBLE
	P-40R-1	WARHAWK	(70)		SHORT-FUS. F TO ALLISON.
	P-40R-2	WARHAWK	(53)		P-40L CONV. TO ALLISON.

SEE ALSO TABLE 29 ON FOLLOWING PAGE FOR EXPORT DISTRIBUTIONS

TABLE 29
P-40 EXPORT DISTRIBUTIONS

TOMAHAWK IIA—23 to RUSSIA, 1 TO CANADA.

P-40C—38 TO RUSSIA, 10 TO RAF.

TOMAHAWK IIB— 100 TO AVG IN CHINA, 146 TO RUSSIA, 15 TO
TURKEY, A FEW
TO EGYPT, 31 LOST AT SEA.
P-40G—21 TO RUSSIA

H87A-3/KITTIHAWK I— 72 TO CANADA, 6 TO RUSSIA,
17 TO TURKEY.

P-40E-1/KITTIHAWK IA— (—) TO RUSSIA, 163 TO AUSTRALIA,
12 TO CANADA,
117 TO NEW ZEALAND.
KITTIHAWK II— NONE TO UK, 100 TO RUSSIA, 25 TO FREE
FRENCH IN NORTH
AFRICA, (—) LOST AT SEA, 81 BACK TO U.S. IN
NORTH AFRICA, 1 TO NEW ZEALAND
P-40N-40—586 TO UK, (—) TO RUSSIA, (—) TO DUTCH.

added aft of the pilot. The last of the line, the XP-40Q test airplanes, had modifications quite different from all the rest, and never
entered production.

P-40 types were exported to US allies, mostly for British Commonwealth and Russian air forces as shown in Table 29. Perhaps
the most famous were the 100 H81 Tomahawks for China sent to
equip an American Volunteer Group known as the Flying Tigers.

Physical data for the P-40 in Table 30 indicates the airplane
was slightly larger than the P-39.

The fuel capacities of various P-40 models are shown in Table
31. The first production P-40 had a 180 gallon capacity in unprotected tanks, one of which was in the fuselage just aft of the cockpit. The rest of the fuel was carried in inboard wing tanks. Later
H81 airplanes had less internal fuel because protected tanks were
incorporated in the same size wing and fuselage spaces. The P-40C
compensated a bit by adding a 52 gallon centerline external drop
tank. The H87 high production models stabilized somewhat on an
internal capacity of 148 to 161 gallons, an approximate one third
increase over that of the P-39. Exceptions were the P-40L and the
P-40N-1 which were stripped down to save weight. As can be seen,
late model P-40 versions could carry considerably more fuel in external drop tanks, this in common with most US fighters.

A three view drawing shows the H81 arrangement as a conventional low wing monoplane with tail wheel, and the nose scoop
and gun fairings mentioned earlier. Main landing gear wheels turned
and laid flat in underwing pockets upon retraction. Other three

TABLE 30
P-40 PHYSICAL DATA

WING SPAN	37'3.5"	FLAP MAXIMUM DEFLECTION	45 DEGREES
LENGTH(XP-40 TO P-40C)	31'8 7/16"	MAX. FUSELAGE WIDTH(P-40B/C/G)	39.6"
LENGTH(D/E/E-1)	31'8.5"	MAX. FUSELAGE WIDTH(P-40F)	3.1'
LENGTH (P-40F EARLY)	31'7.7"	MAX. FUSELAGE DEPTH(P-40B/C/G)	65.7"
LENGTH (P-40F LATE)	33'4"	MAX. FUSELAGE DEPTH(P-40F)	4.8'
LENGTH (P-40L/N-25)	33.22'	MAX. FUSELAGE WIDTH(P-40K)	38.5"
LENGTH (P-40M)	31.67'	MAX. FUSELAGE DEPTH(P-40K)	69'11/16
HEIGHT	12'4"	MAIN WHEEL TIRE SIZE	30"
LANDING GEAR TREAD	8'2.5"	AUXILIARY WHEEL TIRE SIZE	12.5"
PROPELLER DIAMETER	11'0"	MAIN GEAR SHOCK STRUT TRAVEL	7.0"
HORIZ. TAIL SPAN		AUX. GEAR SHOCK STRUT TRAVEL	8 3/4"
GROSS WING AREA	236 SQ.FT.	TOTAL HORIZ. TAIL AREA	48.0 SQ.FT.
NET WING AREA	217.6 SQ. FT.	STABILIZER INCIDENCE	2.0 DEGREES.
WING ROOT CHORD	108"	STAB.AREA(INC.3.56FUS.)	30.86SQ.FT.
WING TIP CHORD	54" (WING STA.197")	ELEV.AREA(INC.BAL.& TAB)	17.44SQ.FT.
WING ASPECT RATIO	5.89	ELEV. BALANCE AREA	3.8 SQ.FT.
WING TAPER RATIO	2.31:1	ELEVATOR TAB SPAN	22 1/8"
WING MEAN AERO.CHORD	81.6"	ELEVATOR TAB CHORD	5.01"
WING ROOT AIRFOIL NACA	2215	ELEV. TAB AREA (BOTH)	1.68 SQ.FT.
ROOT AIRFOIL t/c	15%	ELEVATOR MOVEMENT	30DEG.UP;20DEG.DN.
WING TIP AIRFOIL NACA	2209	ELEV. TAB MOVEMENT	3DEG.UP;26DEG.DN.
TIP AIRFOIL	t/c 9%	TOT.VERT.TAIL AREA	20.74(LATER21.74)
WING INCIDENCE(ROOT/TIP)	BOTH 1DEG.	VERTICAL FIN OFFSET	1.5 DEG. LEFT.
WING DIHEDRAL	6 DEG.	VERTICAL FIN AREA	7.0 SQ.FT.
WING L.E. SWEEP	1DEG.19MIN.	RUDDER AREA(INC.TAB&BAL>)	13.74SQ.FT.
TOTAL AILERON AREA(W BAL)	18.3SQ.FT.	RUDDER BALANCE AREA	1.95 SQ.FT.
AIL.BAL.AREA(BOTH)	4.24 SQ.FT.	RUDDER TAB HEIGHT	14.59"
AILERON AREA(AFT H/L)	11.94 SQ.FT.	RUDDER TAB CHORD	5.43"
AIL.MOVE.(P-40B/C/G)	18.8UP;10.7DN.	RUDDER TAB AREA	0.53 SQ.FT.
AIL.MOVE.(P-40E/F/K)	18>7UP;10.6DN.	RUDDER MOVEMENT	30DEG.LEFT;30DEG.RT.
AILERON TAB AREA	30.59 SQ.IN.	AIL. TAB MOVE.	20DEG.UP; 20DEG.DN.

TABLE 31
P-40 FUEL CAPACITIES
(US GALLONS)

MODEL	MAXIMUM INTERNAL FUEL	MAXIMUM EXTERNAL FUEL
XP-40	158	—
P-40	180	—
P-40B	160	—
P-40C	135	52
P-40D	148	52
P-40E,E-1	148-9	52
P-40F	157	170
P-40G	148	—
P-40K	157	170
P-40L	120	170
P-40M	157	170
P-40N-1	120	170
P-40N-5,-15	161	450
P-40N-20,-30	161	450
P-40N-35,-40	161	450

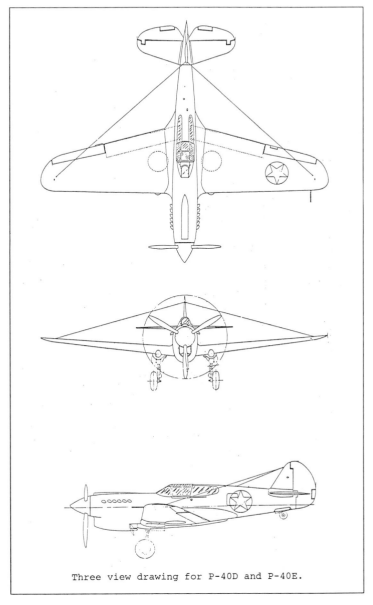

Three view drawing for P-40D and P-40E.

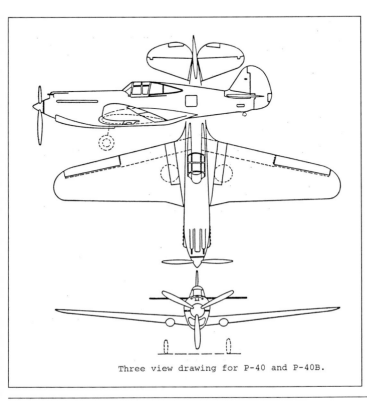

Three view drawing for P-40 and P-40B.

views show the general arrangement of a short fuselage Model 87, the first an

Allison-powered airplane with upper nose carburetor scoop, and then a Merlin-powered version with smooth upper cowl. Here the carburetor scoop was incorporated within the deep chin scoop because the Merlin had an updraft carburetor. The last P-40 three view drawing shows a long fuselage P-40N with a revised cut-down aft deck and squared-off aft Plexiglas covering. All P-40s after the H81 models had wing machine guns only, usually six, but sometimes four .50 caliber weapons.

The inboard profiles show typical P-40 internal arrangements. Forward located engine and liquid cooled powerplant components were conventional and closely grouped. The fuselage fuel tank had to be located aft of the cockpit and of the wing quarter chord line, so fuel burn-off from this tank caused some forward movement of the aircraft center of gravity. The P-40 layout had evolved over a

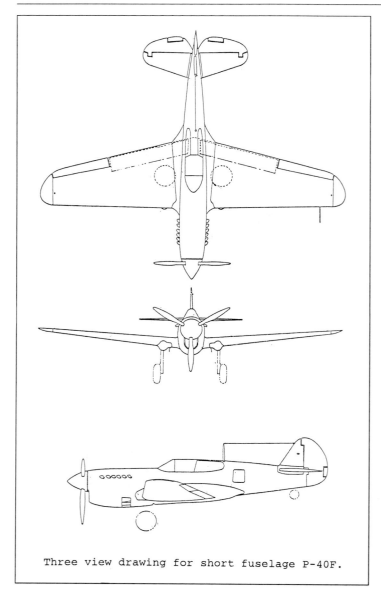

Three view drawing for short fuselage P-40F.

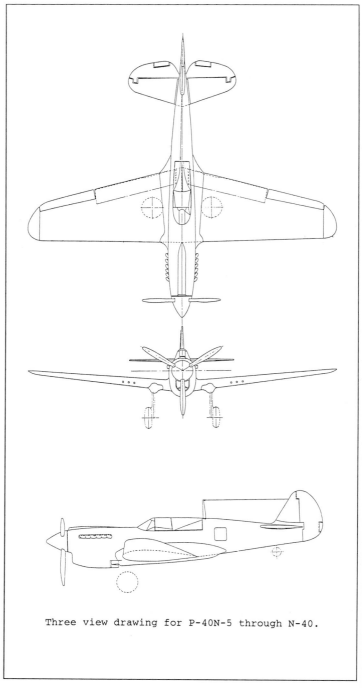

Three view drawing for P-40N-5 through N-40.

considerable period of time (since 1935), and there were no unconventional aspects to the design, a situation quite opposite to that of the P-38 and the P-39. An airplane diagram for a P-40N is also displayed as is a cutaway drawing of an early P-40. Table 32 gives engine rated power data for the various Allison engine models employed and for the Packard Merlin used in the P-40F and P-40L airplane versions. The Allison models in all production aircraft had single stage single speed superchargers similar to those of the P-39. Engine powers increased somewhat in successive P-40 models, but hardly really significantly except with advent of a WAR EMERGENCY/COMBAT power setting. Like the P-39, the P-40 was a middle altitude fighter at best. The Merlin installation in two of the P-40 versions was not the same Merlin fitted into the late P-51 fighters. It had a single stage two speed supercharger as in the Hawker Hurricane, not the two stage supercharger model in the P-51B/C/D and the Supermarine Spitfire IX. As shown in the table, basic ratings of the P-40F/P-40L Merlin were not much different

from the Allison models, but the two stage feature of the Merlin supercharger conferred better altitude performance. This fact is seen in Graph 25 where the powers of Allison and Merlin engines are charted against altitude. The Allison peaked at 1150 MILITARY horsepower at 12000 feet altitude, then fell of sharply. The Merlin first peaked at 1240 horsepower at 10800 feet and started to fall off with increasing altitude, but shifting the supercharger impeller drive gearing to provide higher blower rotational speed yielded another power peak at just over 18000 feet before falling off again. At 18000 feet the Merlin engine in the P-40 delivered almost 200 more horse-

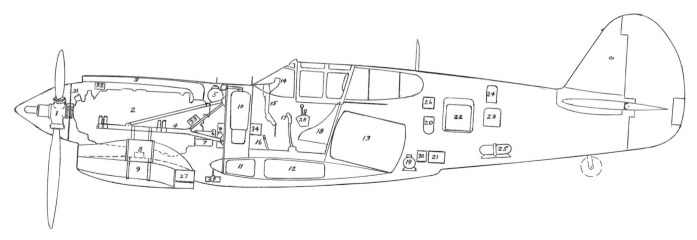

1. Curtiss Electric propeller
2. Allison V-1710 engine
3. Carburetor air intake
4. Engine mount
5. Coolant expansion tank
6. Electric generator
7. Engine starter
8. Coolant radiator (2)
9. Oil cooling radiator
10. Oil tank
11. Wing reserve fuel tank
12. Wing main fuel tank
13. Fuselage fuel tank
14. Gunsight
15. Instrument panel
16. Rudder pedals
17. Pilot's control stick

18. Pilot's seat
19. Electric hydraulic pump
20. Hydraulic fluid tank
21. Battery
22. Radio
23. Radio
24. Hydraulic reserve tank
25. Oxygen bottle
26. Data case
27. Cooling air exit gills
28. Throttle quadrant
29. Fuel selector valve
30. Battery junction box
31. Propeller governor
32. Propeller relay box
33. Booster coil
34. Electrical junction boxes

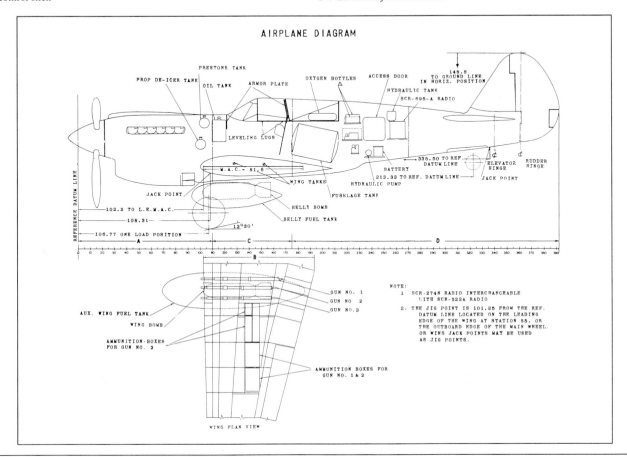

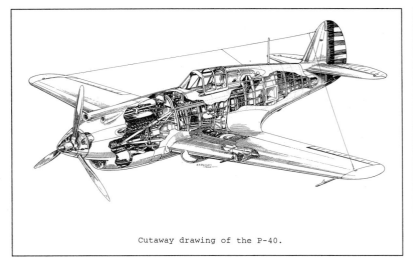

Cutaway drawing of the P-40.

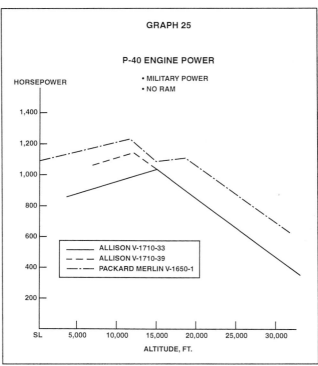

TABLE 32
P-40 ENGINE DATA

AIRCRAFT	ENG.MODEL	RATING	HP	RPM	ALT'	MP"HG.	SUPERCHARGER
XP-40	V-1710-19/C-13	T.O.	1050		S.L.		1-STAGE, 1-SPEED
		MIL.	1150		10000		
		NORMAL	1000		10000		
P-40C/G	V-1710-33/C-15	T.O.	1040	2800	S.L.	44.2	1-STAGE, 1-SPEED
P-40/B	(GR=0.5:1)	MIL.	1040	3000	15000	40.0	
		NORMAL	930	2600	15000	35.3	
P-40D/E	V-1710-39/F3R	T.O.	1150	3000	S.L.	46.2	1-STAGE, 1-SPEED
P-40E-1	(GR=0.5:1)	MIL.	1150	3000	12000		
		NORMAL	1000	2600	11000	38.7	
P-40F/L	V-1650-1	T.O.	1300	3000	S.L.	54.3	1-STAGE, 2-SPEED
	(GR=.447:1)	MIL.	1240	3000	11800	48.2	
		NORMAL	1080	2650	9500	44.2	
P-40K	V-1710-73/F4R	T.O.	1325	3000	S.L.		1-STAGE, 1-SPEED
		WAR EMERG.	1550	3000	S.L.(RAMMED)		
		MIL.	1150	3000	11800		
		NORMAL	1000	2600	11000		
P-40M/N-1	V-1710-81/F20R	T.O.	1200	3000	S.L.		1-STAGE, 1-SPEED
N-20/-35	V-1710-99/F26R	W.E.	1360	3000	S.L.(RAMMED)		
P-40N-40	V-1710-115/F31R	MIL	1125	3000	14600-15500		
		NORMAL	1000	2600	13800-14000		
XP-40Q	V-1710-121	T.O.	1425	3000	S.L.		TWO STAGE
		WAR EMERG.	1800	3000	S.L.(RAMMED)		
		MILITARY	1100	3000	25000		
		NORMAL	1000		21000		

NOTE: For the V-1710-39 engine one source gives: Takeoff-1100 HP at 3000RPM at SL at 42.9 "MP; Military-1090 HP at 13200 ft. at 3000RPM at 38.9 HG.; Normal-960 HP at 12000ft. at 2600 RPM at 35.0" HG.

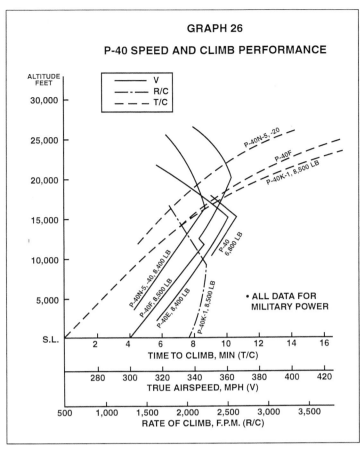

GRAPH 26

P-40 SPEED AND CLIMB PERFORMANCE

overall the speed of these later models was almost 20 mph slower. It is not clear why this speed difference came about. Speeds of P-40 models at COMBAT power were not available.

Graph 26 also shows climb data. Climb rate for an Allison powered P-40K at MILITARY power is typical, starting at just over 2000 feet per minute at sea level, increasing to about 2250 FPM at 9000 feet, and dropping off at the higher altitudes to 1800 FPM at 15000 feet. Climb times are shown as just under five minutes to 10000 feet and 11.5 to 12.5 minutes to 20000 feet, with the better Merlin power at altitude providing the P-40F with the better performance.

P-40 "yardstick" ranges are shown in the chart of Graph 27 for the case of cruising at 10000 feet with no wind and no reserve fuel allowance. It is also noted there is no fuel allocation for takeoff, climbout, combat, or descent, which is why it was called "yardstick" range. It is really practical only for comparison with "yardstick" ranges of other aircraft types. The curves show range versus aircraft weight, the latter varying primarily with amount of fuel initially aboard. On this basis the curve shows P-40 range on internal fuel alone varied between 650 and 750 miles. With maximum internal fuel plus external drop tank fuel aboard, and at a 10000 pound takeoff weight, most P-40s could achieve a range of 1400 to 1500 miles. The final P-40N model, at an extreme takeoff weight of 11400 pounds, corresponding to a 611 gallon fuel load, could make a "yardstick" range of 2500 miles. In the more practical situation of a P-40 with a 75 gallon drop tank giving total takeoff fuel of 232 gallons, combat radius could be about 300 miles.

Various estimates of P-40 takeoff performance are depicted in the curves of Graph 28. There is considerable variation in the data, but at normal takeoff gross weights of the order 8400 to 8600 pounds the takeoff ground run ate up about 1500 to 1750 feet on a dry surface with no wind. An exception appeared to be the Merlin pow-

power than the Allison. Production demands on Packard for newer model Merlins with more supercharging soon cut the P-40 out of the Merlin engine picture, and Allison engines powered all later P-40 types.

The curves of Graph 26 show the speed and climb capability of P-40 models from sea level to 25000 feet. The original pre-war plain P-40 (H81) was fastest of all with a MILITARY power high speed of just over 365 mph at 15000 feet, partly because it was the lightest version at just over 6800 pounds normal gross weight. The first H87 high production model (P-40E) speed-altitude performance is indicated as five miles per hour slower at 15000 feet at a much higher gross weight of 8400 pounds. High speed attainable with the P-40E fell off both above and below the 15000 foot level as shown on the curve. It was the old story, high speed increased, due to decreasing air density, up to where engine power dropped off drastically. The curve of high speed for the Merlin powered P-40F is different, as seen in the graph. From a sea level speed of just 300 mph the capability steadily increased up to 11500 feet and then started to drop off. With the supercharger impeller switched to higher RPM, airplane speed capability again increased up to 20000 feet where it peaked at almost 365 mph before starting to drop off. It can be seen the P-40F was over 30 mph faster than the P-40E at 20000 feet. The late P-40 models of the N-5 to N-40 series had high speed characteristics as shown on the curve. This speed-altitude curve was shaped like that of the earlier Allison powered models. The altitude for peak speed performance was slightly higher, though

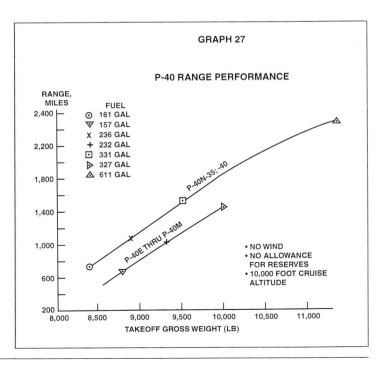

GRAPH 27

P-40 RANGE PERFORMANCE

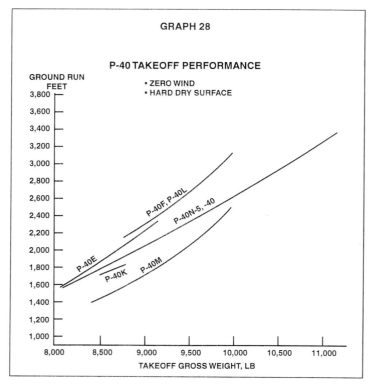

GRAPH 28

P-40 TAKEOFF PERFORMANCE

• ZERO WIND
• HARD DRY SURFACE

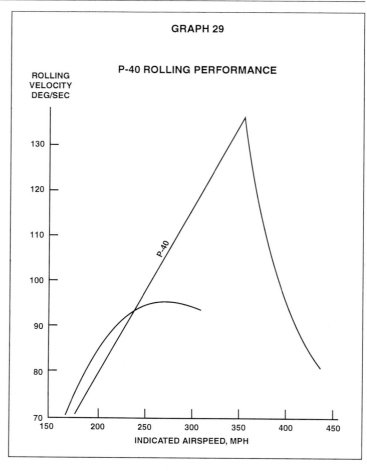

GRAPH 29

P-40 ROLLING PERFORMANCE

TABLE 33
P-40 EMPTY AND BASIC WEIGHTS (LB.)

MODEL	P-40 (#5)	P-40B (#11)	P-40C (#1)
GROUP			
WING	1003	1022	1002
TAIL	142	125	125
FUSELAGE	387	420	420
LANDING GEAR	628	649	649
ENGINE SECTION	293	298	298
ENGINE	1345	1352	1357
ENGINE ACCESS.	114	113.8	114
ENGINE CONTROLS	22	21.4	21
PROPELLER	342	377	337
STARTING	42	46	46
COOLING	291.5	291.5	292
LUBRICATION	59.5	62.3	62
FUEL SYSTEM	171	253.4	420
INSTRUMENTS	48	38.7	38.7
SURFACE CONTROLS	100	104.5	104.5
HYDRAULIC	—	—	—
ELECTRICAL	193	233.4	233.4
COMMUNICATION	71	71	71
ARMAMENT PROV.	—	—	—
FURNISHINGS	115	137	137
EMPTY WEIGHT	5367	5615	5767
TRAPPED OIL	38	38	38
TRAPPED FUEL	—	—	—
CAL.30 GUN INSTL.	47.2 (2)	94.4 (4)	94.4 (4)
CAL.50 GUN INSTL.	150.5 (2)	150.5 (2)	146.9 (2)
GUNSIGHT	2.4	3.5	3.5
ARMOR/BP GLASS	—	93	93
OXYGEN EQUIP'T.	20	—	—
BASIC WEIGHT	5625.1	5990.8	6142.8

ered airplanes at higher takeoff weights which took well over 2000 feet of ground run.

Roll performance of the P-40 series was good. In the curves as shown on Graph 29 data is presented for a pre-war plain P-40 (H81) and a later Merlin powered P-40F. The peak of the typical inverted vee for the P-40 shows 135 degrees per second roll capability at 360 mph IAS (a 2.7 second full roll). This was truly fine performance for the time, noteable not only for the peak rate, but for the high speed at which it was attained. The curve for the P-40F, with greatest rate of 95 degrees per second (a 3.8 second roll) at a lower speed, is more conservative. The reason for the difference is unknown, but World War Two pilots familiar with the P-40 have agreed its rolling capability was very good.

Table 33 gives actual empty and basic weights of some H81 series P-40s, the plain P-40, P-40B, and the P-40C. Actual weights of individual airplanes varied, but those given are typical. As the design progressed weights increased, and group weights can be tracked to see the sources of these increases. A major increase in empty weight resulted from fuel system increases, mostly in changes to protected tanks. Basic weight increases came from two extra .30 caliber machine guns and the installation of armor. A basic weight jump of over 500 pounds was involved.

In Table 34 typical alternate loads for H81 models P-40, P-40B, and P-40C are depicted. The continued increase in gross weight can be noted, gross weights with maximum fuel going up from about

TABLE 34
TYPICAL P-40 ALTERNATE LOADS

A/C & MISSION	P-40 NORMAL	P-40 MAX.FUEL	P-40B NORMAL	P-40B MAX.FUEL	P-40C NORMAL	P-40C MAX.FUEL
PILOT	200	200	200	200	200	200
USEABLE OIL	97	97	86	86	86	86
CAL.30 AMMO.	65	65	127.4	127.4	127.4	127.4
CAL.50 AMMO.	100	100	228	228	228	228
BOMB INSTLN.	—	—	—	—	—	—
OTHER EQUIP.	—	—	—	44	—	44
DROP TANK	—	—	—	—	—	54
EXTERNAL FUEL	—	—	—	—	—	312
INT.FUEL WG.FR.	240	240	240	240	204	204
INT.FUEL WG.AFT	366	366	366	366	312	312
INT.FUEL,FUSE.	114	480	114	342	204	303
TOT.DISPOSE.LD.	1182	1548	1361.4	1633.4	1361.4	1870.4
GROSS WEIGHT	6807.1	7173.1	7352.2	7624.2	7504.2	8013.2
USEFUL LOAD	1440.1	1806.1	1737.2	2009.2	1737.2	2246.2

Note: The 44 pounds of OTHER EQUIPMENT noted above consisted of two M8 flares at 33 pounds and a mooring kit of 11 pounds.

TABLE 35
P-40 EMPTY AND BASIC WEIGHTS (LB.)

MODEL	P-40E	P-40F	P-40K	P-40L	P-40M	P-40N-25
A/C NUMBER	29	400	700	66	300	3901
GROUP						
WING	1126	1132	1120	1126	1122	1131
TAIL	129	154	129	152	131	150
FUSELAGE	449	418	435	437	434	424
LANDING GEAR	695	552	545	549	548	488
ENGINE SECTION	345	349	349	350	345	335
ENGINE	1307	1518	1324	1523	1337	1340
ENG.ACCESSORIES	106	114	73	60	81	92
ENGINE CONTROLS	26	8	36	34	35	29
PROPELLER	383	386	418	418	418	417
STARTING	43	34	45	8	46	45
COOLING	294	306	294	305	294	235
LUBRICATION	61	64	116	116	117	92
FUEL SYSTEM	425	437	425	322	428	366
INSTRUMENTS	41	40	41	41	40	37
SURFACE CONTROLS	101	98	97	100	98	93
HYDRAULIC	—	200	162	169	164	150
ELECTRICAL	229	240	241	237	236	203
ARMAMENT PROV.	—	328	313	321	320	297
FURNISHINGS	235	54	74	60	58	59
COMMUNICATION	74	134	130	157	134	223
EMPTY WEIGHT	6069	6576	6367	6485	6386	6206
TRAPPED OIL	38	38	38	37	38	37
TRAPPED FUEL	—	—	—	—	—	—
CAL.50 GUN INST.	479.9	475	470.9	313.7	470.9	467
GUNSIGHT	4.1	(ABOVE)	4.1	4.3	4.1	7.0
ARMOR/BP GLASS	111	(IN E.W.)	(IN E.W.)	(IN E.W.)	(IN E.W.)	(IN E.W.)
PYROTECHNICS	—	—	—	—	—	—
OXYGEN EQUIP'T.	—	—	—	—	—	—
BASIC WEIGHT	6702	7089	6880	6840	6899	6717

NOTE: The weight format was changed to put the armor weight into the ARMAMENT PROVISIONS category in EMPTY WEIGHT.

TABLE 36
P-40 DISPOSEABLE LOADS, GROSS WEIGHTS, AND USEFUL LOADS (LB.)
MAXIMUM INTERNAL FUEL AND AMMUNITION

MODEL	P-40E	P-40F	P-40K	P-40L	P-40M	P-40N-25
PILOT	180	180	180	180	180	200
USEABLE OIL	97	98	97	98	97	60
CAL.50 AMMO.	423	423	423	282	423	423
INTERNAL FUEL	888	888	942	720	942	954
TOT.DISP.LOAD	1588	1589	1642	1280	1642	1637
GROSS WEIGHT	8290	8678	8522	8120	8541	8354
USEFUL LOAD	2221	2102	2155	1635	2155	2148

NOTE: The following weights were added for a 52 gallon fuselage centerline drop tank installation:

Additional fuel piping _____ 0.5 lb.
Fuel tank rack _____ 5.0 (later reduced to 3.1 on N-25)
Tank sway braces _____ 8.6
Belly tank _____ 40.0
Fuel in tank (52 gallons) _____ 312.0

TOTAL _____ 366.1 lb.

Add 15.4 pounds for wing bomb provisions.

The P-40E above had an empty weight 35 pounds over guarantee.
The P-40F above had an empty weight 109 pounds over guarantee.

7200 to 8000 pounds, an 800 pound increase. There were increases in the amount of ammunition, and a drop tank was added in the P-40C version.

Table 35 shows actual empty and basic weights for sample H87 series models of the P-40 going from E to N versions. These are specific airplanes taken from production and weighed, with individual aircraft numbers specified. After an initial empty weight increase of 300 to 800 pounds, the empty weight of succeeding models stabilized in the 6100 to 6400 pound range with the exception that Merlin powered F and L versions were heavier; the Merlin engine alone being about 200 pounds heavier than the Allison. Areas of weight increases and some of weight savings can be seen in looking through the different models. Note that oxygen equipment had to be added as extra optional equipment at a weight penalty.

The figures of Table 36 give a view of H87 series aircraft loaded with maximum internal fuel and ammunition for comparison. Gross weights under this loading condition run from a minimum of 8120 pounds for the P-40L (the "stripped Gypsy Rose Lee" version) to a high figure of 8678 pounds for the P-40F. Note the "stripping" of the L was done mainly in fuel, guns, and ammunition, hardly a very useful move for a combat aircraft. Some of the airplanes noted were over or under guaranteed empty weight. Two examples of weight overages, for which Curtiss paid a penalty, are noted in the table.

P-40 MAJOR MODEL CHANGES AND IDENTIFYING CHARACTERISTICS
MODEL CHANGES AND CHARACTERISTICS

P-40 (From XP-40) Cooler moved forward, exhaust modified, simplified wing-fuselage and landing gear fairings, fuel capacity change, new gun blast tube fairings.

P-40B Added two wing .30 caliber guns (to make four in wings), added 93 pounds of armor, more ammunition, added externally-protected fuel tanks.

P-40C Revised fuel system with internally self-sealing integral tanks, and 52 gallon external belly fuel tank installation, radio change.

P-40D New fuselage, powerplant, shorter landing gear, (same wing and tail), fuselage centerline rack for 500 pound bomb, wing racks, no fuselage guns four wing .50 caliber guns.

P-40E As D except six wing .50 caliber guns, revised armor, no wing bomb racks. All E models had short fuselage, late aircraft incorporated fin fillet.

P-40E-1 Wings strengthened for bomb racks.

P-40F Merlin engine, no upper carburetor scoop, modified nose lines, greater belly tank capacity, six .50 caliber wing guns, short fuselage, some late versions had dorsal fin fillet.

P-40F-5 Long fuselage (20 inch increase), vertical tail moved aft.

P-40F-10 Change from electrically to manually operated cowl flaps.

P-40F-15 Winterized version.

P-40F-20 Electrical and oxygen system changes.

P-40G As P-40 except H81A-2 Tomahawk four-gun wings, fuel capacity change.

P-40K-1 New Allison engine, automatic manifold pressure regulator. Short fuselage, fin fillet, slight fuel capacity increase over E model.

P-40K-5 Short fuselage, fin fillet, engine rotary valve cooling.

P-40K-10 Long fuselage (20 inch increase), vertical tail moved aft. Some aircraft winterized.

P-40K-15 Long fuselage, emergency hydraulic system eliminated, battery moved forward, many or all winterized.

P-40L-1 Merlin engine, no upper cowl scoop. Short fuselage.

P-40L-5 Long fuselage, four guns only, less armor, fuel, less ammo, rocket kit

P-40L-10 Engine control changes, electrical aileron trim tab, relocated equipment, no coolant tank armor, new drop tank sway braces.

P-40L-15 Permanent carburetor air filter, signal lights added.

P-40L-20 Radio and electrical system changes, provision for destruct grenade.

P-40M-1 As long-fuselage K, but radio mast, carburetor air bypass perforated grill forward, six wing guns, reinforced ailerons.

P-40M-5 Permanent carburetor air filter.

P-40M-10 Air vapor eliminator, fuel pressure warning signal, visual landing gear position indicator (colored pins through wing).

P-40N-1 Lightweight, four guns, aluminum coolers, less fuel, magnesium wheels, less ammo, no battery or starter (restored in service), no wing racks.

P-40N-5 Revised canopy, cut down rear, new pilot seat, radio, recognition lights, bomb racks added on wings.

P-40N-10 Winterized version, rate of climb indicator added, four guns.

P-40N-15 All fuel tanks restored, six guns, battery now forward of firewall.

P-40N-20 Various engine control changes, six guns, capacity for 3 500lb.bombs.

P-40N-25 Changed instrument panel, non-metal self-sealing tanks.

P-40N-30,-35 Minor systems changes on -30; new radio and ADF on -35

P-40N-40 New powerplant controls, engine, new armor, metal-covered ailerons flame-dampening exhaust, revised oxygen system.

XP-40Q New engine, two-stage supercharging, 4-blade prop, wing coolers, bubble canopy, modified fuselage.

P-40 CHRONOLOGY

Mar ,'37-Design work is started on an Allison-powered version of the standard Army P-36A fighter.

Jul30,'37-The XP-40 is ordered as a converted P-36A with the twelve cylinder vee-type Allison V-1710 engine.

Mar 3,'38-Curtiss supplies data to the Army showing an estimated P-40 high speed of 350 mph.

Apr26,'38-A modified contract for the XP-40 prototype is approved.

Oct14,'38-The XP-40 has a first flight with pilot Edward Elliot; high speed is only 299 mph.

Oct16,'38-The prototype XP-40 is delivered to Wright Field, Dayton, Ohio

Oct26,'38-Army Lt. Ben Kelsey flies the new XP-40 from Dayton to Buffalo at an average ground speed of 350 mph and sets a record.

Dec ,'38-The XP-40 is modified with radiator moved forward and other changes; high speed is now 342 mph.

Jan25,'39-A fighter competition is held at Wright Field; the types included are XP-40, XP-37, 75R, AP-4, XP-38, XP-39, and XP-41.

Apr ,'39-The XP-40 is announced as winner of the pursuit competition.

Apr ,'39-Further small modifications up to a production standard are made on the XP-40 type.

Apr ,'39-The US War Department announces a contract for 524 P-40 planes worth $12,872,898 which is $22,929 without GFE each.

Oct 9,'39-The French Purchasing Commision orders 230 Hawk 81A-1 export versions of the P-40 type.

Dec ,'39-Additional modifications made on the XP-40 result in a high speed of 366 mph at 15000 feet altitude.

Jan11,'40-The French request twenty-five P-40s, but this is not allowed by the current military equipment export laws.

Mar25,'40-The P-40 type is released for foreign government purchase and Lend-Lease goes into effect.

Apr 4,'40-The first production P-40 is flown by test pilot Lloyd Child.

Apr ,'40-The US Army agrees to defer delivery of 324 P-40s to allow manufacture of export versions.

May ,'40-The first eleven P-40 production aircraft are accepted.

May ,'40-England orders 560 advanced H87A Kittihawk aircraft.

Jun 6,'40-The French H81A P-40 export version is flown by Lloyd Child.

Jun10,'40-A decision is made to substitute the advanced H87A P-40 type for the planned XP-46.

Jun17,'40-England takes over French H81A orders, and increases the number on order to 1180 aircraft. A total of 140 planes have been produced by this time. The last 90 aircraft on the French order can be modified partially to UK standards and are called the Tomahawk IA.

Jun ,'40-The first P-40s are delivered to the 33rd, 35th, and 36th Sqdns. 8th Pursuit Group, at Langley Field, Virginia.

Jul 1,'40-The first of a group of 20 P-40s and one P-40G are shipped to Russia; shipment is completed by Oct.29, the first of many.

Sep ,'40-The P-40D model is ordered by the US Army.

Sep13,'40-Army contracts are approved for 131 P-40B and 193 P-40C.

Sep17,'40-Initial testing of the H81A type is performed by the British.

Sep18,'40-Between this date and Oct.29 230 Tomahawk aircraft are produced by Curtiss for the British. The first Tomahawk aircraft reaches the UK this month.

Sep30,'40-Two hundred P-40s have now been delivered to the US Army; 114 aircraft in September alone. Besides the 8th Pursuit Group, the 20th Pursuit Gp. at March Field, Cal. and the 31st Pursuit Group at Selfridge Field, Michigan are receiving P-40s.

Oct15,'40-All 199 P-40s are now delivered to the US Army.

Oct30,'40-Between this date and Nov.12 85 H81A aircraft are produced for the United Kingdom at $36,327 each.

Nov ,'40-The British are now receiving the Tomahawk II (H81A-2), and also some Mk.IIB models.

Nov13,'40-Between this date and Aug.21,1941, 694 H81A-2 and -3 aircraft are produced for the UK and for the American Volunteer Group in China—prices are from $35,876 to $36,746.

Dec31,'40-Curtiss has now built 778 P-40 types, of which 558 Tomahawk versions have been accepted during the previous year.

Jan 1,'41-Curtiss employment at Buffalo,NY sets an alltime high of 10000.

Jan 3,'41-Production of the P-40B version for US Army is now starting.

Jan 6,'41-One hundred H81A-2 Tomahawks are sold to China for use by the American Volunteer Group, later to be known as Flying Tigers.

Feb ,'41-The P-40B version begins to reach US Army squadrons.

Apr ,'41-Fifty-five P-40Bs go to Hawaii for the 15th and 18th Pursuit Gps., and 31 P-40Bs are sent for the 20th Pursuit Gp. in the Philippines, the latter batch arriving in June.

Apr ,'41-Initial Tomahawks are sent from England to North Africa-205 through Oct. as well as 89 aircraft shipped right from the US during the same period. They begin to reach the Middle East, brought by ship to the Gold Coast for assembly, and flown across central Africa to Kartoum. Later this is stopped due to frequency of crashes, and unloading is done at Port Sudan on the Red Sea. The aircraft are assembled there and flown toWadi, Haifa, or Cairo for final delivery.

Apr ,'41-In North Africa #3 Sdn.RAAF is the first to be equipped with Tomahawk IIB aircraft. Three hundred and one of the IIBs are ultimately sent three RAF, one RAAF, and three SAAF Squadrons. No more than 90 aircraft will ever be operational at one time.

Apr10,'41-The first P-40C version is flown by Curtiss test pilot Child.

Apr23,'41-The first flight of the H81A-3 export Tomahawk takes place.

Apr24,'41-Deliveries of the 131 P-40B aircraft are now completed.

Apr30,'41-Deliveries of the P-40C version to the US Army begin.

May ,'41-The Army order for P-40C aircraft is completed by Curtiss.

May ,'41-The first P-40D fighter, a considerably revised design, is delivered to the US Army. It has 4 .50 caliber wing guns.

May 7,'41-The first 420 aircraft of the British Lend-Lease P-40E-1 Kittihawk are ordered from Curtiss.

May14,'41-The Tomahawk IIBs in North Africa see their first combat.

May22,'41-The first flight of the UK H87A-2 Kittihawk takes place.

Jun ,'41-The 100 AVG Tomahawks arrive in Rangoon, Burma for use in China by Chenault.

Jun 1,'41-The 6th Air Force in the Carribean includes at this time 6 P-40Bs and 64 P-40Cs.

Jun 8,'41-A Tomahawk of #250 Squadron, RAF scores the first victory for the type over Libya in North Africa.

Jun25,'41-Nine Tomahawks of #250 Sdn., RAF in North Africa engage thirty enemy aircraft of which three are shot down for a loss of two Tomahawks. Four days later seven Tomahawks of 250 Sdn. down six enemy aircraft without any loss to themselves.

Jun30,'41-A second batch consisting of 1080 P-40E-1 aircraft under Lend-Lease is ordered by Britain.

Jun30,'41-The XP-40F, with a Rolls Royce Merlin engine, makes a first flight piloted by Curtiss test pilot Lloyd Child.

Jul ,'41-The British offer 200 Tomahawk aircraft to the USSR, 140 to come from the UK and 60 via the Middle East.

Jul ,'41-#2 SAAF Sdn. are now operational with Tomahawks in No. Africa.

Jul11,'41-Delivery by Curtiss of 22 P-40D aircraft begins.

Jul23,'41-Delivery of the few P-40Ds is completed, and they are sent to the 6th Air Force in the Carribean.

Jul25,'41-The 33rd Sdn. of the 8th Pursuit Gp. with 30 P-40C aircraft is taken to Iceland by the aircraft carrier Wasp, and will remain in Iceland for the duration of the European war.

Aug ,'41-RAF Tomahawk fighters in the UK are being used only for training and with Army Cooperation units.

Aug ,'41-The Flying Tigers are assembling and testing their aircraft at Toungoo in Burma.

Aug ,'41-The USAAF in the Philippines now has one squadron of P-40B aircraft operational.

Aug11,'41-#112 Sdn. RAF is now operational with Tomahawk IIBs, making it the third Tomahawk squadron in the Western Desert, No. Africa.

Aug23,'41-#3 RAAF Sdn. is now in the Western Desert using Tomahawks.

Aug29,'41-Curtiss starts deliveries of the USAAF P-40E model.

Sep ,'41-Arrangements are made for 50 P-40Es direct from the factory and 28 P-40Bs, to be taken from operating units, to be sent to the Philippines to beef up defense forces there.

Sep ,'41-Deliveries from Curtiss of the export P-40E-1 begin; most go to North Africa.

Oct ,'41-The first British P-40E-1 Kittihawks arrive in Egypt.

Oct ,'41-The first Tomahawks in Russia go into action on the Moscow and Leningrad fronts.

Oct ,'41-#4 South African Air Force goes operational with Curtiss Tomahawks in the North African desert.

Oct28,'41-An initial order for 600 P-40K fighters is received by Curtiss .

Nov ,'41-Tomahawk fighters are sent to bolster Turkish neutrality.

Nov15,'41-With the exception of the 34th Sdn. at Del Carmen Field (with 29 P-35As), all squadrons of the 24th Pursuit Gp. in the Philippines are equipped with P-40s. The 17th and 24th Sdns. are at Nichols Field and the 3rd Sdn. at Iba, the former equipped with 18 hastily assembled E models. The 3rd and 17th each have 18 P-40Es; the 20th at Clark Field has 18 P-40Bs. The 21st and 24th Squadrons arrive in the Philippines late in the month.

Nov18,'41-The British launch Operation Crusader in Egypt with the help of five Curtiss Tomahawk squadrons along with Hurricanes operating against the German Africa Corps.

Nov25,'41-In the Western Desert of North Africa, 19 Tomahawks attack 70 enemy aircraft over Sidi Rezegh and claim nine victories against one loss.

Dec ,'41-In the SW Pacific the Royal New Zealand Air Force has one combat squadron of Kittihawks.

Dec ,'41-Seventy-one P-40s of the 16th Pursuit Group are among the aircraft based at Albrook Field in the Canal Zone, Panama.

Dec 1,'41-A total of 74 P-40Es have now been received in the Philippines

Dec 5,'41-In North Africa 22 Curtiss Tomahawks from #250 and #112 Sqdns. encounter 45 Stukas with 30 escort fighters. The Tomahawks destroy 18 enemy aircraft.

Dec 7,'41-In the Pearl Harbor, Hawaii area the 15th and 18th Pursuit Gps of the 14th Wing have 87 P-40B and 12 P-40C aircraft. The 18th Gp. has five newly-equipped P-40 squadrons, the 6th, 19th, 44th, 73rd, and 78th. The 44th Sdn. is the only one not caught on the ground in the Japanese attack. Except for a small detachment of the 47th Sdn., all squadrons of the 15th Gp. (45th, 46th, and 47th) are caught lined up in neat rows at Wheeler Field for the Japanese attack. During the raid only 27 P-40 sorties are made, and after the raid there are 50 P-40Bs left (25 useable) and 7 P-40Cs (with 2 useable)

Dec14,'41-Twenty-five P-40s arrive in the Canal Zone, Panama, from Puerto Rico to reinforce the area. Later in December an additional 80 pursuits arrive in Panama.

Dec20,'41-The first Flying Tiger combat in China takes place. The Tigers down four enemy bombers near Kunming.

Dec22,'41-Eighteen P-40s reach Brisbane Australia on this date. Between now and Feb.4, 138 P-40s are assembled, and comprise five provisional squadrons, the 3rd, 13th, 17th, 20th, and 33rd.

Dec25,'41-Fifteen AVG Tomahawks and eighteen RAF Brewster Buffalos intercept 80 bombers with 28 fighters over Rangoon, Burma, and shoot down 32 enemy aircraft, 25 by the Flying Tiger pilots, who have no losses.

Dec26,'41-In the Philippines there are only 18 P-40s remaining after attrition from Japanese bombing, air fighting, and accidents. The 17th, 21st, and 34th squadrons are made into one umit.

Dec31,'41-Curtiss Airplane Div. now has 45000 employees. Production of P-40 types totals 2246 aircraft in the year of 1941.

Dec31,'41-The Russians claim that 35 of 228 P-40s sent them have generator or other problems, and the others are being operated without generators.

Jan,'42-Fifty P-40Es are allocated to the AVG in China, and water shipment will start in February. Most will be in China by June 1942.

Jan 1,'42-RAF H87A Kittihawks go into action in the North African Desert

Jan 3,'42-Curtiss starts delivery of the P-40F with the Packard Merlin engine which has a single stage two-speed supercharger.

Jan15,'42-Difficulty the Russians are having with P-40 Tomahawk generators is being cleared up with the shipment of three hundred new generators to the USSR.

Jan25,'42-The 17th Provisional Sdn. with 12 P-40Es gets to Java in the Netherlands East Indies from Brisbane Australia. The P-40Es of the 3rd Sdn. will arrive in Java Feb.11, but nine aircraft crash in poor weather. A total of only 36 P-40s ends up reaching Java in spite of the fact that 120 to 124 P-40s are sent up Jan. to Feb.11. In a Japanese raid on Darwin Feb. 14 11 aircraft are destroyed, 14 are lost in transit, including 3 at Timor, 32 P-40s are lost when the old carrier Langley is sunk on Feb.27, and there is no time to assemble P-40s crated on the Sea Witch, so they are dumped in the water.

Feb,'42-The 49th Fighter Gp. equipped with P-40s arrives in Australia.

Feb 4,'42-The P-40s of the 20th Provisional Sdn. arrive to try to defend Bali in the Southwest Pacific.

Feb14,'42-Tomahawks have shot down 56 enemy aircraft in North Africa.

Feb19,'42-The 33rd Provisional Sdn. P-40s are sent to defend Darwin, Australia, but is overwhelmed by a big Japanese raid on the town.

Feb25,'42-Fifteen AVG Tomahawks along with RAF Hurricanes attack over 150 enemy aircraft and claim a total of 24 victories. The AVG has now about 20 flyable P-40s left, and retreats from Mingaladen to Magwe to Lashio, to Loiwing in Burma, and then into China.

Feb26,'42-Thirteen P-40s now remain in Java under Col. E.L. Eubank; some are being flown by Dutch pilots.

Mar,'42-Twelve Kittihawks are delivered to Canada by rail.

Mar,'42-The AVG starts to get 30 P-40Es ferried into China via Africa and India. The first six arrive in late March.

Mar,'42-The 10th Air Force is organized in the CBI and starts out with only 10 P-40s from Australia. Gen. Brereton wants newer aircraft, and is promised P-38s some day, but has to use P-40s for over a year and make do.

Mar,'42-RAAF Kittihawks of #75,76, and 77 Squadrons are in action against the Japanese, operating from Port Moresby and Milne Bay in New Guinea.

Mar,'42-British RAF Sdn.112 experiments using the Kittihawk as a fighter-bomber using a 250 pound bomb in North Africa.

Mar,'42-One P-40 is converted to a P-40A for reconnaisance, but this is an informal designation.

Mar 1,'42-Nine P-40s fly the last mission against the Japanese landings on the island of Java, along with six Hurricanes and four Brewster Buffalos. All Allied aircraft are lost.

Mar15,'42-Part of the 49th Gp. P-40s are moved to assist in the defense of Darwin, Australia.

Mar18,'42-By this date a total of 337 P-40s have reached Australia (along with 190 Airacobras). Of these about 125 P-40s are lost in the Java fighting, others by accident, 75 are turned over to the RAAF, 74 are being repaired, and about 100 await assembly. There are 92 P-40s in commission (and 85 Airacobras).

Mar24,'42-Brig. Gen. HC Davidson of 7th Air Force Fighter Command in Hawaii expresses dissatisfaction with the P-40 (and the P-39) as an interceptor. It cannot operate at high altitudes, and also has an unsatisfactory rate of climb.

Apr,'42-Winterized P-40Es start operations in the Aleutians.

Apr,'42-P-40E-1 Kittihawks start replacing the older Tomahawks in the North African Western Desert.

Apr,'42-Sixty-eight P-40Es are flown to Quonset Point, RI. and with crews are loaded aboard the aircraft carrier Ranger. They fly off safely at Accra in Africa, and fly across Africa. Eventually 58 aircraft reach the 10th Air Force in India.

Apr , '42-The AVG in China now has more P-40Es, making a total of 36 flyable P-40 types, with 39 being repaired, but 22 repairable aircraft have to be destroyed when a move is required.

May , '42-P-40K deliveries are started and will be completed by year end

May , '42-The 49th Fighter Gp. with 90 P-40s is still assigned the defense of Darwin, Australia.

May 6, '42-The five remaining P-40s in the Philippines are destroyed by US forces; in the period Dec.8,1941 to Apr.8,1942 available records indicate at least 103 enemy aircraft have been destroyed by P-40s in the Philippines.

May16, '42-RAF #112 Sdn., after experiments with Curtiss H87 Kittihawk bombing, becomes the 1st Fighter-Bomber Sdn. in the Desert Air Force in North Africa.

May17, '42-The 68th Fighter Sdn., with P-40Es, lands at Tongatabu after leaving Brisbane, Australia, on the 8th; by June 4th all of the squadron aircraft have been assembled and test flown.

May23, '42-Ten P-40Es of the 11th Fighter Sdn. arrive at Unmak Island in in the Aleutians.

May31, '42-The 7th Air Force, with headquarters in Hawaii, has 101 P-40s in commission out of 134 in the area. (also a few P-39s).

Jun , '42-USAAF forces in Alaska and the Aleutians include 21 P-40s of the 11th Fighter Sdn. at Fort Randall, Cold Bay, 12 P-40s at Fort Glenn, Unmak, and 17 P-40s at Kodiak.

Jun , '42-The China Air Task Force is organized with Col. Robert L. Scott in command of the 23rd Ftr. Gp.(ex-AVG) with three squadrons of Allison-powered P-40s, the 74th, 75th, and 76th. They are at full strength by July 4th when the formal AVG-CATF changeover is made. The 23rd Gp., in three years of fighting with P-40s, will maintain a victory-to-loss ratio of 15 to 1.

Jun , '42-RAF and RAAF Kittibombers (Kittihawk bombers) are covering the retreat of the British Army into Egypt by flying 350 sorties per day. Each aircraft is flying three to four low-level missions every day.

Jun 1, '42-The Royal Canadian Air Force dispatches 15 Kittihawk fighters to Fort Richardson in Alaska to aid in defense.

Jun 4, '42-The Japanese attack Dutch Harbor in the Aleutians, and eight P-40s of the 11th Fighter Sdn. get into the action. Four enemy aircraft are downed and two P-40s lost, one pilot saved

Jun11, '42-The decision is made to order more P-40K, L, and M models in place of the new Curtiss P-60A fighter.

Jun15, '42-The US Army orders 700 P-40L aircraft with Packard Merlins.

Jun30, '42-The 10th Air Force in India now has the 16th Fighter Sdn. of the 51st Fighter Gp. in Kunming, China, along with the three squadrons of the 23rd Fighter Gp. The 16th is operational in August, giving the CATF four P-40 squadrons.

Jun30, '42-The total amount of P-40s sent to Russia and available at the factory for shipment has reached 875, close to the agreed-on figure of 900. Due to the lack of transport, however, the number actually exported by this date is 657 aircraft.

Jul , '42-P-40s (and P-39s) based at Port Moresby New Guinea and Darwin Australia are most often unable to intercept the high-flying (over 22,000 feet) Japanese bombers that frequently conduct raids. There are now 80 P-40s of the 49th Ftr. Gp. at Darwin.

Jul 1, '42-P-40F aircraft of the 57th Ftr. Gp., 9th Air Force leave Quonset Point R.I. on the carrier Ranger for North Africa, and 100 miles off the African coast they take off and fly to Accra on the Gold Coast, and then across Africa to the Middle East. By July 31st they will be in Palestine attached to the Western Desert Air Force, and start to see action. The 57th has the 64th, 65th, and 66th Sdns. with a total of 72 P-40 aircraft.

Jul 4, '42-The AVG is formally taken over by Chennault's China Air Task Force. Only five AVG pilots volunteer, but many stay two weeks to assist in the change-over. The AVG has produced 39 aces, has shot down 286 enemy aircraft, with 40 destroyed on the ground, and over 200 probables. Twelve P-40s have been lost in combat, and 61 lost to other causes.

Jul 5, '42-The China Air Task Force starts operations. It has 51 P-40 fighters, 27 of the original Tomahawks, and 24 P-40Es. Twenty-nine of the total are currently flyable.

Jul21, '42-During the Japanese landing at Buna, New Guinea, RAAF Kittihawks use 500 pound bombs to dive-bomb the enemy.

Jul30, '42-In one of the few interceptions over Darwin, Australia, 27 P-40s engage the enemy and shoot down six Zero fighters and two bombers for the loss of only one P-40.

Aug , '42-The P-40K-1 export version is now being produced by Curtiss.

Aug , '42-Gen. MacArthur has now, in Australia, two squadrons of the 35th Fighter Gp. at Port Moresby, New Guinea with about 35 P-40s and two RAAF squadrons with about 30 Kittihawks.

Aug ,'42-Gen. Kenney of the 5th Air Force, SW Pacific, assures Gen.Arnold of the usefulness of the P-40 (and P-39) but wants P-38s.

Aug 9,'42-The first USAAF P-40F victory is scored in North Africa. Two German ME-109s are shot down for the loss of one P-40.

Aug24,'42-A contract is given Curtiss for the P-40M version, a lend-lease model for the United Kingdom.

Aug31,'42-The 57th Fighter Gp., with 72 aircraft total, flies its first combat mission for the 9th (US Army Middle East) Air Force in North Africa as a unit using P-40F and P-40K aircraft. The 57th squadrons have been training with RAF Kittihawk units.

Sep ,'42-Stalin says:"The American Government has furnished the Soviets P-40 fighters, not Airacobras; the British have supplied Hurricanes, not Spitfires. Both of these aircraft are inferior to the German aircraft they have to face."

Sep ,'42-Elements of the 66th Fighter Gp. with P-40s see occasional action in the North African Western Desert Air Force, but are used mainly as a reserve force.

Sep ,'42-P-40Ks from the North African desert fighting are sent to reinforce the China Air Task Force squadrons. The CATF is faced also with a very bad fuel shortage.

Sep ,'42-RCAF Kittihawk Squadrons #14 and #111 return to Canada after having fought in the Aleutians alongside USAAF P-40 squadrons of the 28th Composite Group since February 1942.

Oct ,'42-Brig. Gen. R. Douglas Jr. of the 7th Air Force Fighter Command provides local defense for Central Pacific bases, and now has a total of 319 fighters, all P-40s except for one squadron each of P-39s and P-70s. His fighters are at the Hawaiian Is., Midway, Canton, and Christmas Is. The 73rd Fighter Sdn. with 25 P-40Es, has been sent to Midway from Oahu via carrier Saratoga to replace battered Marine units. The 73rd will fly daily patrols from Midway until replaced in January 1943 by the 78th Squadron.

Oct 3,'42-The India Air Task Force is organized, including the 51st Ftr. Gp. with two P-40 squadrons, the 25th and 26th defending Assam in India. The third squadron is with 14th Air Force in China.

Oct 6,'42-In the North African Western Desert the P-40s of the 66th Sdn. 57th Ftr.Gp. are attached to #239 Kittihawk Wing of the RAF's #211 Group. The other 57th squadrons are attached to #212 Gp.

Oct 9,'42-The first batch of P-40s start delivery to Russia via the northern ALSIB (Alaska-Siberia) route, shortly after this is opened subsequent to torturous US-Russian negotiations.

Oct16,'42-The USAAF can muster only a total of 56 P-40s in Egypt.

Oct26,'42-The 57th Group P-40s claim the downing of four Italian M202s and four German Me-109s in the Western Desert fighting.

Oct27,'42-Sixteen 57th Group P-40s of the 64th and 65th Squadrons carry out a dawn fighter-bomber attack at minimum altitude on a Fuka airfield, and later sucessfully tangle with assorted Fiat CR-42s, JU-87s, Macchis, and Me109s. They shoot down seven enemy aircraft with three probables with no losses themselves.

Oct22,'42-Remaining P-40B aircraft are now put in the restricted category, and thus become RP-40Bs.

Nov ,'42-The US Middle East Air Force becomes the 9th Air Force, and because of Operation Torch has lost the P-40s of the 33rd Ftr. Gp. to Gen. Doolittle's 12th Air Force for use at Casablanca. The 33rd Gp. has the 58th, 59th, and 60th Fighter Squadrons.

Nov 4,'42-The USAAF 57th Ftr. Gp. in No. Africa claims its 20th victory.

Nov 7,'42-Curtiss completes deliveries of its P-40K model.

Nov11,'42-For Operation Torch, the 33rd Fighter Gp., under Major Philip Cochran, launches its 78 P-40F fighters from the escort carriers Chenang and Archer near Casablanca. Two aircraft are lost immediately and 17 are damaged on landing from the Chenang batch. On D+5 35 replacement aircraft for the 33rd come in to Port Lautney from Archer, and four crack up.

Nov12,'42-The 79th Fighter Gp., its 85th, 86th, and 87th Squadrons equipped with Merlin-powered P-40 Warhawks, reaches Egypt.

Dec ,'42-P-40s, mostly K models, are in India with 51st Ftr.Gp. 10th AF

Dec ,'42-Deliveries of the P-40M version with the Allison engine start.

Dec 8,'42-P-40s of the 68th Fighter Squadron arrive at Henderson Field on Guadalcanal, the first of the type to arrive there.

Dec22,'42-The 44th Squadron with its P-40s arrives at Henderson Field.

Dec23,'42-The three squadrons of the 324th Ftr. Gp. (314th, 315th, and 316th) with P-40L aircraft arrive for the USAAF 9th AF in Egypt. The 314th Sdn. will join the 57th Ftr. Gp., and the other two join the 79th Ftr. Gp. in Libya for battle experience. This allignment is employed for the rest of the campaign.

Dec31,'42-By this time a total of 4453 P-40 types have been delivered.

Jan ,'43-Merlin-powered P-40L aircraft are being delivered in the first four months of 1943.

Jan ,'43-The final P-40F-20 model is delivered by Curtiss.

Jan ,'43-At the time of the Casablanca Conference a shortage of P-40s has developed. The 33rd Ftr. Gp. has suffered heavy losses, and on Jan 9 donates 25 P-40F aircraft to re-equip the French Lafayette Escadrille in North Africa. The French unit joins fights with the 33rd. The French have flown 287 sorties and have seven victories. By Mar.15 only five of the French-operated aircraft are left.

Jan 1,'43-In the war against Japan the USAAF has 618 P-40s out of a total of 1118 fighters.

Jan 9,'43-The Japanese succeed in reinforcing Lae, New Guinea, but they suffer heavy losses, including 28 planes shot down by the P-40 fighters of the 49th Ftr. Gp. The P-40s also make dive bombing attacks on enemy transports using 300 pound bombs.

Jan19,'43-P-40Fs and P-40Ls of the 325th Fighter Gp. are flown off the carrier Ranger to Casablanca, French Morocco. All 72 aircraft take off successfully. The three squadrons are the 317th, the 318th, and the 319th, and have been diverted from the 9th AF.

Jan26,'43-The operational strength of the 12th Air Force Air Support Command in North Africa has been built up, and among other types includes 52 P-40s. They double as fighter-bombers, using Spitfires as high cover.

Feb ,'43-Deliveries of the P-40M version are completed.

Feb ,'43-As a result of Gen.Hap Arnold's request for help at the Casablanca Conference, the carrier Ranger ferries in 75 P-40L replacement aircraft.

Feb 1,'43-The 33rd Ftr. Gp. in Tunisia is short of pilots and down to 13 aircraft. The German Me-109Gs at Gabes have given it a very hard time; the group is withdrawn from action.

Feb15,'43-The 9th AF in Tunisia has only the 57th Ftr. Gp. in the combat area with P-40s. However the two new groups (79th and the 324th) are soon to become operational. The 57th is initiating flight leaders of the new groups, which later undertake ground support missions. The 79th and 324th will later be transferred from 9th AF to 12th AF in Italy.

Mar ,'43-One flight from the 49th Ftr. Gp. with P-40Es and P-40Ks arrives at Horn Is. off Queensland, Australia. The rest of the 49th Gp. (35th, 7th, and 9th Sdns.) goes to Port Darwin.

Mar ,'43-The P-40N-1 model is now being delivered from Curtiss.

Mar 4,'43-Air units of the 5th Air Force, SW Pacific, participating in the battle of the Bismark Sea include 43 P-40s of the 7th and 8th Ftr.Sdns. of the 49th Ftr. Gp. along with 17 RAAF Kittihawks of #75 Squadron.

Mar10,'43-The China Air Task Force under Gen.Chennault becomes the 14th Air Force, and Chennault is now a Major General. During it's tenure the CATF P-40s have destroyed 149 enemy aircraft and claimed 85 probables for a loss of 16 planes of their own.

Mar14,'43-After being trained by the 57th Ftr. Gp., the 79th Ftr. Gp. which is the second to join the 9th Air Force, flies its P-40Fs as an independent unit on its first mission against enemy concentrations in Tunisia, North Africa.

Mar15,'43-The 33rd Fighter Group in Tunisia, No. Africa, after having been withdrawn because of heavy losses, returns to action.

Mar25,'43-Groupe Lafayette in North Africa receives 36 new P-40L aircraft just assembled at Oran, West Algeria. The group had lost most all their P-40F aircraft.

Apr ,'43-The USAAF 99th Ftr.Sdn., with all black pilots, enters the No. African fighting using P-40Ns. It is not attached to a group.

Apr ,'43-Gen. Kenney of the 5th Air Force objects to suggestions he may get more P-40s instead of the P-38s (second choice P-47s) that he desires.

Apr ,'43-P-40s of #15 Squadron are the first New Zealand air forces to reach the combat zone when they move up to Guadalcanal.

Apr17,'43-The 325th Fighter Group with P-40s enters No. African combat as an independent group after having trained under the 33rd Ftr. Gp. to whom it initially gave up 44 of its Warhawks. The 325th flies both escort and strafing missions.

Apr18,'43-The Palm Sunday Massacre takes place in Tunisia. Four P-40 squadrons (the 57th Group plus the 314th Squadron of the 324th Group) with Spitfire top cover meet a large German aerial resupply convoy. They destroy 50 to 70 JU-52s along with 16 Macchis and Messersmitts for a loss of only six P-40s and a Spitfire.

Apr22,'43-An entire Me-323 aerial convoy is destroyed over the Gulf of Tunis by four squadrons of South African Air Force Kittihawk aircraft covered by Spitfires. Twenty-one Me-323s and ten enemy fighters are shot down. Four of the Kittihawks are lost.

Apr28,'43-P-40s of the 23rd Fighter Gp. in the SW Pacific intercept 21 bombers and 21 Zero fighters. The P-40s down 11 enemy aircraft confirmed with 8 probables.

Apr28,'43-Production of Merlin-powered P-40s ends with the last P-40L-20 to allow Packard to produce more Merlin engines for P-51s.

May , '43-Forces used during the capture of Attu in the Aleutians include 28 Kittihawks of #14 and #111 Sqdns. of the RCAF.

May , '43-P-40Ks and P-40Ms start arriving in the China Theatre.

May , '43-The 325th Ftr. Gp. P-40s are escorting B-25s near Algiers, and also dive bomb with 500 pound bombs. Later the 325th is to participate in the war over Sicily, Sardinia, and Italy.

May11, '43-The 11th Air Force in Alaska now has 80 P-40s of the 343rd Ftr. Gp. (11th, 18th, and 54th Sdns.), with 35 at Unmak, 22 at Adak, and 23 at Amchitka. It also has 26 P-38s.

May13, '43-Eleven P-40s of the USAAF and 6 of the RNZAF #15 Sdn. are among the many Allied types to intercept an enemy fighter sweep over Guadalcanal, and 19 Japanese aircraft out of about two dozen are shot down by the 102 Allied fighters involved.

May15, '43-P-40s of the 23rd Ftr. Gp. and the 16th Ftr. Sdn. in China engage 36 enemy bombers and 30-40 fighters, and down 16 aircraft at a cost of one P-40 badly damaged.

May22, '43-The 324th Ftr. Gp. P-40 squadrons all come together as a single unit. In June the group is in Tunisia carrying out escort and patrol missions until the Sicily invasion, and then becomes a training unit.

May20, '43-French fliers in their P-40L aircraft participate in the victory flypast over Tunis just after the Axis surrenders in North Africa. They are given a mission of North African coastal patrol and convoy defense. The unit will change to P-47s in December 1943. Their P-40 aircraft are then used as trainers.

Jun 1, '43-USAAF P-40 units of the Northwest African Air Forces are: The 325th Ftr. Gp.(in the Strategic Air Force), and in the Air Support Command the 33rd, 57th, 79th, and 324th Ftr. Gps. The Commonwealth Kittihawk units are not included here.

Jun 2, '43-The 99th Ftr. Sdn. flies its first combat missions in the assault on Pantelleria in the Mediterranean. It will later fight as an all-black unit in Sicily, Italy and Greece, and will end up downing 111 enemy aircraft. It flies P-40 aircraft.

Jul 1, '43-P-40s are engaged in a major air battle over southern Italy in which 21 enemy aircraft are shot down with loss of one P-40.

Jul13, '43-The P-40s of the 18th Ftr. Gp., 5th Air Force have been successful in air battles around Guadalcanal, and claim 57 aerial victories for the loss of three P-40s since Jan.19,1943. During that time the group has operated P-40E,F,M, and N aircraft.

Jul30, '43-Twenty Warhawks of the 325th Ftr. Gp. over southern Sardinia are jumped by 35 Me-109s and Mc 202s. In a swirling air battle at low altitude the Checkertail P-40s shoot down 21 enemy aircraft and claim four probables against only one P-40 lost. The 325th Ftr. Gp. will fly 128 missions in P-40s and shoot down 135 enemy aircraft, including 122 fighters, while losing 35 P-40 aircraft.

Aug , '43-The Chinese-American Composite Wing (CACW) is formed with 8 squadrons of P-40Ks. There are two groups, the 3rd and 5th, each with four squadrons.

Aug14, '43-The P-40Ms and P-40Ns of the 44th Ftr. Sdn., 18th Ftr. Gp. land in New Georgia, Solomon Is. right after US forces capture the island. Between July and September 1943 the 44th Sdn. downs 111 1/2 enemy aircraft for a loss of only eight P-40s.

Aug15, '43-P-40 aircraft, along with P-39s and USMC Corsairs, cover the US invasion of Vella LaVella in the lower Solomon Is. P-40s also covered the invasion of Rendova Island.

Aug20, '43-P-40s in China encounter newer higher-flying enemy fighters which dive on them from above and zoom back up again. On this date P-40s claim two enemy aircraft, but lose three of their own. The P-40 is getting outmoded for aerial combat.

Aug25, '43-All groups, including P-40s, of the 9th Air Force in North Africa are transferred to the 12th Air Force. The 9th is moved to England and re-established there Oct.16, 1943 as an ETO Tactical Air Force. The P-40 groups participate in the battle for Sicily, and prepare for the invasion of Italy.

Aug31, '43-Gen. Paul Wirtsmith of 5th Air Force has 598 fighter aircraft of which 118 are P-40s. But many P-40s are in depot, and all are weary, having 300 to 500 combat hours each-equivalent to about 2000 normal operating hours. Gen. Kenney writes from the Pacific to Hap Arnold-"I don't believe anyone else, with the possible exception of Chennault, is flying stuff as old and worn out as these youngsters out here are—".

Sep , '43-The 49th Ftr.Gp. moves up to New Guinea; the 7th and 35th Sdns keep their P-40s; the 9th Sdn. gets P-38s.

Sep , '43-Being replaced by the 8th Ftr. Gp. in India, the 51st Ftr.Gp. is transferred from there to the 14th Air Force in China. Col. John Barr of the 51st Gp. is the first pilot in the CBI to drop a 1000 pound bomb from a "B-40". The 51st specializes in ground attack, and skip-bombs with delayed-action fuses.

Sep , '43-After operational training in Karachi, India on P-40s (having trained with P-47s), the 80th Ftr. Gp.,USAAF takes the P-40N-1 into action from Assam in Burma with three squadrons, the 88th, 89th, and 90th..

Sep , '43-At Curtiss the production of 1577 P-40N-5,-10, and-15 Warhawks ends, and the line switches to production of P-40N-20s.

Sep 1, '43-P-40M and P-40N-5 Warhawks of the 45th Ftr. Sdn. come to Bakers Is. from Bellows Field in Hawaii. Navigation for the sqadron is done by an accompanying B-24 bomber.

Sep 8, '43-One hundred and twelve P-40s of the 325th Ftr. Gp. attack Pabillonis airfield in Italy, strafing and dropping bombs.

Sep 9, '43-During the invasion at Salerno, Italy, P-40 (and P-39) radius, allowing 10 minutes of combat and using an auxilliary fuel tank, is only about 150 miles, so the type can be used only for duty near Sicily. But prior to the invasion P-40s and RAF Kittihawks bomb and strafe vehicles in southern Italy from nearby Sicilian bases.

Sep11, '43-In the Central Pacific, 19 P-40Ns of the 45th Ftr. Sdn, 7th Air Force fly from Canton Is. to Baker Is. to provide local protection.

Sep18, '43-The 325th Ftr. Gp. in Italy turns its P-40s over to the 324th Ftr. Gp., and is withdrawn to re-equip with P-47D aircraft.

Oct , '43-Curtiss P-40Es, Ks, and Ms fly their last combat mission in Alaska, but some P-40 patrols go on until the end of the war.

Oct , '43-Four of the 12th Air Support Command Tactical Branch Fighter Groups are now in Italy, and three of them are operating P-40 aircraft: The 33rd Gp. in western Italy and the 57th and 79th in the eastern part. The 324th Gp. moves into Italy in late Oct. RAF Desert Air Force Kittihawks are also in eastern Italy along with US and RAF Spitfires.

Oct 1, '43-One hundred and sixty P-40 fighters pave the way for landings at Termoli, Italy on the Adriatic Sea by bombing and strafing enemy troops and vehicles.

Oct 6, '43-P-40s of the 57th and 79th Ftr. Gps. fly many sorties over the battle area near Termoli, Italy, and also interdict enemy shipping in the Adriatic headed for Italy, Greece, and Yugoslavia.

Nov , '43-In the Bougainville campaign, Solomon Is., Gen. Harmon of 5th Air Force considers available fighter aircraft inadequate in both quantity and quality- he regards the P-40 as useful for certain purposes, but unequal to the demands made on it.(He is even harder on the P-39).

Nov 1, '43-During the US invasion of Bougainville, a Japanese counterattack of Val dive bombers is broken up by eight Kittihawks along with eight Lightnings. RNZAF Kittihawks of #18 Sdn. shoot down seven enemy aircraft without loss to themselves.

Dec , '43-A total of 485 Kittihawks has now been received by the Australian RAAF. They will eventually receive a grand total of 863 Kittihawks for the SW Pacific area.

Dec , '43-The 15th Ftr. Gp. of the 7th Air Force with P-40s is sent to the Ellice Is. south of the Marshall Is. in the Pacific.

Dec17, '43-The fighter strength of AIRSOLS (Air Solomons) for the task of air assault on the big Japanese base at Rabaul includes 39 P-40s of US and RNZAF Sdns. of which 36 are operational. There are also 229 other Army, USN, and USMC fighters, 163 are ready

Dec18, '43-Seventh Air Force P-40s of the 45th Ftr. Sdn., along with P-39s, escort A-24 dive bombers from Makin on raids over the bypassed Japanese Is. of Mille and Jaluit. The P-40s are used in a variety of missions—escort, bombing, strafing, patrol, and ship attacks.

Dec25, '43-The P-40s of the 35th Ftr. Sdn., 49th Group, move up from Port Moresby in New Guinea to Finchhaven where a new advanced air base has just been constructed.

Jan , '44-P-40Ks and P-40Ms of the 344th Ftr.Gp. arrive in Shemya, Alaska. The group has a bad time with poor weather and boredom.

Jan 1, '44-In the war against Japan the Army is using 630 P-40s out of a total of 1765 fighters.

Jan14, '44-One hundred and nineteen P-40s of the 79th Ftr.Gp. escort 35 Martin Baltimore bombers, and destroy a major tank-repair depot at Loreto, Italy. Some of the P-40s also carry bombs.

Jan22, '44-P-40s are on patrol at 6000-8000 foot altitudes over the beaches at Anzio, Italy.

Jan29, '44-P-40s of the 45th Ftr.Sdn., along with P-39s, conduct combat patrols over Mille Is. until February 1 in support of the US landings on Kwajalein Is. in the Pacific.

Feb , '44-Reinforcements arrive for the 14th Air Force in China in the form of the 7th and 8th Ftr.Sdns., but only 18 P-40s come with them.

Feb , '44-The 58th, 59th, and 60th Sdns. of the 33rd Ftr.Gp., after fighting a tactical air war in Italy, are sent to Karachi India

Feb14, '44-Another 1000 P-40 Warhawks are ordered; 500 each of -30 and -35 models.

Mar10, '44-A systematic air attack on supply dumps on Rabaul begins with a strike by 24 New Zealand P-40N Warhawks armed with two 500 pound general purpose bombs each.

Mar15, '44-P-40s are being used as air support for US troops on Bougainville in the Solomon Is., SW Pacific.

Apr ,'44-P-40K aircraft in the China-Burma-India Theatre start to be exchanged for P-51B Merlin-powered Mustangs.

Apr ,'44-The total USAAF inventory of P-40s peaks at 2499 aircraft.

Apr ,'44-The 59th Ftr.Sdn. flies into Szechwan Province in China with its P-40s, and is the only local fighter defense when the B-29s start their fuel-stocking activities this month.

Apr 9,'44-RAF #112 Sdn. in Italy receives Kittihawl IV models which they operate with 2000# bomb loads. Missions are almost all ground attack. The squadron will change to Mustangs in July.

May ,'44-The 23rd Ftr.Gp. in China is now exchanging its older P-40s for new P-40N-20 models. They install electric starters.

May ,'44-For support of the hard-pressed Chinese Army against the the enemy, Chennault included among his fighter units the 5th Ftr. Gp. with P-40s, an element of the Chinese-American Composite Wing.

May ,'44-The 88th Ftr.Sdn., with P-40s, is based at Shingbwiang in China, and a flight of P-40s of the 20th Tactical Reconn. Sdn is based at Tingkawk Satan. In Assam there are two more P-40 squadrons.

Jun ,'44-Gen.Whitehead of 5th Air Force reminds Gen.Kenney that his 7th and 8th Ftr. Sdns. need re-equipping. Their P-40s are about on their last legs. Kenney, who calls the plane "the spearhead of the air advance" makes an unsuccessful attempt to obtain more. It is finally decided to make the 49th Ftr. Gp. an all-P-38 outfit, and this will be accomplished in Sept.-Oct. The P-40s of the 7th and 8th Sdns. will then be transferred to the 82nd and 110th Recon. Sdns. until they can receive F-6D reconnaisance Mustangs in November. The P-40s of the 110th Sdn. are to be very busy during the Philippine Campaigns.

Jun 3,'44-The 76th Ftr.Sdn. of the 23rd Ftr.Gp. in China is now equipped with Merlin Mustangs after trading in their P-40s.

Jun22,'44-The 23rd Ftr.Gp. has to evacuate their base at Hengyang, China because of Japanese advances. They bomb their own field with their P-40s using 1000 pound bombs.

Jun26,'44-In China the P-40s of the 74th and 75th Sdns. and the 118th Tactical Recon. Sdn. fly a joint strafing mission just south of Hengyang. A heavy burden is placed on the 14th Air Force fighters defending against the enemy advances. P-40s are averaging three sorties per plane per day. In spite of these efforts, Hengyang falls to the enemy on August 8th.

Jun30,'44-One thousand P-40N-40 models are ordered from Curtiss. This order is later cut back to 220 aircraft.

Aug 5,'44-In China a "major mission" for that theatre is flown. Eight P-40s from the 75th Sdn. and eight from the 16th Sdn. fly a dive bombing attack on enemy installations. It is rare to send more than eight fighters on a mission.

Aug31,'44-The Far East Air Force, in preparing for the Philippines invasion, has 135 P-40s ready out of a total fighter force of 1103 aircraft. This does not include reconnaissance aircraft but does count planes on the way from the US.

Sep ,'44-Battle damage and losses has left the 75th Sdn. of the 23rd Gp. in China with only four serviceable P-40s. They manage to obtain 15 P-40s from another group switching to P-47s.

Sep ,'44-The 23rd Ftr.Gp. in China is now switching from P-40s to the new North American P-51C models powered with Merlin engines.

Oct 6,'44-The 82nd Recon.Sdn. flying P-40Ns in place of their old P-39 aircraft arrives at Wama on Morotai just prior to the Leyte Gulf invasion in the Philippines.

Nov 1,'44-The 75th Ftr.Sdn, 23rd Ftr.Gp. in China flies its last P-40 missions, ferry flights to Luliang.

Nov 3,'44-The P-40s of the 110th Tactical Recon.Sdn. reach Leyte, P.I. They operate from Buri along with P-38s.

Nov22,'44-Curtiss-Wright's 15000th fighter airplane, a P-40N, is delivered to the Army.

Nov23,'44-Elements of the 110th Tactical Recon.Sdn. with P-40s are operating from Elmore and Hill Fields on Mindoro, P.I. shortly after the US invasion. Efforts at reinforcement by the enemy are put down by 20 P-40s along with P-38s, P-47s, and B-25s. Losses are heavy, including six P-40s, but the beach-head has been saved.

Nov24,'44-Eleven P-40s of the 110th Recon. Sdn. on Leyte, P.I. wipe out a convoy hiding in Port Cataingen, and Philippinos report 1500 enemy troops are killed in the attack.

Nov26,'44-Air support for US 7th Division troops attacking on Leyte is provided by several P-40s. Another P-40 support mission is flown on Dec.2.

Nov30,'44-The last production Warhawk, a P-40N-40, Ser.44-47964, leaves the Curtiss Buffalo plant. A total of 13738 Hawk 81 and 87 types have been built of which 5492 have been supplied as Lend-Lease to Allies, 2799 of these to British Commonwealth countries, 2069 shipped to Russia, 377 to China, and 89 to Brazil. A total of 11995 aircraft went to the US Army either for their own use or for Lend-Lease.

Dec ,'44-The China-Burma-India Theatre fighter strength includes 205 P-40s this month. In 1945 the numbers will be: Jan 1945-182, Feb-171, Mar-134, Apr-109, May-95, Jun-76, Jul-62. There are no replacements, and attrition has taken its toll. For the 14th AF in China the numbers of P-40s are: Jan 31,1945-47, Mar31-32, Jul31-13. The 10th Air Force in India has no more than two or three P-40s in 1945.

Dec ,'44-Enemy attempts to bring in reinforcements north of the US invasion force at Ormoc, Leyte, P.I. are hampered by continuous fighter attacks. Among the 153 US fighters so employed are 40 P-40 Warhawks.

Dec ,'44-The, P-40s of the 110th Tactical Recon. Sdn. combine with Marine Corsairs of MAG-12 to provide another 184 sorties by the Leyte garrison attacking enemy installations.

Dec17,'44-Fifteen P-40s bomb and strafe enemy positions at Valencia, Leyte, P. I. ahead of US troops who judge the results "wonderful". On Dec23 12 P-40s attack enemy positions at Matagob.

Dec31,'44-P-40s are now no longer on the Far East Air Force fighter unit lists.

Jan ,'45-All P-40s and P-40Bs are either obsolete or in restricted category.

Jan17,'45-P-40s of the 82nd Tactical Recon. Sdn. along with P-51s arrive on the Lingayan airstrip on Luzon, P.I.

Jul ,'45-The USAAF continues to use the P-40—mainly in the Pacific and Mediterranean areas, and in July there is a single P-40N group in the Pacific.

Jul23,'45-RAAF Kittihawks bomb a final target in Borneo. The RAAF, at its peak, has 14 fighter squadrons, of which eight are equipped with Kittihawks. In addition, Dutch Sdn.120 equipped with Kittihawks, accompanied the RAAF. The RNZAF at its peak has seven Kittihawk squadrons and has received a total of 293 of the Curtiss fighters.

Oct 5,'46-The XP-40 prototype aircraft is surveyed. It has spent its time at Wright Field in Dayton, Ohio.

'47-There are still some flyable P-40s left in France at the Mont de-Marsan base.

'49-P-40N aircraft are being used by the Netherlands East Indies against the Indonesian rebels. This is the last combat use of the P-40.

'58-Some P-40N aircraft are still in service in Brazil.

P-40 HANDLING QUALITIES AND CHARACTERISTICS

HANDLING QUALITIES
GROUND HANDLING
Taxi visibility straight ahead was nil. With the long nose rising up front the view ahead was blocked. One pilot said it was "a little worse than a P-51 and a little better than a P-47". Visibility to the

Fig.40-1 Curtiss XP-40, Ser.38-010, Mfr.photo via J. Schneider. The single prototype in the initial configuration of a P-36 airframe with an Allison V-1710 engine in shiny metal finish. Note the aft location of the Prestone cooler in a position similar to that of the later P-51 airplane. The carburetor air intake is on top of the cowling halfway between propeller and cockpit; the oil cooler intake ducting is low and forward. The landing gear is strictly P-36 type.

forward quarters and sides was generally good however. As with other tail-down fighters, taxiing was done using S-turns, that is, swinging the aircraft from side to side using the forward quarter view to see ahead. Braking was used for turning. Brakes were good, and not too susceptible to overheating. Even a slight turn required some effort. The tail wheel was not lockable, and the airplane was limited to 30 to 40 degree turns when the tail wheel was not in full swivel mode. To go into sharper turns the tail wheel was kicked into full swivel by holding on one brake and applying a fair amount of power. Torque swings were countered by braking and by rudder if taxi speed was high enough. Once the pilot was used to these methods, taxi was not too difficult.

TAKEOFF AND CLIMB
For takeoff the rudder trim tab was set nose right. Flaps were not normally lowered during operational takeoffs; they could be used however if set less than half way down. The book recommended 15 degrees for the P-40 and 30 degrees for the P-40E if their use was chosen. Cockpit checks were made, the aircraft was run up against the brakes, and with brake release the takeoff run was started. Hard right rudder was kicked initially to counteract the powerful torque reaction tending to turn the aircraft to the left. Even with smooth application of power the aircraft tended to swing, and firm right rudder was required. One USAAF pilot noted "An experienced P-40 pilot could be recognized by his muscular right leg". The right rudder requirement decreased almost linearly as speed built up,

Fig.40-2 Curtiss XP-40, Ser.38-010, Mfr. photo via John Schneider. First XP-40 flight was in the fall of 1938, and initial performance was disappointing, but publicity blurbs claimed a speed of 400 mph. To this then-thirteen year old author one look at that sharp pointed nose and it had to be true! The large wing-fuselage fairing was much cut down in later versions.

however the P-40 was probably the most difficult of US contemporary fighters to keep straight on takeoff, and an inexperienced pilot could have his hands full until he got the knack of it. The tail was not to be forced up violently in the early stages of takeoff or the pilot would lose control of the steerable tail wheel before rudder control was gained. The tail was raised slightly after having gained sufficient speed. The P-40 was not to be taken off three-point. In addition to the torque swing, when the tail came up the left wing had to be brought up using right stick, but not too much, or the aircraft increased its tendency to go left.

Depending on model and weight, takeoff speed was 90 to 105 mph IAS using MILITARY power, and lift-off was obtained by allowing the aircraft to fly itself off using some smooth aft stick. Once in the air the P-40 was cleaned up. Flaps, if used, retracted

Fig.40-4 Curtiss XP-40, Ser.38-010, Mfr. photo via F. Dean coll. The XP-40 seen here in late 1939 has evolved into production configuration. The radiator scoop and cooler design has been revised and integrated with the oil cooler system, the carburetor air intake moved forward between gun blast tube fairings, the wing-fuselage fairing has been cut down, and the main landing gear modified to a simpler design. Curtiss was well pleased with the high speed of over 360 mph.

rather quickly, but a standard rule was not to retract them under 500 feet altitude. Landing gear came up more slowly, most often one leg at a time. Climb power was set; best climb speed was 150 to 160 mph IAS, but sea level climb could be made at 140 mph without risk. Best climb speed decreased slightly as altitude was gained. In a P-40E or P-40K a low altitude climb rate of slightly over 2000 feet per minute could be established at MILITARY power and a normal weight. In a climb right rudder pressure increased. A right climbing turn needed extra rudder pressure; a left turn needed little.

TRIMMING

A major aspect of flying the P-40 series airplanes was handling trim changes from power and speed changes. A veteran AAF pilot stated "The trim changes with speed were more than in other con-

Fig.40-3 Curtiss XP-40, Ser.38-010, Mfr. photo via J. Schneider. The same prototype airplane getting a little closer to production configuration with coolant radiator moved forward, according to Project Engineer Don Berlin because the Curtiss Wright Sales Dept. pursuaded management it should be forward. In any case, the XP-40 won the January 1939 pursuit competition and was ordered into production. Note the nose gun blast tubes protruding to close behind the propeller.

Fig.40-5 Curtiss P-40s in Production, Mfr.photo via H.Andrews. An early production picture of P-40s at Curtiss in Buffalo shows fuselages and Allison powerplants lined up on dollys. The photo provides a good view of two coolant and one oil radiators mounted under the engine, the engine mount, reduction gear case, and forward mounting bulkhead.

Fig.40-6. Curtiss P-40 in Production, Mfr. photo via H. Andrews. Another in-plant picture of early P-40 production showing fuselages in various stages of assembly. Certainly a clear production flow line is not obvious at this stage, but Curtiss was the only US fighter manufacturer at this time doing any kind of volume production.

Fig.40-7 Curtiss P-40 photo via R. Besecker. One of the first 200 P-40 aircraft, now in squadron service with an Army paint job and old-style tail stripes. What appears to be an early type of gun camera is externally mounted ahead of the cockpit. Gills for the exit of oil and coolant radiator air are wide open just forward of the wing root area. Provision was made for the pilot to view the rear quarters by aft Plexiglas panels over concave sections of the turtledeck.

Fig.40-8 Curtiss P-40, photo via R. Besecker. Another in-service P-40, the first type to be painted in Army olive drab for some years. Soon the tail stripes would be gone. The photo shows the much simplified main landing gear compared to the earlier P-36. Contrary to some reports the P-40 was armed with four guns as shown here, two .50 caliber weapons in the upper cowl with one blast tube each side of the carburetor air intake, and one .30 caliber gun in each wing.

Fig.40-9 Curtiss P-40, Ser.39-280, USAAF photo. A fine flight view of a "plain P-40" showing off its shark-mouth nose, and most probably used as a fighter trainer stateside. The aircraft looks well used. The pilot is enjoying the fresh air! P-40 deliveries started in the spring of 1940, but this photo was taken much later. Unprotected fuel tanks carried 180 internal gallons; there were no external store stations.

temporary fighters". Typical of many single engine propeller fighters, the vertical tail fin was slightly offset to counter propeller slipstream effect at cruising speed. In a dive, as speed increased, more and more left rudder trim had to be added; slowing down in a climb some right rudder trim was needed. One pilot said "—a drawback was having to virtually stand on the left rudder pedal to keep the ball centered—it could be a real handful in a loop" (where trim reversed from dive to climb and then back again). Although directional trim tab power was available to zero out pedal force, left rudder trim could not be rolled in fast enough with high dive acceleration. No matter what P-40 version was involved, it was the same: "In the air the Tomahawk tended to yaw considerably with speed changes" , needing directional trim, and for the P-40E/H87A:

"Every power and speed change brings an immediate trim change which the pilot must either counteract or trim out". The H87 was, if anything, worse than the H81 Tomahawk.

On the P-40E lowering the landing gear made the aircraft slightly nose heavy; there was no appreciable trim change with flap positioning. Dropping a belly tank resulted in minor tail heaviness. The elevator trim system could take care of these effects as well as longitudinal variations due to speed and power changes.

DIVE AND RECOVERY

If there was one point upon which all pilots seemed to agree; P-40 aircraft could dive well. A manual said "The P-40 is a great diving aircraft. In dives at maximum allowable speeds it has shown no tendency to vibrate, flutter, or break to pieces". One pilot said of a P-40B "Its best characteristic was its dive speed speed. With the nose down the P-40B picked up speed at an unbelievable rate". Another said of later models "We used the strengths of the P-40, one of which was its diving speed". A third noted of an H87A "I shoved the nose down. Within a few seconds speed was picking up

Fig.40-10 Curtiss P-40, photo via F. Dean coll. America's newest pursuit plane in 1940, this production P-40 retains early markings. With full fuel tanks and complement of ammunition the fighter weighed just under 7200 pounds. It was not yet a combat-worthy aircraft because it had no armor. It was also the fastest of the H81 style airplane versions.

Fig.40-11 Curtiss P-40B, Mfr. photo via J. Schneider. A P-40B in the Buffalo, New York winter of 1940-1941 after the British and the US Army reached accord on production standards and schedules. B models started going to US squadrons in February, 1941. This version had four .30 caliber wing guns besides the two .50s in the nose, some armor, and a start at fuel tank protection, and thus could be considered combat-worthy. Most P-40Bs went overseas to Hawaii and the Philippines.

Fig.40-12 Curtiss H81A-2 Tomahawk IIA, Mfr. photo via J.Schneider. An export model for Britain ready for service in late 1940, roughly equivalent to the P-40B with four wing rifle caliber guns besides the nose .50s. The ring and bead sight is readily apparent. This is the type sold to China for use by the Flying Tigers in January,1941. The British did not consider the Tomahawk models suitable for European use, and sent them to the Middle East.

Fig.40-13 Curtiss P-40C, Mfr. photo via H.Andrews. A factory photo shows P-40C aircraft being assembled. This version had internally protected fuel tanks which in the process reduced internal fuel capacity to 135 gallons, down from 180 gallons in the P-40. This reduction was compensated for to an extent by addition of a centerline mounted external tank. The picture shows that planes were "all over the place" in production.

rapidly until I was approaching 400 mph IAS with no effort". Dive speed limit of a P-40E was 485 mph IAS with an engine limit of 3120 RPM, and minimum safe altitude to start pullouts from this speed was 7100 to 8000 feet depending on model. This was because dive acceleration was rapid and initial pullout stick force was inclined to be heavy. The elevator trim tab was very sensitive, and not to be used to assist pullout "unless absolutely necessary".

Normally P-40s would not experience compressibility effects because dives were not started high enough or continued long enough. However by the time a limit speed of 485 mph IAS was reached, say at 10000 feet altitude at the end of a long dive, the Mach number reached would be 0.77, and, like the P-39 with a similar drag divergent Mach number, the P-40 would be well into

compressibility. Operationally this would hardly ever happen. As one experienced P-40 pilot said "I made many high speed dives, but never encountered any of the signs of compressibility". Pilots were advised however that vertical dives from above 20000 feet were not recommended because of danger of compressibility.

A very significant dive characteristic was the strong right yaw tendency requiring more left rudder as speed increased. As one P-40B pilot put it "The need for constant attention was dramatically illustrated during strafing runs; the aircraft had a tendency to skid." In addition there was some right wing heaviness. When diving a P-40 tended to roll to the right; the higher the speed the greater the tendency to roll. As the book said of the P-40E, trim tab action was required to counteract both turning and rolling forces in dives. Pi-

Fig.40-14 Curtiss P-40C, Mfr. photo via H. Andrews. A refueling scene in the Curtiss factory yard with the new P-40C version showing off its external fuel tank. The smooth finish of a factory-fresh airplane is apparent, as is the Curtiss Electric propeller decal on the upside blade. As with most all the fighters, empty weight was growing; that of the C model was about 400 pounds greater than that of the P-40.

Fig.40-15 Curtiss P-40C, Mfr. photo via H. Andrews. Another factory view of a new P-40C with wing tanks being fueled. The background aircraft are also P-40Cs; note the sway braces under the bellies. Famed Curtiss test pilot Lloyd Child made the first P-40C flight in April, 1941. The C model order of only 193 aircraft was completed by the end of May that year.

Fig.40-16 Curtiss P-40D, Mfr. photo via F. Dean coll. One of only twenty-two P-40Ds built, the initial version of the H87A type appearing in the summer of 1941. A substantial change in appearance was effected by revisions in the P-40 sufficient to make it almost a new design. The nose contour changed primarily because of a new Allison engine reduction gear arrangement, but the engine still had only a single stage single speed geared supercharger.

Fig.40-17 Curtiss P-40D, Mfr. photo via F. Dean coll. Flight view of the P-40D shows new nose contours including a much deeper air scoop for Prestone and oil coolers, a larger propeller spinner, and a flattened carburetor air scoop atop the cowl. An important change, masked here by photo retouching, was placement of all guns in the wings and these of .50 caliber. In the P-40D the armament was four wing guns. The P-40D airplanes went to the Panama Canal Zone.

lots had to keep hard on the left rudder pedal to avoid skidding. The rudder required excess pedal pressure in a dive, and as noted earlier, rudder tab action was too slow to completely alleviate the pressure during steep dive bombing attacks.

With the significant design changes making up the P-40E model, major faults in directional stability and control came to the fore. As a NACA test report put it "Difficulties were experienced in P-40 series aircraft in dive demonstrations, and there were inadvertant entries into spins in service operations." Yawing led to snap rolls and then to spins. There were also rudder force reversals in sideslips using rated power at the lower speeds, as noted subsequently. Three new tail configurations were tested to find a fix for these problems, a dorsal fillet on the standard fin, a tail of totally new geometry, and the same tail surfaces on a 20 inch longer fuse-

lage. The initial fix, used in late P-40E and some P-40F and P-40K aircraft, was the dorsal fillet along with a zero-offset fin and a rudder trim tab only, no balance tab. These changes were effected to minimize impact on production lines. Later when a more major change could be reasonably introduced into production, the long-fuselage P-40 was born, first in the later P-40F models. These fixes were successful in taming the very worst of the directional problems, but P-40s could still be a handful (or more accurately perhaps a footful) in diving flight. One pilot who had flown both fuselage versions stated "As far as I could tell there was no flying difference between short and long fuselage models". But pilots were told the short fuselage P-40s had greater rudder and elevator loads and thus required more rudder and elevator pressures.

Fig.40-18 Curtiss P-40Es, Mfr. photo via Hal Andrews. An interesting photo of P-40Es in final assembly almost ready to go out the door. Removed cowl panels show some powerplant details including oil and coolant tanks and a diagonal member of the engine mount. The background P-40E has its baggage compartment open. The high wing monoplanes in the rear are Curtiss O-52 Owl observation planes. Some of these went to Russia.

Fig.48-19 Curtiss P-40Es, Mfr. photo via H.Andrews. This Curtiss plant yard view shows four P-40Es and an O-52 as well as a DC-3 in the background. The only way to easily distinguish E models from the D was the former had six wing guns instead of four, and the facing aircraft appears to have three gun ports in the starboard wing leading edge. It is undoubtedly the summer of 1941 with the US not yet in the war; Curtiss started P-40E deliveries in late August of that year. Note the shirtsleeved employees.

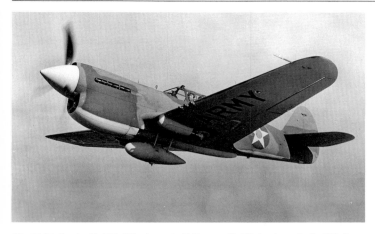

Fig.48-20 Curtiss P-40E, Mfr.photo via F. Dean coll. Flight view of a P-40E shows clearly the three .50 caliber guns in the port wing and also illustrates the manner in which the retracted landing gear wheel laid flat in a wing underside pocket. The 52 gallon belly tank was now a standard item; together with internal fuel the P-40E would carry 200 gallons. The P-40E-1 was the Lend-Lease version . About 2300 Es were built.

Fig.48-21 Curtiss P-40E, photo via R. Besecker. The deep forward airscoop and the shorter landing gear of the P-40E are emphasized in this photo. This early E was marked up for the fall 1941 Louisiana Army War Games, and by appearances got some fairly rough use. Just about this time fifty new P-40Es were sent direct from the factory to reinforce the Philippines, and shortly after British Lend-Lease E-1 Kittihawk versions started arriving in Egypt.

Left: Fig.40-22 Curtiss H87A-2 Kittihawk I, Mfr. photo via J. Schneider. One of the first H87A models, the British export equivalent of the P-40D with four wing guns. England contracted for twenty four-gun and 540 six-gun Kittihawks on a direct buy prior to the Lend-Lease agreement; AK571 was well photographed to illustrate the aid we were giving Britain.

Fig.40-23 Curtiss P-40E-1, Ser.41-25094, Mfr. photo via H. Andrews. Many attempts were made to increase range of fighter aircraft and provide a self-ferrying capability to avoid the submarine menace and quicken deliveries, a prime concern in the global war, and particularly in 1942. This August 1942 photo at Buffalo shows one such experiment with two very large (225 gallon) under-wing tanks on a P-40E-1. Takeoff weight would have been close to 11000 pounds, very high for a P-40. It is doubtful the arrangement ever had any in-service use.

Fig.40-24 Curtiss H87A-3 Kittihawk, Mfr. photo via H. Andrews. A Curtiss test pilot poses a Kittihawk for Britain over the northern New York countryside for the camera plane. He has slowed the fighter and opened the cockpit hatch and lower cooling air exit gills. Most British Kittihawks went to squadrons in the North African desert where they were operated by British, Australian, New Zealand, and South African pilots.

Fig.40-25 Curtiss H87A-3 Kittihawk, Mfr. photo via H. Andrews. Another flight view of the British-named Kittihawk. The US Army P-40 aircraft through the P-40E never had a name. Three of the six .50 caliber wing guns show here. H87A aircraft went into North African combat in January of 1942. In the spring many were turned into "Kitti-bombers".

When pulling out of a dive in the P-40B stick forces grew very heavy with a lot of effort necessary to bring the nose up at diving speeds approaching 400 mph IAS. One pilot commented "A gradual pullup was a fight with very heavy elevators." Another pilot, perhaps more muscular, said "Stick forces per g in dive pullouts were fairly high, but not excessive." Controls stiffened almost linearly with increased airspeed; elevator and rudder forces were high in high speed dive pullouts. In pulling out too suddenly from a dive a pilot could get into a high speed (accelerated) stall, and the aircraft would snap over and start a spin. Pilots were instructed "Pull out of a dive firmly and smoothly".

MANEUVERING

In general P-40 series aircraft were designed to perform most all fighter-type maneuvers. There were restrictions, however. Prohibited maneuvers were outside loops, sustained inverted flight, spins of over three turns (no spins with baggage or external stores), and inverted spins. In addition there were restrictions on rolls; depending on the P-40 version no snap rolls over 140 to 180 mph IAS, and no slow or barrel rolls over 260 to 310 mph IAS were to be performed. These roll limitations were tied to the directional stability and control difficulties noted above.

Fig.40-26 Civil Curtiss "P-40E", Ron McCann photo via F. Dean coll. This fine rehabilitated "P-40E" at a 1980s Oshkosh airshow is probably an ex-Canadian H87A Kittihawk, several of which came back into the US post war. Another is exhibited at the National Air and Space Museum in Washington, D.C. The serial number on the tail appears to be ficticious. Note the electric gunsight on the forward cockpit coaming.

Fig.40-27 Civil Curtiss H87A Kittihawk, R. Besecker photo. A restored latter-day Kittihawk in fine condition with powerplant cowl panels stripped off provides a view of how left and right wing panels carry through the fuselage and are joined at the aircraft centerline. The engine mount and isolators along with Prestone and oil coolers are also clearly shown.

Fig.40-28 Curtiss XP-40F Warhawk, Ser.40-360, Mfr.photo via F. Dean coll. A converted P-40D is tested using the Rolls Royce Merlin engine with a single stage two speed supercharger. Note the two gun wing panel. The Merlin is to be built under license by Packard Motor Car Co. The upper cowl is now smooth because the Merlin had an updraft carburetor. The XP-40F was tested with several different tail configurations.

Fig.40-29 Curtiss XP-40F Warhawk, Ser.40-360, Mfr. photo via F. Dean coll. Another picture of the second P-40D converted to the Merlin engine. This engine conferred some increased altitude performance on the P-40 due to provision of about 200 extra horsepower available over the Allison at altitudes over 20000 feet. The Merlin was heavier than the Allison engine however, and the version in the P-40 was not the one later installed in the Mustang, the latter being a two stage mechanical supercharger instead of single stage two speed.

Fig.40-30 Curtiss P-40F Warhawk, Mfr. photo via H. Andrews, A nose closeup of the new Warhawk, the name officially bestowed on USAAF P-40s starting with the F version. P-40E-1 aircraft with Allison engines are in the background. Production deliveries of the P-40F started in January, 1942 and ran into February of 1943. Details of nose scoop, cooling air exit gills, and external fuel tank installation show up well.

In general P-40 airplanes were very maneuverable for US Army fighters, some said better than a P-51. Early Pacific war reports credited them as being more maneuverable than a P-39, and they were certainly better in this respect than P-38 or P-47 airplanes. The P-40 had few equals among US fighters below 15000 feet; it turned inside nearly all other high performance fighters. Constant use of rudder trim control was recommended in a turn. A higher propeller RPM setting allowed a tighter turn. Before the P-40 reached stall in a turn it gave plenty of warning by shuddering violently, and a tight turn could be made even under shuddering conditions if controls were coordinated smoothly. Like other US fighters the P-40 had too high a wing loading to maneuver close-in with Japanese fighters. A P-40 combat veteran said "We never tried to out-turn a Japanese fighter, but in practice dogfighting other US fighters the P-40 could generally out-turn them. Stick forces were not excessive in wind-up turns". The early P-40s were handed down the light ailerons and well-harmonized controls of their direct predecessor, the P-36. One pilot said "A pretty good airplane for slam-bang maneuvers compared to other US fighters", and another stated "There was nothing pilots wouldn't try in a P-40C. As long as you got airflow over the control surfaces and had enough altitude, it would come out of any maneuver".

These aircraft were both statically and dynamically stable in the longitudinal mode at normal center of gravity locations.

P-40 airplanes were particularly good in roll. An early model was shown in one report as having a maximum roll rate of 135 degrees per second at an indicated airspeed of 360 mph. Later data show a P-40F having a peak rate of 95 degrees per second at about 275 mph IAS. In any case pilots attested to high roll rates. For the P-40C "It had an extremely high rate of roll". For the H87A/P-40E "The rapid roll rate , the most delightful aspect of the P-40". And other comments: "The extremely rapid roll rate—", "Rolls are effortless", "Rolling performance was excellent; I think it was as good as any AAF fighter", "Rapid aileron response; by comparison the P-51 was locked in cement", and "Roll was great".

Fig.40-31 Curtiss P-40F Warhawk, Mfr. photo via H.Andrews. Clean lines of a P-40F in flight are evident. This airplane is a short fuselage F with no fin fillet. With the big scoop up front and the short aft fuselage and tail arm P-40s were experiencing stability difficulties in dives and inadvertant entries into spins. Late P-40F aircraft had either the fin fillet or the longer aft fuselage.

Fig.40-32 Curtiss P-40F Warhawk, Mfr. photo via H. Andrews. Well over 50 P-40 fighters, all F models as far as can be determined, are shown sitting in a Curtiss plant yard at Buffalo. The red circle center has now disappeared from the national insignia on these aircraft. A chain fall hovers over the near Warhawk. In the hands of a good pilot the Warhawk could be a potent adversary at low and moderate altitudes.

Fig.40-33 Curtiss P-40F Warhawks, Mfr. photo via H. Andrews. These Merlin powered Warhawks appear ready for final flight test and delivery to service units; all are short fuselage aircraft. Over 1300 P-40F versions were produced by Curtiss. Many went to North Africa and the Middle East, some delivered by and flown off aircraft carriers.

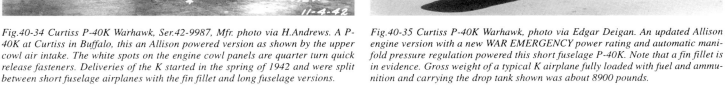

Fig.40-34 Curtiss P-40K Warhawk, Ser.42-9987, Mfr. photo via H.Andrews. A P-40K at Curtiss in Buffalo, this an Allison powered version as shown by the upper cowl air intake. The white spots on the engine cowl panels are quarter turn quick release fasteners. Deliveries of the K started in the spring of 1942 and were split between short fuselage airplanes with the fin fillet and long fuselage versions.

Fig.40-35 Curtiss P-40K Warhawk, photo via Edgar Deigan. An updated Allison engine version with a new WAR EMERGENCY power rating and automatic manifold pressure regulation powered this short fuselage P-40K. Note that a fin fillet is in evidence. Gross weight of a typical K airplane fully loaded with fuel and ammunition and carrying the drop tank shown was about 8900 pounds.

There was good rudder control of adverse yaw due to roll and under sideslip conditions. Rudder pedal forces were about average, as were aileron forces, with ailerons effective through the flight speed range. Elevator forces tended to be a little heavy, but no more than a P-51.

APPROACH AND LANDING

The P-40 was noted for its landing qualities, many of them bad according to pilot's testimony. Among the comments "The H81A aircraft did not take kindly to close-the-throttle and stick-right-back landings, especially in a crosswind; result—a large number of wingtips dug in", and "Avoid crosswind landings whenever possible".". A crosswind landing was hairy", "It was tougher in a crosswind than any of its fighter contemporaries". Finally "The P-40 was the hardest to land of any of the US World War II fighters". P-40s, particularly the short fuselage models, were easy to ground loop because of rather narrow tread main landing gear. A reputation

for ground looping preceeded it with new pilot trainees. Most pilots preferred grass landings which of course were not always possible.

In a P-40 approach maximum gear down speed was 170 mph IAS and maximum flap down speed 140 mph IAS. An approach glide was established at 110 to 115 mph IAS. The throttle was cut and the landing made three point. Landing speed varied with model and loading. Generally the P-40 models handled well in dirty configuration at low approach speeds with all controls effective. If the approach speed was correct there was no tendency to float or sink too fast. A combat pilot related "The visibility in the landing pattern was satisfactory because we approached in a turn, and could see the runway until we lined up and the nose came up into the three point position." Landing the P-40 at night, though seldom necessary, was a problem because the flare from engine exhausts prevented the pilot from seeing much; this was also true for a P-51. In the ground runout the P-40 could be very skittish, particularly in

Fig.40-36 Curtiss P-40K Warhawk, Ser.42-10343, USAAF photo via C. Mandrake One of the later long fuselage K airplanes with a twenty inch length increase and the vertical tail displaced aft of the horeizontal surfaces, making a considerable change in the appearance of the P-40. Note the external ring and bead gunsight used as a backup to the primary electric reflector sight located behind the windshield on the cockpit coaming.

Fig.40-37 Curtiss P-40L Warhawk, photo via F. Dean coll. Another rendition of the Warhawk was the P-40L which combined the Merlin engine of the F with, in all but it's earliest variant, the long fuselage as shown here. Although much has been made of the fact that the P-40L was supposed to be a stripped light weight version, reference to the weight data herein will show little was accomplished in weight reduction with two guns and some armor removed. The L was the last P-40 with a Merlin engine. Like the F, many P-40L airplanes went to North Africa.

Fig.40-37A Curtiss P-40L Warhawk, Mfr. photo via H. Andrews. Flight photo of a P-40L with long fuselage and the smooth upper cowl associated with Merlin engine power along with the ubiquitous 52 gallon centerline drop tank. This was the four gun stripped "Gypsy Rose Lee" version, but all the weight came out of useful load. Merlin Warhawks outweighed Allison versions anyway.

Fig.40-38 Curtiss P-40M Warhawk production line, Mfr. photo via H. Andrews. Appearing in late 1942 with deliveries completed in early 1943 the P-40M reverted to the Allison engine again. Packard production was needed for P-51s. The six gun armament was restored. Most all of the 600 M airplanes were slated for British Commonwealth air forces as Kittihawk IIIs. Changes from the late K versions were minor. The photo shows M production lines at Curtiss. A couple of P-47G Thunderbolts can be seen at the far left.

a crosswind, and such cases had to be very carefully handled right down to low speed. Brakes were effective. For crosswind landings the procedure was to come in slightly hot with no more than 30 degrees of flap with a wing dipped into the wind and land wheels first. The nose tended to swing into the crosswind and corrections were made with rudder and brake. Although very experienced pilots could make three point landings in a crosswind, it required a high degree of skill, and the safer way to land in this case was wheels first. It was also better to land wheels first on a wet surface.

STALLS AND SPINS

P-40 stall characteristics were good. "An honest airplane" noted a pilot. The one g stall warning, both clean and dirty, was a conventional shudder a few miles per hour above stall speed. A typical stall speed was about 84 mph IAS dirty and about 90 mph IAS clean; there was some variation between individual aircraft. The stall was gentle; at the break the nose dropped straight ahead. Low speed one g stalls were considered safe. There was little wing drop unless the aircraft was mishandled and the ball not centered. If there

Fig.40-39 Curtiss P-40N Warhawk, Ser.42-104958, Mfr. photo via J.Schneider. In March of 1943 the first of the P-40N versions was delivered from Curtiss. After the initial variant the remainder of the series could be recognized by the change in aft canopy design. The P-40N was produced in far greater quantities than other versions. Shown here is a factory-fresh N-5 model with the now-standard long fuselage and the standard 52 gallon belly tank. This photo emphasized the relatively narrow landing gear tread of the P-40, assisting in its title of toughest fighter to land.

Fig.40-40 Curtiss P-40N Warhawk, Mfr. photo via H. Andrews. A Curtiss publicity photo of its P-40N with pilot in a typical wartime pose. The picture shows the Curtiss propeller decals on the blades, the large three-section split lower intake, and Allison upper cowl carburetor air scoop, horn-type exhaust stacks, the squared-off aft canopy peculiar to the N, and a wing bomb rack aft of the gun muzzles. The grillwork just aft of the spinner provides for bypass carburetor air through the warm engine compartment.

Fig.40-40A Curtiss P-40N-35 Warhawk, Mfr.photo via H. Andrews. One of 500 N-35 variants production of which started in July of 1944 near the end of the line. This factory-fresh airplane was photographed over upper New York State on July 8,1944 subsequent to a local air show demonstration. Contrasting this flight view with a much earlier one of the prototype XP-40 will show how much the P-40 configuration changed from 1938 to 1944.

was gross mishandling the aircraft would tend to snap roll over on its back and enter a spin. With proper handling there was no tendency to spin from a stall. Stall recovery was effected by dumping the stick forward. With an accelerated stall, such as in a tight turn, there was less warning and more violent action. In this case it could easily snap into a spin. "If a high speed stall develops it usually snaps the aircraft", and "If you get into a high speed stall in a turn it gave plenty of warning by shuddering violently, and a tight turn could be made even under shuddering conditions if controls were coordinated smoothly". The motion at the high speed stall break

Fig.40-41 Curtiss P-40N Warhawk, photo via E. Deigan. Flight photo of P-40N shows well the new squared-off aft canopy arrangement. Beneath the canopy the turtledeck structure sloped down as it went forward. The pilot's view to the rear quarters was enhanced over the earlier arrangement, though vision could not have been as good as with a full bubble canopy.

was the same as a one g stall, but unless the P-40 was caught instantly a severe departure would result. Stall recovery procedure was the same—release stick back pressure at the first shudder. Pilots were advised to avoid high speed stalls because they were dangerous.

Spin qualities differed between P-40 models. Commenting on a P-40C type, a pilot noted "It was almost impossible to spin. This marked tendency of the P-40C to resist spins was very unusual. Even if you tried to snap it, it would simply skid, making only a one eighth or one quarter turn, alternating violently from side to side, but refusing to slide in and wind up". However the P-40E would spin. In the manual the spin was characterized as extremely violent, though one experienced P-40 pilot described it as "A fairly tight spin, but recovery was standard." As to recovery the pilot said "In fact if you let go of the controls it would usually recover by itself". This was true, and was OK as long as the pilot had enough altitude. The airplane would recover in two or three turns with each turn losing about 1000 feet and full recovery taking about 2000 feet after the plane stopped turning. The standard by-the-book recovery procedure was to throttle back and apply opposite rudder, put the stick forward, and not use ailerons against the spin because it blanketed the rudder. One pilot said "Our instructors told us to spin it so we would know the recovery techniques". The manual said, however, "Never spin the P-40 intentionally; spins should be avoided". It also noted it was possible, in short fuselage P-40s, to make the rudder lock full left if the airplane was skidded with almost full left rudder at fairly low speed, and then power suddenly applied. This action could cause a spin. Power reduction would unlock the rudder allowing it to be centered. In the case of an inverted spin the procedure was to change into a normal spin and recover using stan-

Fig.40-42 Curtiss P-40N Warhawk, Mfr. photo via H. Andrews. A P-40N for China with the Nationalist star on the wing sits outside the plant near a C-46A transport. The extent of the wing flap area is shown in this flaps-down photo. P-40s were used by the CACW, the Chinese-American Composite Wing. Towards the end of the war P-40s in China were being outclassed by the newer Japanese fighters.

Fig.40-43 Curtiss P-40N Warhawk, Mfr. photo via H. Andrews. The flavor of a wartime flight test hangar is tasted in this picture where parts of five P-40s can be seen. The bar on the national insignia finally appears under the wing of the near airplane. Curtiss never got a production fighter replacement for the P-40 though they tried all through the war with the XP-60 series.

dard methods. Changing to a normal spin involved retarding throttle, pulling full back pressure on the stick, and applying rudder with the spin.

CHARACTERISTICS
COCKPIT

The cockpit had plenty of room for the average fighter pilot, and "Large pilots did not seem to complain". One pilot was "Impressed with the cockpit roominess; more space than a P-51". The pilot could move his head around easily, and there were both seat and

rudder pedal adjustments, though on P-40N models the seat was ground-adjustable only via re-bolting. Cockpit heating was adequate for the moderate altitudes normally attained by P-40s.

Ventilation was marginal to poor with the canopy closed, and pilots got hot at low altitudes in summer conditions, often flying with open canopies when feasible. The cockpit noise level was not objectionable with the canopy closed. One veteran pilot rated the P-40 cockpit slightly more comfortable than a P-51 and slightly less so than a P-47, but this shows how pilot opinions can differ

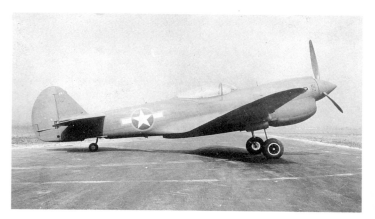

Fig.40-44 Curtiss XP-40N Warhawk, Mfr.photo via F. Dean coll. This photo shows Curtiss did test a bubble canopy on a P-40 with this aircraft carrying the designator XN-1 on its vertical tail. Why the bubble instead of the squared-off rear canopy was not incorporated in any production N airplanes is not known.

Fig.40-45 Curtiss P-40N Warhawk, Mfr. photo via J. Schneider. Throughout the war efforts were made to increase fighter range, including ferry range. Here a company photo dated 6/28/43 shows a P-40N decked out with very large fuel tanks hung on its wing bomb racks and supported with long sway braces. Test results are not known, but the takeoff weight so equipped and fueled up must have been extremely high.

Fig.40-46 Civil Curtiss P-40N Warhawk, photo via P.M. Bowers. A restored P-40N in pristine condition sits painted with a fine shark's mouth, and illustrates the contours and features of the last of the P-40 production line. The last production order for P-40s was given in June 1944, and the last P-40 left Curtiss that November. There was considerable post-war criticism that P-40s were produced so long.

Fig.40-47 Curtiss TP-40N, USAAF photo. A few P-40s were converted to two-seat trainers, some at the factory and some as field conversions. This P-40, probably revised in the field, sidles up to the camera plane with cooling gills wide open.

since others rated a P-51 more comfortable than a P-47 (probably the long-legged ones in the latter case).

Cockpit controls and instrument layout were generally good for the period, pretty much on a par with the P-47, P-51, and P-63. All instruments and displays could be seen and read easily. A modern pilot looking at a P-40E cockpit said "Controls all over the place, but generally straightforward and laid out logically". Adverse comments were "The flap handle seemed to work in the wrong sense for some people", and "The electric bomb release on the stick was not reliable, and the manual cable releases on the floor were awkward to operate".

VISIBILITY
As noted earlier, taxi visibility ahead was non-existant. In the air, except for near stall when the nose was high, visibility was generally good forward and to the side, but poor to the rear compared to the bubble canopy P-47 and P-51 airplanes. In all except the latest P-40N versions vision to the rear was facilitated by concave cutouts in the structure aft of the cockpit covered with transparent panels. In most P-40Ns structure was cut down drastically at an angle to effect improved visibility to rear areas. No production P-40s ever got a full bubble canopy.

POWERPLANT OPERATION
Some pilot comments on the Allison and Packard Merlin powerplants are interesting. For the Allison: "Lost power rapidly above 12000 feet, and not the most reliable of powerplants"; "Lacked automatic manifold pressure controls" (on early models); "Prone to overheating"; "Did not thrive on high power settings, and I was afraid it would come apart"; and "Many pilots avoided using full power with an Allison, even in emergencies". For the Merlin: "The Merlin in the P-40F was more prone to overheating on the ground than the Allison", and "We had more confidence in the Merlin than in the Allison".

VULNERABILITY/ARMOR
The literature is filled with references to the ruggedness and relative invulnerability of the P-40, in fact even those most critical of the type grant these characteristics, if little more. An early official report from the Pacific said "The P-40 fighter was able to absorb a very large number of hits, both cannon and machine gun, in the fuselage skin and armor plating. The P-40E-1 armor plating is believed to be the most satisfactory one observed to date (early 1942); this protection includes pilot, engine, and glycol tank". Of the P-40C it was said "The P-40 could absorb a great deal of punishment and still continue to fly". A pilot summarized the subject pretty well: "A very rugged airplane; it could take a lot of punishment and return unless you were hit in the coolant". A coolant hit would disable the powerplant very quickly indeed. One pilot, in discussing this aspect of the P-40 compared to a P-51C, concluded that the cooling system of the P-40 was much less vulnerable to gunfire than that of the P-51C because it was concentrated in the nose area rather than extending aft to a rear cooler location as in the latter airplane.

GUN PLATFORM AND WEAPON PERFORMANCE
One World War II pilot who had flown them all rated the P-40 gun platform qualities about the same as the P-51, but not as good as a P-47 or a P-38. The P-40 armament, starting with the P-40D, consisted of either four or six wing-mounted .50 caliber machine guns, most often six. The installation was a good one and the guns themselves were reliable; it was extremely rare for a gun to jam. The P-40K, M, and N did not have gun chargers, so if a jam did occur there was no remedy when in the air. There were no ammunition counters either, so you could not tell which gun had stopped when it ran out of ammunition, though you could tell which side. The need to know was academic however since nothing could be done.

Fig.40-49 Curtiss XP-40Q, Mfr. photo via F. Dean coll. The last try at extending the life of the P-40 as a fighter was the XP-40Q of which three were converted from other P-40 airframes. With a higher power Allison engine version having a two stage supercharger, a four blade propeller, a bubble canopy, and other modifications, the Q was nearly a new airplane and bore no resemblance to early P-40s.

Fig.40-48 Curtiss TP-40N, Mfr. photo via H. Andrews. With the P-40 design obsolete as a first-line fighter, but still used extensively as a single place fighter-trainer, Curtiss made efforts in 1945 to keep the line going by selling a two place version as a trainer. Pictured here is the manufacturer's effort in this direction looking somewhat slicker than some of the field conversions. But in any case no production resulted. The day of the P-40 was over.

GENERAL COMMENTS

One pilot who had flown various aircraft indicated the H87A Kittihawk was the most enjoyable to fly of all.

It was not at all tiring to fly, because it became almost part of the pilot, and you flew it without thinking of the pilot per se. Easy to fly formation, very few instruments to worry about; nothing required constant attention. It was a lot of fun to fly. Rat races and simulated dogfights were great sport. Definitely a pilot's airplane. It was a favorite of mine because I have more time in it than any other propeller fighter, and I flew it in combat.

No difference in the air between Allison and Merlin engined models.

You had to remember to kick rudder early in takeoff and then the rest was OK.

The preferred method of bailout was to dive over the right wing, or alternately roll in nose down trim but hold back pressure on the stick, roll inverted, and let go of the stick and drop out. Most all pilots cleared structure successfully.

Even with stiff controls the P-40 had excellent flight characteristics. Pilots could fly it in the stall without a problem if they were careful.

The P-40 was behind the times when introduced and never caught up. But it was the best available fighter at the time.

The P-40 could be very effective, and if well flown could even best an ME-109 at low altitude.

Stalin to Roosevelt, October 7,1942: "It should be borne in mind that the Kittihawk planes do not stand the fight against present German pursuits."

Fig.40-50 Curtiss XP-40Q, Mfr. photo via F. Dean coll. Flight view of a Q model illustrates some physical features including the bubble canopy and the four gun armament. The four blade propeller and the cut down rear fuselage combined would tend to destabilize the airplane compared to earlier three blade propeller high turtledeck models. The shark's mouth did not help to make the airplane operational!

Fig.40-51 Curtiss XP-40Q, Ser.42-45722, Mfr. photo via F. Dean coll. The airframe of this XP-40Q test aircraft is one from the second batch of P-40Ks, but many modifications have taken place. In spite of this Curtiss modernization effort the XP-40Q offered no performance improvement over then-current US fighter production models.

Fig.40-52 Civil Curtiss XP-40Q racer, photo via P.M. Bowers. One of the XP-40Qs was bought from Curtiss and groomed as the racer shown here, but racing success eluded the aircraft which crashed at the 1946 National Air Races. This final P-40 in almost no way except perhaps the basic wing resembled the early H81 type P-40 fighter that Don Berlin's design team started.

The Japanese were loathe to meet the six heavy caliber guns of a P-40 close and head on.

The primary disadvantages of the P-40s were lack of range and altitude capability.

In the Pacific area only the P-47 could out-dive the P-40E.

When you learn to fly the P-40 there won't be a fighter you can't handle. The P-40 is no cinch to fly; its fast and skittish and responds like lightning to controls.

If you are a good P-40 pilot you are a good fighter pilot.

You cannot doze at the controls of a P-40.

Many Commonwealth and American pilots ground looped P-40s.

A belly tank slowed a P-40 about ten mph.

No matter what we did we just couldn't make an ME-109 out of a P-40.

The advantage of the P-40 was an ability to maintain a dive at greater speed than that of the Zero.

After checking out in a P-40 one pilot reported he didn't like having to constantly trim for speed changes, and was concerned about landing, having heard they were hardest to land.

The P-40 was, in the early stages, an excellent fighter against the Japanese fighters below 20000 feet, where it was better than the Hurricane.

A pilot had the following to say about an H81A Tomahawk: No poor flying characteristics, handles well in roll, and lands nice enough, but a little stiff on the controls and not too maneuverable.

A new pilot worried about the rate at which the P-40 speed increased in a dive.

The Japanese Zero didn't seem as fast as the P-40, but was better in lower speed turns.

If an unwary pilot turned off the landing strip at too high a speed he could easily ground loop a P-40.

The split S was the best P-40 defense if attacked, even when as low as 5000 feet. With the ability to quickly roll over and start down it was as quick as a Zero.

Though maximum allowable dive speed of a P-40 was about 480 mph, pilots occasionally dove as fast as 510 mph.

One pilot noted if the H81 was stalled very nose high it would start a tail slide and could drop over 1000 feet before recovery was possible.

If hit and run fighting was used with the P-40 the fact it could not turn with the Japanese Zero did not matter because the P-40 could out-run its opposition.

The P-40 was a good fighter against the Zero.

The Germans in North Africa found that the P-40 turned quickly and well against the ME-109 while the latter was faster and climbed better. The German aircraft could initially dive more quickly as well, but in a long dive a P-40 would catch a ME-109.

P-40 STRUCTURAL DESCRIPTION
(Unless otherwise noted metal refers to aluminum alloy.)

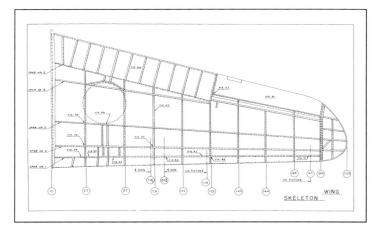

WING SKELETON

WING SEPARATED AT CENTER LINE BULKHEAD

WING GROUP

The wing was a completely separable unit shipped as a full wing assembly. It consisted of left and right panels spliced at the plan centerline of the fuselage by heavy bolted angles and multiple bolts. Each wing panel included three main spars extending across the full span of the panel along with partial span intercostal members for support of internal components. Main spars were built up of a single metal sheet web with punched lightning holes and riveted channel spar caps. The forward main wing spar lined up with the fuselage firewall bulkhead and formed a principal support for the main landing gear, and further inboard formed a forward bulkhead support for the wing section reserve fuel tank. The middle main spar also ran the length of the wing panel and formed a support for main landing gear retraction components, and for both the wing main and reserve fuel tanks inboard. It was also a forward support for .50 caliber wing machine guns and ammunition boxes outboard. A spanwise intercostal beam running between ribs in the inboard area of the panels behind the middle spar provided aft support for guns and ammunition boxes and for the wing main fuel tank. The pocket, or recess, for the retracted main wheel was located aft of the middle spar. The intercostal beam aft was built around the wheel

pocket. The rear spar ran the length of the wing semi-span just ahead of the ailerons and flaps, and provided support for hinges and control surface drive components. Wing ribs ran between spars and intercostals, and were stamped flanged metal sheet members with cut out lightning holes. Metal angles were riveted to join spar and rib webs. Ribs were cut out to accept extruded stiffening stringers running spanwise. Metal sheet skins were flush riveted over the wing panel framing. Cut-outs and access panels were provided in wing skins for landing gear wheel wells, fuel tanks, machine gun installation and ammunition containers, ejection chutes, inspection plates, and covered hand holes.

Flaps were of the split type and extended between ailerons on the wing trailing edge. They were all-metal units constructed of flat sheet riveted to half-ribs on the top surface, and hinged at the flap leading edge. A single on-centerline hydraulic cylinder drove a torque tube to actuate the flaps. Power for the flap cylinder was taken either from the basic hydraulic system or from emergency manual pumping. A flap control was located in the cockpit ; maximum flap-down speed was 140 mph IAS. Flaps could be positioned anywhere from full down to fully retracted.

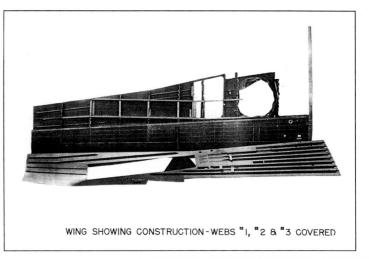

WING SHOWING CONSTRUCTION - WEBS #1, #2 & #3 COVERED

TAIL GROUP

The tail group was composed of a horizontal stabilizer, elevators, a vertical stabilizer/fin, and a rudder.

The horizontal stabilizer was a single piece assembly bolted to fittings on a rear fuselage deck. It was made up of a metal frame with a metal sheet covering flush riveted to the frame. Framing comprised a leading edge member, built up ribs and spanwise stringers, and a spar at the aft edge which mounted elevator hinges. A stabilizer cut-out at each tip made room for the aerodynamic balance portion of the mating elevator surface.

The elevators were statically, dynamically, and aerodynamically balanced, the latter by providing a tip section extending forward of the hinge line. The framework was metal, comprised of leading edge spar, built up ribs, a trailing edge member, and trim tab cut-out framing. The elevators were fabric covered, and a cockpit-controlled trim tab was inset on each elevator. Elevators were driven by bellcrank and torque tube, tabs by flexible shaft drives.

The vertical stabilizer, or fin, was tied to the fuselage via the horizontal stabilizer with six lugs, and was a cantilever all metal structure with flush riveted skins. Navigation lights were installed on each side, and an attachment on the upper leading edge formed an anchor for a radio aerial. The framing was comprised of a leading edge member, ribs, and vertical stringers, a rear spar supporting hinges for the rudder, and metal skins. The tip of the fin was cut back to clear the aerodynamic balance area of the rudder. Fairing skins blended the root areas of both fin and horizontal stabilizer into the fuselage.

The rudder was balanced statically, dynamically, and aerodynamically, and was made up of a metal frame covered with fabric. Framing consisted of forward spar assembly, ribs, tip and trailing edge member, and tab cut-out framing. The trim tab, located in the lower section of the rudder, and controlled from the cockpit, was equipped with a horn driven by a push rod running outside the contour on the right side and connecting with a mechanical drive inside the fuselage. The rudder was driven by a bellcrank and torque tube arrangement.

Ailerons were of all metal frame construction consisting of a metal-covered leading edge section, eleven ribs, and a trailing edge member, and were statically and dynamically balanced by means of lead weights bolted into the overhanging leading edge forward of the hinge line. Aft of the leading edge section the ailerons were fabric covered. The right side aileron contained a sheet metal ground-adjustable trim tab on its inboard trailing edge, and the left aileron carried a trim tab inboard which was adjustable from the cockpit via an adjacent electric motor in the wing driving mechanical linkage. A three-position tab control switch was available for the pilot.

The wing was attached to the fuselage by lowering fuselage over wing and bolting through attach angles on the wing at the sides of the fuselage. Contoured ribs from local fuselage formers and bulkheads provided anchors for large metal fuselage-to-wing fairings to blend the contours of the two assemblies.

FUSELAGE GROUP

The semi-monocoque all metal fuselage was built up as a single assembly from firewall aft with provision made for attachment of engine section components forward, the wing beneath, and the tail surfaces at the aft end.

The fuselage was comprised primarily of transverse frames and bulkheads forming the contours, four primary longerons (closed section on early models, open section on later ones), the upper longerons running along the cockpit edge and aft, longitudinal stringers between the longerons, and Alclad metal skins flush riveted to the framework.

Attach fittings for major components were provided. A cut-out and deck was provided at the aft end to attach the horizontal stabilizer to the fuselage. Cut-outs were also provided in the assembly for the cockpit, aft left side baggage compartment, radio bay, wing attach area, tail wheel assembly, and access panels and hand holds. Reinforcement was provided around cut-out areas. The forward bulkhead of the assembly was constructed as a firewall reinforced

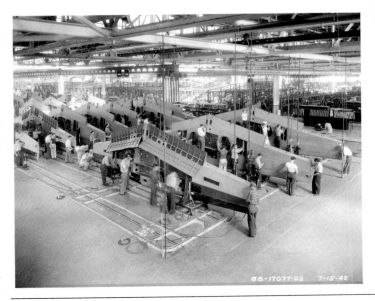

with stainless steel sheet. Four major attach fittings for the engine mount were located on the forward face. The first bay aft provided space and support for an engine oil tank, and was closed off by the cockpit forward bulkhead. The cockpit area was enclosed by a windshield assembly and an aft-sliding canopy. The windshield assembly was made up of four transparent sections set in metal framing. The front panel was of bullet-resistant glass, and the upper and two side panels were of heavy Plexiglass. An external rear view mirror completed the assembly. The sliding canopy was metal framed with Plexiglass transparencies. The left side panel was a knock-out section. The canopy on some aircraft was opened by pressing a flush-type release button located at the top rear frame of the windshield; on others it was held shut by a friction grip and could be opened by a sudden backward push. The emergency canopy release system used a hand crank on the cockpit right side driving a pulley and cable system to release the canopy from its sliding rails. Face-hardened armor plate was located both forward and aft of the pilot compartment. The cockpit seat on models prior to the P-40N version could be adjusted for height via a lock release handle on the right side. A spring-loaded positive lock system was employed. On the N the seat height was ground-adjustable by re-bolting it in a new position. The turtle deck framing and skin aft of the cockpit on models prior to the N had a concave recess on each side for three frame spaces covered with Plexiglass panels at full contour to provide some rear quarter vision to pilots. In most N models this ar-

rangement was revised to a cut-down sloped deck combined with additional large transparency areas. The fuselage aft section included supports for radio equipment, fuselage fuel tank, hydraulic system components, oxygen tank, baggage compartment, and tail landing gear. A lifting tube was built in transversely in the rear fuselage to facilitate handling and assembling the aircraft.

LANDING GEAR GROUP
The landing gear group consisted of two main gears and a tail gear assembly and controls. All gears were fully retractable.

The main gear elements were located just forward of the wing front spar. The oleo shock strut and axle assembly of each was mounted in a collar support allowing the strut to fold aft and also rotate or twist 90 degrees about its own axis. This collar support was attached to fittings mounted off the front spar of the wing. A side load brace ran diagonally inboard from a collar on the shock strut to the spar fitting, and was also capable of swinging aft. At the top of the shock strut a bevel gear segment mated with a fixed bevel gear segment mounted inboard in a manner to twist the shock strut and axle assembly 90 degrees as it retracted aft, thereby allowing the landing wheel to lay flat in a pocket provided in the wing underside. Drag and actuator links with downlock, and the hydraulic retracting actuator were mounted in the bay between front and middle wing spars and supported by the mid-spar. The retracted shock strut and side brace stayed outside and underneath the wing structure. A landing gear fairing assembly consisted of a fixed section running forward of and under the wing, and inner and outer fairing doors hinged to the fixed fairing. Doors were driven by the strut action. The shock struts were equipped with a torque scissors between strut body and piston. The main wheels, thirty inches in diameter, were equipped with hydraulic brakes actuated by cockpit toe pedals.

The 12.5 inch diameter tail wheel was fully retractable and enclosed by a tailwheel door. The wheel and axle were mounted on a single-sided fork at the bottom of an oleo shock strut. The strut was mounted in fuselage structure so that a tail gear retraction hydraulic actuator supported in the lower fuselage could swing the wheel and strut up into the fuselage recess. The tail wheel could normally swivel about 30 degrees either side, and the mechanism allowed it to be switched into full swivel when required.

The landing gear was normally extended or retracted employing a cockpit control lever with a safety latch bolt while using the basic hydraulic system. In an emergency a manually actuated hand hydraulic pump could also be used.

ENGINE SECTION
The engine section consisted of the engine mounting system and powerplant cowlings.

The engine mount was an alloy steel tubular assembly consisting of horizontal and diagonal members running alongside the engine. Rubber shock-absorbing mounts were located between the mount structure and the mounting pads of the engine proper. The tubular mount assembly was attached to the fuselage forward firewall bulkhead at four locations using mount fittings and bolts.

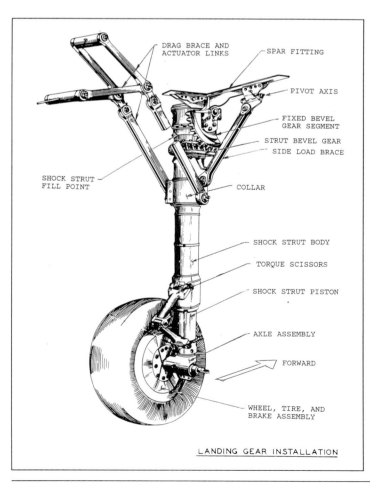

DRAG BRACE AND ACTUATOR LINKS

SPAR FITTING

PIVOT AXIS

FIXED BEVEL GEAR SEGMENT

STRUT BEVEL GEAR

SIDE LOAD BRACE

SHOCK STRUT FILL POINT

COLLAR

SHOCK STRUT BODY

TORQUE SCISSORS

SHOCK STRUT PISTON

AXLE ASSEMBLY

FORWARD

WHEEL, TIRE, AND BRAKE ASSEMBLY

LANDING GEAR INSTALLATION

The engine cowling system was made up of cowl panel support strips running forward from firewall to a mount ring just aft of the propeller spinner and supported by the engine reduction gearbox. Cowl panels differed depending on whether an Allison or Rolls Royce/Packard Merlin engine was used. On the Allison version the upper central cowl assembly included the duct leading to the downdraft carburetor; this ducting was not present on a Merlin engine cowl. Cowl side panels were cut out for the sets of engine exhaust stacks on each side. The lower cowl panel was a single large assembly attached to the lower support strips on either side and included entry ducts for engine cooling radiators on each side and the oil cooler in the center. Structural mounts for these items were supported by the engine mount. Cowl panels were attached to their mounting strips by a series of quickly releasable quarter turn fasteners. Cooling cowl flaps were hinged at the rear end of the lower cowl assembly. These flaps, or shutters, were actuated by a mechanical system driven from a cockpit control (on P-40F-10 and later models).

P-40 SYSTEMS DESCRIPTION

PROPULSION SUBSYSTEMS

ENGINE

The engine was either an Allison V-1710 liquid-cooled twelve-cylinder vee-type inline model of 5.50 inches bore and 6.00 inches stroke, or a Packard-built Rolls Royce Merlin V-1650-1 liquid-cooled twelve-cylinder vee-type inline model. The engines were in the 1100 to 1300 HP class. Several versions of the Allison engine were employed in the various aircraft models; the Merlin was used in the P-40F and the P-40L versions. The Allison engines, except for that in the experimental XP-40Q, all used an integral single-stage single speed supercharger with a 9.50 inch diameter blower driven at 8.77 times crankshaft speed, this running at a maximum of 3000 RPM. The propeller reduction gear ratio was 2:1, and the gearbox was integral with the engine.

The Merlin engine in the F and L airplanes employed an integral single-stage two speed supercharger with blower ratios of 8.151 in low gear and 9.49 in high gear. Compression ratio was 6:1 and maximum takeoff RPM was 3000 with a propeller reduction gear ratio of 0.447:1. The gearbox was an integral part of the engine. The SAE #50 splined output shaft of both engines rotated clockwise looking from the rear.

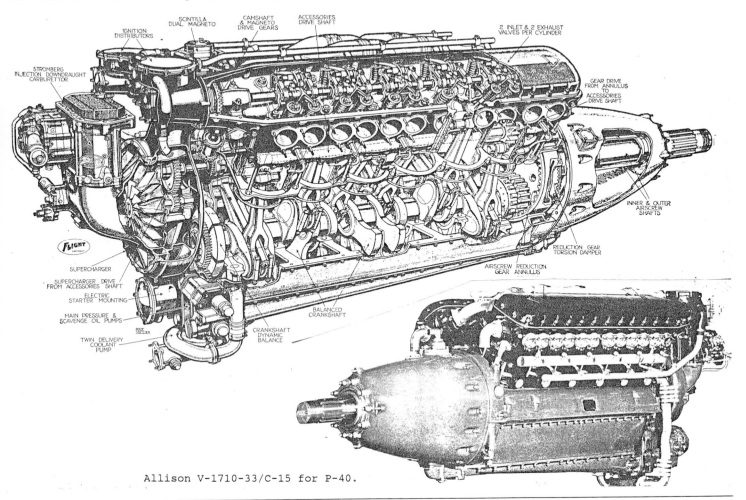

Allison V-1710-33/C-15 for P-40.

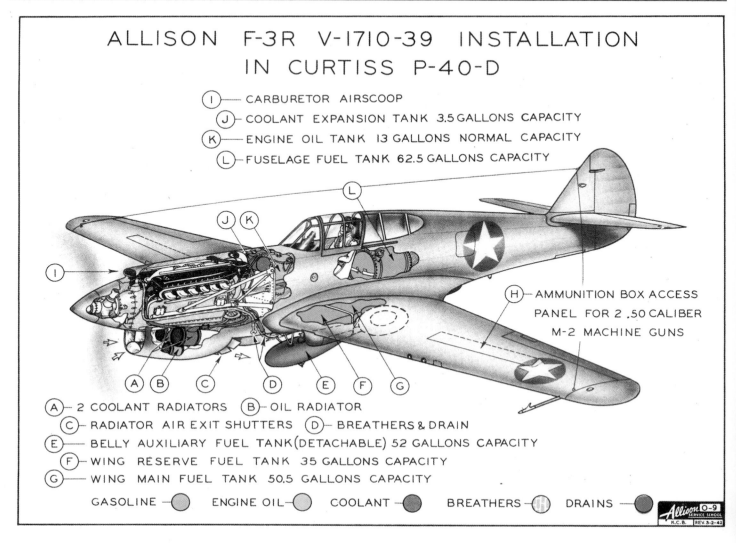

ALLISON F-3R V-1710-39 INSTALLATION IN CURTISS P-40-D

I — CARBURETOR AIRSCOOP
J — COOLANT EXPANSION TANK 3.5 GALLONS CAPACITY
K — ENGINE OIL TANK 13 GALLONS NORMAL CAPACITY
L — FUSELAGE FUEL TANK 62.5 GALLONS CAPACITY

H — AMMUNITION BOX ACCESS PANEL FOR 2 .50 CALIBER M-2 MACHINE GUNS

A — 2 COOLANT RADIATORS   B — OIL RADIATOR
C — RADIATOR AIR EXIT SHUTTERS   D — BREATHERS & DRAIN
E — BELLY AUXILIARY FUEL TANK (DETACHABLE) 52 GALLONS CAPACITY
F — WING RESERVE FUEL TANK 35 GALLONS CAPACITY
G — WING MAIN FUEL TANK 50.5 GALLONS CAPACITY

GASOLINE   ENGINE OIL   COOLANT   BREATHERS   DRAINS

ENGINE INTAKE SYSTEM

A ram intake air scoop located at the top of the forward fuselage directed air via ducting to the downdraft carburetor of the Allison engine models. On late Allison-powered models alternate air could be taken in from a flush screened duct just aft of the spinner on the side and through the warm engine compartment. On the Packard Merlin powered models the engine used an updraft Bendix-Stromberg carburetor. The intake duct was mounted in the middle of the large main air intake duct beneath the propeller spinner of the airplane. Ducting was such that alternate warm air could be taken from the engine compartment via a cockpit-controlled hinged vane in the intake path.

ENGINE EXHAUST SYSTEM

The exhaust system consisted of six stainless steel stacks mounted to engine exhaust ports on each side of the aircraft and protruding from the skin line. The stacks were curved and shaped to direct exhaust gases aft and provide jet thrust.

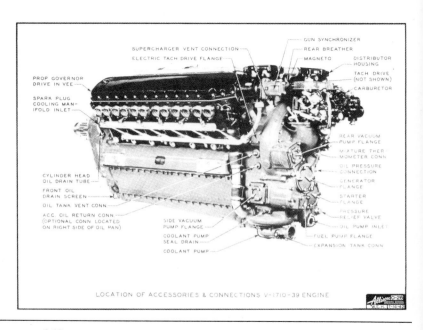

LOCATION OF ACCESSORIES & CONNECTIONS V-1710-39 ENGINE

ENGINE-MOUNTED ACCESSORIES

Accessories mounted directly on the engine included a fuel pump, lubrication oil pump, coolant pump, vacuum pump, electrical generator, tachometer, propeller speed governor, starter, and carburetor.

ENGINE CONTROLS

Cockpit-located engine controls were provided for throttle, fuel mixture, oil dilution, priming, and carburetor heat. All controls were mechanically operated and ran from the cockpit directly to the engine or engine compartment. The carburetor heat control operated a hinged vane in the intake duct. The Merlin-engined aircraft were equipped with automatic manifold pressure control with an on-off control lever on the bottom of the throttle quadrant which controlled the two speed supercharger. Allison powered P-40s starting with the K had a manifold pressure regulator. Its effectiveness decreased above 12000 feet altitude.

PROPELLER

The propeller was a Curtiss Electric C5315S model with three steel 614-1C1.5-12 design blades in 11'0" diameter. The propeller was a constant speed type with the alternate of selective fixed pitch, and electric power for blade pitch change was supplied by the aircraft system. With electric power failure the propeller would revert to fixed blade pitch. Under constant speed control the propeller operated from a low pitch at takeoff to high pitch at a high speed condition. Propeller blade angle varied from a low of 24.5 degrees to a high of 54.5.

PROPELLER CONTROLS

The propeller cockpit controls consisted of a governor control lever on the throttle quadrant and a three-way toggle switch on the front panel. With the switch in the AUTO mode the propeller was in automatic constant speed control with the speed determined by the position of the lever on the control quadrant. The lever connected via a mechanical linkage to the engine-driven speed governor mounted on the engine nose section which provided electrical output control signals to the propeller as required. Moving the cockpit switch to INCREASE or DECREASE would bypass the governor and directly increase or decrease blade angle via an electrical signal to the propeller. P-40N models had propeller and throttle controls linked.

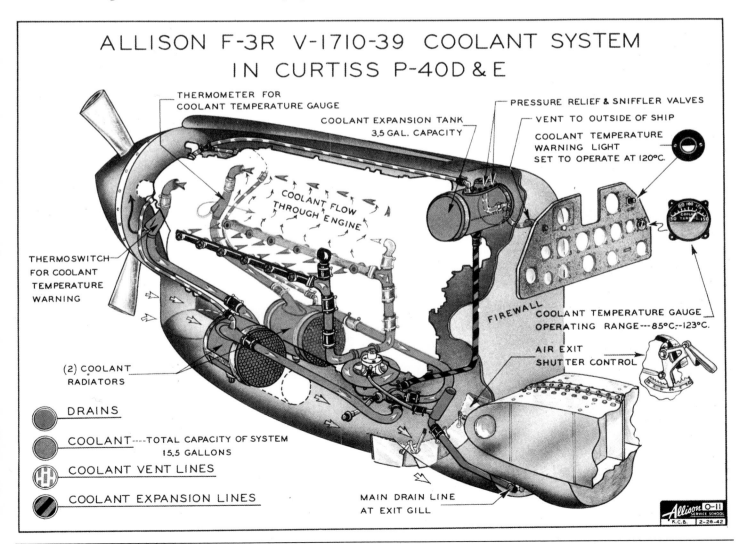

ALLISON F-3R V-1710-39 COOLANT SYSTEM IN CURTISS P-40D & E

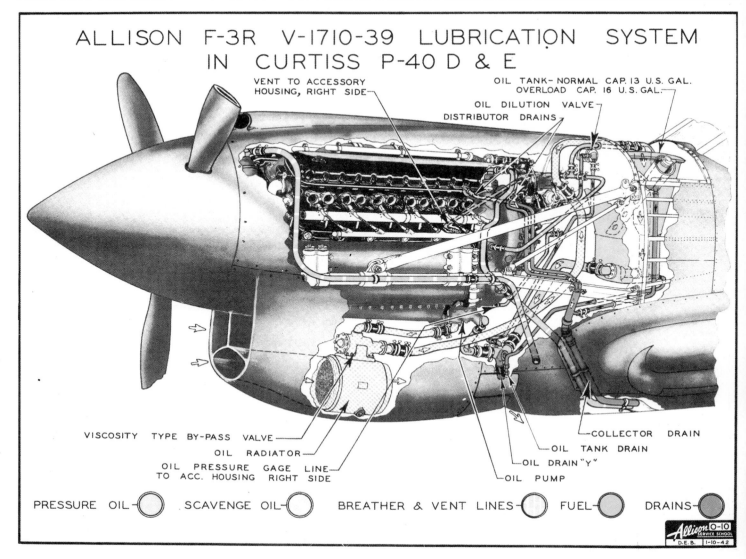

ALLISON F-3R V-1710-39 LUBRICATION SYSTEM IN CURTISS P-40 D & E

VENT TO ACCESSORY HOUSING, RIGHT SIDE

OIL TANK— NORMAL CAP. 13 U.S. GAL. OVERLOAD CAP. 16 U.S. GAL.

OIL DILUTION VALVE
DISTRIBUTOR DRAINS

VISCOSITY TYPE BY-PASS VALVE
OIL RADIATOR
OIL PRESSURE GAGE LINE TO ACC. HOUSING RIGHT SIDE

COLLECTOR DRAIN
OIL TANK DRAIN
OIL DRAIN "Y"
OIL PUMP

PRESSURE OIL— SCAVENGE OIL— BREATHER & VENT LINES— FUEL— DRAINS—

ENGINE STARTING SYSTEM
The engine starting system was an inertia type. An electric motor was turned on to spin up a flywheel; upon attaining maximum speed the flywheel was clutched to the engine to turn it over while acting through a reduction gear train. The engine was primed during the starting operation. The starter control was on the floor, and foot-operated. The heel was pressed to wind up the flywheel, and when the whine was loudest the toe was pressed to engage the starter and crank the engine.

ENGINE WATER INJECTION SYSTEM
No water injection system was fitted.

ENGINE COOLING SYSTEM
(Allison and Merlin systems were generally similar)
The Etheleyne Glycol liquid cooling system for the engine had all its components located forward of the firewall. These consisted of two cylindrical coolant radiators in the large duct under the engine with controllable exit shutters at the rear end of the ducting, a cool-

ant thermometer, a coolant pump driven by the engine, an expansion tank high and behind the engine with pressure relief and sniffler valves, connecting lines, and a temperature gage and warning light on the instrument panel. Main flow of the coolant was from the engine headers at the forward end of the V-12, aft and down to the coolers, left side to left cooler and right side to right, out of the coolers and into the pump, then back into the engine. A control linked mechanically to the shutters, or cowl flaps, was located at the right side of the cockpit, and incorporated a lock. It was operated manually to maintain desired coolant temperature. The radiator shutters were not to be extended over a speed of 175 mph IAS. On the Merlin-powered P-40F the exit shutters were operated electrically using a cockpit toggle switch control. Coolant capacity was 3.7 gallons. The filler was on top of the cowl.

ENGINE LUBRICATION SYSTEM
(Allison, Merlin generally similar.)
The lubrication system was totally contained in the powerplant area forward of the firewall. The engine oil cooler, a cylindrical assem-

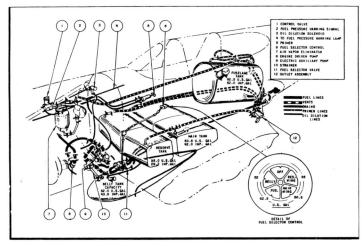

Fuel system diagram for P-40E.

sure and scavenge lines connected the above components, and vent and drain lines were directed overboard.

ENGINE FIRE SENSING/FIRE EXTINGUISHING SYSTEMS

There were no sensing or extinguishing systems on the airplane.

FUEL SYSTEM

The fuel system included the internal protected tanks, two in the wings inboard, and one in the fuselage. The main tank, with a capacity of 50.5 US gallons (capacities varied between models), was located astride the aircraft centerline between the central main wing spar and an aft intercostal beam. Another tank in the wing, designated the reserve tank, was also at the aircraft lateral centerline between the central and forward wing spars. The tank had a capacity of 35 US gallons. The fuselage tank with a capacity of 62.5 US gallons was located just behind the cockpit. This tank was of cylindrical shape and canted slightly down aft. It was filled via a filler neck extending up into the overturn structure. The other tanks were filled at over-wing points. The normal external drop tank was located on the aircraft centerline and had a capacity of 52 US gallons; it was not protected like the internal tanks. A fuel selector control in the cockpit with tank options indicated on its face drove through shafting, universals, and gearing, a fuel selector valve in the for-

bly with integral bypass valve and oil temperature regulator, was located in the large air intake duct below the engine and between the two coolant radiators. The engine-driven oil pump, which scavenged the oil into the cooler, was located at the lower aft end of the engine. The oil tank was located in a bay between engine and cockpit and had a normal capacity of 13 US gallons with a maximum of 18 gallons. An oil dilution valve was mounted on the firewall. Pres-

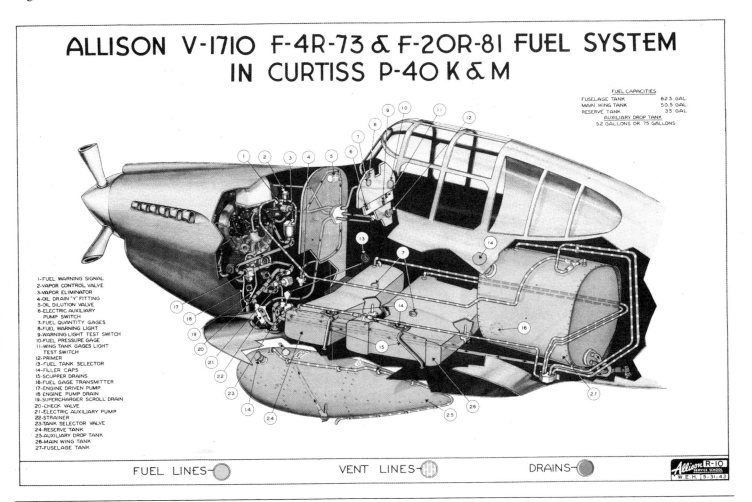

271

ward fuselage belly which directed the flow from selected tank to engine. Vent and drain lines for all tanks were routed to a location on the fuselage bottom aft of the wing trailing edge. The main fuel pump was driven by the engine, and an electrically driven auxiliary fuel pump was located in the engine compartment. An engine prim-ing hand pump was placed in the cockpit, and a fuel strainer, oil dilution solonoid, air vapor eliminator, and control valve were all located in the engine compartment. A fuel pressure signal was carried to a cockpit warning light, and fuel gages were on the instrument panel. Normal fuel pressure was 15 to 16 psi.

FIXED EQUIPMENT SUBSYSTEMS

INSTRUMENTS

Flight instruments included: Altimeter, clock, compass, turn indicator, turn and bank indicator, airspeed meter, flight indicator, and climb indicator. Engine instruments included: Engine gage unit, fuel quantity gages, tachometer, manifold pressure gage, and coolant temperature gage. The engine gage unit included indications of oil temperature and pressure along with fuel pressure. Other instruments were an ammeter and a flap and wheel indicator.

SURFACE CONTROLS

The aircraft was equipped with conventional stick control for elevators and ailerons and pedal control for the rudder. Elevator controls ran from the stick to the elevator torque tube drive horn, and consisted of pre-stretched steel cables running over pulleys supported on the airframe. The rudder controls ran from the pedals to control horns on the torque tube at the base of the rudder, and also consisted of cables running over pulleys fixed to the fuselage. Aileron control runs extended from the lower end of the stick via a cable and pulley system running in the wing section aft of the landing gear wheel pocket out to the aileron control drum which drove control links near the inboard end of the aileron.

Trim tabs on elevators, rudder, and the left wing were controlled from the cockpit, the elevator and rudder tabs by control wheels at the left side of the pilot. The mechanical drive to the tail surface tabs consisted of chain, cable, and flexible drive shafts to the tab actuators. The push rod from the actuator driving the rudder tab protruded from the right side of the aircraft. A ground-adjustable metal tab was mounted on the right aileron. The left aileron trim tab was electrically controlled via a cockpit switch and a local trim tab drive electric motor in the aft section of the wing just ahead of the tab.

CURTISS P-40 D & E
INSTRUMENT PANEL & CONTROLS

1—THROTTLE
2—MANUAL MIXTURE CONTROL
3—FUEL TANK SELECTOR
4—PROPELLER GOVERNOR CONTROL
5—FUEL SIGNAL
6—FUSELAGE FUEL TANK GAGE
7—PARKING BRAKE
8—ELECTRIC FUEL PUMP SWITCH
9—PROPELLER CIRCUIT BREAKER
10—PROPELLER CONTROL SWITCH
11—IGNITION SWITCH
12—OIL DILUTION SWITCH
13—PRESTONE AND FUEL TEST SWITCH
14—GENERATOR SWITCH
15—FUEL GAGE LIGHTS CHECK SWITCH
16—STARTER SWITCH
17—MAIN FUEL TANK GAGE
18—ENGINE PRIMER
19—RESERVE FUEL TANK GAGE
20—TACHOMETER
21—MANIFOLD PRESSURE GAGE
22—COOLANT WARNING LIGHT
23—COOLANT TEMPERATURE GAGE
24—OIL TEMPERATURE GAGE
25—OIL PRESSURE GAGE
26—FUEL PRESSURE GAGE
27—CARBURATOR HEAT CONTROL
28—CIRCUIT BREAKERS
29—OIL-COOLANT SHUTTER CONTROL

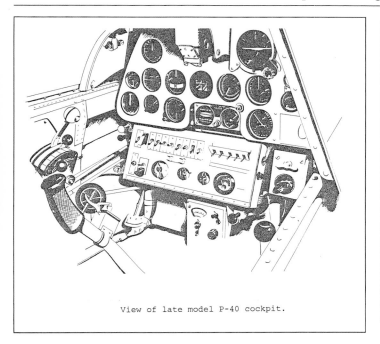

View of late model P-40 cockpit.

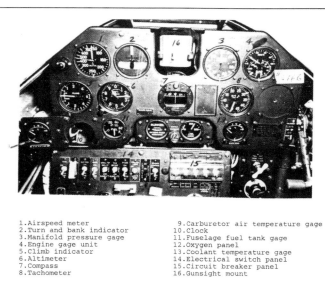

1. Airspeed meter
2. Turn and bank indicator
3. Manifold pressure gage
4. Engine gage unit
5. Climb indicator
6. Altimeter
7. Compass
8. Tachometer
9. Carburetor air temperature gage
10. Clock
11. Fuselage fuel tank gage
12. Oxygen panel
13. Coolant temperature gage
14. Electrical switch panel
15. Circuit breaker panel
16. Gunsight mount

Instrument panel of P-40N

ALLISON V-1710 F-3R-39 ELECTRICAL SYSTEM IN CURTISS P-40 D AND E

1- L.H. COCKPIT JUNCTION BOX
2- GENERATOR SWITCH
3- COOLANT AND FUEL WARNING SWITCH
4- OIL DILUTION SWITCH
5- PROPELLER CONTROL SWITCH
6- PROPELLER CIRCUIT BREAKER
7- IGNITION SWITCH
8- AMMETER
9- CIRCUIT BREAKERS
10- FUEL PRESSURE WARNING
11- COOLANT TEMPERATURE WARNING
12- COOLANT TEMPERATURE GAGE
13- IGNITION STOWING PLUG
14- OIL DILUTION SOLENOID
15- FUEL PRESSURE WARNING SIGNAL
16- MAGNETO JUNCTION BOX
17- BOOSTER COIL

18- COOLANT TEMP. WARNING BULB
19- PROPELLER GOVERNOR
20- PROPELLER RELAY BOX
21- PROPELLER BRUSH ASSEMBLY
22- COOLANT TEMPERATURE BULB
23- COOLANT WARNING THERMOSWITCH
24- STARTER ENGAGING SOLENOID
25- STARTER
26- GENERATER
27- FIREWALL JUNCTION BOX
28- CONTROL COLUMN JUNCTION BOX

29- STARTER SWITCH
30- BATTERY JUNCTION BOX
CONTAINS VOLTAGE REGULATOR,
VOLTMETER AND STARTER AND
BATTERY SOLENOID SWITCHES
31- BATTERY
32- BATTERY VENTS
33- JUNCTION BOX

ELECTRICAL CIRCUITS { STARTER— BATTERY & GENERATOR— FUEL— / IGNITION— PROPELLER— COOLANT— }

Allison S-6 SERVICE SCHOOL
DEB JWB 4-19-43

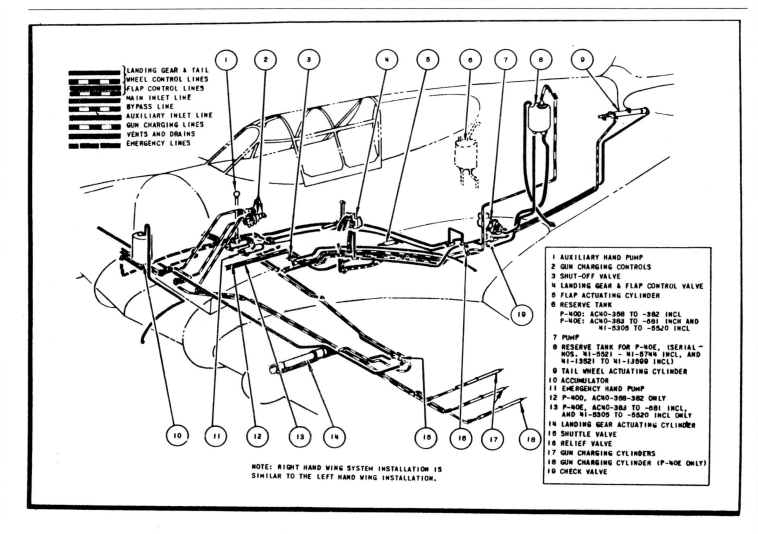

LANDING GEAR & TAIL WHEEL CONTROL LINES
FLAP CONTROL LINES
MAIN INLET LINE
BYPASS LINE
AUXILIARY INLET LINE
GUN CHARGING LINES
VENTS AND DRAINS
EMERGENCY LINES

1 AUXILIARY HAND PUMP
2 GUN CHARGING CONTROLS
3 SHUT-OFF VALVE
4 LANDING GEAR & FLAP CONTROL VALVE
5 FLAP ACTUATING CYLINDER
6 RESERVE TANK
 P-40D: AC40-358 TO -382 INCL
 P-40E: AC40-383 TO -681 INCH AND
    41-5305 TO -5520 INCL
7 PUMP
8 RESERVE TANK FOR P-40E, (SERIAL NOS. 41-5521 - 41-5744 INCL, AND 41-13521 TO 41-13599 INCL)
9 TAIL WHEEL ACTUATING CYLINDER
10 ACCUMULATOR
11 EMERGENCY HAND PUMP
12 P-40D, AC40-368-382 ONLY
13 P-40E, AC40-383 TO -681 INCL, AND 41-5305 TO -5520 INCL ONLY
14 LANDING GEAR ACTUATING CYLINDER
15 SHUTTLE VALVE
16 RELIEF VALVE
17 GUN CHARGING CYLINDERS
18 GUN CHARGING CYLINDER (P-40E ONLY)
19 CHECK VALVE

NOTE: RIGHT HAND WING SYSTEM INSTALLATION IS SIMILAR TO THE LEFT HAND WING INSTALLATION.

Hydraulic system diagram for P-40E.

ELECTRICAL SYSTEM

The electrical system was a 24 volt DC single wire airframe ground return type. A DC generator was driven by the engine at the accessory housing location. A battery was located in the lower fuselage aft of the wing trailing edge.

The electrical system powered aircraft cockpit, landing, and navigation lights, the auxiliary fuel pump, radio gear, propeller controls, engine starter, cockpit switches, pitot heater, hydraulic pump motor, electric gun sight and gun controls, and the aileron trim tab motor.

HYDRAULIC SYSTEM

A hydraulic system was installed to perform the functions of landing gear extension and retraction, wing flaps operation, and charging of the wing guns on the P-40D and later models. The landing gear, including tail wheel, could be operated either automatically using an electrically-driven hydraulic pump located in the lower aft fuselage, or a hand pump in the cockpit. Control was effected using a landing gear position lever with a safety latch and an elec-

tric motor control switch button on top of the stick. A warning horn tied to throttle position was also in the system, as was a position indicator in the cockpit. In late airplanes a new position indicator consisted of colored pins protruding through the wings. If the electrical system was inoperative the landing gear could be operated using the position lever and pumping the auxiliary hand pump. If this pump failed the gear could still be operated using an emergency hand pump. This was done by opening shut-off valves on the cockpit floor, removing the handle from the auxiliary hand pump, and attaching it to the emergency hand pump. The emergency system would not operate the tail wheel however. Hydraulic lines ran out to the main landing gear actuators in the bay between front and middle wing spars on each side, and to the tail wheel retraction actuator in the aft fuselage.

The flaps could be operated, like the landing gear, using either the electrically-driven hydraulic pump or, with electrical failure, by the auxiliary hand pump. The emergency hydraulic hand pump would not operate the flaps. They were operated by a flap control lever in the cockpit, and the same button on top of the control stick used for the landing gear (which turned on the pump motor). A flap position indicator was located on the instrument panel. Hydraulic lines ran to a single flap actuating cylinder in the lower part of the fuselage on centerline which drove an arm on the flap torque tube. The flaps could be put in any intermediate position as well as full up or down.

Hydraulic lines ran from the fuselage outboard through the wings to the three gun charging cylinders on each side (for each of the six .50 caliber machine guns used on the P-40E and most subsequent models.) A gun charging control for a charging valve was located on the left side of the cockpit.

Other major components in the hydraulic system were the accumulator in the engine compartment, a landing gear and flap control valve, a shut-off valve, and a reserve tank for hydraulic fluid mounted in the aft section of the fuselage.

PNEUMATIC SYSTEM
The only pneumatic system was the vacuum system for instruments. A vacuum pump was mounted on the engine.

ARMAMENT PROVISIONS
The initial P-40 airplanes had two M-2 synchronized .50 caliber machine guns mounted in the forward fuselage with breeches in the bay just ahead of the cockpit. Ammunition containers and ejection chutes were in the same bay just below the guns. Cooling louvres were cut in the skin outside the bay. The guns fired through blast tubes at the forward end. Guns were mounted on A-3 trunnion and bracket assemblies and A-4 post assemblies. They was equipped with E-2A control solonoids, A-1 plunger assemblies, and trigger motors. An ammunition load of 400 rounds was carried. Two .30 caliber wing guns , one on each side, were installed, each with a C-4B gun control solonoid. The gun breeches protruded through the web of the center main spar with barrels poking through the forward spar web. Ammunition trays were installed between the spars, and carried 500 rounds in each wing. There was no armor on the P-40. A N-2A gunsight was provided.

The P-40B fuselage gun installation was the same as for the P-40 except 760 rounds of amminition were carried. Wing armament was increased to four .30 caliber guns, two on each side, with C-4B control solonoids and 980 rounds of ammunition carried in each wing. A type N-3 optical gun sight was provided. In this model armor plate was added in the cockpit area. Two steel plates were placed aft of the pilot, the lower 7.5mm thick and the upper 9.5mm thick. A single plate was located just forward of the cockpit and was 9.5mm thick. The weight of the armor plate totaled 93 pounds.

The P-40C armament, gunsight, and armor plate installation were the same as those of the P-40B. The C model could also carry a 500 pound bomb on centerline.

The P-40E, a major revision of the P-40 design from the "Tomahawk" type above, had a change of armament eliminating the fuselage guns and providing for three .50 caliber M-2 machine guns in each wing. The installation included, for each gun, a G-4 solonoid, front and rear adapters and blast tube along with the hydraulic gun charging cylinders. The guns were charged by placing the control valves "ON". They were fired by placing the selector switch "ON" and pressing the trigger switch on the control stick grip. All guns were either on or off.

A total of 1410 rounds of ammunition was carried in wing trays. An N-2A gun sight with reflector was installed.

The P-40E was protected by two pieces of armor plate, one forward and one aft of the pilot. The forward piece was a steel plate 3/8 inches thick, the rear a 5/16 inch steel plate. The two totaled 111 pounds. A bullet proof glass windshield weighed 36 pounds. The P-40E could carry a 500 pound bomb on centerline; a bomb release handle was located at the left side of the cockpit. The release was electrical, with a mechanical backup.

The guns and armor on the P-40F were the same as the E, but armor weight was increased to 149 pounds. The P-40K was the same except for an armor weight of 136 pounds. The L model was like the F except the total number of .50 caliber rounds was reduced to 940. The M duplicated the K in guns and armor. The P-40N-25 had 130 pounds of armor, a 34 pound one and one half inch thick bulletproof glass windshield, and an N-3B gunsight with the same gun installation as previous models.

FURNISHINGS
A metal bucket-type seat with safety harness was provided in the cockpit. In the P-40E the seat could be adjusted in height by lifting a lock release handle and moving it up or down. A spring-loaded locking device was provided. In later N models the seat was adjustable only by unbolting and rebolting in another position. A relief tube was fitted on all models.

HEATING/VENTILATING/COOLING SYSTEMS
Pick-off tubes were run from outside and aft of the radiator in the ducting to the cockpit with a mixing control lever in the cockpit on the lower right side. Closing the radiator exit shutters increased the air temperature entering the cockpit. There was no cooling system.

ICE PROTECTION SYSTEM
A cockpit control operated a vane in the carburetor air inlet ducting that could switch incoming air from cold outside flow to warm air taken from inside the engine compartment.

A windshield defrosting system included a hand-operated pump in the cockpit, a glycol container, and a line and nozzle directed at the windshield outer surface. No other ice protection system was incorporated.

HOISTING/TOWING/LEVELING EQUIPMENT
A tow ring was provided at the inboard side of each main landing gear axle. Retractable tiedown rings were located under each wing near the tip. Means were provided for hoisting and leveling the aircraft.

FLOTATION/ARRESTING GEAR
None was provided.

USEFUL LOAD SUBSYSTEMS
GUNS/BOMBS/ROCKETS

See section above. Bombs up to 500 pounds could be carried on a centerline rack starting with P-40C. In the field larger loads were sometimes carried after modifications. Structural provision was made to carry two 100 pound bombs under the wings, but this was seldom if ever done. No rockets were carried.

GUNSIGHT/GUN CAMERA

For gunsights see the earlier section. A gun camera could be installed in the cockpit adjacent to the gun sight. It was operated by the gun trigger switch on the stick. On early P-40s a gun camera could be mounted externally on the cowling for gunnery practice. On later models the gun camera was an N-2 or N-6 in the right landing gear fairing.

PYROTECHNICS

Early models carried flares. The P-40C carried two M-8 models in the rear fuselage.

OXYGEN SYSTEM

The P-40 carried a Type C-1 oxygen cylinder weighing 20 pounds; piping ran from the cylinder in the aft fuselage to the cockpit. A regulator was provided. The normal gross weights of P-40E,F,K,L,M, and N versions did not include an oxygen system, but one could be carried on all. The cylinder was stowed in the aft fuselage and a line carried forward to the cockpit. The normal P-40E bottle was a low pressure F-1 type. Flow was controlled by an A-9 regulator on the cockpit floor. In addition an adjusting knob and a gage were provided. A connector for a pilot oxygen mask was provided in the cockpit. The supply was good for up to two and three quarter hours at a 25000 foot altitude.

REFERENCES, P-40

1. *Hawks*, Page Shamburger and Joe Christy, Wolverine Press, Kalamazoo, Mich.,1972.
2. *Into The Teeth of The Tiger*, Donald S. Lopez
3. *Curtiss Single Seat Fighter Monoplanes*, Louis Kessler Billing Books Curtiss Airplane Div. Contract and Order Dept. Buffalo, NY.
4. *Airplane Engine Performance Data*, Allison Engineering Report 7939 on V-1710-15, Dec.7,1939
5. *Airplane Engine Performance Data*, Allison Engineering Report on V-1710-39.
6. *Engine Performance Chart*, Packard Motor Car Co. V-1650-1 Engine.
7. *Tactical Planning Characteristics and Performance Chart*, P-40, 8/21/44
8. *Tactical Planning Characteristics and Performance Chart*, TSEAL-6-AI AAF Air Technical Service Command, P-40, June 29, 1945.
9. *SAE Journal (Transactions)* Vol.49,No.5, Nov.1941,Allison Engines
10. *Air International Magazine*, Jan.1977 and Feb.1977.
11. *RAF Flying Review*, Vol.XVII, No.10, Old War Hatchet.
12. *Air Age Technical Library*, Group1, No.4, Curtiss P-40 Warhawk, Air Age, Inc.,NY, 1944.
13. *Three View Drawings*, P-40, Curtiss-Wright Corp.
14. *Journal of the American Aviation Historical Society*, Winter 1964 P-40s in the US Army Middle East Air Force.
15. *JAAHS*, Fall 1965, Checkertails.
16. *JAAHS* Fall 1968, Summer 1969, Spring 1972, Winter 1974, Fall 1975, and Spring 1974.
17. *Air Progress Magazine*, March/April 1989, Jeff Ethell
18. Curtiss Aeroplane Div., Buffalo, NY, Report 7939, *Flight Tests of P-40 Airplane No.1*, June 24,1940.
19. Curtiss Report 8780, *Determination of High Speed at Sea Level of P-40F Airplane*, July 22, 1942.
20. Curtiss Report 8988, *Flight Tests for Pilot's Handbook of P-40K* Feb.12, 1943.
21. Curtiss Report 8950, *Summary of design Features of P-40 Series E.* Foster, undated.
22. *Curtiss Reports on Actual Weight and Balance:* 7936 for P-40 #5, June 28,1940; 8303 for P-40B #11, March 11,1941; 8336 for P-40C #1, Apr.3 1941; 8500 for P-40E #29, Aug.15,1941; 8763 for P-40F #400, June 24, 1942, 8899 for P-40K #700, Dec.1,1942.; 8976 for P-40L #66, Jan 20, 1943; 8970 for P-40M #300, Jan.4,1943; 9329 for P-40N-25 #3901, Mar. 27,1944; 9420 for P-40N-35, #4907, Sept.20,1944.
23. *Operating Instructions Data Sheet*, P-40, Sept.26,1940.
24. *Operating Instructions Data Sheet*, P-40, Sept.11,1941.
25. *Operating Instructions Data Sheet*, P-40D, Nov.18,1941.
26. *Operating Instructions Data Sheet*, P-40E, Nov.18,1941.
27. *Characteristics Sheet CA-47*, Curtiss Wright Corp., Airplane Div. Buffalo NY,P-40E, Aug.23,1941.
28. *Characteristics Sheet CA-48*, Curtiss Wright Corp., Airplane Div. Buffalo NY, P-40F, Aug 23,1941.
29. NACA Memorandum Report L-547, *Flight Characteristics of the Rudder Control and Sideslip Characteristics of Four Vertical Tail Arrangements on P-40 Series Aircraft.*
30. *The Curtiss P-40 Tomahawk*, Ray Wagner, Profile Publications #35
31. *Warbirds International Magazine*, July/Aug. 1988, Bound for Glory, Salute to the P-40, Michael O'Leary.
32. *War Dept. Bureau of Public Relations*, Press Release, May 23, 1943 Details of Apr.18, 1943 Air Victory, 57th Fighter Group P-40s.
33. *Informational Intelligence Summary*, Asst. Chief Air Staff, Feb.29, 1944, P-40s against Jap Fighters, SW Pacific Area.
34. *Air Force Magazine*, Oct.1943, The "B-40"Over Burma, Capt. Luther Davis.
35. *Journal of the American Aviation Historical Society*, Winter,1967, The Early Curtiss P-40s, Eric Hart.
36. *Air International Magazine*, Jan/Feb. 1977, Hawk Monoplanes, The Second Generation.
37. *The Curtiss P-40 Kittihawk I-IV*, Ray Wagner, Profile Publications.
38. *JAAHS*, Winter, 1966, Curtiss P-40 in French Service, J. Cuny.
39. *Air Progress Magazine*, Warbirds, Mar./Apr. 1989, National Warplane Museum and the Kittihawk., Jeff Ethell.
40. *Pilot's Manual/Flight Operating Instructions*, Curtiss P-40D and E Airplanes, TO 01-25CF-1, Revised Apr.10, 1943.
41. *Letter*, Donald S. Lopez-F.H. Dean, Dec.18, 1990 (Answers to P-40 Questions)
42. *God Is My Copilot*, Col. R.L.Scott, Ballantine Books, NY, 1956.
43. *Curtiss Aircraft 1907-1947*, Peter M. Bowers, Putnam, London, 1979.
44. *Wings Magazine*, Feb.1973, Hawkman, Joe Christy.
45. *Airpower Magazine*, Mar.1983,May,1983, and Wings Magazine, Apr. 1983; Heritage of the Hawks, P.M.Bowers.
46. *Roosevelt and Hopkins, An Intimate History*, Robert E. Sherwood Harper and Brothers, New York, 1948.
47. *Days of the Ching Pao*, by Malcomb Rosholt, Rosholt House II Appleton, Wisc. 1978.
48. *The Pictorial History of the Flying Tigers* by Larry Pistole, Moss Publications, Box 729, Orange, Va. 22960, 1981.
50. *Way of a fighter*, by C. L. Chennault
51. *Crosswinds, An Airman's Memoir*, by Najeeb E. Halaby, Doubleday and Co.Inc. Garden City, New York.
52. *Pacific Sweep* by William N. Hess, Doubleday and Co.Inc.Garden City, New York,1974.
53. *Pilot Training Manual For The P-40*, Published by Headquarters, AAF Office of Flying Safety, 1943.
54. *Destiny, A Flying Tiger's Rendevous With Fate*, by Eric Shilling, 1993.

THE P-47

Model sub-types and numbers of each produced are shown for the big P-47 Jug in Table 37. Almost sixteen percent of America's Hundred Thousand were Republic Thunderbolts. By far the largest number were in the P-47D series; these split into "razorback" and bubble canopy versions. About the same number, roughly 6300 each of these D versions, were built. The 770-odd P-47Bs and P-47Cs started high production levels, then about 12600 P-47Ds came along; the special 130 "hot rod" P-47Ms followed, and finally about 1800 long range P-47Ns for the Pacific closed out production. Very few were sent to Russia because the P-47 was one of the three "premier" USAAF types. The table also shows 1944 was the big Thunderbolt production year with over 7000 coming off the lines, an average monthly production of almost 600 P-47 airplanes.

Table 38 confirms the P-47 as a relatively large fighter airplane, certainly the largest Army single engine type. It was imposing to stand next to a Jug, if only because of its maximum fuselage depth of over seven feet.

Table 39 gives maximum internal and external fuel capacities of various P-47 models. Early versions had internal fuel capacity only, and even the 200 gallon external centerline slipper tank for P-47C aircraft was unwieldy for use in the combat areas. Only when P-47D models were produced did the Thunderbolt start to get practical centerline or underwing drop tanks so total capacity could climb to 710 gallons. More internal fuel capacity was badly needed, and late bubble canopy P-47Ds gained an additional 65 gallons of fuel in a larger main forward fuselage tank. This capacity was also pro-

TABLE 37
REPUBLIC P-47 THUNDERBOLT MODELS

CO.MODEL	MILITARY DESIGNATION	NO.OF AIRCRAFT	FIRST DEL.	NOTES
	XP-47B	1	FF.MAY,'41	PROTO.CRASHED AUG.'42
	P-47B	171	DEC.21,'41	ENGINE CHANGE
	P-47C(to-5)	602	SEP.14,'42	LONGER,QEC,BELLY RACK
AP-16	P-47D(to-5)	1463	FEB. '43	WING RACK
	P-47D(-6 &-10)	850		
	P-47D(-11&-15)	1053		
	P-47D(-16&-20)	768		
	P-47D(-21,22,23)	2179		
	P-47D(-25 to-28)	3024	APR. '44	BUBBLE,MORE FUEL,PROP
	P-47D-30	2600		
	P-47D-40	665		
	XP-47E	(1)	SEP. '42	P-47B W.PRESS. CABIN
	XP-47F	(1)	SEP.17 '42	B W.LAMINAR FLOW WING
	P-47G(to-5)	120	OCT. '42	CURTISS BUILT
	P-47G(-10&-15)	234		
	TP-47G-16	(2)		TWO-PLACE TRAINER
	XP-47H	(2)	FF JUL.27'45	D-15 W. CHRYSLER ENG
	XP-47J	1	NOV. '43	SPEED RECORD HOLDER
	XP-47K	1	JUL. 3,'43	LAST D-5 WITH BUBBLE
	XP-47L	1	'43	D-20 W. ADD'L FUEL
	YP-47M	3		D A/C W.UPRATED ENG.
	P-47M	130	DEC. '44	ANTI BUZZ BOMB
	XP-47N	1	FF.JUL.'44	LONG RANGE PROTO.
	P-47N(-1&-5)	1100	SEP. '44	NEW WING; FOR PACIFIC
	P-47N-15	200		
	P-47N-20	349		
	P-47N-25	167		
	TOTAL	15683		

P-47 EXPORTS TO RUSSIA

ROUTE	DELIVERED AT FACTORY	LOST EN ROUTE	DELIVERED TO RUSSIA
ALSIB	3	0	3
NO.RUSSIA,WATER	4	0	4
PERSIAN GULF,WATER	196	8	188
TOTALS	203	8	195

ACCEPTANCES BY YEAR AND MANUFACTURER

YEAR	1941	1942	1943	1944	1945	TOTALS
LOCATION						
FARMINGDALE	1	516	3026	3901	1643	9087
EVANSVILLE	—	10	1131	3087	2014	6242
BUFFALO	—	6	271	77	—	354
TOTALS	1	532	4428	7065	3657	15683

TABLE 38
P-47D PHYSICAL DATA

WING SPAN	40'9 15/16"	AUXILIARY WHEEL TIRE SIZE	
LENGTH	34.833'	MAIN WHEEL SHOCK STRUT TRAVEL	
HEIGHT		AUX GEAR SHOCK STRUT TRAVEL	
LANDING GEAR TREAD	15'7"	TOTAL HORIZ. TAIL AREA	59.6 SQ.FT.
WHEELBASE		HORIZONTAL TAIL ASPECT RATIO	4.30
PROPELLER DIAMETER	13'0"	STABILIZER INCIDENCE	+2 1/2 DEG.
TAIL SPAN	16' 0 13/16"	STABILIZER AREA	37.6 SQ.FT.
GROSS WING AREA	300 SQ.FT.	ELEVATOR AREA(INC.TAB&BAL)	22.SQ.FT.
WING ROOT CHORD	109 1/4"	ELEVATOR BALANCE AREA	3.6 SQ.FT.
WING TIP CHORD	3.575'(CONSTR.)	ELEVATOR TAB SPAN	175/8"
WING ASPECT RATIO	5.61	ELEVATOR TAB CHORD	8.1"
WING MEAN AERODYNAMIC CHORD	87.46"	ELEVATOR TAB AREA (BOTH)	
WING ROOT AIRFOIL	REPUBLIC S-3	ELEVATOR MOVEMENT	30 DEG. UP, 20 DN
WING ROOT THICKNESS RATIO		HORIZ. TAIL MAXIMUM CHORD	
WING TIP AIRFOIL	REPUBLIC S-3	STABILIZER MAXIMUM CHORD	47 3/16"
WING TIP THICKNESS RATIO		ELEVATOR MAXIMUM CHORD	18 3/32"
WING INCIDENCE ROOT/TIP	1 DEG./1DEG.	ELEVATOR TAB MOVEMENT	
WING DIHEDRAL	TOP 4DEG.BOT 7.5 MEAN 6.	TOTAL VERTICAL TAIL AREA	
WING LEADING EDGE SWEEP	3 DEG.	VERTICAL FIN OFFSET	
TOTAL AILERON AREA	25.7 SQ.FT.	FIN AREA	13.6 to 13.9 SQ.FT
AILERON SPAN, EACH	90 15/16"	RUDDER AREA(INC.TAB&OFFSET)	11.9'
AILERON BALANCE AREA (BOTH)	6.7 SQ.FT.	RUDDER BALANCE AREA	1.91 SQ.FT.
AILERON AREA,AFT OF H/L,BOTH,	19SQ.FT.	RUDDER TAB HEIGHT	17"
AILERON MOVEMENT	16 DEG.UP,12 DEG.DN.	RUDDER TAB CHORD	9 3/8"
LEFT AILERON TAB AREA	0.89 SQ.FT.	RUDDER TAB AREA	0.87 SQ.FT.
AILERON TAB MOVEMENT	16 DEG.UP,12 DN.	RUDDER MOVEMENT	28 DEG.L.; 28 DEG.R
TOTAL FLAP AREA	39.6 SQ.FT.	FIN ROOT CHORD	4' 0 7/8"
TOTAL FLAP SPAN	209"	RUDDER MAXIMUM CHORD	28 3/4"
MAXIMUM FUSELAGE WIDTH	53.5"	RUDDER O/A HEIGHT(@H/L)	7'2 7/8"
MAIN WHEEL TIRE SIZE	34"	MIN.PROP. TIP GROUND CLEAR.	4.15"
MAXIMUM FUSELAGE DEPTH	88"		

TABLE 39
P-47 FUEL CAPACITIES
US GALLONS

MODEL	MAXIMUM INTERNAL FUEL	MAXIMUM EXTERNAL FUEL
XP-47B	305	—
P-47B	305	—
P-47C	305	200
P-47D thru -23	305	710
P-47D-25,-40	370	710
P-47G	305	200
XP-47H	305	—
XP-47J	270	600
P-47M	370	110
P-47N	556	600

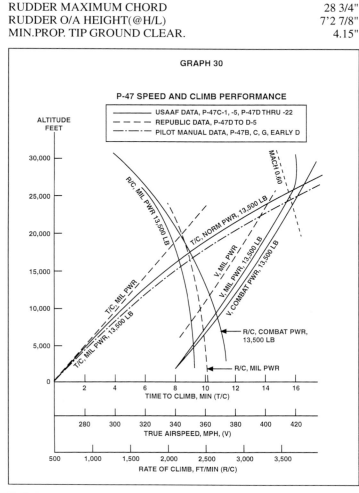

GRAPH 30

P-47 SPEED AND CLIMB PERFORMANCE

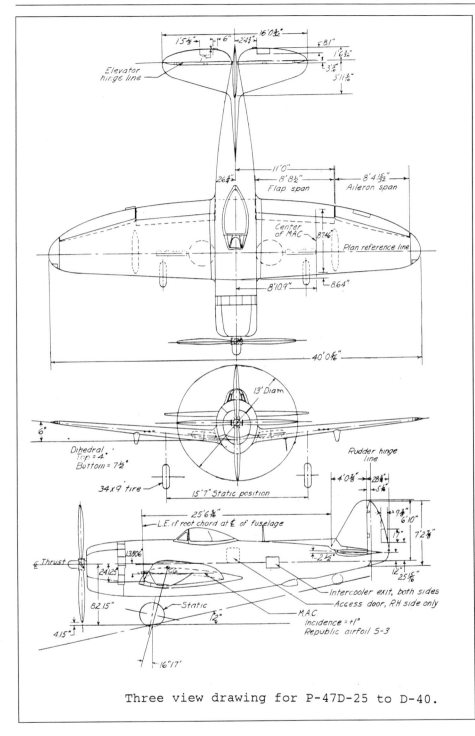

Three view drawing for P-47D-25 to D-40.

The P-47 three view drawing, a D-30 model, depicts a rather graceful conventional looking fighter characterized by a stubby oval-section radial-engined nose preceding an exceptionally deep-bellied fuselage and a wing of eliptical planform. The stubby nose resulted from a USAAF desire to incorporate the relatively new, large, and very powerful R-2800 radial engine in a new Army fighter. The deep belly was necessitated by internal air ducting required to service an aft-located turbosupercharger system. The eliptical wing plan , as on the British Spitfire, was one way of achieving good aerodynamic span loading efficiency to reduce drag. Other distinguishing features of the P-47, aside from pure bulk, were a wide tread conventional (for the time) tail wheel type landing gear, and a large four blade propeller.

The inboard profile drawing provides reasons for a bulky fuselage on the P-47. The section forward of the firewall enclosed a large (53 inches in diameter and six feet long) R-2800 radial engine with eighteen cylinders, its accessories and mount, with other components such as oil, water, and hydraulic fluid tanks and the battery. Just aft of the firewall resided a deep forward (main)fuel tank which together with a smaller rear (auxiliary) tank formed an "L" shape and carried all internal fuel. A space just forward of the front tank and another between the two tanks allowed a fuselage structural carrythrough for left and right wing panel spars. The cockpit was located within the space enclosed by the legs of the tank "L". A deep belly running well below the wing lower surface line housed air intake and exhaust ducting running aft to the turbosupercharger. Compressed air from the supercharger ran forward in ducts along each side of the cockpit to the engine carburetor. The turbosupercharger and the intercooler unit, the latter a big box-like heat exchanger structure, along with associated ducting took up most all space in the middle and lower aft fuselage. Radio equipment and oxygen bottles were placed in the upper central fuselage. Other components located in the middle or aft fuselage included tail flight control runs and a retract-

vided in the P-47M. Because the P-47D was still limited in combat radius, particularly with respect to late P-51s, and not considered appropriate for flying long Pacific distances, Republic redesigned the aircraft with a new larger wing incorporating additional internal fuel to bring that total to 556 gallons. Adding 600 gallons of external drop tank fuel capacity provided a total maximum load of 1156 gallons, about three and one half tons of fuel, giving the P-47N model very long range.

able tail wheel. A cutaway drawing of a late model P-47D is also shown.

Table 40 lists major power ratings of the various R-2800 engines used in P-47 models. All versions employed turbosupercharging. Improvements in horsepower came steadily, and the altitudes at which certain powers could be developed rose as well. A water injection system was incorporated along the way and kit retrofitted into earlier models to provide COMBAT power,

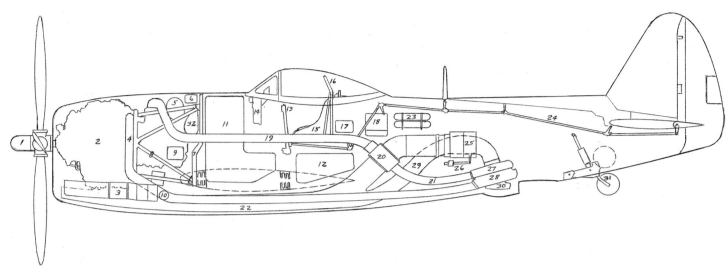

1. Hamilton propeller
2. P&W R-2800 engine
3. Oil cooler (2)
4. Exhaust manifold
5. Oil tank
6. Hydraulic reservoir
7. Firewall
8. Engine mount
9. Battery
10. Exhaust bypass valve
11. Main fuel tank
12. Auxiliary fuel tank
13. Control stick
14. Instrument panel
15. Pilot seat
16. Rear armor plate

17. Radio
18. Radio
19. Pipe for air to caburetor
20. Intercooler
21. Pipe to intercooler from turbo
22. Air intake pipe
23. Oxygen bottle
24. Elevator control run
25. Intercooler air exit duct (2)
26. Exit duct actuator
27. Turbosupercharger compressor
28. Turbosupercharger turbine
29. Compressor intake duct
30. Turbine waste gate
31. Retractable tail wheel
32. Water tank

REPUBLIC P-47D "THUNDERBOLT"

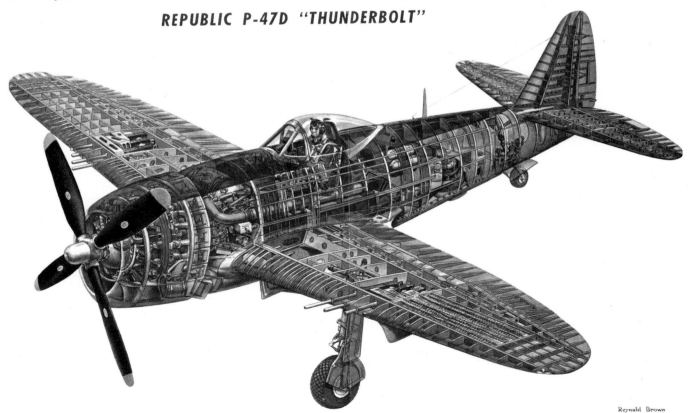

Reynold Brown

TABLE 40
P-47 ENGINE DATA

AIRCRAFT	ENG.MODEL	RATING	HP	ENG.RPM	ALTITUDE'	MAN.PRESS.	SUPERCHARGER
XP-47B	R-2800-17,	T.O.	2000	2700	SEA LEVEL	52"HG.	TURBO
P-47B	-21	MIL.	2000	2700	25000	52"HG.	
		NORMAL	1525	2550	25000		
P-47C	R-2800-21,	T.O.	2000	2700	SEA LEVEL	52"HG.	TURBO
P-47G	-58,-63	COMBAT	2300 RAM	2700	27000		
		MIL.	2000	2700	27000	52"HG.	
		NORMAL	1625	2550	29000	42"HG.	
P-47D	R-2800-21	T.O.	2000	2700	SEA LEVEL		TURBO
		MIL.	2000	2700	25000		
		NORMAL	1625	2550	6500-25000		
P-47D-5	R-2800-21	T.O.	2300	2700	SEA LEVEL		TURBO
(TO -10)	WATER INJ.KIT	COMBAT	2300	2700	27000		
		MIL.	2000	2700	25000		
		NORMAL	1625	2550	6500-25000		
P-47D	R-2800-63	T.O.	2300	2700	SEA LEVEL		TURBO
(TO -20)		COMBAT	2300	2700	27000		
		MIL.	2000	2700	25000		
		NORMAL	1625	2550	6500-25000		
P-47D-20	R-2800-59	T.O.	2300	2700	SEA LEVEL		TURBO
(TO -27)		COMBAT	2300	2700	31000		
		MIL.	2000	2700	25000		
		NORMAL	1625	2550	6500-25000	42.5"HG.	
P-47D-27	R-2800-59	T.O.	2600	2700	SEA LEVEL		
(THRU-40)		COMBAT	2600	2700	25000	64"HG.	
		MIL.	2000	2700	25000-27000	52"HG.	
		NORMAL	1625	2550	6500-29000	42.5"HG.	
XP-47H	XIV-2220-1	T.O.	2500		SEA LEVEL		TURBO
		MIL.	2500	25000			
XP-47J	R-2800-61	T.O.	2100	2800	SEA LEVEL	54"HG.	TURBO
		COMBAT	2800	2800	30000	72"HG.	
		MIL.	2100	2800	30000	54"HG.	
		NORMAL	1700	2600	30000	43"HG.	
P-47M	R-2800-57	T.O.	2100	2800	SEA LEVEL	54"HG.	TURBO
P-47N	-73, -77	COMBAT	2800	2800	32600	72"HG.	
		MIL.	2100	2800	30000-37000	54"HG.	
		NORMAL	1700	2600	30000	43"HG.	

which in the latest versions yielded 2800 horsepower at over 30000 feet for short periods.

Graphs 30 through 33 show speed and climb performance curves for early P-47C and D, late P-47D, P-47M, and P-47N Thunderbolt models respectively. Except for climb times, data are shown for cases of MILITARY and COMBAT power settings. For the early models high speed varied from about 325-335 mph at sea level up to well over 400 mph at high altitudes, the speed capability steadily increasing with altitude up to about 30000 feet. Data from both the USAAF and the manufacturer are shown, and in this case the latter indicates more conservatism. From the Army figures use of COMBAT power increased high speed by about five mph over MILITARY power at medium to high altitude. The reason speed increased smoothly with altitude is that power available was essentially constant with altitude using turbosupercharging. Climb rates at MILITARY power were in the 2400-2500 foot per minute range at low altitude, with manufacturers figures showing somewhat higher performance. Rates dropped off to around 1800 FPM at 25000 feet. Application of COMBAT power boosted climb rate at low altitude considerably to about 2750 FPM. Climb times are provided from several sources on the graph. They vary from 4-5 minutes to 10000

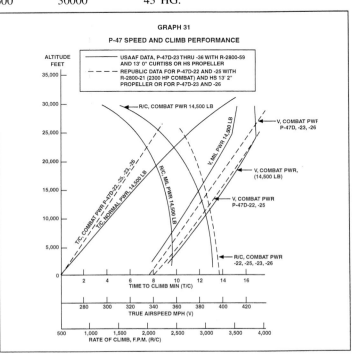

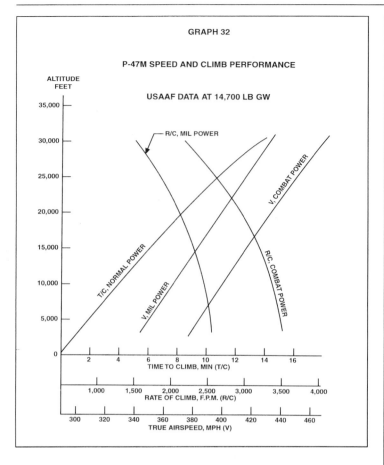

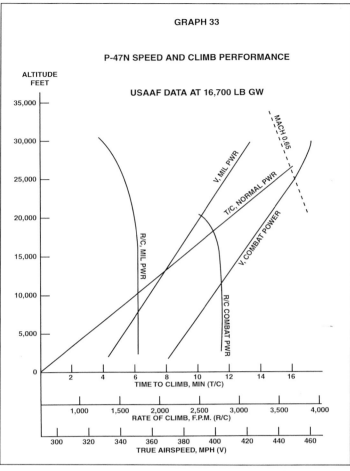

feet, and from eight and one half to eleven and one half minutes to 20000 feet. Some of these differences can be attributed to variations in propeller performance in climb.

Graph 31 gives performance of later P-47D variants. Generally the curves show small improvements in speed capability over earlier models. The big increase in performance appears in the climb rate figures where COMBAT power climb stayed over 3000 FPM up to medium altitudes. Along with this Republic's COMBAT power time to climb figures show commensurate improvement with time to 10000 feet slightly over three minutes and to 25000 feet just over eight minutes. These aircraft were equipped with new "paddle blade" high activity factor propellers which, while giving little if any improvement in high speed performance, were instr-umental in significantly improving climb capability, something sorely needed in the P-47.

The performance of the P-47M buzz bomb chaser with a new more powerful engine version is shown in the curves of Graph 32. High speed with this hot rod got to 400 mph quickly at 10000 feet using COMBAT power and at 20000 feet using MILITARY power settings, and speed kept increasing with altitude. In spite of greater aircraft weight COMBAT power climb rates touched 3500 FPM low down and stayed above 3000 FPM almost to 20000 feet. This

version was the limited production hot rod version of the Thunderbolt line used by just one European Theatre group.

P-47N performance is depicted in the curves of Graph 33. Speed performance of the N model was down five to ten mph from the P-47M because the P-47N was bigger and heavier with the same engine, but the real difference was in climb performance which at COMBAT power was less than that of early Thunderbolts, and at MILITARY power hardly exceeded 1700 FPM up to 20000 feet. The ton and one half of extra combat weight affected climbing performance to a much greater degree than it did speed capability.

The curves of Graph 34 provide a picture of "yardstick" range for Thunderbolt models at takeoff weights corresponding to various amounts of fuel on board at takeoff. Data are shown for P-47Cs and early P-47Ds, late P-47Ds, and for the P-47N. Note all ranges are based on 10000 foot cruise altitude, zero wind, and no fuel reserves. In addition there is no fuel allocation for takeoff, climbout, or descent to a landing. On this basis early airplanes with internal fuel only had a range of about 900 miles and late P-47Ds slightly over 1000 miles with more internal fuel and a higher takeoff weight. Loaded with maximum allowable total fuel of 680 gallons early P-47s could make a yardstick range of about 1700 miles; the later Ds with a maximum of 780 gallons could do slightly better at about

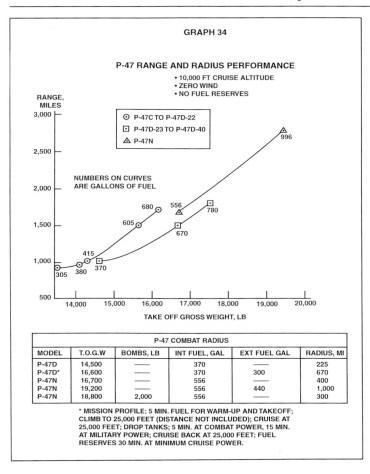

GRAPH 34

P-47 RANGE AND RADIUS PERFORMANCE
- 10,000 FT CRUISE ALTITUDE
- ZERO WIND
- NO FUEL RESERVES

RANGE, MILES

⊙ P-47C TO P-47D-22
⊡ P-47D-23 TO P-47D-40
△ P-47N

NUMBERS ON CURVES ARE GALLONS OF FUEL

TAKE OFF GROSS WEIGHT, LB

P-47 COMBAT RADIUS					
MODEL	T.O.G.W	BOMBS, LB	INT FUEL, GAL	EXT FUEL GAL	RADIUS, MI
P-47D	14,500	———	370		225
P-47D*	16,600	———	370	300	670
P-47N	16,700	———	556	———	400
P-47N	19,200	———	556	440	1,000
P-47N	18,800	2,000	556	———	300

* MISSION PROFILE: 5 MIN. FUEL FOR WARM-UP AND TAKEOFF;
CLIMB TO 25,000 FEET (DISTANCE NOT INCLUDED); CRUISE AT
25,000 FEET; DROP TANKS; 5 MIN. AT COMBAT POWER, 15 MIN.
AT MILITARY POWER; CRUISE BACK AT 25,000 FEET; FUEL
RESERVES 30 MIN. AT MINIMUM CRUISE POWER.

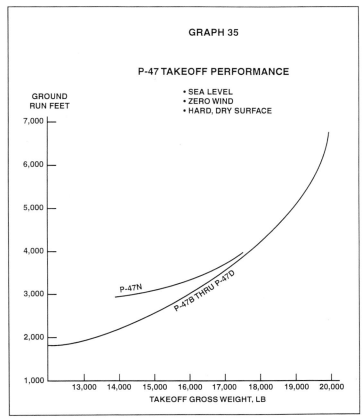

GRAPH 35

P-47 TAKEOFF PERFORMANCE
- SEA LEVEL
- ZERO WIND
- HARD, DRY SURFACE

GROUND RUN FEET

P-47N

P-47B THRU P-47D

TAKEOFF GROSS WEIGHT, LB

1800 miles. The long range Pacific P-47N Thunderbolt curve shows tremendous improvement. It could make almost the same range on just internal fuel as the Ds could handle with maximum internal and drop tank fuel. With maximum allowable fuel, including 440 gallons in drop tanks, this final "Jug" model ranged out to 2800 miles on a yardstick basis; this was probably close to a 2200-2400 mile practical range. The table enclosed in Graph 34 provides some figures on practical P-47 combat radius, allowing for midpoint combat time, fuel reserves, and cruising at high altitude. Under the conditions stated late model D airplanes had a radius capability from 225 miles on internal fuel only to 670 miles with two 150 gallon drop tanks. Under similar conditions the P-47N had radius capability of 400 to 1000 miles. The P-47 airplanes were always limited by modest range and radius capability until the advent of the P-47N very late in the war. The N was too late for Europe and just made it to the Pacific Theatre to participate in the last stages there.

In Graph 35 takeoff ground run information is provided for Thunderbolts on the basis of zero wind conditions at sea level and a hard dry runway. The P-47 was noted for requiring a long takeoff run, and the data shows with full internal fuel load takeoff distances were well over 2000 feet for early models, 2500 feet for late D versions, and about 3500 feet for a P-47N. Thunderbolt operations in forward areas were sometimes limited by long takeoff distances required.

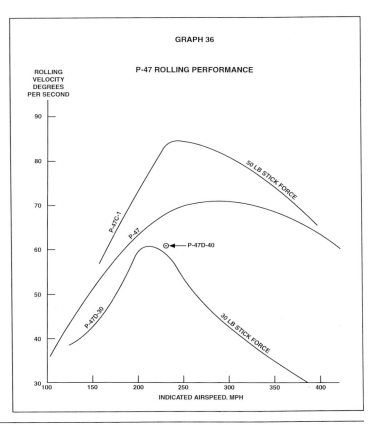

GRAPH 36

P-47 ROLLING PERFORMANCE

ROLLING VELOCITY DEGREES PER SECOND

50 LB STICK FORCE

P-47C-1

P-47

P-47D-40

P-47D-30

30 LB STICK FORCE

INDICATED AIRSPEED, MPH

TABLE 41
P-47 EMPTY AND BASIC WEIGHTS
POUNDS

MODEL	P-47D-RE	P-47D-25
GROUP		
WING	1459.6	1447.4
TAIL	250.5	250.5
FUSELAGE	1443.5	1425.5
LANDING GEAR	1123.0	1125.0
ENGINE SECTION	379.0	383.0
ENGINE	2265.0	2283.2
ENGINE ACCESSORIES	954.0	977.0
ENGINE CONTROLS	57.8	57.8
PROPELLER	541.3	659.3
STARTING	56.0	56.0
COOLING	—	—
LUBRICATING	117.9	138.1
FUEL SYSTEM	332.3 (305 GAL.)	422.2 (372 GAL.)
INSTRUMENTS	53.4	52.2
SURFACE CONTROLS	137.1	127.4
HYDRAULIC	110.0	97.5
ELECTRICAL	209.1	214.1
COMMUNICATION	146.0	151.1
ARMAMENT PROVISIONS	183.2	203.1
FURNISHINGS	103.2	115.2
ANTI-ICING EQUIPMENT	34.8	13.1
EMPTY WEIGHT	9956.7	10198.7
TRAPPED OIL	—	73.9
TRAPPED FUEL	—	9.0
BASIC .50CAL INSTL.(6)	428.1	428.1
ADDIT'L.50CAL INSTL.(2)	145.0	145.0
GUN SIGHT	2.3	3.5
PYROTECHNICS	6.0	6.0
OXYGEN EQUIPMENT	7.0	—
BASIC WEIGHT	10545.1	10864.2

OTHER MODEL EMPTY AND BASIC WEIGHTS (LB.)

MODEL	EMPTY WEIGHT	BASIC WEIGHT
XP-47B	9190	
P-47B	9346	
P-47C	9900	10700
P-47G	10000	10700
P-47M	10423	11100
P-47N	11000	11600

P-47 rolling performance is shown in the curves of Graph 36, and was far from sensational. With a 50 pound pilot lateral force on the control stick a P-47C at 240 mph IAS would roll at about 85 degrees per second (a 4.2 second full 360 degree rotation). This performance dropped to about 65 degrees per second at a fast 400 mph IAS. If gs were being pulled at the same time roll rate could drop significantly from the figures shown. There also tended to be some difference between roll capability to the left or to the right.

Table 41 gives a breakdown of empty weights and then items adding up to basic weight from empty for both an early and a late version of the P-47D airplane. With about five tons of empty weight the "Jug" was certainly a heavy fighter aircraft. The P-47D-25 empty weight increased almost 250 pounds over the earlier D model. Addition of water injection added some powerplant weight, a new paddle blade version increased propeller weight, as did a new main fuel tank holding almost 70 gallons of additional internal fuel. The lower tabulation shows how much empty and basic weights of the final P-47N model increased over earlier versions. A larger wing and greatly increased fuel capacity provided most of that weight increase. Table 42 shows typical loading alternates for P-47D models using the empty and basic weights of the previous table. It is seen the Jug could easily be loaded to takeoff gross weights of 16000-17000 pounds.

P-47 MAJOR MODEL TO MODEL CHANGES

P-47B (FROM XP-47B) New engine version, redesigned sliding canopy, repositioned radio mast, metal-covered rudder and elevators (the latter on late B models), metal-covered ailerons, reinforced tail fin.

P-47C (After first 57 short-fuselage aircraft) New engine version with provision for water injection on C-5 version, quick-engine-change (QEC) mounting, forward fuselage extended eight inches at firewall and with new engine mount fuselage overall length increased thirteen inches, redesigned elevator and rudder balances, radio change and new radio mast, belly shackles added under fuselage for a 200 gallon external belly fuel tank or a 500 pound bomb. Bobweight in elevator system.

P-47D-1 TO -20 Additional cockpit armor, engine water injection standard, redesigned turbosupercharger exhaust, redesigned vents for engine accessory section, wing reinforced (starting with P-47D-15) to allow external wing loads, wing pylons added, -20 introduced "universal wing" to carry a variety of drop tanks or bombs, longer tail wheel strut, paddle blade propeller.

P-47D-25 TO -40 New engine version on some, bubble canopy, larger main internal fuel tank, revised cockpit switches, stronger belly shackles, extra oxygen bottles, dorsal fin (-27 and on), dive flaps (-30 and on), under-wing rocket provisions (-35 and on).

XP-47E P-47B with pressurized cabin.

XP-47F P-47B with longer-span laminar flow wing, armament removed.

P-47G The P-47G was like the P-47C; the P-47G-5 was like the P-47D-1.

P-47G 2-seat trainer-Reduced main fuel tank size, second cockpit added.

XP-47H A P-47D-14 with an experimental Chrysler liquid-cooled engine.

XP-47J New engine model, engine cooling fan, revised cowling, new turbosupercharger, only six guns, no external stores provisions, shortened fuselage, smaller fuel tank, new larger diameter propeller.

XP-47K A P-47D-5 with a Hawker Typhoon bubble canopy. Tested wing internal fuel for P-47N.

XP-47L A P-47D-20 with a larger fuel tank.

P-47M New engine version, new turbosupercharger, automatic engine controls, dive flaps, automatic intercooler and oil cooler doors, revised aileron design.

P-47N New wing with fuel added, new engine model and turbosupercharger like the P-47M, more oxygen supply, additional automatic engine controls, wider tread main landing gear, strengthened structure.

TABLE 42
TYPICAL P-47 DISPOSEABLE LOAD ALTERNATIVES (LBS.)
P-47D UP TO P-47D-25

A/C MODEL MISSION	DESIGN	COMBAT	BOMBER	MAX. FUEL
PILOT	200	200	200	200
USEABLE OIL	143	143	143	143
EXTRA OIL	—	72	72	72
WATER	124	124	124	124
CAL.50 AMMO.,NORMAL	498	498	498	498
CAL.50 AMMO.,ADDIT'L.	—	166	—	—
GUN CAMERA	—	4	4	—
(2)1000LB.BOMB INSTL.	—	—	2033	—
FUEL, MAIN INT'L TANK	1230	1230	1230	1230
FUEL, AUX.MAIN INT.TANK	—	—	—	—
FUEL, AUX.INT'L TANK	—	600	600	600
DROP TANKS,2 300 GAL.	—	—	—	314
BELLY TANK,1 75 GAL.	—	—	50	—
DROP TANK FUEL	—	—	450	3600
TOTAL DISPOSEABLE LOAD	2195	3037	5404	6781
GROSS WEIGHT	12740	13582	15949	17326
USEFUL LOAD	2783	3625	5992	7369

P-47D-25 AND UP

A/C MODEL MISSION	DESIGN	COMBAT	BOMBER	MAX. FUEL
PILOT	200	200	200	200
USEABLE OIL	143	143	143	143
EXTRA OIL	—	72	72	72
WATER	—	248	248	248
CAL.50 AMMO.,NORMAL	498	498	498	498
CAL.50 AMMO.,ADD'L	—	166	—	—
GUN CAMERA	—	—	—	—
(2)1000LB.BOMB INSTL.	—	—	2000	—
FUEL, MAIN INT'L TANK	1230	1230	1230	1230
FUEL, AUX.MAIN INT.TANK	—	390	390	390
FUEL, AUX.INT'L TANK	—	600	600	600
DROP TANKS,2 150 GAL.	—	—	—	175
DROP TANK FUEL	—	—	—	1980
TOTAL DISPOSEABLE LOAD	2071	3547	5381	5536
GROSS WEIGHT	12935	14411	16245	16400
USEFUL LOAD	2736	4212	6046	6201

P-47 CHRONOLOGY

Oct ,1939-The Seversky Aircraft Co. is reorganized into the Republic Aviation Corp.

Jun ,1940-At a Wright field meeting with the Army Republic is told that their planned P-44 pursuit and the Allison-engined XP-47 and XP-47A models are to be dropped, and that a new pursuit with a Pratt and Whitney R-2800 engine is desired quickly.

Sep 6,1940-Authorization for an XP-47B with an R-2800 is given as a change on the XP-47 contract.

Sep ,1940-Seven hundred and thirty three production P-47B and P-47C models are ordered by the US Army from Republic.

May 4,1941-The prototype XP-47B aircraft is rolled out.

May 6,1941-The first flight of the XP-47B takes place—20 minutes from Republic to Mitchell Field, L.I. Piloting is Lowery Brabham.

Sep ,1941-In a reply to a British request, Gen. Hap Arnold notes the P-47 is not ready for operations in the Middle East.

Oct14,1941-Eight hundred and fifty P-47D models are ordered from Republic at Farmingdale, L.I. by the US Army.

Oct16,1941-The XP-47E model is ordered as a conversion of a P-47B with a pressurized cockpit.

Dec21,1941-The first aircraft of the 169 P-47B models comes off the assembly line, but changes are required.

Dec31,1941-At this time only the XP-47B prototype has been accepted by the US Army.

Jan ,1942-One thousand and fifty P-47Ds are ordered from the planned Evansville, Indiana facility, and 354 P-47Gs are ordered from Curtiss at Buffalo, NY.

Mar,1942-Construction of Republic's Evansville plant is initiated.

Mar18,1942-Five P-47B aircraft come off the line this month; one is used as a service test aircraft.

May ,1942-The P-47 is supposed to become operational on this date originally.

May ,1942-The delivery of P-47B aircraft is stopped to change to metal covered ailerons.

May26,1942-The British test a P-47 in the US.

Jun ,1942-The Army's 56th Fighter Group receives a few P-47B aircraft. One is allocated for pilots to fly and is based at Mitchell Field. Later the available P-47s are split among the three squadrons—61st and 63rd at Bridgeport, Conn.(headquarters) and the 62nd at Bradley Field near Hartford, Conn.

Jun ,1942-The 56th Group loses its first P-47 in flames—the pilot bails out safely. They also encounter compressibility problems in high speed dives. Several fatal accidents occur.

Aug ,1942-Production of the P-47C model is getting started.

Aug 8,1942-Republic test pilot Fil Gilmore bails out of the burning XP-47B prototype airplane.

Sep ,1942-Production of the last P-47B airplane is completed.

Sep14,1942-The first P-47C with the longer fuselage is completed at Farmingdale, Long Island.

Sep17,1942-An XP-47F test model with a new laminar flow wing is delivered to the Army at Wright Field, Ohio.

Sep19,1942-The first Evansville, Indiana P-47D-1 is flown by test pilot Walter Pixey.

Sep23,1942-In an almost unprecedented feat of construction, the Evansville, Indiana P-47 plant is fully completed.

Oct ,1942-Curtiss rolls out its first P-47G aircraft at Buffalo, NY.

Oct ,1942-The improved P-47C-1 is coming off the Republic assembly lines, and three aircraft are sent to Eglin Field, Fla. for comparative tests against the P-38F, P-39D, P-40F, and the Allison-powered P-51 running from Oct 27 to Nov. 26.

Nov ,1942-The 56th Fighter Group goes operational with the P-47.

Nov ,1942-The XP-47J project is initiated at Republic.

Dec ,1942-Curtiss begins production of the P-47G airplane.

Dec ,1942-The first P-47Cs are assembled in Liverpool, England for 8th Air Force testing. They arrived on the 20th as deck cargo.

Dec27,1942-Personnel of the 56th Fighter Group are ready to start the trip to England; they sail Jan.6, 1943 on Queen Elizabeth.

Dec31,1942-A total of 532 P-47s have so far been produced, including ten at Evansville and six at Curtiss. Two US Army fighter groups are now using the P-47.

Jan ,1943-The 78th Fighter Group in 8th Air force starts re-equipping with P-47Cs. The 78th had come to the UK earlier with P-38s but all its aircraft and all but 15 of its pilots had gone to North Africa to fill in for losses there.

Jan ,1943-The plan is to have the first P-47 group, the 4th, which is unhappily switching from Spitfires, operational by Mar.1, 1943, the 56th Group two weeks later, and the 78th Group all ready by the end of March.

Jan ,1943-The first flight of a P-47C-2 is made in the UK piloted by Col. Cass Hough.

Jan24,1943-The first P-47 aircraft arrive crated for the 56th Fighter Group. They are P-47C-2 and-5 versions. Planes are assembled by 56th mechanics. Test flying shows engine plug fouling and distributer ignition leak problems.

Feb ,1943-By this time 602 P-47C aircraft have been delivered at the Republic Farmingdale plant.

Feb ,1943-Gen. Kenney of the 5th Air Force, SW Pacific gets the word—no more P-38s until summer because of North African requirements—next he prefers P-47s—in May he will get assurance from Gen. Marshall that he can have the 348th Fighter Group with P-47s by June 12. The group had been for Europe.

Feb ,1943-The initial P-47D-1 Thunderbolt aircraft is put out by the Farmingdale Republic plant.

Feb ,1943-The three 8th Air Force fighter groups, 4th, 56th, and 78th, are training and working out bugs. Radio interference and engine problems predominate.

Mar 1,1943-US-made 205 gallon resinated paper P-47 belly tanks arrive in the UK, but are not satisfactory. They leak, will not feed at high altitude, and cannot be pressurized.

Mar10,1943-The 4th Fighter Group goes operational in the 8th Air Force using P-47C aircraft when a group of 14 P-47s and 12 Spitfires goes on an offensive sweep over France. This was not effected without pain. Some 4th pilots deprecate the P-47 and a few even refuse to fly it. There are crashes, dead stick landings, mid-air fires, bailouts, and gear collapses on the runway. Some pilots die in operational accidents. On this first sweep radio interference problems are encountered. Plane-to-plane communication is impossible.

Apr 5, 1943-The 56th Fighter Group with P-47s moves to its new station near Norwich; all serviceable aircraft fly to the new base.

Apr 8, 1943-The P-47 officially goes into action with the 8th Air force. The three fighter groups (4th, 56th, 78th) are all operational. Twenty-four P-47s from all three groups, with the experienced 4th Group pilots in the lead, make a fighter sweep which turns out to be uneventful.

Apr13, 1943-Thirty-six P-47s of the 4th and 78th Fighter Groups go on a sweep over St. Omer, France.

Apr13, 1943-Elements of the 4th and 56th Fighter Groups fly a fighter sweep over Pas de Calais. They have no external tanks.

Apr15, 1943-Twelve P-47s of the 4th Fighter Gp. make a sweep and get their first P-47 victory. Maj. Don Blakeslee shoots down an FW-190 near Dieppe. There is little fighter opposition. Engine problems continue to occur.

Apr29, 1943-The 56th Fighter Gp. loses two P-47 aircraft to enemy FW-190 fighters. They have radio difficulties.

Apr, 1943-The P-47C is tested against captured ME-109G and FW-190 fighters. The enemy aircraft have generally better performance under 15000 feet, but the P-47 improves with altitude and is faster at 30000 feet. The Thunderbolt steady rate of climb is relatively poor however; dive and zoom capability is good.

May, 1943-The complement of the 56th Fighter Gp. squadrons is increased from 18 to 25 aircraft per squadron. Most of the new aircraft are early P-47D versions, though little different from P-47Cs.

May 4, 1943-P-47s of the 4th and 56th Groups and RAF fighters escort B-17s to Antwerp, Belgium. One P-47 is lost due to an engine problem, and there are more radio problems.

May14, 1943-P-47s of the 78th Fighter Gp. escort bombers to Antwerp; they get a first victory and two probables, but lose three planes.

May31, 1943-The 56th Fighter Gp. makes a 50 aircraft sweep of P-47s over the Belgian coast, but meet no enemy aircraft. One pilot is lost due to an oxygen failure. The 56th has flown 26 missions and has no victories, while the 4th and 78th Groups each claim several enemy aircraft.

Jun , 1943-The early P-47D versions are now reaching all three fighter groups in the 8th Air Force Fighter Command.

Jun , 1943-P-47Cs of the 348th Fighter Gp. are the first Thunderbolts to arrive in the SW Pacific. They are for the 5th Air Force.

Jun11, 1943-The P-47s of the 56th Fighter Gp. get their first victory during a fighter sweep near Rouen, France. The 78th Group also scores on this date.

Jun18, 1943-A contract for the experimental XP-47J is approved by the US Army.

Jun30, 1943-The 56th Fighter Gp. in the UK gets beat up by German fighters. They lose five aircraft with four others badly damaged for a claim of two enemy aircraft destroyed.

Jul , 1943-Range deficiencies of the P-47 are exasperating the 8th Air Force, and there is feverish work to extend combat radius.

Jul , 1943-The XP-47K with a British Typhoon bubble canopy makes its first flight.

Jul , 1943-The cabin of the experimental XP-47E model is pressurized for the first time.

Jul , 1943-Gen. Kenney writes Gen. Hap Arnold that his 5th Air Force P-47s have less range than a P-40, and knocks the "engineers back home" for their short-sightedness. The depot at Port Moresby receives a rush order to convert the 110 gallon tank used on P-39s and P-40s as a belly tank for the P-47s. The depot soon is converting seven tanks per day.

Jul , 1943-The 56th Fighter Group is losing about one plane of their own for every enemy aircraft shot down. The 4th and 78th Groups are doing better.

Jul 7, 1943-Tests are made of a British cylindrical reinforced paper drop tank for the UK P-47s, and the first few production examples are obtained July 12.

Jul27, 1943-The three 8th AF P-47 fighter Gps., 4th, 56th, and 78th, have a combined total score of 33 enemy aircraft destroyed.

Jul28, 1943-The 4th and 78th Groups use the unpressurized 200 gallon paper drop tanks, fill them only half full, and drop them after climbing out, thus extending range somewhat.

Jul28, 1943-One hundred and five P-47s using the 200 gallon drop tanks are put up to cover bomber withdrawal from a raid, and meet them about 260 miles out. They catch about 60 German fighters picking off bombers, shoot down nine, and lose one P-47.

Jul30, 1943-P-47s of 8th AF destroy 22 enemy aircraft, with the 78th Ftr. Gp. getting 16 of the victories, but it loses three pilots.

Jul31,1943-The P-47Cs of the 348th Fighter Group, 5th AF, have now all made the 1200 mile flight from Brisbane, Australia to Port Moresby in New Guinea, and start combat operations.

Aug ,1943-Ten P-47D-5 aircraft with two 165 gallon P-38 type external fuel tanks adapted are air-ferried to the UK. They are part of the 356th Ftr. Gp. All the group has arrived by the 25th, but only some came by air.

Aug ,1943-The XP-47H project with liquid-cooled Chrysler engine starts.

Aug ,1943-The escort radius of the 8th AF P-47s has now been extended to 340 miles, but the lack of really deep fighter escort is hampering the execution of Operation Pointblank. The bomber losses are high.

Aug ,1943-P-47s of the 348th Ftr.Gp, 5th AF, assist in repulsing a Japanese raid on Tsili-tsili, about 60 miles from Lae in New Guinea.

Aug ,1943-USAAF engineers in Brisbane, Australia develop a 200 gallon external belly fuel tank for the SW Pacific P-47s. Manufactured locally, it becomes a P-47 standard in this area, except it cannot be manufactured in enough quantity. The Service Command in Australia proposes use of a 150 gallon wing drop tank made in the US, but aircraft modifications would take 300 man-hours for each aircraft to adapt. Gen. Kenney orders attempts made to install a protected internal tank behind the cockpit, but this is not really satisfactory.

Aug ,1943-The combat efficiency of 8th AF P-47 groups is growing. The ratio of German to US fighter losses is now better than 6:1. The 56th Group claims 29 victories, the 4th 21, the 78th seven, and the new 353rd two.

Aug ,1943-The cost of a P-47 is now $104,258.

Aug 9,1943-An additional P-47 group, the 353rd, becomes operational in the ETO, and assisted by the 56th, flies a mission the 12th.

Aug12,1943-The 56th Fighter Group, 8th AF, all use the awkward and troublesome 200 gallon belly fuel tanks for the first time, dropping them at 22000 feet. Three groups (4th, 56th, and the new 353rd) put up 131 P-47s to escort B-17s. The 4th downs 18 ME-109s and FW-190s for a loss of one P-47.

Aug16,1943-The first P-47D version goes into combat in the SW Pacific.

Aug16,1943-The 4th Fighter Group escorts bombers going to Paris, and shoots down a record 18 enemy aircraft. The 56th Group loses one pilot and gets no kills.

Aug17,1943-On the day of the first Schweinfurt ball bearing plant raid P-47s of the 56th Ftr. Gp., meeting the returning bombers, end up shooting down 17 enemy aircraft for a loss of three P-47s, their best day yet.

Aug19,1943-While escorting bombers on a raid over Holland, P-47s of the 56th Group destroy nine enemy aircraft; one Thunderbolt pilot is forced to ditch.

Aug24,1943-P-47s of the 56th Ftr. Gp. are being fitted for use of the new pressurized metal 75/85 gallon teardrop tank on a two point centerline bomb shackle. The tank is pressurized using the exhaust of the engine-driven vacuum pump. The tanks will extend the range of P-47 fighter escort to 340 miles. The tanks were first tested on August 12.

Aug25,1943-The 356th Fighter Group arrives in the UK. Ten of the unit's P-47D-5 aircraft are air-ferried over the Atlantic using two 165 gallon P-38 external fuel tanks adapted. One of the pilots is Barry Goldwater.

Aug31,1943-The 75/85 gallon pressurized metal tanks (originally designed for P-39 and P-40 aircraft and adapted for the P-47) arrive from the US. Ten thousand tanks are being shipped, and these will become a mainstay. The new tanks are used on a combat mission for the first time by the 56th Group. With them the P-47s are in the air for a new record time of two hours and forty minutes. The 4th Group also uses them.

Sep ,1943-Three P-47D-10s go to Russia via Alaska. These will be followed by 200 more P-47Ds shipped in 1944.

Sep ,1943-Two new groups equipped with P-47D fighters become operational this month; the 352nd on the 9th, and the 355th on the 14th of September.

Sep ,1943-In the UK locally-produced 108 gallon metal drop tanks for the P-47 start to become available, and also the locally-produced 108 gallon paper fuel tanks are now being delivered in increased quantity. These tanks give the P-47 a theoretical escort radius of about 375 miles.

Sep27,1943-P-47s with drop tanks escort B-17s all the way to Emden, Germany, and destroy 21 enemy aircraft for a loss of one.

Oct ,1943-P-47D aircraft are shortly to replace P-40s in the Mediterranean Theatre.

Oct ,1943-It is planned that all P-38s, and P-51s with Merlins, be sent to the ETO instead of the Mediterranean Theatre during Oct./Nov./Dec. 1943, and that the North African (12th) Air Force receive P-47 Thunderbolts in their place. This is because greater fighter escort range capability is needed in the 8th Air Force in England, and the P-38 and P-51 have that capability.

Oct 4,1943-P-47s provide escort on another Emden raid and destroy five enemy fighters.

Oct 4,1943-P-47s of the 56th Ftr. Gp., using new 108 gallon drop tanks support bombers raiding Frankfort, Germany, and shoot down 15 ME-110 aircraft with no losses of their own.

Oct10,1943-Maj. Dave Schilling and Lt. Robert Johnson become P-47 aces and Capt. Gerald Johnson has 7 victories in the 56th Group; Major Eugene Roberts of the 78th Group has 8 victories; Capt. Walter Beckham of the 353rd Group has 6 victories in only 6 missions.

Oct14,1943-On the date of the infamous second Schweinfurt raid where 60 B-17s are lost, the 56th Ftr. Gp. goes along as far as possible before dropping their 108 gallon tanks. The group is in the air for a record two and three quarter hours. The P-47s were avoided and destroyed only three enemy aircraft.

Oct15,1943-Seven P-47 fighter groups are now operating with the 8th AF Fighter Command as the 356th Group becomes operational.

Oct16,1943-The 9th Air Force is activated in England as a tactical air force, but has only the skeleton of an air arm. The P-47s it will receive in December are not yet assigned.

Oct20,1943-The 56th Fighter Group P-47s using the 75/85 gallon drop tanks escort bombers, but get very low on fuel coming back. The group as of this date has a total score of 94 E/A.

Nov ,1943-Additional P-47s arrive for the 5th Air Force in the SW Pacific. In place of P-38s for the 5th, Gen. Hap Arnold authorizes an allocation of 350 P-47s to the Pacific. But there is a transportation shortage, so that from October to December 1943 only 207 P-47s actually arrive in Australia.

Nov ,1943-P-47s also equip the 5th Emergency Rescue Squadron of the 8th AF, and show location of downed pilots using markers.

Nov ,1943-P-47 aircraft arrive for the 325th Ftr. Gp. (Checkertail Clan) to replace their P-40 aircraft. The 325th is attached to the 5th Bomb Wing, 15th (Strategic) Air Force , and is its only P-47 equipped bomber escort group. There are no P-47s in the 12th Air Force at this point.

Nov ,1943-Large numbers of P-47s are reaching England, and the strength of each group is now increased to 100 aircraft.

Nov ,1943-Republic is fitting water injection systems on all P-47Ds from D-20RE models onward, and in England modifications are started to add the system on older aircraft of the fighter groups. Most mod work is completed by the end of the year.

Nov 1,1943-The combat record of the P-47s in the ETO is now a total of 237 enemy craft downed for a loss of 73 P-47s, for a ratio of better than three to one.

Nov 5,1943-The 56th Ftr. Gp., 8th AF, UK, is the first 8th Fighter Command group to reach 100 enemy aircraft destroyed, nearly twice as many as the 4th Group. The 56th is called the Wolf Pack.

Nov25,1943-P-47s are used for bombing for the first time. The 56th and 353rd Groups do the bombing supported by the 78th and 356th Groups. The P-47s fly formation with a B-24 which does the sighting; each Thunderbolt carries a 500 pound bomb. Only "fair" results are obtained. More bombings are done on Dec. 4 and Dec.23.

Nov26,1943-The XP-47J model of the Thunderbolt is completed and makes its first flight on this date.

Dec ,1943-With the addition of the 358th and 359th Ftr. Groups with P-47Ds going operational this month ten P-47 groups are now with the 8th Air Force in England.

Dec ,1943-The 9th (Tactical) Air Force in England is now joined by the 362nd and 365th Fighter Groups with P-47s.

Dec ,1943-The 325th Ftr. Gp. (Checkertails) moves its P-47s up from bases in North Africa to Foggia, Italy, and on the 14th goes on its first P-47 mission escorting bombers to Greece.

Dec ,1943-The 35th Fighter group arrives in the Pacific with P-47 fighters. They will use the type until March 1945. Single squadrons of the 8th and 49th Groups in the Pacific switch to P-47s, and will use the type for a few months. The 9th Squadron of the 49th Group is very unhappy to switch from their P-38s to the P-47s.

Dec ,1943-While escorting bombers to Emden, Germany, 56th Fighter Gp. P-47s get 17 victories.

Dec ,1943-Fitting of "paddle-blade" propellers (Curtiss 836 design blades in place of the 714 "toothpick" blades) starts on P-47s, a squadron at a time. This modification, together with the water injection system on the engine, provides a very greatly improved climb rate for the P-47 such that below 15000 feet it can beat the FW-190 in climb.

Dec17,1943-348th Fighter Group P-47s move forward to their new advanced fighter base at Finchhaven in New Guinea along with P-40s.

Dec26,1943-P-47s assist in providing air support during the New Britain invasion in the Pacific. Seventy-five Japanese planes, including 50 Zeros, come to attack the invasion fleet at Cape Gloucester. They are met by P-40s of the 35th Sdn., P-47s of the 36th Sdn., and P-38s of the 431st. Later two Sdns. of the 348th Ftr. Gp. P-47s intercept 15 enemy bombers with fighter escort, and down 14 bombers and two fighters.

Dec30,1943-The 325th Ftr. Gp. of the 15th Air Force flies out ahead of Allied bombers slated to hit the Udine area, and manages to down 28 enemy aircraft..

Dec31,1943-At years end a total of 4428 P-47s have been produced, including 1131 from the Evandale, Indiana plant, but only 271 from Curtiss at Buffalo, New York.

Dec31,1943-P-47s of the 342nd Sdn., 348th Ftr. Gp., SW Pacific claim a total now of 79 enemy aircraft destroyed.

Dec31,1943-The P-47s in the ETO are proving to have a remarkably high reliability now that early engine problems are solved.

Dec31,1943-There are now 12 fighter groups in the 8th Air Force in England, ten P-47 and two P-38. This is three groups short of planned total strength, but the 8th can now field a force of 550 fighters, or an escort of one for one for the heavy bombers.

Jan ,1944-A program is started to equip all P-47C and P-47D aircraft with wing racks to carry either two 108 gallon drop tanks or two 1000 pound bombs.

Jan ,1944-The 8th Air Force swaps the 358th (P-47) Ftr. Gp. to the 9th AF for the 357th (P-51) Ftr. Gp.

Jan ,1944-The first unit in the 12th (Tactical) AF in the Mediterannean Theatre to get the P-47 is the 57th Ftr. Gp. which turns in its P-40s. The 57th starts flying interdiction missions behind enemy lines in Italy.

Jan ,1944-The 58th Ftr. Gp. arrives to join the 5th Air Force in the SW Pacific, and is the third P-47 organization there.

Jan21,1944-The 361st Ftr. Gp. goes operational with P-47s in the 8th AF and this will be the last P-47 unit in the 8th.

Jan24,1944-US and British commanders agree that the 8th AF is to be equipped almost exclusively with Merlin-powered P-51s, and that most P-38s and P-47s will be transferred to the 9th (Tactical) Air Force. The agreed fighter allocation is: For 8th AF-four P-47 groups, four P-38 groups, and seven P-51 groups; for 9th AF: thirteen P-47 groups, three P-38 groups, and two P-51 groups.

Jan30,1944-The P-47s of the 56th Fighter Group (Zemke's Wolf Pack) get their 200th aerial victory; the 4th Fighter Group P-47s are second with 100 victories.

Feb11,1944-The 56th Ftr. Gp., 8th AF, after escorting bombers, does its first ground strafing of enemy airfields.

Feb19,1944-The 8th AF in England now has eight groups of P-47s, the 9th AF has five (including the new 358th Group, operational February 3), and the 15th AF has one group.

Feb20,1944-The 150 gallon metal belly drop tank, locally made, is introduced for 8th AF P-47s just in time for Big Week-the bombing campaign taking place between the 20th and the 25th. During this time 8th AF fighters, mostly P-47s, shoot down 218 enemy aircraft. The new tank adds 15 minutes flying time, and the P-47s can now escort 350 miles from base.

Feb22,1944-The 61st Ftr. Sdn. of the 56th Group is the first ETO squadron to destroy a total of 100 enemy aircraft in the air.

Feb25,1944-The 4th Fighter Group, 8th AF, converts from P-47s to P-51B models. The movement towards P-51s in the 8th AF and P-47s in the 9th AF in England has started.

Mar ,1944-Production of P-47s in this month alone will total 641 A/C.

Mar ,1944-The Curtiss contract to build P-47s is cancelled after only 354 P-47Gs are built in about a year and a half. A total of 4220 Curtiss P-47 aircraft are cancelled.

Mar ,1944-With the decision to invade Saipan in the Mariannas the 318th Ftr. Gp. of 7th Air Force in the Pacific, which had flown P-47Ds since October, 1943 is selected in planning to assist USN and USMC fighter units. Two of the 318th squadrons, the 19th and 73rd, with 73 aircraft, will be employed.

Mar ,1944-The 355th Ftr. Gp. in the 8th AF, UK, converts from the P-47 to P-51s.

Mar ,1944-The 79th Ftr. Gp., 12th AF in the Mediterranean area is now re-equipping from P-40 to P-47 fighters.

Mar 8,1944-The 56th Fighter Group, Zemke's Wolf Pack, shoots down 23 enemy aircraft for a loss of five along the route of the bombers going to Berlin.

Mar14,1944-The new P-47 groups, the 366th and the 368th, join 9th AF and are operational.

Mar15,1944-Ninth AF P-47s of the 366th Ftr. Gp. go on a dive bombing mission over the German airfield at St. Valery, France.

Mar15,1944-The 56th Ftr. Gp. claims 24 victories during a bomber raid on Brunswick, Germany. First Lt. Robert S. Johnson claims three enemy aircraft and is now the ETO leading ace with a total of 21 victories.

Mar15,1944-In the ETO the 353rd Ftr. Gp. experiments using two 1000 lb. bombs dropped from a shallow dive.

Mar22,1944-Using two 100 gallon drop tanks, the 56th Ftr. Gp. 8th AF P-47s are able to extend their flight endurance to over four hours for the first time in escorting the B-17s part way on a Berlin raid.

Mar26,1944-Ninth AF P-47s attack many targets in France, including V-1 Buzz Bomb launch sites.

Mar27,1944-P-47s of the 80th Ftr. Gp., 10th Air Force intercept and break up a large Japanese attack on the oil refineries at Assam, India.

Mar30,1944-CVEs Mission Bay and Wake Island ferry 100 P-47s and arrive at Karachi, India. Fifty more P-47s are to arrive by regular transport. The flight echelons of the 33rd and 81st Ftr.Gps, veterans of the Mediterranean campaigns, had arrived the previous month. Transitional training is to begin Apr.15. The 81st will join the 14th Air Force in China.

Apr,1944-Both Republic plants change over from "razorback" to "bubble canopy" type design with the P-47D-25 model.

Apr,1944-The 33rd Fighter Group moves from India to Shwangliu, China after being assigned to the 14th Air Force with P-47s. It had previously been in the Mediterranean. Training on the P-47 aircraft type starts for the 33rd.

Apr,1944-P-47 groups in England are being positioned for the coming cross-channel invasion. They are seeing less air combat and doing more strafing. The restricting factor on P-47 combat radius is internal fuel capacity for the return trip. The most that can be squeezed out is about an hour and a half on the return.

Apr,1944-Three more P-47 fighter groups come aboard as operational in the 9th Tactical Air Force, the 405th Ftr. Gp. on the 11th, the 371st Group on the 12th, and the 48th on the 20th.

Apr 8,1944-Another 8th AF unit in the UK now switches from the P-47 to the P-51; the 352nd Fighter Group.

Apr26,1944-Twenty-four B-24s escorted by 10 P-51s and also accompanied by 12 of the first P-47 Thunderbolts to appear in China attempt to bomb bridges, after which the P-47s retire to Chengtu.

May,1944-Two P-47 squadrons of the 33rd Fighter Group, the 58th and 60th, fly into Szechwan Province in China. On the 15th of the month the 92nd Squadron, 81st Ftr. Gp., arrives in Kwanghan, China with P-47s.

May,1944-In preparation for the cross-channel invasion, British airfields are loaded with 9th AF P-47 Thunderbolts. In May no less than five new P-47 Groups become operational in the 9th; the 50th and 404th on the first, the 36th and the 373rd on the 8th, and the 406th on May 9th. Thirteen groups in five fighter wings are ready for the invasion; the 9th AF now has 1500 fighters with the vast majority being P-47s.

May,1944-The 359th and the 361st Groups, 8th AF, convert from P-47s to P-51s.

May,1944-In the SW Pacific P-47s of the 342nd Sdn., 348th Fighter Gp. shoot down five Zeros during the invasion of Biak Island off the New Guinea coast.

May,1944-The two fighter squadrons (5th and 6th Air Commando Sdns.) attached to the First Air Commando Group in Burma replace their P-51A Allison Mustangs with P-47s. The First Air Commandos had been formed in India in March.

May,1944-The 80th Fighter Group receives P-47s and starts flying ground support missions in Burma as well as providing air defense capability.

May 8,1944-Major Robert Johnson gets two of the six victories obtained by the 56th Ftr. Gp. over Germany this date, and raises his total to 27 enemy aircraft destroyed.

May12,1944-The 56th Ftr. Gp., 8th AF, operates in the area of Frankfurt and claims 18 enemy planes downed for a loss of three P-47s. Captain R. Rankin gets five victories over ME-109s.

May19,1944-The XP-47N model of the Thunderbolt is ordered as a conversion of a YP-47M with a new wing and more fuel for long range.

May21,1944-In one of the softening-up raids prior to invasion, approximately 500 P-47 fighters strafe rail targets in France; 46 locomotives are claimed destroyed.

May22,1944-A few P-47D-25 Thunderbolt models are getting into UK fighter groups. Sometimes labelled the "Superbolt", there are only three in the 56th Ftr. Gp. at this time. The major changes involve an extra 65 gallons of internal fuel in the fuselage and a "bubble" canopy.

May24,1944-The 325th Fighter Group (Checkertails, in Italy) trade in their P-47s for P-51 aircraft. Their last P-47 mission is flown on this date.

Jun,1944-The 332nd Fighter Group, 15th AF, in Italy converts from P-40s to P-47s. The 306th Fighter Wing now has this one P-47 group along with three of P-38s and three of P-51s.

Jun,1944-The 27th Fighter-Bomber Group (which has been flying A-36As) and the 86th Ftr. Gp. of the 12th (tactical) AF are now re-equipping with P-47 aircraft.

Jun,1944-US fighter pilots are starting to obtain G-suits, including most 9th Air Force P-47 units.

Jun,1944-Many of the old P-47s rendered surplus from the 8th AF conversion program are sent as replacements to 9th AF groups which often complain about their condition, and sometimes reject them as unserviceable.

Jun 6,1944-On D-day between 8th and 9th Air Forces twenty P-47 groups are available to the Allied Forces in England.

Jun 6,1944-The P-47 fighter groups left in the 8th AF are used to provide a screen forward of the invasion area. The groups are the 56th and the 78th. There is also a 495th Fighter Training Group with P-47s.

Jun12,1944-The 353rd Group P-47s are attacked by ME-109s while on a fighter-bomber mission and lose eight P-47s, but later the 353rd and 56th Groups together destroy 14 enemy planes in the Paris area. The 56th Group is acting as "flying artillery."

Jun19,1944-The 336th Fighter Group of 9th Air Force moves from England forward to an airfield on the continent less than two weeks after the invasion.

Jun22,1944-Twenty-four P-47s of the 318th Ftr. Gp. 19th Squadron from Hawaii are catapulted from two CVEs, and land at Aslito (later Isley) Field on Saipan during the Pacific invasion. Within hours they go on a rocket attack against nearby Tinian Is. Within two days they are reinforced by P-47s of the 73rd Sdn. and the rest of the 19th. The P-47s provide daily air patrol and ground attack missions until Japanese resistance ceases July 9th.

Jun30,1944-A contract for 1900 P-47N long range Thunderbolts is given to Republic.

Jul ,1944-The XP-47E with a pressure cabin is delivered by Army Capt. Colchagoff to Wright Field in Dayton, Ohio for testing.

Jul ,1944-In China the other two squadrons (91st and 93rd) of the 81st Fighter Group arrive in Kuanghan to join the 92nd Sdn. Later, though, General Chennault exchanges the P-47 Group for the 311th Fighter Group using P-51Bs in the interest of fuel economy. Fuel is a scarce commodity in China.

Jul 4,1944-The 56th Ftr. Gp. 8th AF on a dive bombing mission downs 20 ME-109s, bringing the group total to 500 aerial victories. There are now 38 aces in the 56th. They are still in P-47s.

Jul17,1944-The two squadrons of the 318th Ftr. Gp. in the Pacific have flown 2500 P-47 sorties since June 22nd.

Jul18,1944-The third squadron of the 318th Ftr. Gp. brings their P-47Ds to Saipan, thus filling out the Group in the Mariannas. They continue ground attack support on Tinian and Guam. Late in the month the P-47s use a new weapon in ground attack—the napalm fire bomb.

Jul22,1944-The first flight of the XP-47N aircraft takes place.

Jul25,1944-Eight fighter-bomber groups bomb a concentrated area assisting a troop breakout from the Normandy beachhead in France. After heavy bombers attack, another seven fighter-bomber groups renew the attacks. Five hundred and fifty fighters, mostly P-47s, drop over 200 tons of bombs. During the next few days P-47s provide close air-to-ground support.

Jul31,1944-Practically all 9th Air Force fighter units and their P-47s are now based in France.

Aug ,1944-Various efforts had been and are being made to increase P-47 range in the Pacific. The 5th Air Force had designed a 220 gallon belly tank in Australia, the AAF had, in later models,(P-47D-25 and on) added 65 gallons to internal fuel, and two 150 gallon wing drop tanks are being used as in the ETO; the Far East Air Force Service Command experiments with a 42 gallon fuel tank in the fuselage just below the pilot together with a form-fitting belly slipper tank of about 70 gallons. But the 5th Air Force fighter pilots, having seen crashes due to overload, are not willing to carry more than a total of 505 gallons. Gen. Kenney, realizing that the P-47 has reached a load limit without impractical heavier-ply tires, has cancelled both the aft-fuselage fuel cell and the slipper tank. Cruise control techniques are helping to increase P-47 range.

Aug ,1944-P-47s of the 57th, 86th, and 324th Fighter Groups fly flak supression missions over the airfields of southern France prior to the invasion of that area.

Aug ,1944-The 324th and 350th Ftr. Gps. are re-equipped with P-47 A/C.

Aug 4,1944-The 56th Ftr. Gp., 8th AF, is about one third equipped with bubble canopy P-47D-25 aircraft. As penetration of Allied forces into the continent increases, the lack of P-47 radius from England keeps the group from finding enemy fighters, and more P-47 missions are the bombing and strafing type.

Aug 5,1944-Republic test pilot Mike Richie flies the XP-47J version to 505 mph at 34450 feet, the fastest speed so far by a piston engined airplane.

Aug13,1944-P-47s of the 12th Air Force Tactical Air Command team up with P-38s of the 15th Air Force for a total of 180 fighters, and dive bomb and strafe seven airfields in the Rhone River delta and in northern Italy with great success.

Aug15,1944-For the invasion of southern France there are based on the island of Corsica a large number of fighter units. Of the twenty-one USAAF fighter squadrons fifteen are equipped with P-47s, and of four Free French Air Force squadrons three have Thunderbolts. In addition Coastal Air Force has the 350th Group with P-47s and P-39s.

Aug15,1944-In Operation Dragoon southern France is invaded. P-47s of 12th Air Force provide close air support for the landings and for some time after.

Aug17,1944-Rockets are used by the P-47s of the 56th and 78th Fighter Groups in the European Theatre of Operations. They are found to be difficult to aim to hit the target. The three-tube chutes are found to be unwieldy.

Aug26,1944-The 348th Ftr. Gp., less its 342nd Sdn., left to fly cover at Wadke and Hollandia, New Guinea, arrives at Noemfoor with its new P-47D-23 Thunderbolts as part of an air buildup prior to the Phillipine invasion. On Sept. 3 the 348th is augmented by arrival of the newly-activated 460th Squadron, and thus is now the only four-squadron group in the Southwest Pacific.

Aug29,1944-Eight P-47s of the 78th Ftr. Gp. flying top cover for strafing aircraft see their first German ME-262 jet fighter, and are able to force it down and destroy it.

Aug31,1944-Among the fighters available for the initiation of the Philippines campaign in the Pacific are 429 P-47s; this out of a total of 1103 fighter aircraft. The figures include planes enroute from the US.

Sep ,1944-The first production P-47N-1 aircraft is delivered by Republic Aviation.

Sep ,1944-The RAF begins to use the P-47 in Burma.

Sep ,1944-The 350th Fighter Group of Coastal Air Force in the Mediterannean area has now been fully re-equipped from P-39 to P-47 aircraft, and changes from defensive coastal patrol work to offensive operations in northern Italy.

Sep ,1944-The P-47s of the 33rd Fighter Group return from China to India and join 10th Air Force for the rest of the war, flying ground support missions over Burma.

Sep 1,1944-Four P-47 groups of 8th Air Force (138 aircraft) destroy 94 locomotives, damage 20, and destroy or damage 537 items of rolling stock and 382 vehicles including 15 tanks.

Sep 5,1944-Fifty-sixth Ftr. Gp., 8th AF P-47s strike at airfields, destroying 60 enemy aircraft on the ground, losing three aircraft of their own, and three others down in France with the pilots later rescued.

Sep17,1944-P-47s of the 56th, 78th, 353rd, and 356th Fighter Groups, 8th Air Force, 200 aircraft in all, go on flak-suppression missions during the Allied thrust at Arnhem.

Sep18,1944-P-47s again go on strafing missions near Arnhem. Of 39 P-47s of the 56th Ftr. Gp., 16 aircraft are brought down by enemy fire.

Sep21,1944-P-47s of the 56th Ftr. Gp., 8th AF, shoot down 15 German FW-190s for a loss of three of their own near Nijmegan.

Sep25,1944-In the battle for Arnhem the 8th AF has lost 73 fighters; 45 of these are P-47s.

Sep31,1944-Three P-47 groups, (50th, 358th, and 371st) are transferred from 9th Air Force to the First Tactical Air Force in France, along with units from the 12th Air Force (324th Group), and the entire French Air Force. The Allied troops from southern France have joined with those from Normandy, and the 12th Air Force returns to operations in northern Italy, losing the 324th Group.

Oct ,1944-Tenth AF P-47s begin a very active two months supporting the Allied offensive moving through central Burma. In eastern Burma the 14th Air Force's 25th Fighter Squadron P-47s support Gen. Dorn's Yunnan ground forces.

Oct ,1944-Sixteen P-47s of the 40th and 41st Squadrons from Morotai conduct a fighter sweep over enemy airfields at Negros for indirect support of the big invasion at Leyte, Philippines.

Oct 2,1944-The 8th AF 353rd Ftr. Gp. starts switching from P-47s to Merlin powered Mustangs in the European Theatre.

Oct 5,1944-Two squadrons of P-47s from the 35th Fighter Group come in to Wama at Morotai along with other fighters (P-40s and P-61s) in readiness for the Leyte Gulf invasion in the Philippines.

Oct 8,1944-Raids are made on Balikpepan oil refineries in Borneo on this date and the two days following. Fifth Air Force P-47s from Morotai (40th and 41st Sdns.,35th Group) go in first on a fighter sweep followed by B-24s escorted by P-38s. The P-47D-28s carry a 310 gallon drop tank on one wing and a 165 gallon tank on the other, and keep a 75 gallon belly tank on all the way. The trip from Morotai to Balikpepan is 835 miles. The P-47s come in from high altitude and can only make a few passes, but shoot down 15 Japanese on each mission. Two pilots are lost on these missions.

Oct21,1944-Twenty P-47Ds of the 318th Fighter Group at Saipan escort B-24s on a raid to Iwo Jima and shoot down an enemy aircraft.

Nov ,1944-The 356th Fighter Group of 8th Air Force is now switching from P-47s to P-51s.

Nov10,1944-P-47s of the 460th Squadron, 348th Ftr. Gp. reach Leyte in the Philippine Islands, and are basing there.

Nov11,1944-A Brazilian P-47D squadron starts operating with the 12th Air Force in Italy.

Nov15,1944-A new 200 gallon (actually 215 gallon) drop tank is now available to extend P-47 range.

Dec ,1944-There are now 31 P-47 fighter groups in combat all over the world.

Dec ,1944-Republic delivers 130 P-47M "hot rods" along with 24 P-47N long range Thunderbolts.

Dec ,1944-The combat career of the P-47 in the 8th Air Force is ending. Only one fighter group, the 56th Wolf Pack retains the P-47. But in the 9th (Tactical) Air Force there are now 14 P-47 Thunderbolt groups.

Dec ,1944-P-47 strength in the China-Burma-India Theatre is 417 aircraft. Thunderbolt strength in the months following is: Jan. 1945—379, Feb.—344, Mar.—372, Apr.—350, May—336, June—296. The distribution of P-47s among CBI forces in 1945 is: Jan.31 IBT-97, 10th AF-140, 14th AF-51. Mar.31 IBT-110, 10th AF-132, 14th AF-55. For July31, 1945, IBT-41, 10th AF-73, and 14th AF-59.

Dec ,1944-New P-47 combat pilots received by the Far East Air Force total 220 in the last six months. In the next six months (Jan. to June, 1945) 165 new P-47 pilots will arrive.

Dec ,1944-The 9th AF has been complaining to the 8th AF about the poor condition of the many P-47s made surplus by the changeover of the 8th to the North American Merlin-powered P-51.

Dec ,1944-As the miserable weather starts lifting to allow flying, the 406th Fighter Group, 9th AF, provides direct support to the encircled US troops at Bastogne, knocking out enemy tanks, vehicles, and gun positions.

Dec 2,1944-Two more P-47 fighter groups come in to base at Leyte in the Philippines, the 342nd Group on this date and the 341st Group four days later.

Dec 4,1944-During the US landings at Ormoc on Leyte, P.I., P-47s of the 460th Squadron shoot down two enemy Sally bombers over an Allied destroyer. Attempts by the Japanese to unload their troops north of Ormoc are hindered by continuous attacks of 86 P-47s as well as P-40s and Corsairs.

Dec 4,1944-The 56th Fighter Group, 8th AF, encounters very bad weather, and after conducting a strafing mission nine of its P-47s crash due to cloud and fog. The 1944-45 European winter is to be the worst in years.

Dec 7,1944-P-47s of the 348th Ftr. Gp. are still providing fighter cover for the US invasion forces at Ormoc, Leyte, P.I.

Dec17,1944-The P-47 Thunderbolts of the 460th Ftr. Sdn. make a sweep of the coastal Luzon area in the Philippines, and are the first US fighters to reappear over Manila.

Dec23,1944-P-47s of the 58th Ftr. Gp. arrive on Mindinoro Is. P.I. about a week after the invasion, moving in by squadrons on the 23rd 25th, and 27th of the month. On the 25th P-47s take part in attacks on a Japanese fleet attempting to break up the US invasion forces. Twenty-eight P-47s along with P-38s and P-40s participate in a wild melee that saves the beachhead, but 10 P-47s are lost.

Dec23,1944-After several days of terrible weather the 56th Ftr. Gp. is now able to go on a mission. The 61st, 62nd, and 63rd Sdns. encounter large numbers of German fighters near Bonne, and destroy 37 enemy aircraft for a loss of four P-47s, a record.

Dec23,1944-Five P-47s of the 341st Squadron along with P-40s attack Palompan on Leyte, P.I. with bombs and gunfire in preparation for US landings.

Dec24,1944-P-47s of the four squadrons of the 348th Ftr. Gp. (this group was unique in having four squadrons instead of the usual three) escort US bombers raiding Clark Field on Luzon P.I. The 348th downs 32 enemy aircraft for the loss of four Thunderbolts.

Dec31,1944-A total of 7065 P-47s have been produced in the last year—including 3087 in Indiana and 77 by Curtiss.

Dec31,1944-Two hundred and fifty-seven P-47s are now available to the Far East Air Force, including those enroute from the US. P-47s are slowly being replaced by P-51s.

Dec31,1944-The 78th Fighter Group, 8th Air force, gets its 400th and final victory using the P-47, and is almost complete in its conversion to P-51 Mustangs.

Jan ,1945-Ninth Air Force P-47 fighter-bombers defend themselves during heavy German Air Force attacks on Allied air bases. P-47s of the 336th Fighter Group claim a total of twelve enemy aircraft destroyed.

Jan ,1945-The 81st Ftr. Gp.,14th Air Force, has been training with P-47s, and is finally considered combat-ready this month. The 81st flies tactical support for the Chinese ground forces.

Jan 3,1944-The 56th Ftr. Gp., 8th AF, gets its first new P-47M Thunderbolt with a new version of the R-2800 engine. The M is 40 mph faster than the D, and reaches 30000 feet nearly five minutes quicker than the D, but does not increase range; in fact the aircraft proves to use more fuel than the D.

Jan14,1945-The 56th Ftr. Gp. in England shoots down 19 enemy aircraft for the loss of three P-47s over Germany.

Jan15,1945-Fifth Air Force P-47s are in action in ground-strafing missions from Lingayen on enemy troops after the US invasion of Luzon in the Philippines.

Mar ,1945-Gen. Kenney of 5th Air Force, temporarily in Washington, agrees to retain the 58th Ftr. Gp. as a P-47 organization at least until he can test the conbat capability of the new P-47N model offered him as a replacement.

Mar ,1945-A buildup of aircraft in the Pacific Ocean Area is taking place. Between now and July, 451 P-47 aircraft will arrive.

Mar ,1945-The 348th Ftr. Gp., Far East Air Force, squadron by squadron has been exchanging its P-47s for P-51 Merlin-powered Mustangs, and completes the switch this month. The 35th Ftr. Gp. also makes the transition in March. Many pilots are reluctant to part with the Jug, which Gen. Whitehead thinks "the best fighter which our country posesses". But the P-47's weight requires long runways, and Gen. Whitehead figures it will be late getting forward.

Mar 4,1945-The 56th Ftr. Gp. has been getting the new P-47M, but is having difficulties. The 62nd Squadron sends out 14 P-47Ms, but six have to return because of engine trouble. Several pilots are killed. After this incident all engines on M model aircraft with over 50 hours of flight time are changed. Causes of trouble include faulty ignition and poor engine pickling.

Mar 5,1945-Twelve P-47s of the 460th Ftr. Sdn. assault Japanese positions during the US forces retake of Corregidor Island off Luzon, P. I. with great success.

Mar10,1945-During the Allied assault on Mandelay in Burma P-47s of the 224th Ftr. Gp. drop 14 tons of bombs on a defensive strong point; the next day Thunderbolts of the 221st Ftr. Gp., each carrying two 500 pound bombs, eliminate other enemy strong point positions.

Apr ,1945-The 56th Ftr. Gp., 8th AF, finally gets its P-47Ms operational.

Apr ,1945-The initial shipment from San Francisco of a total of over 400 P-47Ns on aircraft carriers is made. They go first to Hawaii. From there the aircraft go out on carriers or are island-hopped to Saipan, then to Ie Shima near Okinawa. Three fighter groups are involved, the 413th, 414th, and the 507th. The 318th Ftr. Gp. is also re-equipping with P-47Ns.

Apr ,1945-The 350th Ftr. Gp. of the 12th Air Force sends its P-47s in attacks on heavily defended airfields in northern Italy.

Apr ,1945-The 318th Ftr. Gp. gets new P-47Ns and gets ready to move to Ie Shima, three miles off the coast of Okinawa, and only 325 miles from Japan.

Apr 5,1945-The P-47 equipped Mexican 201st Squadron reaches Clark Field in the Philippines. It is attached to the 58th Ftr. Gp. which will keep its P-47s through the end of the war. The planes of the 58th provide ground support for US troops on Luzon.

Apr10,1945-The 56th Ftr. Gp., after destroying two ME-262 jets, strafes German airfields and claims destruction of 45 enemy aircraft on the ground.

Apr13,1945-The 56th Ftr. Gp. P-47s strafe an airfield near Kiel, and claim 95 aircraft destroyed on the ground. The group now claims they have destroyed a total of 1000 enemy aircraft.

May ,1945-Peak inventory of AAF P-47s has been reached; 5595 aircraft are now with USAAF units.

May ,1945-The 318th Ftr. Gp. on Ie Shima, after arriving on the 14th and 15th, starts operations with its P-47N aircraft; on May 25th the group destroys 34 enemy aircraft over Kyushu, Japan.

May ,1945-After operations in support of Allied ground forces with P-47s, the First Air Commando Group switches back to late model P-51 Mustangs in order to save fuel.

May 8,1945-Ninth Air Force P-47 fighter-bombers in the ETO have flown, since Mar.25th, 29200 sorties, and during that time are credited with 240 enemy aircraft destroyed in the air and 1495 more on the ground. The last P-47 lost in the ETO comes just one day before Germany surrenders when a 405th Group aircraft crashes while buzzing a prisoner of war camp. The European war officially ended on the 7th of the month.

May16,1945-At the battle of Ipo on Luzon, Philippines, the 5th AF assists ground troops by sending P-47s, together with P-38s and P-51s in a total of 673 fighters against six square miles of Japanese positions. The P-47s and P-38s drop napalm and the P-51s strafe, decimating the defenders.

May17,1945-Two 17th Air Force P-47Ns from Okinawa, though lacking radar and homing aids, conduct night intruder missions over Kyushu Japan, and continue this until June 10 when P-61s arrive at Ie Shima. The night of the 16th they hit Kagshima, firing rockets, and fly down the lit-up streets strafing along the way.

May25,1945-The score is high for the newly-arrived 318th Ftr. Gp. of 20th Air Force whose long range P-47Ns tangle with enemy kamakazes 100 miles north of Okinawa. The group had no victories at the start of the day; at the end they had downed 34 enemy aircraft out of a 165-plane attack.

Jun ,1945-The Evansville, Indiana plant of Republic is ready to stop producing P-47Ds, and starts working on the P-47N type for the Pacific war.

Jun ,1945-The last fighter group to receive P-47Ns is the 414th. There are now four fighter groups operating the P-47N in the Pacific.

Jun10,1945-The 318th Ftr. Gp. P-47s have now destroyed 102 enemy planes. Later the same day the total goes to 108 victories.

Jun13,1945-Japanese defensive action is intensive over Kyushu. During the previous week the P-47Ns of the 318th Ftr. Gp. from Ie Shima are intercepted by 244 aircraft of which the Thunderbolts down 48 for a loss of three of their own.

Jun14,1945-P-47s of the 413th Ftr. Gp. arrive at Okinawa and contribute nine kills, seven in the kamakaze attack of June 22.

Jun21,1945-P-47s of the 413th Ftr. Gp., 20th AF, join in on fighter sweeps over Japan.

Jun28,1945-The 507th Ftr. Gp. brings in 48 more P-47N aircraft, becomes operational July 1, and shoots down ten enemy planes on July 9, most all of them enemy training planes attempting to make interceptions.

Jun30,1945-Fighters in the Tactical Air Force against Japan include 144 P-47s, also 288 F4U-s and other fighters. Next to the Corsairs the Thunderbolts are most numerous.

Jul 5,1945-One hundred and two P-47Ns escort B-24s and B-25s on another Kyushu raid.

Jul22,1945-The 414th Ftr. Gp., now based on Guam with P-47Ns, has been flying missions against Truk since July 11. Later in the month the 414th is transferred to Iwo Jima.

Jul27,1945-The first flight of the XP-47H model using a 16 cylinder Chrysler engine takes place.

Aug ,1945-P-47Ns of the 301st Ftr. Wing (318th, 413th, 414th, and 507th Groups) are transferred from 20th to 8th Air Force. But before the 8th AF B-29 heavy bombers get into action with P-47N escort the war ends on August 15.

Aug 5,1945-A combined 5th and 7th Air Force mission hits Tarumizi, Japan where rocket suicide planes are made. Among the large group of planes (including B-24s, B-25s, 32 A-26s, and 49 P-51s) are 97 P-47 fighters with GP and napalm bombs.

Aug 8,1945-Bombers attack Yawata, Japan, the most important industrial city left after the destruction at Hiroshima. One hundred

and fifty one P-47Ns of the 301st Ftr. Wing, 413th and 507th Groups fly their only escort mission over Japan. There are 400 bombers. Sixty enemy fighters appear, and in fierce air battles 13 enemy planes are downed for loss of five P-47Ns.

Aug11,1945-P-47Ns of the 318th Ftr.Gp. bomb a critical rail bridge on the east coast of Kyushu, Japan, and finish the job the big bombers started.

Aug13,1945-P-47Ns of the 507th Ftr. Gp. on Ie Shima fly a fighter sweep to Korea and meet 50 aircraft. They down 20 of these and destroy two on the ground, losing one P-47N.

Aug15,1945-World War II ends with the surrender of Japan.

Dec ,1945-P-47 production lines are closed. Republic has produced 13329 fighters in about 45 months, including 1667 P-47N models. In 1945 3657 P-47s are delivered, including 2014 from Indiana.

1945-About two of every three P-47s produced get into action, and 5222 aircraft are lost. The combat losses are quite low, less than 0.7%. Eight hundred and twenty six Thunderbolt I and II models serve with the UK, mostly in Asia. P-47 aircraft during the war claim destruction of 3572 enemy planes in the air and 3315 on the ground. From D-day in Europe to V-E day P-47s have destroyed 86000 railway cars, 9000 locomotives, 6000 armored vehicles and tanks, and 68000 trucks.

Apr ,1946-AAF Ftr. Gps. are still equipped with P-47 and P-51 aircraft. Only three P-80 jet fighters are available.

Late 1940s-From now through the early 1950s P-47Ds are sent to various countries: Iran-160, Portugal-50, Turkey and Yugoslavia-126, China-one Group, Peru-100, and Italy are included. In the 1950s France is still flying some P-47Ds. They are also used in a Guatamalan revolution. In the 1960s a few P-47s are still in use in South and Central America. In the late 1980s a few civilian P-47s are being flown as hobbyist aircraft, and several are contained in museum collections.

P-47 HANDLING QUALITIES AND CHARACTERISTICS

HANDLING QUALITIES
GROUND HANDLING

The P-47 was considered a good ground handling aircraft with of course the usual reservation as to forward visibility which, like other tail down fighters, was nonexistant. Thus the aircraft was taxied using the usual S-turns to unmask a view of obstacles in its path via a pilot's look at the forward quarters. The bulk of the big R-2800 radial engine up front made even more of an S-turn necessary than with some other fighters. The lockable tail wheel was unlocked for free castoring during taxi and S-turning. Directional control was

gained by a combination of engine power application and differential braking as required. The brakes were very good, and the aircraft was easy to taxi with the wide tread main landing gear being a helpful feature; however, the fully castoring tail wheel required riding the downwind brake. There was no tendency for the plane to nose over with a sudden application of power. One wartime pilot's evaluation was "Easy to taxi, good brakes".

Fig.47-1 Republic XP-47B Thunderbolt, Ser.40-3051, Mfr. photo via Jon Davis. The single prototype of the big Thunderbolt. Compare the small size of the man's head in the cockpit with the rest of the airplane. Size and weight of the selected powerplant system determined those characteristics of the aircraft. The turbosupercharged R-2800 with supporting powerplant subsystems, including fuel tanks but no fuel, weighed about 4300 pounds, well over two tons. The equivalent weight for a Curtiss P-40E was about 60% of that figure.

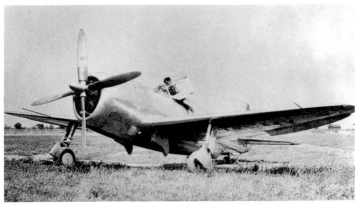

Fig.47-2 Republic XP-47B Thunderbolt, Ser.40-3051, Mfr. photo via F. Dean coll. Another picture of the unpainted prototype on the Republic grass field. First flight was in May of 1941, almost exactly seven months before Pearl Harbor. No P-47s had been accepted by the US Army by the time of the Japanese attack. The car-type door shown in the photo was unique to a very few early aircraft. The cuffs on the inner portion of the Curtiss propeller blades were there to assist in cooling the engine.

TAKEOFF AND CLIMB

For takeoff the P-47 was turned to point down the runway and moved straight forward to line up the tail wheel, which was then locked to prevent a swing developing on the takeoff run. Five degrees of right rudder trim was rolled in to provide good control of the initial torque swing with application of MILITARY power; it also allowed pedal forces to be trimmed out during climbout. Flaps could be left full up or be set halfway down to shorten the takeoff distance. The takeoff could be made with or without the turbosupercharger, but its use made for a shorter run. During takeoff the aircraft had satisfactory handling qualities, with good rudder control of torque swing, and was very stable with the wide tread landing gear. The gear was retracted as soon as the aircraft left the ground. A typical pilot's comment was "Good control on takeoff, but a long run required". On early models the takeoff was indeed long; a pilot checking out a

P-47B related "On takeoff I wondered if we were going to leave the runway, the roll being so much longer than other fighters." Later models, P-47D-25 and on, with a change from "toothpick" to wide chord "paddle" propeller blades had improved takeoff performance capability, but were heavier, which countered the improvement in propeller thrust. P-47s operating in all war theatres were loaded up with more and more fuel and ordnance, and takeoff performance on forward airstrips, as well as weight limits on tires, became critical. One pilot noted "People in the Pacific in the P-47D-25 used 2535 horsepower WAR EMERGENCY power rating to better advantage for takeoff". In just about all cases and in all versions the P-47 was noted for eating up large chunks of real estate on takeoff.

Best climb speed of the P-47 was 140 to 155 mph IAS. In long climbs in hot weather cowl flaps were opened and climb speed was increased to cool the engine. The legacy of the P-47 was that climb

Fig.47-3 Republic P-47B Thunderbolt, Ser. 41-5905, USAAF photo via F. Dean coll. A very early P-47B showing showing the distinctive forward-sloping radio antenna. The oval shape of the engine cowl resulted from not only enclosing the engine but the lower air intakes for the induction system and the oil cooler. The fuselage underbelly and the wing undersides were clear of any fittings for external stores. The B airplane flew on 305 gallons of fuselage internal fuel alone. The covering of moveable tail surfaces soon had to be changed from fabric to aluminum. P-47B production was completed in September, 1942.

Fig.47-4 Republic P-47C Thunderbolt, Mfr. photo via Jon Davis. A P-47C sits outside the Republic plant in a view emphasizing the wide tread of its landing gear, the shock strut of which was shrunk in length to fit into wing recesses upon retraction. P-47C models arrived in England at the end of 1942. They had, after the first fifty-seven aircraft, a longer fuselage forward due to a revision in engine mounting to facillitate changes. Along the way in production provisions were made for adding water injection for the engine and for attaching a large slipper-type belly fuel tank on centerline.

Fig.47-5 Republic P-47D Thunderbolt, Ser.42-74987, photo via P.M. Bowers. Perhaps a new arrival in light of its seeming good condition and lack of markings, this P-47D-10 razorback Jug sits on the crushed stone hardstand of an Italian airfield. Water injection was standard on the D aircraft. P-47s started arriving in the Mediterranean Theatre for the 12th Air Force in January, 1944 to replace P-40 aircraft.

rate, particularly on early models was, in the words of a P-47B pilot "Decidedly poor". Others commented in a similar vein "Mediocre rate of climb" and "The rate of climb was the main concern". But the classic and much repeated comment was "And its climbing ability was almost equal to that of a brick". Another pilot said "The P-47 had good performance if you could get it to altitude". The new paddle blade propeller, specifically designed to improve climb performance, was of considerable help on the later models of the aircraft. One report indicated "Engine water injection and a paddle blade propeller gave the P-47 a vastly improved rate of climb, and allowed it to outclimb an FW-190 below 15000 feet".

TRIMMING
There were some differences in trimmability between models "The P-47D-25 trimmed harder than the D-15", but generally longitudi-

nal and lateral trimmability was satisfactory on the P-47, and the tabs were very sensitive. There was very little trim change with gear retraction and initial acceleration; dropping flaps made the airplane slightly nose heavy. Longitudinal trim changes with power and speed changes were small, and elevator tab power was sufficient to trim stick forces to zero at all speeds and all normal center of gravity locations. The aileron trim tab action was sufficiently powerful for all flight conditions, and the rudder tab could trim pedal forces to zero at all speeds above 120 mph IAS in the power on clean condition. But as with other fighters, like the P-40, the rudder trim force change with changing power or speed was objectionally high.

DIVE AND RECOVERY
Probably the most outstanding and most remembered capability of the P-47 airplane was its diving performance. What it lacked in

Fig.47-6 Republic P-47D Thunderbolt, Ser.42-75568, Mfr. photo via F. Dean coll. Running up at the Republic Farmingdale, Long Island plant a D-11 version shows the eliptical curve of its wing, a characteristic of all Seversky and Republic aircraft through the Thunderbolt series. Like the British Spitfire the P-47 eliptical wing planform design was one effective method of obtaining good spanwise distribution of aerodynamic loading. The louvre on the side of the fuselage aft was an intercooler cooling air exit. One was on the other side also.

Fig.47-7 Republic P-47D Thunderbolt, photo via P.M. Bowers. In the "dirty" landing condition a razorback (as opposed to a bubble canopy) Jug comes in "over the fence" at an Italian airfield, causing a couple of the locals to duck a bit. Wing pylons appear noteably absent; this is strange for a tactical support aircraft. This D was probably coming in at a weight of about 13500 pounds if most fuel and ammunition was still aboard.

Fig.47-8 Republic P-47D, Ser.42-27666 etc., Air Force Museum photo. These razorback D-23 models are equipped with the standard Jug underwing pylons which could carry an array of different external stores, those on the near airplane apparently being tanks for spraying chemicals. These pylons were much criticized for their bulk; some called them monstrosities, and in-the-field attempts were made for redesign. As with these aircraft, most P-47 models seemed to use the Curtiss Electric propeller.

climb it made up in diving, and with a turbosupercharged engine it could easily start the dive from a high altitude. One expressive pilot quote was "I have never seen a plane that could get rid of such appalling hunks of altitude in such a short time". Another pilot said "Our evasive action (in combat) was to dive until you saw 500 mph IAS and you could be sure there was no one behind you any longer". The 500 mph IAS was the dive limit speed (400 mph above 25000 feet), and it was recommended dive recovery be made no lower than 12000 feet. At this altitude the limit dive speed corresponded to 601 mph TAS (true airspeed) and a Mach number of 0.82. At this speed the P-47 was well into compressibility with a drag coefficient of at least two and one half times the value at moderate speeds. A pilot described a long almost vertical high speed dive by two

early P-47B versions into compressibility. He said they could not pull out because the stick would not move and chopping throttle didn't help. Only when they got into warmer air at a lower altitude were they able to recover. In dives the P-47D-30 had neutral to negative static longitudinal stability with stick fixed above a speed of 300 mph IAS, and was unstable stick free above 260 mph IAS. The P-47 also had an inclination to reverse controls in a high speed dive, particularly in thin air, and aileron forces became high at speeds over 350 mph IAS. High speed dives from altitude produced a tendency for the plane to nose down, the so-called "tuck-under". If very high indicated airspeeds were reached the elevator tab had to be used for recovery. Using much nose-up trim could be dangerous, however. The combined effect of this trim and heavy pilot pull

Fig.47-9 Curtiss P-47G Thunderbolt, Mfr. photo via J. Schneider. This Curtiss-built P-47G sits for a picture as a Curtiss employee leaning against the tail of a P-40 doesn't quite get out of the way. Curtiss was selected to provide a third source besides the Republic Farmingdale and Evansville plants, and began production of the G in late 1942, but it was a very poor effort in contrast to the other sources.

Fig.47-10 Curtiss P-47G Thunderbolt, Mfr. photo via H. Andrews. Another Curtiss-built G version in flight. These Curtiss airplanes, in three or four sub-variants, were based on Republic P-47C and early P-47D models. The Curtiss effort appeared to be a half-hearted one, and in March, 1944 the contract was cancelled after only 354 aircraft had been produced. Note this aircraft had no external store stations apparent. Curtiss really wanted to produce one of their P-60 series fighters.

Fig.47-11 Curtiss TP-47G Thunderbolt, Ser.42-25266, photo via Jon Davis. As with just about all the other USAAF wartime single seat fighters two place trainer versions were attempted with the P-47. Here a two place Jug is pictured, one of two Curtiss-built P-47Gs, though it is believed Republic did the modifications. Since the cockpit extension is forward it is clear there had to be a reduction in internal fuel capacity as reference to the P-47 inboard profile shown elsewhere will demonstrate.

Fig.47-12 Civil Republic P-47D, N5087V, photo via P.M. Bowers. A beautiful example of a post-war restored P-47D except for the markings. Later on restorers benefitted from regulation changes allowing civil N numbers on World War II aircraft to be much less conspicuous. The restoration was done for a reunion at the Republic plant. Post-war civil Jugs often operated without benefit of complicated and unnecessary turbosupercharger installations.

force could impose a g overload on the airplane as it reached the denser air of lower altitudes, and a tail structural failure could result. On late model airplanes dive recovery flaps, hinged under each wing, were installed to aid the P-47 in coming out of high speed dives where compressibility was encountered. The words of a Republic test pilot on the flaps in 1944 are quoted "The P-47 (now) has dive flaps which lift the restriction on dive speed. You will get compressibility without the dive flaps, but they are to be used for recovery. At high altitudes, up around 25000 to 27000 feet, you

will recover at about four to four and a half g without any trouble to the pilot. At lower altitudes, down around 17000 to 18000 feet, the recovery is about six g, and then it progressively modifies itself because of the natural tendency of the aircraft to come out of compressibility at low altitudes, so it would be about three g at 10000 feet. So you actually have no restrictions as far as a dive and compressibility are concerned. It is very much similar in compressibility and not in compressibility. The angle of the flaps when extended is 20 to 22 degrees." Several pilots checked out recovery flap op-

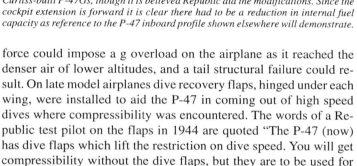

Fig.47-13 Civil Curtiss P-47G Thunderbolt, Ser.42-8476, Ron McCann photo. Another example of a restored P-47, this photo taken at a 1980s Oshkosh air show. The aircraft is believed to be a refurbished P-47G with a P-47D-5 serial number. Today it is unusual to see a flyable P-47 airplane. The propeller is a Hamilton Hydromatic type.

Fig.47-14 Civil Curtiss P-47G-15 Thunderbolt, Ser.42-25234, photo via R. Besecker A clean looking civil Jug in beautifully restored condition. This flight view shows off trim basic lines in spite of that big R-2800 engine up front when unadorned by external pylons and stores. The trouble was without the external stores the fighter could often not get to the war.

Fig.47-15 Republic P-47D Thunderbolt, Don Campbell photo. A postwar D model in the USAF. P-38s were discarded relatively quickly postwar, but P-47s and P-51s soldiered on several years in peacetime, first in the regular Air Force and then in the Air National Guard. The aircraft pictured has those much criticized over-large wing stores pylons and is also fitted with five zero-length rocket standoffs under each wing. The printing on the cowl says simply "Keep off!"

eration and all liked them. Typical comments were "Dive flaps a help in 400 mph IAS pullouts", and "Dive recovery normal". Dive stick forces were considered satisfactory. A Vought test pilot tried the flaps and said "I checked them out at 400 mph IAS, and I liked them so much I just let the stick go and let it pull me out. It is very nice for maneuvering. If you ever lose your elevators I think you have got something". So the P-47 dive flap installation appeared to be a success and allowed Thunderbolt pilots to go into high speed dives with assurance of being able to pull out. One interesting tale concerning P-47 dive and zoom capabilities was related by a Jug pilot "I was told if you tangle with an FW-190 or ME-109 at 25000 feet and want to beat him to 30000 feet, then dive to 20000 feet and zoom, and you'll be waiting for him up there. It really was true; the Jug's zoom capabilities (out of a dive) were tremendous."

MANEUVERING

All normal acrobatics were allowed with the P-47, but not outside loops or sustained inverted flight. Slow rolls were permitted up to 313 mph IAS, but snap rolls were not allowed; in any case they were not to be done over 150 mph IAS. Other prohibited maneuvers were intentional spins of more than half a turn, whip stalls, and violent maneuvers and high speed dives with belly or wing tanks aboard. On very early P-47B airplanes violent maneuvers with over 15 gallons of fuel in the auxiliary tank, which was somewhat aft, were prohibited. But after the nose extension provided on P-47C and on this restriction was lifted.

The general verdict of pilots on P-47 maneuverability was "fair" to "poor". There were comments such as "Poor maneuverability", "The P-47 was nothing to shout about in a turn", and "Has a large

Fig.47-16 Republic P-47D-25 Thunderbolt, Ser.42-26389, Mfr. photo via F. Dean coll. In the spring of 1944 Republic started producing a new Thunderbolt version, sometimes called the Superbolt that year. There were significant changes in the D-25 including a bubble canopy and a larger internal main fuel tank raising the capacity internally from 305 to 370 gallons. The photo shows a new P-47D-25 version posing at the plant. Note there is no dorsal fin on the aircraft.

Fig.47-17 Republic P-47D-25, Ser.42-26422, F. Dean coll. An operational D-25 Jug, Anne, with Hamilton paddle blade propeller sits in a field alongside a C-47 transport with empty centerline and wing store stations. In May, 1944 P-47D-25s started getting to operational groups in the UK, though in late May there were only three in the 56th Fighter Group. This photo is believed to have been taken in Italy where D-25s would have arrived much later.

Fig.47-18 Civil Republic P-47D-25, Ser.42-26424, R. Besecker photo. With the serial number of a D-25 version this Confederate Air Force Jug appeared at the Reno Air Races of 1974. It has the dorsal fin of later variants and is decorated with "invasion stripes". The low down exit just aft of the cowl flaps was a waste pipe with a gate valve to control exhaust flow. The remainder of the exhaust gas flow was piped aft internally to the turbine of the turbosupercharger, though it is doubtful such was installed on this civil version. The supercharger flight hood aft on the belly is in place, however.

Fig.47-20 Republic P-47D-28 Thunderbolt, Ser.42-29002, photo via P.M. Bowers Taken in Italy, this picture shows "Ponnie" with its four staggered port wing .50 caliber machine guns and the large store station pylon. The guns were charged manually on the ground before takeoff. Ammunition boxes were located outboard in the wing, and maximum capacity per gun was 425 rounds. Sway braces at the fuselage centerline store station can be seen beneath the aircraft.

turning circle". But one pilot said "At high altitude it had the most amazing maneuverability of any plane I have flown. She seemed to thrive on thin air". Pilots rated elevator trim forces in turns as good probably because stick longitudinal forces were on the low side. On the P-47D-30 at forward centers of gravity stick force per g was within design requirements except at 350 mph IAS at low altitude where it was slightly high. At rearward center of gravity locations and low altitude stick force per g was low, and force reversals occurred. In high altitude turns stick force reversals occurred at speeds below 250 mph IAS and stick force per g above that speed was dangerously low. Stick forces were higher in right turns than in left. A modern evaluation of the P-47D-40 at a nominal center of gravity location gave a stick force per g in turning of seven and a half

pounds. It is not clear whether this airplane had a bobweight installed in the elevator control system as did some P-47s. The aircraft had a light buffet in a 4.8 g turn and moderate buffet at 5.2 g.

Nobody raved about aileron performance of P-47s, though data for the P-47C-1 showed a peak roll rate of about 85 degrees per second (a 4.2 second full roll) at 250 mph IAS with a 50 pound pilot force on the stick. Other information, for a P-47D-30 or D-40 indicated a peak of about 60 degrees per second (a six second roll) at around 220 mph IAS using a stick force of 30 pounds. Roll rate dropped to half that value at 400 mph IAS.

On early bubble canopy P-47D versions there was no dorsal fin. With the additional destabilizing effect of a new paddle (wide chord) blade propeller directional stability and control problems

Fig.47-19 Civil Republic P-47D-25, Ser.42-26424, R. Besecker photo. Another photo of the D-25 belonging to the CAF and appearing at Reno, Nevada. A good view of the partially lowered single slotted plain wing flap on the P-47 is provided. This aircraft is equipped with the Curtiss propeller having 836 design paddle propeller blades. Installation of the new propellers with higher activity factor blades started in December of 1943, and together with additional power available with engine water injection yielded a large and sorely needed increase in airplane rate of climb.

Fig.47-21 Republic P-47D-30 Thunderbolt, Ser.44-32927, photo via R.Besecker. A post-war Rhode Island Air National Guard P-47 sits on the line with other Jugs. Throughout the war almost to the end P-47s struggled with a problem of limited combat radius, and with that big R-2800 engine up front pilots kept a wary eye on the fuel gage. The extra 65 internal gallons starting with the P-47D-25 helped, but it seemed the Jug never had enough legs as an escort fighter, particularly as escort distance requiremants increased, until the P-47N came along late in the Pacific war.

Fig.47-22 Republic P-47D-40 Thunderbolt, Ser.45-49355, USAAF photo. "Big Stud" was the last P-47 airplane of Lt.Col. Robert Baseler. The D-40 block was the final variant of the D series, and had all the improvements made to that time, including the dorsal fin (-27 and on), dive flaps (-30 and on), and provisions for carrying rockets. This D-40 has a wing clear of stores attachments however. The picture shows how big the Thunderbolt was in comparison to the pilot. The cockpit was large, but big pilots did not have enough leg room.

would be encountered similar to those found on early P-51D airplanes. The problem is illustrated by the instructions of a Republic test pilot to a group ready to fly a P-47D-30 without the dorsal fin, apparently an early version. "However on the D-30 you don't have the fin and there is the possibility, by (using) rough uncoordinated flight, of an outside snap roll. Don't yaw the airplane over ten degrees at high speed and high power". And later "Again I want to warn you about all our P-47s. Don't use full rudder force. Plain coordinated flying is all that is required, and you won't get into trouble with the P-47. On the P-47M we have the dorsal fin which

eliminates the unsatisfactory yaw condition". After the dorsal fin fix the P-47D-30 aircraft still had weak directional stability, rudder fixed or free, in all low speed power on conditions. Directional stability at higher speeds was satisfactory. Stability decreased slightly at high altitude. A later report on a P-47D-40 noted positive static directional stability with the dorsal fin. Other aspects of the D-40 affecting maneuvering characteristics were a positive dihedral effect, high side forces, almost no adverse yaw due to roll, and a large pitching moment due to sideslip.

Fig.47-23 Republic P-47D-40 Thunderbolt, Ser.45-49355, USAAF photo. Another fine flight view of Col. Baseler's Big Stud emphasizes the brawn of the big fighter and the eliptical planform of the wing. With maximum fuel the Jug could get to a gross weight of 16400 pounds or more. On one Pacific mission in October, 1944 P-47s took off with three external tanks of 310, 165, and 75 gallons. The 75 gallon belly tank stayed on for the whole mission as a substitute for lack of sufficient internal fuel capacity.

Fig.47-24 Civil Republic P-47D-40 Thunderbolt, F. Dean photo. A nicely restored D-40 at an air show in the late 1980s done up in mottled camouflage and invasion stripes, seemingly to duplicate the aircraft of Col. Gabreski. Like many P-51s, some operational D-40 aircraft were equipped with the new K-14 British-invented gunsight, but by this time most all Thunderbolts were used as tactical ground support fighters rather than primary air combat fighters. This aircraft is equipped with the extended trailing edge high activity factor propeller blades.

Fig.47-25 Republic XP-47E Thunderbolt, Ser.41-6065, Mfr. photo via Jon Davis. The last of the early P-47B airplanes shown here was designated as an XP-47E to test a pressure cabin design. Fighters with particularly high altitude capability such as the P-38 and the P-47 were considered appropriate candidates for installation of a pressure cabin. These designs proved difficult to execute without considerable penalties, and no production fighter aircraft was so equipped.

Fig.47-26 Republic XP-47JThunderbolt Ser.43-46952, Mfr. photo via Jon Davis. Appearing in the fall of 1943 the single J variant included many changes from standard Jugs, including powerplant revisions with less fuel and only six guns. The photo shows the large propeller spinner and a geared cooling fan just behind with a lower separate recessed air scoop. It was claimed the test aircraft achieved level flight speeds of about 500 mph true airspeed near 35000 feet. Such performance would correspond to the very high Mach number of about 0.76 in a standard atmosphere, making one wonder a bit about the numbers.

APPROACH AND LANDING
The word on aproach and landing for a Thunderbolt was summarized as fast coming in but settling very well after touchdown. Maximum allowable gear down speed was 250 mph IAS and for flaps down 195 mph IAS. Approach speed was 115 to 130 mph IAS with the turbosupercharger operating. In the approach condition the D-30 airplane had neutral stick fixed static longitudinal stability above 130 mph IAS if the center of gravity was aft; in the dirty landing condition stability was satisfactory. The elevator control available met landing requirements, but because of some longitudinal instability in a low power on approach test pilots considered the aircraft unsatisfactory. Touchdown speeds for the C and D versions varied, depending on weight, from 92 to 105 mph. On ground runout

"The aircraft had satisfactory handling qualities" according to a test pilot. This view was pretty much echoed by a large group of pilots at a conference where typical comments were "Fast landing, but comfortable", "Stable easy landing", and "Needs a large airfield". The wide tread landing gear of the P-47 "Was a good feature", and contributed greatly to safe landing qualities of the airplane. Another factor which helped: brakes were excellent.

STALLS AND SPINS
Typical one g stall speeds for a P-47D-30 aircraft at a normal weight were 115 mph IAS clean and 100 mph IAS dirty. The warning was a mild buffet about four to five mph above stall. Other warnings were decreasing aileron effectiveness, increased elevator stick force,

Fig.47-27 Republic XP-47K Thunderbolt, Ser.42-8702, Mfr.photo via Jon Davis. The last P-47D-5 airplane , redesignated XP-47K, was used as a test vehicle for design features planned for use on future production Thunderbolts. As pictured here it was testing a bubble canopy, reputed to be borrowed from a British Hawker Typhoon fighter. A bubble was later employed in production starting with the P-47D-25. Another job for the K airplane was testing of a new wing incorporating fuel tanks, something later employed on the long range P-47N.

Fig.47-28 Republic YP-47M Thunderbolt, Ser.42-27386, Mfr. photo via Jon Davis. The P-47 probably never looked better than in this shot of M2, the second prototype of the P-47M, a real "hot-rod" version with the new R-2800C engine providing a COMBAT power of 2800 HP at 32600 feet at 72 inches of manifold pressure. The P-47Ms were produced only to the extent of 130 airplanes, these delivered at the end of 1944, and started going to the crack 56th Fighter Group in the ETO in January, 1945. After initial problems with the engines the group finally got going with their new aircraft in April. These were the fastest operational Thunderbolts.

Fig.47-29 Republic P-47N Thunderbolt, Ser.44-88335, Mfr.photo via F. Dean coll. A well known Republic publicity photo shows a gun, bomb, and rocket loaded P-47N, the final major variant of the Jug, taxiing out to a company runway. This was the Thunderbolt reworked for Pacific long distance flying, bigger and heavier than ever, and, as this picture shows, a very imposing machine.

Fig.47-30 Republic P-47N Thunderbolts, Ser.44-88576 (near aircraft), Mfr. photo via Jon Davis. A dramatic duo of new P-47Ns show off their revised wing planform in this Republic photo. Over 1800 of this last version were produced as Republic's answer to criticism of P-47 range and radius limitations. Over 550 gallons of internal fuel was packed in, some in new tanks in the wing, and maximum external fuel capacity was 600 gallons, making a total of 1156 gallons. This Thunderbolt had legs.

and rearward stick movement. The usual pilot rating for stall warning characteristics was "good'. This was true regardless of flight condition, gliding, approach, landing, or waveoff. If the aircraft was one g stalled power on and clean there was a strong buffet and a tendency to roll right, then left, but this could be controlled. This was also true in a power off glide. In the approach with low power and gear and flaps down, the control forces to hold the aircraft level at stall were high and irregular, and if the stall was allowed to continue a rapid and uncontrollable roll would ensue. Recovery from a one g stall by standard methods was described variously by pilots as "straightforward", "normal", and "good", and "The plane recov-

ered from a stall pretty well". With an accelerated stall in a turn or pullout (a high speed stall) characteristics were generally similar. There was plenty of warning via buffeting and control sloppiness. It was noted as "Predictable and controllable", and "Characteristics were satisfactory", and "It could be held at near the maximum useable lift coefficient with ease". An NACA pilot indicated "Mild lateral instability which could be very easily controlled with aileron". In the absence of gross mishandling there was little tendency to depart, but if the stall was held "There was a pronounced tendency to snap to the left".

Fig.47-31 Republic P-47N Thunderbolts, Ser.44-88576 (near aircraft), Mfr. photo via Jon Davis. Shiny new, a trio of P-47N fighters pose for the company photographer. The increase in size of the dorsal fin is evident, as are the squared off wingtips. Here again Thunderbolt bulk shows up in comparison to pilot size. Increased loaded weight of the N version sharply reduced rate of climb at MILITARY power again. With about 1000 gallons of fuel the P-47N could fly a realistic combat radius of 1000 miles. In one case takeoff weight was well over 19000 pounds.

Fig.47-32 Republic P-47N Thunderbolt, photo via P.M. Bowers. A P-47N on postwar display, probably at the USAF Museum with guns removed, dummy bombs and rockets aboard, and looking a bit weary. The name below the cockpit canopy is Col.Dave Schilling, top man in the famous 56th Fighter Group. The original contract was given to Republic for 1900 P-47N aircraft at the end of June, 1944. It appears that 1816 Ns were built. First flight of the XP-47N took place in late July of 1944. Twenty four aircraft had been delivered by years end.

Fig.47-33 Republic P-47N Thunderbolt, Ser,44-89422, photo via P.M. Bowers. One of the last batch of 167 N-25 models looking to be in the final stages of life sits without any special markings at a civilian field. The photo illustrates the larger dorsal fin. With advent of the bubble canopy and resulting loss of of aft turtledeck side area and the installation of a new wide chord paddle blade propeller increasing propeller destabilizing effect, the dorsal was needed to help restore directional stability.

Fig.47-34 Republic P-47N Thunderbolt, Ser.44-88680, photo via P.M. Bowers. A post-war P-47N, probably at Selfridge Field in Michigan, is decorated with pre-war tail marks, bringing a touch of nostalgia to aeronautical buffs. This was in 1946, and the aircraft carries the then-new buzz markings on the fuselage sides. Wartime P-47Ns operated in the Pacific in 1945 and eventually equipped four fighter groups. Many were shipped out on aircraft carriers to Hawaii, then island-hopped west to where the action was.

Spin characteristics were normal with a light clean aircraft having a forward center of gravity except for a vertical acceleration of the nose during a spin. The aircraft would never spin of its own accord, but had to be forced into a spin by use of rudder and elevator. Once a stable spin was attained it was necessary to apply full elevator and rudder at all times. The recovery technique was full opposite rudder, neutral elevator, and ailerons set against the spin, with all control movements rapid but smooth. This procedure would usually provide spin recovery in a half turn. If not half throttle was applied. With a clean aircraft a single turn spin could lose 3000 feet in altitude; with two turns it would be 4000 feet, and so on. Deliberate spinning in excess of one half turn was prohibited.

CHARACTERISTICS

COCKPIT

The World War II pilot evaluation of the P-47 cockpit started with words like "Plenty of room", "The Ritz", "Inordinately spacious", "Roomy", and so on. There was one caveat, however, and this was noted both years ago and in a modern evaluation. There was not enough leg room for large pilots so they had to sit in an awkward knees-up position. Seat and pedals were adjustable, but not enough for long legs. In spite of this a large group of the "old" pilots voted the P-47D-30 cockpit the most comfortable of eleven fighter types at a wartime meeting, whereas the modern pilot evaluation was "cramped and uncomfortable". Perhaps pilots were more easily satisfied in World War II. The P-47 cockpit was also relatively quiet. One Navy pilot who got to fly it said "I wish we had a Navy fighter as quiet as the P-47". As to cockpit layout a P-47B pilot said "Controls pretty standard except for the turbo". The throttle and turbosupercharger control were normally linked together, but could be disconnected for individual use. There were mixed ratings, as usual, from pilots. Some controls were considered hard to see and identify, some hard to tell apart by feel, and the tail wheel lock was considered hard to reach. In a 1944 meeting it got some poor rat-

ings in voting for best and worst "all-around" cockpit of several fighter types. One could conclude since the same group voted it "best" in comfort it must have been considered quite poor in arrangement to get the poor all-around rating. One item on the P-47D-30 that got excellent reviews was the electric operation of the bubble canopy; pilots liked the power actuation. There were some complaints about the bubble; it got to be a hothouse in warm weather conditions in the South Pacific.

VISIBILITY

Pilot visibility in the older "razor-back" P-47 models was not particularly good. Although there was adequate space for pilot head movement, the forward view was poor because the aircraft nose was long and the big radial engine also made it wide, so sight with the nose even slightly raised was poor. As noted earlier, on the ground in three point attitude there was no forward visibility. Forward quarter and side visibility was fair in the razorback, and limited rear quarter visibility was facilitated by cut-outs of turtledeck contour aft of the cockpit covered by transparencies. With advent of the bubble canopy in later P-47D models visibility was very much better. A pilot said "Bubble canopy (was) a tremendous improvement in visibility". It improved almost everywhere, side, rear, upwards, except over the nose, where it remained pretty much as described earlier.

VULNERABILITY/ARMOR

Of eight fighter types ranked in 1944 pilots put the P-47D-30 first in a category "best armor". Between the armor, a very rugged airframe, and an air cooled radial engine without problems of leaking coolant and freezing up from a projectile hit, the Thunderbolt was no doubt the best single engine Army fighter in terms of low vulnerability to weapons fire. There were no liquid heat exchangers other than the oil cooler; the rest were of the air-to-air type. There are many reports of damaged Jugs heading for home being ham-

Fig.47-34 Republic P-47N Thunderbolt, photo via P.M. Bowers. Another view of a post war P-47N with the old tail stripes and the new buzz numbers on the fuselage. Along with some D models the long range N hung in with the Air Force, Air Force Reserves, and the Air National Guard for several years after the war, gradually giving way to the jets. By the mid-50s they had passed from the scene.

Fig.47-35 Republic P-47N Thunderbolt, F. Dean photo. A 1946 picture of an N taxiing in after an air show fly-past with the striped tail in evidence. The author took the photo in Massachusetts at his first post-war air show shortly after leaving the service, and remembers P-51H and P-47N airplanes in attendance, but the new "star of the show" was a gray painted Lockheed P-80A Shooting Star screaming past to announce the jet age.

mered unmercifully by enemy aircraft and making it back to safety. The same was true of battle damage from ground fire while in the fighter bomber and strafer roles. The P-47 in many instances could return after being severely damaged.

GUN PLATFORM AND WEAPON PERFORMANCE
Most pilots considered the P-47 a good gun platform though some said only fair. One veteran pilot said it was better than a P-40 or P-

51. It was rated first of nine fighter types in "best strafer" category by one pilot group. A modern evaluation came up with similar results based on good air to air tracking, light control forces without retrimming, and crisp and deadbeat control responses, along with good dynamic stability characteristics.

Performance of the eight .50 caliber machine guns on the P-47 was generally good. The gun was considered reliable, and the installation was a good one.

Fig.47-36 Republic P-47N Thunderbolt, Ser.44-89308, USAF Museum via F. Dean coll. P-47s were used in a variety of peacetime roles for a few years after the war. This Jug was employed on loan to the US Forestry Service as part of water bombing tests on forest fires. Water tanks were carried on the standard under-wing pylons.

GENERAL COMMENTS

A Thunderbolt pilot reported his aircraft gained 15 mph in speed at 1000 feet after a fine sandpapering of the surfaces.

Best at high altitude; not so good at low altitude.

Not for a dogfight; best as a fighter-bomber.

The enormous and unnecessary size of the bomb releases (wing pylons) could be narrowed to reduce drag.

My P-47D-16 was exactly 50 mph slower with the same throttle setting due to those monstrosities (wing pylons) they used on it.

The P-47 turned out to be a loveable and forgiving beast.

Many considered the P-47 an excellent plane because it could take lots of punishment and dish it out too. It was dependable; no worrying about coolant leaks, easy to maintain, just a good all-around airplane.

Other noted P-47 attributes were a comfortable cockpit, a low internal noise level, little vibration, and excellent control response.

Its visibility on the ground was poor. The large barrel-like nose protruded far out ahead of the pilot and obscured flight visibility too. (With paddle propeller blades) the improvement in rate of climb was quite drastic.

The bubble canopy provided excellent all-around visibility.

Pilots reported the Thunderbolt was faster than anything they would run up against.

By God it ought to dive; it certainly won't climb.

With the P-47 the way to evade an enemy was to roll over and dive. According to pilots there was nothing that could catch the airplane in a dive.

Some pilots considered the P-47 very versatile because though it was known as a high altitude fighter it could dive swiftly and attack at very low altitude.

P-47s were better suited for strafing than the more vulnerable P-51s.

The Thunderbolt could absorb more punishment than other fighters and still make it home using that dependable engine.

Luftwaffe Gen. Galland, after flying the P-47, said he initially felt the cockpit was big enough to walk around in.

It was said a P-47 pilot diving in from over 20000 feet could feel the nose tuck under.

After reaching compressibility in a high altitude dive and going out of control a P-47 pilot could finally start moving the controls at 13000 feet and was even shooting his guns to slow down.

Compressibility could kill not only P-38s and some P-51s but even P-47s. The latter type could lose its empennage in a dive, earning in some cases the name "widow-maker".

One pilot noted he didn't dislike the P-47 and had some success as a Jug pilot, but was glad to make the transfer to P-51s.

Gen. Arnold told Gen. Kenney of the 5th Air Force he was to get three more fighter groups. One flew P-47s, which no one else wanted. Kenney said he would take them.

On internal fuel tankage alone the P-47 did not have enough range to get into the war.

Fifth Air Force personnel had pre-judged the P-47 as follows: It was no good as a combat aircraft. It did not carry enough fuel, took up too much runway to take off, had no maneuverability, would not pull out of a dive, had a weak landing gear, and used an unreliable engine.

Cockpit heating was adequate.

P-47 firepower was a sight to behold. And it could also take a great deal of punishment.

Initially the ME-109 could out-turn and out-climb the P-47.

When a Jug dropped on you from a long dive there was no escape. The Thunderbolt could really punish a target as well as still fly after being badly shot up. nothing can catch a Thunderbolt. I eluded them.

One German pilot flew a captured P-47. He didn't like it-too big an airplane and a huge cockpit with everything out of reach.

P-47 STRUCTURAL DESCRIPTION
(Metal is aluminum alloy unless otherwise noted)

WING GROUP

The wing was a full cantilever type employing two main spars, stressed skin, and multi-cellular construction. The primary wing structural members were the two main spars attached to the fuselage and three auxiliary spars, one supporting the aileron, another supporting the wing flap, and the third, a short inboard spar, providing support for the main landing gear. The main spars, running on each side from fuselage to wingtip, were constructed of E-shaped cap strips riveted to webs of thicknesses varying from a maximum of 0.25 inches (inboard on the forward main spar) to .032 inches (outboard on both main spars). Both main spar webs were reinforced at intervals by vertical extruded angles which also served as anchors for wing rib installations. The inboard ends of the main spars of each wing were equipped with a pair of wing hinge fittings which were pinned to the mating fuselage hinge fittings by split bushings; tapered bolts expanded these bushings to assure a tight fit to secure positive attachment. The aft auxiliary spars supported the moveable surfaces, and were constructed of angle cap strips with webs varying in thickness from .072 to .025 inches. The landing gear auxiliary spars, subjected to heavy landing loads, had webs .091 inches thick and caps similar to the main spar. Flanged ribs were secured between spars at the angle stiffener locations. The rib web thicknesses varied from .051 to .032 inches except for the ribs at the wing root and the gun bay partitions where web thicknesses were .064 inches. The nose and trailing edge sections of the wing were formed by flanged rib sections. The wing covering metal skins were butt jointed, flush riveted stressed skin reinforced by extruded angle spanwise stringers. The skins had reinforced cut-out areas for inspection access, and maintenance doors and larger cut-out areas for landing gear wells and ammunition bays, all of which comprised about 16 percent of the total main panel area. Separable wingtips were formed by a tip inboard rib attaching to the main panel, five tapering spanwise formers, and an edge member.

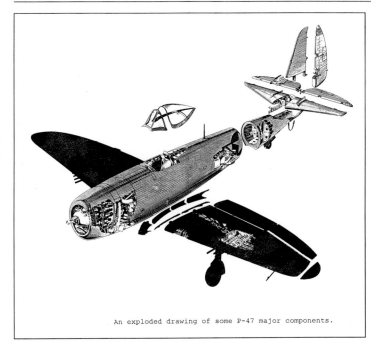

An exploded drawing of some P-47 major components.

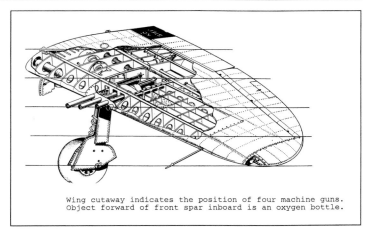

Wing cutaway indicates the position of four machine guns.
Object forward of front spar inboard is an oxygen bottle.

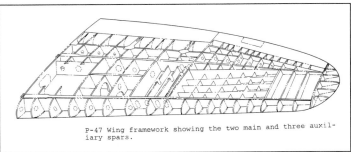

P-47 Wing framework showing the two main and three auxiliary spars.

controlled by a system of push-pull rods. An all-metal controllable trim tab was provided on the left aileron. Flanged nose and tail ribs were attached in staggered fashion to a single main aileron spar, and metal sheet was flush riveted to the spar and ribs. Aileron hinges were of forged alloy.

The landing flaps, representing 13 percent of the total projected wing area, were NACA slotted types. They were hydraulically operated, and during extension moved first aft and then down, and during retraction moved first up and then forward. The movement was synchronized by three trapezoidal linkage hinges to ensure accurate positioning of the flap against the main wing panel to

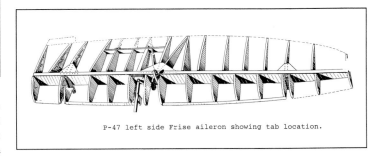

P-47 left side Frise aileron showing tab location.

The four guns in each wing had conical shaped front mounts, and guns were locked to these by rotating the locking ring of a gun bracket assembly. The rear mounts were locked by simple levers in the mount assemblies. Ammunition was stored just outboard of the gun bays.

Ailerons, representing about 11.4 percent of the projected wing area, were the Frise type, aerodynamically and dynamically balanced with 16 inch-pounds overbalance. They were hinged to steel forgings attached to the outboard auxiliary wing spar, and were

maintain the proper airfoil. The links were synchronized by attachment to a torque tube, and the assembly was attached to the inboard auxiliary wing spar. Independent units either side were synchronized by the hydraulic system. The flap linkage assembly was bolted to the flaps. The double-cambered external surfaces of the flaps were formed by flanged nose and tail ribs attached to a single spar. Additional light nose ribs were provided between basic rib locations.

Late P-47 models had in addition wing flaps to aid in recovery from high speed dives where compressibility might be encountered. These flaps were flat metal sheets .188 inches thick hinged to the wing undersurface at the landing gear auxiliary spar location just forward of the landing flaps on both sides of the aircraft. In the retracted position they laid flush with the wing lower surface contour. Extension and retraction of these surfaces was effected by two reversible electric intermittant-acting motors synchronized by flexible shafting. Magnetic brake and clutch assemblies were incorpo-

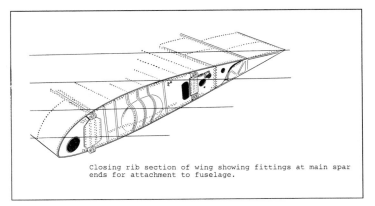

Closing rib section of wing showing fittings at main spar
ends for attachment to fuselage.

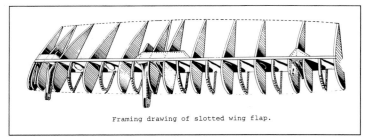

Framing drawing of slotted wing flap.

rated to prevent overtravel, and switches limited flap extension to a maximum of 22 1/2 inches.

TAIL GROUP

The tail group consisted of the vertical fin, or stabilizer, the horizontal stabilizer, the rudder, and the elevators.

The vertical fin was an all-metal structure built up of flanged ribs between a forward and aft spar and flanged nose ribs covered with Alclad skin. The hinges for the rudder and the chain-actuated worm and screw units for trim tab operation were attached to the rear spar of the fin. The lower ends of the fin spars straddled the horizontal stabilizer assembly spars, and at this juncture were bolted to common splice plates, thus forming a complete vertical and horizontal stabilizer unit. The horizontal stabilizer assembly was of similar construction to the vertical stabilizer, being a two spar system with flanged ribs between and flanged nose ribs, all metal covered. To install the complete stabilizer unit, vertical and horizontal, the stabilizer forward spar was bolted to fittings on the horizontal web of the aft fuselage section, and the aft spar was fastened to the last frame of the fuselage.

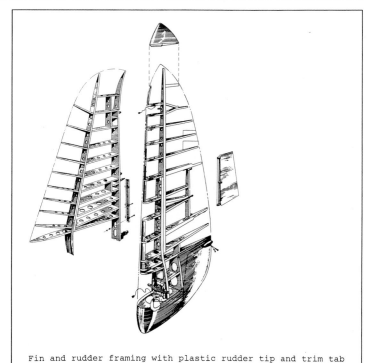

Fin and rudder framing with plastic rudder tip and trim tab

The rudder was a Handley-Page type and was statically and dynamically balanced. The dynamic balance coefficient was less than zero, and the static balance was 25 inch-pounds under balance. The rudder trim tab provided dynamic balance as well as selective trim, and the P-47 was the first airplane to reduce rudder pedal loads by use of a balanced trim tab. The rudder employed a single main spar and flanged ribs, and was covered with Alclad metal.

The elevators were of the Handley-Page type with a dynamic balance coefficient of zero or less and a static balance of 10 inch-pounds under balanced. The elevators were manufactured singly and then assembled into a unit by splicing torque tubes extending from the inboard nose sections of the elevators. The elevators were constructed of a single spar and stamped flanged ribs; the torque tubes were secured to the first three inboard nose ribs of each elevator. The entire elevator surface was metal covered. The elevators were hinged to the rear stabilizer spar, and a torque tube pivot was provided by roller bearings staked into hinge brackets attached to the rear fuselage frame. The last control rod was linked to the

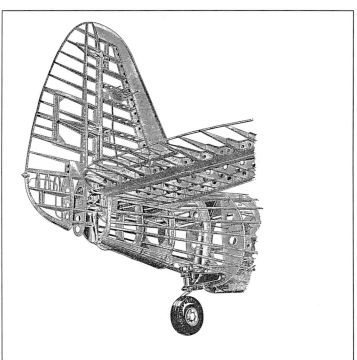

Framing of empennage assembly and fuselage aft end. Tail wheel assembly and tail warning radar antenna are on fin.

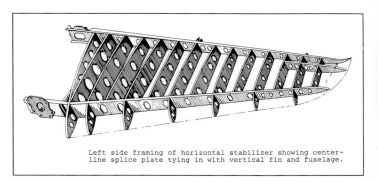

Left side framing of horizontal stabilizer showing centerline splice plate tying in with vertical fin and fuselage.

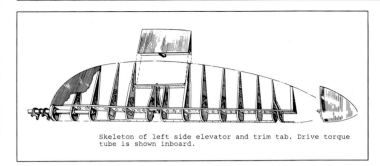

Skeleton of left side elevator and trim tab. Drive torque tube is shown inboard.

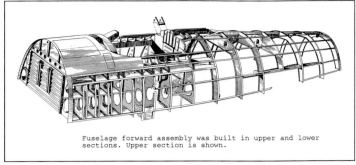

Fuselage forward assembly was built in upper and lower sections. Upper section is shown.

elevator system at a bracket that was part of the torque tube splice sleeve.

FUSELAGE GROUP

The fuselage was of semi-monocoque, all-metal stressed skin construction, composed of transverse bulkheads or frames and longitudinal stringers. It was made up of a main forward structure divided into upper and lower halves extending aft to fuselage station 302.5, and the tail cone or fuselage aft section, comprising the fuselage aft of station 302.5, which was constructed as a unit.

The upper and lower main fuselage halves were bolted together at reinforcing angles built into the parting surfaces of the structures, and joggled extensions on the upper half frames were spliced by riveting to the lower half frames. Assembly of the fuselage was completed by joining the aft fuselage section to the main section at the 302.5 station. Here, the facing frames of the forward and aft sections were riveted and bolted while the skin extension of the aft section was butt jointed to the main section skin and riveted to the last frame of the forward section.

Major structural units of the fuselage, two wing supporting bulkheads, were contained in the main lower half section. Each of these two bulkheads was constructed around a pair of 3.5 inch wide E-section steel beams which extended across the width of the bulkheads and served as cross-ties or carry-through structure. The wing support hinges, X4130 steel forgings mating with the wing beam end fittings, extended into each end of the cross-tie/carry-over beams, and were secured to the ties by 3/8 inch bolts. The forward, or firewall, bulkhead was faced with stainless steel sheet over Alclad sheet of .091 gage, and the aft side was faced with similar flat sheet, reinforced by corrugated sheet and channel sections, all of Alclad metal. The aft bulkhead incorporated the aft wing support hinge fittings. The structure was similar to that of the forward bulkhead except for the absence of stainless steel facing and corrugated sheet. The outboard ends of both the wing hinge fitting bulkheads supported trapezoidal-shaped forgings; longeron components were riveted to these forgings, thus providing the foundation for the remainder of the lower half fuselage structure. The lower longeron extended the entire length of the forward fuselage section, and provided support for the remaining transverse frames and bulkheads. Stringers were located at suitable intervals up from the longerons to the angle-reinforced parting surface of the lower half structure. Lower half-frame segments were riveted to longerons and stringers, and then flush riveted skin of various gages with additional reinforcing skins at the wing hinge fitting openings completed the

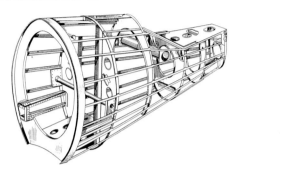

Framing of aft fuselage section shows flat deck for the empennage attachment.

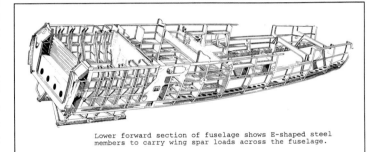

Lower forward section of fuselage shows E-shaped steel members to carry wing spar loads across the fuselage.

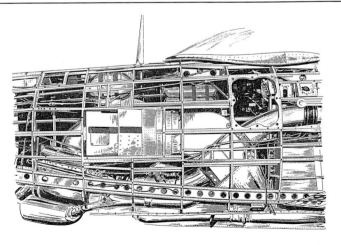

A cutaway view of P-47 aft fuselage showing the great amount of space taken up by items associated with turbo-supercharging, including the unit itself (at left), the intercooler (tilted box), and connecting air ducts.

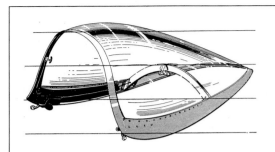

Bubble canopy assembly of metal-framed Plexiglass used in the later P-47 models.

structure of the main lower half fuselage section.

The upper half of the forward fuselage section was constructed similar to the lower half section. The upper half forward bulkhead had , due to the absence of the 3.5 inch steel channel, less depth than the matching lower half and thus was stepped back so as to present a flush surface on the aft face of the firewall. A corrugated sheet faced on either side extended to the engine mount upper cross-tie which was an angle section member. The section above this cross-tie was of single sheet thickness. Trapezoidal-shaped forgings similar to those employed in the bulkheads of the lower half section were bolted to the engine mount cross-tie to serve as a structural base for the upper longerons. The upper fuselage portion of the main aft bulkhead consisted of .064 inch flanged segments extending to the upper longeron, spliced with .064 inch splice plates to both faces of the bulkhead. Frame 180, the aft partition of the cockpit, had heavy construction in its upper half section because the frame supported the rear armor plating. The lower portion of 180 was of standard flanged bulkhead construction. The remaining upper half frames aft of station 180 were flanged semi-circular segments tied together by stringers.

The aft fuselage section, since it was constructed as a unit, employed complete frames and was tied with stringers. The tail wheel supporting frame was reinforced by vertical and horizontal extrusions and webs. The frame was also braced at the bottom by a box-like structure extending to frame 302.5. A transverse web was

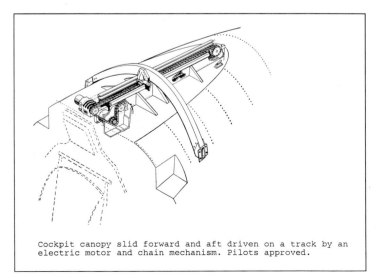

Cockpit canopy slid forward and aft driven on a track by an electric motor and chain mechanism. Pilots approved.

riveted along the upper area of the last three frames of the aft section, forming the support structure for the tail assembly.

P-47 models beginning with the later D versions were changed from the earlier types in the cockpit area by removing the raised aft turtledeck structure that blended in with the cockpit canopy (the so-called razor-back), and providing instead a "bubble" canopy arrangement having a flattened aft turtledeck. The cockpit enclosure for the later models consisted of a forward fixed windshield of three panels set in heavy metal framing. The front transparent panel was of 1.5 inch thick bullet-resistant glass which complemented the 3/8 inch face-hardened armor plate located at the forward end of the cockpit. A combined armor plate and crash overturn protector was located just behind the pilot's bucket-type seat. A sliding aft canopy section was made of formed Plexiglas set into a metal frame. An upward-bowed cross-member connected the framing sides about half-way back on the assembly. Attached to the cross-member was a follower on an endless chain running in a channel built up on the aft deck. The chain was driven by an electric motor fixed on the deck just behind the pilot. The motor drove the chain, follower, and cross-member of the aft canopy in a manner providing the required opening and closing motion of the canopy. Rollers in the canopy

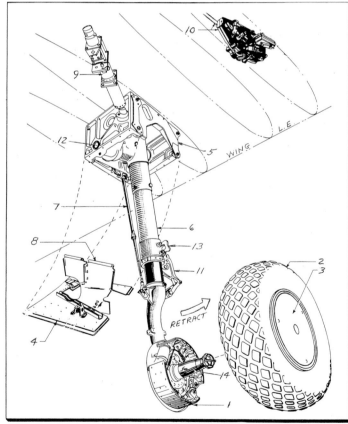

Landing Gear Installation

Landing Gear Installation Legend

1.	Brake	8.	Dust Cover
2.	Tire and Inner Tube	9.	Downlock Assembly
3.	Wheel	10.	Uplock Assembly
4.	Bottom Plate	11.	Torque Scissors
5.	Bearing Box	12.	Pivot Axle
6.	Shock Strut	13.	Tow Fitting
7.	Shrinkage Strut	14.	Axle

lower framing slid in tracks built into the fuselage structure. An emergency release handle located on the right side of a frame could be pulled such that a cable released the rollers from the track. This action would permit the sliding canopy to be pushed up and lifted free by the force of the airstream.

LANDING GEAR GROUP

The full cantilever hydraulically controlled retractable main landing gear consisted of independent left and right hand units of combination air-oil shock strut assemblies and extra high pressure cast magnesium wheels of the drop center rim type. A hydraulically retractable tail wheel assembly was also provided. The tail wheel was free-castoring but lockable.

On the main gear the shock struts were supported by a box-like structure of four cast magnesium plates, two of which served as trunnions. The box assembly fitted into a well in the wing underside formed by wing rib 86, wing rib 84, and the landing gear auxiliary spar, and was attached by four bolts through each of the ribs and adjacent plates. Before the main gear retraction cycle was started, hydraulic pressure was applied to withdraw a steel downlocking pin from a housing in the downlocking arm of the strut; a mechanically operated sequence valve was thus opened to admit pressure to the landing gear retraction cylinder. During retraction the shock strut piston was telescoped to the bottoming position so at cycle completion the gear would fit into a wing well nine inches shorter than would be necessary otherwise. The telescoping would be accomplished by the geometry of the system which employed a shrinkage strut or rod where one end was attached to the shock strut piston and the other pivoted about an axis outboard of and below that of the landing gear pivot axis. As the piston telescoped the air in the air-oil chamber of the shock strut was displaced by the oil and was transferred to an auxiliary air chamber higher in the strut assembly. The auxiliary chamber was opened by a push rod following a cam track above the shock strut.

ENGINE SECTION

The engine section was made up of the engine mounting system and the engine cowling. The engine mount was constructed of chrome molybdenum steel tubing and sheet welded into a single unit. This unit also supported the engine oil reservoir, and was attached to the forward fuselage by four bolts. The engine was attached through Lord shock absorber mounts.

The NACA cowling consisted of a group of four quick-detacheable panels fastened to supporting rings attached to the rocker box covers of the engine. Hydraulically-operated cowl flaps for controlling cooling air exit flow were provided at the upper section of the secondary engine cowling.

P-47 SYSTEMS DESCRIPTION

PROPULSION SUBSYSTEMS

ENGINE

The engine was a 2000 to 2300 HP class Pratt and Whitney R-2800 Double Wasp air-cooled 18 cylinder two row radial model of 5.75 inches cylinder bore and 6.00 inches stroke. The propeller reduction gear ratio was 0.5 to 1. The installation used two-stage supercharging; the engine had an integral single-stage single speed mechanical supercharger with an 11.5 inch impeller diameter and a 7.29:1 gear ratio, and the second stage was a remote exhaust-driven turbosupercharger built by the General Electric Company. Maximum engine speed for takeoff was 2700 RPM, and engine compression ratio was 6.7 to 1. The engine was about 73 inches long and 52.5 inches in diameter, and by itself weighed more than a ton. The SAE 60A splined propeller drive shaft rotated clockwise looking from the rear.

ENGINE INTAKE SYSTEM

Air for the engine entered the aircraft via a scoop built into the lower section of the engine cowling which formed the front end of the main duct. This large duct ran aft along the fuselage belly to near the middle of the fuselage length where it split into upper and lower ducts. The upper duct lead the cool air directly to the intercooler, a box-like unit located in the center of the aft fuselage. The intercooler was an air-to-air heat exchanger where the cool intake air passed by the heated compressed air from the turbosupercharger exit and cooled it. From the intercooler exit the upper duct air was drawn into two ducts, one on each side of the fuselage, and then dumped overboard through an intercooler exit door on each side.

The doors were electric motor-controlled to vary exit areas and thus the flow of cooling air through the intercooler. The exit door motors were controlled from the main switch panel in the cockpit. A cockpit indicator showed the doors as either in closed, open, or neutral position.

The lower duct of the main intake led air through a filter to the upper, or compressor, section of the turbosupercharger assembly where the centrifugal compressor wheel, driven by the turbine right below on the same shaft, compressed and heated the charge air. The air filter in the compressor intake line had a bypass when filtering was not required, and a pull tee handle was provided on the rear bulkhead of the cockpit to provide pilot control. The compressed air from the supercharger was ducted back through the intercooler to be cooled down and exited in two ducts running forward along the sides of the fuselage with both looping up to merge again at the engine carburetor intake. Pressure in the system was maintained at the proper level by a supercharger regulator.

ENGINE EXHAUST SYSTEM

The engine exhaust was collected by two half ring pipes, one on each side, and each half tied into a single pipe running aft down the lower quarter of the fuselage section. An exit, or waste pipe, came off each main pipe just forward of the firewall and ran overboard. Each waste pipe was equipped with a gate valve to control exit flow. Valves were controlled via a crank and mechanical rod drive from the supercharger regulator. The two main exhaust pipes running aft were housed in stainless steel shrouds with asbestos covering to confine exhaust heat. The two pipes converged at the turbosupercharger inlet in the lower rear fuselage, and exhaust gases impinged on the turbine wheel which drove the intake air compressor, then exited overboard from the flight hood under the rear of the fuselage.

TURBOSUPERCHARGER CONTROL SYSTEM

Supercharging was controlled to maintain the manifold pressure value selected by the pilot by means of an oil-operated supercharger regulator located in the engine compartment on the firewall under the oil tank. The regulator was set, through linkage from the supercharger control on the throttle quadrant on the left side of the cockpit, to vary the position of the gate valves in the exhaust system waste pipe exit overboard. It thus controlled the volume of exhaust gases directed aft to the turbine wheel of the turbosupercharger. The position of a piston in the regulator was balanced by exhaust pressure and a compression spring; the spring was mechanically loaded to correspond to the desired exhaust pressure value by the input from the cockpit supercharger control lever on the quadrant. When exhaust pressure varied from the selected value, the piston moved in the direction of the greater pressure and opened a port admitting oil to the side of the piston, moving the waste gate valves to reach a new balanced piston position. The linkage between controller and gate valves was mechanical. When turbine RPM reached 18250 an overspeed light went on.

ENGINE-MOUNTED ACCESSORIES

The engine-mounted accessories included: Oil pump, fuel pump, hydraulic pump, propeller governor, starter, carburetor, magnetos, electrical generator, vacuum pump, and tachometer.

ENGINE CONTROLS

The engine controls consisted of the throttle, the mixture control, and a supercharger control. All three levers were mounted on a quadrant on the left side of the pilot seat. On most models of the aircraft the supercharger, or boost, control could be linked with the throttle control and the propeller control, and moved as a single lever with power and RPM mechanically coordinated through the full range of the control quadrant. The propeller RPM selector lever was correlated by use of a cam; throttle and boost levers were correlated by adjustment of push-pull rods. Controls could be disconnected from each other by releasing a spring-loaded clip on the throttle lever. The supercharger lever was mechanically linked to the supercharger regulator as noted above. The throttle control was a mechanical linkage from cockpit lever to the engine carburetor, and the mixture control was a similar mechanical run.

PROPELLER

Early P-47 versions used the Curtiss Electric four blade 12 foot 2 inch diameter C642S propeller with 714-1C2-12 design hollow steel blades.

Later P-47D aircraft used either the Curtiss Electric four blade C642S propeller with design 836 hollow steel blades in 13 feet diameter or a Hamilton Standard four blade Hydromatic 24E60 propeller with model 6507-2 blades in 13 feet diameter. The later propellers with slightly increased diameter and wider chord "paddle

Pratt and Whitney 18 cylinder R-2800 two row radial engine.

AIR FILTER CONTROL
AIR FILTER
TO CARBURETOR
INTERCOOLER
(BOTH COOLING AIR AND SUPER-CHARGED AIR GO THROUGH THIS UNIT)
SUPERCHARGER TURBINE
INTERCOOLER COOLING AIR EXIT
EXHAUST PIPES
WASTE GATE
COLLECTOR RING
MAIN AIR DUCT INTAKE
FLIGHT HOOD

A reason for fuselage bulk was the supercharging system, shown schematically viewed from above and below.

blades" were used to improve the airplane climb performance over the earlier "toothpick" blades. Both propeller types, Curtiss and Hamilton, were constant speed models with an alternate selective fixed blade pitch mode. There were no feathering or reverse features on either model.

PROPELLER CONTROLS

The Curtiss propeller controls comprised an on-off switch and an automatic constant speed/ manual increase, manual decrease pitch three way selector switch on the cockpit main switch box, and the propeller speed selection lever for RPM set on the throttle quadrant. As noted above the propeller lever could be linked mechanically with the throttle and supercharger control for coordinated use. The propeller lever was mechanically linked to the propeller governor mounted on the engine nose by control rods and bell cranks. The Curtiss propeller governor output was sent to a propeller junction box and from there to the electrical brush assembly mounted on the engine nose with brushes bearing on propeller hub slip rings. Power was supplied by the aircraft electrical system. The Hamilton propeller was a hydraulic unit using engine oil. The propeller governor controlled the flow of oil through a hydraulic oil transfer system to the propeller hub and pitch change mechanism.

ENGINE STARTING SYSTEM

The engine was started by means of a fuel primer system with a control handle in the cockpit, and an inertia starter system using an electric motor-powered flywheel and a clutch to crank over the engine starter gearing. The flywheel was spun up to full speed using at least fifteen seconds. A switch in the cockpit energized the starter.

ENGINE WATER INJECTION SYSTEM

Later models of the P-47 were equipped with a water injection system to safeguard the engine from detonation when operated considerably above MILITARY power. Water was pumped via an electrically-driven pump from a 30 gallon tank strapped to the firewall, and was admitted through a water regulator by operation of a solonoid valve. Pressurized water beyond the regulator reset the

carburetor mixture so the fuel-air ratio was decreased, thus increasing power without a corresponding rise in manifold pressure. The power increase, however, was developed by high manifold pressure attained through a boost reset mechanism also actuated by water pressure; the reset over-rode the supercharger regulator setting of the exhaust waste gates, permitting the turbosupercharger to develop the higher RPM required to attain WAR EMERGENCY (or COMBAT) manifold pressure.

ENGINE COOLING SYSTEM

The R-2800 was an air-cooled engine; cooling was effected by passing cowl intake air closely over baffled and finned cylinders, and providing air exit passages after the air passed over the engine. A series of cowl flaps controlling the exit air passage were provided around the aft upper edge of the powerplant compartment. These flaps were manually controllable from the cockpit using a pull handle at the right side of the instrument panel. The flaps could be controlled from full closed to full open and also could be set for any intermediate angle. They were hydraulically operated; the cockpit control provided direct input to a hydraulic valve controlling flow to a single cowl flap linkage actuating cylinder on the upper right hand side of the engine compartment. A coordinating mechanical linkage system extending around the upper section of the cowl drove the individual cowl flaps.

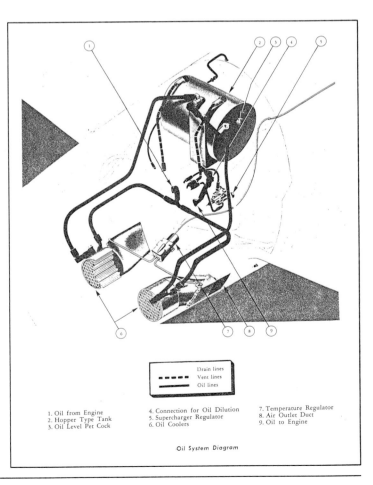

Drain lines
----- Vent lines
Oil lines

1. Oil from Engine
2. Hopper Type Tank
3. Oil Level Pet Cock
4. Connection for Oil Dilution
5. Supercharger Regulator
6. Oil Coolers
7. Temperature Regulator
8. Air Outlet Duct
9. Oil to Engine

Oil System Diagram

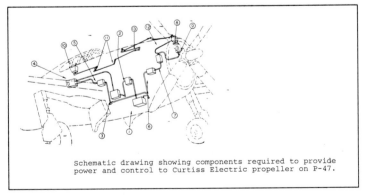

Schematic drawing showing components required to provide power and control to Curtiss Electric propeller on P-47.

1. Battery
2. Battery junction box
3. Generator control box
4. Propeller switches
5. Filter
6. Relay
7. Propeller junction box
8. Governor
9. Brush assembly
10. Cockpit control lever
11. Bell cranks
12. Governor springback adjustment
13. Push pull rods

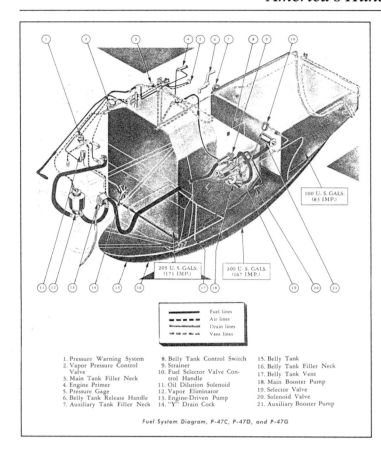

1. Pressure Warning System
2. Vapor Pressure Control Valve
3. Main Tank Filler Neck
4. Engine Primer
5. Pressure Gage
6. Belly Tank Release Handle
7. Auxiliary Tank Filler Neck
8. Belly Tank Control Switch
9. Strainer
10. Fuel Selector Valve Control Handle
11. Oil Dilution Solenoid
12. Vapor Eliminator
13. Engine-Driven Pump
14. "Y" Drain Cock
15. Belly Tank
16. Belly Tank Filler Neck
17. Belly Tank Vent
18. Main Booster Pump
19. Selector Valve
20. Solenoid Valve
21. Auxiliary Booster Pump

Fuel System Diagram, P-47C, P-47D, and P-47G

ENGINE FIRE SENSING/FIRE EXTINGUISHING SYSTEMS

The aircraft did not include such systems.

FUEL SYSTEM

In versions prior to the P-47D-25 and in the P-47G (that is, prior to the bubble canopy airplanes), the main fuel tank was an L-shaped self-sealing unit in the fuselage forward of and partly under the cockpit. Capacity was 205 US gallons and the tank was baffled to minimize surge. On later D models and on the P-47M the main tank capacity was increased to 270 US gallons, mainly by adding space at the top of the tank. The other internal fuel tank was a unit of 100 US gallon capacity aft of the main tank and under the rear portion of the cockpit. This tank was also self-sealing, and was called the auxiliary fuel tank; its size did not change with airplane model changes. To prevent vapor lock at high altitude, both internal tanks were equipped with electrically-operated booster pumps of capacity sufficient to ensure adequate fuel pressure and flow in the event of failure of the G-9 engine-driven fuel pump.

Early versions of the P-47 (through D-23 and G) could be equipped with a large external slipper-type droppable fuselage belly fuel tank of 200 US gallon capacity, and that was the only external tank. The main tank was filled at a point on the right side ahead of the cockpit; the auxiliary tank filler was further aft and lower on the same side. Tank vent and drain lines were provided. Other system components were fuel lines running forward to the engine, a vapor pressure control valve, a fuel strainer, an oil dilution solonoid, a vapor eliminator, an engine primer system, fuel pressure indication, and a fuel selector valve. The belly external tank was filled near the nose of the tank. In later models the slipper tank was not used as it was unpressurized and tended to be unwieldy, and various sizes of external drop tanks were carried on bomb shackles on fuselage centerline and/or in large pylons under the wings. These external fuel tanks were pressurized by the exhaust of the vacuum pump. The belly-mounted drop tank, if used, was normally of 75 or 110 US gallon capacity. Wing-mounted drop tanks each side were normally 150 or 300 US gallon capacity. In these later models through P-47M fuel lines were run in the wings to the drop tank locations.

The P-47N long range Pacific version had the same 370 US gallon total internal fuel capacity in the two fuselage tanks. In a new wing, however, two auxiliary 93 US gallon total wing tank systems were added. Wing fuel was placed in leading edge cells just inboard of the gun ports and in cells between spars just inboard of the gun bays. Four interconnected self-sealing fuel cells were incorporated to make up the 93 gallons in each wing panel. The total internal capacity of the N model was 556 US gallons. External drop tank capacity of the N was similar to late D models.

ENGINE LUBRICATION SYSTEM

Two cylindrical core-type oil coolers were located just behind the inlet of the lower portion of the engine forward cowling. They were on either side of the large central inlet air duct. Air entered the coolers and then passed through exit ducting leading to outlets overboard on the sides of the cowl, with the exit areas being controlled by moveable shutters both actuated by mechanical linkage from an oil temperature regulator unit located centrally in the powerplant bay. Surge valves were in the system to permit cold air to bypass the radiators. The regulator unit included an electrically-operated motor to power the exit shutters. The motor was operated by a cockpit switch, and shutter position indicators were located on the left side of the cockpit. A twenty-eight US gallon oil tank was located in the upper part of the engine compartment with a filler accessible through a cowl door. Oil from the engine was pumped through the lines to both coolers, from these back to the tank, and out of the tank to the engine again. Engine oil also operated the supercharger regulator. A connection was made to the oil line going into the engine for the oil dilution system. Vent lines were run overboard from the oil tank.

FIXED EQUIPMENT SUBSYSTEMS

INSTRUMENTS

A typical flight instrument complement was: Altimeter, turn indicator, airspeed indicator, bank and turn indicator, artificial horizon, compass, clock, and rate of climb indicator. Engine instruments included: Fuel gage, suction gage, carburetor air temperature gage, oil temperature and pressure gage, turbo tachometer, manifold pressure gage, tachometer, fuel pressure gage, and cylinder head temperature gage. Other instruments included a hydraulic pressure gage, oxygen cylinder pressure gage, and oxygen flow indicator.

SURFACE CONTROLS

The elevator control runs from stick aft to the surface consisted of a series of control rods tied together with swing links pivoted on structure. The run was routed back from the stick assembly to behind the cockpit, then angled up to the top area inside the fuselage and aft. The aft rod tied to a control horn located inboard on the elevator torque tube. Elevator trim tabs were driven by mechanical runs from the cockpit left side tab control going aft. The runs consisted of a series of cables, pulleys, control rods, and chains.

The rudder controls consisted of cables and pulleys from the pedal assemblies running aft in a continuous system with a cable on each side of the fuselage interior to control horns driving a rudder torque tube. The mechanical drive to the rudder tab was similar to the elevator.

The aileron control system ran from the cockpit control stick out to the ailerons, and was an all-mechanical linkage. Stick lateral

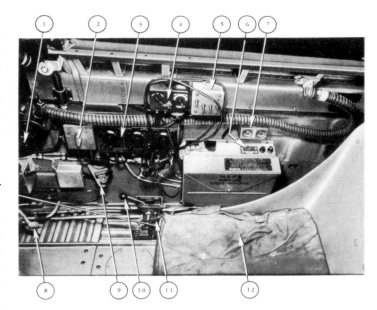

1. Oxygen Regulator
2. Crystal Filter Selector Switch
3. Command Receiver Control Box
4. Command Transmitter Control Box
5. Identification Lights Switches
6. Contactor Heater Switch
7. IFF Radio Destroyer Buttons
8. Rudder Pedal Adjustment Lever
9. Cockpit Vent Control
10. Tail Wheel Lock
11. Belly Tank Release
12. Pilot's Seat

Figure 33—Cockpit—Right Side View—P-47C, P-47D, and P-47G

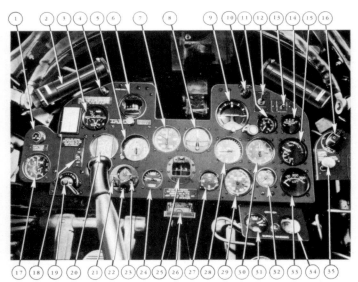

1. Propeller Anti-Icer Control
2. Fluorescent Light
3. Landing Gear Tail Wheel and Flap Position Indicator
4. Fuel Level
5. Altimeter
6. Turn Indicator
7. Air-Speed Indicator
8. Bank and Turn Indicator
9. Artificial Horizon
10. Fuel Pressure Warning Lamp
11. Suction Gage
12. Vacuum Gage Selector Valve
13. Starter Switch
14. Carburetor Air Temperature Gage
15. Oil Temperature and Pressure Gage
16. Engine Primer
17. Turbo Tachometer
18. Master Battery Switch
19. Ignition Switch
20. Fuel Quantity Gage
21. Contactor Switch
22. Contactor (Pip Squeak)
23. Contactor Clock Switch
24. Hydraulic Pressure Gage
25. Compass
26. Parking Brake Handle
27. Clock
28. Rate of Climb Indicator
29. Manifold Pressure Gage
30. Tachometer
31. Oxygen Cylinder Pressure Gage
32. Fuel Pressure Gage
33. Cylinder Head Temperature Gage
34. Oxygen Flow Indicator
35. Cowl Flap Control

Figure 31—Instrument Panel—P-47C, P-47D, and P-47G

1. Cockpit Spotlight
2. Wing Flap Control Handle
3. Intercooler Shutter Indicator
4. Oil Cooler Shutter Indicator
5. Landing Gear Control Safety Latch
6. Gun Safety Switch
7. Throttle
8. Supercharger Control
9. Microphone Push-to-Talk Button
10. Mixture Control
11. Propeller Control
12. Landing Gear Warning Horn Switch
13. Propeller Anti-Icing Control
14. Rudder Trim Tab Control
15. Elevator Trim Tab Control Crank
16. Aileron Trim Tab Control
17. Landing Gear Control Handle
18. Fuel Selector Valve
19. Hydraulic Hand Pump
20. Main Switch Box
21. Circuit Breakers
22. Belly Tank Control Switch
23. Control Stick Grip

Figure 35—Cockpit—Left Side View, P-47C, P-47D, and P-47G

motion was transferred through rods to bellcranks at the fuselage sides and from there via long push-pull control rods and swing links supported on the aft auxiliary wing spar out to the ailerons. There motion was transferred to an aileron drive link. The drive for the all-metal trim tab on the left aileron was a cable and pulley system running to the rear of the aft auxiliary wing spar, and connecting to the tab through a chain and cable drive and a screw actuator.

ELECTRICAL SYSTEM

The sources for electrical power were a generator mounted on the rear of the engine and a storage battery mounted in the engine compartment. The system was a 24 volt DC single wire airframe ground return type. The electrical components in the engine compartment were an induction vibrator, starter, and firewall and battery junction boxes. Electrically powered items included intercooler exit doors, Curtiss propeller, starter, water injection pump, oil cooler

exit shutter drive motor, fuel tank boost pumps, instruments, radio gear, machine gun solonoids, aircraft lights, gunsight, and on the bubble canopy versions, the canopy drive motor. A main electrical switch box and circuit breakers were located on the left side of the cockpit.

HYDRAULIC SYSTEM

A hydraulic system was installed to power the cowl flaps, main landing gear retraction and extension, tail wheel retraction and extension, and wing flaps. A hydraulic pump was driven by the engine, and a fluid reservoir and valve unit were located in the engine compartment. Further back in the fuselage on the floor to the right of the pilot's seat an equalizer valve was installed, and a selector valve and hand pump were also provided in the cockpit. A pressure gage was located on the instrument panel. A control handle at the right side of the instrument panel operated the cowl flaps by admitting pressure to a single flap actuating cylinder which drove the flap linkage. The landing gear was normally operated using the pressure from the engine-driven hydraulic pump, but a backup hand pump was available to the pilot in case of engine pump failure. A landing gear control lever with safety latch and button on the left side of the cockpit controlled the action of the landing gear actuating cylinders, one each on both main gear assemblies for unlocking the downlock, retracting the gear, and closing the gear door. A single actuator was provided at the aft end of the fuselage for retracting the tail wheel assembly. Some early aircraft had an indicator showing wheel position located on the instrument panel, and on early models a warning horn indicated gear up when the throttle was closed. The throttle arm controlled a horn shut-off switch which was automatically closed when the throttle was opened. On later types the gear indicator and horn were removed, and a red warning light for gear not down and locked or not fully retracted was located on the instrument panel. The wing flaps were normally operated using engine pump pressure, but could also be operated from auxiliary hand pump pressure. Left and right flap hydraulic pressure was equalized by the equalizer valve on the cockpit floor so the two flaps would operate strictly in unison. A hydraulic actuating cylinder in each wing drove its own flap. Actuation was initiated by a flap control switch in the cockpit. On early airplanes only a wing flap position indicator was placed on the instrument panel.

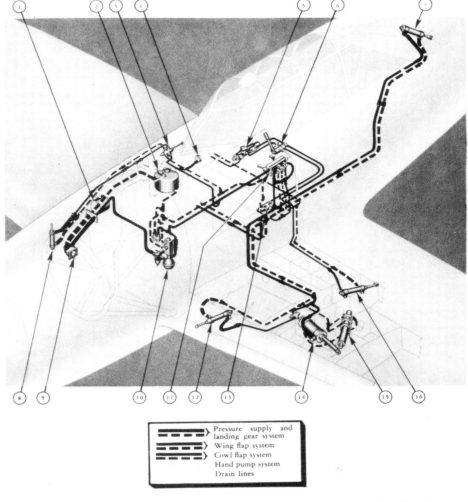

Pressure supply and landing gear system		
Wing flap system		
Cowl flap system		
Hand pump system		
Drain lines		

1. Carburetor Air Duct
2. Tank
3. Cowl Flap Valve
4. Pressure Gage
5. Equalizer Cylinder
6. Hand Pump
7. Tail Wheel Cylinder
8. Cowl Flap Cylinder
9. Engine-Driven Pump
10. Hydraulic Units
11. Selector Valve
12. Landing Gear Door Cylinder
13. Relief Valve
14. Landing Gear Cylinder
15. Downlock Cylinder
16. Flap Cylinder

Figure 27—Hydraulic System Diagram

PNEUMATIC SYSTEM

The only pneumatic system was the vacuum system powered by an engine-driven pump and used for some instruments and to pressurize drop tanks.

COMMUNICATION/NAVIGATION /IDENTIFICATION SYSTEMS

These systems varied, however a typical installation on early aircraft models used an SCR-274N or SCR-522A command radio with an RC-96 "pip squeak", located in the fuselage baggage compartment. Three receivers and one transmitter were placed in that location. Transmission by CW or voice could be made. In addition an SCR-535 IFF set was installed with an explosive detonator in the aft fuselage baggage compartment. Radio set remote controls were on the right side of the cockpit.

ARMAMENT PROVISIONS

Provisions were made in each wing panel for installation of four .50 caliber machine guns, their ammunition, and supporting equipment. The guns were located side by side in a staggered-back arrangement going outboard with breeches located between forward and middle wing spars and barrels poking through the web of the forward spar and the leading edge. Blast tubes were incorporated forward of the wing leading edge. Guns were mounted on trunnions at the forward end and on cradles aft. The guns were locked at the forward end by rotating the locking ring of the gun bracket assembly. The rear mounts were locked by simple levers which were part of the rear mount assemblies. A large access panel in the top skin was provided for gun installation and removal, and ejection chutes were located beneath each gun position. Electrical wiring carried firing signals to the gun solonoids. Guns were charged manually on the ground before takeoff. Ammunition boxes were carried in the wing section outboard of the guns. No round counting indicators were provided. The guns could be bore-sighted in a horizontal plane from parallel to converging at 250 yards. Usually they were set to converge at 250 to 350 yards. Maximum ammunition storage capacity per gun was 425 rounds. The fire rate was such that 300 rounds were equivalent to about 20 seconds of fire. Since guns were loaded and charged on the ground they were ready to fire when the cockpit safety switch was "on". The squeeze trigger on the control stick fired all guns simultaneously. If one gun jammed the others would continue to fire.

Early aircraft models were equipped with an N-3A gunsight. The brilliance of the sight reticle was adjustable by means of a rheostat on the main switch panel in the cockpit. The reticle was visible only when the pilot's eyes were in the proper position just behind the sight.

Heat was supplied to the machine gun bays through flexible metal gun-heater tubes running through the wing structure just ahead if the flaps.

Early models could carry a single bomb only, up to 500 pounds, on a centerline bomb rack. Many C and D aircraft were updated to carry bombs on wing racks mounted in large pylons. The maximum bomb size for these pylons was 1000 pounds each side. Bomb release was electrical with a mechanical backup.

Starting on the P-47D-35RA version provision was made in production for a maximum of ten five-inch High Velocity Aircraft Rockets (HVARS) under the wings (without bombs or drop tanks). Kits were made available for various rocket installations on some earlier models.

PASSIVE DEFENSE SYSTEM

Passive defense system items consisted of a forward-located 3/8 inch thick face-hardened steel armor plate running from the top of the main fuel tank to the bottom of the windshield, a 1.50 inch thick bullet-resistant glass panel behind the forward windshield (the built-in flat forward panel was found in later bubble canopy models), and a large 3/8 inch thick face-hardened steel armor plate behind the pilot at the rear of the cockpit.

FURNISHINGS

The seat was a metal bucket type which could be adjusted for height by lifting a lock release handle at the right of the seat, and raising or lowering it. The locking mechanism was spring-loaded. The seat was equipped with a standard shoulder harness with the spring release or lock control on the left side.

A relief tube was located under the seat and a first aid kit was provided in the cockpit.

HEATING/VENTILATION SYSTEM

Fresh air was let into the cockpit vent using a push-pull control at the right side of the seat. Heat from the engine compartment was supplied by use of a hot air defroster control mounted on the right side of the cockpit just behind the windshield.

ICE PROTECTION SYSTEM

A glycol windshield spray system with a supply tank was installed, pressurized by an electrically-driven pump controlled from the cockpit. A propeller blade deicing system using a glycol spray ring could be installed on the propeller if required.

AIRCRAFT HANDLING

Tow rings were provided on the main landing gear. Hoisting hardpoints and leveling means were provided. Lugs for mooring were installed inside a flush door on the lower wing surface ahead of the forward spar. The doors could be opened and the lugs pulled out for tiedown attachment. A lift tube could be inserted laterally through the aft end of the fuselage to raise the tail.

FLOTATION GEAR

No flotation gear was provided.

ARRESTING GEAR

No arresting gear was included.

USEFUL LOAD SUBSYSTEMS
GUNS/BOMBS/ROCKETS
See earlier description

GUNSIGHT/GUN CAMERA
See earlier description. A gun camera could be fitted.

PYROTECHNICS
In early versions a signal pistol and ammunition were provided in the cockpit.

PHOTOGRAPHIC EQUIPMENT
No photographic equipment other than a gun camera was carried.

OXYGEN SYSTEM
On bubble canopy aircraft supply bottles for the oxygen were located in the leading edge section of the wing ahead of the forward spar and just outboard of the fuselage, one on each side. On earlier "razorback" aircraft before the aft turtledeck was cut down oxygen supply bottles were located in the turtledeck area just aft of the canopy. An oxygen pressure and flow indicator and an oxygen regulator were located in the cockpit. The oxygen system filler valve was located in the fuselage baggage compartment. Provisions were made in the cockpit for attachment of the pilot's oxygen equipment to the system.

REFERENCES, P-47
1. Thunderbolt in Action, by Gene Stafford
2. The Mighty Eighth, by Roger Freeman
3. Thunderbolt, by R.S.Johnson.
4. Zemke's Wolf Pack, Told to Roger Freeman by Hub Zemke, Pocket Books, Div. of Simon and Shuster, New York, 1988.
5. USAAF in World War II, edited by Craven and Cate.
6. Journal of the American Aviation Historical Society, Winter,1963, P-47 in the European Theatre of Operations
7. JAAHS,Fall,1965, Checkertails.
8. JAAHS, Spring 1964, Spring 1971, Spring 1972, Winter 1978, Spring 1985.
9. Fighter Aces, by Col.R.F.Tolliver and Trevor Constable, The Macmillan Company, New York, 1965
10. Minutes of the Fighter Conference at Patuxent River, Md. Oct. 1944.
11. NACA Report ACR L4L07, Dec.1944, Climb and High Speed Tests of Curtiss Propeller on Republic P-47C airplane.
12. Air Corps Technical Report 4677, Test of Scale Model of Republic XP-47B Pursuit Type Airplane, Sept.11,1941
13. Ending the Argument, Society of Experimental Test Pilots Paper, J.M. Ellis and C.A. Wheal, 1988.
14. NACA War Report L-439 (ARR3E25), Investigation of Tail Pressure Distribution on P-47B, R.C. Dingledein
15. Tactical Planning Characteristics and Performance Chart, P-47 Airplane, USAAF, July 28,1945.
16. Airplane Engine Characteristics, R-2800-57,-73,-77, and -81. Apr.6, 1953.
17. Republic Aviation Corporation Report 411, Model P-47D.
18. Pilot's Manual, P-47B and C; Pilot's Flight Operating Instructions, P-47B,C, and G Airplanes, TO 01-65BC-1, Jan.20,1943.
19. P-47 Series Airplanes Basic Weight Check List and Loading Data, AN-01-1B-40.
20. Industrial Aviation Magazine, Jan.1945. Some Details of the Republic P-47 Thunderbolt, N. Mastrangelo.
22. Air Tech Magazine, Dec.1943, P-47 Thunderbolt.
23. Aircraft Designers Data Book, Neville, Mcgraw Hill, NY.,1951
24. Journal of the American Aviation Historical Society, Winter, 1963. Fighter Markings, Pacific Area of Operation.
25. NACA Report TN2675, Measurements of Flying Qualities of an F47D-30 Airplane to Determine Lateral and Directional Stability and Control Characteristics, July, 1952.
26. NACA Report TN2899, Measurements of Flying Qualities of an F-47D-30 Airplane to determine Longitudinal Stability and Control and Stalling Characteristics, Feb.1953.
27. The Thunder Factory, by Joshua Stoff, Motorbooks International, Osceola, Wisconsin, 1990.
28. Wings Magazine, Special Edition No.1, Thunderbolt, by Warren Bodie.
29. Wings Magazine, Apr.1974, Aug.1974; Airpower Magazine May 1974, July 1974, Whine from the Jug, by Warren Bodie.
30. Cross-Winds, An Airman's Memoir, by Najeeb E. Halaby, Doubleday and Company, New York, 1978.
31. Pacific Sweep, by William Hess, Doubleday and Co. Inc.Garden City New York, 1974.
32. General Kenney Reports, A Personal History of the Pacific War, by George C. Kenney, Duell, Sloan, and Pierce, New York, 1949.
33. Thunderbolt, A Documentary History of the Republic P-47, by Roger Freeman, Motorbooks International, PO Box 2, Osceola, Wisc.54020.

THE P-51

A list of P-51 Mustang variants with numbers built is provided in Table 43. If the P-51H and the F-6 photo versions are included Mustangs counted for about fifteen and one half percent of America's Hundred Thousand. P-51 production was divided into Allison powered and the later Merlin powered models. Almost nine out of ten Mustangs were equipped with the two stage supercharged Merlin. Production of these later versions started in 1943. The most-produced Mustang by far was the six gun bubble canopy Merlin engined P-51D. This airplane was known as the Spam Can by US forces and as the Mustang IV in RAF and Commonwealth service. Table 43 also gives notes on distribution of some Mustang types.

The physical data given in Table 44 shows the Mustang about average in fighter size with a wing span like the P-40. A major difference was use of a new North American/NACA laminar flow wing section design conferring excellent low drag characteristics on the airplane.

Mustang fuel capacities are shown in Table 45. The Allison powered models and the two XP-51Bs (which were modified Allison powered aircraft using Merlins for test) had 180 gallons of internal fuel in the wings with the P-51A having drop tank carrying capability up to 300 gallons. Soon after a production start on P-51B Merlin engined aircraft with many design modifications, fuel capacity was

TABLE 43
P-51 MODEL DESIGNATIONS

CO.MODEL	MIL.DESIG.	EXP.DESIG	NO.OF A/C	1ST.DEL.	NOTES
NA-73X	—	—	1	OCT.'40	PROTOTYPE
NA-73,-83	—	MUSTANG I	620	AUG.'41	3 STAYED NAA,6 MERLIN
					FOR USAAF TEST.
NA-73	XP-51	—	2		
NA-91	P-51	MUSTANG IA	150	JUL.'42	20mm CANNON,2 TO XP-78
NA-97	A-36A	—	500	OCT.'42	DIVE BOMBER,ONE TO RAF
NA-99	P-51A	MUSTANG II	310	MAR.'43	UPRATED ENG.-1,-5,-10
NA-101	XP-51B(XP-78)		(2 CONV.)		2 P-51, MERLIN TESTS
NA-102,-104	P-51B	MUSTANG III	1988	'43	1ST MERLIN PRODUCTION
NA-103,-111	P-51C	MUSTANG IIIB	1750	AUG.'43	DALLAS BUILT P-51B
NA-106	P-51D	MUSTANG IV	2	JAN.'44	6-GUN,BUBBLE CANOPY
NA-109	P-51D-5-15	MUSTANG IV	2500		" "
NA-110	P-51D-1	MUSTANG IV	100		TO AUSTRALIA
NA-122	P-51D-20	MUSTANG IV	1600		
NA-122	P-51D-25	MUSTANG IV	1600		
NA-122	P-51D-30	MUSTANG IV	800		
NA-111	P-51D-5	MUSTANG IV			DALLAS PRODUCTION
NA-111	P-51D-20	MUSTANG IV	1454		" "
NA-124	P-51D-25	MUSTANG IV			" "
NA-124	P-51D-30	MUSTANG IV			
NA-105	XP-51F	—	3		LIGHTWEIGHT,ONE TO UK
NA-105A	XP-51G	—	2		" "
NA-126	P-51H	—	555	FEB,'45	FASTEST,1-USN,1-UK
NA-105B	XP-51J	—	2		LIGHT, NEW ALLISON ENG
NA-111	P-51K	MUSTANG IVA	1337		D WITH AEROPROP.
NA-129	P-51L	—	0		CANC., H W. ENG. CHG.
NA-124	P-51M	—	1 JUN-AUG'45		64 AIRFRAMES SCRAPPED
	TP-51D	—	10		DALLAS 2-PL.TRAINER
		TOTAL FIGHTERS	15187		

PHOTO VERSION	NO.OF A/C	
F-6A	(55 CONV.)	1942 MODIFIED P-51-1
F-6B	(35 CONV.)	1943 MODIFIED P-51A
F-6C	(91 CONV.)	1943 71 MOD.B & 20 MOD.C
F-6D	136	NOV.'44 RECONN. P-51D
F-6K	163	APR.'45 RECONN. P-51K
TOTAL	15486	

PRODUCTION BY YEAR: 1941-136; 1942-632; 1943-1711; 1944-6904; 1945-6103
        MUSTANG DISTRIBUTIONS
MUSTANG I: Six aircraft were used for various experimental purposes in the UK.
P-51: Of the 150 P-51 aircraft 93 went to the UK as Mustang IA aircraft
and 55 were converted to F-6A photo reconnaisance aircraft. Two airframes were later converted to Merlin powered XP-78 types which became the XP-51B prototypes listed.
P-51B: Of the 1988 P-51B aircraft 308 went to the RAF. Most all were revised to use the Malcomb hood type of canopy for better visibility in that service, as were some retained in the USAAF.
P-51C: Of the 1750 P-51C models 636 went to the British and were modified as noted above.
P-51D: Of these versions 282 went to the UK forces and 40 went to the Dutch.
P-51K: The British received 595 of this version, Australia 84, and 10 went to the Dutch.

TABLE 44
P-51 PHYSICAL DATA (THROUGH P-51D)

WING SPAN	37.03'	STABILIZER SPAN	13'2"
LENGTH OVERALL	32'2 5/8"	STABILIZER AREA (INC.TAB)	27.98 SQ.FT.
HEIGHT (TAIL DOWN)	12'8"	STABILIZER INCIDENCE	2DEG.(LATER 0.5)
TREAD	11'10"	STABILIZER MAX.CHORD	2'6"
PROPELLER DIA.P-51,-51A	10'9"3-BL.	STABILIZER DIHEDRAL	0 DEG.
PROPELLER DIA.P-51B,C,D	11'2"4-BL.	ELEV.TOTAL AREA(INC.TABS)	13.05SQ.FT.
TAIL SPAN	13'2.13"	ELEV.MAX CHORD(AFT H/L)	17"
GROSS WING AREA	235.75SQ.FT.	ELEV.TRIM TAB SIZE,EA.	4 3/8"x31 1/2"
WING ROOT CHORD(@C/L)	103.99"	ELEV.BALANCE AREA,TOT.	0.24 SQ.FT.
WING TIP CHORD,STA. 215	50.0"	ELEV.TRAVEL	25-30DEG.UP,20-25DEG.DN.
WING ASPECT RATIO	5.815	ELEV.TAB TRAVEL	10DEG.UP,25DEG.DN.
WING TAPER RATIO	2.16:1	HORIZ.TAIL ASPECT RATIO	4.14
WING MEAN AERO. CHORD	79.60"	HORIZ.TAIL ROOT AIRFOIL NACA	0010.22
WG.ROOT AIRFOIL	NAA/NACA LAM.FLOW	HORIZ TAIL TIP AIRFOIL NACA	0009.65
WG. TIP AIRFOIL	NAA/NACA LAM.FLOW	VERTICAL FIN AREA	8.83SQ.FT.,LATER9.61
WING ROOT INCIDENCE	1.0 DEG.	RUDDER AREA,INC.TAB	10.7 SQ.FT.
WING TIP WASHOUT	-1.25DEG.	RUDDER TAB SIZE	5.25"x 22"
WING DIHEDRAL, MEAN	5 DEG.	VERTICAL TAIL SPAN	74.25"
WING ROOT t/c	16.5%	MAX.RUDDER CHORD,AFT H/L	26.0"
WING TIP t/c	11.5%	FIN OFFSET	1.0 DEG. NOSE LEFT
WING L. E. SWEEP	3 DEG.35'32"	RUDDER TRAVEL	30 DEG.L,30 DEG.R.
WING ROOT CAMBER	3% @ 42%CHORD	RUD.TAB TRAVEL,REV.BOOST,	18DEG.R.12L.
WING TIP CAMBER	0.8% @ 51%CHORD	VERT.TAIL ROOT AIRFOIL NACA	0010
WING SURF.EXPOSED TO AIR	452.19SF.	VERT.TAIL TIP AIRFOIL NACA	0007.63
WHEELBASE	142"	VERT. TAIL ASPECT RATIO	1.17
MAX.FUSELAGE WIDTH	35"	MAIN WHEEL DIAMETER	27"
MAX.FUS.DEPTH,INC.SCOOP	133.6"	TAIL WHEEL SIZE	12.5"x 4.5"
MAX.FUS.CROSS-SECT.AREA	11.54SQ.FT.	MAIN GEAR SHOCK STRUT TRAVEL	8.0"
TOT.A/C WETTED SURF.AREA	862.12 SF.	TAIL GEAR SHOCK STRUT TRAVEL	7.5"

TABLE 45
P-51 FUEL CAPACITIES

MODEL	INTERNAL FUEL (US GAL.)	EXTERNAL FUEL (US GAL.)
XP-51	170	—
P-51	180	—
P-51A	180	300
XP-51B	180	—
P-51B, P-51C	269	300
P-51D	269	220
XP-51F	180	150
XP-51G	180	150
P-51H	255	220
XP-51J	180	150
P-51K	269	220

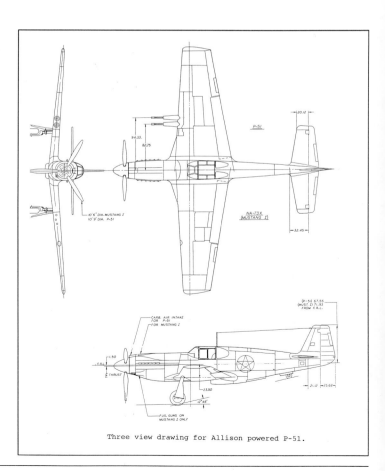

Three view drawing for Allison powered P-51.

greatly increased by 85 gallons giving the airplane additional range/radius capability sorely needed for bomber escort duty. The new fuselage tank had to be placed where space was available aft of the airplane center of gravity behind the cockpit. This addition caused the P-51 to go unstable when the new tank was full, but the wartime need to increase combat radius was pressing indeed, and pilots had to cope with control difficulties thus presented.

General arrangement drawings show, respectively, the Allison powered early Mustang, the first Merlin powered P-51B/C type with four wing machine guns, and the six gun P-51D with bubble canopy. The Allison powered versions were characterized by particularly lean slim lines, a shallow aft belly scoop, an upper cowl carburetor intake scoop, a three narrow chord blade propeller, and a low-set cockpit canopy fairing into the aft turtledeck. The plain P-51 version was distinguished by large wing leading edge protuberances enclosing four 20 mm cannon. Appearance of the Merlin P-51B/C was changed by new nose contours enclosing the Merlin engine, a larger aft ventral air scoop, and a four wide chord blade propeller of slightly larger diameter. The definitive P-51D, and P-51K, Mustangs changed configuration again, this mainly confined to a full blown cockpit canopy and cut down aft fuselage. A dorsal fin, not shown in the figure, was soon added to the D model.

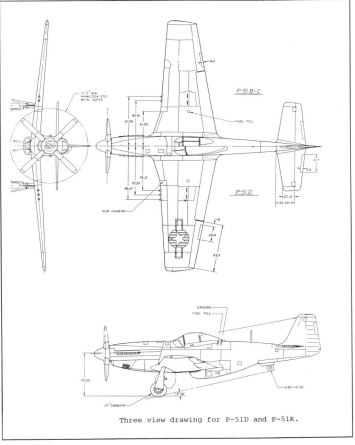

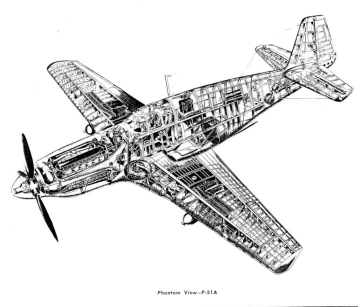

Three view drawing for P-51D and P-51K.

An inboard profile drawing showing major fuselage contents of a P-51D Mustang is also depicted. The engine compartment ahead of the firewall contained the big Merlin, oil and coolant tanks, engine mount, and many other powerplant items not shown. The cockpit was placed just behind the firewall, and beneath it was space for the left and right side wing panels to pass through and tie together

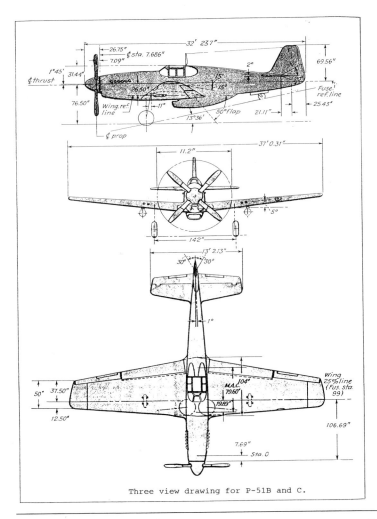

Three view drawing for P-51B and C.

Phantom View—P-51A

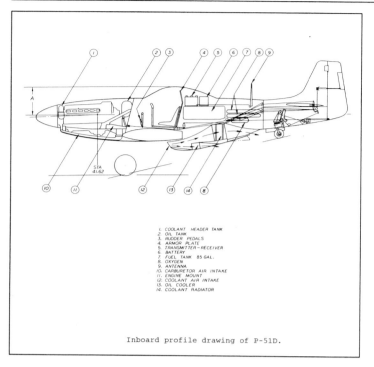

1. COOLANT HEADER TANK
2. OIL TANK
3. RUDDER PEDALS
4. ARMOR PLATE
5. TRANSMITTER-RECEIVER
6. BATTERY
7. FUEL TANK 85 GAL.
8. OXYGEN
9. ANTENNA
10. CARBURETOR AIR INTAKE
11. ENGINE MOUNT
12. COOLANT AIR INTAKE
13. OIL COOLER
14. COOLANT RADIATOR

Inboard profile drawing of P-51D.

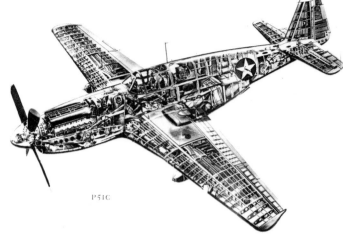

P-51C

on centerline while preserving lower outside contours. Just aft of wing structure was the large scoop that ducted outside air through coolant, aftercooler, and oil cooling radiators. This cooling air exited through the variable area aft end of the duct. The fuselage fuel tank was located just aft of the pilot's seat with oxygen bottles behind. Radio equipment was mounted on a shelf just above the tank. Cables ran from the cockpit aft to tail control surfaces, and a retractable tail wheel assembly was supported by the aft fuselage section. In addition cutaway drawings are shown of a P-51A, P-51C, and P-51D.

Table 46 displays rating figures for the engines powering various Mustang models. It is clear the Allison engines with their single stage single speed superchargers were strictly for low to medium altitudes. On the P-51A the Allison had a MILITARY power critical altitude of only 14600 feet, where it developed 1125 horsepower. In contrast the Merlin in the P-51B with its two stage supercharger in high blower setting, put out 1210 MILITARY horsepower at almost 26000 feet. Graph 37 shows pictorially the available power advantage the Merlins had over Allison engines in production Mus

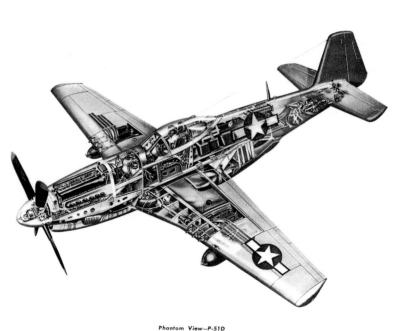

Phantom View-P-51D

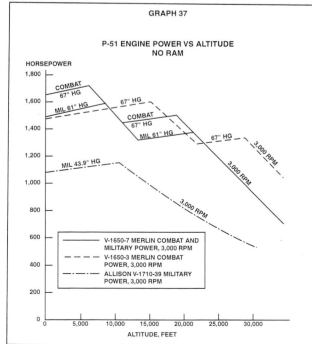

GRAPH 37

P-51 ENGINE POWER VS ALTITUDE
NO RAM

HORSEPOWER

V-1650-7 MERLIN COMBAT AND MILITARY POWER, 3,000 RPM
V-1650-3 MERLIN COMBAT POWER, 3,000 RPM
ALLISON V-1710-39 MILITARY POWER, 3,000 RPM

ALTITUDE, FEET

TABLE 46
P-51 ENGINE RATINGS

MODEL	ENGINE	RATING	HP	ENG.RPM	ALTITUDE'	MP"HG.	SUPERCHARGER
XP-51;P-51	V-1710-39	TO	1150	3000	SEA LEVEL	44.5	1-STAGE,1-SPEED
	(GR=.5:1)	MIL.	1150	3000	10800	43.9	
		NORMAL	1000	2600	11000	39.5	
P-51A	V-1710-81	TO	1200	3000	SEA LEVEL	52.0	1-STAGE,1-SPEED
	(GR=.5:1)	COMBAT	1330	3000	11800	57.0	
		MIL.	1125	3000	14600	44.2	
		NORMAL	1000	2600	13800	38.3	
A-36A	V-1710-87	TO	1325	3000	SEA LEVEL	47.0	1-STAGE,1-SPEED
	(GR=.5:1)	COMBAT	1500	3000		52.0	
		MIL.	1325	3000	5400	47.0	
		NORMAL	1100	2600	3700		
XP-& P-51B	V-1650-3	TO	1380	3000	SEA LEVEL	61.0	2-STAGE,2-SPEED
P-51C,-51D	(GR=.479:1)	COMBAT	1600	3000	15600	67.0	LOW BLOWER
XP-51F		COMBAT	1330	3000	29000	67.0	HIGH BLOWER
		MIL.	1490	3000	13750	61.0	LOW BLOWER
		MIL.	1210	3000	25800	61.0	HIGH BLOWER
		NORMAL	1110	2700	17400	46.0	LOW BLOWER
		NORMAL	950	2700	29500	46.0	HIGH BLOWER
P-51B,-51C	V-1650-7	TO	1490	3000	SEA LEVEL		2-STAGE,2-SPEED
P-51D,-51K	(GR=.479:1)	COMBAT	1720	3000	6250	67.0	LOW BLOWER
		COMBAT	1505	3000	19250	67.0	HIGH BLOWER
		MIL.	1590	3000	8500	61.0	LOW BLOWER
		MIL.	1370	3000	21400	61.0	HIGH BLOWER
		NORMAL	1180	2700	11300	46.0	LOW BLOWER
		NORMAL	1065	2700	23400	46.0	HIGH BLOWER
P-51H	V-1650-9	TO	1380	3000	SEA LEVEL	61.0	2-STAGE,2-SPEED
	(GR=.479:1)	COMBAT	1930	3000	10100	80.0	LOW BLOWER, (WET)
		COMBAT	1630	3000	23500	80.0	HIGH BLOWER,(WET)
		MIL.	1490	3000	13750	61.0	LOW BLOWER
		MIL.	1210	3000	25800	61.0	HIGH BLOWER
		NORMAL	1110	2700	17400	46.0	LOW BLOWER
		NORMAL	950	2700		46.0	HIGH BLOWER
P-51D	V-1650-9A	(RATINGS AS -9 EXCEPT NO WATER INJECTION FOR COMBAT PWR)					
XP-51J	V-1710-119	TO	1500	3200	SEA LEVEL	58.0	2-STAGE,2-SPEED
		COMBAT	1720	3200	20000		

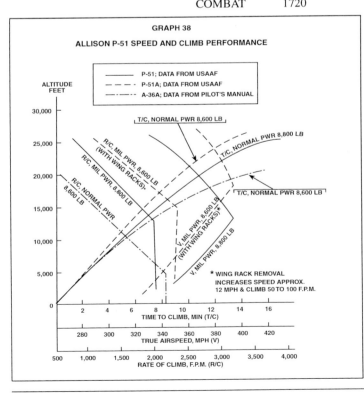

GRAPH 38

ALLISON P-51 SPEED AND CLIMB PERFORMANCE

tangs. This graph, using the V-1650-7 Merlin as an example, and MILITARY power, indicates the Merlin had a 400 horsepower advantage at sea level, 350 horsepower at 10000 feet, 550 horsepower at 20000 feet, and an almost 400 horsepower margin at 30000 feet where the Allison put out only 540 horsepower. At 25000 feet the Merlin developed about twice the MILITARY power of the Allison engine. These figures show dramatically the power boost the Mustang received when mated with the two stage Merlin engine.

Graph 38 shows the performance of Allison engined Mustangs in high speed and climb. From about 320 to 335 mph at sea level Mustang high speed capability rose steadily with altitude to a peak of over 390 mph due to its sleek low drag design. The P-51A version attained that speed about 5000 feet higher in altitude than the P-51 because of a higher altitude rating for its Allison engine. Even with the power fall-off at higher altitudes the P-51 could touch 375 mph at 25000 feet, a very respectable performance. Climb rates at MILITARY power were moderate, 2000 feet per minute at low altitude for the P-51 and 2300 feet per minute low down for the P-51A, part of the difference being weight changes shown. Climb times were thus unspectacular, under 2.5 minutes to 5000 feet, 4.5 to 5 minutes to 10000 feet, and 9 to 11 to 20000 feet, these all at NORMAL rated power, a setting lower than MILITARY. Climb

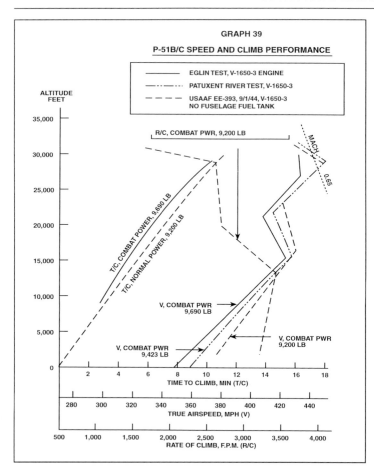

GRAPH 39

P-51B/C SPEED AND CLIMB PERFORMANCE

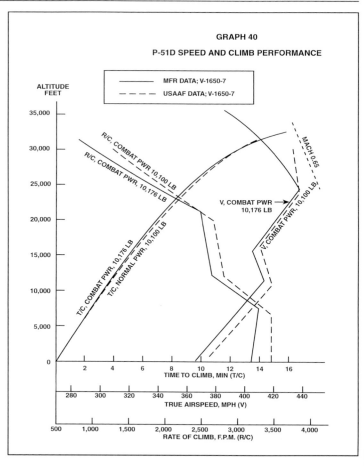

GRAPH 40

P-51D SPEED AND CLIMB PERFORMANCE

data for the low altitude dive bomber version of the Allison Mustang, the A-36A, are also shown. The A-36A used a particularly low altitude rated version of the Allison befitting a dive bomber and climb capability was moderate.

Speed and climb data for the first Merlin powered versions, the P-51B and P-51C, are given in Graph 39. The boost in performance is immediately apparent. Data are for COMBAT power settings, the short term WAR EMERGENCY rating. High speeds attained varied from 350 to 370 mph on the deck to about 425 mph at 15000 feet, holding well above 400 mph through 20000 feet, and making 430 to 450 mph at 30000 feet. This performance was excellent for the time. COMBAT power climb rate peaked over 3400 feet per minute at medium altitude, then dropped, but was still above 2500 feet per minute at 25000 feet. Climb time was 6 to 7 minutes up to 20000 feet and 11 minutes to 30000 feet. P-51D performed similarly, (Graph 40) though perhaps not quite as spectacularly, with high speed at COMBAT power exceeding 400 mph starting well under 10000 feet and a speed of over 435 mph at 25000 feet. COMBAT power climb rates were 3200 to 3300 feet per minute at medium altitudes, falling to about 2000 feet per minute at 25000 feet. Climb times were just over 3 minutes to 10000 feet , around 7 to 20000 feet, and 13 minutes to 30000 feet. The speed performance of Merlin Mustangs was excellent and as good or better than enemy types; climbing performance was not as competitive.

The curves of Graph 41 illustrate "yardstick" range capability of Allison powered Mustangs. This is the somewhat unrealistic range based on expending all fuel cruising and allowing no fuel reserves. Even so the curves make it clear the clean Mustang design yielded

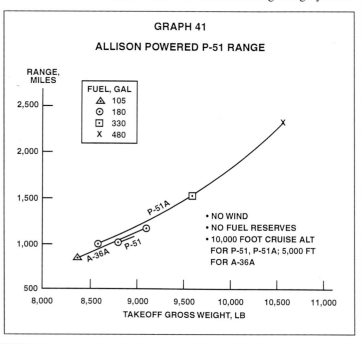

GRAPH 41

ALLISON POWERED P-51 RANGE

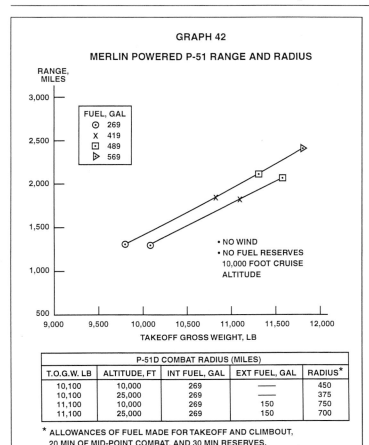

GRAPH 42

MERLIN POWERED P-51 RANGE AND RADIUS

RANGE, MILES

FUEL, GAL
⊙ 269
X 419
⊡ 489
▷ 569

• NO WIND
• NO FUEL RESERVES
  10,000 FOOT CRUISE
  ALTITUDE

TAKEOFF GROSS WEIGHT, LB

P-51D COMBAT RADIUS (MILES)				
T.O.G.W. LB	ALTITUDE, FT	INT FUEL, GAL	EXT FUEL, GAL	RADIUS*
10,100	10,000	269	—	450
10,100	25,000	269	—	375
11,100	10,000	269	150	750
11,100	25,000	269	150	700

* ALLOWANCES OF FUEL MADE FOR TAKEOFF AND CLIMBOUT, 20 MIN OF MID-POINT COMBAT, AND 30 MIN RESERVES.

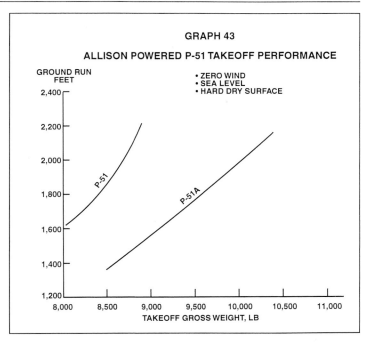

GRAPH 43

ALLISON POWERED P-51 TAKEOFF PERFORMANCE

GROUND RUN FEET

• ZERO WIND
• SEA LEVEL
• HARD DRY SURFACE

P-51

P-51A

TAKEOFF GROSS WEIGHT, LB

very good range performance. With full internal fuel a yardstick range of 1000 miles could be obtained; with normal external tanks aboard the figure was about 1500 miles. Ferry range on the same basis was over 2300 miles. Reducing these figures about 20 percent to be more practical, allowing for reserves and takeoff, climb, and descent fuel, they would become 800, 1200, and 1800 miles respectively, very good performance.

Graph 42 shows "yardstick" range performance for the Merlin Mustangs was even better. With just internal fuel aboard on takeoff 1300 miles was achieved, and with two 150 gallon drop tanks the aircraft could go over 2400 miles. The inserted table in Graph 42 provides P-51D combat radius performance at two different cruise altitudes with and without drop tanks. The resulting practical radii, where time is allowed for both midpoint combat and fuel reserves, show the superior capability of the Merlin Mustang which allowed it to escort bombers all the way in to targets and back out on many long missions over Europe, and later in the Pacific.

The curves of Graph 43 give takeoff ground run estimates under conditions stated for Allison powered P-51 aircraft. At a weight of 8800 pounds the P-51 took over 2000 feet to break ground. The run for the slightly more powerful P-51A at 8600 pounds was substantially less at 1400 feet. For all practical weights takeoff ground runs well over 1000 feet were indicated, much more distance than Navy fighters required to get off.

Graph 44 provides the same data for Merlin powered Mustangs, but the ground run estimates from different sources vary widely. For a gross weight of 10000 pounds three sources give distances of 1150, 1250, and 1800 feet. The most optimistic is manufacturers data while the greatest distance is quoted by the USAAF.

Rolling velocity in degrees per second against indicated airspeed is plotted in the curves of Graph 45. Three curves are for the original Allison powered XP-51 prototype tested by the NACA where ailerons had cusp-shaped trailing edges. Efforts were made to improve roll performance by changing trailing edge shape; a

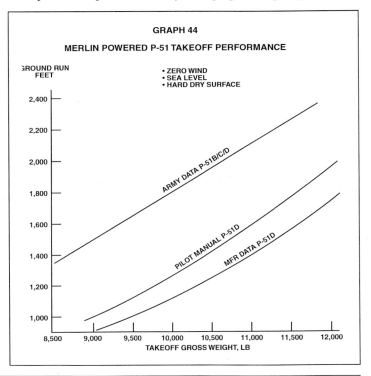

GRAPH 44

MERLIN POWERED P-51 TAKEOFF PERFORMANCE

GROUND RUN FEET

• ZERO WIND
• SEA LEVEL
• HARD DRY SURFACE

ARMY DATA P-51B/C/D

PILOT MANUAL P-51D

MFR DATA P-51D

TAKEOFF GROSS WEIGHT, LB

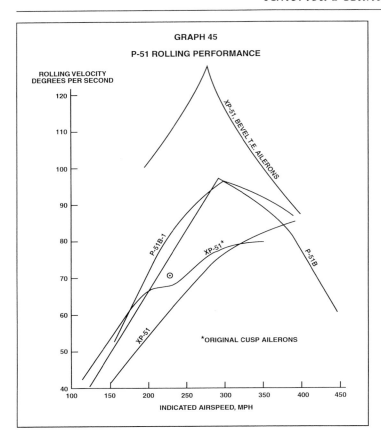

GRAPH 45

P-51 ROLLING PERFORMANCE

ROLLING VELOCITY
DEGREES PER SECOND

XP-51, BEVEL T.E. AILERONS

P-51B-1

XP-51*

P-51B

XP-51

*ORIGINAL CUSP AILERONS

INDICATED AIRSPEED, MPH

TABLE 48
MERLIN P-51 EMPTY AND BASIC WEIGHTS
(POUNDS)

MODEL	P-51B & P-51C
GROUP	
WING	1066
TAIL	183
FUSELAGE	509
LANDING GEAR	781
ENGINE SECTION	274
ENGINE (INCL.ACCESSORIES)	1670
ENGINE CONTROLS	30
PROPELLER	483
STARTING	25
COOLING	663
LUBRICATING	101
FUEL SYSTEM	320
INSTRUMENTS	48
SURFACE CONTROLS	108
HYDRAULICS	57
ELECTRICAL	176
COMMUNICATION	163
ARMAMENT PROVISIONS	246
FURNISHINGS	85
EMPTY WEIGHT	6988
TRAPPED FUEL AND OIL	61
CAL.50 GUN INSTALLATION	(4) 270
PYROTECHNICS	6
BASIC WEIGHT	7325

NOTE: An average basic weight for a P-51B or a P-51C with a fuselage fuel tank was 7580 pounds.

TABLE 47
ALLISON P-51 EMPTY AND BASIC WEIGHTS(LB.)

MODEL	XP-51	P-51	P-51A	A-36A
EMPTY WEIGHT	6278	6550	6433	6650*
TRAPPED FLUIDS			165	165
PYROTECHNICS			4	4
OXYGEN			1	1
GUNSIGHT			4	4
GUNS,.50CAL.			278 (4)	416 (6)
BASIC WEIGHT		`7050	6885	7240

*INCLUDES 2 WING BOMB RACKS AT 26 LB.

ALLISON P-51 TYPICAL DISPOSEABLE LOAD ALTERNATES

MODEL	P-51A			A-36A-1			
MISSION	FIGHTER	LG.RG.FIGHTER	FERRY	NORMAL	LG.RG.COMBAT	BOMBER	FERRY
PILOT	200	200	200	200	200	200	200
USEABLE OIL	60	90	90	60	90	90	90
CAL.50 AMMO.	378	378	—	420	420	420	—
BOMB INSTLN.	—	—	—	—	—	1010	—
MISC.EQUIPT.	—	—	80	—	—	—	80
DROP TANKS	—	120	210	—	120	—	210
INTERNAL FUEL	630	1080	1080	630	1080	1080	1080
DROP TANK FUEL	—	900	1800	—	900	—	1800
TOT.DISP.LOAD	1268	2768	3460	1310	2810	2800	3460
BASIC WEIGHT	6885	6885	6885	7240	7240	7240	7240
GROSS WEIGHT	8153	9653	10345	8550	10050	10040	10700
USEFUL LOAD	1720	3220	3912	1900	3400	3390	4050

TABLE 49
TYPICAL P-51D USEFUL LOAD ALTERNATIVES(LB.)

MISSION	FTR.	FTR M.FUEL	FTR.LR1	FTR.LR2	FTR.LR3	FTR.B1	FTR.B2	ROCK.FTR.LR.
EMPTY WT.	7205	7205	7205	7205	7205	7205	7205	7205
FUS.TANK	—	55	55	55	55	55	55	55
TRAP.FLU.	61	61	61	61	61	61	61	61
6 .50 CAL.	401	401	401	401	401	401	401	401
PYROTECH.	6	6	6	6	6	6	6	6
BOMB RKS.	—	32	32	32	32	32	32	32
RKT.PODS	—	—	—	—	—	—	—	21
BASIC WT.	7673	7760	7760	7760	7760	7760	7760	7781
PILOT	200	200	200	200	200	200	200	200
USE.OIL	94	94	94	94	94	94	94	94
CAL.50AMMO	564	564	564	564	564	564	564	564
BOMBS	—	—	—	—	—	1004	2000	840
ROCKETS	—	—	—	—	—	—	—	230
DROP TANKS	—	—	120	180	230	—	—	230
INT.FUEL	1080	1590	1590	1590	1590	1590	1590	1590
EXT.FUEL	—	—	900	1320	1980	—	—	1104*
GROSS WT.	9611	10208	11228	11708	12418	11212	12208	12403
USEFUL LD.	2406	2948	3968	4448	5158	3952	4948	5143

* Partial external fuel; a higher gross weight (over 12403) results in combat ceiling under 25000 feet aqltitude.

beveled trailing edge design provided much improved roll as shown. For reasons unknown this design was not adopted in production airplanes, but another was. Allison powered production airplane roll performance is shown in the third XP-51 curve which shows poor roll at low speed and very good rolling performance near 400 mph IAS. The two curves for Merlin powered P-51B aircraft are quite similar and indicate substantial improvement in low speed roll rate while the rate at near 400 mph IAS was still good. Peak performance is shown as 96 degrees per second at 300 mph IAS, a 3.75 second complete roll.

Table 47 provides weight data for Allison engined models. Empty and basic weights stayed quite stable at around 6300 to 6500 pounds and 6900 to 7200 pounds respectively, the heaviest version being the A-36A dive bomber. Typical alternate loads are given for fighter and dive bomber versions of the Allison Mustang. With full internal fuel both versions had a gross weight near 10000 pounds, the fighter being 400 pounds lighter without bomb racks and dive brakes.

The group weight breakdown of the first Merlin powered Mustang versions, P-51B and P-51C, is provided in Table 48. Empty weight originally increased about 550 pounds above the P-51A, and when the fuselage fuel tank was added in the P-51B/C it was about 700 pounds greater in basic weight. The fuel system weight in the table is for an airplane without the 85 gallon fuselage tank. A very large portion of the weight increase was attributable to powerplant items. The Merlin engine weighed considerably more than the Allison, and the new propeller with four wide chord blades also substantially increased empty weight. The airframe was not extensively redesigned structurally for the Merlin version of the Mustang. Such redesign had to wait for the P-51H, essentially a post-war airplane as far as USAAF operations went.

Table 49 gives gross weights resulting from several alternate useful loads aboard the P-51D bubble canopy version. Empty weight of the D model increased about 200 pounds as did basic weight. One source of the increase was incorporation of six instead of four .50 caliber machine guns. It is seen the P-51D gross weight, depending on mission loading, could vary all the way from 9600 to 12400 pounds, a difference of almost a ton and a half.

P-51 MAJOR MODEL-TO-MODEL CHANGES
P-51(from XP-51) Armament changed to four 20mm cannon in wings, bullet-proof windshield added, radio change, detail aileron changes.
A-36 New engine variant, change to aluminum blades on Curtiss propeller from steel, greater propeller diameter, dive flaps added, armament changed to six .50 caliber machine guns (two in fuselage; four in wings), wing shackles added for bombs or drop tanks.
P-51A New engine variant, engine induction system changes, radio change, propeller ice protection system added, armament change to four wing .50 caliber guns only, new tail wheel locking arrangement.
P-51B/C Powerplant change to Merlin engine with two-stage supercharging from previous Allison, new radiator and ducting, sealed balanced ailerons, Hamilton four wide chord bladed propeller with larger diameter, gun camera moved from nose to left wing. Changes along the way or retrofitted: Fuselage fuel tank added, elevators changed from fabric to metal covering, horizontal stabilizer incidence reduced, rudder anti-balance (reverse-boost) tab added, elevator control system bobweight added.
P-51D Engine model change, armament change to six wing guns in a new installation, bubble canopy added, increased capacity wing bomb racks, aileron modifications, including three hinges in place

of two, New gunsight-N-9 then K-14. Dorsal fin added after D-5 with kits for earlier versions, battery moved forward to engine compartment on late versions, electrical system revisions, D-20 added rocket capability, tail warning radar added.

P-51K As D model with Aeroproducts propeller having hollow steel blades. Nose ballast added to compensate for lighter propeller.

XP-51F Completely revised lighter experimental aircraft. Allison engine with two-stage supercharger, no fuselage fuel tank, three blade Aeroproducts propeller, four wing guns, reduced capacity bomb racks.

XP-51G New lightweight design. Tested with five-blade Rotol propeller. Four guns only.

P-51H New completely revised production design with revised airframe, propulsion systems, and subsystems.

P-51J New lightweight experimental design with Allison engine and two-stage supercharger.

P-51M New Merlin-powered version, one experimental aircraft only.

P-51 CHRONOLOGY

Jan '40-A British Purchasing Commission visits the US looking for an American fighter to buy, and suggests North American build the Curtiss P-40. After North American reviews British requirements they propose to build a superior new design instead.

Apr24'40-The North American design proposal for a new NA-73X fighter is accepted by the BPC; North American is to secure pertinent P-40 fighter data from Curtiss.

May 4'40-The British approve the preliminary design of the NA-73X.

May '40-The US Army releases the NA-73 design for sale to the UK, but requires two of the aircraft for USAAF testing.

May29'40-The British order 320 NA-73 aircraft with the name Mustang. The price per aircraft is $50,000. The next day a contract is signed with the US Army for two aircraft. The 5th and 10th aircraft are to be delivered to the US Army as the XP-51.

Sep '40-The British place another order for 300 NA-83 Mustang IIs.

Sep 9'40-The first NA-73 aircraft is rolled out of the North American plant without an engine and with wheels from a trainer.

Oct 7'40-The Allison engine for the NA-73X arrives at North American.

Oct11'40-The Allison engine has been installed and ground tests start.

Oct26'40-The first flight of the NA-73X takes place at Mines Field with Vance Breese as the test pilot.

Nov20'40-On the ninth test flight of the NA-73X with pilot Paul Balfour the engine stops (the selected fuel tank had run dry) and the aircraft crashes gear-down in a field, nosing over. The pilot is not badly hurt, but the aircraft damage is considerable.

Apr16'41-The first Mustang I for the UK, AG345, is rolled out.

Apr25'41-Mustang I, AG345, makes a first flight piloted by Louis Wait.

May20'41-The first flight of AG348, which becomes an XP-51, takes place piloted by Robert Chilton.

Jul '41-Propeller blade cuffs are tested on an XP-51.

Jul 7'41-North American Aviation obtains a contract for 150 Allison powered P-51 Apache fighters as part of the Lend-Lease program. These are modified Mustangs designated by the British as Mustang IA, and are to be armed with four 20mm cannon. Ninety-three of this order are eventually delivered to the RAF. Of the fifty-seven remaining fifty-five are taken over by the USAAF as F-6A photo planes, and two are held back to become Merlin test XP-78s.

Jul20'41-NAA test pilot Bob Chilton flies a Mustang in a demonstration before North American employees.

Aug24'41-The first XP-51 arrives at Wright Field, Dayton, Ohio and is placed in storage.

Sep '41-The second UK Mustang, AG346, is shipped to England by sea through the Panama Canal.

Oct24'41-The AG346 aircraft arrives in Britain and is ready for flight at the end of October. British radio gear and guns are fitted. It is shortly test flown at 382 MPH at 14000 feet altitude.

Nov11'41-Four more Mustang Is arrive in England.

Dec 7'41-North American Aviation now has over 15000 employees as the Japanese attack Pearl Harbor and America enters the war.

Dec16'41-The second XP-51 is delivered to the US Army at Wright Field.

Jan '42-Flight tests of a Mustang I are made at Boscombe Downs, UK.

Jan '42-Peak monthly output for Mustang I is reached at 92 aircraft.

Feb13'42-First flight of the Mustang II (NA-83) for the RAF takes place when Robert Chilton takes AL958 into the air.

Mar 1'42-The XP-51 Serial 41-038 starts tests at NACA Langley. The tests will include performance and lateral control and aileron improvement aspects. Testing lasts through June, and the aircraft stays at Langley through 1943.

Apr '42-The Mustang I gets its first assignment in the British Army Cooperation Command. British #2 Squadron is the first military unit to use the Mustang I. They are located at Sawbridgeworth in the UK.

Apr16'42-A contract is awarded NAA for 500 A-36 (NA-87) dive bomber versions of the P-51 with dive brakes and bomb racks.

May10'42-British #2 Squadron raids a German airfield in France just across the channel, the first Mustang operational mission.

May29'42-First flight of the P-51 (NA-91) version takes place with Louis Wait as pilot. The aircraft has four 20mm cannon and is procured for the RAF and the USAAF.

Jun '42-Development of the A-36 version is started.

Jun23'42-A contract is let for 1200 Allison-powered P-51A models (NA-99). The order is cut back to 310 aircraft in December. Fifty P-51A aircraft will be furnished to the British as replacements for the 57 P-51s held back from the Lend-Lease contract. These will be Mustang II versions.

Jul '42-The last Mustang I aircraft comes off the NAA lines and these are being followed by P-51s. AG-351 is being tested by the British.

Jul14'42-Rolls Royce in the UK makes a preliminary study of installing a Merlin 61 engine in a Mustang airframe.

Jul25'42-A contract is given North American for conversion of two Lend-Lease P-51 aircraft to XP-78s using Packard Merlin engines with two-stage superchargers. (Later to be XP-51B aircraft.)

Jul27'42-Sixteen Mustang I aircraft of #2 Squadron make a fighter sweep into the Ruhr area in Germany, the first time an Allied fighter had gone over German territory.

Aug '42-A prototype installation is made of the Packard-Merlin in the P-51 airframe.

Aug '42-Five Mustang I aircraft are sent to Rolls Royce for the development of "Mustang X", and modifications start.

Aug18'42-Four British squadrons are now equipped with Mustang Is. At the peak the British will operate 21 Mustang I squadrons.

Aug19'42-British Mustang Is are involved in the Dieppe raid. One FW-190 is shot down and one Mustang lost. The Mustang I shows up well against the FW-190 at low altitudes.

Aug26'42-An order is placed with NAA for 400 P-51B-1NA aircraft (NA-102). Later 1350 more are ordered.

Sep '42-The XP-78 Mustangs are officially redesignated as XP-51Bs.

Sep '42- The first A-36A Mustang dive bomber flight is made.

Oct '42-Deliveries start on the first models of the A-36A airplanes.

Oct 8'42-The North American Aviation Dallas plant receives an order to produce 1350 Merlin-powered Mustangs to be designated P-51C.

Oct13'42-The first of the five Mustang Is converted to the Merlin engine has a first flight in England. The flight is aborted when a piece of cowling leaves the aircraft.

Oct16'42-The sixth test flight of the first Mustang X takes place. Powerplant changes are made and the aircraft hits 422 MPH at 22000 feet. Later a speed of 432 MPH is reached.

Oct16'42-Winston Churchill advises presidential aide Harry Hopkins that The Merlin-powered Mustang should be developed.

Nov30'42-The first XP-51B aircraft flies in the US piloted by NAA pilot Robert Chilton. The plane lands due to engine overheating. The radiator and the cooling air scoop must be redesigned.

Dec '42-Flight tests of the XP-51B resume with a new radiator design.

Jan '43-Fifteen RAF squadrons now use the Allison-powered Mustang I.

Jan '43-The USAAF orders over 2000 P-51B aircraft. P-51A contracts are to be completed as P-51Bs.

Jan 2'43-Lightweight Mustang versions (XP-51F,G, and J) are started as part of an RAF program.

Jan19'43-US data on the XP-51B is put together in a study to be sent to the UK. It is decided not to modify existing Allison Mustangs in England, but to wait for US production of the P-51B.

Feb '43-All five Mustang Xs in the UK are completed. Numbers four and five are being tested by the USAAF in England.

Feb 3'43-The Allison-powered P-51A has a first flight at North American as the NA-99, Serial No. 43-6009, piloted by Robert Chilton.

Feb27'43-The 201st and 202nd P-51B-10 aircraft are assigned as manufacturing prototypes (NA-106) for the new D-model planned.

Mar '43-Production is started on the P-51A Mustang version; deliveries are now complete on the A-36A dive bomber version.

Apr '43-A-36A dive bomber Mustangs, sometimes called Invaders, are with the 27th and 86th Fighter-Dive Bomber Groups of the NW African Air Force at Rasel Ma in French Morocco.

Apr 9'43-The first mission by a USAAF P-51 over enemy territory takes place. Lt. Alfred Schwab of the 154th Observation Sdn. at Sbeitla, Tunisia flies a sucessful reconnaisance mission over Kairouan airfield. The RAF #225 Sdn. repeatedly borrows two P-51s from the 68th Observation Sdn. for use on long range missions their Spitfires can't handle.

Apr13'43-The first production order for P-51Ds is placed with North American when 2500 aircraft are contracted for.

Apr23'43-The first loss of a P-51 occurs when a 154th Observation Sdn. Mustang is shot down by US forces. The P-51 resembles a ME109.

Apr23'43-An additional order is placed for 100 Merlin-Mustangs for Australia. The first four aircraft will be B models with the remainder being P-51Ds.

May '43-Three hundred and ten P-51A aircraft have been produced up to this time when production is shifted to P-51B manufacture.

May '43-Finished Mustang airframes are accumulating without engines due to a shortage of Packard-Merlins.

May '43-The F-6A reconnaisance version equips the 111th Photo Recon. Sdn. in North Africa and is used to spot for artillery and to direct air strikes.

May '43-P-51A acceptances reach a peak rate of 120 per month. First production aircraft are delivered to Drew and Lakeland Fields in Florida for operational training units.

May 3'43-A contract is awarded to the Dallas, Texas NAA plant for 2500 Mustangs. It provides for 400 P-51Cs, 800 D models, and the remainder to be P-51K versions.

May 5'43-The first production P-51B-1 is flown by NAA test pilot Robert Chilton. It is serial number 43-12093.

Jun '43-Fifty Mustang IIs and one A-36A join the RAF.

Jun 6'43-First missions are flown by A-36A aircraft of the 27th Fighter Bomber Group as part of the air assault on Pantelleria Island.

Jun11'43-British Flight Lt. Hollis Hills becomes the first Mustang ace flying a IA version.

Jun20'43-A-36A aircraft are operating against the enemy in Sicily. A-36s of the 27th and 86th Fighter Bomber Groups fly over a thousand sorties in the first 35 days after A-36 combat introduction. The aircraft are based on Pantelleria.

Jul '43-Production P-51As reach the 311th Fighter Bomber Group in India. The group has A-36As, so the introduction of the P-51A causes no problems. Eventually the 311th will have two P-51A squadrons and one of A-36As.

Jul '43-The A-36A groups, 27th and 86th, are now based on Sicily after its conquest, and are ready to attack Italy.

Jul '43-Only 173 Merlin engines have been received by North American when 534 P-51B airframes have been completed.

Jul20'43-A contract is signed for five prototypes in the light weight P-51 program (XP-51F, G, and J).

Aug '43-The first production P-51B aircraft are being readied for shipment to England.

Aug '43-The job of protecting ground troops during the invasion of Italy falls on P-38s, Spitfires, and the two groups of A-36s.

Aug '43-Twelth Air Force A-36As attack rail and road junctions and marshalling yards in Calabris, Italy. After bombing they strafe trains and transport vehicles.

Aug 5'43-The P-51C makes its first flight at the NAA Dallas, Texas plant, and the plant begins deliveries this month.

Sep '43-The 23rd Fighter Group in Kweilin, China, formed with a Flying Tigers nucleus, obtains some P-51A aircraft and uses them in fighter missions.

Sep '43-The first Merlin-powered P-51B arrives in the United Kingdom.

Sep '43-The 27th Fighter Bomber Group with A-36As is awarded a Distinguished Unit citation for its ground attack work in Italy.

Sep '43-A-36 Mustangs hinder enemy movement by bombing a road junction at Catanzaro, Italy.

Sep '43-During Operation Avalanche at Salerno, Italy through daylight hours twelve A-36s fly low cover, P-38s fly medium cover, and twelve Spitfires fly top cover to maintain air protection. The A-36s operate from bases on the Catania plain in Sicily.

Sep '43-Gen. Hap Arnold urges the RAF to put as many of its Mustang-equipped squadrons as possible at the disposal of the US 8th Air Force for long range escort.

Sep13'43-Many A-36s are shifted back to fighter-bomber operations against enemy transport.

Sep14'43-US P-51s provide spotting direction for naval gunfire from the USS Philadelphia during Operation Avalanche.

Sep14'43-In Italy the ground situation enters a critical phase for the US 5th Army, and A-36s and P-38s go all-out attacking troops, vehicles, bridges, and marshalling yards.

Sep21'43-A large number of aircraft are now moved to the Italian mainland. The three A-36 squadrons of the 86th Fighter Bomber Group are flying from Paestum, Italy.

Oct '43-P-51B aircraft are arriving steadily in England.

Oct '43-It is decided that all P-51 aircraft (and P-38s) scheduled to go to the Mediterranean will instead go to the 8th Air Force in the UK for at least the period through the end of 1943. Gen. Kepner of 8th Fighter Command refers to the P-51 as "disinctly the best fighter we can get over here", and "they are going to be the only satisfactory answer".

Oct '43-It is becoming very evident that the P-51B can be developed into a more maneuverable, and even more important, a longer range fighter than the P-38.

Oct30'43-A compromise is reached in England where the 9th AF Mustangs of their 354th Ftr. Gp. will provide escort for 8th AF bombers until further notice, and all incoming P-51s will be assigned to 8th Air Force units.

Nov '43-Allison-powered P-51As of the 311th Fighter Bomber Group arrive in India to go into operations in Burma. The group also operates A-36s in one of its three squadrons.

Nov '43-The 354th Ftr.Gp., 9th AF, begins training at Colchester, England with P-51B aircraft after getting its first plane Nov.11.

Nov '43-The A-36A dive bomber Mustang is operated by only three groups (27th and 86th in Italy, and 311th in Burma) in combat. In this role the A-36A proves excellent; they together fly 23373 combat missions, deliver more than 8000 tons of bombs on enemy targets in the Mediterranean and the Far East. They shoot down 84 enemy aircraft, and destroy 17 on the ground. A total of 177 A-36As are lost from all causes of enemy action.

Nov '43-Lt. Col. Don Blakeslee, deputy CO of the 4th Ftr.Gp.,8th AF is sent to Colchester to check out in the new P-51B since he is to lead the 354th Ftr.Gp.,9th AF on its first missions.

Nov '43-P-51As are taken from Florida bases and put aboard ship to go to India. They are to be used by the 538th Provisional Unit to assist Gen. Wingate's Raiders with air support.

Nov 1'43-As of this date the Mustangs available in the 12th (tactical) AF in the Mediterranean/Italy Theatre are the A-36As of the 86th and 27th fighter Bomber Gps. of the 64th Fighter Wing, and the Allison P-51s in the 111th Recon. Sdn. of same wing. There are no P-51s in the recently formed 15th (strategic) Air Force in Italy.

Nov17'43-The XP-51D (NA-106), a modified P-51B-1 aircraft, makes a first flight piloted by Robert Chilton.

Nov26'43-The 23rd Ftr.Gp. in China sends its P-51As on their first mission; eight P-51As and eight P-38s escort B-25s to Formosa.

Dec 1'43-The P-51Bs of the 354th Ftr.Gp. are being "de-bugged". They also are not yet operating with the extra fuselage fuel tank or with external tanks.

Dec 1'43-Twenty-four P-51Bs of the 354th Ftr.Gp. take their first fighter sweep over Belgium and France led by Lt.Col. Don Blakeslee of the 4th Ftr.Gp. There is no enemy action and they do some ground strafing.

Dec 5'43-On an uneventful mission some P-51Bs of the 354th Ftr.Gp. go as far as Ameins on a fighter sweep. Two squadrons of P-51Bs escort B-17s from the French coast to Paix, where P-47s reieve them for the rest of the mission.

Dec 9'43-In Italy in the last two days over 400 A-36As and P-40s, along with 60 A-20s, fly sorties in support of the 5th Army against troop concentrations, gun positions, and communication centers.

Dec13'43-Along with P-47s, the first long range escort mission to Kiel is undertaken by the P-51Bs of the 354th Ftr.Gp. in the UK. The P-51s carry 75 gallon drop tanks, giving them a six hour endurance and a 650 mile escort range. P-38s of the 55th Ftr. Gp. are also on this raid and use 75 gallon drop tanks, giving them an escort range of 520 miles. There are 1462 aircraft, including 710 bombers on the raids to Kiel, Bremen, and Hamburg. There are 46 P-51s; one is lost to unknown causes and a ME-110 is shot down.

Dec17'43-Good weather in southern Italy permits over 1100 attack sorties by A-36A and P-40 aircraft supporting the 5th Army.

Dec20'43-Forty-four P-51s and 35 P-38s protect bombers on another raid to Bremen. P-47s escort to and from the target with the P-51s and P-38s protecting over the target. P-51s destroy three enemy aircraft and lose three Mustangs.

Dec31'43-At this time 60 P-51A aircraft are in overseas service in the CBI and North Africa. The 107th Tactical Reconnaisance Sdn. of the 67th Recon.Gp. is using the P-51A in North Africa.

Dec31'43-By this time the value of the Merlin-powered P-51 as an escort fighter is fully apparent, and fighter allocations are to be revised accordingly.

Jan '44-P-51B operations so far confirm the feeling that the P-51 is the answer to the long range bomber escort problem. Without external tanks the aircraft can escort to a 475 mile distance from base (roughly equal to a P-47 with two 108 gallon drop tanks); with two 75 gallon drop tanks it has an escort distance capability of 650 miles, and with two 108 gallon drop tanks it can escort to 850 miles.

Jan 5'44-The 354th Ftr.Gp. P-51Bs return from escort over target at Kiel after destroying 18 enemy aircraft with no losses, and repeat this performance with another score of 15 E/A and no losses. But there are problems: gun jams during maneuvers, transparencies frosting over, radios, coolant leaks, and engine spark plugs.

Jan18'44-A P-51A Mustang is tested with retractable skis, but the conversion is never used operationally.

Jan21'44-The 354th Ftr.Gp. P-51Bs have shot down 103 enemy aircraft in their first 83 days of combat.

Jan24'44-US and British commanders agree to place most Merlin P-51 units in the 8th Air force in the UK.

Jan31'44-It is decided to allocate to the 8th AF seven P-51 groups (plus four each P-38 and P-47), and the 9th Tactical AF two P-51 groups (along with thirteen P-47 and three P-38).

Jan31'44-In Europe during the month P-51Bs fly 325 effective missions (36 less than in December). The firing defect in the guns is causing many aborts. By the end of the month corrective action is initiated.

Feb '44-The RAF starts operations with Merlin-powered Mustang IIIs. They will be allotted a total of 308 B models and 636 P-51Cs under Lend Lease; some will later be repossessed by the USAAF.

Feb '44-The British test the Malcomb hood on a Mustang III, and later retrofit all these to gain better cockpit visibility.

Feb '44-F-6C Mustangs of the 8th Reconnaisance Group are assigned to the 10th AF in Bally, India. They are also assigned escort and ground attack missions.

Feb '44-The 15th AF in Italy is up against bitter opposition, and needs more P-51s, but none are available.

Feb 2'44-The 8th AF in England receives its first P-51B by exchanging its 358th Group, with P-47s, for the 9th AF second P-51 group, the 357th. The two groups have exchanged their bases Jan.31.

Feb 3'44-The 5318th Provisional Unit supporting Gen.Wingate in Burma sends its Mustangs on their first combat mission. Later in the month they carry a 1000 pound bomb for the first time.

Feb11'44-On the first operation of Mustangs assigned to 8th AF, 41 aircraft of the 357th Ftr. Gp. go on a sweep of the Rouen area in support of B-24s.

Feb14'44-The initial P-51F model flies for the first time, piloted by test pilot Robert Chilton.

Feb19'44-The 8th AF in the UK now has two groups of Mustangs, along with two of P-38s and eight of P-47s.

Feb22'44-The 363rd Ftr.Gp. joins the 9th AF in the UK with its P-51s, and is the last P-51 group to be assigned to the 9th.

Feb28'44-The 4th Ftr.Gp. under Lt.Col.Don Blakeslee, having received its first Mustangs on the 24th, has converted from P-47Ds to P-51Bs and goes on a first Mustang mission, a sweep of 22 aircraft over France. The change is not easy. There are losses due to failures in aircraft systems and to heavy fighting with deep penetrations. There are initial doubts about the Mustang and one group pilot calls the P-51B "an experimental aircraft". The 4th Group is fully converted on the 29th.

Mar '44-P-51As are supporting Gen.Wingate's drive into Burma.

Mar '44-The P-51D model replaces the B in NAA Englewood production.

Mar '44-The P-51D with bubble canopy and six guns is introduced into the 8th Air Force in England, and the last of the B and C models go into service.

Mar '44-To the amazement of many seasoned observers (including Herman Goering) US P-51 fighters fly with the bombers to Berlin and even beyond.

Mar 2'44-The 4th Ftr.Gp. escorts bombers on a mission to Frankfurt with their new Mustangs; two enemy aircraft are downed for a loss of one P-51.

Mar 2'44-The thirty P-51As attached to Wingate's forces in Burma under Col. Phil Cochran use 3-cluster rockets for the first time and there are no undue troubles. The P-51As fly often with two drop tanks or 500 pound bombs. Sometimes two 1000 pound bombs are carried , or two 325 pound depth charges. They are up against Japanese Oscar fighters in the air. On March 29 the name of the unit is changed to "First Air Commando Group".

Mar 6'44-The 4th Ftr.Gp. P-51Bs spearhead the escort of bombers over Berlin, and destroy at least 15 E/A. There is a large air battle with 803 US fighters of all types involved. The new 357th Mustang Group has a big day with 20 E/A destroyed. But of 48 P-51s taking off 15 had to turn back, mostly because of engine coolant problems.

Mar 9'44-The 355th Ftr.Gp., which has been operating in England since September 9, 1943, converts from P-47Ds to Mustangs.

Mar31'44-P-51s of the 4th Ftr.Gp. claim 100 enemy aircraft shot down from March 18th to this date.

Mar31'44-By this time three P-51 groups, the 4th, 355th, and the 357th, have 140 aircraft completely operational. This is in addition to the 9th AF 354th Group on loan to the 8th Air force.

Apr '44-More than 300 Mustangs have been converted to F-6 photo aircraft, and Merlin-powered F-6Cs are being used to help plan the Normandy invasion. Planes of the 10th Recon. Group are being used to find suitable landing beaches.

Apr '44-In addition to other orders, 6000 P-51Ds are ordered from the North American plant in California.

Apr '44-The fighter section of the First Air Commando Group in Burma receives five P-51B aircraft. The rocket installation is not made on this aircraft version.

Apr 1'44-The 4th Ftr.Gp. gets their 300th victory. Ace Don Gentile has a score one ahead of the 56th Ftr.Group's Robert Johnson.

Apr 5'44-P-51s of the 4th and 355th Ftr.Gps. go on airfield strafing missions in the Berlin and Munich areas, destroying almost 100 enemy aircraft. Seven aircraft are lost from the two groups.

Apr 7'44-The 352nd Ftr.Gp. converts from P-47s to Mustangs.

Apr 8'44-Mustangs and other fighters destroy 128 enemy aircraft.

Apr16'44-The 31st Ftr.Gp., changing over from A-36s and Spit-fires, starts operating the P-51B in Italy, adding 156 aerial victories to the previous 192 in the first seventy-five days of Mustang operation.

Apr22'44-The 4th Ftr.Gp. destroys 17 German aircraft trying to "bounce" them.

Apr25'44-P-51s of the 23rd Ftr.Gp. in China, along with B-24s, are moved up to Chengtu in hope of stalling a Japanese offensive.

Apr30'44-The 4th Ftr.Gp. of 8th AF in England now has a score of more than 500 E/A destroyed. In April alone they have destroyed

222 enemy planes. The 355th Ftr.Gp. has a total of 153 E/A destroyed; the newly operational 352nd Group has a total score of 140 E/A destroyed. But losses in the 8th AF fighter groups are high-67 aircraft, almost the equivalent of an entire group lost. The six P-47 groups lose only 42 aircraft. The conclusion can be drawn that the P-51 is less able to accept battle damage.

Apr30'44-The 339th Ftr.Gp. with P-51B and P-51C Mustangs joins 8th AF on the 4th of the month and is now operational as a new unit.

May '44-The weary P-51As of the First Air Commando Group in Burma are flown back to Karachi, India, and P-47D-23 Thunderbolts replace them.

May '44-The 528th Fighter Sdn. with both P-51s and A-36s is located at Tingkawk, Sakan, and there are two squadrons of P-51s at Assam, India.

May 5'44-P-51Bs of the 31st Ftr.Gp. participate, along with RAF Mustangs and Kittihawks, 200 total aircraft, in a raid on the Pescara Dam in Italy and destroy it.

May 8'44-The 352nd Ftr.Gp. Mustangs, on an escort mission, shoot down 27 E/A for a loss of only one P-51 in the ETO fighting.

May13'44-Using the UK-made 108 gallon paper drop tanks which are now standard on P-51s in Europe on long range missions, the 355th Group flies escort on a record trip of 1480 miles to Politz and back, the 357th flies a 1470 mile escort trip to Poznan in Poland and return, and the 359th Group meets the bombers 645 miles from its base.

May21'44-The 361st Group, newly converted from P-47Ds to P-51s shoots up and destroys 23 locomotives in strafing runs.

May29'44-The new 339th Ftr.Gp. goes for a distance of 1420 miles escorting bombers to East Germany.

Jun '44-P-51D Mustang models start to reach the 8th AF fighter groups in quantity.

Jun '44-Five RAF squadrons still use Allison-powered Mustang Is. Two squadrons will retain them until the end of the war.

Jun '44-G-suits are issued to the 4th and 339th Fighter Groups.

Jun 3'44-The P-51B Mustang appears in the China/Burma/India Theatre. The 23rd Ftr.Gp. in China starts replacing their P-40 and P-51A aircraft with the Merlin-powered Mustangs.

Jun 6'44-On the day of the European invasion the following Mustang groups are stationed in England: the 4th Ftr.Gp. at Debden,

339th Ftr.Gp. at Fowlemere, 355th Ftr.Gp. at Steeple Morden, 357th Ftr.Gp. at Leiston, and the 496th Fighter Training Group at Goxhill with P-51s and P-38s.

Jun '44-The 52nd Ftr.Gp. of the 15th AF in Italy is in the process of being equipped with Merlin-powered Mustangs. On June 15 the 15th has the 306th Ftr.Wing which includes the 31st, 52nd, and 325th Ftr.Gps. with P-51s. It also has three P-38 and one P-47 group.

Jun13'44-The 354th Ftr.Gp. moves a detachment to a Normandy coast airfield just seven days after D-day.

Jun21'44-Seventy P-51s of the 4th Ftr.Gp.,8th AF plus a squadron of the 352nd Group escort a shuttle bombing mission to Russia. The mission takes seven and one half hours and covers 1470 miles.

Jun26'44-Seventy-sixth Squadron P-51Bs fly top cover for a joint strafing mission with P-40s of the 74th, 75th, and 118th Sqdns. of the 23rd Ftr.Gp. south of Hengyang, China. For support of the hard-pressed Chinese army, Chennault has these P-51s and P-40s of the veteran 23rd Group and P-40s of the 5th   Ftr.Gp., Chinese American Composite Wing (CACW).

Jun29'44-P-51s of the 357th Ftr.Gp. claim 21 E/A destroyed during their bomber escort mission to German targets, including Leipzig.

Jun30'44-One thousand P-51H aircraft are ordered from NAA, Englewood.

Jun30'44-The third XP-51F, RAF FR409, is sent to Boscombe Downe in England to start testing.

Jun30-44-The second XP-51F has been flown seven times by NAA test pilot Robert Chilton; its last flight is to Vultee in Downey, Cal.

Jul '44-It is the end of active service for the A-36A Mustang dive bomber version after over a year.

Jul '44-Ground strafing by the 355th Ftr.Gp.,8th AF Mustangs destroys 118 enemy aircraft and damages 130 of them.

Jul '44-Three of the 8th AF P-38 groups convert to Mustangs, the 55th Ftr.Gp. on July 14, the 20th Group on July 17, and the 364th Group on July 28.

Jul 2'44-The 4th Ftr.Gp. and part of the 352nd Group P-51s, after having flown on the shuttle mission to Russia, now fly from Russia to Italy and support the 15th Air Force over the Balkans. Six P-51s are lost in air battles near Budapest in Hungary.

Jul 3'44-The entire 354th Ftr.Gp.is now based in France.

Jul21'44-A flight of P-51s from the 352nd Ftr.Gp. goes into a thunder cloud over the North Sea and all are lost.

Jul25'44-P-51s of the 31st Ftr.Gp., 15th Air Force return from a shuttle flight to Russia and strafe German airfields.

Jul28'44-German ME-163 rocket fighters dive on and shoot down three P-51s of the 352nd Ftr.Gp.

Aug '44-P-51s of 8th AF fly many strafing missions, but losses are high because of the sensitivity of the liquid cooling system to flak hits.

Aug '44-Modification kits become available to install the dorsal fin and modify the rudder tab on P-51s.

Aug '44-P-51s of the 10th, 67th, and 363rd Fighter Groups are operating from French airfields.

Aug 8'44-A second bomber shuttle mission to Russia is made escorted by the 357th Ftr.Gp. with 72 Mustangs.

Aug 9'44-The first XP-51G model flies with an imported Merlin engine and a five-blade propeller. The test pilot is Robert Chilton. Three days later the aircraft is flown with a four-bladed Aeroproducts propeller.

Sep '44-P-51K propeller vibration problems result in many rejections.

Sep '44-Fifteen cases of Mustangs breaking up in flight have occurred in the last three months, and some flight restrictions are put in place. Many result from tail surface failures. The horizontal stabilizer is beefed up and metal-covered elevators are installed.

Sep '44-P-51Ks using Aeroproducts propellers go into operating squadrons. Propeller balancing problems have held up delivery of the K models.

Sep '44-In the 8th Air Force in England the 479th Ftr.Gp. converts from P-38s to P-51s on the 27th of the month and the 353rd Ftr.Gp. switches from P-47Ds to P-51s on the 30th.

Sep 1'44-Mustangs of the 15th AF (325th, 31st, and 52nd Groups), along with RAF Mustangs, a total of 193 aircraft, go on strafing missions over German airfields. They destroy or damage a total of 342 E/A for one of the most destructive missions of the entire war.

Sep11'44-P-51s escorting B-17s meet heavy opposition near Leipzig. Planes of the 339th, 55th, and 359th Ftr.Gps. destroy 116 E/A in big air battles. Fifteen US planes are lost, and others make emergency landings in France.

Sep11'44-P-51Cs are assigned to the 75th Sdn.23rd Ftr.Gp. in China, and start to replace their P-40N aircraft.

Sep12'44-The 354th Ftr.Gp.,9th AF has 48 Mustangs assigned to dive-bomb German airfields. They encounter over 100 enemy aircraft, drop their bombs near the Rhine River, and in the subsequent aerial battle destroy 23 E/A for a loss of one Mustang.

Sep16'44-The 75th Sdn.23rd Ftr.Gp. in China flies its first mission in P-51C Mustangs as top cover for CACW P-40s and then strafe enemy installations in the Hengyang area. The guns jam on at least three of the P-51Cs.

Sep18'44-In an air battle with ME-109s and FW-190s the P-51s of the 357th Ftr.Gp. down 26 E/A for a loss of two Mustangs. In the Arnhem area the 359th Gp. encounters 35 FW-190s, and shoots down two of them while losing two Mustangs.,

Oct '44-Introduction of the new K-14 gyroscopic gunsight is being made on P-51s of the 8th AF starting with the 357th Ftr.Gp. This sight is to replace the N-9 model, and greatly improves pilot shooting accuracy.

Nov '44-At the Dallas, Texas NAA plant manufacture is underway of 136 F-6D and 163 F-6K recon Mustang versions. These are armed.

Nov '44-The 311th Fighter-Bomber Group, in Merlin Mustangs, are released from protecting B-29 Chinese bases and start to escort B-24s. They also go on ground attack missions against Japanese fighter bases.

Nov '44-Fourteenth AF units now equipped with the P-51 include: The 68th Composite Wing having the 23rd Ftr.Gp. with 74th, 75th, and 76th Sdns. mostly if not fully equipped; the 69th Composite Wing with headquarters at Kunming, China having the 51st Ftr.Gp. with 16th, 25th, 26th, and 449th Sdns., and the 312th Fighter Wing with the 311th Ftr.Gp. with 528th, 529th, and 530th Sdns, along with the 81st Ftr.Gp. with 91st and 92nd Sdns. The Chinese-American Composite Wing (CACW) has two groups, each with four squadrons (3rd and 5th Groups) equipped with P-40s in Central China.

Nov '44-In the Pacific area only eight P-51s with Merlins have arrived up to this date.

Nov '44-The 82nd Recon.Sdn. at Morotai in the Pacific receives their first F-6D aircraft and is the initial unit in the SWPA to use the type. The squadron has previously had P-40Ns and before that P-39s.

Nov1'44-Sixteen Merlin Mustangs are available at Kunming, China for the 75th Sdn. 23rd Ftr.Gp., and the last flights in P-40s are made to go and pick up the new aircraft.

Nov2'44-During a raid on oil refineries at Merseburg heavy German fighter opposition is encountered by hundreds of P-51 escorts of the 20th, 55th, 352nd, 359th, and 364th Ftr.Gps. The Mustangs down 134 E/A for a loss of about eight P-51s and 27 B-17 Flying Fortresses.

Nov 6'44-The 356th Ftr.Gp.,8th AF gives up its P-47s and converts to P-51 aircraft.

Nov15'44-The US Navy tests a hooked version of the P-51D aboard an aircraft carrier.

Nov18'44-Three hundred and fifty-five P-51s and 47 P-47s attack the German ME-262 jet fighter development center at Lechfeld.

Nov21'44-Six hundred and fifty P-51 Mustangs escort 700 B-17s to Merseberg, Germany, and are met by several hundred E/A. Seventy-three of the German aircraft are destroyed; several Mustangs are lost. The P-51 pilots are using G-suits and have the new K-14 gunsights.

Nov26'44-On a raid to Hanover, Germany 110 out of about 400 enemy aircraft are destroyed. The 339th Group downs 29, the 355th 27, the 361st 19, and the 356th 23 without any P-51 losses. This is accomplished despite widespread jamming of guns on P-51s.

Nov26'44-In a blow to the 354th Ftr.Gp. 9th AF their Mustangs are being replaced by P-47 Thunderbolts, and the P-51s are assigned to the 8th Air force in England.

Nov27'44-Three Mustang groups of 8th AF, 357th, 353rd, and 359th, engage large numbers of German fighters. In furious air battles 98 enemy aircraft are claimed destroyed for a loss of 11 Mustangs.

Nov27'44-The largest number of German interceptors to date, about 750 aircraft, are up over Europe to fight. The Germans mistake a very large force of P-51s for bombers and attack. The bombers raid Bingen and Offenburg without seeing an enemy plane. The P-51s claim 98 E/A downed for a loss of eleven of their own.

Dec '44-New P-51 pilots received by Far East Air Force total only 27 in the period July to December, 1944. For the period January to June, 1945 the figure will increase to 397.

Dec '44-From this time until war's end the average number of Mustangs per month available to fighter units in the China-Burma-India Theatre is 531 aircraft.

Dec '44-The P-51D-20NA Mustang with rocket capability becomes available, and is provided to three fighter groups assigned to the Pacific islands, the 35th Ftr.Gp., the 71st Recon.Group, and the 3rd Air Commando Group.

Dec '44-The first P-51D model arrives for the 23rd Ftr.Gp.,14th Air Force, in China.

Dec '44-The number of P-51s in the China/Burma/India Theatre is 417 aircraft. In 1945 the number of P-51s in the theatre is: Jan-492, Feb-510, Mar-482, Apr-527, May-518, Jun-556, Jul-753. During 1945 the distribution of P-51s among the principal CBI units is: For the AAF IBT-Jan31-40 aircraft; Mar31-35 aircraft. For the 10th AF-Jan31-no aircraft; Jul31-82 P-51 aircraft. For the 14th AF-Jan31-324 aircraft; Mar31-317 aircraft Jul31-228 P-51 aircraft.

Dec21'44-The 78th Ftr.Gp.,8th AF is the last to switch to Mustangs, and now starts to give up their P-47Ds. From now until the end of the war in Europe the 8th Air Force will have 14 P-51 and one P-47 groups. The two P-51 groups in the 9th (tactical) AF complain almost constantly of a lack of adequate P-51 aircraft replacements during the 8ths conversion period.

Dec23'44-The Mustangs of the 479th Ftr.Gp. encounter FW-190s and down 12 E/A for a loss of one P-51.

Dec31'44-There are now 95 P-51 aircraft in the Far East Air Force, Pacific, including planes on the way from the US.

Jan '45-The P-51K starts to enter 8th AF squadrons. Performance appears slightly inferior to that of the P-51D, and pilots think the Aeroproducts propeller slower-acting than the Hamilton Standard type.

Jan 1'45-P-51s of the 352nd Ftr.Gp.'s.487th Sdn. shoot down 13 FW-190s and 10 ME-109s in the course of defending their own airfield at Asch in France. The 361st Ftr.Gp. is also stationed in France. Both groups are part of the 9th Air Force.

Jan 7'45-The P-51s of the 3rd Air Commando Group arrive at Leyte in the Philippine Islands, six days after group personnel arrive. They are assigned to the 5th Air Force Fighter Command and begin combat operations.

Jan 7'45-Mustangs of the 82nd Reconnaissance Sdn. arrive at the Lingayen airstrip on Luzon, P.I., and the next day F-6 Mustangs of the 26th Photo Sdn. also arrive there.

Jan11'45-Two F-6D Mustangs of the 82nd Recon.Sdn. meet 12 Japanese fighters and a Betty bomber flying down the Cagayon Valley in Luzon,P.I. The Japanese apparently identify the F-6Ds as friendly Tony fighters. One F-6D easily shoots down the bomber and six fighters; the other Mustang gets three fighters, all in 15 minutes.

Jan31'45-In the month of January the California NAA plant production of P-51Ds reaches a peak of 570 aircraft; the Dallas plant reaches a peak of 728 Mustangs in the same month.

Feb '45-The 110th Recon.Sdn. replaces its P-40s with F-6D Mustangs after using the Curtiss aircraft through the Leyte and Mindoro campaigns in the Philippines.

Feb 3'45-The first P-51H model flies with pilot Bob Chilton.

Feb17'45-The 354th Ftr.Gp.,9th AF, converts back partly from P-47 to P-51D-20NA Mustangs (the first batch). The 36 aircraft received are divided up among the three squadrons. The 354th Group will finish the war with the highest number of aerial victories of any USAAF fighter unit-701 enemy aircraft.

Feb20'45-On this day, and the day before, the P-51s of the 55th Ftr.Gp. 8th Air Force attack 170 enemy locomotives, a group specialty.

Feb25'45-The 55th Ftr.Gp. shoots down six German ME-262 jet aircraft as they are taking off.

Mar '45-Fifty P-51D aircraft are supplied to Sweden. Together with internments of USAAF P-51 aircraft the Swedes have 161 Mustang fighters.

Mar '45-One P-51H goes to the RAF for evaluation, and another goes to the US Navy for testing.

Mar '45-Because P-51s are in short supply the 5th AF's General Kenney agrees in Washington to retain the 58th Ftr.Gp. as a P-47 organization, at least until he can test the combat suitability of the new P-47N aircraft offered him as replacements.

Mar 6'45-With ground fighting still going on, 28 P-51D aircraft of the 15th Ftr.Gp. arrive at South Field, Iwo Jima. The aircraft are quickly used for ground support, starting on the 8th, and by the 10th they stay on station in flights of eight aircraft, bombing and strafing upon request.

Mar 6'45-The 35th Ftr.Gp. of 5th AF in the Pacific receives its first P-51s early in the month, converting from P-47s. The 348th Ftr.Gp. begins converting to P-51s from its P-47s, squadron by squadron, late in March. Many pilots are reluctant to make the change.

Mar19'45-The 78th Ftr.Gp.,8th AF, on a sweep ahead of the bombers, has its first big air battle using Mustangs. The 45 P-51s destroy 32 enemy aircraft for a loss of five P-51s.

Mar21'45-The 78th Ftr.Gp. P-51s claim six ME-262 jets shot down, and the next day three more. By the end of the month they claim 13 German jets destroyed in air combat.

Mar21'45-The 21st Ftr.Gp. P-51Ds arrive at Central Field on Iwo Jima. These aircraft aid in attacks on Chichi Jima nearby.

Mar31'45-In a fierce rivalry for victory totals, the 4th Ftr.Gp. with P-51s claims 867 E/A destroyed as against 865.5 for the 56th Ftr.Gp. with P-47s.

Apr '45-P-51 groups strafe German airfields and destroy hundreds of enemy planes on the ground, but many Mustangs are lost from flak hits.

Apr 7'45-P-51s of the 15th and 21st Ftr.Gps. fly their first long range mission over Japan.

Apr10'45-P-51s of the 78th and 339th Ftr.Gps. strafe German aircraft on the ground and together claim 157 aircraft destroyed.

Apr16'45-On a fighter sweep over Kyushu, Japan weather is poor and only 57 out of 108 P-51s are able to attack.

Apr19'45-P-51s strafe airfields on Honshu Is.,Japan, and then do the same on the 23rd of the month.

Apr23'45-A P-51D first flies with an Aerojet rocket motor added.

Apr23'45-The first XP-51J, with a two-stage Allison -119 engine, is test flown by NAA pilot Joe Barton.

Apr23'45-The Mustangs of the 506th Ftr.Gp. are relieved from patrol duties at Tinian, and are assigned to North Field on Iwo Jima.

May '45-The 25 Mustang groups in the European area are split as: Nine groups at bases in Belgium, France, and Germany; five groups in Italy; and eleven groups at English airfields.

May 7'45-VE-Day is celebrated. Victory in Europe has been attained. The USAAF in Europe claims destruction by P-51s in the air of 4950 enemy aircraft and 4131 more on the ground for a loss of 2520 Mustangs, better than for any other US fighter.

May 8,45-The last German fighter, an FW-190, is destroyed in the European war by an F-6C Mustang.

May18'45-P-51s of the 5th Fighter Command are part of a force of 673 Mustangs, Thunderbolts, and Lightnings doing low-level bombing and strafing of Japanese forces in the Ipo area on Luzon, PI.

Jun 1'45-A mission ends in disaster after a 148 aircraft force of Mustangs from Iwo Jima attempts to form up in poor weather. Mid-air collisions cause the loss of 27 P-51s, the greatest operational loss of the war.

Jun '45-Twelve P-51 groups are assigned to the CBI Theatre. Four groups are in the Philippines and Okinawa; two groups are at Iwo Jima, two are in China, and four are in India and Burma.

Jun22'45-The P-51 effort over Japan is not considered very successful. From April 26 until this date they make 832 strike sorties, but only 374 are effective. The P-51s claim 64 enemy aircraft destroyed and 180 damaged on the ground plus 10 aircraft shot down in combat. Mustang losses are 11 lost in combat and seven from other causes.

Jun26'45-One hundred and forty-eight P-51s form an escort force for B-29s on a bombing raid of southern Honshu Is., Japan.

Jul '45-By this time NAA, California has built 6502 P-51Ds, and NAA, Texas has built 1454 P-51Ds, 1337 P-51Ks, 136 F-6Ds, 163 F-6K versions, and 10 TP-51D trainers.

Jul '45-The number of P-51Ds in the Pacific Ocean Area has now increased to 348.

Jul 2'45-The 77 P-51s of the 35th Ftr.Gp. move forward and arrive at Yontan in the Ryukyus. Other groups arriving there are the 348th on July 14, the 58th Ftr.Gp., and the 8th Ftr.Gp. on August 10, 1945, all with the 5th Air force.

Jul28'45-From this date until August 14 five P-51 anti-shipping sweeps are made off the China coast and on up to the coasts of Korea.

Aug '45-Production of P-51Ds ends at Dallas; the last aircraft is completed as a P-51M (a Dallas-built H model) with a Merlin engine. Of the 1700 P-51L aircraft with Packard Merlins ordered none are completed before cancellation.

Aug 5'45-Forty-nine P-51s are with a combined 5th and 7th AF group of 63 B-24s, 84 B-25s, 32 A-26s, and 97 P-47s on a strike to Tarumizu, Japan where a suicide rocket factory is reported. The town and factory are covered with general purpose and napalm bombs.

Aug15'45-The war ends; it is VJ-Day. The total of all Mustangs produced is 15,484; 5541 Mustangs are in the USAAF at war's end. By this date 370 P-51H model aircraft have been produced.

Sep '45-The nine groups of Mustangs on the European continent assume occupation duty. Five Mustang groups are assigned occupation duty in Japan.

Sep '45-After VJ-Day 1000 P-51D aircraft are cancelled, the P-51H order is reduced to 555 aircraft, 1700 P-51Ls are cancelled, as are 1628 P-51Ms.

Nov 9'45-The last P-51H leaves the NAA Inglewood, California production line.

'47-Mustangs in service are now designated F-51s; the Air National Guard operates fifteen wings of these.

'47-One hundred P-51 aircraft go to Switzerland and 48 go to Italy.

Jun '47-The first of 151 F-51s are delivered from US stocks to Canada; they phase out by 1956.

Jun '50-At the start of the Korean War Air Guard and stored P-51 aircraft total 1804. Many are called to active service.

'51-The Air Force has ten F-51 wings; three of these serve in Korea.

'52-Sweden sells 25 P-51s to Israel, 42 to the Dominican Republic, and 25 to Nicaragua.

Jan '53-At the end of the Korean War F-51 aircraft have flown 62,607 sorties, and 194 aircraft are lost to enemy action.

Jul '55-The US force of F-51D and F-51H aircraft is down to 260; by June of the next year it is down to 150 aircraft.

Oct '56-F-51s are used by Israel in the Sinai Campaign.

Mar 1, '57-The last Air National Guard F-51D-30NA goes to the Air Force Museum.

P-51 HANDLING QUALITIES AND CHARACTERISTICS

HANDLING QUALITIES
GROUND HANDLING
The ALLISON powered Mustangs were good ground handling aircraft. They had a wide tread gear, good brakes, and a tail wheel lock with a control alongside the seat. The tail wheel was unlocked for turning during taxi, was locked for takeoff, and stayed locked for the later landing run. With the poor forward vision common to tail-down fighters during taxi, the pilot used S-turns to see where he was going. Toe brakes were used as required for turning. Before taxi the rudder trim tab was set nose right and the elevator tab set slightly up in preparation for takeoff.

The MERLIN powered Mustangs were similar in ground handling. Here the tail wheel lock was on the stick. Stick pushed forward with neutral rudder unlocked it for turning. Again the view ahead was very poor and S-turns were required to check the runway.

TAKEOFF AND CLIMBOUT
ALLISON powered Mustangs were taken off with locked tail wheels and either no flaps or flaps down 10 to 20 degrees, the latter for the shortest run. A no-flaps takeoff was normal. The tail was held down until rudder control was gained, then raised slowly. Elevator power was sufficient to raise the tail at about one half takeoff speed. With flaps down the aircraft was taken off in three point attitude. As with all powerful US single engine fighters, strong right rudder was required to counteract torque during takeoff.

The more powerful MERLIN Mustangs produced even greater torque reaction which had to be carefully countered with rudder to prevent rolling off the edge of the runway.

On Mustang climbout gear was retracted and flaps, if used, were pulled up gradually. Best climbout speed, reached quickly with airplane cleanup, was 160 to 170 mph IAS.

TRIMMING
ALLISON powered Mustangs were particularly noteable for lack of required trim changes. Power or flap setting changes gave only small trim variations, and the same was true of gear retraction. The changes in tab settings for climbing and diving were negligible. Tab controls were sensitive and had to be used carefully.

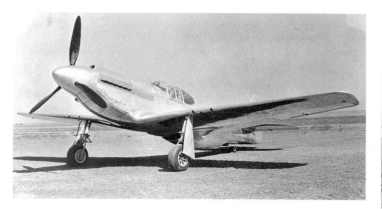

Fig.51-1 North American NA-73X, Mfr.photo via F. Dean coll. The prototype airplane of the Mustang series, ordered by the British Purchasing Commission in late May of 1940 and flying first in late October of that year. Five months from first order to first flight is fast time, even for 1940. The prototype was powered by essentially the same Allison engine with single stage single speed mechanical supercharger as the P-39 and the P-40.

Fig.51-2 North American XP-51, Mfr.photo via F. Dean coll. When the British ordered 320 NA-73 fighters in May, 1940 the US Army approved the sale, but made a requirement that two of the aircraft be delivered to them as XP-51s. The photo shows one of these in Army markings and heavily retouched so any indication of armament is missing. For some reason the retoucher heavily emphasized an antenna wire.

Fig.51-3 North American XP-51, F. Dean coll. One of the two XP-51 aircraft showing a revised carburetor intake duct atop the engine cowl and indicating the armament complement. This was two .50 caliber nose machine guns in an unusual low mounting and two .30 caliber and one .50 caliber machine gun in each wing, pretty heavy armament for the period.

Fig.51-4 Civil North American Mustang I, photo via R. Besecker. A beautifully restored aircraft painted up as a British Mustang I photographed at Reno, Nevada. The British order for a total of 620 aircraft set up North American as a fighter producer whereas they had been previously known mainly as a manufacturer of trainer aircraft. Mustang I first flight took place in late April of 1941, about eight months before the US entered the war, and the first operational mission for the British was in May, 1942 on a cross-channel raid. English pilots liked the fighter; it had excellent performance at low to medium altitudes and handled well.

Trimmability was also quite good in the MERLIN Mustangs, and tabs were sensitive. In these versions directional trim changed more with speed and power changes. When the rudder trim system was changed and rigged as an anti-balance tab to give opposite boost, a resulting disadvantage was more tab was required to trim the aircraft from a climb into a dive.

Along with trimming the airplane for longer term steady flight conditions, some pilots trimmed their aircraft almost continuously to wash out any high stick or pedal force during maneuvering in combat.

DIVE AND RECOVERY

The ALLISON Mustangs had a limit dive speed of 505 mph IAS. Up to the normally attained diving speeds of the airplane very little trouble was encountered with instability or other peculiar flight characteristics generally inherent in most airplanes of the period at

higher Mach numbers. This was due principally to low airplane drag, relatively moderate engine power, and the favorable characteristics of the three blade narrow chord propeller. Maximum allowed engine speed in a dive was 3120 RPM. Low elevator forces were encountered in dive recovery, and elevator tab use was not required. These light control forces caused the structural failure of a few airplanes where pilots failed to realize the easy attainability of very high load factors.

The P-51B and P-51C airplanes with MERLIN engines were considerably heavier, and used a propeller with four wide chord blades to efficiently utilize the increased engine power, particu-

Fig.51-5 North American P-51, Ser.41-37324, Mfr.photo via F. Dean coll. With the new Army drab paint job and the red center now missing from the national insignia, a cannon-equipped P-51 is shown in this photo where the lean appearance of the aircraft is emphasized. First appearing in the summer of 1942, 150 of this version came off North American production lines with a substantial number converted to F-6A reconnaissance aircraft.

Fig.51-6 North American P-51, Mfr.photo via F. Dean coll. A heavily retouched flight photo of the P-51 with all indications of armament obliterated by the censor whose highlighting near the leading edge of the wing has distorted the curve of the new laminar flow airfoil shape. The forward station of the carburetor scoop has been moved up close behind the propeller. P-51 aircraft could touch 380 to 390 miles per hour at a medium altitude. Two P-51 airframes were to be converted to XP-78 aircraft using Merlin engines with two stage superchargers; later the two were redesignated XP-51Bs.

Fig.51-7 North American P-51, Mfr.photo via F. Dean coll. The four 20mm cannon of the P-51 model are well shown here. Each cannon had a maximum supply of 125 rounds of ammunition. A good deal of testing was done to assure a minimum effect of the cannon installation on wing airflow. P-51 production took place after that of the British Mustang I and prior to the A-36A dive bomber version.

Fig.51-8 North American A-36A, Ser.42-83795, photo via P.M. Bowers. This is a boneyard photo of a handsome airplane. Unlike the Lockheed A-29 Hudsons and Curtiss A-25 Helldivers in the background this Mustang still has its (Allison) engine. The story has it the Army ran out of fighter funds temporarily but had plenty of money for attack/dive bombers, so to keep the line going Dutch Kindleberger of North American, ever inventive, decided to equip the Mustang with bomb racks and dive brakes and sell it as a dive bomber. In any case he was successful to the extent of producing 500 airplanes for the Army starting in October, 1942 and lasting into early 1943.

larly for high altitude flight. The new propeller caused a marked decrease in directional stability which became serious at high speeds such that in dives rudder pedal forces tended to decrease, rather than increase as is normal, at yaw angles greater than ten degrees. If the pilot did not apply sufficient opposite rudder the airplane tended to increase the slip or skid by itself, and eventually got into a nasty snap roll or a spin entry. Horizontal tail failures were occurring as a result until the forward spar of the stabilizer was strengthened. Early P-51D aircraft were still directionally unstable ; as one pilot said "Directional stability is bad as speed increases in a dive."

A dorsal fin was added to increase directional stability and a rudder anti-balance tab provided to keep pedal forces acting in the proper manner. The tail changes were made separately on in-service aircraft, and incorporated simultaneously on new airplanes. Several pilots used the directional instability on their unmodified P-51B and C airplanes to provide an evasive maneuver in combat. In a steep high speed dive a pilot deliberately pushing the controls to give the consequent series of violent snap rolls was quite sure of losing a pursuer as well as getting bruised himself from being thrown

Fig.51-9 North American A-36A Mustangs, Ser.42-83707 etc., Mfr. photo via F. Dean coll. A trio of A-36As pose for the North American photographer. First flight of this version took place in September of 1942 with delivery starting the next month. In April of 1943 two groups of Mustangs, sometimes unofficially called Invaders, were operating with the Northwest African Air Force in Morocco. In June of 1943 they carried out many dive bombing missions against the Mediterranean island of Pantelleria prior to the Sicily invasion. They were also operated in Italy later and in India.

Fig.51-10 North American P-51A Mustang, photo via P.M. Bowers. This Mustang appeared in March of 1943 with a new variant of the Allison engine having a COMBAT rating of 1330 horsepower at 11800 feet. Labeled Mustang II by the British the P-51A achieved its greatest speed a few thousand feet higher than the P-51. Importantly, wing store stations for 150 gallon fuel tanks or bombs were incorporated. The first P-51As went to operational training units in Florida, and later some of these aircraft moved to India and operated together with A-36A airplanes.

Fig.51-11 Civil North American P-51A Mustang, photo via R. Besecker. This P-51A lasted long enough to obtain a civil NX licence just post-war. At the end of 1943 sixty of the 310 P-51A fighters produced were operational in North Africa where they were used mainly for reconnaissance, and in the China/Burma/India Theatre. The only Allison powered Mustangs used in the European Theatre were operated by Britain. Besides the Mustang I versions fifty P-51As were furnished to the British as Mustang IIs. They had four .50 caliber wing guns with an option to install two .50 caliber fuselage synchronized guns low alongside the engine.

Fig.51-14 North American P-51C Mustang, Ser.42-103751, Mfr. photo via Bill Vance The P-51C was in all essentials the same as the P-51B but built in North American's Dallas, Texas plant instead of in California. This C model, purchased with War Bond sales of the Milwaukee Boy Scouts, shows off the elegant lines of the Merlin Mustang. The Texas plant built 1750 Cs and the California plant 1988 Bs. Unfilled P-51A contracts were finished as Merlin B and C versions. The perforated cowl panel in the nose area served as an alternate carburetor air inlet.

around. There were some complaints about losing this evasive capability on the modified airplanes.

In P-51B, C, D, and K aircraft incorporating the aft fuselage fuel tank, added for range extension, longitudinal stability was lost with that tank more than half full, since this condition moved the airplane center of gravity aft. The instability was particularly dangerous in that a dive pullout at high speed was always accompanied by a stick force reversal which, unless opposed by the pilot, would quickly carry the plane into an extreme accellerated condition where the wings would fail. The incidence of structural wing failures rose sharply because it was difficult for a pilot who had always flown a stable airplane to revise his flying technique to handle a dangerously unstable one. To meet this situation a twenty pound bobweight was added to the elevator control system of all airplanes. This fix

eliminated the stick force reversal in dive pullouts and made the airplane marginally stable with about 35 gallons of fuel in the 85 gallon fuselage tank.

From the structural strength viewpoint, because the airplane was heavier than earlier models the allowable dive pullout g loading of a P-51D with full internal fuel was 6.3 with ultimate breaking loads occurring at one and a half times this figure, or 9.5g. Maximum permissible dive speed for a P-51D was 505 mph IAS below 9000 feet and 300 mph IAS (539 mph TAS and Mach .81) at 35000 feet. If these diving limits were exceeded compressibility would be experienced. Maximum allowed engine overspeed in a dive was 3300 RPM, or 10 percent over normal maximum. In a dive compressibility effects were indicated by instability, uncontrollable rolling or pitching, stiffness of controls, or combinations

Fig.51-12 North American XP-78/XP-51B Mustang, Mfr. photo via F. Dean coll. One of the two P-51 airframes held out to be fitted with a Packard-produced Rolls Royce Merlin engine. It still retains the four wing cannon armament of the P-51, later to be changed in production to four .50 caliber machine guns, quite a reduction in hitting power. The nose intake just below the propeller spinner serviced the updraft carburetor of the Merlin. Britain did much of the early work with regard to a P-51/Merlin engine combination and made initial studies as early as July, 1942. The English also did test work on five airframes starting in August that year.

Fig.51-13 North American P-51B Mustang, Mfr. photo via F. Dean coll. An early P-51B Mustang with its Merlin engine and two stage mechanical supercharger providing considerably improved performance at higher altitudes, and a four bladed Hamilton propeller of much higher total activity factor with blade cuffs all to absorb the extra power. The ports for the two .50 caliber guns can be seen in the starboard wing. The whole powerplant, including the cooling radiator and air ducting, had to be redesigned compared to the Allison Mustang installation. The cockpit enclosure of the earlier Mustangs was retained.

Fig.51-15 North American P-51C Mustang, Ser.43-25148, Mfr. photo via F. Dean coll. A Dallas-produced Merlin powered Mustang flies over a flat Texas country-side. The Texas plant started turning out Merlin Mustangs in early August, 1943, just three months after the first production B model flew. As with all new aircraft there were bugs in early planes to the extent one combat pilot complained he was flying "an experimental aircraft". Most problems were cleared up fairly quickly under wartime pressures, but armament difficulties persisted, and when the fuse-lage fuel tank was installed special precautions had to be taken by the pilot when that tank was full.

Fig.51-16 Civil North American P-51B or C Mustang, photo via R. Besecker. A civil Merlin Mustang photographed in the 1980s at the Reno Air races. Though there are even today many P-51D or P-51K airplanes still in flight status, Mustangs with the original canopy arrangement are rare. Pilot visibility was lacking in this model; the British refitted their aircraft with a "Malcomb Hood", a bulged frameless arrange-ment that provided considerable visibility improvement. US Navy tests indicated this Mustang had unsatisfactory pilot vision, though their own Corsair was cer-tainly no standard to go by!

of these along with vibration. Nose-heaviness (tuck-under) was noticeable, and became more severe with speed increases. The lon-gitudinal characteristics remained normal until Mach .72 to .74. Dive recovery procedure was to reduce power and pull up as gradu-ally as possible depending on aircraft altitude. The elevator trim tab was not normally used to aid recovery.

In July 1944 Wright Field test pilots explored the high speed dive characteristics of a MERLIN powered Mustang. A series of dive tests were made starting from about 35000 feet in a test air-plane equipped with a Mach meter. The idea was to explore the effects of compressibility such as buffeting, vibration, control force

changes, and so on. Initial dives showed the onset of the problem to occur at just under Mach .75. Additional dives were made, using three test pilots, which carried the aircraft successively to Mach .77, then .79, and on up to Mach .81, and finally to Mach .83 (605 mph). As the dive Mach number was increased the compressibility effects became more violent, but the aircraft was still controllable, and it was possible to fly it out of the problem when desired. At Mach .83 the shaking and buffeting of the aircraft was so strong that it was decided to explore no further. The airplane had suffered considerable structural damage and was written off.

Fig.51-17 Civil North American P-51C Mustang, photo via R. Besecker. A typical civil conversion of the Mustang with the CBS Television "eye" logo photographed sometime in the 1950s. This airplane has the dorsal fin incorporated to counter destabilizing effects of the wide chord four bladed propeller, and chances are the fuselage fuel tank added for extra combat radius capability on military machines was either removed or carefully restricted as to use. From an exterior viewpoint the airplane looks pretty much "stock", but no doubt was considerably lighter than an armed military counterpart.

Fig.51-18 North American P-51D Mustang, Ser.44-14214, Mfr. photo via F. Dean coll. A factory flight photo of the P-51D Mustang showing two of the major changes from earlier versions, the new frameless "bubble" canopy and cutdown rear deck-ing along with the three machine guns in each wing. In addition the D incorporated a new Merlin version, higher capacity bomb racks, and aileron modifications.

Fig.51-19 North American P-51D Mustangs, Ser.44-13719 etc.USAAF photo via Pete Howell. D model Mustangs are shown in European skies. Note the far airplane hasn't yet had the dorsal fin installed nor, probably, the rudder anti-balance tab. These changes were usually made separately on in-service aircraft and together on factory-new airplanes. Since P-51D airplanes were substantially (about 550 pounds in empty weight) heavier than early Allison models, flight limit maneuver load factor allowed was less.

Fig.51-20 North American P-51D Mustang, Ser.44-14017, US Navy photo via H. Andrews. What? A sea-going Mustang? Yes, this P-51D version with a tail hook installed was tested aboard a Navy aircraft carrier. Note the interesting vortex patterns set up off the the propeller blade tips in the damp air as the Mustang readied for takeoff. In head-to-head tests of a P-51B/C against F4U-1D aircraft the Navy found they preferred the Corsair. One of the items criticized by the Navy was the less than desireable low speed lateral control of the P-51 for carrier approaches.

At airspeeds over 450 mph IAS longitudinal porpoising often occurred on MERLIN powered P-51 airplanes with fabric covered elevators, particularly with some nose up trim. The porpoising resulted from fabric bulging at the high speed, resulting in airflow breakdown and elevator oscillation. On the P-51D-30 airplane, and as a modification to other P-51D aircraft metal covered elevators were installed to improve high speed flying qualities. Since the metal covered elevators did not bulge, the normal tendency was for the aircraft to become increasingly nose heavy at very high speeds, and to compensate for this undesireable characteristic, most noticeable at high altitudes, the incidence setting of the horizontal stabilizer was decreased from one and a half degrees nose up to only one half

degree nose up, done at the same time as the change to metal covered elevators. Without the incidence change of the stabilizer the pilot would have observed a sharp pitch forward of the airplane, and a sharp reversal of control stick forces from push to pull as the high speed placard limits were reached. With these changes the pitch tendency was hardly noticeable, however the airplane required not only additional nose heavy trim for stabilized level flight, but even further nose heavy trim as the airplane was maneuvered from a climb into a dive. It was recommended that at speeds above 400 mph IAS the pilot should never fully trim the elevator for hands off flight, but should always maintain a slightly tail heavy trim requiring a forward pressure on the stick. By this procedure porpoising of

Fig.51-21 North American P-51D Mustang, F. Dean photo. A D-25 Mustang sits for a picture at a 1946 air show with "buzz" markings on the fuselage and underwing bomb/tank racks along with rocket standoffs. The author remembers the P-51D took a back seat to the then-new P-51H versions that performed flight demonstrations. More P-51Ds were produced by far than any other versions, over 8000 airplanes.

Fig.51-22 North American P-51D Mustang, Ser.44-72948, photo via P.M. Bowers An Air Force "Spam Can" cruises just off shore in post-war "buzz" marks, so called because the letters and numbers were large enough to provide a ground observer relatively easy airplane identification during any illegal low altitude buzz jobs. Pilots agreed the bubble canopy instituted on the P-51D provided them a marvelous overall visibility bonus compared to earlier P-51s.

Fig.51-23 North American P-51D Mustang, photo via P.M. Bowers. Excellent flight photo of a P-51D emphasizing attractive overall lines. The P-51 had the lowest equivalent flat plate drag area of any US World War II production fighter, certainly due in part to the North American-NACA low drag laminar flow airfoiled wing. Use of these wing section profiles delayed the drag rise due to Mach number significantly more than the drag rise of other US aircraft with older style airfoil sections.

Fig.51-24 Civil North American P-51D Mustang, F. Dean photo. Done up in wartime markings and converted to a two place airplane by removal of the fuselage fuel tank, this beautifully restored P-51 is run up at a 1980s air show in Atlantic City, New Jersey. Even with the 85 gallon fuel tank missing the P-51D still had 184 gallons of internal wing tank fuel, suficient for a very practical civilian cruising range.

the airplane could be avoided, even at the limit airspeeds. However with fuel in the fuselage tank more caution had to be used in the transition from dives to pullout or into a sharp turn because the normal stick reversal would still occur.

MANEUVERING

The maneuvering qualities of the ALLISON powered airplanes were exceptional. All normal acrobatics were permitted, but inverted flying was limited to ten seconds. Because the airplane was light compared to later models it was good for an allowable flight limit load factor of eight g and of 12 g ultimate breaking load factor. The

airplane was positively stable under all flight conditions both stick fixed and stick free, and dynamic stability was satisfactory. The pilot had to apply a pull force on the stick to produce positive g, had to push on the rudder pedal to produce yaw, and had to apply side force on the stick to produce roll, and all of these required pilot forces were proportional to the result obtained through the speed range of the aircraft. There were no control force reversals. Pilots liked the aircraft because, in addition to its good low to medium altitude performance and flying characteristics, its working limits of speed and acceleration could be obtained with a minimum of physical effort on the part of the pilot. The control forces were un-

Fig.51-25 Civil North American P-51D Mustang, F. Dean photo. A civil P-51D taxiing in after an air show flying demonstration in the late 1980s, done up in invasion stripes and combat markings. A passenger is easily visible aft of the pilot. Modified canopies were built for a few in-service two seaters, but this canopy is stock, and provides little clearance for a tall passenger when closed. Since the Merlin P-51s were unstable with a full fuselage tank it was a wise move to remove that tank for any non-wartime use.

Fig.51-26 Civil North American P-51D Mustang, F. Dean photo. This airplane could almost be a Mustang in wartime if it were not for the give-aways of the small civil N-number beneath the horizontal stabilizer and the hard helmet perched atop the windshield. With dummy gun muzzles and bomb racks in place the airplane looks warlike enough. According to the writing on the canopy Ge Ge was piloted, and probably owned, by a Mr. Scott P. Smith. Cooling radiator exit air was dumped overboard via the exit chute seen wide open just below the fuselage star.

Fig.51-28 Civil North American P-51D, Ser.44-73586, F. Dean photo. Piloted by Col. John Trainer of New Hampshire, this civilian P-51D flew down to Pennsylvania to attend an air show in the late 1970s. Looking a bit worn, but quite serviceable, Gentle Libby put on a fine display. After the last day of the show Col. Trainer took off in marginal weather to return home, but the aircraft crashed locally, killing the pilot. P-51s were never the easiest plane to handle and needed experienced piloting.

Fig.51-29 Civil North American P-51D Mustang, Ser.44-73856, F. Dean photo. Gentle Libby taxis out for takeoff. Pilots had somewhat different views of Mustang flight characteristics; it seemed the wartime pilots were more forgiving in their evaluation than some of the late comers flying civil P-51s. An experienced modern military test pilot condemned the P-51D for its vicious stall-spin characteristics. A wartime combat ace noted that perhaps the P-51 didn't have as much stall warning as a pilot might like, but didn't recall it as any problem for pilots.

usually light. One pilot commented "Stick forces on the old original ALLISON P-51 were about as nice as anybody ever had". It is true that these light control forces indirectly caused the loss of a few airplanes.

In turns elevator control of the ALLISON version was sufficient to develop either the allowable eight g limit load factor or maximum lift coefficient throughout the speed range, and the variation of elevator angle with normal acceleration in steady 180 degree turns was stable. The aircraft was sensitive to small stick movements, but stick force gradients were satisfactory. Normal acceleration in steady 180 degree turns varied linearly with stick force, as was desireable. On the XP-51 with forward centers of gravity

the stick force per g was 8.3 pounds. At more rearward centers of gravity the value was somewhat less.

The maneuvering qualities of the MERLIN powered P-51B/C and D/K airplanes were more complex than those of the ALLISON engined versions. In turning flight these Mustangs could be stable or unstable longitudinally depending on how much fuel was in the fuselage tank added on to increase range. Pulling high g levels in a quick turn with considerable fuel in that tank would mean stick reversal where the pilot would have to brace himself to oppose backward travel of the stick. The actual motion of the stick was much less apparent than the reversal of force obtained. The pilot definately had to apply a push force to prevent a further tightning of the turn

Fig.51-27 Civil North American P-51D, Ser.44-72308, R. Besecker photo. Showing its classic side elevation, Ridge Runner was photographed at the Reno Air Races several years ago and appears in stock condition with very careful restoration apparent. Among the civilian signs are the N-number at the rear fuselage and lack of a gunsight on the cockpit forward coaming. Looking at the wing tip an indication can be seen of maximum airfoil thickness more aft than on conventional airfoils of the wartime period. After the aerodynamacists carefully worked out the detailed technical aspects of the laminar flow wing section they found it matched almost perfectly the contours of a trout looking at the fish from the top.

Fig.51-31 Civil North American P-51D Mustang, photo via P.M. Bowers. Another well kept civilian Mustang with a race number on its tail, Seattle Miss strikes a fine pose for the photographer. Here again the maximum thickness of the wing airfoil is shown to be well back on the chord. The plain flap is deflected full down. It can be seen the upper lip of the main air scoop is set down off the fuselage enough to avoid slower moving boundary layer air. The substantial dorsal fin is very apparent in this picture.

which, if unopposed, could result in a high speed stall and possible wing structural failure. Turns at speeds above 250 mph IAS and above four g were particularly dangerous. In these cases a pilot not equipped with an anti-g suit could be at least partially blacked out, and consequently less alert to the stick reversal. As noted earlier the addition of a 20 pound bobweight helped, though it was by no means a cure-all. At a 1944 conference the comment was made that as the P-51 developed the aircraft, by admission of the Army and the British and North American itself, had gotten to be a less nice flying machine.

The experimental ALLISON powered prototype airplane was disappointing in roll rate performance, but further experimentation with details of aileron design geometry improved the situation. One British pilot said "Yes I did like the ailerons on the P-51 with the ALLISON engine. But the US Army universally didn't like them. The original P-51 ailerons had restricted throw because they were of the internal balance type. But I was enthused about the rolling characteristics of these ailerons at high speed. They were quite low in rolling response at low speed, though they were light". A US pilot agreed "They stank on the original ALLISON P-51. Those ailerons were as good as the later P-51B at high speed though. The Brits liked the ailerons because they were operating at high speed, and the US Army was operating at low speed".

Fig.51-30 Civil North American P-51D Mustang, F. Dean photo. Awaiting clearance to get in line for takeoff and hoping he will not overheat, with radiator duct exit full open, a civil Mustang shows off for an appreciative 1980s crowd. The rearing Mustang symbol on the fin was a favorite of hobbyist owners. The patch just under the Miss Kat Brat name up front is the logo of the British Rolls Royce Company, fathers of the Merlin V-12 engine. There are many accounts of the "terrific yaw" tendency due to propeller torque reaction when the power was poured to the Mustang on takeoff.

Fig.51-31A Civil North American P-51D Mustang, R. Besecker photo (5x7). A Mustang with racing number and civil registration, otherwise unadorned. The photo was taken at Reno, Nevada in November of 1971. The bare metal seems to emphasize the rakish P-51 lines. Much has been made of the fact layout of the fuselage was accomplished using all second degree mathematical curves.

Fig.51-32 Civil North American P-51D Mustang, R. Besecker photo. A P-51D painted up in what appears to be British colors as a Mustang IV is present at the Reno Air Races. With no obvious modifications for racing and absence of a racing number, this Mustang, apparently owned by Mr. Jimmy Leonard of Ocala, Florida may have just come in to watch. This aircraft has the wartime standard retractable tail wheel; some post-war Air Force Mustangs operated with the tail wheel fixed down. Note the civil Bell P-63F airplane in the background, a type easily distinguished by the shape of its vertical tail.

Fig.51-33 Civil North American P-51D Mustang, F. Dean photo. Showing handsome lines with its Merlin ticking over in slow taxi, the Mustang of a well-heeled hobbyist comes in after an early 1980s air show. Pilot's hard hat, absence of wing guns, and lightplane background assure that this P-51 is a latter-day peaceful fighter. The aft location of the coolant radiator resulted in long coolant line runs from the engine and back, increasing aircraft vulnerable area over an airplane like the P-40. The P-51 was considered quite vulnerable during ground attack missions.

Fig.51-34 Civil North American P-51D Mustang, F. Dean photo. At the Cape May, New Jersey airport this beautifully restored civil P-51D sits on the hardstand in the 1980s. The relatively simple wide tread main landing gear arrangement is well shown here, designed to retract neatly into wells formed by a forward-raked inboard wing section ahead of the wing front spar. The shock strut took vertical, side, and drag landing loads up into wing structural fittings. A landing light was in the wheel well.

The MERLIN powered P-51B/C and D/K airplanes had internally sealed and balanced ailerons which tended to keep stick forces light. Generally the roll rate performance of these ailerons at high speeds equalled or was slightly improved over the earlier P-51, but low speed performance was substantially increased. Although one pilot at a conference rated P-51D ailerons as "best in the show", another noted "weak ailerons at low speed", and a US Navy evaluation of a P-51B airplane said "The P-51B lateral control at low speeds is marginal, and would not be sufficient for carrier operations". The P-51D flight manual indicated lateral control at low speeds tended to be slightly mushy, but control was still good.

Even after the horizontal tails of P-51B/C airplanes were strengthened to withstand the very high speed snap maneuvers resulting from the directional instability noted earlier, slow rolls were prohibited. This was because the inverted snap maneuver which often occurred during the portion of the slow roll where controls were well crossed was catching the pilot unawares, and the violence of the maneuver was causing many bumps and bruises, scratches, and torn flying suits. This is where the dorsal fin and reverse boost rudder tab were incorporated, and the slow roll restriction was then lifted.

APPROACH AND LANDING

On the approach the ALLISON Mustang limit speed for gear down was 170 mph IAS and for flaps 165 mph IAS. In clean configuration at best glide speed of 140 mph IAS the glide was fairly flat due to low airplane drag with nose very high and poor forward visibility. Dropping gear and flaps steepened the glide angle, and best over the fence speed was 100 to 110 mph IAS.

Approach characteristics of the MERLIN Mustangs were similar; a typical over the fence speed was 120 mph IAS with touchdown at 90. Although the pilot's manual called for continuous back pressure on the stick to obtain a tail low attitude for touchdown, it was common for combat pilots landing in flights to make tail up level landings to see better for as long as possible.

As noted in the earlier section on ground handling, because of the wide landing gear tread and locked tail wheel the Mustang landing characteristics were good. Although one pilot mentioned a lack of directional stability on the landing rollout, a large number of pilots rated P-51D approach and landing characteristics good.

As to refused landing or waveoff characteristics, an experienced combat pilot noted "If you opened the throttle too fast it would roll to the left, and you could lose it".

STALLS AND SPINS

One g stalls in ALLISON Mustangs were characterized as follows: With a clean airplane, power on, warnings were mild tail buffet and light aileron snatching. The stall break motion was a right roll which quickened with more aft stick, and then a steep spiral. With a dirty airplane there was no warning, but a mild and easily controlled rolloff. Recovery was "entirely normal by release of back pressure on the stick and application of rudder opposite from the dropping wing". There was a time element involved. In the NACA flight test report of the XP-51 airplane "By use of the rudder or aileron control it was possible to check or correct the airplane movement (at stall break), but such control was possible for only a short time, after which the airplane tended to roll violently".

For high speed (accelerated) stalls of the ALLISON Mustangs there are notations varying from "no stall warnings" (XP-51) to "sharp buffeting at the elevators and wing root"(A-36). For general high speed stall characteristics those of the XP-51 "compared favorably with other modern fighters", and the A-36 "recovered immediately when back pressure on the stick was released".

One g stalls in MERLIN Mustangs were characterized generally the same as their predecessors. At one time the aircraft was restricted from power on stalls, but with the dorsal fin addition the restriction was lifted. At a fighter conference pilots rated P-51D stall warning characteristics "good to fair". Three pilots noted a shake and three more a shudder. Of twenty five pilots flying the P-51D seventeen labeled recovery characteristics good, seven said fair, and one noted poor.

MERLIN Mustangs accelerated stall behavior is labeled anywhere between "Sharp buffet warnings and almost immediate recovery with stick pressure release" (1940s) to a modern pilot's "totally inadequate stall warning and vicious departure".

On the ALLISON Mustangs there was a difference between left and right spins. The left spin oscillated from 80 degrees below the horizon back to the horizon during the first turn, dampening out to 50 degrees during the second turn, and then became stable, smooth, and quiet with the nose 30 to 40 degrees below the horizon. The right spin started exactly like the left spin, but the oscillations continued without increasing or decreasing. Spin recovery procedure was the same for both ways. Upon application of opposite rudder the nose dropped slightly and the spin speeded up rapidly for one and a quarter turns after which it stopped. Recovery was made normally using full opposite rudder followed by neutral stick.

For the MERLIN powered P-51D spins were not to be performed intentionally. In a power on spin the nose remained 10 to 20 degrees above the horizon, and recovery control had no effect on the aircraft unless the throttle was completely retarded. Power on spins were considered extremely dangerous in the P-51D. The recovery procedure was to close the throttle and apply flight controls as in a power off spin recovery. Power off spins in a P-51D were uncomfortable because of heavy oscillations which usually would not dampen out. When a spin was started the aircraft snapped a half turn in the spin direction with the nose dropping to near vertical. At the end of one turn to or above the horizon the spin slowed down,

Fig.51-35 Civil Racer North American P-51D Mustang, R. Stukey photo via Joe Weathers. One of many Mustang racers seen at the Reno Races in past years, Miss Candace runs up on the tarmac. An obvious modification is the cut-down canopy, but P-51 racers had many changes under the skin. Special tuned Merlin racing engines and exotic fuel mixtures along with special cooling systems were incorporated for low altitude high speed closed course racing.

Fig.51-36 North American TP-51D Mustang, Ser.44-84662, photo via P.M. Bowers
One of the very few two place trainer Mustangs acquired by the Air Force. The new canopy gave the back seat man more room than the average converted civil two place P-51s as can be seen. This aircraft illustrates the use of the fixed tail wheel on some post-war Air Force Mustangs. Gun and store station provisions are incorporated. Whether a full set of controls and displays was provided is not known. Ten of these aircraft were put out by the Dallas plant.

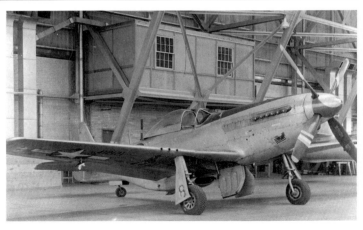

Fig.51-37 North American P-51K, Ser.44-12121, Don Campbell photo via F. Dean coll. A P-51K version of the Mustang, essentially the same as the D. Over 1300 were built, and used the Aeroproducts propeller instead of a Hamilton unit; both propellers were hydraulically operated. The K version started into operations in the fall of 1944 after some propeller balance and vibration problems got sorted out. Armed reconnaissance versions of the P-51K were labeled F-6Ks.

occasionally coming to a complete stop. The aircraft then snapped a half turn with the nose dropping to 50 to 60 degrees below the horizon and continued as during the first turn. Some rudder buffet was noticeable. When controls were applied for recovery the nose dropped to near vertical position and the spin speeded up, and then stopped in one to one and a quarter turns. About one thousand feet of altitude was lost for every spin turn. Recovery took as many as five or six turns after the rudder was applied, and 9000 to 10000 feet of total altitude could be lost.

CHARACTERISTICS
COCKPIT
The Mustang cockpit was small for a US fighter. One pilot thought it was "cramped for space". There was less space than in a P-40 cockpit, and it was slightly less comfortable, according to a pilot

who had flown both. Of one large group of US service, British, and contractor pilots almost two thirds rated the P-51D cockpit comfort good and another 20 percent said fair. One modern evaluation reported a P-51D cockpit more comfortable than a P-47D, a Hellcat, or a Corsair. These pilots were not evaluating comfort under extreme hot or cold conditions. Some in-theatre pilots complained the bubble canopied P-51D cockpit was very warm in low and moderate altitude summer flying conditions; many others suffered from the cold resulting from inadequate cockpit heating during long high altitude and/or winter flying conditions in escort missions over Europe.

MERLIN Mustang cockpit arrangements were usually considered good by pilots, and the P-51D-5 cockpit was "cleaned up a good bit" from the P-51B. On the P-51D-15 the seat was modified

Fig.51-38 North American CTF-51D Mustang, photo via P.M. Bowers. Set up as a post-war Air National Guard aircraft, 01-Z sports a tall vertical tail modification quite similar to that on the P-51H. The higher aspect ratio of the vertical surface substantially increased tail effectiveness and the increased area aided directional stability, something that Merlin P-51 aircraft could always use. Early short vertical tailed P-51Ds without a dorsal fin encountered stability difficulties.

Fig.51-39 North American XP-51F Mustang, Ser.43-43333, Mfr. photo via F. Dean coll. One of three experimental F models built as part of a cooperative US-British light fighter program. Built generally along standard Mustang configuration lines, this aircraft was a major redesign in all respects. The contract for five lightweight fighter prototypes was signed in July of 1943. Besides the F the program included an XP-51G and and XP-51J. By June, 1944 the second XP-51F had made seven flights and the third aircraft had been sent to Britain for tests.

Fig.51-40 North American P-51H Mustang, photo via P.M. Bowers. Essentially an all new Mustang with redesigned structure and a new version of the Merlin engine providing no less than 1930 horsepower COMBAT rating at 10000 feet at a manifold pressure of 80 inches of mercury, the P-51H was ordered to the extent of 1000 airplanes in June of 1944. First flight occurred in February, 1945, and in March one P-51H was sent to the UK for tests. Though there has been considerable discussion as to whether this model ever got into Pacific combat it is now generally conceded that it did not.

to increase pilot comfort. Seat and pedal adjustments were adequate to accomodate various pilot sizes.

VISIBILITY

Three different cockpit canopies were utilized on various P-51 models. The original canopy, the so-called "birdcage", was used on ALLISON engined aircraft and MERLIN powered B and C Mustangs. The US Navy evaluation of the birdcage was "Vision in the P-51B is notably poor forward because of the low pilot position and heavy framing. Vision aft is also poor because of limited head travel allowed by the narrow cockpit". P-51Bs supplied to the British as Mustang III aircraft had the same canopy arrangement, and the RAF agreed with the US Navy. A new bulged frameless sliding hood was designed in England by a Mr. R. Malcombe and fitted to most British Mustangs. Some of these new canopies were acquired by Americans in the UK and, as attested by one combat veteran "The visibility was excellent". The third Mustang cockpit canopy was introduced with the extensive redesign of the B and C into the P-51D. Here a change was made to a frameless full "bubble" aft of the windshield which gave really good visibility. Pilots made comments as "Best all-around visibility (of eight different fighters)", "Had the best field of view (of four US fighters)", "It was a delight to fly in that bubble canopy", and "The all-around view was excellent". So from the visibility perspective North American got it right on the second try, and for once all pilots agreed.

VULNERABILITY/ARMOR

Mustang aircraft were more vulnerable to projectile strikes than some other US fighters, particularly during ground attack runs. The liquid cooled powerplant would overheat and shut down quickly with a hit in the cooling system. The P-51 system was strung out under the fuselage from the engine area back under the wing trail-

ing edge to the cooler, and presented a larger vulnerable area than that of the P-40. The latter had its liquid cooling system parts grouped in the nose area. The P-51 was considerably more vulnerable than the air cooled radial engined fighters such as the P-47 and Navy types. A large group of service and test pilots ranked the P-51D last of eight US and British fighters in the category "best all-around armor".

GUN PLATFORM AND WEAPON PERFORMANCE

In ALLISON powered Mustangs the pilot could obtain high maneuverability with minimum effort; his ability to track and aim on a target was improved as a result of unusually light control forces. MERLIN powered Mustang gun platform qualities were about the same as a P-40, but not as good as a P-38 or P-47. At a conference four pilots rated P-51D gun platform qualities good, sixteen pilots rated them fair, and nine gave a poor rating. The group was a mixture of US Army, Navy, Marine Corps, and US fighter contractor test pilots.

As to weapon performance, one experienced combat pilot of MERLIN Mustangs remarked "Gun trouble was hardly uncommon on the P-51". On the four gun P-51B and P-51C aircraft the guns did not sit upright in their mounts, but were inclined partly on their sides. The ammunition cans were just outboard and ammunition belts crossed over the top of the gun and entered the feed mechanism in a sharp curve. There was a great deal of trouble in combat; belt links broke from combat maneuvers and guns often jammed from poor feeding and ejection provisions. It was not uncommon for Eighth Air Force P-51Bs to return from a mission with half or more of their guns out of action. Another common problem was freezing of oil on gun bolts and of firing solonoids. In the 357th FG the latter problem was solved by covering the solonoid with a heavy wrapping of tape and a coat of shellac.

Fig.51-41 North American P-51H Mustang, Ser.44-64192, photo via P.M. Bowers Pretty near at the peak of piston engine and propeller fighter design, the P-51H was produced in quantity, though not to full wartime standards. A total of 370 airplanes had been put out by North American by war's end, and after V-J Day the H order was reduced to 555 aircraft total. They became a standard Air Force first line fighter until the jets came in. The aircraft pictured was used for airfoil testing post-war.

Fig.51-42 North American P-51H Mustang, Ser.44-64192, photo via Herb Fyfield, Even more rakish than the P-51D, though certainly showing its lineage, the P-51H poses for a fine camera shot. The structure of this model met the full 8.0 g positive flight maneuver load factor of the Air Force requirements at design weight, whereas that of the P-51D at full gross weight reached limit loading at about 6.3 g. This result came about because the D had the same airframe structurally as the much lighter earlier Allison powered P-51s. Note the high aspect ratio tall tail of the H and the revised air inlet contour. Here again the farther aft maximum thickness of a new laminar flow airfoiled wing design can be seen.

Designers corrected the poor gunnery system with the advent of the P-51D model. Now there were six guns mounted in an upright position and much less trouble was encountered.

GENERAL COMMENTS
(FOR ALLISON POWERED P-51s)
As the ALLISON Mustang operated by the British proved itself in the war the USAAF became interested, but by the time they made up their minds to make a purchase they found the funds for fighters depleted. The ingenious Dutch Kindleburger found a solution to the Air Force problem. The company would add bomb racks and dive brakes and call the airplane an attack bomber. Sure enough, the Air Force had funds for attack airplanes. And thus was born the A-36.
Below 22000 feet the Allison P-51 had the best all-around fighting qualities of any fighter.
The two XP-51s didn't generate much enthusiasm at Wright Field. Gen. Kenney noted the XP-51 aircraft parked behind some puddles of oil in the rear of a hangar.

(FOR MERLIN POWERED P-51s)
Powerplant automatic features relieve pilot work load.
When the P-51 dove down to medium altitude the noise of the aneroid-controlled supercharger dropping out could be easily heard by the pilot.
It had fine turning ability.
Best of 1944 US fighters in all-around combat.
The best way to get out of a Mustang was to roll over and simply fall out.

The P-51 flew beautifully if the fuselage tank was emptied of at least half its fuel.
I don't recall a Mustang as having high stick force per g.
A P-51 was a different matter from a P-40. With its sensitivity and wing design, an insensitive pilot could have spin trouble.
I am sure a P-51 didn't have as much stall warning as one might like to have. But I don't recall it being a problem. I do not recall a lot of stalling and spinning in combat situations. I personally never stalled or spun a P-51 in combat.
The P-51 was different from a P-40 because Mustang pilot laxity could more easily cause a spin.
General Keptner, 8th Air Force Fighter Command: Distinctly the best fighter we can get over here (ETO). They are going to be the only satisfactory answer.
The laminar flow wing design of the P-51 gave the aircraft a diving advantage. It could reach higher speeds than many other types without incurring compressibility effects.
By January 1944 the value of the Merlin P-51 as a long range bomber escort had become so apparent that aircraft allocations were completely revised. Operations during January with limited numbers further confirmed the feeling that this plane was the answer to the long range escort problem.
The P-51 became the top-notch all-around fighter (in the Pacific) even as it proved to be the best all-purpose fighter in Europe. The statistical record, as well as post-war testimony of Japanese pilots, leaves little doubt that the P-51 was the superior of the three (P-38, P-47, and P-51).

Generally speaking the P-51 did not require above normal maintenance.

A pilot who had converted from P-47 to P-51 noted initially he was dubious about the switch, mainly with concerns over vulnerability. He was reassured after air combat victories quickly increased. He felt the P-51 was the better fighter below 30000 feet, but above that altitude the P-47 gained ascendency.

Its long range characteristics made the P-51 special. Pilots often went on missions lasting at least five hours. This long range capability was a major attraction of the aircraft.

Pilots had to be alert to the heavy yawing tendency of the P-51 under high power takeoff conditions, and pay heed to the infamous torque effect.

One pilot felt the Merlin P-51 was the finest propeller fighter aircraft ever, and claimed he could defeat any pilot who differed.

An ex-P-40 pilot was thrilled to change into a Merlin P-51 and considered he now had unrivaled advantages in combat.

Gen. Spaatz told Gen. Arnold what he wanted was the Mustang with the Merlin engine. Gen. Arnold told him if that was what he really wanted he would get it.

Never never spin a P-51 because it might not come out.

Few if any airplanes can turn with a P-51 at 400 mph.

Goering: "The reason for the failure of the Luftwaffe against Allied Air Forces was the success of the USAAF in putting out a long range escort fighter airplane (the P-51)". Goering knew Germany would lose the war when he saw Mustang fighters over Berlin.

Merlin P-51s had many problems early on: the familiar gun problems, the wheel well doors tending to drop down, structural failures, and handling troubles with a full 85 gallon fuselage tank.

At years (1943) end the P-51, a fighter pilot's dream, finally became available.

It was the Mustangs that took the heart out of Herman Goering when he saw them shooting down his best fighter pilots over Berlin.

Gen. H. H. Arnold: The P-38 and the P-47 were excellent airplanes, there is no argument about that, but the P-51, with its Merlin engine, was the airplane for that (bomber escort) job.

It was an awful antagonist—and we (Germans) hated it.

It was hard (for German flyers) to recognize. Except from the side it looked like an ME-109. An enemy pilot commented it was surprising American P-51 pilots had time to fight considering the cockpit complexity.

P-51 STRUCTURAL DESCRIPTION
(All metal is aluminum alloy except where noted)

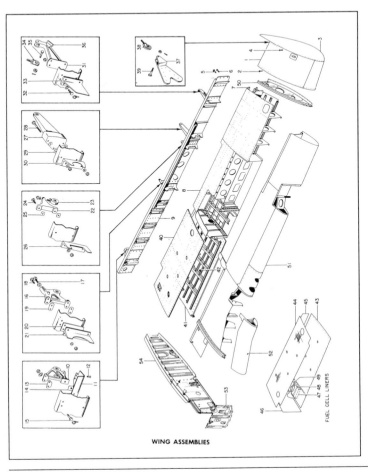

WING ASSEMBLIES

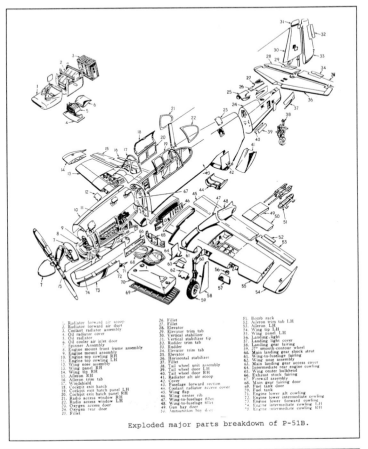

Exploded major parts breakdown of P-51B.

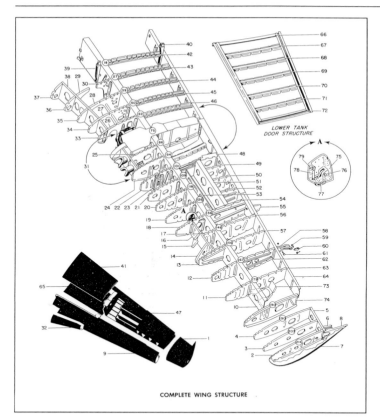

COMPLETE WING STRUCTURE

LOWER TANK
DOOR STRUCTURE

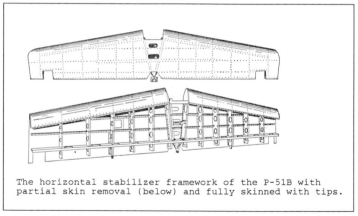

The horizontal stabilizer framework of the P-51B with
partial skin removal (below) and fully skinned with tips.

WING GROUP

The wing was a cantilever stressed skin structure in two sections,
bolted at the airplane centerline. Each side consisted of a main panel,
a removeable tip, aileron, and trailing edge flap. The 25% chord
line was perpendicular to the airplane centerline.

Each basic wing panel consisted of a main spar, a rear spar,
twenty-one pressed ribs and a center joining rib, and spanwise extruded stringers covered with flush-riveted alloy sheet. Space was
provided at the inboard end for a self-sealing fuel cell, part of which
was located under the fuselage area. A bay was provided in each
wing panel to accomodate guns, ammunition containers, and ejection chutes. Space was also provided for the main landing gear to
retract into wheel bays in the inboard leading edge. The main structural member of the wing was the forward, or main, spar built of
two sections of sheet spliced together. The inboard spar web section was fabricated of 0.129 inch thick metal with spar upper and
lower caps made up of angle sections. A 0.25 inch thick metal bar
was riveted to the inner side of the upper cap between wing stations
0 and 85.5 (airplane centerline to 85.5 inches outboard). The rear
spar was formed of two sheets of metal spliced at wing station 128.6.
The upper spar cap was reinforced by an 0.091 inch thick angle
between stations 0 and 92.5. Wing ribs and formers were approximately 12.5 inches apart.

Each aileron had two spars and twelve flanged ribs and was
metal-covered. The forward spar was U-shaped Alclad metal. The
trailing edge was sheet metal reinforced with supports and plastic
ribs. Three aileron hinge brackets were bolted to the forward spar
to provide bearing attachment points. The ailerons were dynami-

cally and statically balanced. Internal aerodynamic balance was
obtained by a diaphragm attached to the forward edge of the aileron and sealed to the rear spar by a fabric strip. Phenolic fiber trim
tabs were mounted in each aileron by three hinge bearings. A metal
horn provided an attachment point for the tab actuating rod. The
left tab, adjustable in flight, was operated from the cockpit. Angular travel was limited by stops on the control cables. The ailerons
were conventionally controlled, and could be adjusted for angular
travel of 10, 12, or 15 degrees.

The framing of the metal covered plain flaps included two
Alclad spars, thirteen nose ribs, fifteen main ribs, and a series of
rolled-section stringers, all of metal. The flap trailing edge was
formed from a single sheet reinforced with twenty-seven tapered
hat-section supports. Flaps were hinged on three sealed ball bearings, and were hydraulically controlled by a cockpit lever; the lever
position held any corresponding flap position.

Wing tips were removeable, being attached to the main panels
by screws.

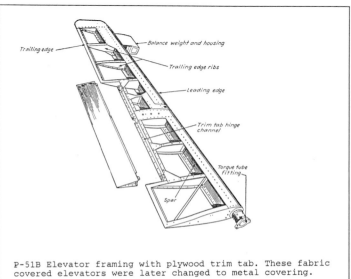

Trailing edge

Balance weight and housing

Trailing edge ribs

Leading edge

Trim tab hinge
channel

Torque tube
fitting

Spar

P-51B Elevator framing with plywood trim tab. These fabric
covered elevators were later changed to metal covering.

TAIL GROUP

The tail group consisted of the horizontal stabilizer and elevators along with the fin, or vertical stabilizer, and the rudder.

The horizontal stabilizer, attached to the fuselage aft section by four bolts, was a one-piece full cantilever surface, non-adjustable, with detacheable tips. It was fixed to the fuselage at a positive two degree angle (later revised downward) of incidence relative to the longitudinal axis of the airplane. The surface had two Alclad spars, flanged formed ribs, and six spanwise extruded stringers. Dual stringers were used with the lower covering and all skins were metal. Stabilizer tips contained two ribs, were removeable, and were attached with screws. The elevators incorporated eighteen flanged ribs, a front spar, a trailing edge member, and a short intercostal channel-section beam acting as a trim tab hinge support. The covering for the elevators was initially fabric with an Alclad sheet leading edge except for sections cut out for the elevator hinge fittings. Late models had metal-covered elevators, and some aircraft were retrofitted with these. The elevator leading edges terminated in torque tube drive fittings inboard. Right and left elevators were interchangeable and fastened to the stabilizer with five sealed ball bearing hinges. They were statically and dynamically balanced. Static balance was achieved using a 13 1/4 pound lead weight attached to the outboard end of the leading edge. Each elevator had an adjustable trim tab.

The vertical stabilizer, or fin, was made up of Alclad front and rear spars and ribs all covered by Alclad metal sheet. The tip had two ribs and was not detacheable, and the skin was stiffened by spanwise light rolled stringers. The fin was set at one degree to the left of the centerline of the rear beam. On most D models a dorsal fin was added forward of the vertical stabilizer. The rudder consisted of a single metal spar, twenty flanged Alclad ribs, a vee trail-

Rudder framing for P-51B showing tab cut-out.

ing edge member, and a short beam for attachment of the trim tab hinge. The rudder was covered with mercerized cotton fabric except the leading edge back to the spar was metal-covered. The leading edge was cut out for hinge fittings. The rudder was hinged to the fin with three sealed ball bearing fittings, and was dynamically balanced by means of a 16.6 pound lead weight at the tip. An additional balance weight at the bottom of the leading edge reduced static unbalance. The phenolic fibre trim tabs on elevators and rudder were hinged by three sealed needle bearings. The rudder and elevator tabs were controlled from the cockpit. Tab travel was limited by stops on the cables. The rudder tab was revised to a reverse-boost (anti-balance) type on later models, and retrofitting was also done on some aircraft.

FUSELAGE

The fuselage was of semi-monocoque construction and was divided into two parts, the main section and the rear section, joined by bolts. With the exception of the forward and aft cockpit armor and the firewall the fuselage was made up entirely of Alclad and other metal extrusions. The main fuselage section was constructed around four extruded longerons and included intermediate frames , stringers, and Alclad covering.

The forward bulkhead was formed by a stainless steel sheet and armor plate firewall. A turnover truss of extrusions and formed sheet aft of the cockpit protected the pilot. The upper longerons of

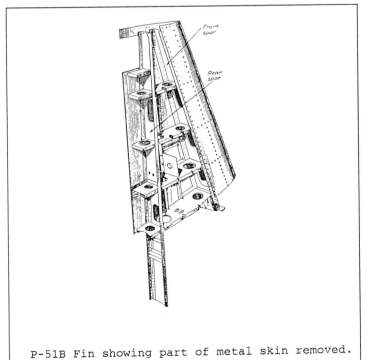

P-51B Fin showing part of metal skin removed.

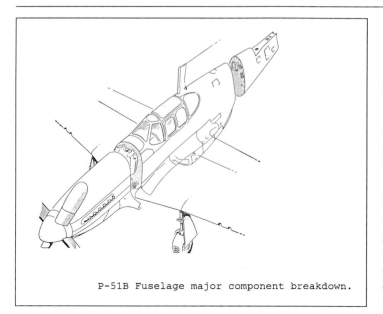

P-51B Fuselage major component breakdown.

Plexiglas. The windshield cowling extended from the lower forward end of the glass to the firewall and down to the upper longeron. Over the instrument panel a shroud, integral with the windshield, extended aft with an integral rubber extrusion to protect the pilot. This shroud supported the windshield defroster, the optical gunsight and handholds, and it also eliminated instrument glare in the windshield glass. The cockpit enclosure of standard B and C models consisted of upper and side plastic panels, each in two sections, the forward one forming a sliding window with locking handle. The right upper panel hinged upward; the left panel hinged downward against the fuselage. Both had locks controlled from outside and inside. The hood was attached by four hinges mounted on the upper longerons. An emergency release permitted the enclosure to be removed or jettisoned in an emergency. Aft windows of moulded Lucite fit the fuselage contour and were removeable for access to the radio behind the pilot. Aft of the radio a plywood bulkhead prevented draft and kept objects from rolling aft and fouling the controls. Nut plates at the center of the bulkhead secured the oxygen bottles. Starting with the D model a new cockpit canopy and aft deck arrangement was provided. A full bubble canopy and a cut down aft deck replaced the faired-in cockpit and aft turtledeck of earlier models. Aft of the fixed three-panel windshield, the moveable canopy was a one-piece blown plastic unit within a metal frame. The canopy was hand-crank operated, and slid forward and aft on tracks built into the fuselage. A flush external button on the right side of the fuselage could be pushed to allow manual sliding of the canopy aft for entrance to the cockpit. The canopy hand-crank was located on the right side of the cockpit near the windshield side panel. An emergency release handle, operable from either inside or outside, was provided just forward of the normal hand-crank. Pulling the handle aft released the canopy latches and permitted the slipstream to carry it clear of the aircraft.

The rear section of the fuselage consisted of two longerons, a shelf, and five formers, three solid bulkheads, and Alclad metal skin.

the main section were extruded H-sections which extended aft from the firewall, tapering to a T-section, and terminating near the rear section. The lower longerons, an H-beam and a U-channel, extended the full length of the main section. The eight riveted and bolted assemblies which made up the main fuselage section could be removed and replaced as units. These eight were : firewall, turnover truss, upper deck, left and right side panel sub-assemblies, radio shelf, web assembly, and the lower section with the air scoop. The cockpit seat accomodated a seat-type parachute, and had a kapok back cushion life preserver; provisions for heating and cooling the cockpit were included, and two pieces of armor plate were located behind the seat. The forward flat section of the cockpit windshield was bullet-proof five-ply laminated glass one and one half inches thick and slanted thirty-one degrees back from the vertical. The side and upper panels of the windshield were of 3/16 inch thick

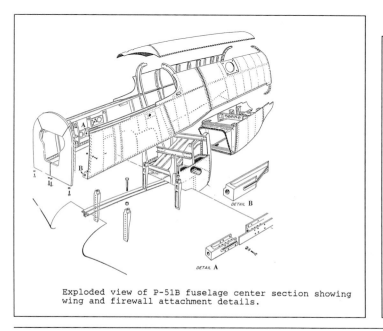

Exploded view of P-51B fuselage center section showing wing and firewall attachment details.

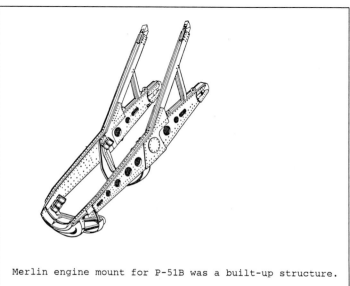

Merlin engine mount for P-51B was a built-up structure.

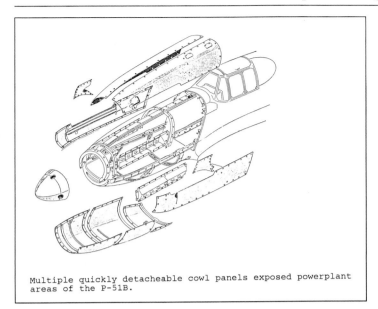

Multiple quickly detacheable cowl panels exposed powerplant areas of the P-51B.

LANDING GEAR

The landing gear was of the hydraulically retractable main and tail wheel type. The main wheels retracted into wing wells and the tail wheel into the aft fuselage. All wheels were fully enclosed when retracted.

A magnesium main landing gear support casting was bolted to the wing front spar at the outboard end of the wheel well. Hydraulic actuators on the front spar retracted the gear inboard. An oleo shock strut assembly was attached to the gear support casting with a half-fork on the piston end connecting to the axle of the magnesium wheel and the 27 inch diameter tire. A torque scissors assembly connecting piston and oleo housing was located at the rear of the gear. A two-piece fairing, the outer section carried by the gear and the inner hinged at the fuselage, provided smooth closure for the main gear after retraction. The main gear was equipped with multiple disc brakes. A hydraulic cylinder, connected to the brakes by metal tubing, furnished pressure for the brakes via a separate and independent system controlled by the rudder pedals. Hydraulic pressure was relieved by a spring when a pedal was released. A parking brake was controlled by depressing the brake pedals and pulling a knob below the instrument panel. The pressure was maintained until released by depressing both brake pedals.

The tail landing gear was mounted on a magnesium casting bolted to thelower longerons. The shock strut assembly included cylinder, piston, torque tube, and post housing which supported the wheel axle. The tail gear was steered by cables from the rudder bellcrank. Fairing doors were hinged at the side, and a link pulled them up as the gear was retracted. The tail wheel was unlocked with the stick placed in a forward position during parking and taxiing.

ENGINE SECTION

The engine section was made up of the engine mounting and cowling components. The engine mount was designed so the engine could be removed as a unit. The mount was attached at the firewall by four bolts. It was made up of box-type beams of Alclad sheet and extruded parts. Two lower main horizontal beams, separated by two bowed cross members, were supported by another two angled support beams tied into the upper support fittings of the firewall. The whole assembly formed a cradle for the engine, which was attached to its mount structure through Lord anti-vibration units.

Engine cowl upper, lower, and side panels were attached to framing strips by multiple quick-detach quarter-turn fasteners. The strips were supported on frames tied to the engine mount.

P-51 SYSTEMS DESCRIPTION

PROPULSION SUBSYSTEMS

ENGINE

The engine for the earlier models of the airplane, P-51, P-51A, and A-36A, was a version in the 1200 HP class of the Allison V-1710 liquid-cooled twelve-cylinder vee-type inline model of 5.5 inches bore and 6.0 inches stroke with a 6.65:1 compression ratio. It employed an integral single stage single speed mechanical supercharger with 9.5 inch diameter impeller driven at an 8.8:1 gear ratio, and maximum engine speed was 3000 RPM. The propeller reduction gear ratio was 2:1. Later versions of the aircraft, P-51B/C and P-51D/K, used a Packard-built Rolls Royce V-1650 Merlin engine in the 1500 HP class. This was a liquid cooled twelve-cylinder vee-type inline powerplant of 5.4 inch bore, 6.0 inch stroke, with a 6.0:1 compression ratio, and used an integral two stage two speed mechanical supercharger. Maximum engine speed was 3000 RPM and the propeller reduction gear ratio was 0.479:1. The two speed supercharger (on the -3 engine, -7 was different) had a low gear ratio of 6.391:1 and a high ratio of 8.095:1. First stage impeller diameter was 12.0 inches and the second stage 10.1 inches. The Merlin weighed about 1690 pounds and was 87 inches long. The Allison weighed about 1335 pounds and was 86 inches long.

ENGINE INDUCTION SYSTEM

On Allison powered airplanes, P-51, P-51A, and A-36A, the induction system was made up of a ram air scoop on top of the engine cowl just behind the propeller spinner which ducted air aft past a valve to the downdraft carburetor of the engine. The valve in the duct was mechanically controlled by a push-pull handle on the left side of the instrument panel to change from outside air taken into the carburetor to warm air from inside the engine compartment.

The induction system of the Merlin powered airplanes was designed so the pilot could choose between cold rammed intake air, cold un-rammed filtered air, or un-rammed hot air. Cold outside ram air entered a scoop and duct under the fuselage just aft of the propeller spinner. Under normal operation the air would pass straight through the duct aft and then turn upward in the duct to enter the up-draft carburetor which was a double-throated injection type with a double-diaphragm acceleration pump, automatic mix-

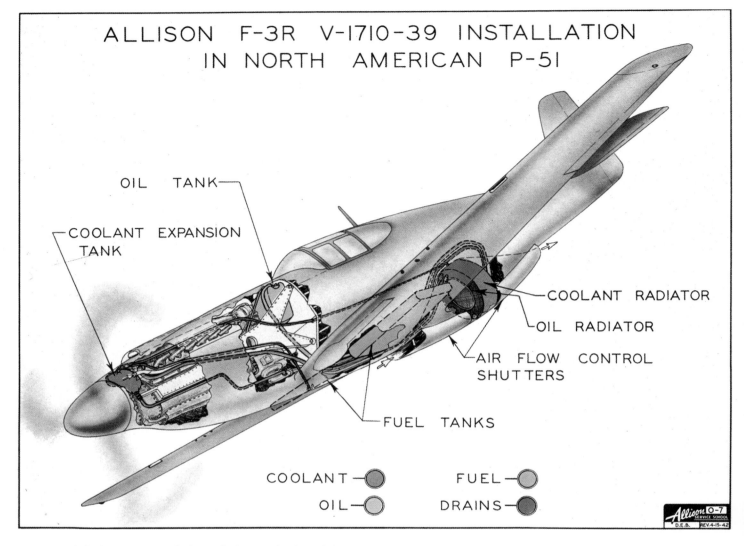

ALLISON F-3R V-1710-39 INSTALLATION
IN NORTH AMERICAN P-51

OIL TANK

COOLANT EXPANSION
TANK

COOLANT RADIATOR

OIL RADIATOR

AIR FLOW CONTROL
SHUTTERS

FUEL TANKS

COOLANT

OIL

FUEL

DRAINS

ture control, fuel pressure regulation, a fuel control unit, and throttle. A door at the forward end of the duct could be closed mechanically using a cockpit left side control to force the air to enter through a perforated side panel with a filter. For cold weather operation these perforated panels could be blocked off. With blocking panels in place, the induction system pulled warm air from the engine compartment through an entry door. On early models the door was spring-loaded; on later aircraft the door position was mechanically controlled from the cockpit. After the fuel-air mixture left the carburetor it was compressed by the supercharger impellers, cooled by the aftercooler system, and entered the intake manifold.

ENGINE EXHAUST SYSTEM
The exhaust system consisted of six individual stainless steel jet exhaust stacks on each side curved to face aft and narrowing in section. Other parts on each side included an exhaust shroud to keep heat from the spark plugs, lock plates holding the stacks in place, and a single piece fairing with six holes fitting over all the stacks.

Flame dampening exhaust stacks were used on export Mustang I airplanes.

ENGINE-MOUNTED ACCESSORIES
Items mounted on or driven by the engine (either Allison or Merlin) included a carburetor, two rotating-magnet type magnetos, propeller governor, fuel pump, oil pump, coolant pump, hydraulic pump, electrical generator, vacuum pump, starter, and tachometer.

ENGINE CONTROLS
For the Allison powered versions the engine controls, mechanically or electrically linked to the engine from the cockpit, consisted of throttle, carburetor air control, engine primer, starter switch, mixture control, and ignition switch.

For the Merlin powered aircraft, engine controls included the throttle located on the left longeron and mechanically linked to the automatic manifold pressure regulator. This regulator, made either by Packard or Simmons, was an engine oil-operated unit maintaining constant manifold pressure, as selected, over a wide range of

ALLISON F-3R V-1710-39 COOLANT SYSTEM IN NORTH AMERICAN P-51

TOTAL COOLANT CAPACITY-20.4 GALLONS

SNIFFLE VALVE OPENS AT 3/4 LB. PRESSURE

PRESSURE RELIEF VALVE OPENS AT 3 LBS. PRESSURE

COOLANT TEMP GAGE

INSTRUMENT PANEL

HYDRAULIC AIRSCOOP CONTROL

AIRSCOOP OPERATING MECHANISM- (SCOOPS OPEN)

THERMOMETER WELL FOR TEMP GAGE

VENT LINE ON RIGHT SIDE OF SHIP

TO DRAIN BOX

EXPANSION TANK VENT VALVE

COOLANT EXPANSION TANK

FIREWALL

RADIATOR AIR OUTLET SHUTTER

COOLANT DRAIN

COOLANT RADIATOR

RADIATOR AIR INTAKE SCOOP

FILLER CAP

DRAIN BOX

COOLANT PUMP DRAIN PLUG IN PUMP OUTLET

TO RIGHT CYLINDER BANK OUTLET

COOLANT — EXPANSION-SUPPLY LINE — VENT LINES — FREE AIR FLOW — DRAINS

Allison P-8 SERVICE SCHOOL W.E.H. 10-26-42

throttle settings. The throttle had a gate which allowed up to 61 inches of mercury pressure up to critical altitude. When the throttle was moved past the gate, breaking the light lockwire, a manifold pressure up to 67 inches of mercury could be provided for War Emergency (Combat) power. The mixture control lever was located on the aft side of the throttle quadrant. There was no shift lever for the supercharger; an electrical aneroid-actuated pressure switch automatically controlled the shifting of supercharger speed. If the aneroid failed, backup switches to shift speed could be used. Other engine controls were provided for the primer system and the ignition system. On early aircraft a hand-operated primer was used; on late versions there was an electric primer switch. In the manual system the primer pump drew fuel from the fuel strainer on the firewall and directed it to the engine induction manifold. On later planes a solonoid valve on the carburetor opened to permit fuel into primer lines to the induction manifold. The ignition system supplied electricity to the one magneto booster coil to intensify the spark.

PROPELLER

The earlier Allison powered P-51 airplanes used a Curtiss Electric C532D propeller of 10 foot 9 inch diameter with three solid aluminum 50700 design blades, a change from the prototype XP-51 which had employed a Curtiss C532S three blade propeller with design 614-1C1.5-18 blades of hollow steel construction in 10 foot 6 inch diameter and 88.5 activity factor per blade. The propellers were both constant speed variable pitch type, electrically controlled.

The later Merlin powered aircraft, starting with the P-51B, were equipped with a four-bladed Hamilton Standard 24D50-65 or -87 Hydromatic propeller of 11 feet 2 inches diameter using design 6547-6, 6547A-6, or 6523A-24 aluminum blades. The P-51K version of the D used an Aeroproducts A542S Unimatic hydraulic propeller with four H20-156P-23M5 hollow steel blades of 11 feet 1 inch diameter. These propellers were also of the automatic constant speed variable pitch type. All the propeller types were equipped with aluminum spinners mounted to their hubs by attaching bulkheads.

PROPELLER CONTROLS

On Allison powered aircraft the Curtiss propeller electric control switch was mounted on the central switch panel below the instrument panel where automatic constant speed under governor control or manual increase or decrease pitch modes could be selected. The constant speed propeller control lever was on the throttle quadrant at the left side of the cockpit, and was connected directly through mechanical linkage to the propeller governor mounted on and driven by the engine.

The Merlin engined airplanes had the same arrangement of a propeller control on the throttle quadrant linked mechanically to the speed governor on the engine. The control setting determined the engine RPM which was maintained constant by the governor.

ENGINE STARTING SYSTEM

With the Allison powered aircraft the engine was primed in the starting procedure and the starter switch was energized to initiate the rotation of the flywheel of an inertia starter mounted on the engine. When this switch, located below the center of the instrument panel, was pressed upward to the "crank" position after the flywheel had reached maximum speed it was clutched in to crank the engine. Provision was made for connecting an external electrical supply at a location on the right side of the fuselage. Provision was also made for hand-crank starting the engine using a starter crank and extension stowed in the right wheel well. The crank was set in a hole in the lower aft engine cowl.

The later Merlin powered aircraft were started by pressing then holding the starter switch. This action energized an electric direct-cranking starter and a booster coil on the right magneto. On late Merlin aircraft an electric engine primer was used instead of a manual pump.

ENGINE WATER INJECTION SYSTEM

No water injection system was used on any production models prior to the P-51H.

ENGINE COOLING SYSTEM

On the P-51, P-51A, and A-36A airplanes with the Allison engine the curved coolant tank with sniffler valve for the Ethylene Glycol liquid cooling system was located on the inside top of the engine nose ring behind the propeller spinner, and was protected by armor plate between tank and spinner. The radiator was located in a duct under the fuselage near the aft portion of the wing. It was annular in shape and surrounded the oil cooler. Coolant was forced through the system by an engine-driven pump. Coolant lines ran from forward on the engine on both sides to a "Y" connection, and through a single line splitting again at cooler entry. Lines returned along the bottom of the fuselage to the pump and into the engine case. Vent

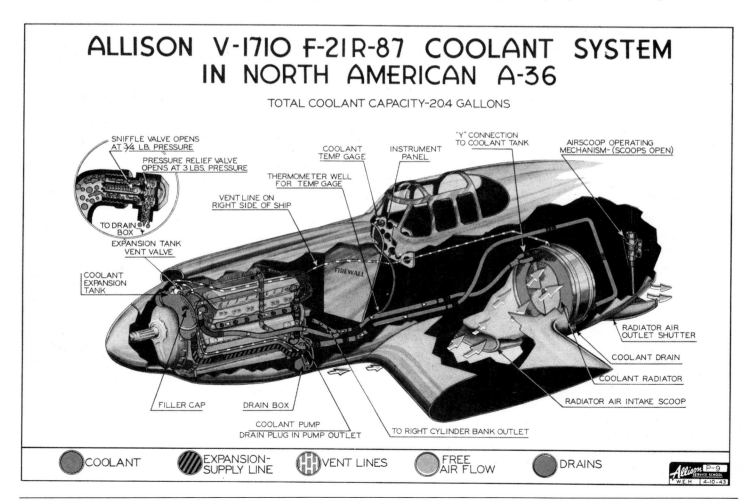

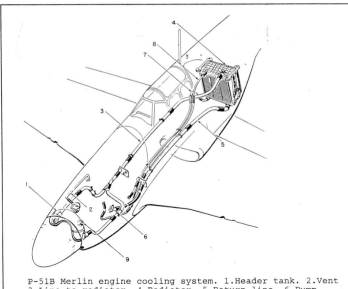

P-51B Merlin engine cooling system. 1.Header tank. 2.Vent 3.Line to radiator. 4.Radiator. 5.Return line. 6.Pump. 7 and 8.Supercharger cooler. 9.Filler.

Cooling
SYSTEM

■ ENGINE COOLING SYSTEM LINES
▨ AFTERCOOLING SYSTEM LINES
▭ OIL SYSTEM LINES
┄ VENT LINES
─ ─ ELECTRICAL
─ ─ MECHANICAL

and drain lines completed the system. A fill point was incorporated in the tank, and coolant temperature was indicated on an instrument panel gage. The scoop for the radiator had an adjustable exit flap moved by a hydraulic actuator. The actuator was controlled using a handle at the left of the pilot seat.

On the Merlin powered models there were two complete and separate cooling systems. One cooled the engine; the other, the aftercooling system, cooled the supercharged fuel/air mixture. Coolant from each system passed through its respective portion of a dual radiator located in the modified air duct under the fuselage.

The engine cooling system consisted of the radiator, an engine-driven pump, a kidney-shaped coolant header tank just aft of the propeller spinner, a relief valve, and connecting lines. A coolant temperature gage was located on the instrument panel. The system had a capacity of 16.7 gallons including header tank capacity of 5.2 gallons. The system was filled at the tank. Coolant ran from the tank to the radiator and back from the radiator to the pump and engine, and out to the tank.

The aftercooling system for the charge mixture consisted of its separate radiator, an aftercooling header tank in the engine compartment, an engine-driven centrifugal pump, and coolant lines. It was a low pressure system with a 4.8 gallon capacity including tank capacity of 0.5 gallons. The coolant was forced by the pump through the radiator to the supercharger cooling jacket and then returned through the lines to the tank.

The airflow through the underside radiator duct was controlled by varying exit area with a flap driven by an electric actuator. A four-position switch (auto, open, close, and off) in the cockpit controlled the actuator with "automatic" being the normal setting in which coolant temperature governed flap position. In case of actuator failure an emergency release handle on the cockpit floor could open the flap mechanically on a one-time only basis.

ENGINE SUPERCHARGING SYSTEM CONTROL

The supercharger of the Allison Mustangs was a single stage single speed integral unit that ran at a single multiple of engine speed at all times and required no control. The supercharger of the Merlin powered P-51s was a two stage two speed type and was under automatic control using an aneroid-operated switch tied to air pressure at the carburetor entrance. The supercharger shifted from low to high between 16000 and 25000 feet depending on engine version and aircraft speed. A cockpit switch allowed a manual alternate to the automatic mode.

ENGINE LUBRICATION SYSTEM

For the Allison Mustangs the lubrication system was made up primarily of an oil tank mounted on the firewall forward face, an engine-driven oil pump, oil lines, and a cylindrical oil cooler housed in the under-fuselage duct directly in the center of the annular coolant radiator. Oil exited the engine and ran through a line low in the fuselage to and through the oil cooler, then back to the tank and to the pump and engine. An automatic relief valve was provided to permit the oil, with excessive pressure due to being cold, to bypass the oil cooler.

P-51D

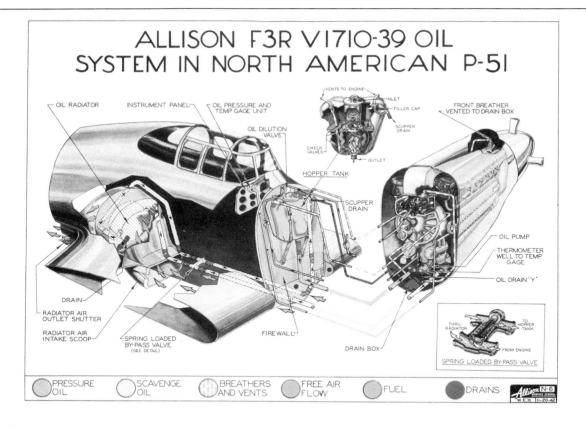

ALLISON F3R V1710-39 OIL SYSTEM IN NORTH AMERICAN P-51

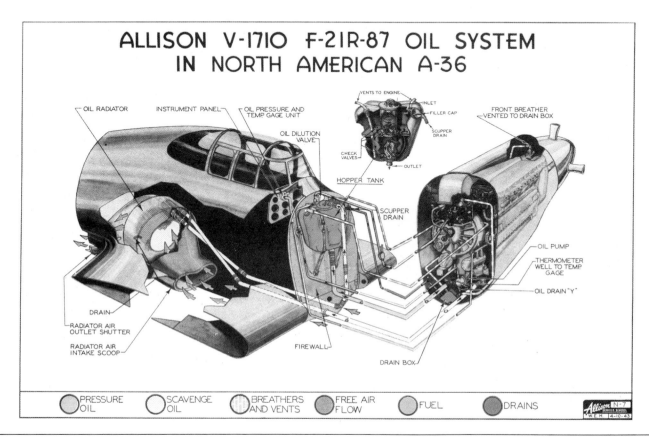

ALLISON V-1710 F-21R-87 OIL SYSTEM IN NORTH AMERICAN A-36

On the Merlin Mustangs oil for engine lubrication was supplied from a 12.5 gallon tank strapped to the front of the firewall. It was pumped by an engine-driven pressure pump through the engine with a scavenge pump return through the oil cooler and back to the tank. In this case the oval section oil cooler was mounted in the lower duct, but forward of and separated from the coolant and aftercooler radiators. The oil temperature was normally regulated automatically, with the oil going through the cooler when required, or bypassing it and flowing directly back to the tank. The oil cooler sub-duct had its own exit flap which was driven by an electric actuator controlled by a cockpit switch. With the switch in automatic mode the actuator was thermostatically controlled. The other switch positions were for manual backup to open or close the flap. Limit switches stopped the actuator travel when full open or full closed position was reached. An oil dilution system was also included, and oil temperature and pressure were recorded in the cockpit.

ENGINE FIRE SENSING/FIRE EXTINGUISHING SYSTEMS

No such systems were included in the Mustangs.

FUEL SYSTEM

The Allison powered airplanes had two protected internal fuel tanks each of 90 US gallon capacity located inboard between the main and rear wing spars. The left tank included a supply designated as reserve (31 gallons of the 90) using the high and low standpipe system. There were no provisions for external drop tanks on the P-51, but the P-51A and the A-36A provided for a 75 or 150 US gallon drop tank on a bomb rack under each wing. The 75 gallon size was a combat drop tank; the 150 gallon tank was a slipper-type for long range ferry operation. An engine-driven fuel pump powered the system with a manually -controlled electrical booster pump also provided in the engine compartment, as was a fuel strainer. The engine primer system picked fuel off from the strainer. A main fuel selector valve was located in the cockpit, and an auxiliary fuel selector valve connected the fuel lines running across the wing to drop tank positions to the rest of the system. The two selector valves and the boost pump switch were on a center console just ahead of the control stick. A fuel quantity gage was included.

The later Merlin powered aircraft had two protected internal fuel tanks each of 92 US gallons in the inboard wing locations. The

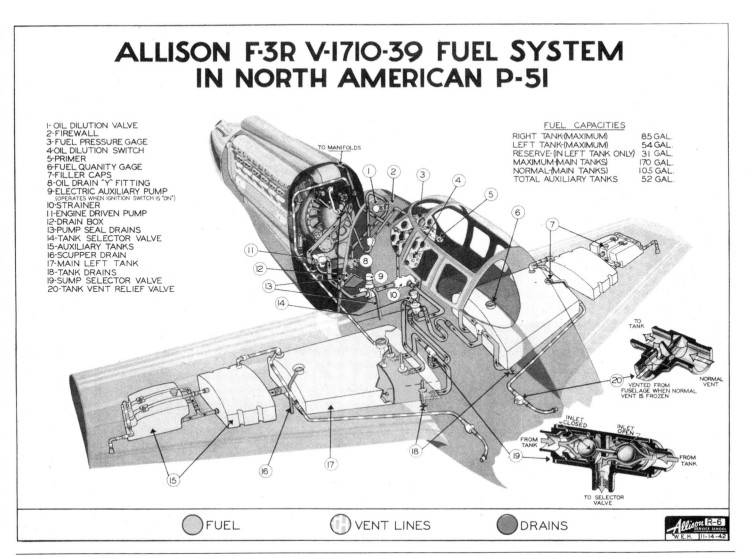

ALLISON F-3R V-1710-39 FUEL SYSTEM IN NORTH AMERICAN P-51

1- OIL DILUTION VALVE
2- FIREWALL
3- FUEL PRESSURE GAGE
4- OIL DILUTION SWITCH
5- PRIMER
6- FUEL QUANITY GAGE
7- FILLER CAPS
8- OIL DRAIN "Y" FITTING
9- ELECTRIC AUXILIARY PUMP
   (OPERATES WHEN IGNITION SWITCH IS "ON")
10- STRAINER
11- ENGINE DRIVEN PUMP
12- DRAIN BOX
13- PUMP SEAL DRAINS
14- TANK SELECTOR VALVE
15- AUXILIARY TANKS
16- SCUPPER DRAIN
17- MAIN LEFT TANK
18- TANK DRAINS
19- SUMP SELECTOR VALVE
20- TANK VENT RELIEF VALVE

FUEL CAPACITIES
RIGHT TANK-(MAXIMUM)	85 GAL.
LEFT TANK-(MAXIMUM)	54 GAL.
RESERVE-(IN LEFT TANK ONLY)	31 GAL.
MAXIMUM-(MAIN TANKS)	170 GAL.
NORMAL-(MAIN TANKS)	105 GAL.
TOTAL AUXILIARY TANKS	52 GAL.

TO MANIFOLDS

TO TANK
NORMAL VENT
VENTED FROM FUSELAGE WHEN NORMAL VENT IS FROZEN

INLET CLOSED
INLET OPEN
FROM TANK
FROM TANK
TO SELECTOR VALVE

FUEL   VENT LINES   DRAINS

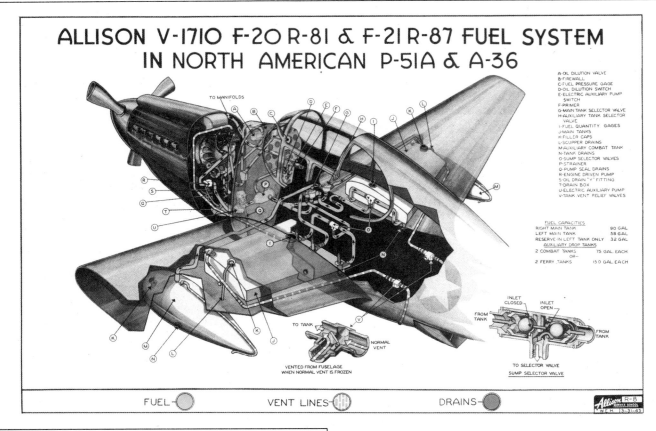

ALLISON V-1710 F-20 R-81 & F-21 R-87 FUEL SYSTEM
IN NORTH AMERICAN P-51A & A-36

A-OIL DILUTION VALVE
B-FIREWALL
C-FUEL PRESSURE GAGE
D-OIL DILUTION SWITCH
E-ELECTRIC AUXILIARY PUMP
    SWITCH
F-PRIMER
G-MAIN TANK SELECTOR VALVE
H-AUXILIARY TANK SELECTOR
    VALVE
I-FUEL QUANTITY GAGES
J-MAIN TANKS
K-FILLER CAPS
L-SCUPPER DRAINS
M-AUXILIARY COMBAT TANK
N-TANK DRAINS
O-SUMP SELECTOR VALVES
P-STRAINER
Q-PUMP SEAL DRAINS
R-ENGINE DRIVEN PUMP
S-OIL DRAIN "Y" FITTING
T-DRAIN BOX
U-ELECTRIC AUXILIARY PUMP
V-TANK VENT RELIEF VALVES

FUEL CAPACITIES
RIGHT MAIN TANK   90 GAL
LEFT MAIN TANK   58 GAL
RESERVE IN LEFT TANK ONLY 32 GAL
AUXILIARY DROP TANKS
2 COMBAT TANKS   75 GAL EACH
        OR
2 FERRY TANKS   150 GAL EACH

TO MANIFOLDS

FUEL— VENT LINES— DRAINS—

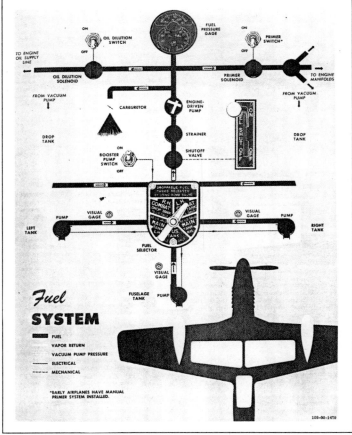

Fuel **SYSTEM**

— FUEL
— VAPOR RETURN
— VACUUM PUMP PRESSURE
— ELECTRICAL
--- MECHANICAL

*EARLY AIRPLANES HAVE MANUAL
PRIMER SYSTEM INSTALLED.

P-51B-5 aircraft became B-7 types (and P-51C-1s became C-3s) after installation of an 85 US gallon protected fuselage fuel tank aft of the cockpit area. Kits were made available for fuselage tank installation on earlier B models, and all subsequent production Merlin powered aircraft had the 85 gallon fuselage tank except for some P-51C-5 reconnaissance aircraft. Filling the fuselage tank sent the aircraft center of gravity aft and resulted in stability and control problems, so various restrictions were set up at various times, depending on the combat situation as to how much fuel was placed in that tank. Late models were sometimes placarded at a 65 gallon limit. The system was powered by an engine-driven pump, but in addition each of the main wing tanks had its own gravity-fed submerged type of booster pump powered by the electrical system. The drop tanks provided had no boost pumps, but fuel was forced out of them by a controlled pressure of five PSI from the exhaust side of the vacuum pump. If this pressure failed the engine-driven fuel pump could draw fuel from the drop tanks up to about 10000 feet altitude.

Priming and oil dilution components were also part of the system, as was a strainer, fuel pressure and fuel quantity gages, and a fuel shut-off valve. Cockpit controls included the shut-off lever, tank selection switch, boost pump switch, and mechanical drop tank salvo levers which provided selective release of the tanks as a backup for electrical release of bombs or tanks.

(Left) P-51D

FIXED EQUIPMENT SUBSYSTEMS

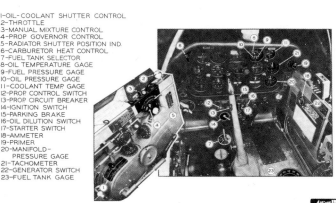

NORTH AMERICAN P-51 INSTRUMENTS AND CONTROLS

1-OIL-COOLANT SHUTTER CONTROL
2-THROTTLE
3-MANUAL MIXTURE CONTROL
4-PROP GOVERNOR CONTROL
5-RADIATOR SHUTTER POSITION IND.
6-CARBURETOR HEAT CONTROL
7-FUEL TANK SELECTOR
8-OIL TEMPERATURE GAGE
9-FUEL PRESSURE GAGE
10-OIL PRESSURE GAGE
11-COOLANT TEMP GAGE
12-PROP CONTROL SWITCH
13-PROP CIRCUIT BREAKER
14-IGNITION SWITCH
15-PARKING BRAKE
16-OIL DILUTION SWITCH
17-STARTER SWITCH
18-AMMETER
19-PRIMER
20-MANIFOLD-
     PRESSURE GAGE
21-TACHOMETER
22-GENERATOR SWITCH
23-FUEL TANK GAGE

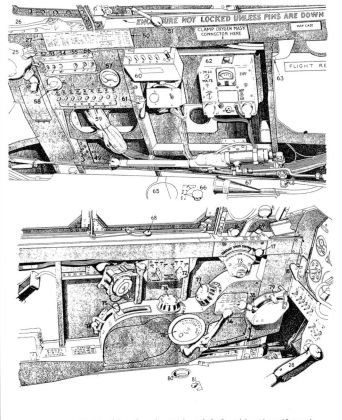

Right side view (upper) and left side view (lower) of P-51B cockpit.

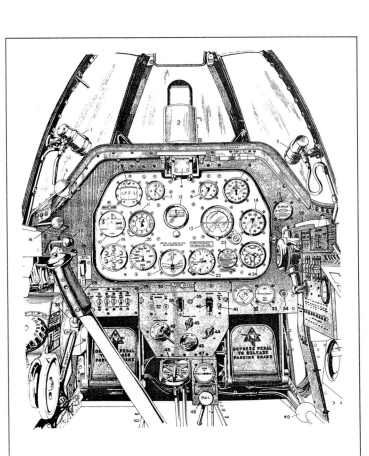

Forward view of P-51B cockpit instrument panel.

P-51B COCKPIT ITEMS

1. Fluorescent light.
2. Crash pad.
3. Fluorescent light.
4. Gunsight
5. Throttle.
6. Compass.
7. Clock.
8. Suction gage.
9. Manifold pressure gage.
10. Remote contactor.
11. Altimeter.
12. Directional gyro.
13. Flight indicator.
14. Tachometer.
15. Oxygen flow blinker.
16. Mixture control.
17. Propeller control.
18. Boost control.
19. Landing gear indicator.
20. Airspeed indicator.
21. Bank and turn indicator.
22. Rate of climb indicator.
23. Coolant temperature indicator.
24. Oil temp./fuel & oil gage.
25. Oxygen regulator.
26. Emergency release handle encl.
27. Engine instruction plate.

28. Control stick grip.
29. Gun & bomb control panel.
30. Parking brake control handle.
31. Parking brake instruction plate.
32. Engine primer.
33. Oxygen pressure gage.
34. Oxygen system warning light.
35. Bomb control handle.
36. Landing gear control.
37. Booster pump switches.
38. Supercharger control.
39. Supercharger warning light.
40. Starter switch.
41. Oil dilution switch.
42. Ignition switch.
43. Compass light control.
44. Gunsight light control.
45. LH fluorescent light control.
46. Fuel valve control.
47. (blank)
48. Emergency fairing door control.
49. Hydraulic hand pump.
50. Airplane restriction plate.
51. Cockpit enclosure handle.
52. Generator disconnect switch.
53. Battery disconnect switch.
54. Pitot heater switch.

55. Landing light switch.
56. Position light switches.
57. Ammeter.
58. RH fluorescent light control.
59. Circuit breaker buttons.
60. SCR522 Radio control box.
61. Cockpit light.
62. SCR535 Radio control box.
63. Map case.
64. (Restricted item).
65. Right fuel tank gage.
66. Hot air control.
67. Pilot's relief tube.
68. Sliding window lock handle.
69. Carburetor mixture control.
70. Signal pistol discharge tube.
71. Cooland radiator scoop control.
72. Oil radiator scoop control.
73. Quadrant friction control.
74. Flap control handle.
75. Carburetor air control.
76. Rudder trim tab control.
77. Aileron trim tab control.
78. Elevator trim tab control.
79. Bomb control anti-salvo guard.
80. Left fuel tank gage.
81. Defroster control.

Cockpit *** LEFT SIDE

1. Side Air Outlet Control Knob
2. Signal Pistol Storage Case
3. Signal Pistol Mount
4. Armrest
5. Cockpit Light
6. Coolant Radiator Air Control Switch
7. Oil Radiator Air Control Switch
8. Landing Light Switch
9. Fluorescent Light Rheostat
10. Mixture Control
11. Propeller and Mixture Control Friction Lock
12. Propeller Control
13. Throttle
14. Microphone Button
15. Bomb-Tank Salvo Levers
16. Landing Gear Handle
17. Throttle Friction Lock
18. Aileron Trim Tab Control Knob
19. Elevator Trim Tab Control Wheel
20. Rudder Trim Tab Control Knob
21. Shoulder-harness Lock Handle
22. Carburetor Ram-air Control Lever
23. Carburetor Hot-air Control Lever
24. Anti-G Suit Connector
25. Wing Flap Handle
26. Map Case
27. Drop Message Bag Holder

P-51D

Cockpit *** RIGHT SIDE

1. Oxygen Regulator
2. Canopy Emergency Release Handle
3. Circuit-breaker Reset Cover
4. Recognition Light Keying Switch (Disconnected)
5. Fluorescent Light Rheostat
6. Ammeter
7. Canopy Handcrank
8. VHF Control Box
9. DF Tone Switch
10. IFF Radar Control Panel
11. Side Air Outlet Control Knob
12. Oxygen Hose
13. Coolant Flap Emergency Release Handle
14. First-aid Kit
15. Circuit Breakers
16. Seat Adjustment Lever
17. Cockpit Light
18. VHF Volume Control Knob
19. Range Receiver Control Box
20. Right Switch Panel
21. Battery-disconnect Switch
22. Generator-disconnect Switch
23. Spare Bulb Compartment

P-51D

INSTRUMENTS

Allison powered P-51s had the following complement of instruments: Flight instruments were clock, accelerometer, altimeter, turn indicator, flight indicator, airspeed indicator, bank and turn indicator, rate of climb indicator, and magnetic compass. Engine instruments included suction gage, manifold pressure gage, tachometer, coolant temperature indicator, oil temperature and fuel and oil gage. Other instruments were an oxygen flow indicator, a hydraulic pressure gage, and an ammeter.

Merlin powered aircraft carried an instrument complement as follows: Flight instruments were the airspeed indicator, remote-reading compass indicator, directional gyro, clock, rate of climb indicator, flight indicator, accelerometer, and altimeter. Engine instruments included a suction gage, manifold pressure gage, coolant temperature gage, tachometer, carburetor air temperature gage, and engine gage unit. Other instruments were the oxygen pressure gage, hydraulic pressure gage, and ammeter.

SURFACE CONTROLS (P-51B/C AIRCRAFT)

The surface controls consisted of stick, rudder pedals, and trim wheels in the cockpit and the runs from these to elevators, ailerons, and rudder, and to the respective trim tabs.

The elevators were operated by the fore-aft motion of the stick mounted on a pivot supported by a tube set in pillow blocks. The stick motion was transferred aft by a rod running through the tube to a bellcrank system just aft of the cockpit. Here the motion was

(Right) P-51D

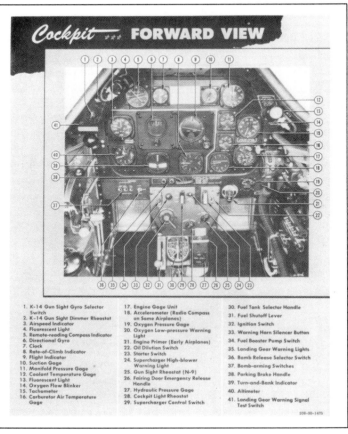

Cockpit *** FORWARD VIEW

1. K-14 Gun Sight Gyro Selector Switch
2. K-14 Gun Sight Dimmer Rheostat
3. Airspeed Indicator
4. Fluorescent Light
5. Remote-reading Compass Indicator
6. Directional Gyro
7. Clock
8. Rate-of-Climb Indicator
9. Flight Indicator
10. Suction Gage
11. Manifold Pressure Gage
12. Coolant Temperature Gage
13. Fluorescent Light
14. Oxygen Flow Blinker
15. Tachometer
16. Carburetor Air Temperature Gage
17. Engine Gage Unit
18. Accelerometer (Radio Compass on Some Airplanes)
19. Oxygen Pressure Gage
20. Oxygen Low-pressure Warning Light
21. Engine Primer (Early Airplanes)
22. Oil Dilution Switch
23. Starter Switch
24. Supercharger High-blower Warning Light
25. Gun Sight Rheostat (N-9)
26. Fairing Door Emergency Release Handle
27. Hydraulic Pressure Gage
28. Cockpit Light Rheostat
29. Supercharger Control Switch
30. Fuel Tank Selector Handle
31. Fuel Shutoff Lever
32. Ignition Switch
33. Warning Horn Silencer Button
34. Fuel Booster Pump Switch
35. Landing Gear Warning Lights
36. Bomb Release Selector Switch
37. Bomb-arming Switches
38. Parking Brake Handle
39. Turn-and-Bank Indicator
40. Altimeter
41. Landing Gear Warning Signal Test Switch

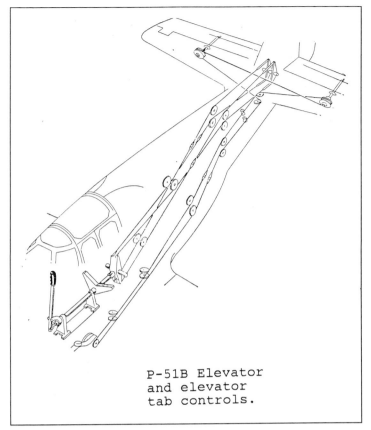

P-51B Elevator
and elevator
tab controls.

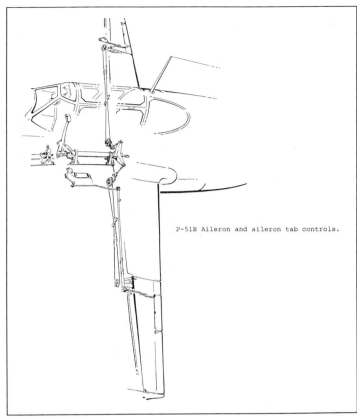

P-51B Aileron and aileron tab controls.

transferred to a dual set of preformed tinned steel cables running over pulleys to the rear end of the fuselage where the cables were tied to two bellcranks. These were attached to the torque tubes at the inboard end of each elevator at the nose. On late airplanes and with retrofits to earlier models a 20 pound bobweight was introduced into the elevator control system to increase required pilot stick forces and lessen the tendency to overcontrol. The bobweight was tied in with the bellcrank just aft of the cockpit. The cockpit elevator trim wheel drove a closed system of cables over pulleys aft in the fuselage and out through the stabilizer on each side to cable drums on the forward ends of mechanical screw actuators translating rotary into linear motion. The actuators drove control horns on the plywood trim tabs.

The ailerons were operated by the lateral motion of the pilot's stick turning the lower tube set in pillow blocks. Two crank arms fastened to the aft end of the tube drove linkages on each side connecting to pulleys at the inboard wing areas. From there the control motion was carried out each wing on pulley and cable systems just behind the aft spar. At the inboard end of the aileron the driven pulley's motion was translated into linear motion to drive the ailerons. The left aileron trim tab drive from the cockpit trim wheel started in the fuselage with bevel gears and shafts translating aft to the rear spar area where a cable drum and pulley system took over running out the wing. The driven cable drum was located on a screw actuator translating rotary to linear motion where the output drove a trim tab horn to move the surface.

The rudder pedal motion was translated aft through the fuselage by a pulley and cable system to drive the rudder torque tube control horns. The runs were also connected to bell cranks at the rear fuselage which implemented tail wheel steering. Rudder trim tab action was obtained by rotating the cockpit trim wheel whose motion actuated a continuous system of drums, pulleys, and cables extending aft through the fuselage and up the vertical fin to a screw actuator driving the tab via a control horn. On most aircraft a reverse-boost rudder tab was installed. Reverse action of the tab was obtained by a linkage that caused the tab to move slightly in the same direction as the rudder, making it necessary to increase rudder pedal pressure to obtain an increase in yaw of the aircraft.

ELECTRICAL SYSTEM

The Allison powered aircraft electrical system was a 24 volt DC single wire ground return type with power supplied by a battery or an engine-driven generator. The battery was located on a shelf just aft of the cockpit rear bulkhead. Items powered by the electrical system included the magnetos, propeller and propeller governor, starter, fuel booster pump, instruments, radio gear, aircraft lights, gun solonoids, gunsight, and drop tank and bomb release systems.

The electrical system for the Merlin powered P-51D aircraft was a 24 volt DC single wire ground return type with the airframe providing the return. It was powered by a 28 volt 100 ampere engine-driven generator with a 24 volt 34 ampere-hour battery supplying current when generator output dropped below 26.5 volts.

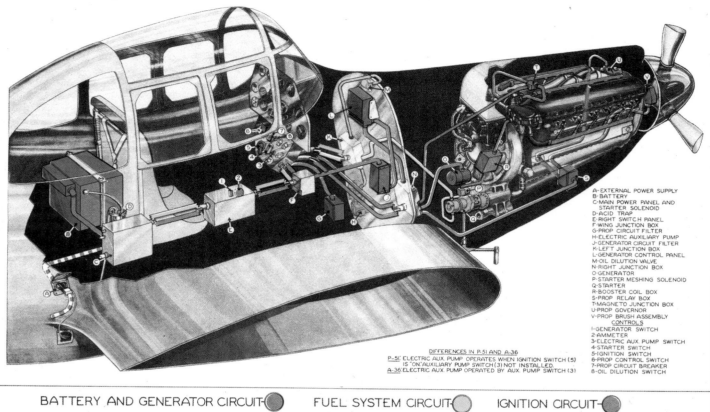

ALLISON V-1710 F-3R-39 & F-21R-87 ELECTRICAL SYSTEM in NORTH AMERICAN P-51 & A-36

A- EXTERNAL POWER SUPPLY
B- BATTERY
C- MAIN POWER PANEL AND STARTER SOLENOID
D- ACID TRAP
E- RIGHT SWITCH PANEL
F- WING JUNCTION BOX
G- PROP CIRCUIT FILTER
H- ELECTRIC AUXILIARY PUMP
J- GENERATOR CIRCUIT FILTER
K- LEFT JUNCTION BOX
L- GENERATOR CONTROL PANEL
M- OIL DILUTION VALVE
N- RIGHT JUNCTION BOX
O- GENERATOR
P- STARTER MESHING SOLENOID
Q- STARTER
R- BOOSTER COIL BOX
S- PROP RELAY BOX
T- MAGNETO JUNCTION BOX
U- PROP GOVERNOR
V- PROP BRUSH ASSEMBLY

CONTROLS
1- GENERATOR SWITCH
2- AMMETER
3- ELECTRIC AUX. PUMP SWITCH
4- STARTER SWITCH
5- IGNITION SWITCH
6- PROP CONTROL SWITCH
7- PROP CIRCUIT BREAKER
8- OIL DILUTION SWITCH

DIFFERENCES IN P.51 AND A-36
P-51: ELECTRIC AUX. PUMP OPERATES WHEN IGNITION SWITCH (5) IS "ON." AUXILIARY PUMP SWITCH (3) NOT INSTALLED.
A-36: ELECTRIC AUX. PUMP OPERATED BY AUX. PUMP SWITCH (3)

BATTERY AND GENERATOR CIRCUIT
EXTERNAL POWER CIRCUIT
FUEL SYSTEM CIRCUIT
PROPELLER CIRCUIT
IGNITION CIRCUIT
STARTER CIRCUIT

An external power receptacle was located on the fuselage right or left side just below the cockpit. The battery was located just aft of the pilot rear armor on a shelf. In late models it was moved to the engine compartment. All electrical circuits were protected by circuit breakers. An inverter was provided to supply 26 volt 400 cycle AC power for the remote-reading compass. The main electrical switch panel was on the cockpit right side as were the circuit breakers. An ammeter was provided. Items powered by the electrical system included the pitot heater, aircraft lights, gunsight, gun heaters, armament controls, fuel primer, oil circulation system, supercharger control, oil cooler and coolant scoop exit flap actuators, radios, boost pumps, and engine starter.

HYDRAULIC SYSTEM

On the Allison powered P-51, P-51A, and A-36A the hydraulic system was used to power landing gear extension and retraction including tail wheel, radiator scoop exit flap operation, wing flaps, and on the A-36A version the dive flaps. The basic system was made up of a reservoir mounted in the engine compartment, an engine-driven pump, filter and accumulator also in that compartment,

a hand crank on the cockpit floor, pressure gage on the instrument panel, and control valves, lines, and couplings. The operation of the landing gear was controlled by a selector valve in the cockpit, and seven actuating cylinders powered the gear, three on each side for the main gear and one for the tail gear. Separate cylinders operated retraction of the main gear, the downlock, and also the gear fairing door. Another cylinder operated tail wheel retraction. A hydraulic cylinder in each wing moved a piston, connecting link, and bell crank on the A-36A to open and close the perforated dive flaps employed on that airplane. The control was a dive flap selector valve in the cockpit. A single hydraulically-operated actuator powered the exit flap of the radiator duct in the belly, and another single hydraulic actuator in the fuselage drove the wing flaps. The flap actuator piston drove a link and bellcrank on a lateral tube, and another crank arm on the tube on each side drove the flaps through linkage at the inboard ends. A valve in the cockpit controlled the hydraulics. If the engine-driven hydraulic pump failed the emergency hand pump could be used to keep system pressure up and operate the above items. A handle was provided to release pressure and drop the landing gear in case of hydraulic failure.

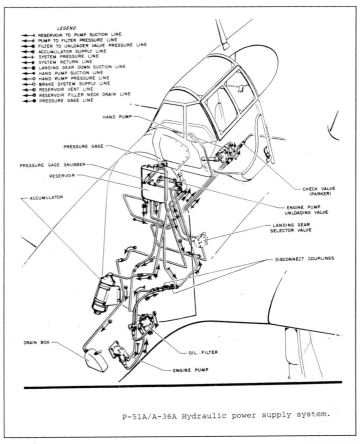

LEGEND
- RESERVOIR TO PUMP SUCTION LINE
- PUMP TO FILTER PRESSURE LINE
- FILTER TO UNLOADER VALVE PRESSURE LINE
- ACCUMULATOR SUPPLY LINE
- SYSTEM PRESSURE LINE
- SYSTEM RETURN LINE
- LANDING GEAR DOWN SUCTION LINE
- HAND PUMP SUCTION LINE
- HAND PUMP PRESSURE LINE
- BRAKE SYSTEM SUPPLY LINE
- RESERVOIR VENT LINE
- RESERVOIR FILLER NECK DRAIN LINE
- PRESSURE GAGE LINE

HAND PUMP
PRESSURE GAGE
PRESSURE GAGE SNUBBER
RESERVOIR
ACCUMULATOR
CHECK VALVE (PARKER)
ENGINE PUMP UNLOADING VALVE
LANDING GEAR SELECTOR VALVE
DISCONNECT COUPLINGS
DRAIN BOX
OIL FILTER
ENGINE PUMP

P-51A/A-36A Hydraulic power supply system.

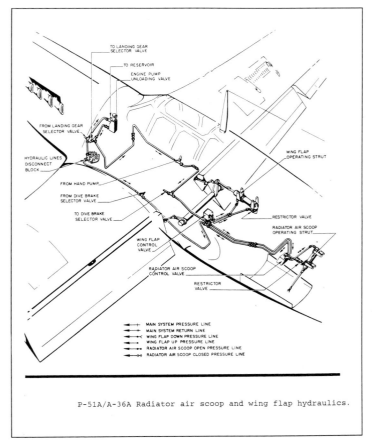

TO LANDING GEAR SELECTOR VALVE
TO RESERVOIR
ENGINE PUMP UNLOADING VALVE
FROM LANDING GEAR SELECTOR VALVE
HYDRAULIC LINES DISCONNECT BLOCK
FROM HAND PUMP
FROM DIVE BRAKE SELECTOR VALVE
TO DIVE BRAKE SELECTOR VALVE
WING FLAP CONTROL VALVE
RADIATOR AIR SCOOP CONTROL VALVE
RESTRICTOR VALVE
WING FLAP OPERATING STRUT
RESTRICTOR VALVE
RADIATOR AIR SCOOP OPERATING STRUT

- MAIN SYSTEM PRESSURE LINE
- MAIN SYSTEM RETURN LINE
- WING FLAP DOWN PRESSURE LINE
- WING FLAP UP PRESSURE LINE
- RADIATOR AIR SCOOP OPEN PRESSURE LINE
- RADIATOR AIR SCOOP CLOSED PRESSURE LINE

P-51A/A-36A Radiator air scoop and wing flap hydraulics.

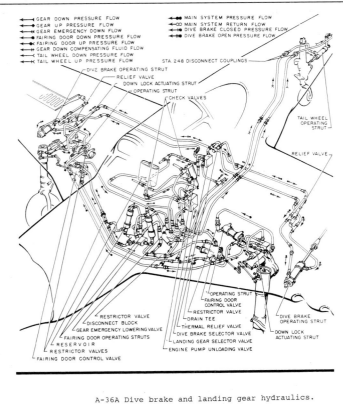

- GEAR DOWN PRESSURE FLOW
- GEAR UP PRESSURE FLOW
- GEAR EMERGENCY DOWN FLOW
- FAIRING DOOR DOWN PRESSURE FLOW
- FAIRING DOOR UP PRESSURE FLOW
- GEAR DOWN COMPENSATING FLUID FLOW
- TAIL WHEEL DOWN PRESSURE FLOW
- TAIL WHEEL UP PRESSURE FLOW
- MAIN SYSTEM PRESSURE FLOW
- MAIN SYSTEM RETURN FLOW
- DIVE BRAKE CLOSED PRESSURE FLOW
- DIVE BRAKE OPEN PRESSURE FLOW

STA 248 DISCONNECT COUPLINGS
DIVE BRAKE OPERATING STRUT
RELIEF VALVE
DOWN LOCK ACTUATING STRUT
OPERATING STRUT
CHECK VALVES
TAIL WHEEL OPERATING STRUT
RELIEF VALVE
RESTRICTOR VALVE
DISCONNECT BLOCK
GEAR EMERGENCY LOWERING VALVE
FAIRING DOOR OPERATING STRUTS
RESERVOIR
RESTRICTOR VALVES
FAIRING DOOR CONTROL VALVE
OPERATING STRUT
FAIRING DOOR CONTROL VALVE
RESTRICTOR VALVE
DRAIN TEE
THERMAL RELIEF VALVE
DIVE BRAKE SELECTOR VALVE
LANDING GEAR SELECTOR VALVE
ENGINE PUMP UNLOADING VALVE
DIVE BRAKE OPERATING STRUT
DOWN LOCK ACTUATING STRUT

A-36A Dive brake and landing gear hydraulics.

The hydraulic system for the Merlin powered airplanes was a closed-center arrangement that incorporated an accumulator and a relief valve to prevent excess pressure. A hydraulic reservoir was located in the engine compartment, and supplied fluid to the toe brakes and parking brake system as well as for landing gear and wing flap operation. A hydraulic pressure gage was located in the cockpit. The hydraulic system operated at a normal pressure of 1000 to 1100 PSI. Early versions had a 1.8 gallon reservoir, later ones a 1.2 gallon size. Landing gear and flap handles in the cockpit operated gear and flap selector valves respectively to direct fluid to actuators. A landing gear fairing door emergency handle operated an emergency release valve to allow the gear to lower in event of hydraulic failure. The plane was then yawed to engage the gear downlocks. Normal operation of the gear was effected by the main gear retraction actuating cylinder, the downlock actuator, and the fairing door actuator on each side. In the P-51B and P-51C the tail wheel was retracted by a hydraulic actuator; on the P-51D the tail wheel was not retractable on late models. Flaps had a total downward travel, but the flap handle could be used to obtain any of four intermediate angles. There was no emergency means of lowering the flaps; however, if the engine-driven hydraulic pump alone failed the hydraulic accumulator had enough pressure to lower them if the gage showed at least 800 PSI.

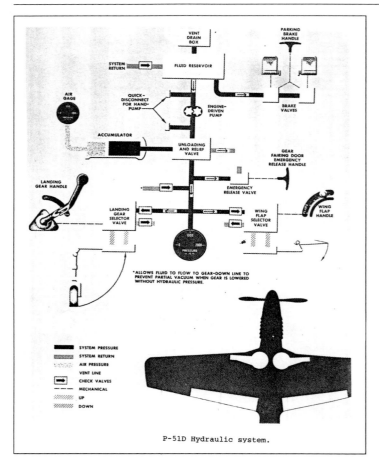

P-51D Hydraulic system.

PNEUMATIC SYSTEM

An engine-driven vacuum pump was used to provide vacuum for instruments and to assist in drawing fuel from external drop tanks. It was also used on late airplanes to provide pressure for an anti-g suit.

COMMUNICATION/NAVIGATION/IDENTIFICATION SYSTEMS

For the Allison powered P-51 versions and the A-36A, a typical radio installation was the SCR-274 Command Set which included a transmitter and three receivers. An alternate installation was the newer SCR-522 set. Other alternatives were the SCR-535, SCR-515, or the SCR-695. Radio equipment was carried on shelves in the turtledeck area aft of the cockpit. A direction finding system with external loop antenna was carried in some operational theatres. An IFF transponder was often carried in P-51A aircraft.

The P-51D models used either an SCR-522A or an AN/ARC-3 Command Radio set, a BC-453B range receiver installed in conjunction with the command set, and the AN/ARA-8 homing adapter. An alternate IFF transponder was the AN/APX-6. On airplanes with the fuselage fuel tank and battery behind the pilot seat the IFF set was not installed. If, however, either the fuselage fuel tank had been removed or the battery had been moved forward of the firewall the IFF equipment could be installed. Control panels for radio gear were located at the right side of the cockpit.

ARMAMENT PROVISIONS

The armament provisions varied significantly between various models of the P-51 and A-36A Mustang airplane.

The P-51 version was unique in carrying four M2 20mm cannon, two in each wing, with barrels and their fairings extending well ahead of the wing leading edge. Each cannon installation had a maximum of 125 rounds of ammunition storage capability in the wing. The aircraft had no provision for carrying bombs or rockets.

The P-51A model was equipped basically with four .50 caliber wing guns with the option of adding two more .50 caliber guns under each side of the engine in the nose, and synchronized to fire through the propeller. The A-36A dive bomber version had the six .50 caliber machine guns, four wing and two fuselage, as basic equipment. Thus the P-51A and A-36A installations will be described together. With the six .50 caliber guns installed normal provisions were made for 200 rounds of ammunition per gun, but a maximum load of 1100 rounds could be carried. The two fuselage guns were mounted at a rolled angle on structural hard points adjacent to the engine mount low in the cowled area. Blast tubes covered the inner portion of the barrels with barrel ends protruding to a point just aft of the propeller spinner. Ammunition boxes and shell case and link containers were located directly adjacent under the cowling. An impulse tube synchronization system was used, and guns were not to be fired under 1000 and over 3000 RPM. The fuselage guns fired parallel and were adjusted vertically so that fire converged with the line of sight at 300 yards. Charging these fuselage guns was done mechanically by pulling back and releasing the gun charging handles at the upper right and left sides of the instrument panel support. No gun heating system was required for these weapons. If the fuselage guns were removed there was no need to ballast the aircraft since it tended to be nose heavy with them installed. The four wing .50 caliber guns were adjusted horizontally and vertically so fire converged with the line of sight at 300 yards. These guns were charged manually prior to flight. The wing guns were located in bays just outboard of the landing gear support with breeches between front and rear spars and barrels and blast tubes protruding through the front spar web to leading edge ports. Wing inboard .50 calibers had storage capacity for 250 rounds of ammunition each, outboard for 350 rounds. Gun trays were laid in troughs in the bay outboard of the guns, and warm air heating was supplied to the gun bays. The guns were fired electrically by lifting a safety switch on the armament control panel and then depressing the trigger switch on the control stick.

In some export Mustangs the wing gun arrangement was made up of one .50 caliber gun inboard in each wing bay and two .30 caliber machine guns just outboard on each side. The installation was generally the same as in the Allison P-51A and A-36A. These export aircraft normally carried the two fuselage .50 caliber weapons.

The Allison powered airplanes were provided with an optical reflector-type gunsight with rheostat for the sight lamp and an auxiliary external ring and bead sight. The bead was permanently installed on the firewall forward of the cockpit; the ring could be removed from local stowage in the cockpit and installed in flight.

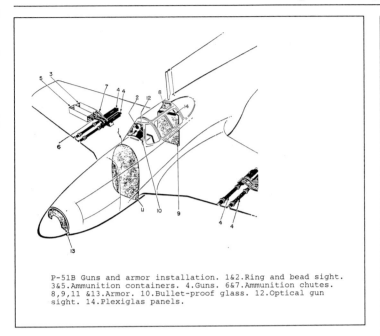

P-51B Guns and armor installation. 1&2.Ring and bead sight. 3&5.Ammunition containers. 4.Guns. 6&7.Ammunition chutes. 8,9,11 &13.Armor. 10.Bullet-proof glass. 12.Optical gun sight. 14.Plexiglas panels.

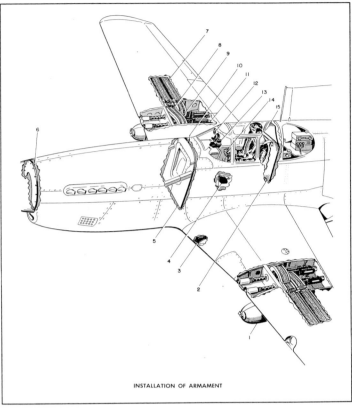

INSTALLATION OF ARMAMENT

The P-51A airplanes could be equipped with wing bomb racks, one on each side, to carry either two 100, 250, 325, or 500 pound bombs, as could the A-36A. The bombs were released simultaneously either manually or electrically in either safe or armed condition. The bomb control handle was on the forward left side of the cockpit. Bombs were released electrically via arming switches and a bomb release button on the top of the stick grip, and manually via the bomb control handle. Bombs could be released in any attitude from a 30 degree climb to a vertical dive, but sideslipping more than five degrees in a vertical dive was dangerous since the propeller could be hit by a bomb.

Rockets were fitted in the field to some Allison powered Mustangs.

The Merlin powered P-51B and P-51C airplanes were provided with a new installation of four .50 caliber guns in the wings and had no fuselage guns. The two guns in each wing were mounted in a rolled or canted position, rotated 60 degrees. They were normally adjusted to converge fire with aircraft centerline at 300 yards. A lateral adjustment of one half degree either side was provided. Guns were quickly removeable through doors in the upper wing surface over the weapons and between spars. Ammunition was fed to the top sides of the guns through curved stainless steel chutes, with cases and links being ejected through metal chutes in the lower wing skin. All four guns were fired simultaneously by a control stick switch. A reflector-type gunsight was used. This optical or an auxiliary ring and bead sight could be employed. Electric heaters were attached to each gun. Ammunition capacity was 250 rounds for each inboard gun and 350 rounds for each outboard weapon. A removeable streamlined wing bomb rack with integral sway braces was provided for bombs up to 500 pounds on each side. Rockets could be installed via a field change using kits.

KEY, P-51B INSTALLATION OF ARMAMENT

1. Bomb Rack and Bomb	9. Outboard Gun Feed Chute
2. Pilot's Rear Armor Plate	10. Auxiliary Bead Sight
3. Camera, 35 mm. or 75 mm. Lens	11. Machine Gun, .50 Caliber M2
4. Bomb Rack Handle Assembly	12. Auxiliary Ring Sight
5. Firewall Armor Plate	13. Gunsight
6. Coolant Tank Armor Plate	14. Type B-5 Gun Control Switch
7. Rear .50 Caliber Ammunition Box	15. Pilot's Head Rear Armor Plate
8. Inboard Gun Feed Chute	

The P-51D version had six .50 caliber machine guns , three mounted upright in each wing with each gun having a type J-1 or J-4 electric gun heater. Either of two gun installations was possible: three mounted in each wing with 500 rounds (400 rounds on late airplanes) for each

inboard gun, and 270 rounds for each center and outboard gun; or, the center gun could be removed allowing the inboard guns to carry 500 rounds (400 rounds in late airplanes), and the outboard guns to carry 500 rounds each. Ammunition containers were mounted in the wings. Empty cases were ejected through the bottom of the wings. Gun charging was done manually on the ground before flight. A gun charger handle was stowed in each gun bay for this purpose. The guns were normally boresighted with a point of convergence at 250 or 300 yards. A gun safety switch was located to the right of the gunsight and a trigger switch was mounted on the control stick. The gun heater switch was mounted on the right switch panel.

Early P-51D airplanes were equipped with the N-9 gunsight, a non-computing type with a fixed reticle, the only control being the

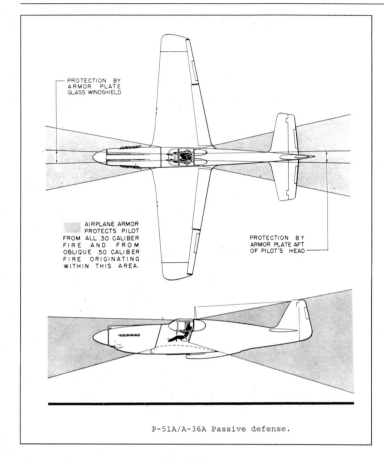

P-51A/A-36A Passive defense.

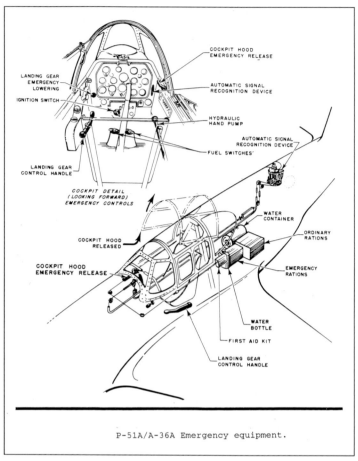

P-51A/A-36A Emergency equipment.

dimmer rheostat to vary reticle brilliance. A ball bank indicator was mounted right on the sight. Later airplanes were equipped with the K-14A or K-14B computing sight with both a fixed and a gyro optical system. The sight gyro motor was turned on by a switch on a control panel. A throttle twist grip on late models was used to adjust sight range.

External removeable bomb racks , one on each wing, could carry one 100, 250, or 500 pound bomb. The bomb system electrical control was backed up by two bomb salvo handles providing for mechanical release. Bombs were aimed using the gunsight. Late airplanes were equipped to carry ten zero-rail rockets attached to two pads on the wing underside. Rockets were aimed using the gun sight. If bombs or drop tanks were carried only six rockets could be installed. The rocket armament switches were located on the front switch panel in a special rocket panel insert.

The gun armament was most often kept aboard the aircraft in the F-6 photo variants.

PASSIVE DEFENCE SYSTEM
The Allison powered P-51 aircraft incorporated an armor plated firewall as basic integral equipment to protect the pilot from the front along with a forward windshield section made up of bullet-resistant glass. Provision was made, as overload equipment, for armor plate behind the pilot seat to protect his head and back. All armor was sufficient to counter .30 caliber fire from any angle and .50 caliber fire from oblique angles.

On the P-51B a combination armor plate-firewall was installed forward made of face-hardened steel except for a section at the center of stainless steel to provide room for the oil tank. Rear protection was provided by two plates of face-hardened steel aft of the cockpit. The forward flat section of the windshield was a bullet-proof five ply piece of laminated glass one and one half inches thick slanted 31 degrees aft from the vertical. All internal fuel tanks were self-sealing.

The armor complement of the P-51D and P-51K was similar to that of the P-51B.

FURNISHINGS
On the Allison powered airplanes the cockpit seat was made of plywood and accomodated a seat-type parachute. The back cushion was kapok-filled to make it buoyant and useful as a life preserver. The seat had a type B-11 safety belt and a shoulder harness attached to a spring-loaded mechanism. A control lever for the harness was located to the left of the seat, and a seat vertical adjustment lever was located on the right side. The relief tube horn was stowed under the seat. The tubing extended along the lower inboard side of the fuselage to where it emerged through a metal scoop outlet beneath the rudder. A first aid kit was on the left fuselage side panel in the radio compartment. A water container and bottle and two rations kits were stowed in the radio compartment.

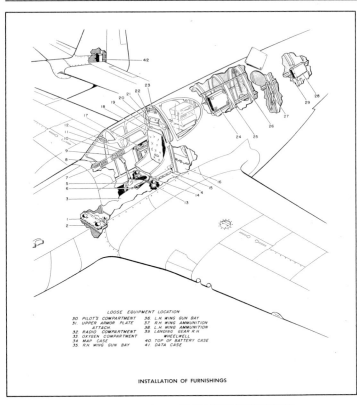

LOOSE EQUIPMENT LOCATION
30. PILOT'S COMPARTMENT
31. UPPER ARMOR PLATE
    ATTACH.
32. RADIO COMPARTMENT
33. OXYGEN COMPARTMENT
34. MAP CASE
35. R.H. WING GUN BAY
36. L.H. WING GUN BAY
37. R.H. WING AMMUNITION
38. L.H. WING AMMUNITION
39. LANDING GEAR R.H.
    WHEELWELL
40. TOP OF BATTERY CASE
41. DATA CASE

INSTALLATION OF FURNISHINGS

P-51A/A-36A INSTALLATION OF FURNISHINGS

The Merlin powered P-51D had a seat with vertical adjustment; pins could snap into any of nine holes. The pilot's parachute was used as a seat cushion, and the kapok-filled seat back could be used as a life preserver. Shoulder straps and a safety belt were attached to the seat and secured by a quick-release safety buckle. A first aid kit was located on the right side of the seat. Provision for an anti-g suit connection was made by an air pressure outlet at the left side of the seat with pressure taken from the exhaust side of the engine-driven vacuum pump. A data case with a drop message bag was carried at the left of the seat. An arm rest was located on the left longeron aft of the engine control quadrant, and a relief tube was stowed on the floor to the left of the seat.

HEATING/COOLING/VENTILATION SYSTEMS

Wooden bulkheads were provided aft of the cockpit on the Allison powered airplanes to aid in the heating of the cockpit and to minimize drafts. A hot air valve directing air from aft of the radiator was located to the right rear of the pilot's seat; a cold air valve was located to the left of the control stick. A windshield defroster was controlled by a handle over the instrument panel.

On the Merlin powered P-51D warm air was routed to the cockpit from a scoop aft of the coolant radiator. The warm air passed through a flexible duct to a point behind the pilot's seat; from there a duct led to the hot air outlet valve at the right side of the cockpit. Air from the forward side of the radiator air scoop was used to cool the cockpit. Hot and cold air control handles and knobs were on the floor near the stick. Some of the hot air was directed to the wind-

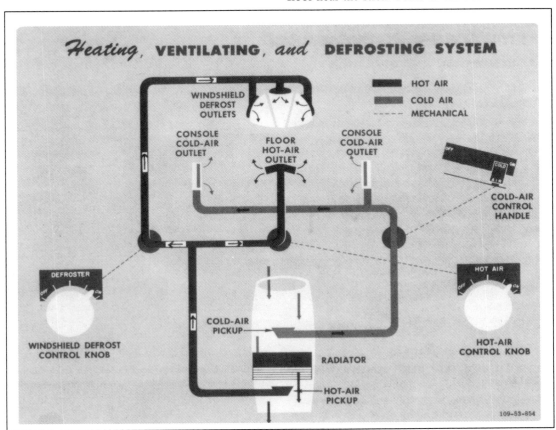

P-51D

shield and side glass panels. The defroster control knob was on the floor. Heating for the pitot tube was electrical with a cockpit control switch, and electrical heating was supplied for the guns.

ICE PROTECTION SYSTEM

The Allison powered P-51s had a carburetor anti-ice system which on some aircraft consisted of a reservoir aft of and below the pilot's seat, and a hand pump to the left of the seat. On other aircraft the system used a temporary tank in the right hand wing ammunition box, along with an electrically-driven pump operated by a cockpit switch. A spray jet provided fluid for the windshield from the coolant system, controlled by a valve above the instrument panel. A glycol slinger ring type of deicing system could be installed for the propeller blades. A wing and tail deicer shoe set could be supplied at an additional weight of 51 pounds.

As noted above, the P-51D airplane windshield was hot air defrosted.

HOISTING/TOWING/LEVELING/TIEDOWN EQUIPMENT

Allison Mustangs had provision for a 21 pound mooring kit for tiedown. Two airplane hoist rings could be supplied where required. Tow rings were provided on the main landing gear.

On the P-51D Mustang tiedown points were provided on each wing, each main landing gear wheel axle, and on the fuselage. A flush mooring ring was located on the lower surface of each wing, and could be pried out for use. The mooring rings were on the inboard side of the wheel axles. For fuselage tiedown rope was passed through the lift tube in the aft fuselage.

FLOTATION/ARRESTING/CATAPULTING GEAR

No gear of these types was carried. The P-51D would sink in about two seconds after ditching in the water.

USEFUL LOAD SUBSYSTEMS
GUNS/BOMBS/ROCKETS

See the earlier section.

GUNSIGHT/GUN CAMERA

Gunsights were mentioned earlier. In the Allison P-51s an N-1 gun camera was located low in the nose in front of the engine.

In Merlin P-51D airplanes a Type N-4 or N-6 gun camera was installed in the leading edge of the left wing. The camera could be set for 16, 32, or 64 frames per second. On early airplanes the camera opening was covered by glass; on later planes the opening was covered by a spring-loaded metal plate attached by a cable to the left landing gear. A heater in the camera functioned automatically when the temperature was low. The camera was controlled by the gun safety switch and the gun trigger on the switch.

PYROTECHNICS

On the Allison airplanes an automatic signal recognition device was located aft of the radio compartment with a control at the pilot's right. The control had a selector so flares of any color could be put in firing position.

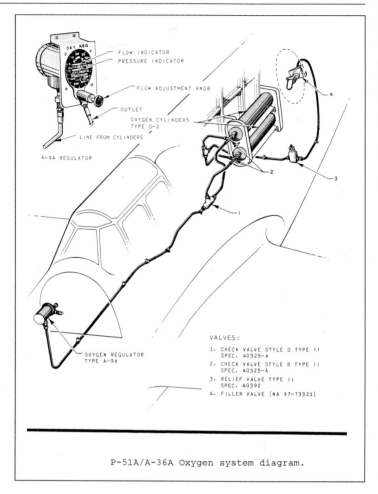

P-51A/A-36A Oxygen system diagram.

The P-51D carried a Type M-8 pyrotechnic pistol stowed in a canvas holster strapped to a pistol cartridge stowage bag at the left of the pilot.

PHOTOGRAPHIC EQUIPMENT

The only photo equipment in the fighter versions was the gun camera. The F-6 airplanes were the photo versions. Two K-24 camera installations were provided in the early versions of P-51A aircraft. Later Merlin powered airplanes of the F-6 series carried one each K-17, K-22, and K-24 cameras.

OXYGEN SYSTEM

On Allison Mustangs a low pressure oxygen system was provided with the A-9A regulator located on the right hand side of the instrument panel. Two D-2 oxygen cylinders were in the fuselage aft of the cockpit, and could be recharged without removal from the aircraft.

On the P-51D two type D-2 and two Type F-2 low pressure oxygen cylinders were carried in the aft fuselage. They could be filled without removal using a filler valve on the lower left side of the fuselage. Normal full oxygen pressure was 400 PSI. Early D aircraft used the AN6004 oxygen regulator; later versions used the

A-12 diluter-demand regulator on the right side of the cockpit. Oxygen system controls and a pressure gage were located in the cockpit.

REFERENCES, P-51

1. *P-51 in Action*, Larry Davis
2. *The Mighty Eighth*, Roger Freeman.
3. *Mustang, The Story of the P-51 Fighter*, Robert W. Gruenhagen, Arco Publishing Co. Inc. NY
4. *US Army Air Forces in World War Two*, Craven and Cate, ed.
5. *Journal of the American Aviation Historical Society*, Summer,1964 Mustangs of the Eighth Air Force.
6. *JAAHS*, Summer,1961; Summer 1979; Winter 1978; Winter 1969; Fall 1985; Summer, 1980; Fall, 1980; Spring 1965.
7. *JAAHS*, Fall,1968, The First Air Commando Group.
8. Fighter Aces, Tolliver.
9. *To Fly and Fight*, Col.(Ret.) Clarence Anderson with Joseph Hamlin, St. Martins Press, NY, 1990.
10. *Minutes of Fighter Conference*, NAS Patuxent River, Md., Oct.1944.
11. *Tactical Planning Characteristics and Performance Chart*, P-51, Aug. 22, 1944, and July 8, 1945.
12. *Weights Archives*, J.J. Schneider.
13. *Air International Magazine*, Sept/Oct.1983, Mustang, The Willing War Horse.
14. *NAS Patuxent River Flight Test Report*, FT44086, Jan./Feb.1944.
15. *NACA Wartime Report MR L-6F-12 (L-741)*, June,1946, Flight Measurements of Drag Characteristics of the XP-51 Airplane.
16. *NACA MR*, Apr.1943, Flying Qualities and Stalling Characteristics of the North American XP-51 Airplane.
17. *Janes All The World's Aircraft*, 1945-1946.
18. Chapter XIV, *P-51 Laminar Airfoil, The Real Stuff*, E. J. Horkey (unpublished)
19. *North American Aviation Report 8679*, Briefing for P-51 Pilot Instructors, Louis S. Wait, Aug.8,1945.
20. *Duels in the Sky*, Eric Brown.
21. *Pilots Manual, A-36A Airplane/ A-36A-1-NA Airplane Pilots Flight Operating Instructions*, TO-01-60HB-1, Mar.20, 1943.
22. *Pilots Manual, F-51D Airplane, TO 1F-51D-1*, Jan.20,1954.
23. *Letters*, Col.(Ret.)"Bud" Anderson to F. H. Dean.
24. *Aviation Magazine*, July, 1944, Design Analysis #7, The North American P-51 Mustang.
25. *Aircraft Designer's Sketchbook*, Neville, McGraw Hill, NY, 1951.
26. *NorthAmerican Aviation Report 5723*, May 5, 1943, Aerodynamic Load Calculations, P-51B.
27. *NACA Report ACR 4K03*, Figure 22, Variation of Drag Coefficient with Mach Number, P-51B Airplane.
28. *NACA MR*, Aug.5,1944, Tests of Three Airfoil Sections for the North American XP-51F Airplane.
29. *NACA MR L4L18*, Flight Tests of the High Speed Performance of a P-51B Airplane.
30. *North American Aviation Report 8449*, Dec.1,1944, Performance Calcula tions for Model P-51D-5NA Airplane (NA-109).
31. *North American Aviation Report NA-46-130*, Feb.6,1946, Performance Calculations for Model P-51D Airplane (NA-122).
32. *NACA Wartime Report MR*, Dec.1943, Flight Tests of Beveled Trailing Edge Ailerons with Various Modifications on a North American XP-51.
33. *Mustang At War*, Roger A. Freeman, 1974.
34. *Test Flying at Old Wright Field*, by Ken Chilstrom, Westchester House Publishers, Omaha, Nebraska.
35. *Airpower Magazine*, November,1971, NA-73, The Forgotten Mustang, by Robert Waag.
36. *Air Classics Magazine*, July 1974, NA-73X, First of a Famous Breed, by Michael O'Leary.
37. *Heritage of Valor, The 8th Air Force in World War II*, by Budd J. Peaslee, Col.USAF, Ret.,J.B.Lippencott, Philadelphia Pa. and NY,1964
38. *Cross-Winds, An Airman's Memoir*, by Najeeb E. Halaby, Doubleday and Company, Inc.,NY, 1978.

THE P-61

TABLE 50
NORTHROP P-61 BLACK WIDOW MODELS

MILITARY DESIGNATION	NO.OF AIRCRAFT	FIRST DELIV.	NOTES
XP-61	2	F.F.MAY 1942	
YP-61	13	AUGUST 1943	SERVICE TEST;BECAME P-61.
P-61A-1	45	OCTOBER 1943	POWER TURRET IN FIRST 37 A/C ONLY. BUFFET TROUBLE
P-61A-5	35		NO TURRET, NEW ENGINE
P-61A-10	100		WATER INJECTION ADDED.
P-61A-11	20		WING RACKS ADDED.
P-61B-1,2,5,6,11	155	JULY 1944	EXTENDED NOSE, NO TURRET. WING RACKS ON -2,6,AND 11
P-61B-10	45	1944	FOUR WING RACKS
P-61B-15 TO -25	250	1944	TURRET BACK; 2 OR 4. WING RACKS; 2 on -16.
P-61C-1,5,10	41	JULY 1945	TURRET, TURBOSUPERCHARGERS, and AIR BRAKES
XP-61D	(2 CONVERTED)	NOVEMBER1944	P-61A-1;NEW ENG.,TURBO. FOUR WING RACKS
XP-61E	(2 CONVERTED)	APRIL 1945	P-61B, NO TURRET, MORE FUEL. 2-CREW, BUBBLE CANOPY
XP-61F	—	(CANC. 10/45)	PROJECT CANCELLED, AIRCRAFT COMPLETED AS P-61C-1
P-61G	(16 CONVERTED)	1945	P-61B-20 A/C MODIFIED FOR WEATHER RECON. NO ARMAMENT.
	TOTAL 706		

NOTES: -THE TOTAL ABOVE DOES NOT INCLUDE THE 36 F-15A REPORTERS, RECONN. AIRCRAFT BUILT IN 1946..
-THERE WERE 62 P-61B-1;38 B-2;3 B-5;47 B-6; AND 5 P-61B-11 AIRCRAFT.
-THERE WERE 153 B-15;6 B-16; 84 B-20; AND 7 B-25 AIRCRAFT.
-IN SEPTEMBER, 1945 THE USMC OBTAINED 12 P-61B AIRCRAFT FROM THE USAAF DESIGNATED F2T-1. THEY WERE USED TO TRAIN F7F- TIGERCAT CREWS FOR NIGHT-FIGHTING.
-OF THE TOTAL OF 706 AIRCRAFT ABOVE, 674 WERE PRODUCED BY THE END OF THE WAR.

TABLE 51
P-61 PHYSICAL DATA

SPAN	66'0"
LENGTH (P-61A)	48'11"
LENGTH (P-61B)	49'7"
HEIGHT (OVER RUDDER)	14'8"
HEIGHT TO PROP HUBS	7'0"
HEIGHT TO WING TIP	9'2"
TREAD	206.4"
WHEELBASE	180.7"
HORIZONTAL TAIL SPAN	16'8"
PROPELLER ARC DIAMETER	12'2"
PROPELLER TIP TO FUSELAGE CLEARANCE	11"
AIRCRAFT NOSE TO C/L PROPELLER HUB	10'6"
CREW NACELLE LENGTH	33'10"
CREW NACELLE WIDTH	49"
C/L AIRCRAFT TO C/L ENGINE NACELLE	8'11"
WING AREA	664 SQ.FT.
WING ROOT CHORD	144"
WING TIP CHORD (AT TIP ATTACHMENT)	80"
MEAN AERODYNAMIC CHORD	126.3"
INNER WING DIHEDRAL	4 DEG.
OUTER WING DIHEDRAL	2 DEG.
INNER WING FLAP SPAN	4'5"
OUTER WING FLAP SPAN	16'7"
AILERON SPAN	4'9"

TABLE 52
P-61 FUEL CAPACITIES
(US GAL.)

MODEL	INTERNAL FUEL CAPACITY	EXTERNAL FUEL CAPACITY
XP-61	646	—
YP-61	646	—
P-61	646	—
P-61A-1	646	—
P-61A-5,-10,-11	646	620 (A-11 only)
P-61B-1,-5	646	—
P-61B-2,-6,-11	646	620
P-61B-10	646	1240
P-61B-15,-20,-25	646	1240
P-61B-16	646	620
P-61C-1,-5,-10	646	1240
XP-61D	646	1240
XP-61E	1158	1240

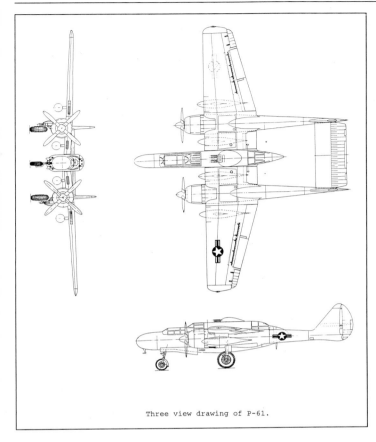

Three view drawing of P-61.

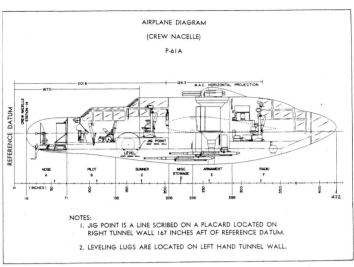

AIRPLANE DIAGRAM

(CREW NACELLE)

P-61A

NOTES:
1. JIG POINT IS A LINE SCRIBED ON A PLACARD LOCATED ON RIGHT TUNNEL WALL 167 INCHES AFT OF REFERENCE DATUM.

2. LEVELING LUGS ARE LOCATED ON LEFT HAND TUNNEL WALL.

Inboard profile drawing of P-61A crew nacelle.

Table 50 shows how few Black Widows were made compared to most other US production fighters. They made up less than one percent of America's Hundred Thousand. Some reasons: A late start, with production getting under way only in October 1943, the problem of a large relatively complex twin engined aircraft with considerable equipment sophistication for the period, and the need for large numbers of night fighters receding as the war went on. There were no massed enemy night bomber attacks on Allied territories to compare with the almost nightly operations of RAF Bomber Command over occupied Europe. So Widows tended to be used in squadron strength only. The data also shows well over half the aircraft were delivered without a power turret atop the crew nacelle. And the P-61C models with turbosupercharged engines added for better altitude performance were too late for wartime combat use, these versions built because of the "too low and slow " criticism of A and B models.

The physical data of Table 51 show the P-61 fighter compared in size to major wartime light and medium bombers of the USAAF. Span was greater than an A-20 attack bomber, and compared with that of both the B-25 and B-26 medium bombers. In addition P-61 wing area was greater than that of all three bombers. Large size and twin engined layout immediately put the P-61 at an agility disadvantage with smaller single engine fighters.

Table 52 indicates internal fuel capacity of the P-61 remained the same for all wartime versions, but shows how total capacity doubled, and then tripled by use of external drop tank capacity added

under the wings at two, then later four, store stations. This was a typical trend for wartime fighters.

The general arrangement drawing shows a graceful looking airplane except for the rather bulky and lumpy crew nacelle, or fuselage, this appearance generated mainly by placing the gunner cockpit a level above that of the pilot, and the bulge of the belly cannon installation. A noteable departure from convention can be seen in the wing plan where the flap span is large and the ailerons unusually small. This arrangement was allowed by use of spoilers for lateral control, and the location of these can be seen just forward of the flaps on the outer wing panels. A modern tricycle landing gear was utilized, and four blade propellers incorporated to absorb the high power of the R-2800 engines. Noteable also was the four-gun turret atop the fuselage and the bulbous radar nose..

The inboard profile of the P-61A crew nacelle provides a look at interior arrangement of this big three-crew fighter. The key to the whole night fighting problem was the radar carried in the nose with the dish antenna up front. The nose section was housed in a large fiberglass cover. Behind the nose radar came the pilot's compartment with his yoke and wheel controls inside a considerable amount of glass. The large nose gear assembly retracted into a well beneath this station. The gunner sat in a compartment just aft which was raised to provide a view forward over the top of the pilot compartment. A weapons control and sighting apparatus was provided the gunner. Armament of the P-61 was located centrally behind the gunner station and consisted of a four-gun turret and ammunition storage assemblies above, and four fixed 20 mm cannon and ammunition containers mounted in the central belly beneath floor level. The rearmost compartment was set up for the radio operator with radio gear, seat, and alternate weapons control and sighting equipment. The tail end of the crew nacelle was made up of large transparent areas, and the radio operator could face either looking forward or aft. Access to crew stations was gained through folding doors and ladders on the underside of the aircraft forward and aft.

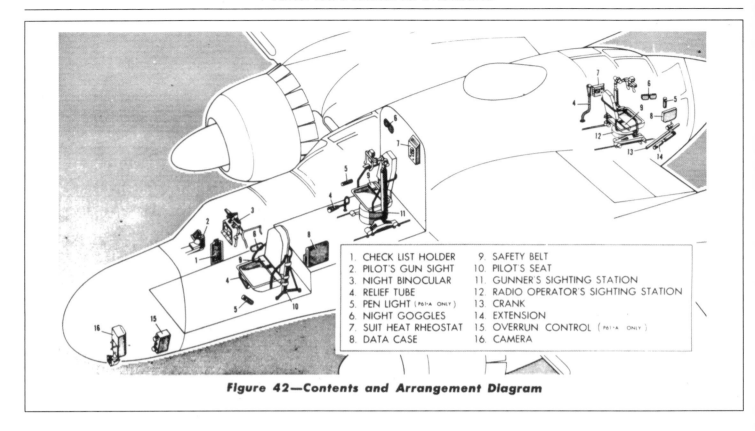

Figure 42—Contents and Arrangement Diagram

1. CHECK LIST HOLDER
2. PILOT'S GUN SIGHT
3. NIGHT BINOCULAR
4. RELIEF TUBE
5. PEN LIGHT (P61-A ONLY)
6. NIGHT GOGGLES
7. SUIT HEAT RHEOSTAT
8. DATA CASE
9. SAFETY BELT
10. PILOT'S SEAT
11. GUNNER'S SIGHTING STATION
12. RADIO OPERATOR'S SIGHTING STATION
13. CRANK
14. EXTENSION
15. OVERRUN CONTROL (P61-A ONLY)
16. CAMERA

Further details of crew station equipment, of emergency features, and nacelle basic arrangemant are also shown.

With all versions powered, as shown on Table 53, by two Pratt and Whitney R-2800 eighteen cylinder Double Wasp engines each in the 2000 horsepower class the P-61 had much more installed power than other US production fighters and, again, equalled or exceeded the total power available from USAAF light and medium bombers. With the installation of turbosupercharged engines in the C and D models the chart shows how power available at high altitude improved over earlier versions. Increased propeller size and activity factor was employed to handle this additional power up high.

Graph 46 of available power for the two stage mechanically supercharged engines in the P-61B shows typical variation with

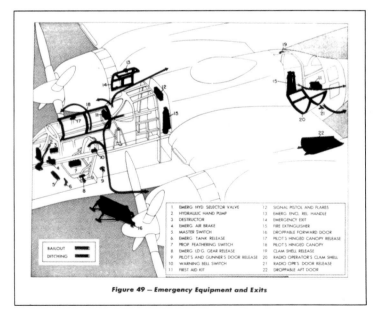

1. EMERG. HYD. SELECTOR VALVE
2. HYDRAULIC HAND PUMP
3. DESTRUCTOR
4. EMERG. AIR BRAKE
5. MASTER SWITCH
6. EMERG. TANK RELEASE
7. PROP. FEATHERING SWITCH
8. EMERG. LD'G. GEAR RELEASE
9. PILOT'S AND GUNNER'S DOOR RELEASE
10. WARNING BELL SWITCH
11. FIRST AID KIT
12. SIGNAL PISTOL AND FLARES
13. EMERG. ENCL. REL. HANDLE
14. EMERGENCY EXIT
15. FIRE EXTINGUISHER
16. DROPPABLE FORWARD DOOR
17. PILOT'S HINGED CANOPY RELEASE
18. PILOT'S HINGED CANOPY
19. CLAM SHELL RELEASE
20. RADIO OPERATOR'S CLAM SHELL
21. RADIO OPR'S DOOR RELEASE
22. DROPPABLE AFT DOOR

BAILOUT
DITCHING

Figure 49 – Emergency Equipment and Exits

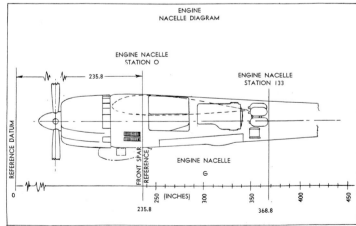

Inboard profile of engine nacelle/forward boom of P-61A.

TABLE 53
P-61 MODELS PROPULSION DATA

MODEL	ENG.MODEL	RATING	HP	RPM	ALT.'	MAP"HG.	SUPERCHARGER
XP-61	R-2800-10	T.O.	2000	2700	SEA LEVEL	54.0	2-STAGE, 2-SPEED
P-61		COMBAT	2000	2700	19000	60.0	
P-61A		MILITARY	2000	2700	1000		
		MILITARY	1650	2700	22500	53-54	
		NORMAL	1675	2550	5500		
		NORMAL	1500	2550	21500	44.5-49.5	
P-61A	R-2800-65	T.O.	2000	2700	SEA LEVEL	54.0	2-STAGE, 2-SPEED
P-61B		COMBAT	2040 RAM.	2700	12800		
XP-61E		COMBAT	1930	2700	17000	60.0	
		MILITARY	2000	2700	1000		
		MILITARY	1650	2700	22500	53-54	
		NORMAL	1675	2550	5500		
		NORMAL	1550	2550	21500	44.5-49.5	
P-61C	R-2800-73	T.O.	2100		SEA LEVEL		TURBO
		COMBAT	2800		32500		
		MILITARY	2100		30000		
		NORMAL	1700		30000		
XP-61D	R-2800-77	T.O.	2100		SEA LEVEL		
		COMBAT	2800		30000		
		MILITARY	2100		30000		
		NORMAL	1700		30000		

NOTES: -The propeller for the P-61A and P-61B models was the four bladed Curtiss Electric of 12'2" diameter using Curtiss blade design 714-7C2-12. Vibration characteristics restricted operation of the engine between 1800 and 2300 RPM.
-The P-61C and XP-61D propeller diameter was increased to 12'8".

altitude. Without the second stage blower operating engine power drops off, then as the second stage is clutched in at the lower of its two speeds (low blower) power available increases again until it reaches a limit. It then begins to fall off again until the speed of the second stage blower is increased (high blower), and for a small increment in altitude power again increases. Then the supercharger

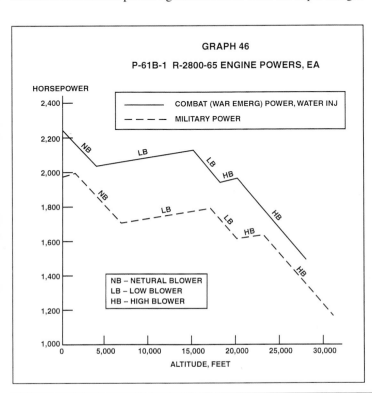

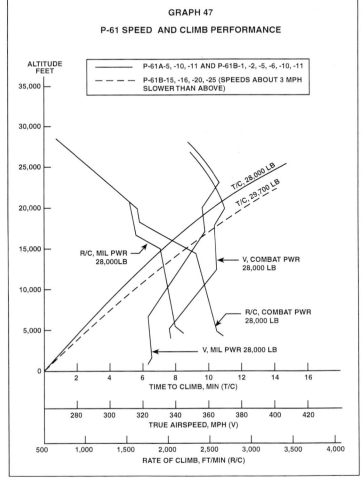

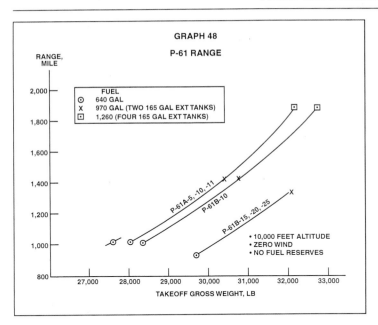

GRAPH 48

P-61 RANGE

FUEL	
⊙	640 GAL
X	970 GAL (TWO 165 GAL EXT TANKS)
▣	1,260 (FOUR 165 GAL EXT TANKS)

P-61A-5, -10, -11
P-61B-10
P-61B-15, -20, -25

• 10,000 FEET ALTITUDE
• ZERO WIND
• NO FUEL RESERVES

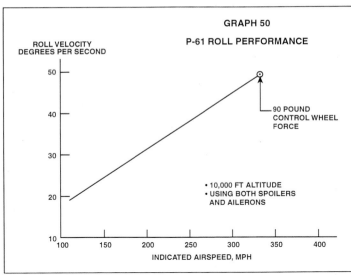

GRAPH 50

P-61 ROLL PERFORMANCE

90 POUND
CONTROL WHEEL
FORCE

• 10,000 FT ALTITUDE
• USING BOTH SPOILERS
  AND AILERONS

limit is reached at the 20000 to 24000 foot level with power falling off quickly when higher altitude flight is attempted.

Graph 47 shows the high speed of the P-61 production versions as about 365 mph at altitudes depending on whether MILITARY or COMBAT power setting of the engines is used. The variation of speed with altitude was very much dependent on the power available based on supercharging as shown previously. Speed started falling off at 20000 to 23000 feet. The COMBAT power climb rate fell steadily with increase in altitude, again depending on supercharged power available, from over 2500 feet per minute at low altitude to around 1500 feet per minute at 20000 feet. At 30000 feet it was down to 500 feet per minute. Time to climb curves show the

effect of aircraft weight, where time to get to 20000 feet increased almost two minutes for 1700 pounds of extra aircraft weight.

"Yardstick" range of the P-61 fighter is presented in the curves of Graph 48 against takeoff weight. This is the theoretical range based on the rather impractical assumptions of no allowances for fuel reserves and zero wind. A more practical range at 10000 feet would be about 75 to 80 percent of the range taken from the curves. The yardstick range shown for internal fuel only is about 1000 miles. Two 165 gallon drop tanks underwing could increase this range to near 1400 miles. If four external tanks were emnployed in an overload condition a maximum yardstick range of 1900 miles was theoretically possible.

Black Widow takeoff ground run requirements from a sea level hard dry surface with no wind are shown against takeoff gross weight in Graph 49. The minimum practical weight was between 28000 and 29000 pounds, so a ground run under the stated conditions would take almost 2000 feet of runway. At a high gross weight of 32000 to 33000 pounds a run of near 3000 feet was in order. The big P-61 needed a good-sized airfield from which to operate. Takeoff run data for the later P-61C version is not available.

An indication of Black Widow rolling performance is seen in Graph 50 where roll rate is plotted against indicated airspeed. The P-61 was a large airplane and used an unusual and unboosted lateral control system consisting of very small ailerons to give the pilot control feel along with spoilers to give most of the roll located ahead of the wing flaps. These were plates that could be raised differentially from a flush position into the airstream to spoil lift on one side and and thus create a rolling moment. Resulting roll performance was not very good, particularly at low speeds, as shown in the figure. If the pilot was able to exert a pretty hefty 90 pound force on the control wheel at about 330 mph IAS the P-61 would roll at a rate of 49 degrees per second, taking seven and one third seconds to complete a full roll, poor fighter performance.

The buildups in three P-61 versions from empty to operating weights are depicted in Table 54. It is seen the large twin engined Widow, depending on model, had an empty weight from ten and one half to twelve tons, about the same or more than maximum

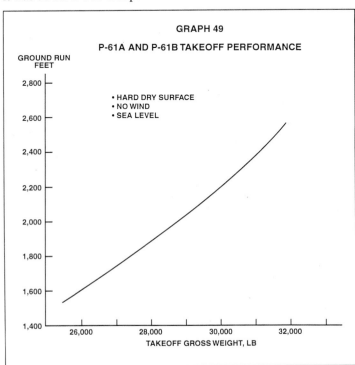

GRAPH 49

P-61A AND P-61B TAKEOFF PERFORMANCE

• HARD DRY SURFACE
• NO WIND
• SEA LEVEL

TABLE 54
P-61 EMPTY AND BASIC WEIGHTS
(LBS.)

MODEL	P-61A	P-61B	P-61C
EMPTY WEIGHT	20965	22000	24000
TRAPPED FLUIDS	(IN E.W.)	(IN E.W.)	(IN E.W.)
(4).50CAL.GUN INSTL.	797	795	769
(4)20mm CANNON INSTL.	589	638	667
(2)GUN SIGHTING STA'S.	206	228	228
GUN CAMERA	5	3	3
PROV.FOR DROP TANKS	0	196	190
ARMOR	445	400	400
PYROTECHNICS	5	6	6
NAVIG. EQUIP'T.	0	0	0
PHOTO EQUIP'T.	0	0	0
OXYGEN EQUIP'T.	64	64	64
EMERGENCY EQUIP'T.	76	80	86
MISC. EQUIP'T.	6	3	5
BASIC WEIGHT	23158	24413	26418

loaded gross weight of a twin engined P-38. It can also be seen when the items listed were added to make up operating weight, those totaling well over another ton, that the weight of a Black Widow before any disposeable items like crew, fuel, oil, and ammunition were added could total over twelve to thirteen tons.

Tables 55 and 56 show typical alternate loads of disposeable items for the P-61A, P-61B, and P-61C models. In the case of the two versions that got into some action, the B and A, typical gross takeoff weights were substantial, running from a minimum of 28000

to a maximum of almost 37000 pounds. In the case of the P-61C version gross weight was in some cases about 40000 pounds. Clearly the P-61 was not only the size of a medium bomber but also as heavy. This size and weight was what it took to fulfill the then-existing Army requirements for a night fighter airplane.

P-61 MAJOR MODEL TO MODEL CHANGES

YP-61 & P-61 (from XP-61) Booms changed from welded magnesium alloy to aluminum alloy construction. Redesigned horizontal tail surface. Zap flap changed to near full span trailing edge type. Retractable spoilers and small ailerons added.

P-61A-1 Engine model change on 46th aircraft. Upper gun turret removed after 37 aircraft are produced. Aircraft used as two-place after turret removal. Cockpit canopy strengthened.

P-61A-5 to -11 Engine model change. Revised fuel system. Water injection added in later versions. No upper gun turret or provisions for gunner. Wing racks for two drop tanks or two bombs added. Additional oil capacity.

P-61B-1,-2,-5,-6,-11. Eight inch nose length increase. Increased powerplant water capacity. Wing racks on -2,-6, and -11 versions. No aileron trim tabs; revised trim controls. Revised hydraulic system. Changes in cockpit controls and displays. Electrical instead of hydraulic cowl flap operation. Completely revised heating system. New radar. Split landing gear doors.

P-61B-10 Racks for four wing drop tanks or bombs.

P-61B-15 through -25 Upper turret and gunner restored. The -16 version had only two wing store stations. Automatic cowl flaps, oil cooler exit flaps, and intercooler flaps.

TABLE 55
P-61A TYPICAL ALTERNATE LOADINGS (LB.)

MISSION	FIGHTER	ALTERNATE FUEL	ALTERNATE AMMO.	MAX. ALTERNATE
BASIC WEIGHT	23158	23158	23158	23158
CREW	690	690	690	690
CAL.50 AMMO.	496	496	620	620
20mm AMMO.	420	420	560	560
USEABLE OIL	270	345	270	345
WATER	0	0	0	0
BOMB INSTL'N.	0	0	0	0
INTERNAL FUEL	3168	3876	3168	3876
DROP TANKS	0	0	0	0
EXTERNAL FUEL	0	0	0	0
GROSS WEIGHT	28202	28985	28466	29249

P-61B TYPICAL ALTERNATE LOADINGS

MISSION	FIGHTER	ALT.FIGHTER	LG.RG.FIGHTER#1	LG.RG.FIGHTER#2	BOMBER
BASIC WEIGHT	24413	24413	24413	24413	24413
CREW	690	690	690	690	690
CAL.50 AMMO.	496	620	496	496	496
20mm AMMO.	420	560	420	420	420
USEABLE OIL	300	330	563	630	330
WATER	299	614	299	299	299
BOMB INSTL'N	0	0	0	0	6384
INTERNAL FUEL	3168	3876	3876	3876	3876
DROP TANKS	0	0	544	888	0
EXTERNAL FUEL	0	0	3600	7344	0
GROSS WEIGHT	29876	31103	34901	39056	36908

TABLE 56
P-61C TYPICAL ALTERNATE LOADINGS(LB.)

MISSION	FIGHTER	ALT.FIGHTER	LG.RG.FTR.1	LG.RG.FTR.2	BOMBER
BASIC WEIGHT	26418	26418	26418	26418	26418
CREW	690	690	690	690	690
CAL.50 AMMO.	496	694	496	496	496
20mm.AMMO.	420	560	420	420	420
USEABLE OIL	345	375	608	675	375
WATER	531	531	531	531	531
BOMB INSTL'N.	—	—	—	—	6384
INTERNAL FUEL	3168	3876	3876	3876	3876
DROP TANKS	—	—	538	688	—
EXTERNAL FUEL	—	—	3600	7344	—
GROSS WEIGHT	30068	33144	37177	41138	39190

P-61C New engine model with turbosuperchargers. New wide chord "paddle blade" propellers. Turbo air inlets under engines. Revised carburetor air inlets. Additional internal fuel. Fighter-type air brakles added on wings.

XP-61D Development aircraft with turbosupercharged engines.

XP-61E Two place escort day fighter version. Turret omitted. Crew nacelle cut down flush with wing. Bubble canopy added (two different versions). Additional internal fuel tank capacity added located in the crew nacelle. New radio equipment. Nose radar omitted; four .50 caliber fixed nose machine guns added.

P-61G Weather reconnaissance version; armament removed. Revised electronics.

P-61 CHRONOLOGY

Oct21'40-Northrop receives US Army preliminary requirements for a twin-engined night fighter.

Nov '40-Discussions are held by Northrop with Wright Field personnel on night fighter design characteristics.

Dec17'40-Northrop presents the Army with a quotation for construction of two prototype night fighter aircraft.

Jan30'41-The contract for a new night fighter is approved by the Army. It calls for two prototype aircraft and two wind tunnel models and is in the amount of $1,367,000.

Mar10'41-A contract is approved for construction of 13 YP-61s and a static test airframe with a value of $5.5 million.

Apr 2'41-An initial mockup inspection of the XP-61 arrangement is held at Northrop.

Sep17'41-A contract is awarded for 150 P-61 night fighter aircraft.

Feb26'42-A supplemental contract from the Army calls for production of 410 additional P-61s with 50 of these to go to the UK. The contract is worth $63.0 million. A total of 560 P-61 airplanes are now on order.

May 8'42-The two XP-61 prototypes are completed by Northrop.

May26'42-The XP-61 makes its first flight from Northrop Field with Vance Breese as test pilot. The aircraft employs a Zap flap arrangement.

May '43-The first YP-61 is ready for Army testing.

Jul 8'43-The first YP-61 is accepted by the Army.

Aug 6'43-The remaining YP-61 aircraft are started in delivery to the Army.

Sep '43-All YP-61 deliveries are now completed. A severe tail buffet is found to occur when the top turret is moved.

Oct '43-The first P-61A-1 Black Widow is delivered and accepted. The first 37 aircraft include the dorsal turret, but the remaining aircraft of the first 200 are delivered without the turret and as two-place airplanes.

Jan 8'44-The P-61 Black Widow night fighter is "unveiled" to the public in the night sky over the Los Angeles Coliseum during a show for war workers.

Mar '44-A P-61A is delivered to England for British evaluation.

Apr17'44-The 423rd Night Fighter Squadron arrives in England and is attached to the 9th Air Force.

May '44-The 6th Night Ftr.Sdn. in Hawaii is the first USAAF outfit to receive P-61s in the Pacific.

May '44-The 419th Night Ftr.Sdn. on Guadalcanal starts to receive P-61 aircraft and becomes the second unit to receive the Black Widow in the Pacific.

May '44-P-61s are coming by sea to Brisbane, Australia for the 5th Air Force, and crews of the 421st Night Ftr.Sdn. are arriving there to pick them up. The 421st is based in New Guinea.

May23'44-P-61s are now in the hands of the 422nd Night Ftr.Sdn., 9th AF in England.

May31'44-A first combat mission is flown by the 419th Night Ftr.Sdn. in their new P-61s over Green Island in the Solomons, SW Pacific.

Jun '44-The 419th Night Ftr.Sdn., the only one in the 13th Air Force, is changing over from P-38s and P-70s to the P-61. The squadron is then split. Detachment A is sent to Nadzab, New Guinea under 5th AF, and Detachment B goes to Los Negros in the Admiralties. The Headquarters Detachment remains on Guadalcanal.

Jun '44-At Wadke, New Guinea, the 421st Night Ftr.Sdn. flies in five new P-61s to replace the obsolescent P-70s.

Jun12'44-The 425th Night Ftr.Sdn., 9th AF gets their new P-61 aircraft.

Jun21'44-Six P-61s of Detachment A, 6th Night Ftr.Sdn, 7th AF arrive at Isley Field on Saipan; their first mission is flown three days later. Soon they move to Aslito Field nearby and provide night protection for B-29s based there.

Jun28'44-A detachment of the 421st Night Ftr.Sdn. with P-61s, along with Airacobras of the 82nd Recon.Sdn., move up to Owi in New Guinea.

Jul '44-The first P-61B aircraft is accepted by the Army.

Jul '44-Detachment A of the 419th Night Ftr.Sdn. moves from Nadzab, New Guinea up to Noemfoor Island.

Jul 5'44-A P-61 from the 422nd Night Ftr.Sdn. is evaluated against the British Mosquito. The results are uncertain and open to question.

Jul 6'44-The 6th Night Ftr.Sdn. CAP over Saipan scores its first P-61 victory, downing a Japanese Betty bomber. This is the first for a P-61 in any theatre.

Jul 7'44-A P-61 0f the 421st Night Ftr.Sdn. trails and shoots down a Japanese Dinah bomber to score the first Black Widow victory in the Southwest Pacific area. Another enemy bomber is shot down later over Japen Island in the Solomons.

Jul16'44-A detachment of the 422nd Night Ftr.Sdn. is assigned the task of shooting down German buzz bombs and scores a first victory.

Jul31'44-The 422nd Night Ftr.Sdn. goes to a new base near Cherbourg in France, and has a score of three enemy aircraft destroyed and one probable as of this date.

Aug '44-Production deliveries of the P-61B model are being made by Northrop.

Aug 5'44-The P-61s of the 419th Night Ftr. Sdn. get their first aerial victory by shooting down a Japanese bomber.

Aug 7'44-The 422nd Night Ftr.Sdn. scores its first aerial victory by shooting down a German JU-88 aircraft.

Aug18'44-The 418th Night Ftr.Sdn., now relieved of B-25 night intruder missions, moves to Hollandia, New Guinea, to train with P-61 Black Widow aircraft.

Aug18'44-The 425th Night Ftr.Sdn. arrives in France and goes into action strafing German troops.

Aug31'44-The Far East Air Force has forty-two P-61 night fighters at this time.

Sep '44-The 422nd Night Ftr.Sdn. moves its P-61s to Belgium.

Sep '44-The 548th Night Ftr.Sdn., 7th Air Force, arrives in Hawaii with P-61 aircraft and trains there.

Sep '44-P-61s of the new 547th Night Ftr.Sdn., 5th AF, arrive at Oro Bay, New Guinea, then move to Owi in the Schouten Islands to relieve the 418th Night Ftr.Sdn.

Sep 1'44-A P-61 destroys a "bogie" over Biak in the Pacific.

Oct '44-The new 549th Night Ftr.Sdn. of 7th Air Force arrives in Hawaii with P-61 aircraft.

Oct 5'44-The air echelon of the 418th Night Ftr.Sdn., newly equipped with P-61s, arrives at Wama on Morotai as part of the deployment there just prior to the invasion of Leyte gulf in the Philippine Islands.

Oct 6'44-The first P-61s of the 426th Night Ftr.Sdn. come in to Chengtu China.

Oct 7'44-A P-61 of the 418th Night Ftr.Sdn. scores the squadron's first Black Widow victory over Morotai, and later has shot down a total of seven aircraft while based at Morotai.

Oct31'44-Six P-61s of a detachment of the 421st Night Ftr.Sdn. fly into Tacloban airstrip on Leyte, Phillipine Islands to provide a night defense capability. They are assigned dawn and dusk patrols.

Nov '44-Four P-61s of the 421st, on dusk patrol over Leyte, encounter seven enemy fighters and destroy four of them.

Nov 8'44-The XP-61D version of the Black widow is flown for the first time.

Nov 9'44-Two P-61s of the 547th Night Ftr.Sdn., 5th AF, arrive at Tacloban, Leyte, along with two specially-equipped radar P-38s. The P-61s are adapted with shackles for external fuel tanks.

Nov10'44-A P-61 on dawn patrol at Leyte destroys two Japanese Tony fighters.

Dec '44-The P-61 strength in the China/Burma/India Theatre is 33 aircraft. For the next year, 1945, the number of Black Widows in this theatre will be: Jan-32, Feb-33, Mar-32, Apr-36, May-33, Jun-53, July 1945-53.

Dec '44-The 425th Night Ftr.Sdn., 9th AF, is involved in ground strafing missions and is using 5" HVARs.

Dec '44-The 422nd Night Ftr.Sdn.loses three P-61s in the battle of the Ardennes in Europe.

Dec '44-A detachment of the 548th Night Ftr.Sdn. moves to Saipan to reinforce the 6th Night Ftr.Sdn.

Dec '44-Late this month the 418th Night Ftr.Sdn. goes forward to San Juse, Mindoro, P.I. from Leyte after being relieved by the 419th. Later, in January, it is joined by the 547th Squadron.

Dec 4'44-The P-61s of the 421st Night Ftr.Sdn. are deemed to be not functioning well against fast enemy night raiders over Leyte. Gen.Kenney exchanges the P-61 squadron for the night fighter F6F-5Ns Hellcats of Marine Air Squadron 541 who came in from Peleliu to Tacloban on December 3rd. The Black Widows go to Pelelieu. Reasons for this switch have long been debated.

Dec20'44-Five days after the US invasion of Mindoro Island in the Philippines, the 418th Night Ftr.Sdn. arrives at Hill Field on the island with its P-61 aircraft.

Dec26'44-A P-61 of the 422nd Night Ftr.Sdn.,9th Air Force, destroys two German JU-88s.

Dec30'44-A P-61 of the 418th Night Ftr.Sdn.,5th Air Force, destroys four Japanese aircraft in one night and another P-61 destroys one E/A, giving a total of eight downed in five days.

Dec31'44-The 5th Air Force in the Southwest Pacific now has three P-61 squadrons, and there are two Black Widow squadrons in the CBI Theatre, one of which is the 427th in Burma. In the European Theatre the 9th AF has two squadrons, the 422nd and the 425th. The 12th AF in the Mediterranean has the 414th Night Ftr. Sdn.of P-61s which has just replaced British Beaufighters.

Dec31,44-The 6th Night Ftr.Sdn. in the Pacific has downed a total of six enemy aircraft, but has lost two P-61s from operational causes.

Jan '45-The 414th Night Ftr.Sdn. now is fully equipped with P-61s at Pontedera, Italy, and sends a detachment to support the 422nd in Belgium to gain combat experience.

Jan '45-The 12th Air Force P-61s of the 415th and 417th Night Ftr. Sdn. are now based in France.

Jan '45-In the European Theatre the 414th, 422nd, and 425th Night Ftr. Sdns. each have only one confirmed enemy aircraft destroyed in this month.

Jan '45-Many P-61 aircraft in the Pacific have their range extended by removal of the top turret and installation of a fuselage fuel tank in the cavity thus provided.

Jan16'45-Right after the invasion of Luzon in the Philippines, P-61s of the 547th Night Ftr.Sdn. move in from Mindoro.

Feb '45-In the Pacific P-61 squadrons are equipping their aircraft to carry drop tanks and bombs.

Feb21'45-The P-61s of the 6th Night Ftr.Sdn. land at Iwo Jima to provide night air defense.

Feb28'45-The P-61s of the 548th Night Ftr.Sdn. also arrive on Iwo Jima and take over night patrols on the first of March.

Mar '45-Ten P-61 squadrons are now deployed in the Pacific.

Mar '45-The 550th Night Ftr.Sdn. is now at Morotai, and later goes to Tacloban in Leyte, P.I. They have equipped their P-61s to carry rockets, as has the 419th and the 548th Sdns. The 427th Night Ftr.Sdn. of the 10th Air Force in India has now also modified their P-61 aircraft to carry rockets.

Mar '45-The 6th Night Ftr.Sdn. leaves Iwo for Saipan and then goes back to Hawaii.

Mar20'45-The 549th Night Ftr.Sdn. with P-61s arrives on Iwo Jima to reinforce the 548th, and stays until war's end.

Mar29'45-P-61s fly nightly harassing intruder raids until April 20 on Haha Jima and Chichi Jima near Iwo Jima in the Pacific.

Mar31'45-In this month the scores of European-based P-61 squadrons are: 414th-zero E/A; 422nd-4 E/A; and 425th- 1 E/A.

Apr '45-Two XP-61E prototype aircraft are converted from P-61Bs. One cracks up in a takeoff accident on Apr 11.

Apr20'45-Five P-61s along with three PBJ-1 aircraft crash in the Iwo Jima area due to a heavy ground fog.

Jun '45-P-61 detachments from the 418th, 419th, and 550th Night Ftr.Sdn. stage out of Sanga Sanga in the Sulu Archipelago in support of the Allied invasion of Balikpapan, Borneo. The P-61s provide pre-invasion strikes and a night patrol from June 21-30. Auxiliary fuel tanks (four 160 gallon drop tanks) are used as well as rockets. Some missions last six to eight hours.

Jun 8'45-The 548th Night Ftr.Sdn. with P-61s arrives at Ie Shima, just off Okinawa, from Iwo Jima to take over night intruder attacks on the Japanese island of Kyushu. The 548th is attached to the 318th Ftr.Gp. with P-47Ns. While with the 318th Group the 548th shoots down five enemy aircraft.

Jul '45-The first P-61C model is delivered by Northrop and is accepted by the Army.

Jul '45-The 6th night Ftr.Sdn.,7th Air force, is back in Hawaii preparing to take part in the invasion of Japan.

Jul '45-The 421st and 547th Night Ftr.Sdns.,5th AF, join the 7th AF Night Ftr.Sdn. on Ie Shima, and the 418th Night Ftr.Sdn. arrives on Okinawa. The P-61s fly night intruder missions over Kyushu, Japan.

Jul '45-The 13th AF 419th NFS and 550th NFS are in the Philippines, the 419th at Palawan and the 550th at Tacloban.

Jul '45-There are now 74 P-61 fighters employed in the Pacific Ocean area.

Aug14'45-A P-61 of the 548th NFS pursues a Japanese Oscar fighter which crashes into the sea during an evasive maneuver. No shots are fired; this is probably the last enemy aircraft downed in World War II.

Aug15'45-By VJ-Day 674 P-61-type aircraft have been completed by Northrop.

Aug15'45-At war's end fifteen of the USAAF's sixteen night fighter squadrons have been equipped with P-61 aircraft. The single squadron having other aircraft is the 416th NFS of 12th Air Force using British Mosquitos..

Aug15'45-By the end of the war two P-61 squadrons are based in the Ryukyus; the 418th NFS had come in on July 28, and the 421st on August 8.

Sep '45-The USN obtains 12 P-61Bs from the USAAF, redesignated F2T-1 and used in training for Navy F7F- twin engine fighters.

Oct24'45-The XP-61F program is cancelled.

Jun '48-Ten USAF squadrons are still equipped with P-61 Black Widows.

'50-P-61s are being replaced by jet aircraft.

P-61 HANDLING QUALITIES AND CHARACTERISTICS

GROUND HANDLING

The tricycle landing gear equipped Black Widow handled well on the ground. In a group of twenty-one pilots who tested it fifteen gave it a good rating. The Widow was a big twin engine airplane, and thus required some space to maneuver on the ground. During taxi rolling motion was necessary to castor the nose wheel. The slower the taxi speed the greater the aircraft turning ability. But it was very important not to let the inside wheel stop rolling in a turn. As with all aircraft it was wise to avoid excessive brake use. Directional changes during taxi were accomplished by combined or separate use of differential braking, differential engine power, and rudder action. On the P-61A model taxi was done with flaps up; wheel brakes lost effectiveness when flaps were operated. Aileron and rudder tabs were left at zero or neutral setting, and the elevator tab was set according to aircraft weight.

TAKEOFF AND CLIMB

For takeoff the aircraft was lined up and engines run up, then brakes were released and the roll started. Flaps were either left up or set one third down depending on aircraft load and runway length. Flaps down would decrease takeoff roll distance. Takeoff speed was 100 to 110 mph IAS. As was usual with twin engine aircraft, the P-61 had a spread between this speed and single engine minimum control speed. The latter varied from 120 mph IAS at a light 27500 pound gross weight to 140 mph IAS at a very heavy 37000 pound

weight. There was thus a gap of about 10 to 40 mph where an engine failure meant a takeoff accident because the airplane could not be controlled. The unsafe speed band depended on many factors, including how quickly the failed engine lost power, how fast the pilot reacted to the problem by sensing which engine had failed and feathering the proper propeller, and how quickly he could control

Fig.61-1 Northrop XP-61 Black Widow, Ser.41-19509, Mfr. photo via H. Andrews One of the two Widow prototypes at the factory before the flat black night fighter paint job was applied. The leading edge intake for carburetor induction air and oil cooler air are well shown just outboard of the engine nacelle. The lower cannon bay and the upper machine gun turret are apparent as well. The two tail booms were made from welded magnesium alloy on the prototype, but this construction proved impractical for production, and more conventional aluminum alloy structure was later selected. The airplane looked as if it should have been a medium bomber.

Fig.61-2 Northrop XP-61 Black Widow, Ser.41-15509, Mfr. photo via F. Dean coll. The prototype now in black paint seemingly befitting its mission, but certainly doing nothing for the appearance of the aircraft. The big Double Wasp engines with two stage two speed mechanical supercharging drove four bladed Curtiss Electric propellers with spinners and blade cuffs. The wing of the XP-61 incorporated a Zap type flap; this was changed on later aircraft. The original contract for two aircraft was approved in January of 1941; the first prototype flew in May, 1942. Note the Northrop-built Vultee Vengeance dive bomber in the background.

aircraft roll, yaw, and the power of the good engine. The P-61 normally had good acceleration after leaving the ground, and passed quickly through the critical speed band however. Thirteen pilots rated takeoff qualities generally good; none said fair or poor. Several pilots mentioned the good directional control on takeoff, though eight noted takeoff as long. This pilot group ranked the P-61 only eighth of eleven fighter types in a category "Best overload takeoff from a small area." In contrast however, one enthusiastic pilot, not at the above meet, said "The first P-61 takeoff was incredibly short. I was airborne in 1000 feet. Thats right, only 1000 feet for takeoff even though the aircraft weighed 30000 pounds."

After leaving the ground the P-61 was cleaned up, power reduced to climb setting, and airspeed set about 160 mph IAS for best climb rate. One pilot commented "It lacks rate of climb."

TRIMMING

Trimmability of the aircraft was very good as rated by eleven pilots evaluating the P-61B. Trim tab power was also adequate to zero out pilot control forces for single engine cruising flight above approximately 130 mph IAS.

Fig.61-3 Northrop YP-61 Black Widow, photo via F. Dean coll. The thirteen service test Widows, with many changes from the experimental prototypes, appeared in the spring and summer of 1943. This photo emphasizes the tricycle landing gear now coming into vogue and the size of the whole aircraft. The large tail booms were now of conventional aluminum construction, the horizontal tail was redesigned, and the Zap flap of the prototypes was redesigned into a long trailing edge flap with lateral control effected by spoilers and small ailerons.

Fig.61-4 Northrop YP-61 Black Widow, Ser.41-18877, photo via H. Andrews. A flight view of one of the service test airplanes shows the general contours of the Widow, including the twin booms and vertical tails and the lower 20mm. cannon bay. The radar scanner was in the nose of the aircraft; note the antenna alongside the forward fuselage. Powerplant induction air came in from leading edge intakes on both inboard and outboard sides of the engine nacelles. The YP-61 airplanes became P-61s.

Fig.61-5 Northrop P-61A Black Widow, Mfr. photo via F. Dean coll. A Widow runs up its engines with a crewman access ladder still down and engine cowl flaps full open for maximum cooling. It appears the upper turret is still aboard; it was removed after thirty-seven aircraft were produced because its presence in some positions was causing a tail vibration from disturbed airflow. The Army Air Force accepted the first P-61A in October of 1943; squadrons of Widows started serving in operational areas in the spring of 1944.

Fig.61-6 Northrop P-61A Black Widow, Ser.42-5608, photo via H. Andrews. An operational P-61A airplane in flight showing the step-up of the tandem seated pilot and gunner with both able to see directly ahead. The white nose is the result of a large unpainted Fiberglas radome over radar components up front. The rear area of the fuselage was occupied by a radio operator. The gun turret is still aboard this P-61A. One wonders if a much higher horizontal tail would have solved the turret/tail problem.

DIVE AND RECOVERY

Prior to a dive the aircraft was trimmed for level flight at 275 mph IAS, and no further trimming was necessary for a dive recovery. The P-61 was not to be trimmed nose-heavy prior to a dive as some aircraft were to make pullout control forces greater. Normally elevator trim was not to be used in dive pullouts, but if it was employed the word was use it very slowly and carefully. After trimming, the aircraft was pushed over into the dive. By the book limit diving speed was 420 or 430 mph IAS depending on the aircraft static line arrangement in the particular aircraft, or Mach .70, whichever was less. Buffeting and tuck-under would start to occur outside these limits. Maximum engine speed was limited to 3060 RPM

allowed up to 30 seconds. One pilot said of diving the P-61 however "I would be indicating 450 to 475 mph, but the Widow easily went over that with no problems. This was around 10000 to 15000 feet." If this pilot was indicating 450 mph at 15000 feet and 475 mph at 10000 feet he was well outside the redline envelope. He would be doing 599 mph true airspeed and Mach .83 at 15000 feet, but would be coming back inside the Mach envelope at 512 mph true airspeed and Mach .70 by the time he got to 10000 feet. If buffeting occurred during a dive it was best to immediately begin a gradual pullout. Buffet did occur near a 2g start of pullout above Mach .60, but the P-61 could be pulled up through the buffet region until an accelerated stall was produced. The buffet might increase

Fig.61-7 Northrop P-61A Black Widow, Ser.42-5631, photo via H. Andrews. A P-61A flying with the upper gun turret removed, usually flown as two-place aircraft with the gunner eliminated. There was a lot of transparency area on the Widow both front and rear. With a wingspan of 66 feet, an empty weight of eleven and a half tons, and a gross weight of well over fourteen tons, the P-61A was a lot of airplane. In spite of criticism about performance its high speed of over 350 mph at medium altitudes was very creditable for its size.

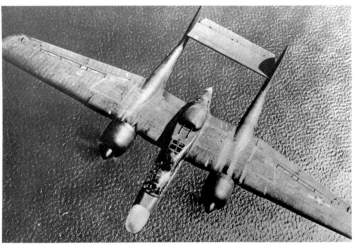

Fig.61-8 Northrop P-61A Black Widow, photo via F. Dean coll. A good view of the P-61 twin boom twin tail configuration and wing planform. It appears the upper turret on this airplane has been reduced from four guns to two. The long span of the wing flaps is shown along with the small ailerons near the wingtips. The black outlines forward of the flaps are the recesses for the spoilers used for lateral control. The spoilers were plates curved in section rising from the recesses to spoil wing lift on one side or the other. Such devices were unique to the P-61 among US World War II fighters.

Fig.61-10 Northrop P-61B Black Widow, W. Larkins photo via H. Andrews. After 200 production P-61As had been delivered the P-61B appeared in the summer of 1944. Some B variants had two wing store stations and others had four. In the Pacific where long range was so important some P-61 squadrons operated with extra internal fuel tanks mounted in place of the machine gun turret and its ammunition spaces. The four 20mm. cannon were fixed in a belly installation to fire forward.

Fig.61-9 Northrop P-61B Black Widow, Mfr. photo via F. Dean coll. A P-61B on the ramp at Northrop is so black it is difficult to photograph. As with the A model there were several sub-variants of the P-61B. Among the changes in various Bs were an eight inch longer nose, wing store racks added, cockpit revisions, increased water capacity for engine water injection, new radar, and revised subsystems including a new heating system. There was also a new landing gear door design and aileron trim tabs were eliminated in some variants. Taxi lights were added on the nose gear.

in severity, but the Widow could pull up to about 2g at 30000 feet, and to increased g levels at lower altitudes before stall. So the pilot had considerable leeway. However if external loads were carried caution had to be used in high speed dives and pullouts. The word was to avoid violent control movements if the aircraft was buffeting. Another pilot said of the Widow in diving "The redline was 420 mph IAS , but I have exceeded this by a considerable margin and never experienced the slightest tendency to buffet." Several pilots at a fighter meet test dove a P-61B airplane. Most rated dive acceleration, control forces, and recovery characteristics good, but placed the Widow only eighth of eleven fighter types in the category "Best stability and control in a dive." To think of the big three place twin engined Black Widow hurtling towards the earth at well over 500 mph true airspeed tends to boggle the mind, but

for it to finish off with a successful thundering pullout must have been something to see!

MANEUVERING

For an airplane with the size and weight of a medium bomber, maneuverability of the P-61 was surprisingly good. But thinking of it as a fighter, pilots rated maneuverability fair to poor, mostly the latter. Maneuvers permitted at 28220 pounds and under included half rolls, normal inside loops, Immelmans, chandelles, slow rolls at 350 mph IAS and under, barrel rolls, vertical reversements at 250 mph IAS and under, and just about any precision maneuver. Well coordinated barrel rolls could be done with ease; slow rolls were somewhat tougher to do well. Starting at about 260 mph IAS in level flight, the aircraft could be pulled around in a loop and come out of it higher than the initial altitude. A few pilots performed quite exotic maneuvers with the large P-61 fighter. Maneuvers prohibited were outside loops, other than momentary inverted flight, spins, and snap rolls, along with very high speed slow rolls and vertical reversements.

With heavy engines out on the wings, the P-61 rolling capability was nothing to write home about. But lateral control forces with the small ailerons and the spoilers were light, even up to high speed. One pilot said "I was surprised at the ease of lateral control. The spoiler-type ailerons were incredibly easy to operate at high speeds. Over 400 mph IAS the "ailerons" could still be moved quickly and with ease with just one finger on the control wheel." Things were not quite as nice at speeds around 150 mph IAS where control was sloppier. A group of pilots ranked the P-61B seventh of ten fighter types in "Best ailerons at 350 mph IAS", no doubt because the big Widow was hampered by high lateral inertia characteristics. They also ranked it tied for last of twelve fighters in "Best ailerons at 100 mph IAS."

The P-61 was good in turning flight. "It could turn with the best of the fighters; it could definately out-turn an F6F-; I'd be on his tail so fast it was incredible." The Widow, with its small conventional ailerons and spoilers ahead of these, came closest to having full span flaps of any US fighter.

Fig.61-11 Northrop P-61B Black Widow, P.M. Bowers photo via H. Andrews. This photo of a P-61B was taken in Calcutta, India four months before war's end. Drop tanks are on the store stations and the gun turret is back on top of the fuselage. Decals on the propeller blades show them to be on a Curtiss Electric propeller. Since the numbers of Widows were relatively small the airplanes were operated in squadron rather than group strength. A total of 450 B versions were produced; by war's end a total of 674 P-61 type night fighters had been produced.

Fig.61-12 Northrop P-61B Black Widow, Ser.42-39713, Martin and Kelman photo via H. Andrews. A similar view of a P-61B Widow with what appears to be several stored P-51s in the background. The P-61 had quite delightful flight characteristics and many pilots were convinced it could do most any maneuver well. It was considered maneuverable for its size, but of course its size was large! A typical evaluation pilot comment would be: Too big for a night fighter; lacks speed and climb rate.

Fig.61-13 Northrop P-61C Black Widow, Mfr. photo via F. Dean coll. The P-61C airplane was Northrop's answer to criticism that earlier models were too low and slow, and had many changes. This model did not appear until a month before the end of the war however, and with resulting production cut-backs only 41 P-61C aircraft were built. Changes included a new turbosupercharged powerplant, wider chord propeller blades, more internal fuel, and fighter-type air brakes on the wings, these latter shown deployed in the Northrop photo of their new P-61C.

Pilots rated the P-61B a very stable airplane about all axes. Pilots testing the aircraft also rated elevator and rudder force requirements and surface effectiveness as good.

APPROACH AND LANDING
When the P-61B was checked out by a pilot group thirteen of twenty-one gave an unqualified "good" rating to approach and landing characteristics. They also ranked the night fighter second of eleven types in "Best characteristics five mph above stall"; this was somewhat strange in view of the sloppy low speed aileron control characteristic noted above. Maximum flaps and gear down speed was 170 mph IAS. Landing gear was lowered during the downwind leg of the approach. It was recommended flaps be lowered in two stages. At the half-way point of the approach base leg flaps were put down half way, and on the final leg lowered fully. Typical over the fence speeds were 100 to 110 mph IAS power on and 115 mph IAS power off.

Waveoff characteristics were considered fair. One pilot said "Much better waveoff than an F7F-, but somewhat slow and sluggish."

STALLS AND SPINS
The Black Widow was exceptional in this area. Because the airplane had such gentle stall characteristics using either two engines or just single engine power, pilots were encouraged to try stalling it just for practice. Ample stall warning was given by a strong tail buffet. Controls remained effective up to and into the stall. No control deflections were required to prevent roll in a normal two engine stall. It was "Straightforward and with no tendency for a wing to drop." There would be some shake of the airplane, the nose would drop slightly, and then rise again. A pilot said "Every stall results in the nose dropping forward with never any tendency to fall off on one wing."

Fig.61-12A Civil Northrop P-61B Black Widow, photo via P.M. Bowers. A civil P-61 was something of a rarity. With the three place arrangement of the military P-61 it is difficult to see the civilian use it could be put to. Nevertheless civil registration N30020 can be seen on the vertical tail.

Fig.61-14 Northrop P-61C Black Widow, Ser.43-8353, photo via P.M. Bowers. A Black Widow survivor in the yard of the Air Force Museum at Wright Patterson AFB again painted up so that many details are obscured. The large air scoops under the engine nacelles reflect major powerplant changes from previous models. The Widow is considered a significant aircraft because it was the first Air Force type designed from the start as a night fighter.

With one engine at high power and the other propeller windmilling the stall of the Widow was still not a problem. Ninety to one hundred percent of full rudder deflection was required to compensate for the yaw, and rudder forces were somewhat high, but only five to ten percent "aileron" was required to hold the airplane level. In a similar case with gear and flaps down the only difference was that up to ninety percent of full lateral control input was needed to hold things level. As one pilot said of the clean high power on one engine case "Nothing, just the same gentle dropping of the nose, and a wings-level attitude was easily maintained with rudder and opposite aileron."

Stall speeds on the P-61B ranged from about 110 to 112 mph IAS clean and power off to a dirty power on 70 to 80 mph IAS, depending on several factors but mainly aircraft landing weight.

The high speed accelerated stall of the Widow was similar to the normal one g low speed stall except buffeting might occur before stall was reached, and the pitching motion in the stall was considerably more violent. At a fighter meet the three g accelerated stall speed of the P-61B was listed at 137 mph IAS. One Black Widow pilot related how you could "safely and conveniently" make continuous accelerated stalls with one engine out.

Whether in clean or dirty configuration there was no tendency for the P-61 to spin inadvertantly. It had to be snap rolled into a spin. The book did prohibit deliberate spinning of the aircraft, even though it would recover from a spin up to the half turn mark almost instantly when pressure was reduced on either rudder or elevator controls. The prohibition was based on the fact that past the half turn mark the spin tended to tighten, and acceleration increased, with the plane losing about 2000 feet of altitude per turn. In the clean condition the big Widow fell off slowly and deliberately, and at the end of a 180 degree turn the nose would be nearly straight down. The descent rate was high, but forward speed did not increase appreciably during a half turn. With gear and flaps down spin conditions were similar, but continuous and quite severe buffeting occured. Here the spin was oscillatory in nature and recovery was considerably slower. Conventional recovery methods were used to stop a spin. Recovery was easy during the first one to one and a half turns, and could be made without great difficulty after two and a half turns by reversal of rudder and elevator. But if there was no definite indication of regaining control in a fully-developed spin below 5000 feet altitude it was time to try and leave the airplane.

CHARACTERISTICS
COCKPIT
The cockpit of the P-61 was evaluated by a mixed group of pilots. Most thought it was reasonably comfortable; fourteen of twenty-one said comfort was good and three said fair. But they were not impressed by the cockpit arrangement. Only two of the twenty-one said the arrangement was good. Eight called it "cluttered" while ten said the instrument panel was too far away from the pilot. Other comments included "Cockpit too complicated", "Needs improvement in the cockpit", and "Poor cockpit." To make their point this group ranked the P-61B third of eleven fighter types in the category "Worst cockpit."

VISIBILITY
Pilots were not pleased with P-61 visibility. Five indicated that cabin restricted visibility and another commented "Visibility not good." In this airplane, however, the pilot had two additional sets of eyes to help him see. A postwar version of the Widow had a bubble canopy installed, but no wartime versions were so arranged.

VULNERABILITY/ARMOR

With two big radial aircooled engines, self-sealing fuel tanks, and armor plating scattered all over the crew pod, the Widow should have had quite good resistance to enemy weapons fire. Probably because of its relatively limited usage and night fighting mission no specific data has been found regarding these qualities.

GUN PLATFORM AND WEAPON PERFORMANCE

The P-61 was a big fighter airplane with generally good stability characteristics about all axes. Out of fourteen pilot evaluations in one case five rated it a good gun platform, eight rated fair, and one pilot said gun platform qualities were poor.

On early models there was a major problem with use of the flexible gun turret equipped with four .50 caliber machine guns. The turret was designed to swivel and cover the full 360 degrees of azimuth as well as a considerable range of elevation. This turret and the four fixed 20 mm cannon in the fuselage belly comprised the total armament of the P-61. When the turret was slewed into certain positions on early aircraft it set up air turbulance causing

heavy buffeting of the tail surfaces. A large number of airplanes were therefore delivered without the turret. After a great amount of testing a fix was found, and the turret insttallation went back on later aircraft.

GENERAL COMMENTS

The Widow was terrific; it could lick many other fighters.
Had a flight in a P-61. An exceptionally fine aircraft. Excellent, except short on performance.
Lacks speed; not enough performance.
Combat qualities poor; lacks speed and climb rate.
Not enough performance for a night fighter.
Just too big for a night fighter.
Has a wobble that detracts from it as a night fighter.
Cumbersome as a night fighter; hopeless as a day fighter.
Useful combat aircraft. Needs improvement in speed.
One pilot noted he had great confidence in the P-61.
It was a forgiving airplane.

P-61 STRUCTURAL DESCRIPTION

(Metal is aluminum alloy unless otherwise noted)

WING GROUP

The complete wing assembly, except for the wingtips, was of fully cantilever riveted metal stressed skin construction with the loads concentrated on two main spars. The wing skin carried the chord bending and torsional loads, and was supported by chordwise ribs and stiffeners, and spanwise stringers to prevent wrinkling.

The wing group consisted of two each inner panels, outer panels, and wingtips. Each inner panel contained an engine nacelle, two fuel tanks, and a section of the wing flaps, and was built in two sections-the main section containing the two spars, and the aft sec-

tion which included the inboard flaps. The main section extended from leading edge to rear spar, and from the crew nacelle inboard to just outboard of the engine nacelle. The forward spar of the inner panel was a dual-web box section; the rear spar was a single web type with flanged cap strips. Bathtub and lug-type fittings at the spar ends were used to bolt-connect to the crew nacelle carry-through spar extensions inboard, and to the outer wing panel spars. Vertical channel-section spacers were placed between front spar webs. A stainless steel firewall was built into this spar in the nacelle area. The space between spars was employed for fuel tanks and only bay

Fig.61-15 Northrop P-61C Black Widow, Ser.43-8353, photo via P.M. Bowers. Another view of the P-61C residing at the USAAF Museum. The wide chord of the propeller blades is notable with trailing edge strips added to increase the propeller activity factor and thus its ability to absorb efficiently the increased power of the Double Wasp engine which by this time had a COMBAT power rating of 2800 horsepower at 30000 feet! The turret is missing from the museum's P-61C.

Fig.61-16 Northrop XP-61D Black Widow, Ser.42-5559, photo via H. Andrews. The XP-61D in the picture was one of two P-61A airframes converted in late 1944 as development test aircraft for the turbosupercharged Double Wasp engine installation to be utilized in the P-61C production aircraft. Part of the new turbo installation is shown in the photo as the large duct and fairing under the engine nacelle.

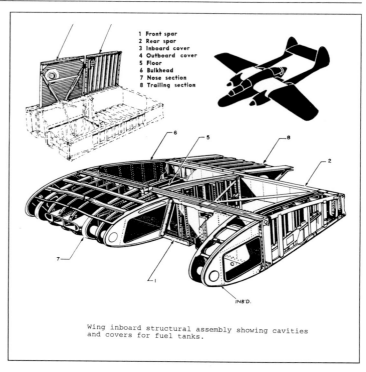

Wing inboard structural assembly showing cavities and covers for fuel tanks.

closure ribs inboard and outboard of the tanks were used. Two large reinforced structural covers, hinged at their forward edges, were located over the fuel tanks. Covering outer skins in these areas were backed up by corrugated under-skins or hat section stiffeners. Similar stiffening was provided on the fixed lower skins under the fuel bays. Diagonal braces laced to the fuel cells were located over the nacelle tank. The nose section forward of the front spar was made up of ribs of flanged sheet and lateral stringers except in the area over the nacelle. Nose section space was provided inboard for air intake

ducting from the leading edge and outboard for an oil tank. Skins were flush riveted.

The aft section behind the rear spar was made up of flanged ribs shaped and cut back on the lower side to mate with the inboard flap contour. Flush riveted sheet metal skins were employed.

The outer wing panels were each built in two sections: The main section containing the two spars and nose section, and the detacheable trailing edge section which included wing flaps, spoiler panels, and ailerons. The outer panel forward spar was a single sheet web design with tapering extruded upper and lower cap strips having forged attach fittings for bolting at the inboard end. Vertical stiffener angles were riveted along the spar web. The rear spar was of similar design. Inter-spar and nose ribs were of reinforced flanged

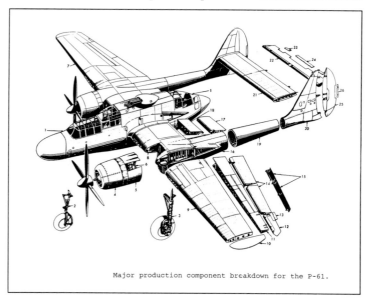

Major production component breakdown for the P-61.

1. Crew Needle	14. Outer wing flaps
2. Nose landing gear	15. Spoilers
3. Main landing gear	16. Engine nacelle
4. Powerplant assembly	17. Inner wing flap
5. Engine accessory cowling	18. Inner wing trailing section
6. Engine mount support	19. Tail boom
7. Outer wing, complete	20. Vertical boom
8. Inner wing panel	21. Horizontal stabilizer
9. Outer wing panel	22. Elevator
10. Wing tip	23. Elevator spring tab
11. Outer wing trailing section	24. Elevator trim tab
12. Aileron	25. Rudder
13. Aileron tab	26. Rudder tab

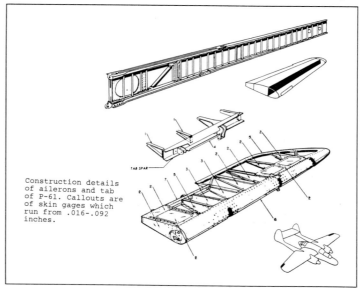

Construction details of ailerons and tab of P-61. Callouts are of skin gages which run from .016-.092 inches.

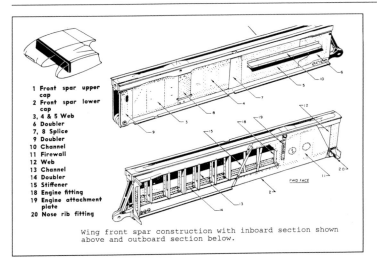

1 Front spar upper cap
2 Front spar lower cap
3, 4 & 5 Web
6 Doubler
7, 8 Splice
9 Doubler
10 Channel
11 Firewall
12 Web
13 Channel
14 Doubler
15 Stiffener
18 Engine fitting
19 Engine attachment plate
20 Nose rib fitting

Wing front spar construction with inboard section shown above and outboard section below.

sheet metal. Space was provided for air ducting from the inboard section of the leading edge and an oil cooler with exit shutters. Flush riveted skins reinforced with spanwise stringers covered the outer panel main section.

There were six single slotted type flaps mounted on the after-sections of the wings- two on each outer panel and one on each inner panel. They were of all-metal construction, and were linked so as to move aft and down when extended. Full deflection was 60 degrees. Flaps were operated by hydraulic actuators and linkages.

Small ailerons were located outboard of the flaps and extended to the wingtips. They were employed to provide normal "feel" to the pilot. Ailerons were supported from the wing after section at three hinge locations. A closed nose D-section of sheet metal made up the principal structure. Flanged ribs were attached to the nose section. An edge member and flush riveted metal skin completed the assembly. On early aircraft models a combination trim and booster tab, controllable from the cockpit, was fitted to the inboard end of the left aileron. The tab was single spar with four ribs and metal covering, and was mounted on two hinges. A booster tab was

located on the right aileron with no cockpit control. On late models there were no aileron tabs fitted.

Spoilers were housed in the outer wing panel trailing sections aft of the rear spars and ahead of the outer flaps. The spoilers were curved metal panels arranged to extend into the airstream from slots in the wing, or retract so as to be flush with the wing upper surface. The spoilers were used differentially for aircraft lateral control, and, like the ailerons, were mechanically driven from the pilot's control column.

Late models of the aircraft were equipped with air brakes, slotted panels which extended from both upper and lower surfaces of the wings to provide symmetrical drag on the airplane. Removeable welded magnesium alloy wingtips were provided which screwed to the outer sections of the wing panels.

FUSELAGE, OR CREW NACELLE

The crew nacelle contained the pilot's cockpit and stations for a gunner and radio operator. The nacelle was a semi-monocoque structure composed of transverse bulkheads and channel-section frames, longerons at the upper and lower quarters, longitudinal bulb-angle stringers, and flush-riveted stressed skin. The structure was cut out for crew station enclosures, a gun turret, a nose wheel well, and an entrance door with extra stiffeners provided around the cut-outs. Cut-outs were also made for the wing front and rear spar extensions which were structural carry-throughs between left and right inner wing panels. These were located ahead of and behind the gun turret location about half-way up on the crew nacelle, and were tied into the nacelle structure by heavy forged fittings on each side. Major nacelle bulkheads were at fuselage stations 71, 150, 205, 236, and 284. The bulkhead at station 71 provided support for the airborne interception radar components. From this station forward the nose section was enclosed in a large resin-impregnated fiberglass shell attached to the crew nacelle by four locating studs and four toggle latches. At approximately station 150 a door in a bulkhead connected the pilot's and gunner's compartment. Station 205 bulkhead closed off the rear of the gunner compartment, and station 236 bulkhead lined up with the forward spar extension and also formed the forward support for the gun turret assembly. The bulkhead at station 284 lined up with the rear spar extension and was the closing bulkhead for the radio operator's compartment.

The pilot and gunner station transparent enclosure was made up of moulded Lucite sheets within extruded metal framing. The forward windshield panels at both forward crew stations were made

Fig.61-17 Northrop XP-61E Black Widow, photo via H. Andrews. Two P-61B airframes were converted to an XP-61E configuration, one of which is shown here in an overhead view. The conversions were made in the spring of 1945 and almost immediately one XP-61E crashed. The changes were extensive, and meant to make the Widow into a two place escort day fighter. The new fuselage had guns up front instead of radar, a bubble canopy over the two crewmen, and extra internal fuel aft.

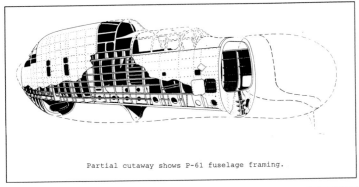

Partial cutaway shows P-61 fuselage framing.

of thick bullet-resistant glass. A panel directly over the gunner was supported by square-section steel tubing. An access panel was located over the pilot's seat, and there was an emergency kick-out panel to the right of the gunner's seat which could be opened from inside or outside. The pilot's and gunner's entrance door was located just aft of the pilot's seat and combined with the nose wheel well. The door frame and folding ladder formed a welded steel structure hinged at the forward end, and the wheel well was riveted to the door structure. The flexible gun turret assembly was mounted between the two wing spar extensions and protruded through the top of the crew nacelle.

The radio operator's station was in the aft section of the crew nacelle separated from the other two compartments by the turret and radio equipment and a bulkhead. Access to this station was gained via a flush type door on the underside of the tail cone. An integral ladder was built into the door which hung down vertically when open. the transparencies for the compartment were formed of moulded Lucite sheets in extruded metal frames. The transparent tail cone forming the aft end of the crew nacelle was made from two moulded sheets of Lucite cemented together at the vertical centerline and bolted to the last frame of the nacelle.

Provision was made in the bottom section of the nacelle just aft of the gunner's station for installation of four 20mm cannon and associated subsystems.

TAIL BOOMS
The two tail booms extended aft from the engine nacelles to the vertical stabilizer assemblies, and were of all-metal monocoque construction, consisting of riveted metal frames, longitudinal stiffening stringers, and flush-riveted metal skins. Bolts through forged steel brackets attached the tail boom structures at each end to the engine nacelles forward, and empennage vertical stabilizers aft. The booms housed communucation and identification equipment antennas, the remote indicating compass transmitter, and flight control system cables to rudders, elevators, and tabs.

NACELLE GROUP
Engine nacelles were semi-monocoque structures consisting of stressed skin, longitudinal stringers, and transverse frames. The loads applied directly to the engine mount from engines, main landing gear, fuel tank, and tail boom were transferred to the basic wing structure through the structural strength of the engine nacelle. The

Fig.61-18 Northrop XP-61E Black Widow, Ser.42-39549, Mfr. photo via Jon Davis. A flight view of the XP-61E conversion to long range fighter shows the nose armament of four .50 caliber machine guns which, along with the four 20 mm. cannon still in the belly, made made up a formidable array of fixed forward firing armament. The crew of two sat under a spacious bubble canopy and the aircraft had two store stations under the wings. The E model was one step in Northrop's desire to extend life of the Widow, and played no part in the war.

forward nacelle structure was made up of three sections-inboard, outboard, and lower foward. The upper and lower ends were built as integral parts, respectively, of the bulkheads and keel structure on each side of the landing gear wheel well cut-outs. The aft structure of the nacelle was attached directly to the forward structure by riveted keel and stringer splices, and to the rear spar by two fittings. All nacelle stringers were extruded bulb angles. Nacelle frames were built up or formed single channel sections, or double channel sections riveted back to back.

TAIL GROUP/EMPENNAGE
The tail group included the horizontal stabilizer and elevator, two vertical stabilizers which were faired into the tail booms, and two rudders. The horizontal and vertical stabilizers were of all-metal construction.

Two spanwise spars supported the horizontal stabilizer structure, and the contour was formed by metal ribs and skin. It was bolted to the vertical stabilizers at the ends of the spars and faired with light removeable metal fairing strips. The closing channel at the trailing edge of the vertical stabilizer formed the main spar. An auxiliary spar was located just aft of the leading edge of the vertical stabilizer, and extended downward from the tip. The lower portion of each vertical stabilizer formed the aft end of one of the tail booms. It was fastened to the boom by an elliptical internal attaching angle.

The elevator and rudders were constructed of fabric covered metal framing. Each was statically and dynamically balanced. All-metal combination trim and booster tabs, controllable from the pilot's cockpit, were built into the trailing edges of the rudders. A combination trim and de-booster tab, also controllable from the cockpit, and two all-metal pre-loaded spring tabs were built into the trailing edge of the elevator.

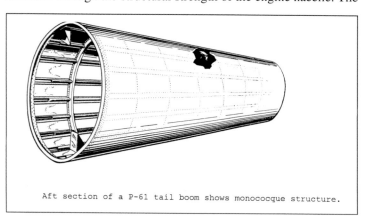

Aft section of a P-61 tail boom shows monococque structure.

LANDING GEAR

The aircraft was equipped with retractable tricycle-type landing gear. The two units of the main gear extended from the engine nacelles, and the nose gear extended from the lower forward portion of the crew nacelle. When retracted the landing gear elements were completely enclosed by doors which closed to conform to the contours of the engine and crew nacelles.

Each main landing gear was supported by two steel castings which were bolted, one on each side of the nacelle, to closed box keel structures built into the nacelle on each side of the cut-out provided to accomodate the retracted gear. Landing gear loads were transmitted through the shock strut to the two support trunnions, the side load brace, the downlock, and the main supports. The main gear retracting cylinder and uplock, and their fittings, were attached to a diaphragm or bulkhead structure installed transversely across the engine nacelle at the aft end of the gear cut-out. The diaphragm served to reinforce the nacelle frame as well as to support retracting cylinder and uplock assemblies.

Upon retracting the gear was hinged on two trunnion pins at the two steel castings. Both pins were secured by lockbolts. One end of the actuating cylinder was attached to the drag arm, or head, of the shock strut. A side load brace was mounted between the inboard end of the trunnion and the shock strut. The main gear was held in position, both when extended and retracted, by mechanical latching mechanisms. If the gear failed to latch in the down position and the throttle was closed to less than 1000 RPM, a warning horn would sound. An emergency system was installed to extend the gear in the event of hydraulic system failure.

The nose gear was supported by two brackets, one on each side of the crew nacelle, and hinged on trunnion pins which passed through needle bearings and into the trunnion structure. Both pins were secured in place by lockbolts. A folding drag link assembly also supported the gear when it was in the extended latched position. A warning horn, similar to that provided for the main gear, sounded when the nose gear was not latched down and the throttle was closed to 1000 RPM. A micro-switch wired to the gear and the flap position indicator registered when the gear was latched down. The nose gear was equipped with a shimmy damper to prevent rapid wheel oscillations. Torque scissors were placed between shock strut body and piston assembly. The nose wheel was self-castoring to a limit of 50 degrees either side, but was not steerable.

ENGINE SECTION

The engine sections each consisted of the engine mount, a built-up welded steel tube structure bolted to the nacelle and wing forward spar and to the engine mounting points through vibration isolators, and the engine cowling panels. These consisted of a forward cowl ring, an engine cowling with adjustable cowl flap segments at the aft end, and the engine accessory compartment cowl. Cowl sections were fastened to engine-supported mounting strips by quickly-detacheable quarter-turn fasteners, and were removeable in large sections to provide maintenance access to the powerplants. The hinged engine cooling flaps on the cowlings were controllable from the cockpit via a hydro-mechanical actuating system.

P-61A/P-61B SYSTEMS DESCRIPTION

PROPULSION SUBSYSTEMS

ENGINES

The aircraft was powered by two 2000 HP class Pratt and Whitney R-2800 Double Wasp air cooled eighteen cylinder two row radial engines of 5.75 inches bore and 6.00 inches stroke. The engines

Fig.61-19 Northrop F-15 Reporter, Ser.43-8335, Mfr. photo via H. Andrews. Not really included in Black Widow production for wartime, but interesting as a finale to the Widow story are the three dozen Reporter airplanes based on the P-61C but revised for a mission of high altitude photo reconnaissance. These aircraft were produced after the war in 1946. The photo shows they included turbosuperchargers on the engines, a bubble canopy like the XP-61E, and a camera nose in place of guns.

were equipped with mechanically-driven two stage two speed superchargers. Engine compression ratio was 6.7:1; maximum engine speed was 2700 RPM. The SAE#60 splined output shaft rotated clockwise looking from the rear on both engines.

ENGINE INDUCTION SYSTEM

Induction air for the engines was taken in from wing leading edge inlets on either side of the engine nacelles. For low altitude flight, under approximately 6500 feet, the auxiliary blower of the supercharger would be in neutral (inoperative); the intake air came directly from the wing inlets through ducting with spring-loaded flapper valves into the carburetor and then into the main blower. At higher altitudes the auxiliary blower was normally engaged by moving a cockpit lever control, and wing inlet air passed through ducting either directly, or via an air filter, to this blower and then to an intercooler. The intercoolers were air-to-air heat exchangers where cool outside air was passed by the compressed and heated intake air, thus cooling it sufficiently to enter the carburetor. From the intercooler charge air was lead to the carburetor and on into the engine main, or first stage, blower and the intake manifold. Intercooler cooling air was dumped overboard through exit doors controlled by hydraulic actuators.

Alternate heated inlet air from the engine compartment could be introduced into the intake system; a selector control or switch

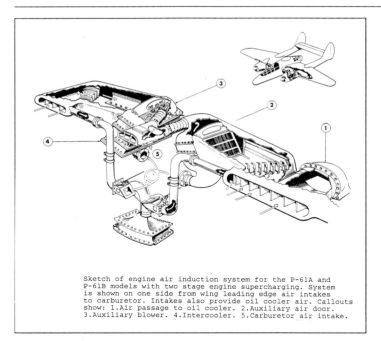

Sketch of engine air induction system for the P-61A and P-61B models with two stage engine supercharging. System is shown on one side from wing leading edge air intakes to carburetor. Intakes also provide oil cooler air. Callouts show: 1.Air passage to oil cooler. 2.Auxiliary air door. 3.Auxiliary blower. 4.Intercooler. 5.Carburetor air intake.

was in the cockpit and temperature was registered on cockpit gages. Carburetor filters were controlled by a cockpit electric switch moving filter insertion actuators. These could be used only when the auxiliary blower was not operating.

ENGINE EXHAUST SYSTEM
The engine exhaust exited the aircraft via individual stainless steel exhaust stacks distributed around the periphery of the nacelle. A flame dampening design was employed to reduce the nightime signature of the aircraft. Stack exits were located just aft of the cowl flaps on the engine nacelle.

ENGINE-MOUNTED ACCESSORIES
Accessories mounted on the engine included magnetos, carburetor, fuel pump, oil pumps, vacuum pump, starter, generator, tachometer generator, hydraulic pump, and propeller governor.

ENGINE CONTROLS
Basic engine controls operated throttle, mixture, and auxiliary blower. The throttle and mixture control levers for both engines were on a quadrant on the left side of the cockpit alongside the two propeller controls. The supercharger control levers for each engine were located on a separate quadrant low on the left side of the cockpit, and had a neutral, low speed, and high speed position. All engine controls were mechanically linked to the engines via runs in the fuselage, wing, and engine compartments. Throttle assemblies included detents past which levers could be pushed forward to operate water injection systems to give COMBAT power in emergencies.

PROPELLER
The propellers for P-61A and P-61B models were Curtiss Electric four blade constant speed selective pitch full-feathering types. Hubs

were the C642S design with model 714-7C2-12 blades in 12 feet 2 inches diameter. Engine speeds between 1800 and 2300 were restricted from use because of a propeller vibration in that range. Large metal spinners enclosed the propeller hubs and the inboard blade shank sections. The spinners were mounted on bulkheads supported on the hub.

PROPELLER CONTROLS
The two propeller control levers were located on the inboard side of the throttle quadrant next to mixture and throttle levers. These levers were mechanically linked to the propeller governors mounted on the engines via runs through fuselage, wing, and engine compartments. Power for blade pitch change was taken from the aircraft electrical system. Switches for control of the propellers from automatic constant speed to manual increase or decrease pitch and covered switches for feathering were located on a propeller control panel in the cockpit.

ENGINE STARTING SYSTEM
The engines were cranked over by inertia starting systems. Electric motors on the accessory cases were energized from the cockpit starter switches and battery, and spun up inertia flywheels. After reaching highest speed in about 20 seconds, the flywheel was clutched into engine starter gearing to crank it over. On early airplanes a backup starter hand crank and extension was stowed in the left wheel well. On later planes the crank was stored on the radio operator's entrance door. If the engine was cold it was primed for starting, and fuel booster pumps were switched on.

ENGINE WATER INJECTION SYSTEM
Water injection systems were included for the engines. They were activated by placing throttles in the extreme forward position and pressing the system power-on switch. The water pumps, electrically-powered, were automatically turned on by the throttle advancement. Water was carried in outer wing panel tanks; late P-61A and early P-61B versions carried 26 US gallons which would last for about 15 minutes. In early airplanes water was carried in engine ring cowl metal tanks. Late P-61B aircraft had capacity for 34 US gallons , good for 20 minutes of use. Some airplanes had a capacity of as much as 74 US gallons. A water pressure gage was located in the cockpit.

ENGINE COOLING SYSTEM
The radial engine was cooled by cowling it, forcing air around and through the two rows of finned and baffled cylinders, and exiting the air in the rear of the cowling aft of the engine. Exit area and cooling airflow were controlled by an upper and lower series of hinged cowl flaps. These were actuated by crank and rod assemblies for each flap powered by a ring and a local hydraulic actuator using the main hydraulic system. On P-61A models the cowl flaps were controlled, upper and lower sets individually, by manually operated selector valves in the lower part of the cockpit. On late P-61B airplanes they were controlled by cockpit switches that operated solonoid control valves in the hydraulic sysyem.

ENGINE LUBRICATION SYSTEM
A separate oil system was provided for each engine, and each engine accessory section carried an oil pump. P-61A airplanes and some B's had a self-sealing oil tank of 22 to 23 US gallons capacity located in each wing panel. Later P-61B versions had metal tanks, each of 42 US gallon capacity, located in the main landing gear wheel well area. Oil coolers were installed in the outer wing panels just outboard of the oil tank on early planes. Air was taken in at the outboard sections of outer leading edge intakes and ducted to the cooler. Air flow through the coolers was controlled by hydraulically operated air outlet doors in the lower skin of the wing. P-61B airplanes had automatically controlled doors with a manual backup cockpit control. Door position indicators were provided in the cockpit.

ENGINE FIRE SENSING/EXTINGUISHING SYSTEMS
No such systems were incorporated in P-61 airplanes.

FUEL SYSTEM
The internal fuel system provided for a total of 646 US gallons carried in four self-sealing tanks, two on a side. The two inboard tanks were located in the inboard wing sections between the fuselage and nacelles and between spars. Each had a capacity of 118 US gallons. Outboard tanks were placed over the nacelles between spars, and the top of each nacelle tank was laced to the V-brace between front and rear spars. Nacelle tanks had a capacity each of 205 US gallons. Each tank contained a Thompson variable speed electric fuel booster pump. The pump in each tank was individually controlled, and was used for transferring fuel between tanks at any altitude, and for supplying fuel to the engine-driven pumps at six to eight PSI pressure to prevent vapor lock.

The right side wing fuel tank was designated as the reserve. A cross-feed line was provided so fuel from any tank could be used for either one or both engines. A type G-9 rotary vane positive displacement fuel pump was mounted on each engine. A fuel primer valve was located in each engine compartment, as were fuel strainers. Fuel lines ran in the wing leading edge sections inboard and fuel selector valves were located in each nacelle. A central low point drain with valve was provided, and a cross-flow control valve was also in the center of the interconnecting line. On late P-61B models a fuel dump system was provided with an exit at the bottom of the rear end of the crew nacelle. Vents were provided at central high points in the lines. Primer switches, boost pump switches, and tank and cross-feed valve controls were provided in the cockpit as well as a fuel quantity gage with selector switch.

Late P-61A and early P-61B aircraft had provisions for installation of two external pressurized auxiliary droppable tanks under the outer wing panels. These tanks could be either of the 165 US gallon or the 310 US gallon capacity each. On these aircraft additional fuel selector switches were in the cockpit to turn on drop tank fuel. Late P-61B aircraft were equipped for two additional external pressurized droppable tanks, one under each inner wing panel between nacelles and fuselage. These tanks could be of either 165 or 310 US gallon capacity. External tank pressurization was provided by the vacuum system of the aircraft. On these late P-61B airplanes the fuel controls were incorporated in fuel selector valves mounted on the throttle quadrant. These valves had positions as: outboard main tank, inboard main tank, outboard auxiliary (droppable) tank, inboard auxiliary tank, and off. Tanks could be dropped electrically using the bomb control switch and a release button on the control wheel.

FIXED EQUIPMENT SUBSYSTEMS

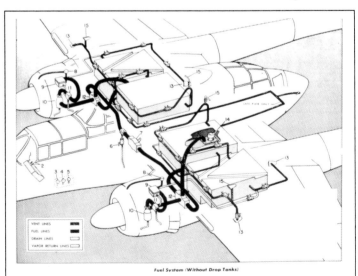

Fuel System (Without Drop Tanks)

1. Primer switch
2. Booster pump switches
3. Cross feed control
4. R.H. tanks control
5. L.H. tanks control
6. Drain cock
7. Cross flow valve
8. Fuel primer
9. Carburetor
10. Strainer
11. Fuel pump
12. Fuel selector valve
13. Air scoops
14. Booster pump
15. Siphon breaker

INSTRUMENTS (P-61B)
Flight instruments included an airspeed indicator, turn and bank indicator, altimeter, radio compass, gyro horizon, radio altimeter, clock, bank and climb gyro, and turn gyro.

Engine instruments were manifold pressure gage, tachometer, oil temperature gage, cylinder head temperature gage, fuel level gage, water quantity gage, fuel pressure gage, carburetor air temperature gage, oil pressure gage, and vacuum gage.

Other instruments included pilot's radar indicator, wheel and flap position indicator, hydraulic pressure gage, water pressure gage, autopilot oil pressure gage, and de-icing pressure gage.

SURFACE CONTROLS
Ailerons, spoilers, and the elevators were controlled in the conventional manner by a torque tube type control column in the pilot's cockpit. The torque tube was attached at the base of the column, and extended completely across the cockpit. Four control lines at the extreme ends of the tube were attached to the four elevator control cables. Ailerons and spoilers were controlled by the wheel on the control column by means of an enclosed sprocket and chain attached to cables. From the chain ends cables ran aft along the left

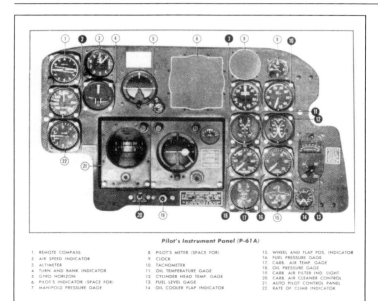

Pilot's Instrument Panel (P-61A)

1. REMOTE COMPASS	8. PILOT'S METER (SPACE FOR)	15. WHEEL AND FLAP POS. INDICATOR
2. AIR SPEED INDICATOR	9. CLOCK	16. FUEL PRESSURE GAGE
3. ALTIMETER	10. TACHOMETER	17. CARB. AIR TEMP. GAGE
4. TURN AND BANK INDICATOR	11. OIL TEMPERATURE GAGE	18. OIL PRESSURE GAGE
5. GYRO HORIZON	12. CYLINDER HEAD TEMP. GAGE	19. CARB. AIR FILTER IND. LIGHT
6. PILOT'S INDICATOR (SPACE FOR)	13. FUEL LEVEL GAGE	20. CARB. AIR CLEANER CONTROL
7. MANIFOLD PRESSURE GAGE	14. OIL COOLER FLAP INDICATOR	21. AUTO PILOT CONTROL PANEL
		22. RATE OF CLIMB INDICATOR

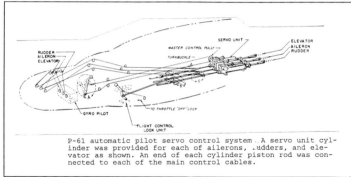

P-61 automatic pilot servo control system. A servo unit cylinder was provided for each of ailerons, rudders, and elevator as shown. An end of each cylinder piston rod was connected to each of the main control cables.

and right walls of the cockpit, and outboard through the wings to the spoiler quadrants and then to the aileron quadrants. From the spoiler quadrants push-pull rods connected to differential bell-cranks which caused the spoilers on one wing to rise 65 degrees while those on the other side lowered to 28 degrees. Adjustable push-pull rods connected the differential bell-cranks to the spoilers. Aileron quadrants connected directly to the ailerons by means of adjustable push-pull rods.

Conventional adjustable foot pedals controlled the rudders. Two cables extended aft from each of the two pedals, providing an independent system for each rudder. A buss cable connected the two pedals. The cables were installed on both sides of the cockpit and ran through wings and both tail booms to bellcranks in the empennage, from which they extended aft to the rudder horns. The right rudder cable system was connected through the autopilot servo unit.

The automatic pilot servo unit consisted of three hydraulic cylinders cast en bloc with piston rods extending at each end. The piston rods were connected directly to the main control cables of the aircraft. A manually operated bypass valve was employed to engage or disengage the autopilot. Spring-loaded relief valves (overpower valves) were built into each hydraulic surface control to permit the pilot to overpower the automatic pilot by applying increased force to the controls. The servo unit was located on the right hand side of the crew nacelle below the floor of the gunner's compartment. Bank and climb, and turn gyro control units were located on the main instrument panel.

The elevator incorporated two spring-loaded balance tabs, not controlled by the pilot, which were self-operating at high speeds to reduce pilot control forces.

On P-61A airplanes the trim tabs on the flight controls were moved by three trim wheels, one for each surface, at the left of the pilot's seat. The tab for roll trim was on the left aileron. The right aileron tab acted as a booster and was adjustable on the ground only.

On P-61B airplanes the ailerons were not equipped with trim tabs. The trim controls in the cockpit on early P-61Bs were two conventional trim wheels. On late P-61B aircraft a dial knob controlled rudder tabs while the control for the elevator was a wheel aft of the knob.

ELECTRICAL SYSTEM

The electrical system was a 24 volt direct current type with an airframe ground return. The power supply was from two 28 volt 200 ampere-hour engine-driven generators along with a 24 volt, 34 ampere-hour storage battery installed in each engine nacelle just aft of the landing gear well. Electrical power from a battery cart could also be applied to the system from a power supply terminal on the outboard side of the left engine nacelle. Main electrical switches were on the pilot's electrical panel located at the left of the instrument panel.

Among the elements powered or controlled by the electrical system were the radar, armament control systems, primers, starters, electrical instruments, lights, selector valves, aiming point camera control, fuel boost pumps, oil dilution system, crew nacelle heaters, anti-icers, de-icers, radio, warning bell, landing gear position warning system, and propeller pitch change power and control.

HYDRAULIC SYSTEM

Hydraulics consisted of a main pressure system and an emergency hand pump system. The main pressure system, which included the

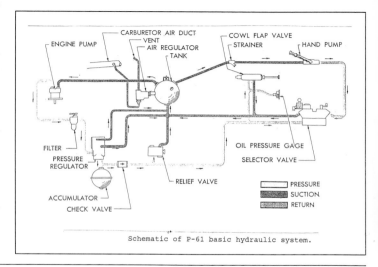

Schematic of P-61 basic hydraulic system.

automatic pilot, provided pressure for the accumulator system. On the P-61A the wing flaps, landing gear brakes, ejection chute doors, and carburetor air filters operated on the accumulator system. On P-61B aircraft only the brakes and ejection chute doors operated on the accumulator system.

On P-61As the oil cooler flaps, carburetor air heat, intercooler doors, and upper and lower cowl flaps were controlled by manually-operated selector valves. On P-61Bs the oil cooler flaps and intercooler doors operated automatically from electrically controlled hydraulic valves. Late P-61Bs had no intercooler doors. The automatic control could be over-ridden by moving the switch in either direction from "automatic." Upper and lower cowl flaps were actuated by switches located near the oil cooler flap and intercooler flap switches. On all P-61B airplanes the carburetor air heat and air filter were controlled by switches on the accessory instrument panel, and operated by hydraulic cylinders actuated by solonoid control valves.

A double acting hydraulic hand pump was mounted on the pilot cockpit floor. Use of hand pump and selector valve would direct fluid pressure to any hydraulically operated unit except the autopilot. Hydraulic pressure and accumulator pressure indicators were provided in the cockpit.

The main pressure system operated the landing gear, main gear up and down latches, and wheel doors, engine upper and lower cowl flaps, carburetor air heat valves, intercooler exit flaps (on P-61As), wing flaps (on B models), and the autopilot. Fluid under pressure from both engine pumps converged and flowed through a filter to an unloading valve which maintained 850 to 1000 PSI in both main and accumulator systems. The valve also supplied fluid through the autopilot pressure regulator to the autopilot and to the hydraulic reservoir. Major units of the system, including reservoir, accumulator, main pressure regulator, and surge chamber were mounted on a bulkhead aft of the gunner's position.

PNEUMATIC SYSTEM

The pneumatic system consisted of engine-driven vacuum pumps to supply instruments and to provide pressure for expelling fuel from drop tanks. It was also used for the wing and tail ice protection system to inflate and deflate the de-icer boots.

ELECTRONIC EQUIPMENT

Electronic equipment was extensive for a World War II fighter aircraft. The primary pieces of equipment were the SCR-720 radar and SCR-729 radio mounted in the extreme nose of the aircraft. A dish-type antenna was provided. This was an airborne intercept radar system with the antenna assembly mounted inside a large fiberglas enclosure tied to the forward bulkhead of the crew nacelle. A radar range of up to 16 miles could be achieved under good conditions.

For command radio the P-61 was equipped either with two sets of SCR-522 or one set of AN/ARC-3 equipment. In addition, provisions were made for the installation of one SCR-274N equipment. The number one SCR-522 set was installed on the floor of the radio operator's compartment. The number two set on P-61A and early P-61B aircraft was installed beneath the crew nacelle floor

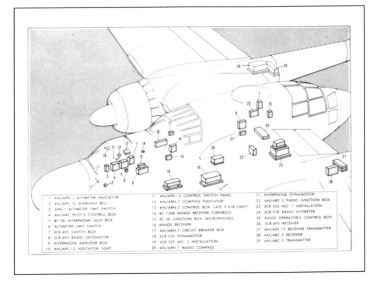

between two 20mm cannon, and on late P-61Bs in the right hand tail boom. Controls were in the pilot's cockpit. The AN/ARC-3 transmitter-receiver was installed in the right hand tail boom with control box in the pilot's cockpit. An SCR-695 IFF set was also installed, as was an RC-36 interphone system for communication between the three crew stations. P-61A and early P-61B airplanes had the SCR-718 radar altimeter, and late P-61B models had the later AN/APN-1 set installed. These were located at the radio operator's station. In addition, an AN/APS-13 radio with indicator and warning bell and a MN-26C radio compass were installed alomg with a BC-1206A range receiver.

ARMAMENT PROVISIONS

The P-61 aircraft was equipped with four fixed 20mm cannon firing forward and mounted on supports beneath the crew nacelle floor structure, and, on early P-61A and late P-61B models, a rotatable turret mounting four .50 caliber machine guns atop the crew nacelle aft of the gunner station.

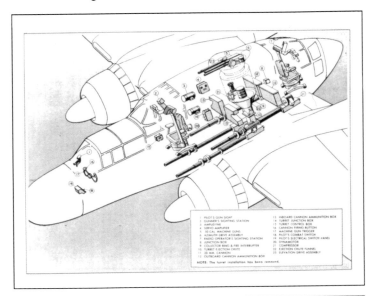

The 20mm cannon were controlled by cockpit switches and electrically fired by a switch button on the pilot's control wheel. Each cannon was provided with a 200 round ammunition box. The outboard cannon ammunition boxes were accessible only from the ground through outside doors. The inboard ammo boxes were located behind the front wing spar location on the crew nacelle floor and were accessible from the gunner's compartment. The cannon were charged manually while the aircraft was on the ground. If one or more cannon jammed the others would continue to operate. The cannon were controlled by the pilot, and could be set to fire forward through a horizontal angle range of plus or minus 1/4 degree from dead ahead and a vertical range of plus 1/4 to minus 1 degrees from the horizontal, making possible converging, diverging, elevated, or depressed lines of fire. There was a hydraulically operated ejection chute door for each cannon. The door was automatically controlled by a solonoid wired into the cannon firing circuit so the doors opened only during the time the cannons were being fired.

The pilot was provided with a gunsight and night binocular. The sight was mounted on the coaming above the instrument panel. On the P-61A the sight was an L-1 type; on the P-61B an LY-3N sight was provided. Sights were the reflector type with sight lamps controlled by a rheostat. The night binocular was mounted on an arm permitting it to swing into place aft of the pilot's armor glass windshield. The assembly was stored at the left of the gunner's armor glass windshield by sliding it aft on a track mounted on the cockpit rail.

The four .50 caliber machine guns in the top turret fired simultaneously at about 800 rounds per minute each. The turret had full 360 degree rotational capability in azimuth and the guns could be elevated up to 90 degrees from the horizontal. Electric motor amplidyne drives powered and controlled the turret and guns. Control was from either one of two sighting stations located forward and aft of the turret in the gunner's and radio operator's compartment respectively. The gunner, radio operator, or pilot could control the firing of the guns. Links and shells were collected at the bottom of the turret assembly and were dropped through a chute in the belley of the airplane. The gunner had full control of the turret at all times unless he chose to transfer control to the radio operator. On early P-61A aircraft the gunner could transfer control to the pilot by rotating the turret to point the guns forward and turning off the turret power switch, thus latching the turret, and then throwing a switch to "pilot." On late P-61B airplanes the turret automatically returned to the forward strafing position when the action switches on all sighting arm grips were open. Each gun was provided with an ammunition case with a maximum capacity of about 560 rounds of ammunition. Gunner and radio operator sighting stations each consisted primarily of a crew seat assembly, a rotating housing mounting a support column which in turn supported a sighting arm, all supported by a base mounted on tracks. Firing controls at the sighting station were mounted on two grips attached to the sighting arm, including turret movement control and weapons firing. Adjustments could be made to the sighting elements to fit individual gunners.

External Armament Control System

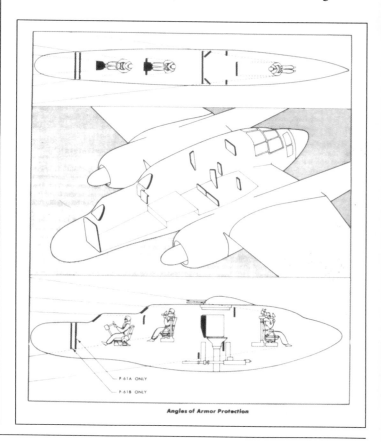

Angles of Armor Protection

The sight itself was attached to the arm between the two grips; the sights were N-6 models of the reflector type. The sight and arm could be moved to the stowed position.

Bombs could be mounted on the wing racks, either two or four, used alternately for fuel drop tanks, depending on aircraft mission. Bomb release controls were different depending on airplane version. Generally release was controlled electrically with a mechanical backup. Bombs weighing from 100 to 1600 pounds could be carried on each bomb rack.

PASSIVE DEFENSE SYSTEM
The crew members and ammunition boxes were protected from machine gun fire by a number of armor plates, bullet-resistant glass on forward windshields, and deflector plates.

Bullet resistant glass formed the forward windshield panels of both the pilot and the gunner. Plates of armor were located at the forward bulkhead behind the nose radar, ahead of the gunner below his windshield, ahead of the turret ammunition containers and cannon ammunition containers, and behind the radio operator.

FURNISHINGS
The P-61A pilot seat was mounted on tracks and rollers and could be moved to the right of center on its track for easier entrance and exit. A track adjustment lever was located below the seat. The P-61B pilot seat was bolted to the floor. Pilot seats in both cases could be adjusted vertically by a local control lever. Another lever allowed the seat pan to be tilted up or down, and in addition the complete seat could be tilted back to facilitate entrance and exit.

The gunner's seat was mounted on a fore-aft track, however it was normally not necessary to move it in flight. The seat could be rotated through 360 degrees and could be locked in forward or aft facing position.

The radio operator's seat was mounted on a post assembly held in the seat base by a locking pin. It could be locked in either the gun firing (aft) or the radio operating (forward) position.

All seats had a metal pan, padded back, and a seat belt; relief tubes were provided at the three crew positions, and hand fire extinguishers were installed.

HEATING, COOLING, AND VENTILATING SYSTEMS
The system for the P-61A consisted of four fuel-air mixture heaters, a manifold to provide heat to the 20mm cannon and the turret section, and three crew ventilators. The pilot's heater was at the forward end of his compartment, the gunner's on the bulkhead aft of his seat, and the radio operator's under the floor of his compartment. The gun heater was aft in the cannon bay. The left engine supplied the fuel-air mixture for gun and radio compartment heaters, and the right engine for pilot and gunner heaters. Burned gases were exhausted overboard. Local crew controls were provided. For ventilation a manually-operated louvre type ventilator opening into the airstream was provided at each crew station.

The P-61B airplanes were equipped with two fuel-air type surface combustion heaters. The forward heater was mounted on the right side of the bulkhead in the gunner's compartment, received fuel from the right engine, and provided heat for the forward com-

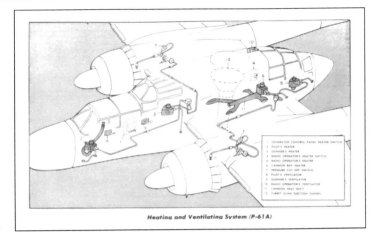

Heating and Ventilating System (P-61A)

partments. The aft heater was below the radio operator's floor and received fuel from the left engine. It provided heat for the radio operator and the guns. Local control was provided for the heaters. Ventilation was provided through the heating system. On late P-61B aircraft a hinged Plexiglas ventilating window was located in the radio operator's enclosure.

ICE PROTECTION SYSTEM
Anti-icing equipment for the propellers included a six gallon fluid tank with a built-in electrically-driven pump located beneath the floor just forward of the radio operator's entrance door, two spinners and fluid slinger rings, and a rheostat control switch and anti-icer fluid gage forward of the pilot's control column.

The windshield defroster system on the P-61A consisted of a flexible tube held in a bracket on the right cockpit rail opposite the pilot's seat which provided warm air. The heater had to be operated to provide the warm air.

On the P-61B fixed defroster tubes were installed below the pilot's and gunner's windshields, and flexible defrosting tubes were installed at each of the three crew stations.

De-icer boots were provided for the leading edge of the outer wings and the vertical and horizontal tail surfaces. Air for operation was supplied from the pressure side of the engine-driven

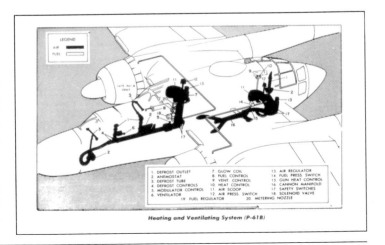

Heating and Ventilating System (P-61B)

vacuum pumps. If one pump failed the other could drive the system alone. A de-icer control handle was located at the right of the pilot.

HOISTING/TOWING/LEVELING/TIEDOWN

Provisions were made to accomplish all these functions.

FLOTATION GEAR/ARRESTING GEAR

No provision was made for flotation or arresting the aircraft.

USEFUL LOAD SUBSYSTEMS
GUNS/BOMBS/ROCKETS

See earlier section.

GUNSIGHT/GUN CAMERA

Gunsights were described earlier. A gun camera was located low in the extreme nose of the aircraft, and was controlled electrically at the pilot's switch panel. The camera worked in conjunction with the cannon.

PYROTECHNICS

A pyrotechnic pistol and flares were mounted on a bulkhead aft of the gunner.

PHOTOGRAPHIC EQUIPMENT

No photographic equipment other than the gun camera was carried.

OXYGEN SYSTEM

The P-61 was equipped with a low pressure oxygen system operated at 425 PSI. The oxygen supply was carried in twelve cylinders, six in each engine nacelle, aft of the wheel well at the tail boom attaching angle. The two upper cylinders in each nacelle provided oxygen to the pilot, the two middle cylinders to the radio operator, and the two bottom cylinders to the gunner. Three demand-type regulators, one at each crew station, automatically supplied the required mixture and volume of oxygen. Regulator assemblies included pressure gages and signal lamp except the lamp was deleted on late P-61B aircraft. A blinker flow indicator was also on the regulators. Local crew station controls were provided.

REFERENCES, P-61
1. Tactical Planning Characteristics and Performance Chart, P-61 June 29, 1945.
2. P-61 Pilot's Manual/Pilot's Flight Operating Instructions, P-61A and P-61B Aircraft.
3. Minutes of Fighter Conference, NAS Patuxent River, Md. Oct.1944
4. Air Classics Magazine, March 1971, The Spider's Sting, Bob Davidson.
5. Memo, P-61 Basic Weights, Hdqtrs Army Air Base, Hammer Field, Fresno, Cal. Feb.1945.
6. Basic Weight Check List and Loading Data, P-61A,B,C. TO 01-15F-5 Feb.25,1948.
7. Northrop Corp. Publicity Release Data, P-61 Black Widow.
8. Aero Digest Magazine, Nov.1/Dec.1 1945, Design Details of the Northrop P-61.
9. Wings Magazine Oct.1976/Dec.1976 and Airpower Magazine Nov.1976/Jan. 1977, Dark Lady, Gary Pape and Ronald C. Harrison.
10. Airpower Magazine, July 1973, Night Creature, Bob Grinsell.
11. Northrop P-61 Black Widow, The Complete History and Combat Record, by Gary R. Pape with John M. and Donna Campbell, Motorbooks International P.O.Box 2, 729 Prospect Ave. Osceola, WI. 54020.

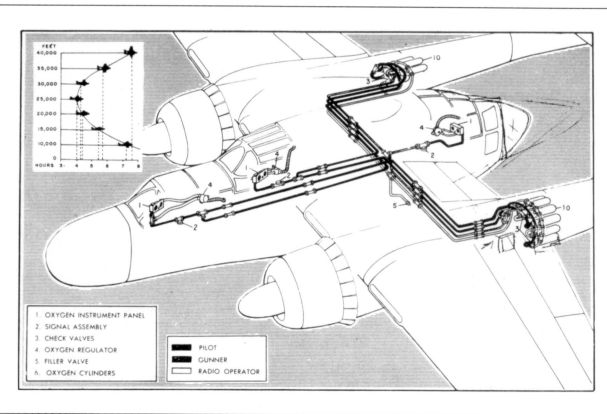

1. OXYGEN INSTRUMENT PANEL
2. SIGNAL ASSEMBLY
3. CHECK VALVES
4. OXYGEN REGULATOR
5. FILLER VALVE
6. OXYGEN CYLINDERS

PILOT
GUNNER
RADIO OPERATOR

THE P-63

Information on variants and numbers built of the P-63 Kingcobra is provided in Table 57. These P-39 Airacobra follow-ons from Bell made up about three and one half percent of America's Hundred Thousand. Of the Kingcobra total two thirds got to Russia as shown in the table. The USAAF confined use of the others to training; none served in American operational combat groups. Almost all of the Kingcobras for Russia were ferried by US pilots to Alaska and there handed over to USSR pilots who continued the ferry procedure into Siberia and further west.

TABLE 57
BELL P-63 KINGCOBRA MODELS

COMPANY MODELS	MILITARY DESIGNATION	NO.OF A/C	1ST.DEL.	NOTES
24	XP-63	2	MAY 1943	PROTOTYPES; 2-STAGE SUPERCH.LAM.FLOW WG.
24A	XP-63A	1	MAY 1943	ENGINE CHANGE
33A-1	P-63A-1	50	OCT.1943	FIRST PRODUCTION
33A-5	P-63A-5	20		
33A-6	P-63A-6	130		
33A-7	P-63A-7	150		
33A-8	P-63A-8	200		
33A-9	P-63A-9	445		
33A-10	P-63A-10	730		
33A-11	RP-63A-11	5		TARGET A/C,NO ARM.
33A-12	RP-63A-12	95		
33C-1,-5	P-63C-1,-5	1227	DEC.1944	
33C-2	RP-63C-2	200		TARGET AIRCRAFT
37	P-63D-1	1		BUBBLE CANOPY
41	P-63E-1	13	MAY 1945	INTENDED PRODUCTION
43	P-63F-1	2		
41G	RP-63G-1	32		

TOTAL 3303

EXPORTS TO RUSSIA

ROUTE	NO.DELIV.AT FACTORY	NO.LOST EN ROUTE	NO.DELIV.TO RUSSIA
NO.RUSSIA BY WATER	3	0	3
ALSIB; ON UK ACCOUNT	85	0	85
ALSIB*	2333	21	2312
TOTALS	2421	21	2400

* ALASKA-SIBERIA ROUTE

Physical data in Table 58 shows the Kingcobra to be somewhat larger all around than the P-39. It also shows the wing airfoil sections were of the new laminar flow type.

One startling aspect of the P-63 is shown in Table 59 concerning aircraft fuel capacities. It carried only six more gallons of internal fuel than the noteably short-legged Airacobra at a time when fighter range was of paramount importance. Though it has been alleged there was some sort of political conspiracy to limit internal fuel capacity there were practical design reasons for this limit. Fuel tanks were located only in the wings; there was no fuselage space available, the same situation as with the earlier Airacobra. Space behind the cockpit used for a fuselage fuel tank in the P-40 and Merlin P-51 fighters was taken up in this case by an engine installation in Bell fighter design. And space beneath the cockpit on the Kingcobra was used for wing center section structure and cooling

components for the powerplant. Other fuselage spaces for fuel were too far away from the center of gravity to be practical. An option would have been to deepen the fuselage which Bell chose not to do. As the table shows, a large amount of fuel could be carried in external drop tanks , but this fact did not increase return distance capability after combat at midpoint (with external tanks dropped) in a radius mission. So internal fuel, placed in wings only, seriously limited Kingcobra radius capability.

Tthree view drawings of a P-63A and a P-63E are shown. The Kingcobra shows as a larger more angular version of the P-39 Airacobra with the same tricycle landing gear scheme and a look-alike cockpit enclosure having similar auto-type side doors. Another look shows some differences, a four blade propeller, cockpit moved forward relative to the wing compared to the P-39, and podded guns for wing armament like the final P-39 models. The P-63E

TABLE 58
P-63 PHYSICAL DATA

SPAN (P-63A,C)	38'4"	WING FLAP AVG.CHORD	13.7"
SPAN (P-63E)	39'2"	WING FLAP MAX.DEFLECTION	45 DEG.
LENGTH (P-63A)	32'8"	WING AILERON SPAN (H/L)	120.75"
LENGTH (P-63C)	32'10.4"	TOTAL AILERON AREA	16.286 SQ.FT.
LENGTH (P-63E)	32'8.25"	TOT.AILERON TAB AREA(1)	0.43 SQ.FT.
HEIGHT,FIN TOP(P-63A)	10'6.25"	A/C C/L TO CTR.AILERON,P-63A	156"
HEIGHT,FIN TOP(P-63E)	10'7.5"	AILERON TRAVEL(P-63A)	+15,-15 DEG.
HEIGHT,PROP.TOP(P-63E)	12'3.5"	AILERON TRAVEL(P-63E)	+17,-17 DEG.
WHEELBASE	129.2"	AILERON TAB TRAVEL(P-63E)	+15,-15DEG.
TREAD (P-63A)	171.0"	TOTAL HORIZ.TAIL AREA	46.53 SQ.FT.
TREAD (P-63E)	181.5"	HORIZ.TAIL THEO.MAX.CHORD	54.5"
TAIL SPAN	175"	TOTAL STABILIZER AREA	33.70 SQ.FT.
PROPELLER DIA.(P-63A)	11'0"	TOTAL ELEV.AREA(2)	INC.BAL.12.83SQ.FT.
PROPELLER DIA.(P-63E)	11'6"	STABILIZER SETTING	+1.0 DEG.
WING AREA (P-63A/C)	248 SQ.FT.	ELEVATOR MOVEMENT	+35,-15 DEG.
WING AREA (P-63E)	255 SQ.FT.	TOT.ELEV.TAB AREA	0.80 SQ.FT.
WING ROOT CHORD(@C/L)	100.0"	ELEV.TAB MEAN CHORD	5.5"
WING TIP CHORD	50.0"	ELEV.TAB MEAN SPAN	23.0"
WING TAPER RATIO	2:1	ELEV.TAB MOVEMENT	+14,-21 DEG.
WING ASPECT RATIO(P-63A)	5.93	TOTAL VERT.TAIL AREA	23.73 SQ.FT.
WING ASPECT RATIO(P-63E)	6.02	VERTICAL FIN AREA	13.47 SQ.FT.
WING MAC (P-63A)	82.54"	RUDDER AREA(INC.BAL.)	10.265 SQ.FT.
WING MAC (P-63E)	83.01"	FIN SETTING(REL.TO C/L)	0 DEG.
WING ROOT AIRFOIL	NACA66,2X-116(a=.6)	RUDDER MOVEMENT	30 DEG.R & L.
WING TIP AIRFOIL	NACA66,2X-216(a=.6)	RUDDER TAB AREA	0.75 SQ.FT.
MAX.WING RIB SPACING	16.0"	RUDDER TAB SPAN	21.68"
WING ROOT INCIDENCE	+1DEG.18MIN.	RUDDER TAB MEAN CHORD	5.0"
WING TIP INCIDENCE	-0DEG.27MIN.	RUDDER TAB MOVEMENT	15DEG.L&R.
WING DIHEDRAL(TOP,.35c)	3DEG.40MIN.	MAIN WHEEL TIRE DIA.	27"
WING SWEEP @ L.E.	5DEG.6MIN.17SEC.	NOSE WHEEL TIRE DIA.	22"
WING FLAP TYPE	PLAIN, SEALED	MAIN GEAR MAX.OLEO TRAVEL	7"
TOTAL FLAP AREA(2)	12.9 SQ.FT.	NOSE GEAR MAX.OLEO TRAVEL	7"
WING FLAP SPAN(EA.)	67.75"		

TABLE 59
P-63 FUEL CAPACITIES (US GAL.)

MODEL	INTERNAL FUEL CAPACITY	EXTERNAL FUEL CAPACITY
XP-63	136	75
XP-63A	136	75
P-63A-1,-10	126	325
P-63A-11,-12	126	—
P-63C-1,-2,-5	128	225
P-63D	168	225
P-63E	126	295

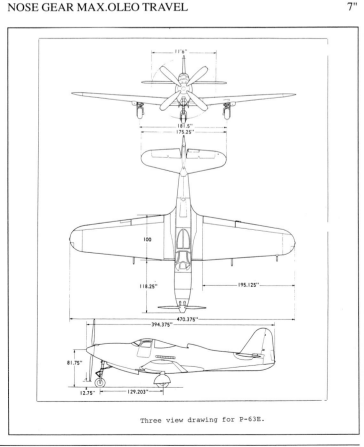

Three view drawing for P-63E.

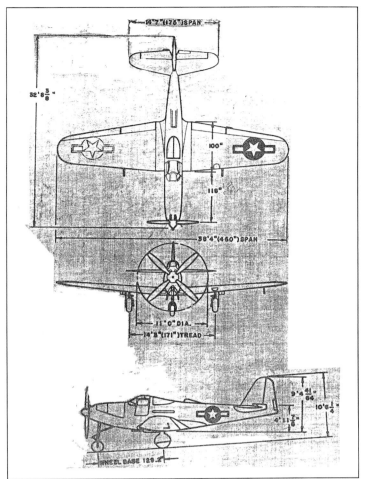

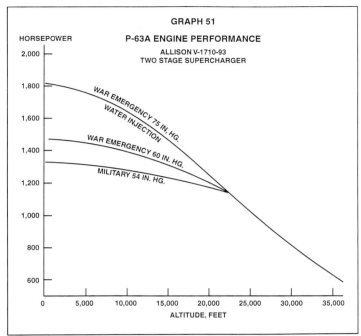

differed from the P-63A in using increased wing area and span along with use of a ventral fin, the latter first added on the P-63C version.

Additional P-63 drawings show interior arrangement of major items, again quite similar to the Airacobra. A large armament bay forward housed the cannon and two .50 caliber machine guns and supporting equipment; the engine drive extension shaft ran under the pilot forward to a remote propeller reduction gearbox, and the engine compartment started just behind the cockpit. The overall powerplant bay in this case was longer than that of the P-39 because a separately mounted second stage supercharger blower assembly, driven from the rear of the engine, was placed between engine and oil tank. Radio equipment was located both behind the pilot's head and aft of the oil tank. The cutaway view of the overall airplane, this a P-63E, further illustrates the overall arrangement of a Kingcobra. The second stage or auxiliary supercharger can be clearly seen; the carburetor was part of this assembly. The view also shows location of all internal fuel was well out in the outer wing panels where the tank cavity is indicated.

Powerplant ratings for engines in the Kingcobra models are given in Table 60. The figures for the two major production airplanes, P-63A and P-63C, are quite similar. Use of the two stage supercharging provided means of

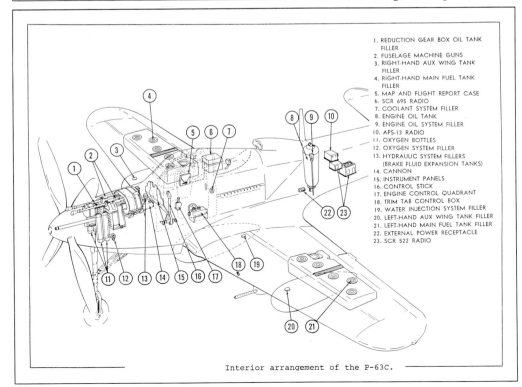

1. REDUCTION GEAR BOX OIL TANK FILLER
2. FUSELAGE MACHINE GUNS
3. RIGHT-HAND AUX WING TANK FILLER
4. RIGHT-HAND MAIN FUEL TANK FILLER
5. MAP AND FLIGHT REPORT CASE
6. SCR 695 RADIO
7. COOLANT SYSTEM FILLER
8. ENGINE OIL TANK
9. ENGINE OIL SYSTEM FILLER
10. APS-13 RADIO
11. OXYGEN BOTTLES
12. OXYGEN SYSTEM FILLER
13. HYDRAULIC SYSTEM FILLERS (BRAKE FLUID EXPANSION TANKS)
14. CANNON
15. INSTRUMENT PANELS
16. CONTROL STICK
17. ENGINE CONTROL QUADRANT
18. TRIM TAB CONTROL BOX
19. WATER INJECTION SYSTEM FILLER
20. LEFT-HAND AUX WING TANK FILLER
21. LEFT-HAND MAIN FUEL TANK FILLER
22. EXTERNAL POWER RECEPTACLE
23. SCR 522 RADIO

Interior arrangement of the P-63C.

P-63E Cutaway

TABLE 60
P-63 PROPULSION DATA

MODEL	ENGINE	POWER SETTING	HP	RPM	ALTITUDE'	MAN.PRESS"HG.	SUPERCHG.
XP-63	V-1710-47	TAKEOFF	1325	3000	SEA LEVEL	54.0	TWO-STAGE
XP-63A	V-1710-93	TAKEOFF	1325	3000	SEA LEVEL	54.0	TWO-STAGE
P-63A	(-E11)	COMBAT	1500	3000	SEA LEVEL	60.0	
RP-63A		COMBAT(H2O)	1820	3000	SEA LEVEL	75.0	
		MILITARY	1180	3000	21500	52.0	
		MILITARY	1150	3000	25000	50.0	
		NORMAL	1050	2600	10000	43.0	
		NORMAL	1000	2600	20000	42.5	
P-63C	V-1710-117	TAKEOFF	1325	3000	SEA LEVEL	54.0	TWO-STAGE
RP-63A	(-E21)	COMBAT	1500	3000	SEA LEVEL	61.0	
		COMBAT(H2O)	1820	3000	SEA LEVEL	76.0	
		MILITARY	1150	3000	25000		
		MILITARY	1100	3000	27000	52.0	
		NORMAL	1000	2600	23000	43.0	
P-63D	V-1710-109	TAKEOFF	1425	3000	SEA LEVEL		TWO-STAGE
P-63E		COMBAT	1500		SEA LEVEL		
		COMBAT(H2O)	1750	3200	SEA LEVEL		
		MILITARY	1100	3200	28000		
		NORMAL	1050	2600	SEA LEVEL		
		NORMAL	950	2600	24000		

NOTE 1. The weight of the -93 engine was 1620 pounds; the weight of the -117 was 1660 pounds.,
NOTE 2. The P-63F used an Allison V-1710-133 engine; the RP-63G the V-1710-135.
NOTE 3. The propeller for the P-63A was an Aeroproducts Unimatic Model A642S-D3 with four hollow steel A-20-156-24M design blades in either 11'1" or 11'7" diameter. The P-63C had a Unimatic in 11'0" diameter; the P-63D had 11'1" and the P-63E 11'6" diameter, all four-bladed.

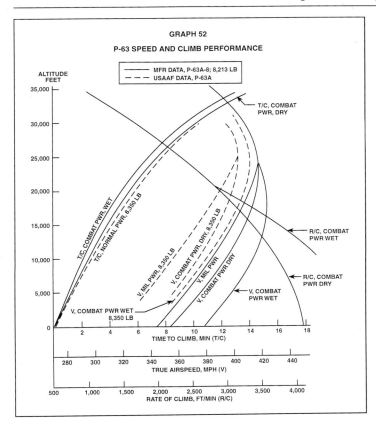

GRAPH 52

P-63 SPEED AND CLIMB PERFORMANCE

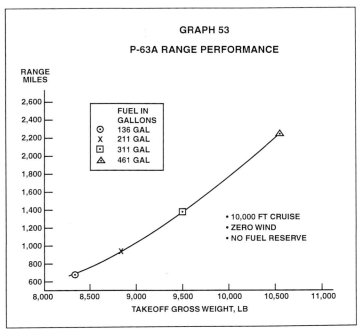

GRAPH 53

P-63A RANGE PERFORMANCE

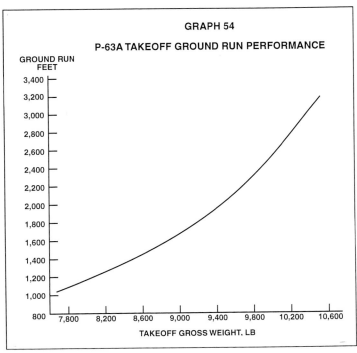

GRAPH 54

P-63A TAKEOFF GROUND RUN PERFORMANCE

keeping MILITARY power up as altitude increased. This result is portrayed in Graph 51 where MILITARY and WAR EMERGENCY powers are plotted against altitude. MILITARY power drops quite slowly from 1325 to 1150 horsepower going from sea level to 22000 feet altitude, and then falls much more rapidly above that altitude. The power curves are smoothly variable because a hydraulic coupling in the second stage input allowed a smooth variation of impeller speed with altitude.

The curves of Graph 52 illustrate high speed and climbing capability of the Kingcobra. Two sets of information are shown for high speed at various altitudes, that put forth in a manufacturer specification and that used by the USAAF. As is often the case manufacturer's data were more optimistic, these showing high speed five to fifteen mph faster under COMBAT power conditions. The P-63 could exceed 400 mph at 13000 to 17000 feet depending on whose data one believed, with speed increasing to just under 25000 feet, after which it fell off, but holding at 400 mph at 30000 feet. Speed at MILITARY power was about ten mph slower most of the way up. Two versions of WAR EMERGENCY, or COMBAT, power were introduced here, the one without water injection (dry) and the other incorporating this (wet) feature which allowed higher manifold pressure without incurring engine detonation. In the detail specification Bell indicates a sea level high speed of over 375 mph could be achieved using the 1820 horsepower gained by water injection. High speed is shown as over 420 mph at medium altitudes. Manufacturer's data on climb at dry COMBAT power shows Kingcobra rates in the 3500 to 4000 foot per minute range at low altitude, and even better with water injection. A rate of 2800 feet

per minute is shown at 21000 feet and over 1600 feet per minute at 30000 feet. There is no doubt the P-63 was a fast-climbing US fighter; whether manufacturer's data was borne out in full may be in question since the supercharging system of the engine was reputed to not always work as intended. Climb times at dry COMBAT power are shown at about two and a half minutes to 10000 feet and seven and a half to 25000 feet.

Range of the P-63 is indicated, on a "yardstick" basis, plotted against takeoff gross weight in Graph 53. Yardstick range assumes all fuel is consumed in cruise flight at the conditions indicated, in this case 10000 feet altitude, no wind, and no fuel reserve allowance. It is thus quite impractical for any use other than airplane-to-airplane comparison on the same basis. On the curve anything above the first point, 136 gallons of fuel (the major production aircraft had less than that, 126 to 128 gallons) means a drop tank or tanks had to be carried. It is seen yardstick range is less than 700 miles on internal fuel only; this could easily correspond to a practical range of 500-600 miles allowing fuel for takeoff, descent, and reserves. No P-63 data has been found in a practical radius mission, but it is clear the return leg of such a mission would have to be accomplished on full internal fuel less that used in mid-point air combat, assuming external tanks were dropped just prior to combat. The radius attainable would therefore be very limited. Only the Russians had that to worry about, however, since the P-63 never found combat in US service, only operational training.

Takeoff ground run performance of the P-63A is shown in Graph 54 for sea level dry surface conditions in zero wind. Distance required is plotted against airplane takeoff gross weight which in practical cases could vary from about 8500 to 10500 pounds. The curve indicates a ground run requiremant for this weight range of 1400 to 3100 feet, fairly long distances for a relatively light fighter aircraft.

Roll performance of the Kingcobra was relatively good as the data of Graph 55 indicates. Peak roll rate between 250 and 300 mph IAS reached 110 degrees per second, the equivalent of a 3.27 second full 360 degree roll. Above 300 mph IAS the rate fell off quickly, limited by the maximum lateral force a pilot could exert on the control stick; in the case shown this was 50 pounds. At the low speed end roll rate fell off as well, limited by the "bite" generated with maximum aileron deflection.

Empty and basic weight items are laid out in Table 61 for the P-63A. Quite typically the empty weight increased between the

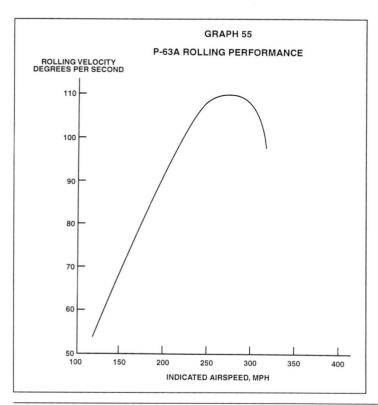

GRAPH 55

P-63A ROLLING PERFORMANCE

ROLLING VELOCITY
DEGREES PER SECOND

INDICATED AIRSPEED, MPH

TABLE 61
P-63A EMPTY AND BASIC WEIGHTS
(LB.)

MODEL	XP-63A	P-63A-10	P-63C
GROUP			
WING	1027	1139.6	1152
TAIL	141	159.9	178
FUSELAGE	598	628.7	676
LANDING GEAR	641	619.2	607
ENGINE SECTION	4	—	—
ENGINE	1681	1620.0	1710
ENGINE ACCESSORIES	(INCL.W.ENGINE)	105.3	114
ENGINE CONTROLS	40	40.7	41
PROPELLER	475	460.0	460
STARTING	58	57.6	58
COOLING	349	347.4	346
WATER INJECTION SYSTEM	—	50.0	—
LUBRICATION	137	134.9	135
FUEL SYSTEM	298	342.7	343
INSTRUMENTS	46	46.5	46
SURFACE CONTROLS	116	140.8	141
HYDRAULIC	—	—	—
ELECTRICAL	170	200.1	202
COMMUNICATION	124	144.4	146
ARMAMENT PROVISIONS	206	333.5	378
FURNISHINGS	62	86.5	93
ICE PROTECTION	—	5.9	—
SERVICE PICKUP	—	30.0	30
OTHER	15	—	—
EMPTY WEIGHT	6188	6693.7	6856
TRAPPED OIL	33	33.0	
TRAPPED FUEL	9	9.0	
CAL.50 GUN INSTLN.	141 (2)	361.4	(4) (141.4 FOR 2)

37mm.CANNON INSTLN.	245.0
GUNSIGHT	6.2
PYROTECHNICS	—
GUN CAMERA	3.3
OXYGEN	—
MISC. EQUIP'T.	—
BASIC WEIGHT	7351.6*

*(7131.6 with 2 cal.50 fus.guns & cannon only)

NOTE: ADD 15 LB.PER BOMB RACK; 12 LB.PER ROCKET LAUNCHER (KITS)

experimental model and a production version; in the case shown the increase was about 500 pounds, or over eight percent. With the exception of the landing gear all airframe weights increased. The total of engine and accessories weight increased as did the fuel system, and a water injection system was added with a 50 pound penalty (not including the water). All fixed equipment groups also incurred weight increases.

Table 62 depicts some typical mission loadings for a P-63A-10 aircraft. Note the normal armament and normal fuel mission is really a stripped down case where only the nose armament is included (the two podded wing guns are left off), and .50 caliber ammunition carried is just for nose guns; also less than full internal fuel and oil is carried. This would appear an impractical case, especially where full internal fuel is such a small amount anyway. In the next mission the aircraft is fully loaded internally with ammunition

TABLE 62
P-63A-10 TYPICAL DISPOSEABLE LOAD ALTERNATES(LB.)

MISSION	NORMAL ARM. NORMAL FUEL	COMBAT ARM. NORMAL RG.	FTR-BOMBER NORMAL RG.	FTR-BOMBER LONG RANGE	FTR-DESTROYER NORMAL RANGE
NO.50CAL'S	2	4	4	4	4
PILOT	200	200	200	200	200
USEABLE OIL	72	87	87	118	87
CAL.50 AMMO.	124	279	279	279	279
37mm.AMMO.	128.4	128.4	128.4	128.4	128.4
BOMBS	—	—	1488 (3x500#)	496 (1x500#)	—
ROCKETS	—	—	—	—	640
DROP TANKS	—	—	—	120	—
INTERNAL FUEL	600 (100GAL.)	756 (126GAL.)	756	756	756
DROP TANK FUEL	—	—	—	900 (150GAL.)	—
WATER/ALCOHOL	186.5 (25GAL)	186.5	186.5	186.5	186.5
TOT.DISPOS.LD.	1310.9	1636.9	3124.9	3183.9	2276.9
BASIC WEIGHT	7131.6	7351.6	7393.6	7366.6	7375.6
GROSS WEIGHT	8442.5	8988.5	10521.5	10550.5	9652.5
USEFUL LOAD	1748.8	2294.8	3827.8	3856.8	2958.8

and fuel. The third mission loading case is similar except three 500 pound bombs are loaded under the aircraft. The fourth case shows the weight of the P-63A carrying one 500 pound bomb and two 75 gallon drop tanks. Here is a case where the airplane might be limited in a radius mission on the return leg by internal fuel depending on how much extra drag the external stores created on the outbound leg. In the last case the P-63A is assumed to carry only internal fuel because the wing store stations are loaded with rockets. These sample loadings out of the many possible combinations show how aircraft takeoff gross weight can vary widely from about 8500 pounds to over 10500 pounds. Loading for a ferry range mission is not shown in the tabulation, but would consist of no ammunition, full internal fuel, and a maximum load of drop tank fuel.

P-63 MAJOR MODEL-TO-MODEL-CHANGES

P-63A-1 (From XP-63) Engine model change; propeller diameter increase by one inch to 11'7";horizontal tail area and flap span increases; provision made for carrying one centerline 500 pound bomb.
P-63A-5 Additional armor plate;no wing guns on Russian versions; dorsal antenna added.
P-63A-6 Horizontal tail area reduced.
P-63A-7 Wing bomb shackles added; capacity for three external drop tanks; no camouflage on USAAC aircraft.
P-63A-8 Propeller diameter reduced to 11'0"; first installation of engine water injection system; more armor.
P-63A-9 Cannon ammunition increased from 30 to 58 rounds; additional armor; new bullet-resistant windshield; new M-10 37mm cannon in place of M-4 model.
P-63A-10 Additional armor and bullet-resistant glass; provision for two wing-mounted three-tube rocket launchers.
RP-63A-11 The A-10 version converted to a target plane. Carburetor air inlet changes; armament removed; water injection system removed; covered externally with 1470 pounds of dural armor plate.
RP-63A-12 Production A-11 target aircraft; additional armor plating.
P-63C-1 New engine version; ventral fin or strake added; slightly longer.

RP-63C-2 Target aircraft version of C-1
P-63C-5 Three external bomb or tank racks added over C-1.
P-63D-1 New engine version; bubble canopy incorporated; increased wing span and wing area; propeller diameter increased one inch; cannon ammo rounds reduced to 48; additional internal fuel.
P-63E-1 Intended production version of D; standard canopy used.
P-63F-1 New engine version; new higher vertical tail; dorsal fin.
RP-63G-1 Target aircraft with new engine version and more armor.

P-63 CHRONOLOGY

Feb '41-Work is started at Bell Aircraft on the Model 33 fighter.

Jun27'41-Two XP-63 prototype aircraft are ordered by the US Army.

Jun '42-A third prototype , the XP-63A, is ordered from Bell.

Sep29'42-A first production order is given Bell for P-63A airplanes.

Dec 7'42-The first flight of an XP-63 airplane takes place.

Jan28'43-The first prototype airplane is damaged beyond repair during testing when the landing gear will not extend. Test pilot Jack Woolams burns off fuel, and in the disorientation of dusk lands in a field of small trees.

Feb 5'43-The second prototype airplane is rolled out.Mar 4'43-The second prototype XP-63 takes to the air for a first flight.

Apr26'43-The first flight of the XP-63A airplane takes place.

May '43-The US Army formally accepts an XP-63 airplane.

May25'43-The second prototype XP-63 crashes after suffering an engine failure.

Jul '43-A prototype XP-63D Kingcobra model is accepted by the Army.

Oct '43-Production deliveries of the P-63A model are started with the type supplanting the P-39Q Airacobra fighter on Bell production lines.

Jan '44-Model testing is done to predict spin characteristics of a heavily loaded P-63 to supplement earlier NACA 1942 testing.

May '44-The first of two P-63As is delivered to the RAF for testing.

May16'44-A report on operational suitability of the P-63 from Eglin Field concludes the aircraft cannot in current form be an operationally suitable front line fighter.

Aug '44-The USAAF has a total of 339 P-63A aircraft on hand.

Aug15'44-Gen. Hap Arnold suggests that the Russians take as many used P-39s and P-63s as are in the US, this prompted by Soviet requests for more and more fighters.

Oct '44-Extensive full-scale stability and control testing on a P-63A-1 aircraft is continuing at NACA. Four different sets of elevators and two different vertical tail surfaces are tested.

Oct '44-The P-63A is one of several US and British fighters evaluated by company and service pilots at a Patuxent River Fighter Conference. It gets mixed reviews.

Dec '44-Delivery of P-63C versions start after 1725 A models have been produced with most of these having been sent to Russia.

Apr '45-The Russians express dissatisfaction with the P-63, saying the plane is weak. The aft fuselage is beefed up in a field modification. Many P-63Cs are on the way to Russia at this time.

Apr '45-The P-63F version of the Kingcobra is accepted by the US Army.

May '45-Testing begins on the P-63E version, and it is accepted by the Army shortly after.

Jul '45-The P-63G is now being delivered to the US Army.

'46-RP-63 piloted target versions of the Kingcobra are being used to train bomber gunners, who fire special frangible bullets at these specially armored fighters during practice attacks.

P-63 HANDLING QUALITIES AND CHARACTERISTICS

HANDLING QUALITIES
GROUND HANDLING

Like its older brother the P-39, the P-63 airplane had good forward visibility for taxi by virtue of its tricycle landing gear. The near level attitude thus imparted made S-turning unnecessary. One Army test pilot noted "Excellent taxi visibility". Steering was accomplished using engine power, rudder, and wheel brakes as required. One problem during taxi involved a powerplant that ran rough at certain RPMs. The pilot would increase RPM to get past the rough spot, increasing taxi speed unduly, and then have to ride the wheel brakes. One pilot complained "Required excessive use of brakes in taxi". Another said "When you started the engine the drive shaft vibrated so much that the instrument panel was a blur, and the liquid in the compass turned into a froth until the RPM was increased". However a large number of pilots rated ground handling good, though wheel brakes were considered weak.

Fig.63-1 Bell XP-63 Kingcobra, Ser.41-19511, Mfr. photo via F. Dean coll. One of the two Kingcobra experimental prototype aircraft. Though of the same general configuration as the earlier P-39 Airacobra, the P-63 was a new fighter featuring a version of the Allison V-1710 engine with a two stage supercharger and a wing using the then-new laminar flow airfoil sections. The first flight of an XP-63 took place exactly one year after Pearl Harbor, and the airplane was damaged beyond repair in a landing a few weeks later. The second prototype was in the air by early March, 1943.

Fig.63-2 Bell XP-63A Kingcobra, Ser.42-78015, Mfr. photo via F. Dean coll. Shortly after the second XP-63 took to the air a third Kingcobra first flew on April 26,1943. The XP-63A illustrated had powerplant, wing flap, and horizontal tail area changes. The Kingcobra looked like a longer leaner more angular version of the Airacobra. Interestingly, in spite of the fact the earlier P-39 was criticized as a very short range fighter the Kingcobra was provided with only sixteen (later reduced to six) gallons more internal fuel than its predecessor. Speed and height capabilities were considerably improved; mission radius capability hardly at all.

Fig.63-3 Bell P-63A Kingcobra, Ser.42-68871, Mfr. photo via F. Dean coll. A view of an early P-63A shows some additional features, including a podded .50 caliber gun under each wing and a good-sized four blade Aeroproducts Unimatic propeller of eleven feet seven inches diameter using hollow steel blades. There were at least seven sub-variants of the P-63A with many design changes between them for a total of 1725 aircraft, most going to Russia.

Fig.63-5 Bell P-63A Kingcobra, Ser.42-68894, photo via P.M. Bowers. An interesting photo of an early P-63A in later years. There is no 37mm. cannon installed based on the pointed spinner nose, a ventral fin normally associated with the later P-63C has been installed in a retrofit, and the future is clearly seen just behind the P-63A in the form of a new Lockheed P-80A jet fighter. The P-63A had space for internal fuel only in the wing because the powerplant arrangement did not allow for correct placement of a fuselage fuel tank.

During taxi trim tabs were set for takeoff. The rudder tab was set to right rudder four graduations and the elevator tab to three graduations nose up.

TAKEOFF AND CLIMB

In the P-63 flaps were not normally used for takeoff. Propeller torque reaction imparted a severe yaw to the left if throttle was opened full before sufficient speed was attained to provide rudder control. In addition it was not possible to hold the airplane with brakes at 60 inches manifold pressure. So the best method of takeoff was to start with the nose pointed somewhat to the right side of the runway. This action aided inherently weak brakes in offsetting the initial torque reaction tending to swing the airplane to the left. Brakes were held at 40 inches of manifold pressure and takeoff checks

made. Upon brake release throttle was advanced slowly to the 60 inch position, holding right rudder as required to maintain course. It was important not to overheat the right brake by dragging it to keep straight. Elevator power was sufficient to raise the nose wheel from a concrete runway long before 80 percent of takeoff speed was reached, even with a forward center of gravity. The aircraft lifted off the runway at 90 to 100 mph. Landing gear was then retracted as quickly as possible. Some pilots were not particularly pleased with takeoff performance of the Kingcobra. Six of them said "A long slow takeoff". Three complained about "Not enough rudder control". Another said "On takeoff a strong torque and swerve

Fig.63-4 Bell P-63A Kingcobra, Ser.42-68871, Mfr. photo via B. Matthews. A flight photo of the same Kingcobra airplane shows a very clean fighter except, perhaps, for the podded wing guns which, incidently, adversely affected spin characteristics. The pilot sat slightly more forward with respect to the wing than on the P-39, giving somewhat better visibility forward and down. Early P-63As were fitted with one centerline store; later two wing store stations were added.

Fig.63-6 Bell P-63A Kingcobra, Ser.42-68941, Mfr. photo via F. Dean coll. A P-63A poses nicely for the cameraman in a Bell publicity shot. Armament of the Kingcobra consisted of the 37mm. nose cannon, two synchronized nose .50 caliber machine guns, and two podded .50 caliber wing guns, the same as the earlier P-39Q Airacobra. The Kingcobra could attain a high speed at MILITARY power of from 400 to 420 mph at 25000 feet depending on whose performance data, the manufacturer or the military, one tended to believe.

Fig.63-7 Bell P-63A Kingcobra, Mfr. photo via F. Dean coll. This flight photo shows two wing store stations just outboard of the wing gun pods and the portion of the retracted wheels not masked by cover plates along with the inboard wing leading edge air intakes. These intakes served a single central engine oil cooler and two coolant radiators, one on each side of the oil cooler. The air exited through rear belly shuttered openings. These systems were similar in configuration to those of the P-39. A pitot tube hangs down from the outboard portion of the port wing.

Fig.63-10 Bell RP-63C Kingcobra, Ser.43-11074, photo via P.M. Bowers. Clean angular lines are shown in this target version of the P-63C. Interestingly there is no ventral strake or fin , usually attributed as a modification used with C models, on this aircraft. Never used in operational US fighter groups, P-63s were sent to Russia or employed in training functions. The RP-63C versions, 200 of which were built, were employed as training targets for bomber gunners, a most unique function.

tendency with sudden power application". Testing of a P-63 take-off at Eglin Field in Florida seemed to differ, with one report noting "Comparatively short takeoff run makes it suitable for operation from small combat fields". Reports from this testing indicated "An average distance of 2100 feet is required for takeoff if the brakes are released at 40 to 50 inches of manifold pressure. The minimum distance measured was 1700 feet".

Best initial climb speed was 165 mph IAS with optimum climb speed easing off slightly with increasing altitude. Climb characteristics were considered good. One pilot said "Full throttle produced an exhilerating rate of climb".

TRIMMING
Very little change in P-63 elevator trim was required with power or speed changes. In addition rudder trim changes due to these factors were desireably low; in fact directional trim characteristics of the aircraft were considered excellent. Initially P-63 aircraft had no aileron trim tab which was criticized during Army testing "A definite need for an aileron trim tab. It was impossible to get equal fuel flow from both wing tanks. One wing gets heavy". Later aircraft got the aileron tab after NACA also recommended its addition while testing a P-63A-1 airplane.

Fig.63-8 Bell P-63A Kingcobra, Ser.42-69421, W.E. Johnson photo via B. Matthews. A late variant of the P-63A in natural metal finish sits on the hardstand. The cockpit enclosure was in some ways like a bubble canopy, however the heavy framing just aft of the pilot needed with the auto-type door design did obscure some vision. The P-63A-9 version shown had a new model of the 37mm. cannon with ammunition supply almost doubled to 58 rounds along with additional armor and a new windshield. Production deliveries of the P-63A started in October, 1943 and finished up near the end of 1944.

Fig.63-11 Bell RP-63C Kingcobra, Ser.43-11074, photo via P.M. Bowers. Another view of a target RP-63C airplane showing substantial beef-up around the cockpit area to protect the pilot from frangible bullets fired at the aircraft by trainee gunners aboard US bombers. It is hard to realize how more realistic training could be accomplished.

Fig.63-12 Bell RP-63C Kingcobra, Ser.43-10948, R. Besecker photo via B. Matthews. A somewhat weary looking Kingcobra target aircraft sits at Newark Airport, New Jersey in the spring of 1946. With 128 gallons of internal fuel and external drop tanks not allowed on target aircraft, the Kingcobra did not have a lot of flight endurance, but pilots made realistic slashing attacks on bombers. Considerable armor plating was distributed around critical areas of the fighter for this mission.

Fig.63-14 Bell RP-63G Kingcobra, Ser.43-11724, photo via F. Dean coll. The final version of the target aircraft concept, only 32 of which were manufactured just postwar, carried the idea a step further by imitating a pinball machine, and were thus labeled "pinball" aircraft. Sensors responding to frangible bullet hits on the reinforced aircraft skin lit up a light in the aircraft nose to register the strike. This was not an elegant end for a promising World War II fighter type.

DIVE AND RECOVERY

The P-63, in common with other Army fighters, was designed for a positive flight maneuver limit load factor of 8.0 g (ultimate load factor being 12.0 g), and would satisfactorily withstand an 8.0 g dive pullout. Bell conducted dive tests and got an approximate top Mach number of 0.80 at which time the aircraft started to porpoise slightly. If they went a little faster it porpoised more and more. At this time it was decided they had gone far enough. Army tests showed a nose heavy trim (tuck under) in high speed dives above 400 mph IAS. The limiting dive speeds set up for the aircraft were 525 mph IAS at sea level, 400 mph IAS at 15000 to 20000 feet, and 250 mph IAS at 30000 to 35000 feet. Above these speeds the nose down tendency became increasingly apparent in dives, and a reversal of stick forces was noticed in pullouts. In addition, during pullouts the P-63 had a tendency to roll, particularly at high altitudes, and application of opposite aileron was not immediately effective. When aileron input did take effect the aircraft would roll in the opposite direction, and a wallowing motion would result. A forward push on

the stick to relieve g forces would correct this condition. The tendency to roll and hunt would not get too alarming if the limiting dive speeds above were observed. A group of pilots rated P-63A-9 dive acceleration good, calling it "rapid". They also rated dive stick forces and dive recovery good. Army testing of a P-63 diving against other fighters rated it just equal to the P-38J, slightly inferior to a P-47D-20 in long dives, and not as good as a P-51B-5 in diving.

As noted later there were several changes made to the tail of the P-63. Lowering horizontal stabilizer incidence angle eliminated stick force reversals in high speed dives, and reducing elevator rib spacing to eliminate fabric ballooning also helped dive characteristics, including the porpoising tendency. Horizontal tail area changes were also made in various models.

Zoom climbing out of dives was considered good, slightly better than a P-38J or a P-47D-20, but not quite as good as the P-51B.

MANEUVERING

Acrobatic maneuvers in the P-63A were found by the Army to be "Exceptionally easy to perform at all altitudes at which the aircraft would normally operate, and a new pilot would quickly feel at ease doing them". A World War II pilot said "In regard to maneuverability the Kingcobra was particularly outstanding". Maneuvers restricted or prohibited were: Intentional spins, inverted spins, outside loops, inverted flying over ten seconds, and high speed snap rolls. Maneuvers were not permitted in models with external wing tanks; only normal flight attitudes were allowed. Army Air Force testing of an early P-63A concluded "Desireable features included handling qualities and maneuverability". At a fighter conference pilots were not as kind in their evaluation; sixteen of nineteen (a mixed group of US and British service and US contractor test pilots) rated P-63 maneuverability just fair or poor, eight in each category. One pilot noted "Heavy controls and instability". Because of changes between models like different tail areas handling qualities such as control forces did tend to differ.

P-63 rolling performance was outstanding. Army tests showed Kingcobra ailerons were excellent; all test pilots agreed. Action

Fig.63-13 Bell RP-63C Kingcobra, Ser.43-11031, P.M. Bowers photo. Another postwar photo of a highly protected RP-63C target aircraft. Late in World War II when the Russians were receiving P-63 aircraft they complained the airframe was weak, apparently after some accidents. A modification was instituted to strengthen the aft fuselage and many Kingcobras were beefed up in Alaska as they proceeded along the ALSIB (Alaska-Siberia) delivery route to Russia.

Fig.63-15 Civil Bell P-63C Kingcobra Racer, photo via P.M. Bowers. A modified P-63C in racing form, possibly a civil RP-63C since the aft section of the cockpit canopy is done over in metal. Several P-63C aircraft were employed in post-war racing, including the 1946 and 1947 Bendix Trophy Races and the 1946 and 1949 Sohio Trophy Races. The P-63 pictured was flown to fourth place, behind three other P-63s, in the all-P-63 1947 Tinnerman Trophy Race. Major outward modification is the clipped wing. Some P-63s were severely modified.

was rapid with light but positive forces, and good control feel was present at all times without any dead spot or overbalance. Roll performance was tested against other aircraft; it was much better than a P-38, and also better than the P-51B. Peak rolling speed was about 100 degrees per second at approximately 275 mph IAS. One ferry pilot complimented the steady rolling capability of the P-63. "You could do rolls, and I mean slow rolls, continuously while going cross-country with no effort; it would roll exactly on its longitudinal axis, and you could maintain perfect altitude". Another report commented "The aircraft responds rapidly to the ailerons at all

Fig63-16A Civil bell P-63C Kingcobra, Milt Sheppard photo. A civil P-63C of the Confederate Air Force at an air show in markings of the Free French Air Force celebrating the fact a batch of Kingcobras were supplied to France late in the war. The ventral strake added to the C version is shown under the aft fuselage.

speeds". NACA said "Aileron characteristics compare favorably with other US contemporary fighter aircraft. They were exceptionally effective per unit area and deflection". NACA felt roll performance could even be improved by stiffening the system and increasing aileron maximum deflection angle. But on the P-63A-1 there was a problem. Directional stability was inadequate with excessive inadvertant yawing taking place during abrupt rolling maneuvers, a problem not uncommon in US World War II fighters. In fact early P-63A-1 aircraft tended to oscillate directionally even with controls fixed in steady flight. Testing indicated vertical tail height should be increased, and a small dorsal fin added to improve behavior at large sideslip angles and high power. It was felt if later on a larger wider chord blade propeller was installed to cater for a future engine power increase even more serious directional instability could be anticipated, and that a ventral fin could then be installed to counter the problem by adding a further directional stability contribution. A ventral fin was placed on the later P-63C version.

There were also longitudinal stability and control characteristics affecting maneuverability that had to be fixed in the P-63A-1 aircraft. The stick fixed stability in both straight and turning flight was satisfactory, but stick free stability at aft centers of gravity was marginal to negative, particularly at high altitudes. A new enlarged production horizontal tail was fitted and this improved stability, but tended to make stick forces in turns undesireably high with a forward center of gravity at low altitude. A small bobweight was added in the elevator control system, and the new elevators were highly balanced. This combination gave more desireable maneuvering stick forces at various center of gravity locations and flight altitudes. Elevator control feel characteristics were still considered unsatisfactory by some pilots, mainly because the large amount of aerodynamic balance made the stick control over-sensitive during rapid movement. However at a fighter conference most pilots found elevator force reflected at the stick and elevator effectiveness of a P-63A-9 (incorporating these changes) to be good.

Army testing of an early P-63A at Eglin Field indicated reversal of stick forces in a tight turn (similar to the reversals noted in dive pullouts above, both at high g levels). In these turns stick forces lightened up, and an intentional 3g turn might suddenly increase to 5g, this similar to P-51 Mustang problems under certain conditions. Turning tests against other US fighters showed the P-63 to be relatively good. It was better than a P-38J if the latter did not use a maneuver flap setting, and about the same if the P-38 did. Against a P-51B the P-63 could get on the Mustang's tail in three to four turns and P-63 performance got relatively better with increasing turning speed. Against a P-47D the P-63 could get into a stern shot position after two turns. But the stick had to be handled carefully because of potential force reversals. As noted above changes in the tail surfaces and the elevator control system improved longitudinal and directional characteristics of later P-63 models to the point they were considered very nice airplanes to fly.

APPROACH AND LANDING
On approach the highest speed allowed for lowering gear and flaps was 180 mph IAS. The normal landing approach was a glide, and when in clean condition the P-63 had a fairly flat gliding angle. Minimum gliding speeds were typically 120 mph IAS power off and 110 mph IAS power on for safe control. At lower speeds the aircraft settled quite rapidly. Recommended speed for the turn into

Fig.63-15C Civil Bell P-63C Kingcobra racer, R, Besecker photo. A Kingcobra much revised for racing at Reno in 1971. Major external modifications were the clipped wings and practical elimination of the standard cockpit and canopy with replacement by a tiny bubble.

final was 140 mph IAS. Speed reduced to 115 mph IAS with flaps down going over the fence. The P-63 was landed in conventional nose high attitude for tricycle gear aircraft with main wheels touching first. As speed decreased the nose wheel settled to the ground. Brakes were applied intermittantly to prevent excess tire and brake wear. Army testing showed a landing could be made with a roll of approximately 1600 feet without excessive use of brakes, but it was also noted wheel brakes were unsatisfactory. Test pilots also felt the small flap area resulted in flaps having little effect on landing characteristics. The P-63 tricycle gear was considered "an excellent and desireable feature" with wide tread main gear making

Fig.63-15B Civil Bell P-63C Kingcobra, photo via P.M. Bowers. Another civil Kingcobra attached to the CAF post war, its fuselage blackened by exhaust from the stacks of the mid-located engine. Wing root air intakes fed two coolant radiators and a single engine oil cooler between them. The upper aft air intake fed the carburetor supercharger blowers.

Fig.63-15D Civil Bell P-63C Kingcobra racer, R. Besecker photo. A clipped wing P-63C racer at the 1973 Reno Air Races. "Tipsy Miss" was a revision of an airplane that dropped out of a Bendix race back in 1947.

Fig.63-15E Civil Bell P-63C Kingcobra, R. Besecker photo. The "Tipsy Miss" back at Reno, Nevada in September, 1974 in a photo emphasizing the clean lines of the aircraft. The clipped wingtip shows clearly the laminar flow airfoil contour of the wing with maximum thickness well aft.

for good anti-ground looping tendencies. A Bell test pilot noted to prospective P-63 pilots "In making a good landing try and keep the nose wheel off and try to drag the tail. Just let the nose wheel fall down of its own accord". Most pilots rating P-63 approach and landing characteristics indicated they were good. Pilots were split on refused landing, or waveoff, characteristics. Three said they were good, two said fair, and five poor. One Navy Commander commented "I don't know who the contractor pilot was who said "good" for waveoff, but I personally would hate to have a waveoff in that plane".

STALLS AND SPINS
One g stall characteristics of P-63 aircraft were variously described as "normal", "good", "milder than a Cessna 150", and by the NACA

Fig.63-15F Bell P-63E Kingcobra, photo via P.M. Bowers. The remaining E model of the Kingcobra displayed at the US Air Force Museum. The P-63E was to have been the 1945 production model of the series with increased wing span and area and uprated Allison engine. Only thirteen were built before the war ended and contracts were cancelled. Reasons for the absence of aft air intake and presence of the radio mast forward are unknown.

"excellent". As the stall was approached (82 to 96 mph IAS dirty, depending on aircraft weight and power setting), elevator buffet gave a warning, the aircraft "mushed", and mild rolling occurred. Ailerons were still effective at or somewhat below stall speed. The NACA indicated "Inadvertant spinning would not ordinarily be encountered. As stall was approached, buffet and rolling motions occur warning the pilot of impending stall in sufficient time so corrective action could be applied before spinning had a chance to develop. Nosing down and gaining speed would take the aircraft out of stall.

Starting in 1942 extensive model tests of P-63 spin characteristics were undertaken. NACA flight tests did not involve spinning the full scale airplane however. Model tests predicted rapid spin recovery could be made in any condition if ailerons were deflected against the spin and rudder partly deflected against it, followed by downward elevator movement. Later, full scale spin tests of the P-63 were made by Bell test pilots. These agreed well with model test results except recoveries with wing guns aboard appeared even more critical than model tests had predicted. The shape of the wing gun fairings had a pronounced effect on spin characteristics. Satisfactory recoveries could be made for aircraft gross weights under about 7700 pounds without wing guns installed. For higher gross weights and/or wing guns installed a very precise sequence of corrective control action was required. After these tests it was recommended that spin recoveries be made less critical by adding ventral fin and/or rudder area below the fuselage. This was done on the P-63C aircraft.

On the P-63C, five turn spins were sucessfully demonstrated; both left and right hand spins oscillated violently, but recovery was prompt. Entry into a right hand spin was more difficult than into a left hand spin, and recovery took more time. During the spin there was considerable rudder buffet, and once during each oscillation a force was felt on rudder and elevator tending to throw them against the spin. The recommended spin recovery, regardless of airplane loading or whether wing pod guns were carried was: From a steady

Fig.63-16 Civil Bell P-63F Kingcobra, R. Besecker photo. A photo of one of the only two P-63Fs as a civil racer taken at the Reno Air Races in September, 1976. Originally delivered to the USAAF in April of 1945, four months before war's end, the P-63F was distinguished externally by a new tall vertical tail. It started a civil racing career flying to tenth place in the 1946 Thompson Trophy Race.

spin condition of power off, full rudder with the spin, elevator up, and ailerons neutral, apply full rudder and ailerons against the spin simultaneously, then about one half turn later move the stick quickly full forward maintaining rudder and ailerons against the spin.

CHARACTERISTICS
COCKPIT
After both pilots had flown a P-63A-9 Navy Cdr. Ramsey said to a large Britisher "Commodore, could you get into that plane and shut all the windows? Just as a matter of interest, could you get into that plane?" The Commodore replied "I could get into the P-63 with a

Fig.63-15G Civil Bell P-63F Kingcobra, R. Besecker photo. One of two experimental aircraft that survived photographed at Reno in 1976. The tall tail with dorsal fin combined with the ventral strake introduced earlier to provide solutions to earlier Kingcobra stability problems.

chute, but I had to leave out the chute in getting into the P-39." The older brother of the P-63, the P-39 was designed for a pilot five foot eight inches tall. The P-63, depending on the data source, was designed for a pilot either 5 foot 8 inches or 5 foot 10 inches tall. The Army evaluation noted "The cockpit was designed for a man five foot 10 inches tall, and would feel a little crowded for a larger pilot." Bell specifications indicated: "—shall provide for pilots not over 5 feet, 8 inches tall; the fuselage shall be streamlined to fit this size pilot". In either case the cockpit of the P-63 was definitely one on the small side. In a later evaluation 13 of 21 pilots noted the P-63 cockpit to be "small and cramped".

As to layout of instruments and controls, the official Army evaluation was "Instrument and switch panel arrangements quite desireable, and the cockpit arrangement is generally satisfactory". There were gripes on cockpit heating and ventilation, however. The cockpit was "cold, and hot air ventilation inadequate and difficult to adjust. A cockpit heater redesign was needed". This was amplified in some late 1944 testing "Cockpit heater no good above 12000 feet". In a vote for "worst cockpit" a group of pilots ranked the P-63A-9 fifth of eleven fighter types.

VISIBILITY
As noted earlier, taxi visibility forward was facilitated by the tricycle landing gear layout. From there on pilots had some good to say about P-63 flight visibility, but not very much. Perhaps they were comparing it to potential visibility from a full blown bubble then coming into style on such planes as late P-47 and P-51 models. An Army evaluation noted "Combat visibility is limited by canopy frames. The cockpit of the P-63 is further forward with respect to the wing leading edge than the P-39, and thus the visibility

Fig63-17 Civil Bell P-63F Kingcobra, R. Besecker photo. About as handsome as an ex-fighter aircraft can be, the remaining P-63F sits at the Reno Races in the 1970s. Note the very high activity factor bladed propeller used to absorb the high power generated by a late model Allison engine. Bell stuck with their standard cockpit canopy arrangement except in the single P-63D test aircraft which used a bubble canopy.

down and to the front is improved. However the doors and door frames are still the most objectionable feature of the cockpit enclosure, and greatly restrict pilot visibility up and to the side. In formation flying this is particularly tiring since it is necessary for the pilot to change his position constantly to see around the frame. (Also) the clear vision panel provided is no longer required; it obstructs forward visibility. Rearward vision is poor due to the armor plate, and it is believed the bullet-resisting glass on the P-39 was more satisfactory. A bubble canopy would be desireable". At a fighter meet pilots agreed. The P-63A-9 ranked last of eight fighter types in "Best all-around vision". Some remarks were "Visibility obstructed by door frames" (five pilots), and "Poor visibility rearward and all around".

VULNERABILITY/ARMOR
The P-63 carried various amounts of armor in different versions, and no specific assessment can be made. Further, the only combat use of the Kingcobra was by the USSR, and no reports of combat vulnerability have been found.

GUN PLATFORM/WEAPON PERFORMANCE
One group of pilots rated the P-63A-9 as a fair to poor gun platform. Test reports of early P-63A models indicated the value of the aircraft as a gun platform could be greatly increased by adding vertical tail height and area, or by adding a ventral tail surface. This fix was to increase stability as noted earlier, and such changes were incorporated in later versions, thereby making them improved gun platforms.

With the benefit of P-39 combat experience on the 37mm cannon the installation on the P-63 was more reliable. In the P-63 case

however, contrary to the P-39, the design did not cater for alternate installation of a 20mm weapon. The Army Eglin Field test evaluators did not like the externally podded .50 caliber wing gun installation well out on each wing, and recommended internal wing guns be substituted as with other US fighters. This was never done.

GENERAL COMMENTS
A pilot who flew the P-63 found it easy to handle and responsive, quite delightful all around.

The P-63 was an entirely different flying machine than the P-39.

The USAAF Eglin Field evaluation team recommended that their suggested changes be made to the P-63, and that it then be returned to Eglin for comparison with the latest model of the P-51 airplane. If the comparative test results were then unfavorable to the Bell aircraft, P-63 production should be cancelled immediately.

Much better than the old P-39, but not up to most fighters. This is what the P-39 ought to have been.

The limited range and ceiling were serious liabilities for combat flying.

Not operationally suitable because high speed is not up to that of contemporary fighters.

The P-63 proved a real improvement (over the P-39) with more cockpit room, more power, and more maneuverability.

It was a dream to fly.

The P-63 was a good fighter against the P-38, P-47, and P-51. At low altitude it could out-maneuver and out-climb the P-51. Higher up performance suffered against the others. Though all the aircraft had two stage supercharging of one sort or another that of the P-63 was less effective.

A huge deficit for the P-63 was its limited combat radius capability due to the small amount of internal fuel capacity.

The P-63 controls were stiffer than those of the Airacobra. With flaps down part way the P-63 was superior in turning to most anything else in the air.

An honest aircraft.

There was no place in the fuselage to put needed fuel with the mid-engine arrangement; if it got to the war it couldn't come back.

In a climb it was absolutely excellent, especially low down. I don't know who it was that said the P-63 was good in wave-off; I certainly wouldn't want to take a waveoff in that plane.

The single largest modification project carried out during the ALSIB project was the reinforcement of the aft fuselage of the P-63. On October 7, 1944 all enroute P-63s were grounded. The total number modified was 111 at Fairbanks, Alaska, 60 at Nome, and 62 at Edmonton.

P-63 STRUCTURAL DESCRIPTION
(Metal is aluminum alloy unless otherwise noted)

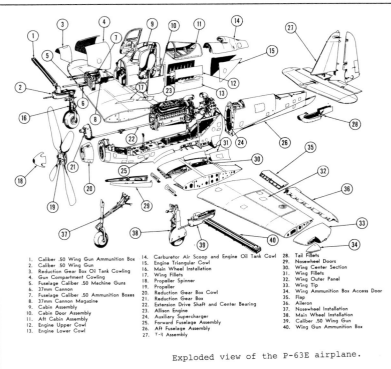

1. Caliber .50 Wing Gun Ammunition Box
2. Caliber .50 Wing Gun
3. Reduction Gear Box Oil Tank Cowling
4. Gun Compartment Cowling
5. Fuselage Caliber .50 Machine Guns
6. 37mm Cannon
7. Fuselage Caliber .50 Ammunition Boxes
8. 37mm Cannon Magazine
9. Cabin Assembly
10. Cabin Door Assembly
11. Aft Cabin Assembly
12. Engine Upper Cowl
13. Engine Lower Cowl
14. Carburetor Air Scoop and Engine Oil Tank Cowl
15. Engine Triangular Cowl
16. Main Wheel Installation
17. Wing Fillets
18. Propeller Spinner
19. Propeller
20. Reduction Gear Box Cowl
21. Reduction Gear Box
22. Extension Drive Shaft and Center Bearing
23. Allison Engine
24. Auxiliary Supercharger
25. Forward Fuselage Assembly
26. Aft Fuselage Assembly
27. T-11 Assembly
28. Tail Fillets
29. Nosewheel Doors
30. Wing Center Section
31. Wing Fillets
32. Wing Outer Panel
33. Wing Tip
34. Wing Ammunition Box Access Door
35. Flap
36. Aileron
37. Nosewheel Installation
38. Main Wheel Installation
39. Caliber .50 Wing Gun
40. Wing Gun Ammunition Box

Exploded view of the P-63E airplane.

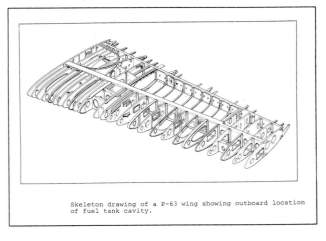

Skeleton drawing of a P-63 wing showing outboard location of fuel tank cavity.

WING GROUP

The wing was an all-metal cantilever stressed skin structure of laminar flow design contour made up of a center section of constant chord bolted to and becoming part of the forward fuselage, two tapered outer panels, ailerons and flaps, along with wing-fuselage and intake duct fairing pieces.

The wing center section was a single assembly consisting of a front main spar, rear spar, and four main bulkheads or ribs, carrying through beneath the fuselage structure. The two spars provided primary bending strength, and were bolted in through four fittings on the front beam and two on the rear beam to the longitudinal beams of the fuselage. The section leading edge was open for, and the spar webs were cut to provide for air ducting to oil and coolant radiators located in the center section aft of the front spar. Duct exit shutter doors formed part of the center section lower surface. A closing rib of extra heavy construction provided for steel fittings at the spar cap locations for bolt attachment of the outer wing panels on each side of the center section. Metal skin covering material locally reinforced with stiffeners was provided except for cutouts directly under the fuselage. Wing fillet fairings of sheet metal provided a smooth streamlined transition from the wing to the fuselage contour. On late airplane versions fittings were installed on the lower surface of the center section on centerline for a bomb shackle.

The outer wing panels incorporated two spars, a forward and an aft beam. The aft beam supported the flaps and the ailerons. At

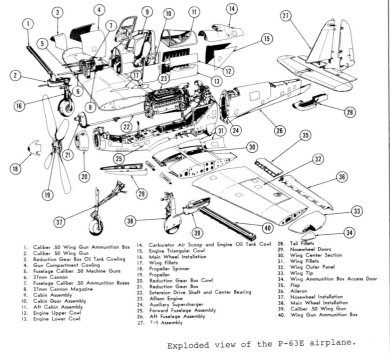

the inboard end the spars lined up with those of the center section and the spar caps were bolted together through attach fittings. Spars were made up of reinforced sheet webs and extruded caps. At the mid-section of the wing panels space was provided between front and rear spars for removeable self-sealing fuel cells, and three access holes were provided at the top surface for fuel bag inspection and repair. Stamped chordwise ribs were provided at a maximum spacing of sixteen inches along the span of the panel, and spanwise reinforcing stringers were employed under the flush-riveted sheet metal skins covering the panel from leading edge to rear spar on both surfaces. Space was provided aft of the forward spar for a trunnion mount for the main landing gear assembly and for a wheel well. Wing structural reinforcement was provided for a gun pod under each wing, and space was made for ammunition containers within the wing leading edge section.

The wing surfaces were smoothed by covering rivet heads, openings around access doors, and other irregularities with glazing putty; there were to be no ridges or depressions greater than .008 inches from the laminar flow design wing section contours.

Metal flaps of the plain full-contour type were employed, and were supported off the rear spar by three hinge fittings, and driven to a maximum deflection of 45 degrees by an electrically actuated inboard torque tube. A flap position indicator consisting of a paint stripe along the flap near the leading edge was visible to the pilot. No maneuver position was provided for the flap system. Flaps were of the stiffened single spar multiple rib type, and were skinned with magnesium alloy sheet and flush riveted on exterior surfaces. Flaps incorporated a balance seal of the same type as used on the ailerons.

Ailerons ran all the way from the outer flap section to the tip of the wing. There was no separable wingtip. Aerodynamic balance was of the NACA pressure differential type, and the surfaces were statically and dynamically balanced. The ailerons were hinged on four brackets to fittings on the aft spar, and consisted of a single spar, multiple formed leading and trailing edge ribs, a trailing edge member, and flush riveted magnesium skins. There was no controllable trim tab on either aileron of early aircraft, but P-63C-1 and P-63C-5 airplanes had an electrically-operated trim tab inboard on the right aileron. The tab was of metal and phenolic construction. A ground-adjustable tab was provided on the inboard end of the left aileron to correct rigging errors. There was no differential motion of the ailerons. A fabric balance seal was attached to the leading edge, to the inboard end of the aileron, and to the wing rib to reduce pilot stick forces and to increase aileron effectiveness and airplane roll rate.

TAIL GROUP

The tail group consisted of the fixed horizontal stabilizer, two elevators, a fixed vertical stabilizer or fin, a rudder, and sheet metal empennage fillet pieces used for root fairings.

The cantilever horizontal stabilizer, set at plus one degree relative to the airplane horizontal axis, was a fixed single piece surface bolted onto cast fittings on a flat deck at the rear of the aft fuselage section. The structure was comprised of two spars, stamped inter-

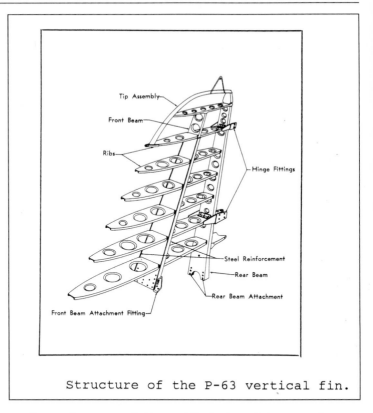

Structure of the P-63 vertical fin.

mediate and nose metal ribs, and flush riveted sheet metal covering.

There were no separable tips. Fittings for two elevator hinges were employed on each side of the surface.

The elevators, two separate surfaces connected by flanged torque tubes at the elevator hub quadrant on the inboard ends across the fuselage, were of the modified Frise type statically and dynamically balanced by weights and areas forward of the hinge line. The elevator construction was metal framing with a single channel-shaped spar along with ribs and trailing edge member with a fabric covering. Fabric attachment to the framing was reinforced with pinked strips of fabric. A controllable tab was located at the inboard end of the trailing edge on the left hand elevator. The tab was mounted on an auxiliary beam for hinges and actuator mounting. A ground-adjustable tab was installed on the inboard end of the right elevator. Two hinge fittings were provided on the main beam of each elevator. Elevators were electrically bonded to the stabilizer with braided wire.

The vertical fin or stabilizer was set on the airplane centerline and was a fixed cantilever all-metal surface using two channel shaped spars and chordwise ribs. The front spar was reinforced with steel strips. Fittings were provided at the lower ends of the two spars for a bolt attachment through the horizontal stabilizer to fittings on the rear deck of the aft fuselage. The fin was metal covered with flush riveted skins. The rear spar provided support for two rudder hinge fittings.

The rudder was a single assembly of the modified Frise balanced type supported off the aft spar of the fin on two hinges, and

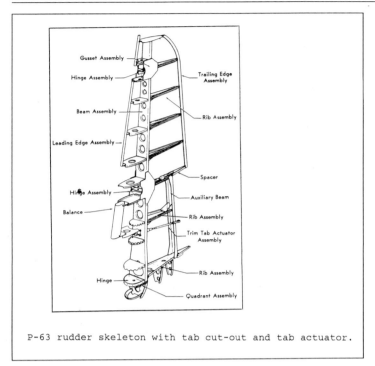

P-63 rudder skeleton with tab cut-out and tab actuator.

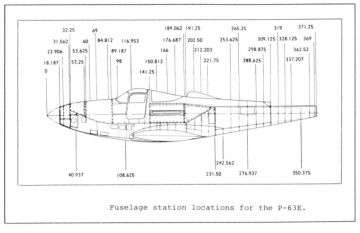

Fuselage station locations for the P-63E.

was both statically and dynamically balanced. The rudder framing was similar to that of the elevators, consisting of a single channel-shaped spar, ribs, and edge members. Covering was fabric with pinked reinforcing strips where required. The rudder assembly included a controllable trim tab located at the lower trailing edge section.

FUSELAGE GROUP

The all metal fuselage consisted of a forward section and an aft section. The two sections were joined together at station 231.5 by 38 attaching bolts and nuts through splice bulkheads

The forward section included the cabin enclosure, the wing center section, and the armament and engine compartments. The

aft fuselage housed the engine oil tank and the radio compartment, and supported the tail group.

The main structure of the forward fuselage consisted principally of two built-up longitudinal beams. Each beam was constructed of web sheets heavily reinforced by extruded angle stringers and vertical stiffeners. Frames, bulkheads, and longitudinal stiffeners were assembled to the outboard side of each beam, and the Alclad outer skin was attached by flush rivets. The two beams were joined at the forward end by a circular bulkhead. The beams supported the nosewheel strut fittings, the reduction gearbox mounting fittings, and the cannon mounts. Further aft the beams supported the cabin structure, the wing center section, and the engine mounts. Beams were joined together at the aft end by upper and lower stiffeners. Plating which extended from the top of the built-up beams to the outer skins provided three pairs of decks. These included a left and right forward inclined deck. left and right aft inclined deck, and two intervening horizontal decks. The horizontal and aft inclined decks were reinforced by a steel channel extending between station 189 and 231.5. The beams and decks supported several installations. The reduction gearbox oil tank, armament, oxygen bottles, and battery were supported at the forward inclined decks. The cabin, extension drive shaft center bearing, engine cowl formers, and elevator bellcrank were supported by the level decks. The engine was mounted between the decks aft of the cabin and bolted to fittings attached to the inboard sides of the longitudinal beams. The aft

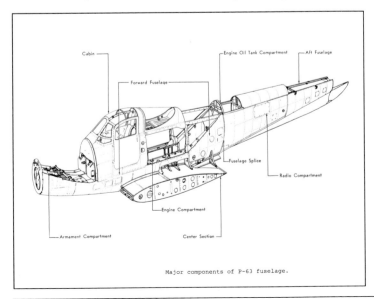

Major components of P-63 fuselage.

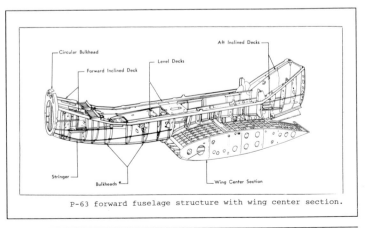

P-63 forward fuselage structure with wing center section.

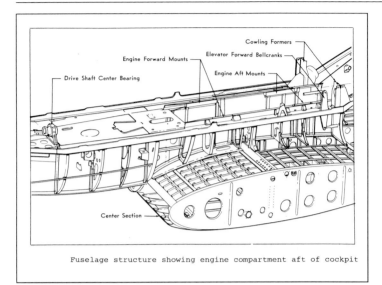

Fuselage structure showing engine compartment aft of cockpit

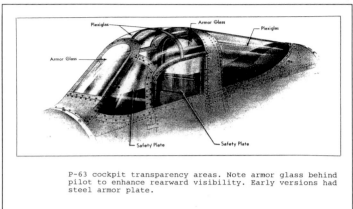

P-63 cockpit transparency areas. Note armor glass behind pilot to enhance rearward visibility. Early versions had steel armor plate.

inclined decks supported lateral leveling lugs, vacuum system oil separator, and oil dilution and engine primer valves.

The wing center section was attached to the fuselage beams with four fittings on the front beam (spar) and two on the aft beam. Matching fittings were on the fuselage beams.

The cabin section consisted of a forward cabin, an integral part of the forward fuselage, and a removeable aft cabin directly over the engine compartment. The main structure of the forward cabin was an arch-shaped turnover beam aft of the pilot's seat. The forward wall of the cabin was a fume-tight bulkhead sealing against firing gases from the gun compartment. This bulkhead served as a

support for the forward armor plate, hydraulic brake reservoirs, longitudinal braces for machine gun aft tripod mounts, and the vacuum system air cleaner. The cabin structure also included tubular metal frames supporting the windshield and Plexiglas canopy, outer skin, automobile-type doors, and a firewall behind the pilot's seat. Cabin doors were hinged for normal entrance and exit, and could be opened from inside or outside. Doors were provided with safety latches to prevent opening at high speeds. Emergency release handles allowed door release from the aircraft in an emergency. The safety glass windows in the doors could be raised or lowered by the pilot. The firewall behind the pilot was made of two dural sheets with layers of aluminum foil between the sheets. The windshield was made of one and one half inch thick armor glass. A two and one half inch thick piece of armor glass was located behind the pilot's head, after

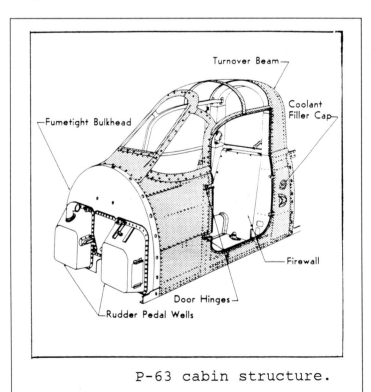

P-63 cabin structure.

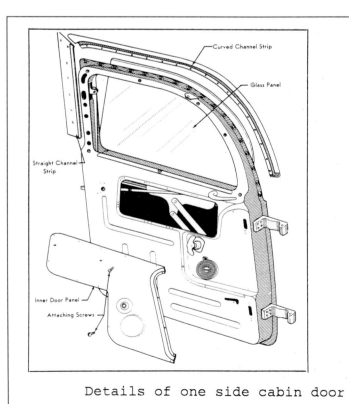

Details of one side cabin door

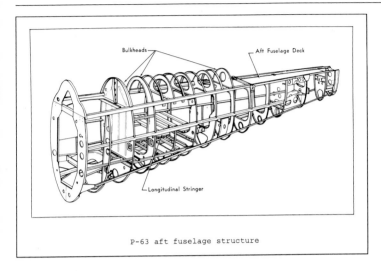

P-63 aft fuselage structure

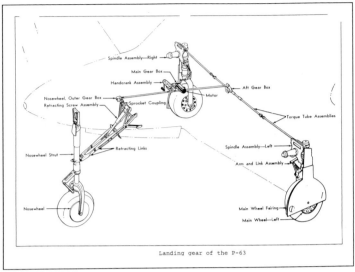

Landing gear of the P-63

there had been complaints about poor visibility aft from pilots testing early aircraft versions with a piece of steel armor plate in this location. Side windshield panels and door windows were laminated plate glass. The upper canopy was made of Plexiglas.

Cowling panels were provided over compartments as required, and were constructed of Alclad sheet reinforced by stringers and edge members. They were secured to a framework of formers by Dzus quarter-turn fasteners and screws. Six removeable cowl panels surrounded the reduction gearbox forward. A forward, left, and right panel covered the fuselage gun compartment, and three fuselage belly access panels were employed.

The aft fuselage section started at station 231.5, and was electrically bonded to the forward section. This section was a semimonocoque structure built up of a forward splicing bulkhead, formers, longerons, and longitudinal stringers covered by flush riveted Alclad sheet. A flat deck at the aft end provided for attachment through fittings of the tail assembly. Access panels were provided on the left side to the radio compartment, and on top over the engine oil tank compartment, the latter attached by screws. On late model aircraft, starting with the P-63C, a long ventral strake was attached to the belly of the aft fuselage, and was comprised of former sections covered with Alclad sheet.

LANDING GEAR GROUP

The aircraft was equipped with a fully retractable tricycle-type landing gear consisting of a main gear under each outer wing panel and a nose gear under the forward fuselage. Each wheel was mounted on an oleo pneumatic shock strut. Independently operated hydraulic brakes were provided for each main wheel. The electro-mechanical retraction system was composed of three gearboxes, worm and sector gears, and a nose wheel screw actuator all of which was connected by metal torque tubes. The main wheels retracted inboard and upward into the outer wing panels; the nose wheel retracted aft and upward into the underside of the forward fuselage. Fairings covered the retracted gear to present a smooth flush exterior surface.

Normal operation of the gear was accomplished via a one and three quarters HP electric motor with magnetic brake activated by a cockpit toggle switch and controlled at the extreme positions by limit switches located on the left main wheel spindle. A manual crank provided a means of emergency operation in event of electrical system failure. A ratchet pawl on the crank inboard face permitted selection of rotation to raise or lower gear.

The landing gear warning system consisted of warning lights and a horn. A squat switch on the left main wheel protected against gear retraction while on the ground.

The electric motor, main gearbox, and hand crank assembly were all located to the right of the pilot's seat and drove a fuselage torque tube running forward to a nose wheel gearbox and rearward to an aft tee-gearbox. The nose wheel gearbox turned the drive 90 degrees and provided mechanical input to a nose wheel retracting screw jack. The aft tee-gearbox drove lateral torque tubes within the wings which in turn powered worm and sector gears at the main wheel spindles to extend or retract the main landing gear elements.

The nose wheel was self-castoring and non-steerable. A self-centering cam in the strut centered the nose wheel when the strut was relieved of aircraft weight. A hydraulic shimmy damper was located inside the lower end of the strut piston. The nose wheel could swivel sixty degrees either side of center. A torque scissors was incorporated forward of the strut, and a tow attachment was provided on the strut. A nose wheel upper fairing which closed the forward end of the wheel well on retraction was bolted to the forward side of the strut cylinder. The upper end of the nose wheel strut was pinned to a casting bolted between the fuselage longitudinal beams at the forward end of the nose wheel well. The piston end of the strut was attached to a double fork supporting the wheel and axle. A magnesium nose wheel with a 22 inch diameter tire was mounted on the axle. The nose wheel drag link was attached to the aft side of the strut cylinder, and the strut was retracted by the combined action of the retracting screw jack and drag link. Two metal closure doors were hinge-mounted one at each side of the nose wheel well. The doors were actuated by cams on the drag linkage and

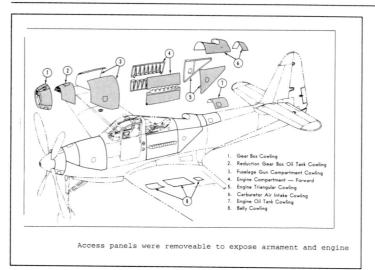

1. Gear Box Cowling
2. Reduction Gear Box Oil Tank Cowling
3. Fuselage Gun Compartment Cowling
4. Engine Compartment — Forward
5. Engine Triangular Cowling
6. Carburetor Air Intake Cowling
7. Engine Oil Tank Cowling
8. Belly Cowling

Access panels were removeable to expose armament and engine

rollers on the doors in a manner to close the nose wheel well, along with the strut upper fairing, when the nose gear was retracted.

The main gear spindle assemblies were mounted on the aft side of each wing main spar by ten bolts. The aft end of the spindle formed a socket and flange to which the main gear shock struts were attached. The forward extension end of the spindle was mounted in needle bearings tied to the spindle beam. Each spindle assembly contained a sector gear splined to the spindle and a worm gear on a fitting above the sector gear. When the worm gear was turned by a wing torque tube it rotated the sector gear and spindle

to extend or retract the main gear. Limit switches mounted on brackets at the left spindle controlled the landing gear electric motor.

An upper and lower main wheel fairing was attached to the outboard side of each main wheel strut. The upper fairing attached near the top of the strut body slightly inboard of the lower fairing, and the lower fairing attached to the piston portion of the strut. The fairings together closed the strut tunnel and all but a very small portion of the main wheel when the gear was retracted.

Torque scissors were located on the front side of the main gear struts. A 27 inch heavy duty main wheel of magnesium alloy was mounted on the axle of a single fork leg. Tires with special treads were provided on Russian-allocated aircraft to make them more suitable for use on snow.

ENGINE SECTION

The engine section consisted of the engine mounting system and the cowling panels surrounding the engine. The engine was mounted to the two main beams of the forward fuselage section aft of the cockpit via isolators and steel supports. A sandwich type of vibration isolator was located at each of the four engine hold-down positions. The isolators were bolted to steel supports which were in turn bolted to the main beams.

The engine compartment cowling was in seven sections. Two were located on each side of the engine, one above and one below the exhaust stacks. In addition two triangular cowl sections covered the sides of the engine accessory compartment, and the carburetor air scoop cowling was installed directly above the triangular cowl pieces. Cowls were tied to aircraft structure by a series of quick-disconnect fasteners for easy compartment access.

P-63 SYSTEMS DESCRIPTION

PROPULSION SUBSYSTEMS
ENGINE
The P-63 was powered by a 1300 horsepower class Allison V-1710 liquid cooled vee-type engine with automatic manifold pressure and supercharger control. Cylinder bore and stroke were 5.5 inches and 6.0 inches respectively. The propeller reduction gear ratio was

.449 to 1.0. The engine was equipped with a two stage mechanical supercharging system, one stage integral with the engine with a 9.5 inch diameter impeller geared at 8.1:1, and the other stage , mounted separately aft of the engine, with a 12.18 inch diameter impeller (blower). The separately-mounted stage was capable of being driven by the engine from a rear pad at a variable speed through a fluid

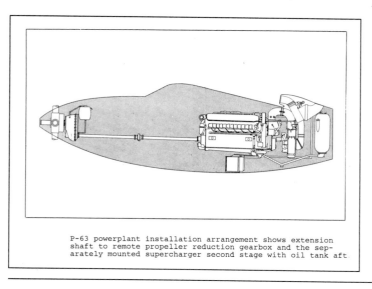

P-63 powerplant installation arrangement shows extension shaft to remote propeller reduction gearbox and the separately mounted supercharger second stage with oil tank aft.

Allison V-1716-93 Model E-11 Engine-One-Quarter Left Front View

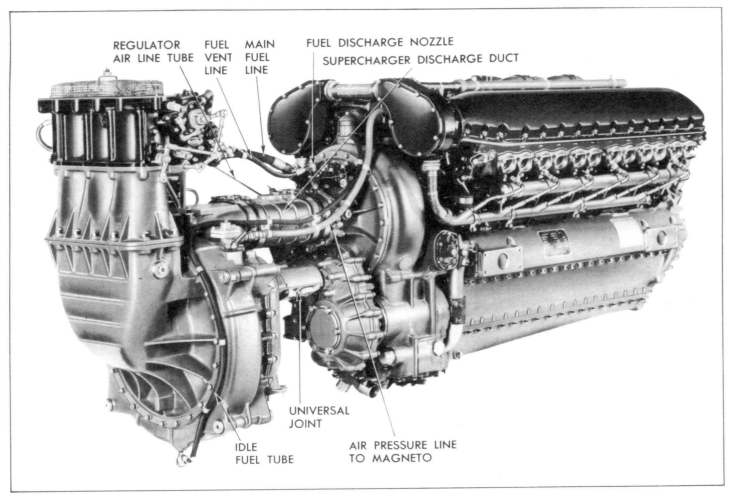

REGULATOR
AIR LINE TUBE

FUEL
VENT
LINE

MAIN
FUEL
LINE

FUEL DISCHARGE NOZZLE

SUPERCHARGER DISCHARGE DUCT

UNIVERSAL
JOINT

IDLE
FUEL TUBE

AIR PRESSURE LINE
TO MAGNETO

Fig. 60—Connections Between Auxiliary Stage Supercharger and Engine

drive. A carburetor air regulator assembly was mounted on top of this separate auxiliary stage supercharger intake air duct. Maximum engine speed was 3000 RPM. The propeller reduction gearbox was a forward remote unit also separately mounted several feet forward of the engine and driven by a two-section shaft with a center bearing supported on airframe. This gearbox incorporated an oil system separate from that of the engine and provided drives for two E-8 impulse-type machine gun synchronizers and a propeller governor. The governor drive was not used because the governing mechanism of the Aeroproducts propeller was self-contained in the propeller assembly. The SAE #60 splined propeller drive shaft rotated right-handed looking from the cockpit.

ENGINE INDUCTION SYSTEM

Air into the engine carburetor could be obtained either as cold rammed unfiltered flow, cold un-rammed filtered flow , or heated un-rammed filtered flow. The cold rammed air came from an intake scoop built into the removeable fuselage top cowling just aft of the cabin. With a cockpit carburetor air switch in the ram position an actuator opened doors in the top of the carburetor air regulator allowing scoop rammed air to enter first the auxiliary supercharger and then the carburetor through a cross-over duct. The air was not filtered in this case. If the cold intake air was to be filtered the cockpit control switch was put to the FILTER position, the actuator opened doors at the rear of the regulator, allowing cold fil-

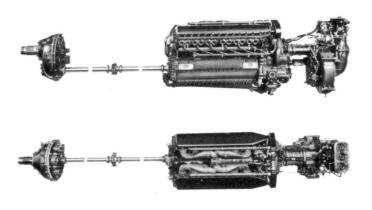

Allison V-1716-93 Model E-11 Engine-One-Left side and Top views

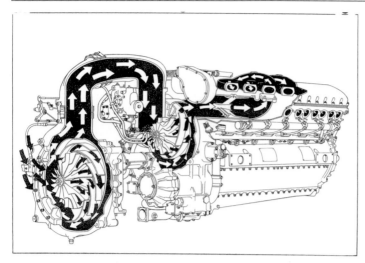

The two stage supercharged Allison engine of the P-63E. In this version the initial blower stage compressed air prior to fuel mixing.

tered air into the auxiliary supercharger and then into the carburetor. This un-rammed flow was obtained from a flush screened opening in the cowling of the aft fuselage over the main engine oil tank. The filter was in a housing aft of the regulator. If warm air was required the cockpit switch was moved to the HOT position. This action provided for warm air to be taken from the exit side of the right hand coolant radiator duct and up through the fuselage to the auxiliary supercharger and carburetor. Two electrically powered actuators were in the system, one to control the regulator doors and another for duct doors. System controls varied with the aircraft version, including switches, tee-handles, and levers. In all cases the intake air, after leaving the carburetor, entered the built in supercharger in the engine and from there went to the intake manifold and the cylinders of the engine.

ENGINE EXHAUST SYSTEM
The engine exhaust system was composed of six dual-exit stainless steel stacks, one for each cylinder, on each side of the aircraft protruding through the skin line and turned aft to provide jet thrust. Flame dampening exhausts were not provided.

ENGINE-MOUNTED ACCESSORIES
These engine-mounted items included a Stromberg injection-type carburetor, magnetos, fuel pump, oil pump, coolant pump, vacuum pump, starter, generator, tachometer generator, and hydraulic pump.

ENGINE AND PROPELLER CONTROLS
A split-lever synchronized throttle/propeller control was located at the left side of the cockpit. The throttle and propeller levers could be used in unison as a synchronized control giving an automatic optimally-scheduled coordination of the two via a cam system in the throttle quadrant. They could also be used independently by releasing a snap catch. The output of the propeller lever adjusted the propeller governor via a mechanical linkage running forward to the propeller. The throttle lever mechanically operated the PC-9 manifold pressure regulator mounted on the auxiliary supercharger.

The regulator automatically maintained the desired manifold pressure. Linkage was such that if the regulator failed manual control of the carburetor could be maintained. The mixture control lever was also on the quadrant and was linked mechanically to the carburetor. Both throttle and mixture levers had a wire stop across their forward travel which had to be broken to go into WAR EMERGENCY settings.

PROPELLER
The propellers on all P-63 aircraft were four blade Aeroproducts Unimatic hydraulically operated constant speed self-contained types using hollow steel blades. In the case of the P-63A the Aeroproducts A642S-D3 model with design A20-156-24M blades in 11'0" was used. The P-63E used the A642S-E2 propeller with blades giving an 11'6" diameter. In both cases the blade angle range was about 35 degrees, from 24.5 minimum to 60 maximum. The propeller hub was a machined steel forging. The propeller was controlled by a donut-shaped regulator unit just aft of the hub, and this unit hads its own oil system separate from any engine component. The propeller governor was part of the regulator.

ENGINE STARTING SYSTEM
The engine starting system was an electric inertia type where the engine-mounted starter consisted basically of an electric motor, a flywheel, and a clutch. A backup system used hand cranking of the flywheel using a crank stowed on the cockpit floor. Normal electric starting connected either the battery or an external source via a cockpit starter switch to the starter motor. The switch was held in one position until the starter reached maximum speed, then moved to another position to engage the clutch until the engine fired regularly then released to a central position. In the backup manual start the hand crank was used to spin the flywheel, then removed, and a loop pulled in a clutch engagement cable.

ENGINE WATER INJECTION SYSTEM
Some P-63 airplanes were equipped with water injection systems. The system capacity was 25 US gallons which was sufficient for 15 minutes of operation at a manifold pressure of 75 inches of mer-

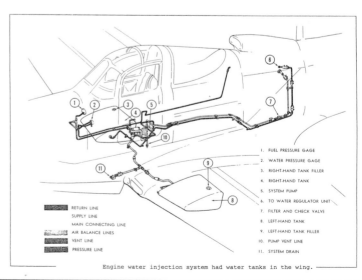

	1. FUEL PRESSURE GAGE
	2. WATER PRESSURE GAGE
	3. RIGHT-HAND TANK FILLER
	4. RIGHT-HAND TANK
	5. SYSTEM PUMP
RETURN LINE	6. TO WATER REGULATOR UNIT
SUPPLY LINE	7. FILTER AND CHECK VALVE
MAIN CONNECTING LINE	8. LEFT-HAND TANK
AIR BALANCE LINES	9. LEFT-HAND TANK FILLER
VENT LINE	10. PUMP VENT LINE
PRESSURE LINE	11. SYSTEM DRAIN

Engine water injection system had water tanks in the wing.

cury. Two water/alcohol tanks were located in the inboard leading edges of the wings. An electrically-driven water pump in the fuselage drew the fluid from the tanks and forced it aft into the engine. A system vent and drain were provided, and a water pressure gage was installed in the cockpit. The water injection system was activated when the coordinated throttle lever was advanced full forward past the mechanical detents.

ENGINE COOLING SYSTEM

The aircraft was equipped with a liquid Ethylene Glycol engine cooling system with a 13 US gallon capacity. Major components included an engine-driven coolant circulation pump, a coolant expansion tank of 1.5 US gallons capacity located between cylinder banks, two coolant radiators, air ducts and exit shutters with actuators for the radiators, coolant lines, and system controls. The expansion tank was equipped with a vacuum relief valve and an aneroid-controlled pressure relief valve to maintain a tank pressure of 23 PSIA, and three vent lines. The two coolant radiators were located one installed in each side of the wing center section held by bolts to structure through Lord isolation mounts. The coolers were box-shaped and located in air ducts fed by wing leading edge air scoops. Cooling air exit ducts aft of the radiators directed the air downward to shuttered exits. Warm air for wing gun heating was picked off each exit duct at the outboard side. Additional warm air was picked off the right side exit duct to direct heat to the cabin, fuselage guns, and carburetor. The exit duct shutters to control cooling air flow were operated by an electric actuator which drove both via a cross-shaft and connecting bell-cranks and push rods. A control switch in the cockpit could select automatic mode so the actuator would maintain desired coolant temperature. The automatic action of the shutter actuator was controlled by a temperature bulb assembly. With the switch in manual open or close the exit shutters would assume any desired position.

Coolant lines ran from the engine to each radiator, through the coolant pump and expansion tank, and back to the engine. A fluid filler port was located high on the left side of the fuselage. A coolant temperature gage was on the instrument panel.

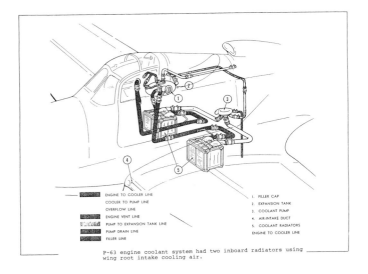

ENGINE TO COOLER LINE
COOLER TO PUMP LINE
OVERFLOW LINE
ENGINE VENT LINE
PUMP TO EXPANSION TANK LINE
PUMP DRAIN LINE
FILLER LINE

1. FILLER CAP
2. EXPANSION TANK
3. COOLANT PUMP
4. AIR-INTAKE DUCT
5. COOLANT RADIATORS
ENGINE TO COOLER LINE

P-63 engine coolant system had two inboard radiators using wing root intake cooling air.

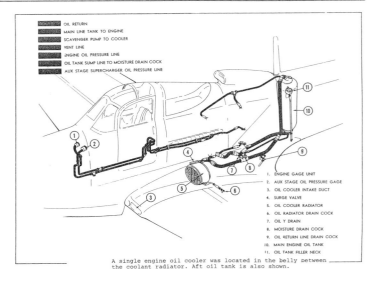

OIL RETURN
MAIN LINE TANK TO ENGINE
SCAVENGER PUMP TO COOLER
VENT LINE
ENGINE OIL PRESSURE LINE
OIL TANK SUMP LINE TO MOISTURE DRAIN COCK
AUX STAGE SUPERCHARGER OIL PRESSURE LINE

1. ENGINE GAGE UNIT
2. AUX STAGE OIL PRESSURE GAGE
3. OIL COOLER INTAKE DUCT
4. SURGE VALVE
5. OIL COOLER RADIATOR
6. OIL RADIATOR DRAIN COCK
7. OIL Y DRAIN
8. MOISTURE DRAIN COCK
9. OIL RETURN LINE DRAIN COCK
10. MAIN ENGINE OIL TANK
11. OIL TANK FILLER NECK

A single engine oil cooler was located in the belly between the coolant radiator. Aft oil tank is also shown.

ENGINE LUBRICATION SYSTEM

Two lubrication oil systems were incorporated on the airplane. The main engine oil system was located primarily in the engine section of the fuselage and lubricated the engine. A maximum of 13.7 US gallons was carried. Another separate oil system lubricated the engine-propeller reduction gearbox in the nose of the airplane. That system had a capacity of 2.0 US gallons. Operation of both systems was automatic and could not be controlled in flight by the pilot except oil temperature for the main engine oil system could be regulated by using the oil cooler exit shutter control switch in the cockpit. The shutter was moved by an electrically powered actuator. Engine oil pressure and temperature were registered on the engine gage unit in the cockpit as was the oil pressure of the auxiliary stage supercharger unit on its own gage. The oil cooler was located centrally under the fuselage with cooler air fed by a duct from the wing leading edge on the other side of the fuselage, and after flowing through the cooler exited under the fuselage with flow controlled by the exit shutter. The oil cooler was equipped with a surge valve which could bypass oil if required. Drains were provided in the system. The magnesium oil tank for the main engine was mounted in the fuselage aft of the engine with a fill point high on the left side of the fuselage. Oil was circulated by a pressure pump and a scavenge pump.

The separate oil system for the reduction gearbox had a magnesium alloy oil tank mounted high and just behind the gearbox. The system included a sump and an integral pump.

ENGINE FIRE SENSING AND EXTINGUISHING SYSTEMS
The aircraft was not equipped with these systems.

FUEL SYSTEM
The internal fuel system included two removeable self-sealing tanks inboard in the wing between forward and rear spars. The tank capacity was 63 to 66 US gallons each side (63 on P-63A; 66 on P-63C and P-63E). External tanks could be carried on three stations on the later versions, a centerline location under the fuselage and two outboard locations under the wing, one on each side. On the

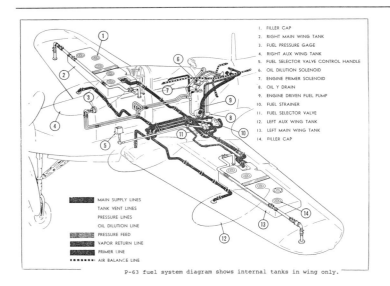

1. FILLER CAP
2. RIGHT MAIN WING TANK
3. FUEL PRESSURE GAGE
4. RIGHT AUX WING TANK
5. FUEL SELECTOR VALVE CONTROL HANDLE
6. OIL DILUTION SOLENOID
7. ENGINE PRIMER SOLENOID
8. OIL Y DRAIN
9. ENGINE DRIVEN FUEL PUMP
10. FUEL STRAINER
11. FUEL SELECTOR VALVE
12. LEFT AUX WING TANK
13. LEFT MAIN WING TANK
14. FILLER CAP

MAIN SUPPLY LINES
TANK VENT LINES
PRESSURE LINES
OIL DILUTION LINE
PRESSURE FEED
VAPOR RETURN LINE
PRIMER LINE
AIR BALANCE LINE

P-63 fuel system diagram shows internal tanks in wing only.

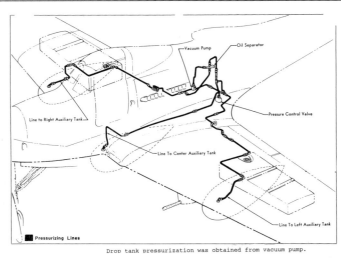

Drop tank pressurization was obtained from vacuum pump.

centerline station either a flush-fitting slipper type tank of 64 US gallons or a teardrop shaped droppable 75 US gallon tank could be carried. On each outboard wing panel station provision was made for a 75 US gallon auxiliary drop tank. The centerline 64 gallon external tank was self-sealing and included a booster pump. The 75 gallon tanks were not self-sealing.

Selection of fuel from all sources was made by a fuel selector valve to the left of the pilot on the cockpit floor. The fuel flowed through an electric boost pump located in each internal wing tank when the selector valve was set for that tank. A mechanical drive was provided between the fuel selector handle in the cockpit and the selector valve in the engine compartment. Boost pump switches

were on the instrument panel and could be set for either normal or emergency pump speed. A type G-9 engine-driven pump was employed. Fuel filler points for external tanks were provided on the wing upper surface. Other elements in the system were a fuel strainer, an engine primer solonoid, an oil dilution solenoid, and a fuel pressure gage in the cockpit. A low fuel warning light was provided as were vents and drains.

The 75 gallon external fuel tanks were mounted on bomb racks and were dropped using the bomb release system. These external tanks were pressurized using piping connected to the pressure side of the vacuum pump on the engine. The line from the engine-driven fuel pump to the carburetor was made of self-sealing material.

FIXED EQUIPMENT SUBSYSTEMS

1. Ammeter
2. Landing Gear Warning Horn Release Switch
3. Carburetor Filter Switch (P-63C-1)
4. Cannon Loading Handle
5. Suction Gage
6. Fuselage Gun Charging Handle
7. Airspeed Indicator
8. Altimeter
9. Turn Indicator
10. Rate of Climb Indicator
11. Gunsight Spare Bulbs Stowage
12. Turn and Bank Indicator
13. Flight Indicator
14. Compass
15. Engine Gage Unit
16. Oil Shutter Control Switch
17. Fuselage Gun Charging Handle
18. Cannon Charging Handle
19. Oxygen Flow Indicator
20. Oxygen Cylinder Pressure Gage
21. Landing Gear Switch
22. Landing Gear Warning Light (Red)
23. Wing Bombs or Tanks Salvo Switch
24. Landing Gear Warning Light (Green)
25. Wing Bomb Arming Switch (Right)
26. Wing Bomb Arming Switch (Left)
27. Cannon Switch
28. Gunsight Rheostat
29. Pitot Heater Switch
30. Oil Dilution Switch
31. Carburetor Air Temperature Gage
32. Booster Pumps Switch
33. Engine Primer Switch
34. Starter Switch
35. Aux. Stage Supercharger Oil Pressure Gage
36. SCR 695 Radio Demolition Switches
37. Fluorescent Light Rheostat
38. SCR 695 SW-180 Switch
39. SCR 695 ON-OFF Switch
40. SCR 695 IFF Switch
41. SCR 695 Emergency Switch
42. Fluorescent Light Rheostat
43. Landing Light Switch
44. Wing Navigation Lights Switch
45. Tail Navigation Light Switch
46. Ignition Switch
47. Master Armament Switch
48. Battery Switch
49. Wing Guns Switch
50. Generator Switch
51. Fuselage Guns Switch
52. Fuel Low Level Warning Light
53. Fuel Level Gage
54. Fuel Low Level Warning Light
55. Manifold Pressure Gage
56. Clock
57. Tachometer
58. Gear Box Oil Pressure Gage
59. Coolant Temperature Gage
60. Coolant Shutter Control Switch

INDICATES POWER-PLANT INSTRUMENTS AND CONTROLS

Figure 14—Instrument Panels

INSTRUMENTS

A typical instrument complement included: For flight, airspeed indicator, altimeter, turn indicator, rate of climb indicator, turn and bank indicator, flight indicator, clock, and compass; for the engine,

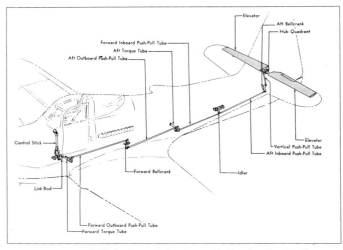

P-63 elevator control system used bellcranks and push-pull rods instead of cables.

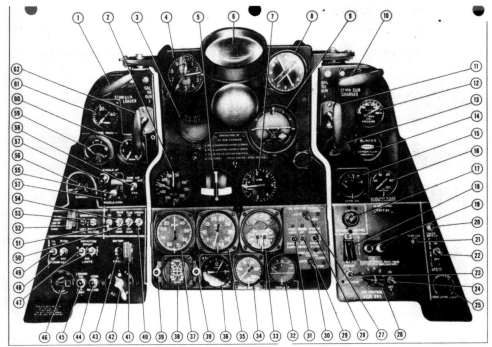

P-63E instrument panel.

Key to Figure

1. 37mm Gun Loader
2. Air Speed Indicator
3. Directional Indicator
4. Altimeter
5. Turn and Bank Indicator
6. Gunsight
7. Rate-of-climb Indicator
8. Compass Indicator
9. Flight Indicator
10. 37mm Gun Charger
11. Right Caliber .50 Fuselage Gun Charger
12. Oxygen Pressure Indicator
13. Right Fluorescent Light Rheostat
14. Oxygen Flow Indicator
15. Carburetor Air Temperature Indicator
16. Auxiliary Stage Supercharger Oil Pressure Indicator
17. ARC-3 Radio Volume Control
18. SCR-695 Radio Emergency Switch
19. SCR-695 Radio Detonator Push-Button Switches
20. APS-13 Radar Check Switch

21. SCR-695 Radio Test Pilot Light
22. APS-13 Radar Power Switch
23. SCR-695 Steady-Momentary Switch
24. SCR-695 Power Switch
25. APS-13 Radar Indicator Light Rheostat
26. SCR-695 Signal Selector Switch
27. Oil Shutter Control Switch
28. Starter Switch
29. Engine Primer Valve Solenoid Switch
30. Coolant Shutter Control Switch
31. Auxiliary Fuel Pumps Switch
32. Coolant Temperature Indicator
33. Engine Gage Unit
34. Gear Box Oil Pressure Indicator
3S. Tachometer
35. Tachometer
36. Clock
37. Manifold Pressure Indicator
38. Fuel Level Indicator
39. Fuel Level Warning Lights
40. 37mm Cannon Switch
41. Generator Switch
42. Ignition Switch

43. Battery Switch
44. Landing Gear Warning Horn Release Switch
4S. Landing Light Switch
46. Left Fluorescent Light Rheostat
47. Position or Navigation Light Switches
48. Pitot Tube Heater Switch
49. Oil Dilution Valve Solenoid Switch
50. Fuselage Caliber .S0 Guns Switch
51. Master Armament Switch
52. Wing Bomb Salvo Switch
53. Wing Bomb Selector Switches
54. Wing Caliber .50) Guns Switch
55. Landing Gear Control Switch
56. Gunsight Rheostat
57. Landing Gear Warning Lights
58. Carburetor Air Control Switch
59. Ammeter
60. Vacuum or Suction Indicator
61. Water Pressure Indicator
62. Left Caliber .50 Fuselage Gun Charger

fuel gage unit, carburetor air temperature gage, auxiliary stage oil pressure gage, fuel level gage, manifold pressure gage, tachometer, gearbox oil pressure gage, and coolant temperature gage; others were, ammeter, suction gage, and oxygen cylinder pressure gage.

SURFACE CONTROLS

A conventional cockpit stick and rudder pedal control system was employed to actuate elevators, ailerons, and rudder. Trim tab controls were mounted on a tab control box at the left side of the cockpit. Adjustable stops were provided for all cockpit primary controls. The wing flap controls were electrically operated through a screw jack actuator driving a bellcrank on a torque tube which passed laterally through the wing center section to drive the flaps.

The elevator controls started with the cockpit stick motion driving a lower-end link which in turn drove a crank on a forward torque tube. On some P-63 aircraft a bobweight in the system provided an 80 inch-pound moment to increase stick force for any given value of aircraft acceleration. The elevator drive was a single push-pull tube , bellcrank, and idler swing-link system running through the lower fuselage. A bellcrank and vertical push-pull tube drove a quadrant on the elevator torque tube to move both elevators. A trim tab was located on the left elevator. The tab drive ran from the cockpit control box via a drive chain and control cables and pulleys. A drive sprocket and screw jack actuator completed the drive to the tab.

The aileron control system was similar in using bell cranks and push-pull rods to transfer stick motion aft through the fuselage and out the wings to the ailerons. The output of the outboard bellcrank on each wing drove an aileron horn to move the surfaces differentially. Early aircraft had no cockpit controlled trim tab, using only a ground-adjustable tab on each aileron. Later aircraft employed an electrically-operated aileron trim tab on the right wing side. A cockpit toggle switch controlled the tab electric actuator.

The rudder pedals were adjustable to any of five positions using a spring-loaded lever outboard of each pedal. A rudder balance cable controlled relative pedal position and was attached to the aft outboard side of each pedal. The control system was of the closed-loop dual cable type with the cables running aft through the lower fuselage through fairleads and over pulleys. Turnbuckle adjustment was provided. The cable was attached at the aft end of the fuselage to a rudder drive quadrant tied rigidly to the lower section of the rudder. The rudder trim tab drive was similar to that of the elevator tab system, using a chain and cable from the cockpit control box to a tab screw jack actuator.

ELECTRICAL SYSTEM

The electrical system was a 24 volt DC single wire type with aircraft structure serving as a common ground return. Electrical circuits were protected by breakers located in the aft section of the nose wheel well. An engine-driven generator supplied power to charge the battery and power the system. The battery was installed on the left hand forward deck of the fuselage gun compartment, and was accessible by removing cowling. Russian aircraft had an

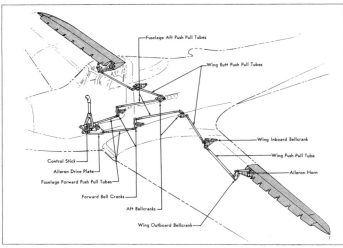

Separated tube and crank systems drove P-63 ailerons.

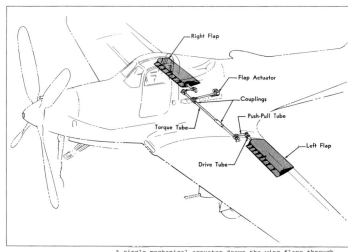

A single mechanical actuator drove the wing flaps through a torque tube and gearing system.

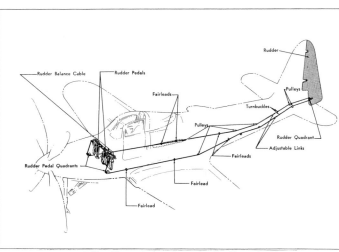

P-63 rudder control system employed cables and pulleys.

asbestos battery enclosure for protection against the cold. The battery had vent and overboard drain lines, and a disconnect relay and cockpit switch. On P-63C airplanes an external power socket was located on the left side of the fuselage aft of the engine. Other electrical system components included a generator current control relay switch near the generator, a carbon pile voltage regulator, and a thermostatic protector. A guarded generator switch was provided in the cockpit. A starter assembly and starter relay were provided along with a high capacity booster coil with a filter in the booster primary lead to minimize radio noise level.

Items requiring electrical power from the system included instrument, position, and recognition lights and a signal lamp, air intake filter actuator, intake air duct doors, magnetos, starter, water injection pump, coolant radiator shutter actuators, oil cooler exit shutter actuator, fuel boost pumps, aileron trim tab actuator, landing gear motor, flap actuator, gun controls, gunsight, gun camera, and radio equipment.

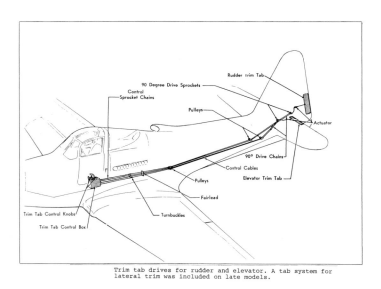

Trim tab drives for rudder and elevator. A tab system for lateral trim was included on late models.

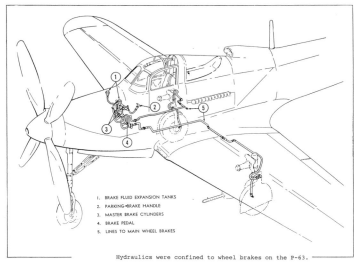

1. BRAKE FLUID EXPANSION TANKS
2. PARKING-BRAKE HANDLE
3. MASTER BRAKE CYLINDERS
4. BRAKE PEDAL
5. LINES TO MAIN WHEEL BRAKES

Hydraulics were confined to wheel brakes on the P-63.

HYDRAULIC SYSTEM

The only hydraulic system in the aircraft controlled the main wheel brakes which were operated on the pedals, and a parking brake handle in the cockpit.

PNEUMATIC SYSTEM

An engine-driven vacuum pump provided a vacuum for the instruments as required, and pressure to force fuel from drop tanks.

COMMUMICATION, NAVIGATION, AND IDENTIFICATION SYSTEMS

Alternate installations of equipment could be used in P-63 aircraft. One installation consisted of an SCR-274N command set consisting of two transmitters and three receivers with independent controls for each group and an antenna switching relay. Controls were in the cockpit; transmitters and receivers and relay were located in the aft fuselage. In addition an SCR-695 identification radio was mounted on the deck just aft of the pilot seat with controls in the cockpit on the right side. An APS-13 tail warning radar set could also be installed as well as a Bendix MN-26 radio compass. Another installation was similar except the SCR-522A command set was substituted for the SCR—274N.

ARMAMENT PROVISIONS

The P-63 was equipped with a Type M-10LH automatic 37 mm aircraft cannon located in the forward section of the aircraft. It was mounted on the aircraft thrust centerline and was rolled nine degrees to the left to reduce the possibility of ejected cases jamming in the chute. The cannon fired through the center of the reduction gearbox and the hollow propeller hub. It depended on a long movement of its recoiling parts for automatic operation. Recoil and counter-recoil were controlled hydraulically by a piston tied to the recoiling portions and a cylinder mounted to a stationary trunnion block. The cannon was fed by a disintegrating belt; the system had a maximum capacity of 58 rounds with 30 in the ammunition box on the inclined deck of the right longitudinal beam assembly, and 28 on the oval-shaped magazine curving around over the .50 caliber nose machine guns. The weapon was equipped with a G-15

electrical firing solonoid assembly. The projectiles had a muzzle velocity of 2000 feet per second and the firing rate was 165 rounds per minute. The cannon was charged and loaded using handles at the top of the instrument panel; a trigger on the cockpit control stick fired the gun after moving a selector switch on the panel to the proper position. An average cannon burst was considered to be five rounds, and a maximum burst was to be limited to 15 rounds at a time. Empty cases and links passed through separate chutes and were collected in fuselage compartments between longitudinal beams and outer skins, cases to a left compartment and links to a right one. The compartments were later emptied on the ground.

Additional nose armament on the aircraft consisted of two .50 caliber M-2 machine guns mounted on tubular welded tripods secured to airframe. Each gun had a maximum ammunition capacity of 200 rounds. Synchronization was of the impulse tube type driven off the reduction gearbox. The guns were charged remotely by cable control from two cockpit charging handles in the upper corners of the instrument panel. They were fired by arming a switch on the panel and using a trigger on the pilot's stick. Guns could be adjusted so fire was parallel to the aircraft centerline or anywhere in to a convergence at minimum range of 200 yards. Flame suppressors were installed on these guns. A feed container for 200 rounds maximum was provided and case ejection led to compartments in the nose structure of the fuselage. Compartment doors allowed removal of spent cases and links on the ground.

As an alternate load two fixed .50 caliber unsynchronized M-2 machine guns, one on either side of the fuselage outside the propeller arc, were mounted on their sides. The guns, mounts, and ejection chutes were contained in a separate streamline fairing mounted on the underside of each wing panel by quick-disconnect fasteners. These guns were arranged for manual charging on the ground only. Removal of the entire fairing was required to load and unload. Guns were electrically fired by G-9 or G-11 solonoid assenblies. Space was provided in each wing for 250 rounds of ammunition carried in a box which could be removed through the wingtip. An ammunition feed booster was installed in the feed chute of each gun. Case ejection chutes and link ejection chutes were provided extending from guns to the surface of the fairing where cases and links were

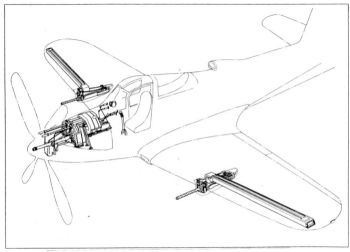

P-63 armament installation showing podded wing guns.

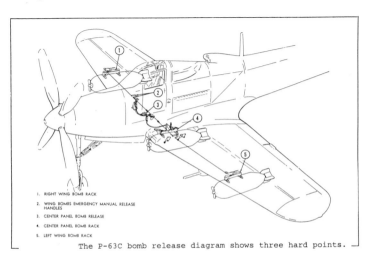

1. RIGHT WING BOMB RACK
2. WING BOMBS EMERGENCY MANUAL RELEASE HANDLES
3. CENTER PANEL BOMB RELEASE
4. CENTER PANEL BOMB RACK
5. LEFT WING BOMB RACK

The P-63C bomb release diagram shows three hard points.

ejected from the aircraft. Wing guns were not installed on P-63A aircraft destined for Russia. No rounds counters were installed.

Gun heating was provided. The fuselage nose guns were heated by diverting cockpit air; wing guns were heated by air taken from behind the coolant radiatiors.

A type N-9 gunsight with a G-9 bulb and rheostat was installed without reflector and sun filter. A spare lamp container was installed on the instrument panel. Provision was made for allignment of the sight. No other gunsight was installed.

A GSAP (gunsight aiming point) camera was located outboard on the right wing which operated in conjunction with the guns.

Provisions were made in later models of the P-63 for carrying three 300 or 500 pound bombs as overload in place of the external fuel tanks. One bomb rack was on centerline, and one was under each wing. The fuselage bomb rack was mechanically controlled only. Cockpit arming and release controls were provided. The wing bomb shackles were normally controlled electrically by cockpit switches with an emergency mechanical release system also provided. An alternate installation under the wings of a three-tube rocket installation on each side could be provided in late P-63A models. The P-63E aircraft were able to carry M-10 4.5 inch rockets. Three ten foot long plastic tubes were mounted beneath each outer wing panel. The launcher tubes were fired in a sequence by setting a selector switch on an intervalometer and depressing a button on the pilot's stick. A single or automatic mode could be selected. Wing and fuselage machine guns could not be fired during rocket launch, but the 37mm cannon could be fired.

PASSIVE DEFENSE SYSTEM

Armor installations varied with the P-63 model. A typical installation consisted of reduction gearbox armor plate, fume-tight bulkhead armor plate, cabin armor plate, center windshield armor glass, pilot's head rear armor glass, and pilot's seat armor plate. The reduction gearbox armor plate was installed in the nose section of the forward fuselage just aft of the propeller. It consisted of six sections of 5/8 inch thick homogeneous steel plate. Upper sections had double thickness; lower sections had a single thickness of plate. The plates were bolted on, and also provided needed ballast for the

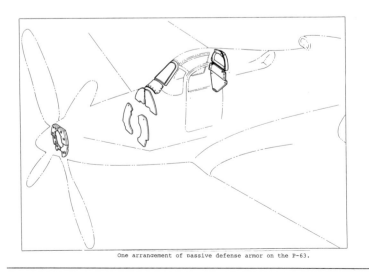

One arrangement of passive defense armor on the P-63.

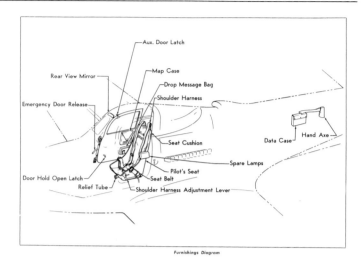

Furnishings Diagram

nose of the aircraft. The fume-tight bulkhead armor plate was installed in the gun compartment directly forward of the cockpit forward fume-tight bulkhead. The installation was made up of 1/4 inch thick face-hardened steel plate. The cabin armor plate was mounted directly below the forward windshield armor glass; it was a single piece of 1/4 inch thick face-hardened steel plate. The windshield armor glass was directly forward of the pilot. It was a single piece of 1 and 1/2 inch thick bullet-resisting glass held in a plastic-cushioned frame. The aft armor glass was installed in the arch of the turnover beam just aft of the pilot's head. It was a solid piece of 2 and 1/2 inch thick armor glass held in a plastic-cushioned frame. Glass and frame were held in place by thick steel retainer plates at top and bottom. The pilot's seat armor plate was a V-shaped section of 1/4 inch thick hardened steel plate installed behind the seat.

FURNISHINGS

A bucket-type non-adjustable seat was provided with a safety belt and shoulder harness. A pilot's relief tube was stowed in a bracket under the left forward section of the seat. An adjustable rear view mirror was installed on the upper center windshield bracket and a map case was on the floor. The data case, first aid kit, and an axe were located in the aft fuselage accessible from the radio compartment door. A mooring kit was provided on the aft cabin deck. A kapok-filled seat back cushion could also serve as a life preserver. A drop message container was clipped to the right side cabin door.

HEATING, COOLING, AND VENTILATION SYSTEMS

The cockpit was heated by air taken from the right side cooler air exit duct. The air entered the cockpit through a duct at the right side of the pilot's seat. Air temperature was regulated by a push-pull control at the right of the seat, forward of the heater duct, which operated a damper. Cold air was taken from the intake duct leading to the right hand coolant radiator. The handle was pulled up for heated air and pushed down for cool air. The flow of air was controlled by heat deflector vanes in the mouth of the heater duct.

The aircraft was equipped with a defrosting system which conducted heated air forward from the left hand coolant radiator air

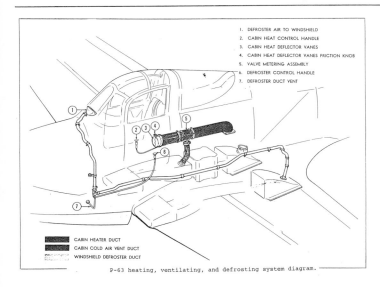

1. DEFROSTER AIR TO WINDSHIELD
2. CABIN HEAT CONTROL HANDLE
3. CABIN HEAT DEFLECTOR VANES
4. CABIN HEAT DEFLECTOR VANES FRICTION KNOB
5. VALVE METERING ASSEMBLY
6. DEFROSTER CONTROL HANDLE
7. DEFROSTER DUCT VENT

CABIN HEATER DUCT
CABIN COLD AIR VENT DUCT
WINDSHIELD DEFROSTER DUCT

P-63 heating, ventilating, and defrosting system diagram.

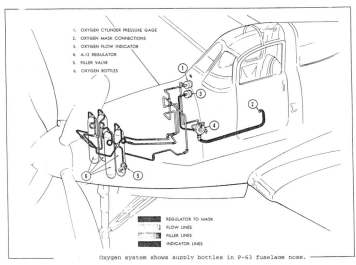

1. OXYGEN CYLINDER PRESSURE GAGE
2. OXYGEN MASK CONNECTIONS
3. OXYGEN FLOW INDICATOR
4. A-12 REGULATOR
5. FILLER VALVE
6. OXYGEN BOTTLES

REGULATOR TO MASK
FLOW LINES
FILLER LINES
INDICATOR LINES

Oxygen system shows supply bottles in P-63 fuselage nose.

exit duct under the cabin floor, and to the base of the windshield armor glass where the duct divided, half the air being conducted to the outside of the cockpit windshield and half to the inside. The flow of air was regulated by a control handle in the cockpit. The handle was connected to a flexible cable which operated a control valve in the duct system under the left hand cockpit deck slightly aft of the fume-tight bulkhead.

Wing machine guns were heated by hot air taken from both right and left coolant radiator air exit ducts and routed through flexible hoses in the wings to the gun fairings. Fuselage machine guns were heated using warm air delivered from the right rudder pedal well via a heater duct located between the two gun receivers. Heat was delivered to the 37mm cannon by two fabric duct openings in the inboard sides of each rudder pedal well. The duct openings allowed cabin heat flow to the receiver of the cannon.

Heating was provided for the engine water injection system. Elbow pickoff ducts from wing gun heater tubes led to the water supply tanks and the water injection pump.

AIRCRAFT HANDLING EQUIPMENT

Mooring points included: Two tiedown rings were attached to the upper aft side of each main wheel strut; a mooring line could be passed through the hollow axle of the nose wheel. In addition, mooring lines could be passed through the aft hoist tube holes in the fuselge. A mooring kit was located on the aft deck of the cockpit area.

PYROTECHNICS/PHOTOGRAPHIC EQUIPMENT

A pyrotechnic pistol and holder, flare container, and flares were provided in the cockpit. No photographic equipoment was installed aside from the gun camera.

OXYGEN SYSTEM

Oxygen was supplied from four low pressure D-2 bottles, two on each forward inclined fuselage deck. On some aircraft an additional F-1 cylinder was located in the left wing panel, or in the right panel on export aircraft. Standard regulator, indicator, and gage were supplied. Oxygen could be added at a filler valve on the left side of the cowl.

P-63 REFERENCES

1. *Statistical Characteristics-Bell P-63 Fighter Aircraft*, Birch Matthews
2. *Erection and Maintenance Instructions*, Bell P-63E-1.
3. *Pilot's Manual*,P-63C/Pilot's Flight Operating Instructions for Airplane Army Model P-63C, AN 01-110FQ-1, Mar.30, 1945.
4. *Tactical Planning Characteristics and Performance Chart*, P-63, Aug. 21, 1944.
5. John J. Schneider archives.
6. *Minutes of Fighter Conference*, NAS Patuxent River,Md. Oct.1944.
7. NACA ACR L5A30.
8. NACA Wartime Report CMR L4J19, *Resume of NACA Stability and Control Tests of the Bell P-63 Airplane*, Oct.19,1944.
9. NACA Wartime Report MR L6E20 (L-730), *Flight Investigation to Improve the Dynamic Longitudinal Stability and Control Feel Characteristics of the P-63A-1 with Closely Balanced Experimental Elevators.*
10. *Bell Aircraft Corp. Report 33-947-001-8*, Dec.8,1944, P-63A-8 Performance/RP-63A-12 Performance.
11. *Aircraft Engine Normal Performance*, Allison V-1710-109 in P-63D, Jan.6,1944.
12. *Engine Power Curves*, Allison V-1710-93(E-11), Nov.2,1944.
13. Bell Aircraft Corp. *Model Specification for P-63A-10(33A-10)*, Report 33-947-001-10, Apr.15,1944.
14. Army Air Forces Proof Dept.,Eglin Field, Fla. *Final Report, Test of Operational Suitability of P-63A-1 Airplane*, May 16, 1944.
15. NACA MR L4LO8, *Flight Tests of the Effect of Several Modifications on the Maximum Speed of the P-63A Airplane.*
16. Airpower Magazine, Sept.1973, Kingcobra, *America's Great Giveaway Fighter*, by Robert J. Wang.
17. *Operation Pinball*, by Ivan Hickman, Motorbooks International, 1990.

THE F2A-

The various Navy F2A- and export Buffalo fighter versions, along with numbers involved, are laid out in Table 63. Certainly the numbers of aircraft are small, constituting only half of one percent of America's Hundred Thousand. And exports numbered more than twice those used by the US Navy, the latter totaling only 163 aircraft. The tabulation also shows most all were delivered before the US entered the war, with production stopped shortly after. And so perhaps this Brewster fighter should be classed as "interesting" rather than important to the fortunes of the US and its allies in World War II. One reason for interest might be the fact that it was held in such poor regard by so many. Another would be it was one of only two "modern" US Navy fighter types ready for war when the US entered. Yearly production totals are also shown.

TABLE 63
BREWSTER F2A- BUFFALO MODELS

COMPANY MODEL	MILITARY DESIGNATION	EXPORT DESIGNATION	NO. OF A/C	FIRST DELIVERY	NOTES
B-139	XF2A-1	—	1	DEC.1938	F.F.JAN.'38, TO XF2A-2
B-239	F2A-1	—	11	JUN.1939	54 ORD. REST TO FINLAND 8 -1s UPGRADED TO -2
B-239	—	B-239	44	JAN.1940	CIVIL G-5 ENG. JAN./FEB.
B-139	XF2A-2	—	(1)	JUL.1939	XF2A-1 A/C UPDATED
	F2A-2	—	43	SEP.1940	
B-339B	—	B-339B	40	APR.1940	BELGIAN, MOST ALL TO UK.
B-339E	—	BUFFALO I	170	MAY 1940	BRITISH, LAND-BASED
B-339D(-16)	—	B-339D	72	MAR.1941	FOR DUTCH EAST INDIES
B-339	F2A-3	—	108	JUL.1941	USN; DEL.JULY TO DEC'41
B-439/339-23	—	B-439	20	LAST MAR.'42	2ND.N.E.I.ORDER; 17 TO RAAF.
	XF2A-4		(1)	SEP.1941	-3 WITH PRESS.COCKPIT
			TOTAL 509		

NOTE: THE FOLLOWING TOTAL AIRCRAFT SETS OF SPARE PARTS WERE PRODUCED: USN-33, UK-34, BELGIUM-8, NETHERLANDS EAST INDIES-9, FINLAND-4.

AIRCRAFT PRODUCTION BY YEAR

	1938	1939	1940	1941	1942	TOTAL
US NAVY	1	11	42	108	1	163
EXPORT	0	0	124	201	21	346
TOTAL	1	11	166	309	22	509

TABLE 64
F2A-/239/339 PHYSICAL DATA

SPAN	35'0"	WING FLAP LENGTH, EA.	8.47 FT.
LENGTH (XF2A-1/-2)	25'7 3/8"	WING FLAP AREA,EA.	8.22 SQ.FT.
LENGTH (339)	26'0 1/16"	WING FLAP MAX.CHORD	1.06 FT.
LENGTH (F2A-3)	26'4 3/8"	WING FLAP MAX.DEFL.	58 DEG.
HEIGHT (LEVEL A/C)	11'11 7/8"	AILERON AREA,AFT H/L	15.3SQ.FT.
TAIL SPAN	12' 6 1/4"	AIL. TAB AREA	0.55 SQ.FT.
TREAD		AILERON THROW	26 DEG.UP,15DN.
PROP.DIA.XF2A-1/239	9'0"	AIL. TAB THROW	8 DEG.UP,8 DN.
PROP.DIA. 339E	10'1"	FIXED TAIL SURF.AIRFOIL	N-69
PROP.DIA. F2A-3	10'3"	STABILIZER INCIDENCE	+.75 DEG.
WING AREA, GROSS	208.9 SQ.FT.	HORIZ.TAIL AREA	39.5 SQ.FT.
WING AREA,LESS FUS.	178.1 SQ.FT.	HORIZ.STAB.AREA,TOT.	22.6 SQ.FT.
WING ASPECT RATIO	5.864	ELEV. AREA, AFT H/L	16.9 SQ.FT.
WING ROOT CHORD,C/L	7'0 1/2"	ELEVATOR TAB AREA	1.0 SQ.FT.
WING TIP CHORD	60.4"	ELEVATOR THROW	28 DEG.UP,20DN.
WING MEAN AERO.CHORD	74.88"	ELEV.TAB THROW	5 DEG.UP,22.5DN.
WING ROOT SECTION	NACA 23018	VERT.TAIL AREA,F2A-3	19.2SQ.FT.
WING ROOT t/c	18%,(WG.STA.0)	FIN AREA, F2A-3	10.3 SQ.FT
WING TIP SECTION	NACA 23009	RUDDER AREA,AFT H/L	8.9 SQ.FT.
WING TIP t/c	9%	RUDDER TAB AREA	0.45 SQ.FT.
WING ROOT INCIDENCE	0 DEG.	RUDDER THROW	30 DEG.LEFT,30 RT.
WING TIP INCIDENCE	0 DEG.	RUDDER TAB THROW	12DEG.L, 4 RT.
WING DIHEDRAL	5 DEG.30 MIN.	RUDDER CABLE TENSION	70 LB.
WING SWEEPBACK	1.41 DEG.	MAIN WHEEL TIRE DIA.	27"
TAIL WHEEL TIRE DIA.	6.0"	TAIL WHEEL WIDTH	2.5"

FIGURE 65
F2A-/239/339 BUFFALO FUEL CAPACITIES

MODEL	MAXIMUM INTERNAL FUEL (GAL.)
XF2A-1	110
F2A-1	160
B239	160
XF2A-2	110
F2A-2	160
B339B (Belgium)	160
B339E (Britain)	160
B339D (Dutch NEI)	160
F2A-3	240
B439/339-23 (NEI)	160

Note 1: No external drop tanks were carried on any model.
Note 2: The XF2A-2 was the XF2A-1 airframe modified.
Note 3: On the F2A-3 version a 40 gallon fuselage protected fuel tank and two 20 gallon wing leading edge protected fuel tanks were incorporated, adding 80 gallons to the basic 160 gallon capacity to make a total of 240 gallons.

Table 64 provides physical information for the Brewster fighter showing it as the smallest of Navy wartime fighters and the one with the least wing area. The wings did not fold, and it was necessary to limit fighter size to fit a maximum number on aircraft carriers with their severe space limitations.

Fuel capacities of the Brewster fighter models are given in Table 65. The Navy experimental types, XF2A-1 and XF2A-2 (the latter the same airframe revised), had a fuel capacity of only 110 gallons located in the wing torque box on each side outboard of the fuselage. This amount was later increased to 160 gallons in the same wing location on the early Navy F2A-2 and all export versions. When the US Navy finally decided to provide fighters with self-sealing gunfire-protected tanks the Brewster fighters presented a difficult if not impossible task as tanks were so closely integrated with basic wing structure. Thus on the F2A-3 three additional small protected fuel tanks were added, one in the lower fuselage and one in each wing inboard leading edge. The overall addition totaled 80 gallons, thereby increasing full internal capacity to a hefty 240 gallons. In some cases one of the 80 gallon wing tanks was sealed off and labeled not to be used except with special permission, this to reduce aircraft vulnerability. How or whether lateral trim could then

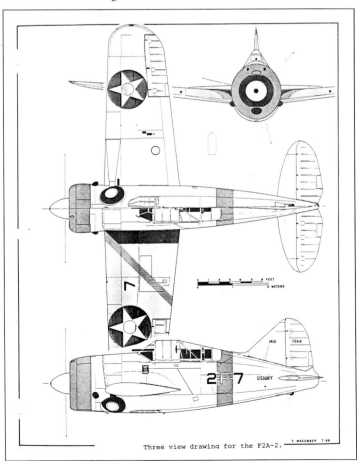

Three view drawing for the F2A-2.

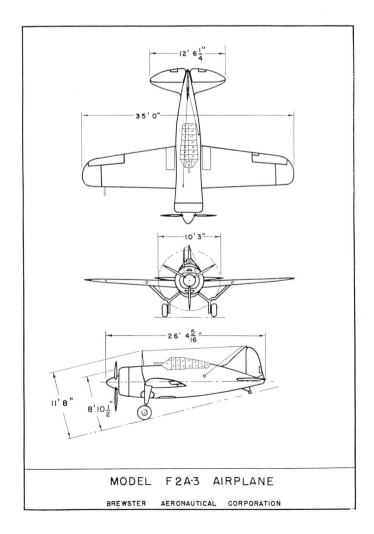

MODEL F2A-3 AIRPLANE
BREWSTER AERONAUTICAL CORPORATION

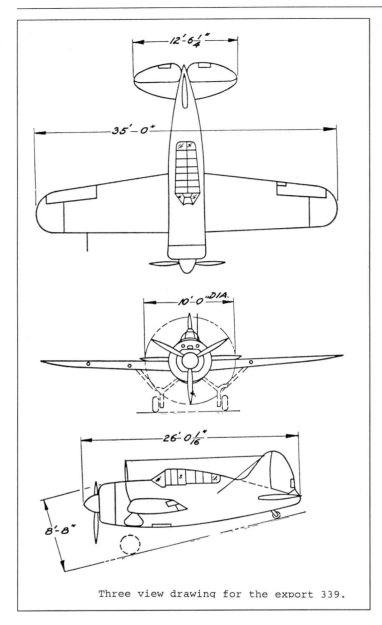

Three view drawing for the export 339.

radial engine with accessories and steel tube engine mount. In addition this area contained the nose machine guns with their ammunution boxes and ejection chutes, the oil tank located high in the firewall stepped-back section just forward of the cockpit, and major components of the main wheel retraction system including wheel pockets. The oil cooler with associated air ducting was mounted low down in the area. The fuselage structure was steel tubing forward of the firewall. In the F2A-2 inboard profile the fuselage belly fuel tank is missing. In the section just aft of the firewall space was provided for the central part of the wing structural section to pass through, since the wing was a one piece design on a mid-wing airplane. The cockpit was located aft of the firewall and the central structural area of the wing. Aft of the pilot's head was a headrest, a large cylindrical container for a life raft, and an ADF antenna. The large volume inside the aft fuselage contained oxygen and fire extinguisher bottles, radio gear with antenna connections, and an equipment stowage compartment as well as mechanical control runs from cockpit to tail surfaces. A retractable tail wheel assembly and a retractable arresting gear hook assembly occupied the far aft end of the fuselage.

Table 66 provides power ratings for engines of the Brewster fighter variants. TAKEOFF rating increased from 950 to 1200 horsepower as development progressed on the Wright Cyclone which for production types used a single stage two speed supercharger. Details varied but it was the same basic engine on all the Brewster fighters. As noted in the table, both Hamilton and Curtiss propellers were used with some variations in diameter.

Speed and climb performance of US Navy F2A-2 and F2A-3 airplanes is given by Graph 56 in the form of curves and additional tabular data. High speeds of these two aircraft models are shown as essentially the same for all altitudes at the respective weights noted. There is less than a five mph difference up to 25000 feet. A maxi-

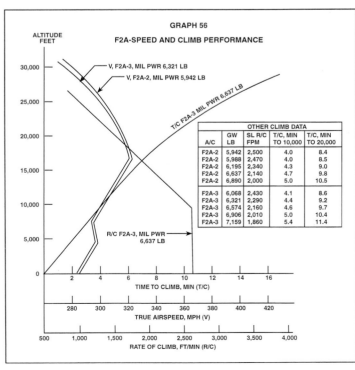

be achieved is a question.Three view drawings of the Brewster fighter are provided. The immediate impression is one of a squat, compact, rather chubby mid-wing aircraft with little to recommend it aesthetically; it was sometimes called a "flying barrel." The fuselage cross-section was pretty much determined by the large diameter of a big single row nine cylinder Wright Cyclone engine up front. Propeller spinners were sometimes used, but normally dispensed with. Another distinguishing feature was a large amount of canopy transparency area with the purpose of providing good vision to the rear quarters, but perhaps the most unique Buffalo feature was the main landing gear "W" arrangement with wheels retracting into forward fuselage pockets. The mid-wing aircraft configuration required long landing gear struts.

An inboard profile of the F2A-2 aircraft is also shown. The forward compartment, ahead of a stepped-back firewall, housed the

TABLE 66
BREWSTER F2A- MODELS PROPULSION DATA

MODEL	ENGINE	RATING	HP	RPM	ALTITUDE'	MAP,"HG.	SUPERCHARGER
XF2A-1	XR-1820-22	TAKEOFF	950	2200	SEA LEVEL		1-STAGE
		MILITARY					
		NORMAL	850	2100	SEA LEVEL		
		NORMAL	750	2100	15200		
F2A-1	R-1820-34	TAKEOFF	950	2200	SEA LEVEL		
		MILITARY					
		NORMAL	850	2100	SEA LEVEL		
		NORMAL	750	2100	15200		
239	R-1820-G5	TAKEOFF	950	2200	SEA LEVEL	39.5	1-STAGE,2-SPEED
FINLAND	G.R.=1:1	MILITARY	1000	2200	SEA LEVEL		
		MILITARY	800	2200	16000		
		NORMAL	850	2100	6000 LOBLO.36.5		
		NORMAL	750	2100	15200 LOBLO.34.0		
XF2A-2	R-1820-40	TAKEOFF	1200	2500	SEA LEVEL	45.5	1-STAGE,2-SPEED
F2A-2	G.R.=3:2	MILITARY					
F2A-3		NORMAL	1000	2300	S.L.-4500 L.B.37.3		
		NORMAL	900	2300	9800-14000 HI.B.40.0		
339B,BEL.	R-1820-G105A	T.O.	1100	2350	SEA LEVEL		1-STAGE,2-SPEED
339D,NEI.	G.R.=16:11	MILITARY	1100	2350	1500 LO.BLO.		
339E,U.K.		MILITARY	800	2350	17100 HI.BLO.		
		NORMAL	900	2300	6700 LO.BLO.		
		NORMAL	775	2300	17300 HI BLO.		
339-23	R-1820G-5E	TAKEOFF	1200	2500	SEA LEVEL		1-STAGE,2-SPEED
	G.R.=16:11	MILITARY	1200	2500	4200 LO.BLO.		
		MILITARY	1000	2500	14200 HI.BLO		
		NORMAL	1000	2300	6900 LO.BLO.		
		NORMAL	900	2300	15200 HI.BLO.		

NOTE: The propeller for the XF2A-1, F2A-1, and export 239 for Finland was a 9.0 ft. diameter Hamilton Standard 3D40-235 type with three design 6101A aluminum blades. The propeller for the XF2A-2, F2A-2, and F2A-3 models was a three blade Curtiss Electric C5315S design with hollow steel blades in 10'3" diameter. The export British 339E had a Hamilton Standard three blade propeller in 10'1" diameter; the 339B and 339D Belgian and Dutch models had Curtiss C5315D propellers with aluminum blades in 10'3" diameter.

mum speed of just over 320 mph was achieved at a critical altitude of 14500 feet. Starting at a sea level maximum of about 285 mph high speed capability increased up to just under 5000 feet where maximum performance using low supercharger blower speed was obtained, after which airplane speed fell off. At around 7500 feet the supercharger was switched to high blower RPM, and with the additional power thus available airplane high speed increased with altitude again to 16500 feet. Here the supercharger reached the limits of its capability. Engine power and resultant high speed capability fell off again. At about 28000 feet sea level high speed was again achieved. Climb capability from one set of data reported for the F2A-3 airplane is plotted in terms of rate and time. The information indicates the Brewster low altitude climb rate at 6637 pounds was 2600 feet per minute up to about 10000 feet, then decreased quickly to 1000 feet per minute at 25000 feet. Climb time was shown as four minutes to 10000 feet and nine minutes to 20000 feet. The tabular data within the chart presents other more conservative information on climb performance for the aircraft. Here F2A-3 sea level climb rate at 6321 pounds is 2290 feet per minute (over 300 fpm less), and times to climb at the same weight were 4.4 minutes to 10000 feet and 9.2 minutes to 20000 feet (under half a minute greater).

"Yardstick" range characteristics are provided for the F2A- in Graph 57 cruising at 4500 feet altitude in zero wind with no fuel reserves for gross weights corresponding to different amounts of initial fuel. The aircraft have quite similar range characteristics, but the F2A-3 as a heavier airplane for a given amount of fuel aboard yielded slightly less distance performance. Apparently at least some

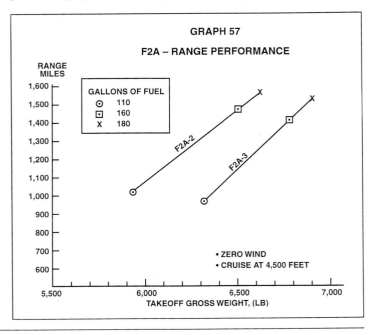

GRAPH 57

F2A – RANGE PERFORMANCE

RANGE MILES

GALLONS OF FUEL
⊙ 110
⊡ 160
✕ 180

F2A-2
F2A-3

• ZERO WIND
• CRUISE AT 4,500 FEET

TAKEOFF GROSS WEIGHT, (LB)

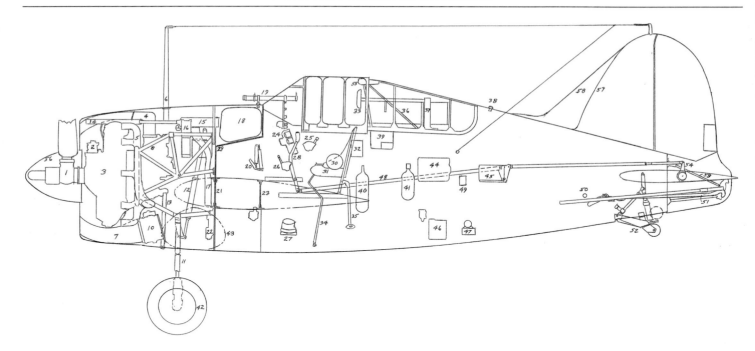

Inboard profile of Brewster fighter.

1. Curtiss Electric propeller
2. Propeller governor.
3. Wright R-1820 engine.
4. Carburetor air intake.
5. Engine exhaust manifold.
6. Radio antenna mast.
7. Oil cooler intake duct.
8. Engine mount.
9. Steel tube forward structure.
10. Oil cooler.
11. Landing gear inboard strut.
12. Landing gear retraction actuator.
13. Drain.
14. Machine gun blast tube.

15. Machine gun (left hand).
16. Machine gun ammunition box.
17. Shell ejection chute.
18. Engine oil tank.
19. Telescopic sight.
20. Rudder pedal.
21. Wing forward spar.
22. Fuel valve.
23. Wing aft spar.
24. Instrument sub-panel.
25. Engine control.
26. Bomb control.
27. Fuel pressure regulator.
28. Pilot's control stick.

29. Firewall
30. Elevator trim wheel.
31. Pilot's seat.
32. First aid kit.
33. Pilot's head rest.
34. Relief tube.
35. Very pistol assembly
36. Life raft container.
37. Radio direction finder.
38. Section light.
39. Water and ration compartment.
40. Oxygen bottle.
41. Fire extinguisher system bottle.
42. Landing gear wheel (extended).
43. Main wheel pocket.

44. Radio receiver.
45. Radio transmitter.
46. Battery.
47. Dynamotor.
48. Elevator control rod.
49. Antenna relay.
50. Lift tube.
51. Tail hook (retracted).
52. Tail wheel assembly (extended)
53. Tail hook support structure.
54. Elevator torque arm.
55. Turnover structure.
56. Propeller spinner.
57. Early fin profile
58. Later fin profile.

F2A-2 airplanes were brought up to the F2A-3 standard of 240 gallons maximum internal fuel, though in such cases one 80 gallon tank was restricted from use in a combat area. In this case maximum internal fuel would return to 160 gallons, giving F2A-2 and F2A-3 a yardstick range of about 1450 and 1400 miles respectively. Practical ranges would be 75 to 80 percent of these numbers, or perhaps 1050 miles. No combat radius figures have been found, but allowing for takeoff and forming up along with midpoint combat time about one third of that figure, or 350 miles, would not be unreasonable. If a full load of 240 gallons were carried, resulting in an overload takeoff gross weight of near 7300 pounds, the cruising range would be considerably extended, but no data has been found for such a case.

Graph 58 plots F2A-2 and F2A-3 takeoff distance required for sea level zero wind conditions against gross weight, which would be in the 6000 to 7000 pound range. The takeoff distances were extremely short, particularly compared to those of the USAAF fighters. Assuming a 6600 pound gross weight aircraft at takeoff the distance to lift-off is shown as about 560 feet. And this is in a zero wind condition; there is no carrier wind over the deck to shorten takeoff run distance.

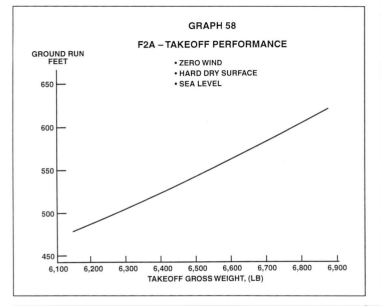

GRAPH 58

F2A – TAKEOFF PERFORMANCE

- ZERO WIND
- HARD DRY SURFACE
- SEA LEVEL

GROUND RUN FEET (y-axis: 450, 500, 550, 600, 650)

TAKEOFF GROSS WEIGHT, (LB) (x-axis: 6,100 to 6,900)

TABLE 67
WEIGHTS OF VARIOUS BREWSTER FIGHTERS
POUNDS

DATE	5/16/39	11/30/39	11/6/39	1/2/40	11/31/40
SERVICE	USN	USN	USN	USN	USN
MODEL	XF2A-1	F2A-1 #1	F2A-1	XF2A-2	F2A-2
WING	698.52	739.2	732.8		723.0
TAIL	104.17	106.4	107.0		107.0
BODY (2)	955.15(1)	818.3	820.3		846.9
ENGINE SECTION	—	142.9	143.4		135.4
POWERPLANT	1540.50	1552.8	1555.3		1893.6
FIXED EQUIP'T.	423.21	423.4	426.3		443.9
EMPTY WEIGHT	3721.55	3783.0	3785.1	4131.2	4149.8
CREW	200.0	200.0	200.0	200.0	200.0
EQUIPMENT	128.7	128.0	128.1	128.7	126.7
ARMAMENT	221.3	214.0	214.0	221.3	214.0
OIL	68.0	68.0	68.0	68.0	68.0
FUEL	660.0	660.0	660.0	660.0	660.0
USEFUL LOAD	1278.0	1270.0	1270.1	1278.0	1268.7
NORM.GROSS WT.	4999.55	5053.0	5055.2	5409.2	5418.5

NOTE (1) Includes landing gear and engine section. (2) Includes landing gear.

No information has been found citing specific rolling performance of Brewster fighters, though there are several comments concerning excellent general maneuverability for the earlier lighter weight models.

The data in Tables 67 and 68 show weights of both US Navy and export versions of the Brewster fighter taken from manufacturer's aircraft characteristics sheets. Dates of the information are shown in each case. Table 69 provides the addition of airframe, propulsion, and fixed equipment weight groups of the export Model 239 version supplied to Finland, this being essentially a landplane version of the Navy F2A-1 airplane. It is interesting to note the empty weight increase in the basic airplane from May 1939 until two years or more later in 1941. The XF2A-1 experimental model had an empty weight of only 3722 pounds with the export 239 version almost the same at 3744 pounds. The F2A-3 empty weight in May 1941, seven months before Pearl Harbor, had increased to 4765 pounds, over half a ton more. Everything increased in weight, the airframe by 280 pounds, the powerplant by 547, and the fixed equipment by 215 pounds. Wing weight alone went up 172 pounds, and the area remained the same. Part of the powerplant weight increase can be explained by the later airplane's use of a newer Cyclone engine version with a two speed super-

TABLE 68
WEIGHTS OF BREWSTER MODELS (CONT'D)

DATE	5/2/41	5/29/40	11/13/40	——
SERVICE	USN	BELGIAN	BRITISH	DUTCH,2ND ORD.
MODEL	F2A-3	339B	339E	339D
WING	870.9	701.5	843.5	866.9
TAIL	107.0	107.0	107.0	107.0
BODY (2)	895.7	783.0	809.7	816.4
ENGINE SECTION	165.1	127.6	127.6	163.4
POWERPLANT	2087.9	1838.9	1896.4	1819.8
FIXED EQUIP'T.	638.7	461.7	484.0	508.5
EMPTY WEIGHT	4765.3	4019.7	4268.2	4282.0
CREW	200.0	200.0	200.0	200.0
EQUIPMENT	132.8	86.2	160.7	89.8
ARMAMENT	692.5	403.0	755.3	794.7
OIL	68.0	68.0	68.0	68.0
FUEL	660.0	660.0	660.0	660.0
USEFUL LOAD	1753.3	1417.2	1844.0	1812.5
NORMAL GROSS WT.	6518.6	5436.9	6112.2	6094.5

TABLE 69
FINNISH MODEL 239 AIRCRAFT WEIGHTS
(POUNDS)

WING	738.0
TAIL	107.0
FUSELAGE	410.2
LANDING GEAR	383.6
ENGINE SECTION	143.4
ENGINE	1100.0
ENGINE ACCESSORIES	86.2
ENGINE CONTROLS	11.8
PROPELLER	262.0
STARTING SYSTEM	41.6
COOLING SYSTEM	—
LUBRICATING SYSTEM	26.7
FUEL SYSTEM	27.6
INSTRUMENTS	39.8
SURFACE CONTROLS	73.7
HYDRAULIC SYSTEM	—
ELECTRICAL SYSTEM	139.0
COMMUNICATION SYSTEM	(IN USEFUL LOAD)
ARMAMENT PROVISIONS	"
FURNISHINGS	143.8
AUXILIARY GEAR	9.7
EMPTY WEIGHT	3744.1

TABLE 70
MODEL 239 TYPICAL ALTERNATE USEFUL LOADS
POUNDS

MISSION	2-GUN FIGHTER 110 GAL.FUEL	BOMBER 110 GAL.FUEL	2-GUN FIGHTER 160 GAL.FUEL	4-GUN FIGHTER 110 GAL.FUEL
EMPTY WEIGHT	3744.1	3744.1	3744.1	3744.1
TRAPPED FLUIDS	—	—	—	—
CREW	200.0	200.0	200.0	200.0
1 CAL.50,1 CAL.30	108.7	108.7	108.7	—
3 CAL.50,1 CAL.30	—	—	—	251.1
PROV. FOR BOMBS	—	30.0	—	—
PYROTECHNICS	3.9	3.9	3.9	3.9
COMM.EQUIP'T.	92.3	92.3	92,3	92.3
NAVIG.EQUIP'T.	3.2	3.2	3.2	3.2
MISC.EQUIP'T.	35.1	35.1	35.1	35.1
FIXED USEFUL LOAD	443.2	473.2	443.2	585.6
BASIC WEIGHT	4187.3	4217.3	4187.3	4329.7
USEABLE OIL	68.0	68.0	83.0	68.0
CAL.50 AMMO.	59.8	59.8	59.8	179.4
CAL.30 AMMO.	39.0	39.0	39.0	39.0
INTERNAL FUEL	660.0	660.0	960.0	660.0
EXTERNAL FUEL	—	—	—	—
BOMBS	—	232.0	—	—
DISPOSEABLE LOAD	826.8	1058.8	1141.8	946.4
USEFUL LOAD	1270.0	1532.0	1585.0	1532.0
GROSS WEIGHT	5014.1	5267.0	5314.1	5276.1

TABLE 71
F2A-3 EMPTY WEIGHT
POUNDS

WING	811
TAIL	105
FUSELAGE	350
LANDING GEAR	451
ENGINE SECTION	237
ENGINE WITH ACCESSORIES	1370
ENGINE CONTROLS	12
PROPELLER	339
STARTING SYSTEM	40
COOLING SYSTEM	4
LUBRICATION SYSTEM	87
FUEL SYSTEM	286
INSTRUMENTS	55
SURFACE CONTROLS	80
HYDRAULIC SYSTEM	36
ELECTRICAL SYSTEM	157
COMMUNICATION SYSTEM	(IN USEFUL LOAD)
ARMAMENT PROVISIONS	230
FURNISHINGS	56
OTHER/MISC.	26
EMPTY WEIGHT	4732

NOTE: The empty weight of F2A-3 airplane No.01516, but including oil contained in the sumps and coolers, was 4879 pounds.

charger and a new propeller of 15 inches greater diameter. Armor plate could account for some of the fixed equipment weight increase. In the case of the design mission useful load, even with equal weights of pilot, fuel, and oil, total weight increased 475 pounds from XF2A-1 to F2A-3. There was little increase in useful load equipment weight, about four pounds; the big 471 pound increase came in armament. This result came primarily from a change to four .50 caliber machine guns from one .50 caliber and one .30 caliber weapon. As seen in the tables noted, the result was an increase in gross weight, with design useful load, from 5000 pounds for the XF2A-1 prototype to over 6500 pounds on the F2A-3, a huge increase for a small fighter aircraft. Performance and flying qualities deteriorated severely; increased engine power could not make up the difference.

Table 70 provides a look at typical alternate useful loads for a Model 239, the airplane exported to Finland. The relatively light gross weights, from 5000 to 5300 pounds, are to be noted; at these weights it was a delightful airplane to fly, and it performed well for the Finns. Table 71 details group weights adding to the significantly increased empty weight compared to earlier models. Comparisons can be made in each group area. Tables 72 and 73 detail typical alternate useful loads for F2A-2 and F2A-3 types respectively. They show the gross weights of these aircraft varying in the range 6000 to over 7000 pounds. These are the weights that contributed so significantly to the demise of the Brewster fighter.

TABLE 72
F2A-2 TYPICAL ALTERNATE MISSION LOADS

MISSION	2-GUN FIGHTER	4-GUN OVERL'D. FIGHTER	2-GUN BOMBER	4-GUN OVERL'D BOMBER	ZERO-GUN FERRY
EMPTY WEIGHT	4576	4576	4576	4576	4501
TRAPPED FLUIDS	—	—	—	—	—
CREW	200	200	200	200	200
CAL.50 GUNS	139	277	139	277	—
COMM./NAV.EQUIP.	134	151	163	180	124
FIXED USEFUL LD.	473	628	502	657	324
BASIC WEIGHT	5049	5204	5078	5233	4825
USEABLE OIL	83	83	83	83	83
CAL.50 AMMO.	150	270	150	270	—
BOMB RACKS	—	—	24	24	—
BOMBS	—	—	200	200	—
INTERNAL FUEL	660	1080	660	1080	1080
EXTERNAL FUEL	—	—	—	—	—
DISPOSEABLE LOAD	893	1443	1117	1657	1163
USEFUL LOAD	1366	2061	1619	2314	1487
GROSS WEIGHT	5942	6637	6195	6890	5988

TABLE 73
F2A-3 TYPICAL ALTERNATE MISSION LOADS

MISSION	4-GUN FIGHTER	4-GUN OVERL'D. FIGHTER	4-GUN BOMBER	4-GUN OVERL'D BOMBER	0-GUN FERRY
EMPTY WEIGHT	4732	4732	4732	4732	4590
TRAPPED FLUIDS	—	—	—	—	—
CREW	200	200	200	200	200
CAL.50 GUNS	277	277	277	277	—
COMM./NAV.EQUIP.	129	144	158	173	115
FIXED USEFUL LD.	606	621	635	650	315
BASIC WEIGHT	5338	5353	5367	5382	4905
USEABLE OIL	83	83	83	83	83
CAL.50 AMMO	240	270	240	390	—
BOMB RACKS	—	—	24	24	—
BOMBS	—	—	200	200	—
INTERNAL FUEL	660	1080	660	1080	1080
EXTERNAL FUEL	—	—	—	—	—
DISPOSE. LOAD	983	1553	1207	1777	1163
USEFUL LOAD	1589	2174	1842	2427	1478
GROSS WEIGHT	6321	6906	6574	7159	6068

F2A- MAJOR MODEL TO MODEL CHANGES

F2A-1 (from XF2A-1): New version of Wright R-1820 engine; revised engine cowl; raised cockpit canopy; larger vertical tail.

XF2A-2 Another version of the R-1820 engine with single stage two speed supercharger. Modified vertical fin. Curtiss propeller with spinner and blade cuffs in place of Hamilton model. Fuel and carburetion systems revised. Integral flotation arrangement modified. Cockpit escape hatch added.

F2A-2 (30th and subsequent aircraft) Late aircraft updated with combat modifications. Additional armor and new protected fuel tanks added. Armament increased to four .50 caliber machine guns, two in the forward fuselage and one in each wing.

F2A-3 Additional armor plate and an armored windshield. Engine moved forward. Modified fuel system. New radio.

F2A-/BUFFALO CHRONOLOGY

'32-The Brewster Corporation is formed.

Nov15'35-The US Navy approves two new fighter designs-a Grumman biplane and a Brewster monoplane.

Jun22'36-The USN orders a prototype aircraft as the XF2A-1 (Brewster Model 139). The aircraft design team is headed by Dayton T. Brown and R.D.McCart.

Feb10'37-Brewster and Work Engineering are legally consolidated under the name of Brewster Aeronautical Corporation.

Dec '37-The first flight of the XF2A-1 prototype takes place.

Jan '38-The XF2A-1 airplane is delivered to NAS Anacostia, Md. for testing by the US Navy.

Mar 1'38-Comparative tests are run at Anacostia between the XF2A-1, the Grumman XF4F-2 monoplane, and the Seversky NF-1.

Apr '38-Deck landing tests are conducted on the XF2A-1 airplane. During a hard landing the landing gear is severely damaged, and the plane is returned to the manufacturer.

Apr21'38-The XF2A-1 is shipped to NACA, Langley Field, Va. and is tested in the 40'x80' wind tunnel, the first full-size aircraft to be so tested in the US. Cowl, canopy, and tail modifications are made as a result of the testing. Three days are spent determining what surface irregularities slow the airplane. Several NACA recommendations are followed, and speed increases 20 mph.

Jun11'38-A production order for 54 F2A-1 (Brewster Model 239) aircraft is placed by the Navy.

Jul29'38-Brewster purchases the vacant Pierce-Arrow building in Long Island City, Queens, NY, a four story structure with a central elevator.

Dec '38-The repaired XF2A-1 aircraft is delivered for further USN testing.

Dec31'38-During the year, besides the XF2A-1 work, Brewster has been making wings, tail surfaces, and tip floats for US Navy aircraft, parts for Canadian aircraft, and also obtained USN acceptance of their XSBA-1 monoplane dive bomber.

Mar22'39-The USN orders conversion of the XF2A-1 prototype aircraft to XF2A-2 standard.

Jun20'39-Deliveries of F2A-1 models to the US Navy begin; the first production aircraft is rolled out. One F2A-1 goes to NAS Anacostia for engine cooling tests.

Jul '39-The XF2A-2 (the XF2A-1 with an engine change and other modifications) is rolled out and begins flight tests.

Aug '39-The British Purchasing Commission considers ordering a Model 339 export version as a land-based fighter for the RAF, and a contract is prepared for an order of 120 aircraft. The export model compares to the USN F2A-2.

Aug '39-Poland orders 250 F2A-type fighters for $15.0 million. The order is never filled since Poland is invaded by Germany the next month and overwhelmed.

Oct '39-The British Air Ministry says the Brewster fighter "is not suitable for the Royal Air Force."

Dec '39-Eleven F2A-1 aircraft have been accepted by the US Navy, and enter service with Squadron VF-3. The remaining 43 aircraft on Navy order are released to Finland using commercial model engines. The Finnish order is valued at about $3.0 million.

Dec 8'39-Nine F2A-1 aircraft are received by Navy squadron VF-3 on board aircraft carrier Saratoga. They are operated along with Grumman F3F-1 biplanes.

Dec11'39-Belgium orders 40 Model 339 export fighters at $2.2229 million plus spares, and an option to manufacture the plane under license.

Jan '40-The British Purchasing Commission gives Brewster a $9.6 million order for 120 Model 339E aircraft, later increased to 170 airplanes.

Feb '40-Seventeen aircraft are delivered in January and 27 in February for Finland. They are shipped to Sweden, assembled and tested at SAAB in Trollhatten, and then placed in service in Finland.

Apr '40-Production of the 40 339B export aircraft for Belgium is started. One plane is produced this month and six more in May.

Apr '40-All the 44 Brewster 239 fighters have reached Finland. They are operated very successfully by Nr.24 and Nr.26 Squadrons of the Finnish Air Force against the Russians.

May10'40-The first Belgian 339B aircraft is delivered just as the Germans invade that country, and falls into German hands. France is to assume the undelivered portion of the contract.

May16'40-Brewster Aeronautical leases additional plant space at Newark Airport, NJ. using a new large hangar with 217000 square feet of space. The last of a $10.0 million USN PBY- flying boat parts contract is finished at Newark, and final assembly, flight test, and packing for shipment of Brewster fighters is done at Newark also.

Jun '40-Brewster acquires an eight story Ford building with 482000 square feet of space diagonally across from the original plant in Long Island City.

Jun '40-Ten F2A-1 airplanes are in service with USN Squadron VF-3 on USS Saratoga. Several problems arise, including failures of a weak landing gear.

Jun30'40-Model 339E aircraft for Britain are being produced; two in May, 22 in June, and nine more will be put out in July. Production is stopped in August to change over to make planes for the US Navy.

Jul '40-Six Belgian 339B aircraft are diverted to Martinique on the French aircraft carrier Bearne, and are left there. With the fall of Belgium and France to Germany the remainder of the order, 38 airplanes, is taken over by Britain's Fleet Air Arm.

Jul '40-The first British Buffalo Is, as the 339Es are called, are assembled at Burtonwood, Lancashire, England.

Sep '40-The RAF gets Buffalo I aircraft delivery from assembly points. Flight trials are made of the planes by No.71 Squadron at Church Fenton, and the type is rejected for use in Europe.

Sep '40-Production delivery of F2A-2s for the USN begins to replace those allocated to Finland. Six F2A-2s are produced in September, 26 in October, and 10 in November, when the USN order is completed except for one aircraft delivered January, 1941.

Oct 7'40-Navy Squadron VF-2 gets their first F2A-2 aircraft. They ferry them from Anacostia to San Diego. The last aircraft arrives on November 28th.

Nov '40-USN Squadron VF-3 now has 15 F2A- aircraft, some being the -2 version.

Dec '40-Production of RAF 339E/Buffalo I airplanes is restarted after completion of the USN order, and 40 are produced in December and 38 more in January, 1941.

Dec31'40-Along with the fighter work in the last year, Brewster made outer wings, ailerons, and tip floats and outer braces for Consolidated PBY- flying boats.

Jan21'41-The US Navy orders 108 F2A-3 models to keep the Brewster production line going since the Grumman F4F-3 cannot be produced fast enough.

Feb '41-Twenty-two 339E Buffalo I aircraft are manufactured for the British this month.

Mar '41-Navy Squadron VF-2 goes aboard the carrier Lexington with 18 F2A-2s and three spares.

Mar '41-Along with British aircraft, production starts on the first of 72 339D Buffalos ordered by the Netherlands East Indies in 1940 at a cost of $3.177 million. These planes will employ used (re-manufactured) Wright G105 Cyclone engines from the TWA fleet of DC-3s.

Mar '41-Six of the Belgian Brewster 339B airplanes go to the British #805 Squadron and are operated with Fairey Fulmars in Crete by the Fleet Air Arm.

Mar28'41-Work is started on a new large assembly plant on a 400 acre site at Johnsville, Warminster Township, Pa. Upon completion the plant will bring total Brewster factory space to 1,334,000 square feet.

Mar31'41-The production for the month at Brewster is 19 Buffalos for the British, and 18 for the Dutch.

Apr31'41-Buffalo production in April totals 35 339Es and nine 339Ds for the British and Dutch respectively.

May '41-The last of the British Buffalo order is completed. Most of these go to Singapore, but 32 are sent to Rangoon in Burma.

May '41-In this month Brewster updates eight US Navy F2A-1s to F2A-2 standard, and puts out 27 Buffalos for the Netherlands East Indies.

Jun '41-With completion this month of the final 18 Dutch Buffalos of the original 1940 72-plane order Brewster has completed its export model production for the year. An order from the Netherlands East Indies for an additional 20 more powerful Model 439D Buffalos will not be filled until 1942, but by then the NEI. will have been lost to the Japanese.

Jul '41-Deliveries of the F2A-3 to the USN begin with the initial aircraft being accepted.

Aug '41-Navy Squadron VF-2 get off the carrier Lexington with their F2A-2s, and in September turn them in for F2A-3 models. The F2A-2s go to operational training units. VS-201 uses them on the east coast until February, 1942.

Aug31'41-Brewster delivers 26 F2A-3s to the USN in August. In September 39 more are delivered.

Sep '41-An F2A-3 is to be reworked as an F2A-4 with a pressurized cabin, but the project is soon abandoned.

Sep12'41-Navy Squadron VF-2 now has 18 F2A-3s and is the only USN squadron to use the F2A-3.

Oct '41-With delivery of 23 more F2A-3s this month the Brewsters are getting into Navy and USMC squadron use. Besides VF-2 with its 18 F2A-3s and a few F2A-2s, VF-3 has five F2A-3 aircraft and nine F2A-2s, and Marine Squadron VMF-221 is operating 11 F2A-3 and three F2A-2 airplanes.

Oct14'41-The carrier Lexington and VF-2 are on their way to Pearl Harbor with 17 F2A-3s and five spares.

Nov '41-Nine more F2A-3s are delivered to the Navy by Brewster.

Dec 3'41-VF-2 reports to the Navy Bureau of Aeronautics that they had "ceased all operations until enemy contact became iminent." It is reported that three more F2A-3 landing gear struts failed on normal landings, and that progressive landing gear failures had started in 12 of the 17 aircraft. VF-2 also loses three planes in operational accidents, but no pilots are lost.

Dec 7'41-At the time of the Japanese Pearl Harbor attack the USN has approximately 90 F2A-3 aircraft on hand. They are encountering landing gear and arresting hook failure problems. On this date the carrier Saratoga is at San Diego with 18 F2A-3s of VMF-211 aboard. The next day the carrier heads towards Wake Island, but is later turned around to let the Marines off at Ewa, Hawaii. VF-2 is aboard carrier Lexington with F2A-3s.

Dec 8'41-Thirty of the Dutch 339D aircraft are in service in the Netherlands East Indies. One squadron is sent to Malaya to assist the British defenders against the Japanese.

Dec25'41-Eighteen RAF Buffalos with 15 AVG Curtiss Tomahawks encounter 80 Japanese bombers and 28 fighters over Rangoon, Burma. The Buffalos shoot down seven E/A and the Tomahawks 25. Some of the Brewsters are lost, but no AVG airplanes fall.

Dec25'41-Midway Island receives its first fighter planes -14 F2A-3s of Marine Squadron VMF-221 are dropped off from the carrier Saratoga after returning from the aborted relief mission to Wake.

Dec31'41-With the production of nine more F2A-3s this month US Navy Brewster fighter deliveries are complete , with the exception of one aircraft delivered early in January, 1942. Further production of the F2A-3 is abandoned by the USN, in part because satisfactory gunfire-protected fuel tanks cannot be installed. Some F2A-3s are being delivered directly to training units.

Dec31'41-At this time the USN has one F2A-1 and one XF2A-2 at Norfolk, 49 F2A-2s (three at San Diego, seven at Miami, others scattered), and 107 F2A-3s (five at San Diego, 37 at New York, 19 with VF-2 on Lexington, 14 with Marine VMF-221 at Midway, seven at Pearl Harbor, seven with jeep carrier Long Island, eight at Miami, three at Cape May, NJ., and the rest scattered).

Jan '42-The first 11 export Model 439D Buffalos of the order for 20 are produced at Brewster for the NEI. and service tests begin.

Jan '42-British 339E Buffalos are being used in Malaya for the defense of Singapore by two RAF squadrons, #67 and #243, two RAAF squadrons, #21 and #453, and one RNZAF squadron, #433. Buffalos are rated as having very poor performance. The five surviving Dutch 339D Buffalos are shortly withdrawn to Sumatra.

Jan 3'42-The F2A-s of VF-2 land at Ewa in Hawaii.

Jan 7'42-The VF-2 F2A-3s are now back on the carrier Lexington. They bomb and claim damage on a submarine.

Jan27'42-VF-2 F2A-3 airplanes go back to MCAS Ewa, Hawaii, where all 18 are transferred into the Marines VMF-211 Squadron. Navy VF-2 Squadron gets new F4F-3A Wildcats.

Feb15'42-After the fall of Singapore to the Japanese 16 Brewster Buffalos of #67 Squadron at Mingaladon join with 24 AVG Curtiss Tomahawks to act as the only air defenses of Burma.

Mar 1'42-On the island of Java, N.E.I. four Dutch Buffalos, the only flyable ones, combine with six Hawker Hurricanes and nine Curtiss P-40s to fly the last mission against Japanese landings. All the Allied aircraft are lost.

Mar '42-Ten US Marine F2A-3s are sent to the island of Kauai in the Hawaiian Islands to practice night fighter interceptions to guard against another raid on the islands. They are kept at this northern outpost of the islands until after the Midway battle.

Mar10'42-Four F2A-3s of Marine Squadron VMF-221 shoot down a Japanese flying boat off Midway Island.

Mar31'42-Brewster is not doing any real production of Buffalos. None were produced in February and only one 439D for the N.E.I. is put out this month.

Apr '42-Total production of US Navy F2A- and export Buffalo aircraft reaches 509 with the final nine of the second order from the Netherlands East Indies being delivered. Of the 20 439D aircraft 17 are shipped to Australia and used by the RAAF. With no more orders Brewster terminates production.

Apr18'42-Fourteen F2A-3s of Marine VMF-211 fly off carrier Lexington to Palmyra Island to form an air defense there.

May26'42-Cdr.C.Fischer successfully demonstrates the use of JATO (Jet Assisted Takeoff) at NAS Anacostia,Md. using five solid rocket motors on an F2A-3 fighter. Takeoff distance reduces 49%.

May31'42-The original 14 F2A-3 aircraft on Midway Island have now been augmented by seven more, along with seven F4F-3 Wildcats. The Midway Marines now have a total of 28 fighter aircraft.

Jun 4'42-As the Battle of Midway starts , seven F2A-3s and five F4F-3s in one US group and 12 F2A-3s and one F4F-3 in another group attack a 108 aircraft Japanese strike force at 12000 feet 30 miles out of Midway. The Marines claim 34 E/A downed, but later the enemy admits only to losing nine with 34 planes damaged. Thirteen F2A-3s and two F4F-3s are lost. Of the remaining ten US fighters only two are in condition to fly again, and VMF-211 is essentially wiped out. One of the surviving Brewster pilots is quoted as: "It is my belief that any commander who orders pilots out for combat in an F2A- should consider the pilot lost before leaving the ground." The F2A-3 is considered a failure in combat, and is subsequently withdrawn from combat areas.

Jun '42-USN Brewster fighters are used as fighter-trainers, some at Opa Locka, Florida.

Nov30'42-There are no Brewster F2A- fighters on strength with the US Marine Corps.

Aug '44-The last of the Finnish Brewster Model 239 fighters are now out of service, replaced by Messerschmitt ME-109s.

*(Current)*One Brewster 239 fighter still survives in a Finnish museum. Brewsters in Finnish service are credited with shooting down 477 enemy aircraft.

BREWSTER FIGHTER HANDLING QUALITIES AND CHARACTERISTICS

HANDLING QUALITIES
GROUND HANDLING
When taxied the aircraft allowed only a poor view forward because of the somewhat aft location of the pilot, and a nose high position with the tail down. The airplane was easy to taxi; the tail wheel could be unlocked into swivel for turning and parking. It was adviseable to lock the tailwheel in allignment if the aircraft had to be taxied straight and fast for any distance. This action prevented tail wheel shimmy; it could then be unlocked for S-turning. While the tail wheel was satisfactory for hard runways, The Finns operating the Model 239 had problems sinking into soft airfield surfaces. Otherwise they found no taxi difficulty. There was a complaint on a British Buffalo also "The tailwheel wobbled on its center and ripped the rubber off its tire." The US Navy found the F2A-3 aircraft to be controllable and stable for taxi, but noted there was insufficient braking capacity. The wide tread main landing gear provided good stability for the aircraft during all phases of ground handling.

In preparation for takeoff the rudder tab was turned about three and a half divisions to provide right rudder, and the elevator tab moved to make the aircraft slightly nose heavy.

TAKEOFF AND CLIMB
After trimming as noted the airplane was positioned straight down the runway, into the wind if possible for takeoff, and the tailwheel was locked in neutral position. Flaps could be lowered for a minimum takeoff run. After engine runup and checks brakes were released. Because engine manifold pressure was not automatically regulated care was taken with the throttle to stay within the pressure limit. The takeoff run was normal and stable, but as with all powerful single engine US propeller fighters the aircraft tended to swing to the left. This torque swing could be countered by application of right rudder which became more effective as speed increased. During the takeoff stick forces were rather heavy, and the stick had to be forced forward to raise the tail. The takeoff run was short, and climb was quickly initiated with wheels retracted immediately and flaps, if used, coming up at 500 feet or above. The best initial speed for climbout, about 138 to 145 mph IAS depending on model, was set up. Optimum speed for climb reduced slowly as altitude was gained. During high power climbs, particularly at the high gross weights of later versions, the Brewster showed signs of static lateral instability. If the center of gravity was well aft the airplane was

Fig.2A-1 Brewster XF2A-1, No.0451, USN photo via H. Andrews. The prototype of the Brewster fighter series, the XF2A-1 ordered by the US Navy in the spring of 1936, shortly before they ordered another prototype from Grumman. These aircraft represented a serious step by the Navy towards moving finally from biplanes towards monoplane carrier fighters to improve performance. The Brewster first flew near the end of 1937, a few weeks after the Grumman aircraft initially took to the air.

Fig.2A-2 Brewster XF2A-1, No.0451, USN photo via H. Andrews. Another flight view of the XF2A-1 showing it as a rather corpulant fighter with considerable transparency area around and behind the cockpit, and, in this picture viewing windows in the belly too. Openings in the leading edge of the engine cowl are for two machine guns, a carburetor central air intake up top, and an oil cooler air intake duct below.

Fig.2A-3 Brewster XF2A-1, No.0451, Photo via F. Dean coll. Level the ground in this photo and note the Brewster prototype is rolling to port. It was light, maneuverable, and according to reports, fun to fly. Early in 1938 the XF2A-1 was turned over to the Navy for testing, and in the spring it was the first full scale aircraft tested in the big new NACA wind tunnel at Langley Field in Virginia after which suggested improvements were implemented to increase performance.

Fig.2A-4 Brewster XF2A-2, No.0451, USN photo via H. Andrews. An excellent flight photo of the Brewster Navy prototype revised to XF2A-2 configuration. Among the changes were a new version of the Wright Cyclone engine with a two speed geared supercharger, a Curtiss propeller with spinner and blade cuffs in place of the Hamilton model, increased vertical fin area, and subsystems modifications. Empty and gross weight increased by 410 pounds, the start of a long climb in weight. Note how neatly the main landing gear wheel flushed into the aircraft fuselage. The catapult hook is below and just to the left of the wheel.

statically unstable longitudinally with stick fixed as well. With the center of gravity more forward longitudinal stability became neutral or positive.

TRIMMING

The trim tabs were very effective. The Finns reported "Trim tab adjustment was sufficient to maintain perfect balance in flight", and the British reported "Tabs were efficient; the rudder tab allowed feet-off flying at all speeds." The elevator tab was powerful and thus had to be used with care; and on no account was it to be used for dive recovery. With increasing speed left rudder trim was required. The aircraft became nose-heavy when flaps or landing gear was lowered.

Fig.2A-5 Brewster F2A-2, Curtiss Propeller Div. photo via F. Dean coll. Since all but eleven of the initial US Navy order for fifty-four fighters were exported as B-239s to assist Finland in defending itself against Russian invasion in early 1940, the F2A-2 was the first Brewster to get to the USN in any quantity with just about all -2 versions delivered in the fall of 1940. This ground shot of an F2A-2 at Caldwell, New Jersey shows well the Curtiss propeller and the main landing gear arrangement. Note the vertical landing loads had to be taken in strut bending and distance between the drag load reaction points at the wing was short, a real compromise in basic structure. Though not showing in this photo armament was two cowl and two wing guns of .50 caliber. With these guns and updated combat design provisions gross weight climbed to over 6600 pounds where the prototype design gross weight was just about 5000 pounds.

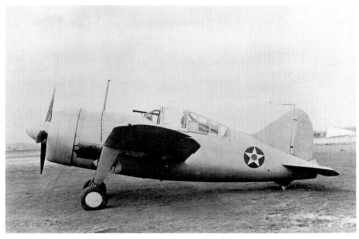

Fig.2A-6 Brewster F2A-3, NACA photo via H. Andrews. An F2A-3 aircraft under test by NACA, the final US Navy Brewster fighter and one produced in greatest numbers at 108 airplanes. Deliveries to the Navy took place from July, 1941 until years end. Thus Brewster production for the Navy stopped just about the time of the Pearl Harbor attack and US entry into World War II. Empty weight of the -3 version again increased over 150 pounds from the -2. With fuel of 180 gallons the F2A-3 grossed out above 6900 pounds, almost a ton greater than the XF2A-1 prototype, and there was no increase in wing area.

Fig.2A-7 Brewster F2A-3, photo via H. Andrews. The F2A-3 got to Navy Squadron VF-2 in August and September of 1941 after this squadron had operated F2A-2s from October 1940 on. Their -2 aircraft were then given over to training units. By the time of the Pearl Harbor attack the Navy and Marines had about ninety F2A-3s, but landing gear and arresting gear problems were prevalent. VF-3 also had Brewsters as did Marine Squadron VMF-221. The propeller of the aircraft in this photo is equipped with both blade cuffs and spinner.

DIVE AND RECOVERY

An old Navy pilot recalled with evident relish "We used to dive those things; the Brewster would pick up speed in a hurry." Diving characteristics, particularly if the aircraft center of gravity was not too far aft, were considered good, though the Finns reported "Ailerons became a little twisted while diving." Maximum engine speed allowed in a dive was 2730 RPM, and the calculated terminal velocity in a dive was 450 knots (518 mph) IAS. Normal Brewster fighter operations were at moderate altitudes, and such a dive speed was probably never reached, this indicated speed corresponding to 576 mph true airspeed (TAS) at a pullout altitude of 7000 feet.

During a dive the aircraft required considerable left rudder or left rudder trim to keep the nose headed straight. In addition, as speed in the dive increased the aircraft became tail heavy, and this inclination could be trimmed out with the elevator tab. Stick forces for dive recovery were on the light side, particularly when the airplane was heavily loaded and the center of gravity was aft. In such a case considerable care had to be taken to avoid excessive g loading by pulling out too quickly. NACA tests had shown that an F2A-2 airplane with a center of gravity well aft would encounter a dangerous instability at about 400 mph IAS in a dive. On the F2A-3 model with an extreme aft center of gravity diving was dangerous because

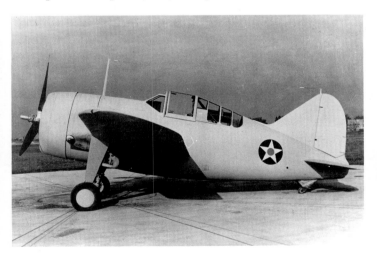

Fig.2A-8 Brewster F2A-3, USN photo via H. Andrews. Another side view of an F2A-3; this machine has its Curtiss Electric propeller installed without a spinner. An overturn structure and a life raft container tube are located just behind the pilot. There is no gunsight on the aircraft. Both F2A-2 and F2A-3 airplanes had two cowl and two wing .50 caliber guns. Wing guns of the -3 had 400 rounds each, double the -2 quantity.

Fig.2A-9 Brewster F2A-3, USN photo via H. Andrews. A three quarter front view of the F2A-3 shows details of propeller, engine cowl and exhaust, and landing gear. The wing ports for the .50 caliber guns do not show here and bomb racks are not installed. All fuel for the F2A-3 was carried internally, a whopping 240 gallons if all five tanks were filled. Because the main fuel tanks between wing spars could not be adequately protected against gunfire three additional protected tanks totaling 80 gallons were added to the airplane, no doubt in some desperation.

Fig.2A-10 Brewster F2A-3, USN photo via H. Andrews. This three quarter rear view shows the fairing atop the wing used to enclose the butt end of the .50 caliber wing gun. The ammunition container for the wing gun was inboard of the weapon, the ejection chute just outboard. The dark spot aft of the fuselage insignia is a hole for a tail lifting bar. At the end of 1941 nineteen F2A-3s were aboard carrier Lexington, fourteen were at Midway Island, and USMC VMF-221, seven at Pearl Harbor, and seven on the small carrier Long Island. The remainder of the 107 total aircraft were scattered between east and west coast bases in the US.

Fig.2A-11 Brewster F2A-3, USN photo via H. Andrews. The -3 version had a bullet-resistant windshield with a hole for the telescopic sight. In this view the wing gun port can be seen just outboard of the main gear strut. The wing of the aircraft was built in one piece and the main structural section was continuous through the fuselage. Assembly was effected by lowering the fuselage over the wing; a piece of lower fuselage was carried with the wing to fill out the lower contour. One of the added protected fuel tanks was located just aft of the fuselage pocket for the landing gear. One central actuator retracted the main gear.

of a stick force reversal during four to five g pullouts. In any case, if the aircraft had not been trimmed correctly for diving, tail heaviness during the dive made it necessary to hold the stick firmly to avoid too rapid a pullout with the attendent excessive g level incurred. The "book" was adamant about disallowing use of the elevator trim tab for dive recovery.

MANEUVERING

The Brewster fighter was initially a very maneuverable machine, though much less so in later versions having significantly increased weight. This maneuverability was due in part to a near neutral static stability characteristic. Reports on the F2A-1/239 and early F2A-2

versions were enthusiastic about maneuverability. These reports were particularly interesting when they came from pilots who had been flying the quite maneuverable Grumman F3F- biplane fighter series of airplanes. The Finns reported "Its inherent quality of high maneuverability was successfully demonstrated." A US Navy pilot said "When first produced the F2A-1 was an excellent aerobatic aircraft, a delight to fly." The British stated "The aircraft was excellent for all acrobatics. It behaves with the ease of a Gloster Gladiator, and is just as simple to acrobat." And perhaps the greatest accolade of all, for an F2A-2 (presumeably before modifications) by a Navy pilot "I think it would have matched the Zero (in maneuverability)." This pilot thought of the F2A-3 as "a different air-

Fig.2A-12 Brewster F2A-3, USN photo via H. Andrews. Starting almost immediately in 1942 production of F2A- fighters was discontinued, leaving Grumman F4F-production as the sole source of US Navy fighters since newer types were not ready. Except for a few Brewsters defending Pacific islands the remainder were sent to training units, some production airplanes being sent there directly. The photo shows a rather weary looking F2A-3 over an area flat enough to be Florida. The Brewsters in the training units were not held in high regard.

Fig.2A-13 Brewster F2A-3, USN photo via H. Andrews. The chunky F2A-3 is shown in flight with hatch open, sight installed, and a rear view mirror added. About the time these aircraft were being used in training their twenty-one brothers operated in mid-1942 by the Marines on Midway Island were taking a well-reported drubbing by a large force of attacking Japanese aircraft. Surviving F2A- airplanes were shortly withdrawn from combat areas.

Fig.2A-14 Brewster F2A-3, USN photo via H. Andrews. A dramatic peel-off of Brewster fighter-trainers looks like all could be ready to go into action. The pilots would go, but the aircraft would stay at training bases until it was time for the boneyard. By the end of November, 1942 the USMC had no Brewsters left; it is probable the Navy had none either unless a few trainers survived.

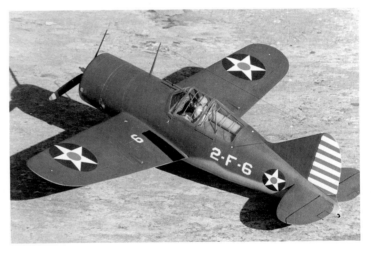

plane; I wasn't as impressed with the F2A-3." Another bit of praise, this for the 339 export version "The Buffalo could almost match the Zeke 22 for maneuverability."

On the F2A-1/239 airplane and the British Buffalo just about all maneuvers could be performed, including vertical banks, loops, slow rolls, aileron rolls, snap rolls, sideslips, chandelles, Immelman turns, dives, stalls, and spins in both normal and inverted flight, although deliberate spinning was officially prohibited and prolonged inverted flight was not possible. As usual there was a caution to allow ample height for recovery from any maneuver because acceleration was rapid. The aircraft controls were rated as highly effective during maneuvering "Elevators were very effective", "Ailerons were highly effective throughout the speed range", and "Rudder performance was good." On early F2A-3 aircraft ailerons oscillated and buffeted at large displacements during rolls, but modifications, including reduced aileron throw, corrected the problem.

APPROACH AND LANDING
In the approach the self-centering tail wheel was checked to assure it was locked in the trail position to lessen possibility of a ground loop in an airfield landing runout. Normal approach was made at about 110 mph IAS and the final made with flaps lowered. Limit flaps-down speed was 140 to 160 mph IAS depending on model. Final approach was done at 80 to 90 mph IAS, again depending on version, loading, and engine power. During an engine-assisted approach the lateral instability noted earlier was quite obvious; there was also a distinct lack of stick feel of the elevators, though they

OPPOSITE: Fig.2A-15A,B,C,and D Brewster F2A-3, Model and photos by J. Weathers. The four photos of a beautifully built F2A-3 model in the markings of VF-2 provide excellent views of various aspects of the Brewster aircraft. The F2A-3 girth was often described in uncomplimentary terms, this due to starting up front with a Wright Cyclone single row nine cylinder engine of fifty-five inches in diameter. Of course some Wildcat versions has essentially the same engine, but somehow managed to look a bit less corpulent.

Fig.2A-16 Brewster 339D Buffalo Cockpit, Mfr. photo via Carl Schaub. The cockpit of a 1941 fighter, the 339D export version of the Navy F2A- for the Dutch East Indies. There was a central main instrument panel and port and starboard auxiliary sub-panels. Pilot complaints included a problem of scratching hands on the small panels while charging the guns, and placement of flap and landing gear handles on the right side of the cockpit instead of the left side. In general the cockpit was considered roomy and comfortable.

STALLS AND SPINS

Stalling the Brewster under one g conditions was quite a mild experience, both power on and power off. Stall speed varied with weight, engine power, and configuration, and thus could run from 70 to 90 mph IAS. A good stall warning just above stall speed was provided by shuddering of the aircraft, and the British reported the stall itself was generally preceeded by "quite a loud bang", the source apparently unknown, or at least unexplained. In the stall aileron reversal to the left was encountered with a mild wing drop. Recovery could be made by bringing the nose down and increasing speed. The altitude lost in a recovery was quite moderate, being estimated at only 200 to 300 feet.

An accelerated stall could be encountered in high speed pullouts or turns by pulling too much g. Under these conditions the action was much more exciting. There was the same aileron reversal to the left, but the accompanying roll-off was violent and uncontrollable with the quite possible result of a spin.

The F2A-/239 aircraft was restricted to spins not exceeding two turns because of a delay in recovery and an urgent need for precision in the spin recovery. Recovery technique was similar to that noted below, and after the technique was applied correctly recovery could be effected from a ten turn spin, with wing guns installed, in two to three and a half turns. The altitude loss for a total of twelve and a half spin turns was about 7000 feet.

With the later 339 airplanes spinning was prohibited. If the aircraft was spun inadvertently the following aspects were noteable: The rotation of the spin was extremely erratic; for recovery complete reversal of the rudder against the spin had to be applied before the stick was moved forward, which required considerable strength. Just when recovery was imminent the spin would start to smooth out. Flaps were not to be lowered during a spin.

were still effective. Aft elevator trim was required, and speed had to be held down. There was some tendency to float. Touchdown was normal at a typical speed of about 75 mph, throttle was chopped, and aft stick could produce a tail down landing. The aircraft had to be held straight after the landing, and brakes were to be applied gently. One veteran of F2A-2 flying said "We didn't have much trouble on landing. For example I never heard anything about anybody who could ground loop a Brewster." There were a couple of ground loops however. The official verdict by the US Navy on the heavy F2A-3 was "While the maximum power off speed on landing was 3.9 mph over guarantee, the landing characteristics were found to be very good." As a result of F2A-3 testing the aircraft was accepted for carrier arrested landings at weights up to 6400 pounds. Upon completion of the landing runout on land the tail wheel was unlocked into full swivel and the aircraft could be turned for taxi.

One aspect of Navy Brewster landings that must be mentioned is the frequent landing gear failures when operating at sea, particularly those of the heavier F2A-3 versions. In the harsh environment of landing aboard a carrier there were unusually large numbers of main landing gear strut failures. In addition "Coming aboard the carrier the tail wheel was prone to collapse."

Fig.2A-17 Brewster 339D Buffalo Accessory Bay, Mfr. photo via Carl Schaub. With piano hinged upper cowl panels open and other panels removed powerplant and armament components of the Dutch Buffalo are revealed. The starboard side nose machine gun is mounted atop forward tubular structure with blast tube, ammunition storage boxes, and feed. A wire runs back to the cockpit charging handle. At left is the oil tank, and the curved duct inboard of the gun barrel is the carburetor air intake.

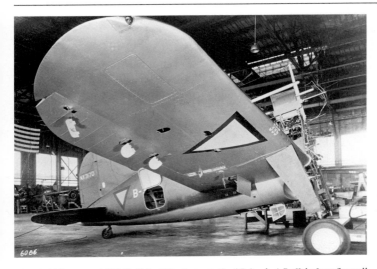

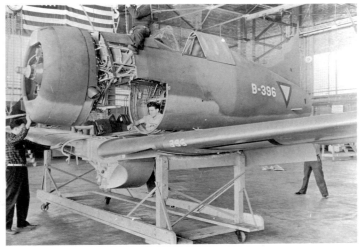

Fig.2A-18 Brewster 339D Buffalo, Mfr. photo via Carl Schaub. A Buffalo from firewall aft at a Brewster facility with access panels and hand holes open. Clearly there was not a real production line. The landing gear outer strut is shown, called the dog-leg drag strut. It was a built up box beam with a shock strut on the lower end. Note the large access door at the aft fuselage and the civil NX3170 marking on the rudder, the latter a requirement for doing flight test work in the US.

Fig.2A-19 Brewster 339D Buffalo, Mfr. photo via Carl Schaub. This photo provides a revealing view of how Buffalo fuselage and wing were assembled. The structural torque box of the wing, spar-to-spar, carried through the fuselage after assembly. The fuselage was lowered over the single piece wing which carried a fuselage-contoured portion on its lower center section. In the photo a cover has been placed over the wing leading edge gun port. The man inside the fuselage is just about where the forty gallon protected fuel tank was located on the Navy F2A-3. This Dutch airplane had no fuselage fuel tank.

CHARACTERISTICS

COCKPIT

The cockpit of the Brewster fighter was considered roomy and generally quite comfortable. There were complaints, however. These included: Carbon monoxide fumes from the engine exhaust tended to seep into the cockpit on both US Navy and British export models; the seat adjustment lever was too small and not smooth-acting; both flap and landing gear handles were on the right side of the

cockpit, "The worst possible place , when it would have been so easy to put them on the left", and the handles were too small and sharp, and thus difficult to operate. Also the positioning slots were too small and hard to find. In addition the fuselage gun charging handles were placed in a poor position. "The backs of my hands still carry scars from scrapes on the edges of the instrument sub-panels."

VISIBILITY

As noted the taxi view ahead for the pilot, typical of tail-down fighters, was poor. One British pilot said it was average, but for this type of aircraft average meant poor. As for in-flight visibility, the Finns said it was "good" on the 239 airplane. The British criticized the pilot's view on their 339, saying the inclination of the bullet-proof windshield and its green tinting interfered with a clear sighting view, but one pilot indicated the "searching view was good, including the view downward and to the rear." Another comment, during night flying tests, "The air view was spoiled by the windscreen frame, particularly on the landing approach."

POWERPLANT OPERATION

Aside from problems of lower power output at the higher altitudes common to engines with only a single stage supercharger, there were certain areas of complaint about the Wright Cyclone engine in the Brewster fighters. The British did not like the inertia starting system, saying "It was not too good for quick takeoffs", nor did they like the fact, not uncommon with American engines of the time, that the Cyclone had no automatic manifold pressure control. Another engine problem was mentioned by both British and American operators. An American pilot said "In hot weather we had an engine in the F2A- which overheated rapidly as soon as any power

Fig.2A-20 Brewster 339D Buffalo, Mfr. photo via Carl Schaub. With a practice bomb underwing on its rack, but no gunsight, a 339D poses for a Brewster photographer in camouflage paint and Dutch-specified markings along with the required NX number for temporary operation in the US. The window in the belly of the fuselage is shown in this photo. Ordered in 1940, production of a batch of seventy-two 339Ds for Netherlands East Indies using re-manufactured US airline Wright Cyclone engines started in March, 1941 with completion of the final airplane in June of that year. British and Dutch export Buffalos were produced together for a time.

Fig.2A-21 Brewster 339D Buffalo, Mfr. photo via Carl Schaub. Another manufacturer's photo of a Dutch 339D Buffalo with bombs underwing and wing guns installed. Recesses in the wing leading edge and in the fuselage for flush re-traction of the main landing gear are well shown. What appears to be an early type of gun camera is temporarily mounted off the forward fuselage. By the time of Pearl Harbor thirty of the Brewsters were serving in the Indies with one squadron going to Malaya to help the British resist the Japanese invasion.

Fig.2A-22 Brewster 339D Buffalo, photo via P. M. Bowers. A Dutch Buffalo with a large airport crowd in the background. The location may be Newark, New Jersey airport where Brewster leased a new large hangar for extra plant space to do final assembly, testing, and packing for shipment of export Buffalos. A second order from N.E.I. for twenty Buffalos started into production only in March, 1942; most all of these went to Australia as Allied forces were being soundly beaten in the Pacific. Had the Buffalo been a much better fighter than it was the overwhelming superior-ity of the Japanese forces would still have doomed the meagre Allied forces.

was applied." A British pilot agreed "The oil and cylinder head temperature were higher in warm climates. This made for prob-lems in tropical areas." Buffalos in Southeast Asia combat were limited by engine overheating in high power climbs.

VULNERABILITY/ARMOR

The original F2A-1/239 airplane had no armor. One item noted by the Finns "Needs an armor plated pilot's seat back." The US Navy started updating its F2A-2 airplanes with armor, and it was pro-vided on later F2A-3 models along with a significant weight in-crease. Airplanes exported to the British had armored windshields and armor behind the pilot. The British complained however "The rear armor plate behind the pilot was not thick enough nor high enough up behind the head." They were also unhappy about certain percieved vulnerabilities "The elevator was operated by a bullet-vulnerable push-pull rod. Twin cables would be preferred", and "The rudder had only one instead of two control cables, and had only two instead of three hinges (no redundancy)." The fuel tanks were so integrated with the wing beam structure that it was almost im-possible to make them into a satisfactory self-sealing types, and this was cited as one reason why the US Navy dropped the type and ceased ordering F2A- aircraft from Brewster.

GUN PLATFORM AND WEAPON PERFORMANCE

There was certainly a difference of opinion between the Finns and the British in gun platform evaluation. Of the Model 239 the Finns said "The plane loses its equilibrium during the firing of its guns." Of the 339B the British commented "The effect of firing the guns on the aircraft was nil", and "Handling qualities for gun firing were good." But to counter this "Considerable vibration of the (gun) sight at all airspeeds and RPMs was experienced; it became serious when firing."

Fig.2A-23 Brewster 339D Buffalo, Mfr. photo via Carl Schaub. A flight test view of a Buffalo before delivery to the Netherlands East Indies. More Brewster fighters were exported than delivered to the US Navy. Britain got 170 plus most all of the forty ordered by Belgium. In Malaya and the Indies British and Dutch 339s fought the Japanese together and were overwhelmed to the last airplane. In Burma British Buffalos fought alongside American Volunteer Group P-40s.

Fig.2A-24 Brewster 339D lineup, photo via Carl Schaub. Fourteen Dutch Buffalos are lined up in perfect order after delivery to the Netherlands East Indies. Dutch and British aircraft had approximately the same design gross weight of 6100 pounds, about 1100 pounds greater than the original F2A-1 gross weight of just over 5000 pounds, and 800 pounds greater than the approximate 5300 pounds of the Finnish 239 aircraft. These large weight increases engendered severe performance and flying quality penalties for the British and Dutch versions notwithstanding some increase in engine power.

Fig.2A-25 Brewster 339 Buffalo, photo via Carl Schaub. A weary looking Dutch Buffalo in the Indies seems to reflect the fate of Allied efforts to defend the Southeast Asia territories threatened by the Japanese expansion in 1942. On March 1, 1942 in Java four remaining 339D Buffalo fighters along with six British Hurricanes and nine American P-40s went to their demise fighting the invading Japanese and signalled the end of air resistance in that area.

Finnish experience with Model 239 weapons installation was satisfactory "Armament was good. Locations and mountings for machine guns were good; easy manipulation." The British were less complimentary in some areas. They noted "The fuselage gun adjustment (range) was very limited." The gun installation in the Buffalo was satisfactory for service use after modifications (several minor hardware items) were put into effect "An illuminated sight installation would be preferable to the telescopic sight", and "All guns fired satisfactorily at an acceleration of plus five g (pullout or turn). All guns stopped firing when a negative acceleration of minus one g (pushover) was applied."

Gun stoppages in British and Dutch Buffalos during combat over the Malay Peninsula were not uncommon.

GENERAL COMMENTS

(239) Flying characteristics were good. No unusual flying or stalling characteristics were evident in the airplane.

(239) The Finnish aircraft with low gross weight had a reasonably lively performance below 10000 feet altitude.

(F2A-) One pilot considered the aircraft difficult to handle and full of gremlins.

(F2A-) Radio masts on all VF-2A's F2A-s were removed because they vibrated at high speed.

(F2A-) It was our first monoplane fighter and had deficiencies normal to a first plane.

(F2A-) It was a nicer flying plane than the F4F-4. However it wasn't as tough and rugged as the F4F-4. In my opinion the F2A- was not constructed as well as the Wildcat.

(F2A-) The much-maligned F2A-s were by then well-liked as far as handling qualities were concerned, (but) the performance was not as expected.

(F2A-2) Now while I was with the chiefs (VF-2) I flew simulated

dogfights and whipped the F4F-s, probably the F4F-3 with no folding wing, but I could also outfly the F2A- when in an F4F-. It all depended on who was in the pilot's seat.

(F2A-2) Teething problems with VF-2 included life raft inflation in the sun and landing gear collapse or deformation.

(F2A-3) Of 17 F2A-3s (on the carrier) there were landing gear failures on twelve.

(F2A-3) Because of the landing gears failing VF-2 stopped normal F2A-3 operations until contact with the Japanese became imminent.

(F2A-3) In the month of America's entrance into World War II production of the F2A-3 was abandoned because satisfactory leak-proof fuel tanks could not be installed.

(F2A-3) The other trouble with F2A-3s: Landing on the carrier deck the gear struts would twist, more because of the extra gas on board meaning extra weight. This was maybe the reason we had strut failures. The landing gear wheels landed pretty hard; negative three g. The struts had a tendency to move forward. When you retracted the gear on the next flight the box strut scraped on the wheel well, so the mechanics would file some off, and get closer to the rivets.

(F2A-3) Capt. Philip White, USMC, VMF-221, Midway: It is my belief that any commander that orders pilots out for combat in an F2A-3 should consider the pilot lost before leaving the ground.

(339E) It was strongly recommended that the type should on no account be considered a fighter without considerable modification.

(339E) Wings were one piece through the fuselage. Changing a whole wing was uneconomical and slow. The fuel tanks were of the integral type built into the spars. A bullet hole in the tank would therefore mean changing the whole wing.

(339E) As a trainer the aircraft was a delight. It behaved with the ease of a Gloster Gladiator, and was just as simple to acrobat. So far we have found no vices.

(339B) The airplane handled well but performance was not impressive.

(339) The Buffalo could almost match the Zeke 22 for maneuverability.

(339E) Let England have the "super" Spitfire and the "hyper" Hurricane; Buffalos are quite good enough for Malaya. (Air Chief Marshall Sir Brook-Popham, Commander in Chief, Far East, 1940.)

(339E) The Zero could out-pace, out-climb, and out-maneuver the Buffalo but could not out-dive it.

(339E) A 1942 mock fight between a Buffalo and a Hurricane showed the former as inferior below 16000 feet, equal at 16000 feet, and superior to the British aircraft at 20000 feet and above.

BREWSTER BUFFALO STRUCTURAL DESCRIPTION
(Metal is aluminum alloy unless otherwise mentioned)

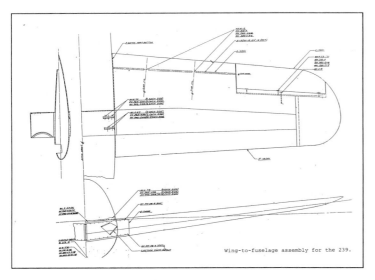

Wing-to-fuselage assembly for the 239.

WING GROUP

The wing group was arranged to provide a mid-wing cantilever monoplane. It consisted of a single piece panel extending through the fuselage structure, and two removeable wingtips to facilitate damage repair. The prime structural component of the wing was the main torque box beam which ran continuously from wingtip to wingtip. This all metal box structure consisted of forward and aft spars of built-up web and cap construction connected by chordwise ribs of formed material and covered with reinforced metal sheet on upper and lower surfaces. The inboard portions of the torque box beam contained the completely integral fuel tanks. Handhole inspection plates were provided for each fuel tank compartment. The shell and chordwise sections of the tanks were metal. The beam was sealed over its entire length to provide water-tightness for buoyancy. Portions of the wing both forward and aft of this beam were also sealed to provide buoyancy in case of a forced water landing. Structural provision was made at wing station 84 on either side for the installation of a .50 caliber machine gun and ammunition container just aft of the main torque box with gun barrel running forward through the box. Metal fairings enclosed the rear portions of the guns. Structural provision was also made under each side of the main box just outboard of the wing guns for installation of a supporting rack for a 100 pound bomb.

The box section alone passed through the fuselage; leading and trailing edge sections terminated at each side of the fuselage.

The center of the box, coincident with the airplane longitudinal centerline, included on its bottom side a built-up structure conforming to the lower fuselage contour so as to blend in with fuselage lines. The wing-fuselage assembly was made by suspending the fuselage over the wing box, lowering it, and bolting the attach fittings which were jig drilled to give positive allignment. With the assembly completed the lower fuselage section was then continuous.

The wing leading edge section was covered by metal skin in several sections extending continuously from the main beam upper surface around the leading edge to the under surface of the beam except where the cut-out for the main landing gear wing-attached strut assembly retracted. Fitting plates to support the main gear outboard struts were located in the leading edge section, and were attached to the forward spar of the wing main beam structure. At the point of juncture between skins and box beam the beam was provided with machined off-sets so there was a continuous smooth exterior contour in the chordwise direction.

The fixed wing portion aft of the main box was of metal rib and metal covered construction. Closing intercostal members running spanwise provided mounts for aileron and flap hinges. On the upper sections of the wing skin adjacent to the fuselage walkways covered with Corprene set in cement were provided.

A single split-type flap piano-hinged to the underside of the main surface outboard of the fuselage was employed on each side. The flaps were made of sheet metal with a leading edge reinforce-

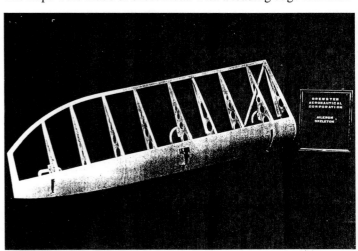

Aileron framing on the Model 239.

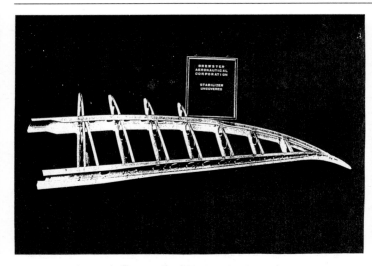

Horizontal stabilizer framing on the model 239.

Elevator framing on the Model 239.

ment running spanwise, eighteen tapered hat section sheet stiffeners riveted on the inner side, and a trailing edge member. The flaps were controlled hydraulically and were operable up to 150 mph IAS. A position indicator was included. Flaps were driven by hydraulic cylinders with output to two control horns on each side.

The ailerons were located just outboard of the flaps at the wing trailing edge and were driven by push rods to aileron horns. Ailerons had an all-metal frame consisting of leading edge spar, nine punched metal forming ribs, a diagonal brace inboard, and a trailing edge and tip closure member. The leading edge 25 percent was metal covered with the remainder covered in fabric. Ailerons were fastened to the main wing with two hinge bolts in fittings. There was no provision for drooping the ailerons. They were both statically and dynamically balanced. The left aileron included a trim tab controllable from the cockpit via a mechanical drive system.

Wingtips were separable and made up of metal framing consisting of five stamped and flanged ribs and three similarly constructed spanwise formers.

TAIL GROUP
The tail group consisted of a fixed stabilizer, an elevator, a fixed fin, and a rudder, all of which were readily removeable for storage or replacement. The horizontal stabilizer was constructed in left and right halves, each removeable from the fuselage. On each stabilizer side framing consisted of a straight rear spar curved back slightly at the tip and of tapered channel section with cap flanges aft, a front channel spar continuously curved back and mating with the rear spar at the tip, eight channel section forming ribs between spars, and four nose forming ribs. All members had stamped lightning holes in the web sections. The stabilizers were bolted to fuselage bulkheads at station 201 and 214 for front and rear spar ends respectively using six bolts at each location with matching holes jig drilled at the factory. Stabilizer surfaces were covered with metal sheet. Two elevator hinge fittings were provided on the rear spar of each surface. The stabilizer was set 0.75 degrees down at the leading edge with reference to the fuselage horizontal centerline.

The elevators were attached to the stabilizer by two hinges on each side and were driven by inboard torque tubes acted on by central elevator horns and push rods. The elevators were statically and dynamically balanced. The framing of each elevator consisted of a single forward spar, eight ribs with lightning holes, a curved trailing edge member, and a tip section. The upper and lower parts of the leading edge were metal covered while the remainder of the surfaces were fabric covered. Each elevator incorporated a cockpit-adjustable trim tab driven by a mechanical system. The tab hinge

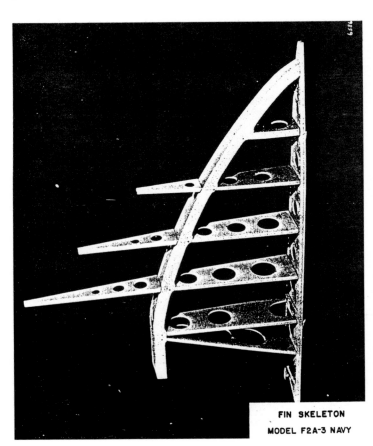

FIN SKELETON
MODEL F2A-3 NAVY

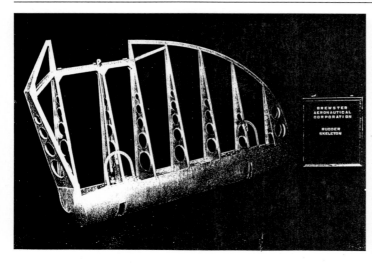

Rudder framing on the Model 239.

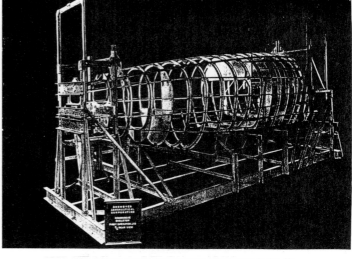

Aft monococque section of Model 239 fuselage in its jig.

support was an intercostal member running between the third and fifth rib. Diagonal bracing supported the intercostal.

The vertical fin was a cantilever surface of all metal two spar construction. the rear spar was a straight tapered aft-facing channel section which carried two hinge fittings for the rudder and which was bolted to the fuselage frame at station 201. The forward spar was a curved aft-facing tapered channel section which joined the rear spar at the fin tip. It was bolted to fuselage frame 214. Six intermediate fin ribs and four nose ribs were employed. Flush riveted metal skins covered the entire fin surface.

The rudder construction was the same as that of the elevators, and a controllable trim tab was mechanically moved from the cockpit. The tab was located near the base of the rudder. The rudder was driven by a torque tube and horn assembly at the base of the hinge line, and was statically and dynamically balanced.

FUSELAGE GROUP

The fuselage proper was made up of two sections. The forward section consisted of the portion aft of the engine mount and forward of the wing beam, where the structure was made up of welded steel tubing. This welded structure supported the firewall and engine mount, the fuselage-mounted machine guns, the radio mast, the inboard part of the landing gear assembly, and various powerplant items. The portion of the fuselage between the forward web of the wing beam and below its rear web, and below the main beam was built as part of wing structure and was moveable with it upon disassembly. Covering of this welded tubing forward section of the fuselage was made up of quickly detacheable metal cowling panels.

The aft fuselage section was of all-metal semi-monocoque construction and was bolted to the steel tube forward section. It consisted of sixteen flanged formers of zee section and bulkheads which framed out the contour and four heavy king stringers, or longerons, along with intermediate bulb-angle stringers running the length of the structure. The aft fuselage was covered with metal stressed skin fastened to the framing with flush rivets. A large access door was

provided on the right side of the aft fuselage which opened to a compartment for baggage and for access inside the fuselage. The aft fuselage included the cockpit section which was enclosed by a sliding hood of framed transparent panels. The front portion of the pilot's windshield was of laminated plate glass; the other panels were of Plexiglass. The windshield had a cut-out for a sight, and an insert was used when the sight was not employed. The canopy locking system was designed to hold the canopy in any of several positions from fully closed to full open, and provision was made for locking and unlocking from the outside. A turnover structure of metal tubes was provided on the deck behind the pilot's seat, and four sections of Plexiglas transparencies with metal framing were provided aft of the cockpit for rearward visibility. A window of curved Plexiglass was provided in the bottom of the fuselage at the cockpit location to provide a downward view for the pilot. The cockpit flooring was kept at a minimum to allow maximum possible vision downward. On the US Navy F2A-2 and F2A-3 versions provision was made in the most forward part of the monocoque section of the fuselage for an oval section fuselage fuel tank having a lower portion matching the contour of the inside of the lower framing. On these navy airplanes a heavy bulkhead near the aft end of the fuselage provided the location for four arresting hook support truss attach fittings. Four truss members ran aft to join at another fitting located at the extreme aft end of the fuselage.

LANDING GEAR GROUP

The landing gear consisted of main and tail wheel elements all hydraulically retractable to positions flush with the exterior contour. The hydraulic system was served by an engine-driven pump with a mechanical stand-by. An electrical landing gear position indicating system was included which showed the pilot when the gear was not fully locked anytime engine RPM was below 1200. On the British 339E airplane the warning system was a vibrator horn located just aft of the pilot's head. In addition a mechanical indicator showed main wheel position anywhere from fully retracted to completely

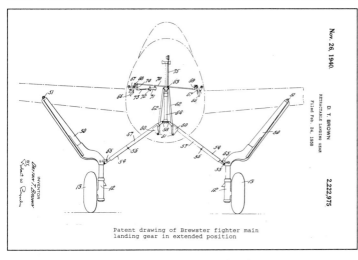

Patent drawing of Brewster fighter main landing gear in extended position

LANDING GEAR CALLOUTS

12. SHOCK ABSORBER	58. PIVOTS
13. WHEEL	60. ARM
50. DOG-LEG DRAG STRUT	62. LINK
51. PIVOT AT WING	63. PISTON
54. STRUT	64. HYDRAULIC CYLINDER
55. PIVOT, LOWER SECTION	66. LATCH
56. TOGGLE JOINT	67,68, 69 UPLOCK SYSTEM
57. STRUT, UPPER SECTION	71. UPLOCK CYLINDER

extended. Downlocks and uplocks were included, and the gear could be operated up to an airplane speed of 120 mph IAS.

The main gear on each side consisted of both an inwardly and outwardly sloped strut arrangement as seen in a view from ahead. The inwardly sloping "dog-leg" strut pivoted at two chordwise upper support locations outboard on the wing just ahead of the main beam, and took landing drag as well as vertical loads. The oleo shock strut carrying carrying axle and main wheel assembly was socketed into the lower section of this structure. In addition an outwardly sloping strut, pivoted at both ends, extended from inside the fuselage on centerline to the upper end of the shock strut. Retraction of the main gear was effected by breaking a toggle or knuckle joint on the inboard sloping strut and making it fold, or jacknife, so as to pull the wheel and shock strut into a lower forward fuselage well. With full retraction the outboard strut and its attached fairing

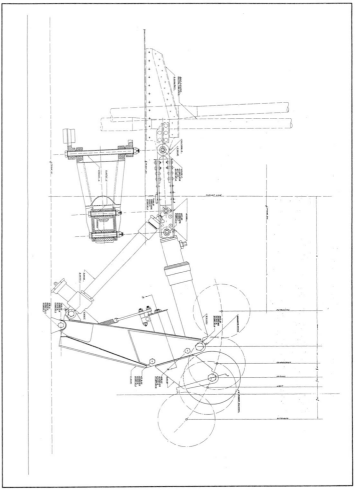

Tail wheel, Model 239

then lay folded flush along the inboard section of the wing leading edge. Breaking and folding the inboard strut was accomplished by a link and arm folding the knuckle and driven by the piston of a single double-acting hydraulic retraction cylinder serving both gears and mounted vertically in the fuselage on the aircraft centerline. An uplock actuated by another hydraulic cylinder latched the gear in the retracted position. Release of the uplocks, gravity, and the evacuation of the hydraulic cylinder allowed the gear to drop to the extended position. In this position the inboard strut straightened out again , and assisted the outboard strut in together taking vertical and side landing loads. A hard point formed by the steel tube structure of the forward fuselage absorbed loads from the inboard strut.

Twenty-seven inch streamline wheels and tires were mounted on roller bearings over the axles at the piston end of the shock struts. Main gear wheels were equipped with expander tube brakes operated by an independent brake hydraulic system. Brake controls were incorporated with the rudder pedals and were connected to a brake cylinder by flexible lines.

The tail wheel was hydraulically retractable and of the 360 degree free swiveling type but was restrained to trail in flight before retraction. It could be locked in the trailing position from the

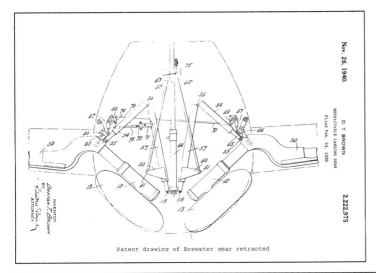

Patent drawing of Brewster gear retracted

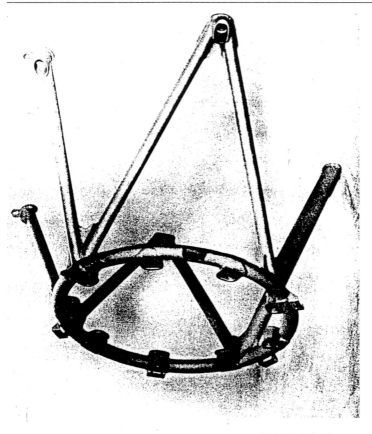

ENGINE MOUNT
MODEL F2A-3 NAVY

cockpit. The solid rubber tail wheel tire was six inches in diameter and two and one half inches wide. The tail gear was supported at fuselage frames 191 and 201. The elements of the tail wheel system were a trailing arm pinned at station 191 into which a swiveling castored wheel assembly was set, a shock strut between the trail arm and a pivoted support at station 201, and a hydraulic retraction actuating cylinder attached so as to retract trail arm, wheel, and shock strut into a fuselage recess.

ENGINE SECTION

The engine section consisted of the engine mount and the powerplant cowlings.

The engine mount was of welded chrome molybdenum steel tubing bolted to the forward fuselage welded tube section by straight bolts in tension at five points, and was thus detacheable. Shock-absorbing rubber bushings were incorporated between the engine proper and the engine mount. The engine was attached to the engine mount at nine points.

The engine cowling was made up of quickly detacheable metal panels secured by quarter-turn fasteners. A ring cowl was fitted in separate sections around the forward portion of the engine. The cowl was removeable without having to remove the propeller.

SYSTEMS DESCRIPTION

PROPULSION SUBSYSTEMS

ENGINE

The aircraft was powered by a 950 to 1200 HP class Wright R-1820 Cyclone nine cylinder single row air cooled radial engine of 6.125 inches bore and 6.875 inches stroke. The propeller reduction gear ratio was either 1:1 or 3:2 depending on engine model. The engine was equipped with a single stage two-speed integral supercharger with impeller gear ratios of 7.14:1 and 10:1 at low and high blower settings respectively. Maximum engine RPM was 2350, and the propeller drive shaft rotated clockwise looking from the rear.

ENGINE INDUCTION SYSTEM

The engine cowl was fitted with an air scoop in the upper section leading edge which conducted cold intake air in a duct to an air mixture valve and on to the carburetor. The engine cowl was designed to prevent hot air from spilling out and entering the cold air duct at high angles of attack. An alternate source of protected carburetor air supply was provided if required which took warm air from inside the engine accessory section. The air mixture valve controlled the intake of air from either outside or accessory section. A push-pull knob on the right side of the main instrument panel mechanically controlled the air mixture valve.

ENGINE EXHAUST SYSTEM

The exhaust system was constructed of corrosion and heat resistant steel. It consisted of two collector tube assemblies. The right hand assembly was composed of four sections connected to each other by slip joints and bolted to the engine cylinder studs. The left hand assembly consisted of five sections. Both assemblies exited through the skin line low on the cowling. On the F2A-3 airplane the manifold was shrouded with a cowling which collected hot air for the carburetor air intake.

ENGINE MOUNTED ACCESSORIES

Accessory items mounted on or driven off the engine accessory pads included two magnetos, carburetor, electrical generator, propeller governor, fuel pump, oil pump, vacuum pump, and tachometer drive.

ENGINE CONTROLS

The engine control unit was located at the left side of the cockpit, and consisted of a throttle knob and lever with a sea level stop set at takeoff power, a supercharger knob and lever control with latches for high and low blower speed positions, and a mixture control with

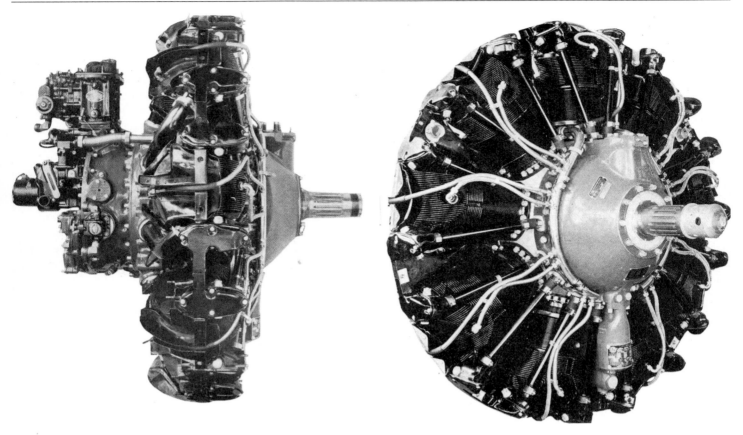

Wright R-1820 Cyclone engine (clockwise from top left) side view, 3/4 Front view, and 3/4 Rear view)

a lock at the top of the control assembly. The mixture control had an idle fuel cut-off and a serrated stop. A primer pump with a built-in shutoff valve was mounted on the right side of the main instrument panel. The engine controls were of the self-lubricating mechanical push-pull rod type running from the cockpit to the levers on the engine.

PROPELLER

The propeller on the Finnish Model 239 was a Hamilton Standard hydraulic constant speed Model 3D40-235 three blade type using design number 6101A-12 solid aluminum blades in 9'0" diameter. The normal blade angle range was 16.4 degrees. On the F2A-3 airplane version the propeller was a 10'3" diameter Curtiss Electric three blade model with a 25 degree minimum pitch range. Blade angles were 22.3 degrees low and 46 degrees high at the 42 inch blade radius station.

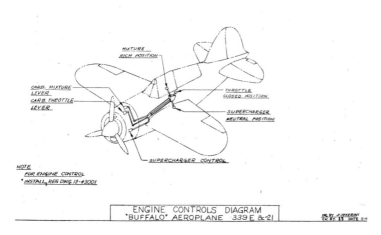

MIXTURE
RICH POSITION

CARB. MIXTURE
LEVER
CARB. THROTTLE
LEVER

THROTTLE
CLOSED POSITION

SUPERCHARGER
NEUTRAL POSITION

SUPERCHARGER CONTROL

NOTE
FOR ENGINE CONTROL
* INSTALL REF DWG. 13-43001

ENGINE CONTROLS DIAGRAM
"BUFFALO" AEROPLANE 339 E & -21

DR. BY J. OFFERINI
CK. BY ___ DATE 11-4

PROPELLER CONTROLS

The propeller was controlled by an engine-mounted speed governor. The governor speed was set by a mechanical linkage running from a push-pull unit with a vernier adjustment on the left side of the main instrument panel. On the Hamilton propeller installation the governor controlled the flow of engine oil into the propeller hydraulic pitch change mechanism to adjust blade angle for the set constant speed. On the Curtiss propeller the governor was electric in operation but was set in the same manner as above. The electric propeller could be set by a cockpit switch eith increase or decrease RPM positions.

ENGINE STARTING SYSTEM

The starting system for Model 239 consisted of an Eclipse hand-cranked inertia starter with a built-in booster coil. The starter clutch and booster controls were mounted near the center of the instrument panel and were mechanically connected to the starter. The starter included an integrally-mounted crank extension shaft with a lubricated bearing which was replaceable. A stowage position for the hand crank was provided on the deflector plates forward of the wing spar.

On the Navy F2A-2 and F2A-3 types an Eclipse type II cartridge starter was provided. The breech was mounted on the lower right engine mount brace, and was accessible through the right wheel well opening. The operating switch was on the right side of the main instrument panel. A box for eight cartridges was located at the right side of the cockpit. A container for forty more cartridges was in the baggage compartment.

ENGINE WATER INJECTION SYSTEM

No such system was included.

ENGINE COOLING SYSTEM

The engine was cooled by ram air from the central cowl opening passing over the single row of nine radially arranged cylinders and exiting overboard at the aft edges of the cowl ring. The aft section of the cowl was louvered to permit circulation of air around the oil tank and engine accessories, and the cowling was designed to direct cooling air to the magnetos. On the British 339E airplanes cowl shutters were provided. The shutter control was a push-pull type located under the main instrument panel.

ENGINE LUBRICATION

The system was made up of an oil tank, an automatic oil temperature control valve, engine-mounted oil pump, oil cooling radiator, temperature and pressure gages, and aluminum oil feed lines and fittings. Vent and drain lines were also provided. The tank was equipped with a screened filter, a sounding rod, and a drain plug. It was of welded aluminum alloy with an eleven US gallon capacity plus allowance for three and one quarter gallons of expansion space, and was mounted just forward of the firewall on the engine mount. The temperature control valve with bypass was mounted on the bottom of this tank. The oil cooler was a nine inch diameter unit on the Model 239, eleven inches on the F2A-3, mounted on a cradle under the engine accessory compartment. An air scoop ran from the engine cowl leading edge directly to the front of the oil cooler. Exit air went overboard at the aft edge of the cowl. The oil cooler incorporated a drain plug. A dial on the left auxiliary instrument panel contained an oil pressure gage and an oil temperature gage along with fuel pressure indication. The temperature gage was connected to a sensor at the engine oil outlet.

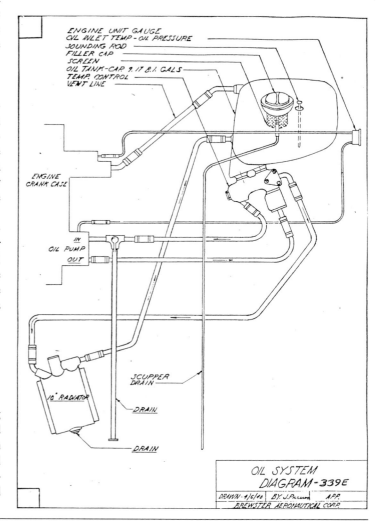

ENGINE UNIT GAUGE
OIL INLET TEMP - OIL PRESSURE
SOUNDING ROD
FILLER CAP
SCREEN
OIL TANK - CAP. 9.17 8.1 GALS.
TEMP. CONTROL
VENT LINE

ENGINE
CRANK CASE

IN
OIL PUMP
OUT

SCUPPER
DRAIN

10" RADIATOR

DRAIN

DRAIN

OIL SYSTEM
DIAGRAM - 339E

DRAWN - 4/6/40 | BY J. PICCININ | APP.
BREWSTER AERONAUTICAL CORP.

FIRE SENSING AND FIRE EXTINGUISHING SYSTEMS

No automatic fire sensing system was used.

A pressure fire extinguishing system was provided for the powerplant. A five pound carbon dioxide bottle was mounted at the right side of the fuselage interior between frames 96 and 108 behind the cockpit, and was accessible through the radio access door. The bottle was activated by pulling a cockpit handle at the top of the right auxiliary instrument panel. The handle was attached to a cable and pulley system running aft from the cockpit to the bottle valve. The bottle exhausted through a line running forward to the engine compartment where a nozzle and perforated ring ejected the carbon dioxide into the compartment. The discharge ring encircled the engine just aft of the cylinder row and the end of the tubing was attached to the carburetor intake duct. The cylinder and valve were considered special equipment not included in normal weight empty, but as an overload.

FUEL SYSTEM

In the Finnish Model 239 the fuel system consisted of two unprotected tanks built into the wing beam system between spars, a hand emergency pump with a built-in relief valve, an engine-driven pump with a bypass and relief valve, two hydrostatic fuel quantity gages with pumps and check valves, and a fuel shut-off valve. Each wing tank held 80 US gallons. The right tank outlet was located several inches above the bottom of the tank which left 25 gallons of reserve fuel available when the fuel selector valve was turned to reserve. The multiple-position selector valve was mounted below the tank with a remote control on the left side of the cockpit. The pilot could select right or left tank, the reserve, or shut off all tanks. The tanks could be drained using two drain cocks on the selector valve. A combination hand pump, relief valve, and strainer was mounted on the firewall below the wing. The hand pump lever was mounted on the left side of the cockpit. The fuel strainer was accessible through the wheel well. The fuel gages and pumps were mounted on the right side instrument panel. Tank vent lines ran from the tanks inside the fuselage to the top and then aft to a tee and down to outside the fuselage. Flapper valves were located in the lines. Fuel lines were aluminum alloy tubes connected with Duprene hose where flexible joints were needed.

The fuel tanks were filled at the leading edge of the wing just inboard of the outer landing gear strut attach point. In the F2A-2 and F2A-3 airplanes for the US Navy additional fuel tankage was included, and three additional tanks were provided with leakproof rubber fuel cells, while the two original 80 US gallon unprotected (and apparently almost unprotectable) inboard tanks were retained, but with a carbon dioxide purging system to blanket them against fire. A new tank of 20 US gallon capacity was built into the inboard leading edge section of each wing, and a new single 40 US gallon tank was mounted in the bottom of the fuselage forward of the pilot. This was a tank of oval section matched to the inner contour of the forward end of the fuselage monocoque section. The total fuel capacity of these USN versions was thus 240 US gallons. The three

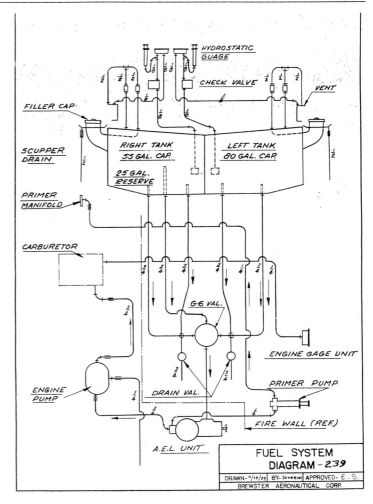

new protected tanks were filled through hinged access plates at the forward top surface of the wing at station 162 each side. The new fuselage tank was filled via a hinged access plate on the fuselage right side just aft of the sliding canopy.

The left wing unprotected fuel tank was to be used for operations only in the overload fighter condition, and the filler neck cover plate was sealed off with the legend stenciled on: "Not to be filled except on special authority of Commanding Officer."

A five-way fuel selector valve was mounted on the forward face of the firewall, controlled from the left side of the cockpit. Pressure regulators, one for protected and one for unprotected tanks, were used to provide pressure over the fuel. Vented to outside under 16000 feet altitude, they closed the vents at 18000 feet and built up pressure over the fuel by admitting manifold pressure from the engine.

On the British 339E version the fuel tanks in the main wing beam were protected by armor plate on the forward face of the beam, and by a covering of Linatex and horsehide leather on all sides of the tank so as to provide self sealing in case of puncture.

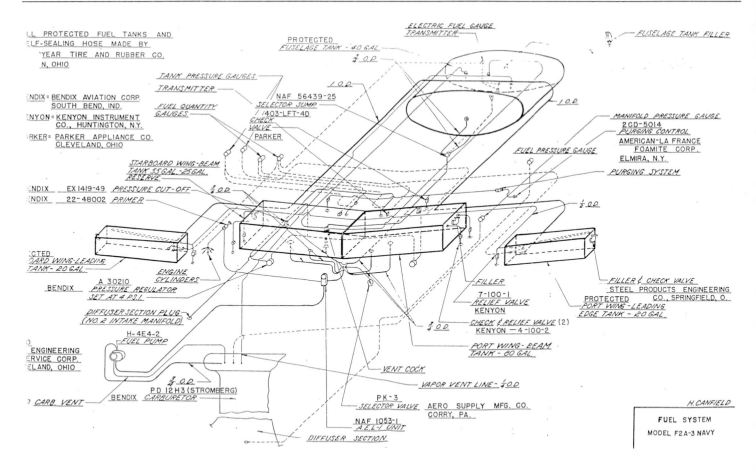

LL PROTECTED FUEL TANKS AND
ELF-SEALING HOSE MADE BY
YEAR TIRE AND RUBBER CO.
N, OHIO

NDIX = BENDIX AVIATION CORP.
SOUTH BEND, IND.
NYON = KENYON INSTRUMENT
CO., HUNTINGTON, N.Y.
RKER = PARKER APPLIANCE CO.
CLEVELAND, OHIO

ELECTRIC FUEL GAUGE
TRANSMITTER

FUSELAGE TANK FILLER

PROTECTED
FUSELAGE TANK - 40 GAL.

TANK PRESSURE GAUGES
TRANSMITTER

NAF 56439-25
SELECTOR SUMP
1403-LFT-4D
CHECK
VALVE
PARKER

FUEL QUANTITY
GAUGES

MANIFOLD PRESSURE GAUGE
2 GD-5014
PURGING CONTROL
AMERICAN-LA FRANCE
FOAMITE CORP.
ELMIRA, N.Y.

FUEL PRESSURE GAUGE

PURGING SYSTEM

STARBOARD WING-BEAM
TANK 55 GAL. - 25 GAL.
RESERVE

NDIX   EX 1419-49   PRESSURE CUT-OFF
NDIX   22-48002   PRIMER

CTED
DARD WING-LEADING
TANK- 20 GAL.

ENGINE
CYLINDERS

A 30210
BENDIX   PRESSURE REGULATOR
SET AT 4 P.S.I.

DIFFUSER SECTION PLUG
(NO. 2 INTAKE MANIFOLD)

FILLER

7-100-1
RELIEF VALVE
KENYON

FILLER & CHECK VALVE
STEEL PRODUCTS ENGINEERING
PROTECTED   CO., SPRINGFIELD, O.
PORT WING-LEADING
EDGE TANK - 20 GAL.

CHECK & RELIEF VALVE (2)
KENYON — 4-100-2

PORT WING-BEAM
TANK - 80 GAL.

H-4E4-2
FUEL PUMP

ENGINEERING
ERVICE CORP.
LAND, OHIO

VENT COCK

VAPOR VENT LINE - 4 O.D.

PD 12H3 (STROMBERG)
BENDIX   CARBURETOR

CARB. VENT

PK-3
SELECTOR VALVE   AERO SUPPLY MFG. CO.
CORRY, PA.

NAF 1053-1
A.E.L-1 UNIT

DIFFUSER SECTION

H. CANFIELD

FUEL SYSTEM
MODEL F2A-3 NAVY

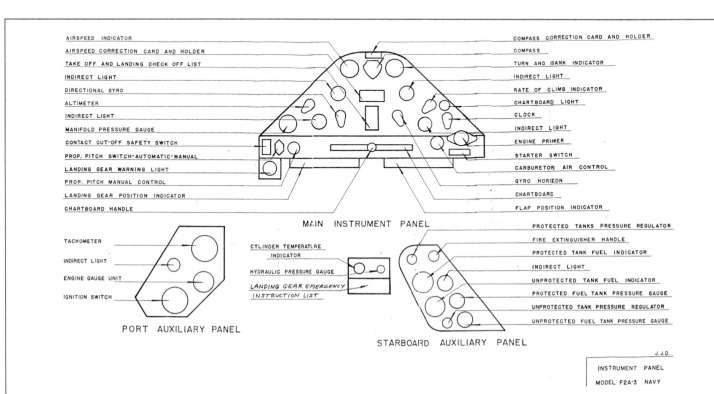

AIRSPEED INDICATOR
AIRSPEED CORRECTION CARD AND HOLDER
TAKE OFF AND LANDING CHECK OFF LIST
INDIRECT LIGHT
DIRECTIONAL GYRO
ALTIMETER
INDIRECT LIGHT
MANIFOLD PRESSURE GAUGE
CONTACT CUT-OFF SAFETY SWITCH
PROP. PITCH SWITCH-AUTOMATIC-MANUAL
LANDING GEAR WARNING LIGHT
PROP. PITCH MANUAL CONTROL
LANDING GEAR POSITION INDICATOR
CHARTBOARD HANDLE

COMPASS CORRECTION CARD AND HOLDER
COMPASS
TURN AND BANK INDICATOR
INDIRECT LIGHT
RATE OF CLIMB INDICATOR
CHARTBOARD LIGHT
CLOCK
INDIRECT LIGHT
ENGINE PRIMER
STARTER SWITCH
CARBURETOR AIR CONTROL
GYRO HORIZON
CHARTBOARD
FLAP POSITION INDICATOR

MAIN INSTRUMENT PANEL

TACHOMETER
INDIRECT LIGHT
ENGINE GAUGE UNIT
IGNITION SWITCH

CYLINDER TEMPERATURE
INDICATOR
HYDRAULIC PRESSURE GAUGE
LANDING GEAR EMERGENCY
INSTRUCTION LIST

PROTECTED TANKS PRESSURE REGULATOR
FIRE EXTINGUISHER HANDLE
PROTECTED TANK FUEL INDICATOR
INDIRECT LIGHT
UNPROTECTED TANK FUEL INDICATOR
PROTECTED FUEL TANK PRESSURE GAUGE
UNPROTECTED TANK PRESSURE REGULATOR
UNPROTECTED FUEL TANK PRESSURE GAUGE

PORT AUXILIARY PANEL

STARBOARD AUXILIARY PANEL

J.J.D.

INSTRUMENT PANEL
MODEL F2A-3 NAVY

FIXED EQUIPMENT SUBSYSTEMS

INSTRUMENTS

Flight instruments included: Artificial horizon, directional gyro, airspeed indicator, altimeter, clock, compass, turn and bank indicator, rate of climb indicator, and radio compass. Engine instruments included: Manifold pressure gage, tachometer, engine gage unit, carburetor air temperature indicator, fuel quantity gages, and engine cylinder temperature gage. Other instruments were: hydraulic pressure gage.

SURFACE CONTROLS

Surface controls were of the conventional stick and pedal type. The rudder was connected to the pedals using extra-flexible cables and pulleys. Pedal position was adjustable. Stops to limit rudder movement were located on the cables below and aft of the pilot's seat. Two cables ran aft over pulleys in the rear fuselage to arms on the lower end of the rudder torque tube. The elevators were linked to the stick with a push-pull tube system. Motion stops were provided on the stick torque tube in the cockpit. The elevator push-pull tube system was in two sections connected by a fuselage-mounted swing link. The aft tube drove an arm on the elevator torque tube on the fuselage centerline. The ailerons were operated by a torque tube with arms driving independent push-pull and swing-link sections

running outboard from the stick to each aileron. A differential movement of ailerons was incorporated giving a movement of 26 degrees up and 15 down. Aileron stops were provided on the stick torque tube on the fuselage centerline.

Trim tabs for the rudder, the two elevators, and the left aileron were adjustable from wheel controls on the left side cockpit shelf. The rudder tab drive started as a chain which connected to a cable and pulley system. The cable drove a drum mounted to the fin which in turn drove a shaft with a universal at the hinge line. The shaft was part of a screw jack acting on the tab arm to provide desired motion. The drive for the elevator tabs was similar, but added a right-angle bevel gearbox in the horizontal stabilizer. The aileron tab control started as a chain around the control sprocket which drove shafting, more chain, and a right-angle gearbox to a screw jack acting on the tab arm.

ELECTRICAL SYSTEM

The electrical system was a single wire airframe ground return type except in the vicinity of the compass where twisted pairs were used. It was provided with an engine-driven generator and a storage battery. The battery was enclosed in an aluminum alloy container on the left side of the aircraft just inside the radio access door.

Items powered by the electrical system included the engine magnetos, wingtip and tailcone running lights, a retractable landing light on the lower left wing, cockpit lights, and machine gun controls.

The British 339E model had two retractable landing lights, one on the undersurface of each wing. They could be raised and lowered individually and were controlled by two cockpit switches. They were not to be lowered over 140 mph IAS.

HYDRAULIC SYSTEM

A hydraulic system was provided for main and tail landing gear retraction and for operation of the wing flaps. The major components of the system were a tank with a vent, filter, drain plug, and fill and return line connections, a Pesco engine-driven hydraulic pump, relief valve, pressure gage in the cockpit, landing gear and flap control valve with levers in the cockpit, bypass valve, hand

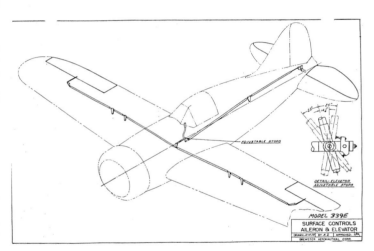

MODEL 339E
SURFACE CONTROLS
AILERON & ELEVATOR

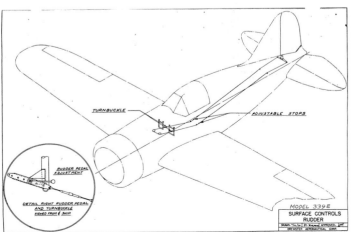

MODEL 339E
SURFACE CONTROLS
RUDDER

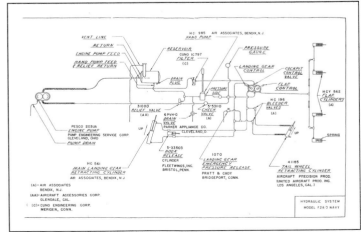

HYDRAULIC SYSTEM
MODEL F2A-3 NAVY

pump, and system actuating cylinders. The main landing gear was retracted by a double-acting cylinder on the aircraft centerline forward which was connected to the inboard landing gear struts by two lift struts. The tail wheel was retracted by a double-acting cylinder that broke the tail wheel oleo strut. A small oleo cylinder on the firewall disengaged the main gear uplock hooks. A landing gear operating lever was located in the cockpit to retract and extend the gear. An emergency release bypass valve wheel in the cockpit operated together with an emergency manual release handle and emergency downlock handle could be used for a last-ditch lowering of the landing gear by releasing hydraulic pressure from the gear actuating cylinders.

The wing flaps were operated by two single-acting cylinders in each wing with a spring return of the actuator piston. The cockpit flap actuator lever was operated to allow hydraulic pressure into one side of the cylinders to lower the flaps. The springs in the other side aided outside air pressure in retracting the flaps when hydraulic pressure was relieved. Normal operation of the system was obtained using the engine-driven hydraulic pump. If that pump failed the emergency hand pump in the cockpit could be used by the pilot. A landing gear position indicator was placed below the main instrument panel, and a flap position indicator was also included. An emergency release bypass valve wheel in the cockpit operated together with an emergency manual release handle and emergency downlock handle could be used for a last-ditch lowering of the landing gear by releasing hydraulic pressure from the gear actuating cylinder.

PNEUMATIC SYSTEM
A vacuum pump was driven by the engine to supply a vacuum to instruments as required.

COMMUNICATION, NAVIGATION, AND IDENTIFICATION SYSTEMS
In the export Model 239 provision was made for installation aft in the fuselage of a Westinghouse WE52B aircraft radio receiver and an RCA AVT-7B aircraft transmitter. The equipment was accessible through a door in the aft fuselage.

The radio for the British 339E model was a TR9D or TR1133A transmitter-receiver as well as an R3003 radio. All were located aft of the baggage compartment.

On the USN F2A-3 airplanes provision was made for installation on shelves in the aft fuselage of a Model GF8 radio set which consisted of a transmitter, receiver, homing loop, fixed antenna, junction, control, and switch boxes, and a dynamotor. Controls were located at the right side of the cockpit.

ARMAMENT PROVISIONS
The armament installation of the Finnish Model 239 consisted of one fixed .50 caliber Browning M-2 synchronized machine gun installed forward on the right top side of the fuselage with 200 rounds of ammunition, one fixed synchronized .30 caliber Browning M-2 machine gun forward on the upper left side of the fuselage with 600 rounds of ammunition, and two .50 caliber Browning machine guns, one in each wing outside the propeller arc, with a total of 400

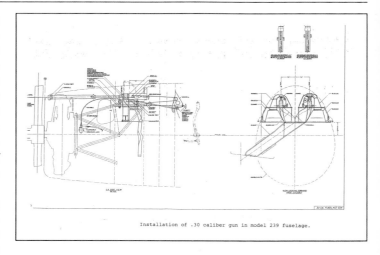
Installation of .30 caliber gun in model 239 fuselage.

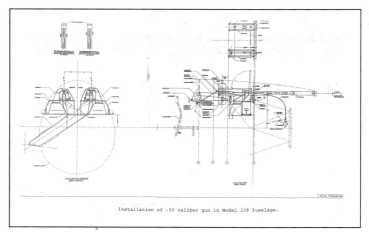
Installation of .50 caliber gun in Model 239 fuselage.

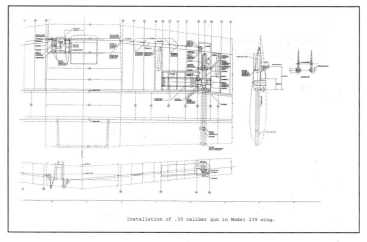
Installation of .50 caliber gun in Model 239 wing.

rounds of ammunition. The fuselage guns were synchronized with propeller rotation using an impulse generator system to control the gun firing solonoids with impulse cables leading back from the engine to the guns. Electric trigger motors were employed. Guns were mounted on the airframe using forward trunnion fittings and rear mounting posts with boresighting graduations. Ammunition boxes were mounted adjacent to the guns and ejector chutes were led through the fuselage to dump casings overboard at the wing

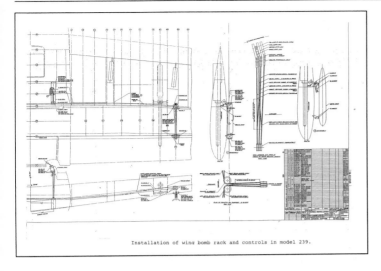

Installation of wing bomb rack and controls in model 239.

root areas. Links were discharged into metal containers. Rounds counters were provided in the cockpit. Gun charging handles were located high and forward in the cockpit and operated the weapons via cable and pulley systems running to the guns. Doors and removeable panels provided access to the fuselage gun installation. The wing .50 caliber guns were located at wing station 84 with breeches behind the rear spar and ahead of the flap. The gun barrels poked through the two wing beams to the leading edge. Fairings were provided over the slightly protruding rear sections of the guns. Ammunition was contained in trays inboard of the guns just behind the rear spar. Access doors were provided over trays and guns. The weapons were supported by the rear spar and reinforced ribs on each side. Ejection chutes for cases were located just outboard of the guns and led to the wing lower surface from which the cases were ejected. The wing guns were fired electrically through trigger motors; guns were charged mechanically. Gun charge tee-handles were over a pedestal located to the right of the seat, and were connected to cables running out to the guns via the aft section of the wing. An electric gun trigger switch was mounted on the pilot's control stick for all guns. A C-4 ring and bead gunsight was installed on Mark III sight mounting brackets on aircraft centerline forward of the windshield. The bomb sight was mounted in the windshield using a grommet. A bomb rack could be mounted under each wing at station 94 with structural attachments to the spars. The capacity of each rack was 116 pounds. Bombs were released using a mechanical system of cables and pulleys running outboard to the racks just aft of the rear spar and controlled by a release lever forward on the left side of the cockpit within reach of the pilot with his eye at the sight. On the 239 provision was made for mounting a gun camera externally on the right side of the fuselage just forward of the wing leading edge position mounted on tubular supports. A similar installation could be made on other versions. The gun camera was electrically controlled.

The armament on the US Navy F2A-2 and F2A-3 was similar to that of the 239 except that both synchronized fuselage guns were .50 caliber M-2 models with a total round capacity of 500. The F2A-2 .50 caliber gun installation with 200 rounds in each wing

was the same as the 239; however, the F2A-3 installation doubled the ammunition capacity to 400 rounds per gun.

On the USN airplanes a telescopic sight was located on the aircraft centerline. The front mounting hole for support was just forward of the windshield with the rear mount on top of the main instrument panel. A hole, plugged with a transparent cover plate when the sight was not used, was provided in the forward windshield panel for the telescope tube.

On the F2A-3 airplanes the wing guns were jacketed, and hot air could be furnished to the jackets.

The British 339E airplanes also used two .50 caliber cowl guns and two .50 caliber wing guns.

PASSIVE DEFENSE SYSTEM
No armor or self-sealing fuel tanks were mounted in the Model 239 airplanes. One of the disadvantages noted by Finland in operating the 239 was the lack of an armor-plated seat back for the pilot.

The US Navy F2A-2 airplanes were retrofitted with armor, and the F2A-3 models were fitted up as follows: Two pieces of 3/8 inch thick armor plate were located just forward of and above the oil tank to protect the pilot from forward fire, and five pieces of 3/8 inch thick armor plate was placed just aft of the oil tank. The two bottom pieces were hinged on their top sides so they could be lifted for fuselage gun removal, and were latched in position with a lock pin. Two pieces of 5/16 inch thick armor were placed aft of the pilot's seat. One piece covered the seat back and the other was in back of the pilot's head. The two pieces were hinged together so the upper one could be swung down to give access to the life raft. The moveable upper piece was latched or unlatched from its position by a slider. A one and one half inch thick bullet proof windshield panel was mounted aft of the 1/4 inch thick laminated glass windshield. This panel was perforated for the gun sight.

On the 339E British model the pilot was protected by two sheets of armor plate forward and another sheet of armor plate aft of the seat. In addition the sides of the fuselage between stations 39 and 47 had armor plate protection. A one and one half inch thick armor glass windshield was provided. Fuel and oil tanks were protected by being sealed with Lenotex and horsehide leather.

FURNISHINGS
The pilot's seat was the metal bucket type with provision for five and 5/8 inches minimum vertical adjustment. Seat height could be adjusted by pulling back on a lever at the right side of the seat. The seat of the British 339E Buffalo I was constructed to take an English-type Mark V-S parachute with safety shoulder harness. A seat belt was included on the 239. A pilot relief tube was provided near the seat. A small flat stowage locker was provided in the cockpit along with a map case. A baggage compartment was located in the aft fuselage. Provision was also made for a one quart carbon tetrachloride hand fire extinguisher for use during engine starts. On the F2A-3 airplane a chart board was provided under the main instrument panel and a map case was installed on the left side of the cockpit.

HEATING/COOLING/VENTILATING SYSTEMS
On the Model 239 a cockpit ventilator was provided with a control to direct fresh air flow to the pilot's face. On the British 339E ventilation was provided via fixed louvres just under and aft of the pilot.

On the US Navy F2A-3 airplane heated air, obtained from a manifold muff, was supplied to the space between the regular windshield and the bullet-proof windshield. The cockpit was not heated directly, but the warm air, after passing over the windshield, was exhausted to the cockpit. The control was located at the forward right side of the cockpit. The British version was similar; warm air taken from the muff around the engine exhaust manifold could be supplied to the cockpit, the windshield, the wing guns, or shut off completely using a four-way cockpit control.

CARBON DIOXIDE SYSTEM
On the export Model 239 for the Finns the only system was that for engine fire extinguishing as described earlier.

On the F2A-3 USN airplanes carbon dioxide was used in the airplane fire extinguishing system (an overload item), and was also used as a fire suppressant over the unprotected wing beam fuel tanks. The carbon dioxide bottle for this purpose was located on the left side of the airplane aft of and below the pilot's seat. The control was mounted on a bracket on the left side of the cockpit. One pound of carbon dioxide was provided for each 9.1 cubic feet of fuel tank space. A safety blow-off for the bottle led to a discharge port on the left side of the fuselage.

ICE PROTECTION SYSTEM
An alternate warm air source was provided for the carburetor intake as noted earlier. No other ice protection system was installed on the 239.

On USN airplanes as previously noted the windshield was heated by hot air.

HOISTING/TOWING/LEVELING/TIEDOWN EQUIPMENT
Jack pads were provided at the inboard side of the main landing gear oleo struts to lift the airplane. Jack points were also provided at the outboard landing gear strut fittings so the airplane could be supported when the entire landing gear was removed.

The hoisting sling was of the single pendant type and was folded into the top of the fuselage forward of the windshield. It was reached through a door in the top of the fuselage cowling.

A cable could be attached to the lower ends of the inboard landing gear struts for towing.

Tiedown fittings were provided in the forward wing beam shear web near the tip. A bar through the rear lift tube could be used to secure the tail. A ring was provided in the tail wheel assembly for tiedown. Controls could be held in neutral by a parking harness.

For airplane handling, strong points, painted black, were provided on each wingtip. A hand grip was provided on each side of the fuselage near the edge of the cockpit.

The aircraft could be leveled laterally by placing a spirit level on a straight edge across the leveling buttons provided on the two top longerons with the canopy open. Longitudinal leveling could be accomplished by placing the level on the two buttons provided on the left hand longeron.

FLOTATION GEAR
Flotation was provided by watertight compartments in the wing beam between forward and aft spars and in the leading and trailing edge sections of the wing. The compartments were vented to atmosphere inside the fuselage. In the US Navy airplanes a life raft was housed on the deck just aft of the cockpit seat in a cylindrical phenolic tube container.

ARRESTING/CATAPULT GEAR
The Model 239 export version for Finland carried no arrestor or catapult gear, nor did the British or Dutch landplane versions.

The arresting gear for the carrier-based USN F2A-3 airplane was a retractable hook unit located at the extreme tail end of the fuselage. Support was provided by a heavy mounting brace structure tied to fittings on the rearmost bulkhead. The fittings were tied in to the ends of the fuselage longerons at the bulkhead. The mounting structure was covered by a removeable streamlined tailcone with a hole in the end for the hook. The hook retrieving mechanism consisted of a carriage to which the inboard end of the hook was fastened and a grooved retrieving drum around which flexible steel cable was wrapped. The cable ends were fastened to the carriage to form a continuous circuit. The hook had a standard "niblick" point and an integral self-centering cam and roller device at its upper end. An oleo strut with a spring cut down on hook bounce tendencies during carrier landings. Turnbuckles regulated cable tension.

ARRESTING HOOK
RETRACTED
MODEL F2A-3 NAVY

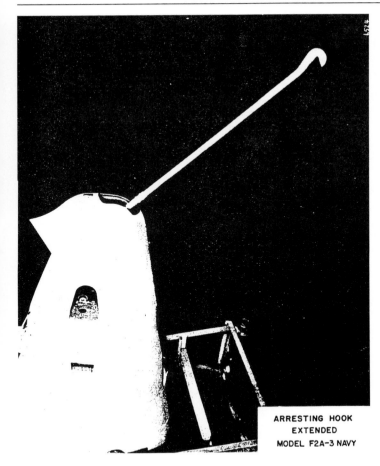

ARRESTING HOOK
EXTENDED
MODEL F2A-3 NAVY

The cables ran through the aft fuselage. The retrieving drum was located at the left side of the cockpit. The hook was extended by pressing a thumb button in the handle, and the handle was rotated about three times to get the hook locked down.

A barrier crash guide was provided on the forward face of each main landing gear strut.

The F2A-3 airplane was designed for land catapulting. It was provided with a single hook on centerline just forward of the main landing gear wheel wells. The hook was bolted on and could be removed. A bridle length of 75 inches hook to hook was used. A hold-back ring was provided on the tail assembly.

USEFUL LOAD SUBSYSTEMS
GUNS/BOMBS/ROCKETS
See the previous armament section. No rockets were carried.

GUNSIGHT/GUN CAMERA
See the earlier armament section. The British 339E model had a gun camera installed in the left wing leading edge outboard of the gear strut controlled by cockpit switch and gun button.

PYROTECHNICS
A Very pistol installation was located in the cockpit, including pistol, 12 cartridge containers, bracket, and firing tube out to the fuselage skin. In addition, on the F2A-2 and F2A-3 USN airplanes two smoke grenades were carried in a left side stowage compartment just aft of the pilot's seat. A smoke grenade handle was mounted on the deck aft of the cockpit.

PHOTOGRAPHIC EQUIPMENT
Except for a gun camera on some models there was no photographic gear.

OXYGEN SYSTEM
Provision was made for mounting an oxygen cylinder at the right side of the fuselage aft of the seat. A bracket was also provided for the installation of an oxygen regulator on the left side in the cockpit. Piping was run from the cylinder to the regulator. On the British Buffalo I two oxygen bottles were mounted in a wire mesh enclosure to prevent scattering of bottle fragments if struck. They were located behind the pilot and within reach. An oxygen regulator was included.

REFERENCES, F2A-/239/339
1. *Journal of the American Aviation Historical Society*, Summer,1985
2. *JAAHS*, Fall 1969,
3. NACA Report ACR, Oct.1940.
4. NACA Report ACR 3I30,Sept.1943, *Calculated and Measured Turning Performance of a Navy F2A-3 Airplane.*
5. *The First Team*, John B. Lindstrom, Naval Institute Press, Annapolis, Md.
6. John J. Schneider Archives, weights.
7. Data Sheet, *Finland's Experiences With Brewster Airplanes.*
8. *Duels in the Sky*, Capt. Eric M. Brown, RN, Naval Institute Press Annapolis, Md.
9. Washington DC Navy Yard Aerodynamical Laboratory Report 559, Oct.19, 1937, *Air Force and Moment for XF2A-1 Airplane Model.*
10. *Erection and Maintenance Instructions for Model F2A-3 Airplane*, Navy BuAer Report 512.
11. Brewster Aeronautical Corp. Report 353, Dec.26,1939, *Pilot's Handbook for Model 239 Airplane.*
12. *Fighter Weight and Performance Comparison*, AN-58973, Dec.11, 1941.
13. JAAHS, March 1983, *Brewster Aeronautical Corp. Production*, Jim Maas.
14. *Brewster Aircraft Model Numbers*, Engineering Manual, Brewster Aeronautical Corp.
15. *Brewster Airplane Characteristics Sheets*, Revised May 13, 1941, Brewster Aeronautical Corp.
16. Brewster Aeronautical Corp. Report 350, Dec.15,1939, *Detail Specification for Model 239 Airplane.*
17. Patent 2,222,975, *Retractable Landing Gear*, Applied Feb.24,1938; Patented Nov.26,1940, Dayton T. Brown, assignor to Brewster Aeronautical Corp.
18. *Erection and Maintenance Instructions for Model 239 Airplane*, Brewster Aeronautical Corp. Report 350, Dec.26, 1939.
19. Interview of Lt.Cdr. John Thatch, USN, at BuAer on Aug.26, 1942.
20. Excerpts from Conversation with Gordon Firebaugh, VF-2 NAP, later Capt,USN, Jan.17,1983.
21. *Final Report of Production Inspection Trials on Model F2A-3 Airplanes* Oct.22, 1941 to Jan.29, 1942.
22. Letter, Henry Miller, Rear Adm. (Ret.) to Jim Maas, Jan.22, 1982.
23. Air Publication 1806A, Vol.I, Pilot's Notes, *The Buffalo I Airplane*, Wright GR-1820-G105A Engine, Contract A-71, Dec.3, 1940.
24. Aeroplane and Armament Experimental Establishment, Boscombe Down, *Brewster 339B, Night Flying trials and Gunnery Trials*, 1941.
25. RAF Station Church Fenton, Oct.28,1940, *Brewster Aircraft* (Evaluation).
26. Air Classics Magazine, July,1967, *Requiem For a Pint-Size Pioneer*, Brewster F2A- Buffalo, by Anson McCullough.
27. Airpower Magazine, March,1972, *Farewell to the Fleet's Forgotten Fighter*, Brewster F2A-, by Joe Mizrahi. (Text the same as Item 26. above).
28. *The US Marine Corps in World War II*, Compiled and Edited by S.E. Smith, Random House, NY,1969.
29. *Bloody Shambles*, Christopher Shores and Brian Cull with Yasuho Izawa, Grub Street, London, 1992.

THE F4F-

TABLE 74
GRUMMAN F4F- WILDCAT MODELS

CO.MODEL	MIL.DESIG.	EXPORT DESIG.	NO.OF A/C	FIRST DEL.	NOTES
	XF4F-2	—	1	F.F.SEP.'37	SINGLE STAGE SUPERC.
	XF4F-3	—	(1 CONV.)	F.F.NOV.'39	NEW WG. 2-STAGE SUP.
	F4F-3	—	285	AUG.'40	FIXED WG. F.F.FEB.'40
	F4F-3A	—	65	(ALL BY 12/41)	MOST TO USMC.
G-36A	—	MARTLET I	81	JUL.27,'40	R-1820, 1-STAGE SUPER.
G-36B	—	MARTLET II	100	MAR.'41	R-1830;LAST 90 W.FOLD.
	—	MARTLET III	30	MAR.18'41	GREECE, THEN UK
	XF4F-4	—	1	MAY '41	POWER-FOLDING WINGS
	F4F-4	—	1169	DEC.'41	MANUAL WING FOLD
	XF4F-5	—	2	JUL.'40	-3 W. R-1820 SUPERCH.
	XF4F-6	—	1	NOV.'40	ENGINE TEST BED
	F4F-7	—	21	JAN.'42	LONG RANGE PHOTO A/C
	F4F-4B	MARTLET IV	220	JUL.15,42	R-1820 ENG.1-ST.2-SP.
	—	MARTLET V	311	DEC.'42	AS EASTERN FM-1
	XF4F-8	—	2	DEC.'42	GRUM.PROTO.FOR FM-2
	FM-1		839	F.F.AUG.31'42	EASTERN 4-GUN F4F-4
	FM-2		4437	SEP.'43	R-1820; ESC.CARRIERS
	—	WILDCAT VI	340	1944	BRITISH VERSION FM-2
			TOTAL 7905		(1978 GRUMMAN; 5927 EASTERN)

ACCEPTANCES BY YEAR

	1939	1940	1941	1942	1943	1944	1945	TOTAL
GRUMMAN	1	106	324	1447	100	0	0	1978
EASTERN	0	0	0	23	1437	3130	1337	5927
TOTAL YEARLY	1	106	324	1470	1537	3130	1337	7905

NOTES ON WILDCAT DISTRIBUTIONS
The original order was for 185 F4F-3 aircraft; 100 additional were ordered as trainers early in 1943.
50 Martlet II aircraft were delivered in the fall of 1941; 36 0f these went to the UK, the others to the Far East.
An F4F-4A aircraft with a single stage supercharged R-1830-90 engine was planned, but was never built.
A twin-float seaplane version, the F4F-3S, first flew on February 29, 1943, but no more were built.

TABLE 75
F4F- PHYSICAL DATA

WING SPAN	38'0"	FLAP SPAN (EACH)	119.63"
WING SPAN, FOLDED (F4F-4)	14'6"	FLAP AVG.CHORD, AFT H/L	21.38"
OVERALL LENGTH	28'9.38"	MAXIMUM FLAP DEFLECTION	43 DEG.
HEIGHT, LEVEL THRUST LINE	11'10.38"	AILERON TRAVEL (F4F-3)	19DEG.UP;15DN.
HORIZONTAL TAIL SPAN	13'8"	AILERON TRAVEL (F4F-4)	17DEG.UP;13DN.
PROPELLER DIAMETER	9'9"OR 10'0"	AILERON TAB TRAVEL(L.)	20DEG.UP;20DN.
PROP.STATIC GROUND CLEAR.	8.75"	TAIL SURFACE AIRFOILS	SYMMETRICAL
WHEEL TREAD	6'4.97"	HORIZ.STABILIZER INCIDENCE	+1.5 DEG.
WING AREA, GROSS	260 SQ.FT.	TOT.PROJ.HORIZ.TAIL AREA	49.05SQ.FT.
WING ROOT CHORD (AT C/L)	103.081"	TOT.HORIZ.STAB.AREA (INCL.1.81 FUS.	
WING ROOT CHORD (30"OUT)	97.629"	AREA & 4.96 BAL.AREA)	30.43SQ.FT.
WING TIP CHORD	61.437-61.64"	TOT.ELEV.AREA,AFT H/L	18.62SQ.FT.
WING MEAN AERO.CHORD	84.14"	HORIZ. TAIL CHORD,MAX.	60.91"
MAC,AFT LE.@ ROOT CHORD	3.33"	ELEV.CHORD, AFT HG.LINE	22.06"
MAC,ABOVE THRUST C/L	9.52"	ELEVATOR TRAVEL	26DEG.UP;20DN.
WING INCIDENCE	0 DEG.	ELEVATOR TAB TRAVEL	6DEG.UP;11DN.
WING DIHEDRAL,MEAN LINE	4DEG.54MIN.	TOT.PROJ. VERT.TAIL AREA	22.58SQ.FT.
WING DIHEDRAL,UPPER SUR.	3DEG.30MIN.	FIN AREA,INCL.RUDDER BAL.	13.2 SQ.FT.
WING DIHEDRAL,LOWER SUR.	6DEG.17MIN.	RUDDER AREA,AFT HG.LN.	9.38SQ.FT.
WING AIRFOIL, ROOT	NACA 23015	RUDDER MAX. CHORD	23.625"
WING ROOT THICKNESS RATIO	15%	RUDDER HT.,T/L TO TOP	6'2.875"
WING AIRFOIL, TIP	NACA 23009	RUDDER TRAVEL (F4F-3)	27DEG.R.27L
WING TIP THICKNESS RATIO	9% .	RUDDER TRAVEL (F4F-4)	31DEG.R.31L.
WING ASPECT RATIO	5.56	RUDDER TAB TRAVEL	22.32DEG.L.16.43R.
TOTAL AILERON AREA	13.26 SQ.FT.	MAIN WHEEL TIRES	26x8 HEAVY DTY.
TOTAL FLAP AREA (2)	27.70 SQ.FT.	TOTAL OLEO DEFLECTION	12.5"
AILERON SPAN, EACH	60.062"	TAIL WHEEL TIRE SIZE	6x2.50
AILERON MEAN CHORD	15.9"		

TABLE 76
F4F- FUEL CAPACITIES (GALLONS)

MODEL	MAXIMUM INTERNAL		MAXIMUM EXTERNAL
F4F-3/F4F-3A (Unprotected Tanks)	160		—
F4F-3/F4F-3A (Protected Tanks)	147		—
F4F-4/FM-1	144		116
F4F-7	685*		—
FM-2 (Early)	117	(With liner)	116
	130	(No tank liner)	
FM-2 (No.2401 and Subsequent)	126		116

* 555 Gallons of which was in a "wet" wing.

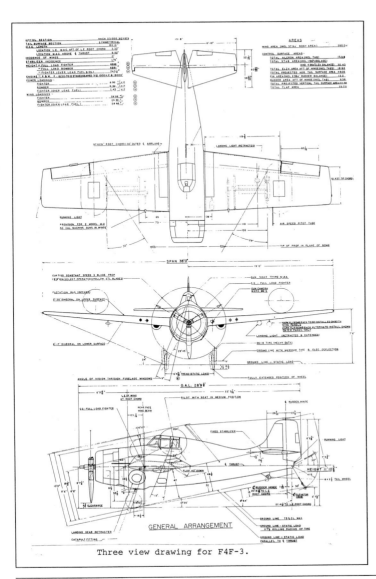

Three view drawing for F4F-3.

Wildcat fighter variants from both Grumman and Eastern Division of General Motors, and numbers built of each, are itemized in Table 74. Notes on the distribution of Wildcats are also given in this table.

Perusal of first delivery dates shows production deliveries of the British Martlet version started about the same time as those to the US Navy. Wildcat and Martlet airplanes constituted almost eight percent of America's Hundred Thousand. Close to 1100 of the total went to the UK. About 75 percent of all Wildcats were built by Eastern, with the large majority of these being the final FM-2 model used on small escort carriers. One of the more interesting aspects of Wildcat orders is noted in Table 74 where 100 F4F-3 fixed wing versions were ordered late as fighter trainers.

Table 75 provides physical data for the Wildcat where it is seen how much wing folding reduced airplane width for easier stowage and handling aboard carriers.

Fuel capacities of various Wildcats are itemized in Table 76. The early pre-war Wildcats had no fuel tank protection and carried 160 gallons in the fuselage tanks. With advent of war protection for fuel tanks was hurriedly installed, and capacity was thereby reduced to 147 gallons for fixed wing F4F-3 airplanes. The fuel quantity situation worsened slightly in the folding wing F4F-4 models with fuselage tank capacity dropping to 144 protected gallons, and Eastern FM-1 airplanes were similar. The only airplane with an increase in fuel was the wet wing F4F-7 photo reconnaissance type with the tremendous capacity of 685 gallons. The Eastern FM-2 Wildcat had even less fuel than earlier versions; with a protected tank arrangement the internal capacity went down to 117 gallons. A new tank design upped this figure to 126 gallons. From the F4F-4 on, however, two 58 gallon drop tanks, one under each wing inboard, were part of the Wildcat repetoire.

Two three view general arrangement drawings of Wildcats are depicted. The F4F-3 and F4F-4 are shown; the later FM-2 was distinguished chiefly by a somewhat taller vertical tail and a larger diameter cowl. The Wildcat was a chubby mid-wing monoplane with a radial engine, squared-off wingtips, narrow tread landing gear, and a distinctly "Grumman" look, even though it was the company's first monoplane fighter.

An inboard profile drawing of the FM-2 is also laid out. The engine compartment ahead of the firewall contained the big nine cylinder radial Cyclone engine mounted on a steel tube framework, and engine accessories including water injection controls. The engine oil tank was mounted high in the compartment just ahead of the firewall, and below it sat a large water tank for the water injection system. Low within the compartment just aft of the engine and mounted sideways was a cylindrical oil cooler with air intake and exit ducting. In the lower portion of the compartment aft of the oil cooler space was provided for steel tube structure acting as support for the main landing gear retraction linkage, the linkage itself, and pockets for retracted main wheels. Wing primary structural loads from forward and aft spars were carried through the fuselage using major bulkheads, the firewall forward and cockpit closing bulkhead aft. The upper section of the bay aft of the firewall contained the cockpit with pilot's seat, controls, and indicators; just below in a deep-bellied fuselage was the single fuel tank. This was a change

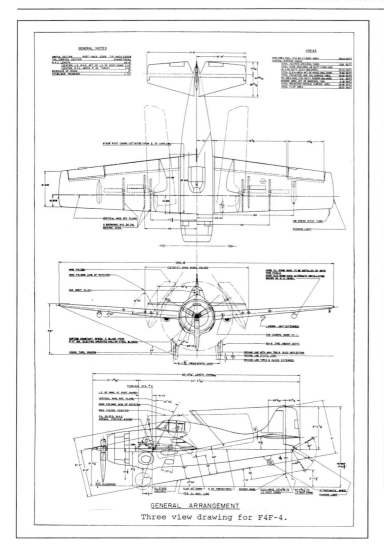

GENERAL ARRANGEMENT
Three view drawing for F4F-4.

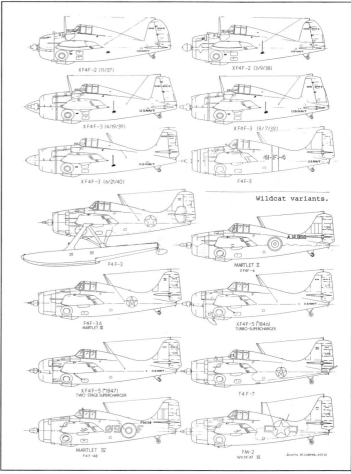

Wildcat variants.

Wilcat Variants

from the F4F-4 which had a large tank with a small tank just aft; the FM-2 omitted the small tank. The fuselage aft of the cockpit contained an oxygen bottle. Another item used on earlier Wildcats was a life raft stowed in the turtledeck area just aft of the cockpit, but this was done away with on the late models. An item unique to the Wildcat type, the large vacuum tank for a pneumatic wing flap operating system, sat high in a bay aft of the cockpit. Other items in the rear fuselage were radio and electrical system components, including the battery, and flight control runs from cockpit to tail surfaces. A fixed tail wheel assembly with shock strut and a retractable arresting hook completed the major items located far aft in the fuselage.

Table 77 provides information on engines and their major power ratings for various Wildcat models. Some Wildcats had Pratt and Whitney Twin Wasps and some were powered by Wright Cyclones. Both Curtiss Electric and Hamilton Standard propellers were used, the Curtiss type predominating. Takeoff power progressed from 1050 on the first prototype to 1350 horsepower on late FM-2 models having a Cyclone with strengthened crankshaft. The F4F- airplane was the pioneer fighter utilizing a Navy/Pratt and Whitney devel-

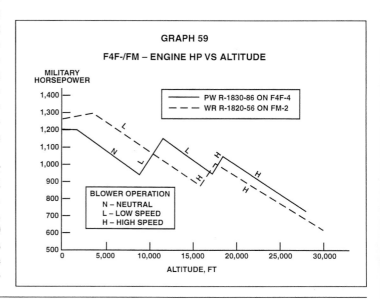

GRAPH 59

F4F-/FM – ENGINE HP VS ALTITUDE

MILITARY HORSEPOWER

PW R-1830-86 ON F4F-4
WR R-1820-56 ON FM-2

BLOWER OPERATION
N – NEUTRAL
L – LOW SPEED
H – HIGH SPEED

ALTITUDE, FT

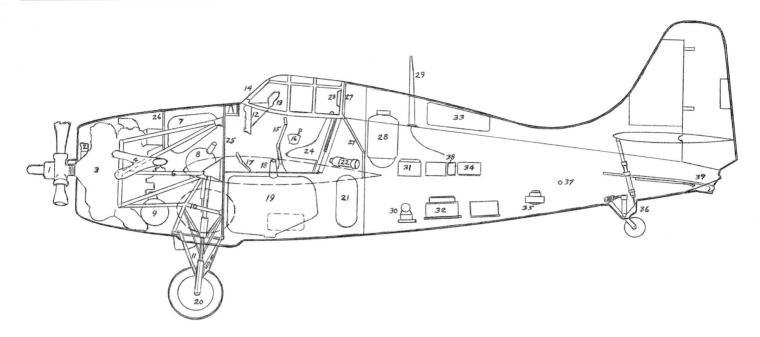

Inboard profile drawing of the FM-2.

1. Curtiss Electric propeller.
2. Propeller governor.
3. Wright R-1820 engine.
4. Engine exhaust stacks.
5. Water injection controls.
6. Steel tube engine mount.
7. Engine oil tank.water tank.
8. Water injection water tank.
9. Oil cooler.
10. Steel tube landing gear support.
11. Retractable landing gear.
12. Instrument panel.
13. Gunsight.
14. Armor glass windshield.
15. Pilot's control stick.
16. Throttle quadrant.
17. Rudder pedals.
18. Main fuel tank filler neck.
19. Main fuel tank.
20. Main landing gear wheel.
21. Reserve fuel tank.
22. Oxygen cylinder.
23. Pilot's headrest.
24. Pilot's seat.
25. Firewall.
26. Oil tank armor plate.
27. Rear armor plate.
28. Flap system vacuum tank.
29. Radio mast.
30. Dynamoter.
31. Battery.
32. Radio installation.
33. Life raft compartment.
34. Tool kit.
35. Remote indicating compass transmitter.
36. Fixed tail wheel assembly.
37. Lift tube.
38. Antenna relay.
39. Tail hook (retracted).

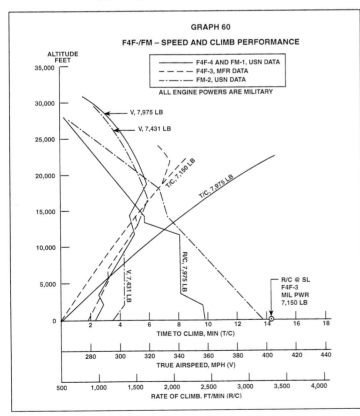

GRAPH 60

F4F-/FM – SPEED AND CLIMB PERFORMANCE

ALTITUDE FEET

	F4F-4 AND FM-1, USN DATA
	F4F-3, MFR DATA
	FM-2, USN DATA

ALL ENGINE POWERS ARE MILITARY

V, 7,975 LB
V, 7,431 LB
T/C, 7,150 LB
T/C, 7,975 LB
R/C, 7,975 LB
V, 7,431 LB

R/C @ SL
F4F-3
MIL PWR
7,150 LB

TIME TO CLIMB, MIN (T/C)

TRUE AIRSPEED, MPH (V)

RATE OF CLIMB, FT/MIN (R/C)

oped two stage mechanical supercharger which kept engine power up at high altitudes. Graph 59 shows the variation of MILITARY power with altitude, and illustrates the effect of this two stage supercharging. Other versions of the Wildcat with the Wright Cyclone, including the final FM-2 version by Eastern, had single stage two speed supercharging, and this is also illustrated as to power variation with altitude. It is seen the Cyclone in the FM-2 put out more power up to about 10000 feet, whereas above that altitude the Twin Wasp was more powerful most of the way up. The difference at high altitude was only about 50 horsepower, however.

High speed and climb performance of Wildcat models is depicted in the curves of Graph 60. The curves for F4F-3 and F4F-4 indicate that up to 15000 feet there is not more than five mph difference in high speed between the two. Above that altitude speed differences widened to as much as 20 mph with the lighter F4F-3 being faster. Up to about 10000 feet the later Cyclone powered FM-2 was noteably faster than the earlier Grummans, but at higher altitudes there was little difference between the FM-2 and F4F-4. Late Wildcats could make about 285 to 295 mph with MILITARY power at sea level, and high speed topped out to 320 mph at medium altitude. The fastest and lightest Wildcat was the early F4F-3 which touched 335 mph at 22000 feet. In addition the climb rate of the early F4F-3 was over 3300 feet per minute at sea level, very sprightly performance for the time. The heavier F4F-4, in contrast, could

TABLE 77
GRUMMAN F4F- MODELS PROPULSION DATA

MODEL	ENGINE	RATING	HP	RPM	ALTITUDE'	MAP"HG.	SUPERCHARGER
XF4F-2	R-1830-66	TAKEOFF	1050		SEA LEVEL		
	(SC-G)	MILITARY	1050				
		NORMAL	900		12000		
XF4F-3	R-1830-76	TAKEOFF	1200	2700	SEA LEVEL	48.5	2-STAGE 2-SPD.
F4F-3	(SC2-G)	MILITARY	1100	2550	3500	43.0	
XF4F-4	(G.R.3:2)	MILITARY	1000	2550	19000		
		NORMAL	1000	2550	19000		
F4F-3A	R-1830-90	TAKEOFF	1200	2700	SEA LEVEL		1-STAGE 2-SPD.
XF4F-6	(S3C4-G)	MILITARY	1200		4900		
MARTLET	(G.R.16:9)	MILITARY	1000	2700	14500		
II & III							
F4F-4	R-1830-86	TAKEOFF	1200	2900	SEA LEVEL		2-STAGE 2-SPD.
XF4F-7	(S5C7-G)	MILITARY	1200	2700	1800		
FM-1&		MILITARY	1040	2550	18400		
MARTLET V		NORMAL	1100	2550	3300		
		NORMAL	1030	2550	13000		
XF4F-5	R-1820-40	TAKEOFF	1200	2500	SEA LEVEL		1-STAGE 2-SPD.
MARTLET	(G205A)	MILITARY	1200	2500	1800		
I & IV		MILITARY	1000	2500	13500		
		NORMAL	900	2300	15200		
XF4F-8	R-1820-56	TAKEOFF	1300	2600	SEA LEVEL	46.5	1-STAGE 2-SPD.
FM-2	-56W,-56A	COMBAT	1360	2600	SEA LEVEL	52.0	
MARTLET	-56WA	MILITARY	1300	2600	4000 LOBLO.	46.5	
VI		MILITARY	1000	2600	17000 HIBLO.	44.0	
		NORMAL	1200	2500	5000 LOBLO.	43.5	
		NORMAL	900	2500	19000 HIBLO.	39.0	

NOTE: THE A MODELS OF THE R-1820 ENGINE ON THE FM-2 AIRPLANES HAD A REVISED CRANKSHAFT ALLOWING A TAKEOFF RPM OF 2700 WITH 1350 HP.

NOTE: THE PROPELLER ON THE XF4F-2 WAS A HAMILTON THREE BLADE MODEL.
ON THE F4F-3 A CURTISS THREE BLADE C5325D WITH 109354-1 SOLID ALUM. BLADES OR A C5315S WITH 512 DESIGN HOLLOW STEEL BLADES PROPELLER WAS USED, BOTH IN 9'9" DIAMETER.
ON THE F4F-4 AIRCRAFT A CURTISS THREE BLADE C5315S PROPELLER WITH 512-1CL5-15 HOLLOW STEEL BLADES IN 9'9" DIAMETER WAS INSTALLED. AN ALTERNATE INSTALLATION FOR THE -4, FM-1, OR MARTLET V WAS A HAMILTON 23E50 THREE BLADE PROPELLER.
FOR THE FM-2 AIRPLANES A CURTISS C5325D PROPELLER WITH THREE 109354-12 ALUMINUM BLADES IN 10'0" DIAMETER WAS PROVIDED.
THE MARTLET I AND IV AIRPLANES WERE EQUIPPED WITH THREE BLADE HAMILTON PROPELLERS.

make less than 2500 feet per minute at sea level and, as the curve shows, this performance decreased rapidly at the higher altitudes to little over 1500 feet per minute at 15000 feet in spite of using the two stage supercharged engine. The FM-2, at a lighter weight than the F4F-4, managed to recover a lot of the early F4F-3 climbing ability, particularly at sea level. With its two speed single stage supercharger the FM-2 climb rate drop-off with altitude was faster than that of the Twin Wasp powered airplanes, however. Curves of climb time are also shown in Graph 60. They illustrate again the great reduction in climb performance from F4F-3 to F4F-4. Time to 20000 feet was almost five minutes more for the latter. Though not shown on the chart, the final FM-2 model from Eastern retrieved most all the F4F-3 climb time performance; it took 3.7 minutes to make 10000 feet and 8.0 to 20000. It is clear the attributes of the Wildcat, particularly the F4F-4 and the almost identical FM-1, came in areas other than those of flashy speed and climb performance.

Ideal maximum range capability of Wildcats is shown in Graph 61. Ranges are given with no fuel reserves and under zero wind conditions cruising at the altitudes noted. The F4F-3, after installation of protected fuel tanks, could achieve ranges of almost 1100 miles at 3500 feet cruise altitude and 1275 miles if cruising was done up high at 19000 feet. F4F-3 takeoff weights with full internal fuel (there were no external tanks for this model) were in the area of 7400 to 7550 pounds. The F4F-4 range capability at 5000 foot cruise altitude is shown at approximate takeoff weights from just under 8000 pounds to 8750 pounds. The first instance reflects a case with full internal fuel of 144 gallons where the -4 could make just over 800 miles, quite a come-down from -3 performance. The

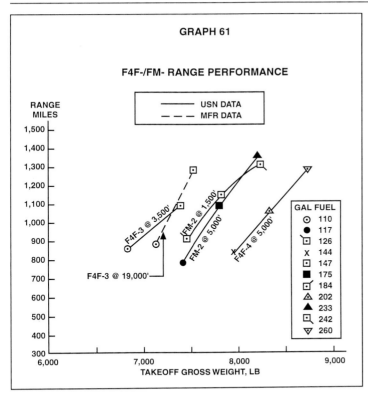

GRAPH 61

F4F-/FM- RANGE PERFORMANCE

RANGE MILES

USN DATA
MFR DATA

GAL FUEL
⊙ 110
● 117
☐ 126
X 144
☐ 147
■ 175
☐ 184
△ 202
▲ 233
☐ 242
▽ 260

F4F-3 @ 3,500'
FM-2 @ 1,500'
FM-2 @ 5,000'
F4F-4 @ 5,000'
F4F-3 @ 19,000'

TAKEOFF GROSS WEIGHT, LB

middle point indicates carriage of a single 58 gallon drop tank under one wing of the F4F-4 where a maximum range of 1050 miles could be attained. With two of these drop tanks added to full internal fuel the -4 Wildcat could labor off to achieve 1275 miles range cruising at 5000 feet altitude. The comparative range of the final FM-2 model is also shown in the figure, and the data shows for a full internal fuel case a range of 780 to 900 miles depending on whether the FM-2 was an early model with 117 gallons or a late one with 126 gallons of fuel and the cruising altitude employed. Maximum FM-2 range with drop tanks is shown as just over 1300 miles.

Graph 62 indicates takeoff ground run requirements of Wildcats versus gross weight. Practical weights were in the 7500 to 8300 pound area. Navy Wildcat fighters got off the ground in considerably less distance than most Army fighters. Distances for the above gross weights were about 600 to 700 feet. The figures reflect a land takeoff without the aid of carrier wind over the deck.

Rolling performance of an F4F-3 Wildcat is shown in the curve of Graph 63 plotted against indicated airspeed. Peak roll rate of about 69 degrees per second occurred at just under 250 mph IAS, meaning a full roll could be made in 5.22 seconds, not exactly inspiring performance. At higher indicated speed roll rate at a constant pilot lateral stick force of 50 pounds dropped off quite slowly to about 60 degrees per second at 350 mph IAS, a six second full roll.

An interesting comparison of Wildcat empty weights, broken down into the various standard airframe, propulsion, and fixed equipment groups, is provided in Table 78. The F4F-3, F4F-4, and FM-2 models are shown left to right in chronological order of their appearance. One can see the groups where weight increased or decreased. Provision of manual wing folding increased wing weight from -3 to -4 and FM-2. A taller vertical tail on FM-2 increased tail weight slightly. The FM-2 landing gear weight increase may have

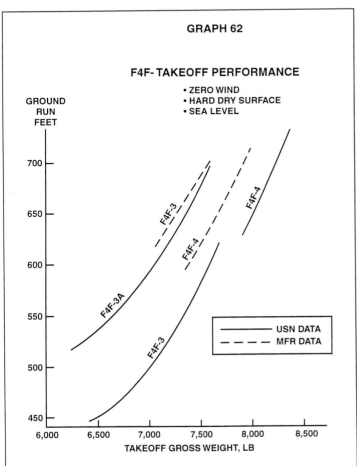

GRAPH 62

F4F- TAKEOFF PERFORMANCE

• ZERO WIND
• HARD DRY SURFACE
• SEA LEVEL

GROUND RUN FEET

F4F-3
F4F-4
F4F-4
F4F-3A
F4F-3

USN DATA
MFR DATA

TAKEOFF GROSS WEIGHT, LB

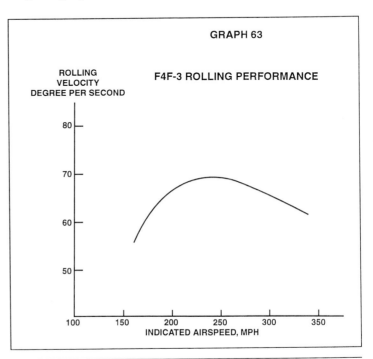

GRAPH 63

F4F-3 ROLLING PERFORMANCE

ROLLING VELOCITY DEGREE PER SECOND

INDICATED AIRSPEED, MPH

TABLE 78
F4F- AND FM-2 EMPTY WEIGHTS
POUNDS

MODEL	F4F-3	F4F-4	FM-2
GROUP			
WING	893	1181	1154
TAIL	144	148	150
FUSELAGE	525	517	470
LANDING GEAR	351	351	442
ENGINE SECTION	294	335	253
ENGINE	1565	1568	1401
ENGINE ACCESSORIES	242	242	(INCL.W.ENG.)
ENGINE CONTROLS	22.5	25	20
PROPELLER	314	315.5	394
STARTING SYSTEM	43	43	30
LUBRICATION SYSTEM	30	35	99
FUEL SYSTEM	233.5	264.5	232
OTHER	—	—	8
INSTRUMENTS	58	61	52
SURFACE CONTROLS	113	161.5	126
HYDRAULIC	—	—	—
ELECTRICAL	140	143	162
COMMUNICATION	(IN USEFUL LOAD, ALL CASES)		
AUXILIARY GEAR	30	30	42
FLOTATION GEAR	90	—	—
ARM.PROV.,INCL.ARMOR	155	162.5	223
FURNISHINGS & EQUIP.	183	195.9	80
EMPTY WEIGHT	5426	5778.9	5328

PER NAVAIR DATA, THE EMPTY WEIGHT OF FM-2 AIRPLANES
AS OF 9/1/44 WAS 5448 LB.

been simply from a structural beef-up but this is unclear. Note the major weight savings in engine and accessories for the FM-2, due to a change from Twin Wasp to simpler Cyclone engine. Part of the reason for an FM-2 propeller weight increase was the slightly larger diameter unit; propeller weight varied with more than the square of the diameter. It is believed the large increase for FM-2 under "lubrication system" is somewhat of a mis-nomer, and that a major part of the increase reflected installation of a water injection system for the Cyclone engine. Part of the increase in surface controls weight on the F4F-4 was due to wing fold complications. Flotation gear in early F4F-3 airplanes was removed and never used again, replaced either by stowed lift rafts or pilot's personal life jacket. Armor protection of Wildcats steadily increased, and this fact is reflected in the weights. The reason for a large reduction in FM-2 furnishings and equipment is unknown. All in all an approximate 350 pound increase in empty weight accrued to the F4F-4 over the F4F-3. This increase was pretty well zeroed out with advent of the final Eastern FM-2 however. Table 79 shows typical alternate mission loads for the early fixed wing four gun F4F-3 and F4F-3A models, the latter differing primarily in use of a Twin Wasp engine with only single stage two speed supercharging making for less weight. Table 80 shows typical mission weight alternatives for the later Wildcats, F4F-4, FM-1, and FM-2. The data indicates how much greater F4F-4/FM-1 weights were than those of earlier models using the empty weights of the previous table. Note how much heavier the weight of guns and ammunition became in the six gun F4F-4 as shown in the overload fighter mission column. The first column, fighter, omitted two of the six guns.

TABLE 79
TYPICAL MISSION WEIGHTS
POUNDS

MODEL		F4F-3				F4F-3A		
MISSION	FTR.	OVERL'D FIGHTER	BOMBER	FTR.	OVERL'D FIGHTER	BOMBER	OVERL'D BOMBER	FERRY
TRAP.FLUID	—	—	—	—	—	—	—	—
CREW	200	200	200	200	200	200	200	200
CAL.50 GUNS	286	286	143	286	286	143	286	—
BOMB RACKS	—	—	13.3	—	—	13.3	13.3	—
PYROTECH.	7.9	7.9	7.9	7.9	7.9	7.9	7.9	7.9
GUN CAMERA	13.7	13.7	13.7	13.7	13.7	13.7	13.7	13.7
COM/NAV/MISC	129.1	129.1	129.1					
FIXED U.L.	636.7	636.7	507					
BASIC WT.	6062.7	6062.7	5933					
USEABLE OIL	68	82.5	68	68	82.5	68	82.5	82.5
CAL.50 AMMO	360	516	225					
BOMBS	—	—	200	—	—	200	200	—
INTERN.FUEL	660	882	660	660	882	660	882	882
DROP TANKS	—	—	—	—	—	—	—	—
EXTERN.FUEL	—	—	—	—	—	—	—	—
DISPOS.LD.	1088	1480.5	1153					
GROSS WT.	7150.7	7543	7086	6783	7320	6779	7573	6244
USEFUL LD.	1724.7	2117.2	1660	1599	2136	1595	1060	1289

NOTE: F4F-3A EMPTY WEIGHT-5184 POUNDS NORMAL; 4955 POUNDS FERRY.

TABLE 80
TYPICAL MISSION WEIGHTS (CONT'D)
POUNDS

MODEL MISSION	FTR.	F4F-4 OVERL'D FTR.	FTR.1	FTR-1 EXT.TK.	FTR-2 EXT.TK.	FM-1 FTR.	FTR.	FM-2 FTR-2 EXT.TK.	BOMBER
TRAP.FLUID	—	—	—	—	—	—	—	—	—
CREW	200	200	200	200	200	200	200	200	200
CAL.50 GUNS	288.7	433.0	433.0	433.0	433.0	288.7	288.7	288.7	288.7
EXT.RACKS	—	—	—	20	20	—	—		
PYROTECH.	11.8	11.8	11.8	11.8	11.8	11.8			
GUN CAMERA	13.7	13.7	—	—	—				
COM/NAV.	164.9	156.6	56.7	30.7	27.7	192.0			
FIXED U.L.	679.1	815.1	701.5	695.5	692.5	692.5			
BASIC WT.	6458	6594	6596.5	6590.5	6587.5	6587.5			
USEABLE OIL	68	82.5	82.5	82.5	82.5	82.5	82.5	82.5	82.5
CAL.50AMMO	240	432	432	432	432	516	516	516	516
BOMBS	—	—	—	—	—	—	—	—	500
INTER.FUEL	660	864	864	864	864	864	756	756	756
DROP TANKS	—	—	—	50	100	—	—	100	—
EXTER.FUEL	—	—	—	348	696	—	—	696	—
DISP. LOAD	968	1378.5	1378.5	1776.5	2174.5	1462.5	1354.5	2150.5	
GROSS WT.	7426	7972.5	7975	8369	8762	8050	7487	8271	8011
EMPTY WT.	5778.9	5778.9	5895	5895	5895	5895	5448	5448	5448
USEFUL LD.	1647.1	2193.6	2080	2472	2867	2155	2039	2823	2563

F4F- MAJOR MODEL-TO-MODEL CHANGES

XF4F-1 Biplane, never built.

XF4F-2 Completely new mid-wing monoplane. Wing span 34 feet; rounded wingtips, no wing fold, leading edge flotation bags. P&W R-1830 engine with single stage single speed supercharger. Hamilton Standard propeller. Two .50 caliber cowl machine guns.

XF4F-3 Actual fuselage and landing gear of the XF4F-2 with completely new design square-tip 38 foot span non-folding wings, and new tail surfaces. P&W R-1830 engine with two stage two speed supercharger and Curtiss Electric propeller. Many revisions during testing. Two .50 caliber cowl guns; two wing .50 caliber guns.

F4F-3 Initial production version. New R-1830 engine version with two stage two speed supercharging. Self sealing fuel tanks and armor added in late aircraft. Four .50 caliber wing guns. Provision for gun camera. Radio homing added. Forged steel arrester hook. Gun heating added. Electric gun sight to replace telescope type.

F4F-3A F4F-3 with another R-1830 engine model having a single stage two speed supercharger. Martlet III similar.

XF4F-4 F4F-3 with hydraulic power folding wings.

F4F-4 New production model. Manually folding wing. Self sealing fuel tanks standard. Provision for two underwing 58 gallon drop tanks. Two more .50 caliber wing guns added for a total of six, with less ammunition per gun. More armor. Pneumatic in place of solid tail wheel.

XF4F-5 F4F-5 with engine changes to various Wright R-1820 models to test supercharger variations.

F4F-7 F4F-3 with fuel-filled wing, no armor or guns. Camera in aft fuselage for reconnaissance.

XF4F-8 F4F-4 with Wright R-1820 engine. Tested with slotted flaps and taller vertical tail. Prototype for FM-2.

FM-1 Eastern-built F4F-4 with only four .50 caliber wing guns. Martlet V similar.

FM-2 Production XF4F-8 by Eastern. Larger and taller vertical tail. R-1820 engine with single stage two speed supercharger. Fuselage auxiliary fuel tank omitted. Most aircraft had water injection engines. Two drop tanks available. Oil cooler transferred behind engine lieu under wing. New Curtiss propeller. Four .50 caliber wing guns. Late models were equipped to carry six rockets underwing. Martlet VI similar.

G-36A Export F4F-3 with Hamilton propeller and Wright R-1820 engine. Four .50 caliber wing guns. Became Martlet I.

F4F-4B F4F-4 with R-1820 engine with a single stage two speed supercharger and Hamilton propeller. Six .50 caliber wing guns. This was export model for Britain and became the Martlet IV.

F4F-/FM- WILDCAT CHRONOLOGY

Mar 2'36-The US Navy awards the Grumman Aircraft Engineering Co. a contract for a new biplane fighter, the XF4F-1.

Jul10'36-The US Navy Bureau of Aeronautics approves a change of design from the XF4F-1 biplane to an XF4F-2 monoplane since the new biplane will not provide sufficient performance increase over existing service aircraft.

Jul28'36-Grumman is given a contract for the XF4F-2 and drops work on the XF4F-1.

Sep 2'37-The first flight of the XF4F-2 monoplane takes place at Bethpage, L.I.N.Y. piloted by Robert L. Hall.

Dec23'37-After completion of initial Grumman testing the XF4F-2 is flown for further tests at NAS Anacostia, MD. by the Navy.

Feb14'38-The XF4F-2 has an in-flight fire over Bethpage, but lands successfully.

Feb16'38-The XF4F-2 is tested at NAS Dahlgren, including dive pullouts up to 8.5g and spins.

Mar 1'38-At NAS Anacostia competitive testing begins of the XF4F-2 versus the Brewster XF2A-1 and the Seversky NF-1.

Mar11'38-Over 16 hours of flight test time have been accumulated on the XF4F-2 aircraft. The maximum speed is 290 mph, short of the 300 mph goal.

Apr 6'38-The XF4F-2 flies to NAF Philadelphia for further testing, including catapult and deck-landing tests.

April11'38-The engine of the XF4F-2 fails and a forced landing is made on New Jersey farmland. The aircraft is salvageable, and is returned to Grumman on Long Island.

Jun '38-Grumman loses the production contract with the award going to the Brewster F2A-1 aircraft.

Aug '38-The XF4F-2 is back at Grumman ready to be reworked and repaired.

Oct '38-Grumman receives a Navy contract for a modified version of the airplane, the XF4F-3. There are many significant changes in the design, including a new wing, engine, and tail.

Jan '39-A new two-stage supercharged Pratt and Whitney R-1830 engine is installed in the XF4F-3.

Feb12'39-Grumman test pilot Robert Hall takes the "new" XF4F-3 on a first flight. The airplane is a much-modified XF4F-2.

Mar '39-The XF4F-3 is delivered to NAS Anacostia, MD. for USN testing.

May '39-The XF4F-3 is returned to Grumman for wing and tail modifications.

May18'39-The XF4F-3 prototype airplane is flown to NAF Philadelphia for catapult and deck landing tests. A speed of 333.5 mph is attained. Engine cooling is a constant problem, but after much effort this is finally solved.

Aug 8'39-Grumman is awarded a production contract for 54 F4F-3 airplanes.

Oct '39-France orders 100 export versions of the F4F- with civil Wright R-1820 Cyclone engines.

Dec '39-The F4F-3 static test airframe is delivered to NAF, Philadelphia.

Feb '40-The first production F4F-3 aircraft, #1844, makes its first flight.

Mar '40-A contract change by the Navy provides for installation of a wing folding feature on one of the ordered F4F-3 airplanes.

Apr '40-The first production F4F-3 is used as a chase plane for the experimental Grumman XF5F-1 Skyrocket aircraft.

Apr '40-The USN orders the third and fourth production aircraft to be equipped with Wright R-1820 engines and designated as XF4F-5.

May11'40-Flight tests begin on the export version of the F4F- with the Wright R-1820 civil engine for the French.

Jun '40-The two XF4F-5 aircraft with the Wright Cyclone engine make their first flights.

Jul '40-The two XF4F-5s are delivered to NAS Anacostia, MD. and are kept there for test work on engine superchargers.

Jul '40-The second production F4F-3 airplane, #1845, has its first flight.

Jul27'40-Since France has fallen to Germany, the British take over the French order and accept delivery of the first French aircraft.

Aug '40-The first production USN airplane, #1844, is flown to Pratt and Whitney, East Hartford, Ct. for engine testing.

Oct '40-The first flight of a British Martlet II version with a Pratt and Whitney R-1830 single-stage two speed supercharged engine takes place.

Oct31'40-By this time 81 Martlet aircraft have been delivered to the British Royal Navy Fleet Air Arm.

Nov '40-The USN XF4F-6 version using an R-1830 single-stage two-speed supercharged engine is flown to NAS Anacostia for tests. The airplane is used as a test bed.

Dec '40-A total of 578 F4F-3s and F4F-3As (the latter redesignated XF4F-6s) are on order, but only 22 F4F-3 aircraft have been accepted by the US Navy.

Dec 4'40-The first F4F-3 goes to a Navy fleet squadron, VF-41 (was VF-4) in Norfolk, VA., later to go on the aircraft carrier Ranger and work out in the Carribean.

Dec16'40-The XF4F-3 airplane is destroyed in a crash at Norfolk, VA.

Dec25'40-A British Martlet fighter on patrol near Scapa Flow off Scotland shoots down a German JU-88 for a first F4F- type "kill" of the war.

Dec31'40-A total of 103 F4F-s and Martlets have been completed by Grumman.

Jan '41-F4F-3 aircraft replace the F3F-1 biplanes of Navy Squadron VF-7 (later VF-72) which subsequently heads to the Pacific.

Mar '41-The first production F4F-3 airplane crashes near Anacostia due to a pilot oxygen system failure.

Mar '41-The first British Martlet II is delivered by Grumman. The first few aircraft have fixed wings, but the remainder get the foldable wing feature incorporated.

Mar 1'41-Eighteen F4F-3s replace Vought SBU-1 and SB2U-1 scout bombers in Navy Squadron VF-71, which had been VB-7.

Mar18'41-The first aircraft intended for Greece, an F4F-3A, is ready for delivery. Because Axis forces have invaded Greece this airplane and another of the original order are made UK planes.

Apr14'41-The first flight of the power folding wing six-gun XF4F-4 takes place. (The F4F-3 has four guns and fixed wings.)

May '41-Navy Squadron VF-6 receives F4F-3A aircraft.

May '41-The XF4F-4 airplane is turned over to Navy Squadron VF-42 for carrier deck trials on the USS Yorktown.

Sep20'41-British Martlet aircraft of #802 Sdn. shoot down an FW-200 Condor German four-engine patrol airplane while operating from the escort carrier Audacity. On a later voyage of this carrier its Martlets will shoot down four more FW-200s.

Oct '41-The US Marine Corps now has 16 F4F-3A and 41 F4F-3 fighters.

Nov28'41-Marine squadron VMF-211 with 12 F4F-3 airplanes, leaving 10 at Ewa in Hawaii, goes on board the carrier Enterprise for transfer to Wake Island in the Pacific.

Dec '41-The First Marine Air Wing and MAG-21 are forced to surrender their F4F-3s to the Navy aircraft carrier squadrons.

Dec '41-The USN and USMC squadrons now have a total of 181 F4F-3s and 65 F4F-3As.

Dec 4'41-Marine Sdn. VMF-211 fly their Wildcats off carrier Enterprise to Wake Island to provide an aerial defense force there.

Dec 6'41-On the day before the Japanese Pearl Harbor attack the USMC fighter disposition is: At Quantico, VA. the First Marine Air Wing, MAG-11, consisting of Sdn. VMF-111 with 15 F4F-3A aircraft and VMF-211 with 20 F4F-3 airplanes; and at Ewa, Hawaii the Second Marine Air Wing, MAG-21, consisting of Sdn. VMF-211 with 12 F4F-3s at Wake Island and 10 F4F-3s at Ewa, and VMF-221 with 14 F2A-3s on carrier Saratoga at San Diego.

Dec 7'41-In the Japanese attack on Pearl harbor nine out of 11 F4F-3 aircraft of VMF-211 are damaged or destroyed at Ewa in Oahu and no F4F-s get to fight.

Dec 8'41-The first enemy attack on Wake Island destroys seven Wildcats; another is destroyed in a taxi accident. Four airplanes are on patrol.

Dec11'41-The four remaining Wildcats at Wake Island bomb and strafe Japanese invasion forces causing considerable damage. Later two remaining F4F-3s shoot down three enemy bombers out of a thirty plane raid.

Dec20'41-After salvage and rebuilding two Wildcats are flyable on Wake Island. Two days later both aircraft are lost and the next day Wake is taken by the Japanese.

Dec30'41-The first flight of the F4F-7 long range photo version takes place.

Dec31'41-Folding wing F4F-4s are starting to be delivered to US Navy squadrons. The first five airplanes have been accepted.

Dec31'41-A total of 323 Grumman fighter monoplanes are produced in 1941 including 107 F4F-3s and the five F4F-4s.

Jan21'42-The Eastern Aircraft Division of General Motors Corp. in Linden, NJ. is revised from automobile to aircraft production.

Feb 1'42-USN Wildcat fighters participate in the first US carrier raid by Enterprise and Yorktown on islands in the Marshalls and Gilberts groups. F4F-3s of Squadron VF-6 destroy two E/A.

Feb20'42-Lt.Edward O'hare of carrier Lexington becomes the first Navy ace in a Wildcat by shooting down five enemy bombers.

Feb24'42-Wildcats on carrier Enterprise are part of a strike made against enemy-held Wake Island in the Pacific.

Mar 4'42-Wildcats on the Enterprise take part in the first raid on Marcus Island in the Pacific.

Mar 8'42-Nineteen F4F-3s of VMF-111 leave San Diego as part of a force to defend the island of Samoa. They are now part of MAG-13.

Mar10'42-USN Wildcats are part of a strike launched from carriers Lexington and Yorktown on islands in the Marshalls and Gilberts groups in the Pacific.

Mar29'42-The forward echelon of Wildcat Squadron VMF-212 arrives at Efate and prepares an airstrip.

Apr18'42-Eastern Aircraft of G.M. receives a contract to build 1800 FM-1 Wildcat fighters, a variant similar to the Grumman F4F-4.

Apr20'42-Seven F4F-3s are brought to the Marines at Midway Island by USS Kittihawk to bolster its defenses.

May 4'42-Carrier fighter aircraft available to US Task Force 17 at the start of the Battle of the Coral Sea are: On Yorktown VF-42 with 20 F4F-3s and the Air Group Cdr. with one F4F-3; on Lexington VF-2 with 22 F4F-3s and the Air group Cdr. with one F4F-3.

May11'42-Twenty-one F4F-3 aircraft of VMF-212 fly off carriers Enterprise and Hornet to land at Tontouta airfield, thirty miles NW of Noumea, the capital of Caledonia in the SW Pacific.

May10'42-A demonstration is made at the Naval Aircraft Factory in Philadelphia of a BD-2 Havoc light bomber towing two Wildcats for an hour at 180 knots at 7000 feet altitude.

May27'42-Some F4F-3 Wildcats of VMF-212 initiate operations from Efate in the Pacific, but all squadron planes are not yet ready.

Jun 1'42-Just before the Battle of Midway the fighters on US aircraft carriers are: Yorktown-25 F4F-4 of VF-3; Enterprise-27 F4F-4 of VF-6; and Hornet-29 F4F-4 of VF-8. Total combat and operational losses of Wildcats in the Midway Battles are: Yorktown-10 aircraft; Enterprise-one aircraft; and Hornet-12 aircraft. Shore-based Marines have seven F4F-3s of which two are lost.

Jun 9'42-The remaining F4F-3 Wildcats of VMF-212 arrive at Vita Field on Efate.

Jun15'42-By this time the manually folding wing F4F-4 Wildcats are being produced in sufficient numbers that after the Battle of Midway they carry the brunt of the carrier-based fighter action as F4F-3s are transferred to land bases.

Jun30'42-Admiral Nimitz sums up the situation as: "Our F4F- is markedly inferior to the Jap Zero in speed, maneuverability, and climb. These characteristics must be improved, but not at the cost of reducing the overall superiority that, in the Battle of Midway, enabled our carrier fighters to shoot down about three Zero fighters for each of our own lost. However much of this superiority may exist in our splendid pilots, part at least rests in the armor, armament, and leakproof tanks of our planes.

Jul15'42-British Navy Squadron #892 is the first to get the Martlet IV type of which the British have ordered 220 for their escort aircraft carriers.

Jul28'42-The airfield at Espirito Santo is completed and ready to receive Marine Wildcat fighters.

Aug '42-Navy and Marine Corps land-based fighters in the SW Pacific include: 18 USMC F4F-3 Wildcats at Efate, 16 F4F-3 aircraft at New Caledonia, 12 USMC Wildcats at Fiji, 24 USMC Wildcats at Tongatabu, and six USMC VMF-111 Wildcats at Samoa.

Aug 1'42-Among the forces ready for the Guadalcanal invasion in Task Force 61 are: From carrier Saratoga-VF-5 with 34 F4F-4 fighters, from carrier Enterprise-VF-6 with 36 F4F-4s, and from carrier Wasp-VF-71 with 29 F4F-4s.

Aug 2'42-Just before sailing on the escort carrier Long Island for the Pacific Marine VMF-223 receives brand-new F4F-4s.

Aug11'42-Sixteen F4F-3P long range photo planes of VMO-251 arrive at Espirito Santo, but have to wait until August 20 to receive their wing tanks to achieve long range.

Aug15'42-VMF-224 sails with 19 Wildcats from Pearl Harbor to the SW Pacific on the airplane transports Kittihawk and Hammondsport.

Aug20'42-Nineteen USMC F4F-4s of VMF-223, MAG-23, land on Henderson Field, Guadalcanal in the Solomon Islands. They are the first US fighters to arrive, and 19 hours later they have their first combat.

Aug24'42-Marine VMF-223 Wildcats intercept an enemy raid of 15 bombers and 12 fighters from Japanese carrier Ryujo and shoot down 16, including three Zero fighters.

Aug26'42-Twelve Marine Wildcats from Henderson Field, Guadalcanal shoot down 13 enemy raiders.

Aug29'42-VMF-223 F4F-4s on Guadalcanal destroy four bombers and four fighters; the next day 14 more Japanese aircraft are shot down.

Aug30'42-Nineteen F4F-4s of VMF-224 arrive, in the middle of an air raid, as reinforcements at Henderson Field on Guadalcanal.

Sep 1'42-The Eastern Aircraft Division of General Motors test flies its first FM-1 aircraft.

Sep 2'42-VMF-223 and -224 Wildcats intercept a raid of 40 enemy aircraft near Henderson Field and shoot down seven planes.

Sep 3'42-Six Wildcats and two Bell P-400s strafe enemy craft landing reinforcements on Guadalcanal.

Sep10'42-The "Cactus Air Force" on Guadalcanal has high combat and operational attrition. The current effective fighter strength is 11 F4F-s and three P-400s.

Sep11'42-Twenty-four F4F-4s of USN Sdn.VF-5 from carrier Saratoga, which has been torpedoed, fly in to Henderson Field on Guadalcanal.

Sep12'42-Twenty-one of the VF-5 Wildcats with 11 Marine F4F-s intercept 42 Japanese aircraft and shoot down 15 with a loss of only one of their own.

Sep13'42-Navy pilots from carriers Hornet and Wasp ferry in 18 additional F4F-s for use by VMF-223 and VMF-224. This effort is timely since on this day Cactus Air Force loses six aircraft while shooting down 11 enemy planes.

Sep17'42-Twenty-nine F4F-s and three P-400s now constitute the total fighter strength at Henderson Field, Guadalcanal.

Sep28'42-Navy and Marine Wildcats take a big toll of Japanese aircraft during an enemy raid on Henderson field. A total of 23 bombers and one fighter is downed. VMF-223 gets seven, -224 gets eight and Navy VF-5 downs nine of the enemy.

Oct '42-For Operation Torch, the invasion of North Africa, the Western Naval Task Force is to employ US Naval fighter forces as follows: Sdn.VF-9 from carrier Ranger with 27 F4F-4s, Sdn.VF-41 from Ranger with 28 F4F-4s, Sdn.VGF-19 from escort carrier Santee with 14 F4F-4s, Sdn.VGF-26 from escort carrier Sangamon with 14 F4F-4s, and Sdn.VGF-27 from escort carrier Suwanee with 12 F4F-4 airplanes.

Oct '42-Many Wildcat pilots of VMF-223, -224, and VF-5 are relieved when replacements come in. More than half the US fighter pilots shot down around Guadalcanal are saved to fight again.

Oct 1'42-The Guadalcanal Cactus Air Force has the following operational fighters: 34 F4F-4 and three Army Bell P-400s.

Oct 9'42-USMC Sdn. VMF-121 of MAG (Marine Air Group)-14 arrives on Guadalcanal to raise F4F-4 strength from 26 to 46 aircraft.

Oct13'42-The enemy achieves surprise in a destructive raid on Henderson and Fighter 1 fields. Enemy battleships and cruisers shell Henderson day and night. Many aircraft are lost, including six F4F-4s and four Army P-39s. There are now only nine Wildcats left on Guadalcanal. Then VMF-212 comes up from Efate with 19 Wildcats.

Oct17'42-Fresh fighter squadrons VMF-121 and VMF-212 and Navy VF-5 are are now on Guadalcanal. On this day they manage to shoot down nine Japanese aircraft and then 20 the next day, then 12 the two days after that. The air battles are furious.

Oct23'42-Twenty-four F4F-4s from two Marine and one Navy Squadrons break up a heavy Japanese air attack on Guadalcanal, destroying 20 enemy fighters and four bombers. Marine Capt. Joe Foss shoots down four Zero fighters.

Oct25'42-Enemy raids on Guadalcanal continue almost all day. Twenty-two E/A are shot down; Capt. Joe Foss gets four more victories.

Oct26'42-The Cactus Air Force is again in desperate trouble. Fighters available on Guadalcanal are 12 F4F-4s, one F4F-7 photo recon plane, three Army P-400s and three P-39s.

Nov '42-The first F4F-4B aircraft is delivered to the British Navy at Speke in England.

Nov '42-There are now two F4F-7 long range photo Wildcats on Guadalcanal with guns removed and unprotected internal wing fuel tanks bringing total capacity to 685 gallons of fuel. The two planes are flown on reconnaissance missions daily. The F4F-7 camera installation is not fully satisfactory, however, and it is soon replaced by other aircraft. The F4F-7s are later converted to F4F-4s.

Nov 8'42-The first XF4F-8 test airplane is flown. This is a precursor to the later FM-2 Wildcat model.

Nov11'42-After a week of no raids on Guadalcanal fields, the Japanese come again. They lose 11 planes, but the Cactus Air Force loses seven. The next day 33 enemy planes raid US ships unloading; F4F-4s and P-39s down 21 planes, but lose three F4F-s and one P-39.

Nov14'42-In the last four days Wildcats of the Cactus Air Force participate in the Sea Battle of Guadalcanal. The worst of the air battles are now over, and reinforcements have now arrived.

Nov20'42-Fighter strength on Guadalcanal has now increased, though Wildcats still predominate. The planes consist of: 35 F4F-4s, 17 P-38s, 16 P-39s, and one P-400. On the 29th the number of Wildcats increases to 71.

Dec '42-During Operation Torch in North Africa British Martlets of #802 Sdn. have operated from the carrier Victorious. Martlets of #805 Sdn. have operated in the North African Western Desert from Dekheila.

Dec '42-Flight tests commence on two XF4F-8 Wildcats, the prototypes for the later Eastern FM-2 model.

Dec24'42-Wildcats assist P-38s and P-39s in escorting nine Dauntless dive bombers on a raid of the enemy base at Munda, catch the Japanese by surprise, and destroy 24 Zero fighters, 10 on the ground. That afternoon Wildcats go on another bomber escort mission.

Dec31'42-A total of 1164 F4F-4 aircraft have been delivered in 1942, bringing the total of -4s to 1169 manufactured by Grumman. Eastern Aircraft has produced 23 FM-1 Wildcats so far. The total in 1942 is 1445 Wildcats and Martlets produced, including 21 F4F-7s and two XF4F-8s. Along with the FM-1s Eastern has produced two Martlet Vs. The FM-1s have four guns and are 75-100 pounds heavier than the F4F-4.

Jan31'43-Nine F4F-4 Wildcats are sent to defend Funafuti Island in the Central Pacific, but after three weeks return to Tutuila, leaving Funafuti unprotected.

Feb '43-Marine Capt. Joe Foss obtains his 27th victory, all obtained while flying Wildcat fighters.

Feb 7'43-The Japanese evacuate Guadalcanal. During the time on the island through January, 1943 the Marines claim destruction of 427 enemy aircraft while losing 118 planes to the enemy and 30 operationally. Most all losses are Wildcats. The Japanese say they have lost only 136 aircraft.

Feb12'43-A dozen Marine Corsairs of VMF-124 come in to Guadalcanal to assist the Wildcats.

Feb28'43-An F4F-3S equipped with twin Edo floats is flight tested by Grumman pilot Hank Kurt, but no more are made as there is now no operational requirement for a seaplane Wildcat version.

Mar '43-Grumman has produced a further batch of 100 F4F-3 versions to be used as trainers.

Mar22'43-Six F4F-s from VMF-441 are sent up again to Funafuti Island for defensive purposes. On the 27th they shoot down one of four raiding Japanese bombers.

Apr 4'43-Marine Air Group MAG-21 with three Wildcat squadrons moves up to Banika in the Russell Islands to intercept enemy planes and ships heading down the Slot towards Guadalcanal, and to escort US bombers heading north.

Apr 7'43-The big Japanese "I" Operation is underway and 177 enemy aircraft detached from carriers come south to attack US bases at Tulagi and Guadalcanal. In big air battles the enemy loses 12 Val bombers and several Zero fighters. Seven F4F-s are downed, but all pilots are saved. A few days later the big "I" operation is cancelled by the Japanese.

Apr23'43-A night raid on Funafuti by enemy bombers destroys one VMF-441 Wildcat and damages eight others there on temporary duty.

May11'43-Among forces supporting the operation capturing Attu in the Aleutian Islands is the escort carrier Nassau with 26 F4F-4 Wildcats and three F4F-3P reconnaissance models aboard. One section of four Wildcats sinks an enemy landing barge.

May '43-Production of F4F-4 aircraft is ended at Grumman so efforts can be concentrated on the new Hellcat fighter. In 1943 100 F4F-4s have been produced; Grumman has now turned out 1971 aircraft of the Wildcat/Martlet type.

Jul17'43-Thirty-five F4F-4 Wildcats are among the 114 fighters escorting 78 US bombers which hit Kahili area shipping in a surprise attack (other fighters are 23 P-40s, 12 P-38s, and 44 F4U-1s). Forty-one enemy aircraft are claimed shot down in this raid.

Sep '43-Deliveries start from Eastern Aircraft of the FM-2 Wildcat with the Wright Cyclone engine, the production version of the XF4F-8. The FM-2 is intended for escort carriers. The propeller design is optimized for good takeoff characteristics.

Nov '43-Two USN squadrons are conducting accelerated service tests of FM-2 aircraft, and five FM-2s are under test at various Navy facilities.

Nov10'43-Among the forces supporting Operation Galvanic against the enemy-held Gilbert Islands in the Pacific are escort carriers Liscome Bay with 16 FM-1 Wildcats, Coral Sea with 16, and Corregidor with another 16 FM-1s. The other five escort carriers and the eleven fleet carriers employed now have Grumman Hellcat fighters aboard.

Dec31'43-During this last year Eastern Aircraft Division of GM has built 1127 Wildcats with 312 going to the UK as the Martlet V. Three hundred and ten FM-2 models have also been produced.

Jan '44-The name Wildcat is now standard in the British Navy.

Jan29'44-Included with the carrier support group for the Navy's Marshall Islands operations against the Japanese are the CVEs Manilla bay with 16 FM- Wildcats, Coral Sea with five FM-1 and nine F4F-4, and the Corregidor with three F4F-4 and six FM-1s, also the Nassau with Sdn.VC-66 having 14 FM-1s and Natoma Bay with Sdn.VC-63 having 12 FM-1 Wildcats. The other CVs, CVLs, and CVEs totaling 15 ships carried Hellcats.

Jul '44-Eastern FM-2 aircraft are now operational on escort carriers, and are equipped with water injection systems for the engines.

Jul '44-Wildcat VIs are operational with British #881 Sdn. aboard CVE HMS Pursuer.

Dec31'44-Eastern has built 3130 FM-2s in 1944; 370 are Wildcat VIs.

May '45-Eastern Wildcat production ceases.

May '45-A total of 7905 Wildcats have been built altogether with 1082 of these for others than the US Navy.

Aug '45-The USN credits Wildcat fighters, in 1941 through 1943, with the destruction of 905 enemy planes for a loss of 178, a victory-to-loss ratio of 6.9:1.

F4F-/FM- WILDCAT HANDLING QUALITIES AND CHARACTERISTICS

HANDLING QUALITIES
GROUND HANDLING
The ground handling characteristics of the Wildcat were often called "tricky", due mainly to a narrow tread landing gear equipped with rather soft mushy shock struts which on occasion could collapse. Under certain conditions, such as a crosswind, a sudden power application, a sharp taxi turn, a strut collapse, or some combination the aircraft could take quite a roll, and pilots had to be careful not to dig in a wingtip. In spite of this the "book" noted there were no unusual ground handling characteristics, and turns of 360 degrees in either direction could be made. Yet one pilot said in referring to his F4F-3 "It had terrible ground handling characteristics". Pilots at a fighter conference were divided on FM-2 Wildcat ground handling. Eight of sixteen said it was good; another eight said fair or poor.

During taxi the tailwheel was unlocked to allow the S-turns required to see ahead. The aircraft was turned by a combination of engine power and brake application, and care was taken not to overheat the brakes. They were applied with caution since there was a tendency to nose over if they were jammed on.

In preparation for FM-2 takeoff the elevator trim tab was set neutral or slightly nose up, and the rudder tab set for strong right rudder about two and a half units.

TAKEOFF AND CLIMB
On land, where some considered taking off more difficult than lifting from a carrier, the tail wheel was locked and checked by moving straight forward. If flaps were lowered for a shorter takeoff the normal tendency for a torque swing to the left seemed to increase. If the aircraft was held with brakes and power increased the tail

Fig.4F-1 Grumman XF4F-2, Mfr. photo via J.Weathers. The initial version of Grumman's first effort to produce a monoplane carrier fighter for the Navy; the XF4F-1 had been proposed as a biplane but Grumman was directed in the summer of 1936 to initiate design of an XF4F-2 monoplane. The result is shown in the photo; it looked a bit like Grumman removed the wings from one of their biplanes and inserted a monoplane wing through the middle of the fuselage.

Fig.4F-2 Grumman XF4F-2, USN photo via H. Andrews. With rounded wingtips and a forward-sloping rudder hinge line, the XF4F-2 is shown during flight testing that started in September of 1937. Powered by a Pratt and Whitney R-1830 Twin Wasp engine of 1050 horsepower with a single stage single speed supercharger, the XF4F-2 had a thirty-four foot wingspan and two cowl machine guns. High speed was projected at 290 mph at 12000 feet. In April, 1938 the XF4F-2 made a forced landing in a New Jersey field after engine failure with substantial damage resulting.

Fig.4F-4 Grumman XF4F-3, USN photo via H. Andrews. Major changes characterized the new prototype XF4F-3, two of the most important being installation of a new Twin Wasp engine version with a two stage two speed mechanical supercharger giving greater altitude power, and a new square-tipped wing of greater span and area. Powerplant cooling problems during development resulted in prototype use of propeller blade cuffs and a spinner. The photo was taken in August of 1939.

Fig.4F-3 Grumman XF4F-3, USN photo via J. Weathers. The XF4F-2 (along with the Seversky XNF-1) lost the initial fighter competition to Brewster's XF2A-1 with the latter being awarded a production contract. The Navy wanted a backup, however, and provided a new contract to Grumman for an XF4F-3 prototype in October, 1938. This new aircraft, formed around part of the fuselage from the XF4F-2, had many new features and flew first in mid-February of 1939.

Fig.4F-5 Grumman XF4F-3, USN photo via H. Andrews. Another photo of the XF4F-3 taken in August of 1939 shows the airplane still retained a vertical tail with a forward-slanting rudder hinge line and a low horizontal tail mounted on the fuselage aft end in a perfect position to be unduly influenced by downwash from the wing. The fire was at the far side of the airfield, not in the cockpit!

Fig.4F-6 Grumman XF4F-3, USN photo viA H. Andrews. Along with some other fighter aircraft of the period, including the Brewster fighter prototype, the XF4F-3 was placed in the then-new NACA full scale wind tunnel at Langley Field, Virginia for aerodynamic evaluations, this testing taking place in late 1939. The photo illustrates the set-up for power-off tests.

would start jumping at about 30 inches of manifold pressure, so brakes were released gradually at about 25 inches, then on an FM-2 the throttle was opened slowly to 45 and a half inches. Since powerful propeller torque reaction could cause an inexperienced pilot to ground loop to the left on takeoff, "The airplane had an awsome tendency to ground loop", full right rudder was applied along with the right brake used to keep the aircraft straight. On early Wildcats with the shorter vertical tail and small solid rubber tail wheel tire rudder action was partly blanketed by the fuselage until the tail raised; on late aircraft with the taller tail and larger pneumatic tire on the tail wheel the rudder became more effective early on. Tail wheel changes were made on F4F-3s in early 1942, but the taller tail had to wait for the FM-2 model. As speed in-

Fig.4F-7 Grumman XF4F-3, USN photo via H. Andrews. Flight view of the XF4F-3 in July, 1939 shows the new larger wing. The two stage supercharger on the Twin Wasp engine reflected a Navy/Pratt and Whitney cooperative development program started in 1934 and flight tested on two Navy types in 1935 and 1936. Based on the aircraft cowling discoloration it appears some gunnery tests have taken place. Testing continued on the prototype until the aircraft crashed in December, 1940.

Fig.4F-8 Grumman XF4F-3, photo via J. Weathers. A fine banking flight shot of the XF4F-3 showing the wing planform. Action shots of this type were a bit unusual. Giving away the fact this is the X prototype is the horizontal tail planform with that surface still mounted off the fuselage. The belly windows for pilot vision below are shown. Bumps inboard on the wing underside are oil coolers.

Fig.4F-9 Grumman F4F-3, Mfr. photo via J. Weathers. The first production F4F-3 shown here first flew in February, 1940 and first underwent tests at the Grumman plant and then later in the summer went to Pratt and Whitney at East Hartford, Connecticut. The armament was two .30 caliber cowl guns and two .50 caliber wing guns (the ports for the latter obliterated in the photo. The Curtiss propeller blades were equipped with cuffs to assist in engine cooling; the spinner had been eliminated as unnecessary. The cowl lip scoop was for carburetor air.

Fig.4F-11 Grumman F4F-3s, USN photo via H. Andrews. A trio of early F4F-3 fighters showing the national insignia still with the red center circle, the crosses used for markings during war maneuvers, and racks for a 116 pound bomb under each wing. The tail wheel gear is fixed; no Wildcat model ever had a retractable tail wheel. These airplanes were fitted for the new arrangement of four .50 caliber wing machine guns only; shell casing ejection ports can be seen just outboard of the starboard oil cooler.

creased and the rudder took hold less brake action was required. During the takeoff run motion of the aircraft was variously described, but was sometimes likened to a drunken sailor waddling down the street on its soft-sprung landing gear. The run was short, acceleration was good, and an FM-2 would unstick from a three point attitude at about 81 to 85 mph IAS. Flaps, if used, were raised with landing gear retraction initiated as quickly as possible in climb via pilot manual labor, the required effort increasing if too much speed was gained. Hand cranking was started at 150 to 160 mph IAS, often resulting in a porpoising flight path of the airplane caused by the pilot reaction on the stick during cranking until about twenty-seven crank rotations were completed.

Optimum climbout speed varied with model from 144 to 154 mph IAS with higher speed providing better engine cooling. On earlier lightweight models an excellent initial climb rate, well over 3000 feet per minute, could be established, but this dropped way down on the clunky F4F-4 version, picking up to its original value on the final more powerful FM-2.

Takeoff procedure differed somewhat aboard the carriers. Runup was made against the brakes to the extent possible without slipping or nosing over forward, or getting too much left shock strut compression from torque reaction and reducing right brake effectiveness. Flaps were either put down initially or dumped suddenly near the end of the deck run. Since the high torque reaction

Fig.4F-10 Grumman F4F-3, USN photo via Joe Weathers. A flight photo of the second production F4F-3 aircraft shows it still carried cowl guns. This airplane was the last F4F- with machine guns in the fuselage. The horizontal tail has been raised to mount in the lower portion of the vertical fin rather than on the fuselage to remove it from the influence of wing downwash air thus making the surface more effective.

Fig.4F-12 Grumman F4F-3, Mfr. photo via Joe Weathers. A fine portrait of an F4F-3 with the pilot taking some fresh air by cracking the canopy open a bit. This aircraft is somewhat worn as evidenced by the wing panel replacement disfiguring the nation insignia. The center red circle is now gone from the marking to avoid any possibility of getting it mixed up with the Japanese "meatball". That the airplane is a -3 Wildcat is confirmed by the pitot tube located at the wing leading edge and the four gun armament along with absence of a wing fold parting line indication.

Fig.4F-13 Grumman F4F-3s, USN photo via H. Andrews. An interesting photo of two F4F-3s, the lead aircraft being the second (and last) production machine with cowl guns, and having the old unarmored windshield. The earlier propeller spinner has been removed to disclose a Hamilton Hydromatic propeller hub. An interesting aspect is the late style national insignia with bars on the fuselage. The rear aircraft has a Curtiss propeller and an armored windshield, but where is the carburetor air intake?

that went with slow early climb made a right turn difficult with rudder throw already used up, either a straight or a left turn climbout was generally employed. Most pilots testing the FM-2 rated its take-off characteristics good; a few had some reservations.

TRIMMING

The Wildcat always had sufficient trimming power in its controllable tabs, and the fixed tab on the right aileron of early models could be reset after an initial flight to compensate for any wing heaviness. Test pilots flying the F4F-3 model reported the aircraft would balance satisfactorily at all useful load conditions without ballast, and that elevator trim tab power was sufficient to maintain perfect trim in flight, and also to permit getting the tail down when landing in any loading condition. Rudder tab action was also reported as satisfactory. Yet there were reports on the F4F-4 that it was almost impossible to trim the controls so the plane would fly hands off. For the FM-2 "The trim tabs had sufficient range to maintain stability". All sixteen pilots flying this late Wildcat at a fighter

Fig.4F-14 Grumman F4F-3 Wildcats, USN photo via H. Andrews. War has come to the US, and these F4F-3 Wildcat fighters are running up on the deck of carrier Enterprise in mid-May of 1942. The Wildcat had to hold the fort as the only acceptable US carrier fighter for many months to come. As can be seen the F4F-3 wing did not fold. Douglas Dauntless dive bombers run up behind the Wildcats. These are most probably Marine aircraft ready to fly off to reinforce New Caledonia in the Southwest Pacific.

Fig.4F-15 Grumman F4F-3 Wildcats, USN photo via Joe Christy. A famous photo of Wildcats being flown by two early war aces, Lt.Cdr. Jim Thatch, the originator of the Thatch Weave air combat tactic, and Lt.Edward O'hare (rear aircraft). In February, 1942 Lt. O'hare became the first Navy Wildcat ace by downing five Japanese bombers, one of very few bright spots of early wartime.

Fig.4F-16 Grumman F4F-3A Wildcat, Mfr. photo via H. Andrews. Due to a temporary shortage of two stage supercharged Pratt and Whitney Twin Wasp engines Grumman installed another version with a single stage two speed supercharger in some Wildcats, thereby losing some altitude power and resulting speed and climb performance, though weight was down. These fighters were designated F4F-3As, and by the time of Pearl Harbor all sixty-five had been delivered, most all to the Marines.

Fig.4F-17 Grumman F4F-3 Wildcatfish, Mfr. photo via J. Weathers. In an attempt to copy Japanese fighter floatplanes like Rufe the US Navy decided in late 1942 to provide an F4F-3 to the Edo Corporation for installation of floats. First flight took place in February, 1943.The result of the experiment is shown in the photo where the twin floats are equipped with detacheable beaching gear. It turned out there was no operational need for such a floatplane and the project was abandoned.

meet rated trimmability good. Trim changes due to variations in speed and power were present but moderate.

DIVE AND RECOVERY

On the earliest model F4F-3 the required vertical dive and pullout tests were demonstrated successfully. The airplane terminal velocity was approximately 410 mph IAS (483 mph true airspeed at 10000 feet) with the Curtiss propeller at 45.5 degrees pitch angle. The maximum Pratt and Whitney R-1830 engine RPM allowed in a dive was 3060. Prior to the dive the propeller was set for 2100 RPM with supercharger put in neutral (auxiliary blower inoperative), the

rudder set one and a quarter divisions nose down and rudder tab neutral. The aircraft was quite steady while diving; there could be a slight roll tendency and some longitudinal instability however. The nose down trim helped prevent the pilot from incurring excessive g loading by requiring higher stick forces in a pullout. The Wildcat hardly had to worry about compressibility effects since terminal velocity at 10000 feet represented only Mach 0.66. There was a slight nose heavy tendency at the higher speeds.On the latest model, the FM-2, there were no particular diving limits; terminal velocity dives were allowed with or without wing stores. In this version, with dives not approaching zero lift, some slight forward stick force

Fig.4F-18 Grumman G-36 Martlet, Mfr. photo via Joe Weathers. In October, 1939 France ordered one hundred export versions of the F4F-3 for their navy and in May, 1940 flight tests of such a variant were initiated. When France fell to the Germans Britain took over the order and named the type Martlet. The Grumman G-36A was the Martlet I powered by a Wright Cyclone engine and the G-36B a Martlet II using a Pratt and Whitney Twin Wasp. An early Martlet is shown in brand new condition at the plant.

Fig.4F-19 Flight shot of a G-36A Martlet I powered by a Wright R-1820 Cyclone driving a Hamilton Standard propeller. The airplane is number ten in line of eighty-one produced in the summer and fall of 1940. Like the F4F-3 for the US Navy the wings did not fold, but folding was incorporated in later Martlets. The French-ordered fighters were revised for the British and mounted four .50 caliber wing guns like the F4F-3.

Fig.4F-20 Grumman F4F-4 Wildcat, USN photo via H. Andrews. One of the first of many F4F-4 Wildcats with changes not immediately meeting the eye, but including a manually-foldable wing and six wing machine guns. Also included as standard were self-sealing fuel tanks and pilot armor. The new F4F-4 was initially greeted with howls of protest from pilots because the changes meant increased weight, reduced performance, and less gun firing time because of reduced rounds per gun. There were underwing fittings for external fuel tanks, but the airplane was overloaded and labeled as a real dog when these were carried.

was required. In a zero lift dive there was no longitudinal stick force. Maximum engine RPM in a dive for the Wright Cyclone was 3100. When diving the FM-2 had a tendency to become left wing heavy, and like many other US fighters tended to yaw nose-right. Aileron tab action and some left rudder, or left rudder trim, would correct these inclinations, which increased in magnitude with an increase in speed. During a dive pullout the tendencies decreased. It was recommended that any attitude deviations taking place during the dive be corrected with stick and rudder pedals; that meant keep the aircraft going straight. Most fighter pilots rated dive char-

acteristics of the FM-2, acceleration, stick forces, and recovery, all good. One comment was "Needs better dive capability", meaning it needed to be able to dive faster. Others rating it poor in diving had generally the same feeling.

MANEUVERING
The earlier and lighter Wildcats were quite maneuverable, but the pilot had to work at it, and the aircraft was considered by many as less responsive than early F2A- models. Pilots had comments like "Needed plenty of stick handling to get the best out of it", and "It

Fig.4F-21 Grumman F4F-4 Wildcat, Mfr. photo via J. Weathers. A fine flight portrait of the main Grumman production item in early wartime. The F4F-4 was the only carrier fighter available to the US Navy in quantity during the early months of the war. Though nowhere near as agile and poorer in speed (except at low altitude) and climb than the Japanese Zero fighter opposition, it was rugged, armored, and had plenty of firepower.

Fig.4F-22 Grumman F4F-4 Wildcat, USN photo via H. Andrews. With flaps and gear down and the tail hook catching a wire a Wildcat comes aboard a carrier. Characteristics during carrier approach and landing were considered very good. Though the narrow tread landing gear made the aircraft prone to ground looping on field landings, its soft energy-absorbing features and the alligning effect of a caught wire on the tail hook made the Wildcat a real honey for carrier landings.

Fig.4F-23 Eastern FM-1 Wildcat, Henry Mcgraw photo via J. Weathers. A Wildcat built by Eastern Aircraft Division of General Motors serving in VMF-112 is shown on a training flight over California in 1944 with the late design of the national insignia about as large as could be fit on the fuselage. Note this pilot is truly "behind the eight ball". The FM-1 was the Eastern equivalent of the F4F-4 except it went back to four gun armament.

Fig.4F-24 Grumman F4F-4 Wildcat, USN photo via Joe Christy. A Wildcat in position to come aboard the escort carrier Suwanee (CVE-27) in 1943 just after receiving the "cut" signal. On final approach speed was down to about 80 mph. With an escort carrier, slower than the big fleet carriers, relative speed at touchdown was 55 to 60 mph. One particularly experienced pilot noted that for carrier landings the Wildcat was nothing less than superb.

was truly a Wildcat; if you didn't fly it, it flew you!. One had to maintain control of that plane or you ended up in a heap. It was not too forgiving when you made mistakes". Peak roll rate of an F4F-3 was just under 70 degrees per second at about 250 mph IAS. At 350 mph IAS roll capability fell off to about 50 degrees per second.

The F4F-4, with lots of added weight, was much less maneuverable, and was called uncomplimentary names by its pilots, such as "A TBD-1 with a torpedo; has the feel of a fully-loaded torpedo plane", "Unresponsive", "Generally sluggish, compared even to

F4F-3s and F4F-3As", "Pitifully inferior to the (Japanese) Zero in maneuverability", and "An overloaded clunker".

The FM-2, though more powerful and agile than an F4F-4, had generally similar characteristics. Although the controls were considered effective, it was "Heavy to maneuver; needs lighter controls", and had "Heavy controls; heavy elevators in a turn". In addition "Heavy ailerons and slow rolling", and again "Heavy rudder in a turn". So the general consensus was the controls, while generally effective and nicely harmonized, were "heavy". The aircraft was reported by all to have good stability "It was stable to fly; displayed good stability".

At normal fighter loadings the early F4F-3 performed most all maneuvers including left and right vertical banks, loops, snap rolls, Immelmans, and power-off stalls, and could be maneuvered within its total flight envelope without problems. The same was true of the FM-2 final model. Without external stores there were no standard maneuvers prohibited. With external stores like drop tanks maneuvers such as wingovers, vertical turns, and (for entering a dive) aileron rolls and limited time inverted flight were allowed. Under these conditions loops, snap rolls, chandelles, Immelmans, and spins were prohibited maneuvers however. For the FM-2 maximum maneuver g limits were 7.5 g up to 7700 pounds and 7.0 g up to 8200 pounds gross weight.

APPROACH AND LANDING

On a land approach flaps were lowered, landing gear cranked down, the wheel castor was locked out, the hook left up, and the cockpit canopy locked open. Depending on the model an approach speed was set up, 90 mph IAS or slightly under (pilots cut the speed down as they got more proficient) for an F4F-3, and 98 mph IAS for the later and heavier FM-2. There was no particular speed for flaps or landing gear down, however the flaps would not lower above 150

Fig.4F-25 Eastern civil FM-2 Wildcat, R. Besecker photo via F. Dean coll. When Grumman gave up Wildcat production in favor of the Hellcat Eastern aircraft took over and kept producing Wildcats in the FM-2 version, a development of Grumman XF4F-8 prototypes. Starting in the fall of 1943 Eastern put out a total of over 4400 FM-2 Wildcats, many of which survived the war and were purchased by private owners. This aircraft has wing mounts for rockets.

Fig.4F-26 Eastern civil FM-2 Wildcat, J. Weathers photo. A beautifully restored civil FM-2 Wildcat, number five, photographed at New Orleans in 1969 shows the Curtiss Electric propeller with bullet-shaped power unit cover, the narrow tread landing gear, and two gun ports in the wing leading edge. The FM-2 had also reverted to four .50 caliber wing machine guns. Its wings folded in the same manner as the F4F-4 and FM-1, back along the fuselage.

mph IAS as they were the blow-up type. Since flaps were pneumatically operated lowering them could cause the engine to cough and lose up to 200 RPM, but this was normal and only temporary. Gear was lowered well below 172 mph IAS since above that speed the landing gear mechanism would overtravel, and the cockpit handle would spin and knock at the pilot's shin. There was very little tendency for the aircraft to overshoot because high flap drag gave it a steep glide angle, eliminating any floating. The top of the cowling sloped upwards about four degrees when in a three point landing attitude. This attitude was to be maintained to within a few feet of the ground as speed was quickly lost when the nose was brought up. In approaches at very low power and speed an FM-2 had a tendency to nose down and lose stick control. Upon touchdown careful control with rudder and wheel brakes was required. The soft narrow tread gear made the aircraft susceptible to ground looping. One Navy Commander said "The F4F- has long been known as the best ground looping plane we have. They say there are only two kinds of F4F- pilots, those who have ground looped, and those who are going to". The British pilots had similar problems at times. During the landing run the aircraft could sway on its gear. Some pilots got into PIO (pilot-induced oscillations) in attempting to make corrections, which could worsen the situation. After the landing runout the tail wheel was unlocked to allow turning during taxi.

On a carrier approach with an early Wildcat the downwind leg was flown at about 92 mph IAS where flaps, gear, and canopy were adjusted as above, but here the tail hook was lowered and the tail

wheel left in swivel mode. Many felt the aircraft was easier to land aboard a carrier than on a field. A pilot experienced in carrier landings in the war period said "For carrier landings it was superb". On final approach speed was cut down to about 80 mph. The Wildcat dropped to the deck and sank firmly on its soft shock struts with little rebound, and its trailing hook caught a wire raised across the

Fig.4F-27 Eastern civil FM-2 Wildcat, R. Stuckey photo via J. Weathers. Another view of civil Wildcat number five shows a smooth camouflage paint job and a civil N number carefully hidden under the horizontal stabilizer. FM-2 Wildcats could be picked up for fantastically low prices just after the war during War Assets Administration sell-offs. One of the major external configuration changes was the taller vertical tail which provided considerably better effectiveness via the increased aspect ratio and area and tended to help counteract propeller torque reaction.

Fig.4F-28 Eastern civil FM-2 Wildcat, F. Dean photo. Another fine example of a civil FM-2 as shown in this 1980 picture of N315E taken at Coatsville, Pennsylvania. The airplane was (and perhaps is) owned by Mr.Alexi Dupont of Delaware. Unfortunately the national insignia and tail stripes are wrong (too early); the FM-2 went into production in September, 1943. In addition the N number could have been hidden under the tail. The antennas indicate modern avionics installations for which Mr. DuPont can certainly be forgiven.

Fig.4F-29 Eastern civil FM-2 Wildcat, photo via R. Besecker. This civil FM-2 is marked as a Wildcat of Marine Squadron VMF-211 of the First Marine Air Wing which on December 7, 1941 was operating F4F-3 aircraft. The much later FM-2s were normally operated from escort carriers and were particularly effective in anti-submarine work equipped with rockets. Everything looks "stock" except the antenna fairing under the belly and the early version of the national insignia. The manner in which Grumman and Eastern applied skins wrapped around the fuselage is quite apparent here.

deck. With a thirty knot carrier speed the aircraft speed relative to the deck at touchdown was only about 45 mph. At a fighter pilot gathering eleven said FM-2 approach and landing characteristics were good; none said just fair or poor.

STALLS AND SPINS

The Wildcat, whether in early or later versions, had stall characteristics described variously as "Completely innocuous", "Good", and "Fairly gentle". The F4F-3 with gear and flaps down could be stalled by adjusting the elevator tab to the full tail heavy position, and pulling aft on the stick with a force of ten to fifteen pounds. The stall was evidenced by a definite dropping of the nose and the left wing. The F4F-3 would recover immediately upon release of the stick. Any tendency to spin was thus immediately counteracted by the forward stick movement.

In the FM-2 stalls were quite gentle regardless of flight configuration. Warning of stall appeared as a shudder of the aircraft just prior to full stall development. The FM-2 tended to drop one wing or the other rather than mush after stalling. Aileron control was adequate five mph above, but not at the stall. Dumping the stick forward would bring the aircraft out of a stall. The rudder could then be used to raise a low wing after ailerons became effective.

The F4F-3 Wildcat was checked out very carefully in both left and right spin tests, and from one and a half up to ten turns. After ten turns to the left a recovery took only one half turn; after ten to the right under two turns were required. The spins were done with closed throttle throughout, including during recovery. The stick was held full back and the rudder full over. The recovery was effected by an abrupt rudder reversal followed by full forward stick which required a stick force of forty to fifty pounds. Ailerons were not moved during the spin or the recovery. Recovery from a left hand

spin was almost immediate; from a right hand spin it was slower but positive. The character of the spin changed immediately upon start of the recovery procedure; the nose dropped and the speed of rotation increased before recovery. During the spin the airspeed was about 184 mph IAS.

In addition to normal spins testing was done on inverted spins, both to the left and the right. After stalling the F4F-3 inverted, the stick was held full forward and rudder hard over for the duration of the spin. Recovery was effected by an abrupt reversal of rudder followed by a backward stick movement. There was no aileron movement at any time. Two spin turns were made with recovery in one quarter to one half turn after control reversal. The throttle was closed throughout.

Fig.4F-30 Eastern civil FM-2 Wildcat, W. Larkins photo via R. Besecker. Another civil FM-2 painted in glossy dark blue with authentic markings, the national insignia on the fuselage being the final version. The taller tail of the FM-2 was effective in counteracting propeller torque reaction in low speed high power conditions. The FM-2 used a Wright R-1820 Cyclone engine with a single stage two speed supercharger. Water injection was provided in the later versions.

In spite of all this intentional test spinning of the Wildcat, prior to the FM-2 model spinning in service aircraft was officially not permitted because, among other things, a lot of stick force was required for recovery. In the FM-2 recovery from normal fully developed spins to left or right could be effected in one and a half to two turns by using full opposite rudder and forward stick. Right spins had an erratic motion at times, but eventually became normal; however during the first five or six turns of an abnormal spin recovery was difficult and required about four turns. If the abnormal spin was allowed to continue it would become normal after five or six turns, and recovery could then be made in two turns. Inverted spins were normal, and recovery was easy. In the dirty condition (gear and flaps down) the FM-2 had a tendency to start its rotation gently, and then after about one third of a turn, whip into a spin. The spin was gentle enough, but had a peculiar whip in the early stages of rotation.

CHARACTERISTICS

COCKPIT

The Wildcat cockpit was fairly roomy to UK pilots, and compact but comfortable to US Navy pilots. Seat and pedals were adjustable for different pilot sizes. At a meeting ten pilots rated FM-2 cockpit comfort good while only one rated it fair and two said poor. Some FM-2 pilots said the cockpit was noisy, and mention was made of carbon dioxide leaking in, but the most criticism appeared to be of controls arrangement. One pilot thought controls were confusing. The FM-2 was ranked near poorest of US fighters in location and arrangement of engine, landing gear, and flap controls by the pilots noted above. Criticism of the landing gear control was understandable; stories are legion about pilots getting hurt by this handcrank "Shins could get knocked hard if the crank handle got away from the pilot", "The handle was awkwardly located just behind the pilot's right knee; that landing gear retraction handle was a bit much", and "The handle could spin out of control against the pilot's right leg. Broken bones and cracked shins were common".

VISIBILITY

Like the rest of the tail down fighters, forward visibility was poor in taxi, but better than some types. In the air the view from the Wildcat cockpit was good for an early US fighter type, though visibility aft was pretty well blocked. The larger diameter Wright Cyclone powered models had poorer forward visibility than the versions with the smaller diameter twin row Pratt and Whitney engine.

POWERPLANT OPERATION

The Wildcat was powered by either a Pratt and Whitney R-1830 Twin Wasp, usually with a two stage supercharger, or a Wright R-1820 Cyclone with a single stage two speed supercharger. Strangely perhaps, the P&W engine drove a Curtiss Electric propeller while the Wright engine swung a Hamilton Standard. The first combination was noted by some as quieter with less engine-propeller vibration. The Cyclone, with only nine cylinders, was never a very smooth powerplant. Pilots at a meet said the Cyclone engine in the FM-2 was good, though vibration was criticized. The Curtiss propeller on the P&W models was often criticized for poor reliability, especially with respect to electrical problems at high altitude.

VULNERABILITY/ARMOR

Original production F4F-3 Wildcats had no pilot armor or self-sealing fuel tanks. Just after the US entered the war these items were added to the fighters, and later models had protective systems put in at the factory. The use of self-sealing tanks reduced fuel capacity, which was a sore point, but vulnerability was also significantly reduced. Wildcats had an excellent reputation for standing up well under enemy fire. "It was a tough little fighter", "It could take a lot of punishment", "We stayed in business after being hit repeatedly". Again "The F4F- was as solid as a brick outhouse, almost a flying tank".

Fig.4F-31 Eastern civil FM-2 Wildcat, F. Dean photo. Mr. DuPont is running up his FM-2 Wildcat prior to a takeoff for an air show at New Garden, Pennsylvania in the mid-1970s. The nine cylinder Wright Cyclone had a unique rough staccato sound. Takeoff was effected from grass alongside the runway and the run was very short, particularly with this lightly loaded civilian aircraft.

Fig.4F-32 Eastern civil FM-2 Wildcat, F. Dean photo. With the seat adjusted to full up position and with a cockpit placed high on the fuselage the Wildcat pilot had a very good forward view for taxi compared to many tail-down fighters as illustrated by this pilot taxiing the DuPont Wildcat. Pilots did complain that FM-2s gave off more noise and vibration than the F4F-4. The big reason was that nine cylinder Wright Cyclone versus the smoother two row fourteen cylinder Twin Wasp!

Fig.4F-33 Eastern civil FM-2 Wildcat, F. Dean photo. Another FM-2 photo illustrating the narrow landing gear tread of a Wildcat. Pilots who flew the airplane never forgot that landing gear. It was hand cranked and the work started right after takeoff, often leading to an erratic flight path as the pilot worked the crank. In cranking down for a landing though the mechanism was supposed to be irreversible under certain conditions the gear could drive the hand crank and give the pilot some terrific whacks with the crank handle.

GUN PLATFORM AND WEAPON PERFORMANCE

The F4F- "made a good gun platform" according to most accounts. It was more stable than the Brewster F2A- airplanes. Another comment "The F4F-, a marvelous gun platform". Yet another view "The F4F- could be tricky as a gun platform; it tried to skid while firing".

An F4F-3 carried four .50 caliber guns with lots of ammunition per gun.

The main problem on early airplanes was gun jamming under maneuvering conditions. This was quite common and exasperating. It was found belting was shifting in the ammunition containers and hanging up on rough spots in the feed chutes. These problems were later corrected. In addition during the early part of the war there was a shortage of incendiary rounds for the guns. The F4F-4 was the new model redesigned for folding wings and six wing .50 caliber guns instead of four with considerably less ammunition per gun. With wings folded the guns were somewhat more difficult to service, but the main problem was the shorter firing time allowed which greatly upset pilots. There were comments such as "The F4F-4 ammo supply of (only) 240 rounds per gun was insufficient; the gun battery was unsatisfactory", "Very disappointed with the length of sustained firepower of the F4F-4", and "The reduction of rounds per gun cut the firing time by at least five seconds. That doesn't seem like much, but it can be a lifetime in combat". Also "Weaknesses of the F4F-4 (included) reduced ammo capacity", "Reduced ammo capacity (was) the glaring deficiency in this battle", and so on. The FM-1 and the FM-2 versions by Eastern went back to four guns with more ammunition per gun. The British, who instigated the six gun arrangement the -4 version used for commonality of manufacture, stayed with this configuration.

GENERAL COMMENTS

The F4F-4 was noted as very inferior to the best Japanese fighters as performance was not satisfactory.

One of the reasons for the low opinion held of the F4F-4 concerned limited range and endurance which adversely affected operations from a carrier. Pilots felt it had increased fuel consumption rates compared to earlier versions.

Other factors cited against the F4F-4 versus the earlier F4F-3 and F4F-3A were lower climb rates and poorer maneuverability.

Many pilots felt the F4F-4 was completely outclassed by the Japanese Zero.

Pilots also felt the F4F-4 when carrying two external fuel tanks was a particular dog.

What the F4F-4 lacks in climb and maneuverability is more than compensated for by its excellent armament, protective armor, protected fuel system, and greater strength; let us not condemn our equipment; it shoots down the enemy in flames, and gets most of us back to our base.

The upkeep and general maintenance of the F4F-4 airplane was excellent.

One squadron suffered the usual fate of F4F- pilots who tried to dogfight the Japanese.

The narrow tread of its landing gear made the Wildcat a strange looking bird during taxi. It made for difficulty in cross wind taxi and also on the takeoff run.

The Grumman F4F-4 Wildcat was not a superior aircraft by 1942 standards.

One of these types (P-38 or F4F-) should be replacement planes for P-400 and P-39 aircraft in the South Pacific.

F4F- attributes frequently cited included ruggedness and an ability to dive and run.

A pilot on Guadalcanal noted the Wildcats were able to climb to over 34000 feet to await a Japanese attack on Henderson field.

Fig.4F-34 Eastern civil FM-2 Wildcat, F. Dean photo. A low speed fly-over shows an unusual view of an FM-2. The generous wing area led to a moderate wing loading compared to some other US production fighters and the FM-2 could therefore out-turn them. The type could give a good account of itself in aerial combat properly flown; one Corsair pilot found it hopeless to try and stay with an FM-2. But escort carriers with FM-2s never purposely sought combat with Japanese fighters.

F4F-4 STRUCTURAL DESCRIPTION
(Metal is aluminum alloy unless otherwise noted)

WING GROUP

The wing group was arranged to provide a cantilever mid-wing configuration, and consisted of two inboard sections, two foldable outboard panels, flaps, and ailerons. Flap sections were carried on both the fixed inboard and the outboard panels, and ailerons were located on the outboard ones. The inboard non-folding panels, of all-metal construction, were made principally of two spars, front (main) and rear, formed rib sections, and a covering of stringer-reinforced stressed metal skin. The forward spar, of conventional built-up caps and shear web metal structure, was bolt-attached through heavy fittings to the fuselage bulkhead at station two containing the stainless steel firewall and ran outboard to the wing fold pivot location. The rear spar, of similar but lighter construction, was bolted to the major bulkhead just aft of the pilot's seat at fuselage station five, and ran outboard angled forward to form the support for the inboard flap sections on each side. The wing torque box was formed by the forward spar and the reinforced leading edge "D" section of the wing, and constituted the primary structure.

The fold pivot hinge at the front spar was skewed in a manner allowing outer panels to fold along the sides of the fuselage. Wing folding was manual. A heavy closing nose rib at the end of the center section on each side mounted a fold locking pin cylinder which mated with a lug on the leading edge closing rib of the outer wing panel when the wing was spread. A hand crank was supplied to screw the locking pin through the lug for securing the wing in the spread position. When this was accomplished a signal flag protruding above the wing surface was retracted to give the pilot assurance that the wing sections were locked on the spread position. A wing fold jury strut could be placed between wing tip and horizontal stabilizer on each side when wings were folded. Required electrical service lines passed through the fold joint just ahead of the hinge in the form of pigtail loops to allow slack for fold motion. These included pitot tube lines and electrical conduit. Gun heater tubes in both wing sections matched up when wings were spread.

Mechanical services passed through the joint using various swing links as required. These services included aileron cables, aileron tab control shafts, and gun charging cables. A pneumatic flap operating tube passed close to the hinge. The fold parting line between fixed and outboard sections was contoured to suit the fold geometry requirements as was the canting of fold joint closing ribs of both sections.

The metal outboard, or foldable, panel of each wing consisted of a forward main spar, an aft spar supporting outer flap section and aileron, appropriately spaced ribs, and stressed skin and spanwise stringer covering. As with the inboard sections, the structural torque box was the "D" section made up of the main spar and the leading edge portion ahead of it. Multiple ribs and spanwise stringers under flush riveted stressed skin comprised the leading edge section.

Most of the inner part of the space between wing spars was taken up by the installation of three .50 caliber machine guns at wing stations 77.625, 86, and 122 on each side, along with their accessories such as ammunition boxes, feed chutes, ejection chutes, gun charging controls, trigger motors, and supporting structure. Gun barrels ran forward through the main spar web to the wing leading edge. Guns were mounted between ribs and large access panels were located over each of them, hinged at the main spar location. Access panels ran chordwise from spar to spar and were secured by quarter-turn fasteners.

The outer wing panels were closed at the tip by a metal cap running full chord and containing a navigation light.

Wing flaps were in four sections, one each on inboard and outboard panels. They were of the split type normally recessed under the fixed trailing edge of the wing and hinged to fittings on the rear spars of each section. Two hinges were provided for inboard sections and three for each outboard section. Flaps were all-metal, made up of a leading edge spar, stamped forming ribs, trailing edge member, and metal covering. They were operated by a pneumatic system. Flap actuating cylinders in the inter-spar location on outboard panels acted on flap horns to deflect them. Return springs worked the flaps in the opposite direction. The operating partial vacuum was obtained from the carburetor intake manifold or from a vacuum tank in the fuselage. Maximum flap down angle was 43 degrees. An operating valve was located in the cockpit. Due to an overlap at the wing fold joint the inboard flap sections were driven by the outboard ones so as to act as a unit.

The ailerons were statically and dynamically balanced units located at the outboard trailing edges and supported by the aft spars via three hinges on each side. The hinges incorporated self-alligning bearings. Ailerons were metal framed with a single forward spar, formed ribs and diagonal braces, and a trailing edge closing member. The leading edge sections were metal covered with the remainder of the aileron covered in fabric. The right aileron included a fixed ground-adjustable metal tab about mid-span; the left aileron had a cockpit-controlled trim tab located on its inboard trail edge driven by a mechanical linkage.

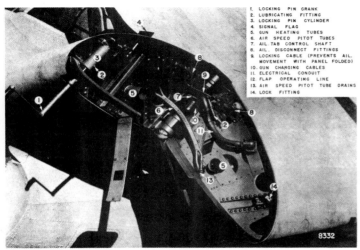

1. LOCKING PIN CRANK
2. LUBRICATING FITTING
3. LOCKING PIN CYLINDER
4. SIGNAL FLAG
5. GUN HEATING TUBES
6. AIR SPEED PITOT TUBES
7. AIL. TAB CONTROL SHAFT
8. AIL. DISCONNECT FITTINGS
9. LOCKING CABLE (PREVENTS AIL. MOVEMENT WITH PANEL FOLDED)
10. GUN CHARGING CABLES
11. ELECTRICAL CONDUIT
12. FLAP OPERATING LINE
13. AIR SPEED PITOT TUBE DRAINS
14. LOCK FITTING

8332

WING FOLDING AXIS

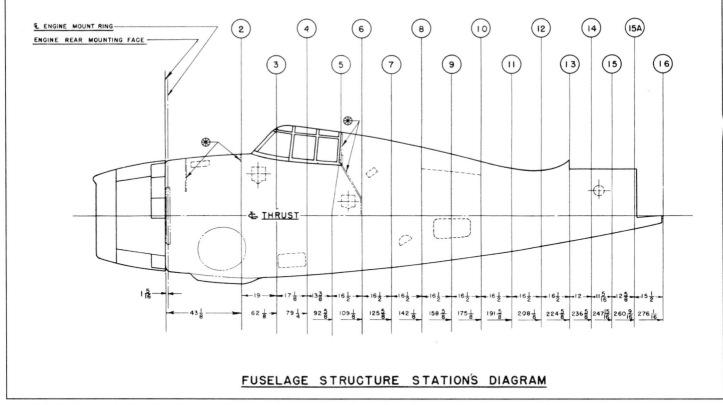

FUSELAGE STRUCTURE STATIONS DIAGRAM

Note: The "star symbol" positioned at two points around the canopy mark the locations of armor plating.

A bomb rack could be installed on the wing outboard sections ahead of the ailerons. The bomb capacity was 100 pounds each side. Provision was made for two oil coolers to be supported under the wing inboard sections, and for a gun camera to be installed in the leading edge of the left inboard wing section. A pitot tube was located at the left wingtip.

TAIL GROUP

The tail group was made up of a horizontal stabilizer, left and right elevators, a vertical fin or stabilizer, and a rudder. All surfaces were cantilever and metal framed.

The horizontal stabilizer was a one piece assembly bolted to fuselage fittings. Its structure consisted of an aft spar, a leading edge and tip member, and stamped forming ribs including reinforced inboard tie-in ribs. The stabilizer tips were recessed to match with the elevator balance sections outboard. Covering was of all-metal stressed skin with flush rivets employed.

Elevators were statically and dynamically balanced units consisting of a leading edge spar, metal nose section covering, ribs and diagonal braces, and fabric covering aft of the nose section. Balance area was located at the elevator tip. Framing was included for an elevator trim tab on each side controlled from the cockpit via a mechanical drive, including flexible shafting located in the elevator. Elevator control was mechanical via torque tube.

The vertical fin was contoured to match up with and bolt tie to a dorsal fin which was an integral part of the fuselage, and to aft fuselage deck structure through the center of the horizontal stabi-lizer. It was an all metal structure using an aft spar to support the rudder, a leading edge former, a tip member, and pressed horizontal forming ribs. Flush riveted metal skin was used over the fin surfaces. Two hinge fittings were bolted to the aft face of the rear spar using self-alligning bearings.

The rudder was constructed in a manner similar to the elevators, was fabric covered, and contained a trim tab mid-span on the trailing edge, controllable from the cockpit. The tab was actuated by a flexible mechanical shaft drive located in the vertical surface. The rudder was driven by a torque tube at the base of the assembly. It was statically and dynamically balanced and had an aerodynamic balance area at the outer tip. The tip section carried a stand-off for a radio aerial.

FUSELAGE GROUP

The fuselage group consisted of two parts, one forward of the firewall at fuselage station two, and the major assembly extending from the firewall aft to the tail.

The forward section was bolted to the firewall bulkhead at station two, and was a built up steel tube and fitting assembly in the lower part of the powerplant bay arranged to support, on aircraft centerline, the inboard ends of the main landing gear upper and lower drag link assemblies. It also provided a hard point to support the aircraft catapult hook mounted in a lower fairing.

The major fuselage section, an all metal stressed skin semi-monocoque structure, ran from the forward firewall, station two, to the rear end of the fuselage, station 16, and was composed of fifteen transverse frames or bulkheads tied with longitudinal longerons or stringers and plated over with circumfirential strips of skin between frames. The two upper longerons ran from the firewall along the cockpit edges to the tail, and formed a crease between the lower rounded fuselage section and the upper turtledeck area to the rear of the cockpit. The monocoque structure was cut out and locally reinforced for access panels over the life raft compartment in the turtledeck, baggage compartment in the aft fuselage, and framing of the observation windows in the fuselage bottom area below the cockpit.

The forward bulkhead at station two was made up of heavy aluminum alloy reinforced with stainless steel on the forward side, and was a solid barrier in front of the cockpit area. Frames three and four were lighter flanged formers spaced, respectively, 19 and 36.125 inches aft of the firewall. The bulkhead at station five was a heavy double flange and web type canted slightly aft which supported the wing rear spar, seat, aft armor plate, and overturn structure. The next nine frames were of angle section and spaced 16.5 inches apart, extending to aft fuselage station 13 at the start of the fin assembly. The frames at station 13 and aft were reinforced to mount the tail wheel landing gear, tail hook, and the tail group elements. The cockpit section between frames two and five were enclosed by a windshield assembly and a sliding canopy. The wind-

shield consisted of four transparent areas-front, two side, and upper. The front windshield was a flat section of bullet-resistant plate glass. The other sections were of Plexiglas, and all were set in metal framing attached to the firewall and upper longerons. The sliding canopy was composed of two sections framed in metal and riding in longitudinal rails. It was operated using a large handle mounted in a slide on the right side of the cockpit. The handle could be latched in any of four positions from closed to fully open. The handle could be operated from outside via a small door just below the windshield. Pins joining slide and canopy could be released in an emergency. The pilot's bucket seat was adjustable to any one of seven height positions, and provision was made for a standard shoulder harness.

LANDING GEAR GROUP

The landing gear group consisted of two forward main gear elements, a tail wheel, and an arresting hook. The main gear was fully retractable by manual mechanical means, and the tail wheel was fixed. The main gear retracted into wheel wells and space within the fuselage just ahead of the firewall. Wheels and forged steel axle members, along with two drag link assemblies tied to a fixed tubular steel framework on centerline in a double-vee arrangement to take drag loads, were pinned to the lower end of oleo shock struts.

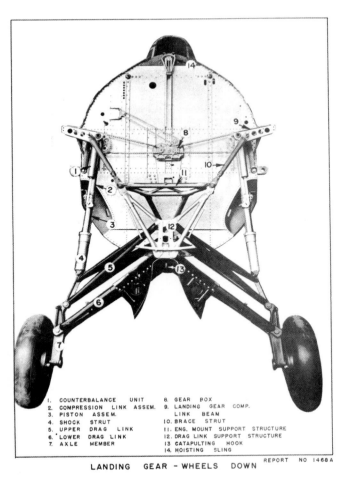

1. COUNTERBALANCE UNIT	8. GEAR BOX
2. COMPRESSION LINK ASSEM.	9. LANDING GEAR COMP.
3. PISTON ASSEM.	LINK BEAM
4. SHOCK STRUT	10. BRACE STRUT
5. UPPER DRAG LINK	11. ENG. MOUNT SUPPORT STRUCTURE
6. LOWER DRAG LINK	12. DRAG LINK SUPPORT STRUCTURE
7. AXLE MEMBER	13 CATAPULTING HOOK
	14. HOISTING SLING

REPORT NO 1468A

LANDING GEAR - WHEELS DOWN

GRUMMAN AIRCRAFT ENGINEERING CORPORATION

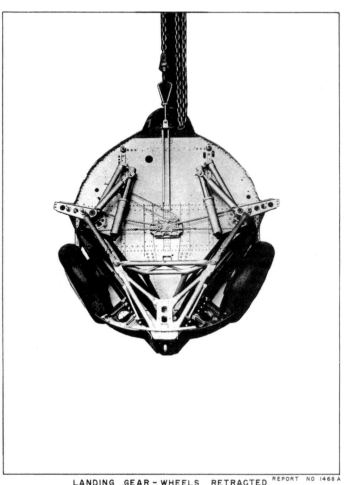

LANDING GEAR - WHEELS RETRACTED REPORT NO 1468A

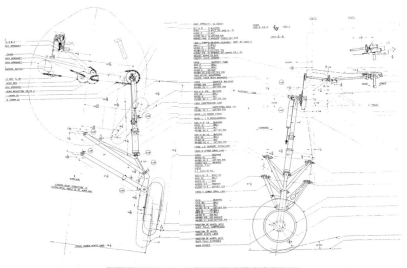

Wildcat main landing gear mechanism.

The upper ends of the shock struts were pinned to a compression link assembly, the upper ends of which were fixed to the center shafts of chain-driven sprockets mounted on either side of the firewall. Turning the sprockets folded the compression link assemblies and thereby pulled shock struts, pivoting drag link assemblies, and wheels upwards and inwards so that the wheels stowed in recessed pockets with all linkage contained within the fuselage contour in front of the firewall. Sheet metal fairing assemblies tied to the lower drag linkage faired over the fuselage underside in the landing gear area to provide a smooth outer contour with gear retracted. The chain sprockets on the firewall were driven from a crank in the cockpit and the mechanical drive system consisted of gearboxes, torque tubes, sprockets, and chains. The reduction ratio was such that the pilot could crank 28 turns and retract the gear. The system was not supposed to over-run and back-drive the pilot's crank, but sometimes it did.

Main gear tires were 26 inch diameter six inch wide smooth contour types. Hydraulic brakes were included and were operated by toe pressure on the rudder pedals. With the wheels cranked to full-down enough force was generated by the chain drive system, in conjunction with spring counterbalancing units, to prevent wheels inadvertantly retracting, thus providing a downlock.

The tail wheel was initially a small solid rubber type later replaced with a 10 inch diameter pneumatic wheel carried on a single side axle fork. The protruding mechanism was shrouded by a fairing fixed to the fuselage. The tail wheel castor strut was pivoted and mounted so it could swivel within the constraint of centering springs. An oleo shock strut was pinned to the wheel strut and to fuselage structure. The tail wheel mechanism was equipped with a

swivel lock pin controlled from the cockpit by a cable. When the pin was inserted the tail wheel was locked in trail position; when the pin was pulled the unit was free to swivel.

A 41 inch long forged steel retractable arresting hook was mounted to fuselage structure in a manner such that it could be stowed inside the fuselage or extended for use during carrier landings. When extended the hook pulled from a point right at the end of the fuselage and one inch below the aircraft thrust line, and it could swing from 30 degrees above horizontal to 60 degrees below. The hook was operated through a system of cables by a pilot control in a slide under the cockpit left hand rail. An approximate 20 pound push on the control was required to retract the hook.

ENGINE SECTION

The engine section group was made up of the engine mount and the engine cowling parts.

The engine mount was a conventional alloy steel tube structure mounted to the upper firewall at four locations. Tubes ran forward to support an engine mount ring which directly supported the engine through rubber shock mounts. A dished cowl former was attached to and surrounded the mount ring, and two support rings for cowling panels were mounted on engine rocker box covers, the rear of these supporting hinged cowl flap assemblies over part of the periphery. Cowl flaps were manually operated by a hand crank on the instrument panel and a mechanical drive system. Enclosing metal cowl sections, along with carburetor and cooling air ducting located above and alongside the engine respectively, were attached to the support rings by quick-detach quarter-turn fasteners.

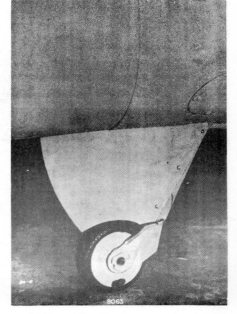

SOLID & PNEUMATIC TAIL WHEEL - SIDE VIEW

F4F-/FM- SYSTEMS DESCRIPTION

PROPULSION SUBSYSTEMS

ENGINE

The various versions of the Wildcat were powered by either a two-row 14 cylinder Pratt and Whitney R-1830 Twin Wasp radial engine or a single row nine cylinder Wright R-1820 Cyclone radial, both in the 1200 HP class. The definitive version of the Twin Wasp incorporated a two stage two speed mechanical supercharger, although some early aircraft had a version with a single stage two speed unit. The two stage engine had a main stage impeller gear

P&W R-1830 14 cylinder twin row engine in the F4F-3, and -4.

ratio of 8.08 :1 with a 9.5 inch diameter impeller (blower) and an auxiliary stage impeller gear ratio of 8.48:1 with an 11 inch diameter impeller. Engine bore was 5.50 inches and stroke was also 5.5 inches; the engine compression ratio was 6.7:1. The propeller reduction gear ratio was 3:2. Maximum engine RPM was 2700 or 2900. The propeller rotated clockwise looking from the cockpit.

The Wright Cyclone engine had a single stage two speed supercharger. Engine cylinder bore was 6.125 inches and stroke was 6.875 inches. The maximum engine RPM was 2600 or 2700, the latter figure for later engines with redesigned crankshaft. The propeller rotated clockwise looking from the cockpit with this engine too.

ENGINE INDUCTION SYSTEM

Carburetor air entered from an intake at the forward end of the upper cowling. It was ducted to a valve actuated mechanically by a tee-handle push-pull control below the left side of the instrument panel. One position of the valve allowed the outside intake air to pass directly to the carburetor unobstructed; the other position blocked this air passage and allowed the carburetor to obtain warm air from the engine accessory section compartment to reduce the possibility of carburetor icing.

ENGINE EXHAUST SYSTEM

On the Twin Wasp engined aircraft cylinder exhaust was directed into a stainless steel collector ring and exhausted at two points low on the outside of the cowling. On FM-2 airplanes with the Wright engine cylinder exhaust was taken by individual short pipes to be exhausted at three locations at the aft edge of the engine cowl, one low and centered and the other two left and right just above the longitudinal centerline of the aircraft and the wing location.

ENGINE-MOUNTED ACCESSORIES

Engine accessories included in all cases the carburetor, magnetos, electrical generator, fuel pump, oil pump, vacuum pump, propeller governor, starter, and tachometer generator.

ENGINE CONTROLS

Throttle and mixture controls were levers on a quadrant at the left side of the pilot's seat and were directly connected via rods and links to the engine carburetor. In models where a water injection system was installed throttle movement all the way forward past a detent or joggle selected COMBAT POWER. The supercharger control was a lever in a quadrant just aft of the throttle quadrant and was mechanically linked by rods directly to the engine. The Wright Cyclone engine models lever had two positions-low and high- to shift between the two blower speeds. The Twin Wasp powered models had levers with three positions- neutral, low, and high- the first position making the auxiliary blower inoperative.

PROPELLER

The aircraft was most often equipped with a Curtiss Electric constant speed variable pitch propeller with three blades. Some export models and a few USN models used a Hamilton Standard constant speed three blade 23E50 Hydromatic hydraulic propeller. The Curtiss propeller was a C532D or a C5315S model using respectively either design 109354-12 solid aluminum blades or design 512-1C1.5-15 hollow steel blades. Propeller diameter was 9'9" except for the FM-2 where it was 10'0".

PROPELLER CONTROLS

The Curtiss Electric propeller was controlled in the cockpit by a mode selector switch for either automatic governor-controlled constant speed operation or manual increase or decrease blade pitch (and thus manual RPM control). With governor control use was made of the push-pull knob under the left side of the instrument panel to select desired RPM. Push-pull gave large selected RPM changes, and knob rotation provided a vernier control. Output of this control was linked directly to the propeller governor on the engine nose. Controls were generally similar for the Hamilton propeller.

ENGINE STARTING SYSTEM (FM-2)

For priming the engine an electrically controlled system drew fuel from the carburetor and injected it into two places in the diffuser section of the engine. The primer switch was next to the starter switch at the right side of the cockpit. The starter was a Breeze Type I cartridge model where the Type C cartridge was fired electrically by the starter switch. Gases from the cartridge acted on a piston in a cylinder which drove a gear train to crank the engine. The starter breech was located on the right side of the engine mount, and was accessible from the right landing gear well. A box with extra cartridges was located on the engine mount. No backup starting system was provided.

ENGINE WATER INJECTION SYSTEM

Late model FM-2 aircraft versions with the Wright Cyclone engine had a water injection system provided. The water tank, located in the accessory compartment, contained a ten minute supply of water/alcohol mixture, pressurized via a boost pressure supply line. A check valve in the line prevented tank pressure loss when manifold pressure was reduced after takeoff. The manifold pressure regulator and water injection control unit were mounted together. The solenoid valve controlling start of water injection was actuated by two switches in series. One switch was on the supercharger control quadrant and the second was on the throttle control lever. Both had to be actuated in water injection.

ENGINE COOLING SYSTEM

The engine was cooled by air entering the front of the engine cowling, passing over the finned and baffled cylinders, and exiting through cowl flap openings at the aft edge of the cowl. Some models had upper and lower cowl flap sets and some upper only. The hinged flap segments were operated together by a hand crank mechanically attached to a ganged flap linkage at the cowl location. The pilot-operated crank varied the air exit area and thus the cooling airflow over the engine.

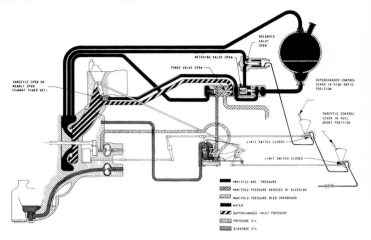

Water Injection System Schematic Diagram

ENGINE LUBRICATION SYSTEM (FM-2)

Oil for lubrication was carried in a nine to eleven US gallon tank attached to the upper engine mount. It was distributed by an engine-driven oil pump and returned by scavenger pumps in the engine nose sump and rear case. In the Twin Wasp powered airplanes an oil cooler was located under the inboard fixed section of each wing in a semi-submerged installation with oil lines running through the wing. In the Cyclone-powered FM-2 a single oil cooler was located low and sideways in the engine accessory compartment. A blast tube took cowl intake air and turned it 90 degrees through the cooler from where it dumped into the engine compartment to be then vented overboard. Airflow through the coolers reduced oil temperature in the cooler tubes. A thermostatic control valve mounted on the cooler determined, based on oil temperature, whether oil flowed through the cooler or bypassed it.

Late FM-2 airplanes incorporated an oil dilution system consisting of a solenoid valve controlled from a cockpit switch, a single restricted fitting, and a safety shut-off cock located in the dilution line between carburetor and oil tank suction outlet leading to the oil pump.

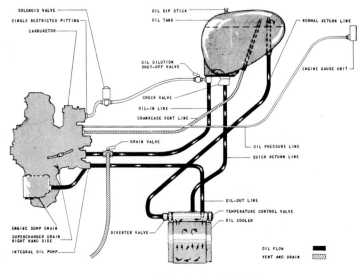

Oil system diagram for FM-2.

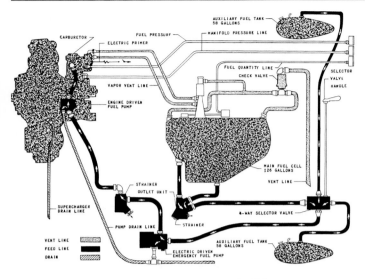

Fuel system diagram for FM-2.

one just aft of the first tank carrying 27 US gallons. Two 58 US gallon drop tanks could also be carried under the inboard wing sections.

On the FM-2 the fuel system consisted principally of a single internal tank with strainer, fill and vent lines, a fuel selector valve (in later models with external under-wing tanks), an engine-driven fuel pump, and an electrically-driven emergency fuel pump along with connecting fuel lines. In late FM-2s a drop tank could be carried under each wing.

The fuel tanks in the fuselage were unprotected in early pre-war Wildcat models. Protection from gunfire was first achieved by using a self-sealing liner inside the aluminum tank. Later FM-2 airplanes had a rigid self-sealing fuel cell with no aluminum shell. Main tank capacity was 117 US gallons with a liner, 130 US gallons without a liner, and on the late airplanes with a rigid self-sealing cell 126 US gallons. The capacity of the wing drop tanks was 58 US gallons each. The tank selector valve handle was located on the left hand cockpit shelf and it was attached mechanically to the valve. The electrically-driven emergency pump was controlled by an electric switch set in the left hand side of the instrument panel. An electric fuel quantity gage for the main tank was located in the cockpit. No gage was provided for the drop tanks. On late FM-2 airplanes a low fuel level warning light was installed. Pull rings, one on each side of the cockpit, were provided for releasing the drop tanks using mechanical cables through the wings to the bomb racks.

ENGINE FIRE SENSING/FIRE EXTINGUISHING SYSTEMS
No such systems were incorporated.

FUEL SYSTEM
The F4F-4 and FM-1 airplanes had two protected internal fuselage fuel tanks, a large one forward carrying 117 US gallons, and a smaller

FIXED EQUIPMENT SUBSYSTEMS

INSTRUMENTS
Flight instruments consisted of altimeter, directional gyro, airspeed indicator, turn and bank indicator, rate of climb indicator, gyro horizon, compass, and clock.

Engine instruments included were: cylinder head temperature gage, manifold pressure gage, tachometer, fuel quantity gage, and engine gage unit.

1. CLOCK
2. CYLINDER HEAD TEMPERATURE GAGE
3. RUDDER PEDAL ADJUSTMENT LEVER
4. PROPELLER CONTROL
5. IGNITION SWITCH
6. GUN SIGHT LIGHT SWITCH
7. EMERGENCY ELECTRIC FUEL PUMP SWITCH
8. CHECK- OFF SWITCH
9. WINDSHIELD DEFROSTER
10. ALTIMETER
11. DIRECTIONAL GYRO
12. PADDED ELECTRIC GUN SIGHT MOUNT
13. AIRSPEED INDICATOR
14. TURN & BANK INDICATOR
15. RATE OF CLIMB INDICATOR
16. GYRO HORIZON
17. MANIFOLD PRESSURE GAGE
18. TACHOMETER
19. OUTSIDE AIR TEMPERATURE
20. FUEL QUANTITY GAGE
21. PRIMER PUMP
22. COWL FLAPS HANDCRANK
23. ENGINE GAGE UNIT
24. COMPASS
25. OIL DILUTION SWITCH
26. RADIO SIGNAL LIGHT

Other instruments included an oxygen flowmeter and an outside air temperature gage.

SURFACE CONTROLS
The ailerons and elevators were controlled by a standard type stick and the rudder by standard underhung pedals. The pedals were adjustable to four different positions.

Elevator control cables ran from the cockpit stick aft over pulleys through the fuselage to the upper and lower input arms of a bellcrank, an aft output arm of which drove a link and crank arm fixed to the elevator torque drive tube.

Rudder controls were similarly of the pulley and steel cable type running from pedals in the cockpit aft to control horns driving a rudder torque tube at the base of the vertical tail.

Ailerons were driven from the control stick via cables, pulleys, and linkage in the

INSTRUMENT PANEL
F4F-4

8977

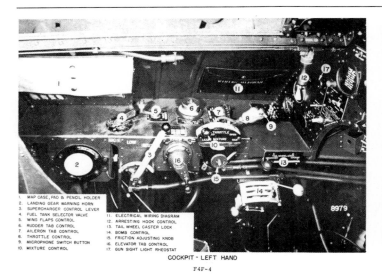

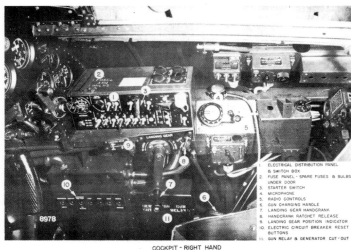

COCKPIT - LEFT HAND
F4F-4

1. MAP CASE, PAD & PENCIL HOLDER
2. LANDING GEAR WARNING HORN
3. SUPERCHARGER CONTROL LEVER
4. FUEL TANK SELECTOR VALVE
5. WING FLAPS CONTROL
6. RUDDER TAB CONTROL
7. AILERON TAB CONTROL
8. THROTTLE CONTROL
9. MICROPHONE SWITCH BUTTON
10. MIXTURE CONTROL
11. ELECTRICAL WIRING DIAGRAM
12. ARRESTING HOOK CONTROL
13. TAIL WHEEL CASTER LOCK
14. BOMB CONTROL
15. FRICTION ADJUSTING KNOB
16. ELEVATOR TAB CONTROL
17. GUN SIGHT LIGHT RHEOSTAT

COCKPIT - RIGHT HAND
F4F-4

1. ELECTRICAL DISTRIBUTION PANEL & SWITCH BOX.
2. FUSE PANEL - SPARE FUSES & BULBS UNDER DOOR
3. STARTER SWITCH
4. MICROPHONE
5. RADIO CONTROLS
6. GUN CHARGING HANDLE
7. LANDING GEAR HANDCRANK
8. HANDCRANK RATCHET RELEASE
9. LANDING GEAR POSITION INDICATOR
10. ELECTRIC CIRCUIT BREAKER RESET BUTTONS
11. GUN RELAY & GENERATOR CUT-OUT

wing. The upper and lower cable assemblies running through the fixed inboard section of the wing were routed to the fold joint where the local cable and pulley arrangement right at the joint allowed folding without any break in the cable runs which then ran outboard in the folding panel to the ailerons. Elevator tabs, one for each unit, were controlled using a hand crank on the side of the left hand shelf. A cable and pulley tab drive ran aft through the fuselage

to a point where motion was picked up by flexible shafts running in tubes placed diagonally in the stabilizer surfaces from which the drive was carried past the hinge to the tab horn.

The rudder trim tab was controlled by a wheel at the left of the pilot's seat on a shelf. The tab drive through the fuselage and fin was similar to that of the elevator tab system.

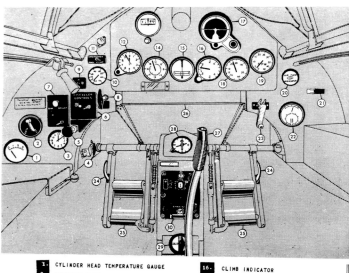

1.	CYLINDER HEAD TEMPERATURE GAUGE	16.	CLIMB INDICATOR
2.	IGNITION SWITCH	17.	GYRO HORIZON
3.	CLOCK	18.	MANIFOLD PRESSURE GAUGE
4.	WINDSHIELD DEFROSTER CONTROL	19.	TACHOMETER
5.	PROPELLER GOVERNOR CONTROL	20.	OXYGEN FLOW METER
6.	PROPELLER SELECTOR SWITCH AND CIRCUIT BREAKER	21.	OIL DILUTION SWITCH
7.	GUN SIGHT SWITCH AND RHEOSTAT	22.	ENGINE GAUGE UNIT
8.	CARBURETOR AIR CONTROL	23.	COWL FLAP CONTROL HANDLE
9.	LOW LEVEL FUEL WARNING LIGHT	24.	PEDAL ADJUSTMENT LEVERS
10.	FUEL QUANTITY GAUGE	25.	RUDDER PEDALS
11.	EMERGENCY FUEL PUMP SWITCH	26.	CHART BOARD
12.	ALTIMETER	27.	CONTROL STICK
13.	DIRECTIONAL GYRO	28.	COMPASS
14.	AIRSPEED INDICATOR	29.	CABIN AIR INTAKE CONTROL
15.	TURN AND BANK INDICATOR	30.	MARK 3 STATION DISTRIBUTOR

Forward view of FM-2 cockpit.

1.	MAP CASE	10.	AILERON TAB CONTROL
3.	FUEL TANK SELECTOR VALVE	11.	THROTTLE AND MIXTURE CONTROL QUADRANT
4.	LANDING FLAP CONTROL	12.	OXYGEN OR LIP MICROPHONE SWITCH
5.	SUPERCHARGER CONTROL QUADRANT	13.	RECOGNITION LIGHT SWITCHES
6.	DROPPABLE FUEL TANK RELEASE HANDLE	14.	ARRESTING HOOK CONTROL HANDLE
7.	RUDDER TAB CONTROL	15.	TAIL WHEEL LOCK CONTROL
8.	ELEVATOR TAB CONTROL	16.	GUN CHARGING HANDLES
9.	WIRING DIAGRAM POCKET	17.	CHECK OFF LIST

Left side view of FM-2 cockpit.

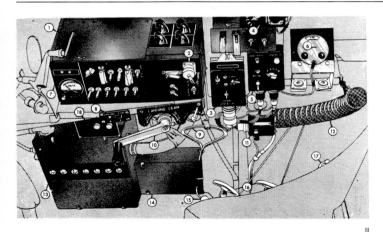

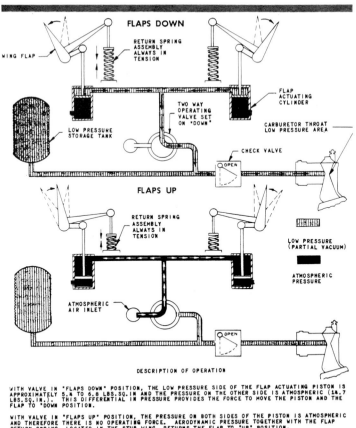

1- PILOT'S DISTRIBUTION PANEL
2- POWER RECEPTACLE (FOR ELECTRI-
   CALLY HEATED SUITS)
3- COMMUNICATION EQUIPMENT CONTROL UNIT
4- IFF CONTROL BOX AND SELECTOR SWITCH
5- NAVIGATION EQUIPMENT CONTROL UNIT
6- RANGE RECEIVER
7- VOLTAMMETER OR VOLTMETER
8- LANDING GEAR POSITION INDICATOR
9- DROPPABLE FUEL TANK RELEASE HANDLE
10- LANDING GEAR HANDCRANK
11- JACK BOX
12- COCKPIT VENTILATOR
13- MAIN JUNCTION BOX AND CIRCUIT
    BREAKER RESET BUTTONS
14- GENERATOR CUT-OUT
15- PILOT'S SEAT ADJUSTMENT HANDLE
16- RIGHT HAND GUN CHARGING HANDLES
17- OXYGEN BOTTLE SHUT-OFF VALVE
18- CIRCUIT BREAKER BOX AND RESET
    BUTTONS FOR ROCKETS

Right side view of FM-2 cockpit.

DESCRIPTION OF OPERATION

WITH VALVE IN "FLAPS DOWN" POSITION, THE LOW PRESSURE SIDE OF THE FLAP ACTUATING PISTON IS APPROXIMATELY 5.4 TO 6.8 LBS.SQ.IN AND THE PRESSURE ON THE OTHER SIDE IS ATMOSPHERIC (14.7 LBS.SQ.IN.). THIS DIFFERENTIAL IN PRESSURE PROVIDES THE FORCE TO MOVE THE PISTON AND THE FLAP TO "DOWN POSITION.

WITH VALVE IN "FLAPS UP" POSITION, THE PRESSURE ON BOTH SIDES OF THE PISTON IS ATMOSPHERIC AND THEREFORE THERE IS NO OPERATING FORCE. AERODYNAMIC PRESSURE TOGETHER WITH THE FLAP RETURN SPRING, LOCATED IN THE STUB WING, RETURNS THE FLAP TO "UP" POSITION.

Wildcat pneumatic flap operating system.

A fixed tab on the right aileron was ground-adjustable by crimping. A cockpit wheel controlled tab was located on the left aileron. The tab drive was taken through the wing fold joint at the forward spar by a Kenyon flexible shaft.

ELECTRICAL SYSTEM

The electrical system was of the conventional 24 volt DC single wire ground return type using an engine-driven generator and a battery.

The battery was located in the fuselage behind the cockpit just forward of the radio installation, and was accessible through a fuselage access door. The pilot's electrical distribution panel was at the right side in the cockpit, and provided storage for spare electrical items. All other electrical system controls, and an ammeter, were at the right side of the pilot. These included a junction box with circuit breaker reset buttons and generator cut-out. A receptacle in which to plug a pilot's heated suit was provided. Electrical switches included those for exterior and cockpit lights, guns, rocket firing (if fitted), gun camera, pitot tube heater, starter, primer, and battery.

HYDRAULIC SYSTEM

Other than the landing gear braking system no hydraulic system was provided.

PNEUMATIC SYSTEM

A pneumatic system was installed to operate the wing flaps. A partial vacuum for the system was obtained from the low pressure throat area of the engine carburetor intake manifold and could be applied via a control valve directly to a flap operating cylinder in each wing. This partial vacuum could also be stored in a large vacuum tank in the baggage compartment aft of the cockpit. The tank had enough capacity to operate the flaps at least twice with the engine inoperative.

The actuating cylinders were single acting in the direction to have their pistons drive the flaps to the down position via crank arms. Return springs located in the stub wings acted on separate flap drive horns and together with outside dynamic air pressure tended to push the flaps into the retracted position. With the operating valve in the flaps up position both sides of the cylinder pistons were at atmospheric pressure and no operating force was provided. The inboard flaps were driven by the outboard sections through an overlap. Flexible hose lines were provided to go through the wing fold joint without disconnection.

COMMUNICATION/NAVIGATION/IDENTIFICATION SYSTEMS

Various radio installations were used in the Wildcat series. The FM-2 alone was equipped with three different installations depending on airplane serial munber, and exported airplanes often had equipment different from U.S. Navy types. Late FM-2 aircraft had the

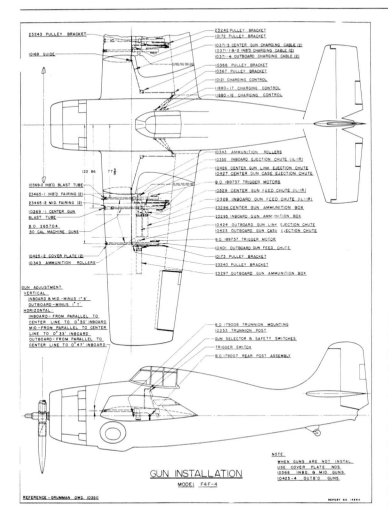

REFERENCE - GRUMMAN DWG. 10350

GUN INSTALLATION
MODEL F4F-4

NOTE
WHEN GUNS ARE NOT INSTAL.
USE COVER PLATE NOS.
10368 INBD. & MID. GUNS
10425-4 OUTB'D. GUNS

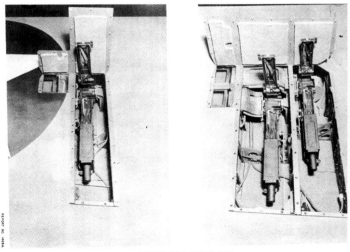

OUTBOARD, MID & INBOARD GUNS

following systems installed: AN/ARC-1 communications set, AN/ARR-2a navigation equipment, BC1206 range equipment, AN/APX-1 IFF set, and provisions for ABA-1 identification gear.

ARMAMENT PROVISIONS

Armament of the various Wildcat models varied between a four and a six .50 caliber Browning M-2 machine gun installation in the wings. The earliest USN aircraft had four guns; the British export models had six, and the later -4 Navy aircraft had six. The Eastern FM-1 and FM-2 versions had just four. Guns were located in the outer folding wing panels centered on wing stations 77.625 and 86 with the outboard gun at station 122 if carried. The reason for the outboard gun being far from the inboard two was to leave space for the ammunition trays which ran outboard from those two guns. Gun breeches were aft of the main spar with barrels protruding through the spar web and structural "D" section to blast tubes in the leading edge. A total of 1720 rounds of ammunition could be carried in the four gun airplanes, and a total of 1440 rounds in the six gun types. Gun mounts were the standard forward trunnion and rear post type. Ammunition was fed from container boxes over rollers to feed chutes, all outboard of their respective guns. Case and link ejection chutes on the inboard side of the weapons led to the lower

wing surface for overboard dumping. Guns were charged manually using a pull handle for each gun in the cockpit floor on each side of the pilot's seat. Handles were connected to a system of cables and pulleys running outboard to each wing. Pulling a handle would put a shell under the gun hammer ready to be fired. Charging cables were routed through the wing fold pin location on each side. Controls for firing the guns were electrical. Gun switches were located on the right side of the cockpit and a trigger switch was incorporated in the control stick handle. Electrical cables were routed through the wing fold hinges out to trigger motors used to fire the guns. Gun bays were covered by individual access panels hinged forward at the main spar location and tied down by quarter turn fasteners. Ammunition loading doors were provided just outboard of the guns. In the FM-2 a Mark 8 gunsight of the reflector type was mounted above the instrument panel center, controlled by a switch and rheostat on the panel. An electrically heated and operated AN-N-4 gun camera was mounted in the leading edge of the FM-2 left stub wing. Pictures were taken whenever the guns were fired by the trigger switch on the pilot's stick. Electric gun heaters of the pad type could be installed over each gun breach. On late FM-2 airplanes three MARK V rockets could be carried under each wing. Rocket firing was accomplished electrically. Each rocket launcher consisted of two streamlined posts; the forward post contained a fuse aiming control and the aft post contained both a receptacle for the rocket firing lead and a latch to restrain the rocket until fired. A bomb up to 250 pounds could be carried on each wing rack as an alternate load. As noted earlier the same mechanical release system was used for bombs or drop tanks.

PASSIVE DEFENSE SYSTEM (F4F-4 AND FM-1)

Passive defense items consisted of self-sealing fuel tanks, a large piece of armor plate in the upper portion of the engine accessory compartment just ahead of the oil tank, armor plate just below the front windshield panel, a bullet-resistant glass forward windshield, and two large sections of armor plate behind the cockpit, one extending up behind the pilot's head, and the other protecting the pilot's back down to the cockpit floor.

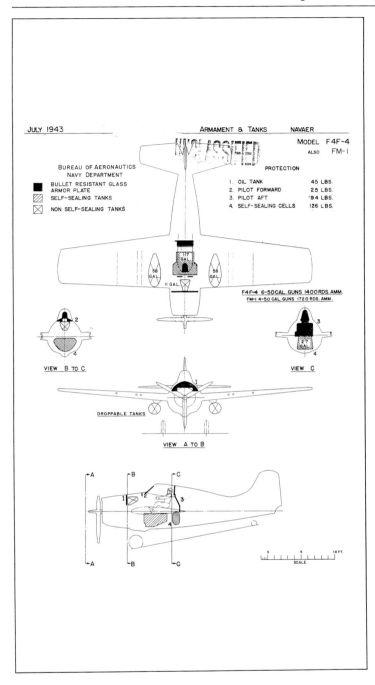

JULY 1943 — ARMAMENT & TANKS — NAVAER

MODEL F4F-4
ALSO FM-I

BUREAU OF AERONAUTICS
NAVY DEPARTMENT

■ BULLET RESISTANT GLASS
ARMOR PLATE
▨ SELF-SEALING TANKS
⊠ NON SELF-SEALING TANKS

PROTECTION
1. OIL TANK   45 LBS.
2. PILOT FORWARD   25 LBS.
3. PILOT AFT   94 LBS.
4. SELF-SEALING CELLS 126 LBS.

F4F-4 6-50CAL. GUNS 1400 RDS. AMM.
FM-I 4-50 CAL. GUNS 1720 RDS. AMM.

VIEW B TO C
VIEW C

DROPPABLE TANKS
VIEW A TO B

SCALE 0 5 10 FT.

FURNISHINGS

A bucket-type seat was provided for the pilot. The seat could be adjusted to any of seven positions using a control lever at the right side which operated a locking pin. With the pin out the seat was counterbalanced by shock cord. A shoulder harness with locking lever was provided with the seat. A canvas map case was located at the left side of the cockpit, and an extensible chart board was located beneath the instrument panel. A relief tube was stowed on the floor.

HEATING/COOLING/VENTILATION SYSTEMS

A cabin air intake control was located in the cockpit low and centered just forward of the control stick. The control was a toe-operated air valve which allowed introduction of fresh outside air via ducting from an intake in the right side stub wing. No heating or cooling equipment was installed.

ICE PROTECTION SYSTEM

A tee handle control for warm air directed into the air space between the double windshield panels was located near the left rudder pedal. The control valved air to the windshield from the accessory compartment.

A carburetor air control allowed use of warm accessory compartment air to feed the carburetor and prevent icing.

HANDLING EQUIPMENT

A parking harness for the stick, located in the baggage compartment, was provided to lock elevators and ailerons. For tiedown with wings spread, rings were provided at wing station 154. With wings folded the rings at station 73 were used. The tail wheel was locked, and a tail tiedown was attached to the catapult hold-back bolt.

FLOTATION GEAR

Very early development airplanes had an inflatable flotation bag system installed in the wings before folding was incorporated. The system was discarded after difficulties with inadvertant inflation arose. No other airplane flotation system was employed. The pilot depended on his personal life preserver. The F4F-4 would sink in a very few seconds after ditching.

ARRESTING GEAR

The arresting gear consisted of a hook located at the aft end of the fuselage. It was extended and retracted through use of a system of cables connected to a push-pull control handle in a slide under the cockpit left side rail.

USEFUL LOAD SUBSYSTEMS
GUNS/BOMBS/ROCKETS/GUNSIGHT/GUN CAMERA

See the earlier section on armament provisions.

PYROTECHNICS

Early aircraft through some of the FM-2 models had a Mark 8 pyrotechnic pistol, a holster assembly, and a holder for four extra cartridges all located on the left hand cockpit shelf. The pistol had to be fired overboard out of the aircraft.

PHOTOGRAPHIC EQUIPMENT

The normal Wildcat fighter had no photographic equipment other than a gun camera on some models as described earlier.

A special highly modified F4F-7 long range photographic version was built in small numbers.

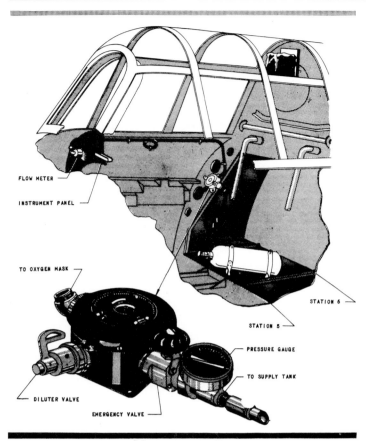

FLOW METER

INSTRUMENT PANEL

TO OXYGEN MASK

STATION 6

STATION 5

PRESSURE GAUGE

TO SUPPLY TANK

TO DILUTER VALVE

EMERGENCY VALVE

FM-2 Oxygen system.

trol wheel at the forward end. The regulator and gage were to the right rear of the pilot and the flowmeter was at the far right side of the instrument panel.

REFERENCES, F4F-/FM-
1. Minutes of Fighter Conference, NAS Patuxent River, Md. Oct. 1944.
2. NACA Report ACR Oct. 1940.
3. John J. Schneider Archives (weights).
4. The Wildcat in World war II, Barrett Tillman,
5. Wings of the Navy, Capt. Eric Brown, RN.
6. Duels in the Sky, Capt. Eric Brown, RN.
7. The First Team, John B. Lindstrom, Naval Institute Press, Annapolis, Md.
8. Journal of the American Aviation Historical Society, Winter,1961, The Wildcat Story, Frank L. Greene.
9. Aero Engine Lab. Naval Aircraft Factory, Philadelphia, Pa., Project 3498, Engine Performance Curves, PW XR-1830-76 for F4F-3.
10. Engine Calibration (Performance) Curves, Operating Limits, R-1820-56 Engine for FM-2.
11. Report 1468A, Grumman Aircraft and Engineering Corp. (Erection and Maintenance Manual).
12. Detail Specification, F4F-3 Airplane, Report SD-235-3-1A (1469), Grumman Aircraft and Engineering Corp.
13. Zero, Masatake Okimita and Jiro Morikoshi with Martin Caidin, Ballantine Books, NY, 1957.
14. Fighter Development, Lee M. Pearson, Naval Aviation Confidential Bulletin, Oct.1948/Apr.1949.
15. Pilot's Manual, Section IV, Flying Characteristics (F4F-3), Revised 1/22/41, Grumman Aircraft and Engineering Corp.
16. Detail Specification, F4F-4 Airplane, Report SD-235-4-3A (1471C revised 10/21/42), Grumman Aircraft and Engineering Corp.
17. NAVAIR Airplane Characteristics and Performance, Model F4F-4, July 1, 1943.
18. NAVAIR Airplane Characteristics and Performance, Model FM-2, Sept. 1, 1943.
19. Pilot's Manual, FM-2 (AN-01-190FB-1), Pilot's Handbook of Flight Operating Instructions, Navy Model FM-2/Wildcat VI, June 15, 1945.
20. Ace-A Marine Night-Fighter Pilot in World War II, Col. R. Bruce Porter and Eric Hammel, Pacifico Press.
21. Grumman Guidebook, VolI., Mitch Mayborn et al, Flying Enterprise Publications, Dallas Texas, 1976.
22. History of Marine Corps Aviation in World War II, Robert Sherrod.
23. Wings Magazine, Feb.1972, F4F-, Foreman of the Iron Works Gang, Joe Mizrahi.
24. The Cactus Air Force, by Thomas G. Miller Jr. Harper and Rowe, New York, 1969.
25. The US Marine Corps in World War II, Compiled and Edited by S.E. Smith, Random House, New York, 1969.

THE F4U-

The Navy Corsair, produced during the war by three companies, Vought, Goodyear, and Brewster as the F4U-, FG-, and F3A- respectively, made up about eleven and one half percent of America's Hundred Thousand. This total represents those produced during the war; several hundred later model Corsairs were also produced after the war ended. The figures of Table 81 provide data on numbers produced of the variants. The -1 models fought most of the Corsair war; -4 airplanes did not reach the war zone until April of 1945, four months before the end of hostilities.

The list of physical data provided in Table 82 shows the Corsair to be one of the larger single engine US fighters. It was approximately the size of the Thunderbolt and Hellcat.

Table 83 gives fuel capacities of Corsair models. The prototype had all fuel in wing tanks, 273 gallons worth. The first production models, -1, -1A, and -1C had a much modified arrangement. Here the primary fuel tank was a protected installation in the fuselage just ahead of the cockpit with 237 gallons capacity. Added to this were two unprotected internal wing tanks each of 62 gallons,

TABLE 81
VOUGHT/GOODYEAR/BREWSTER CORSAIR VERSIONS

CO. MODEL	MIL.DESIG.	EXPORT DESIG.	NO.OF A/C	FIRST DELIV.	NOTES
V-166B	XF4U-1	—	1	F.FLT.MAY'40	FUS/WG.GUNS,WG.FUEL
	F4U-1	—	1734	OCT. 1942	ARM./FUEL,COCKP.CHGS.
	F4U-1"A"	—			NEW CANOPY,SEAT UP
	—	CORSAIR I	95		AS F4U-1, TO BRITAIN
	—	CORSAIR II	510		AS F4U-1"A", TO UK.
	—	CORSAIR II	238		" , TO RNZAF
	F4U-1C	—	200		-1"A" WITH 4 20 MM.
	F4U-1D	—	1685		TWIN PYLONS
	—	CORSAIR IV	126		TO RNZAF
	F4U-2	—	(32)	DEC. 1942	NIGHT FTR.,CONV.-1.
	XF4U-3	—	2	F.FLT.APR'44	HI-ALT.,ONE TO -3B.
	F4U-4X	—	(2)	F.FLT.MAY'44	CONV.-1 W.R-2800C.
	XF4U-4	—	5	F.FLT.SEP'44	ONE W.DUAL PROP,1945
	F4U-4	—	2050	DEC. 1944	PRODUCTION, NEW PP.
	F4U-4B	—	297		
	F4U-4N	—	1		NIGHT FTR. VERSION
	F4U-4P	—	9	1947	RECON. VERSION
	F3A-1	—	305		MFG. BY BREWSTER
	—	CORSAIR III	430		BREWSTER A/C TO UK.
	FG-1	—			GOODYR.-1,NO WG.FOLD
	FG-1"A"	—	3018		GOODYR.-1"A", "
	FG-1D	—			GOODYR.-1D
	—	CORSAIR IV	929		BRITISH GOODYR.-1D.
	—	CORSAIR IV	60		RNZAF GOODYR.-1D.
	F2G-1		5		R-4360 ENG. LAND-BASE
	F2G-2		5		" CARRIER-BASE

POST-WAR CORSAIR VERSIONS

MILITARY DESIG.	NO. OF AIRCRAFT
XF4U-5	(2)CONV.-4
F4U-5	226
F4U-5N	315
F4U-5NL	101
F4U-5P	30
F4U-6/AU-1	111
F4U-7	97
TOTAL, ALL CORSAIRS	12582
TOTAL, THROUGH ALL -4s	11705
TOTAL, -4s ACCEPTED THRU END OF WAR	11514

PRODUCTION BY YEAR

	1942	1943	1944	1945	TOTAL
VOUGHT F4U-	178	1785	2665	2046	6674
GOODYEAR FG-	—	377	2108	1532	4017
BREWSTER F3A-	—	136	599	—	735
TOTALS	178	2298	5372	3578	11426

NOTES. The "A" designation, as F4U-1A, was widely used, but was entirely unofficial.
There were 1859 F4U-4 aircraft accepted by the end of August, 1945 (essentially the end of the war); 2050 was the total F4U-4 production through April, 1946.

TABLE 82
F4U- PHYSICAL DATA

WING SPAN	40'11.73	AILERON CHORD (TO H/L)	15.34"
WING SPAN (FOLDED)	17'0.61"	AILERON AREA,TOT.(AFT H/L)	18.1SQ.FT.
LENGTH (F4U-1)	33'4.13"	TOTAL FLAP AREA (AFT H/L)	36.36SQ.FT.
LENGTH (F4U-4)	33'8.25"	MAX.FLAP DOWN ANGLE	50 DEG.
HEIGHT (TAXI POSITION)	15'1.25"	AILERON TRAVEL	19 DEG.UP,14DN
HEIGHT (FOLDED) (F4U-1)	16'2.3"	LEFT AIL.TAB TRAVEL	15 DEG.UP,15DN
HEIGHT (FOLDED) (F4U-4)	16'4.5"	TOT. HORIZ. TAIL AREA	57.9 SQ.FT.
TAIL SPAN	16'6"	STABILIZER AREA(INC.FUS.)	36.0 SQ.FT.
LANDING GEAR TREAD	12'1"	TOTAL ELEV.AREA	21.9 SQ.FT.
PROPELLER DIAMETER	13'4"	ELEV.BALANCE TAB AREA	0.74SQ.FT.
SPAN TO FOLD HINGE	14'10.5"	ELEV.TRIM TAB AREA	1.36SQ.FT.
MINIMUM PROP GND. CLEAR.	9.1"	HORIZ. STAB.ROOT CHORD	33.84"
WING AREA(INC.FUSELAGE)	314 SQ.FT.	ELEVATOR ROOT CHORD	22.5"
WING DIHEDRAL(OUTER PANEL)	8.5 DEG.	TOTAL VERTICAL TAIL AREA	22.0 SQ.FT.
WING SWEEPBACK (30%CHORD)	0 DEG.	TOTAL VERTICAL FIN AREA	9.0 SQ.FT.
WING INCIDENCE(ROOT & TIP)	2 DEG.	RUDDER AREA	13.0 SQ.FT.
WING ASPECT RATIO	5.35	VERTICAL FIN OFFSET	2.0 DEG.LEFT
WING MEAN AERO. CHORD	94"	RUDDER TRAVEL	25 DEG.L.25 R.
WING CENTER SECT.AIRFOIL	NACA 23018-15	RUDDER TAB TRAVEL	18 DEG.L.18 R.
WING OUTER PANEL AIRFOIL	NACA 23015-08	TAIL SURF.AIRFOILS	VOUGHT SPECIAL
WING ROOT THICKNESS RATIO	18%	HORIZ.STABILIZER INCIDENCE	+1.25DEG.
WING TIP THICKNESS RATIO	8%	MAIN WHEEL TIRE SIZE	32x8
AILERON SPAN, EACH	7'6"	PNEU.TAIL WHEEL TIRE SIZE	12.5x4.5

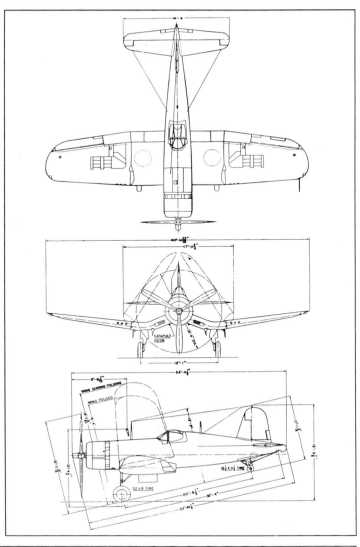

making a total of 361 internal gallons. These models could also carry a centerline external tank of 175 gallon capacity. Another major fuel arrangement change was effected in the -1D Corsair variant where wing internal tanks were eliminated, making the total internal capacity just a 237 gallon fuselage tank. But more external drop tank fuel was added in the -1D. Two 150 gallon external tanks could be carried on wing inboard store stations. In the -2 night fighter internal fuel was reduced to 178 gallons. The late -4 version had a fuel arrangement similar to the -1D.

A three view drawing of the F4U-1D Corsair fighter is shown. The immediately apparent hallmark of Corsair identification is the gull or "bent " wing which in front view dips down from an almost circular fuselage to meet the main landing gear on each side. A large propeller and clean long chord radial engine cowl are also major features. Another Corsair recognition point was a cockpit located well aft on the fuselage; the pilot's eye lined up approximately with the wing trailing edge. An inboard profile drawing of a Corsair shows major contents of the fuselage. The engine compartment up front housed a big R-2800 Double Wasp engine with ac-

TABLE 83
F4U- FUEL CAPACITIES (US GALLONS)

MODEL	MAXIMUM INTERNAL	MAXIMUM EXTERNAL
XF4U-1	273	—
F4U-1, F4U-1"A"	361	175
F4U-1C	361	175
F4U-1D	237	300
F4U-2	178	175
F4U-4	234	300

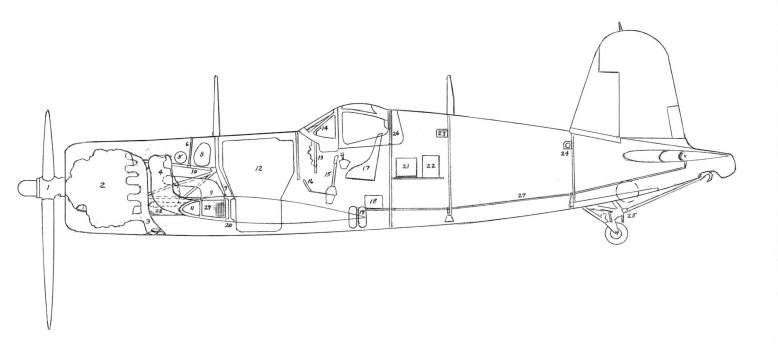

1. Hamilton propeller	9. Auxiliary blower to intercooler pipe
2. P&W R-2800 engine	10. Engine mount
3. Engine exhaust collector	11. Wing air intake passage
4. Auxiliary stage blower input pipe (2)	12. Fuel tank
5. Fire suppressant container	13. Instrument panel
6. Oil tank armor plate	14. Gunsight
7. Firewall	15. Pilot's control stick
8. Oil tank	16. Rudder pedals

17. Pilot's seat	25. Tail wheel and hook assembly
18. Battery	26. Rear armor plate
19. Oxygen bottles	27. Elevator control rods
20. Fuselage carrythrough spar	28. Carburetor air Y duct
21. Radio	29. Intercooler
22. Radio	
23. Antenna junction box	
24. Tail lift tube	

cessories, including components of a two stage mechanical supercharging system. Some parts of this system extended into the accessory compartment just forward of the firewall, these including supercharger intercooling and ducting. Other major components comprised exhaust manifolding and a steel tube engine mount running between firewall and engine mounting points. The engine oil tank was conventionally situated high and just ahead of the firewall. The most distinctive feature of a Corsair interior was the tandem arrangement of fuselage fuel tank and cockpit. This design kept the fuselage relatively slim compared to other Double Wasp powered fighters like the P-47 and F6F- Hellcat, but dictated choosing between best locations of fuselage fuel and cockpit. If the cockpit was placed forward over the wing fuel had to be situated well aft of the center of gravity. If fuel was placed over the wing in optimum position the cockpit had to go well aft. The latter choice was made. A large deep fuel tank, carrying all internal fuel in the F4U-1D, occupied a bay directly over the wing just aft of the firewall. Wing main beam carrythrough structure lined up with the firewall location. The next bay contained the pilot's cockpit, and just aft or below were items such as the battery, oxygen tank, and radio equipment. Tail controls ran from the cockpit aft through the fuselage,

and at the far aft end mechanisms resided for tail wheel and arresting hook retraction.

A cutaway drawing of an F4U-1D model is also shown.

Major power ratings of the R-2800 Double Wasp engine models in Corsair variants are presented in Table 84. Powers are shown for cases where the auxiliary stage supercharger is inoperative, in low blower, and in high blower. The R-2800 started off in the Corsair prototype at an 1850 horsepower TAKEOFF and MILITARY rating, later increased for production F4U-1 fighters to 2000 horsepower. At the same time MILITARY rating in high blower was increased from 1500 horsepower at 14000 feet to 1650 horsepower at 21000 feet. A significant advance was made in the -8W engine version where a water injection system allowed a new COMBAT rating providing up to 2135 horsepower at 12400 feet for a short time in the F4U-1D. In the later F4U-4 model a new R-2800C water injected engine, the -18W version, provided an extra 100 horsepower for takeoff along with higher COMBAT and MILITARY ratings at altitude. To absorb the additional power a new four blade Hamilton propeller was employed on the -4 Corsair. Graph 64 shows how R-2800 MILITARY and COMBAT power varied with altitude using the new two stage mechanical supercharger at various blower

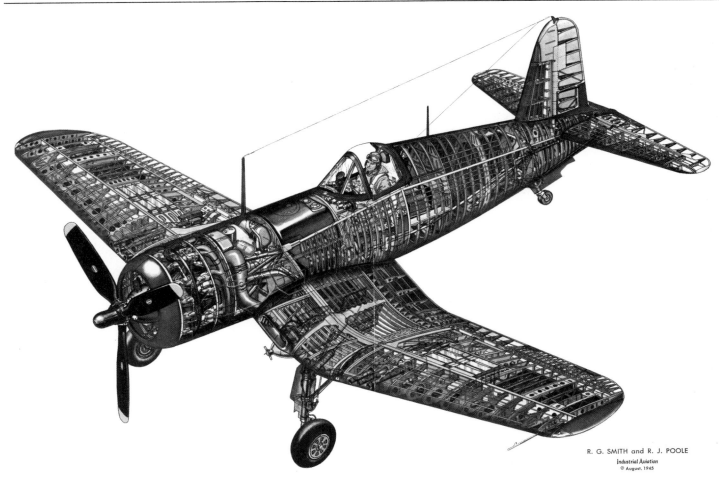

R. G. SMITH and R. J. POOLE
Industrial Aviation
© August, 1945

F4U-ID Cutaway

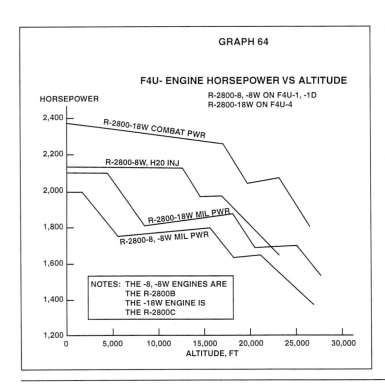

GRAPH 64

F4U- ENGINE HORSEPOWER VS ALTITUDE

R-2800-8, -8W ON F4U-1, -1D
R-2800-18W ON F4U-4

HORSEPOWER

R-2800-18W COMBAT PWR
R-2800-8W, H20 INJ
R-2800-18W MIL PWR
R-2800-8, -8W MIL PWR

NOTES: THE -8, -8W ENGINES ARE
THE R-2800B
THE -18W ENGINE IS
THE R-2800C

ALTITUDE, FT

settings. With auxiliary stage blower in neutral power drops off with altitude until the blower is put in low speed, slightly increasing power with altitude until at a certain height it drops again. Switching to high blower speed arrests the power drop for an additional 4000 foot increase, then power falls off again in spite of operation in high blower.

The curves of Graph 65 show high speed and climbing performance available from F4U-1 Corsairs at various altitudes. The jagged changes in the plots represent points where the supercharger is switched in operational mode as noted above. High speed of the first production F4U-1 at MILITARY power was in the 340 to 360 mph range up to 10000 feet, increasing to 385 to 395 mph from 16000 to 23000 feet where highest speed was attained. From there on up speed capability fell off; the supercharger could no longer hold power up. The more powerful F4U-1D airplane had a speed edge of about 10 mph all the way up in altitude at MILITARY power compared to the earlier version; the -1D got over 400 mph at 22000 to 26000 feet. With COMBAT power applied the F4U-1D was much faster to almost 25000 feet, with a maximum speed of 417 mph at 20000 feet. The first production F4U-1 climbed 2800 feet per minute at sea level using MILITARY power, but dropped to under 2000 feet per minute at 20000 feet and under 1000 at 30000 feet altitude.

TABLE 84
F4U- MODELS PROPULSION DATA

MODEL	ENG.MODEL	RATING	HP	RPM	ALTITUDE	MAP,"HG.	SUPERCHARGER
XF4U-1	XR-2800-4	TAKEOFF	1850	2600	SEA LEVEL		TWO STAGE TWO SPEED
	GR=2:1	MILITARY	1850	2600	2700 LO.BLO.		
		MILITARY	1500	2600	14000 HI.BLO.		
		NORMAL	1500	2400	7500 LO.BLO.		
		NORMAL	1450	2400	13000 HI.BLO.		
F4U-1	R-2800-8	TAKEOFF	2000	2700	SEA LEVEL		TWO STAGE TWO SPEED
F4U-1A	GR=2:1	MILITARY	2000	2700	1700 LO.BLO.		
F4U-2		MILITARY	1650	2700	21000 HI.BLO.		
		NORMAL	1675	2550	5500 LO.BLO.		
		NORMAL	1550	2550	22000 HI.BLO.		
F4U-1A	R-2800-8W	TAKEOFF	2000	2700	SEA LEVEL	54.0	TWO STAGE TWO SPEED
F4U-1D	GR=2:1	COMBAT	2135	2700	12400	59.0	
F4U-1C		COMBAT	1975	2700	16900	59.5	
		MILITARY	2000	2700	1700	52.5	
		MILITARY	1650	2700	21000	52.5	
		NORMAL	1675	2550	5500	45.0	
		NORMAL	1550	2550	22000	49.5	
XF4U-3	XR-2800-16	TAKEOFF	2000		SEA LEVEL		
F4U-4	R-2800-18W	TAKEOFF	2100	2800	SEA LEVEL		TWO STAGE TWO SPEED
F4U-4B	GR=20:9	COMBAT	2380	2800	SEA LEVEL		
		COMBAT	2080	2800	23300		
		MILITARY	2100	2800	4300		
		MILITARY	1710	2800	25000		
		NORMAL	1700	2600	9000		
		NORMAL	1550	2600	26600		
F2G-1	R-4360-4	TAKEOFF	3000		SEA LEVEL		ONE STAGE VAR.SPEED
F2G-2		MILITARY	2400		13500		

NOTE ON PROPELLERS: THE F4U-1 SERIES HAD A HAMILTON 3-BLADE 23E50 MODEL IN 13'4" DIAMETER; THE F4U-4 SERIES HAD A HAMILTON 4-BLADE 24E60 MODEL WITH 6501A-0/4 DESIGN BLADES IN 13'2" DIA.

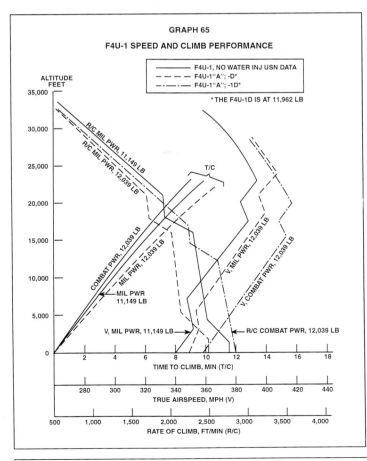

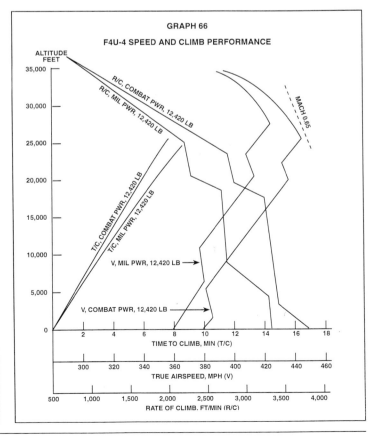

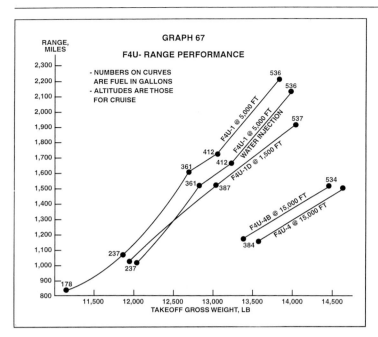

GRAPH 67

F4U- RANGE PERFORMANCE

- NUMBERS ON CURVES ARE FUEL IN GALLONS
- ALTITUDES ARE THOSE FOR CRUISE

with increasing altitude. At COMBAT power setting speed was considerably greater, going from 380 mph at sea level to a maximum of about 445 mph at 25000 feet. The -4 was a "hot" Navy fighter for that time; it is unfortunate it got into combat so late in the Pacific war. Climb rate at sea level and MILITARY power was 3400 feet per minute and almost 3900 feet per minute using COMBAT power. The rate was still 2500 feet per minute at 20000 feet with MILITARY power and the same to over 25000 feet using COMBAT power. Climb took about three minutes to 10000 feet and six to seven minutes to 20000 feet depending on power setting.

The maximum ideal ranges of Corsair airplanes are given in Graph 67. Amounts of takeoff fuel and resulting gross weights are indicated. The ranges are ideal because there is no provision for takeoff and climbout fuel, the flight is in zero wind conditions, and there are no fuel reserves. A practical range might be 75 to 80 percent of the numbers shown. The curves show ranges of 1000 to 1100 miles on fuselage tankage of 237 gallons alone, about 1500 to 1600 miles by adding fuel to internal wing tanks of the F4U-1 or in one F4U-1D external drop tank, and between 1900 and 2200 miles with all external tanks aboard and full at takeoff. The latter meant addition of a big centerline external tank on the -1, and loading two wing drop tanks on the F4U-1D.

It is seen F4U-4 range is considerably less than that of -1 airplanes. This -4 Corsair could make over 1100 miles with one drop tank and and 1500 miles with two when cruising at 15000 feet.

Graph 68 gives plots of Corsair takeoff ground run performance from a hard surface under sea level zero wind conditions, obviously a land takeoff rather than one from a carrier. Curves from two different sources for an F4U-1 fighter show at a typical lift-off weight

At the same power setting the heavier -1D model climbed more slowly as shown by the climb rate curve, but use of COMBAT power picked up this rate to a flashier 2900 feet per minute at sea level. Above 14000 feet rate of climb reduced to about F4U-1 levels. Similar relationships are shown in the time-to-climb curves. The F4U-1 could reach 10000 feet in just under four minutes and 20000 feet in 8.4 minutes. Again the -1D climb times are somewhat poorer at the same MILITARY power setting and a little better using the new COMBAT (was WAR EMERGENCY) power.

F4U-4 high speed and climb capability is denoted in the curves of Graph 66. Performance is generally superior to -1 models. At MILITARY power the -4 could reach 400 mph at about 17000 feet and 425 mph at just over 27000 feet before speed capability fell off

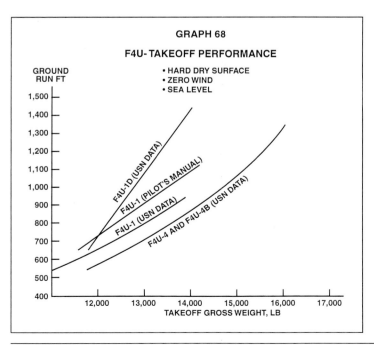

GRAPH 68

F4U- TAKEOFF PERFORMANCE

- HARD DRY SURFACE
- ZERO WIND
- SEA LEVEL

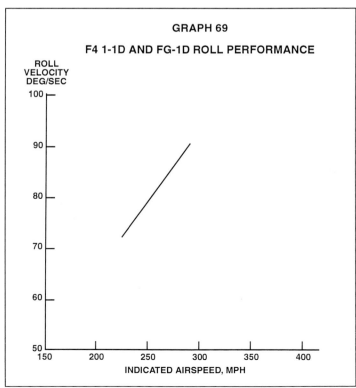

GRAPH 69

F4 1-1D AND FG-1D ROLL PERFORMANCE

TABLE 85
F4U-1 ALTERNATE USEFUL LOADS (LBS.)
THE FOLLOWING IS FOR AN EARLY F4U-1; NO WATER INJECTION

MISSION	NORMAL FIGHTER	BOMBER	OVERLOAD FIGHTER1	OVERLOAD FIGHTER2	OVERLOAD FIGHTER3	OVERLOAD FIGHTER4
EMPTY WEIGHT	8762.7	8762.7	8762.7	8762.7	8762.7	8762.7
TRAPPED FUEL/OIL	88.0	88.0	88.0	88.0	88.0	88.0
CREW	200.0	200.0	200.0	200.0	200.0	200.0
CAL.50 GUN INSTN.	398.5	398.5	398.5	398.5	398.5	398.5
GUNSIGHTS	4.2	4.2	4.2	4.2	4.2	4.2
GUN CAMERA	3.9	3.9	3.9	3.9	3.9	3.9
PYROTECHNICS	11.5	11.5	11.5	11.5	11.5	11.5
PROV.FOR DROP TANK & LARGER OIL TANK	—	—	—	—	27.2	27.2
COMM./NAV. EQUIP.	126.5	126.5	126.5	126.5	126.5	126.5
OXYGEN EQUIP.	27.5	27.5	27.5	27.5	27.5	27.5
EMERGENCY EQUIP.	22.7	22.7	22.7	22.7	22.7	22.7
FIXED USEFUL LOAD	882.8	882.8	882.8	882.8	910.0	910.0
BASIC WEIGHT	9645.5	9645.5	9645.5	9645.5	9672.7	9672.7
USEABLE OIL	90.0	90.0	150.0	150.0	193.5	193.5
CAL.50 AMMO	358.0	358.0	702.6	702.6	702.6	702.6
BOMBS	—	257.2	—	—	—	—
FUEL, FUSELAGE TK.	1068.0	1068.0	1422.0	1422.0	1422.0	1422.0
FUEL, WING PANEL	—	—	438.0	756.0	—	756.0
DROP TANK	—	—	—	—	78.5	78.5
FUEL, DROP TANK	—	—	—	—	956.0	956.0
TOTAL DISPOS.LOAD	1516.0	1773.2	2712.6	3030.6	3352.6	4108.6
USEFUL LOAD	2398.8	2656.0	3595.4	3913.4	4262.6	5018.6
GROSS WEIGHT	11161.5	11418.7	12358.1	12676.1	13025.3	13781.3

NOTE: BY AUG.1,1943 THE EMPTY WEIGHT HAD INCREASED TO 8873 LB.
BY MAR.1,1944 THE EMPTY WEIGHT HAD INCREASED TO 8982 LB. (WATER INJECTION WAS ADDED ALONG WITH 10 GAL.
OF WATER/ALCOHOL IN DISPOSEABLE LOAD)

TABLE 86
F4U-1 ALTERNATE USEFUL LOADS (LBS.)
LATE MODEL, WITH WATER INJECTION

MISSION	FIGHTER	FIGHTER	FIGHTER ONE EXT.TK.	FIGHTER ONE EXT.TK.	FERRY ONE EXT.TK.
EMPTY WEIGHT	8982	8982	8982	8982	8982
OPERATING EQUIPMENT	744	744	792	737	423
BASIC WEIGHT	9726	9726	9774	9719	9272
WATER/ALCOHOL	90	90	90	90	—
USEABLE OIL	98	150	180	180	180
CAL.50 AMMUNITION	703	703	703	703	—
BOMBS/ROCKETS	—	—	—	—	—
FUEL, INTERNAL	1422	2166	2166	2166	2166
FUEL, EXTERNAL	—	—	306	1050	1050
DROP TANK	—	—	40	95	95
GROSS WEIGHT	12039	12835	13259	14003	12763

F4U-1D ALTERNATE USEFUL LOADS (LBS.)

MISSION	FIGHTER	FIGHTER ONE EXT.TK.	FIGHTER TWO EXT.TK.	BOMBER 1-BOMB,1TK.	BOMBER 2-BOMBS
EMPTY WEIGHT	8971	8971	8971	8971	8971
OPERATING EQUIPMENT	678	717	755	750	744
BASIC WEIGHT	9649	9688	9726	9721	9715
WATER/ALCOHOL	90	90	90	90	90
USEABLE OIL	98	165	180	165	98
CAL.50 AMMUNITION	703	703	703	703	703
BOMBS/ROCKETS	—	—	—	1000	2000
FUEL, INTERNAL	1422	1422	1422	1422	1422
FUEL, EXTERNAL	—	900	1800	900	—
DROP TANK(S)	—	79	158	79	—
GROSS WEIGHT	11962	13047	14079	14080	14028

TABLE 87
F4U-4 ALTERNATE USEFUL LOADS (LB.)

MISSION	COMBAT	FIGHTER ONE EXT.TK.	BOMBER TWO EXT.TK.	BOMBER 1-BOMB,1-TK.	ROCKET 1-TK. 8 HVAR
EMPTY WEIGHT	9205	9205	9205	9205	9205
OPERATING EQUIP.	871	927	912	863	912
BASIC WEIGHT	10076	10132	10117	10068	10117
WATER/ALCOHOL	122	122	122	122	122
USEABLE OIL	98	173	173	98	173
CAL.50 AMMUNITION	720	720	720	720	720
BOMBS/ROCKETS	—	—	1000	2000	1155
FUEL,INTERNAL	1404	1404	1404	1404	1404
FUEL, EXTERNAL	—	900	900	—	900
DROP TANK(S)	—	79	79	—	79
GROSS WEIGHT	12420	13530	14515	14412	14670

of about 12500 pounds the run was 650 to 750 feet, a pretty snappy performance. The run for an F4U-1D was somewhat longer; at 13500 pounds it was around 1250 feet. At the same 13500 pound takeoff weight the F4U-4 broke ground at just under 800 feet; at 14500 pounds the -4 took about 950 feet.

Rolling performance of Corsairs was reputed to be excellent for World War II. Only a small amount of data is available however. Graph 69 shows rolling velocity in degrees per second versus indicated airspeed. The highest rate shown is 90 degrees per second at 290 mph IAS, or a four second full roll. How high the curve rises and where it breaks off and turns downward as limited by available pilot lateral stick force is unknown.

No information has been found for the Corsair as to a typical breakdown of empty weight into the normal airframe, powerplant, and fixed equipment groups , but Tables 85, 86, and 87 provide breakdowns for various missions of some Corsair alternate useful loads for an early F4U-1, late F4U-1, an F4U-1D, and an F4U-4 respectively. The tables show how empty weight of the early F4U-1 started out at 8763 pounds, rose over 200 pounds to 8982 on the later F4U-1 aircraft (due partly to addition of a water injection system), stayed about the same at 8971 on the F4U-1D, then rose another 200 pounds to 9205 on the F4U-4. This kind of weight creep-up was typical and not relatively excessive compared to other fighters. Addition of the useful load items listed in the tables brought normal fighter gross weight to 11162 pounds on the early -1 (without full wing fuel tanks), 12039 pounds on a late -1 (quite an increment, but about 350 pounds of this was additional internal fuel), 11962 pounds on the F4U-1D, and 12420 pounds on the F4U-4. Highest gross weights shown in the tables run from about 13800 pounds for early Corsairs to almost 14700 pounds for the F4U-4 version. This range of gross weights pretty much coincided with that of the Grumman F6F- Hellcat.

F4U- MAJOR MODEL-TO-MODEL CHANGES

F4U-1 (Early,from XF4U-1) Fuselage guns omitted; all six guns in the wings. Most fuel in new fuselage tank, displacing cockpit three feet aft. Aileron modifications, including span increase and balance tabs added. New engine version. Wing bomb cells removed. Longer fuselage.

F4U-1 "A" (Late) Pilot seat raised, canopy completely revised, new tail wheel and tail gear. Engine equipped with water injection. Larger engine oil tank. Centerline fittings for external drop tank provided. Revised cowl flap actuation system and cowl flaps removed from upper section. Wing spoiler added. Landing gear shock struts modified to alleviate "bounce" characteristic. Reworked horizontal stabilizer. Provision for additional radio gear. Improved gun feed. Improved engine ignition harness. New tail hook. Additional aileron design modifications.

F4U-2 (From early F4U-1) Radar installation added. Fuel capacity reduced. One outboard gun removed. New cockpit instrumentation and lighting and autopilot added. Higher output electrical generator. Radio altimeter. Flame dampening exhaust system.

F4U-1C Four 20 mm cannon replace six machine guns of D model.

F4U-1D Unprotected internal wing fuel tanks removed. Two underwing pylons for bombs or external fuel tanks replace single centerline installation. Provisions added to carry eight rockets. Anti-shimmy device added to tail gear. Several cockpit controls relocated for improved access.

F4U-4 New uprated powerplant installation with revised air intake system, larger intercoolers and oil coolers, revised exhaust system. Automatic controls for intercooler and oil cooler. Revised carburetor inlet system. Four blade propeller in place of three. New wing fold mechanism. Redesigned cockpit, including new armor plated seat, raised deck and rudder pedals, and new controls and displays.

F4U- CORSAIR CHRONOLOGY
Feb 1'38-The US Navy holds a design competition for a new fighter.

Apr '38-Vought submits two proposals, one with an R-1830 engine and one with the new R-2800 Double Wasp engine.

Jun '38-Vought wins the fighter competition.

Jun11'38-A contract is given to Vought for a prototype XF4U-1 airplane with a Pratt and Whitney R-2800 Double Wasp engine.

Feb10'39-A mockup of the new XF4U-1 is ready for inspection at Vought.

May29'40-A first flight of the new XF4U-1 prototype is made, piloted by Lyman A.Bullard,Jr. Elevator spring tabs flutter and leave the airplane, but it lands safely.

Jul11'40-During testing the XF4U-1 makes an emergency landing on a golf course with test pilot Boone Guyton aboard, and is damaged. The aircraft is rebuilt in less than three months.

Oct 1'40-The rebuilt XF4U-1 airplane attains a speed of 404 mph during a flight from Stratford to Hartford, Ct. It is claimed to be the first US fighter to exceed 400 mph.

Oct24'40-The XF4U-1 is flown to NAS Anacostia, Md. for US Navy flight testing.

Nov '40-Difficulties encountered with the XF4U-1 include propeller RPM surging, lateral stability, and spin recovery.

Nov28'40-Vought receives a US Navy request for a production aircraft proposal with changes in fuel location, armament, armor, and an aileron design to attain a higher rate of roll.

Jan '41-Vought conducts dive tests on the XF4U-1 up to 515 mph. The critical Mach Number is determined to be 0.73.

Feb25'41-Final acceptance demonstration tests of the XF4U-1 are completed for the USN at NAS Anacostia, Md.

Mar 3'41-The Navy issues a letter of intent to enter into a production contract for the F4U-1 airplane.

Apr '41-Vought concludes contract negotiations with the Navy.

Jun14'41-The Navy requests a design study for a special high-altitude version with a new two-stage Turbo Engineering 1009A supercharged engine with the airplane to be designated XF4U-3.

Jun30'41-A contract for 584 F4U-1 fighters is placed with Vought by the US Navy.

Nov 1'41-Brewster Aeronautical Corporation is designated as a associate contractor for the new aircraft type, labeled the Corsair.

Nov 8'41-The USN requests Vought to study a version of the Corsair as a night fighter, this to be designated the F4U-2.

Dec '41-Goodyear is named as a second associate Corsair contractor.

Dec 7'41-When war breaks out with Japan the Corsair is still well away from production; it will be almost seven months before a production airplane is ready to fly.

Jan 6'42-The night fighter version design study results are presented.

Jan28'42-Mockup inspection of an F4U-2 night fighter is held at Vought. Development is not started immediately; later a dozen F4U-1 production aircraft will be modified as night fighters.

Jun25'42-The initial production F4U-1, Bureau Number 02153, considerably changed from the XF4U-1, makes its first flight.

Jul31'42-The US Navy has accepted its first two production Corsairs.

Aug31'42-The USN has now accepted nine more F4U-1s. In addition, 13 more are accepted in September and 31 in October.

Sep 7'42-The first Corsair squadron is commissioned in California, Marine VMF-124. It starts to receive aircraft late in the month.

Sep25'42-Initial carrier tests are performed on the 7th production aircraft aboard USS Sangamon, CVE-26, with four landings made. Problems surface immediately; cowl flap actuator leaks, engine oil leaks from valve push rods, fouling the windshield, the forward view is very poor, the aircraft bounces on landing and swings because the low tail wheel puts flaps very close to the carrier deck.

Oct 3'42-The first USN squadron slated to get the Corsair, VF-12, is ready to receive their F4U-1 airplanes.

Nov '42-The 5th production F4U-1 is modified to raise the pilot seat eight inches to improve visibility, and a modified canopy is added. This modification is later added in production on the 689th aircraft in mid-1943.

Dec '42-The cowl flap actuating system is changed, and the upper section of the cowl now has no cowl flaps.

Dec28'42-After very hasty preparations, VMF-124 is declared operational with 22 F4U-1 airplanes, and in early January sails from San Diego bound for Guadalcanal via Espirito Santo in the Pacific.

Dec31'42-With the acceptance of 55 aircraft in November and 68 in December, the USN has now accepted a total of 178 F4U-1 aircraft.

Jan '43-F4U-1 aileron design is improved for improved roll rate after extensive testing. Test pilots are pleased.

Jan14'43-The first ten F4U-1s of USN Squadron VF-12 are operational, and eight days later the squadron has 22 aircraft.

Feb12'43-Two dozen F4U-1 Corsairs of Marine VMF-124 arrive on Guadalcanal. Problems arise with limited visibility out of the "birdcage", engine ignition faults, and nose-high attitude on landing with the short tail wheel strut. Twelve aircraft go on a first covering mission an hour after landing.

Feb13'43-Marine VMF-124 F4U-1s on Guadalcanal escort USN Liberators on a raid to Buin, but see no action.

Feb14'43-The VMF-124 Corsairs join other fighters escorting Liberators on a raid to Kahili, Bougainville. They meet 50 enemy fighters and only three Zeros are shot down while ten US aircraft are lost: four P-38s, two P-40s, two Liberators, and two of the Corsairs. This engagement becomes known as the Saint Valentines Day Massacre, an inauspicious debut for the Corsair.

Feb15'43-A single F4U-1 is ready for Navy Sdn.VF-17 pickup at Bridgeport,Ct. The poor ground visibility is noticed quickly.

Feb25'43-The first flight of a Goodyear FG-1 Corsair takes place.

Mar '43-Marine Sdn.VMF-213 now becomes the second F4U-1 Corsair squadron in the Southwest Pacific.

Mar '43-Larger tail wheel bearings are now being used on F4U-1s.

Mar '43-Navy Sdn.VF-17 now has a full complement of F4U-1s and is in training. They do not like the shotgun starters, the leaking cowl flap cylinders, the flap blow-up feature, or the battery installation.

Mar4'43-Two Corsairs, the 81st and 154th, are equipped with pneumatic tail wheels on longer struts and tested by Sdn.VF-12 on escort carrier CVE-13, USS Core. There is some improvement on carrier landings, but tail wheels tend to blow out. During VF-12's training on F4U-1s 14 pilots are killed. It is considered tricky to fly, with a bad stalling characteristic. VF-12 later switches to Grumman F6F- Hellcats. They name the F4U-1 the "Hog" because "it is cooperative as a hog on ice".

Apr '43-Two night fighter squadrons using F4U-2 Corsairs are commissioned, VF(N)-75 at Quonset Point, RI., and VMF(N)-532 at MCAS Cherry Point, NC.

Apr '43-VF-17 Squadron moves their training base from NAS Norfolk to NAAS Mantao near Kitty Hawk, NC.

Apr '43-Goodyear is now delivering the first FG-1 type Corsairs with two accepted this month and seven the next.

Apr '43-Navy Sdn. VF-12 hands over their Corsairs to the Marines at Espirito Santo in the Pacific and gets Hellcats.

Apr 1'43-The Japanese "I" Operation starts. Corsairs of Marine Sdn. VMF-124 and other fighters engage 58 Zero fighters over Guadalcanal in the Solomon Islands. Corsairs and Wildcats destroy 18 enemy aircraft, but six US airplanes are lost.

Apr15'43-Wildcat Sdn. VMF-121 drops out of action temporarily to change over to Corsairs, going down to Espiritu Santo to pick them up. They get 10 to 15 hours training, and then are the third Corsair squadron to go into combat.

Apr25'43-Four F4U-1s of Marine VMF-213 meet 16 enemy bombers and over 20 enemy fighters; they destroy five fighters, but two Corsairs are lost.

Apr26'43-The first Brewster F3A-1 version of the Corsair has a first flight.

May10'43-Between the Russell and Florida Islands in the Solomons, Army fighters and USMC F4U-s run into an enemy reconnaissance aircraft escorted by 25 Zero fighters. Sixteen enemy planes are shot down for a loss of three Corsairs, but the VMF-124 Sqadron Cdr.,Major Case, is one of the losses.

May13'43-A large formation of enemy aircraft on a raid towards Guadalcanal is intercepted by Corsairs of VMF-112 and -124. Fifteen Zeros are claimed, but three Corsairs are also downed.

May19'43-Marine Sdn. VMF-221 starts flying Corsairs.

Jun '43-The first two Brewster F3A-1 Corsairs are accepted by the USN. The start is slow, however. In July three more will be accepted, but none are accepted in August.

Jun '43-Marine Sdn. VMF-122 is now equipped with Corsairs, and VMF-214 also converts to F4U-s this month.

Jun 1'43-Royal Navy Sdn.#1830 is formed at Quonset point, RI. using Vought Corsair Is.

Jun 7'43-Corsairs are among US fighters intercepting 112 enemy aircraft on a raid to Guadalcanal. Sdn.VMF-112 downs seven of the enemy but four Corsairs are lost. All US pilots are rescued however.

Jun16'43-Approximately 120 enemy planes conduct a last daylight raid on Guadalcanal. Among many defending US fighters, Corsairs of VMF-121. -122, and -124 claim eight Japanese planes destroyed. A total of 107 enemy aircraft are downed, 80 by defending fighters, and the remainder by anti-aircraft fire. A Navy squadron gets 31 of the 80. Six US aircraft and five pilots are lost.

Jun30'43-USMC squadrons support the US landings in the New Georgia Island group. Four Corsair squadrons claim a total of 58 enemy airplanes downed, and Navy Sdn.VF-21 claims 30 aircraft, while P-40s down 11. Fourteen US fighters are shot down with seven of the pilots lost.

Jul '43-The XF4U-3 high altitude fighter project gets under way with three F4U-1 airframes converted. Also 27 FG-3 conversions are started.

Jul '43-Corsairs are continuing to successfully engage enemy planes in the New Georgia area, SW Pacific, and shoot down many E/A.

Jul 2'43-Marine VMF-123 flies a first mission after converting to Corsairs; now all eight Marine squadrons in the Solomon Islands are equipped with the Corsair fighter.

Jul 7'43-Twelve Japanese bombers covered by 60 Zero fighters try to hit the US invasion ships off Rendova in the New Georgia group, but are met by US fighters of VMF-122, -121, and -221, and the raid is thwarted. On July 11, 14, and 15 there are more enemy raids, and VMF-213 adds to the score. The fighters are very successful in fending off attacks on shipping, and many Japanese aircraft are downed.

Jul15'43-Navy Corsair Squadron VF-17 goes aboard the new carrier Bunker Hill and heads for a shakedown cruise in the Carribean. They encounter tail hook problems; hooks snap off and are replaced. Vought promises that VF-17 will have the new raised-cockpit Corsairs (informally dubbed F4U-1As) upon the squadron's return to Norfolk.

Jul17'43-Seventy-eight US bombers hit the Kahili area shipping at Bougainville in a surprise attack covered by 113 fighters, among which are 44 F4U-1 Corsairs. The others are P-38s, P-40s, and F4F-4 Wildcats.

Jul26'43-Ten B-24s bomb Kahili airfield on Bougainville after 21 Marine Corsairs strafe the area with their machine guns.

Jul30'43-Nine B-24s, escorted by 62 fighters including F4U-1s, hit Ballale Island, a few miles south of Kahili near Bougainville.

Aug '43-Navy Squadron VF-17, in testing out their new Corsairs, dives them from high altitude and encounters some compressibility problems; they are shedding elevator fabric and losing control in the dives. Vertical dives from above 20000 feet are banned in Squadron VF-17.

Aug 9'43-The first raised-cockpit aircraft appear starting with the 950th, the informally-designated F4U-1As, used by Vought, but never officially approved by Navy Bureau of Aeronautics.

Aug14'43-Corsairs of VMF-123 and -124 start operating from the former Japanese base of Munda on New Georgia Island nine days after it is captured by US forces.

Aug15'43-These Corsairs provide cover for the US invasion of Vella Lavella Is., staving off heavy attacks and downing 17 E/A.

Aug20'43-Upon return from the Carribean, Navy Sdn.VF-17 picks up 36 new raised-cockpit F4U-1As. They are to be the first squadron to take the new Corsair models to the SW Pacific.

Aug22'43-Vought produces their 1000th Corsair.

Aug30'43-Vought produces the first F4U-1C model armed with four 20mm cannon in place of the usual six machine guns.

Sep '43-Modifications are all completed on the 32 F4U-1 aircraft to make them into F4U-2 night fighter versions.

Sep '43-Sdn.VMF-124 completes its tour of duty on the Solomon Islands in the Pacific and returns to the US with 68 aerial kills in seven months. The squadron has lost 32 Corsairs, eleven of them to enemy action, and has lost seven pilots.

Sep 7'43-Marine Sdn.VMF-214 is re-organized under command of Maj. G. Boyington with replacement pilots flying Corsairs.

Sep11'43-Navy VF(N)-75 Night-Fighter Sdn. arrives at Espirito Santo, and in two weeks gets to Munda with six F4U-2 Corsairs.

Sep15'43-Marine Sdn.VMF-214, Black Sheep Squadron, arrives at Munda.

Sep16'43-VMF-214 escorts bombers to Ballale, shoots down 11 enemy aircraft (Boyington getting five) while losing one Corsair.

Sep28'43-The carrier Bunker Hill leaves San Diego for the South Pacific with Navy Corsair Sdn.VF-17, The Jolly Rodgers.

Oct 2'43-The Bunker Hill docks at Pearl Harbor; VF-17 and its F4U-1As are off-loaded with orders for Espirito Santo. They are replaced on the carrier by VF-18 equipped with Grumman Hellcats. VF-17 has so far been the only Corsair squadron on a carrier.

Oct 2'43-Operational patrols of F4U-2 night fighters are started on Munda.

Oct 5'43-The first Corsair with a centerline drop tank fitting, #1302, is accepted by the Navy.

Oct12'43-Navy Sdn.VF-17 leaves Pearl Harbor with their Corsairs aboard CVE Prince William. On October 25th they are catapulted off the ship to Espirito Santo; on the 25th they arrive at Guadalcanal, then go to Odonga, New Guinea, and on the 28th fly 34 operational sorties, but see no action.

Oct15'43-Air strikes are made to soften up Bougainville in the Solomons. Sixteen F4U-1s and 12 P-38s escort 21 B-24s to Kahili, and six intercepting Zeke fighters are downed. Two days later 21 Corsairs hit Ballale, engage 30 to 40 enemy airplanes, and shoot down 14. One Corsair is lost operationally.

Oct20'43-Twenty-four Corsairs hit Kahili and meet 20 Japanese Zero fighters, shooting down three and losing two Corsairs. Japanese airfields on Bougainville are now useless as bases.

Oct31'43-An F4U-2 night fighter of VF(N)-75 makes the Navy's first successful radar-guided interception over New Georgia Island.

Nov '43-Production Corsairs now incorporate the spoiler on the right wing, and the extended tail wheel strut is a production item.

Nov 1'43-All five Marine fighter squadrons in AirSols are to see action from the beginning of the action against Bougainville. These are VMF-211,-212,-215,-221, and VMF(N)-531. Corsairs along with P-38s are available in the Russell Islands (27 total); F4U-s are on Munda along with P-39s (31 total); they are at Odonga with P-39s and New Zealand Kittihawks (103 total); and 60 Marine Corsairs are at Bara Koma.

Nov 1'43-During the US invasion at Empress Augusta Bay on Bougainville Allied fighters down 22 enemy planes for an AirSols loss of four aircraft. Navy VF-17, using eight Corsairs, gets five Japanese planes and incurs no losses.

Nov11'43-Land-based Navy Sdn.VF-17 with Corsairs and VF-33 with Hellcats go on CAP to protect aircraft carriers Essex and Bunker Hill as they make strikes on Rabaul. Corsair arrester hooks were installed two days before. The VF-17 F4U-1As land on the carriers to refuel and go back to their land base. VF-17 gets 18 and one half victories and loses two planes. This action is   called the Battle of the Solomon Sea.

Nov25'43-An F4U-1A aircraft, the 1551st Corsair by Vought, is fitted with an engine incorporating water injection.

Nov25'43-For the last month VMF(N)-531 Marine squadron Corsairs have flown night fighter patrols around Bougainville. On November 13 the sqadron made the first successful enemy aircraft interception by a Marine Corsair night fighter.

Nov30'43-VF-17, The Jolly Rodgers, returns to Espirito Santo with a total of 45 victories. Five F4U-1As have been lost, two in combat.

Nov31'43-During November the USN has accepted 235 Vought-produced Corsairs, 82 from Goodyear, and 68 from Brewster.

Dec '43-Seven British Fleet Air Arm squadrons are training on Corsair Is and IIs. Sixteen inches is clipped from the British Corsair wingtips to fit their carriers, and Corsair Is have slightly bulged canopies.They are later equipped with provisions for rockets and a belly drop tank.

Dec '43-Marine Sdn.VMF-213 completes its SW Pacific tour of duty; it has over 100 victories and includes seven aces.

Dec '43-F4U-2 night fighting Corsairs destroy two enemy planes while operating from the Torokino base on Bougainville. The Corsair squadrons start to use Torokino on the northern end of Bougainville Is. December 9th as a base from which to strike the big Japanese base at Rabaul.

Dec10'43-Seventeen F4U-s of Marine VMF-216 land at Torokina on Bougainville, the first US aircraft to be based there.

Dec17'43-Among the fighters available to the AirSols (Solomons Air Forces) for an assault on Japanese-held Rabaul are Marine and Navy Corsairs; 71 are on hand of which 47 are operational. The first AirSols fighter sweep over Rabaul takes place using 31 F4U-s along with 22 F6F-s and 23 RNZAF P-40 Kittihawks. The fighting is at low altitude by the P-40s which shoot down five Japanese planes and lose three of their own.

Dec23'43-Corsairs and other fighters sweep over Rabaul and destroy 30 enemy airplanes. VMF-214 gets 12 with "Pappy" Boyington destroying four of these, raising his total to 24 enemy planes. A total of 93 fighters are employed, some as bomber escorts.

Dec28'43-Four Corsair squadrons have downed 33 Japanese planes in the Rabaul area in the last two days.

Dec31'43-Vought has delivered 1958 Corsairs, Goodyear 377, Brewster 136. Contracts are let for 4699. Some FG-1s have no wing fold. The US Navy still refuses to accept Corsairs on carriers.

Jan '44-A Marine Corsair squadron, VMF-422, in a flight from Tarawa to Funafuti in the Pacific, gets lost over the ocean; of 23 F4U-s starting the flight 22 aircraft and six pilots are lost. Thirteen of the planes ditch together and are rescued, as are three others elsewhere.

Jan '44-F4U-2 night fighters shoot down five enemy planes this month.

Jan '44-Eight F4U-1As of VF-17 Squadron are being re-fitted with water injection equipped engines.

Jan 1'44-A total of 147 enemy aircraft are claimed as air victims since December 17 in fighter sweeps in the Pacific, 52 of these on the 27th and 28th, and 33 of them by the four Marine Corsair squadrons (VMF-214, -216, -223, and -321) staging through Torokina.

Jan 3'44-Major "Pappy" Boyington of the Black Sheep and his wing man are both shot down, and Boyington is captured.

Jan 8'44-Corsair Squadron VMF-214 completes its tour of duty with 97 enemy aircraft downed along with 32 probables.

Jan 9'44-Four F4U-2 night fighter Corsairs of VF(N)-101 go aboard the carrier Enterprise, and are the first Corsairs assigned to a carrier. The landing gear "bounce" is remedied by a local solution. The leaky wing fuel tanks are not used.

Jan14'44-US fighters claim 29 E/A downed in dogfights over the Japanese base of Rabaul, 19 of these by Corsairs of VMF-215 operating from Torokina. VMF-215 has previously operated from Guadalcanal, Munda, and Vella Lavella in the Southwest Pacific.

Jan21'44-The south Piva airfield (Yoke) begins operations on Bougainville in the Solomons and VMF-211 Corsairs move to it from Torokina. Three days later Navy Squadron VF-17 moves there, then VMF-321 and a New Zealand P-40 squadron.

Jan24'44-VF-17 transfers to Torokina on Bougainville with beer stored in one aircraft ammunition container. A new unit, VMF-216, is also at that base.

Jan26'44-Corsairs escort SBD-s on a raid to Rabaul. VF-17 shoots down eight enemy planes and loses three Corsairs with several others damaged.

Jan25'44-Vought receives a letter of intent from the Navy for development of an F4U-4 version. Five F4U-1 airframes are to be converted, the first and second to be F4U-4XA and F4U-4XB, and the other three XF4U-4s.

Jan30'44-VF-17, The Jolly Rodgers, have shot down a total of 54 and one half enemy planes in the last three days.

Jan31'44-For the month Navy VF-17 has a total of 60 and a half E/A destroyed in the air (in only six days!), lost five pilots shot down and killed, had one killed in a mid-air collision, had 13 F4U-1As destroyed (five by enemy planes, four in crashes after being shot up by the enemy, three operational landing crashes, and one in the mid-air collision.)

Feb '44-Marine Air Group (MAG) 24 has the following fighter squadrons in the Solomon Islands: VMF-211, -212, -215, -218, -222, and -223.

Feb '44-After the capture of Roi Island in the Marshalls, 14 F4U-2s of VMF(N)-532 come in from Tarawa to help defend against night intruders. Later some F4U-2s go to Engebi Island on Eniwetok as a defense force.

Feb '44-Navy VF-17 Squadron, with its F4U-1As, is ready to finish its tour as a premier Airsols fighter outfit with 152 E/A shot down for a loss of 20 airplanes of their own in combat and four lost due to accidents.

Feb '44-Marine Corsairs of MAG-13, MAG-22, and MAG-31, all in the 4th Marine Air Wing, are based in the Marshall Islands. In all ten squadrons are involved.

Feb '44-No more VF-17 Corsairs are fitted with water injection; only the eight aircraft modified in January are so equipped.

Feb10'44-Marine Corsair squadron VMF-215 completes a tour of duty. The Fighting Corsairs have shot down 137 enemy planes and have ten aces, but only fourteen of the original pilots are left to go home.

Feb15'44-Eight Marine Corsair squadrons fly cover for New Zealand units occupying Green Island north of Bougainville.

Feb17'44-F4U-2 night fighters of VFM(N)-531 flying from Green Island get two night interceptions and destroy two enemy planes. Three nights later another enemy aircraft is downed.

Feb19'44-The last important Japanese opposition at Rabaul is encountered; 50 enemy planes meet a 145-plane formation of 44 F4U-s along with F6F-3s, P-40s, SBD-s and TBF-s; 23 of the enemy are shot down. The US formation includes 26 Corsairs from VF-17, which itself shoots down 13 Zekes, two Tojos, and one Rufe. Next day the remaining enemy aircraft are pulled back from Rabaul to the big enemy base at Truk.

Feb23'44-Corsairs of VMF-115 destroy a midget Japanese submarine while skip-bombing with 1000 pound bombs at Cebu City.

Mar '44-Goodyear is awarded a contract for 418 fixed wing F2G-1 aircraft and ten folding wing versions with the R-4360 engine.

Mar '44-MAG-14 Corsairs fly ground attack missions near Mindanao prior to US landings on March 10.

Mar '44-Marine Corsairs fly air cover for US landings in the Philippines at Panay on March 18, Cebu on Mar 26, and Negros on March 29, and during the next month provide close air support for troops on Cebu and Negros.

Mar '44-The Chief of Naval Operational Training at NAS Jacksonville is preparing a letter indicating that Corsair carrier deck landing characteristics are dangerous and the accident rate, especially with young pilots, is unacceptably high. The recommendation is side-tracked after further testing.

Mar 4'44-Marine Corsairs of ten different squadrons in the 4th MAW, together with bombers, start attacks on the Japanese-held bypassed islands in the Marshalls group-Wotje, Maloelap, Mille, and Jaluit. Many are hit by anti-aircraft fire. These operations continue for the rest of the war.

Mar 7'44-Navy Squadron VF-17 is officially released by Squadron VF-34, and starts the trip back to the US to be decommissioned.

Mar10'44-US troops invade Mindanao at Zamboanga with Marine Corsairs of MAG-12 flying cover. Four days later F4U-s of VMF-115 land at San Rogue airfield and fly two missions the next day. The airfield is renamed Moret field, and eventually many aircraft of various types are based there including 96 Corsairs.

Mar18'44-The Corsair is first used as a dive bomber. Eight F4U-s of VMF-111 based on Makin drop 1000 pound bombs on Mille. It is found the aircraft can be used safely in dives up to an angle of 85 degrees.

Mar28'44-Six Corsairs of VMF-113 escort B-25s to Ponape atoll in the Carolines, and shoot down eight of 12 intercepting enemy aircraft, ending Japanese resistance there in the air. This is the last real dogfight in the Central Pacific area.

Apr '44-The F4U-1D Corsair model goes into production; the plane has two pylons for bombs or tanks. Goodyear and Brewster also produce the model as FG-1D and F3A-1D. The first Navy acceptance of an F4U-1D takes place on April 22.

Apr '44-New carrier trials with Corsairs modified with the new longstroke landing gear oleo shock strut ("de-bounced") aboard the escort carrier Gambier Bay are pronounced sucessful after 113 landings, and the Corsair is finally cleared for USN carrier operations.

Apr '44-In this month the USN accepts 230 Corsairs from Vought, 220 from Goodyear, and 119 from Brewster; in May the numbers will be, respectively, 254, 220, and 122, and this is the peak production month.

Apr 3'44-British Fleet Air Arm Corsair IIs from #1834 Squadron on Victorious provide fighter cover for bombers attacking the German battleship Turpitz in Norway.

Apr14'44-Marine F4U-2s of VMF(N)-532 at Engebi make their first sucessful night interception. Two enemy aircraft are shot down and one probable is recorded during a Japanese night raid.

Apr17'44-Marine Corsairs support US landings in the Malabang-Parang area of Mindanao in the Philippines.

Apr19'44-The F4U-4XA test airplane makes its first flight.

Apr24'44-An F4U-2 night fighter shoots down its first enemy plane at night operating from the carrier Enterprise off Hollandia in New Guinea.

Apr26'44-The first flight of an XF4U-3 version takes place; development problems shortly arise with the powerplant. The number of the Goodyear version, FG-3, to be made is reduced to 13 airplanes.

Apr '44-British Corsair IIs of #1830 and #1833 Squadrons on the carrier Illustrious go on a sweep of the Indian Ocean area along with the USS Saratoga using VF-12 with Grumman Hellcats. On the 19th of the month they strike at Sabang Island, north of Sumatra.

May '44-The new landing gear oleo struts are now put on production Corsair aircraft, and new strut filling procedures are being used. Corsairs no longer have to be "de-bounced" by using field modifications.
May '44-An F4U-1D costs about $75000.

May '44-Charles Lindbergh starts flying missions in the Corsair with USMC pilots at Green Island and Emirau in the Pacific. His

last mission with an F4U- in the area will be to Rabaul on the ninth of June.

May '44-The first RNZAF Corsair squadron starts operations from Bougainville.

May16'44-After a series of comparative flight tests a Navy Evaluation Board concludes the F4U-1D is the best all-around Navy fighter available and a suitable carrier aircraft. It is recommended that carrier fighter and fighter-bomber units be converted to the F4U- type.

Jun27'44-An F4U-2N from carrier Enterprise shoots down a Japanese bomber at night; the next night two more enemy planes are downed by the F4U-2Ns of VF(N)-101.

Jul '44-The Brewster Corsair production line is closed after 735 F3A-1 aircraft have been produced.

Jul '44-Vought begins building 200 F4U-1C versions of the Corsair with four 20mm cannon instead of the usual six machine guns.

Jul '44-Corsair Squadron #1841 on British carrier Formidable strike again at the German battleship Tirpitz.

Jul12'44-The F4U-4XB prototype makes its first flight.

Jul12'44-Twelve USMC F4U-2 aircraft of VMF(N)-532 are flown off a carrier to Saipan, but are later pulled back to Guam and return to the US in September.

Jul25'44-British Corsairs of carriers Illustrious and Victorious provide air cover during the bombardment of Sabang and shoot down seven Japanese aircraft.

Aug '44-At a high level meeting of Marine and Navy officials at Pearl Harbor it is decided that Marine air squadrons will be assigned to CVEs.

Aug '44-Corsair Squadrons #1841 and #1842 provide top cover for another British strike at battleship Tirpitz.

Aug 4'44-Marine MAG-21 gets to Guam right after its capture with F4U-s of VMF-216, -217, and -225.

Sep '44-The 4th Marine Air Wing in the Marshalls has lost 36 F4U-s to enemy anti-aircraft fire while dive bombing enemy-held atolls.

Sep 3'44-C.A.Lindbergh visits MAG-31, and for the first time carries three 1000 pound bombs on a Corsair while raiding Wotje Atoll.

Sep 8'44-After working on a new bomb rack, Lindbergh drops the first 2000 pound bomb ever carried on a Corsair on Wotje.

Sep12'44-Lindbergh takes off with 3000 pounds of bombs on his Corsair and drops them on Wotje. The next day he carries 4000 pounds with a 2000 pounder on the centerline rack. CAL then departs for Hawaii.

Sep16'44-VMF-114 Corsairs provide close air support in the battle for Peleliu in the Palaus group.

Oct '44-Two additional Marine Corps squadrons arrive on Peleliu, VMF122 on October 1st and VMF-121 October 25th. The two squadrons along with VMF-114 use napalm and 1000 pound bombs in support of US ground actions.

Oct '44-Marines start training for CVE duty. Each group will consist of one sqadron of 18 F4U-s and one of 12 Avenger bombers.

Oct '44-British Corsairs and Hellcats from carriers Victorious and Indomitable attack the Nicobar Islands and shoot dowm seven enemy planes, but lose two Corsairs and a Hellcat.

Oct '44-The advent of the Japanese kamakazes pushes the USN into increasing the proportion of fighters on US aircraft carriers. A shortage of Navy carrier pilots allows USMC squadrons to get on carrier flight decks. Ten Marine F4U- fighter squadrons are authorized for carrier qualification. Preparations are quickly made to put two F4U-1D aircraft on each of five fleet carriers.

Nov26'44-A Navy conference in San Francisco finalizes the decision to put a 73 fighter-per-carrier complement on fleet aircraft carriers and to put Marine fighters aboard.

Dec 3'44-Sixty-six of the fixed wing FG-1 Corsairs arrive at Tacloban airfield in Leyte from Emirau with nine more the next day, and now five Marine squadrons are ready for combat from the muddy crowded field.

Dec 7'44-Corsairs of VMF-211, -218, and -313 together with Army P-40s attack enemy destroyers and transports and help sink four of them with 500 pound bombs near San Isidro, Leyte, Phillipines.

Dec11'44-Thirty F4U-s of VMF-115, -211, -218, and -313 again attack a Japanese convoy aided by 16 Army P-40s near Palompom on the west coast of Leyte, and repeat the attacks on supply ships the next day. They are also assigned to protect the US resupply convoy for the Ormoc, Leyte beachhead. Six Corsairs are lost to enemy anti-aircraft fire and seven are damaged badly enough to be surveyed.

Dec13'44-Thirty-five Corsairs of MAG-12 help cover the US landings on Mindoro Island, Philippines.

Dec15'44-VMF-211 Corsairs, VMF(N)-541 Hellcats, and Army aircraft shoot down several Japanese suicide planes in the Mindoro beachhead area.

Dec28'44-Marine Squadrons VMF-124 and VMF-213 are the first to go on fleet carriers as they arrive aboard carrier Essex at Ulithi. The Essex leaves on the 30th. The two squadrons have three fatal landing crashes in training soon after.

Dec31'44-The USN has accepted 2665 Corsairs from Vought, 2108 from Goodyear, and 599 from Brewster during the year.

Jan '45-Marines from Green Island move into Guiuan, Samar, P.I. VMO-251 with 22 Corsairs arrives January 2 and flies conbat patrol the next day. On January 8 VMF-212 begins to arrive and shortly after VMF-222 and -223 come in. The MAG-14 movement is complete by January 24.

Jan '45-The Marine squadrons on carrier Essex lose 13 Corsairs and seven pilots since the start of the cruise; all are operational losses, mainly weather.

Jan 2'45-Twenty-two Corsairs of VMF-251 in MAG-14 arrive on Samar, P.I. Later, three other squadrons, VMF-212, -222, and -223, arrive. Between MAG-12 and MAG-14 there are seven F4U- squadrons in the Philippines.

Jan 3'45-F4U-1D Corsairs from Essex go on their first strike-escorting bombers to Okinawa. They shoot down one E/A and lose a plane.

Jan 6'45-Fifteen F4U-s of MAG-12 assist Army aircraft in softening up enemy positions prior to the invasion of Lingayen, P.I. Key bridges are destroyed. Ground attacks continue all through January and 15 MAG-12 and -14 pilots are lost on strafing missions.

Jan10'45-The US Navy orders 300 F4U-4C aircraft equipped with four 20mm cannon.

Jan12'45-The carrier Essex with Marine Corsair fighters goes into the South China sea with ten other carriers. On this date Corsairs escort TBM- bombers on a raid in the Saigon area. Considerable damage is done and the fighters claim 10-12 aircraft destroyed on the ground. One F4U- is lost to anti-aircraft fire.

Jan24'45-Four British carriers attack oil refineries in southern Sumatra; among the attacking aircraft are 32 Corsairs to escort bombers and hit airfields. Several Japanese planes are downed but five Corsairs are lost during strafing, one in air battles and one crashes in the ocean near the carriers.

Jan25'45-In the tour on Essex in the last month VMF-124 and -213 have downed 10 enemy planes, destroyed 16 on the ground, and damaged several ships. But a total of 17 F4U-1Ds and eight pilots have been lost, mostly from operational accidents.

Jan29'45-Corsairs from carrier Illustrious escort Avengers on a raid over Sumatra oil refineries. Considerable damage is inflicted.

Feb '45-Three other fleet carriers besides Essex get Marine Corsairs as follows: Bennington has VMF-112 and -123; Wasp on February 3rd with VMF-216 and -217, and Bunker hill with VMF-221 and -451. The total is eight Marine squadrons with 144 Corsairs, or 16% of the fighter strength of the Fast Carrier Task Force.

Feb '45-Thirteen RNZAF squadrons are flying Corsairs, having transferred from Curtiss Kittihawks. At this time there are three on Bougainville, one on Guadalcanal, two at Espirito Santo, one on Emirou, two on Green Island, one on Los Negros in the Philippines, and two in New Zealand. Overall the RNZAF is to lose 150 Corsairs, but only 17 from enemy action. Altogether between May 1944 and the end of the war the RNZAF gets 364 F4U-1A and F4U-1D and 60 FG-1D aircraft.

Feb 3'45-The USMC is assigned its first aircraft carrier, the CVE Block Island. The first fighter squadron on board is VMF-511. Three more CVEs are assigned at monthly intervals, the Gilbert Island, Vella Gulf, and Cape Gloucester. The four CVEs are assigned to Carrier Division 27 on May 21,1945.

Feb 2'45-The last of 1685 F4U-1D airplanes is delivered by Vought, which has built 4699 F4U-1 series Corsairs including 95 Corsair Is and 510 Corsair IIs, along with 370 RNZAF Corsairs.

Feb16'45-Marine Corsairs take part in extensive carrier raids on the Tokyo, Japan area. They are credited with 21 enemy planes destroyed in the air, and 60 on the ground. Several Corsairs are lost.

Feb19'45-The attack starts on Iwo jima, and eight Corsair squadrons provide close air support, along with Army and Navy planes. They continue air strikes through the 22nd of February.

Feb24'45-A mockup inspection is held of an XF4U-5 Corsair version.

Feb25'45-The Corsairs of the Fast Carrier Task Force (58) strike again at the Tokyo area. The weather is bitter cold, and some of the fighter's guns freeze up.

Mar '45-Carrier Franklin arrives at Ulithi with VMF-214 (the old Black Sheep Squadron with new pilots) and VMF-452 to join the task force.

Mar '45-Other Corsair units now flying aboard carriers are Squadrons VBF-83 and -86 on Essex and Wasp respectively, VF-5, VMF-214 and VMF-452 on Franklin, VBF-10 on Intrepid, and VBF-6 on the Hancock. There are now 13 Corsair squadrons in the task force with seven being USN and six USMC.

Mar 1'45-Task Force 58 carrier aircraft, including Corsairs, strike at Okinawa. VMF-124 and -213 on Bennington shoot down 23 enemy airplanes and destroy 24 on the ground for a loss of 24 Corsairs and nine pilots.

Mar 4'45-F4U-s of VMF-216 and -217 in five weeks aboard the carrier Wasp have destroyed 19 Japanese planes, five in the air, losing nine Corsairs and five pilots.

Mar10'45-VMF-124 and -213 leave the carrier Essex and return to the US on escort carrier Long Island. In two months they have shot down 23 Japanese airplanes, destroyed 64 on the ground, and damaged many land targets. Losses of the two squadrons total 24 aircraft and nine pilots.

Mar13'45-Corsair Squadrons VMF-216 and -217 are relieved on Wasp. They have destroyed four E/A in air combat, 15 on the ground, and had sunk a destroyer. Their losses were nine planes and five pilots. The 36 Corsairs and deck crews stay aboard.

Mar18'45-Carriers Bennington, Franklin, and Bunker Hill send off Marine Corsairs on raids over the Japanese island of Kyushu.

Mar18'45-Task Force 58 returns off the coast of Japan, and F4U-squadrons find little air combat on this day.

Mar19'45-Carrier Franklin is hit by kamikazi suicide aircraft and is put out of action. Very badly damaged, squadrons VMF-214 and -452 are out of the war. Only four squadrons of Marine Corsairs are left-these on Bunker Hill and Bennington.

Mar19'45-Japanese bombers and kamikazes strike at the Task Force 58 carriers, and cause heavy damage to three of them, forcing their withdrawal. These attacks reduce total Corsair fighter strength (USN and USMC) to nine squadrons on six carriers.

Mar24'45-Corsairs from Intrepid use the larger Tiny Tim rockets for the first time on Okinawa caves. These rockets are considered inaccurate and unreliable and are later withdrawn from use.

Mar26'45-British carriers Illustrious, Victorious, and Formidible operate in the Pacific with the US 5th fleet, using among other types a total of over 100 Royal Navy Corsairs.

Apr '45-By this date Vought has delivered 500 of the new production F4U-4 models with many changes including an uprated engine. In this month some of the new models are received by MAG-14 in the Philippines.

Apr 1'45-Corsairs of VMF-221 and -451 off Bunker Hill bomb and strafe beaches as the Okinawa invasion starts. The invasion force includes 548000 men, 1457 ships, and thousands of planes.

Apr 3'45-The kamakaze attacks around Okinawa begin. Bunker Hill Corsairs shoot down 11 of them.

Apr 6'45-Corsairs from Bunker Hill and Bennington shoot down 17 kamikazes. Three hundred and fifty-five suicide planes are launched. All except 22 are shot down, but these have hit 22 ships, sinking three and badly damaging the others.

Apr 7'45-Corsair fighters assist in attacking and destroying the Japanese super-battleship Yamato.

Apr 9'45-More Corsairs come to Okinawa. Aircraft of VMF-312, -322, and -323 land at Kadena airfield, making a total of over 100 F4U-s on the island.

Apr12'45-Bennington and Bunker Hill Corsairs shoot down 51 kamikazes off Okinawa. Land-based Corsairs down 16 more.

Apr16'45-Land-based Corsairs on Okinawa shoot down 38 enemy airplanes, many of them on suicide missions, and some with Baka bombs.

Apr16'45-British carriers support the Okinawa invasion, and by this date British-operated Corsairs have downed five kamikazes.

Apr16'45-Big air battles take place over Okinawa where carrier Combat Air Patrol aircraft down 29 enemy planes without a loss. One Corsair pilot, Ens.Alfred Lerch, shoots down seven of the enemy. The same day two kamikazes put the carrier Intrepid out of action with severe losses; it starts back to the US after patching its deck and landing its planes.

Apr22'45-Ground-based Marine Corsairs shoot down 33 and three quarters enemy airplanes that were trying to get at radar picket destroyers off Okinawa. On April 27-28 they shoot down 35 and one half more Japanese planes.

May '45-The first operational F4U-4s reach Okinawa and go into action.

May '45-Contracts for the Goodyear F2G- models are cut back to five each of the F2G-1 and the F2G-2.

May 4'45-Okinawa-based Corsairs shoot down 60 and three quarters Japanese aircraft, most of them kamikazes, the second highest single day total for the USMC in the war.

May 9'45-British carriers Formidible and Victorious are hit by kamikazes and lose many airplanes, including Corsairs.

May10'45-The escort carrier Block Island is the first of the CVEs to go into action in the Okinawa area. It carries eight F4U-s, eight F6F-5Ns and six F6F-5Ps. Later in May two more CVEs carrying Corsairs come into the combat area.

May10'45-A Corsair piloted by Lt.R. Klingman chases a Japanese Nick reconnaissance aircraft to 38000 feet, but his guns freeze. Klingman chews away the enemy's tail surfaces with his propeller, and it crashes. Klingman manages to land deadstick.

May11'45-Carrier Bunker Hill is hit by kamikazes and badly damaged, putting VMF-221 and VMF-451 out of the war.

May15'45-MAG-14 is familiarizing pilots with the new F4U-4 model. The first flight of aircraft from VMF-212 arrives at Kadena airfield on Okinawa June 8 by way of Clark Field, P.I.

May21'45-Marine Corsairs of MAG-22, VMF-113, -314, and -422 begin arriving at Ie Shima from Engebi; three F4U-s are lost on the wayup due to weather.

May25'45-Four F4U-s of VMF-312 kill 12 out of 20 kamikazes near Ie Jima. Later VMF-422 gets six out of 12. The Marines shoot down a total of 39 Japanese planes this day.

May27'45-Suicide planes conduct raids all day long on the ships around Okinawa. There are 56 separate raids of two to four planes each. Marine Corsairs destroy 32 airplanes on this and the next day, and Army P-47s get 17 more.

May31'45-The USN accepts 302 Corsairs from Vought and 195 from Goodyear in the month of May.

Jun '45-The only Corsairs on the fast carriers are VBF-83 on Essex and Air group 85 on carrier Shangri La.

Jun '45-Several Corsair units are operating on CVEs; One is VMF-511 with eight F4U-s on Block Island. Others operating Corsairs are the Gilbert Islands, Cape Gloucester, and Vella Gulf.

Jun 8'45-The last two Marine Corsair squadrons aboard a big carrier, those on Bennington, perform a final mission of bombing Kyushu airfields with special 500 pound bombs. After this the Bennington sails south for Leyte and home. The two squadrons have lost 31 aircraft in combat and 17 in operational crashes, 18 pilots killed, but 15 others rescued. Bennington is the only carrier of the original ten not to be hit by the kamikazes.

Jun10'45-The F4U-4s of VMF-212 get their first victory.

Jun22'45-One day after Okinawa is secured MAG-14 with F4U-4s scores its ninth and last victory. The kamikaze threat is reduced. The twelve F4U- squadrons have shot down a total of 436 enemy aircraft; the leader is VMF-323 with 124 victories.

Jun30'45-Fighters now in the Pacific Tactical Air Force are 288 F4U-s, 36 F6F-5Ns, 144 P-47s, 12 P-51s, 16 P-38s, and two F6F-5Ps.

Jul '45-The remaining carrier Corsairs conduct strikes over Japan and at Japanese warships.

Jul '45-The USN accepts 303 Corsairs from Vought (the highest of any month) and 180 from Goodyear.

Jul 1'45-Okinawa-based Corsairs escort Army B-25s in the first medium bomber attack on Japan since the Doolittle raid.

Jul17'45-British Corsair fighters strike the Japanese island of Honshu.

Jul24'45-Royal Navy Corsairs assist in heavily damaging a Japanese light carrier at Kure.

Jul31'45-British carrier Corsairs have destroyed nearly 50 enemy A/C.

Aug15'45-Two carrier plane strikes are sent against Tokyo, but are recalled. Japan has surrendered.

Sep 2'45-On this date, VJ Day, there are nine F4U- Corsair squadrons on seven CVs in the area of Japan. Additional carriers headed to the area are: Intrepid, Boxer (with F4U-4s), and Antietam (with F4U-4s).

Sep '45-Corsair production is cut way back with the Navy accepting only 41 from Vought and 68 from Goodyear, and after this month

Goodyear production is stopped. A contract for 2500 FG-4s is cut, and only 12 are produced, then scrapped. Vought continues low level F4U-4 production until mid-1947, producing a total of 2356, with 1912 -4s before VJ Day. The Vought -4 contract is reduced from 3149 to 2356 aircraft. In the Pacific, Corsairs are credited with the destruction of 2140 enemy aircraft in aerial combat for the loss of 189 F4U-s. Operational sorties from February 13, 1942 add to 64051, of these 54470 being from land bases and 9581 from aircraft carriers. Additional F4U- losses: 349 from anti-aircraft fire, 230 from other causes, 692 on non-operational flights, and 164 in crashes on carriers or airfields. The United Kingdom received a total of 2012 Corsairs which equipped 19 squadrons. The Royal New Zealand Air Force was allocated 370 F4U-1Ds, but actually received 238 F4U-1As and 126 F4U-1Ds.

Apr ;46-The first F4U-5 model is flown. The test aircraft is a modified F4U-4.

F4U- CORSAIR HANDLING QUALITIES AND CHARACTERISTICS

HANDLING QUALITIES
GROUND HANDLING

Taxi characteristics of the Corsair were fairly typical of other high powered tail-down USA fighters. Visibility ahead over the long nose was non-existant in early "birdcage" versions, improving somewhat with the design changes to the higher canopy, seat, and tail gear models, but never good. S-turns were used to taxi with the tail wheel lock disengaged. Wheel brakes, which were very good, could be used with power for steering. If there was a stiff crosswind it was better to use the tail wheel lock as much as possible to avoid excessive braking. But seeing ahead required S-turning, which needed tail wheel swiveling. This in turn required braking in any wind. With hard braking the aircraft could nose over, or it could get into a ground instability. As the book said it was important to use

low power during taxi, and to avoid riding on and overheating the brakes. Dropping the big wing flaps could make a sail in ground winds, particularly on early aircraft with the original low tail wheel, and cause directional instability problems. It took practice for a pilot to become adept in Corsair ground handling.

Pilot comments showed variability of opinion on handling an F4U-1D "Visibility was poor because of the long nose, the nose high attitude, and the rearward cockpit location with respect to the wing", Excellent brakes and visibility good due to adjustable seat", "Brakes made the ground handling very good", "Visibility was good except dead ahead", and "Fair visibility with seat in top position". In another group five pilots said "Forward visibility poor in ground handling".

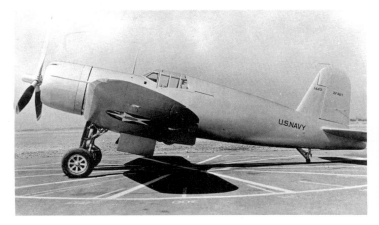

Fig.4U-1 Vought XF4U-1 Corsair, Mfr. photo via F. Dean coll. The single XF4U-1 prototype pictured in 1940. A clean long chord cowling housed a very new Pratt and Whitney R-2800 eighteen cylinder two row radial engine with a two stage two speed supercharger. The Double Wasp was rated at 1850 horsepower for TAKEOFF and low altitude MILITARY ratings, far more power than had ever been installed in a Navy single engined aircraft.

Fig.4U-2 Vought XF4U-1 Corsair, Mfr. photo via F. Dean coll. A three quarter front view of the new fighter prototype shows the cranked wing. Ground clearance needed during takeoff and landing for a large propeller combined with desire for main landing gear of reasonable length dictated the cranked wing design. The gear was located at the wing low point. A derivative advantage accrued in a wing-fuselage juncture without need for heavy filleting.

Fig.4U-3 Vought XF4U-1 Corsair, Mfr. photo via F. Dean coll. The Navy contract for the new fighter was dated June,1938. Almost two years later, in May of 1940, the XF4U-1 had a first flight. The event occurred two and a quarter years after that of the Grumman XF4F-2 and slightly over two years before Grumman Hellcat first flight. The swept disc of the Corsair propeller loomed large in the photo; it was thirteen feet four inches in diameter.

Fig.4U-4 Vought XF4U-1 Corsair, Mfr. photo via Joe Weathers. Flying over Long Island Sound, the big Vought shows off in a well publicized photo. After an emergency landing incurring damage in July, 1940 the prototype was rehabilitated and less than three months later attained a speed of slightly over 400 mph during tests, a widely acclaimed feat at the time. The photo shows prototype armament was two cowl and two wing machine guns. All fuel was in the wings. Leading edge intakes fed air to the oil coolers.

When lined up for takeoff the tail wheel was locked in the neutral or alligned position. Before takeoff the rudder tab was set about six degrees nose right and the aileron tab about six degrees right wing down. If there was to be a full flaps takeoff the elevator tab would be set one degree nose up.

TAKEOFF AND CLIMB
Upon runup of the Corsair for magneto checks prior to takeoff the stick had to be held aft to keep the tail from jumping. With flaps down the tail could not be held on the ground, even with stick back, at manifold pressures over 44 inches of mercury. On a wooden car-

rier deck with 44 inches manifold pressure the wheels would start slipping even with brakes held on. Takeoff, like landing, was one of "the most troublesome stages of flight for inexperienced pilots", and "The Corsair would always require a pilot's attention and a firm hand on the controls". Because of very high torque reaction of the big propeller the rudder tab setting noted above had to be made, or rudder force needed for a straight takeoff run could be very high. In addition the aileron tab setting noted was important because, if not made, considerable left wing heaviness would occurr just as the aircraft became airborne. Proper tab settings could vary somewhat between individual aircraft. Settings were particularly important

Fig.4U-5 Vought F4U-1 Corsairs, Mfr. photo via J. Weathers. Flight photo of four early F4U-1 Corsairs shows them equipped with the "birdcage" type of early cockpit canopy. To provide more head clearance for large pilots the upper forward canopy panel was bumped out. The "birdcage" limited pilot visibility, particularly on landings. Like the Curtiss P-40, recessed turtledeck areas were provided aft of the pilot to allow a degree of rear quarter vision.

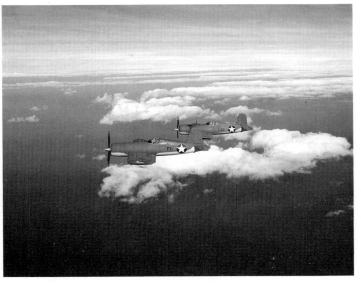

Fig.4U-5A Vought F4U-1s, photo via H. Andrews (8x10).
Two early F4U-1 Corsairs cruise over broken clouds; their fuselage national insignia has the earlier central red circle removed to avoid mis-identification. A total of 688 production aircraft were delivered with the low "birdcage" canopy of these fighters. The F4U-1 became operational in the first months of 1943, entering Pacific combat in February.

Fig.4U-6 Vought F4U-1 Corsair, Mfr. photo via H. Andrews. Three quarter rear view of an F4U-1 Corsair used as a test airplane provides a good view of just how much the wing was cranked. This aircraft, photographed in July, 1944, has the old style low cockpit canopy. Grid marking on elevators is interesting; these surfaces tended to pose problems in high speed dives. Many pilots came back with shredded elevators after diving in the early going; some did not come back.

the lower down the flap setting and the higher the engine power used. A normal flap setting was 20 degrees, however any value from zero to 50 degrees could be used, the greater depression giving the shortest takeoff run. In the latter case the elevator tab was set at the one degree nose up position noted to counter aircraft pitch-down due to flap effect. Zero flap takeoffs could be easily made, with the longer takeoff run traded for avoiding the inconvenience of having to retract flaps. A typical lift-off speed without flaps at slightly over 11000 pounds (light) gross weight on a warm day was

about 98 mph IAS, and the takeoff run about 1200 feet on a hard runway. The tab setting on the rudder used for takeoff was just about right for initial climbout.

At a pilot conference twenty-two of twenty-eight rated takeoff characteristics of F4U-1C and F4U-1D aircraft good, and the Corsairs were ranked high in a category "Best overload takeoff from a small area". In a head-to-head competition between F4U-1 and P-51B airplanes the Navy said the Corsair was better in takeoff.

Fig.4U-6A Vought F4U-1, USN photo via H. Andrews. Navy Squadron VF-17, the Jolly Rodgers, went aboard the new aircraft carrier Bunker Hill for sea-going tests in June-July, 1943. A squadron airplane is shown being catapulted from the carrier. Many problems were encountered during this shakedown, including breaking tail hooks. VF-17 was then operating with early low canopy airplanes.

Fig.4U-6B Vought F4U-1As, USN photo via H. Andrews. Raised-cockpit F4U-1As are shown operating from an advanced base at Majuro in the Marshall Islands. The photo provides a vivid picture of conditions confronting land-based Marine Corsairs in the Pacific area. Centerline bombs are mounted emphasizing the important ground support role of the Corsairs.

Fig.4U-6C Vought F4U-1A, USN photo via H. Andrews. The skull and crossbones on this F4U-1A denotes an aircraft of Navy Squadron VF-17; the time is March,1944. Piloting is the leading Navy ace of the period, Lt.Jg. Ira Kepford, with a record of his sixteen aerial victories displayed on the fuselage.

Fig.4U-6D Vought F4U-1C, photo via H. Andrews. An excellent photo of the F4U-1C Corsair armed with four 20mm. wing cannon in place of the more usual six .50 caliber machine guns. One of 200 built, the first cannon version appeared at the end of August, 1943, and was an initial indication of the Navy's trend towards the 20mm. weapon.

The later F4U-4 with a more powerful engine version needed increased settings for the rudder tab on takeoff "I'd swear that for takeoff on the F4U-4 it took sixteen degrees of rudder trim. The right rudder setting on the trim knob didn't go to twenty degrees for nothing".

The F4U-1D aircraft speed for best initial climb was about 144 mph IAS. This speed stayed constant up to medium altitude, and handling of the aircraft in climb was good. The fast acceleration to climb speed could be felt by the pilot, and the climb rate was "impressive".

TRIMMING

The Corsair was easy to trim out for climb. Trim changes from landing gear and flap retraction were minimal, and those for speed

Fig.4U-7 Vought Corsair I, Mfr. photo via Joe Weathers. One of ninety-five early Corsairs allocated to the British and generally equivalent to the US Navy F4U-1. Shown in a May, 1943 photo, the aircraft has the low canopy, but the tail gear has been lengthened to reduce nose-up ground angle. In June, 1943 the initial Royal Navy squadron, #1830, was formed using Corsairs and trained at Quonset Point, Rhode Island.

Fig.4U-8 Vought Corsair I, National Archives photo via Joe Weathers. A fine photo of a British Corsair I at Brunswick, Maine in September, 1943 being loaded with ammunition by Royal Navy ratings. The bulged Plexiglas panel in the canopy can be seen clearly on this airplane. Wingtips on the plane do not appear to have been clipped to fit British carriers as was done on later UK Corsairs. By December seven Fleet Air Arm squadrons were training on Corsairs.

Fig.4U-8A Vought Corsair I, National Archives photo via H. Andrews. Another September,1943 photo of a British Corsair I. The top of the large fuselage fuel tank can be seen in outline between the cockpit windshield and the forward radio mast. The upper portion of the tank was protected by a .11 inch thick curved aluminum plate; the fuel fill location can be seen at top center.

Fig.4U-9A Vought F4U-1D, USN photo via H. Andrews. Corsairs finally got aboard carriers at the end of 1944. These Marine F4U-1D fighter-bombers are running up ready to launch from carrier Bunker Hill in early 1945. Each carries what is probably a napalm bomb on the belly starboard store station and a load of four HVARs under each wing.

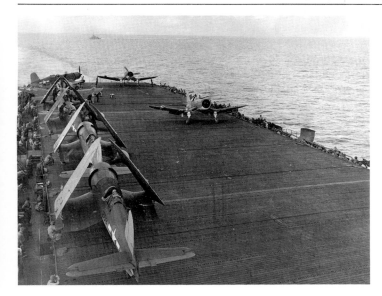

Fig.4U-8B Vought F4U-2, USN photo via H. Andrews. In November,1941 Vought started study of a Corsair night fighter, and a mockup inspection was held the next January. It took until April,1943 to commission two night fighter squadrons, one each USN and USMC, using thirty-two F4U-1 airplanes with a radar installation. The photo shows one squadron, VMF(N)-532 during flight operations aboard escort carrier Windham Bay in July,1944. However the Navy preferred the Hellcat night fighter.

and power changes quite handleable. In a cruise condition the airplane could be trimmed for hands and feet off flying with little trouble. Pilots almost universally rated F4U-1C and F4U-1D trimmability as good. In a dive, as with some other US fighters, a considerable amount of rudder trim was required to zero out pedal force which was high if this was not done.

DIVE AND RECOVERY
Like most US fighters of the time the Corsair could be dived to very high speeds, and in so doing get into compressibility. Diving clean meant closing the canopy, going to neutral blower, keeping engine RPM under 3060 (a figure allowed for 30 seconds), closing all flaps, and trimming rudder six degrees nose right with elevator tab one and a half degrees nose down. Throttle was pulled back to a low power setting. If desired dive speed could be limited by using a dive brake control to extend the main landing gear. The gear was not to be extended over 300 mph IAS or retracted over 400 mph IAS. Gear extension gave a considerable pitch down moment in the dive.

Steep dives in clean condition soon got service pilots in trouble. In typical cases they would come screaming down from about 30000 feet, build up to a very high speed, and get into compressibility buffet with the airplane shaking and vibrating while also trying to tuck under. When they started to pull out they found the stick force reduced instead of increased because their horizontal tail was starting to shred. "I returned with my elevators tattered". As a Vought test pilot related

"We have all had compressibility problems. We have lost elevators on both sides from the tabs on out, and have landed the airplane successfully. I have never heard of a pilot who didn't land

it. We also had one that lost a rudder, and he didn't have any trouble. One fellow landed, and he didn't even know he had lost one side of the elevator until he looked at it". But it was not always so rosy. "Other men in other squadrons died learning the lesson." The problem was widespread. "VMO-251 recently encountered difficulty with compressibility at high diving speeds". Some squadrons barred vertical dives above 20000 feet altitude, the area where the higher Mach numbers were reached.

Vought test pilots performed many high speed dive tests. On some early ones Mach 0.75 was reached, and considerable buffeting and tuck-under was encountered. True airspeeds of up to 575 mph were attained. A limiting envelope for F4U-1D was defined based on the testing, and service pilots were instructed to stay within it. At 30000 feet they were restricted to 299 mph (260 knots) IAS corresponding to 489 mph TAS (true airspeed) which was Mach 0.72; at 20000 feet the restriction was 368 mph (320 knots) IAS corresponding to 504 mph TAS, and about the same Mach number. At 10000 feet, near where the pilot would expect to pull out of the dive, limits were set for more than one g flight, and the speeds allowed were slower, since pulling g tended to make compressibility effects nastier. The Corsair was here restricted to 443 mph IAS/ 516 mph TAS/ Mach 0.70 at 3.5 g and 403 mph IAS/469 mph TAS/ Mach 0.63 at a rather gut-wrenching 6.5 g pullout. Staying under these speeds kept the pilot out of the compressibility troubles noted above. A Vought test pilot counciled "Avoid using the elevator trim tab, which could induce a violent pitch-up maneuver in the denser air at lower altitude, and overstress the airframe." He recommended a reduction in power and a slow steady back pressure on the stick to avoid a high g pullout. At normal weight the maximum design flight limit load factors were 7.5 positive, as in a pullout, and 3.5 negative, which would rarely be achieved, even in a severe nose-down

Fig.4U-9 Vought F4U-1D Corsair, F. Dean photo. "Sun Setter", an obvious reference to the Japanese rising sun, is the F4U-1D fighter restored for display at the National Air and Space Museum. Some of the many changes on the F4U-1D version involved removal of all wing fuel, provision of two underwing pylons for fuel tanks or bombs, and a new raised canopy initially introduced on the F4U-1"A" for better pilot visibility. Note the wing was fabric covered over about the aft two thirds of its area.

Fig.4U-9B Vought F4U-1D, USMC photo via H. Andrews. A well worn Marine F4U-1D Corsair carrying napalm bombs and rockets flies over a desolate Okinawa landscape ready for a bombing run to support Marine ground forces. Corsairs were used extensively for close support work in the latter part of the Pacific war.

Fig.4U-10 Goodyear FG-1 Corsair, Mfr. photo via F.Dean coll. In December, 1941 Goodyear was designated as a second production source for Vought Corsair fighters, and the first Goodyear FG-1 flew in late February of 1943. Shown is a fixed wing FG-1 with the new raised canopy. Some feared this canopy change would cause a substantial drag penalty, but in fact it made little if any difference.

pushover. Pilots were advised to avoid steep dive angles because of the difficulty in attempting to reduce speed and acceleration quickly if buffet occurred. Buffet increased loads on the whole airframe, but the horizontal tail surfaces were the most sensitive items.

The F4U-1D in a dive was characterized by one pilot "Acceleration did not seem to be too fast. Considerable rudder was needed." Navy testing showed that a P-51B out-dove the F4U-1. A more modern evaluation at low altitude indicated the Corsair was somewhat slower in diving than a P-51D, a Hellcat, and a P-47D Thunderbolt. Corsair stability and control in a dive was rated excellent by many pilots, and stick forces were light. The later F4U-4 model of the Corsair was a considerably different and improved airplane, and one Navy pilot claimed he could catch a P-51D aircraft in a dive with this aircraft.

MANEUVERING

Basic restrictions in maneuvering were few for the Corsair. Inexperienced pilots were not to enter loops or Immelmans at less than 322 mph IAS or slow rolls at less than 207 mph IAS; speed could be lowered somewhat as experience in the aircraft was gained. The limit on inverted flight was a typical ten seconds. Pilot's general views on Corsair maneuverability seem to vary. "It is a tough competitor in anything involving maneuvering", "Was superior in maneuverability and response (to the P-51B)", "Couldn't stay on the tail of an FM-2", and "It left much to be desired as a fighter from the viewpoint of maneuverability". One group of twenty-six pilots rated F4U-1D maneuverability Good-6, Fair-17, and Poor-3. Like other US fighter manufacturers Vought worked hard to get the best possible aileron performance, high roll rate from reasonable pilot

Fig.4U-11 Goodyear FG-1D Corsair, R. Stuckey photo via Joe Weathers. An excellent photo of the Goodyear equivalent of a Vought F4U-1D taken post-war. This airplane, part of Minneapolis Naval Air Reserve, has rocket launchers underwing. The leading edge spoiler on the starboard wing is shown clearly, this being Vought's solution to a sudden port wing drop tendency at high angles of attack on early airplanes.

Fig.4U-12 Goodyear FG-1D Corsair, R. Stuckey photo via Joe Weathers. Another view of a Naval Reserve FG-1D airplane illustrates how far aft the cockpit was located on the fuselage, this a result of placing all fuel in the fuselage over the wing. With fuel and cockpit in tandem the fuselage was slim, there was no center of gravity travel with internal fuel burnoff, but pilot visibility was penalized.

Fig.4U-13 Civil Goodyear FG-1D Corsair, F. Dean photo. A nicely restored Goodyear Corsair in the 1970s, later used in the television drama "Black Sheep Squadron". The old hog nose has the raised canopy and flatter ground angle of later airplanes. Note the large flap down angle. Author watched the left aileron drop completely off this airplane during flight; it was able to land safely.

Fig.4U-14 Civil Goodyear FG-1D Corsair, F. Dean photo. "Whistling Death" was supposedly a name given the Corsair by the Japanese as a result of its unique noise pattern in flight. Main landing gear retracted aft with wheel twisting ninety degrees to lie flat in the wing under two large gear bay doors. This action was similar to Curtiss P-40 gear retraction except in that aircraft the retracted wheels were not covered.

lateral stick force. Considerable redesign and testing was done to improve prototype roll performance, including use of balance tabs. A company test pilot claimed "Throwing the stick hard would roll the airplane more than 180 degrees in a second". (An under two second full roll; no speed noted). A more conservative claim by another pilot "Four second aileron rolls at 288 mph IAS". In any case at a fighter meet the Vought test pilot said "The ailerons, Chance Vought thinks, are some of the best in the country". He later noted "Pilots would revel in the Corsair's phenomenal rate of roll; I would hear so often 'Oh those beautiful ailerons'." If there was a two second roll at any speed the ailerons were indeed beautiful. There is no question, however, that the Corsair roll performance was very good for a US World War II fighter. Another pilot said "The roll rate was

terrific". The Vought pilot noted "We had worked out the aileron controls so the stick force was extremely light, enabling the pilot to roll the airplane to its maximum rate even at extremely high diving speeds." The book indicated full stick throw on the ailerons was not to be used above 345 mph IAS, and at higher speeds only the same lateral stick force should be applied. A company test pilot stated however "I think everyone believes they are restricted to 345 mph IAS. Sometimes at full throttle we get a slight buffet (of the ailerons) if you push hard (laterally) against the stops. Most of the time you can't feel it." So much for that restriction! A group of pilots rated aileron control forces and aileron effectiveness good, and ranked the Corsair second of twelve fighter types in "Best ailerons at 350 mph IAS."

Fig.4U-15 Civil Goodyear FG-1D Corsair, F. Dean photo. The FG-1D and F4U-1D were the first Corsairs with ability to carry more fuel externally than internally. The single big internal fuselage tank could carry 237 gallons; each wing store station between fuselage and landing gear locations could handle a 150 gallon drop tank or a 1000 pound bomb.

Fig.4U-16 Civil Goodyear FG-1D Corsair, F. Dean photo. Decision to use an inverted gull, or cranked, wing on the Corsair complicated the structural design. Main wing beam inboard of the folding panels was carried through the fuselage in sweeping curves and had to be specially built up in a series of small pieces to make beam caps.

Fig.4U-17 Civil Goodyear FG-1D Corsair, F. Dean photo. Rather complex flap system on the Corsair is shown in the photo. Plain flaps were in six sections, three on a side. Four inboard portions were part of the non-folding wing center section; outer two were on the outboard folding panels. Gap between each inner and middle flap was filled upon deflection by a special gap-closing panel.

Fig.4U-18 Civil Goodyear FG-1D Corsair, F. Dean photo. Beautifully restored Goodyear Corsair taxis out for a field takeoff at a 1970s air show in Pennsylvania. Until late in the war, December of 1944, all Corsairs were land-based; early testing aboard carriers indicated unsuitability.

Although the Corsair had a slightly higher wing loading than the Hellcat at equivalent loaded weights with peak wing lift coefficient reduced by the small spoiler strip on the right wing and thus a little poorer turning radius, it had very moderate stick forces in windup turns. One modern test indicated a stick force of about five pounds per g in turns which meant a pilot could pull g with little effort. To aid in turning the F4U-1D and later models incorporated a "maneuver" setting on the flaps, 20 degrees down, this to increase lift coefficient and reduce turn radius. Maximum flap down speed was 230 mph IAS. An F4U-4 could apparently turn inside a P-51D and stay on its tail. "In high speed turns when the Mustang pilot would pull up and drop full flaps, I could just drop 20 or 30 degrees

maneuvering flap, and gain on him while still turning well inside him". Corsair longitudinal stability was good, as were elevator charateristics. Pilots rated elevator force and effectiveness good. One pilot group ranked the Corsair first of fourteen fighter types in "Best elevators". One wartime pilot mentioned F4U- elevators as "Heavy", but a modern evaluation noted then "Light and pleasant in maneuvers", the latter for an FG-1D version. The later F4U-4 airplane was a "delight to fly with its light control forces".

The airplane also had positive directional stability and dihedral effect, but some adverse yaw due to roll. Just about all in one pilot group rated Corsair lateral and directional stability good, and ranked the aircraft second of nine fighter types in the category "Best

Fig.4U-19 Civil Goodyear FG-1D Corsair, F. Dean photo. A Corsair without a carrier hook on final field approach for landing shows darker paint on underside of outboard foldable wing panels. These panels folded directly over the fuselage with undersides matching the paint on the upper fuselage.

Fig.4U-20A Vought XF4U-3B, Mfr. photo via H. Andrews. In mid-1943 a high altitude Corsair project was started with three converted F4U-1 aircraft, later cut back to two airframes. First flight took place in April, 1944, but development work on the turbosupercharged R-2800 powerplant installation was slow, and the need for a very high altitude fighting capability never appeared. The XF4U-3B version shown in this September, 1944 photo could reportedly achieve a high speed of well over 400 mph at 30000 feet, but the F4U-4 version coming along could also achieve such performance.

Fig.4U-20 Civil Vought F4U-1D Corsair, O'Dell/Stuckey photo via Joe Weathers. Side view of -1D Corsair shows off slim fuselage lines allowed by tandem arrangement of fuselage fuel tank and cockpit. Main landing gear on early versions had stiff oleo shock struts resulting in very bouncy landings, a fault that was slow in being corrected. Southwest Pacific Corsairs had to be greased in to avoid landing troubles.

all-around stability". A pilot said "It was a solid stable aircraft. Its stability was positive at all times at cruising or high speed flight, and during high powered climbing". Compliments were also paid to Corsair rudder control characteristics, though there were maneuvering cases where rudder forces were high. "Extremely high in steady heading sideslips and in countering adverse yaw during maneuvering", also in a "3.5 g rolling pullout", and "during aggressive lateral corrections".

APPROACH AND LANDING
If the P-40 was the most difficult Army fighter to land, its counterpart in the Navy was certainly the Corsair. Pilot comments varied from "The most troublesome stage of flight" to "Really bad", and "Potentially disastrous". Most of the adverse comments referred to early production aircraft; corrective measures were taken to alleviate landing problems on later aircraft with considerable success, though pilots always had to be very much on the ball when landing the Corsair. A test pilot said "To some pilots it was difficult to fly at slower speeds. To many it was hard to land properly and comfortably".

For landing approach maximum gear down speed was 230 mph IAS. The best power off gliding speed clean was 160 mph IAS, with normal approach at about 104 to 110 mph IAS, and a typical touchdown speed of about 92 mph. Pilots were supposed to avoid flat approaches. Immediately after flaring out a landing in the three point attitude was made by stalling the airplane in. The flap setting for airfield landings was 30 degrees down; less flap would produce a longer runout. After pilots gained experience full down flap land-

ings could be made. Full down flap position was used in carrier landings. Initial production aircraft had blow-up flaps, but after some inadvertant flap retractions at critical moments the design was changed.

Fig.4U-21 Vought F4U-4 Corsair, USN photo via Joe Weathers. Shortly after catching a carrier deck wire a new F4U-4 starts a power wing fold. The F4U-4 version did not enter Pacific action until the spring of 1945. It included many improvements including a rearranged cockpit and new powerplant version along with a four blade propeller. It was considered by many the best of all Corsairs.

Fig.4U-22 Vought F4U-4 Corsair, USN photo via Joe Weathers. Wings neatly folded, an F4U-4 taxis to a parking spot with a centerline fuel tank aboard and empty rocket mounts on a folded wing panel. The British operated Corsairs from carriers well before the US Navy. The latter service used Wildcats and Hellcats exclusively at sea until 1945.

There were many problems along the way however. Approach visibility was particularly poor on early aircraft. As a Vought test pilot said "Raising the long nose near the stall blanked out the runway ahead; it was disconcerting". A more severe critic said the view was "appalling" and "frightful". Even on the F4U-1D one pilot noted "Blind when leveling off", and this was after the seat had been raised and a new canopy provided. On very early models there was likely to be oil spray on the windshield from leaking cowl flap actuators which did not help visibility; an actuating system redesign fixed the problem rather quickly. On early airplanes aileron and elevator control was "sluggish" at 95 mph IAS in the approach as noted by one pilot; however later a group of pilots selected the F4U-1D second of twelve fighter types in a category "Best ailerons at 100 mph landing speed", so that item also got fixed. Another problem on early Corsairs: Tests of stalling characteristics showed a serious left wing dropping tendency during power-on landings. A pilot could get flipped over on his back rather suddenly. Wind tunnel tests indicated above a 17 degree airplane angle of attack a sharp increase in rolling moment occurred, causing serious instability. To correct this characteristic a sharp leading edge strip, or spoiler, was installed inboard on the right wing near the "crank" section. This fix worked; it eliminated the large assymetry of left and right wing stalling and thus the left wing drop. But there was a cost. The airplane maximum lift coefficient was reduced from 2.30 to 1.88, thereby increasing the stall speed. It is interesting , however, to note a Vought pilot's comment on the spoiler "I found the device had more of a psychological effect for apprehensive pilots than a positive cure for unsymmetrical stall'. Another problem, just as serious, was the "bounce" tendency. Main gear oleo shock struts were too stiff, and unless a landing airplane was absolutely greased onto the runway it would bounce up again, often dangerously. An example: "A bad accident today. A Marine pilot stalled down pretty

hard. The plane bounced high and out of control". A Vought pilot said "The oleo metering problem (giving the bounce) caused the most alarm for the green pilot, especially during field landings". A service pilot noted "My first landing confirmed the Navy's decision (not to allow Corsairs on carriers). The rigid landing gear oleo strut caused a potentially disastrous bounce on anything but a smooth touchdown". The word was "Expect the airplane to bounce". Vought eventually sorted out the oleo strut problem, but it was long after Corsairs were in Pacific combat service. The "debounced" aircraft "felt like falling into a feather bed when you stalled in".

Yet another problem peculiar to aircraft with the early "low" tail wheel was a sudden yaw, or "kick" when that wheel touched on landing. A new pilot might not be ready to quickly provide the required corrective yaw control of rudder and brakes, and could get into trouble. The "kick" was described by many pilots as "a sudden directional instability or swing needing immediate correction". To add to the new pilot's discomfort near touchdown a sudden swish of air swept through the cockpit. The changes Vought made to enhance pilot visibility included extending the tail wheel strut which reduced the nose-up ground angle a couple of degrees. In so doing they cured this characteristic of sudden yaw on touchdown which had occurred previously even with the tail wheel locked in neutral.

Other pilot complaints, particularly on early aircraft but even on later models during the landing operation concerned further directional instability on the ground after the tail wheel was unlocked as noted earlier, a rough and noisy tail wheel, and a tail wheel strut that was "hard". These came along with gripes about the great amount of rudder needed in a 45 degree crosswind.

By 1944 things seemed to be much better. There were pilot comments on Corsair landing such as "No tendency to ground loop", "Greatly improved with raised tail wheel", "Characteristics quite acceptable", "A straight-ahead ship, short roll, no trickiness", "Landing was normal with very little tendency to ground loop","Raised tail facilitates good landing", and "Landings easy, three point". These aircraft had been spoiler-equipped, de-bounced, and had the raised tail and new seat and canopy. There were still some complaints about rolling directional stability with an unlocked tail wheel, and one very honest pilot said:"I personally felt more at ease on the takeoff than on the landing". Most pilots would probably say "amen".

STALLS AND SPINS
Stalling characteristics of the Corsair were considered quite normal, at least after the spoiler strip was installed inboard on the right wing to keep the stall reasonably symmetric. Stall warnings consisted of a tail buffet, an abnormal nose-up attitude, a lightening of stick forces, and increasing left wing heaviness with an additional requirement for right rudder if power was on. The warnings came only about five knots before actual stall in landing configuration, so later airplanes were equipped with a warning light in the cockpit to signal impending stall to pilots not fully proficient in the Corsair. The light, located on the instrument panel, was connected to an airflow sensor on the wing center section. A breakdown of wing airflow sent a signal to illuminate the light. The sensing system gave a more advanced warning, about 15 knots above stall speed in

Fig.4U-23 Vought F4U-4C Corsair, AAHS photo via Joe weathers. A late model Corsair equipped with four 20mm. cannon in place of the more usual six .50 caliber machine gun arrangement. Earlier two hundred F4U-1C airplanes were produced in a four cannon version. As the war progressed the US Navy turned increasingly towards use of the 20mm. weapon.

the clean condition of the airplane. After considerable experience with the aircraft pilots could sense an impending stall without the aid of the warning light.

The actual stall was quite abrupt, particularly with flaps down, and was accompanied by a relatively sharp left roll, or in some cases a sharp right wing drop and a nose down pitch. If the stick was quickly dumped forward a tendency to spin could be avoided. Stall speed was in the range of 70 to 90 knots IAS depending on aircraft model, weight, power level, and configuration.

An accelerated stall while pulling g in a high speed turn or dive pullout was preceded by aircraft buffeting a few knots above the actual stall. As with the landing condition, the spoiler on the right wing succeeded in stalling out the wings quite evenly in the high speed case. A Vought test pilot said "We found the wedge most effective in improving flight characteristics during a high speed accelerated stall". The stall was characterized by a quick right wing drop with considerable shaking of the aircraft, which could easily flick out of the turn unless back stick pressure was quickly released. When this was done a rapid recovery could be made.

Stall warning and stall recovery characteristics of both F4U-1C and F4U-1D Corsairs were rated "good" by a group of pilots. Interestingly though, the Corsair was ranked ninth of eleven fighter types in "Best characteristics five mph above stall".

No intentional spinning was permitted by the book in Corsairs, and Vought test pilots advised service pilots not to try. The reason was it got tougher to recover as the number of spins added up. If a spin developed inadvertently the pilot was to apply the standard procedure of full opposite rudder followed by full forward stick

with ailerons held neutral. Recovery from the incipient stage of a spin was quick with standard procedures being used promptly, and with a one turn spin recovery could be made within a quarter turn. Letting it really wind up was the problem. In testing the later F4U-4 airplane though, Vought pilots explored spin behavior, including inverted spins, and found no particular difficulty in recovering from normal four turn spins with a clean airplane. This model was usually considered the very best flying of all the Corsair aircraft versions.

CHARACTERISTICS
COCKPIT
The Corsair cockpit was roomy for a simple reason. It was designed around the six foot four inch Vought project pilot Boone Guyton. This was great for large men, but left the small man hanging-literally. If he sat up high enough to see anything his feet could hardly reach the rudder pedals. This put the shorter pilots in an uncomfortable almost standing position with the seat up high or seat cushions added. It was also a stretch to apply full forward stick. The Corsair had no cockpit floor, only the seat rails and the pedal troughs. New pilots had to get used to the "black hole" beneath them, remembering not to drop anything in the bowels of the fuselage. They could also get beaned by anything dropped by previous occupants during the first slow roll of the aircraft. One of the items large pilots complained about on early "birdcage" canopy models was the framing of the enclosure being too narrow up top. They kept hitting their head on it during maneuvers. This problem was rectified with the later canopy. But the cockpit arrangement was the same on the F4U-

1D as on early F4U-1 airplanes, and there was considerable criticism of this layout. "Arrangement poor for many reasons", "Switches poorly arranged", "Instruments and switches scattered over too much of an area", "Did not feel at ease because of poor cockpit arrangement", "Needs major cockpit redesign", and so on. In another case comments on the F4U-1D were "Cockpit untidy, messed up, too many gadgets". A few changes were made for improvement along the line; the stick was moved aft about four inches for one, but there were still complaints about instruments and levers being so far away. Perhaps the unkindest cuts were references to the relatively excellent arrangement of the Grumman Hellcat cockpit. In the later F4U-4 the cockpit was completely redesigned with considerable improvement resulting. It had a newly designed seat (though the means of adjustment was not appreciated), and raised deck and rudder pedals to incline the pilot back more. There were a few complaints by large pilots who, in this case, were less favored.

VISIBILITY

Corsair versions were made with two quite different cockpit canopy designs. The early models had the "birdcage", and later ones a raised frameless semi-bubble. As its name implied, the birdcage was heavily framed and low down. Many unkind words have been used to describe visibility from the birdcage, but "atrocious" will do. One pilot commented of the birdcage that the only reasonable vision was straight up. Another remarked "The first thing I noticed in my first takeoff was the very limited visibility from the cockpit. This was due in part to the birdcage canopy, and also to the Corsair's nose high three point attitude in taxi". One of the first major modifications was to raise the pilot seat seven inches, completely revise the canopy to a new frameless bubble type, and raise the tail of the airplane as it sat on the ground two degrees nearer a level attitude.

The latter was accomplished by increasing tail wheel strut height and using a new wheel. Pilot view was thus improved both on the ground and in the air. To gage the improvement pilot comments regarding the new arrangement on an F4U-1D are noted: "Was not at ease airborne because of poor visibility", "Its main drawback, and hardest to correct, is poor forward and rearward visibility", "The rear view is distorted" (three pilots). One pilot was a bit kinder "The raised canopy and seat did marginally improve the forward view". One pilot group ranked the F4U-1D seventh of eight fighter types in "Best all-around visibility". It seems clear that efforts to improve visibility were only partially successful.

POWERPLANT OPERATION

Early production Corsairs had cartridge starters which were not popular. After it stood out on a cold night starting an engine this way was no picnic "A monster to fire up; the shotgun starter was a failure". Later aircraft employed electric starting.

The engine of an F4U-1D was generally quite smooth, however there were some rough spots, one from 1750 to 1950 engine RPM, and another at 2200 RPM and 30 to 35 inches of manifold pressure. One pilot said at Eglin Field "The engine changes tone and runs rough as power is reduced near the cruise range". Later four pilots noted the powerplant was rough, "with vibration at certain RPMs". A modern evaluation of an FG-1D noted manifold pressure response to throttle movement was instantaneous and response of the Hamilton Standard propeller was good. On F4U-1D airplanes the pilot was fully in the loop for engine control, and that included manifold pressure. Some pilots complained about this. "Needs more labor-saving devices", particularly "Would like to see automatic blower shifting". Another noted "A lunge when blower is shifted; seems more violent than it should be". Automatic powerplant controls were not introduced on wartime Corsairs.

Fig.4U-24 Vought F4U-4P Corsair, USN photo via H. Andrews. Actually a post-war version of the Corsair, this photo reconnaissance airplane pictured at NAS Patuxent river, Maryland was one of only nine manufactured. Vought took over production of all -4 airplanes. Goodyear and Brewster produced -1 variants only with a -4 Goodyear version cancelled.

Fig.4U-25 Goodyear XF2G-1 Corsair, Mfr. photo via Jon Davis. One of a few Goodyear FG-1 aircraft converted to XF2G-1 configuration using the new 3000 horsepower Pratt and Whitney R-4360 Wasp Major engine to increase low altitude speed capability. A long cowl for the new four row radial engine and a bubble canopy are noteable. Only ten F2G-1 and F2G-2 fighters were produced.

VULNERABILITY/ARMOR

One experienced World War II pilot said of the Corsair "It could absorb a lot of punishment". Another, during an Eglin field evaluation, noted "I like the armor protection". The F4U-1D was ranked second of eight fighter types in the category "Best all-around armor" by a 1944 pilot group.

GUN PLATFORM AND WEAPON PERFORMANCE

There were differences of opinion about the relative merits of the Corsair and Hellcat as a gun platform. One reference flatly states

the Corsair was steadier in this respect. Another said though most pilots thought the Hellcat a more stable gun platform, he could not favor one over the other. Interestingly, of twenty fighter pilots who test flew the F4U-1D seventeen rated gun platform qualities either fair or poor with five of them rating it poor. As to weapon performance, a World War Two pilot experienced in several types said "I liked those six free-firing guns, and I was particularly well impressed by the hydraulic gun chargers. In the F4U- you could quickly and easily charge all the guns, and then concentrate on looking, flying, and shooting".

GENERAL COMMENTS

One pilot who considered himself very competent found difficulty acclimating to the F4U-.

A very good fighter with excellent performance for its type, and very efficient considering the gap between stalling speed and top speed.

Very much impressed with the power and ease of handling. Very good acrobatics. Felt completely at ease after ten minutes of flight. Upon flying the Corsair an experienced pilot was impressed with its power and acceleration capability.

While not pleased with Corsair ground handling one pilot felt it was comfortable and pleasant to fly once he was airborne.

A modern evaluation of a Corsair found it to be the "weapon of choice" over a P-51D, a P-47D, and an F6F-5. A World War II pilot noted the Corsair as a "high strung predator" while the Hellcat was a "nice safe pussycat".

One report indicated the USMC was pleased with Corsair performance and did not feel the type was a maintenance hog.

Lindbergh said the Spirit of St. Louis was no more blind in forward visibility than the F4U-1.

Fig.4U-26 Goodyear XF2G-1 Corsair, photo via F. Dean coll. Flight view of the souped up Corsair shows pleasingly clean lines. Bubble canopies had been tested on earlier Corsairs, but were not used on production aircraft. F2G- airplanes were sold after the war and converted into pylon racers where they achieved a degree of fame, winning the 1947 and 1949 Thompson Trophy Races with engine providing over 4000 horsepower.

Pilots found the Corsair could be very unforgiving if not handled with care.

There was great enthusiasm for the F4U-4; it was considered an outstanding aircraft.

A pilot felt the F4U-4 cockpit was uncomfortable on long flights with seat cushions somewhat of a help.

Some felt the Corsair was over-engineered and hard to maintain.

The F4U- was the champion in the poor ground visibility department.

A pilot took a Corsair up to 37000 feet and went into a series of dives, reaching speeds of Mach 0.67 where it shook badly (carrying certain external stores). The solution was to extend the store pylons.

A pilot described a very difficult landing on the narrow airstrip at Munda in the Pacific. He felt he had the worst type of plane, a Corsair, to accomplish this.

On May 21,1943 a fighter evaluation meeting took place at Eglin AAFB in Florida. Army pilots flying the Corsair for the first time were high in their praise. Dogfights were held with the P-47, P-51, P-38, and P-39 fighters, and all resulted favorably for the Corsair. Many considered the Corsair a "hydraulic monster".

Corsair controls were harmonized better than those of the Hellcat. Early Corsairs were called "Ensign Eliminators".

F4U-1D STRUCTURAL DESCRIPTION
(METAL NOTED IS ALUMINUM ALLOY UNLESS OTHERWISE STATED)

WING GROUP

The wing group consisted of a center section in a single assembly, two outer wing panels, and removeable wingtips, along with the means for wing folding.

The center section incorporated the inverted gull curvature and also provided support and housing for the main landing gear and support for the inner sections of the flaps. It also housed the air intakes and related ducting for intercooler, oil coolers, and ventilation of the cockpit. The center section mated to the fuselage, and at its outboard end provided a folding hinge system and support for the outer wing panels.

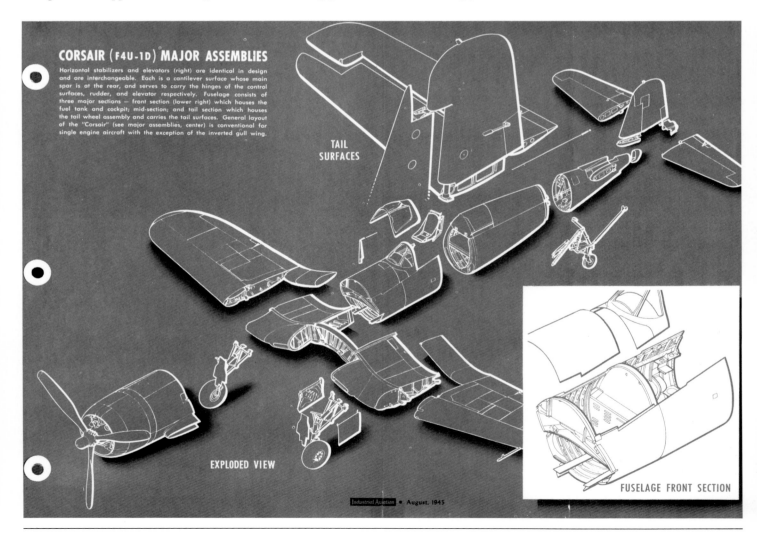

CORSAIR (F4U-1D) MAJOR ASSEMBLIES

Horizontal stabilizers and elevators (right) are identical in design and are interchangeable. Each is a cantilever surface whose main spar is at the rear, and serves to carry the hinges of the control surfaces, rudder, and elevator respectively. Fuselage consists of three major sections — front section (lower right) which houses the fuel tank and cockpit; mid-section; and tail section which houses the tail wheel assembly and carries the tail surfaces. General layout of the "Corsair" (see major assemblies, center) is conventional for single engine aircraft with the exception of the inverted gull wing.

TAIL SURFACES

EXPLODED VIEW

FUSELAGE FRONT SECTION

Industrial Aviation • August, 1945

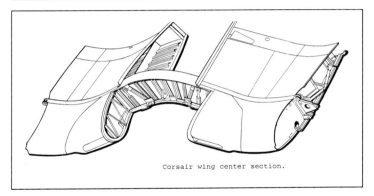

Corsair wing center section.

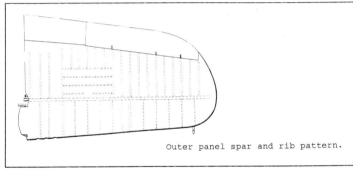

Outer panel spar and rib pattern.

The structure consisted of a leading edge torque box just outboard of the fuselage on each side, and also an interbeam torque box just aft together with a fuselage carrythrough section. The primary structural member was the main beam, or spar, which formed the backbone of the center section and extended for the full section span. It was the aft component of the leading edge torque box and the forward component of the interbeam torque box. The beam was in the shape of a curved flat W. Its curved flanges or caps could not be formed from a single ordinary extrusion so they were built up from a series of flat strips and smaller extrusions, formed to the gull contour and bolted together. The spar web was made of heavy metal sheet reinforced by vertical stiffeners. Items mounted directly to the main beam included the main hinge fittings for the outer wing panels, catapult hooks for launching the aircraft, landing gear drag link attachment fittings, and mount fittings for pylons carrying drop tanks or bombs. The leading edge torque box was formed by a series of chordwise ribs, spanwise stringers and skin, and the main beam or spar; the interbeam torque box was formed by the main beam forward, a rear beam or spar, chordwise ribs, and skins with spanwise reinforcing stringers. These boxes had metal skins of .091 inches thickness. The boxes stopped at the sides of the fuselage where they were tied in by angle fittings; the main spar carried directly through the fuselage and made the center section a single assembly. The rear spar supported the inboard flaps, and was of generally similar construction to the main spar though of lighter construction.

The wing outer panels were of the single spar and leading edge D section design with the D forming the torque box. The spar, at 30% chord, was built up of metal web and cap strips, and was an extension of the center section main beam. The leading edge structure consisted of chordwise ribs, spanwise stringers, and metal skin covering. The nose torque box carried the torsional, drag, and lift loads. All structure aft of the beam was cantilevered from it, and consisted mainly of chordwise metal ribs and a trailing edge subspar to carry outboard flaps and ailerons. The after section was fabric covered except for an area inboard under the gun bay which was metal covered. Provision for installation of three .50 caliber machine guns was made in the inboard section of each panel. Barrels and blast tubes went through the D section to the leading edge. Provision was also made for the ammunition boxes; these were removeable via the upper surface of the aft section, and the guns were accessible through a door in the upper surface. The undersurface of the wing in later versions mounted standoffs for rockets.

Wing tips were of plastic, and were expendable units. They were easily removed via a series of screws, and were interchangeable. British and USN tips were different, but structure inboard of the tips was the same.

The wing folding system was hydraulically operated and was controlled from the cockpit. In the extended position the wing outer panel was connected to the center section by three steel fittings. The forwardmost fitting was mounted just aft of the leading edge, and took torsion and side loads. Fittings at the top and bottom caps of the main spar took the wing bending loads. The fittings at the leading edge and upper spar cap were designed as hinges about which the outer panel could be swung upward. With the aircraft in the three point position the wings folded approximately straight up; if the airplane longitudinal axis was level the wings could be said to fold slightly forward. The third fitting at the lower spar cap was designed as a lock with the wing being held in place by a large sliding pin. The folding procedure consisted of the pilot releasing a mechanical lock on the control and moving it to the "fold' position. This action admitted hydraulic fluid to the hinge lock pin pulling actuator to retract the pin from the lock fitting. As the pin retracted it released a spring loaded mechanism causing a small "flag" door on the top wing surface to spring open. The door cleared a space just above the main spar where wing folding would otherwise crush the skin, and served as a warning the pin was out. A sequence valve

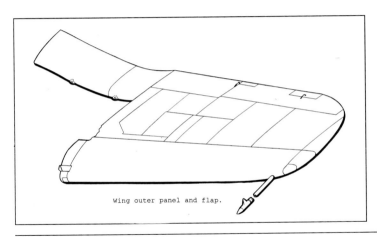

Wing outer panel and flap.

then directed hydraulic fluid to the wing fold actuator located in the outer panel, and the wing folded upwards. When the cockpit control was moved to the spread position the fold actuator in the outer panel lowered it into place, a load and fire valve diverted hydraulic pressure from fold actuator to lock pin actuator, and the pin was powered into "lock' position, thus locking the wing. When the lock pin was near the end of its travel a linkage pulled the flag door closed, completing the spreading action. The pilot then locked the pin from a separate cable-actuated locking control in the cockpit. The design problem of carrying various service controls outboard through the fold joint was solved by running them through the exact wing folding hinge line. For hydraulic services swiveling joints mounted on the exact wing folding line were used.

Ailerons were constructed entirely of wood, including plywood skinning. The plywood skin was covered with fabric for weatherproofing. Three hinge fittings were attached to the aileron front spar and were supported by mating parts on the outer wing panel. Ailerons were dynamically balanced to prevent flutter. A trim tab was provided on the left aileron and was controllable from the cockpit. Both ailerons also incorporated balance tabs at inboard trailing edges, linked to operate in the opposite direction to the aileron.

The plain flaps on each side of the aircraft were sub-divided into three separate sections. One of the sections was carried by the outer wing panel, and was separated from the other sections by the wing fold.

The other two flap sections were carried by the wing center section, one on the down-sloping portion and one on the up-sloping portion. Because of the gull shape, those two flap sections diverged from each other as they deflected, thus opening a gap at the trough of the gull shape. The gap was closed by a "gap-closing door" which was a sliding panel hinged to the inner flap section and sliding telescopically within the center flap section. The flaps were metal framed and metal covered, and were driven by a hydraulic actuator located in the wing center section. To carry the flap actuating mechanism across the wing fold, the hydraulic actuator was at the wing fold line, and the outer flap section connected with it by a rod which incorporated a swiveling universal joint. The cockpit flap control was designed so any desired flap angle in ten degree steps down to 50 degrees full down could be obtained. Flaps would "blow up" or back up from the set angle with excessive aircraft speed (90 to 100 mph IAS for full flap, and greater speed if less than full flap). Even so, the lowering of flaps to 50 degrees was prohibited above 130 KT.IAS and 200 KT.IAS at 20 degrees flap. The flaps could be used in maneuvering; usually maneuver settings were 20 degrees or less.

A small fixed spoiler strip was attached to the right wing leading edge.

TAIL GROUP

The tail group consisted of two horizontal stabilizers, two elevators, a vertical stabilizer, or fin, and a rudder.

The stabilizers were of full cantilever all metal construction. The structure consisted of a single spar at the aft edge to which ribs, elevator hinge fittings, and the stabilizer main attachment fittings were fixed. Hat shaped stringers, parallel to the spar, were spot welded to the skin which was riveted to the bulkheads and the spar. A cut-out area was provided in each stabilizer area at the tip to provide clearance for the elevator balance area. Left and right stabilizers were identical and could be interchanged. Stabilizers were connected to the fuselage by three attachment fittings, two at the spar and one at the leading edge, which took bending loads, while torsional loads were taken through a structural fairing between stabilizer and fuselage. The fairing was attached to the skins by screws and anchor nuts.

Elevators were of fabric covered metal frame construction. They were attached to the stabilizer at three hinge points on each side, and were connected by a torque tube. The tip of each elevator projected eleven inches forward of the hinge line to provide aerodynamic balancing of the surface. The left and right elevators were identical and could be interchanged. Cut-out framing inboard on the trailing edge of each elevator provided for attachment of both a trim tab controllable from the cockpit and a balance tab linked to the elevator only and moving in a direction opposite to it.

The vertical stabilizer, or fin, was of full cantilever all metal stressed skin construction. It contained a single spar aft, ribs, and stringers and skins, and was attached to the fuselage by two main fittings at the spar and a structural fairing to the fuselage around the fin bottom contour. The fin leading edge was offset two degrees tothe left to counteract propeller slipstream effects.

The rudder was similar in construction to the elevators, being metal framed and fabric covered. It also carried an aerodynamic balance area forward of the tip section, and accomodated a short mast on the hinge line to support one end of the radio antenna. The rudder framing provided a cut-out at the lower trailing edge for a cockpit controlled rudder trim tab. No balance tab was used on the rudder.

FUSELAGE GROUP

The structure of the fuselage differed from conventional all metal aircraft fuselage structure mainly by making use of comparatively large metal skin sheets and employing spot welding of aluminum to a larger extent than attempted previously in aircraft. The largest skin sheet was part of the fuselage mid-section, and measured 43 inches by 102 inches. Each of these sheets was pre-shaped by stretching over forms, and some incorporated compound curvatures. There were thus few external fastening seams with a resulting smooth exterior surface. Before the skin sheets were put together to form larger sub-assemblies, stiffeners were fixed to the inboard side of each sheet. The stiffeners were almost exclusively spot welded, rivets being employed only as stoppers in certain critical areas. After assembly the sheets then formed the skin of the airplane, while the stiffeners joined to form the transverse frames of the fuselage or similar internal members. In many cases hydraulic lines, controls, and similar items were installed on these panels before assembly.

The fuselage consisted of three major sections, each of which was replaceable. The forward section extended from the firewall at the forward end to the aft end of the cockpit. The firewall was reinforced with stainless steel sheet and had heavy fittings at four places on its forward side to support the engine mount. The four fuselage longerons terminated at the same locations on the aft face. The wing

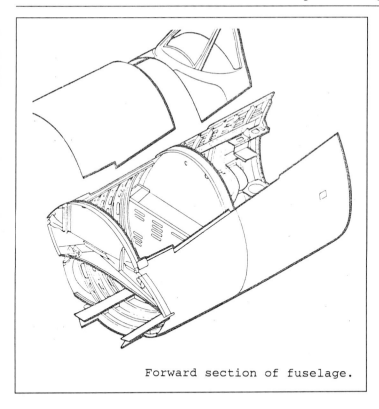

Forward section of fuselage.

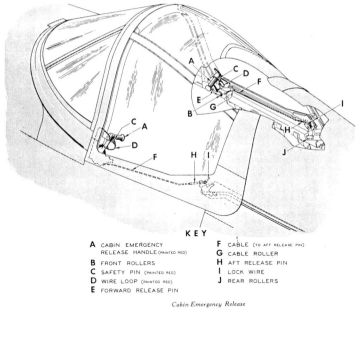

KEY

A CABIN EMERGENCY
  RELEASE HANDLE (PAINTED RED)
B FRONT ROLLERS
C SAFETY PIN (PAINTED RED)
D WIRE LOOP (PAINTED RED)
E FORWARD RELEASE PIN

F CABLE (TO AFT RELEASE PIN)
G CABLE ROLLER
H AFT RELEASE PIN
I LOCK WIRE
J REAR ROLLERS

Cabin Emergency Release

center section main spar carry-through structure lined up and was tied in with this firewall bulkhead. The forward portion of this fuselage section was occupied by the main fuel tank, and the top of it was protected by a 0.109 inch thick aluminum deflection plate acting as armor. Armor plate of the same variety also extended aft to just forward of the cockpit. The rear portion was the cockpit area, and was covered by a windshield assembly and a bulged canopy. The windshield was metal framed into three sections, the center portion being a thick bullet-resistant piece of glass. Four longerons ran through the length of the forward section, terminating in forged aluminum attach fittings. Side covering consisted of large stiffened metal sheets made up as was noted earlier. The cockpit bucket seat

was adjustable in height. The cockpit was not floored over. The sliding canopy was made up of three Plexiglas transparency sections, two side and one upper, framed in metal. A piece of heavy hardened aluminum alloy covered the rear portion of the upper section. The cockpit was entered from the aircraft right side via walkway, steps, and handgrips. The canopy was controlled externally by a push button on the upper forward end of the sliding section. Internally the canopy was controlled by a pull handle. An emergency canopy release system was incorporated where a handle on either side of the sliding canopy could be moved to release four pins, freeing the canopy from the aircraft. At the back end of the fuselage forward section two large pieces of face-hardened steel

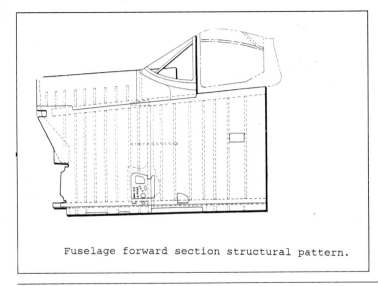

Fuselage forward section structural pattern.

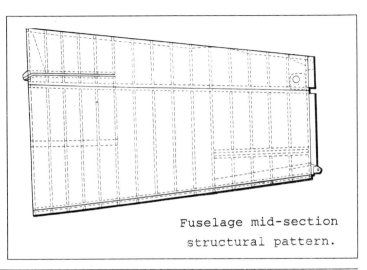

Fuselage mid-section
structural pattern.

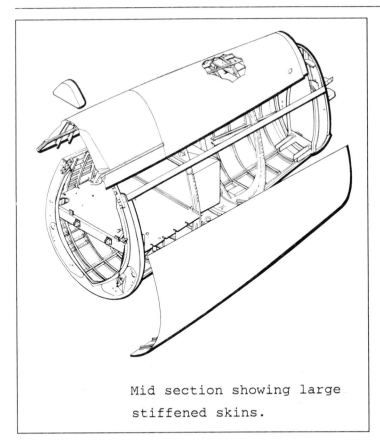

Mid section showing large stiffened skins.

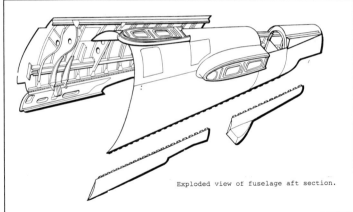

Exploded view of fuselage aft section.

skins was effected by riveting two shear plates together. Skins were up to .072 inches thick.

The aft or tail section of the fuselage supported the tail surfaces, tail wheel assembly, and the tail hook. The structure was made up of a four longeron continuation of those forward with their forged attach fittings, partial frames, and large sections of skin along with reinforced areas mounting the fixed tail surfaces. Retractable tail gear closure doors on the bottom were mounted on piano hinges.

LANDING GEAR GROUP
The landing gear group included the two main landing gear assemblies, the tail wheel, and their mechanisms.

The main landing gear was supported from the wing center section, and retracted aft into the wing, being completely enclosed by doors when retracted. The tail wheel and arresting gear were integrated mechanically and structurally; they were supported from the aft section of the fuselage, and retracted upward into the fuselage. They were almost entirely enclosed by doors when retracted. Power for extension and retraction was normally furnished from the main hydraulic system. The gear could be extended by an emergency system if the hydraulic system failed and if the hand pump would not work. Emergency operation was provided by actuation of a carbon dioxide blowdown system on the main gear and a spring system on the tail wheel. Main landing gear wheel brakes were powered by an independent hydraulic system controlled by toe brakes. The tail wheel was self-centering and could be locked in the fore-aft trailing position.

The main landing gear consisted of 32"x8" wheels with multiple disc brakes, oleo strut, lifting device, linkage, retracting cylinder, and dive brake fairing. The hydraulic retraction operated through a linkage which was self-locking in both the extended and retracted positions. In retracting, the hydraulic retraction cylinder shortened, pulling the cylinder links that were pivoted on the oleo

armor plate were provided just aft of the seat to protect the pilot's back and head. An overturn structure was included back of the pilot.

The fuselage mid-section was comprised of four I-section longerons at the shoulder points ending in dural forged attach fittings and bolts to fit up with forward and aft sections, two heavy end frames, and two major mid-frames, along with large area integrally-stiffened skins covering the top section above the longerons and large side and bottom skins. The mid-section supported radio gear on a large deck in the forward portion. The skins of the mid-section ended in shear plates, and connection between fuselage sections of

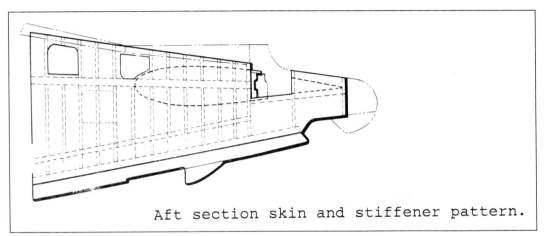

Aft section skin and stiffener pattern.

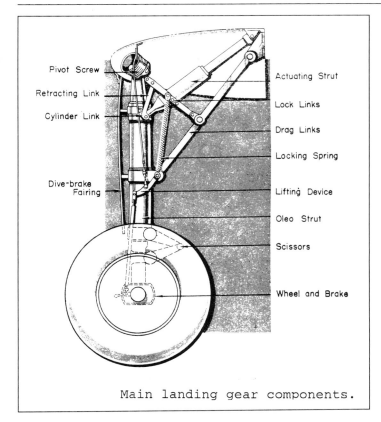

Main landing gear components.

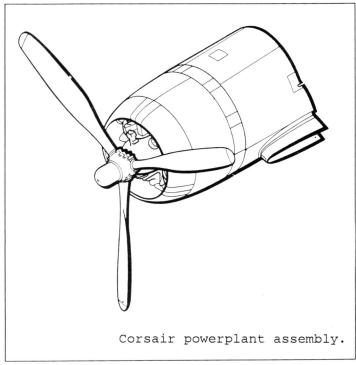

Corsair powerplant assembly.

strut aft, and pushing the lock links up. This action caused the link locks to break upward at their toggle joints, and in turn, to break the drag links upward at their joints. As the retracting cylinder continued to shorten, it pulled the collar of the oleo strut aft and upward, pulling the strut aft. The pivot fitting of the oleo strut, which was set at an angle to the plane of rotation of the strut, rotated as the strut was pulled aft, rotating the strut within a collar. This action permitted the retracted wheel to lie within the wing. Shock struts of both main and tail wheels were of the compound oleo-pneumatic type. The units were specially designed by Vought to correct an early strut problem of excessive stiffness and provide acceptable aircraft carrier landing capability.

The tail wheel linkage carried the arresting hook which was raised and lowered by a separate hydraulic actuator controlled from the cockpit. A dashpot served to prevent the hook from bouncing upon contact with the flight deck of a carrier.

ENGINE SECTION
The engine section consisted of engine mounting and engine cowling components.

The engine mount was an alloy steel tube structure bolted to the firewall fittings at the fuselage forward section and supporting the engine through vibration isolator mounts.

Quickly detacheable skin panels covered the engine accessory bay. Forward cowl panels were supported by the engine, and were also of the quickly-detacheable type. The engine cowl was equipped with adjustable exit flaps which were opened by spring action and closed by a cable drawstring running around the cowl and pulled in or let out by a single hydraulic actuator. The system replaced an earlier and unsuccessful multi-actuator hydraulic system where each flap segment had its own actuator.

F4U-1 SYSTEMS DESCRIPTION

POWERPLANT SUBSYSTEMS
ENGINE
The aircraft was powered by a 2000 horsepower class Pratt and Whitney R-2800 Double Wasp eighteen cylinder two row aircooled radial engine with a bore of 5.75 inches and stroke of 6.0 inches. The engine compression ratio was 6.7:1 and the propeller reduction gear ratio was 2:1. The engine was equipped with a mechanically-driven two stage two speed supercharger. The second stage blower had gear ratios of 6.46:1 in low blower and 7.93:1 in high blower. Maximum engine speed was normally 2700 RPM, and the splined propeller drive shaft rotated clockwise looking from the rear.

ENGINE INDUCTION SYSTEM
For takeoff and low altitude flight the cockpit supercharger control on the throttle quadrant was set to neutral which took the auxiliary blower out of the system. In this case engine charge air entered through doors at each side of the engine compartment, bypassed

Pratt and Whitney 18 cylinder R-2800 two row radial engine.

ENGINE EXHAUST SYSTEM

Six separate stainless steel exhaust manifolds, each serving three engine cylinders, discharged the exhaust aft and produced a jet thrust at full throttle of about 190 pounds.

ENGINE ACCESSORIES

The engine-driven or engine-mounted accessories included fuel pump, oil pump, vacuum pump, hydraulic pump, electrical generator, Bendix-Stromberg injection carburetor, propeller speed governor, and magnetos.

ENGINE CONTROLS

Mechanical engine controls were provided, and an engine control unit at the left side of the cockpit contained levers for throttle (with a forward water injection setting included on all -8W engine versions), mixture, propeller governor RPM set, and supercharger. Additional controls were provided in the cockpit for alternate carburetor air (mechanical), cowl flap positioning, intercooler flap setting, and oil cooler flap positioning-the three latter being controlled by cockpit hydraulic valves and local actuators.

PROPELLER

The propeller was a Hamilton Standard Hydromatic hydraulic three blade 24E60 hub using either 6501A-0 or 6541A-0 design solid aluminum blades in 13'1" diameter. It was an "engine-oil" propeller used with an engine gearbox-mounted propeller governor for constant speed control and a propeller accumulator.

PROPELLER CONTROLS

The propeller control in the cockpit was part of the engine control unit at the left side. The propeller lever was mechanically linked to the propeller governor on the engine, and set the desired speed of the engine-propeller combination.

the intercoolers, and was ducted directly to the carburetor. From there the fuel-air mixture entered the main supercharger stage blower and was then manifolded into the engine cylinders.

For medium or high altitude flight the cockpit supercharger control was moved from neutral to low or high setting, thereby engaging the auxiliary blower at one of the two gear ratios to the crankshaft. Engine charge air entered through the same doors and into ducting through control gate valves to the auxiliary blower. It exited from the blower into two intercoolers alongside, and then passed through Y ducting to the carburetor, and on to the main stage blower and intake manifold. Intercooler cooling air was taken aboard through the same lower doors, passed through the intercooler, and was then dumped overboard through an exit flap under the fuselage. The exit flap position could be controlled from the cockpit by a hydraulic actuator.

Alternate warm air from the engine compartment could be selected with mechanical control of a valve in the intake Y duct. A push-pull knob on the instrument panel moved the valve through a mechanical linkage. It was used in neutral blower only.

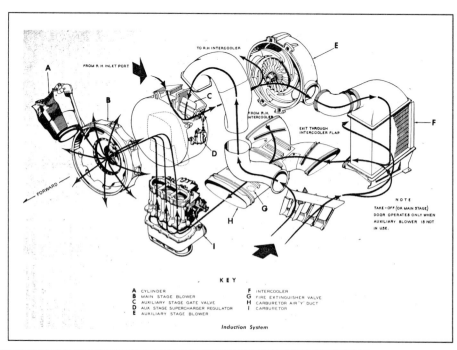

NOTE
TAKE-OFF (OR MAIN STAGE) DOOR OPERATES ONLY WHEN AUXILIARY BLOWER IS NOT IN USE.

KEY

A CYLINDER
B MAIN STAGE BLOWER
C AUXILIARY STAGE GATE VALVE
D AUX STAGE SUPERCHARGER REGULATOR
E AUXILIARY STAGE BLOWER

F INTERCOOLER
G FIRE EXTINGUISHER VALVE
H CARBURETOR AIR 'Y' DUCT
I CARBURETOR

Induction System

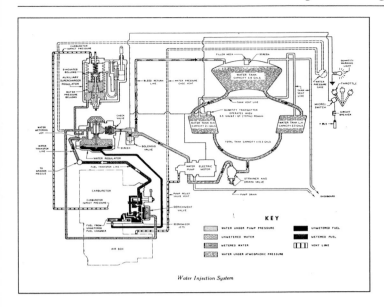

Water Injection System

ENGINE STARTING SYSTEM

The starting system was originally a cartridge type. An Eclipse type III unit was employed along with Type D cartridges for normal use and type E for cold weather. Cartridge gases drove a piston in a cylinder which rotated a gear train that drove the engine. An ignition booster was operated by a cockpit starter switch. In some airplane versions a booster coil was used; in others induction vibrators were employed. An engine primer switch was located next to the starter switch. The auxiliary electrical fuel pump was used to supply pressure for priming before starting the engine.

On the later F4U-1D airplanes electric inertia starters were employed.

ENGINE WATER INJECTION SYSTEM

Late F4U-1 and subsequent airplanes (with the -8W engine model) provided this system to give WAR EMERGENCY or COMBAT power. This was done by injecting a water-alcohol mixture into the engine cylinders. Passage of the throttle lever through a safety-wire

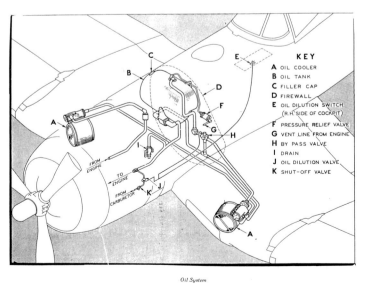

KEY

A OIL COOLER
B OIL TANK
C FILLER CAP
D FIREWALL
E OIL DILUTION SWITCH (R.H. SIDE OF COCKPIT)
F PRESSURE RELIEF VALVE
G VENT LINE FROM ENGINE
H BY PASS VALVE
I DRAIN
J OIL DILUTION VALVE
K SHUT-OFF VALVE

Oil System

detent called for the resulting higher power. The water injection system employed three water tanks with a total capacity of 10.3 US gallons tied to a common supply line, an electrically powered water pump, a flow-metering water regulator, and piping. The water-alcohol combination mixed with the fuel-air mixture in the main stage supercharger area.

ENGINE COOLING SYSTEM

The R-2800 engine was air cooled. The air entered the cowl annulus, passed over the finned cylinders and around the baffles directing the flow, and exited the rear of the cowling through a series of peripheral cowl flap segments. On very early airplanes these segments were each actuated by a small hydraulic cylinder. This proved unsatisfactory due to a high probability of leakage with the many actuators. A new system was used in which a single hydraulic actuator drove a cable and pulley arrangement where all the flap segments were linked by cable. A cowl flaps control lever was located with the intercooler and oil cooler control levers on a panel at the right side of the cockpit. The lever controlled valving to the cowl flap cylinder. A pressure relief valve was incorporated in the cowl flaps master cylinder to blow towards either open or closed position under excessive air loads.

ENGINE LUBRICATION SYSTEM

The engine lubrication system consisted of a 20 US gallon (alternatively 24 US gallons) oil tank mounted high and just forward of the firewall, two oil coolers, one in the leading edge air duct provided at each wing root, an engine-driven oil pump, and valves and piping. Each oil cooler had a thermostatic regulator valve, and pressure relief and bypass valves were included. The air for the oil coolers entered the leading edge ducts, passed through the coolers, and exited through the under-wing flaps which could control airflow and were actuated by hydraulic cylinders. The actuators were controlled by a lever at the right side of the cockpit next to the cowl flap and intercooler levers. The lever actuated a hydraulic control valve. An oil dilution system was included in the lube system with dilution switch located on the right hand panel in the cockpit.

ENGINE FIRE SENSING AND EXTINGUISHING SYSTEMS

Early aircraft did not have either a fire sensing or built-in fire extinguishing system. If a fire started in the duct system during starting a carbon dioxide fire extinguisher nozzle was to be pressed firmly against an air duct valve hole in the bottom of the accessory compartment cowl panel. Later airplanes incorporated a fire suppressor carbon dioxide cylinder and distribution system in the engine accessory bay.

FUEL SYSTEM

On early airplanes, like F4U-1s, the internal fuel system included a self-sealing fuselage main tank of 237 US gallon capacity, including a 50 US gallon standpipe reserve, and two 57 US gallon capacity wing tanks built integrally into the outer panels and unprotected. The wing tanks had a carbon dioxide vapor dilution system available with a supply cylinder in the fuselage. The external tank system (very early airplanes had no external tank capability) was an

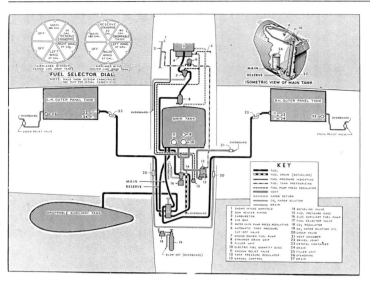

F4U-1 fuel system.

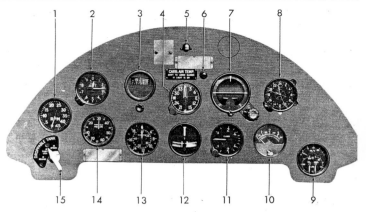

MAIN INSTRUMENT PANEL

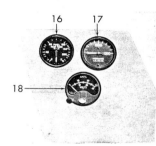

RIGHT HAND SUB-INSTRUMENT PANEL

Instrument Panels

1. Tachometer	10. Cylinder Temperature Indicator
2. Altimeter	11. Climb Indicator
3. Directional Gyro	12. Turn and Bank Indicator
4. Compass	13. Airspeed Indicator
5. Chartboard Light	14. Manifold Pressure Gage
6. Carburetor Air Temperature Warning Light	15. Centerline Droppable Fuel Tank Switch
7. Gyro Horizon	16. Fuel Quantity Gage
8. Clock	17. Hydraulic Pressure Gage
9. Engine Gage Unit	18. Voltammeter

optional single centerline droppable non-self-sealing teardrop tank of 170-175 US gallons capacity. On later airplanes, like F4U-1D models, the original internal main tank was the same along with provisions for mounting the centerline external tank, but the two wing tanks and their vapor dilution system were eliminated. Two under-wing center section pylons for a pair of drop tanks were added, one on each side. Either standard USN 154 US gallon or Lockheed 165-170 US gallon drop tanks could be hung on those pylons.

A tank selector control was provided at the left side of the cockpit and drove the selector valve. The release for the centerline drop tank was a switch located on the left side of the main instrument

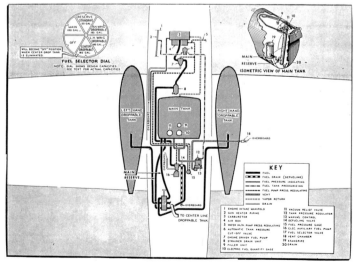

F4U-1D fuel system

Cockpit—Forward

1. Gun Switch Box	4. Bomb Switch Box
2. Gun Sight	5. Main Instrument Panel
3. Defroster Control	6. Cockpit Ventilator
	7. Right Hand Sub-Instrument Panel

panel operating an electrical shackle. For the twin pylon airplanes switches on the cowl above the instrument panel selected the tank to be dropped, and a thumb switch on the pilot's stick released the tank. A backup manual release control for twin pylon drop tanks was located to the left of the pilot's seat. This control was mechanically connected via cables to the shackles.

An electric fuel quantity gage was provided in the cockpit for the main tank only. A vapor return line ran from the carburetor to the top of the main tank and recovered about two quarts of fuel an hour. The main tank was pressurized by a line taken off the engine intake manifold. An electrically driven auxiliary fuel pump with a control switch on the right hand cockpit panel was included in the system. The pump was used during starting, takeoff and landing, changing tanks, and in case of engine-driven fuel pump failure. It was also often used during high power high altitude operation.

FIXED EQUIPMENT SUBSYSTEMS

INSTRUMENTS

Flight instruments included airspeed indicator, altimeter, climb indicator, directional gyro, gyro horizon, turn and bank indicator, compass, and a clock.

Engine instruments consisted of tachometer, oil temperature indicator, oil pressure gage, fuel pressure gage, fuel quantity gage, cylinder temperature indicator, and manifold pressure and RPM indicators.

Other instruments were a hydraulic pressure gage and a volt-ammeter.

SURFACE CONTROLS

The primary surface controls consisted of runs to ailerons, elevators, and rudder which were all moved manually by the pilot. Aileron and elevator control runs from the pilot's stick were of the push rod type with an arrangement of rods, levers, bellcranks, and idlers transmitting motions to the surface torque tubes and control horns. The rudder control runs consisted of a continuous cable system over pulleys from cockpit pedals to the rudder horn.

To improve stick forces during landing the aircraft was equipped with a heavy bungee spring, connected to the elevator controls and the tail wheel door mechanism, which became effective when the landing gear control moved the gear down. This made for a countering trim change when raising or lowering the landing gear.

Trim tabs were provided on the left wing aileron, on the elevators, and on the rudder; all were controlled by hand wheels at the left side of the cockpit. The runs from cockpit to tabs all consisted of cable and chain assemblies from control wheel sprockets in the cockpit to a sprocket in the control surface. These sprockets turned screw jacks which drove rod assemblies. Motion was transmitted to the trim tabs by a rod and bellcrank.

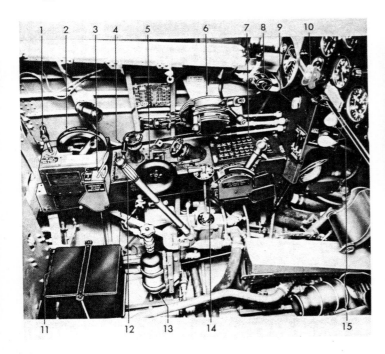

Cockpit—Left Side

1. Wing Hinge Pin Lock Control
2. Wing Folding Control
3. Manual Drop Tank and Bomb Release
4. Tail Wheel Lock Control
5. Trim Tab Controls
6. Engine Control Unit
7. Landing Gear and Dive Brake Control
8. Rocket Launching Switch
9. Ignition Switch
10. Wing Flaps Control
11. Battery
12. Hydraulic System Hand Pump
13. CO. Bottle—Emergency Landing Gear
14. Fuel Selector
15. Gun Charging Controls

Cockpit—Right Side

1. Right Hand Sub-Instrument Panel
2. Rocket Station Distributor Box
3. Cooling Flaps Controls
4. Pilot's Distribution Box
5. Radio and Communications Controls
6. Arresting Hook Control
7. Oxygen Tube
8. Oxygen Bottle
9. Diluter-Demand Regulator
10. Auxiliary Fuel Pump Switch
11. Defroster
12. Battery
13. Map Case

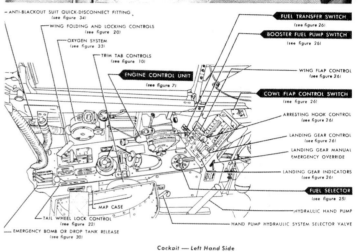

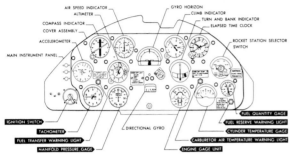

AIR SPEED INDICATOR
ALTIMETER
COMPASS INDICATOR
COVER ASSEMBLY
ACCELEROMETER
MAIN INSTRUMENT PANEL
GYRO HORIZON
CLIMB INDICATOR
TURN AND BANK INDICATOR
ELAPSED TIME CLOCK
ROCKET STATION SELECTOR SWITCH
IGNITION SWITCH
TACHOMETER
FUEL TRANSFER WARNING LIGHT
MANIFOLD PRESSURE GAGE
DIRECTIONAL GYRO
FUEL QUANTITY GAGE
FUEL RESERVE WARNING LIGHT
CYLINDER TEMPERATURE GAGE
CARBURETOR AIR TEMPERATURE WARNING LIGHT
ENGINE GAGE UNIT

Main Instrument Panel

ANTI-BLACKOUT SUIT QUICK-DISCONNECT FITTING (see figure 34)
WING FOLDING AND LOCKING CONTROLS (see figure 20)
OXYGEN SYSTEM (see figure 33)
TRIM TAB CONTROLS (see figure 10)
ENGINE CONTROL UNIT (see figure 7)
FUEL TRANSFER SWITCH (see figure 26)
BOOSTER FUEL PUMP SWITCH (see figure 26)
WING FLAP CONTROL (see figure 26)
COWL FLAP CONTROL SWITCH (see figure 26)
ARRESTING HOOK CONTROL (see figure 26)
LANDING GEAR CONTROL (see figure 26)
LANDING GEAR MANUAL EMERGENCY OVERRIDE
LANDING GEAR INDICATORS (see figure 26)
FUEL SELECTOR (see figure 25)
HYDRAULIC HAND PUMP
HAND PUMP HYDRAULIC SYSTEM SELECTOR VALVE
MAP CASE
TAIL WHEEL LOCK CONTROL (see figure 22)
EMERGENCY BOMB OR DROP TANK RELEASE (see figure 30)

Cockpit — Left Hand Side

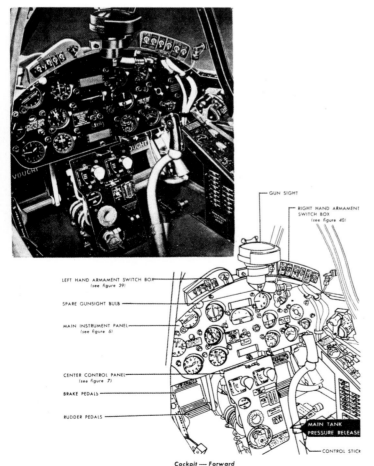

LEFT HAND ARMAMENT SWITCH BOX (see figure 39)
SPARE GUNSIGHT BULB
MAIN INSTRUMENT PANEL (see figure 6)
CENTER CONTROL PANEL (see figure 7)
BRAKE PEDALS
RUDDER PEDALS
GUN SIGHT
RIGHT HAND ARMAMENT SWITCH BOX (see figure 40)
MAIN TANK PRESSURE RELEASE
CONTROL STICK

Cockpit — Forward

Balance tabs on ailerons and elevators were linked directly to the control surfaces and required no pilot control.

ELECTRICAL SYSTEM

Electrical power was supplied by a 24 volt DC installation of the single positive copper wire type with the negative side of all circuits through the aircraft structure where all parts were electrically bonded together. Most of the operation of the system was controlled from the pilot's distribution box on the right hand shelf of the cockpit. A generator was mounted on the engine, and a battery was provided, located under the pilot's distribution box. Circuit breakers of the re-settable type were provided for the various systems.

Items or systems controlled electrically included starter, primer, backup fuel pump, pitot heater, radios, exterior and cockpit lights, armament, cockpit gages, gun heaters, gun camera, and gunsight.

HYDRAULIC SYSTEM

The hydraulic system was a closed-center type operated between pressure limits of 925 to 1150 psi. The system was powered by an engine-driven fixed displacement pump. Oil was supplied to the pump from a reservoir forward of the firewall. Fluid passed from the pump through a filter to a pressure regulator which, in conjunction with an accumulator, maintained pressure within prescribed limits. From the regulator the pressure line entered a main manifold which acted as a distribution center from which pressure lines

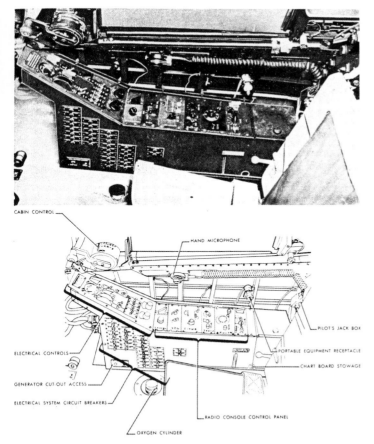

Cockpit — Right Hand Side (Early Models)

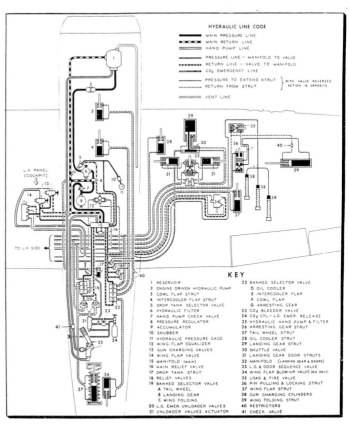

Hydraulic system diagram.

branched to the selector valves controlling the hydraulically actuated units. A main relief valve was provided to keep the pressure at a safe maximum in case of regulator failure. A hand pump at the left side of the cockpit allowed the pilot to actuate a unit in case of an engine pump failure or for a maintenance check when the engine was not running.

The hydraulic system was used to actuate the engine cowl flaps, oil cooler air exit flaps, and intercooler air exit flap, the main landing gear, landing gear doors, and tail wheel, wing flaps, wing folding and locking, the arresting gear, gun charging, and the landing gear acting as a dive brake.

PNEUMATIC SYSTEM
A vacuum pump driven by the engine was used as required to provide suction for instrument use.

COMMUNICATION, NAVIGATION, AND IDENTIFICATION SYSTEMS
The radio sets included AN/ARR-2 and AN/ARC-5 equipment. Mounting facility was also provided for AN/APX-1 or ABA recognition equipment. Controls for this gear were at the right side of the cockpit. All radio equipment was located on a shelf just aft of fuselage station 186 behind the cockpit.

ARMAMENT PROVISIONS
Basic armament consisted of three Colt-Browning M-2 .50 caliber machine guns in the inboard portion of each outer wing panel. Gun breeches were located behind the basic structural D-section of the wing with barrels protruding through the main spar web where they were enclosed by blast tubes near the wing leading edge. Guns were set on forward trunnion and aft post mounts. They were charged hydraulically and had electric trigger controls. Two gun charging knobs were located on the left side just below the main instrument panel. The upper knob controlled the three right guns, and the lower knob the three left guns. Pushing the knobs charged the guns by pressurizing hydraulic lines running out the wing on each side through a swivel joint at the wing fold juncture to the individual gun charging cylinders. Ammunition containers for the guns were located just outboard. Shells were ejected through chutes opening to the bottom of the wing. Access panels for guns and ammunition containers were provided in the upper wing surfaces. Ammunition storage capacity was 400 rounds for each inboard and intermediate gun and 375 rounds for each outboard weapon.

Early airplanes had a centerline mount for a 250 pound bomb. The hook assembly for bomb (or drop tank) release was actuated by a pulley and cable system powered by a drop tank hydraulic

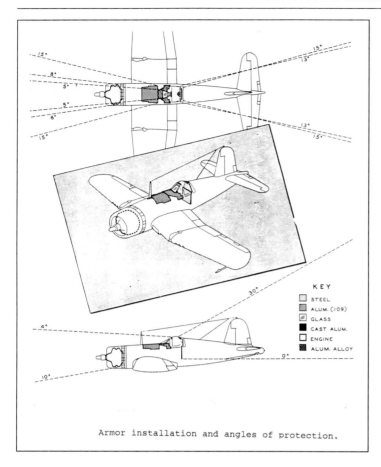

Armor installation and angles of protection.

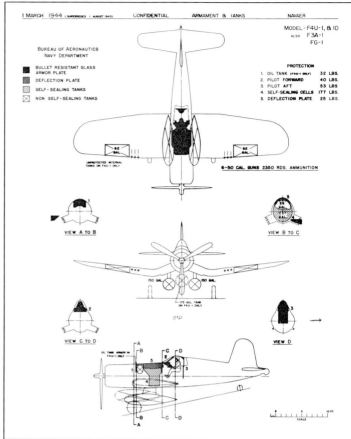

cylinder. The actuator was moved by hydraulic fluid from a forward selector valve. Later aircraft (F4U-1D models) had twin pylons where a set of switches located on the cowl deck above the instrument panel were provided for arming bombs and selecting the bomb to be dropped. A thumb switch on the pilot's stick was used for releasing bombs or tanks. Selection of electrical or manual bomb release depended on the type of bomb rack on the pylon. Bombs up to a maximum of 1000 pounds could be carried on each pylon.

On early airplanes gun control switches were on a sub-panel on the left side. On the F4U-1D airplanes control switches were located on the cowl deck above the instrument panel. The gun trigger was on the stick.

A gun heating system consisted of electrically heated pads attached to each gun and a cockpit switch.

Late aircraft could be equipped with underwing stand-offs for four zero-rail 2.75 inch high velocity aircraft rockets (HVARs) under each wing outer panel.

PASSIVE DEFENSE SYSTEM

The main fuel tank in the fuselage was self-sealing as were the fuel lines. The weight cost of the self-sealing was 177 pounds. A curved cowl deck just forward of the cockpit windshield and forming the outer contour of the fuselage just above the fuel tank acted as a gunfire deflection plate. It was made of .109 inch thick hardened aluminum alloy and weighed 25 pounds. A large piece of armor

plate weighing 53 pounds was located directly behind the pilot for backside protection. A thick piece of optically true bullet-resistant glass was placed directly behind the curved front windshield outer glass in front of the pilot. On early F4U-1 aircraft only, an additional piece of armor plate was placed directly in front of the oil tank in the engine compartment. The big R-2800 engine out front was considered a protection for the pilot from head-on fire. A removeable quarter inch thick steel plate could be placed on the bottom of the pilot's seat.

FURNISHINGS

A bucket type seat was provided with a vertical adjustment of nine inches in one inch increments. The adjustment was controlled by a handle on the right side of the seat. A shoulder harness was provided with the seat. A locking handle was located at the left side of the seat. A seat belt was also provided as was a relief tube.

HEATING/COOLING/VENTILATION SYSTEMS

A combustion heater, located in the cockpit, supplied heat for defrosting the windshield and for the cockpit. A master heat control switch on the right side panel controlled the system. An individual defroster switch was on the right side panel. A regulator control on the cowl deck just below the windshield bullet-proof glass operated a butterfly valve to control the flow of hot air for windshield defrosting. The remainder of the heating flow was bypassed into the cockpit.

Cockpit fresh air ventilation was gained via an opening forward of and between the foot troughs . The amount of fresh air could be varied by rotating a butterfly valve using the pilot's foot.

CARBON DIOXIDE SYSTEM

Emergency landing gear extension was accomplished using a carbon dioxide blowdown system for the main gear and a spring system on the tail wheel. It was to be used in the case of complete hydraulic failure where even the emergency hydraulic hand pump was not effective. A carbon dioxide bottle was located just aft of the seat. When a valve was turned (or on early aircraft a handle was pulled) carbon dioxide was released through a series of valves to the top of the main landing gear shock struts, thus extending the gear.

On early airplanes with unprotected wing fuel tanks a second carbon dioxide bottle was stored in the same location. This supply was used to purge the tanks and dilute fuel vapor.

ICE PROTECTION SYSTEM

The ice protection systems consisted of the alternate warm air supply to the carburetor and the hot air heating of the windshield noted earlier.

HANDLING EQUIPMENT

Tiedown links were provided in the outer wing panels and on the tail wheel mechanism. The towing links on the landing gear, and the drag links at the base of the landing gear provided additional tiedown points if required. Attachment for a hoisting sling was provided ahead of the cockpit.

FLOTATION GEAR

No flotation gear was provided apart from the pilot's life preserver.

ARRESTING GEAR

The tail wheel linkage carried the arresting hook. The hook was raised and lowered by a separate hydraulic cylinder actuated from a control at the right side of the cockpit. A dashpot prevented the hook from bouncing upon contact with the carrier flight deck and missing the deck arresting cables.

USEFUL LOAD SUBSYSTEMS
GUNS/BOMBS/ROCKETS

See the armament provisions section.

GUNSIGHT/GUN CAMERA

An illuminated reflector-type gunsight was located just above the instrument panel. On early airplanes the gunsight switch and light rheostat were on a sub-panel on the forward left side. On later F4U-1D aircraft the sight switch and the sight light rheostat were on the cowl deck above the instrument panel.

A gun camera was provided. A master switch was located on the gun switch box.

PYROTECHNICS

A Molin AN-M8 signal discharger (pyrotechnic pistol) and six cartridges were carried. The pistol was fixed to fire down and located to the right of the seat. A blast tube exited at the bottom of the aircraft. The cartridges were carried in a container just below the main instrument panel.

PHOTOGRAPHIC EQUIPMENT

No such equipment, other than the gun camera, was carried.

OXYGEN EQUIPMENT

A diluter demand type oxygen system was carried. It consisted of an oxygen bottle in the cockpit to the right side of the seat and a diluter demand regulator consisting of dilution valve, bypass valve, and pressure gage located just ahead of the bottle. An oxygen mask connector was provided on the regulator.

REFERENCES, F4U-/FG-
1. *Fact Sheet on F4U-*, Ling Temco Vought Aerospace and Defense, Vought Aero-products Division.
2. *Duels in the Sky*, Capt. Eric Brown.
3. *History of Marine Corps Aviation in World War II*, Robert Sherrod.
4. *Corsair-The F4U- in World War II and Korea*, Barrett Tilman.
5. *The Jolly Rodgers*, Tom Blackburn.
6. *Journal of the American Aviation Historical Society*, Spring 1961, Fall 1972, Spring 1973, Summer 1988.
7. *Fighter Development*, Lee M. Pearson, Naval Aviation Confidential Bulletin, Oct.1948/Apr.1949.
8. *Zero*, Masatake Okimita and Jiro Morikoshi with Martin Caidin, Ballantine Books, NY, 1957.
9. *Minutes of Fighter Conference*, NAS Patuxent River, Md., October, 1944.
10. *Ending the Argument*, SETP Paper, J.M. Ellis and C. A. Wheal.
11. Industrial Aviation Magazine, Aug.1945, *Design Analysis of the Vought Corsair*.
12. Erection and Maintenance Instructions, Model F4U-1, FG-1, F3A-1 Airplanes, Weight and Balance Data.
13. *Whistling Death*, Boone Guyton.
14. Design Analysis #5, Vought Corsair F4U-.
15. Profile Publications, *The Chance Vought F4U-1 Corsair*, J.F. Dial.
16. Fortitudine Newsletter, Winter 1986-7, *F4U-4 Corsair*, Maj. A. F. Elzy, USMC.
17. Fortitudine Newsletter, Summer, 1972, *The Corsair in the Marine Corps*
18. Marine Corps Gazette, May, 1981, *Corsair*, Col Frank E. Walton USMC (Ret.), also Col. Bruce Matheson, USMC (Ret.).
19. *Historical Data of AAF Proving Ground Command*, Eglin Field, Fla., Fighter Conference Jan.12-23, 1944, Narrative of Activities.
20. *Report on Evaluation and Comparison Trials of P-51B and F4U-1 Airplanes*, Jan.-Feb. 1944, USNAS Patuxent River, Md.
21. NAVAIR Airplane Characteristics and Performance, Model F4U-1, 8/1/43
22. NAVAIR Airplane Characteristics and Performance, Model F4U-1, 3/1/44
23. NAVAIR Airplane Characteristics and Performance, Model F4U-1D, 3/1/44.
24. NAVAIR Airplane Characteristics and Performance, Model F4U-4, 3/1/46
25. Standard Aircraft Characteristics, F4U-4 Corsair, Aug.15, 1948.
26. Standard Aircraft Characteristics, F4U-4B Corsair, Aug.15, 1948.
27. Pilot's Manual, F4U- Corsair/ Pilot's Flight Operating Instructions F4U-1D, FG-1D, F3A-1D and Corsair I, II, and III Airplanes. AN01-45HA-1
28. *Ace!, A Marine Night-Fighter Pilot in World War II*, Col. R. Bruce Porter and Eric Hammel, Pacifico press.
29. *The P-38, The P-39, and The F4U-*,Paul S. Bechtel, Aeroplane Historian Magazine, Winter/Dec.1986.
30. Air Classics Magazine, Nov. 1966, *Corsair*.
31. Airpower Magazine, Sept. 1971, *Old Hog Nose*, Boone Guyton.
32. *Cross-Winds, An Airman's Memoir*, by Najeeb E. Halaby, Doubleday and Company, Inc. 1978.
33. *The US Marine Corps in WWII*, Compiled and Edited by S.E.Smith, Random House, New York, 1969.
34. *Saga of the Bent-Wing Bird* by Walter Musciano, Aerophile, NY.
35. *Eighty Knots to Mach 2, Forty-Five Years in the Cockpit*, by Richard Linnekin, US Naval Institute Press, Annapolis, Md.1991
36. Pilot's Manual, F4U-4, F4U-4B, AN-01-45HB-1

THE F6F-

Table 88 gives numbers of Hellcat fighters constructed by model and year, provides some identification of each, and notes first delivery dates. It shows Navy Hellcats made up over twelve percent of America's Hundred Thousand. Almost all Hellcats were production models, either of the earlier F6F-3 variety or later F6F-5 type, with a lot more of the latter produced. One of the more interesting aspects of F6F- production was the number of night fighter versions put out, well over 1600 aircraft. This production was more than twice that of the Army's P-61 night fighter, and made the small number of night fighting Corsairs relatively insignificant. It is seen 1944 was the big Hellcat production year when over half the total number were put out.

TABLE 88
GRUMMAN F6F- HELLCAT MODELS

MILITARY DESIGNATION	EXPORT DESIGNATION	NO. OF AIRCRAFT	FIRST DELIVERY	NOTES
XF6F-1	—	2	F.F.JUN 26,'42	ONE A/C COMPL; WR.R-2600
XF6F-2	—	(1)	F.F.JAN.'44	TEST W.BIRMANN SUPERCH.
XF6F-3	—	(1)	F.F.JUL.'42	R-2800;CRASH,THEN TO -4.
F6F-3	HELLCAT I	4156	DEC.'42	
F6F-3E	—	18	JAN.'44	NT.FTR.WITH APS-4 RADAR
F6F-3N	—	229	SEP.'43	NT.FTR.WITH APS-6 RADAR
XF6F-4	—	(1)	APR.'43	XF6F-3 REFURB.;R-2800-27
F6F-5	HELLCAT II	6436	F.F.APR.'44	
F6F-5N	—	1432		NT.FTR.WITH APS-6 RADAR
F6F-5P	—	(?)		PHOTO RECONN. VERSION
F6F-5K	—	(?)		POST-WAR DRONE AIRCRAFT
XF6F-6		2	F.F.JUL.6'44	R-2800C ENG.,4-BL.PROP.

TOTAL   12275

PRODUCTION ACCEPTANCES BY YEAR

YEAR	1942	1943	1944	1945	TOTAL
NO.OF AIRCRAFT	10	2547	6140	3578	12275

TABLE 89
F6F- PHYSICAL DATA

WING SPAN	42'10"	AILERON TAB SPAN	1.375'
LENGTH	33'6.63"	AILERON TAB AREA (EA.)	0.466 SQ.FT.
HEIGHT,3-PT.OVER PROP.	14'5"	AILERON MOVEMENT	17DEG.UP,13.38 DN.
HEIGHT,OVER TAIL,LEVEL	13'0"	AILERON TAB MOVEMENT	8DEG.UP, 8DN.
HORIZ. TAIL SPAN	18'6"	TOTAL FLAP AREA (2)	39.8 SQ.FT.
TREAD	11'0"	FLAP TYPE	NACA SLOTTED
PROPELLER DIAMETER	13'1"	FLAP SPAN/WING SPAN	65%
SPAN FOLDED	16'2"	AVG.FLAP CHORD/AVG.WING CHORD	19.7%
WHEELBASE	21'5.25"	MAXIMUM FLAP DEFLECTION	48 DEG.
T/L CLEAR.ABOVE GND.	7'1.81"	HORIZ. STAB. INCIDENCE	4.5 DEG.
PROP. GND.CLEAR (LEVEL)	7.31"	TOT.HORIZ. TAIL AREA	77.8 SQ.FT.
WING AREA (INCL. FUS.)	334.SQ.FT.	TOTAL STABILIZER AREA (INC. 2.4 SQ.FT.OF\	
WING DIHEDRAL,OUTER PANEL	7.5 DEG.	FUS.& 8.0 SQ.FT.ELEV. BAL.)	52.0 SQ.FT.
WING L.E. SWEEP	5.0 DEG.	TOT.ELEV.AREA, AFT H/L,INC.TABS	25.8 SQ.FT.
WING INCIDENCE,ROOT&TIP	3.0 DEG.	TOTAL ELEV. TAB AREA	2.0 SQ.FT.
WING ASPECT RATIO	5.51	ELEVATOR CHORD, AFT H/L	1'7.5"
WING ROOT AIRFOIL	NACA 23015.6MOD.	ELEVATOR MOVEMENT	26 DEG.UP,15DN.
WING TIP AIRFOIL	NACA 23009	ELEV. TAB MOVEMENT	4 DEG.UP,18DN.
WING ROOT CHORD	119.438"	TOTAL VERTICAL TAIL AREA	23.4 SQ.FT.
WING TIP CHORD(CONSTR.)	63"	TOT.FIN AREA,INC.1.9 RUD.BAL.	14.4 SQ.FT.
MEAN AERODYNAMIC CHORD	97.4"	TOT.RUDDER AREA,AFT H/L,INC.TAB	9.0 SQ.FT.
WING TAPER RATIO	2.0	RUDDER TAB AREA	0.6 SQ.FT.
AILERON SPAN	6'4.5"	RUDDER MOVEMENT	33 DEG.L;33 R.
AILERON CHORD	0.2xWING CHORD	RUDDER TAB MOVEMENT	30 DEG.L; 8 R.
AILERON AREA (EA.)	7.85 SQ.FT.	MAIN WHEEL TIRE SIZE	32" x 8"
		TAIL WHEEL TIRE SIZE	10.5"x4.4"/8.5"x4.0"

TABLE 90
F6F- HELLCAT FUEL CAPACITIES (GAL.)

MODEL	MAXIMUM INTERNAL FUEL	MAXIMUM EXTERNAL FUEL
F6F-3	250	150
F6F-5	250	450

The F6F- was a large aircraft for a single seat fighter, slightly bigger than the Army P-47 and the Corsair, and with greater wing area than either, as borne out by the physical data displayed in Table 89.

The fuel capacities of Hellcat models are given in Table 90. Both F6F-3 and F6F-5 had a total internal fuel capacity of 250 gallons in three fuselage tanks, two main and one auxiliary, or reserve, all of nearly equal capacity, though the reserve tank was a little smaller. The earlier F6F-3 had a single centerline mounting for a 150 gallon drop tank, as did the later -5 airplane. The F6F-5 also had wing store stations capable of handling an additional 150 gallon drop tank on each side, giving a total maximum airplane fuel capacity of 700 gallons. The arrangement of three drop tanks was very seldom used, however.

Since the aircraft versions were so outwardly similar, the five view drawing included here serves well for F6F-3 or F6F-5. It shows a conventional radial engined low mid-wing monoplane with a typically deep Grumman fuselage. The large wing was distinguished by a flat center section joining two foldable outer panels which provided dihedral. Landing gear tread was considerably greater than

GRUMMAN HELLCAT (F6F-5)

R. G. SMITH

the predecessor Wildcat with main gear rotating so wheels folded flat into the wing underside.

The Hellcat cut-away drawings provide a view of internal arrangement. The big R-2800 Double Wasp engine with its powerplant

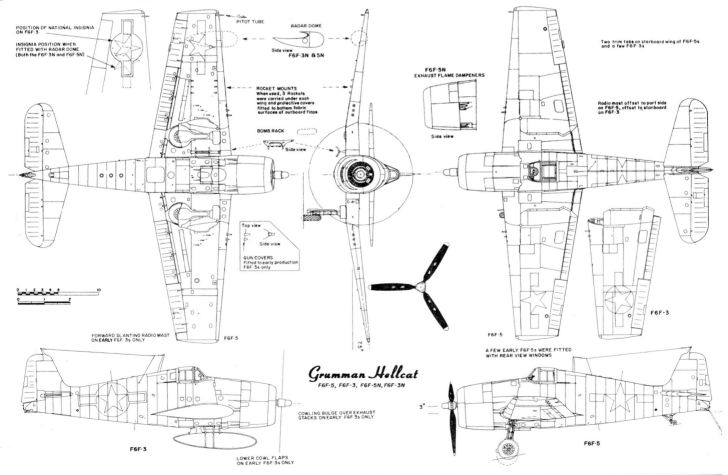

Gruman Hellcat
F6F-5, F6F-3, F6F-5N, F6F-3N

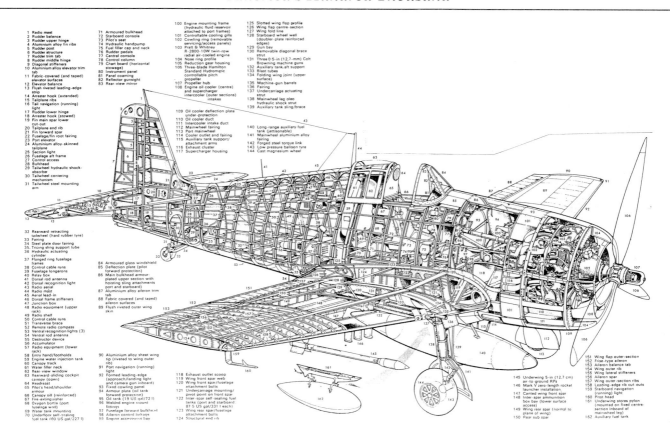

1 Radio mast
2 Rudder balance
3 Rudder upper hinge
4 Aluminium alloy fin ribs
5 Rudder post
6 Rudder structure
7 Rudder trim tab
8 Rudder middle hinge
9 Diagonal stiffeners
10 Aluminium alloy elevator trim tab
11 Fabric-covered (and taped) elevator surfaces
12 Elevator balance
13 Flush riveted leading-edge strip
14 Arrester hook (extended)
15 Tailplane ribs
16 Tail navigation (running) light
17 Rudder lower hinge
18 Arrester hook (stowed)
19 Fin main spar lower cut-out
20 Tailplane end rib
21 Fin forward spar
22 Fuselage/fin root fairing
23 Port elevator
24 Aluminium alloy-skinned tailplane
25 Section light
26 Fuselage aft frame
27 Control access
28 Bulkhead
29 Tailwheel hydraulic shock-absorber
30 Tailwheel centering mechanism
31 Tailwheel steel mounting arm

32 Rearward-retracting tailwheel (hard rubber tyre)
33 Fairing
34 Steel plate door fairing
35 Tricing sling support tube
36 Hydraulic actuating cylinder
37 Flanged ring fuselage frames
38 Control cable runs
39 Fuselage longerons
40 Relay box
41 Dorsal rod antenna
42 Dorsal recognition light
43 Radio aerial
44 Radio mast
45 Aerial lead-in
46 Dorsal frame stiffeners
47 Junction box
48 Radio equipment (upper rack)
49 Radio shelf
50 Control cable runs
51 Transverse brace
52 Remote radio compass
53 Ventral recognition lights (3)
54 Ventral rod antenna
55 Destructor device
56 Accumulator
57 Radio equipment (lower rack)
58 Entry hand/footholds
59 Engine water injection tank
60 Canopy track
61 Water filler neck
62 Rear-view window
63 Rearward-sliding cockpit canopy (open)
64 Headrest
65 Pilot's head/shoulder armour
66 Canopy sill (reinforced)
67 Fire extinguisher
68 Oxygen bottle (port fuselage wall)
69 Water tank mounting
70 Underfloor self-sealing fuel tank (60 US gal/227 l)

71 Armoured bulkhead
72 Starboard console
73 Pilot's seat
74 Hydraulic handpump
75 Fuel filler cap and neck
76 Rudder pedals
77 Central console
78 Control column
79 Chart board (horizontal stowage)
80 Instrument panel
81 Panel coaming
82 Reflector gunsight
83 Rear-view mirror

84 Armoured glass windshield
85 Deflection plate (pilot forward protection)
86 Main bulkhead armour plated upper section with hoisting sling attachments port and starboard)
87 Aluminium alloy aileron trim tab
88 Fabric covered (and taped) aileron surfaces
89 Flush riveted outer wing skin
90 Aluminium alloy sheet wing tip (riveted to wing outer rib)
91 Port navigation (running) light
92 Formed leading-edge (approach/landing light and camera gun inboard)
93 Fixed cowling panel
94 Armour plate (oil tank forward protection)
95 Oil tank (19 US gal/72 l)
96 Welded engine mount fittings
97 Fuselage forward bulkhead
98 Aileron control linkage
99 Engine accessories bay

100 Engine mounting frame (hydraulic fluid reservoir attached to port frames)
101 Controllable cooling gills
102 Cowling ring (removable servicing/access panels)
103 Pratt & Whitney R-2800-10W twin-row radial air-cooled engine
104 Nose ring profile
105 Reduction gear housing
106 Three-blade Hamilton Standard Hydromatic controllable pitch propeller
107 Propeller hub
108 Engine oil cooler (centre) and supercharger intercooler (outer sections) intakes
109 Oil cooler deflection plate under-protection
110 Oil cooler duct
111 Intercooler intake duct
112 Mainwheel fairing
113 Port mainwheel
114 Cooler outlet and fairing
115 Auxiliary tank support/attachment arms
116 Exhaust cluster
117 Supercharger housing
118 Exhaust outlet scoop
119 Wing front spar web
120 Wing front spar/fuselage attachment bolts
121 Undercarriage mounting/pivot point on front spar
122 Inter-spar self-sealing fuel tanks (port and starboard 87.5 US gal/331 l each)
123 Wing rear spar/fuselage attachment bolts
124 Structural end rib

125 Slotted wing flap profile
126 Wing flap centre-section
127 Wing fold line
128 Starboard wheel well (doubler-plate reinforced edges)
129 Gun bay
130 Removable diagonal brace strut
131 Three 0.5-in (12.7-mm) Colt Browning machine guns
132 Auxiliary tank aft support
133 Blast tubes
134 Folding wing joint (upper surface)
135 Machine-gun barrels
136 Fairing
137 Undercarriage actuating strut
138 Mainwheel leg oleo hydraulic shock strut
139 Auxiliary tank sling/brace
140 Long-range auxiliary fuel tank (jettisonable)
141 Mainwheel aluminium alloy fairing
142 Forged steel torque link
143 Low pressure balloon tyre
144 Cast magnesium wheel
145 Underwing 5-in (12.7 cm) air-to-ground RPs
146 Mark V zero-length rocket launcher installation
147 Canted wing front spar
148 Inter-spar ammunition box bay (lower surface access)
149 Wing rear spar (normal to plane of wing)
150 Rear sub spar
151 Wing flap outer-section
152 Frise-type aileron
153 Aileron balance tab
154 Wing outer rib
155 Wing lateral stiffeners
156 Aileron spar
157 Wing outer-section ribs
158 Leading-edge rib cut-outs
159 Starboard navigation (running) light
160 Pitot head
161 Underwing stores pylon (mounted on fixed centre-section inboard of mainwheel leg)
162 Auxiliary fuel tank

Cutaway drawing of F6F-5.

TABLE 91
GRUMMAN F6F- MODELS PROPULSION DATA

MODEL	ENGINE	RATING	HP	RPM	ALT.'	MAP"HG.	SUPERCHARGER
XF6F-2	XR-2600-15	TAKEOFF	2000		SEA LEVEL		BIRMANN
F6F-3	R-2800-10	TAKEOFF	2000	2700	SEA LEVEL	54.0	2-STAGE,2-SPEED
	G.R.=2:1	MILITARY	2000	2700	1000	52.5	
		MILITARY	1800	2700	13500		
		MILITARY	1650	2700	22500		
		NORMAL	1675	2550	5500		
		NORMAL	1625	2550	15000		
		NORMAL	1550	2550	21500		
F6F-3	R-2800-10W	TAKEOFF	2000	2700	SEA LEVEL	54.0	2-STAGE,2-SPEED
F6F-5	G.R.=2:1	COMBAT	2250	2700	SEA LEVEL	57.5	
		COMBAT	2135	2700	15000	59.0	
		COMBAT	1975	2700	20000	59.5	
		MILITARY	2000	2700	1700	52.5	
		MILITARY	1800	2700	15500	53.5	
		MILITARY	1650	2700	22500	52.5	
		NORMAL	1675	2550	5500	45.0	
		NORMAL	1625	2550	18000	49.5	
		NORMAL	1550	2550	24000	49.5	
XF6F-6	R-2800-18W	TAKEOFF	2100	2800	SEA LEVEL		2-STAGE,2-SPEED
	G.R.=20:9	COMBAT	2380	2800	SEA LEVEL		
		COMBAT	2080	2800	23300		
		MILITARY	2100	2800	4300		
		MILITARY	1710	2800	25000		
		NORMAL	1700	2600	9000		
		NORMAL	1550	2600	26600		

The propeller for the XF6F-2 was a Curtiss model; the propeller for the production F6F- aircraft was a Hamilton 23E50 with 3 6501-0 blades in 13'1". The XF6F-6 had a Hamilton 4-bladed 24E50 propeller with the same 6501 blades.

accessories was mounted forward of the firewall with steel tubes of the mount running through the accessory compartment. Air intake ducting for oil cooler, carburetor, and supercharger intercoolers ran beneath the engine. Among items located in the accessory compartment behind the engine were the oil tank and Hydromatic propeller accumulator, both strapped to the engine mount, a piece of armor plate protecting the oil tank, cowl flap actuating system, the intercoolers, a hydraulic fluid reservoir, and engine control runs. The high-set cockpit and enclosing canopy were located just aft of the firewall. Location of the latter coincided with the wing front spar. Fuel tanks were placed below the cockpit. A water storage tank for the engine water injection system and an oxygen bottle were mounted aft of the pilot, and armor plate was provided behind him. Radio equipment was placed on upper and lower racks in the fuselage behind the cockpit area. The aft end of the fuselage was occupied by tail wheel and arresting gear assemblies and their retracting mechanisms.

The figures in Table 91 give major ratings of engines used in Hellcat models. The table shows the switch from a Wright R-2600 engine in the early XF6F-2 prototype to the R-2800 Double Wasp for production Hellcats. The original F6F-3 airplanes had the R-2800-10 engine with TAKEOFF and maximum MILITARY ratings of 2000 horsepower. The latter setting gave 1650 horsepower at 22500 feet with the auxiliary stage supercharger blower at high RPM. With advent of the F6F-5 the R-2800-10W engine was utilized, the W meaning water injection was incorporated to provide a COMBAT power setting for short periods without incurring detonation. Retrofitting was effected on F6F-3 airplanes as quickly as practical. The new COMBAT rating raised power output to 2250 horsepower at sea level and 1975 horsepower at 20000 feet to give the Hellcat a performance boost when critically needed. The new R-2800C engine and a four blade propeller were fitted to the XF6F-

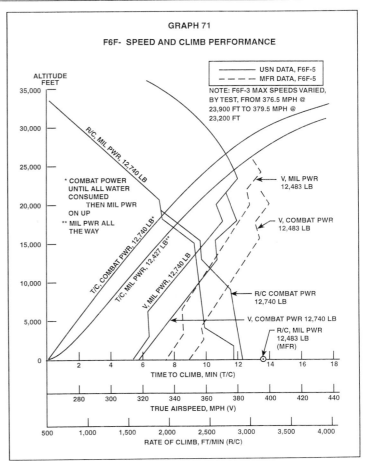

GRAPH 71

F6F- SPEED AND CLIMB PERFORMANCE

6, but this version was too late for war production. Maximum COMBAT power was raised to 2380 horsepower at sea level in this version of the Double Wasp. The engine power curves of Graph 70 show variation with altitude of available MILITARY and COMBAT power of the -10W engine. These curves, or rather series of connected straight lines, indicate how power changed using the supercharger in neutral, low blower, and high blower modes of operation. The two stage supercharger was quite successful in maintaining power until altitudes well over 20000 feet were reached.

In Graph 71 high speed and climb performance versus altitude of the F6F-5 Hellcat is depicted using both US Navy and manufacturer's data on speed. High speeds at MILITARY and COMBAT power differed considerably between data sources with manufacturer's numbers more optimistic. The different aircraft weights noted would make a little but not all the difference in speed capability. All curves show typical abrupt changes reflecting various modes of supercharger operation as noted earlier. Navy data says the -5 Hellcat at MILITARY power was capable of about 314 to 324 mph under 6000 feet after which high speed rose rapidly to 365 to 370 mph at 18000 to 20000 feet. With high blower kicked in the Hellcat reached a maximum speed of 380 mph just over 23000 feet after which capability fell off to 360 mph at 30000 feet. The same data showed COMBAT power setting increased speed capability at all altitudes up to 21000 feet with the airplane touching 380 mph at 18000 feet. Grumman data at 257 pounds less airplane

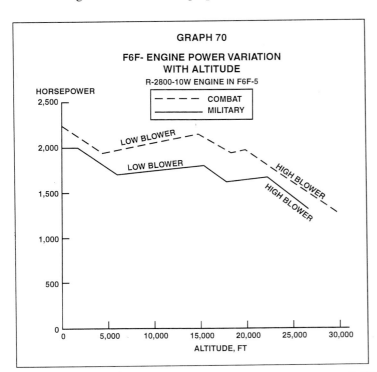

GRAPH 70

F6F- ENGINE POWER VARIATION
WITH ALTITUDE

R-2800-10W ENGINE IN F6F-5

weight and MILITARY power showed the F6F-5 attaining 335 mph at sea level, over 385 mph at 20000 feet, and 390 mph at about 24000 feet. These numbers are 10 to 15 mph greater than the Navy figures. And with COMBAT power the manufacturers indicated the F6F-5 could hit 350 mph at sea level and touch 400 mph at 20000 feet. These figures are 10 to 30 mph increases over Navy numbers.

The curves of climb rate and time are all from Navy sources except one point where Grumman shows the F6F-5 at 12483 pounds could climb 3200 feet per minute at sea level using MILITARY power. The equivalent USN climb rate at 12740 pounds was just over 2800 feet per minute, reducing quickly to under 2500 feet per minute at 5000 feet, 2350 at 10000 feet, and about 1900 at 20000 feet. Application of COMBAT power increased climb rate considerably at low altitudes, but little or no increase was imparted at medium and high altitudes. Time to climb at MILITARY power was just under five minutes to 10000 feet and under 9.5 minutes to 20000 feet.

Though not shown on the curves, using NORMAL power, climb times to 10000 and 20000 feet were 5.2 and 11.2 minutes respectively at a weight of 12740 pounds. As the curves show, use of COMBAT power reduced these times significantly to 3.6 and 7.7 minutes to the same altitudes.

As preface to discussion on F6F- range characteristics, the following is taken from a Navy manual: "In contrast to the record of the F6F- in combat operations, testing of the aircraft for fuel consumption has not gone smoothly. The first tests were run in 1943 with an F6F-3. Analysis of the results of these tests indicated erratic carburetion and probable errors in measurement of fuel flow. Rather than publish results of uncertain accuracy, no report was issued, but information not involving fuel consumption was written into the pilot's handbook. A new series of tests, with an F6F-5, was started in the Fall of 1944, but almost immediately the data took an unsatisfactory trend, particularly in connection with specific fuel consumption." So the Navy had to be somewhat unsure

of Hellcat range capabilities. Graph 72 shows F6F-5 range capability and resulting takeoff gross weight as set down in a manufacturers specification. The data is no doubt ideal maximum range, and it is specified at a cruise altitude of 1500 feet. A range of slightly over 1300 miles on internal fuel only is indicated. In this case the airplane is clean; there are no external appendages. A range figure from a Navy characteristics sheet is also given and shows a "com-

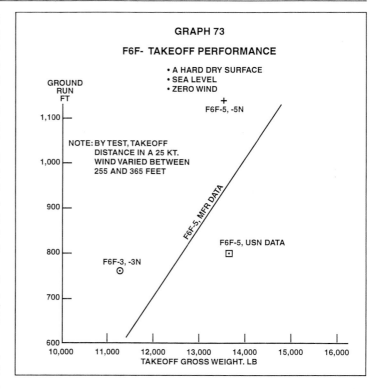

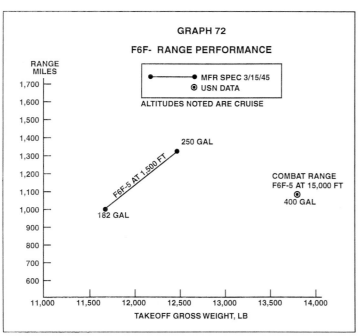

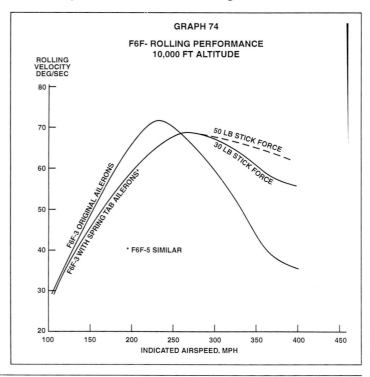

bat range" of almost 1100 miles starting with full internal tankage plus a centerline drop tank. Takeoff fuel in this case is a total of 400 gallons; the external tank dropped when empty. The mission profile is not shown, but it is believed to be a practical one. Though not shown in the figure, combat radius is given by the Navy as 390 miles. This case is a practical one with 20 minutes allowed for warmup and takeoff, 20 minutes for rendevous at sea level, an allowance made for climb to 15000 feet and cruise out at that altitude with external tank dropped at midpoint, an allowance for fuel for 20 minutes of combat at 15000 feet and 10 minutes descent to 1500 feet with cruise back at that altitude, all with a fuel reserve allowance of an hour at speed for best endurance.

Hellcat takeoff distances at various weights are shown in Graph 73.

Rolling performance of the Hellcat is presented in Graph 74. Peak roll rate of the F6F-3 model was slightly over 70 degrees per second at 240 mph IAS. Roll capability fell off quickly to 40 degrees per second at 360 mph IAS. This performance was not considered satisfactory, and efforts were bent towards improvement. An F6F-3 airplane was modified with new ailerons incorporating spring tabs. High speed roll performance was greatly improved with some tolerable loss at lower speeds. The overall improvement was incorporated in the newer F6F-5 Hellcats. As the curve shows, roll rate at 360 mph IAS improved to almost 60 degrees per second with a 30 pound lateral stick force and to 64 degrees per secong with a 50 pound pilot force. Unfortunately this performance cannot be compared to the Corsair at the higher speeds because no F4U-data has been found above 290 mph IAS, but in the 200 to 300 mph speed range the Corsair appears superior.

Table 92 provides breakdowns by group of F6F-3 and F6F-5 Hellcat empty weights. There is a year and a half between dates of the breakdowns, and in that time the Hellcat gained only 128 pounds, a relatively good record in minimizing weight growth. There is nothing dramatic discerned in group weight changes between -3 and -5. A net addition is shown; water injection was added to the later model from the start, and later retrofitted to the -3 aircraft when practical. This retrofit is not shown in the -3 breakdown.

Three alternate useful load possibilities for an F6F-3 Hellcat are seen in Table 93. The first column shows the lowest gross weight of about 11400 pounds, but is probably not realistic for a combat theatre since only a partial load of fuel, oil, and ammunition is carried. The second column, though defined as an overload fighter case, is much more practical. A full ammunition load and 250 gallons of internal fuel are carried (a gallon of gasoline weighs six pounds). In the third case, for a fighter bomber mission, a 150 gallon centerline drop tank and and two 500 pound bombs are carried, jacking up the gross weight to 14335 pounds at takeoff. Some alternate useful loads are shown in Table 94 for the later F6F-5 fighter. Three of these have wartime dates; the other two are from Navy data of 1950 when the airplane was definately a second-line fighter. By the latter date empty weight had grown another 150 pounds. The only difference in operating equipment was that provisions for external loads were standardized. Note again in the fighter case of the first column that the airplane did not carry a full load of fuel and ammunition whereas the overload fighter in the next column did. The last column shows the F6F-5 fighter bomber with the same load as the earlier -3 at a gross weight of 14627 pounds, or about 300 pounds greater than the earlier model. Gross weights of the Hellcat are generally similar to those of the Corsair.

TABLE 92
F6F- EMPTY WEIGHT BREAKDOWNS
(POUNDS)

MODEL GROUP	F6F-3 (SEP.28,'43)	F6F-5 (MAR.15,'45)
WING	2024.5	2039.8
TAIL	271.4	280.8
FUSELAGE	616.0	647.9
LANDING GEAR	733.8	751.2
ENGINE SECTION	411.6	426.2
ENGINE	2469.0	2455.0
ENGINE ACCESSORIES	314.0	318.0
ENGINE CONTROLS	36.5	30.8
PROPELLER	485.2	481.4
STARTING SYSTEM	57.0	43.4
LUBRICATING SYSTEM	144.3	148.5
FUEL SYSTEM	458.5	467.5
INSTRUMENTS	41.0	45.5
SURFACE CONTROLS	171.6	147.2
HYDRAULIC SYSTEM	112.9	126.6
ELECTRICAL SYSTEM	208.4	223.8
ARMAMENT PROVISIONS	288.8	313.6
FURNISHINGS	69.2	54.4
ARRESTING GEAR	37.4	35.7
WATER INJECTION SYSTEM	—	41.5
EMPTY WEIGHT	8951.1	9078.8

TABLE 93
F6F-3 ALTERNATE USEFUL LOADS
(POUNDS)

MISSION	FIGHTER	FIGHTER OVERLOAD	FIGHTER-BOMBER
EMPTY WEIGHT	8951.1	8951.1	8951.1
TRAPPED FUEL & OIL	89.5	89.5	89.5
CAL.50 GUN INSTALL.	433.6	433.6	433.6
PROV.FOR BOMBS,TANKS	—	—	199.2
PYROTECHNICS	3.5	3.5	3.5
GUN CAMERA	4.2	4.2	4.2
COMMUNICATION EQUIP'T.	136.0	136.0	136.0
NAVIGATION EQUIPMENT	3.8	3.8	3.8
MISC. EQUIPMENT	51.7	51.7	51.7
CREW	200.0	200.0	200.0
FIXED USEFUL LOAD	922.3	922.3	1121.5
BASIC WEIGHT	9873.4	9873.4	10072.6
USEABLE OIL	97.5	120.0	142.5
CAL.50 AMMUNITION	360.0	720.0	720.0
INTERNAL FUEL	1092.0	1500.0	1500.0
DROP TANK FUEL	—	—	900.0
BOMBS	—	—	1000.0
WATER/ALCOHOL	—	—	—
TOTAL DISPOSEABLE LOAD	1549.5	2340.0	4262.5
USEFUL LOAD	2471.8	3262.3	5384.0
GROSS WEIGHT	11422.9	12213.4	14335.1

TABLE 94
F6F-5 ALTERNATE USEFUL LOADS (POUNDS)

MODEL		F6F-5 (3/15/45)		F6F-5 (1950)	
MISSION	FIGHTER OVERLOAD	FIGHTER BOMBER	FIGHTER	COMBAT	FIGHTER
EMPTY WEIGHT	9078.8	9078.8	9078.8	9238.0	9238.0
TRAPPED FUEL & OIL	89.5	89.5	89.5	89.5	89.5
CAL.50 GUN INST.	428.1	428.1	428.1	428.1	428.1
BOMB,TANK PROV.	—	—	220.5	96.9	231.4
PYROTECHNICS	—	—	—	—	—
GUN CAMERA	4.2	4.2	4.2	4.2	4.2
COMMUNIC.EQUIP.	164.1	164.1	164.1	164.1	164.1
NAVIG. EQUIP.	3.8	3.8	3.8	3.8	3.8
MISC. EQUIP.	56.0	56.0	56.0	56.0	56.0
CREW	200.0	200.0	200.0	200.0	200.0
FIXED USEFUL LOAD	945.7	945.7	1166.2	1042.6	1177.1
BASIC WEIGHT	10024.5	10024.5	10245.0	10280.6	10035.0
USEABLE OIL	97.5	120.0	142.5	120.0	142.5
CAL.50 AMMUNITION	360.0	720.0	720.0	720.0	720.0
INTERNAL FUEL	1092.0	1500.0	1500.0	1500.0	1500.0
DROP TANK FUEL	—	—	900.0	—	900.0
BOMBS	—	—	1000.0	—	—
WATER/ALCOHOL	119.4	119.4	119.4	119.4	119.4
TOTAL DISPOS.LOAD	1668.9	2459.4	4381.9	2459.4	3381.9
USEFUL LOAD	2614.6	3403.9	5548.1	3502.0	4559.0
GROSS WEIGHT	11693.4	12482.7	14626.9	12740.0	13797.0

F6F- HELLCAT MODEL-TO-MODEL CHANGES

EARLY F6F-3 (FROM F6F-2)
Engine changed from R-2600 with turbosupercharger to R-2800 with two stage two speed mechanical supercharger. Propeller spinner removed. Propeller changed from Curtiss to Hamilton Standard model. Fuselage strengthened. Landing gear door arrangement revised and simplified.

LATE F6F-3
Water injection system added for powerplant. Bulged exhaust stack fairings omitted. Lower cowl flaps omitted. Radio mast changed from forward-slanting to straight.

F6F-5
R-2800 -10W water-injected engine used as original equipment as opposed to retrofit. Provision added for two 150 US gallon capacity underwing drop tanks in addition to the centerline rack. Flat front windshield; two metal braces removed for better visibility. Strengthened canopy. Fuselage windows aft of canopy removed. Red instrument lighting. Closer-fitting engine cowling employed. Spring tabs mounted on ailerons. Additional armor plate area. Strengthened tail structure. Provisions made for carrying underwing rockets. New high-gloss dark sea blue exterior paint used. New gunsight. Some models equipped with mixed armament of two 20 mm. cannon and four machine guns in place of six machine guns. Radio mast offset to port instead of starboard side. Starting system revised from shotgun to inertia type.

F6F- HELLCAT CHRONOLOGY

Jun '41-The US Navy requests Grumman to design an improved F4F- Wildcat version as a backup for the Vought Corsair.

Jun30'41-Navy BuAer awards Grumman a contract for two XF6F-1 aircraft powered with the Wright R-2600 engine.

Jan 7'42-The Navy awards Grumman a large production contract for the F6F-1 fighter.

Apr29'42-A turbosupercharged Wright R-2600 engine is selected for an F6F-2 version of the new fighter.

May23'42-A production order is approved for an F6F-3 version with the Pratt and Whitney R-2800 Double Wasp engine with a two stage mechanical supercharger instead of the XF6F-1 arrangement.

Jun 3'42-The USN decides that the second prototype XF6F-2 aircraft will be equipped later with an R-2800 engine.

Jun26'42-A 25 minute first flight of the prototype XF6F-1 Hellcat takes place piloted by Assistant Chief Engineer-Experimental Bob Hall.

Jul30'42-The second prototype F6F-3 with the R-2800 engine has a first flight lasting 11 minutes.

Aug '42-Work commenses on a new plant (#3) specifically meant for Hellcat production.

Oct 2'42-An XF6F-4 version, modified from the first prototype with an R-2800-27 engine, has a first flight.

Oct 3'42-The first production F6F-3 model makes a first flight piloted by Grumman test pilot Selden Converse.

Dec31'42-Twelve F6F-3 aircraft have now been completed-before the new production plant #3 is finished-and 10 are accepted by the US Navy.

Jan16'43-Navy Squadron VF-9 from carrier USS Essex gets the first F6F-3 aircraft from Bethpage, long Island.

Jan31'43-Twelve F6F-3s have been delivered by Grumman this month.

Feb '43-Thirty-five Hellcats are produced in February; in March this is increased to 81, and in April 131 planes.

Apr '43-The XF6F-4 is delivered to the Navy.

May '43-Deliveries of Hellcats to the British Royal Navy begin.

Jul '43-A radar installation is completed in an XF6F-3N version of the Hellcat and the airplane is ready for tests at Quonset Point, Rhode Island.

Jul 1'43-The first British Hellcat I enters service with #800, the beginning of use in 12 Royal Navy squadrons of World war II.

Aug28'43-Land-based Guadalcanal Hellcats of Sdn.VF-33 enter combat and fly escort for bombers in raids on Kahili and Ballale. The Hellcats are later based at Munda and in three weeks claim 21 Zeros shot down with four F6F-3s lost.

Aug31'43-Carriers Essex, Yorktown, and Independence take F6F-3s of VF-9 and VF-5 into combat in a raid on Marcus Island in the Pacific. Two Hellcats are lost to anti-aircraft fire, and one has to ditch but the pilot is saved.

Sep 1'43-The carriers Princeton and Belleau Wood provide Hellcat air cover for the invasion of Howland and Baker Islands. Lt. Loesch of VF-6 gets the first Hellcat aerial victory, shooting down a Japanese Emily flying boat. Two more Emilys are shot down by Hellcats in the next few days.

Oct '43-Land-based F6F-3 Hellcat Squadrons VF-38 and VF-40 are now operating with VF-33 in the Solomon Islands area in the Pacific.

Oct 5'43-Hellcats on six carriers, including those from VF-5, VF-6, and VF-25 are used in a strike on Wake Island on the 5th and 6th of the month. Twenty-two enemy aircraft are destroyed and 12 Hellcats are lost, six of these to Japanese anti-aircraft.

Nov 5'43-Hellcats from VF-12 on Saratoga and VF-23 from Princeton cover carrier bomber raids on Rabaul. In aerial dogfights the F6F-3s shoot down several of many Zero fighters, but lose five of their own.

Nov10'43-Forces gathered for Operation Galvanic, the attack on the Gilbert Islands in the Pacific include 80 F6F-3 Hellcats aboard five escort carriers of the Air Support Group, along with 371 Hellcats aboard 11 light and fast attack carriers in four separate carrier groups.

Nov11'43-Hellcats of the Southern Carrier Group from Essex, Bunker Hill, and Independence are part of a strike on the Japanese base of Rabaul. There are 72 carrier Hellcats attacking from VF-9, VF-18, and VF-22, assisted in CAP duties by land-based VF-33 F6F-3s from Ondonga and Segi Point and by 24 F4U-1A Corsairs of VF-17. In big air battles US fighters down nearly 50 enemy aircraft.

Nov21'43-Escort carriers Nassau and Barnes launch 44 Hellcats of VF-1 to start raids on Tarawa in the Gilbert Islands.

Nov23'43-During the Tarawa operations 12 F6F-3s of VF-16 from carrier Lexington near Makin Island shoot down 17 Zeros with four more probables and no Hellcat losses. On the next day in another air battle VF-16 downs 13 of the enemy and six probables and loses one aircraft.

Nov24'43-During operations in the Gilbert Islands the F6F-3N night fighter version is employed for the first time. Two F6F-3N aircraft are able to interrupt a Japanese attack.

Dec '43-The first combat of British Royal Navy Hellcats takes place during anti-shipping missions off Norway.

Dec '43-The XF6F-2 Hellcat gets an engine change from the Wright R-2600-15 Double Cyclone with an experimental Birmann turbo-supercharger to a Pratt and Whitney R-2800-21 Double Wasp with a turbosupercharger.

Dec 4'43-Hellcats go into action in the Marshall Islands from carriers Essex, Enterprise, Yorktown, and Lexington. The Lexington is knocked out of action by enemy bombers.

Dec17'43-In the Solomon Islands in the Pacific AIRSOLS (AIR SOLOMONS) has 268 operational fighter aircraft including Army, Navy, Marine, and Royal New Zealand Air Force, of which 199 are operational. There are 58 land-based Hellcats included of which 53 are operational. The F6F-3 has the highest in-commission rate.

Dec31'43-Grumman Hellcats in the Pacific have downed 230 Japanese planes for a loss of less than 30 F6F-3s.

Dec31'43-Grumman has completed 2547 Hellcat aircraft by this date.

Jan '44-The XF6F-2 Hellcat prototype with a turbosupercharged R-2800-21 engine is flown. The project is later dropped and the airplane is delivered as an F6F-3 model.

Jan '44-About 60% of F6F-3 Hellcats are now powered by water-injected P&W R-2800-10W engines.

Jan '44-A modified F6F-3, including some of the features to be included in the later F6F-5 version, is flown at a high speed of 410 mph at 21000 feet altitude.

Jan20'44-Fighter Squadron VF(N)-76 using Hellcat night fighters is commissioned at Quonset Point, Rhode Island.

Jan29'44-Forces engaged in the Marshall Islands operations include F6F-3 Hellcats in the folloWeing units: Carrier Group-CVE Sagamon with VF-37, 12 aircraft; CVE Suwanee with VF-60, 12 aircraft; and CVE Chenango with VF-35, 12 aircraft. Also in the Fast Carrier Group-Enterprise with VF-10, 32 aircraft; Yorktown with VF-5, 36 aircraft; Belleau Wood with VF-24, 24 aircraft; Carrier Task Group 58.2, Essex with VF-9, 35 aircraft, Intrepid with VF-6, 37 aircraft, and Cabot with VF-31, 24 aircraft; Carrier Task Group 58.3, Bunker Hill with VF-18, 37 aircraft, Monterey with VF-30, 25 aircraft, and Cowpens with VF-25, 24 aircraft; Carrier Task Group 58.4, Saratoga with VF-12, 36 aircraft, Princeton with VF-23, 24 aircraft, and Langley with VF-32, 22 aircraft. Enemy air opposition is very light. The Hellcats of light carrier Cabot establish a record of Japanese aircraft shot down for a light carrier.

Feb17'44-With the carrier force essentially as used in the Marshalls, Hellcats and other US aircraft engage in two days of attacks on the huge enemy base at Truk in the Caroline Islands, and destroy 270 E/A including about 200 on the ground. Eight F6F-s are lost in the fighting.

Feb22'44-Hellcats from carriers Yorktown, Essex, and Bunker Hill attack Saipan, Tinian, Rota, and Guam. They destroy a total of about 170 enemy planes of which 67 are victories in the air.

Feb22'44-Hellcat Squadron VF-9 is the first unit to complete a combat tour, and returns to the United States.

Mar30'44-In a two day strike by Task Force 58 on the Palaus in the Pacific 72 Hellcats fight against approximately 30 Japanese airplanes and shoot down 10.

Mar31'44-In the attack on the Palaus VF-5 Hellcats engage about 40 enemy aircraft sent down from the Philippines and claim 29 are downed. The first use of G-suits in the USN is made by F6F-s of VF-8 on Bunker Hill at this time; they destroy 11 of the enemy along with three probables without any losses. Squadron VF-30 from the carrier Monterey claims 25 victories. In all the Hellcats raiding the Palaus claim 95 enemy airplanes shot down.

Apr '44-All F6F-3 aircraft are now powered with the R-2800-10W water-alcohol injected engines giving War Emergency powers.

Apr '44-British Navy #800 Squadron using Hellcat Is provide fighter cover for an attack on the German battleship Tirpitz at Kaafiord,

Norway. The ship is out of action for several months. One Hellcat is lost on the raid.

Apr21'44-The last of 4402 F6F-3 Hellcats aircraft is produced by Grumman. The F6F-5 now replaces the -3 on the production line.

Apr21'44-US carrier air groups including Hellcat fighters attack enemy positions on Hollandia, New Guinea in the Pacific in preparation for landings the next day, and continue these attacks on D-day. Many Japanese planes are destroyed on the ground. Two F6F-s are lost to enemy anti-aircraft fire.

Apr29'44-Hellcats and other US aircraft from carriers Langley, Enterprise, and Lexington hit the Japanese base at Truk again. In two days 59 E/A are downed in air battles, and 34 destroyed on the ground.

May 8'44-An anti-shipping strike by the Royal Navy is supported by British Hellcats of #800 Squadron. In a dogfight with German airplanes three of the enemy are destroyed, but two Hellcats are lost.

May14'44-British Hellcats shoot down two German Heinkel floatplanes over the North Sea.

Jun '44-VF(N)-79 Squadron arrives in Hawaii for further Hellcat night fighter training.

Jun11'44-A force of 541 Hellcats and other USN aircraft from 15 large and five escort carriers are included in Operation Forager, the invasion of the Marianas Islands. On the 11th 208 Hellcats are airborne and claim about 70 enemy aircraft downed for a loss of 11 Hellcats. After these actions the US controls the air.

Jun15'44-A carrier air attack by Hellcats of VF-1 from Yorktown and VF-2 from Hornet is carried out on the enemy island of Iwo Jima with about 35 planes destroyed in the air and some on the ground. More strikes are made the next day. Some Hellcats are lost to Japanese anti-aircraft fire.

Jun18'44-Japanese Zero fighters from Guam attack eight F6F- aircraft of VF-24 from the carrier Belleau Wood near the island. Seven of the enemy are shot down by the Hellcats.

Jun19'44-US aircraft, mostly Hellcats, take part in a very large carrier plane air battle over the Marianas in the Pacific. The Grummans shoot down approximately 300 Japanese planes and lose only 16 F6F-s along with six more in operational accidents, with 13 Hellcat pilots lost. The seven Japanese aircraft carriers withdraw. This battle, called the First Battle of the Philippine Sea, or "The Marianas Turkey Shoot", is the largest carrier battle of the Pacific War to date.

Jun21'44-Navy Hellcat fighters with 500 pound bombs, along with other carrier planes, attack retreating Japanese carriers and supporting ships. One enemy carrier and two fleet oilers are sunk.

Hellcats shoot down 22 enemy planes and lose six of their own. The US aircraft return at night, US carrier lights are put on, and night landings attempted. Many Hellcats are lost through ditching or crashing on deck. A total of 100 planes are lost, including all the Helldivers and half the Avengers.

Jun24'44-Carriers Hornet, Yorktown. Bataan, and Belleau Wood again raid Iwo Jima using, among other aircraft, 51 Hellcats carrying 500 pound bombs. In air battles about half the defending Zero aircraft are destroyed, and an enemy bombing attack on the US carriers is defeated.

Jul 3'44-In another carrier aircraft raid on Iwo Jima in the Pacific the F6F-5 Hellcat model is initiated into combat with zero-length rocket launching rails. The next day attacks are continued, and over 70 enemy Zero aircraft are destroyed in aircombat, while rockets have destroyed several small merchant ships.

Jul 4'44-Hellcat night fighters of Detachment 2, VF(N)-76 from the carrier Hornet on patrol near Chichi Jima destroy eight E/A.

Jul 6'44-The first flight takes place of the XF6F-6 Hellcat model with the "C series" R-2800 engine and a four bladed propeller. This version is the fastest of the Hellcat series at 417 mph at 20000 feet altitude.

Aug '44-Royal Navy Fleet Air Arm Hellcat Is of #1840 Squadron from the carrier Furious go on another strike at the German battleship Tirpitz in Norway.

Aug15'44-Twenty-four Hellcat Is of British Royal Navy #800 Squadron take part in supporting the invasion of Southern France.

Aug15'44-The invasion of Southern France is also supported by two US CVEs, the Tulagi with VOF-1 and the Kasaan Bay with Sdn. VF-74 each squadron having 24 F6F-5 aircraft along with a total of seven F6F-3N night fighters. The latter aircraft provide night protection over the beachhead. In the next few days the US Hellcats down eight German bombers and destroy enemy vehicles and ground installations. Eleven US Hellcats are lost in thirteen days.

Aug24'44-Another attack by Hellcats and other Royal Navy aircraft is made on Tirpitz, but little damage results.

Aug29'44-The carrier Independence leaves Eniwetok in the Pacific with Task Force 38. There are included 14 F6F-5N and five F6F-5 aircraft. The night fighters are not used as such initially.

Sep 9'44-US carrier planes hit airfields in Southern Mindanao in the Philippines during a two day series of strikes. Squadron VF-9 Hellcats off the carrier Lexington destroy 27 enemy aircraft on the ground and Squadron VF-15 F6F-s from carrier Essex sink several ships.

Sep12'44-Hellcat fighter sweeps are conducted over the islands at Leyte, Samar, Negros, and Cebu in the Philippines by Sdn. VF-2 from carrier Hornet, VF-15 from Essex, VF-19 from Lexington, and VF-39 from Cabot on this and the following three days. Many enemy planes are destroyed in the air and on the ground by the fighters.

Sep12'44-An F6F-5N night fighter Hellcat from carrier Independence gets a first night shoot-down of an enemy Dinah aircraft near Samar Island in the Philippines. Most often, however, the -5N planes are used as regular day-fighters.

Sep21'44-The fast carrier groups switch to Luzon in the Philippines, and Nichols, Neilson, and Clark Fields are struck by Hellcats from carriers Princeton, Cabot, Intrepid, Hornet, and Langley. Some Hellcats carry 500 pound bombs. Further strikes are made the next day after which the carrier group retires to Ulithi and Manus Islands to refit and obtain new air groups.

Sep31'44-There are now 17 fast carriers in the task force in the Pacific operating both F6F-3s and F6F-5s. Squadrons VF-17, -18,-20, -21, and -22 are fully equipped with the new -5 aircraft; VF-7 Squadron on the newly-joined carrier Hancock has 41 of them.

Oct '44-Night fighting Hellcats of Squadron VF(N)-41 shoot down 10 Japanese planes during nighttime.

Oct10'44-US carrier groups in the Pacific strike at the island of Okinawa. Hellcats get the advantage of surprise and destroy about 100 enemy planes on the ground.

Oct12'44-The US carriers raid Formosa. In big air battles with a large force of Japanese aircraft Hellcat fighters shoot down 188. The next day there is less resistance. Enemy bombers attack the fleet through the 16th. Two supporting cruisers are disabled and taken under tow. In the total activity over several days around Formosa an estimated 500 Japanese airplanes are destroyed.

Oct18'44-Enterprise VF-20 Squadron Hellcats dogfight with enemy fighters over Clark Field in Luzon, Philippines. Thirty-one of the Japanese are downed for a loss of three Hellcats.

Oct18'44-Navy ace Dave McCampbell becomes the first USN pilot to attain 20 victories.

Oct24'44-Night fighting Hellcats of Sdn.VF(N)-41 and VF-20 destroy two enemy Mavis and one Emily flying boats at night.

Oct24'44-The Battle of Leyte Gulf in the Philippines is initiated. There are 11 US carriers operating in the gulf. On search missions the Hellcats of VF-15 and VF-19 from carriers Essex and Lexington claim a total of 37 victories. The carriers are attacked by Japanese planes and Princeton is sunk. The Combat Air Patrols down

85 of the enemy. Dave McCampbell of VF-15 from the Essex shoots down nine planes in only one sortie, giving him a total of 30 victories.

Oct24'44-Hellcats and Helldivers from Intrepid and Cabot equipped with bombs strike enemy warships, including the superbattleship Musashi, in the Sibuyen Sea. Hellcats from carriers Enterprise and Franklin, along with Helldivers, attack Vice-Admiral Nishimura's seven ships, including two battleships, off Mindanao, Philippine Islands. Battleship Musashi is sunk.

Oct25'44-Hellcats and Helldivers from Essex and Lexington fly 500 carrier sorties, 200 by the Hellcats, in six air strikes and sink four Japanese aircraft carriers and damage other enemy ships.

Oct29'44-F6F- Hellcats from from carriers Hancock, Franklin, Intrepid, and Enterprise attack airfields on Luzon, P.I., and claim 70 aerial victories and about 12 planes destroyed on the ground.

Oct30'44-Hellcat attrition is high, and the first Japanese kamikazes penetrate the CAPs over the carriers operating off Leyte. Carriers Franklin and Belleau Wood are badly hurt and retire to Ulithi.

Oct31'44-Marine Hellcat night fighters from Sdn. VMF(N)-541, based in the Palaus, have shot down one enemy airplane to this date.

Nov '44-Navy Hellcat Sdn. VF(N)-41 obtains eight more victories at night using F6F-5N aircraft. On November 19 two of this squadron's pilots became aces with victories in the Philippines area.

Nov 5'44-F6F-3 and F6F-5 Squadrons of Task Force 38 engage in big air battles with many enemy fighters over Clark field and Manila on Luzon, P.I. The Hellcats claim 58 aerial victories between Squadrons VF-11, VF-14, -15, -19, and VF-80. There is more combat the next day. Sdn. VF-14 is then withdrawn, as is VF-19. The carrier Wasp fighter squadron, VF-14, in six months of combat, has downed 140 of the enemy, destroyed 242 planes on the ground, and lost 20 pilots and 43 aircraft. They like the Grumman F6F- fighter.

Nov11'44-Navy Squadron VF-15 from carrier Essex with 16 Hellcats meets about 20 Japanese fighters near Ormoc Bay, P.I., and destroys 10 of them.

Nov14'44-Squadron VF-15 completes its tour of duty. Dave McCampbell now has 34 confirmed aerial victories, and is the second leading Pacific ace. In six months of Pacific combat VF-15 Hellcats have destroyed a record 313 enemy airplanes in the air and another 313 on the ground. In another record, there have been 26 aces produced. Twenty-one pilots have been lost from the squadron.

Nov19'44-Hellcats from the carrier Lexington, Sdn. VF-20, destroy 70 Japanese planes on a field near Del Carmen, P.I.

Nov25'44-Japanese aircraft come after Task Force 38 near Luzon, P. I. Hellcats knock down 26 of these in aerial combat. Later a kamikaze knocks the carrier Intrepid out of action, ending Sdn. VF-18's tour of duty after having shot down a total of 187 enemy planes in 11 weeks.

Dec '44-Carrier fighter complements are increased to 70 aircraft each because of the kamikaze threat. The number of Helldivers per carrier is reduced as fighter numbers are increased.

Dec '44-F6F-5Ns from carrier Independence get five more night combat victories, but four of the Hellcats and three pilots are lost.

Dec 3'44-VMF(N)-541 Squadron arrives at Tacloban in Leyte, P.I. to trade places with the Army P-61 night fighter squadron there. The P-61s move to the Palaus.

Dec 5'44-VMF(N)-541 obtains a first Leyte victory in the dark, shooting down an Oscar fighter, and gets two more the next night.

Dec14'44-Carrier Hellcats go on fighter sweeps over Mindoro, P.I. a day prior to US landings on the island. VF-80 F6F-s from the Ticonderoga shoot down 19 of 27 enemy planes without a US loss. An additional 46 aircraft are downed by carrier fighters, and about 200 enemy planes are destroyed on the ground. Twenty-seven US carrier planes are lost, mostly to anti-aircraft guns.

Dec30'44-The Hellcat is joined by Corsairs on the carriers—finally. Aboard Essex there are now a mix of 54 Hellcats, 36 Corsairs, and 15 Avengers. Soon there are more F4U-s and less Hellcats.

Jan '45-VF(N)-41 Sdn. completes its combat tour with a total of 46 enemy airplanes destroyed, including both night and day victories.

Jan '45-Fleet carrier Enterprise's fighter squadron, VF(N)-90 now has 19 F6F-5Ns, 11 F6F-5Es and two F6F-5Ps out of a total of 34 Hellcat fighters.

Jan '45-The fast carrier task force undertakes a nearly month-long cruise with Hellcats and other aircraft types striking targets on Formosa, the Ryukyus, Luzon, and then moves into the South China Sea.

Jan '45-British Hellcats go into large scale action against Japan with an attack on oil fields in Sumatra.

Jan12'45-The 14 carriers of the task force mount strikes in the Saigon, Indochina area. Hellcats strafe the airport and destroy 70 Japanese planes; 20 more seaplanes are destroyed at Cam Ranh Bay. Eleven F6F- aircraft are lost in the raids.

Jan16'45-A strike is made at Hongkong by carrier aircraft. Thirteen of the enemy are brought down, but 22 US airplanes are lost to anti-aircraft guns, many of these being Hellcats.

Chapter 4: Fighter Figures

Jan21'45-During carrier aircraft strikes at Formosa targets kamikazes hit carriers Langley and Ticonderoga, forcing the latter to retire to Ulithi.

Jan12'45-Sdn.VMF(N)-541 returns from Tacloban P.I. to the Palaus after having obtained 19 victories on dawn/dusk patrols. Its only night victories are those of December 5-6.

Jan '45-The Fast Carrier Task Force has 12 CVs and six CVLs. There are 820 Hellcats aboard (and 174 F4U-s). Of the Hellcats only 63 F6F-3 models remain; the others are -5 versions. Wasp now has 127 fighters (91 F6F- and 36 Corsairs) and 15 Avengers. Five other CVs are using at least 70 Hellcats.

Feb16'45-Carrier fighter sweeps with Hellcats are made to airfields around Tokyo and encounter heavy opposition. A total of 250 enemy planes are claimed destroyed with more than three quarters of these claimed by Hellcats. But several of the Hellcats are lost, including three in operational accidents.

Feb17'45-Despite terrible weather some strikes are launched over Japan by the carriers. Hellcats and Corsairs down another 70 of the enemy, making a two day total of almost 320 air victories and 190 planes destroyed on the ground. Losses are high, however, as 60 US planes are down in the two days. The fast carrier force leaves the area to support the invasion of Iwo Jima.

Mar18'45-Carrier fighter strikes are made on Kyushu, Japan airfields. At Kanoya VF-17 Hellcats shoot down 25 Japanese aircraft without a loss of their own. The next day Japanese bombers knock the carrier Franklin out of the war with terrific damage done, and severely damage the Wasp.

Mar21'45-Enemy bombers carrying "Baka" bombs and escorted by Zero fighters attack the carriers. Hellcats from Hornet and Belleau Wood destroy 18 of the bombers and 12 Zeros.

Apr 6'45-The invasion fleet off Okinawa is attacked by about 700 enemy planes, half of them kamakazes, and large air battles take place. The enemy loses half the planes, but hits many ships.

Apr 7'45-Marine night fighter squadrons arrive on Okinawa; VMF(N)-542 on this date, and -543 two days later, providing a total of 30 F6F-5N aircraft for night defense. They also fly daytime missions.

Apr16'45-F6F-s from carrier Hornet off Okinawa score a total of 45 aerial victories, and VF-9 from Yorktown gets 14.

May '45-The 10000th Hellcat, an F6F-5, is delivered to fighter-bomber Squadron VBF-87 of the carrier Ticonderoga. The squadron enters combat on May 17.

May 4'45-Squadron VF-9 destroys 11 enemy aircraft in an air battle over the radar picket destroyers off Okinawa.

May31'45-Approximately 3000 enemy planes have attacked the carrier force off Okinawa. Ten carriers are hit by bombs or kamikazes. About 1700 enemy planes have been downed by F6F-s or F4U-s.

Jun '45-The Okinawa operation is over and the carriers of Task Force 38 again start air strikes on the Japanese islands. In the first week of June Hellcats and Corsairs down 77 Japanese planes for a loss of 14 carrier aircraft, the loss being mainly from anti-aircraft fire. The fast carriers now start back to Leyte in the Philippines.

Jun '45-A few F6F-5N aircraft now have the mixed armament of two 20mm cannon and four .50 caliber machine guns instead of the standard six .50s.

Jul10'45-Task Force 38, back in Japanese waters with eight CVs and six CVLs launches air strikes at Tokyo; there is no air opposition and Hellcat and Corsair fighters destroy 100 enemy planes on the ground. More strikes are made on July 14 and 15. The strikes are unopposed in the air and no attacks are made on the carriers though they are less than 100 miles from land.

Jul16'45-Four carriers of the British Pacific Fleet join the US carrier group. The carrier Indomitable has Hellcats in #1844 Sdn.

Jul25'45-British Hellcat IIs destroy three Japanese torpedo bombers in night attacks without radar. The British Hellcats have now shot down 47 and one half enemy planes in the Pacific area, with #1844 Sdn. having 31 of these.

Jul31'45-Hellcats and other carrier aircraft strike at the enemy fleet base at Kure, Japan and also Kobe and Nagoya as well as at small Japanese ships on the Inland Sea. Anti-aircraft fire is heavy; TF-38 loses 133 planes from July 24 to 28.

Aug '45-Marine night fighting Hellcats of the -533, -542, and -543 Squadrons have scored a total of 69 victories over enemy aircraft during their stay in the Okinawa area, with -533 getting 35 0f these.

Aug '45-Ten British Royal Navy squadrons have Hellcats and eight are fully operational. In addition two squadrons have Hellcat II night fighters, a total of 80 aircraft.

Aug 9'45-On the day the second atom bomb is dropped on Nagasaki, F6F-s and F4U-s raid Misawa airfield where Japanese suicide bombers are congregated, and destroy most all of them.

Aug13'45-Carrier Hellcats range over Japan, destroying ground targets.

Aug13'45-Navy VF(N)-91 F6F-5Ns from carrier Bon Homme Richard obtain the final Navy night fighter victories when two Hellcats shoot down five enemy planes in 40 minutes.

Aug15'45-Carrier aircraft strikes are called back as the war ends.

Aug15'45-USN and USMC Hellcats are credited with 5156 enemy airplanes downed in the Pacific, 4948 by carrier units and 208 by land-based units. The British Pacific Fleet is credited with 47 enemy planes destroyed; Hellcats in Europe claim 13 enemy aircraft. The total is 5216 Axis aircraft in the two years, August 1943 to August 1945. About 270 Hellcats have been lost in air combat—a ratio of 19:1.

Sep 2'45-The USN cancels an order for 1677 more F6F-5s. No Hellcats are delivered in September.

Oct31'45-Thirty-two Hellcats are delivered to the USN; 30 more are delivered in November, the last being the 12275th, an F6F-5.

'50-Forty-eight Hellcats go to a French Navy squadron in Indo-China.

Apr '52-F6F-5K drone Hellcats attack bridges in Korea.

Aug '53-The last USN unit to use Hellcats, F6F-5Ns, gives them up.

'59-Hellcat aircraft are serving with the Argentine and Uruguayan navies.

F6F- HELLCAT HANDLING QUALITIES AND CHARACTERISTICS

HANDLING QUALITIES
GROUND HANDLING

Since in the three point attitude the top of the forward cowl was nearly level with the ground or deck, a Hellcat pilot with seat raised had better visibility forward and to the forward quarters than most tail down fighter pilots during taxi, but S-turning was stll desireable on airfields. For this the tail wheel was unlocked into free castoring mode. If there was a significant crosswind however, the aircraft could weathercock, and it was adviseable under such conditions to lock the tail wheel straight whenever possible. The tail wheel was also locked for field landings and landing runouts. It was adviseable to taxi with stick full back to keep the tail down; sudden throttle application tended towards an airplane noseover.

Just about everyone agreed the Hellcat was an easy aircraft to taxi; it was quite stable with the wide tread main landing gear which gave a good pivoting moment arm about a braked wheel using engine power. At a fighter pilot gathering twenty-one of twenty-seven who test flew an F6F-5 aircraft rated ground handling "good'. To get ready for a land takeoff the tail wheel was locked, the rudder tab set two marks nose right, and the other tabs set neutral. The tail wheel was left unlocked for carrier operations.

TAKEOFF AND CLIMB

The runup checks were made "I pushed hard on the brake pedals and pulled the stick into my gut to keep from nosing over". Brakes were then released, and in common with most other US fighters

Fig.6F-0 Grumman XF6F-1, Mfr. photo via H. Andrews. One of the two prototype aircraft ordered by the Navy in June of 1941 as a Wildcat replacement using a twin row Wright R-2600-16 Double Cyclone engine of 1700 horsepower, and the only one so powered. First flight took place a year later. Deflected flaps are in two sections since wing dihedral started only in outer panels.

Fig.6F-0A Grumman XF6F-1, Mfr. photo via H. Andrews. Another view of the Wright powered XF6F-1 shows the general look of later production aircraft except for the propeller and landing gear fairings along with engine cowling details. Discussions with Navy personnel, including combat veterans, resulted in a decision to install additional power in the fighter and obtain increased performance.

Fig.6F-0B Grumman XF6F-2, Mfr. photo via H. Andrews. The single XF6F-2 aircraft in flight. The original powerplant installation was a twin row Wright R-2600 equipped with a Birmann turbosupercharger; later this was changed in December,1943 to a turbosupercharged Double Wasp and first flew so powered in the following January. The turbo experiments were then abandoned and the airframe was converted to a production F6F-3.

Fig.6F-1 Grumman XF6F-3 Hellcat, Mfr. photo via Herb Fyfield. Although the original contract from the Navy in June of 1941 was for two fighters using Wright R-2600 engines of 1700 horsepower a year later the Navy decided one of the planes would use a 2000 horsepower Pratt and Whitney R-2800 engine. This version, shown in the photo, flew first in July, 1942. The propeller spinner did not last, and the landing gear fairing doors were revised.

right rudder was kicked. This action was needed in addition to the rudder tab setting to control the tendency of the aircraft to swing left with torque reaction of the big propeller. Takeoff could be made with flaps in any position from full up to full down, though the latter was less usual. The greater the flap deflection the shorter takeoff run required. With full flap the elevator tab was set slightly nose up to counter the pitch down effect of the flaps. A fairly normal flap setting for a short takeoff was 20 degrees down. The Hellcat accelerated well in takeoff and the tail got up quickly. A typical liftoff speed was anywhere from 80 to 100 mph depending on aircraft weight and flap setting. Pilots evaluating takeoff performance were

almost unanimous in giving a good rating. Further, because of its relatively low wing loading, the F6F-5 in one case was ranked first of eleven fighter types in a category "Best overload takeoff from a small area". This certainly was as it should be for a Navy carrier fighter.

In climb the aircraft was trimmed out and gear and flaps retracted with climb speed set to 150 mph IAS and supercharger auxiliary blower kept in neutral.In a low speed high power climb condition right rudder trim was used. Climb rate was good; when 7000 feet was reached a shift was made to low blower operation of the supercharger. General handling in climb was considered good,

Fig.6F-1A Grumman XF6F-3 Hellcat, USN photo via H. Andrews. Another view of the R-2800 Double Wasp powered prototype with the two stage mechanical supercharger, the powerplant arrangement to be used in production. This prototype retains the Curtiss propeller less blade cuffs and the somewhat awkward looking main landing gear fairings. The flat wing center section is readily apparent; the folding outer panels have the dihedral.

Fig.6F-1B, Grumman XF6F-3 Hellcat, USN photo via H.Andrews (8x10). Runup photo of the XF6F-3 prototype shows further progression towards Hellcat production configuration with substitution of a Hamilton Standard hydraulic propeller for the Curtiss Electric model and addition of camouflage paint. The early type wheel fairings remain. Stubbiness of the Hellcat fuselage is emphasized in this view.

Fig.6F-2 Grumman F6F-3 Hellcat, Mfr. photo via Herb Fyfield. Flight view of an early F6F-3 Hellcat identified by the small rear view window aft of the cockpit hatch, the forward slant of the radio antenna, and cowl flaps on lower as well as upper engine cowling. A relatively quick design, test, and production program under wartime pressure got ten production F6F-3 Hellcats out the door by the end of 1942.

Fig.6F-3 Grumman F6F-3 Hellcat, photo via F. Dean coll. F6F-3 under test with gear down appears to have a wing equipped with a "mixed battery" where two 20mm. cannon replaced the inboard .50 caliber machine guns of the more usual three .50s in each wing. Stubbiness of Hellcat fuselage resulted from placement of fuel tanks beneath the cockpit. There was no fuel in the outer wing panels.

though there was some initial lateral instability. One pilot new to the F6F-5 said "The rate of climb was the most surprising feature; excellent up to 20000 feet". Above that altitude it started to slacken. The F6F-5 was somewhat poorer in climb than a Zeke Model 52 up to 9000 feet, about its equal from there up to 14000 feet, and was better than the Japanese fighter at higher altitudes.

TRIMMING

There were nose up trim changes with gear and flap retraction, though they were minimal, and the same was true of initial acceleration into climb. In general there were substantial trim changes both directionally and laterally with speed and power changes, but tab action allowed trimming out control forces to zero except for the rudder. At low speed and high power rudder pedal force could not be trimmed out fully. Most pilots though trimmability was gen-

erally good, though some made the following comments "Lack of trimmability", Excess rudder trim change", and "Aircraft requires excessive trim" (three pilots). It was noted that in a dive control forces could not be trimmed out quickly enough.

DIVE AND RECOVERY

Diving characteristics of the Hellcat were rated good by most pilots. Stick forces were moderate in the dive, and one group ranked the F6F-5 third of eleven fighter types in a category "Best stability and control in a dive". Further, all these pilots rated dive recovery characteristics good. The Hellcat became tail heavy in a dive and tended, like other US single engine fighters, to yaw to the right. As noted, trim action could not always keep up with these tendencies, but resulting control forces were handleable. Dive limits on the engine were 3060 RPM (though any RPM above about 2200 gave some vibration) and a manifold pressure of 34 inches of mercury. The supercharger was shifted into neutral; neither high nor low speed settings of the auxiliary blower were to be used. To keep the Hellcat out of trouble in a dive speed limits were set: 370 knots (426 mph) IAS above 15000 feet altitude, and 390 knots (449 mph) IAS below 15000 feet altitude. These limits were to be observed for pull-outs up to five g. Because of more severe compressibility effects at higher g levels for a given speed, dive speeds at five to seven g pullouts were restricted to 320 knots (368 mph) IAS at all altitudes. The 390 knot dive speed limit corresponded at 15000 feet to a true airspeed of 566 mph, or Mach 0.78, so that would be really whistling along in the dive, and be well into compressibility. To reach this condition a dive would have to start from high altitude. The nearer the Hellcat was pushed to its diving limits the greater the overall vibration of the aircraft, whether this was in terms of speed or of g level encountered in the pullout, so ample warning of trouble was given the pilot. After a short time into a dive the Hellcat could pull well ahead of a Zeke 52, and would also beat the Zeke in a zoom climb out of a dive.

Fig.6F-3A Grumman Hellcat I, photo via H. Andrews. Flight view of a Hellcat I, an F6F-3 export version under Lend-Lease for the British. The first of this version was delivered in May of 1943. Shortly thereafter British Hellcats started operations with #800 Squadron, the first of a dozen Fleet Air Arm units to use the type. Initially named the Gannet, over 250 were exported. Many more Hellcat II versions of the F6F-5 were later utilized by the British, mainly in the Pacific.

Fig.6F-4 Grumman F6F-3 Hellcat, National Archives photo via Joe Weathers. F6F-3 Hellcat aboard USS Charger, CVE-30, in March of 1943, only two months after the first Navy Hellcat squadron, VF-9, reported aboard the fleet carrier USS Essex. VF-5 and VF-9 were in an August, 1943 strike on Marcus Island in the Pacific; the first combat for the F6F-3 came only fourteen months after prototype first flight.

Fig.6F-4A Grumman F6F-3 Hellcat, USN photo via H. Andrews. An F6F-3 Hellcat sits for an official photo at NAS Patuxent River in Maryland in April,1944 with the FT for flight test marked on the cowl. A good view is provided of the much simpler production main wheel fairings. The standard and much-used 150 gallon external centerline fuel tank is suspended beneath the belly.

Fig.6F-5 Grumman F6F-3 Hellcat, Mfr. photo via Joe Weathers. The Hellcat was a big fighter; compare the size of the pilot with the overall aircraft in this F6F-3 photo. Wing area was the greatest of the Double Wasp powered fighters, 34 square feet more than a P-47 and twenty more than the Corsair, and wing span was also greater. Though not originally so equipped, most F6F-3 aircraft were later retrofitted with an engine water injection system.

Fig.6F-5A Grumman F6F-3 Hellcat, USN photo via H. Andrews. With cockpit canopy open, flaps full down, and tail hook engaged to a wire, an F6F-3 comes aboard a carrier. The F6F- fighter was considered a particularly benign aircraft during the approach and landing phase of carrier operations, a characteristic credited with saving the lives of many combat-weary pilots.

MANEUVERING

The acrobatic qualities of the F6F- airplanes were quite good. All normal acrobatics were permitted with a limitation being only three seconds of inverted flight, this based in consideration of an oil scavenge pump operation. Otherwise nothing was ruled out, and "Aerobatics were easy to perform", Loops, rolls, and Immelmans were among normal maneuvers in the repertoire. A pilot said "You could make abrupt and positive maneuvers, even at high speed".

Rolling performance of the F6F-3 Hellcat needed improvement at high speeds where aileron forces got high. Typically roll rate peaked at about 72 degrees per second at 230 mph IAS, but fell off to under 40 degrees per second at 375 mph IAS. New design ailerons equipped with spring tabs were tested on a -3 airplane. Performance was similar at the lower speeds, but a roll rate of about 60

degrees per second was now attained at 375 mph IAS, a considerable aileron performance increase. The newer F6F-5 incorporated the spring tab ailerons. As with most all fighters, attainable roll rate diminished when also pulling g.

The F6F-5 airplane could out-roll a Zeke 52 at the higher speeds. On this Hellcat most pilots felt aileron forces were "light to moderate, with good effectiveness". In 1944 the -5 Hellcat was voted as having the best ailerons at 100 mph of twelve fighters, and ranked fourth in "Best ailerons at 350 mph IAS".

In turning flight the Hellcat, by virtue of a large wing and resulting moderate wing loading, was superior to most all the later US fighter types with the probable exception of the Bell P-63. One modern test showed an F6F-5 out-turning a P-47D, a P-51D, and an FG-1D Corsair. An analysis at mutually appropriate gross weights

Fig.6F-6 Grumman F6F-3 Hellcat, USN photo via H. Andrews. Stubby F6F-3 aircraft were not quite as fast as the Corsair. In a test of five different production Hellcats off the line high speeds varied from 376.5 mph at 23900 feet to 379.5 mph at 23200 feet. Some criticized the F6F- for lack of performance, but all praised it for excellent carrier compatibility features.

Fig.6F-7 Grumman F6F-3 Hellcat, photo via Joe weathers. A rather beat up F6F-3 sits tied down on the hardstand in 1944. From the end of 1942 until spring of 1944 over 4400 F6F-3 versions of the Hellcat were produced and quickly replaced the Wildcat as the standard fleet carrier fighter. Over 200 of the -3s were put out as night fighters with radar equipment.

Fig.6F-8 Civil Grumman F6F-3 Hellcat, R.O'Dell/R. Stuckey photo via Joe Weathers. A few Hellcats found their way into the hands of civilian hobbyists after the war, but it was unusual to spot one. This picture of a civil version illustrates how high the pilot sat in the fuselage and how forward he was located with respect to the wing, particularly compared to pilot location in the Corsair.

shows this should be true. In common with its predecessor the Wildcat, the F6F- airplane was difficult to turn to the right under conditions of low speed and high power such as early climb, and for the same reason, high torque reaction of the propeller. In a high g turn the Hellcat would warn of impending trouble by exhibiting considerable airframe vibration. Interestingly, a modern evaluation of F6F-5 Hellcat stick force per g in wind-up turns at maximum speed noted a high value of 12.5 pounds, meaning the aircraft had to be really muscled around these turns unless constant longitudinal trimming was effected. This result seemed to run counter to notations of wartime pilots where elevator stick forces were "good", the aircraft ranked high in a category "Best elevator", and a pilot said "Elevator force considered light to moderate".

In comparison with some other fighters the Hellcat was not considered a particularly exciting aircraft to fly and maneuver. It was very stable, both statically and dynamically, about all axes under normal loading conditions. All pilots seemed to agree; they almost invariably noted longitudinal and directional stability "good". In fact the F6F-5 airplane was ranked number one of nine fighter types in a category "Nicest all-around stability". One characteristic noted was rudder forces were high in trying to hold a heading during sideslips, and in correcting adverse aileron yaw. Both in a modern test and in World War II pilots commented on high rudder forces. Yet the F6F-5 was ranked second of twelve fighters in a category "Best rudder", and of seven pilots four said rudder force characteristics were "good". All liked rudder effectiveness.

APPROACH AND LANDING
In this crucially important aspect of carrier fighter operation the Hellcat really starred. A pilot's comment "The low speed flying characteristics were nothing less than superb". One sage wartime pilot, after evaluating the handling qualities of the F6F-5 said in 1944 "Marginal advantage against Japanese front line opposition, but operational accidents should be practically nil". An ace carrier pilot commented "As a deck landing aircraft the Hellcat was steady

as a rock at 80 knots (92 mph) with precise attitude and speed control". What better qualities for a carrier aircraft! Another experienced pilot noted "As with all my carrier landings to date, I marveled at the Hellcat's stability and ease of handling; it was the perfect carrier fighter, at least with respect to its handling characteristics during the critical landing phase. I was able to fly by feel alone".

The approach and landing could be made with or without power. The airplane could be slipped or skidded easily if required. Speed was reduced during the initial circuit to 110 to 120 knots (127 to 138 mph) IAS. In preparation for landing the canopy was opened, flaps extended full down and landing gear lowered, cowl flaps left closed to half open, and propeller put in low pitch. The tail wheel was locked for a field landing and left unlocked for a carrier landing, and for the latter the tail hook was lowered. The book put it simply "The F6F- landing characteristics are excellent", and a group of twenty test and service pilots considered them "good" while none said fair or poor. Final approach to the carrier deck was made at 75 to 80 knots (86 to 92 mph) IAS. With the "cut" signal throttle was chopped, the hook caught, and the Hellcat sank onto a main gear with excellent oleo shock struts upon hitting the deck. With a 30 knot carrier speed the aircraft touchdown speed relative to the deck approximated 50 knots (58 mph).

In addition to fine landing capability the Hellcat possessed good waveoff characteristics according to the majority of one group of evaluation pilots.

STALLS AND SPINS
The book indicated stalling characteristics were "very satisfactory", and pilots seemed to agree. A large group of pilots ranked the F6F-5 first of eleven fighter types in "Best characteristics five mph above stall". A typical comment "Good stall characteristics". Stall speed varied widely depending on configuration, weight, and power level. For one g stalls warnings existed slightly above stall speed for the gliding (clean, engine at idle), landing (dirty), and climbing (clean) conditions in the form of increased vibration, a duct howl in the

Fig.6F-9 Grumman F6F-5 Hellcats, photo via R. Besecker. Two F6F-5 Hellcats pose for a camera plane, the near aircraft equipped for rocket installation. The -5 first flew in April of 1944 and started into combat in early July during a carrier raid on Iwo Jima. In that action over seventy Japanese Zero fighters were destroyed in air combat; a fine introduction for the new fighter version.

lower engine cowl-this in power off condition, and gentle buffeting, the latter only if the approach to stall was slow. No stall warning existed for the approach or waveoff conditions. The initial roll-off was mild in most cases. It varied from a right to a left roll-off depending on the flight condition, and could be checked by use of ailerons and rudder. If no control was used after initial roll-off mild pitching and rolling oscillations set in and continued through the stall. Stall recovery was straightforward using normal techniques.

For accelerated stalls, as in turning flight, some stall warning was afforded by mild buffeting of the whole airplane. Initially the aircraft pitched out of the turn, then pitched into it, also going through a mild rolling oscillation. The final roll-off was mild and easily controlled. Recovery from rolling out of the turn was quickly effected by releasing back pressure on the stick. Spin tests were conducted on the Hellcat. Four turn spins were made with an 11250 pound gross weight aircraft having a center of gravity position at 26 percent mean aerodynamic chord. A normal entry was made with ailerons one half against the spin. In a right spin the nose dropped to a 50 to 60 degree angle. Aileron forces were negligible,

Fig.6F-10A Grumman F6F-5 Hellcat, Martin/Kelman photo via H. Andrews. Classic side view of the F6F-5 Hellcat shows how much further forward the cockpit was with respect to the wing compared with the Corsair. The -5 aircraft used a water injected engine as standard; most -3 airplanes were eventually so retrofitted. External differences in appearance between the two were few.

Fig.6F-10 Grumman F6F-5 Hellcat, USN photo via Joe Weathers. Excellent closeup of -5 Hellcat shows Grumman method of wing folding where outer panels swung aft about a canted hinge to lie along the fuselage driven by a hydraulic power fold system. Lower cowl intakes fed air to oil cooler. carburetor, and two stage mechanical supercharger intercoolers. Landing gear twisted during retraction so wheels lay flat in wing partially covered with fairing plates.

Fig.6F-10B Grumman F6F-5 Hellcat, photo via H. Andrews. The 10000th Hellcat (out of 12275), an F6F-5 so labeled, comes aboard a carrier. For at least sixteen months the Hellcat had sole possession of carrier decks as the only modern US shipboard fighter; in early 1945 the Corsair started to share carrier space. By the end of the war Corsairs were in the ascendency.

Fig.6F-10C Grumman F6F-5 Hellcat, photo via H. Andrews. An F6F-5, distinguished by a flat windshield, an upright forward antenna post on the port side, and under-wing rocket mounts, cruises among the clouds. Engine COMBAT power setting using water injection improved -5 performance over -3 models, and spring tab equipped ailerons increased -5 roll rates. Other -5 improvements included better armor protection and a strengthened tail and cockpit canopy.

and there was a nose rotation at the same frequency as the airplane rate of rotation. After four and one quarter turns of a right spin full rudder reversal was made, followed about a second later by full aileron reversal. The spin then steepened sharply, and the rate of rotation appeared to double. Control forces were light for rudder and heavier for elevators and ailerons. Recovery was effected in one and a half turns to level flight with a 5000 foot altitude loss. In a spin to the left the nose drop was not as steep. Aileron forces were heavier and nose oscillation was greater. After four turns of the left spin recovery was effected in one and three quarter turns. Aileron

Fig.6F-10D Grumman F6F-5E Hellcat, USN photo via H. Andrews. An F6F-5E is stationed at the ready on a catapult of the USS Sagamon while enroute to Okinawa in late April, 1945. A white-nosed radar pod is located under the right wing. The photo appears to belie references (such as this one) that list no F6F-5E, only eighteen F6F-3Es produced.

Fig.6F-11 Civil Grumman F6F-5 Hellcat, Joe Weathers photo. It would be difficult to get a more attractive view of the F6F-5 Hellcat than that of the restored CAF Ghost Squadron aircraft pictured. Among the changes from -3 to -5 models were a new flat windshield, strengthened canopy and tail, water injected engine, closer fitting cowl, aileron spring tabs for better high speed roll, increased armor, and racks for two 1000 pound bombs and six five inch rockets on the wings.

and elevator forces were about double those of a right spin, and rudder forces were about the same. The altitude loss was about 4400 feet.

CHARACTERISTICS

COCKPIT

The Hellcat cockpit was roomy, and evaluating pilots ranked it high in comfort. There was lots of seat and rudder pedal adjustment range to fit pilots of varying sizes, including the largest. One pilot called

it "spacious", and was concerned whether he could see out, but adjustments took care of this. The Hellcat cockpit was rated excellent in terms of gear and flap controls locations, and fair from the viewpoint of engine controls arrangement. The general layout was very good, and this fact was often cited to the builders of the competitive Corsair fighter. A pilot said "The F6F- has a good heater". A group of pilots, Army, Navy, Marine, British, and civilian ranked the Hellcat first of the operational US wartime fighters in "Best all-around cockpit".

Fig.6F-12 Civil Grumman F6F-5 Hellcat, Joe Weathers photo. Another view of the civil Ghost Squadron Hellcat at a 1980s air show. Armament and tail hook are missing and modern avionics added. Like the Corsair the Hellcat had a lot of hydraulics which controlled flaps, landing gear, wing fold, arresting gear, cowl flaps, and oil cooler flaps. In a famous quote one pilot indicated how he felt about the Hellcat by saying if it could cook he'd marry it.

Fig.6F-13 Grumman F6F-5N Hellcat, photo via Joe Weathers. Runup shot of F6F-5N night fighter Hellcat of which over 1400 were constructed, by far the largest number of US night fighting aircraft built during the war. Photo shows podded antenna of the AN/APS-6 radar system on the port wing, mixed armament with the two 20mm. cannon and four .50s, and the zero length rocket standoffs. F6F-5Ns replaced Army P-61 night fighters at one point in the Philippines.

Fig.6F-13A Grumman F6F-5N, Hellcat, USN photo via H. Andrews. Its gloss blue paint shining in the sunlight, an F6F-5N night fighter equipped with a mixed armament complement of 20mm and .50 caliber guns poses for a photo. The -5N was by far the most-produced US night fighter of the war with over 1400 manufactured after more than 200 -3N versions had come of the lines. The F6F-3N first saw combat in November,1943 and the -5N the next September.

VISIBILITY

The F6F- cockpit was well located on the fuselage, being at its highest point and well forward. As noted earlier the pilot had a better view during ground handling than most other tail-down fighters because of his relatively high forward location. However the cockpit canopy design made for blind spots, this reflected when the F6F-5 was ranked sixth of seven fighter types in pilot voting for "Best cockpit canopy". Pilots comments included "Poor visibility". Hellcat cockpit visibility was inferior to that of the Japanese Zeke 52.

POWERPLANT OPERATION

Operation of the Hellcat powerplant was generally good. In one evaluation seventeen pilots gave it this rating while none said fair or poor. There were some conditions of flight conducive to supercharger surging, but this could be easily eliminated. One interesting comment on the F6F- "The aircraft has three fuel tanks, all about the same size, and pilots are notorious for cracking up with

two full fuel tanks and one empty tank, and the indicator on empty-it runs out very rapidly".

VULNERABILITY/ARMOR

In common with its Wildcat predecessor the F6F- airplane was noted for its ability to absorb punishment and keep flying. A combination of an air cooled engine, a very strong airframe, good armor, and protected fuel tanks gave the Hellcat a very good chance to survive in an air combat environment against Japanese opposition. "The F6F- airframe could take a severe beating and still fly if it had no vital part damaged. The airframe was unusually rugged".

GUN PLATFORM AND WEAPON PERFORMANCE

Pilots were really split in their opinion of the F6F-5 as a gun platform. Of one group nine rated that quality good, eight more said fair, and two noted poor as an evaluation. One happy pilot said "As a gunnery platform the F6F- was excellent". A modern evaluation noted "(It) was handicapped by heavy stick forces which interfered

Fig.6F-14 Grumman F6F-5 Hellcats, Mfr. photo via Joe Christy. The two Hellcats are from the New York Naval Air Reserve which operated F6F-5 fighters for a time after the war. Head and back armor plate shows just behind the pilots. Hellcat had armor ahead of the oil tank, forward of the cockpit, behind the pilot's head and back, and near the oil cooler. The windshield was of bullet-resistant glass and the fuel tanks were self sealing.

Fig.6F-15 Grumman F6F-5K Hellcat, R. Besecker photo. Some -5 Hellcats were converted post-war as drone aircraft and designated F6F-5K. Some hung around for several years like the -5K shown at Mustin Field near the old Naval Aircraft Factory in Philadelphia. A few drones were used operationally in the Korean War as remote controlled bombers.

with accurate lateral tracking corrections, and very heavy rudder forces which made coordination difficult". One wartime pilot said "Most experienced pilots considered the F6F- a more stable gun platform than the F4U-, but I personally could not favor one over the other". As to weapon performance "I must mention we used our gun chargers almost constantly. The bolt would bang around in the receiver, and we couldn't time them as well as we would have liked.

By charging the guns after each run we could keep them going pretty well".

GENERAL COMMENTS
Underpowered.
Not enough advantage over Japanese.
With more performance should be one of the best.

Fig.6F-16 Grumman F6F-5K Hellcat, photo via P.M. Bowers. A drone Hellcat survivor photographed at a Navy display many years post-war (note the modern jet behind the F6F-). Aircraft has no armament or landing gear wheel fairings. Large wing and resulting moderate wing loading for a US aircraft made the Hellcat one of the better turning US fighters. Steady roll rate was not too impressive however.

Fig.6F-17 Grumman XF6F-6 Hellcat, USN photo via Joe Weathers. One of two examples of a new Hellcat model using a Double Wasp "C" engine of 2100 horsepower (2450 horsepower with water injection) and a four blade propeller making it the fastest F6F- of all—425 mph at 25000 feet, countering claims the aircraft was lacking performance. But F6F- production was stopped before all trials were completed on the -6.

Fig.6F-18 Grumman NF6F-5 Hellcat, photo via R. Besecker. A special test F6F-5 from NAS St.Louis shows the side profile of a Hellcat with its somewhat hump backed appearance. The "N" in front of the designation meant the plane was permanently modified for certain tests to the point where it would be unreasonable to restore it to original configuration.

Good for the Pacific until speed becomes inadequate.

A little lacking in performance.

Critical altitude too low for Pacific work.

It was superb in the environment of the Pacific.

At a late 1944 fighter meet the Hellcat was ranked by pilots as second, behind the F4U-1D Corsair, in the category "Best carrier-based production fighter".

I love this airplane so much that if it could cook I'd marry it!

A pilot recalled the Hellcat as a high performance fighter that really was easy to fly. You could even be a bit careless with it at times. You couldn't even sit in a Hellcat without smiling.

A Hellcat pilot recounted there were so many advantages for the F6F- type it was just about impossible to know where to start. It was the greatest plane of the war.

Another pilot called the Hellcat "marvelous" and the only type suitable where there could be little training and lots of combat.

Many who favored the Hellcat thought it had excellent flight characteristics which prevented pilots from spinning in while attempting a carrier landing under combat conditions and claimed the same could not be said for "some of our other fighter aircraft".

The Hellcat was considered one of the easier planes to fly.

F6F- aircraft were excellent in ground handling as opposed to the Wildcat.

A pilot said of a Hellcat takeoff just add power and "off you go."

A no-bounce three point landing on a field could be made with the stick held full back.

The Japanese felt the Hellcat was the only US fighter type that could acquit itself very well in a dogfight.

The Hellcat was rated a better night fighter than the Corsair. This included both the operational and the maintenance areas.

Above 250 knots the Hellcat could out-maneuver the Japanese Zero.

The Hellcat was equal to or superior to the Wildcat in carrier compatibility factors and almost as good as the Corsair in fighting performance.

In mock combat with the P-47 an F6F- could usually come out best because of superior turning capability even though the Thunderbolt was a lot faster.

In the view of one test pilot the two best designed US World War II fighters were the Merlin P-51 and the Hellcat.

Fig.6F-19 Civil Grumman F6F-5 Hellcat, Bob Dean photo. Beautifully restored Hellcat at an August, 1990 air show, there to take part in a flight demonstration of all the Grumman "Cats" from Wildcat through to the jet types. A Grumman Bearcat sits behind and the wing tip tank of a Panther or Cougar is at the right.

F6F- STRUCTURAL DESCRIPTION
(Unless stated otherwise metal refers to aluminum alloy)

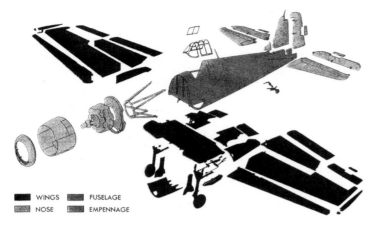

WINGS ■ FUSELAGE
NOSE ■ EMPENNAGE

Exploded view of F6F-5 subassemblies.

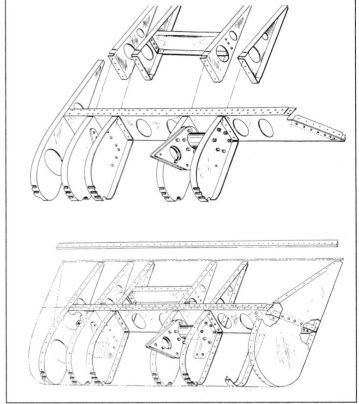

Wing center section flap assembly.

WING GROUP

The wing group consisted of a center panel constructed in one piece and running through the fuselage, and two outer panels. The wing-fuselage assembly was made by lowering the fuselage over the wing center section and attaching the two major assemblies. The outer panels of the wing folded, leading edge nose-down, so the panels lay aft alongside the fuselage; folding was manual.

The wing center section consisted of two beams, or spars, one forward and one aft. Both were built up of conventional web and cap strip construction, but the forward spar was of heavier construction. Both spars extended the full 150 inch nominal span of the center section. The forward spar web was sloped back so its upper cap was aft of the lower cap; this was done to provide the proper tilted axis for the fold hinge, the fitting lugs for which were mounted at the spar caps on the ends of the center section. Locking units to hold the wings spread were located at the ends of the rear spar. The front spar went straight across the panel with no sweep. The center section airfoil was formed by ribs in the nose section and by ribs and spanwise stringers in the inter-spar and aft sections. Flush riveted skin covered the panel. Center section flap segments were located at the trail edge so the rear edge of the fixed section was closed by a sloped concave sheet to properly match contours. The center section housed and supported two fuel tanks, the main landing gear, and the catapult hook structure. It was bolted to the fuselage using an attach angle, reinforcing channel, and two main wing fittings where the main spar passed adjacent to the firewall. Aft of the forward spar the center section was attached to the fuselage by upper and lower bolt angles on each side. Screws and rivets were used through angles at the trail edge aft of the rear spar. At the outboard end of the center section Neoprene strips were cemented to provide a seal at the joints with outer panels in the wings spread condition. Inboard near the fuselage reinforced walkways of trimite carborundum covered cloth, bound with moulding, were provided on the wing upper surface. The center section flaps were of all-metal construction using a single mid-spar, nose and trail edge

flanged rib sections, a drive horn, and a trailing edge strip. There were two sections, one on each side; they were not connected to the outboard panel flaps, and were each moved through use of a hydraulic actuator, torque shaft assembly, and bell crank drive. The space between the inboard and outboard flap sections was faired by a triangular shaped structure extending from the wing center section. When the flaps were up automatic doors closed the gaps between flaps and wing structure.

The foldable outer wing panels were all-metal cantilever structure supporting outboard flap sections and ailerons. They each also supported and housed three .50 caliber machine guns, their accessories, and ammunition trays. An electrically heated pitot tube was mounted on the lower surface of the right wing panel leading edge near the wingtip. Navigation lights were installed in the removeable metal wing tip caps and formation lights were placed on the top surface of the panels out-board. An approach light was installed in the leading edge of the left panel, disappearing tiedown rings were in the lower surface, and a hoisting ring was mounted in the upper surface. The outboard panels were constructed with a front spar extending the length of the surface in line with the inboard section front spar, and with the spar web sloped in a similar manner. A rear spar was in line with the center section rear spar, extending outward just past the inboard end wing station of the aileron. An aile-

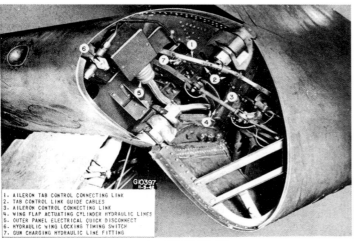

1. AILERON TAB CONTROL CONNECTING LINK
2. TAB CONTROL LINK GUIDE CABLES
3. AILERON CONTROL CONNECTING LINK
4. WING FLAP ACTUATING CYLINDER HYDRAULIC LINES
5. OUTER PANEL ELECTRICAL QUICK DISCONNECT
6. HYDRAULIC WING LOCKING TIMING SWITCH
7. GUN CHARGING HYDRAULIC LINE FITTING

Wing Folding Axis

panel forward spar, nose ribs, and heavy flush-riveted metal skins formed the D-section torque box designed to withstand bending and torsional loads. Large access panels were provided in the upper wing surfaces aft of the main spar to provide for servicing of the guns and ammunition containers in the wings. Guns were supported between spars with barrels extending through the front spar web to the leading edge. Outer panels also supported mounting posts on front and rear hard points for rocket projectiles, or could provide for faired bomb racks supported from the lower cap strips of the front and rear spars. A gun camera installation was provided inboard at the leading edge of the left wing. The end of the wing panel was closed by a formed one piece metal wing tip riveted to the outermost wing rib. Outboard wing flaps were similar in construction to, though longer than, the inboard sections. They were supported on three hinges and driven by three bellcranks operated by a torque tube which itself was driven by a hydraulic actuator operating a torque arm. Automatic doors completely closed the gaps between the flap and the fixed wing structure. Ailerons were statically and dynamically balanced and mounted from three hinges on the aileron intercostal spar. The aileron did not extend to the wing tip. The aileron structural framing consisted of a forward located spar behind a curved metal-covered leading edge and a trailing edge member. The covering was fabric. Both left and right side ailerons were equipped with spring tabs (on the -5 models), and in addition carried a ground-adjustable metal tab protruding aft of the trailing edge. The spring tabs had been added on the F6F-5 to improve Hellcat rolling performance.

ron support spar, or rib intercostal member, extended from the wing tip just past the inboard station of the aileron. Stamped flanged metal ribs were located between spars with vertical stiffeners. Z-section stringers ran spanwise over the wing area aft of the forward spar. Panels were covered by flush-riveted metal skin. The outer wing panel front spar caps contained chrome-nickel steel forged hinge fittings at their inboard ends to match those of the center section front spar, thus providing a fold hinge. Special hinge bolts with lubricators were used through the mating hinge fittings. The outer panel rear spar caps supported latching components at their inboard ends to match those of the inboard section rear spar. The outboard

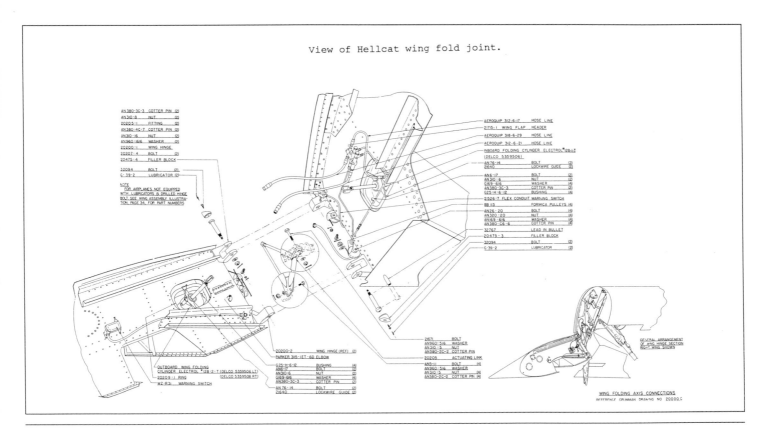

View of Hellcat wing fold joint.

WING FOLDING AXIS CONNECTIONS
REFERENCE GRUMMAN DRAWING NO 20000C

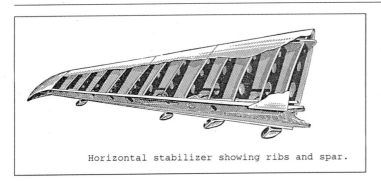

Horizontal stabilizer showing ribs and spar.

TAIL GROUP

The tail group consisted of fixed cantilever horizontal stabilizers, moveable elevators, a fixed vertical stabilizer or fin, and a moveable rudder.

The horizontal stabilizers were of all-metal construction and mounted at one and one half degrees positive incidence angle to aircraft thrust line. The frameworks were made up of stamped ribs riveted to a single aft spar, and these were covered with smooth flush riveted stressed skin. The stabilizers were attached to fuselage structure, including the spar, via fittings on a rear bulkhead. The horizontal stabilizer-fuselage juncture was sealed with rubber edging.

Left and right elevators were identical in construction, and their individual driving torque tubes were connected inboard at a central elevator horn assembly to form an integral unit. Static balance weights were located in the D-section nose cover of the leading edge ahead of the hinge line. The elevator frame consisted of a single flanged spar, a leading edge section with nose ribs and metal covering, a trailing section with ribs, diagonal braces, a trailing edge member, a framed cut-out section for an elevator tab, and a sheet metal tip riveted to the outer rib. Elevator covering was fabric. Each elevator mounted a cockpit-adjustable trim tab.

The fin was a single assembly made up of a rear spar to which stamped ribs were riveted, and it was covered with flush riveted metal skins. The fin spar supported the rudder on three hinge fittings. The aft contour of the tip was recessed to accomodate the balance area of the rudder. The aft radio mast was secured to the tip of the fin. A metal sheet fairing streamlined the lower section of the fin into the fuselage. The fin spar was tied directly into fuselage structure.

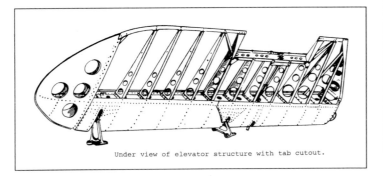

Under view of elevator structure with tab cutout.

Rudder construction was similar to that of the elevators with a metal frame covered with fabric, statically and dynamically balanced, with a trim tab controllable from the cockpit.

FUSELAGE GROUP

The fuselage was built up as a single all-metal semi-monococque stressed skin structure extending from the firewall bulkhead just forward of the cockpit aft to the reinforced bulkheads supporting the fixed tail surfaces, tail wheel, and arresting hook. Frames and bulkheads were of channel or angle cross-section, and were joined by channel-section upper and lower king stringers or longerons and angle-section stringers in between, all running the length of the fuselage. The upper longerons ran along the edges of the cockpit. The forward bulkhead was a primary structural element acting as a firewall with stainless steel facing, as a support for four engine mount fittings, for an armor plated upper section, for two airplane upper hoist fittings, and as a structural tie-in point for the forward spar of the wing center section. Five frames were located at the sides of the cockpit area. A primary solid bulkhead was located aft of the cockpit and tied in with wing center section primary structure. This bulkhead also supported the pilot's head and shoulder area armor plate, and provided a crash turn-over protective structure for the pilot. Steps and hand holds were located on both sides of the fuselage in the cockpit area. The cockpit enclosure was composed of a forward fixed windshield assembly with front and side panels and a sliding canopy. The front transparency of the windshield was a flat armor glass plate; the remaining transparencies were of Plexiglas. All sec-

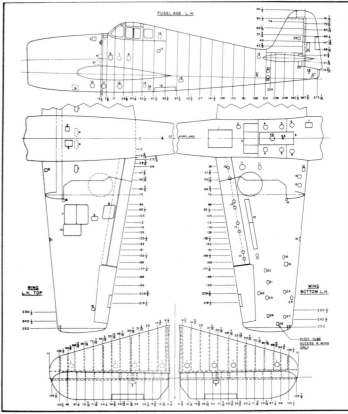

Stations and Inspection Plates Diagram

578

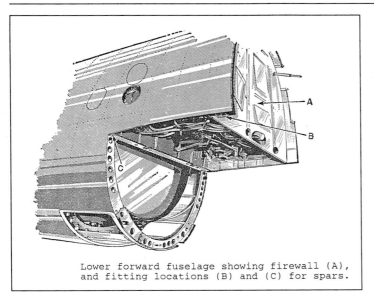

Lower forward fuselage showing firewall (A), and fitting locations (B) and (C) for spars.

tions were framed in metal. A rear view mirror was mounted on the inside of the upper framing. The sliding canopy had four side and one upper Plexiglas panels, was metal-framed, and slid aft in a track. A hand crank, chain and sprocket, and flexible cable system was employed to open and close the canopy. For emergency exit in flight the canopy could be jettisoned by unlocking holding pins and pushing the unit up into the airstream. The cockpit bucket seat was adjustable in height. The fuselage aft of the cockpit was made up of light formers except in the far aft area where bulkhead support for tail items was required. Transverse struts were provided aft of the cockpit inside the fuselage to support radio and other equipment. A large door between lower longerons in the bottom of the fuselage provided access, using quarter-turn fasteners, to this equipment. Baggage could also be stored within the fuselage using this access. A horizontal deck and a bulkhead were employed in the aft fuselage to support the tail wheel assembly. Other bulkheads and decks were provided to support horizontal and vertical stabilizers and the tail hook components.

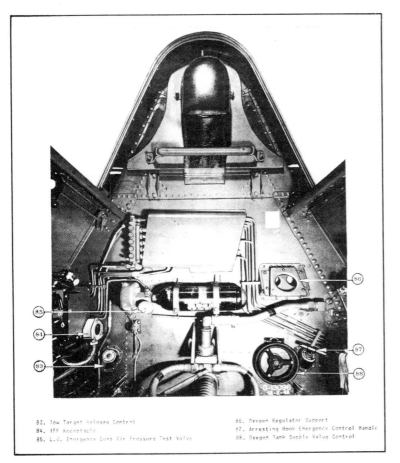

83. Tow Target Release Control
84. IFF Receptacle
85. L.G. Emergency Dump Air Pressure Test Valve
86. Oxygen Regulator Support
87. Arresting Hook Emergency Control Handle
88. Oxygen Tank Supply Valve Control

Cockpit - Rear View

F6F-5 fuselage interior looking aft.

LANDING GEAR GROUP

The landing gear group consisted of two retractable main gear elements mounted at the outboard ends of the wing center section, a retractable tail gear, and an arresting hook.

The main gear consisted of 32x8 inch Goodyear wheels and tires along with Goodyear hydraulic disc brakes mounted on an axle and oleo shock strut assembly. Wheels were on the outboard side of the strut; a metal fairing was attached by three clamps to the strut inboard side. The fairing came flush with the wing under surface in the retracted position and covered the strut and about half the wheel. A torque scissors was located between the strut housing and piston on the forward side of the assembly. The top section of the strut was mounted in a yoke within a sleeve, and contained side load braces with two lateral trunnion bearing housings such that the strut could be retracted aft. The yoke was tied to the center section main spar hinge fittings through which vertical and side loads were taken. A bevel sector gear was mounted on the top of the shock strut, and this was mated to a fixed bevel gear segment on the structure so when the shock strut swung aft for retraction the strut housing, axle, and wheel assembly twisted 90 degrees, thereby assuring that the wheel lay flat in the wing underside recess provided. A drag strut in two linked sections was pinned to the aft side of the shock strut and ran diagonally back to a support formed by a welded steel truss installed between the forward and rear wing spars. At the same time that the hydraulic retraction actuator piston mounted in the wing extended its piston to retract the shock strut

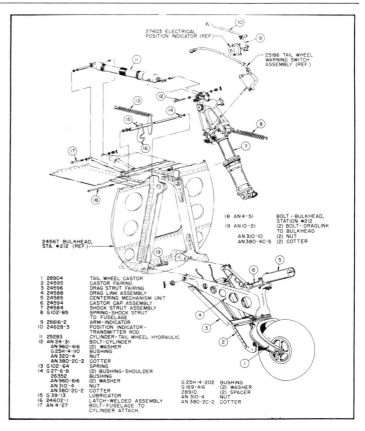

Tail Wheel Assembly

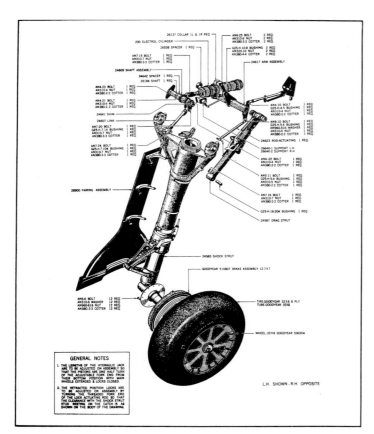

Landing Gear Mechanism

and yoke through linkage, the cylinder body of the actuator moved in reaction to break , or fold, the drag link and allow retraction to take place. At the same time the linkage released the downlock. An uplock was also included in the system. There was a mechanical connection between the cockpit gear control and a "nutcracker" arm on the left side gear shock strut arranged to prevent gear retraction on the ground when the shock strut was compressed. The control lever could not be moved into the retract position unless the left oleo was fully extended after leaving the ground. A wheel position indicator was located in the cockpit.

The tail wheel assembly was mounted to fittings riveted to the aft fuselage bulkhead at station 212. The tail wheel was mounted in a castor supported by a drag link assembly; both castor and drag link had a closure fairing attached. The castor had a centering mechanism mounted between it and the drag link. The whole unit was pivoted off the bulkhead and was held by an oleo shock strut to assist in absorbing tail wheel loads. A double-acting hydraulic retraction actuator was tied to the top of the shock strut assembly. Actuator loads were sheared out on a horizontal deck just forward of the bulkhead. The actuator lifted the tail wheel into the fuselage and the fairings closed over most of the opening. The tail wheel drag link was equipped with a pin which locked the castor in the trailing position, and which was cable-controlled from the cockpit.

The arresting hook was located at the tail end of the fuselage, and in normal operation was extended and retracted electrically with

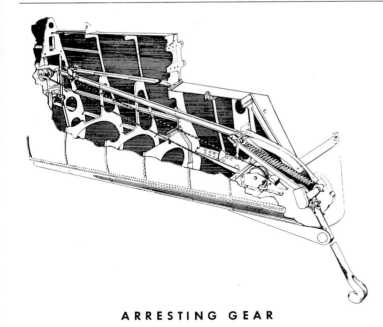

ARRESTING GEAR

the assembly riding on a track in the aft fuselage section. A control switch and a position indicator were located in the cockpit. A backup manual system to extend the hook only was also provided. A tee

handle aft of the seat was pulled and released five times to extend the hook by means of a mechanical chain and pulley system.

ENGINE SECTION

The engine section consisted of the engine mount and engine cowling.

The engine mount was a welded alloy steel tube structure bolted to the fuselage firewall at two upper and two lower locations and extending forward via diagonal members through the engine accessory bay to a circular mount ring just behind the engine. The engine was mounted on the tubular structure through vibration isolator mounts.

The engine cowling consisted of cowl support strips and rings, cowl panels, cowl flaps, and a nose cowl ring. Cowl panels were fastened to the support strips and rings by quick-disconnect quarter-turn fasteners, and formed an outer skin for the forward section of the aircraft. The nose ring was formed to allow cooling air through the engine and provided lower intake lips for carburetor intake air. Cowl flaps were provided just forward of the engine mount and were powered by hydraulic actuators driving mechanical links and bell cranks. A spring-loaded three-position (open, neutral, and closed) cowl flap control lever was located in the cockpit. The backup hydraulic hand pump would operate the flaps in the event of failure of the engine-driven pump.

F6F- SYSTEMS DESCRIPTION

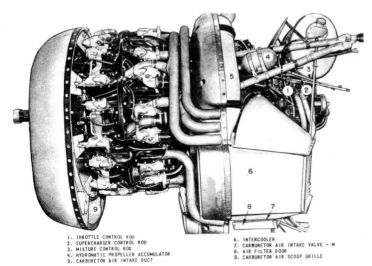

1. THROTTLE CONTROL ROD
2. SUPERCHARGER CONTROL ROD
3. MIXTURE CONTROL ROD
4. HYDROMATIC PROPELLER ACCUMULATOR
5. CARBURETOR AIR INTAKE DUCT
6. INTERCOOLER
7. CARBURETOR AIR INTAKE VALVE - M
8. AIR FILTER DOOR
9. CARBURETOR AIR SCOOP GRILLE

Power Plant L.H. Side View

Power Plant R.H. Side View

PROPULSION SUBSYSTEMS

ENGINE

The engine was a 2000 horsepower class Pratt and Whitney R-2800 Double Wasp twin row eighteen cylinder radial aircooled type with cylinder bore of 5.75 inches and stroke of 6.00 inches. The compression ratio was 6.7:1 and the propeller reduction gear ratio was 2:1. The engine employed a two stage two speed mechanical supercharger with three modes of operation, neutral, low blower, and high blower. The two gear ratios of the second stage blower were

6.46:1 and 7.93:1. Normal maximum engine speed was 2700 RPM; the propeller turned clockwise looking from the cockpit.

ENGINE INDUCTION SYSTEM

With the supercharger in neutral (auxiliary stage inoperative) for low altitude flight operations the path of the intake air to the carburetor was direct. Main supercharger stage air inlet doors were located one each side below the intercooler in the engine accessory compartment. Air entered the doors and was ducted to the carbure-

1. IGNITION INDUCTION BOOSTER
2. OIL SEPARATOR DRAIN - VACUUM SYSTEM
3. HYDRAULIC PUMP - ENGINE DRIVEN
4. AUXILIARY STAGE SUPERCHARGER REGULATOR
5. CARBURETOR AIR INTAKE AUXILIARY STAGE

1. COWL FLAP ACTUATING CYLINDER
2. CARBURETOR BACK-FIRE VALVE
3. OIL TANK ARMOR PLATE
4. PROPELLER ACCUMULATOR
5. OIL TANK

6. GENERATOR BLAST TUBE
7. OIL COOLER AIR SCOOP
8. STARTER CARTRIDGE BREECH
9. CRANKCASE BREATHER LINE
10. TACHOMETER GENERATOR

6. OIL RETURN TO TOP OF TANK
7. OIL RETURN TO WARM-UP COMP'T.
8. ENGINE OIL-IN LINE
9. VACUUM PUMP
10. CARBURETOR ALTERNATE AIR CONTROL

Power Plant with R.H. Intercooler Removed

Power Plant with L.H. Intercooler Removed

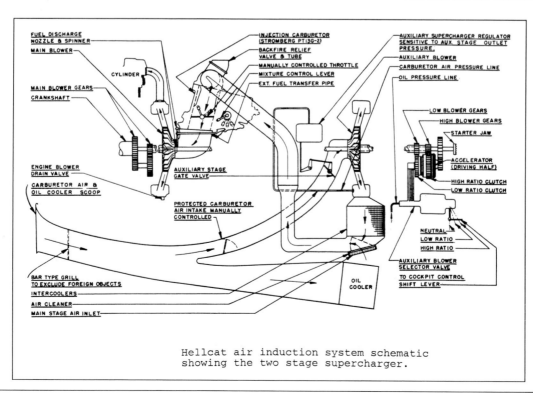

Hellcat air induction system schematic
showing the two stage supercharger.

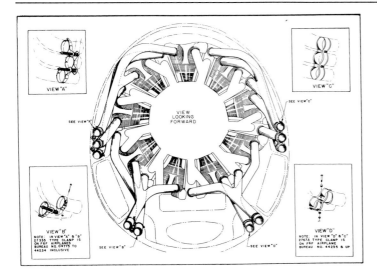

Exhaust System

Engine Control Quadrant

tor inlet. Air filters could be used at the inlets if operations warranted.

With the supercharger control in low or high gear ratio setting (auxiliary stage operating) there were two other modes of air induction to the carburetor, depending on the position of a carburetor air control tee handle on the left side of the instrument panel. With the handle forward in the "direct" position a valve was opened to allow ram air from the lower section of the nose cowling to enter the auxiliary stage blower where it was compressed (and heated). From the blower air passed through two intercoolers mounted low on each side of the accessory compartment. Exit ducts from the intercoolers combined into a carburetor intake duct. With the carburetor air tee-handle control pulled aft to the "protected air" position the valve in the ram air duct from the nose cowl was closed, and alternate warm air was drawn into the auxiliary stage blower from the accessory compartment behind the engine, thus precluding carburetor intake icing.

The cooling air for the intercoolers (air-to-air heat exchangers) was taken in from the forward scoops, passed through them, and exited aft with the flow controlled by variable exit area shutters operated by hydraulic actuators. The actuators were manually controlled by a cockpit lever on the left hand shelf.

ENGINE EXHAUST SYSTEM

Exhaust was collected from the cylinders by a series of stainless steel collector pipes and single pipes, and exited directly aft at the rear of the cowl. Three round pipes were clamped together at each side of the cowl, and two pipes were clamped together at each lower quarter. All pipes pointed directly aft to obtain jet thrust from the exhaust gases.

ENGINE-MOUNTED ACCESSORIES

Engine-mounted or -driven accessories included carburetor, the magnetos, electric generator, fuel pump, oil pump, tachometer generator, vacuum pump, hydraulic pump, and propeller governor.

ENGINE CONTROLS

The engine control quadrant was located on the left hand shelf and had a friction adjustment. The quadrant contained control levers for the auxiliary stage of supercharging (neutral, low blower, and high blower positions), for throttle, mixture, and propeller governor speed setting. These levers were directly connected to the engine and propeller governor by mechanical rods and linkage. In addition there were cockpit controls for auxiliary intake air (instrument panel tee-handle), and intercooler and oil cooler exit air shutters (left side shelf levers), and priming and starting switches.

PROPELLER

The propeller was a Hamilton Standard three blade Hydromatic hydraulically operated 23E50 or 23E60 type of 13'1" diameter using solid aluminum alloy blades of 6501-0 design. The basic blade pitch settings at the 42 inch radius station were: Low pitch 26 degrees and high pitch 65 degrees.

PROPELLER CONTROLS

The propeller RPM control lever was located on the throttle quadrant and included a vernier adjustment. It was directly linked mechanically to a propeller speed governor mounted on the engine nose where the desired speed input from the control was compared with actual engine/propeller speed, and oil was sent to the propeller pitch change mechanism to change blade angle if there was a speed difference between desired and actual RPM. The accumulator in the propeller hydraulic system was strapped to an upper member of the engine mount.

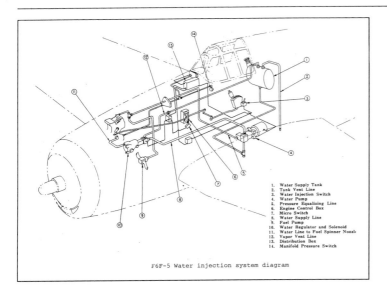

1. Water Supply Tank
2. Tank Vent Line
3. Water Injection Switch
4. Water Pump
5. Pressure Equalizing Line
6. Engine Control Box
7. Micro Switch
8. Water Supply Line
9. Fuel Pump
10. Water Regulator and Solenoid
11. Water Line to Fuel Spinner Nozzle
12. Vapor Vent Line
13. Distribution Box
14. Manifold Pressure Switch

F6F-5 Water injection system diagram

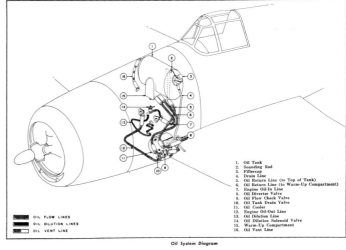

OIL FLOW LINES
OIL DILUTION LINES
OIL VENT LINE

1. Oil Tank
2. Sounding Rod
3. Fillercap
4. Drain Line
5. Oil Return Line (to Top of Tank)
6. Oil Return Line (to Warm-Up Compartment)
7. Engine Oil-In Line
8. Oil Diverter Valve
9. Oil Flow Check Valve
10. Oil Tank Drain Valve
11. Oil Cooler
12. Engine Oil-Out Line
13. Oil Dilution Line
14. Oil Dilution Solenoid Valve
15. Warm-Up Compartment
16. Oil Vent Line

Oil System Diagram

ENGINE STARTING SYSTEM

The ignition switch was on the left side of the instrument panel and the starter switch and primer switches were on top of the electrical panel on the right side of the cockpit. The starter was a Type III cartridge model with the cartridge breech located on the right side of the engine mount and accessible from outside the airplane through a hinged door locked by quarter-turn fasteners. Type D cartridges were normally used, but Type E could be used in colder weather. Cartridge explosive gases forced a piston in a cylinder to move and this action turned engine starting gearing and thus the crankshaft. The ignition induction booster was mounted on an engine mount upper tube.

ENGINE WATER INJECTION SYSTEM

A water injection system to provide extra power short time for combat was provided at the factory on -5 models and fitted retrospectively on most -3 models. The water tank was located in the upper part of the fuselage aft of the pilot between stations 67.5 and 82.5. Access to the filler was gained through a right hand side door held by Dzeus quarter-turn fasteners. Tank capacity was 16 US gallons, and a water quantity gage was located at the right of the instrument panel. A water pump switch was on the left side cockpit shelf; system pressure was about 18 PSI. A water regulator was located in the engine accessory compartment; a line extended from this to the carburetor spray nozzle unit. An electrical solonoid valve in the regulator controlled the line flow. A micro-switch actuated by a tab on the cockpit throttle control rod controlled the solonoid valve so when the throttle lever was moved full forward the water injection system was put into operation.

ENGINE COOLING SYSTEM

The air cooled R-2800 engine obtained cooling flow over the cylinders and past the engine baffles via the engine cowl inlet. The air exited through a series of cowl flaps at the aft edge of the cowling. Flaps were moved in synchronism by a hydraulic actuator and mechanical linkage. The flaps could be powered by the auxiliary hydraulic hand pump if the main engine driven pump failed. A three-

position (open, neutral, closed) flap control lever was on the cockpit left hand shelf with the lever operating a hydraulic valve.

ENGINE LUBRICATION SYSTEM

A single cylindrical oil cooler was located in a duct splitting off from the auxiliary blower ram air duct. After passing through the cooler the air exited through a shutter controlled manually via linkage from the cockpit. On the F6F-3 airplanes the same cockpit lever operated the oil cooler shutter and the intercooler exit flaps; on the F6F-5 model two separate levers were used. An automatic rotary oil temperature control valve was mounted on the oil cooler and could cause the oil to bypass the cooler when the temperature was low. The oil tank was located in the upper part of the engine accessory compartment just forward of the firewall. Fill access was gained through a Dzus-fastened door on the left side of the engine cowling. The maximum filling capacity was 19 US gallons leaving a three gallon foaming space. The oil tank included a warm-up compartment. An oil dilution system was provided with fuel coming from the carburetor via a solonoid-controlled oil dilution valve. An engine-driven oil pump and scavenge pump powered the oil through the system.

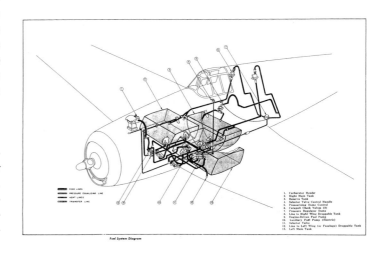

FEED LINES
PRESSURE EQUALIZING LINE
VENT LINES
TRANSFER LINE

1. Carburetor Header
2. Right Main Tank
3. Reserve Tank
4. Selector Valve Control Handle
5. Pressurizing Dome Control
6. Catapult Check Valves (3)
7. Pressure Regulator Dome
8. Line to Right Wing Droppable Tank
9. Engine-Driven Fuel Pump
10. Pressure Fuel Pump (Electric)
11. Selector Valve
12. Line to Left Wing (or Fuselage) Droppable Tank
13. Left Main Tank

Fuel System Diagram

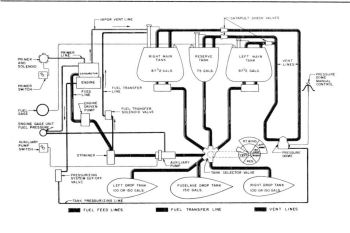

Fuel System Control Diagram

ENGINE FIRE SENSING/FIRE EXTINGUISHING SYSTEMS

No sensing system other than the pilot was provided. A fire extinguisher bottle was located at the right side of the cockpit.

FUEL SYSTEM

The internal fuel tank system was made up of three tanks, a left main and right main cell located respectively to the left and right of the centerline of the aircraft in the wing location, and a reserve tank in the fuselage under the cockpit. Each main tank carried 87.5 US gallons, and the reserve tank capacity was 75 US gallons. The tanks were all of the protected type. External tankage consisted primarily of a droppable 150 US gallon steel tank on a centerline mount. In addition, however, if necessary two 150 US gallon drop tanks could also be installed on the two wing center section bomb racks, one on each side.

When the internal fuselage reserve tank got below 50 gallons a cockpit warning light went on. A fuel tank selector switch at the left side of the cockpit drove a valve controlling fuel feed from the various tanks through a fuel strainer and an engine-driven pump to the carburetor.

An auxiliary electric fuel pump with a switch at the left side of the cockpit was in the system, and was switched on for starting, switching tanks, and as needed to keep fuel pressure up. A vapor return line was run from the carburetor to the right main tank, and could return as much as eight gallons per hour. A Bendix fuel tank pressurization system was used for high altitude flight. A drop tank cockpit switch controlled release of external tanks. Internal tanks were filled on the left side of the fuselage for the left main tank and on the right side for the right main tank and the reserve tank.

FIXED EQUIPMENT SUBSYSTEMS

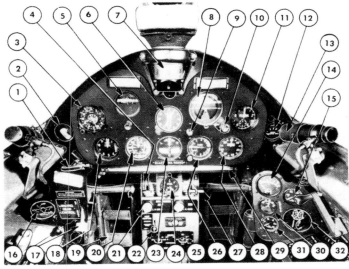

1. Carburetor Protected Air Control (Aux. Stage Only)
2. Ignition Switch
3. Clock
4. Landing Gear Emergency Lowering Control
5. Directional Gyro
6. Compass
7. Gunsight
8. Attitude Gyro
9. Chartboard Light
10. Attitude Gyro Caging Knob
11. Tachometer
12. Water Quantity Gage—A.D.I. System
13. Instrument Panel Fluorescent Light
14. Cylinder Head Temperature Gage
15. Oil Pressure Gage
16. Landing Gear & Wing Flap Position Indicator
17. Landing Gear Control
18. Altimeter
19. Rudder Pedals
20. Airspeed Indicator
21. Gun Charging Controls
22. Cockpit Heater Control
23. Turn and Bank Indicator
24. Ammunition Rounds Counter
25. Fluorescent Lights Control
26. Rate of Climb Indicator
27. Wing Lock Safety Control Handle
28. Manifold Pressure Gage
29. Chartboard
30. Oil-In Temperaure Gage
31. Fuel Pressure Gage
32. Fuel Quantity Gages

Cockpit—Forward View (F6F-3)

33. Lower Left Cockpit Light
34. Tail Wheel Lock Control
35. Rudder Trim Tab Control
36. Cowl Flaps Control
37. Oil Cooler-Intercooler Shutters Control
38. Droppable Fuel Tank Release Switch
39. Mask Microphone Switch
40. Upper Left Cockpit Light
41. Throttle Control
42. Mixture Control
43. Wing Flap Electrical Switch
44. Supercharger Control
45. Water Pump Control Switch
46. Wing Flap Manual Control
47. Map Case
48. Elevator Trim Tab Control
49. Aileron Trim Tab Control
50. Fuel Tank Pressurizing Control
51. Propeller Pitch Control
52. Fuel Selector Valve Dialface
53. Reserve Fuel Tank Warning Light
54. Fuel Tank Selector Valve
55. Oil Dilution Switch
56. Propeller Pitch Vernier Control
57. Engine Control Quadrant Friction Knob
58. Electric Driven Fuel Pump Switch

Cockpit - Left Side View (F6F-3)

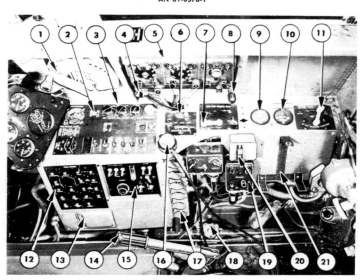

1. Cabin Sliding Hood Control
2. Battery Switch
3. Main Electrical Distribution Panel
4. Electrical Panel Light
5. Radio Controls
6. Recognition Lights
7. Hand Pump Selector Valve
8. Aft Right Cockpit Shelf Light
9. Hydraulic System Pressure Gage
10. Landing Gear Emergency Dump Pressure Gage
11. Wing Locking Hydraulic Control

12. Manual Reset Circuit Breaker Panel
13. Access to Reverse Current Relay
14. Hydraulic Hand Pump
15. Armament Panel
16. Hand Microphone
17. Pyrotechnic Cartridge Clips
18. Pyrotechnic Pistol Retainer
19. Radio Controls
20. IFF Destruction Switch
21. IFF Equipment Support

The F6F-5 differs from the F6F-3 in the following respects:
1. Oil Cooler Shutter Control
2. Fuselage Droppable Tank Manual Release Control
3. Anti-Blackout Regulator
4. Intercooler Shutter Control
5. Removal of the Fuel Level Warning Light

Cockpit—Left View (F6F-5)

Figure 1-32. Cockpit—Right View (F6F-3)

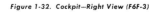

The F6F-5 differs from the F6F-3 in the following respects:
1. Spare Lamps Container
2. Reflector Panel
3. Wing Bomb Rack Manual Release
4. Check-Off Card
5. MK I Rocket Selector
6. Removal of Fluorescent Lights and Control
7. Removal of Cockpit Heat Control Switch to Main
   Electrical Distribution Panel

The F6F-5 differs from the F6F-3 in the following respects:
1. Generator Warning Light
2. IFF Destructor Switch
3. Radio Master Control Switch
4. Rocket Projectile Arming Switch
5. IFF Controls

Cockpit—Right View (F6F-5)

Figure   Cockpit—Forward View (F6F-5)

The F6F-5N differs from F6F-5 in the following respects:
1. Radio Altimeter Indicator
2. Radar Scope

Cockpit—Forward View (F6F-5N)

INSTRUMENTS

Flight instruments included: Clock, directional gyro, compass, artificial horizon indicator, altimeter, airspeed indicator, turn and bank indicator, and rate of climb indicator.

Engine instruments included: Tachometer, water quantity gage, cylinder head temperature gage, oil pressure gage, manifold pressure gage, oil-in temperature gage, fuel pressure gage, and fuel quantity gages.

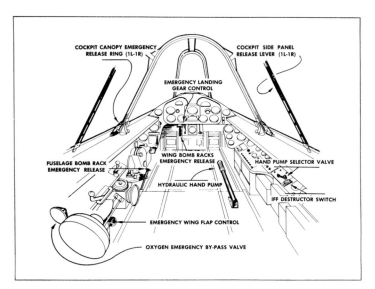

SURFACE CONTROLS

Cockpit controls for the main flight control surfaces were the conventional stick and rudder type. The rudder pedals were suspended from a horizontal bar just below the instrument panel and were adjustable to four positions. Runs from the cockpit controls to the elevator and rudder surfaces were pre-stretched steel cables running over pulleys and through fairleads to horn arms mounted on torque tubes at the surfaces. Elevator cabling was dualized for redundancy. The runs from the stick to the ailerons passed through the wing fold joint at the canted front spar location where links and clevis joints allowed wing folding without breaking any control connections.

Trim tab control wheels for the left aileron, elevators, and rudder were mounted at the left side of the cockpit. Runs to the tabs were chain and cable types with the aileron tab drive passing through the wing fold joint as a non-separating folding link system. Only trim tabs were used on the F6F-3 airplanes; on the F6F-5 models aileron spring tabs were added to lighten control forces. The left aileron tab also operated as a trim tab in this case.

ELECTRICAL SYSTEM

The electrical system included an engine-driven generator and a battery for power, and was of the 24 volt DC single wire airframe ground return type. It was controlled primarily from the distribution panel and switch box located at the right side of the cockpit.

Items operated or controlled by the electrical system included: wing flaps valve, arresting hook, primer, auxiliary fuel pump, lights, cockpit heater, pitot tube heater, gun selector and master controls, gun trigger, gun camera, gunsight, gun heating, droppable fuel tank release, fusing and selecting of bomb release, starter cartridge firing and radio power supplies. Control switches, rheostats, and circuit breakers were on the electrical distribution box which also included a volt-ammeter. All lights were controlled from the panel and included those for cockpit interior, and exterior landing (early airplanes), section, running, and formation lights.

HYDRAULIC SYSTEM

The basic hydraulic system included a 2.2 US gallon reservoir attached to the engine mount, an accumulator in the lower aft section of the fuselage, a strainer and unloader valve, an engine-driven pump to power the system, a main relief valve, a hand pump, and a system pressure gage along with the required hydraulic tubing. The total fluid (red-colored mineral oil) capacity of the system was about four US gallons. Most of the controls for the basic hydraulic system were on the cockpit right side aft of the electrical panel. The emergency hand pump handle was at the right of the seat.

Items powered by the hydraulic system included the wing flaps, gun chargers, wing lock cylinder, main and tail landing gear retraction, intercooler exit flaps, and oil cooler exit shutters.

For normal operation wing flap actuators were moved by a left side toggle switch-operated electric servo motor controlling a hydraulic valve. If the electrical system failed a manual control lever actuating the valve could be used. For landing gear operation a lever on the left hand instrument panel directly operated a hydraulic valve. The wing lock cylinder was controlled by a hydraulic valve

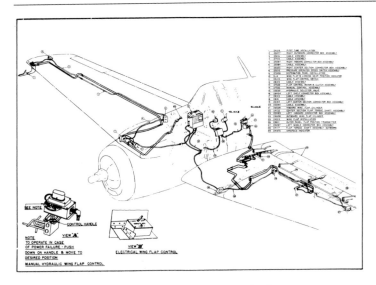

Hydraulic controls diagram for wing flaps.

which was manually operated by a tee handle on the lower center contol panel. The other hydraulically operated items were also controlled from the cockpit by manually-operated levers on hydraulic valves. In the case of failure of the engine-driven hydraulic pump, all the systems noted could be powered by use of the hydraulic hand pump.

PNEUMATIC SYSTEM
An engine-driven vacuum pump was used to supply vacuum for instruments as required.

A one-time emergency air blow-down system was incorporated for the landing gear in case the hydraulic system failed completely. This system lowered and locked main and tail gear. It consisted of a tee-handle control on the lower center panel, a 1950 PSI air bottle clamped to the cockpit rear bulkhead, and valves and lines. When the tee-handle was pulled, gear-up locks were released, the air sys-

1. Wing Flap Cylinder
2. Restrictor
3. Gun Charging Cylinder
4. Wing Lock Cylinder
5. Wing Folding Timer Check Valve
6. Landing Gear Cylinder
7. Shuttle Valve
8. Reservoir
9. Accumulator
10. Filter (Engine-Pump Line)
11. Unloader Valve
12. Engine-Driven Pump
13. Intercooler Flap Cylinder
14. Cowl Flap Cylinder
15. Restrictor
16. Gun Charging Valve
17. Landing Gear Dump Valve
18. Landing Gear Vent Valve
19. Landing Gear Selector Valve
20. Cowl Flap Selector Valve
21. Oil Cooler Selector Valve
22. Wing Flap Selector Valve
23. Air Bottle
24. Check Relief Manifold
25. Wing Lock Selector Valve
26. Air Pressure Gage
27. Air Bottle Filling Valve
28. System Pressure Gage
29. Hand Pump Selector Valve
30. Hand Pump
31. Oil Cooler Flap Cylinder
32. Tail Wheel Cylinder
33. Relief Valve
34. Intercooler Selector Valve
35. Filter (Hand Pump Line)
36. Pressure Snubber

Hydraulic System Diagram

tem vent valve closed; the air bottle valve and the hydraulic dump valve opened simultaneously. As the hydraulic pressure was dumped, air pressure was sent to operate all the gear actuators and lowered the gear.

COMMUNICATION/NAVIGATION/IDENTIFICATION SYSTEMS
Early airplanes were equipped with ATA and ARA communications equipment along with either a ZB adapter or ZBX navigation receiver. Later models were provided with an AN/ARC-5 communications system and AN/ARR-2 navigation receiving equipment. For ferry operations an LF receiver replaced the ARC-5 HF receiver. Equipment controls were on the right side of the cockpit. Transmitters and receivers were installed on racks in the fuselage aft of the cockpit.

ARMAMENT PROVISIONS
Initial basic armament consisted of six fixed .50 caliber Colt-Browning machine guns, three in each wing outer panel. The guns were fired electrically by a trigger switch on the forward side of the pilot's control stick. Gun breeches were located between front and rear wing spars with barrels protruding through the forward spar web and the leading edge. Ammunition trays were located in the wing bays just outboard of the guns. The maximum capacity of the containers in each wing was 1200 rounds. Removeable access panels for the armament bays were provided in the wing upper surface. Electric trigger motors were mounted on the guns, and hydraulic gun charger cylinders were also provided in the gun bays. Gun mountings were of the conventional forward trunnion and rear post types. The guns were supplied with electric heaters clamped over their breeches. The pilot had no control over the heaters; they were wired directly through circuit breakers to the generator. A plug was provided in each wheel well to heat the guns before takeoff if desired.

The gun switches were located on an armament panel at the cockpit right side. Two control handles on the lower center control panel were used to charge or to safety the guns using a push and turn to one side or the other. These controls actuated valves which directed hydraulic fluid flow out to the charging cylinders in the gun bays. The hydraulic lines were carried through the wing fold junctures at front spars by swivel joints at the hinge axes. If the main engine-driven hydraulic pump was inoperative, the hand pump would activate the charging cylinders at about 800 PSI.

A Mark 8 reflector type gunsight was mounted just above the main instrument panel. The control switch and rheostat for the sight was mounted on the armament panel. The sight lamp had two filaments, one as an alternate. A spare lamp was clipped to the sight mount and could be installed in flight.

A gun camera was located in the leading edge of the left side wing center section. The

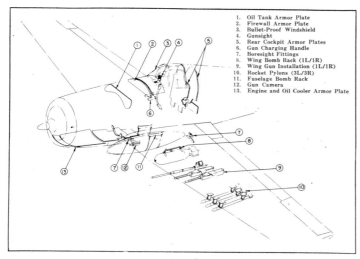

1. Oil Tank Armor Plate
2. Firewall Armor Plate
3. Bullet-Proof Windshield
4. Gunsight
5. Rear Cockpit Armor Plates
6. Gun Charging Handle
7. Boresight Fittings
8. Wing Bomb Rack (1L/1R)
9. Wing Gun Installation (1L/1R)
10. Rocket Pylons (3L/3R)
11. Fuselage Bomb Rack
12. Gun Camera
13. Engine and Oil Cooler Armor Plate

Armament Installation

control switch was on the armament panel. With the switch on the camera would operate whenever the machine gun trigger switch was on.

Two bomb racks, each capable of mounting bombs up to a maximum of 1000 pounds, were provided. A rack was mounted on each side of the wing center section. Bombs were released by an electric button switch on top of the pilot's stick. Bomb selection and fusing was accomplished with switches on the armament panel.

Late airplanes were modified to carry six HVAR 2.75 inch rockets, three under each outer wing panel, mounted on zero-length mount posts. The mounting blocks for the rocket posts were installed at the front and rear spar lower beam cap locations. Rockets were fired electrically; controls were on the armament panel.

Provision could also be made for carrying an aircraft torpedo under the fuselage belly of the aircraft.

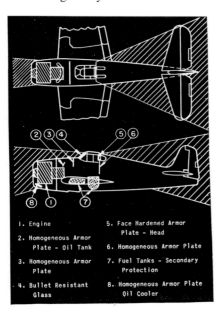

1. Engine
2. Homogeneous Armor Plate - Oil Tank
3. Homogeneous Armor Plate
4. Bullet Resistant Glass
5. Face Hardened Armor Plate - Head
6. Homogeneous Armor Plate
7. Fuel Tanks - Secondary Protection
8. Homogeneous Armor Plate Oil Cooler

Hellcat passive defense features and angles of protection.

Toward the end of Hellcat production some F6F-5 aircraft were equipped with a "mixed battery" of armament where a 20mm cannon replaced the inboard machine gun in each wing. In this case the two cannon were provided with a total of 450 rounds of 20mm ammunition, and the remaining four .50 caliber guns a total of 1600 rounds.

PASSIVE DEFENSE SYSTEM
The passive defense consisted of self-sealing internal fuel tanks and armor. A piece of homogeneous steel armor plate was clamped to the upper engine mount area just ahead of the engine oil tank. Another similar piece of armor was located at the upper section of the firewall just ahead of the cockpit. The forward section of the cockpit windshield was constructed of armor glass. At the rear of the cockpit behind the pilot two sections of armor were in place. A homogeneous steel armor plate protected the pilot's back at the cockpit rear bulkhead, and above that a contoured piece of face-hardened steel armor protected the pilot's head.

At the bottom of the engine compartment a homogeneous steel plate of armor was placed to protect the oil cooler.

FURNISHINGS
The cockpit seat was the standard bucket type and could be adjusted in height up to a maximum of six inches using a control at the right side of the seat. A shoulder harness and seat belt were provided. The control lever for harness adjustment was at the left side of the seat. Harness straps passed over a crossbar mounted on the aft bulkhead behind the seat.

HEATING/COOLING/VENTILATION SYSTEMS
A combustion-type cockpit heater and windshield defroster was provided. An electrical control switch was provided for the heater, on the center panel for the -3 airplanes, and on the electrical panel for the -5 models. A lever on the center panel controlling an air duct valve directed warm air flow from the heater to either the windshield, the pilot's feet, or both.

The flow of outside fresh air into the cockpit for ventilation was governed by a manual control connected to an inlet duct valve. The control was located on the lower central control panel and was foot-operated.

ICE PROTECTION SYSTEM
The only ice protection system for the airframe was the windshield defroster as noted above.

FLOTATION GEAR
Other than the pilot's on-person life preserver no flotation gear was provided.

ARRESTING GEAR
The arresting gear switch, position indicator, and circuit breakers were located on the electrical distribution panel. The switch controlled an electric motor driving a pulley and cable system used to extend and retract the hook. Emergency manual operation of the hook was effected by use of a tee-handle located on the bulkhead

aft of the seat on the lower left hand side. This control would only extend the hook by pulling the tee-handle several times. This action would manually, via the cable and pulley system, run the hook down the guide track to the extended position.

USEFUL LOAD SUBSYSTEMS
GUNS/BOMBS/ROCKETS
See the earlier section on armament provisions.

GUNSIGHT/GUN CAMERA
See the armament provisions section.

PYROTECHNICS
A pyrotechnic pistol retainer and six cartridge clips were located on the right side of the F6F-3 cockpit.

PHOTOGRAPHIC EQUIPMENT
No photographic equipment other than a gun camera was carried on the fighter versions.

OXYGEN EQUIPMENT
A shatterproof oxygen cylinder of 514 cubic inch capacity was located on the aft side of the crash bulkhead behind the pilot. The cylinder was charged to 1800 PSI. The shut-off valve hand wheel extension was located to the left of the pilot's seat. A diluter demand regulator with breathing tube and facepiece was located either on the bulkhead at the left of the pilot's seat or on the lower instrument control panel.

REFERENCES, F6F-
1. *Journal of the American Aviation Historical Society*, Fall,1972.
2. Pearson, Lee M., *Fighter Development-The War Years*, Naval Aviation Confidential Bulletin, Apr.1949.
3. *Zero*, Masatake Okimita and Jiro Horikoshi with Martin Caidin, Ballantine Books, NY, 1957.
4. Minutes of Fighter Conference, NAS Patuxent River, Md. Oct.1944.
5. *Hellcat*, Barrett Tillman.
6. Pilot's Manual F6F- Hellcat/ Pilot's Manual of flight Operating Instructions for Navy Models F6F-3,-3N,-5,-5N Airplanes.
7. *Duels in the Sky*, Capt. Eric Brown, RN.
8. *Skipper-Confessions of a Fighter Squadron Commander*, Capt. Hugh Winters, USN,Ret.
9. *Ace! A Marine Night fighter Pilot in World War II*, Col. R. Bruce Porter and Eric Hammel, Pacifico Press.
10. Industrial Aviation Magazine, June,1945, *Design Analysis of the Grumman F6F-5 Hellcat*, Moss Ringel.
11. *Aircraft Designer's Data book*, Neville, McGraw Hill, NY, 1951.
12. Grumman History Center: F6F- Hellcat, Design 50, (Data on).
13. Data Package, F6F- Hellcat, Grumman Corp. (Excerpts from Manual AN-01-85FB-2).
14. *Wings of the Navy*, Capt. Eric Brown, RN.
15. Model Specification, F6F-3 Airplane, Report SD-286-3B (2422A Revised Sept.28,1943), Grumman Aircraft and Engineering Corp.
16. Model F6F-3 Airplane, Final Report of Production Inspection Trials August 14, 1945.
17. Model Specification, F6F-5 Airplane, Report 2422C, Mar.15,1945, Grumman Aircraft and Engineering Corp.
18. NAVAIR Standard Aircraft Characteristics, F6F-5 Hellcat, Oct.1,1950
19. Manual 01-85FB-1, F6F-5 and -5N Hellcat.
20. *The Pacific War 1941-5*, John Costello, Atlantic Communications. Inc. Quill, NY, 1981.
21. Wings Magazine, Oct.1974, *Hellcat*, Barrett Tillman.
22. *Cross-Winds, An Airman's Memoir*, by Najeeb E. Halaby, Doubleday and Company, Inc.,New York,1978.
23. *Eighty Knots to Mach 2, Forty-Five Years in the Cockpit*, by Richard Linnekin, US Naval Institute Press, Annapolis, Md.1991

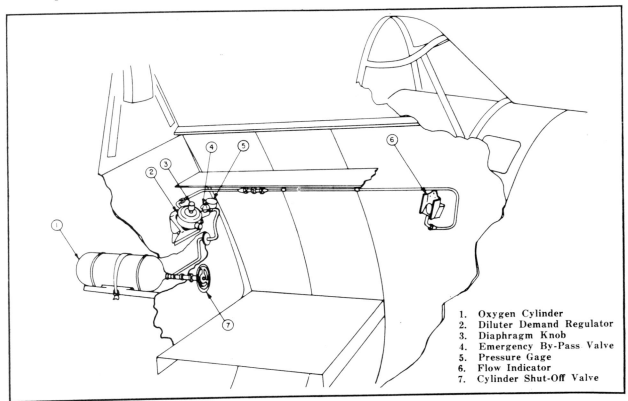

1. Oxygen Cylinder
2. Diluter Demand Regulator
3. Diaphragm Knob
4. Emergency By-Pass Valve
5. Pressure Gage
6. Flow Indicator
7. Cylinder Shut-Off Valve

Oxygen System Installation

5

FIGHTERS COMPARED

MILESTONES COMPARED

Comparison of program milestones for the eleven production fighters is interesting. Table 95 shows major milestone dates from award of initial contract through first flight of the prototype, first production article, first combat in the hands of the US or another nation, and the date when production of the last wartime version ended. With the exception of one type (the F4U- Corsair, produced into 1946 in its -4 version and further in later models) production was stopped either in or before 1945, the last year of the war.

All eleven types were initiated in design before the US entered World War II with six of them started before the war. All except three had prototype first flights before Pearl Harbor, the exceptions being the P-61, Hellcat, and P-63, with these flying first in 1942. Six of the fighters had started in production before US war entry.

There were wide differences between types in development time from first contract to production start. As would be expected,

this time was shortened with the later models under wartime pressures. The two worst cases were the Lockheed P-38 and the Vought F4U- Corsair, both taking four years from first contract to initial production. Reasons in the P-38 case could include an early crash causing destruction of the single prototype, a small initial work force, major redesigns required for high-rate production, and the relative complexity of a twin-engined turbosupercharged fighter. For the F4U- airplane some reasons were similar: Single prototype accidents requiring major repairs, many design changes from prototype to production, and a new two stage supercharged powerplant. For the P-38 the initial development time happened before Pearl Harbor; with the Corsair this slipped six months into war-time for the US. Almost as bad in terms of development time was the Grumman F4F- Wildcat, taking about 43 months from contract to initial production, perhaps reflecting the difficulty of designing a

TABLE 95
FIGHTER MILESTONES COMPARED

TYPE	CONTRACT AWARD	FIRST FLIGHT	FIRST PRODUCTION	FIRST COMBAT	PRODUCTION ENDING	CONTRACT TO PROD.
F4F-/FM-	Jul 28,'36	Sep 2,'37	Feb 1940	Dec 1940	May 1945	43 mo.
F2A-	Jun 22,'36	Dec '37	Jun 1939	Apr 1940	Mar 1942	36 mo.
P-40	Jul 30,'37	Oct 14,'38	Apr 1940	May 1941	Nov 1944	33 mo.
P-38	Jun 23,'37	Jan 27,'39	Jul 1941	Aug 1942	Aug 1945	48 mo.
P-39	Oct 7,'37	Apr 6,'39	Jan 1941	Apr 1942	Jun 1944	40 mo.
F4U-/FG-	Jun 11,'38	May 29,'40	Jun 1942	Feb 1943	Apr 1946*	48 mo.
P-51	May 1940	Oct 26,'40	Aug 1941	Jul 1942	Nov 1945	15 mo.
P-47	Sep 6,'40	May 6,'41	Mar 1942	Apr 1943	Dec 1945	19 mo.
P-61	Jan 30,'41	May 21,'42	Oct 1943	Jun 1944	Dec 1945	33 mo.
F6F-	Jun 30,'41	Jun 26,'42	Oct 1942	Aug 1943	Nov 1945	16 mo.
P-63	Jun 27,'41	Dec 7,'42	Oct 1943		1945	28 mo.

* Production of the last wartime model, the F4U-4, ended that date.
  Production continued on postwar versions for some years.

NOTE For reference purposes World War II started in September 1939; the US entry was in December 1941, and the war ended in August 1945.

pioneer carrier-based monoplane fighter with a two stage super-charged engine. The Wildcat hung around a long time, almost nine years counting Eastern production of FM-2 versions. In contrast, its early competitor for Navy wartime flight decks, the Brewster F2A-, took less development time from near the same 1936 start, got into combat earlier (in Finland) than any other type, but disappeared not long after Pearl Harbor.

Development of the Curtiss P-40 set no records in spite of direct decendency from the earlier Curtiss P-36. Initial contract award to first production took 33 months, most all under a relatively relaxed peacetime atmosphere in the US. Production was initiated a few months after the start of the European war in September, 1939. The P-40 was produced longer than any other US fighter in the war period except the Wildcat, prompting severe criticism later.

The Bell P-39 Airacobra was started the same year as the P-38 and P-40, and development time from first contract to first production was 40 months, seven months longer than the P-40 and eight months less than the P-38, and also under US peacetime conditions. This may have been because the P-39 was a brand new and somewhat unusual fighter compared to the P-40, but not as large and complex as the new P-38. The Airacobra also endured major design changes early on, and the Bell staff was very small at the

time. P-39 production was stopped before the P-40 because of a successor production Bell fighter, the P-63, taking over the lines. There was no successor to the P-40.

The milestones for the two most-produced Army fighters, P-47 and P-51, show development compression in wartime. The P-51 went into production (for the British) about four months before Pearl Harbor and the P-47 (for the US) about four months after Pearl Harbor. The P-51 was a record-breaker in time from first contract to first combat (British), equalled over a year later only by the Navy's Grumman Hellcat. The P-47 took more time, but not by a great amount. The Army's P-61 night fighter was the most complex of the 11 US types, and this fact was reflected in its development time from start to production, though it was no greater than the P-40 three and one half years earlier.

The Grumman Hellcat development program, though a late starter, took only 16 months to first production article, a triumph comparing to the fine P-51 program. Time to first combat was also similar to the P-51.

The Bell P-63 shared with the Hellcat the distinction of obtaining a last wartime fighter production contract award, as well as being a follow-on to a preceding design. It took, however, a full year longer than the F6F- to get a production start. The occasion of its first combat against the Germans in Russia is not known.

DRAG COMPARISON

Table 96 gives a drag comparison of the eleven production fighters in terms of relative equivalent flat plate drag areas at moderate speeds. The drag areas are in square feet, and give an idea of relative cleanliness of the fighter types. The table shows the P-51 as cleanest with an equivalent area of just over four square feet. Next in line are the two Bell fighters, the P-39 and P-63. Note the P-51 and the P-63 are the only types using the then-new laminar flow wing sections to keep drag low. The P-40 is next lowest in drag area, then the Brewster fighter. The drag of the F2A-3 is less than that of the Wildcat because the former has less wing area.

It is seen the large fighters like P-47, Corsair, P-38, and Hellcat have considerably greater drag area, and of course the very large twin-engined P-61 has by far the greatest area. As might be suspected, the drag coefficients of Corsair and Hellcat are quite similar, but the greater Hellcat wing area endows it with considerably larger flat plate area. The twin-engined P-38 has an equivalent flat plate area intermediate between the Corsair and the Hellcat.

A fighter with relatively lower drag area will require less engine power to attain a given speed. So, for instance, the P-51 would require less engine power to cruise at 250 mph at 10000 feet than any of the other types, and the P-61 would require the most power. The high speed attainable by each type depended on the amount of power installed in the airplane and how efficient the propeller was along with the drag rise characteristics as speed increased above moderate values.

TABLE 96
PROFILE DRAG COEFFICIENT SUMMARY

AIRCRAFT	DRAG COEFFICIENT	WING AREA, SQ.FT.	f = EQUIV.FLAT PLATE AREA
P-51D	.0176	233.19	4.10 SQ.FT.
P-39N	.0217	213.2	4.63 "
P-63A	.0203	248.0	5.03 "
P-40	.0242	236.0	5.71 "
F2A-3	.0300	208.9	6.27 "
P-47B	.0213	300.0	6.39 "
F4F-3	.0253	260.0	6.58 "
F4U-1D	.0267	314.0	8.58 "
P-38J	.0270	327.5	8.84 "
F6F-3	.0272	334.0	9.08 "
P-61B	.0244	664.0	15.94 "

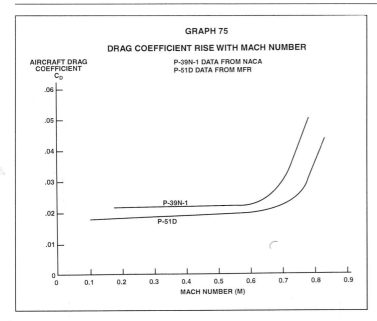

GRAPH 75

DRAG COEFFICIENT RISE WITH MACH NUMBER

AIRCRAFT DRAG COEFFICIENT C_D

P-39N-1 DATA FROM NACA
P-51D DATA FROM MFR

Graph 75 shows drag coefficient increase as speed, expressed in terms of Mach number (flight speed as a percentage of the speed of sound in air) increased. The characteristics of two fighters are shown, the P-39N-1 Airacobra, and the P-51D Mustang. The Mustang incorporated a laminar flow wing design and the Airacobra did not. The curves of drag coefficient for each aircraft are similar in shape; note the very sharp rise at Mach numbers over 60 percent of the speed of sound in both cases. The P-51 curve is not only below that of the P-39 at all speeds, however, but the sudden rise at the higher speeds is delayed. This delay was probably the most important aspect of the laminar flow wing. The so-called drag divergent Mach number (at which the sharp drag rise started) was associated with the onset of compressibility, so the plane that could fly faster and still not encounter these problems had considerable advantage. The P-51 and the P-63, with laminar flow wings, had that advantage over the fighters with older "conventional" wing airfoil shapes.

ENGINE POWERS COMPARED

Graph 76 shows a comparison of available engine power installed in the various fighters, and how these powers varied from sea level to high altitude. The throttle setting used in each case is MILITARY power, the highest setting employed except for the COMBAT, or WAR EMERGENCY, setting used for a very short time in later aircraft models. MILITARY power was meant to be used for a maximum of 15 minutes. A glance will show there was wide variation in available power between models, both at sea level and in changes with altitude.

The most powerful engine used in the US fighters was the Pratt and Whitney R-2800 Double Wasp radial with 18 cylinders giving

2000 horsepower (later 2100) at sea level and used with the Army P-47 and twin-engined P-61 along with the Navy F4U-1 and F6F-. The upper two lines show power variation with altitude of the R-2800 using two different supercharger types. The MILITARY power in the turbosupercharged P-47 engine could be held constant at 2000 horsepower all the way from sea level to over 30000 feet altitude as shown by the upper straight line. For the P-61B, Corsair, and Hellcat a two stage mechanical supercharger provided a power variation with altitude change as shown on the next lower line down. As airplane altitude increased power dropped off until second stage supercharger low blower was kicked in, then dropped off again until that stage was switched to high (speed) blower. This operation held power up fairly well until the plane got over about 23000 feet. It can be seen why the P-47 had superior altitude performance compared to the other Double Wasp-powered fighters.

The next line down shows the power variation of a Packard Merlin engine version in the P-51D Mustang starting at 1490 horsepower at sea level. This line is made up of four segments giving power output changes as altitude increased. The engine had a two stage two speed supercharger and the first two line segments are for low speed blower operation while the second two are for high speed blower use. Power held up well through about 22000 feet with fairly rapid fall-off from there on up. Another version of the two stage Merlin in some Mustangs had better altitude performance. It should be remembered the Mustang was a considerably lighter aircraft than the R-2800 powered types.

Next the figure shows the power variation of the Allison V-1710 turbosupercharged engine in a late model P-38. Again the MILITARY power available is constant to about 30000 feet like the P-47 engine. In this case the airplane had two V-1710s, each with 1425 horsepower, so installed power was greater than in the P-47.

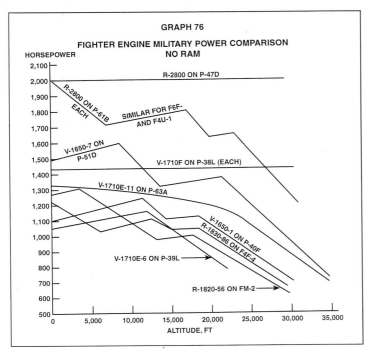

GRAPH 76

FIGHTER ENGINE MILITARY POWER COMPARISON
NO RAM

HORSEPOWER

R-2800 ON P-47D

R-2800 ON P-61B EACH

SIMILAR FOR F6F- AND F4U-1

V-1650-7 ON P-51D

V-1710F ON P-38L (EACH)

V-1710E-11 ON P-63A

V-1650-1 ON P-40F

R-1830-86 ON F4F-4

V-1710E-6 ON P-39L

R-1820-56 ON FM-2

ALTITUDE, FT

TABLE 97
FIGHTER POWER LOADINGS

BASELINE FIGHTER	GROSS.WT.LB.	SEA LEVEL		10000 FEET		20000 FEET		30000 FEET	
		MIL.HP	LB/HP.	MIL.HP	LB/HP	MIL.HP	LB/HP	MIL.HP	LB/HP
P-47D-40	14411	2000	7.21	2000	7.21	2000	7.21	2000	7.21
P-61B	31103	4000	7.78	3490	8.91	3250	9.57	2500	12.44
F4U-1D	12289	2000	6.14	1745	7.04	1625	7.56	1250	9.83
F6F-3	12213	2000	6.11	1745	6.99	1625	7.52	1250	9.77
P-51D	10176	1490	6.83	1500	6.78	1360	7.48	960	10.60
P-38L	17699	2850	6.21	2850	6.21	2850	6.21	2850	6.21
P-63A	8989	1325	6.78	1280	7.02	1190	7.55	865	10.39
FM-2	7487	1260	5.94	1075	6.96	925	8.09	620	12.08
F4F-4	7973	1200	6.64	1075	7.42	990	8.05	650	12.27
P-40F	8678	1100	7.89	1220	7.11	1065	8.15	710	12.22
P-39L	7793	1050	7.42	1130	6.90	850	9.17	—	—

LOWEST POWER LOADING AT:

SEA LEVEL	1.FM-2.	2.F6F-3	3.F4U-1D
10000 FEET	1.P-38L	2.P-51D	3.F6F-3
20000 FEET	1.P-38L	2.P-47D	3.P-51D
30000 FEET	1.P-38L	2.P-47D	3.F6F-3

Below the lines for P-38 and P-51D on the graph is the curved line of power variation for the Allison two stage supercharged engine on the Bell P-63 Kingcobra, an airplane in the Mustang weight class. Starting at 1325 horsepower available at sea level, because of the variable speed second stage supercharger, power dropped off slowly to about 23000 feet altitude, then fell off a lot faster from there on up. At very high altitudes the Mustang and Kingcobra available powers were similar in magnitude.

Two engines used on different versions of the Grumman Wildcat are shown next down, the Wright R-1820 Cyclone with a single stage two speed mechanical supercharger and 1260 sea level horsepower on the FM-2 and the Pratt and Whitney R-1830 Twin Wasp with two stage supercharger and 1200 sea level horsepower on the earlier F4F-4. The Wright engine had more power up to 10000 feet, but from there on up the Twin Wasp had somewhat greater available power because of its two stage supercharging, the latter two segments of the line reflecting high blower operation of the second stage.

Power variations for the other earlier fighters, the P-39 and the P-40, are shown by the final two lines. First, the line for Packard Merlin powered P-40F and P-40L versions is depicted, these Merlins being equipped with a single stage two speed supercharger and rated at 1100 MILITARY horsepower at sea level. This type did a good job of keeping near sea level power up to over 18000 feet, the latter two segments of the line representing high blower speed operation of the single impeller. Above 20000 feet power available dropped rapidly. The variation of power shown for the P-39 also pretty well represented that of Allison-powered P-40 models. The Allison V-1710 with about 1050 sea level MILITARY horsepower for both types used only a single stage single speed mechanical supercharger. Power held up well to the full throttle critical altitude of about 12000 feet and then dropped quickly. This was the reason for the poor high altitude performance of both P-39 and P-40 fighters.

Together these power curves give a picture of how engines in the US fighters stacked up relatively across the altitude spectrum and vividly illustrates the effects of various types and degrees of supercharging. One must be careful, however, and realize that power available alone did not tell the whole story. Weight of the aircraft was very important, and a widely used means of comparison was "power loading", the weight of the airplane divided by the engine horsepower. Of course this loading varied with altitude because the power varied with altitude. Table 97 gives a comparison of some fighter power loadings. In general the lower the power loading, that is, the less weight per each engine horsepower, the better the performance of the aircraft.

SPEED COMPARISONS

Graphs 77 and 78 show, respectively, comparisons of high speed versus altitude at MILITARY rated power of early US wartime fighters at typical weights, and of high speed attainable at COMBAT (WAR EMERGENCY) power for late wartime fighter versions.

The early fighter data represent comparisons for late 1942 where typically the highest power setting for engines was the MILITARY rating. The curves show wide variation of high speed between types and for various altitudes. Typically the speed of each fighter increases with increasing altitude until engine power starts to falter. It is instantly clear the early Navy carrier fighters, F2A-3 and F4F-4, are the slowest airplanes, and remarkably similar, with sea level speed just over 280 mph and greatest speed about 320 mph at medium altitude with a fall-off back to 280 or so at very high altitude. The claim of fastest of the early fighters changed according to altitude. At very low altitudes the early Corsair was fastest at about 340 to 350 mph, but starting just under 5000 feet the Allison-powered P-51 Mustang took the honor, getting to over 390 mph at medium altitude before its single stage supercharger gave up. From medium to high altitude the early turbosupercharged Thunderbolt was fastest, getting to over 400 mph high up. The early P-38 was

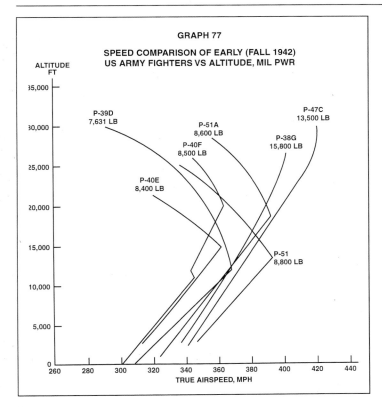

GRAPH 77

SPEED COMPARISON OF EARLY (FALL 1942)
US ARMY FIGHTERS VS ALTITUDE, MIL PWR

ALTITUDE FT

P-39D 7,631 LB
P-51A 8,600 LB
P-40F 8,500 LB
P-47C 13,500 LB
P-38G 15,800 LB
P-40E 8,400 LB
P-51 8,800 LB

TRUE AIRSPEED, MPH

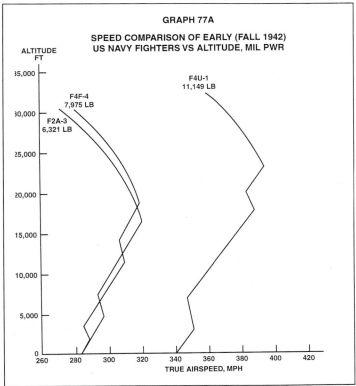

GRAPH 77A

SPEED COMPARISON OF EARLY (FALL 1942)
US NAVY FIGHTERS VS ALTITUDE, MIL PWR

ALTITUDE FT

F4U-1 11,149 LB
F4F-4 7,975 LB
F2A-3 6,321 LB

TRUE AIRSPEED, MPH

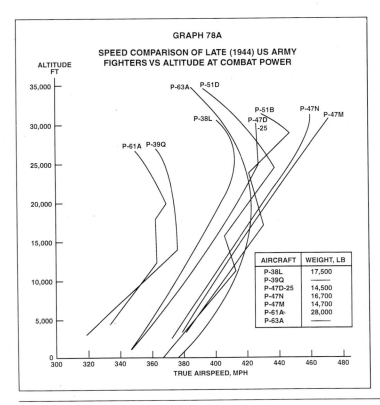

GRAPH 78A

SPEED COMPARISON OF LATE (1944) US ARMY
FIGHTERS VS ALTITUDE AT COMBAT POWER

ALTITUDE FT

P-63A P-51D
P-51B
P-38L P-47D -25 P-47N P-47M
P-61A P-39Q

AIRCRAFT	WEIGHT, LB
P-38L	17,500
P-39Q	—
P-47D-25	14,500
P-47N	16,700
P-47M	14,700
P-61A	28,000
P-63A	—

TRUE AIRSPEED, MPH

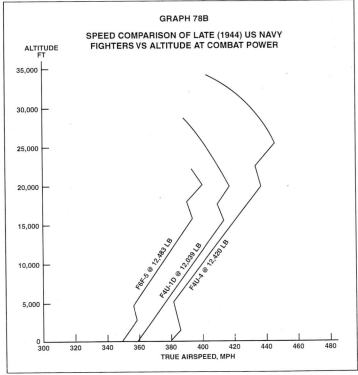

GRAPH 78B

SPEED COMPARISON OF LATE (1944) US NAVY
FIGHTERS VS ALTITUDE AT COMBAT POWER

ALTITUDE FT

F6F-5 @ 12,483 LB
F4U-1D @ 12,039 LB
F4U-4 @ 12,420 LB

TRUE AIRSPEED, MPH

10 to 15 mph behind the P-47s all the way up, and the P-51A, with a higher altitude rated Allison and the F4U-1 with a two stage supercharger was right in there with the P-38 at around 20000 feet, but fell off in speed at greater heights. The early P-39 and P-40 versions were of intermediate speed capability, peaking at between 360 and 370 mph at medium altitudes. The P-39 was the faster of the two except where the Merlin-powered P-40 versions with a two speed supercharger won out at altitudes above 18000 feet.

Comparisons of the late model fighters using COMBAT power are shown in Graph 78. The only two types not making it into the 400 mph area above 25000 feet were the P-39Q and the big twin engined P-61. The main improvement in P-39 speed performance was at the higher altitudes, this provided by a little better supercharging. The P-61 almost got to 370 mph at 20000 feet. The speed merchants, particularly at altitude, were the latest versions of the Thunderbolt, the P-47M and the P-47N, both making 450 mph at about 25000 feet because turbosupercharging kept engine available power up. As shown in the plot this speed represented Mach 0.65, and the airplane was therefore just starting up the drag rise curve representing compressibility. The late model Corsair, the F4U-4, approximated the Thunderbolt high speed up to 25000 feet, but then its speed capability fell off rapidly at higher altitude.

Two versions of the Mustang are shown, the P-51B and the P-51D, with somewhat different engine and supercharger versions between them. Up to medium altitudes they were fastest of all, but

high speed fell off at very high altitudes, particularly that of the D model.

Curves are also shown for the other high-production models, P-38L, P-47D-25, and F4U-1D, where speeds are less than those of P-47M and N and the -4 Corsair. Of these three the F4U-1D speed performance stood out significantly up to 20000 feet, but at higher altitude the bubble canopy P-47D-25 surpassed Corsair performance. Slowest of the three at medium altitudes was the P-38L, though at sea level it matched the P-47D and above 22000 feet exceeded F4U-1D capability. The P-38L at COMBAT power setting just got to Mach 0.60 in the 25000 to 30000 foot range.

The rather unique curved line representing Bell P-63 Kingcobra high speed variation with altitude came about because of variable speed capability of the supercharger second stage. The very clean P-63A was the speed king up to almost 14000 feet, but its supercharging system was less powerful than those of Merlin Mustangs and the latest Thunderbolts, and speed fell off at very high altitudes.

These speed versus altitude graphs show it is often difficult to generalize in comparing speeds of the US fighters because changes with altitude and type of engine supercharging are large. One has to be very specific in talking about fighter maximum speed, being careful to define aircraft configuration, specific variant, altitude, weight condition, and engine power setting as well as the condition of both airplane and engine.

CLIMB COMPARISONS

Fighter climb performances are compared in the time-to-climb curves of Graphs 79 and 80. Two major factors influencing climb capability are aircraft weight and engine power setting, and these are specified on the climb curves for each aircraft type. Since climb is a steady state condition as considered here the use of engine COMBAT power is not practical, and all climb data are for either MILITARY or NORMAL (MAXIMUM CONTINUOUS) engine

throttle setting. In some cases the climb data are for a combination, that is, first MILITARY and then NORMAL. In the case of most fighters performance in climb is shown for both an early and a late version, the latter typically having greater engine power available but also increased gross weight.

Data for early versions of Army fighters, P-38G, P-39D, P-40E, P-47C, and P-51, show the twin engine P-38G as a clear win-

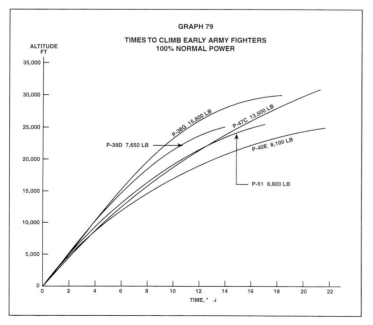

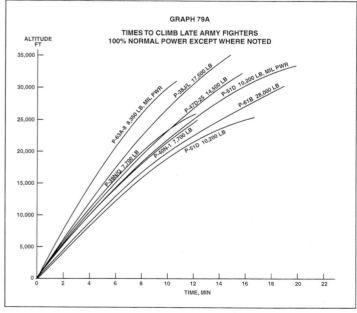

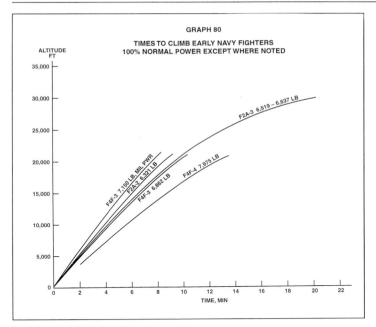

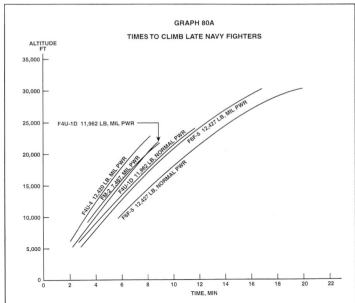

ner in times to climb, it getting to 25000 feet in 11 minutes. The clear loser is the P-40E, taking over 21 minutes to get to the same altitude. The much-maligned P-39D, because of low weight, outclimbed the P-47C and the Allison-powered P-51. The early Thunderbolt was noted for indifferent steady climb characteristics even though its engine was turbosupercharged, this partly due to poor propeller performance in climb. The early P-51 climb data is at a weight over one thousand pounds greater than the P-39D, this being the reason for inferior performance.

Later versions of the same airplanes showed considerable improvement in climb capability. Increases in engine power usually more than made up for the inevitable airplane weight increase. P-38J and P-38L fighters, though near a ton heavier than the early P-38s, took at least six minutes off the time getting to 30000 feet and cut almost two minutes from the time to 25000 feet. Uprated engine performance on the late model Airacobras, P-39N and P-39Q, cut about two and a half minutes from P-39D climb time to 25000 feet, and equalled climb performance of a late P-47D-25 up to about 22000 feet. A huge improvement in climb time was gained by the P-40N-1 over the P-40E; time to 25000 feet was cut to 12.5 minutes instead of the earlier 21.5. The P-47D-25 and P-47M, by virtue of a new paddle blade propeller and increased engine power reduced time to 25000 feet from 15 to 11 minutes, and took six minutes off the P-47C time to 30000. The improved P-47 performance could not match late P-38 versions, however. And the final Thunderbolt, the P-47N for the Pacific, with larger wing and much more fuel, could not better the poor climb performance of the older P-47C until over 25000 feet altitude because of greatly increased weight. Although Merlin-powered P-51D climb times bettered those of the earlier Allison-powered P-51 over 23000 feet, the much greater P-51D weight held down climb performance and surprisingly, perhaps, P-51D climb was poorer than that of a late model Thunderbolt. This was due, no doubt, to the turbosupercharging of the P-47 versus the two stage mechanical supercharging of the P-

51D. Mustang power was only 60% of P-47 power at 25000 feet while its weight was 70% of P-47 weight. The Thunderbolt power loading was therefore lower. As might be expected, the climb times of the big twin-engined P-61 Black Widow night fighter were less than spectacular, though better than the P-51D at the same NORMAL power setting. The fastest climbing fighter in the Army stable, late in the war, was the Bell P-63A Kingcobra (though data is not available for the P-38L at MILITARY power). It could get to 25000 feet in eight minutes or less. This flashy climb performance was achieved by the combination of a two stage Allison engine supercharger and a relatively light weight aircraft (almost a ton less than the P-51D, of which a great deal, it must be said, was less fuel than the P-51.) With almost 90% of Mustang power at 25000 feet and only about 80% of P-51D weight, the P-63 could be expected to outclimb the North American aircraft.

On the Navy fighter side the early types, the F2A- and the F4F-were quite comparable in time to climb performance. The earlier F2A-2 was slightly better than the F2A-3 since the latter had picked up additional weight. At the same NORMAL power setting of their engines time-to-climb performances of F2A-3 and F4F-3 were very close up through 20000 feet, gaining that altitude in about nine and a half minutes, a minute longer than the F2A-2. Performance data shows a heavier F4F-3 at the higher MILITARY power improving this capability to 20000 feet in seven and a half minutes, the best climb performance of the early airplanes. Then came the much heavier six gun folding wing F4F-4 model with inferior climb, taking 12.5 minutes to attain a 20000 foot altitude, a performance almost as bad as that of the Army P-40E. The late Eastern version of the Wildcat, The FM-2, had both more power and greater weight than earlier machines, but succeeded in getting climb time capability almost back to best F4F-3 performance. Climb to 20000 feet in that aircraft took about eight minutes.

The later Navy fighters, Vought F4U-1D and Grumman F6F-5, were generally comparable in climb times, though the curves show the Corsair with a big edge because the F4U-1D gross weight is indicated at about 400 pounds less than the Hellcat. Actually that figure was nearer 200 pounds when each had a full load of ammunition and internal fuel. Interestingly Hellcat climb times were no better than the maligned F2A-3 up to 20000 feet, but bettered the Brewster performance above that altitude. The Hellcat curves show the differences in climb time between NORMAL and MILITARY power at the same weight. The star of the Navy show in climb performance was the late-arriving F4U-4 Corsair which could barely be called a World War II fighter airplane. An up-rated powerplant gave that latest Corsair a time to 20000 feet of 6.8 minutes. The end-of-war F4U-4 could hit 20000 feet just 45 seconds faster than the start-of-war F4F-3!

It can be seen that two of the fastest-climbing fighters had little to do with US fortunes in World war II. The P-63A was used in combat only by the Russians, and the F4U-4 got to the Pacific just before the end of the war. The fastest-climbing fighter in extensive use by US forces was the P-38 Lightning; no other type had particularly flashy performance. The poorest performers in climb were the Army P-40E and the Navy F4F-4, both heavily engaged US types in much of the Pacific fighting.

RANGE AND RADIUS COMPARISONS

TABLE 98
COMPARISON OF ARMY FIGHTER "YARDSTICK" RANGES
ASSUMES ALL WING SPAN EFFICIENCY FACTORS=0.85; ALL PROPELLER EFFICIENCIES=80%
ALL AIRCRAFT SPECIFIC FUEL CONSUMPTIONS=0.5 LB./HP/HR.; AND ALL AIRCRAFT IN CLEAN CONFIGURATION WITH FULL INTERNAL FUEL AND NO EXTERNAL FUEL

AIRCRAFT	P-38J	P-39D-2	P-40E	P-40F	P-47D	P-51D	P-61B	P-63A-10
WG.ASPECT RATIO	8.26	5.42	5.89	5.89	5.56	5.87	6.56	5.93
PROFILE DRAG COOEFFICIENT	.0270	.0217	.0243	.0243	.0251	.0176	.0244	.0203
MAX.LIFT/DRAG	14.28	12.91	12.71	12.71	12.16	14.92	13.39	13.96
EMPTY WT.LB.	12780	5658	6069	6576	10199	7260	22000	6694
USEFUL LD.LB.	4890	2135	2304	2184	4585	2916	8393	2280
GROSS WT.LB.	17670	7793	8373	8760	14784	10176	30393	8974
FUEL WT.LB.	2460	720	888	942	2232	1590	3876	756
GROSS-FUEL WT.	15210	7073	7485	7818	12552	8586	26517	8218
GW/GW-FUEL WT.	1.1617	1.102	1.119	1.120	1.178	1.185	1.146	1.092
LOG TO BASE 10 OF JUST ABOVE	.06521	.04218	.04883	.04992	.07115	.07372	.05918	.03822
RANGE FACTOR	1.4899	0.871	0.993	1.0009	1.3842	1.707	1.268	0.8536
RANGE, MILES	1222	714	814	821	1135	1443	1040	700

TABLE 99
COMPARISON OF NAVY FIGHTER "YARDSTICK" RANGES
ASSUMES ALL WING SPAN EFFICIENCY FACTORS=0.85; ALL PROPELLER EFFICIENCIES EQUAL 80%; ALL AIRCRAFT SPECIFIC FUEL CONSUMPTIONS=0.5 LB./HP/HR.; AND ALL AIRCRAFT IN CLEAN CONFIGURATION WITH FULL INTERNAL FUEL, NO EXTERNAL FUEL.

AIRCRAFT	F2A-3*	F2A-3**	F4F-4	F4U-1D	F6F-5
WING ASPECT RATIO	5.86	5.86	5.55	5.35	5.49
PROFILE DRAG COEFFICIENT	.0300	.0300	.0253	.0267	.0272
MAX. LIFT/DRAG	11.42	11.42	12.10	11.56	11.61
EMPTY WEIGHT,LB.	4781	4781	5779	8971	9079
USEFUL LOAD,LB.	2558	2198	2193	3318	3404
GROSS WEIGHT,LB.	7339	6979	7972	12289	12483
FUEL WT.,LB.	1440	1080	864	1422	1500
GROSS WT.-FUEL WT,LB.	5899	5899	7108	10867	10983
GW/GW-FUEL WT.LB.	1.244	1.183	1.122	1.131	1.137
LOG TO BASE 10 OF JUST ABOVE	.09482	.07298	.04999	.05346	.05576
RANGE FACTOR	1.7320	1.3330	0.9676	0.9890	1.0358
RANGE, MILES	1421	1093	793	811	849

* WITH 240 GALLONS INTERNAL FUEL
* WITH 180 GALLONS INTERNAL FUEL

TABLE 100
ARMY FIGHTER RANGE
STATUTE MILES AT 10000 FEET, CRUISE AT MOST ECONOMICAL POWER

AIRCRAFT	MAX.INTERNAL FUEL,GAL.	T.O.GROSS WEIGHT,LB.	RANGE, MILES
P-38G	300	15800	850
P-38H	300	16300	850
P-38J	410	17500	1170
P-38L	410	17500	1170
P-39D/F/K	120	7650	600
P-39L/M	120	7900	550
P-39N	87	7550	350
P-39Q	110	7700	525
P-40E	149	8700	650
P-40F/K	157	8850/8800	700
P-40L	120	8600	500
P-40M	157	8800	700
P-40N-1	122	7725	520
P-40N	161	8400	750
P-47C/Early D	305	13500	835
P-47D Late/M	370	14500/14700	1020
P-47N	556	16700	1700
P-51	180	8800	1000
P-51A	180	8600	1000
P-51B/C	269	9800	1275
P-51D	269	10100	1250
P-61A	640	27600	1020
P-61B Late	640	29700	940
P-63A	136	8350	700

Accurate information on fighter range and radius, on a truly comparable basis, is difficult to obtain. The so-called "mission profile" must be the same for all the aircraft being compared, and must be carefully defined. The altitude, cruise power settings, allocations of fuel and time or distance for takeoff, climbout, and descent, and amount of fuel for reserves must all be commensurate for good comparisons. The condition of the airplane and engine, piloting techniques, and wind conditions if any are also some of the practical factors that may vary. The drag of external fuel tanks or other stores, if any, must be considered.

Comparisons are made first for the seven Army fighter types and then for the four Navy types. A highly theoretical range comparison, good primarily to see relative values, is given in Tables 98 and 99. Next some USAAF estimated range data is shown in Table 100 and compared with the theoretical data of Table 98. And finally USAAF estimates comparing radius of action of four prominent Army fighters, the P-38, P-47D, P-47N, and P-51, are shown.

The frst range comparison, Tables 98 and 99, is a "yardstick" showing relative capability, that is, which had the longest range, which was next best, next, and so on. It is based on a classic commonly used range formula developed by the Frenchman Louis Breguet. It is theoretical for several reasons, one being the airplane flight starts and ends in mid-air and uses all its fuel between the two points (no fuel reserves). Other assumptions: Each fighter is flown continuously at its peak lift-to-drag ratio (at a minimum drag condition), all propeller efficiencies are continuously the same at 80%, fuel consumption in pounds per horsepower per hour is continuously the same for all at a value of 0.50, and each plane is loaded with full internal but no external fuel. Tables 98 and 99 show relative ranges. The North American P-51D Mustang has the greatest range at 1443 miles, the Lockheed P-38J is next at 1222 miles. Third best is the P-47D-25 at 1135, then the big P-61 night fighter at 1040 miles, and after that the Curtiss P-40E at 814 miles. Bringing up at the short end of the range spectrum are the two Bell fighters, the P-39 and the P-63 at 714 and 700 miles respectively. There are no surprises here.

The next Army fighter range comparison uses USAAF figures, and gets a little more practical, allowing 10 minutes of fuel at NORMAL power for warm-up, taxi, run-up, takeoff, and landing. It allows for fuel needed in climb to cruising altitude, includes climb segment distances in the range (on course climb), and allows 10% of the net ideal range for other factors. The flight condition in each case is use of most economical power speed at 10000 feet altitude. Table 100 shows the USAAF figures on this basis and a comparison with those of Table 98. As would be expected, the ranges are not as great,

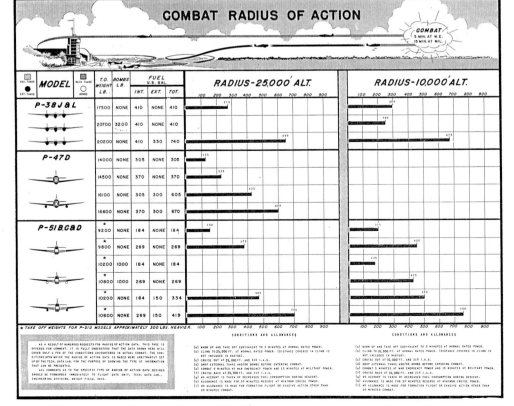

but their order is the same for the first four aircraft types: P-51D, P-38J, P-47D-25, and then the P-61B. There is some variation from Table 98 in results for the last three fighters, but they are all still poorest in range capability. It is indeed strange Bell did not design more internal fuel capacity into the P-63. There were definite internal space problems on this mid-engined aircraft, and this may have been a reason for such limited fuel capacity. It has also been claimed politics played a role. In this comparison the P-51D is best at 1250 miles range, the P-38J next at 1170 miles, the P-47D-25 at 1020 miles, and so on.

The third Army fighter comparison shows the relative practical combat radius performance of the three premier European Theatre of Operations fighters (P-38J/L, P-47D, and P-51D) and the Pacific Thunderbolt (P-47N). All are shown both with and without external stores, and results for the first three are given in two cases of cruising altitude, 10000 feet and 25000 feet. The mission profile is carefully defined in the figure. Of the three ETO fighters the P-51D is again best, the P-38J/L next, and last the P-47D. But the P-47N, redesigned with a new wing and much more fuel, shows up with the longest legs of all. With heaviest fuel load the P-47N provided a combat radius at

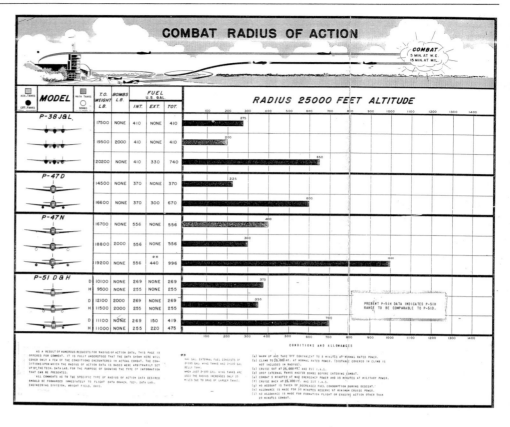

25000 feet of 1000 miles. The P-51D was next; under the same conditions combat radius was 700 miles.

The data for US Navy fighters is shown in Table 101 where ranges on internal tankage only are from Bureau of Aeronautics documents of the World War II era. It is interesting that the Brewster F2A- models are shown with 180 gallons of fuel because maximum internal capacity was normally shown either as 160 gallons or 240 gallons, the former representing the case where the port wing beam tank was not used, and the latter when it was. The 180 gallons would represent all tanks full except only 20 gallons in the port wing beam, or perhaps only 50 gallons in each wing beam tank instead of full to capacity of 80 gallons each side. The light Brewster fighters (relative to the others) achieved over 1500 miles range with 180 gallons of fuel; with 240 gallons the aircraft could have reached a range close to 2000 miles. These aircraft were not designed to carry external fuel tanks.

The various Wildcat models had steadily decreasing maximum ranges on internal fuel alone. From the range of the early F4F-3 version, 1280 miles, capability dropped to 780 miles on early FM-2 aircraft, this because internal fuel capacity went down steadily. Longer ranges had to be achieved by the addition of external tanks.

Early Corsair models got maximum range on internal fuel back to about 1500 miles, but in the F4U-1D version the unprotected wing fuel tanks were left out, reducing internal capacity by a third, and the resulting range a similar amount to about 1000 miles. Additional range could be achieved using two drop tanks on the F4U-1D as opposed to the one on the F4U-1. The much later F4U-4 had about the same basic range capability, as shown.

TABLE 101
NAVY FIGHTER MAXIMUM RANGES
FULL INTERNAL FUEL, NO EXTERNAL FUEL, RANGE IN
STATUTE MILES
MOST ECONOMICAL CRUISE SPEED

AIRCRAFT	GROSS WT.LB.	FUEL,GAL.	CRUISE ALTITUDE,FT.	RANGE, MILES
F2A-3	6637	180*	4500	1565
F2A-3	6906	180*	4500	1530
F4F-3	7399	147	3500	1090
F4F-3	7543	147	19000	1280
F4F-3A	7320	147	6100	1035
F4F-4	7975	144	5000	830
F4F-4	7972	144	19000	925
FM-2	7431	117	5000	780
FM-2	7487	126	1500	900
F4U-1Early	12694	361	5000	1596
F4U-1Late	12836	361	1500	1515
F4U-1D	11962	237	1500	1020
F4U-4	12420	234	1500	1005
F6F-5	12483	250	1500	1322

* Not full internal fuel capacity, which was 240 gallons, 160 in two wing beam tanks, 40 in two wing inboard leading edge tanks, and 40 in a fuselage tank. Unprotected tankage in the left wing beam was restricted for combat operations.

The F6F-5 Hellcat had slightly more internal fuel than the later Corsairs and weighted about the same; maximum internal fuel range is shown as 1322 miles. Again, external tanks could increase this range.

On the same basis, range of the early Navy F4F-4 was significantly greater than the early Army P-39 and P-40, but ranges of the other types, P-38, P-47, and P-51D, were very similar to the Navy F4U-1D and F6F-5, all these aircraft having capability of going a maximum of about 1000 to 1300 miles on internal fuel, and all with capability of adding external tanks for greater range.

TAKEOFF DISTANCE COMPARISONS

TABLE102
TAKEOFF DISTANCE COMPARISON
BASELINE GROSS WEIGHTS (FULL AMMO.& INTERNAL FUEL)
HARD SURFACE, ZERO WIND, SEA LEVEL, AND TAKEOFF POWER

SERVICE	AIRCRAFT	GROSS WEIGHT(LB.)	TAKEOFF GROUND RUN(FT.)	RANKING
USAAF	P-38J	17699	1080	11
USAAF	P-39D-2	7793	1750	16
USAAF	P-39Q-1	7570	1650	14
USAAF	P-40E	8289	1070	10
USAAF	P-40N-1	8354	1760	17
USAAF	P-47C	13582	2220	18
USAAF	P-47D-25	14411	2540	20
USAAF	P-51A	8633	1415	13
USAAF	P-51D	10176	1185	12
USAAF	P-61B	31103	2420	19
USAAF	P-63A	8989	1700	15
USN	F2A-3	6906	620	1
USN	F4F-3	7543	690	4
USN	F4F-3A	7320	650	3
USN	F4F-4	7973	710	5
USN	F4U-1 Early	12676	750	6
USN	F4U-1D	12289	840	8
USN	F4U-4	12281	630	2
USN	F6F-3	12213	950	9
USN	F6F-5	12483	780	7

Table 102 gives takeoff ground run distances of Army and Navy fighters for comparison. Each type is at a takeoff gross weight resulting from a full load of internal fuel and of ammunition. No external stores are carried, and takeoffs are made from a hard dry land surface at sea level with no head or tail wind. The data are from USAAF and US Navy wartime references. Wing flap settings are not specified, but takeoff engine power is used in all cases.

A look at the table shows quickly that Navy fighters had the best ground run performance; all the USN types listed got off the ground faster than the best Army aircraft. The clear winners are the Brewster F2A-3 and the F4U-4 Corsair, the earliest and the latest of USN wartime fighters. The Grumman F4F- Wildcat models are not far behind; none of these much exceeded a 700 foot run.

The most-used Navy and Marine fighters, F6F- and F4U-, were similar in takeoff performance and neither exceeded a 1000 foot run under the stated conditions. It seems quite proper that the Navy aircraft should have the shortest runs since all were intended as carrier types. The big difference between the conditions of the table and carrier conditions is of course the carrier wind-over-deck which could exceed 35 mph. Under carrier takeoff conditions deck runs were considerably shorter since wind-over-deck could be as much as half the relative speed needed for takeoff.

All the Army fighters took over 1000 feet to get off with the Curtiss P-40E and Lockheed P-38J having the shortest runs of 1070 and 1080 feet respectively. It is not at all clear why the P-40N run should be so much longer since weight is little more than the earlier model. Next came P-51 models with the less powerful P-51A requiring a longer run in spite of being lighter than the later P-51D. The Bell P-39 models have relatively long takeoff runs at around 1700 feet, as does the later, heavier, and more powerful Bell P-63A. By far the worst takeoff performers are the P-47 Thunderbolt fighters with runs required of 2200 to 2500 feet. This poor performance is reflected in many comments handed down by World War II airmen.

The takeoff runs shown did not necessarily reflect directly the required airstrip size. Extra length was needed. The major addition would be to account for obstacle clearance at the end of the runway, both in taking off and landing. Normally the landing run-out after touchdown was a large percentage of, but no more than, the takeoff run, and in most cases landing weight was significantly less than takeoff weight. The exception would be an emergency return to the strip.

ROLL RATE PERFORMANCE COMPARISONS

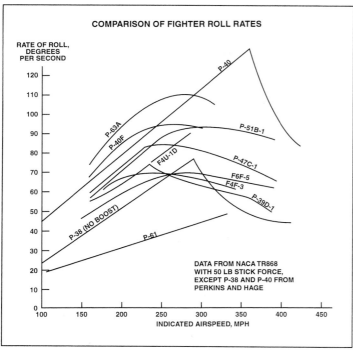

Graph 81

A tremendous amount of wartime effort was made by manufacturers and NACA in research to try and improve fighter aileron performance. But few types met the performance desired by Army specifications.

The roll curves show pre-aileron boost P-38s attaining a maximum rate of about 75 degrees per second at 290 mph IAS then decreasing sharply at higher speeds. The P-39D Airacobra reaches a similar rate at a lower speed, about 235 mph IAS, then roll performance decreases more gradually with speed than the P-38. The early P-40 shows up as a star roll performer, and pilot comments tend to substantiate this. The curve shows a peak rate of over 130 degrees per second at the high speed of 360 mph IAS. Why the later P-40F performance drops off so much is not clear. The early P-47C Thunderbolt shows a peak roll rate of 84 degrees per second, and the rest of the curve falls off as limited by a 50 pound lateral stick force. The P-51B Merlin Mustang shows a much better rate at high speeds, keeping up to 90 degrees per second at 360 mph IAS (a four second roll). The big twin engine P-61 with its spoiler lateral control was poor in roll performance as shown by the graph , but the Bell P-63A had excellent roll rates, peaking at 110 degrees per second at 275 mph IAS. Since no data is shown for the Kingcobra at 350 mph and above, it is unclear whether it could equal the P-51B at the higher speeds.

On the Navy side the F4F-3 Wildcat had mediocre roll rates, never quite reaching 70 degrees per second. The F4U-1D Corsair reputedly had "beautiful" ailerons, and extremely high roll rates have been claimed. The Corsair curve is shown only for a limited speed range. A 90 degree per second roll rate at about 290 mph (a four second roll) is indicated. Nothing is shown to belie statements about very high roll rates at higher speed (about 120 degrees per second at 350 mph IAS has been claimed), but no firm data has been found. The F6F-5 roll rate performance is surprisingly poor on a relative basis, barely peaking at 70 degrees per second, even after the addition of aileron spring tabs to improve performance at the high speed end, one of the changes going from the F6F-3 to the F6F-5 model.

On the premise that the early P-40 was obsolete at the time the US entered the war, the star performers in roll rate of the models shown were clearly the Merlin P-51, the P-40F, and the P-63A. Since the P-63A was not used in combat by US forces, the remaining champions have to be the P-51B Mustang and the P-40F Warhawk. At speeds up to 300 mph IAS the Warhawk was superior; from there on the P-51B took over.

The curves of Graph 81 show comparative steady state rolling performance of all US wartime fighters except the Brewster F2A-, a record of which has not been found. The curves show fighter roll rate at various indicated airspeeds. Remember true airspeed equals indicated at sea level, but gets progressively greater than indicated as altitude increases. A roll performance curve is typically a line representing rate rising with increasing speed and then dropping off at much higher speeds. The rising part of the curve at lower speeds is for full throw of the ailerons where the pilot has no problem with control force. It shows ailerons providing more and more rolling forces on the airplane as their "bite" improves with increasing speed, so the roll gets faster. The top of the curve is where the pilot has reached a strength limit. Constant maximum pilot force into the control system can deflect the ailerons less and less as speed increases further to very high values. All curves shown are for unboosted aileron control systems; everything depends on the pilot's muscle. Though the P-38 had aileron power boost in very late models, the roll rates for that case are not available. Boost increases pilot muscle power and keeps the high speed end of the roll rate curve up, but does not affect the low end.

TURNING PERFORMANCE COMPARISONS

Achievement of the smallest possible radius of turn capability is a very important maneuverability factor for fighter aircraft. The ability to turn inside an enemy aircraft gave the World war II fighter pilot the advantage of better opportunity to draw a bead on the opposition.

Accurate data on minimum turn radius of fighter types is difficult to come by or to estimate. Information is available, however, from one of the World War II US fighter conferences on stall speeds in three g turns for eight of the eleven types considered here. Missing are the Bell P-39, Curtiss P-40, and Brewster F2A-. Data are

TABLE 103
RELATIVE TURNING PERFORMANCE
(NO FLAPS)

AIRCRAFT	FM-2	P-63A-9	P-61B-1	F6F-5	P-51D-15	P-38L	P-47D-30	F4U-1D
Speed for 3g stall, mph,IAS	118.5	132	137	139	159	170	170	172.5
GROSS WT. (LB.)	7420	8780	27000	12500	9500	17488	14300	11803
WING AREA (SQ.FT.)	260	248	664	334	233.19	327.5	300	314
MAXIMUM LIFT COEFFICIENT	2.38	2.38	2.54	2.27	1.89	2.17	1.93	1.48
MINIMUM TURN RADIUS "INDEX NO."	12.0	14.9	16.0	16.5	21.5	24.6	24.7	25.4
RANKING,% RANKING, BEST-WORST	100 1	124 2	133 3	138 4	179 5	205 6	206 7	212 8

provided for the P-38, P-47, P-51, P-61, P-63, FM-2, F4U-, and F6F-. The information is for clean aircraft configuration, that is, gear and flaps retracted, canopy closed, and no external stores aboard. The assumption is made in each case that engine power available is sufficient to keep the plane in level flight (not sinking) during the turn. In such a case the minimum turn radius occurs when the wing develops the maximum possible lift coefficient without stalling.The actual minimum turn radii are not calculated, but Table 103 shows the eight types ranked in order from best to poorest turn radius capability. The radius depends on the airplane wing loading (weight divided by wing area) and maximum wing lift coefficient. A low wing loading tends to make the plane more maneuverable, that is, to have a tighter turning circle capability; if the wing loading is high turning is penalized. There is a direct proportionality. On the other hand if the wing maximum lift coefficient is low the turn capability is poor; if it is high turning can be tighter; the proportionality is inverse.

So minimum turn radius is proportional to how heavily loaded the wing is divided by how efficient the wing is in lifting. Put the same way the minimum radius is proportional to wing loading divided by maximum lift coefficient.

In any of the aircraft, if the control system was suitable, wing flaps could be more or less quickly dropped to a maneuver position to give increased wing lift coefficient and thus provide tighter turns, but these cases are not reflected in the table. For ranking purposes the quickest turning aircraft, the FM-2 Wildcat, is given an arbitrary value of 100%. and the rest are ranked relative to it. The next

tightest turning machine was the Bell P-63 with a 24% greater turn radius capability. It is easy to see why one Corsair pilot commented there was no way he could follow an FM-2 in maneuvers. Review of the P-63 handling qualities section will show the Kingcobra could out-turn other production Army fighters. Next in line, surprisingly perhaps, was the very large P-61B Black Widow night fighter. There are many stories about its good turning ability for such a large aircraft (though it was slow to roll into the turn as noted earlier). The Widow had a minimum radius of 133%, or a third greater than the FM-2. The Navy Hellcat was about the same at 137% of the FM-2, and thus ranks fourth. Fifth ranking of the eight types goes to the P-51D Mustang at 179% of the Wildcat minimum radius. Though one Merlin P-51 pilot said his aircraft could "turn on a dime", the earlier four could apparently "turn on a dime and give you a couple of cents change". Next to poorest in turn performance, ranked sixth and seventh, are the P-38L and the P-47D-30 with a minimum turn radius capability almost the same at just over twice the radius of the FM-2. Of course as noted elsewhere the P-38 could drop its big Fowler flap to an eight degree maneuver setting and do better in turns. The P-47 has often been criticized for lack of tight turning ability. Hauling up in eighth place and last, perhaps surprisingly, is the F4U-1 Corsair with a minimum turn radius 212% of the FM-2, well over twice the Wildcat minimum. This results seems to be due to a relatively low maximum lift coefficient, because wing loading was not overly high. The spoiler placed on the right wing of the Corsair to eliminate an unsymmetric stall problem is suspected of dropping the overall lift coefficient considerably, in fact an NACA test report notes this was indeed the case.

COMPARISONS OF LEVEL FLIGHT ACCELERATION CAPABILITY

Comparisons are shown of initial level flight acceleration capabilities for early and late US fighters in Tables 104 and 105 respectively. The assumption is that each aircraft starts accelerating

from an initial flight condition of 250 mph at sea level. The early fighters get a sudden throttle increase from the initial power setting producing 250 mph to MILITARY power. The later models of Table

TABLE 104
COMPARISON OF LEVEL FLIGHT ACCELERATION
EARLY US FIGHTERS OF WORLD WAR II
(Starting at 250 mph at sea level and applying MILITARY power)

A/C	MIL.HP	WEIGHT,LB.	THRUST,LB.	DRAG,LB.	ACCELERATION.FT/SEC/SEC.	RANK
P-38F	2300	15665	2760	1640	2.30	1
P-47D	2000	13698	2400	1485	2.15	2
P-51	1150	8800	1380	797	2.13	3
P-39D	1150	7759	1380	871	2.11	4
F4U-1	2000	12694	2400	1580	2.08	5
F2A-3	1200	7339	1440	1112	1.44	6
P-40E	1150	8700	1380	1049	1.23	7
F4F-4	1200	7975	1440	1163	1.12	8

105 go suddenly to COMBAT power setting. Propeller efficiency has been assumed constant at 80 percent in all cases.

Table 104 shows the P-38F as best of eight early models in initial acceleration in spite of being the heaviest aircraft. The fighter starts with an acceleration of 2.30 feet per second per second. Close behind, with slightly less MILITARY horsepower available, and a little less weight, thrust, and drag, is the early P-47. The Allison P-51 is third on little more than half the P-47 power and a lot less weight. P-51 figures are about half P-38 numbers except for acceleration. P-39D acceleration is very close to that of the P-51; the Airacobra was lighter with somewhat more drag. F4U-1 Corsair acceleration is a little less than that of the P-39D; it has the same engine and thrust as the P-47D and is 1000 pounds lighter, but has

more drag. The last three fighter types, F2A-3, P-40E, and F4F-4, are comparable in terms of power and weight, but the Brewster airplane comes out best of the three with the Wildcat poorest in initial acceleration because of somewhat higher drag. Weight of the P-40E, almost 1400 pounds greater than that of the F2A-3, makes its acceleration poorer.

Of the eight later fighter models in Table 105 the P-38L is the acceleration leader. The short-time brute COMBAT power of the final Lightning model provides over 1000 pounds more thrust than the early Lightning with little more drag and not much greater weight. The Thunderbolt, this time the P-47M "hot rod" model, is again close behind the Lightning. In third place comes the Merlin powered P-51D Mustang with initial acceleration capability a bit

TABLE 105
COMPARISON OF LEVEL FLIGHT ACCELERATION
LATE US FIGHTERS OF WORLD WAR II
(Starting at 250 mph at sea level and applying COMBAT power)

A/C	COMBAT HP	WEIGHT,LB.	THRUST,LB.	DRAG,LB.	ACCELERATION,FT/SEC/SEC.	RANK
P-38L	3200	16880	3840	1676	4.13	1
P-47M	2800	14700	3360	1527	4.02	2
P-51D	1720	10208	2064	845	3.85	3
P-39Q-1	1420	7570	1704	864	3.57	4
P-63A	1500	8442	1800	926	3.33	5
F4U-4	2380	12420	2856	1569	3.33	5
F6F-5	2250	12740	2700	1673	2.60	6
P-40N	1360	8451	1632	1044	2.24	7

less than the P-47M at 3.85 feet per second per second. Then comes the late-model P-39Q Airacobra with much more power than earlier, nearly the same drag, and even less weight, resulting in an acceleration of 3.57 feet per second per second. Interestingly the ranking of the first four late-model types is the same as that of the early models, P-38, P-47, P-51, and P-39. Tied for fifth place of the late fighter versions, as shown in Table 105, are the P-63A Kingcobra and the F4U-4 Corsair models. Coming up at the rear of the rankings are the F6F-5 Hellcat and lastly the P-40N with accelerations respectively of 2.6 and 2.24 feet per second per second.

DIVE CAPABILITY COMPARISONS

Diving capability of various fighter types is compared in two ways, first in initial diving acceleration from high altitude, and then in limit dive speeds imposed at 10000 feet. The 10000 foot altitude is near where a fighter would have to start pulling out of a high speed dive, and thus near where g levels would start to increase and speeds decrease in the pullout.

A simple analysis of relative vertical diving accelerations of the aircraft starting at about 25000 feet in both 30 degree and 90 degree (vertical) dives results in the ranking shown just below from best to poorest, and pertains only to the initial portions of the dives.

AIRCRAFT	RANK
P-38G	1
P-51D	2 (TIE)
F4U-1D	2 (TIE)
P-47D	3
F6F-5	4
P-39D	5
F4F-4	6
P-40E	7

After a few thousand feet in a vertical dive all the aircraft would be approaching or would have reached their respective one g limit dive speeds as listed below for the altitude of 10000 feet.

AIRCRAFT	LIMIT DIVE SPEED (MPH, IAS, 1g)
P-47D	500
P-51D	500
P-63A	500
P-40E	480
P-39Q	475
F6F-5	449
F4U-1D	443
P-38J/L	440
P-61A	430
FM-2	425

Some wartime and subsequent flight tests seem to add credence to the order shown just above. Flight testing showed a P-51B could out-dive an F4U-1. Flight tests also showed a P-47D-20 and a P-51B-5 could out-dive a P-38J, and a modern test of a P-47D-40, P-51D, F6F-5, and FG-1D (same as F4U-1D) seemed to indicate diving capability to be in just that order.

GENERAL EVALUATION OF FIGHTER TYPES

At the Joint Fighter Conference, Naval Air Station Patuxent River, Maryland held from October 16-20, 1944 a large group of attending pilots evaluated certain characteristics of the fighters present, and by voting ranked the types against the factors noted. When a model was not listed it was not mentioned.

BEST ALL-AROUND COCKPIT:
F6F-5,F4U-4,P-51D,P-47D-30.

WORST COCKPIT:
P-38L,P-61B,F4U-1D,P-63A,P-47D-30,F6F-5,P-51D,FM-2.

BEST ENGINE CONTROLS ARRG'T:
P-51D,P-47D-30,P-63A,F4U-4,P-61B,F6F-5,F4U-1,FM-2, P-38L.

BEST GEAR & FLAP CONTROLS:
F6F-5,P-51D,F4U-1D,F4U-4,P-63A,P-47D-30,P-61B,FM-2.

BEST COCKPIT CANOPY:
P-47D-30,P-51D,F4U-1D,F6F-5.

MOST COMFORTABLE COCKPIT:
P-47D-30,F6F-5,F4U-4,P-61B,P-51D,F4U-1D,FM-2.

BEST ALL-AROUND VISIBILITY:
P-51D,P-47D-30,F6F-5,F4U-1D,P-63A.

BEST ALL-AROUND ARMOR:
P-47D-30,F4U-1D,F4U-4,F6F-5,P-51D.

BEST OVERLOAD TAKEOFF FROM SMALL AREA:
F6F-5,F4U-1D,P-38L,FM-2,F4U-4,P-61B,P-51D.

BEST AILERONS AT 350 MPH:
P-51D,F4U-1D,P-38L,F6F-5,P-47D-30,P-61B.

BEST AILERONS AT 100 MPH:
F6F-5,F4U-1D,P-47D-30,FM-2,P-51D,P-38L,P-61B.

BEST ELEVATORS:
F4U-1D,F6F-5,P-51D,P-47D,P-61B,FM-2,P-38L,P-63A.

BEST RUDDER:
F6F-5,F4U-1D,P-38L,P-51D,P-47D-30,P-61B,P-63A.

NICEST ALL-AROUND STABILITY:
F6F-5,F4U-1D,P-61B,P-47B,P-51D,P-63A,P-38L

BEST CHARACTERISTICS 5 MPH ABOVE STALL:
F6F-5,P-61B,P-38L,FM-2,P-51D, F4U-1D.

BEST DIVE STABILITY AND CONTROL:
F4U-1D,P-47D,F6F-5,P-51D,P-63A,P-61B,FM-2,P-38L.

BEST INSTRUMENT AND NIGHT FLYING QUALITIES:
F6F-5,P-61B,F4U-1D,P-47D,P-38L

BEST ALL-AROUND FIGHTER ABOVE 25000 FT:
P-47D,P-51D,F4U-1D,F6F-5,F4U-4,P-38L.

BEST ALL-AROUND FIGHTER BELOW 25000 FT:
P-51D,F4U-1D,F6F-5,F4U-4.

BEST PRODUCTION CARRIER-BASED FIGHTER:
F4U-1D,F6F-5,FM-2.

BEST FIGHTER-BOMBER:
F4U-1D,P-47D-30,F6F-5,P-51D,P-38L.

BEST STRAFER:
P-47D-30,F4U-1D,P-51D,F6F-5,P-38L,P-63A.

REFERENCES, GENERAL
(See also References for the specific aircraft)
1. *US Army Air Forces in World War II*, Craven and Cate, Editors.
2. Minutes of Fighter Conference, Patuxent River, Md., October,1944.
3. *Dual For The Sky*, Herbert Malloy Mason,Jr. Grosset and Dunlap, NY,1970
4. *Warplanes Of The Second World War-Vol.4, Fighters*, William Green Hanover House, NY,1961
5. *Aircraft Armament, Modern Aircraft Series*, Mearle Olmstead, Sports Car Press, Crown Publishers, NY,1970
6. *US Army Aircraft, 1908-1946*, James C. Fahey, Ships and Aircraft, Falls Church, Va. 1946
7. *Zero* , Masatake Okimita and Jiro Morikoshi with Martin Caidin, Ballantine Books, NY, 1957
8. *The Fighter Aircraft Pocketbook*, Roy Cross,Jarrold and Sons Ltd. London, 1962.
9. *Quest For Performance, The Evolution of Modern Aircraft*, Lawrence Loften Jr. NACA, Washington DC, 1985.
10. US Air Force Museum, US Air Force Museum Foundation, Wright-Patterson Air Force Base, 1980.
11. *A Chronicle Of The Aviation Industry in America, 1903-1947*, Eaton Manufacturing Co. Cleveland, Ohio, 1948.
12. *Air News Yearbook, Vol.2*, Philip Andrews, Ed., Duell, Sloan, and Pierce, NY, 1944.
13. *United States Army and Air Force Fighters*, Bruce Robertson,Ed., Harleyford Publications,Ltd.,1961
14. *Revolution In The Sky*, Richard Sanders Allen, Steven Green Press Brattleboro, Vt.,1964
15. *US Naval Aviation,1910-1960*, NAVWEPS 0080P-1,1960.
16. *US Navy and Marine Corps Fighters, 1918-1962*, Paul R. Matt and Bruce Robertson, Harleyford Publications, Ltd., 1962.
17. *US Naval Fighters*, Lloyd S. Jones, Aero Publishers, Fallbrook, CA 1977.
18. *Janes All The World's Aircraft, 1945-1946*, Compiled by Leonard Bridgeman, Arco Publishing Co. NY.
19. *Aerosphere 1941*, Glen D. Angle, Aircraft Publications,1941
20. *Aerosphere 1942*, Glen D. Angle, Aircraft Publications,1942
21. *The Aircraft Yearbook for 1941*, Aeronautical Chamber of Commerce,Inc
22. *The Aircraft Yearbook for 1943*, Aeronautical Chamber of Commerce,Inc
23. *American Combat Planes, Third Enlarged Edition*, Ray Wagner, Doubleday, Garden City, NY, 1982

24. *The Pacific War 1941-1945*, John Costello, Atlantic Communications Inc., Quill, NY, 1981.
25. *Fighter Aces*, Tolliver and Constable, The McMillan Co. NY, 1965
26. *Famous Fighters Of The Second World War*, Vol.1 and 2, William Green McDonald, London, 1962.
27. *Combat Aircraft Of The World*, W. R. Taylor, G.P. Putnam Sons NY, 1965.
28. *US Military Aircraft Since 1909*, F.G. Swanborough, Putnam, London and NY, 1963.
29. NACA Report 829, Summary of Measurements of Maximum Lift Coefficients and Stalling Characteristics of Airplanes, May 19,1944
30. NACA Wartime Report ACR L5A30, A Summary of Drag Results From Recent Tests of Army and Navy Airplanes, Feb.1945.
31. NACA Report No. 868, Summary of Lateral Control Research, 1947.
32. *Air Force Combat Units of World War II*, Maurer Maurer, Ed. Dept. of the Air Force, US Gov't Printing Office, 1960.
33. *The Mighty Eighth*, Roger Freeman
34. *Eagles West*, The AAF and the Soviet Union, 1941-5, Richard C. Lukas
35. *American Warplanes, Reference Guide to Aircraft*, Hamilton Standard Propellers, East Hartford Conn. (WW2 era.)
36. Air Corps TR#4399, Weights of Air Corps Airplanes, 1938-41, Oct.3,'42
37. *Performance of Aircraft*, Army Air Force School of Applied Tactics, Orlando, Fla., Sept. 1943.
38. Unpublished Data, Statistical Control Office, Air Technical Services Command, Wright Field, Ohio (Aircraft Production Data).
39. *Fighter Development, The Prewar Years*, Naval Aviation Confidential Bulletin, Lee M. Pearson, Naval Historian, Oct.1948.
39. *Fighter Development, The War Years*, Naval Aviation Confidential Bulletin, Lee M. Pearson, Naval Historian, Apr.1949.
40. Performance Characteristics, US Navy service Airplanes, Navy Dept. of Aeronautics, Washington, DC, Aug.1, 1941.
41. Engineering Characteristics and Performance Charts, USAAF Aircraft
42. *Model Designations of Military Aircraft*, Revised Dec.1944, Aircraft Production Board, Resources Control Office.
43. *Fluid Dynamic Drag*, Hoerner, Dr.-Ing.S.F., Hoerner Fluid Dynamics, Brick Town, NJ, 1965
44. *Airplane Performance and Stability and Control*, Perkins and Hage.
45. NACA Report No. 715, Lateral Control Characteristics.

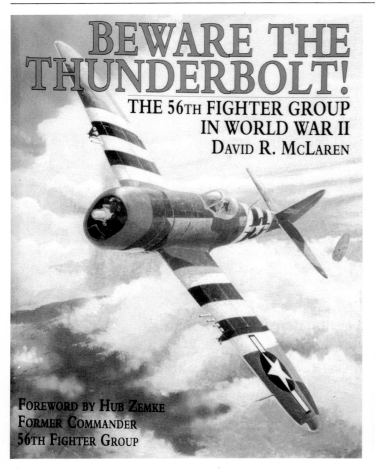

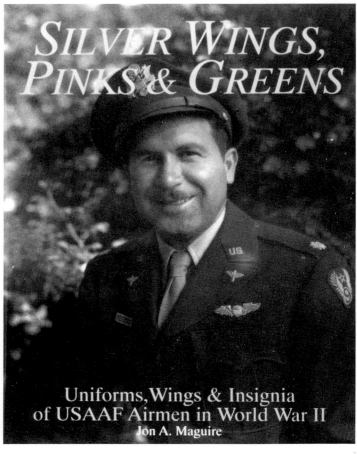

BEWARE THE THUNDERBOLT!: THE 56TH FIGHTER GROUP IN WORLD WAR II

David R. McLaren with Foreword by Hub Zemke

This new book is the story of the legendary 56th Fighter Group in a chronological narrative of their combat missions.
Size: 8 1/2" x 11" over 250 color & b/w photographs, appendices, index
208 pages, hard cover
ISBN: 0-88740-660-2 $39.95

SILVER WINGS, PINKS & GREENS
Uniforms, Wings, & Insignia of USAAF Airmen in WWII

Jon A. Maguire

This look at the uniforms and insignia of the USAAF during the World War II years covers a broad range of clothing, collar insignia, rank insignia, shoulders/sleeve insignia and squadron patches. Additionally, there is a in-depth examination of wing qualification badges.
Size: 8 1/2" x 11"   over 500 b/w and color photos
192 pages, hard cover
ISBN: 0-88740-578-9 $45.00

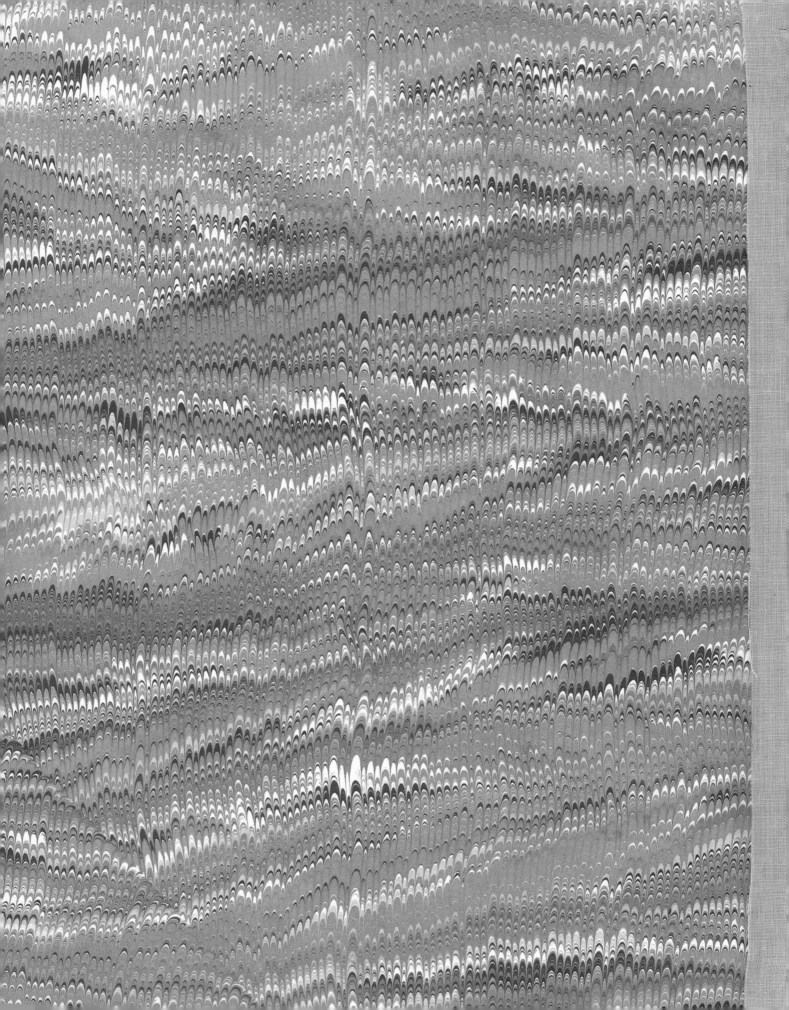